# Handbook of Research on Perspectives on Society and Technology Addiction

Rengim Sine Nazlı
*Bolu Abant İzzet Baysal University, Turkey*

Gülşah Sari
*Aksaray University, Turkey*

A volume in the Advances in Human and Social Aspects of Technology (AHSAT) Book Series

IGI Global
PUBLISHER of TIMELY KNOWLEDGE

Published in the United States of America by
IGI Global
Information Science Reference (an imprint of IGI Global)
701 E. Chocolate Avenue
Hershey PA, USA 17033
Tel: 717-533-8845
Fax: 717-533-8661
E-mail: cust@igi-global.com
Web site: http://www.igi-global.com



Library of Congress Cataloging-in-Publication Data

Names: Nazlı, Rengim Sine, 1980- editor. | Sari, Gülşah, 1984- editor.
Title: Handbook of research on perspectives on society and technology addiction / edited by Rengim Sine Nazlı and Gülşah Sari.
Description: Hershey, PA : Engineering Science Reference, [2023] | Includes bibliographical references and index. | Summary: "Perspectives on Society and Technology Addiction examines every subject of digital addiction in an interdisciplinary way. It discusses the issues about what technology addiction is, how to deal with this addiction, how to use the existing technology in a positive way, how to deal with this technology for disadvantaged groups, and concerns in the fields of social science and communication science. Covering topics such as Consumer 5.0, experience design, and information markets, this premier reference source is an essential resource for sociologists, policymakers, students and educators of higher education, researchers, and academicians"-- Provided by publisher.
Identifiers: LCCN 2023008246 (print) | LCCN 2023008247 (ebook) | ISBN 9781668483978 (h/c) | ISBN 9781668483992 (eISBN)
Subjects: LCSH: Technology--Social aspects. | Industry 4.0. | Digital humanities.
Classification: LCC T14.5 .P4684 2023 (print) | LCC T14.5 (ebook) | DDC 303.48/3--dc23/eng/20230307
LC record available at https://lccn.loc.gov/2023008246
LC ebook record available at https://lccn.loc.gov/2023008247

This book is published in the IGI Global book series Advances in Human and Social Aspects of Technology (AHSAT) (ISSN: 2328-1316; eISSN: 2328-1324)

British Cataloguing in Publication Data
A Cataloguing in Publication record for this book is available from the British Library.

All work contributed to this book is new, previously-unpublished material. The views expressed in this book are those of the authors, but not necessarily of the publisher.

For electronic access to this publication, please contact: eresources@igi-global.com.

# Advances in Human and Social Aspects of Technology (AHSAT) Book Series

Mehdi Khosrow-Pour, D.B.A.
Information Resources Management Association, USA

ISSN:2328-1316
EISSN:2328-1324

## Mission

In recent years, the societal impact of technology has been noted as we become increasingly more connected and are presented with more digital tools and devices. With the popularity of digital devices such as cell phones and tablets, it is crucial to consider the implications of our digital dependence and the presence of technology in our everyday lives.

The **Advances in Human and Social Aspects of Technology (AHSAT) Book Series** seeks to explore the ways in which society and human beings have been affected by technology and how the technological revolution has changed the way we conduct our lives as well as our behavior. The AHSAT book series aims to publish the most cutting-edge research on human behavior and interaction with technology and the ways in which the digital age is changing society.

## Coverage

- Gender and Technology
- Technoself
- Technology and Social Change
- Public Access to ICTs
- End-User Computing
- Information ethics
- Activism and ICTs
- ICTs and social change
- Technology and Freedom of Speech
- ICTs and human empowerment

IGI Global is currently accepting manuscripts for publication within this series. To submit a proposal for a volume in this series, please contact our Acquisition Editors at Acquisitions@igi-global.com or visit: http://www.igi-global.com/publish/.

The Advances in Human and Social Aspects of Technology (AHSAT) Book Series (ISSN 2328-1316) is published by IGI Global, 701 E. Chocolate Avenue, Hershey, PA 17033-1240, USA, www.igi-global.com. This series is composed of titles available for purchase individually; each title is edited to be contextually exclusive from any other title within the series. For pricing and ordering information please visit http://www.igi-global.com/book-series/advances-human-social-aspects-technology/37145. Postmaster: Send all address changes to above address.

## Titles in this Series

*For a list of additional titles in this series, please visit: www.igi-global.com/book-series*

***Exergaming Intervention for Children, Adolescents, and Elderly People***
Shahnawaz Khan (Bahrain Polytechnic, Bahrain) Thirunavukkarasu Kannapiran (S2 Integrators, USA) Arunachalam Muthiah (Karnavati University, India) and Sharad Shetty (Karnavati University, India)
Information Science Reference • © 2023 • 278pp • H/C (ISBN: 9781668463208) • US $215.00

***Handbook of Research on Andragogical Leadership and Technology in a Modern World***
Viktor Wang (California State University, San Bernardino, USA)
Information Science Reference • © 2023 • 474pp • H/C (ISBN: 9781668478325) • US $270.00

***ICT as a Driver of Women's Social and Economic Empowerment***
Pankaj Dhaundiyal (CHRIST University (Deemed), India) and Sana Moid (Amity University, India)
Information Science Reference • © 2023 • 306pp • H/C (ISBN: 9781668461181) • US $215.00

***Handbook of Research on Digitalization Solutions for Social and Economic Needs***
Richard Pettinger (University College London, UK) Brij B. Gupta (Asia University, Taiwan) Alexandru Roja (West University of Timisoara, Romania) and Diana Cozmiuc (West University of Timisoara, Romania)
Engineering Science Reference • © 2023 • 387pp • H/C (ISBN: 9781668441022) • US $380.00

***Digital Psychology's Impact on Business and Society***
Muhammad Anshari (Universiti Brunei Darussalam, Brunei) Abdur Razzaq (Universitas Islam Negeri Raden Fatah Palembang, Indonesia) Mia Fithriyah (Indonesia Open University, Indonesia) and Akmal Nasri Kamal (Universiti Brunei Darussalam, Brunei)
Information Science Reference • © 2023 • 330pp • H/C (ISBN: 9781668461082) • US $270.00

***Frugal Innovation and Social Transitions in the Digital Era***
Muhammad Nawaz Tunio (Mohammad Ali Jinnah University, Karachi, Pakistan) and Atia Bano Memon (University of Sindh, Badin Campus, Pakistan)
Information Science Reference • © 2023 • 208pp • H/C (ISBN: 9781668454176) • US $250.00

***Handbook of Research on Implementing Digital Reality and Interactive Technologies to Achieve Society 5.0***
Francesca Maria Ugliotti (Politecnico di Torino, Italy) and Anna Osello (Politecnico di Torino, Italy)
Information Science Reference • © 2022 • 731pp • H/C (ISBN: 9781668448540) • US $295.00

IGI Global
PUBLISHER of TIMELY KNOWLEDGE

701 East Chocolate Avenue, Hershey, PA 17033, USA
Tel: 717-533-8845 x100 • Fax: 717-533-8661
E-Mail: cust@igi-global.com • www.igi-global.com

# List of Contributors

# Table of Contents

# Detailed Table of Contents



With the development of information technology, societies have become a part of both national and international progress by turning the opportunities using the tools offered by technology. The basic concepts that are important to better understand digital society and its relations with the general framework have been discussed. The 'digital society' consists of institutions, groups, and individuals organized cybernetically around a certain interest relationship, which realize their relations, interactions, connections, and communications with technology via the internet. The structure of the digital society reflects the nature of digital technology as people, technology, business, culture; and social interactions evolve and emerge. There is a need for new frameworks that can transform the complexity of the reshaped world into manageable ideas and shape our perspective.



Emerging technologies have transformed different industrial eras. Recent Industry 5.0 has created various innovative technologies, including big data, artificial intelligence (AI), the internet of things (IoT), virtual reality, cloud computing, and cobots. Industry 5.0 encompasses three core values: human centricity, resilience, and sustainability. Industry 5.0 has various enabling technologies supporting the industrial transformation, including digital twins, cobots, mass customisation, and hyper-personalisation. Digital transformation has affected all areas, including business organisations with all functions and marketing. Marketers have created different and innovative strategies using technological supports stemming from Industrial and societal revolutions. Industry 5.0 proposes a new marketing paradigm with mass customisation, and in this process, a new type of "super-empowered customer" or "consumer 5.0" has been created.

Digital nomadism is defined as "the blending of tourism, leisure and professional activities to create a unique lifestyle based on remote work, global travel and multi-residential practices" (Mancinelli). Considering digital nomadism as a lifestyle, individuals need to be constantly on the move in order to maintain this lifestyle. In this case, lifestyle mobility can be mentioned at the intersection of travel, leisure time and migration. The relevant book chapter will address the issue of digital nomadism from a similar holistic perspective. For this purpose, developments in communication technologies and digitalization will be discussed in the first part, and the prominent features of digital nomadism as a lifestyle mobility will be mentioned in the second part, and finally, critical approaches to digital nomadism will be discussed and whether this lifestyle can be evaluated as a hedonic choice or a necessity.



This study aims to analyze voter-municipality and virtual political communication within the scope of the BLD 4.0 project of the Ankara municipality, which is the first Turkish municipality to join the Metaverse world and to examine the voters' perceptions about the Metaverse world. The study evaluates the comments submitted to the official social media accounts of the Ankara municipality, which has declared it will participate in the Metaverse world. The results of the analysis conducted, the importance of digitalization in governance has emerged, and it has been found that there is awareness among citizens regarding the concepts of industry 4.0 and the Metaverse. In particular, it is understood that the perception of innovative leadership created by the digital municipalism approach creates trust in a political leader.



The objective of this study is to analyze the technology transfer flow in Brazil from 2000 to 2014, considering the domestic and foreign markets, and also the activities carried out by universities and technological institutes from 1972 to 2015. From results, Brazil has been receiving technologies from major economic powers such as the United States, Germany, Japan, France, Italy, the United Kingdom, Switzerland, Canada, and Spain. The barriers regarding cooperation between university-industry are still present, currently there are 27.523 research groups distributed in all areas of knowledge, but only 0.31% develops activities related to technology transfer, and 58% do not establish any relationships with industry. Notwithstanding, the technology supply must depend on the technological diffusion process and the adoption of technology by the society through continuous learning, thereby enabling to increase the performance of services, processes, and products in the domestic market.

Even straightforward objects whose nature we believe we comprehend go through the design process. The task of design is to connect people and technology. Every advance in technology brings about new experiences and ways of life. In this chapter the authors explain how design alters the abilities, motivations, and expectations in daily life, and how graphic design reacts to this shift. If we want to anticipate the future, we need to look closely at the digital technologies that emerged recently and first analyze the transition—how it occurred and how quickly it happened.



The entertainment industry in the digital age is characterized by new technologies as well as a culture embedded in a context of new habits, particularly practiced by Generation Z. These factors result in the emergence of applications such as TikTok and Netflix. TikTok is an indispensable marketing tool and a social media characterized by the rapid viralization of content. The application stands out as a space for creativity and entertainment, where movies and series gain popularity, including content from the streaming platform Netflix. Thus, the impact of the social network in promoting entertainment will be further explored. This chapter synthesizes literature from the past decades to give readers insight into technologies such as streaming and VOD, Netflix's business model, the concept of fandom, and the social media marketing practiced by TikTok. Theory, research, and implications for a better understanding of TikTok's impact on the entertainment industry are outlined.



The use of digital has shifted to a different format, especially with the prominence of interaction with Web 2.0-based social networking sites that developed after internet technology. These environments, which provide users with a platform independent of time and space, have transformed daily and professional life practices, and public spaces have been replaced by virtual communities. Historically, social movements based on class struggle have also been affected by this change. Although the use of media tools in social movements dates back to the 18th century, individuals can easily reach people who think like themselves and organize quickly through social media. Although digital activism, which is one of the trends of digital technology prevailing in the 21st century, has been exposed to criticism such as clicktivism, it has also become an effective force in the political arenas. In this study, changing social movements on the axis of digital technologies will be discussed in general terms to digital activism.

Cyberbullying in organizations refers to the use of technology, such as social media, email, instant messaging, or other digital platforms, to harass, intimidate, or humiliate someone in the workplace. Cyberbullying in organizations can have a significant impact on individuals and the workplace as a whole. It can lead to decreased morale, increased turnover, decreased productivity, and increased absenteeism. Cyberbullying can also have legal and financial consequences for both the victim and the organization. Organizations can take steps to prevent and address cyberbullying, such as establishing clear policies and procedures for online behavior, providing training to employees on appropriate digital communication, and responding quickly and effectively to reports of cyberbullying. By creating a culture of respect and accountability, organizations can work to prevent cyberbullying and promote a safe and supportive workplace for all employees.



For millions of years, mankind has made countless inventions and discoveries. These inventions are basically designed to facilitate humanity's life and serve humanity. So much so that at the cutting edge of technology, there are devices or virtual environments that can listen to people, talk to them, guide them, communicate with them, read, calculate, remember, remind, play, and do many other things on their behalf. Developments that have completely changed people's living habits have brought along many positive and negative developments. With the development of technology, the most widely used technological development is digital objects and virtual environments. Due to the existence of these objects and environments and the possibilities, diversity, and audiovisual richness they offer to people, many of them have deeply affected our perception of life and lifestyle. The basis of these effects is dependent on these devices and environments.



This chapter mainly aims to shed light on a rather overlooked phenomenon of pathological Internet use (PIU). Due to the rise of the technology, the global internet usage is almost inevitable, yet although it has many benefits, the dependency towards the internet usage (where it is specific or general) is an alarming psychological condition, especially for young adults and adolescents. The disorder and its related problems as well as treatment and intervention options that are evidence-based are reported. The results of treatment-outcome studies underlying the positive effects of CBT for PIU are presented. The necessity of more literature in the related field and the need for an official diagnosis for better understanding of etiology and treatment of PIU is underlined.

findings contribute not only theoretically but also practically, highlighting the necessity of implementing school awareness-prevention actions to strengthen early and middle adolescents' social-emotional skills and safe internet use.



The frequency of internet gaming addiction varies between 1-15% in the world. There are some demographic factors, psychosocial factors, and game-related factors in the etiology of gaming addiction. In demographic factors, male gender, adolescent age group, separation of parents, high income, and being a student are seen as risks. Psychosocial factors include low social cohesion, aggressive behavior, anxiety or depression, low academic performance, attention problems, low life satisfaction, problems in family / friend relationships, and low self-esteem. Internet gaming addiction has many health effects, physiological, psychological, and social problems. In addition to determining the diagnostic criteria for gaming addiction, there is a need for national and international studies that will guide protection and intervention efforts, especially for at-risk youth. As a result of these studies, effective and effective evidence-based public health intervention programs should be developed.



This study examines the topic of digital game addiction and children. The study addresses the effects of digital games on children, addiction symptoms, and the impact of addiction on children's social, academic, and psychological development. According to the results of the research, symptoms of digital game addiction include excessive time spent playing games, loss of control, preoccupation with games, developing tolerance, neglecting social and academic responsibilities, and experiencing physical health problems such as sleep disorders and eye strain. Digital game addiction can negatively impact children's social skills, academic performance, and psychological well-being, thus reducing their quality of life. Therefore, it is recommended for parents and teachers to limit children's use of digital games and encourage them to engage in other activities. Parents and teachers should monitor children's use of digital games, recognize addiction symptoms, and take necessary precautions.



In today's digital age, digital games point to an extremely important structure in terms of the audiences they appeal to, and the concept of metaverse, which has experienced a great increase in the speed of development in recent years, is also an area that affects digital games. Therefore, within the scope of this study, the process of digital games becoming metaverse in the near future is discussed. However, the study does not address only these two issues. Within the scope of this chapter, virtual gender creations that can be created in the context of the metaverse, together with the participation of digital games in the metaverse universe, are also examined with SWOT analysis. In addition, attention is drawn to

All the needs for education, social relations, social activities, and personal development are now being provided through digital resources. Based on the fact that studies on digital game addiction are not at the desired level, the main purpose of the study is to investigate the factors affecting digital game addiction in high school students and the relationship between digital game addiction, which has become a growing problem, and mindfulness concepts. According to the results of the survey applied to 181 high school students studying in Istanbul Esenyurt, the general and all sub-dimensions of the Digital Game Addiction Scale do not differ significantly according to gender, grade level and school success. The answer to the question 'I prefer playing games to spend time with my friends physically,' 3.24, 'I discuss the time I spend in the game with people close to me,' is 2.99, 'I postpone my sleep time to reach my goal in the game,' with an average of 2.93. reveals the result that he is addicted to digital games as an indicator of addiction.



Nowadays the usage of digital games has increased a lot. Console games, PC games, and online games are all examples of digital games. Aside from these, it has been observed that digital games are also played with portable technologies such as mobile phones and tablets. Children's play equipment, play habits, and play perceptions have all changed as a result of these changes. As a result, digital games have a significant influence on children. This chapter focuses on the effects of digital games on children and how children became addicted to digital games. It also discusses how to avoid overusing digital games. It also explains the meaning of digital games and discusses their history and future.



Being easy to access and share, social media platforms cause people to spend most of their time in these places. Individuals share pictures, music, and video content in these places; they follow the content shared by others as well. Such appeals of social media lead individuals to become addicted to social media. In this study, social media addiction was evaluated on the basis of the platform, the addicted environment, and the characteristics of the user. In addition, the study is explained with examples, especially on the Instagram platform, through digital storytelling.

While it is known that the COVID-19 epidemic has adversely affected many countries in the world, the stress and anxiety experienced by elderly individuals, especially during pandemic periods, has been more than that of younger individuals. The avoidance of the disease, especially by individuals over the age of 65, has prevented these individuals from communicating face-to-face with other people. In this context, the main purpose of the research is to determine the effect of communication concerns of individuals over the age of 65 on social media addiction. The research question was determined as "Does the communication anxiety seen in individuals over the age of 65 have an effect on social media addiction during the COVID-19 process?" In order to answer the research question, a study was conducted on the population of individuals over the age of 65 living in Konya. 423 individuals who use social media actively participated in the research. As a result of the research, it was determined that communication anxiety strengthens social media addiction behavior.



Research on the negative impact of social media on mental health is extensive and well-documented. However, in this process, relatively little attention has been paid to social media communities oriented around mental health. This study aimed to address this gap by using uses and gratifications theory to analyze the posts and comments related to mental health, anxiety, depression, and self-esteem in the "/r/teenagers" community on Reddit. The results revealed that many users in these communities turn to social media to identify with others and seek advice, while a smaller percentage uses social media for entertainment and escapism. An even smaller minority of users leverage social media platforms to educate others. By exploring the motivations and reasons behind social media use in mental health communities, this study provides valuable insights into the potential benefits and drawbacks of social media use in this context, as well as avenues for future research and intervention.

# Preface

In our age, it has become inevitable to live a life without using technology. However, as technology developed, society has continued to change. Technology, which surrounds humanity in every sense, has become more and more affecting even ordinary activities in today's world. This effect of technology has increased the need for technological tools, moreover, this need has begun to be defined with addiction today. The internet, which has become widespread since the 1990s, is the basic communication tool used in all areas of life today. The changing structure of traditional mass media with the internet has made all communication tools dependent on the internet. As a result of the meeting of mobile phones with internet technology, technology has even affected ordinary activities in people's lives in today's world. Mobile phones are the fastest communication technology in human history (Castells, 2008).

In the light of all these developments, it can be said that people use technological tools to think, socialize, have fun, and meet their various needs. McLuhan (1964) said that the tool is an extension of the person, but every tool brings limitations to people along with new possibilities. The more we use a tool, the more we are likely to get into its shape and pattern. For example, a person who constantly writes on a computer / phone will begin to find it difficult to write by hand (Carr, 2012). Therefore, a society that meets all its needs through a smartphone has also become a matter of social concern. While this situation is increasing day by day, many studies have been started on this subject. Studies on the aforementioned disorder have started to be examined under the title of "addiction" and it is aimed to clarify technological addiction in studies conducted in general terms. In order to draw attention to the importance of this new type of addiction, evocative terms such as "digital heroin," "electronic cocaine," and "virtual drugs" were also used (Hartogsohn & Vudka: 2022). Technology addiction is a worrying situation for the whole society in every aspect. In order to cope with addiction, it is necessary to examine technological innovations.

In this context, the book consists of 31 chapters. In the first chapter, entitled "Digital Society; Basic Framework and Concepts," the digital society and the basic concepts that are important are discussed. In the second chapter entitled "Industry 5.0, Digital Society, and the Consumer 5.0," the concept of Industry 5.0 is discussed in the axis of digital society. The third chapter entitled "Does Digitalization have a Causal Relationship with Economic Development? An Experience from a Country-wise Panel Data Statistical Analysis," has created an information communication technology index (ICTI) for 109 countries between 2010 and 2020 using a composite Z-score method. The fourth chapter, entitled "Theories supporting central bank digital currency development and its usefulness," presents some of the theories supporting the development and usefulness of a central bank digital currency. The fifth chapter entitled "Production and Consumption in the Relationship Between Digital Culture and New Communication Technologies" focuses on the role of new communication technologies in digital culture. The sixth chapter entitled "Changing Society Order With Digitalization: Global Village Global Workers: Digital Nomads," deals with the issue of digital nomadism. Chapter seven entitled "MetaStrategy of MetaCities An Example of Ankara Municipality Project BLD 4.0" analyzes the voter-municipality and virtual political communication within the scope of the BLD 4.0 project of Ankara Municipality, the first Turkish municipality to join the Metaverse world, and examines the voters' perceptions of the Metaverse world. Chapter eight entitled "Technology Transfer process in Brazil: An overview of the national context" analyzes the technology transfer flow in Brazil from 2000 to 2014, taking into account the domestic and foreign markets, as well as the activities carried out by universities and institutes of technology from 1972 to 2015. In chapter nine entitled "Experience Design's Impact on Graphic Design" it is explained that experience design alters the abilities, motivations, and expectations in daily life and how graphic design reacts to this shift. Chapter ten entitled "The Impact of TikTok on the Viralization of the Entertainment Industry: The Netflix's Series Case" provides insight into technologies such as streaming and VOD, Netflix's business model, the concept of fandom, and social media marketing implemented by TikTok. In chapter eleven entitled "New Social Movements and Digital Activism" new social movements and types of digital activism are examined together. Chapter twelve entitled "Cyberbullying in Organizations" examines cyberbullying in organizations. In chapter thirteen entitled "Life in the Digital World" the possibilities offered by technology and its impact on our lifestyle are discussed. Chapter fourteen entitled "The Emerging Psychological Problem of the Digitalized World: Pathological Internet Use" a throws light upon the phenomenon of pathological internet use. In chapter fifteen entitled "The Concept of Addiction and Its Causes" the concept of addiction and its causes are defined, followed by the concept of behavioral addiction and its causes. In chapter sixteen entitled "Digital Addiction and It's Reflections on the Individual and Society" the social and individual reflections of digital addiction are explained. In chapter seventeen entitled "Internet Addiction and Self-esteem Amid the COVID-19 Pandemic: A Preliminary Study in Junior High School Students" while describing a preliminary study of secondary school students' internet addiction during the pandemic period, the role of self-esteem is also examined. In chapter eighteen entitled "Internet Gaming Addiction and Its Health Effects" game addiction and its effects are discussed. In the nineteenth chapter called "Digital Game Addiction and Child: Digital Game Addiction", the issue of digital game addiction and children are examined. In the twentieth chapter titled "A SWOT Analysis of Gender Creations from Digital Games to Metaverse", virtual gender creations that can be created in the context of the metaverse with the participation of digital games in the metaverse universe are also examined by SWOT analysis. The twenty-first chapter titled "Digital Game Addiction: Research About Children and Adolescents" clarifies the meaning of digital game addiction and its effects on child/adolescent life, family functioning, as well as on other areas. In the twenty-second chapter called "A Study on Digital Game Addiction Tendency of Generation Z Individuals", it synthesizes both the measurement of the digital game addiction tendency of the Z generation individuals and the views on addiction. In the twenty-third chapter titled "A Field Research on Digital Playing Tendencies and Addiction of High School Students" considering the fact that the studies on digital game addiction are not at the desired level, the factors affecting digital game addiction in high school students and their relationship with digital game addiction, which has become an increasing problem, are discussed. is being investigated. The twenty-fourth chapter named "Digital game addiction and child" focuses on the effects of digital games on children and how children become addicted to digital games. In the twenty-fifth chapter named "Investigating Social Media Addiction in the Context of Digital Storytelling", social media addiction is evaluated on the basis of platform, addicted environment and user characteristics. In the twenty-sixth chapter named "The Interaction of Social Media Addiction and Communication Anxiety During the COVID-19 Period: The Case of Individuals Over 65 in Konya Province", the relationship between social media addiction and communication is examined through Konya. In chapter twenty seven called "How Adolescents Use Social Media to Navigate Their Mental Health: Examining Reddit's "/r/teenagers" aims to fill this gap by using uses and gratifications theory to analyze posts and comments about mental health, anxiety, depression, and self-esteem in the community. In the twenty-eighth chapter titled "Social Media Addiction and Fear of Missing Out", FOMO, one of the digital diseases, is discussed. "Chapter twenty-nine, called "Negative Impacts of Technology and Digital Diseases", examines disorders such as nomophobia, social media depression, phantom vibration syndrome, and cyber sickness. In chpater thirty called "I am online; therefore, I am! Digital obesity from a sociological perspective" igital obesity is explained sociologically and the situation in Turkey is shed light on. "In the last chapter, titled "An Intergenerational Comparison within the Framework of Digital Minimalism", the approaches of X, Y and Z generations to digital minimalism are examined with in-depth interview technique.

In this book, called *Perspectives on Society and Technology Addiction*, the role of technology in social life will be discussed within the framework of empirical studies on the axis of addiction.

*Rengim Sine Nazli*
*Bolu Abant Izzet Baysal University, Turkey*

*Gülsah Sari*
*Aksaray University, Turkey*

## REFERENCES

Carr, N. (2012). *Yüzeysellik: İnternet Bizi Aptal mı Yapıyor?* (İ. Kapaklıkaya, Trans.). Ufuk Yayınları.

Castells, M. (2008). Afterword, Handbook of Mobile Communications Studies. The MIT Press.

Hartogsohn, I., & Vudka, A. (2022). *Technology and addiction: what drugs can teach us about digital media. Transcult. Psychiatry*. Available.

# Acknowledgment

As editors, we owe a great debt of gratitude to our dear academics who wrote chapters for this book. This book will shed light on researchers, students and academics interested in the field thanks to the contributions of valuable authors. We would also like to express our gratitude to the academics of the editorial advisory board who provided full support in the constitution of the book.

Finally, we would like to thank the IGI Global publishing house for helping us to publish this edited book.

*Bolu and Aksaray / Turkey*
*26.05.2023*

## Editorial Advisory Board

# Chapter 1
# Digital Society:
## Basic Framework and Concepts

**Çağrı Emin Şahin**
*Gulhane School of Medicine, University of Health Sciences, Turkey*

**Metin Hasde**
*Gulhane School of Medicine, University of Health Sciences, Turkey*

## ABSTRACT

*With the development of information technology, societies have become a part of both national and international progress by turning the opportunities using the tools offered by technology. The basic concepts that are important to better understand digital society and its relations with the general framework have been discussed. The 'digital society' consists of institutions, groups, and individuals organized cybernetically around a certain interest relationship, which realize their relations, interactions, connections, and communications with technology via the internet. The structure of the digital society reflects the nature of digital technology as people, technology, business, culture; and social interactions evolve and emerge. There is a need for new frameworks that can transform the complexity of the reshaped world into manageable ideas and shape our perspective.*

## INTRODUCTION

At the beginning of the millennium, the opportunities offered by technology to humans were quite limited. Information technologies, which are used as a universal progress tool day by day, have become an indispensable element of the globalizing world by increasing these opportunities. Nowadays, with the increase in digitalization, it is very difficult to keep up with the speed of technology. The technology century, which is called the digital age, has transformed individuals into technology-dependent individuals by offering innovations while making their lives easier. While technology is used in many areas such as health, education and transportation, with the change of human needs, traditional methods have been left aside and new technological products and services have begun to be preferred. This change has not only been limited to products and services but has also brought along a digitalization process that includes

DOI: 10.4018/978-1-6684-8397-8.ch001

people and society (Balsmeier & Woerter, 2019). With the development of information technology, societies have become a part of both national and international progress by turning the opportunities by using the tools offered by technology. In addition, it is seen that Digitalization and Information Technologies have positive and negative effects on society (Sacco et al.,2021)

The digitalization of many social interactions, the increasing daily use of social media, the development of literature with the definition of internet addiction, and the choice of people to communicate by correspondence instead of face-to-face or telephone are just some of the developments we have seen recently (Cemiloglu et al., 2022). These developments lead to a decrease in the use of traditional urban public spaces of contemporary society, as well as a change in the type of social activities (Kokcu, 2021)

With the new forms of communication of technology, it is necessary to rethink the public sphere within the framework of digitalization. People share photos and videos every day from their homes, which are their most private areas, and use their living rooms as a meeting room to address people they have never met. Space, target audience, inclusiveness, equality-freedom balance, democracy have been among the main topics of discussion in the transformation of the distinction between public and private spheres in parallel with the digitalization process (Floridi, 2015).

In this section, it have been discussed the basic concepts that are important to better understand digital society and its relations with the general framework. Since some concepts are still new, we have conveyed the ongoing discussions about these concepts in their current forms.

## UNDERSTANDING OF DIGITAL SOCIETY

The foundation of the digital society is formed by internet activities. The 'Digital Society' consists of institutions, groups and individuals organized cybernetically around a certain interest relationship, which realize their relations, interactions, connections and communications with technology via the internet. Although the digital society seems to be a result of information technology, many economic, political, cultural and social factors are thought to be effective in the formation of the digital society (Schmidt, 2017). The reflection of digitalization in daily life also creates some problems in terms of the reliability of personal data. The effort to prove that ordinary people are not ordinary posts with excessive exhibitionism makes it difficult to protect the personal data of users. As the limits of time and space are exceeded in digital platforms, users experience unreal virtual satisfaction, which brings many changes in people's face-to-face communication habits (Sezgin, 2018).

Shayo et al. have presented an evolutionary model that aims to delineate the boundaries of the digital society, conceptualizing the driving forces behind the growth of digital societies and the hierarchy of existing arrangements at the individual, group, organizational and community levels (See Figure 1) (Shayo, 2007). Stated that the driving forces in the model are effective in the transformation of individuals and society into the digital society.

### Conceptual Framework

There is a need for new regulations in the digital world, which is a part of every aspect of our lives. Of course, these are challenging and complex. Rather than just a few all-encompassing laws, regulation needs to cover a whole range of different rules, policy makers, and issues. The state of continuous self-regulation in the digital society is declining. A new approach is needed that blends innovation and protection, human dignity and progress. A successful digital transformation can genuinely change the way people interact. Thus, it can eliminate negative criticisms about digital society.

In this case, a framework is needed to develop and evaluate the regulations to be produced. The structure of the digital society reflects the nature of digital technology as people, technology, business, culture and social interactions evolve and emerge. There is a need for new frameworks that can transform the complexity of the reshaped world into manageable ideas and shape our perspective (Katzenbach & Bächle, 2019). In order to create the framework correctly, it is necessary to have a good grasp of key concepts and their explanations. Each will have broader social, political and cultural consequences that follow.

*Figure 1. A framework for digital society*
*(Shayo et al. 2007)*

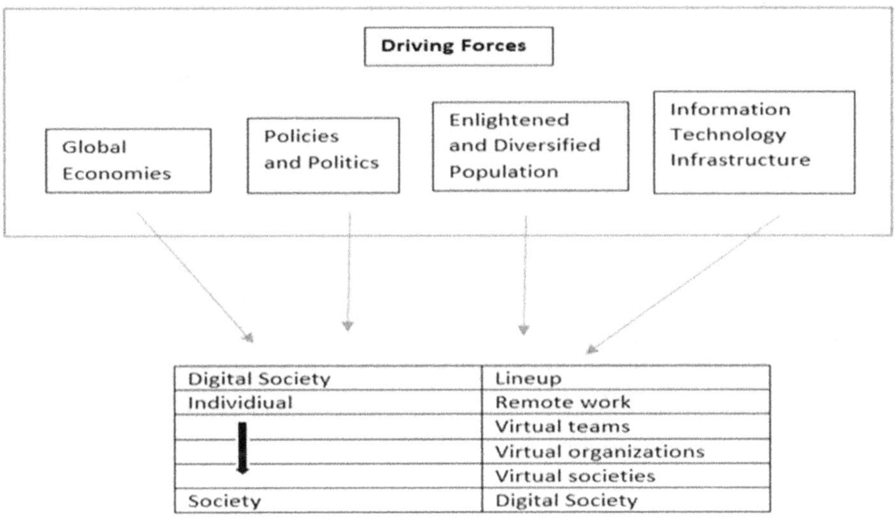


## Privacy

The perception of privacy varies according to the ages. The most obvious reason for the differentiation in the perception of privacy is the polarization in the public and private spheres. With the birth of the bourgeoisie, privacy comes to the fore with modernization and its emphasis, individuality. In traditional societies, people were able to gain an identity within the community, clan or family, and the foundations of their individualization were laid with modernism. The rising phenomenon of individualization has exalted the concept of private space. After modernism, in this age we live in, with the rapid development of information and communication technologies and its impact on social life, the public sphere has completely infiltrated the private sphere, and private lives have become public in internet environments that pave the way for the violation of privacy. The destruction of privacy walls, especially on social media platforms, has brought the concept of surveillance to the agenda (Lahlou, 2008).

It is stated that the private sphere is also included in the transformation in the private and public spheres. While the private sphere has been confined to the nuclear family, which has lost authority, it has been made public, while privacy has infiltrated into the public. In short, it is argued that the private space is made public and emptied. It is also mentioned that the family is idealized as the source of virtuel (Matzner & Ochs, 2019). In this way, the idealization of private life has also increased privacy. However, according to Sennett, the search for autonomy, freedom and individualism have created an isolated, restless and dissatisfied person. At this point, all ideals have led to more and more legal rights to the state in return for non-interference in private life (Habermas, 2003).

According to Sennett, public expansion, which was seen as a result of activities in many areas such as public cafes, theaters, operas or parks in the 18th century, gave way to shrinkage. On the other hand, the public and private spheres have begun to polarize. The feeling of insecurity in the cities created by capitalism and secularization weakened public life, but the importance given to the private sphere increased. This shifting balance has resulted in the erosion of public life (Sennett, 2003).

Today, to think of online and offline as independent fields and to associate them with digital duality means ignoring the intersection and interpenetration between them. The belief that offline and online lives are largely separate and distinct realities has been called digital dualism by social media theorist Nathan Jurgenson. According to the theorist, digital contents are seen as part of a "virtual" world that is separate from a "real" world in physical space. Separating these truly intertwined areas is artificial and unnecessary (Chayko, 2018).

## Datafication

With the rapid increase in the possibilities of data, many areas of life are under surveillance. Individuals become more and more "individual" with each passing day (Han, 2017). Human life has become open to prediction through forms of analysis that can be automated at scale. This poses ample opportunities and risks for creating detailed profiles of individuals, social ranking, discrimination, government repression, and manipulation of consumers and citizens. Uncontrolled surveillance poses a danger to many civil and human rights such as freedom of expression, freedom of assembly and privacy (Mejias & Couldry, 2019).

## Platformisation

Platforms are structures that facilitate personalized interactions. In doing so, it retains the power to shape interaction. It collects data continuously and systematically, processing it algorithmically and basically organizing it to be converted into money. While facilitating software called API can produce various services, social media applications can be counted among these platforms (Plantin, 2018).

The risk that all data can be processed and used against us creates tension. However, it is not without its positive aspects. Platform businesses can create a competitive advantage if they undertake the fundamental analysis function in multilateral markets (McIntyre & Srinivasan, 2017). Especially considering that women can be publishers and bloggers, they also have positive effects on labor.

Its core functions can be summarized as the interrelationships of data infrastructures, markets and forms of governance. These intertwined areas can also change with cultural practices. Only as a result of our understanding of the key mechanisms can platformisation be democratically and effectively regulated by public institutions (Poell et al., 2019).

## Filter Bubble

The metaphor that naturally follows the effects of the reorganization of social life through platforms and data is called the filter bubble. It is a web algorithm that personalizes and predicts which posts the user wants to see in line with digital information about the user (location, search history, etc.). Thanks to filter bubbles, users are isolated from content that is not suitable for their own perspective by encountering content that is suitable for their own cultural or ideological views. These filters cause users to see the world in a representative way. Since people are more inclined to believe the news that fits their views, filter bubbles manipulate the news flow and cause the society to be divided by causing people to become polarized.

In addition, although the idea of an algorithmically arranged filter bubble seems reasonable, scientific studies on this subject have not reached very clear results. There are doubts about how the bone structure formed in the first place emerged (Bruns, 2019).

## Algorithmic Governance

It is argued that digital technologies provide order through algorithms. Algorithms are procedures created by logical and statistical methods. Governance becomes more understandable and powerful as a result of algorithms (Yeung, 2018). A slightly different approach puts technical systems at the center, not social structures and relationships. Relevant studies, especially in computer science, aim to create and optimize algorithmic systems to solve specific social problems. Optimization and guiding user behavior in the most effective way are essential in algorithmically fed services. The public discourse of some ideas has proven more successful than others at stimulating academic thought and economic and political activity. This term also touches on all the other concepts discussed so far and will be discussed later (Just & Latzer, 2017).

## Algorithmic Bias

Over time, as a result of some obvious or cumulative events, some errors caused by overconfidence have been noticed. These are defined as automation bias. (Lee & See, 2004; Parasuraman & Manzey, 2010)

An algorithm that evaluates crimes called ProPublica has detected a decision bias between races. It has been understood that after the obvious inequalities in recruitment or facial recognition, algorithms can also lead to various biases if not paid attention to. A critical approach, including that which has been developed, has begun. Bias in this area has been examined and divided into three categories: technical bias, post-design bias, and pre-existing bias (Barocas & Selbst, 2016).

Technical bias is caused by technical impossibilities or insufficient capacity. The problem with pre-existing biases is in the institutions' ongoing culture and practices. Such biases often enter a system as implicit and unconscious, rather than by conscious effort. Post-design bias is the result of new social knowledge or changing cultural values that are not or cannot be included in the system design. It typically occurs during use, sometimes after a design has been completed. It is an indicator of incompatibility between the assumed experts in the system design and the actual population using the system (Parasuraman & Manzey, 2010).

## Digital Commons

The commons are socio-cultural structures that have legal relations with each other. At the same time, they are holistic social institutions that govern the (re)production of resources, expressed in economic and institutional dimensions. Digital commons is a subset of commons; where resources are data, information, culture and knowledge created and/or maintained online. The concept of the digital commons is an important concept to challenge legal limitations and promote equal access to these resources (Dulong & Stalder, 2020).

One of the main differences between digital and tangible commons is that in the former, the resource is generally unrivaled. There is no danger of overuse. Therefore, loose boundaries exist for the digital commons.

Many people use online connections to interact face-to-face, strengthen these relationships, or add new dimensions. Similarly, communities that come together for different purposes, especially civil society, are also changing. In these structures called virtual community;

1. People interact with others to satisfy their needs.
2. Common goals, common interests, and needs provide reason to form the congregation.
3. It has policies that guide people's interaction.
4. Computer systems facilitate the sense of togetherness and support social interaction (European Economic and Social Committee, 2017).

## Digital Sovereignty

At first glance, the digital transformation of the internet and its global technical infrastructure seem to challenge domination. The dispersed and flexible nature of global digital networks is positioned in opposition to the hierarchy of state principles. In addition, the cumbersomeness of legal governance could not keep up with the speed of digital applications. This has led to the appearance of digital transformation as opposed to legal control. Seeing the risks, the authority states created technical and legal tools to increase their dominance over the digital society (Goldsmith & Wu, 2006). They have also successfully convinced the public that sovereignty and state authority are necessary to protect "vital goods" ranging from security to welfare, from cultural norms to media control. As a result, citizens in many countries today expect their governments to protect their online privacy or combat online disinformation and cybercrime.

The commercial focus of the Internet is on advertising and the use of network effects (Rascao, 2021). Intermediaries and digital platforms play such a dominant role in making content available that open internet protocols on which digital communication is based become meaningless (Hindman, 2018).

A state's digital sovereignty cannot be reduced to its ability to set, communicate and enforce laws. The extent to which regulations subordinate large digital companies to democratic sovereignty continues to be debated. In order to democratize digital sovereignty, it should ensure its accountability and new models should be studied to ensure its sustainability (Bobrowicz-Campos, E. & Matos, AP, 2022).

## FUTURE RESEARCH DIRECTIONS

Some important discussions are pointed out by introducing the concepts. Other concepts that are not mentioned in the article but may become important in the appropriate context need to be well understood. In addition, since the field in question has fast dynamics, the relevant literature should be followed closely, considering that new discussions can be added to the existing discussions.

## CONCLUSION

The digitalization of society is seen as inevitable. In addition to its cultural effects, institutional effects will be systematically investigated and new infrastructures and arrangements will be needed by humanity. In order to propose local, national and global solutions more accurately, the conceptual framework should be agreed.

With the European Union's Declaration of Digital Rights and Principles, it explains its Digital Strategy within the framework of 6 basic principles in order to reduce the possible harms of the digital public sphere (European Economic and Social Committee, 2017). These;

1. Putting people at the center of digital transformation,
2. Solidarity and inclusion,
3. Freedom of choice,
4. Digital public space,
5. Safety, security and authorization,
6. Sustainability.

Since the political conjuncture and cultural structures differ, a global integration without increasing inequalities is only possible with the support of digitalization. In this process, people should be focused, new generations should be educated about these issues and be aware of the dangers involved.

## REFERENCES

Balsmeier, B., & Woerter, M. (2019). Is this time different? How digitalization influences job creation and destruction. *Research Policy*, *48*(8), 1–1. doi:10.1016/j.respol.2019.03.010

Barocas, S., & Selbst, A. D. (2016). Big Data's Disparate Impact. *SSRN*. doi:10.2139srn.2477899

Bobrowicz-Campos, E., & Matos, A. P. (2022). Ageing and Health in the Digital Society: Challenges and Opportunities. In I. Management Association (Ed.), Research Anthology on Supporting Healthy Aging in a Digital Society (pp. 1-17). IGI Global. doi:10.4018/978-1-6684-5295-0.ch001

Bruns, A. (2019). Filter bubble. *Internet Policy Review*, *8*(4). doi:10.14763/2019.4.1426

Cemiloglu, D., Almourad, M. B., McAlaney, J., & Ali, R. (2022). Combatting digital addiction: Current approaches and future directions. *Technology in Society*, *6*, 101832. doi:10.1016/j.techsoc.2021.101832

Chayko, M. (2020). *Superconnected: The Internet, Digital Media, and Techno-Social Life*. SAGE Publications, Inc.

Di Sacco, A., Hardwick, K. A., Blakesley, D., Brancalion, P. H. S., Breman, E., Cecilio Rebola, L., Chomba, S., Dixon, K., Elliott, S., Ruyonga, G., Shaw, K., Smith, P., Smith, R. J., & Antonelli, A. (2021). Ten golden rules for reforestation to optimize carbon sequestration, biodiversity recovery and livelihood benefits. *Global Change Biology*, *27*(7), 1328–1348. doi:10.1111/gcb.15498 PMID:33494123

Dulong de Rosnay, M., & Stalder, F. (2020). Digital commons. *Internet Policy Review*, *9*(4). doi:10.14763/2020.4.1530

European Economic and Social Committee. (2017). *The future evolution of civil society in the European Union by 2030*. EU Press.

Floridi, L. (Ed.). (2015). *The Onlife Manifesto Being Human in a Hyperconnected Era*. Springer Open Press.

Goldsmith, J., & Wu, T. (2006). *Who Controls the Internet?: Illusions of a Borderless World*, 175. Faculty Books. https://scholarship.law.columbia.edu/books/175

Habermas, J. (2003). *The Future of Human Nature*. Polity Press.

Haidi, H. (2023). A Digital Ethnographic Account of a Digital Islamic Society During COVID-19: An Islamic Governance Perspective. In M. Anshari, A. Razzaq, M. Fithriyah, & A. Kamal (Eds.), *Digital Psychology's Impact on Business and Society* (pp. 150–178). IGI Global. doi:10.4018/978-1-6684-6108-2.ch007

Han, C., Wang, H., Hahn, A., Fisher, C., Kandrik, M., Fasolt, V., Morrison, D., Lee, A., Debruine, L., & Jones, B. (2017). Cultural differences in preferences for facial coloration. *Evolution and Human Behavior*, *39*(2), 154–159. doi:10.1016/j.evolhumbehav.2017.11.005

Hindman, M. (2018). *The Internet Trap: How the Digital Economy Builds Monopolies and Undermines Democracy*. Princeton University Press. doi:10.4018/978-1-6684-5295-0.ch001

Just, N., & Latzer, M. (2017). Governance by Algorithms: Reality Construction by Algorithmic Selection on the Internet. *Media, Culture & Society, 39*(2), 238-258. , https://ssrn.com/abstract=3871903 doi:10.1177/0163443716643157

Katzenbach, C., & Bächle, T. C. (2019). Defining concepts of the digital society. *Internet Policy Review*, *8*(4). doi:10.14763/2019.4.1430

Kökcü, M. (2021). Global Transformation of the Public Sphere in the Digital World: From Public to Silent Sphere? *Academia Letters*. *Article*, *3018*. doi:10.20935/AL3018

Lahlou, S. (2008). Identity, social status, privacy and face-keeping in digital society. *Social Sciences Information. Information Sur les Sciences Sociales*, *47*(3), 299–330. doi:10.1177/0539018408092575

Lee, J. D., & See, K. A. (2004). Trust in Automation: Designing for Appropriate Reliance. *Human Factors*, *46*(1), 50–80. doi:10.1518/hfes.46.1.50.30392 PMID:15151155

Matzner, T., & Ochs, C. (2019). Privacy. *Internet Policy Review*, *8*(4). doi:10.14763/2019.4.1427

McIntyre, D. P., & Srinivasan, A. (2017). Networks, platforms, and strategy: Emerging views and next steps. *Strategic Management Journal, 38*(1), 141–160. doi:10.1002mj.2596

Mejias, U. A., & Couldry, N. (2019). Datafication. *Internet Policy Review, 8*(4). doi:10.14763/2019.4.1428

Parasuraman, R., & Manzey, D. H. (2010). Complacency and bias in human use of automation: An attentional integration. *Human Factors, 52*(3), 381–410. doi:10.1177/0018720810376055 PMID:21077562

Plantin, J. C., Lagoze, C., Edwards, P. N., & Sandvig, C. (2018). Infrastructure studies meet platform studies in the age of Google and Facebook. *New Media & Society, 20*(1), 293–310. doi:10.1177/1461444816661553

Poell, T., Nieborg, D., & van Dijck, J. (2019). Platformisation. *Internet Policy Review, 8*(4). doi:10.14763/2019.4.1425

Rascão, J. P. (2021). The Value of Economic Information in the Digital Society. [JTA]. *Journal of Technological Advancements, 1*(1), 1–33. doi:10.4018/JTA.20210101.oa3

Schmidt, F. A. (2017). *Digital labour markets in the platform.* The Friedrich-Ebert-Stiftung.

Sennett, R. (2003). *The Fall of Public Man.* Penguin Books Ltd.

Sezgin, A. A. (2018). Selfies: New Visual Culture of New Digital Society. In S. Hai-Jew (Ed.), *IGI Global.*, doi:10.4018/978-1-5225-3373-3.ch004

Shayo, E. H., Kivuyo, S., Seeley, J., Bukenya, D., Karoli, P., Mfinanga, S. G., Jaffar, S., & van Hout, M. C. (2022). The acceptability of integrated healthcare services for HIV and non-communicable diseases: Experiences from patients and healthcare workers in Tanzania. *BMC Health Services Research, 22*(1), 655. doi:10.118612913-022-08065-4 PMID:35578274

Yeung, K. (2018). Algorithmic regulation: A critical interrogation. *Regulation & Governance, 12*(4), 505–523. doi:10.1111/rego.12158

## ADDITIONAL READING

Aarts, E., Fleuren, H., Sitskoorn, M., & Wilthagen, T. (Eds.). (2021). The New Common. How the COVID-19 Pandemic is Transforming Society. Springer Cham. doi:10.1007/978-3-030-65355-2

Blanchard, A., & Taddeo, M. (2023). The Ethics of Artificial Intelligence for Intelligence Analysis: A Review of the Key Challenges with Recommendations. *DISO, 2*(1), 12. doi:10.100744206-023-00036-4 PMID:37034181

Borges, G., & Sorge, C. (2022). *Law and Technology in a Global Digital Society Autonomous Systems, Big Data, IT Security and Legal Tech.* Springer Cham. doi:10.1007/978-3-030-90513-2

Housley, W., Edwards, A., Montagut, R. B., & Fitzgerald, R. (2023). *The SAGE Handbook of Digital Society.* SAGE Publications. doi:10.4135/9781529783193

Perriam, J., & Carter, S. (2021). *Understanding Digital Societies.* SAGE Publications.

Russo, F. (2023). Digital Society is a Choice. *DISO*, *2*(1), 11. doi:10.100744206-023-00042-6

Wynn, M. G. (Ed.). (2022). *Handbook of Research on Digital Transformation, Industry Use Cases, and the Impact of Disruptive Technologies*. IGI Global. doi:10.4018/978-1-7998-7712-7

Zhou, M., Mahlangu, G., & Matsika, C. (Eds.). (2022). *Digital Transformation for Promoting Inclusiveness in Marginalized Communities*. IGI Global. doi:10.4018/978-1-6684-3901-2

## KEY TERMS & DEFINITION

**Digital Transformation:** It is a concept that needs to find solutions to social and sectoral needs with the application of digital technologies and, accordingly, the speed of work and the developments and consumption they have achieved.

**Digitalization:** It is the name given to the process of transferring accessible information to digital media in a way that can be read by any computer.

**Public Sphere:** The concept used in modern social theories to point to the common social activity area where thoughts, discourses and actions aimed at determining and realizing the common good of society are produced and developed.

# Chapter 2
# Industry 5.0, Digital Society, and Consumer 5.0

**Cüneyd İkbal Sarıoğlu**
*Kocaeli University, Turkey*

## ABSTRACT

*Emerging technologies have transformed different industrial eras. Recent Industry 5.0 has created various innovative technologies, including big data, artificial intelligence (AI), the internet of things (IoT), virtual reality, cloud computing, and cobots. Industry 5.0 encompasses three core values: human centricity, resilience, and sustainability. Industry 5.0 has various enabling technologies supporting the industrial transformation, including digital twins, cobots, mass customisation, and hyper-personalisation. Digital transformation has affected all areas, including business organisations with all functions and marketing. Marketers have created different and innovative strategies using technological supports stemming from Industrial and societal revolutions. Industry 5.0 proposes a new marketing paradigm with mass customisation, and in this process, a new type of "super-empowered customer" or "consumer 5.0" has been created.*

## INTRODUCTION

Technological advancements have continued since Industry 1.0 or the first Industrial Revolution. The starting point of the Industrial development process prior to Industry 5.0 was the Industry 1.0 era in the 1870s. Then assembly lines with electrical energy and mass production were the symbols of Industry 2.0. The Industry 3.0 era started in the 1970s with transistors and microprocessors, and the main actors of this era were electronics and Information Technologies that integrated automation into production lines. Thus, the industry 4.0 era has been related to some technological innovations, namely the Internet of Things (IoT), cloud computing, and Artificial Intelligence (AI), and in this process, the real-time interface of the virtual world and physical world has been possible (Mourtzis, 2016; ElMaraghy et al., 2021). These developments have improved efficiency and product and service quality (Rüßmann et al., 2015). Industry 4.0 has been driven technologically, conceptualising the recent rapid change of technology and emerging new industries with changing social processes and patterns.

DOI: 10.4018/978-1-6684-8397-8.ch002

The pillar technologies of Industry 4.0 focused on the technological developments in production and network areas (i.e., digitalisation and digitisation) through industrial efficiency and flexibility over worker welfare and industrial sustainability (Xu et al., 2021). Consequently, the industrial transformation, utilising the current technological opportunities for the benefit of humankind, including social factors, was aimed. Developed countries, including the European Union countries and the USA, followed the leadership of Japan towards creating Industry 5.0 in a more human-focused manner. The new Industry 5.0 era has also been extended to Society 5.0. It is said that Industry 5.0 is a dynamic technological development process. Hence, Industry 5.0, followed by Society 5.0, has been under construction. Industry 5.0 has been updating the previous versions of Industrial Revolutions by bringing new dimensions (Verma et al., 2022, p.69160). The general understanding of Industry 5.0 has been different from previous industrial revolution eras, proposed that Industry 5.0 as a social and technological phenomenon has transformed old-style profit-based and consumption-driven business models into regenerative, resilient, sustainable, and circular value-creating models (Ghobakhloo et al., 2022, p.718).

In this chapter, the Industry 5.0 era will be reviewed following the Industry 4.0 paradigm, and the connection to Society 5.0 will be made through literature. This chapter focuses on the changing marketing paradigm and its relationship with Industry 5.0 and Society 5.0. Specifically, the new consumer, consumer 5.0, and prosumer profiles created by emerging technologies and applications were analysed through the last divisions of the chapter.

## BACKGROUND: INDUSTRY 5.0

The evolving technologies have transformed different industrial eras, and the incremental process has been accelerated with transistors and microprocessors as Industry 3.0. Computer and communications technologies made it happen more quickly with the automation process as Industry 4.0. Thus, Industry 4.0 is well-known for innovative technologies, including Big Data, artificial intelligence, augmented and virtual realities, cloud computing, adaptive robotics, additive manufacturing, and the Internet of Things (Ustundag & Cevikcan, 2017; Frank et al., 2019; Krishnan, 2021). Also, the organisations of Industry 4.0 are flexible and make their decisions based on data. Industry 5.0 drives the future technology for the next generations that are designed by efficient and intelligent machines (Adel, 2022). The post-industrial society in the 1980s focused on the organisation of information and knowledge, guiding innovation and change, and acting as a social control agent that has been transformed with digitalisation (Mourtzis et al., 2022). The information society has been one of the results of the Industrial Revolution.

The idea of the information society is built on a capitalist system; the modern knowledge society is based on technological transformation and innovations to process data and create new knowledge. Thus, the real World and Cyberspace real world have been increasingly integrated, and further research should focus on finding possible collaborative relationships (Mourtzis, 2018, p.197). Industry 4.0 has shifted from a massive automation approach to a customer-driven paradigm. This transformation process has been related to virtual and extended reality integration, artificial intelligence-based supply chains, twin designs collaborative robots, and digital machinery prototyping (Lu et al., 2020). Although the Industry 4.0 paradigm has yet to be scattered worldwide, technological pioneers and many business and technology investors have been trying to reach Industry 5.0 (Breque et al., 2021).

Industry 5.0 focused on creating a close interaction of the process with cobots (coordinated robots) and also tried to link communication between the supply chain, the factory, the end-user, and transportation. At low cost, manufacturing innovations and digital transformation in different areas are triggered by vast data collection, transmission, analysis, and storage (Mamasioulas et al., 2020). Data analysis is used to make problems more visible and produce potential solutions. The knowledge produced is instantly shared globally to help solve managerial and social problems. There are the Internet of Things (IoT), artificial intelligence (AI), blockchains, 5G, and robotics as examples of digital transformation to make fundamental changes in society (Gill et al., 2019).

Industry 5.0 looks at people at the system's centre through three crucial aspects: inclusivity, sustainability, and quality of life. The primary aim of Industry 5.0 is to create a better world where workers are happy in a better life and are well-trained for higher productivity and automated processes. Industry 5.0 offers penalisation, user-based customisation, cognitive domain integrated into human intelligence, and transition to the natural environment. Thus, the cause for Industry 5.0 is creating innovative societies, and the critical technology of Industry 5.0 is the human and robot interaction with reproducible energy (Verma et al., 2022, p.69163).

Industry 5.0 has been fuelled by digital transformation with creativity and imagination. Digital transformation is not a mere technological change as it shows some aspects of social and cultural dimensions. It represents a reform for establishing new societal values. Thus digital transformation may be considered a paradigm shift more than IT system changes. *Digital transformation* is defined as fundamental changes in society implemented by organisations, industries, and individuals; as a result, exploitation of Digital Technologies (Keidanren, 2022).

## Core Values of Industry 5.0

Industry 5.0 contains three core values, including sustainability, resilience, technology and human-centricity (Leng et al., 2022, p.282);

***Sustainability*** refers to using energy efficiency, renewable energy, energy storage and autonomy, production techniques, and other environmental sustainability means. It is also related to sustainable economic processes for improving the use of materials, reducing waste, and environmental impact. Industry 5.0 has some boundaries for environmental sustainability. The focus of industry 5.0 is on sustainability, and the production process is also related to creative human touch and robots (Demir et al., 2019; Nahavandi et al., 2019).

***Resilience*** represents the need for developing a system having higher robustness in the manufacturing process, precautions against disruptions, and providing and supporting critical infrastructure for crisis management. Industry 5.0 promises that future industries will be resilient to manage natural emergencies and significant political shifts.

***Technology*** is under the control of human factors to serve society, as manufacturing technology is adaptive to the diversity of industrial workers and the needs of society (Lu et al., 2021). Traditional manufacturing paradigms may be developed with new cobots empowering line workers to provide further flexibility in the production area. Industry 5.0 enables cooperation between technology, humans, and machines with technological advances' economic, social, and environmental impacts. Industry 5.0 proposes that the next generation will see cleaner, smarter, and more resilient industries.

***The human-centric approach*** to emerging technologies proposes combining sustainability and competitiveness with emerging tools, including artificial intelligence, cobots, and big data techniques. The human-centric paradigm focuses on core human interests and needs in the production process, being a more human-focused and society-driven approach rather than technology-driven progress (Longo et al.,

2020). Hence, the centrality of human capital in Industry 5.0 includes the collaboration of people and machines, analysing how workers and machines collaborate. Industrial workers may benefit from this collaboration by upskilling and developing themselves for work-life balance and better career opportunities (Breque et al., 2021). The new worker profiles change their value from "cost" to "investment." Society 5.0 is planned as a human-focused society centred around people aiming at reaching sustainable development goals, as stated in the 2030 Agenda for Sustainable Development by United Nations (De Felice et al., 2021). A metric system named Society 5.0 Index (S5I), created to evaluate each country's performance, has helped understand Society 5.0 in different settings (De Hoyos Guevara et al., 2021).

## Enabling Technologies of Industry 5.0

Industry 5.0 has various enabling technologies that combine technologies, including human-machine interaction, intelligent materials, big data analytics, cloud computing, artificial intelligence, and others. Innovative technologies and intelligent systems facilitate transactions to manage networks and privacy (Adel, 2022, p.11). Some of the enabling technologies in the process of Industry 5.0 that ensure the industrial transformation are as follows;

***Mass customisation*** is central to the digital user experience within the Industry 5.0 process. Mass customisation has been a fundamental production paradigm that proposes producing personalised products and services in high volumes at costs close to average mass production costs (Bednarz, 2022). Emerging technologies, such as product family architecture, and reconfigurable manufacturing systems, enable mass customisation and delay differentiation (Hu, 2013).

***Hyper personalisation*** refers to acquiring real-time data on consumer behaviours to personalise product and service experiences for different user preferences. Also, the industrial production area puts hyper-personalisation at the system's centre to ensure a common understanding of the specific goods and services, the users' features, and the technology behind the process. Personalised marketing strategies were based on acquired knowledge of digital technologies using computer vision, machine learning, and artificial intelligence, ensuring industrial processes for specific products.

***Collaborative Robots*** (cobots) integrate enhanced visual and sensor technologies enabling human factors and machines to work together. Industry 5.0 proposes using human factors in production and development processes. Humans' ability to perform critical tasks allows them to individualise the production process. Human inputs develop collaborative robotics in the process of Industry 5.0, and it represents a new age in robotics. The cobot phenomenon is at the heart of the Industry 5.0 paradigm combining human creativity with the power and efficiency of the (Adel, 2022, p.7). Cobots are created to work with humans, and human elements enhance their capacity for production purposes. Northwestern University scientists designed the first cobots in 1996. Cobots are fully personalised for specific processes. Cobots are used for different purposes in different sectors, including healthcare, automotive, construction, and many other industries (Fanibhare et al., 2021).

Cobots can be programmed and trained to work with humans on the production line, and they can be reprogrammed at any time for more complete and different tasks assigned. Four different types of cobots can be classified as "power and force-limiting cobots,"; "speed and separation cobots,"; "hand-guided cobots," and "safety-rated and monitored-stop cobots." In Industry 5.0, collaborative robots involve some human intervention to optimise and maximise their efficiency; on the other hand, robots operate in a fully-autonomous way as there is limited human intervention. Cobots, working with humans, can achieve their objectives, and they help to deliver personalised and mass-customised products and services to customers with accuracy and high speed (Maddikunta et al., 2022, p.15). However, it is predicted that they will not replace human resources and will accomplish routine jobs, leaving critical tasks for human resources. (Elangovan, 2022, p.41).

***Digital twins*** represent the industrial setups created to reproduce the behavioural patterns of physical objects (Dev et al., 2022). The sensors of a specific machine are used to control the motion, power control, and operations, generating data on the actual performance of the process in terms of weather conditions, energy output, and temperature. Digital twins use real-time data as the data is analysed with machine learning and digital twins (Maddikunta et al., 2022, p.16).

***Cloud computing*** includes delivering computing services, including software, databases, intelligence analytics, networks, and others. This emerging technology offers the economics of scale and efficient innovation. This new technology is based on the Internet and is used to store, process and analyse data through all remote servers, and cloud computing creates a supportive framework for various business applications. Cloud computing is used for manufacturing applications through IoT monitoring devices with mobile, web applications, and application programming interfaces (Cioffi et al., 2020).

***Big data analytics*** is an advanced analytic method creating a complex system to manage big data to explore hidden market trends and patterns. It uses diverse data sources to store and analyse using real-time data sets. Big data analytics helps businesses to be more competitive through strategic decisions supported by big data analytics. Big data analytics are used for various business purposes, including marketing area. Customer preferences are analysed to improve customer experiences and build strong customer relationships. Big data analytics has been a powerful tool for enabling Industry 5.0 (Adel, 2022, p.8).

***Blockchain technology*** is another enabling technology of Industry 5.0 as an automated agreement process with various stakeholders. *Blockchain* is a decentralised and distributed technology that keeps digital ledgers, including data, as blocks. Digital ledgers are used to share the data and all transactions by all authorised stakeholders. In marketing, blockchain technology supports customers by monitoring orders, production, payments, and other functions. Smart contracts are stored on a blockchain system to speed up secure transactions (Adel, 2022, p.9). Artificial intelligence integrates human expertise to enhance cognitive abilities and ensure precise control. Industry 5.0 creates a suitable environment to create such manufacturing processes designed for the customised demands of the customers. Thus, Industry 5.0 has been an excellent strategy to increase production quality with the division of labour between robots and humans; as robots are assigned to manage routine and repetitive jobs, people are responsible for intelligent tasks and critical thinking (Demir et al., 2019; Tanwar et al., 2022). Industry 4.0 era and Industry 5.0 transformation are compared from the blockchain technology perspective in table 1.

## Challenges and Responses for Industry 5.0

Industry 5.0 approach posits some unique challenges and responses, including measurement of social and environmental value generation, social heterogeneity of values and acceptance, system complexity and inter-discipline research, integration from value chains of customers in SMEs, agile, outcome-oriented, and ecosystem-based innovation policy. Significant investments and productivity are required (Xu et al., 2021). Also, the European Commission (EC) initiated some policies to promote Industry 5.0 (European Commission, 2022). Also, Industry 5.0 needs substantial investment from various government agencies. Industry 5.0's future depends on the abovementioned core values of resilience: human-centricity and sustainability. Thus, Industry 5.0 has become a major driving force for Society 5.0 (societal progress fuelled by Industry 5.0), as understandable from current government national policies

*Table 1. A comparison of Industry 4.0 and Industry 5.0 features with blockchain*

| Industry 4.0 | Industry 5.0 | Limitations in Industry 4.0 | Limitations in Industry 5.0 |
|---|---|---|---|
| Intelligent supply chain | Distributed supply chain | Administrative access is limited to a single party, which is increases data tampering and misplaced control | Only insertion is allowed which prevents tampering and ensures transparency |
| Mass automation | Collaborative AI | Replaces barriers in networked locations with an increase in cobot communication to yield more productivity | Increased access control is guaranteed with SCs |
| Smart products | Experience activated products | Not customized as per user personal needs | Allow hyper-customization at large scales by ensuring data privacy using BC |
| Focus on connecting machines | Focus on delivering customer experience | End goal (customer experience) often ignored | Trusted and auditable customer-oriented solutions |
| Mass customization | Hyper-personalization | Leaves all the work to the user to generate the best experience for themselves | Immutable ledgers of networked data control processes to streamline the industrial processes |

**Source:** Verma et al., (2022), p.69164.

In the future, Industry 5.0 will develop and expand opportunities for cognitive computing, quantum computing, and human and machine interaction. The main challenges to Industry 5.0 are privacy, security, lack of skilled workers, the need for a large budget, and a time-consuming process. Adopting industry 5.0 for human factors requires following industrial regulations related to working with intelligent machines, especially cobots. Industry 5.0 and Society 5.0 are fuelled by technological developments on a more human-centred perspective through innovation fur sustaining competitive advantages (Aslam et al., 2020). As the importance of AI and robots has increased, IoT, augmented reality, intelligent technologies, innovative ecosystems, and smart societies have enabled human-machine interactions (Nahavandi, 2019; Breque et al., 2021). Thus, Industry 5.0 is related to combining creativity and human brainpower through sustainability and competitive advantage" (Aslam et al., 2020). Industry 5.0 increases the prosperity of investors, workers, society, and all.

## SOCIETY 5.0

The evolving industrial sectors towards the Industry 5.0 paradigm are inevitably related to the parallel development of the study as innovations focus not only on improving productivity but also on solving social challenges (Mavrodieva & Shaw, 2020). Within Society 5.0 concept, some innovations, including IT, IoT, robotics, augmented reality, and AI, are used for the good of society. Innovation represents a long-term strategy initiated by the Japanese Cabinet Office to support innovation in Japanese society. Japanese understanding of the industrial revolution comes with social transformation with the realisation of a Society 5.0 or "super smart society". Thus, the service dimension of the innovation process in Industrial 5.0 has been emphasised with tacit knowledge based on knowledge society (Fujii et al., 2018, p.634).

The society in Industry 5.0 started its transition from focusing on production and profit only to transforming into a post-industrial society based on knowledge. Traditional society has been undergoing a revolutionary structural change due to Industry 5.0. Society 5.0 has been distinguished by values offered by Industry 5.0, including diversity, value creation, problem-solving, resilience, decentralisation, environmental harmony, and sustainability. Society 5.0 is a more humanistic version of the Industry 4.0 environment. Society 5.0 is "a system containing a human-centric society balancing economic transformation through a solution of social challenges integrating physical space and cyberspace" (Huang et al., 2022). Digital transformation creates a diverse society and pursues happiness uniquely (Keidanren, 2022). Society 5.0 creates people typology having diverse values and lifestyles. The people in Society 5.0 focus on solving problems, creating value, and meeting individual needs. Society 5.0 aims to eliminate the danger of cyberattacks, terrorism, natural disasters, poverty, and unemployment. The main goal of Society 5.0 is to design a social structure that value creation is possible from any location and at any time, in harmony and safety, freeing various constraints of today's society (Nakanishi, 2022).

## Emergence of the Society 5.0

The success of the Japanese government and economy has been related to three arrows offered by Japanese Prime Minister Shinzo Abe, including fiscal stimulus, monetary easing, and growth strategy; two arrows supported the Japanese miracle of staying afloat (Roblek et al., 2020). The last arrow, growth strategy, has long-term consequences, and Society 5.0 paradigm was also included in this strategy in 2019. Japan has created an anthropocentric society integrating psychical and cyberspace as a paradigm balancing technological and economic progress with solutions to social problems.

Society 5.0 promoted the Smart Society idea, and digital transformation radically changed society with private and public spheres and industrial areas. Society 5.0 share the same objectives as the 2030 Agenda for Sustainable Development, with the agreement of all the UN member states in 2015. Thus, Society 5.0 helps to maintain these Goals of Sustainable Development. Thus, Industry 5.0 is designed to enable sustainably and a policy-driven innovation discourse. A practical data collection method is made through sensors in Society 5.0 (Syed, 2021).

Society 5.0 approach represents a significant development through national innovation systems as a solution to rapid technological challenges. The required technologies to implement Society 5.0 have yet to develop as Society 5.0 proposes advanced forms of robotics, biotechnology, nano-technology, AI, IoT, and Big Data. The realisation of Society 5.0 will be made possible by employing Big Data to handle the vast quantities of data due to IoT data generation. Also, a "platform of smart society" in Society 5.0 is needed (Gladden, 2019, p.39). Generally, societal priorities should be addressed due to short-term commercial gains (Holroyd, 2022, p.3).

## Theoretical Framework

The Society 5.0 idea is supported by digital transformation, and it creates fundamental changes to society in general, including the economic system, government operations, and employment. The principles of Society 5.0 are followed by Industry 4.0 (between 2011 and 2030, in theory), as Industry 5.0 has yet to be fully developed (Ferreira & Serpa, 2018). Society 5.0 uses emerging production technologies of Industry 4.0 and for integration with society's everyday lives. Industry 4.0 employs evolving technologies to support effectiveness, organisational efficiency, and financial performance. Emerging technologies, including cobots, AI, IoT, augmented reality, VR, and other emerging human-computer technologies, are used to benefit society. The creation of a "smart factory" of the Industry 4.0 paradigm transforms into a "Super Smart Society" in Society 5.0 (Gladden, 2019, p.2). Thus, Society 5.0, as a service-oriented society, uses digital transformation tools of IoT to create a cyber-physical information society environment connecting intangible goods as information networks (Deguchi et al., 2020). So, Society 5.0 creates a sustainable socio-economic structure through big data, AI, IoT, and cobots. Society 5.0 proposes that human productivity is limited, and there should be more resources to end stagnation and thus create a new society type (Narvaez Rojas et al., 2021).

Two concepts offered by Industry 4.0 and then reflected in Society 5.0 paradigm are smart factories and intelligent urbanisation. The first concept is called the *smart factory*, proposing the pure application of technology to manufacturing processes for efficiency with greater flexibility, leaner processes, predictability, reliable productivity, and increased agility. Sustainability, as stressed before, is a part of the Industry 5.0 vision and involves sustainable principles on lower energy consumption and carbon emissions. Smart factories idea is based on the mutual interaction of humans and machines (Abubakr et al., 2020). The intelligent factory vision is very similar to the Society 5.0 idea of a human-centric society; all products and services are in service of people.

The transformation processes of Society 5.0 aims at ensuring lives of all people are comfortable with higher quality living conditions. This strategy includes five principles with ethical standards and answers to questions about how, where, how long, and which organisations should store, generate, and share customer data (Roblek et al., 2020). The Japanese AI Technology Strategy presents that AI is the critical technology for creating Society 5.0. AI may harm social relationships, such as ethical and practical concerns, job loss, social control, the issue of transferring responsibility from people to machines, and other errors (Peeters et al., 2021). The data transactions of private data, ethical issues, and privacy should be considered when offering predictive and customised services to the customer. Japanese government proposed creating universal principles about data sharing, and in 2019, they announced the Social Principles of Human-Centric AI 2019 (Fukuda, 2020).

The second issue is *smart urbanisation*, which is related to city development strategies based on emerging technological solutions transforming the cities into smart cities with AI-based systems. Thus, urban development strategies propose new technological solutions, including the Internet of Everything (IoE), Internet of Services (IoS), IoT blockchain technologies, AI technologies, introducing new economic models such as cycling and sharing economy, new sustainable materials, and the introduction of intelligent processes (e-health, e-mobility, e-government, e-social inclusion and e-education) for continuous development and finally reaching the form of citizens-oriented smart city (Sepasgozar et al., 2019). Thus, Society 5.0 aims for a citizen-centred and prosperous society (Gladden, 2019).

## The Outcomes of Society 5.0

Society 5.0 has also been termed a "humane society" or a "super-intelligent society". Digital transformation has affected many aspects of society through Society 5.0. Recent socio-economic changes take place with the application of innovative knowledge and technologies, such as cobots, sensors, automation, AI, intelligent structure and networks, big data, microelectronics, and real-time databases. Big data analytics is applied as a very effective source in improving customer communication which helps to produce effective outcomes through marketing strategies (Malik & Trivedi, 2022, p.10). Marketers can apply big data analytics to foresight the purchasing behaviour of customers based on their personal and demographic data.

The goals of Society 5.0 focused on the establishment of equal opportunities and maintaining the required environment for all (Serpa & Ferreira, 2019). Society 5.0 paradigm employs evolving technologies to remove social, physical and other barriers for people. That idea is at the core of Society 5.0, that everyone deserves a comfortable and healthy life. The emerging technologies of Society 5.0 provide the conditions to make life more enjoyable and meaningful for all people, including consumers. In Society 5.0, human and technology interaction creates a sustainable and liveable people-centred environment" (Medina-Borja, 2017, p. 235). Industry 5.0 is a developed and evolved version of Industry 4.0, and Industry 5.0 will be fully achieved with the help of Society 5.0. In Society 5.0, societal revolutions are vital for achieving Industry 5.0 in a similar context. In Society 5.0, humans and cobots collaborate to create human-centric design solutions (Huang et al., 2022). However, with more robots and automation systems, the role of people in the system appears to decrease (Gladden, 2019, p.1).

According to experts, Industry 5.0 and Society 5.0 are interconnected, and both objectives will be achieved when AI is created and designed to lead organisational processes as predicted in 2030 (Fukuyama, 2018). It is predicted that the human and technology relationship will help and support evolution in Society 5.0, with the help of the present Industry 4.0 (Shiroishi et al., 2018). The society 5.0 approach was developed for sustainable development in Japan, and the model's components can be applied. Society 5.0 relates to the social domain as experts use some parts of the Japanese paradigm to modernise other social processes. Digital transformation helps create a new society with different people's features and lifestyles. Society 5.0 (super smart society) is described as a new era for the societal framework (Fujii et al., 2018). In Society 5.0, creativity has a special place, and imagination is needed to identify and satisfy people's needs and problems. In this respect, Society 5.0 is also considered a "Creative Society" with digital transformation through creativity and imagination. Figure 1 shows the changes from Society 4.0 Paradigm to Society 5.0 Paradigm.

## NEW CONSUMER IN TRANSITION: CONSUMER 5.0

The marketing paradigm has been changing over the years as marketers' and consumers' relationships adapt and use the Internet for business purposes. Consumers have become content creators in collaboration with some producers and consumers as they were only viewers of the content provided by producers in the past. This transformation directs producers to look for innovative business models for added-value creation for customers (Fukuda, 2020, p.8).

### Industry 5.0 and Changing Marketing Paradigm

Society 5.0 is proposed as a solution to Industrial 4.0 as many believe that Industry 4.0 reduces the human role in the work structure through emerging sophisticated Technologies and applications. Industry 5.0 has been emerging at the same time as Society 5.0 adds value with the help of high technology that is expected to reduce the economic problems of society in the future (Pamudyarini, 2021, p.395). The American Marketing Association explains consumer behaviour as the system of the relationship between awareness and influence, attitude, behaviour, and the dynamic environmental context (Peter et al., 2013, p. 3). Also, Kotler and Keller (2012: 173) propose that some cultural, social, personal, and psychological factors influence consumer behaviour. Technology is one of the most influential environmental factors in recent times.

*Figure 1. The changes from Society 4.0 paradigm to society 5.0 paradigm*

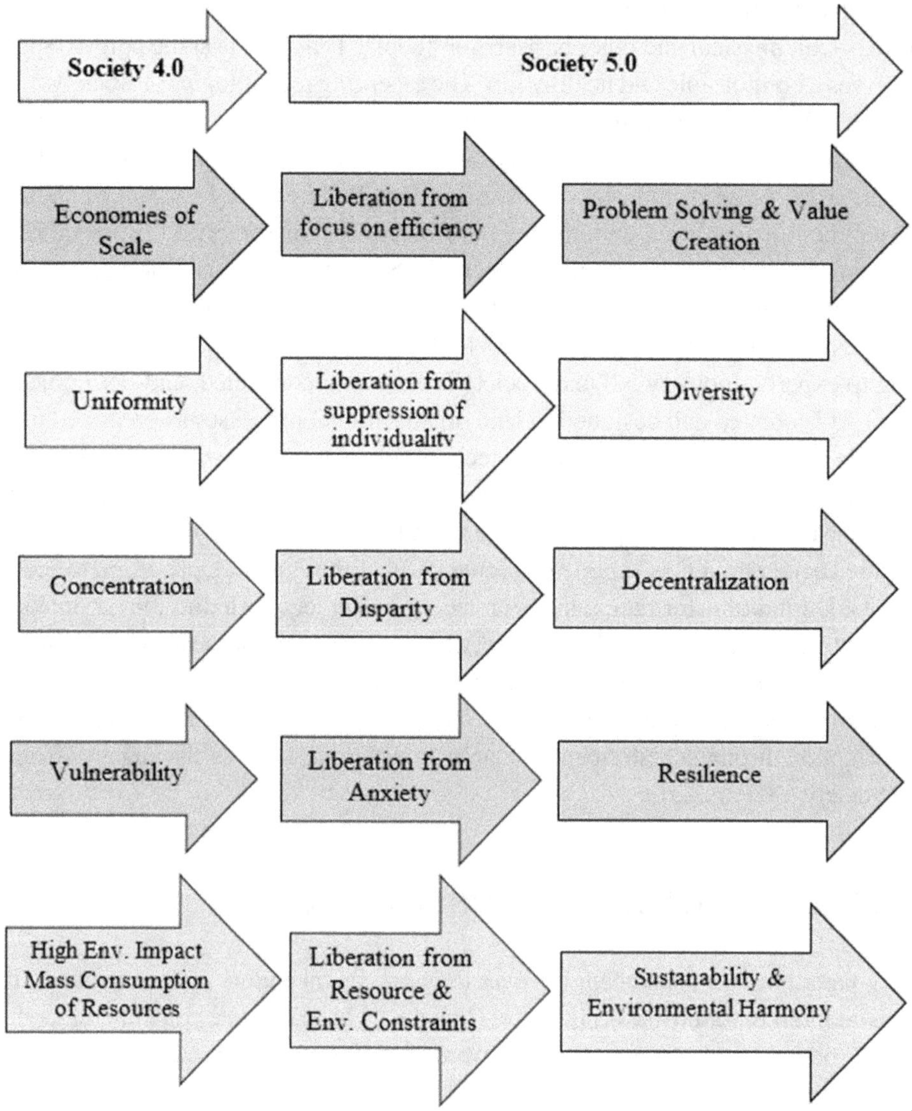


Industry 5.0 offers various benefits for all industries, employees, consumers, and society. Society 5.0 paradigm provides a vision for the future of the contribution of digital and industrial transformation through productivity and efficiency (Mourtzis et al., 2022). At the end of the process, the Society 5.0 paradigm enhances the contribution of the business environment to society. Industry 5.0 supports the environment in various ways. For example, Industry 5.0 supports using circular production technologies that use natural resources more efficiently and are eco-friendly. Digital technologies such as sensors and cloud computing have ensured a 'continuous connectivity' between product providers and consumers in a way that today, selling any product is the beginning of the process, not the end of the relationship (Rosemann et al., 2021). Industry 5.0 will build and strengthen consumers' consciousness of environmental and societal issues in the decision process of consumer purchasing behaviour (Nahavandi, 2019).

Society 5.0 unifies all areas in the economy, including production, market, mass distribution, digital, environmental, and intangible assets (Salgues, 2018).

Supply chain sides have been essential for all industries and customer relationships. Conscious energy consumption and innovative value chains can strengthen industries against disruptive events. Industry 5.0 aligns with three top priorities of the EC, including "An economy that works for people," Europe fit for the digital age", and the "European Green Deal" (De Pablos, 2021). The following principles are also accepted as part of European Commission policy principles (European Commission, 2022);

- ***Skills Agenda and Digital Education Action plan*** includes re-skilling and up-skilling of the European workers, especially skills;
- ***Proposal for AI regulation*** refers to the adoption of a human-centric approach to AI and other digital technologies;
- ***Industrial Strategy*** proposes a globally competitive business World and increasing investment in research and development, particularly innovation initiatives;
- ***Green Deal*** means modern, sustainable, and resource-efficient industries and thus leads to a circular economy.

The marketing paradigm has been evolving with environmental changes happening. Marketing 1.0 focused on product development and production efficiency. Marketing 2.0 is concerned with brand marketing through brand communication and brand experiences. Marketing 3.0 is related to mission marketing by creating human values. Marketing 4.0 considered digital marketing as a tool of marketing strategies, including engagement marketing, content marketing, experiential marketing, community marketing, viral marketing, and social marketing (Jiménez-Zarco et al., 2019). Marketers use digital marketing to reach customers through various channels, including the Internet, mobile devices, social media, and search engines, to attract existing and potential customers (Das, 2021). The marketing 5.0 era witnessed human and machine collaboration with the help of emerging technologies creating a new business ecosystem (Wongmonta, 2021, p.83). Revolutionary changes, emerging technologies, changes in consumer profiles, and changes in brand features have structured the new business ecosystem. The 4 P's marketing mix has become the 4 E's in Industry 5.0: exchange, experience, everyplace, and evangelism (Konhäusner et al., 2021). The marketing 5.0 era is based on the human-centricity of Marketing 3.0 and the technological concentration of Marketing 4.0 (Kartajaya et al., 2021).

## The Effects of Technology on Consumers

Recent technological developments enabled the expansion of social media, social commerce, mobile phones, and AI instruments, including augmented reality and virtual assistants, which have led to new patterns in consumer behaviour (Bartosik-Purgat & Mińska-Struzik, 2022, p.129). These developments are related not only to the transformation of technology but also to the acceptance by consumers (Wang et al., 2021). Accepting new technologies is related to many factors, including generational and cultural differences (Cochoy, et al., 2017). Primarily generational changes influence the acceptance behaviour as younger generations (gen Y and gen Z) are more ready to accept using digital applications to search for products and make purchasing decisions (Calvo-Porral & Pesqueira-Sanchez, 2020). However, old generations also prefer new products.

In Industry 5.0, automation and AI processes produce the specific product and services that customers demand. Customers can specify whatever they want to buy as innovative manufacturing allows greater flexibility and capacity to satisfy new customers (Aslam et al., 2020). Personalisation in marketing enables one to meet all customers' specific needs without delay or additional costs (Grewal et al., 2020). Industry 5.0, in terms of marketing, involves a transformation process from a mass customisation phase to a mass personalisation phase with the help of intelligent data usage data for sustainable development (Tiwari et al., 2022). Mass customisation addresses individual differences in demands involving customers in product and service development. Industry 5.0 creates a suitable environment to make sure that every single customer is satisfied. The mass customisation dimension within industry 4.0 transforms into the mass personalisation dimension of industry 5.0 (Javaid & Haleem, 2020). There is a human touch factor as a societal motive of Industry 5.0. Today, the traditional definition of quality customer is based on something other than friendly salespersons but customised services for customers to support their needs and lifestyles. An example is that Netflix supports and follows the desires and demands of its customers by offering them programs based on their preferences (Lee & Lee, 2020, p.3).

Emerging technologies are planned to support Industry 5.0 in production processes to deliver customers customised and personalised products and services (Maddikunta et al., 2022). Thus, Industry 5.0 aims to satisfy customers with the best customer experience. Sophisticated digital marketing strategies are used with AI and VR and machine-learning personalisation, through the whole process, from supply chain to marketing activities. Thus, Industry 5.0 has various tools in all areas to serve customers with personalisation. Marketing 5.0 is the application of high Technologies to deliver, create, enhance and communicate value to the new customer. Advanced technologies have a central role in Marketing 5.0, including AI, augmented reality, sensors, NLP, blockchain technologies, virtual reality, robotics, IoT, and IoE. IoE in Industry 5.0 was created to enhance customer loyalty and delight and to build customisation experiences based on IoE-based data (Maddikunta et al., 2022, p.15). Primarily AI has been used to replace human cognitive abilities to have customer data that are beneficial for marketing activities (Kartajaya et al., 2021).

Within the Industry 5.0 era, there are increased personalised products and services, green marketing practices, sustainable and environmental-friendly and intelligent products, and using new marketing technologies, which will combine human and technological factors for the new marketing paradigm. (Zengin & Zengin, 2022). Industry 5.0 empowers the most personalised and customised services to the customer through digital Technologies and applications. A study by Javaid and Haleem (2020) proposed some critical factors for Industry 5.0 manufacturing applications. The study concluded that applying Industry 5.0 in the manufacturing industry would increase customer satisfaction and value for the company (Javaid & Haleem, 2020).

Emerging technologies raise consumer issues, including discrimination and choice, transparency and disclosure, interoperability, privacy, security, and accountability (Ronit, 2021). Big data constitutes a new power to analyse customer behaviour. In Industry 5.0, the emergence of industrial robots helps produce mass-customised and personalised products. Industry 5.0 concentrates on the return of human factors to the production scene as the interaction of humans, and AI is a central issue in Industry 5.0 paradigm (Saniuk et al., 2022, p.3). Industry 5.0 enables strong human and machine interaction to predict new consumer behaviour (Tiwari et al., 2022, p.61). Digital activities of the consumers may be analysed by tracking real-time data to plan for the future moves of customers. Big data analytics offer some advantages to marketers for building brand loyalty (Malik & Trivedi, 2022, p.14).

## Consumer 5.0

The Industry 4.0 paradigm has shifted consumers' purchasing behaviours from traditional retailing to electronic and online platforms enabled by advanced digital technologies. Advanced technologies and intelligent digital devices have enabled remote customer services and, thus, a new type of customer (Lee & Lee, 2020, p.1). Recently, radical changes have occurred in the marketing environment, including the economy, high technology, globalisation, and government regulations, as these variables emerge new attitudes and behaviours from customers reflecting their desires and needs (Sanwal, 2022). For a sustainable competitive advantage, marketers must react to the demand changes quickly to satisfy all customer needs and demands to be customer-oriented (Dewi, 2021, p.181). The recent marketing concentration is also moving to green and sustainable marketing; thus, customers' purchasing decisions are affected by this transformation. Customers care for the quality of the goods and services, brand image, product features, and convenience of consumer transactions. Customers consider various transaction varieties through sophisticated business models, as the emergence of the Society 5.0 paradigm (Dewi, 2021, p.186).

When we look at the changes in consumer profiles over industrial revolutions and different industrial eras, digital transformation affected production, distribution, exchange, and consumption due to the new strategies and changing variables in every field in business sectors (Matarazzo et al., 2021). Mass customisation was created due to the first and second Industrial Revolutions and transformed into the "niche customer" with Industry 3.0. In Industry 4.0, a personalised customer type has emerged (Grabowska et al., 2022). In the mass customisation paradigm, consumers are considered integrated with product design and development (Mourtzis, 2016, p.1). Business organisations involve customers for their insights, and also personalisation strategy is created for various customer groups to affect their purchase behaviours through big data (Durmaz & Kitapcı, 2021, p.204). Today, personalisation and customer involvement are intertwined in the Industry 5.0 process.

Industry 5.0 proposes a new marketing model with mass customisation, and this process results in a new "super-empowered customer." Each customer's personalised production solutions through AI-based cognitive systems will be satisfied through hyper-customisation within the production processes (Maddikunta et al., 2022, p.18). Digital devices allow consumers to create and design unique, hyper-specific goods and services. New consumers will enjoy realistic and engaging experiences and use personalised customer experiences with the help of combined high-tech and creativity (Adel, 2022). The virtual world has all the customer's experiences, and service providers follow changes in consumer behaviour to improve real-world marketing performance with the help of digital devices (Leng et al., 2022, p.288). Industry 5.0 allows companies and marketing people to keep their customers in mind and to improve their relationships through some concepts (www.lxahub.com, 2022):

- *Cyber-Physical Cognitive Systems* combine the capabilities of AI and human-based systems to optimise purpose and performance. Thus, the day-to-day tasks of the companies are streamlined, and marketers can focus on their customers.
- *Transparency* can help by combining the human element and highly efficient automation, which can build trust.
- *Enterprise Agility* promotes agility in every function of the business organisation to enhance efficiency. As today's customer demands have been changing rapidly, organisational agility will ensure harmonisation with the rapidly changing environmental factors.

Emerging technologies enabled closer cooperation between consumers and producers, creating a new type of consumer, "the prosumer." The term presumption has been used to describe consumer participation in producing goods and services (Alhashem et al., 2021). Alvin Toffler proposed the prosumption concept in the late 1970s (Toffler, 1981). The term prosumption was the combination of the words production and consumption. However, Alvin Toffler first coined the terms prosumer and presumption in 1980. Prosumption has been described in earlier studies by scholars as "consumer becomes producer" (McLuhan et al., 1972).

Prosumers are more active, demanding, and conscious consumers (Tkaczyk, 2016, p.354). Prosumption is related to customer involvement, and prosumers participate in designing new products and services, improving materials, enhancing product reliability and durability, and being active in designing packaging and other production processes (Bartosik-Purgat & Bednarz, 2021). The possibility of participating in the production process is attractive to consumers, as this will get them involved in the company's activities. This trend is more attractive to younger generations. This idea may be enabled by implementing new IT and social media (Bednarz, 2022, p.32).

Prosumers are different from digital and e-consumers as prosumers are more active in participating in product design and services. Prosumers demand mass customisation and personalisation; thus, human factors cannot be replaced by a robot or any other machine in the industry (Lu et al., 2021). E-consumers are inhabitants of virtual environments, and they purchase online, and digital consumers do not necessarily have to make online purchases as they can take advantage of digital content. Digital consumers may be either active (blogging, commenting) or passive (visiting websites) (Tkaczyk, 2016, p.354). As a result of digital transformation, digital consumer behaviour has been changed with more value creation focus, and new consumers, have become co-creators of value. The collaboration between consumers and businesses has recently increased, and consumers have been more active in value creation (Ipek, 2020, p.183). Figure 2 shows the new prosumer value propositions.

*Figure 2. The new prosumer value propositions*

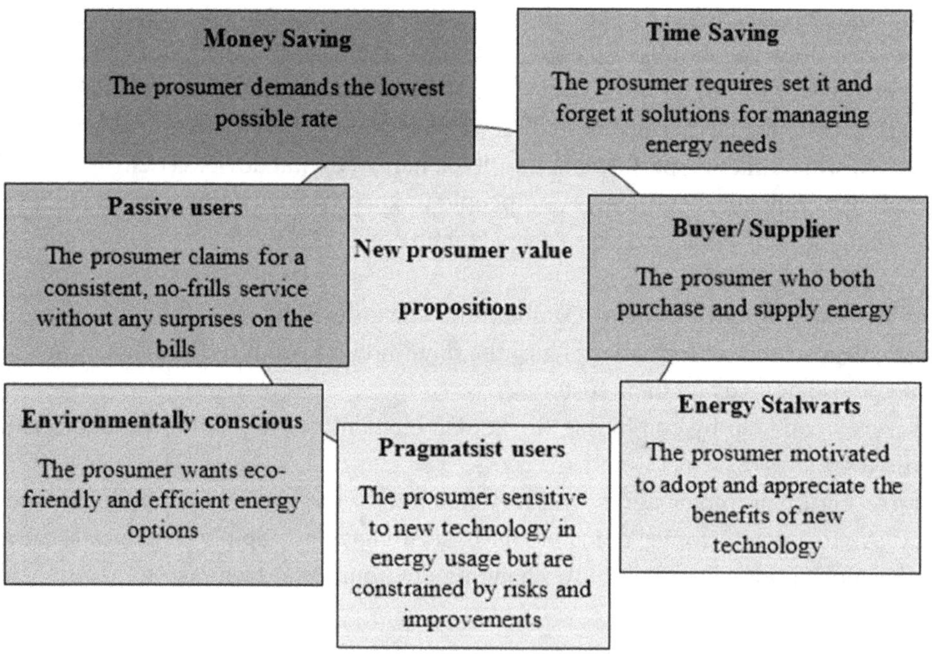

## Future Research and Directions

The applications of Industry 5.0 and Society 5.0 will give a clearer picture of the challenges and future directions for the marketing area. Society 5.0 paradigm set the framework for the Marketing 5.0 era with a new type of consumer, as we call it consumer 5.0, with competencies of using digital technologies to analyse the needs and participate in the design process of the products and services to ensure the satisfaction of the consumers. Industry 5.0 and Society 5.0 revolutions enabled humans to add high value to manufacturing systems. Legalisation and standardisation issues will significantly relate to new technology and transformation in business systems and society in future studies. The adaptation process of the stakeholders will be a new challenge to be investigated by the researchers. The researchers should consider the transparency and trust issues within the context of the new era. Thus ethical considerations of the new society and the new marketing era will be new research areas. Future research should focus on the human side of marketing, concentration on technological advancements.

## CONCLUSION

Industry 4.0 has strongly focused on technological solutions. However, Industry 4.0 is not considered human-centricity, resilience, and sustainability but has technological priority. Industry 5.0 switched from single technologies to more systematic approaches. Industry 5.0 empowers stakeholders to reach social goals more than economic growth and profit. It also focuses on the well-being and happiness of the stakeholders, including workers and consumers of the industry at the system's centre. This point explains why Industry 5.0 has been different from previous Industrial Revolutions. Industry 5.0 has been developed to harmonise human-machine interaction efficiency and working space. Thus, Industry 5.0, enabled by various emerging technologies and applications, is expected to increase customer satisfaction.

Industrial 5.0 is not simply a substitute for Industry 4.0, as Industry 5.0 is a vision of the future and how societal trends will be shaped. Although European Union declared six enabling technologies of Industry 5.0, Industry 4.0 might help realise the social goals of Industry 5.0. Various focused technologies of Industry 5.0 are essential to achieve the objective of Society 5.0, which are the technologies for energy efficiency, energy storage, and renewable energy. In this respect, recent developments in Industry 4.0 research have already contributed to Industry 5.0. Thus, Industry 4.0 as a technology-driven concept and Industry 5.0 as a value-driven concept should be considered together. Industry 5.0 is sometimes called a Techno-Social System.

Society 5.0 proposes a society where people can enjoy life and satisfy. Technological development and economic growth exist for social objectives, not only economic objectives. Although Society 5.0 paradigm originates from Japan, Society 5.0 would serve all societies worldwide with emerging technologies developed. Technological advances and economic and societal consequences drive the industry 5.0 Revolution. Industry 5.0, as a value-driven system, has human-centricity, including customers and consumers. New consumers do not only personalise their demands but also analyse and shape their desires, and their societal values and needs are also at the centre of the new marketing paradigm. Society 5.0 will have the potential to expand and deepen interest in new consumer profiles.

The definitions and tools of industry 5.0 are quite expandable by industrial and academic communities. In this chapter, the theories of Industry 5.0 and Society 5.0 are explained in detail to differentiate the idea of 5.0 from the previous eras. The consumer 5.0 concept may constitute an excellent opportunity to analyse the recent marketing changes; in return, it may provide some information for companies to update their marketing strategies.

## REFERENCES

Abubakr, M., Abbas, A. T., Tomaz, I., Soliman, M. S., Luqman, M., & Hegab, H. (2020). Sustainable and smart manufacturing: An integrated approach. *Sustainability (Basel), 12*(6), 2280. doi:10.3390u12062280

Adel, A. (2022). Future of industry 5.0 in society: Human-centric solutions, challenges and prospective research areas. *Journal of Cloud Computing (Heidelberg, Germany), 11*(1), 1–15. doi:10.118613677-022-00314-5 PMID:36101900

Alhashem, M., Moraes, C., & Szmigin, I. T. (2020). Use and social value in peer-to-peer prosumption communities. *European Journal of Marketing*, 1–55.

Aslam, F., Aimin, W., Li, M., & Ur Rehman, K. (2020). Innovation in the era of IoT and industry 5.0: Absolute innovation management (AIM) framework. *Information (Basel), 11*(2), 124. doi:10.3390/info11020124

Bartosik-Purgat, M., & Bednarz, J. (2021). The usage of new media tools in prosumer activities–a corporate perspective. *Technology Analysis and Strategic Management, 33*(4), 453–464. doi:10.1080/09537325.2020.1820475

Bartosik-Purgat, M., & Mińska-Struzik, E. (2022). Social media and mobile tools in consumers' decisions of Polish consumers. In M. Bartosik-Purgat & F. Nela (Eds.), *European Consumers in the Digital Era* (pp. 129–144). Routledge. doi:10.4324/9781003263685-11

Bednarz, J. (2022). Who is a consumer in the digital era? Still a consumer or a prosumer? In M. Bartosik-Purgat and F. Nela (Ed.), European Consumers in the Digital Era (pp. 27-42). Routledge.

Breque, M., De Nul, L., & Petridis, A. (2021). *Industry 5.0: towards a sustainable, human-centric and resilient European industry*. European Commission, Directorate-General for Research and Innovation.

Calvo-Porral, C., & Pesqueira-Sanchez, R. (2020). Generational differences in technology behaviour: Comparing millennials and Generation X. *Kybernetes, 49*(11), 2755–2772. doi:10.1108/K-09-2019-0598

Cioffi, R., Travaglioni, M., Piscitelli, G., Petrillo, A., & Parmentola, A. (2020). Smart manufacturing systems and applied industrial technologies for a sustainable industry: A systematic literature review. *Applied Sciences (Basel, Switzerland), 10*(8), 2897. doi:10.3390/app10082897

Cochoy, F., Hagberg, J., McIntyre, M. P., & Sörum, N. (Eds.). (2017). *Digitalising consumption: How devices shape consumer culture*. Taylor & Francis. doi:10.4324/9781315647883

Das, S. (2021). A systematic study of integrated marketing communication and content management system for millennial consumers. In *Innovations in digital branding and content marketing* (pp. 91–112). IGI Global. doi:10.4018/978-1-7998-4420-4.ch005

De Felice, F., Travaglioni, M., & Petrillo, A. (2021). Innovation trajectories for a society 5.0. *Data*, *6*(11), 115. doi:10.3390/data6110115

De Hoyos Guevara, A. J., Terra, D. M., Portes, J. H., da Silva, J. L. A., & Magalhães, K. E. (2020). A Ranking of countries concerning progress towards a society 5.0. *Journal on Innovation and Sustainability RISUS*, *11*(4), 188–199. doi:10.23925/2179-3565.2020v11i4p188-199

De Pablos, P. O. (2021). Preface: Intellectual capital, efficiency and organisational performance: some lessons. *Int. J. Learning and Intellectual Capital*, *18*(3), 219.

Deguchi, A., Hirai, C., Matsuoka, H., Nakano, T., Oshima, K., Tai, M., & Tani, S. (2020). What is society 5.0. *Society*, *5*, 1–23.

Demir, K. A., Döven, G., & Sezen, B. (2019). Industry 5.0 and human-robot co-working. *Procedia Computer Science*, *158*, 688–695. doi:10.1016/j.procs.2019.09.104

Dev, K., Tsang, K. F., & Rodríguez, J. M. C. (2022). Guest Editorial: The era of industry 5.0—Technologies from no recognisable hm interface to hearty touch personal products. *IEEE Transactions on Industrial Informatics*, *18*(8), 5432–5434. doi:10.1109/TII.2022.3153833

Dewi, H. P. (2021, June). Determination of green marketing strategies through marketing communication in the business world in the society 5.0 era. In *18th International Symposium on Management (INSYMA 2021)* (pp. 181-187). Atlantis Press. 10.2991/aebmr.k.210628.030

Durmaz, A., & Kitapcı, H. (2021). Revisiting customer involved value chains under the conceptual light of industry 5.0. *Proceedings On Engineering*, *3*(2), 201–210.

Elangovan, U. (2022). *Industry 5.0: The future of the industrial economy*. CRC Press.

ElMaraghy, H., Monostori, L., Schuh, G., & ElMaraghy, W. (2021). Evolution and future of manufacturing systems. *CIRP Annals*, *70*(2), 635–658. doi:10.1016/j.cirp.2021.05.008

European Commission. (2022). *Research and Innovation*. EC. https://research-and-innovation.ec.europa.eu/research-area/industrial-research-and-innovation/industry-50_en

Fanibhare, V., Sarkar, N. I., & Al-Anbuky, A. (2021). A survey of the tactile Internet: Design issues and challenges, applications, and future directions. *Electronics (Basel)*, *10*(17), 2171. doi:10.3390/electronics10172171

Ferreira, C. M., & Serpa, S. (2018). Society 5.0 and social development. *Management and Organizational Studies*, *5*(4), 26–31. doi:10.5430/mos.v5n4p26

Frank, A. G., Dalenogare, L. S., & Ayala, N. F. (2019). Industry 4.0 technologies: Implementation patterns in manufacturing companies. *International Journal of Production Economics*, *210*, 15–26. doi:10.1016/j.ijpe.2019.01.004

Fujii, T., Guo, T., & Kamoshida, A. (2018, August). A consideration of service strategy of Japanese electric manufacturers to realise super smart society (Society 5.0). In *International Conference on Knowledge Management in Organisations* (pp. 634-645). Springer, Cham.

Fukuda, K. (2020). Science, technology and innovation ecosystem transformation toward society 5.0. *International Journal of Production Economics*, *220*, 107460. doi:10.1016/j.ijpe.2019.07.033

Fukuyama, M. (2018). Society 5.0: Aiming for a new human-centred society. *Japan Spotlight*, *27*(5), 47–50.

Ghobakhloo, M., Iranmanesh, M., Mubarak, M. F., Mubarik, M., Rejeb, A., & Nilashi, M. (2022). Identifying industry 5.0 contributions to sustainable development: A strategy roadmap for delivering sustainability values. *Sustainable Production and Consumption*, *33*, 716–737. doi:10.1016/j.spc.2022.08.003

Gill, S. S., Tuli, S., Xu, M., Singh, I., Singh, K. V., Lindsay, D., Tuli, S., Smirnova, D., Singh, M., Jain, U., Pervaiz, H., Sehgal, B., Kaila, S. S., Misra, S., Aslanpour, M. S., Mehta, H., Stankovski, V., & Garraghan, P. (2019). Transformative effects of IoT, blockchain and artificial intelligence on cloud computing: Evolution, vision, trends and open challenges. *Internet of Things*, *8*, 100118. doi:10.1016/j.iot.2019.100118

Gladden, M. E. (2019). Who will be the members of Society 5.0? Towards an anthropology of technologically posthumanized future societies. *Social Sciences (Basel, Switzerland)*, *8*(5), 148. doi:10.3390ocsci8050148

Grabowska, S., Saniuk, S., & Gajdzik, B. (2022). Industry 5.0: Improving humanisation and sustainability of Industry 4.0. *Scientometrics*, *127*(6), 1–28. doi:10.100711192-022-04370-1 PMID:35502439

Grewal, D., Hulland, J., Kopalle, P. K., & Karahanna, E. (2020). The future of technology and marketing: A multidisciplinary perspective. *Journal of the Academy of Marketing Science*, *48*(1), 1–8. doi:10.100711747-019-00711-4

Holroyd, C. (2022). Technological innovation and building a 'super smart'society: Japan's vision of society 5.0. *Journal of Asian Public Policy*, *15*(1), 18–31. doi:10.1080/17516234.2020.1749340

Hu, S. J. (2013). Evolving paradigms of manufacturing: From mass production to mass customisation and personalisation. *Procedia CIRP*, *7*, 3–8. doi:10.1016/j.procir.2013.05.002

Huang, S., Wang, B., Li, X., Zheng, P., Mourtzis, D., & Wang, L. (2022). Industry 5.0 and Society 5.0—Comparison, complementation and co-evolution. *Journal of Manufacturing Systems*, *64*, 424–428. doi:10.1016/j.jmsy.2022.07.010

Ipek, I. (2020). Understanding consumer behaviour in technology-mediated spaces. In *Digital Transformation in Business and Society* (pp. 169–189). Palgrave Macmillan. doi:10.1007/978-3-030-08277-2_11

Javaid, M., & Haleem, A. (2020). Critical components of Industry 5.0 towards a successful adoption in thefield of manufacturing. *Journal of Industrial Integration and Management*, *5*(03), 327–348. doi:10.1142/S2424862220500141

Jiménez-Zarco, A. I., Rospigliosi, A., Martínez-Ruiz, M. P., & Izquierdo-Yusta, A. (2019). Marketing 4.0: Enhancing consumer-brand engagement through big data analysis. In Web Services: Concepts, Methodologies, Tools, and Applications (pp. 2172-2195). IGI Global.

Kartajaya, H., Setiawan, I., & Kotler, P. (2021). *Marketing 5.0: Technology for humanity*. John Wiley & Sons.

Keidanren. (2022). Digital Transformation—Opening up the Future through Co-creation of Values. *Keidanren.* https://www.keidanren.or.jp/en/policy/2020/038.html

Konhäusner, P., Shang, B., & Dabija, D. C. (2021). Application of the 4Es in online crowdfunding platforms: A comparative perspective of Germany and China. *Journal of Risk and Financial Management, 14*(2), 49. doi:10.3390/jrfm14020049

Kotler, P., & Keller, K. L. (2012). *Marketing management* (14th ed.). Pearson Education.

Krishnan, U. (2021). The Industry 4.0 and its associated technologies. *Journal of Emerging Technologies, 1*(1), 1–10. doi:10.57040/jet.v1i1.24

Lee, S. M., & Lee, D. (2020). Untact: A new customer service strategy in the digital age. *Service Business, 14*(1), 1–22. doi:10.100711628-019-00408-2

Leng, J., Sha, W., Wang, B., Zheng, P., Zhuang, C., Liu, Q., Wuest, T., Mourtzis, D., & Wang, L. (2022). Industry 5.0: Prospect and retrospect. *Journal of Manufacturing Systems, 65*, 279–295. doi:10.1016/j.jmsy.2022.09.017

Longo, F., Padovano, A., & Umbrello, S. (2020). Value-oriented and ethical technology engineering in industry 5.0: A human-centric perspective for the design of the factory of the future. *Applied Sciences (Basel, Switzerland), 10*(12), 4182. doi:10.3390/app10124182

Lu, Y., Adrados, J. S., Chand, S. S., & Wang, L. (2021). Humans are not machines-anthropocentric human-machine symbiosis for ultra-flexible smart manufacturing. *Engineering (Beijing), 7*(6), 734–737. doi:10.1016/j.eng.2020.09.018

Maddikunta, P. K. R., Pham, Q. V., Prabadevi, B., Deepa, N., Dev, K., Gadekallu, T. R., & Liyanage, M. (2022). Industry 5.0: A survey on enabling technologies and potential applications. *Journal of Industrial Information Integration, 26*, 100257. doi:10.1016/j.jii.2021.100257

Malik, R., & Trivedi, S. (2022). Big data analytics in predicting consumer behaviour. *Big Data: A Road Map for Successful Digital Marketing*, 9.

Mamasioulas, A., Mourtzis, D., & Chryssolouris, G. (2020). A manufacturing innovation overview: Concepts, models and metrics. *International Journal of Computer Integrated Manufacturing, 33*(8), 769–791. doi:10.1080/0951192X.2020.1780317

Matarazzo, M., Penco, L., Profumo, G., & Quaglia, R. (2021). Digital transformation and customer value creation in made in Italy SMEs: A dynamic capabilities perspective. *Journal of Business Research, 123*, 642–656. doi:10.1016/j.jbusres.2020.10.033

Mavrodieva, A. V., & Shaw, R. (2020). Disaster and climate change issues in Japan's Society 5.0—A discussion. *Sustainability (Basel), 12*(5), 1893. doi:10.3390u12051893

McLuhan, H. M., McLuhan, M., & Nevitt, B. (1972). *Take today: The executive as dropout*. Longman Canada.

Medina-Borja, A. (2017). Smart human-centred service systems of the future. *Future Services & Societal Systems in Society, 5*, 235–239.

Mourtzis, D. (2016). Challenges and future perspectives for the life cycle of manufacturing networks in the mass customisation era. *Logistics Research*, *9*(1), 1–20. doi:10.100712159-015-0129-0

Mourtzis, D. (2018). Development of skills and competences in manufacturing towards Education 4.0: A teaching factory approach. In *International Conference on the Industry 4.0 model for Advanced Manufacturing* (pp. 194-210). Springer, Cham. 10.1007/978-3-319-89563-5_15

Mourtzis, D., Angelopoulos, J., & Panopoulos, N. (2022). A literature review of the challenges and opportunities of the transition from industry 4.0 to society 5.0. *Energies*, *15*(17), 6276. doi:10.3390/en15176276

Müller, J. (2020). Enabling technologies for industry 5.0-results of a workshop with europe's technology leaders. *Europea*. https://op. europa. eu/en/publication-detail/-/publication/8e5de100-2a1c-11eb-9d7e-01aa75ed71a1/language-en.

Nahavandi, S. (2019). Industry 5.0-A human-centric solution. *Sustainability (Basel)*, *11*(16), 4371. doi:10.3390u11164371

Nakanishi, H. (2022) Modern society has reached its limits. society 5.0 will liberate us. *We Forum*. https://www.weforum.org/agenda/2019/01/modern-society-has-reached-its-limits-society-5-0-will-liberate-us/

Narvaez Rojas, C., Alomia Peñafiel, G. A., Loaiza Buitrago, D. F., & Tavera Romero, C. A. (2021). Society 5.0: A japanese concept for a super-intelligent society. *Sustainability (Basel)*, *13*(12), 6567. doi:10.3390u13126567

Pamudyarini, R. A. (2021). The effect of innovation and consumer behaviour towards sustainable fashion in the era of society 5.0 students of fsr ikj product design. *International Journal of Multicultural and Multireligious Understanding*, *8*(2), 394–402. doi:10.18415/ijmmu.v8i2.2353

Peeters, M. M., van Diggelen, J., Van Den Bosch, K., Bronkhorst, A., Neerincx, M. A., Schraagen, J. M., & Raaijmakers, S. (2021). Hybrid collective intelligence in a human–AI society. *AI & Society*, *36*(1), 217–238. doi:10.100700146-020-01005-y

Peter, J. P., Olson, J. C., & Grunert, K. G. (1999). *Consumer behaviour and marketing strategy*. McGraw-hill.

Roblek, V., Meško, M., Bach, M. P., Thorpe, O., & Šprajc, P. (2020). The interaction between Internet, sustainable development, and the emergence of society 5.0. *Data*, *5*(3), 80. doi:10.3390/data5030080

Rodríguez-Molina, J., Martínez-Núñez, M., Martínez, J. F., & Pérez-Aguiar, W. (2014). Business models in the smart grid: Challenges, opportunities and proposals for prosumer profitability. *Energies*, *7*(9), 6142–6171. doi:10.3390/en7096142

Ronit, K. (2021). Business and consumer policy. In *Handbook of Business and Public Policy*. Edward Elgar Publishing. doi:10.4337/9781788979122.00014

Rosemann, M., Becker, J., & Chasin, F. (2021). City 5.0. *Business & Information Systems Engineering*, *63*(1), 71–77. doi:10.100712599-020-00674-9

Rüßmann, M., Lorenz, M., Gerbert, P., Waldner, M., Justus, J., Engel, P., & Harnisch, M. (2015). Industry 4.0: The future of productivity and growth in manufacturing industries. *Boston consulting group, 9*(1), 54-89.

Salgues, B. (2018). *Society 5.0: Industry of the Future, Technologies, Methods and Tools*. John Wiley & Sons. doi:10.1002/9781119507314

Saniuk, S., Grabowska, S., & Straka, M. (2022). Identification of social and economic expectations: Contextual reasons for the transformation process of industry 4.0 into the industry 5.0 concept. *Sustainability (Basel), 14*(3), 1391. doi:10.3390u14031391

Sanwal, R. (2022). How new age technologies are used to identify consumer behaviour and its change during and after a pandemic. In *Handbook of Research on Innovative Management Using AI in Industry 5.0* (pp. 279–290). IGI Global. doi:10.4018/978-1-7998-8497-2.ch020

Sepasgozar, S. M., Hawken, S., Sargolzaei, S., & Foroozanfa, M. (2019). Implementing citizen centric technology in developing smart cities: A model for predicting the acceptance of urban technologies. *Technological Forecasting and Social Change, 142*, 105–116. doi:10.1016/j.techfore.2018.09.012

Serpa, S., & Ferreira, C. M. (2019). Society 5.0 and sustainability digital innovations: A social process. *Journal of Organizational Culture. Communications and Conflict*, (2), 1–14.

Shiroishi, Y., Uchiyama, K., & Suzuki, N. (2018). Society 5.0: For human security and well-being. *Computer, 51*(7), 91–95. doi:10.1109/MC.2018.3011041

Shiroishi, Y., Uchiyama, K., & Suzuki, N. (2019). Better actions for society 5.0: Using AI for evidence-based policy making that keeps humans in the loop. *Computer, 52*(11), 73–78. doi:10.1109/MC.2019.2934592

Syed, M. H. (2021). Digitalisation to society 5.0: the new paradigm. In *A Step Towards Society 5.0* (pp. 1–10). CRC Press. doi:10.1201/9781003138037-1

Tanwar, S., Popat, A., Bhattacharya, P., Gupta, R., & Kumar, N. (2022). A taxonomy of energy optimisation techniques for smart cities: Architecture and future directions. *Expert Systems: International Journal of Knowledge Engineering and Neural Networks, 39*(5), e12703. doi:10.1111/exsy.12703

Tiwari, S., Bahuguna, P. C., & Walker, J. (2022). Industry 5.0: A Macro perspective Approach. In Handbook of Research on Innovative Management Using AI in Industry 5.0 (pp. 59-73). IGI Global.

Tkaczyk, J. (2016). Digital consumer: Trends and challenges. *The impact of the digital world on management and marketing*, 353-367.

Toffler, A. (1981). *The Third Wave*. Bantam Books.

Ustundag, A., & Cevikcan, E. (2017). *Industry 4.0: Managing the Digital Transformation*. Springer.

Verma, A., Bhattacharya, P., Madhani, N., Trivedi, C., Bhushan, B., Tanwar, S., Sharma, G., Bokoro, P. N., & Sharma, R. (2022). Blockchain for industry 5.0: Vision, opportunities, key enablers, and future directions. *IEEE Access : Practical Innovations, Open Solutions, 10*, 69160–69199. doi:10.1109/ACCESS.2022.3186892

Wang, Y., Ko, E., & Wang, H. (2021). Augmented reality (AR) app use in the beauty product industry and consumer purchase intention. *Asia Pacific Journal of Marketing and Logistics*, *34*(1), 110–131. doi:10.1108/APJML-11-2019-0684

Wongmonta, S. (2021). Marketing 5.0: The era of technology for humanity with a collaboration of humans and machines. *Nimitmai Review Journal*, *4*(1), 83–97.

Xu, X., Lu, Y., Vogel-Heuser, B., & Wang, L. (2021). Industry 4.0 and Industry 5.0—Inception, conception and perception. *Journal of Manufacturing Systems*, *61*, 530–535. doi:10.1016/j.jmsy.2021.10.006

Zengin, Y., & Zengin, R. B. (2022). Endüstri 5.0 döneminde pazarlamaya dair genel bir bakış. *Hacettepe Üniversitesi Sosyal Bilimler Dergisi*, *4*(1), 111–138.

## ADDITIONAL READING

Akkaya, B., & Ahmed, J. (2022). VUCA-RR toward industry 5.0. In Agile Management and VUCA-RR: Opportunities and Threats in Industry 4.0 towards Society 5.0 (pp. 1-11). Emerald Publishing Limited.

Dautaj, M., & Rossi, M. (2021, July). Towards a new society: Solving the dilemma between society 5.0 and industry 5.0. In *IFIP International Conference on Product Lifecycle Management* (pp. 523-536). Springer, Cham.

Dewi, H. P. (2021, June). Determination of green marketing strategies through marketing communication in the business world in the society 5.0 Era. In *18th International Symposium on Management (INSYMA 2021)* (pp. 181-187). Atlantis Press. 10.2991/aebmr.k.210628.030

ElFar, O. A., Chew, K. W., & Show, P. L. (2021). What is ındustry 5.0? In *The Prospect of Industry 5.0 in Biomanufacturing* (pp. 57–93). CRC Press. doi:10.1201/9781003080671-4-4

Martynov, V. V., Shavaleeva, D. N., & Zaytseva, A. A. (2019, September). Information technology as the basis for transformation into a digital society and industry 5.0. In *2019 International Conference" Quality Management, Transport and Information Security, Information Technologies"(IT&QM&IS)* (pp. 539-543). IEEE. 10.1109/ITQMIS.2019.8928305

Paschek, D., Mocan, A., & Draghici, A. (2019, May). Industry 5.0—The expected impact of next industrial revolution. In Thriving on future education, industry, business, and society, proceedings of the MakeLearn and TIIM international conference, Piran, Slovenia (pp. 15-17).

Pereira, A. G., Lima, T. M., & Santos, F. C. (2020). Industry 4.0 and society 5.0: Opportunities and threats. *International Journal of Recent Technology and Engineering*, *8*(5), 3305–3308. doi:10.35940/ijrte.D8764.018520

Skobelev, P. O., & Borovik, S. Y. (2017). On the way from industry 4.0 to industry 5.0: From digital manufacturing to digital society. *Industry 4.0, 2*(6), 307-311.

Wongmonta, S. (2021). Marketing 5.0: The era of technology for humanity with a collaboration of humans and machines. *Nimitmai Review Journal*, *4*(1), 83–97.

Yavari, F., & Pilevari, N. (2020). Industry revolutions development from ındustry 1.0 to ındustry 5.0 in manufacturing. *Journal of Industrial Strategic Management*, *5*(2), 44–63.

## KEY TERMS AND DEFINITIONS

**Consumer 5.0:** Consumer 5.0 is new in Marketing 5.0, and they are well educated and trained to use digital technologies to plan and analyse their needs and meet their demands through the satisfaction of the consumers.

**Digital Society:** Digital society has been a progressive society created through the adoption and integration of ICT in every aspect of life.

**Industrial Revolution:** The Industrial Revolution transformed from a handicraft and agrarian economy to one industrial manufacturing and modern economy. The technological changes within Industrial Revolution introduced new ways of working and living and eventually transformed society.

**Industry 4.0:** Industry 4.0 focused on emerging technologies as tools for industrial flexibility and efficiency, maintaining welfare for workers and society.

**Industry 5.0:** Industry 5.0 has been a dynamic technological development process under construction.

**Marketing 5.0:** Marketing 5.0 is a postmodern novel marketing approach that has three components, including data-driven marketing, agile marketing, predictive marketing, contextual marketing, and augmented marketing.

**Prosumer:** Prosumers are the consumers that act as producers as well. They are more demanding, active and conscious consumers, contributing to designing novel products and services, improving materials and product durability reliability, and actively designing all the production and marketing processes.

**Society 5.0:** Society 5.0 is a human-centric society supported by digital transformations and aims to balance economic benefits with social welfare by integrating physical space and cyberspace.

# Chapter 3
# Does Digitalization Have a Causal Relationship With Economic Development?
## An Experience From a Country-Wise Panel Data Statistical Analysis

**Bhim Jyoti**
https://orcid.org/0000-0003-0429-0925
*Department of Seed Science and Technology, College of Forestry, Veer Chandra Singh Garhwali Uttarakhand University of Horticulture and Forestry, Ranichauri, India*

**Ajay Kumar Singh**
*Department of Economics, School of Liberal Arts and Management, DIT University, India*

## ABSTRACT

*The present study created information communication technology index (ICTI) for 109 countries during 2010-2020 using a composite Z-score method. For ICTI estimation, it used 12 different indicators associated with ICT access, ICT use and ICT skills. Statistical values of ICTI were used to explore the comparative performance across countries in digitalization. The correlation coefficient analysis was used to examine the association of digitalization with economic development and other variables. Log-linear regression model (Cobb-Douglas production function model) was employed to observe the causal relationship between economic development and digitalization using a country-wise panel data. Granger causality test was applied to observe the causal association of digitalization and economic development.*

## INTRODUCTION

Any country cannot grow without technological development in the era of globalization and digitalization (Singh & Singh, 2020). Technological development is essential to increase the growth of production activities and human well-being (Hernandez et al., 2016; Aksentijevic et al., 2021). Evidence imply that

DOI: 10.4018/978-1-6684-8397-8.ch003

science and technological development is an essential driver to sustain the economic growth in long-term (Singh & Singh, 2020; Bakari, 2022). Most countries have developed digital technologies, cloud technologies, digital knowledge, information of communication technologies (ICT), digital camera, 3D printer, financial technologies, electronic digital devices, digital devices, artificial intelligence, cloud computing technologies, mobile apps, internet of things, high speed internet devices, computers and broadband devices, appropriate technology, green technology, environmental technology due to science & technological development, R&D activities, technology transfer and commercialization (Aly, 2020; Singh and Kumar, 2022c; Ashraf & Singh, 2022). Furthermore, aforesaid technologies are useful for a country to be a digital economy (Mentsiev et al., 2020; Ahmedov, 2020) and create an infrastructure for it (Magomedov et al., 2020). Digital economy is an integration of digital devices and electronic services which helps to create e-business and e-commerce. Digital economy has a greater contribution to increase communication across individuals, businessmen and government to exchange desired information. Digital technologies and ICT indicators create a process for digitalization that reduce transaction cost, and enhance skills and knowledge of people (Nguyen, 2021; Irtyshcheva et al., 2021). ICT is helpful to increase the economic growth and development as it creates extensive opportunities for job seeker, entrepreneurs, consumers and investors (Rath & Hermawan, 2019; Appiah-Otoo & Song, 2021; Aleksandrova et al., 2021; Habibi & Zabardast, 2020; Irtyshcheva et al., 2021). Furthermore, internet technology sustains a bridge between suppliers, consumers and economic agents as increasing their market accessibility (Hernandez et al., 2016; Kutsuri et al., 2019). Digital economy is also seemed suitable to achieve sustainable economic development (Li & Gospodarik, 2021; Jio & Sun, 2021). Digital economy may be beneficial to increase green growth and green GDP.

Digitalization is also useful to increase product innovation in manufacturing sector (Zhou, 2013; Singh et al., 2019b). It is helpful to transforming most activities such as available information, knowledge, education, entertainment, text, devices, images, factor of production, currency and market in digital forms (Mondejar et al., 2021). Thereupon, these digital forms can be spread across world without any barriers (Dahlman et al., 2016). Consequently, digitalization can contribute to increase social–economic, institutional, science & technological, institutional and environmental development (Dobrota et al., 2012; Gerpott & Ahmadi, 2015; Aly, 2020; Ahmedov, 2020). Most countries are using various digital technologies and ICT indicators in production system to increase economic growth and development (Mentsiev et al., 2020; Irtyshcheva et al., 2021). Accordingly, national and global investors, consumers, producers and government can used digital information to meet their needs (Dahlman et al., 2016; Jio & Sun, 2021). At present the dependency of common people, businessman, entrepreneurs, government and other stakeholders on digitalization, ICT and other digital devices increased consistently (Hernandez et al., 2016; Mentsiev et al., 2020; Aksentijevic et al., 2021).

Accessibility and dissemination of required information for large users associated with health, energy, agriculture, food stuffs, education, transport, weather, climate change, goods and services, product and financial market, exchange rate and social media also increase due to digitalization (Mondejar et al., 2021). For instance, businessmen and market representative can access the requirements of labours, consumers, raw materials and prices of products through digital platforms (Magomedov et al., 2020). Subsequently, digitalization may be supportive to nurture an appropriate business and entrepreneurship ecosystem (Carbo-Valverde, 2017; Ahmedov, 2020; Mentsiev et al., 2020; Aleksandrova et al., 2021; Jio & Sun, 2021; Singh & Kumar, 2022b). New entrepreneurs can use digital technologies and ICT to start new start-ups or business which would enhance appropriate entrepreneurship ecosystem (Jyoti & Singh, 2020). Appropriate entrepreneurship ecosystem would create employment for skilled and unskilled labours (Singh & Ashraf, 2020; Singh & Kumar, 2022b; Singh et al., 2022b). It is projected the digitalization will create 72 million jobs by 2025 at global level (Ahmedov, 2020). Digitalization would help to increase per capita income, purchasing power, and demand of goods and services (Mentsiev et al., 2020; Singh & Kumar, 2022b). Subsequently, manufacturing firms will hire more labours to increase their production scale as per the rising demand of goods and services. Profits and growth of manufacturing sector would also expect to increase due to digitalization. Consequently, digitalization would be supportive to reduce poverty and income inequality (Hernandez et al., 2016; Aly, 2020). Moreover, digitalization would enhance the progress of industrialization, science and technological development, technology transfer and commercialization across firms within and across countries. Digitalization would also enhance human skills and labour productivity (Hernandez et al., 2016; Dahlman et al., 2016; Kutsuri et al., 2019). Furthermore, exports and imports of goods and services across countries may be increased through digitalization. Hence, digitalization would increase foreign trade and the global value chain (Ahmedov, 2020).

Furthermore, digitalization would be positive to reduce monopoly and maintain price stability. Moreover, foreign direct investment (FDI) inflow and outflow also increased significantly across counties due to digitalization and ICT indicators. FDI create physical assets, new venture, infrastructure development and sustain money flows (Singh & Kumar, 2022b). Institutional development and transparency in government policies also improve as digitalization increases. Financial institutions can maintain financial stability through digital technologies (Carbo-Valverde, 2017). Digitalization is useful to reduce waste materials in production industries which would increase environmental development and ecological services. Hence, digitalization would help to increase sustainability in natural and ecosystem services, and develop a favourable path for sustainable future of society. In the abovementioned perspectives, the descriptive and empirical findings of previous studies noticed that digitalization has a positive impact on economic growth and development (Hernandez et al., 2016; Arabi & Allah, 2017; Li and Gospodarik, 2021; Jio & Sun, 2021; Nguyen, 2021; Bakari, 2022). Although, the impact of digitalization on economic growth and development is not uniform across countries (Myovella et al., 2020).

Prior studies used various factors which create or improve digitalization to assess its impact on economic development in empirical investigations. Findings of existing studies, therefore, must be confirmed as examining the integrated impact of digitalization on economic development. Due to aforesaid reasons, earlier studies also could not observe the causal association between digitalization and economic development. Thus, this study seeks to answer on following research questions:

- What is relative progress of digitalization in different income group countries?
- What is the relationship of digitalization with economic development?
- What is the causal relationship between digitalization and economic development and vice-versa?

The chapter realized following objectives:

- To integrate ICT access, ICT use and ICT skills related variables as an information communication technology index (*ICTI*) using a *composite z-score* method.
- To examine the association of digitalization with economic development and other macro level variables using correlation coefficients analysis.
- To assess the causal relationship of digitalization with economic development using a log-linear regression model.

## THEORETICAL AND EMPIRICAL REVIEW

Most researchers found a positive and significant association between internet and economic growth (Mentsiev et al., 2020). It was also reported a positive and significant link between digitalization and economic growth in most countries (e.g., Bougheas et al., 2000; Dutta, 2001; Jacobsen, 2003; Koutroumpis, 2009; Qiang, 2009). Any indicator (e.g., digital technologies, digital communication, digital devices, ICT, broadband connections, internet speed, internet users, etc.) which is useful to create digital platform can be used as proxy variable for digitalization (Myovella et al., 2020). Therefore, Minges (2015) determined that broadband subscribers have a positive impact on economic growth and development. ICT regulate the platform for digital economy and digitalization (Hernandez et al., 2016; Mentsiev et al., 2020). Hence, most studies examined the impact of ICT on economic development and other indicators. Farhadi et al. (2012) investigated the impact of ICT use on economic growth. Rath & Hermawan (2019) reported a positive impact of ICT development on economic growth in Indonesia. Arabi & Allah (2017) explained the role of ICT related indicators like fixed phone line, mobile phone and internet subscribers on economic growth in Sudan. Aksentijevic et al. (2021) examined the impact of ICT on human development in 130 countries. It described that ICT showed a positive impact on human development in lower-middle and low-income countries. Previous evidence also emphasized the factors associated with ICT have a positive impact on social development, social change and economic development (Dobrota et al., 2012; Gerpott Ahmadi, 2015; Mentsiev et al., 2020). Solomon & van Klyton (2020) investigated the influence of ICT related indicators on real GDP in African countries. Nguyen (2021) observed that impact of individual using the internet and fixed telephone subscriptions on per capita GDP in 53 countries. Furthermore, ICT related indicators can be divided in three categories i.e., ICT access, ICT use and ICT skills (Hernandez et al., 2016; Gerpott & Ahmadi, 2015). Accordingly, Raeskyesa & Lukas (2019) examined the impact of ICT related indicators (i.e., fixed-telephone subscriptions, mobile-cellular telephone subscriptions, international internet bandwidth per user, % of households with a computer, % of households with internet access, adult literacy rate, gross enrollment ratio secondary and tertiary level) on GDP per capita growth in ASEAN 8 countries. Myovella et al. (2020) considered broadband internet and telecommunication to examine the impact of digitalization on economic growth in 74 Sub Saharan African countries. Habibi & Zabardast (2020) investigated the impact of internet users and mobile subscriptions on economic growth and education in 10 middle-East and 24 OECD countries. Singh & Kumar (2022b) used internet users to capture the influence of digitalization on economic development and entrepreneurship ecosystem.

Few scholars like Aksentijevic et al. (2021) used only ICT access associated factors (i.e., internet users, mobile broadband subscriptions, mobile telephone subscriptions, fixed telephone subscriptions and fixed telephone line) to investigate the association between ICT with human development. Bakari (2022) used individuals using the internet as a representative variable for digitalization to observe its influence on economic growth in Romania. Rekha et al. (2021) observed the impact of ICT imports and exports on financial inclusion. It claimed that ICT diffusion has a positive impact on financial inclusion. Evangelista et al. (2014); Benjamin & Woerter (2019); Irtyshcheva et al. (2021) observed the contribution of digital technologies in economic growth and job creation in different countries. This study used ICT in production and services related variables to examine the impact of digital technologies on economic growth. Aleksandrova et al. (2021) evaluated the impact of digitalization on per capita GDP in Russia. This study used global competitiveness index, index of digital life, digital adoption index and resilience index as proxy variables for digitalization. Finding of this study claimed that digitalization was seemed as an effective driver to increase economic growth and competitiveness. Aly (2020) examined the relationship between digital evolution index with economic development, labour productivity and employment rate in 25 developing countries. It found a positive impact of digital transformation index on economic development, labour productivity and job employment. Li and Gospodarik (2021) observed the impact of digital economy development index on economic growth in China, Japan, South Korea, Brunei and Cambodia. Tiutiunyk et al. (2021) assessed that impact of digital transformation index on macroeconomic stability in European countries. This study also observed that digital transformation is a key determinant to increase macroeconomic stability. Appiah-Otoo and Song (2021) examined the impact of ICT index on economic growth in 123 countries. It determined that economic growth increases as applications of ICT increases in production activities. Özsoy et al. (2022) detected that impact of ICT development index on technology intensity of exports across countries. It observed that exports of high-tech products increase as digitalization increases.

## MATERIALS AND METHODS

### Summary of *ICTI* Related Variables

Previous researchers and international organizations used three components (i.e., ICT access, ICT use and ICT skills) of ICT to produce *ICTI* which are explained as:

*Table 1. Summary of ICTI associated indicators*

| Indicators | Group of Indicators | Unit | Symbol |
|---|---|---|---|
| Fixed telephone subscriptions (per 100 people) | ICT Access | Numbers | *FTS* |
| Mobile cellular subscriptions (per 100 people) | | Numbers | *MCS* |
| Secure internet servers (per 1 million people) | | Numbers | *SIS* |
| Ratio of ICT goods exports (% of total goods exports) with ICT goods imports (% total goods imports) | | % | *RICTGSEI* |
| Ratio of communications, computer, etc. (% of service exports, BoP) with communications, computer, etc. (% of service imports, BoP) | | % | *RCCEI* |
| Ratio of computer, communications and other services (% of commercial service exports) with computer, communications and other services (% of commercial service imports) | | % | *RCCI* |
| Fixed broadband subscriptions (per 100 people) | ICT Use | % | *FBS* |
| Individuals using the internet (% of population) | | Numbers | *IUI* |
| Automated teller machines (ATMs) (per 100,000 adults) | | Numbers | *ATM* |
| Adjusted savings: education expenditure (% of GNI) | ICT Skills | % | *EE* |
| Compulsory education, duration (years) | | Years | *CED* |
| School enrollment, secondary (% gross) | | % | *SSE* |

**Source:** Farhadi et al. (2012); Dobrota et al. (2012); Gerpott and Ahmadi (2015); Hernandez et al. (2016); Ali et al. (2019); Rath and Hermawan (2019); Raeskyesa and Lukas (2019); Myovella et al. (2020); Aleksandrova et al. (2021); Rekha et al. (2021); Jio and Sun (2021); Appiah-Otoo and Song (2021); Tiutiunyk et al. (2021); Zhang et al. (2021); Li and Gospodarik (2021); Singh and Kumar (2022b); Özsoy et al. (2022).

***ICT Access*** - Fixed-telephone subscription, mobile-cellular telephone subscription, international internet bandwidth (bit/s), percentage of households with a computer, and percentage of households with internet access (Gerpott & Ahmadi, 2015).

***ICT Use*** – Percentage of households using the internet, fixed-broadband subscription per 100 inhabitants and active mobile-broadband subscriptions per 100 inhabitants.

***ICT Skills*** - Mean years of schooling, secondary gross enrolment ratio and tertiary gross enrolment ratio.

As this study also creates *ICTI*, however, it was difficult to use above-mentioned indicators in *ICTI* estimation due to unavailability of their statistics for most countries. Henceforth, in this study most appropriate variables which have significant reflection on digitalization were included to create *ICTI* (Table: 1). These indicators were finalized as per the existing studies.

## Study Area and Data Sources

Information of selected indicators were available for most countries during 2010 – 2020 (Table: 1). This study, therefore, could include the time series of listed indicators during the mentioned period. The statistics for these indicators were derived from the official website of world development indicators (World Bank). Subsequently, this study considers only 109 countries which having the desired information of identified indicators (Table: 2). These countries were belonged to different income groups and regions.

*Table 2. List of undertaken countries in the study*

<table>
<tr><th>Country</th><th>Region</th><th>Income group</th></tr>
<tr><td>Australia, Japan, Korea Rep., New Zealand, Singapore</td><td rowspan="3">East Asia & Pacific</td><td>High income</td></tr>
<tr><td>Indonesia, Mongolia, Myanmar, Philippines, Tonga</td><td>Lower middle income</td></tr>
<tr><td>China, Malaysia, Thailand</td><td>Upper middle income</td></tr>
<tr><td>Austria, Belgium, Croatia, Cyprus, Czech Republic, Denmark, Estonia, Finland, France, Germany, Greece, Hungary, Iceland, Ireland, Italy, Latvia, Lithuania, Luxembourg, Netherlands, Norway, Poland, Portugal, Slovak Republic, Slovenia, Spain, Sweden, Switzerland, United Kingdom</td><td rowspan="3">Europe & Central Asia</td><td>High income</td></tr>
<tr><td>Armenia, Kyrgyz Republic, Moldova, Ukraine</td><td>Lower middle income</td></tr>
<tr><td>Albania, Azerbaijan, Belarus, Bulgaria, Georgia, Kazakhstan, Romania, Russian Federation, Turkey</td><td>Upper middle income</td></tr>
<tr><td>Bahamas, The, Chile, Uruguay</td><td rowspan="3">Latin America & Caribbean</td><td>High income</td></tr>
<tr><td>Bolivia, El Salvador, Guatemala, Honduras, Nicaragua</td><td>Lower middle income</td></tr>
<tr><td>Brazil, Colombia, Costa Rica, Dominican Republic, Ecuador, Jamaica, Mexico, Panama, Paraguay, Peru</td><td>Upper middle income</td></tr>
<tr><td>Israel, Kuwait, Malta, Oman, Saudi Arabia</td><td rowspan="3">Middle East & North Africa</td><td>High income</td></tr>
<tr><td>Egypt, Arab Rep., Morocco, Tunisia</td><td>Lower middle income</td></tr>
<tr><td>Algeria, Jordan</td><td>Upper middle income</td></tr>
<tr><td>Canada, United States</td><td>North America</td><td>High income</td></tr>
<tr><td>Nepal</td><td rowspan="2">South Asia</td><td>Low income</td></tr>
<tr><td>Bangladesh, India, Pakistan, Sri Lanka</td><td>Lower middle income</td></tr>
<tr><td>Benin, Burkina Faso, Gambia, The, Madagascar, Mali, Rwanda, Senegal, Tanzania, Togo, Zimbabwe</td><td rowspan="3">Sub-Saharan Africa</td><td>Low income</td></tr>
<tr><td>Cameroon, Cote d'Ivoire, Ghana, Kenya, Lesotho, Nigeria, Sudan</td><td>Lower middle income</td></tr>
<tr><td>Mauritius, Namibia, South Africa</td><td>Upper middle income</td></tr>
</table>

Linear interpolation and extrapolation techniques were applied to fill the missing values of those variables which have the missing values within or out of sample time frame (Aksentijevic et al., 2021; Singh et al., 2022b).

## Applied Technique for *ICTI* Estimation

In 1990, the United Nations Development (UNDP) created human development index using a simple statistical technique which was based on normalization score or composite score of three variables. Thereupon, previous studies and international organizations used normalization score of desired variables to create different indexes like global food security index, global hunger index, financial inclusion index, entrepreneurship ecosystem index, sustainable livelihood security index, environmental sustainability index, green economy index and digitalization index across countries. Existing studies have created different indexes in the area of digitalization. For instance, Katz et al. (2014) created digitization index as a composition of 24 different indicators. Nhamo et al. (2020) used normalization score of different variables to create *ICTI* index. Li and Gospodarik (2021) developed digital economy development index using a factor analysis. Rath and Hermawan (2019) applied principal component analysis to create *ICDI* in Indonesia. Previous studies assigned equal weightage to all arbitrary variables in measurement of *ICTI*. Hence, previous ICT development index is criticized due to inclusion of equal weights for all indicators (Gerpott & Ahmadi, 2015; Ali et al., 2019). Assigning equal weights for all variables may be incorrect to estimate an index (Kumar et al., 2017; Singh et al., 2019a; Singh et al., 2020; Singh et al., 2021; Singh et al., 2022a). For this, a group of studies assigned weightage using correlation coefficient technique, partial least square structural equation modelling, eigenvalue and eigne vectors (Ali et al., 2019; Singh et al., 2022a,b). As *composite Z-score* method includes the weights for arbitrary variables as per the exist variance across entities. Therefore, *composite Z-score* method has viability to estimate an index (Katz et al., 2014; Kumar et al., 2015; Sharma & Singh, 2017; Nhamo et al., 2020). The technique includes the composite score of a particular variable which converts all values between 0 -1 across entities. In this method, *composite score* (*CS*) of an individual variable was estimated as:

$$(CS)_{ict} = \{[(AV)_{ict} - (MiV)_{ict}]/[(MaV)_{ict} - (MiV)_{ict}]\} \tag{1}$$

Here, *CS* is *composite-score* of $i^{th}$ variables; *AV* is actual value, *MiV* is minimum value and *MaV* is maximum values for $i^{th}$ variable, respectively across countries; *c* is cross-sectional country; and *t* is time period in equation (1). The values of *CS* for respective variable lie between 0 – 1 which examine its relative assessment across countries. Thereupon, weightage for undertaken *n*-indicators is estimated as:

$$Wi = \frac{K}{\sqrt{Var(CS)i}} \tag{2}$$

Here, $W_i$ is the assigned weightage for $i^{th}$ variables; *Var*(*CS*) is the statistical variance among the *composite-score* of a respective variable in equation (2). The statistical value of *K* is estimated as:

$$K = \frac{1}{\left\{\sum_{i=1}^{n}\left(\frac{1}{\sqrt{Var(CS)}}\right)\right\}} \quad (3)$$

Final index (*FI*) is observed as a linear sum of all *composite -score* of *n*-indicators which were multiplied by their respective weightages. Hence, *FI* is assessed as:

$$(FI)_{ct} = W_1 \times (CS\_IND_1)_{ct} + W_2 \times (CS\_IND_2)_{ct} + \ldots + W_n \times (CS\_IND_n)_{ct} \quad (4)$$

Here, *FI* is final index; $W_1$, $W_2$, ..., $W_n$ are the assigned weightages for corresponding variables; the sum of all $W_i$s is 1; and $IND_1$, $IND_2$, ..., $IND_n$ are the indicator 1, indicator 2, ..., indicator *n*, respectively in equation (4). In this study, therefore, *ICTI* is created as:

$$(ICTI)_{ct} = W_1 \times (CS\_FTS)_{ct} + W_2 \times (CS\_MCS)_{ct} + W_3 \times (CS\_SIS)_{ct} + W_4 \times (CS\_RICTGSEI)_{ct} + W_5 \times (CS\_RCCEI)_{ct} + W_6 \times (CS\_RCCI)_{ct} + W_7 \times (CS\_FBS)_{ct} + W_8 \times (CS\_IUI)_{ct} + W_9 \times (CS\_ATM)_{ct} + W_{10} \times (CS\_EE)_{ct} + W_{11} \times (CS\_CED)_{ct} + W_{12} \times (CS\_SSE)_{ct} \quad (5)$$

Here, *ICTI* is information and communication technology index; $W_1$, $W_2$, ..., $W_{12}$ are the assigned weightages for associated variables; and *CS* is *composite-score* of associated variables in equation (5). The explanation of remaining variables is given in Table: 1.

## Functional Relationship Between Variables

Previous studies used per capita gross domestic product (*PCGDP*) as a representative variable for economic development (Singh &d Ashraf, 2020; Magomedov et al., 2020; Singh et al., 2021; Zhang et al., 2021; Singh & Kumar, 2022b). Additionally, prior researchers used different indicators to explain the impact of digitalization on economic development (Aly, 2020; Aleksandrova et al., 2021; Li & Gospodarik, 2021; Tiutiunyk et al., 2021; Appiah-Otoo & Song, 2021; Singh & Kumar, 2022b). In this study, *PCGDP* and *ICTI* were used as proxy variables for economic development and digitalization, respectively.

Economic development is not possible without inflation. Although, the impact of inflation on economic development was not appeared similar in developed and developing countries. Most studies argued that high inflation may be caused to decrease demand of goods and services due to decline in real income of people (Aboudi & Khanchaoui, 2021; Singh & Kumar, 2022b). As a result, gross saving, net investment and consumption pattern may be adversely affected due to increase in inflation. Subsequently, economic development and digitalization may be adversely affected due to increase in inflation increases.

Population growth may be helpful to increase the economic growth and development in several ways (Singh & Kumar, 2022b). Population growth create the demand of goods and services which further provides motivation to the manufacturing and production sector to increase their production scale. Urbanization and infrastructure development are expected to be increased as population growth increases. Accordingly, population growth may be positive to create jobs for skilled and unskilled workers. Thereupon, it may be helpful to increase per capita income and economic development. Population growth also meet the demand of workers in all production units. It also increases the technological need of industries to sustain production scale as per the rising demand of goods and services. However, high population growth may be harmful for economic development and digitalization in largely populated countries (Singh et al., 2021). There are many countries like India, China, Bangladesh and Pakistan are facing several challenges to maintain the pace in economic growth and development.

Infrastructural development has a greater contribution in economic development (Bougheas et al., 2000). Access to electricity, and access to clean fuels and technologies reflect the overall infrastructure development (Singh et al., 2022b). Both the indicators also reproduce the technological development and have a positive implication on environmental development. Furthermore, production activities in all sector and process of digitalization are highly depend on availability of electricity. Hence, above-mentioned indicators are used to detect the impact of infrastructure development on economic development and digitalization in this study.

Vulnerable employment is responsible to increase insufficient salaries, low productivity and difficult conditions of workers (Aly, 2020). Hence, it has a negative impact on economic development and digitalization. Appropriate employment opportunities have a dynamic influence on income, purchasing power, saving, investment and consumption of people. It helps to sustain the overall social-economic prosperity of people. Therefore, wage and salaried workers, and employment to population ratio were used to explain the impact of employment level on economic development and digitalization. Market exchange rate helps to increase money flow and overall financial development in financial market (Singh & Kumar, 2022b). Market exchange rate also determine the trade association between two countries. Also, exchange of ICT related goods and services depend upon market exchange rate. Thus, it is expected that market exchange may produce a positive impact on economic development and digitalization. Therefore, inflation GDP deflator, population growth, access to electricity, access to clean fuel and technology for cooking, vulnerable employment, wage and salaried workers, employment to population ratio, gross savings, and market exchange rate were used as control variables in this study.

This study is proposed to observe the causal association between economic development and digitalization. Thus, it formulates two simultaneous regression equations. For the 1st regression equation, it assumes that economic development depends on digitalization and control variables. For the 2nd regression equation, it accepts that digitalization depends on economic development and mentioned indicators. Mathematically, aforementioned functional forms are defined as:

$$(ED) = f\{ICTI, IGDPD, PGR, AE, ACFTC, VET, WSWT, EPR, GS, MER\} \tag{6}$$

$$(ICTI) = f\{ED, IGDPD, PGR, AE, ACFTC, VET, WSWT, EPR, GS, MER\} \tag{7}$$

The description of underlined variables of equation (6) and (7) is described in Table: 3.

## Formulation of Regression Equations

Previous studies used different models like generalized linear methods of moments estimators (Myovella et al., 2020), OLS fixed-effect and GMM method (Habibi & Zabardast 2020), VAR modeling (Tiutiunyk et al., 2021), GMM Arellano – Bond estimators (Nguyen, 2021), system GMM dynamic estimator (Özsoy et al., 2022), and Cobb-Douglas production function model (Singh & Ashraf, 2020; Singh et al., 2022b) to assess the influence of digitalization, digital technologies, digital transformation, ICT and entrepreneurship ecosystem index on economic growth. Aksentijevic et al. (2021) used a Dynamic

*Table 3. Explanation of dependent and independent variables*

| Indicators | Unit | Symbol |
|---|---|---|
| Information and communication technology index | Number | *ICTI* |
| GDP per capita (constant 2015 US$) | US$ | *ED* |
| Inflation GDP deflator (annual %) | % | *IGDPD* |
| Population growth (annual %) | % | *PGR* |
| Access to electricity (% of population) | % | *AE* |
| Access to clean fuels and technologies for cooking (% of population) | % | *ACFTC* |
| Vulnerable employment total (% of total employment) | % | *VET* |
| Wage and salaried workers total (% of total employment) estimate) | % | *WSWT* |
| Employment to population ratio (15+) total (%) | % | *EPR* |
| Gross savings (% of GDP) | % | *GS* |
| Price level ratio of PPP conversion factor (GDP) to market exchange rate | % | *MER* |

panel data regression analysis and generalized method of moments (GMM) to examine the influence of ICT on human development. Li and Gospodarik (2021) used Pearson correlation coefficient analysis to examine the correlation between digital economy development index and economic growth. The existing studies claimed that functional form of log-linear regression model (Cobb-Douglas production model) produce the rational coefficients of independent variables (*IV*s) with dependent variables (*DV*s) (Solomon & van Klyton, 2020; Singh & Kumar, 2022b). Therefore, Cobb-Douglas production model (C-D model) was used to examine the impact of explanatory variables on digitalization and economic development in following forms:

$$\begin{aligned} ln(ED)_{c,t} &= a_0 + a_1 ln(ICTI)_{c,t} + a_2 ln(IGDPD)_{c,t} + a_3 ln(PGR)_{c,t} \\ &+ a_4 ln(AE)_{c,t} + a_5 ln(ACFTC)_{c,t} + a_6 ln(VET)_{c,t} + a_7 ln(WSWT)_{c,t} \\ &+ a_8 ln(EPR)_{c,t} + a_9 ln(GS)_{c,t} + a_{10} ln(MER)_{c,t} + \mu_{ct} \end{aligned} \tag{8}$$

$$\begin{aligned} ln(ICTI)_{c,t} &= \beta_0 + \beta_1 ln(ED)_{c,t} + \beta_2 ln(IGDPD)_{c,t} + \beta_3 ln(PGR)_{c,t} \\ &+ \beta_4 ln(AE)_{c,t} + \beta_5 ln(ACFTC)_{c,t} + \beta_6 ln(VET)_{c,t} + \beta_7 ln(WSWT)_{c,t} \\ &+ \beta_8 ln(EPR)_{c,t} + \beta_9 ln(GS)_{c,t} + \beta_{10} ln(MER)_{c,t} + \lambda_{ct} \end{aligned} \tag{9}$$

Here, $a_0$ and $\beta_0$ are constant terms; $a_1$, $a_2$, … $a_{10}$ and $\beta_1$, $\beta_2$, … $\beta_{10}$ are the regression coefficients of associated variables; $\mu_{ct}$ and $\lambda_{ct}$ are error terms; *c* is cross-sectional country and t i*s* time period in equation (8) and (9). The significance of remaining dependent variables (DVs*)* and independent variables (IVs) is given in Table: 3. In C-D model, $a_1$, $a_2$, … $a_{10}$ and $\beta_1$, $\beta_2$, … $\beta_{10}$ are the elasticities of respective variables which measure the percentage change in DVs due to one unit or marginal change in IVs. If

1st differentiation of DVs with respect to corresponding IVs is positive or negative, then it infers that the value of DVs is likely to be increased or decreased as the value of IVs increase or decrease by 1%.

## Statistical Tests to Confirm an Appropriate Model

Panel data have several statistically issues such as non-stationarity nature of variables; existence of cross-sectional dependency, heteroskedasticity and serial-correlation across countries. These issues may produce bias results and improper interpretation of regression results which may be unsuitable to take a conducive policy decision. Therefore, it was necessary to use a scientific process to perceive the coefficients of explanatory variables. Hence, this study followed following process to select a statistically sound model:

***Im-Pesaran-Shin Test:*** Non-stationarity form of panel or time series data for an individual variable may provide contradictory result (Tiutiunyk et al., 2021; Aboudi & Khanchaoui, 2021; Bakari, 2022). Therefore, stationarity of time series of individual variable is checked using Im-Pesaran-Shin test. The results based on this test indicate that the nature of most variables was stationarity in nature (Table: 4). However, the time series of *PGR*, *VET*, *WSWT* and *GS* were non- stationarity. Therefore, the 1$^{st}$ difference of these variables was used to make these series in stationarity form (Kumar et al., 2017).

***Random Effect Model (REM):*** REM can be used when cross-sectional countries do not have significant variation (Sahoo et al., 2021; Jio & Sun, 2021). Moreover, diversity across countries has a significant influence on *DV*s and country's error term is uncorrelated with set of explanatory variables. Breusch and Pagan Lagraingian Multiplier (LM) test was used to identify the suitability of REM as assuming that preferred model is ordinary least square (Raeskyesa & Lukas, 2019). However, statistically significant values of $Chibar^2$ for Breusch and Pagan Lagraingian Multiplier (LM) test provide a clarification that REM may be inappropriate to estimate the regression coefficients (Table: 5).

***Fixed Effect Model (FEM):*** The model observes the influence of explanatory variables on output within a country (Sahoo et al., 2021; Jio & Sun, 2021). FEM assumes that each country has individual characteristics which may not be associated with predictors. It is efficient to control time-invariant characteristics across countries. The rationality of this model is analyzed through the Hausman test (Sahoo et al., 2021; Raeskyesa & Lukas, 2019). The $Chi^2$ – values of this test showed that coefficients estimated through FEM was not produced rational results (Table: 5).

***Cross-sectional Dependence:*** The presence of cross-sectional dependence may increase inconsistency in the regression results (Singh et al., 2019). The mentioned problem, therefore, is observed using a Pasaran CD test. The statistical results of this test appeared statistically insignificant which infers that there exists a cross-sectional dependence across countries (Table: 5).

***Autocorrelation:*** Auto-correlation exist when the present and its past (or lags) values of a variable have correlation in a time series. The presence of auto-correlation was detected using Wooldridge test (Singh et al., 2019). The statistically significant $F$ – value under Wooldridge test specify that panel data have autocorrelation (Table: 5).

***Groupwise Heteroskedasticity:*** Existence of heteroskedasticity shows the non-constant variance in the panel data. Therefore, this problem was detected using the Modified Wald test (Singh et al., 2019). The statistically significant $Chi^2$ value of Modified Wald test recommended that panel data have heteroskedasticity (Table: 5).

***Feasible Generalized Least Square (FGLS) Estimation:*** The OLS, random-effect and fixed-effect models were seemed unrealistic to estimate the coefficient of *IV*s with the *DV*s due to presence of cross-sectional dependence, autocorrelation and heteroskedasticity. Hence, the coefficients of variables in the proposed models were estimated using feasible generalized least square (*FGLS*) estimation (Singh et al., 2019; Aly, 2020).

***Existence of Causality among the Variables:*** Granger causality test was used to detect the causality of *DV*s with *IV*s. Proposed descriptive and empirical investigations was completed through SPSS and STATA statistical software.

*Table 4. Panel unit root test results with Im-Pesaran-Shin estimation*

| Variables | *t-bar* | *t-tilde-bar* | *Z-t-tilde-bar* | *p-value* | *Critical values* (1% level) |
|---|---|---|---|---|---|
| *ln(ICTI)* | -2.7108 | -1.7881 | -7.1588 | 0.0000 | -1.740 |
| *ln(ED)* | -1.6531 | -1.3619 | -1.0461 | 0.1008 | -1.740 |
| *ln(IGDPD)* | -2.3042 | -1.7540 | -6.6691 | 0.0000 | -1.740 |
| *ln(PGR)* | -0.6990 | -0.5112 | 11.1570 | 1.0000 | -1.740 |
| *D.ln(PGR)* | -1.8324 | -1.2821 | -0.1176 | 0.0532 | -1.750 |
| *ln(AE)* | -2.3042 | -1.7540 | -6.6691 | 0.0000 | -1.740 |
| *ln(ACFTC)* | -2.3042 | -1.7540 | -6.6691 | 0.0000 | -1.740 |
| *ln(VET)* | -1.2619 | -1.0830 | 2.9544 | 0.9984 | -1.740 |
| *D.ln(VET)* | -2.5755 | -1.7378 | -6.7087 | 0.0000 | -1.750 |
| *ln(WSWT)* | -1.5029 | -1.2152 | 1.0593 | 0.8553 | -1.740 |
| *D.ln(WSWT)* | -2.5238 | -1.7505 | -6.8928 | 0.0000 | -1.750 |
| *ln(GS)* | -1.5986 | -1.3044 | -0.2209 | 0.4126 | -1.740 |
| *D.ln(GS)* | -3.1914 | -2.0404 | -11.0850 | 0.0000 | -1.750 |
| *ln(MER)* | -1.6531 | -1.3619 | -1.0461 | 0.1000 | -1.740 |

**Source:** Author's estimation.

*Table 5. Results of statistical test used for appropriate model finalization*

| Statistical Test/Model | *DV = ED* | *DV = ICTI* |
|---|---|---|
| Hausman test for fixed effect model [$Chi^2$ - Value] | 2733.92[a] | 122.71[a] |
| Breusch and Pagan Lagraingian Multiplier (LM) test for random effect model [$Chibar^2$ - Value] | 2984.13[a] | 3004.64[a] |
| Pasaran CD test for cross-sectional independence | 40.787[a] | 100.152[a] |
| Modified Wald test for groupwise heteroskedasticity [$Chi^2$ - Value] | 22913.65[a] | 11624.80[a] |
| Wooldridge test for autocorrelation [*F* – Value] | 681.006[a] | 58.324[a] |

**Source:** Author's estimation. **Note:** [a] indicate that coefficients are statistically significant at 1% significance level.

## DISCUSSION ON DESCRIPTIVE AND EMPIRICAL RESULTS

### Cross Comparison of Selected Countries in Digitalization in Term of *ICTI*

The relative progress of digitalization of 109 countries is given in Figure: 1. The mean value of *ICTI* during 2010- 2020 lie between 0.049 to 0.58. Hence, there was high diversity in the progress of digitalization across countries. The diversity in digitalization among these countries exist due to variation in 12 indicators listed in Table: 1. Netherlands, South Korea and Malta have 1st, 2nd and 3rd ranks, respectively in digitalization. While, Zimbabwe, Myanmar and Madagascar have 107th, 108th and 109th ranks, respectively in digitalization among the 109 countries. All income group countries were classified in four categories: better, good, moderate and worst performers in digitalization (Table: 6). These categories were determined as per the 4 Quartiles (i.e., 1st quarterlies, 2nd quarterlies, 3rd quarterlies and 4th quarterlies). This study considers, top 25%, 51% to 75%, 26% to 50% and 1% to 25% countries in 1st, 2nd, 3rd and 4th quarterlies, respectively.

*Table 6. Classification of countries as per the values of ICTI*

| Group of countries | Better (0.401 – 0.508) | Good (0.317 -0.398) | Moderate (0.241 - 0.314) | Worst (0.048 -0.232) |
|---|---|---|---|---|
| High income | Netherlands, Korea Rep., Malta, Denmark, Germany, Israel, United States, Iceland, Luxembourg, United Kingdom, Belgium, Switzerland, Canada, Sweden, Austria, Australia, Ireland, Portugal, France, Estonia, Finland, New Zealand, Japan, Cyprus | Norway, Singapore, Uruguay, Hungary, Spain, Italy, Latvia, Slovenia, Lithuania, Czech Republic, Poland, Slovak Republic, Greece, Kuwait, Croatia, Saudi Arabia, Chile | Bahamas, Oman | - |
| Upper middle income | Paraguay, Costa Rica | Russian Federation, Bulgaria, Brazil, Belarus, China, Thailand, Mauritius | Malaysia, Romania, Mexico, Panama, South Africa, Albania, Kazakhstan, Ecuador, Turkey, Colombia, Peru, Georgia, Dominican Republic, Jordan, Azerbaijan | Algeria, Jamaica, Namibia |
| Lower middle income | - | Ukraine, Philippines, Moldova, Honduras | Armenia, Tunisia, El Salvador, Guatemala, Kyrgyz Republic, Morocco, Bolivia, Mongolia, Bangladesh | Lesotho, Indonesia, Nicaragua, Egypt Arab Rep., Tonga, Sri Lanka, Ghana, Cote d'Ivoire, Kenya, India, Pakistan, Sudan, Cameroon, Nigeria, Myanmar |
| Low income | - | - | Nepal | Togo, Senegal, Gambia, Mali, Burkina Faso, Rwanda, Benin,Tanzania, Zimbabwe, Madagascar |

**Source:** Author's estimation.

*Figure 1. Ranking and ICTI values of cross countries*
**Source:** *Author's estimation.*

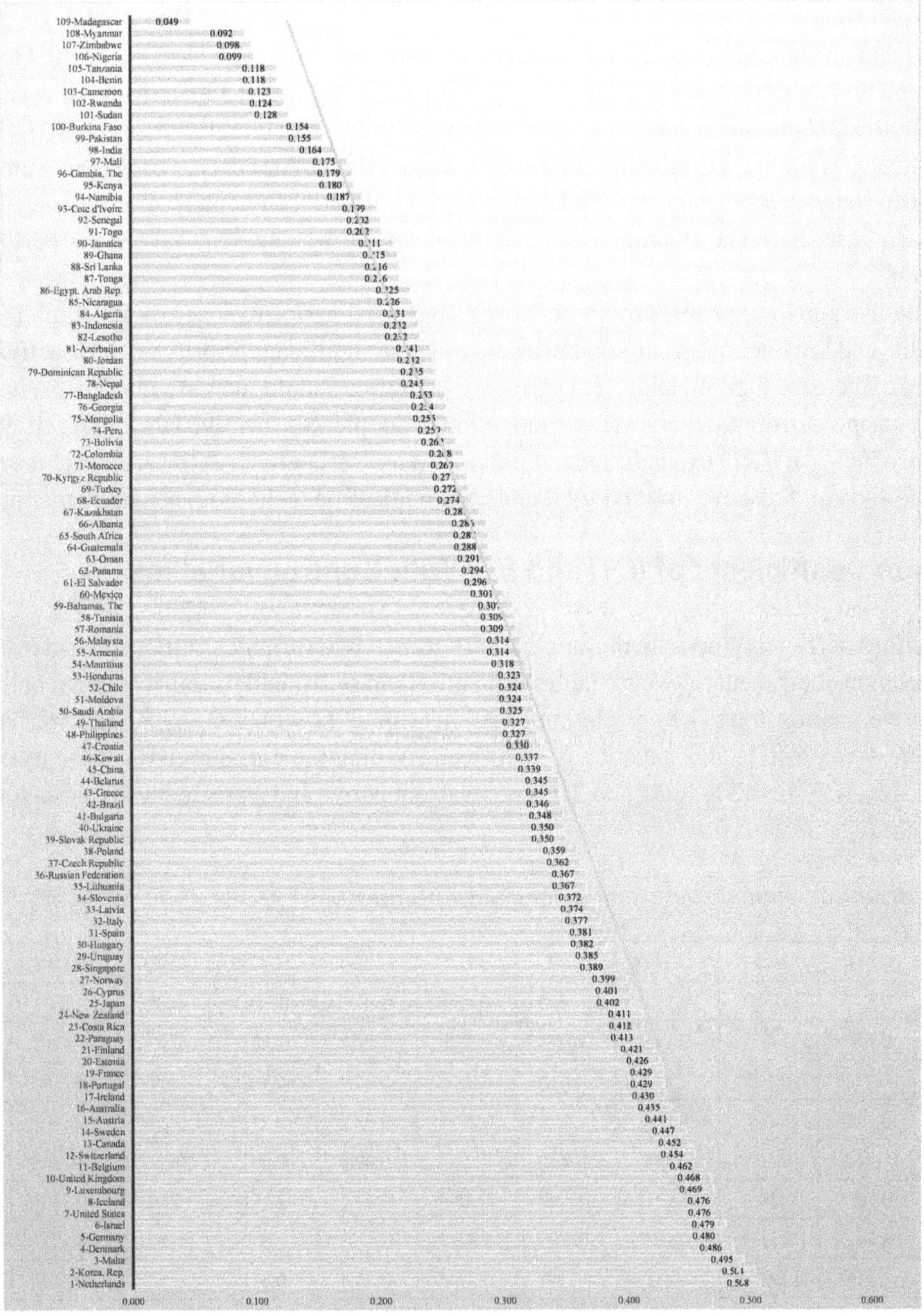


Most high-income group countries have better performance in digitalization. No country from lower-middle- and low-income groups have better performance in digitalization. These countries have adopted ICT instruments in many ways in production activities. Hence, these countries have better position in digitalization. Norway, Singapore, Uruguay, Hungary, Spain, Italy, Latvia, Slovenia, Lithuania, Czech

Republic, Poland, Slovak Republic, Greece, Kuwait, Croatia, Saudi Arabia, Chile, Russian Federation, Bulgaria, Brazil, Belarus, China, Thailand, Mauritius, Ukraine, Philippines, Moldova and Honduras have the good performance in digitalization among the 109 countries. Bahamas, Oman, Malaysia, Romania, Mexico, Panama, South Africa, Albania, Kazakhstan, Ecuador, Turkey, Colombia, Peru, Georgia, Dominican Republic, Jordan, Azerbaijan, Armenia, Tunisia, El Salvador, Guatemala, Kyrgyz Republic, Morocco, Bolivia, Mongolia, Bangladesh and Nepal have the moderate performance in digitalization. Algeria, Jamaica, Namibia, Lesotho, Indonesia, Nicaragua, Egypt Arab Rep., Tonga, Sri Lanka, Ghana, Cote d'Ivoire, Kenya, India, Pakistan, Sudan, Cameroon, Nigeria, Myanmar, Togo, Senegal, Gambia, Mali, Burkina Faso, Rwanda, Benin,Tanzania, Zimbabwe and Madagascar have worst performance in digitalization.

Lower-middle and low-income groups countries have worst performance in digitalization. Therefore, lower-middle- and low-income groups countries should give significant priority on those activities which are essential to increase digitalization. This group of countries should increase internet users, computer users, skills manpower, digital literacy, and motivation of people to be involved in digital activities. These countries also increase R&D expenditure and provide more R&D grants to the scientific research community to develop and discover more digital and communication technologies in the emerging sector.

## Correlation Coefficients of *ICTI* and *EDI* With Control Variables

The correlation coefficients measure the association between two variables without considering *DV*s and *IV*s. If correlation coefficient of two variables is positive and statistically significant than both variables have a positive relationship. The correlation coefficient of *ICTI* with *ED, EPR, AE, ACFTC, WSWT, GS* and *MER* were positive and statistically significant. While, the correlation coefficients of *ED* with *ICTI, EPR, AE, ACFTC, WSWT, GS* and *MER* were also positive and statistically significant (Table: 7).

*Table 7. Pearson correlation coefficient among the variables*

| *Variables* | *ICTI* | *ED* | *IGDPD* | *EPR* | *PGR* | *AE* | *ACFTC* | *VET* | *WSWT* | *MER* |
|---|---|---|---|---|---|---|---|---|---|---|
| *ICTI* | 1 | 0.709$^{b}$ | -0.172$^{b}$ | 0.136$^{b}$ | -0.452$^{b}$ | 0.703$^{b}$ | 0.759$^{b}$ | -0.809$^{b}$ | 0.803$^{b}$ | 0.719$^{b}$ |
| *ED* | 0.709$^{b}$ | 1 | -0.105$^{b}$ | 0.076$^{b}$ | -0.178$^{b}$ | 0.393$^{b}$ | 0.516$^{b}$ | -0.622$^{b}$ | 0.620$^{b}$ | 0.854$^{b}$ |
| *IGDPD* | -0.172$^{b}$ | -0.105$^{b}$ | 1 | 0.076$^{b}$ | 0.060$^{a}$ | -0.121$^{b}$ | -0.102$^{b}$ | 0.099$^{b}$ | -0.094$^{b}$ | -0.136$^{b}$ |
| *EPR* | 0.136$^{b}$ | 0.076$^{b}$ | 0.076$^{b}$ | 1 | 0.208$^{b}$ | -0.333$^{b}$ | -0.345$^{b}$ | 0.299$^{b}$ | -0.291$^{b}$ | 0.060* |
| *PGR* | -0.452$^{b}$ | -0.178$^{b}$ | 0.060$^{a}$ | 0.208$^{b}$ | 1 | -0.488$^{b}$ | -0.467$^{b}$ | 0.374$^{b}$ | -0.367$^{b}$ | -0.257$^{b}$ |
| *AE* | 0.703$^{b}$ | 0.393$^{b}$ | -0.121$^{b}$ | -0.333$^{b}$ | -0.488$^{b}$ | 1 | 0.873$^{b}$ | -0.749$^{b}$ | 0.733$^{b}$ | 0.360$^{b}$ |
| *ACFTC* | 0.759$^{b}$ | 0.516$^{b}$ | -0.102$^{b}$ | -0.345$^{b}$ | -0.467$^{b}$ | 0.873$^{b}$ | 1 | -0.871$^{b}$ | 0.857$^{b}$ | 0.494$^{b}$ |
| *VET* | -0.809$^{b}$ | -0.622$^{b}$ | 0.099$^{b}$ | 0.299$^{b}$ | 0.374$^{b}$ | -0.749$^{b}$ | -0.871$^{b}$ | 1 | -0.996$^{b}$ | -0.579$^{b}$ |
| *WSWT* | 0.803$^{b}$ | 0.620$^{b}$ | -0.094$^{b}$ | -0.291$^{b}$ | -0.367$^{b}$ | 0.733$^{b}$ | 0.857$^{b}$ | -0.996$^{b}$ | 1 | 0.574$^{b}$ |
| *GS* | 0.185$^{b}$ | 0.233$^{b}$ | -0.027 | 0.122$^{b}$ | 0.004 | 0.249$^{b}$ | 0.168$^{b}$ | -0.174$^{b}$ | 0.177$^{b}$ | 0.076$^{b}$ |
| *MER* | 0.719$^{b}$ | 0.854 | -0.136$^{b}$ | 0.060$^{a}$ | -0.257$^{b}$ | 0.360$^{b}$ | 0.494$^{b}$ | -0.579$^{b}$ | 0.574$^{b}$ | 1 |

**Source:** Author's estimation. **Note:** $^{a}$, $^{b}$ and $^{c}$ indicate that coefficients are statistically significant at 1%, 5% and 10% significance level, respectively.

The estimates demonstrated that digitalization and economic development were positive correlated with employment participation rate, access to electricity and fuel technology, wage and salaried workers, gross saving and market exchange rate. Moreover, inflation GDP deflator, population growth and vulnerable employment were negatively correlated with digitalization and economic development.

## Empirical Results

The regression results which explore the impact of *IV*s on digitalization and economic development in given in Table: 8. The regression coefficients of economic development with *ICTI* were seemed positive and statistically insignificant. The estimate infers that economic development may be supportive to nurture a suitable path of digitalization. It is true that those country have high economic development in term of per capita GDP were in better position in digitalization. Thereupon, the coefficient of *ICTI* with economic development demonstrate that digitalization is useful to increase economic development. The result is consistent with prior studies like Billon et al. (2010); Habibi and Zabardast (2020); Irtyshcheva et al. (2021); Jio and Sun (2021); Rekha et al. (2021); Jio and Sun (2021) which have reported a positive impact of digitalization and its associated indicators on economic development. Furthermore, as per the positive coefficient of *ICTI* with *ED* and vice-versa, can be argued that economic development and digitalization have a positive and bi-directional causality.

*Table 8. Regression coefficients of explanatory variables with ICTI and ED*

| *DVs* | *ICTI* | | | *ED* | | |
|---|---|---|---|---|---|---|
| Number of obs. | 1199 | | | 1199 | | |
| Number of groups | 109 | | | 109 | | |
| Wald chi2(10) | 3857.70* | | | 13425.33* | | |
| Log likelihood | 120.1481 | | | -577.0446 | | |
| *VIF* | 4.45 | | | 3.32 | | |
| IVs | *Reg. Coef.* | *Std. Err.* | *P>\|z\|* | *Reg. Coef.* | *Std. Err.* | *P>\|z\|* |
| *ln(ED)* | 0.0026 | 0.0161 | 0.872 | - | | - |
| *ln(ICTI)* | - | - | - | 0.0083 | 0.0517 | 0.872 |
| *ln(IGDPD)* | -0.0226[a] | 0.0057 | 0.000 | -0.0324[a] | 0.0102 | 0.002 |
| *ln(PGR)* | -0.0279[a] | 0.0063 | 0.000 | -0.0097 | 0.0114 | 0.395 |
| *ln(AE)* | 0.2771[a] | 0.0338 | 0.000 | 0.4716[a] | 0.0607 | 0.000 |
| *ln(ACFTC)* | 0.0322 | 0.0136 | 0.018 | 0.1701[a] | 0.0238 | 0.000 |
| *ln(VET)* | -0.0084 | 0.0141 | 0.551 | -0.3461[a] | 0.0232 | 0.000 |
| *ln(WSWT)* | 0.2918[a] | 0.0332 | 0.000 | 0.3303[a] | 0.0605 | 0.000 |
| *ln(MER)* | 0.3005[a] | 0.0325 | 0.000 | 1.5537[a] | 0.0401 | 0.000 |
| *ln(GS)* | 0.0533[a] | 0.0153 | 0.001 | 0.2118[a] | 0.0269 | 0.000 |
| *ln(EPR)* | 0.0609 | 0.0424 | 0.151 | 0.4832[a] | 0.0747 | 0.000 |
| *Con. Coef.* | -3.9967[a] | 0.2656 | 0.000 | 4.2791[a] | 0.5030 | 0.000 |

**Source:** Author's estimation. **Note:** [a], [b] and [c] indicate that coefficients are statistically significant at 1%, 5% and 10% significance level, respectively.

The negative coefficients of *IGDPD* with economic development and *ICTI* that suggested that economic development and digitalization may decline due to increase in inflation. There are many channels in which inflation produce negative impact on economic development and digitalization. As general price of goods and services increase due to inflation. Economic capacity and purchasing power of consumer, therefore, decreases as inflation increases. Accordingly, demand pull and cost-push inflation hamper the domestic demand of household and supply of manufacturing sector. Moreover, level of employment and real income of people also decline due to rise in inflation (Singh & Kumar, 2022b).

The negative coefficient of *PGR* with *ICTI* and *ED* showed that economic development and digitalization are likely to be declined as population growth increases. High population growth is caused to increase additional monetary pressure on government to increase extensive investment towards social-development that increase the fiscal deficit. Hence, it is seemed that highly populated countries have a poor position in digitalization. The result is similar with previous studies like Singh and Kumar (2022b).

Infrastructural development creates jobs and physical assets (Singh & Kumar, 2022b). Thus, the contribution of infrastructural development is positive to improve economic development. In this study, *AE* and *ACFTC* were included as proxy indicators to capture the influence of infrastructural development on economic development and digitalization. The positive coefficients of *AE* and *ACFTC* with *ED* and *ICTI* implies that economic development and digitalization would improve as infrastructural development increases.

Creation of employment for skilled and unskilled labours is positive to increase per capita income and purchasing power of people to buy goods and services (Singh & Kumar, 2022b). Production scale of all sector, therefore, would improve as level of employment increases. The positive coefficient of *WSWT* and *EPR* with *ED* and *ICTI* also indicated that economic development and digitalization would be increased as wage and salaried workers, and employment to population ratio increase.

The negative coefficient of *VET* with *ED* and *ICTI* imply that economic development and digitalization are expected to be declined due to increase in vulnerable employment. Aly (2020) also argued that vulnerable employment is caused to increase low productivity, poor work culture and low wages of workers. Hence, vulnerable employment has an adverse impact on economic development. Consumption, investment and saving are the most influencing factors of sustainable economic growth. Gross saving is effective to increase the long-run investment plan of people. Hence, the impact of gross saving (*GS*) on economic development and digitalization was found positive and statistically significant.

Exchange rate reflect the overall strength of local currency of a country in the international market (Singh & Kumar, 2022b). Import-exports of goods and services may increase or decrease due to variation in exchange rate. Exchange rate also reflect the foreign trade which may be helpful to increase level of employment and foreign direct investment, and infrastructural development. Foreign trade may be useful to increase technology transfer, human skilled and transfer of digital devices across countries (Singh, 2020). Hence, exchange rate may be positive to increase economic development and digitalization. Therefore, the results of this study also found positive impact of exchange rate on economic development and digitalization. Singh and Kumar (2022b) also reported a positive impact of market exchange rate on economic development and entrepreneurship ecosystem across countries.

## Causality of Digitalization and Economic Development With Explanatory Variables

Causality measure that if the value of one variable increases, then the value of another variable also increases and vice-versa. One variable may be cause to change the value of another variable. In this study, the causal relationship between variables were detected using Granger-causality test. The test supportive to examine the prediction of a variable as using past values of *DV*s and *IV*s in regression analysis (Dutta, 2001). Henceforth, the researchers can perceive that how a variable has cause-and-effect relationship with another. For instance, digitalization is a cause for economic development, and economic development is cause for digitalization. This study assumes that explanatory variables does not have causality with *DV*s. The results of Granger-causality test showed that Z-bar and Z-bar tilde values for most variables were seemed statistically significant at 5% significance level. The estimates infer that digitalization, inflation GDP deflator, population growth, vulnerable employment, wage and salaried workers, gross saving, and employment participation rate have a causal relationship with economic development. Furthermore, economic development, population growth, vulnerable employment, wage and salaried workers, gross saving, and employment participation rate have a causal relationship with digitalization. Most importantly, digitalization and economic development have a bi-directional and positive causality with each other.

*Table 9. Statistical results of Granger-Causality test*

| *DV* | **Economic development (ED)** | | | |
|---|---|---|---|---|
| **Hypothesis** | **H0: Explanatory variables does not Granger-cause *ln*(*ED*).<br>H1: Explanatory variables does Granger-cause *ln*(*ED*) for at least one panel** | | | |
| *Indicators* | ***W*-bar** | ***Z*-bar** | ***Z*-bar tilde** | *Conclusion* |
| *ln*(*ICTI*) | 3.5294 | 18.6729[a] | 7.9398[a] | Reject H0 |
| *ln*(*IGDPD*) | 2.2357 | 9.1228[a] | 3.1162[a] | Reject H0 |
| *ln*(*PGR*) | 4.4156 | 25.2152[a] | 11.2441[a] | Reject H0 |
| *ln*(*VET*) | 2.5381 | 11.3552[a] | 4.2437[a] | Reject H0 |
| *ln*(*WSWT*) | 2.7022 | 12.5664[a] | 4.8555[a] | Reject H0 |
| *ln*(*GS*) | 1.8703 | 6.4253[a] | 1.7538[c] | Reject H0 |
| *ln*(*EPR*) | 3.3056 | 17.0209[a] | 7.1054[a] | Reject H0 |

## CONCLUSION AND POLICY SUGGESTIONS

The main aim of this study was to create information and communication technology index (*ICTI*) for 109 countries with different income groups during 2010 – 2020. *Composite Z-score method* was used to integrate 12 indicators associated with ICT access, ICT use and ICT skills as *ICTI*. Accordingly, comparative progress of digitalization of these countries were explained based on estimated values of *ICTI*. The correlation coefficient analysis was used to assess the correlation of digitalization with economic development and other macro level variables. For mentioned investigation, *ICTI* and per capita GDP was used as representative variables for digitalization and economic development, respectively. Log-linear regression equations were also used to observe the causal association of digitalization and economic development as employing a country-wise panel data. Lastly, Granger casualty test was used to examine the nature of causality among the economic development and digitalization.

*Table 10. Table 9 Continued*

| *DV* | **Information communication technology index** *(ICTI)* | | | |
|---|---|---|---|---|
| **Hypothesis** | **H0: Explanatory variables does not Granger-cause** *ln(ICTI)*. **H1: Explanatory variables does Granger-cause** *ln(ICTI)* **for at least one panel** | | | |
| *Indicators* | *W*-**bar** | *Z*-**bar** | *Z*-**bar tilde** | *Conclusion* |
| *ln*(*ED*) | 7.4847 | 47.8727[a] | 22.6879[a] | Reject H0 |
| *ln*(*IGDPD*) | 1.5746 | 4.2419[a] | 0.6510 | Reject H1 |
| *ln*(*PGR*) | 3.9090 | 21.4758[a] | 9.3554[a] | Reject H0 |
| *ln*(*VET*) | 4.7217 | 27.4750[a] | 12.3855[a] | Reject H0 |
| *ln*(*WSWT*) | 4.5823 | 26.4459[a] | 11.8657[a] | Reject H0 |
| *ln*(*GS*) | 4.5734 | 26.3800[a] | 11.8325[a] | Reject H0 |
| *ln*(*EPR*) | 5.0625 | 29.9914[a] | 13.6565[a] | Reject H0 |

**Source:** Author's estimation. **Note:** [a], [b] and [c] indicate that coefficients are statistically significant at 1%, 5% and 10% significance level, respectively.

The descriptive results indicate that there was high diversity in the progress of digitalization among the 109 countries. Netherlands, South Korea and Malta have 1st, 2nd and 3rd position, respectively in digitalization. Zimbabwe, Myanmar and Madagascar have 107th, 108th and 109th position, respectively in digitalization. The diversity in digitalization across countries was presence due to variability in 12 indicators which were used to develop *ICTI*. Undertaken countries were also divided in four groups (i.e., better, good, moderate and worst) as per the statistical values of *ICTI*. Most high-income group countries (except, Bahamas and Oman) were in better and good position in digitalization. Upper-middle income countries also have high diversity in digitalization. None countries from lower-middle income group have the better performance in digitalization. All low-income group countries (except, Nepal) have worst performance in digitalization. Therefore, lower-middle and low-income group countries should give significant priority to increase their position in digitalization.

The results based on correlation coefficient analysis infer that digitalization was positively correlated with economic development, employment participation rate, infrastructural development, wage and salaried workers, gross saving and market exchange rate. Economic development was also positively correlated with underlined indicators. Economic development and digitalization were negative correlated with inflation, population growth and vulnerable employment rate. The results based on log-linear regression model also imply that digitalization, infrastructural development, wage and salaried workers, market exchange rate, gross saving and employment participation rate have a positive impact on economic development. Economic development, infrastructural development, wage and salaried workers, market exchange rate and employment participation rate have a positive impact on digitalization. The impact of inflation GDP deflator, population growth and vulnerable employment rate on economic development and digitalization were reported negative. The results also claimed that digitalization has a positive impact of economic development, and economic development has a positive impact on digitalization. The results based on Granger causality test also provide a confirmation that economic development and digitalization have a positive and causal association with each other. The results of this study increase the attention of lower-middle and low-income groups countries to implement favourable policies to increase their position in digitalization. As high-income group countries were in better position in digitalization which would provide more social-economic benefits to this group of countries. It emphasized that lower-middle and low-income group countries should discover digital technologies, ICT, and develop digital platform to increase digitalization and to be digital economy. Global countries should also control population growth, inflation and vulnerable employment to improve digitalization and economic development. Infrastructural development, creation of employment opportunities and saving would enhance economic development and digitalization in global countries.

In this study, the values of *ICTI* across countries depend on 12 variables of ICT. Therefore, the ranking of these countries may be changed due to inclusion or reducing of number of variables in *ICTI* estimation (Ali et al., 2019). Furthermore, the values of *ICTI* also depend upon applied methods and weightage estimation for included variables (Ali et al., 2019; Gerpott & Ahmadi, 2015). Therefore, this study considered above-mentioned issues as limitations. Further, this study could explain the relative performance of digitalization across 109 countries. It also examined the two-way causal relationship between digitalization and economic development using simultaneous regression equations. Therefore, this study has a methodological, theoretical and empirical contribution in the existing literature. However, this study could not examine the impact of independent and control variables on response variables in high, income, upper-middle and lower and low-income countries. Therefore, existing researchers can address the abovementioned issues in further study.

## Future and Emerging Trend of Digitalization

It is expected that implications of digitalization will be positive in different dimensions in global countries in future. Digitalization would force each country to be digitalized and be a digital economy which reduce green GDP in near future. It would also create a conducive ecosystem of competition in the global market, increase global value chain and greater possibilities of foreign trade. Foreign trade will be positive for transfer of technology, knowledge, green technology, eco-friendly technology, digital technology, ICTs and financial technologies world-wide. Application of these technologies would reduce the dependency of humanity on natural and ecosystem services at a large scale. Digitalization would play a positive role to create new job and business opportunities, and market efficiency. Thus, it would work as key drivers to increase social and economic development. Henceforth, digitalization will develop a conducive path to promote all pillars of sustainable development. Moreover, technological development in the area of digital technology, green technology, appropriate technology and social technology will ensure social equity and health security in future. Hence, it can be concluded that digitalization will increase social prosperity in future. Digitalization would have the greater possibilities to reduce the occurrence of climate change as reducing the GHGs emissions from production activities in near future. Also, be supportive and work as adaptation strategy to mitigate the risk of climate change in most sectors in future. The practices of digitalization would also enhance green entrepreneurial opportunities and the green entrepreneurship ecosystem (Singh et al., 2022b; Singh et al., 2023a,b). In a broad domain, digitalization would increase social justice, transparency and monitoring of government policies, accessibility of information for large users within and across countries, transmission of technology and knowledge which make a sustainable future for society.

High and upper middle-income group countries have a better position in most indicators which create a path of digitalization as compared to lower-middle and low-income group countries. Hence, it would be difficult for lower income group countries to be digitalized due to various reasons. If these countries could not be digitized, then there may be high diversity in factors determining social, economic, environmental and technological development across countries. Lower middle and low income countries will face several issues in the implementation of stated programs to increase digitalization and economic development due to extreme poverty, low per capita income, low infrastructure, low education level of people, low technical skills of people, high population growth, low per capita income, low technology transfer, low technology commercialization, low R&D expenditure, low technological upgradation, low understanding of researchers, scientists and firms towards intellectual property rights.

Therefore, lower-middle and low-income countries should implement effective policies and develop an infrastructure to be digitalized. Most low-income countries have low per capita income, high population growth, high unemployment rate, high vulnerable employment, high inflation, low human skills, low literacy rate, high financial illiteracy of people, poor R&D infrastructure, low scope of technological development, low technological adoption capacity of manufacturing firms, low industrialization, insignificant technology transfer, ineffective mechanism of government policies, poor law and governance system, low entrepreneurial skills of people, inappropriate entrepreneurship ecosystem, financial uncertainty and high dependency of population on agricultural sector. Moreover, most low-income group countries could not create basic infrastructure such as road, transport, electricity, appropriate technologies, digital technologies, education, hospitals, transparency in financial market, banking and other facilities which can assist to increase digitalization. Furthermore, due to technological backwardness of people and ineffective mechanism of government policies, most low-income countries could not develop advance and digital technologies which may be supportive to increase digitalization. These countries also could not attract the foreign direct investment inflows which play a crucial role to increase the technological and economic development, and foreign trade. Also, these countries do not have global networks due to their poor position in science & technological development, innovation and ICT. Hence, it is suggested that extensive investment in R&D will be supportive for low-income and lower ranking countries to develop digital technologies, skills of human resources, ICT platform and online market.

This study creates information and communication technologies development index (*ICTDI*) for selected 118 countries during 2010 – 2020. Thereupon, it examines the causal association between digitalization and economic development. Subsequently, it came with several policy proposals to increase sustainable economic development and digitalization in global countries. Hence, this study has a significant contribution in the existing literature. Further research can be considered to examine the causal-and-effect relationship between economic development and digitalization in high, upper-middle, lower-middle and low-income group countries.

## Future Research Directions

The chapter develop *ICTI* that was an integration of 16 different variables which facilitate the process of digitalization. However, the value of *ICTI* may be changed as inclusion or exclusion any variables it's estimation. Further, research can develop the scientific process to validate the estimated values of *ICEI*. Moreover, the empirical investigation of this chapter is concise to analyzed the causal association between digitalization and economic development in the different income group countries. Accordingly, the findings of this chapter hypothesized that digitalization will create a platform to increase sustainable development and its other components. Thus, it is suggested that existing researchers can observe the impact of digitalization on various drivers (e.g., social development, environmental development, financial development, technological development, sustainable agricultural development, green entrepreneurship, etc.) of sustainable development in further research.

## Consistency of This Book Chapter with the Aim of This Book

The main focus of this chapter is to provide the implications of digitalization in social and economic development. Also, how social-economic activities will be supportive to increase digitalization in future. Furthermore, it also explains the different activities which can be achieved as applications of digitalization. Accordingly, several policies can be implemented a micro level to get significant benefits from digitalization in future. Hence, the findings of this chapter meet the most objectives of the proposed book and would help to increase the insightful understanding of digitalization and its expected impact in a country.

## REFERENCES

Aboudi, S. E. L., & Khanchaoui, I. (2021). Exploring the impact of inflation and external debt on economic growth in Morocco: An empirical investigation with an ARDL approach. *Asian Economic and Financial Review*, *11*(11), 894–907. doi:10.18488/journal.aefr.2021.1111.894.907

Ahmedov, I. (2020). The impact of digital economy on international trade. *European Journal of Business and Management Research*, *5*(4), 1–7. doi:10.24018/ejbmr.2020.5.4.389

Aksentijevic, N. K., Ježic, Z., & Zaninovic, P. A. (2021). The effects of information and communication technology (ICT) use on human development – A macroeconomic approach. *Economics*, *9*(128), 1–12.

Aleksandrova, A., Truntsevsky, Y., & Polutova, M. (2022). Digitalization and its impact on economic growth. *Revista de Economia Política*, *42*(2), 424–441. doi:10.1590/0101-31572022-3306

Ali, M. A., Alam, K., & Taylor, B. (2019). Incorporating affordability, efficiency, and quality in the ICT development index: Implications for index building and ICT policymaking. *The Information Society*, *36*(2), 71–96.

Aly, H. (2020). Digital transformation, development and productivity in developing countries: Is artificial intelligence a cure or a blessing? *Review of Economics and Political Science*, *7*(4), 1–19.

Appiah-Otoo, I., & Song, N. (2021). The impact of ICT on economic growth-comparing rich and poor countries. *Telecommunications Policy*, *45*(2), 1–15. doi:10.1016/j.telpol.2020.102082

Arabi, A. M. K., & Allah, B. A. W. (2017). The impact of information and communication technology (ICT) development on economic growth in Sudan: An application of ARDL bounds testing approach. *Archives of Business Research*, *5*(3), 155–165.

Ashraf, S. N., & Singh, A. K. (2022). Implications of appropriate technology and farm inputs in the agricultural sector of Gujarat: Empirical analysis based on primary data. *Agricultural Economics Research Review*, *35*(2), 59–77. doi:10.5958/0974-0279.2022.00031.3

Bakari, S. (2022). *The impact of digitalization and patent on economic growth in Romania.* MPRA Paper No. 114259.

Benjamin, B., & Woerter, M. (2019). Is this time different? How digitalization influences job creation and destruction. *Research Policy*, *48*(8), 1–10.

Billon, M., Lera-Lopez, F., & Marco, R. (2010). Differences in digitalization levels: A multivariate analysis studying the global digital divide. *Review of World Economics*, *146*(1), 39–73. doi:10.100710290-009-0045-y

Bougheas, S., Demetriades, P. O., & Mamuneas, T. P. (2000). Infrastructure, specialization, and economic growth. *The Canadian Journal of Economics. Revue Canadienne d'Economique*, *33*(1), 506–522. doi:10.1111/0008-4085.00026

Carbo-Valverde, S. (2017). The impact on digitalization on banking and financial stability. *Journal of Financial Management. Markets and Institutions*, *5*(1), 133–140.

Dahlman, C., Mealy, S., & Wermelinger, M. (2016). Harnessing the digital economy developing countries. *OECD Development Centre, Working Paper No. 334*. OECD Publishing, Paris.

Dobrota, M., Jeremic, V., & Markovik, A. (2012). A new perspective of the ICT development index. *Information Development*, *28*(4), 271–280. doi:10.1177/0266666912446497

Dutta, A. (2001). Telecommunications and economic activity: An analysis of Granger causality. *Journal of Management Information Systems*, *17*(4), 71–95. doi:10.1080/07421222.2001.11045658

Evangelista, R., Guerrieri, P., & Meliciani, V. (2014). The economic impact of digital technologies in Europe. *Economics of Innovation and New Technology*, *23*(8), 802–824. doi:10.1080/10438599.2014.918438

Farhadi, M., Ismail, R., & Fooladi, M. (2012). Information and communication technology use and economic growth. *PLoS One*, *7*(11), e48903. doi:10.1371/journal.pone.0048903 PMID:23152817

Gerpott, T. J., & Ahmadi, N. (2015). Composite indices for the evaluation of a country's information technology development level: Extension of the IDI of the ITU. *Technological Forecasting and Social Change*, *98*(1), 174–185. doi:10.1016/j.techfore.2015.03.012

Habibi, F., & Zabardast, M. A. (2020). Digitalization, education and economic growth: A comparative analysis of Middle East and OECD countries. *Technology in Society*, *63*(101370), 101370. doi:10.1016/j.techsoc.2020.101370

Hernandez, K., Faith, B., Martín, P. P., & Ramalingam, B. (2016). The impact of digital technology on economic growth and productivity, and its implications for employment and equality: An evidence review. *Evidence Report No. 207.* Institute of Development Studies, England.

Irtyshcheva, I., Stehnei, M., Popadynets, N., Bogatyrev, K., Boiko, Y., Kramarenko, I., Senkevich, O., Hryshyna, N., Kozak, I., & Ishchenko, O. (2021). The effect of digital technology development on economic growth. *International Journal of Data and Network Science*, *5*(1), 25–36. doi:10.5267/j.ijdns.2020.11.006

Jacobsen, K. F. L. (2003). Telecommunications-a means to economic growth in developing countries? *CMI Report*, (13).

Jio, S., & Sun, Q. (2021). Digital economic development and its impact on economic growth in China: Research based on the perspective of sustainability. *Sustainability (Basel)*, *13*(10245), 1–18. doi:10.3390u131810245

Jyoti, B., & Singh, A. K. (2020). Characteristics and determinants of new start-ups in Gujarat, India. *Entrepreneurship Review*, *1*(2), 1–25. doi:10.38157/entrepreneurship-review.v1i2.154

Katz, R., Koutroumpis, P., & Martin Callorda, F. (2014). Using a digitization index to measure the economic and social impact of digital agendas. *Info*, *16*(1), 32–44. doi:10.1108/info-10-2013-0051

Koutroumpis, P. (2009). The economic impact of broadband on growth: A simultaneous approach. *Telecommunications Policy*, *33*(9), 471–485. doi:10.1016/j.telpol.2009.07.004

Kumar, A., Ahmad, M. M., & Sharma, P. (2015). Carbon emission and global food security: A cross country analysis. *PENCIL Publication of Agricultural Sciences*, *2*(1), 7–24.

Kumar, A., Ahmad, M. M., & Sharma, P. (2017). Influence of climatic and non-climatic factors on sustainable food security in India: A statistical investigation. *International Journal of Sustainable Agricultural Management and Informatics*, *3*(1), 1–30. doi:10.1504/IJSAMI.2017.082917

Kutsuri, G. N., Kamberdieva, S. S., Dedegkaev, V. K. H., Sopoeva, I. A., & Shelkunova, T. G. (2019). Impact of digitalization on improvement of economy, IT and internet of business. *Journal of Physics: Conference Series*, *1399*(3), 1–6. doi:10.1088/1742-6596/1399/3/033008

Li, R., & Gospodarik, C. G. (2021). The impact of digital economy on economic growth based on pearson correlation test analysis. In: J. Jansen, B., Liang, H., Ye, J. (eds) *International Conference on Cognitive based Information Processing and Applications (CIPA 2021), Lecture Notes on Data Engineering and Communications Technologies,* 85. Springer, Singapore.

Magomedov, I. A., Murzaev, H. A., & Bagov, A. M. (2020). The role of digital technologies in economic development. *IOP Conference Series. Materials Science and Engineering*, *862*(052071), 1–4. doi:10.1088/1757-899X/862/5/052071

Mentsiev, A. U., Engel, M. V., Tsamaev, A. M., Abubakarov, M. V., & Yushaeva, R. S. E. (2020). The concept of digitalization and its impact on the modern economy. *Advances in the Economics. Business and Management Research*, *128*(1), 2960–2964.

Minges, M. (2015). Exploring the relationship between broadband and economic growth. *Background Paper, World Development Report 2016*. Digital Dividends.

Mondejar, M. E., Avtar, R., Diaz, H. L. B., Dubey, R. K., Esteban, J., Gómez-Morales, A., Hallam, B., Mbungu, N. T., Okolo, C. C., Prasad, K. A., She, Q., & Garcia-Segura, S. (2021). Digitalization to achieve sustainable development goals: Steps towards a smart green planet. *The Science of the Total Environment, 794*(148539), 1–20. doi:10.1016/j.scitotenv.2021.148539 PMID:34323742

Myovella, G., Karacuka, M., & Haucap, J. (2020). Digitalization and economic growth: A comparative analysis of Sub-Saharan Africa and OECD economies. *Telecommunication Policy*, *44*(2).

Nguyen, V. B. (2021). The digitalization – economic growth relationship in developing countries and the role of governance. *Scientific Annals of Economics and Business*, *68*(4), 481–493. doi:10.47743aeb-2021-0028

Nhamo, G., Nhemachena, C., & Nhamo, S. (2020). Using ICT indicators to measure readiness of countries to implement industry 4.0 and the SDGs. Environmental Economics and Policy Studies, Springer. *Environmental Economics and Policy Studies*, *22*(2), 315–337. doi:10.100710018-019-00259-1

Özsoy, S., Ergüzel, O. Ş., Ersoy, A. Y., & Saygılı, M. (2022). The impact of digitalization on export of high technology products: A panel data approach. *The Journal of International Trade & Economic Development*, *31*(2), 277–298. doi:10.1080/09638199.2021.1965645

Qiang, C. Z. W. 2009. Telecommunications and Economic Growth. Banque mondiale, Washington D.C.

Raeskyesa, D. G. S., & Lukas, E. N. (2019). Does digitalization increase economic growth? Evidence from ASEAN8 countries. *Jurnal Ekonomi Indonesia*, *8*(2), 267–278. doi:10.52813/jei.v8i2.33

Rath, B. N., & Hermawan, D. (2019). Do information and communication technologies foster economic growth in Indonesia? *Bulletin of Monetary Economics and Banking*, *22*(1), 103–122. doi:10.21098/bemp.v22i1.1041

Rekha, G., Rajamani, K., & Resmi, G. (2021). Digital financial inclusion, economic freedom, financial development, and growth: Implications from panel data analysis. *ADBI Working Paper 1244*. Tokyo: Asian Development Bank Institute.

Sahoo, D., Nayak, S., & Behera, J. (2021). Digitalization and economic performance of two fast-growing asian economies: India and the People's Republic of China. *ADBI Working Paper 1243*. Tokyo: Asian Development Bank Institute.

Sharma, P., & Singh, A. K. (2017). Association of state-wise food security index with climatic factors in India: Evidence from state-wise panel data. *Journal of Global Agriculture and Ecology*, *6*(3), 196–205.

Singh, A. K. (2020). Technology transfer and commercialization models and policies in India, USA, China and Malaysia: A conceptual review. *Asian Journal of Sociological Research*, *3*(1), 19–45.

Singh, A. K., & Ashraf, S. N. (2020). Association of entrepreneurship ecosystem with economic growth in selected countries: An empirical exploration. *Journal of Entrepreneurship. Business Economics (Cleveland, Ohio)*, *8*(2), 36–92.

Singh, A. K., Ashraf, S. N., & Arya, A. (2019b). Estimating factors affecting technical efficiency in Indian manufacturing sector. *Eurasian Journal of Business and Economics*, *12*(24), 65–86. doi:10.17015/ejbe.2019.024.04

Singh, A. K., Ashraf, S. N., & Sharma, S. K. (2023). Farmer's perception on climatic factors and social-economic characteristics in the agricultural sector of Gujarat. *Research on World Agricultural Economy*, *4*(1), 36–53. doi:10.36956/rwae.v4i1.788

Singh, A. K., Issac, J., & Narayanan, K. G. S. (2019a). Measurement of environmental sustainability index and its association with socio-economic indicators in Asian economies: An empirical investigation. *International Journal of Environment and Sustainable Development*, *18*(1), 57–100. doi:10.1504/IJESD.2019.098641

Singh, A. K., Jyoti, B., Kumar, S., & Lenka, S. K. (2021). Assessment of global sustainable development, environmental sustainability, economic development and social development index in selected economies. *International Journal of Sustainable Development and Planning*, *16*(1), 123–138. doi:10.18280/ijsdp.160113

Singh, A. K., & Kumar, S. (2022a). Exploring the impact of sustainable and environmental sustainability development on social-economic, science and technological development in selected countries: A country-wise panel data analysis. *Society & Sustainability*, *4*(1), 55–83. doi:10.38157s.v4i1.405

Singh, A. K., & Kumar, S. (2022b). Factors influencing entrepreneurship ecosystem and economic development: Evidence from cross-sectional country-wise imbalanced panel data analysis. *The IUP Journal of Entrepreneurship Development*, *19*(3), 24–47.

Singh, A. K., & Kumar, S. (2022c). Expert's perception on technology transfer and commercialization, and intellectual property rights in India: Evidence from selected research organizations. *Journal of Management, Economics, and Industrial Organization*, *6*(1), 1–33. doi:10.31039/jomeino.2022.6.1.1

Singh, A. K., Kumar, S., & Jyoti, B. (2022a). Does sustainable livelihood security have a relationship with climatic and geographical factors? evidence from a state-wise panel data investigation in India. *The IUP Journal of Applied Economics*, *21*(1), 7–35.

Singh, A. K., Kumar, S., Sharma, A. K., & Sinha, S. (2022b). Does green entrepreneurship have an association with sustainable development and its components? Evidence from country-wise panel data investigation. In M. Magd, D. Singh, D. Spicer, & R. T. Syed (Eds.), *International Perspectives on Value Creation and Sustainability Through Social Entrepreneurship*. IGI Global. doi:10.4018/978-1-6684-4666-9.ch008

Singh, A. K., Sharma, S. K., & Lenka, S. K. (2023a). Causality between green entrepreneurship and sustainable development: A cross country analysis using ARDL model. *The IUP Journal of Applied Economics*, *22*(1), 1–34.

Singh, A. K., & Singh, B. (2020). Implications of intellectual property protection, and science and technological development in the manufacturing sector in selected economies. *Journal of Advocacy. Research in Education*, *7*(1), 16–35.

Singh, A. K., Singh, B. J., & Negi, V. (2020). Does sustainable development have causal relationship with environmental development? Evidence from country wise panel data analysis. *International Journal of Technology Management & Sustainable Development*, *19*(2), 147–171. doi:10.1386/tmsd_00020_1

Solomon, E. M., & van Klyton, A. (2020). The impact of digital technology usage on economic growth in Africa. *Utilities Policy*, *67*(101104), 1–12. doi:10.1016/j.jup.2020.101104 PMID:32904493

Tiutiunyk, I., Drabek, J., Antoniuk, N., Navickas, V., & Rubanov, P. (2021). The impact of digital transformation on macroeconomic stability: Evidence from EU countries. *Journal of International Students*, *14*(3), 220–234. doi:10.14254/2071-8330.2021/14-3/14

Zhang, W., Zhao, S., Wan, X., & Yao, Y. (2021). Study on the effect of digital economy on high-quality economic development in China. *PLoS One*, *16*(9), e0257365. doi:10.1371/journal.pone.0257365 PMID:34547019

Zhou, J. (2013). Digitalization and intelligentization of manufacturing industry. *Advances in Manufacturing*, *1*(1), 1–7. doi:10.100740436-013-0006-5

## ADDITIONAL READING

Dahmani, M., Mabrouki, M., & Youssef, A. B. (2022). ICT, trade openness and economic growth in Tunisia: What is going wrong? *Economic Change and Restructuring*, *55*(1), 2317–2336. doi:10.100710644-022-09388-2

Grahyaia, Z., Abid, M., Sekrafi, H., & Abdelli, H. (2021). The moderating role of ICT diffusion between financial development and economic growth: A bootstrap ARDL approach in Saudi Arabia. *Information Technology for Development*, *28*(4), 816–836.

Kondratenko, N., Papp, V., Romaniuk, M., Ivanova, O., & Petrashko, L. (2022). The role of digitalization in the development of regionsand the use of their potential in terms ofsustainable development. *Amazonia Investiga*, *11*(51), 103–112. doi:10.34069/AI/2022.51.03.10

Nguyen, C. P., & Doytch, N. (2021). The impact of ICT patents on economic growth: An international evidence. *Telecommunications Policy*, *46*(5), 102291. doi:10.1016/j.telpol.2021.102291

Nipo, D. T., Lily, J., Idrisi, S., Pinajaman, S., & Bujang, I. (2022). Information and communication technology (ICT) on economic growth in Asia: A panel data analysis. *International Journal of Business and Management*, *17*(12), 18–23. doi:10.5539/ijbm.v17n12p18

Novikova, O., Khandii, O., Shamileva, L., & Olshanskyi, O. (2022). The impact of digitalization on ensuring economic growth. *Management Theory and Studies for Rural Business and Infrastructure Development*, *44*(2), 223–234. doi:10.15544/mts.2022.23

Pradhan, R. P., Arvin, M. B., & Nair, M. (2021). Urbanization, transportation infrastructure, ICT, and economic growth: A temporal causal analysis. *Cities (London, England)*, *115*(1), 103213. Advance online publication. doi:10.1016/j.cities.2021.103213

Pradhan, R. P., Sarangi, A. K., Maity, C., & Behera, R. R. (2022). ICT infrastructure and economic growth in G-20 Countries: New insights form ARDL modelling. *Journal of Developing Areas*, *56*(1), 47–58. doi:10.1353/jda.2022.0009

Soomro, A. N., Kumar, J., & Kumari, J. (2022). The dynamic relationship between FDI, ICT, trade openness, and economic growth: Evidence from BRICS countries. *Journal of Asian Finance. Economics and Business*, *19*(2), 295–303.

Zhou, A. (2022). Digital infrastructure and economic growth – Evidence for China. *Journal of Infrastructure. Policy and Development*, *6*(1), 1–13.

## KEY TERMS AND DEFINITIONS

**Appropriate Technology:** Any object, method, process, mechanism, etc. which help to fulfil human need and improve sustainability in the system.

**Digitalization:** Process or action to convert available information in digital form.

**Green Economy:** Improved human wellbeing and social equity as increasing sustainability of natural and ecological resources.

**Green GDP:** Consider the environmental consequences due to rising gross domestic product.

**Information and communication evolution index:** Integrated index of factors enhancing digitalization that measure the relative performance of across countries in digitalization.

**Information and Communication Technology:** A diverse set of technological tools and resources used for the transmission, storage, creation, sharing or exchange of information.

**Intellectual Property Rights:** Protect and provide legal security and protection of intellectual of common people, scientists and researchers in science, engineering and medical field.

**Technology Commercialization:** Monetization of technology for using it commercial purpose in the manufacturing sector.

**Technology Transfer:** Dissemination of knowledge, ideas, process, innovation and process across communities, firms and countries.

# Chapter 4
# Theories Supporting Central Bank Digital Currency Development and Its Usefulness

**Peterson K. Ozili**
https://orcid.org/0000-0001-6292-1161
*Central Bank of Nigeria, Nigeria*

## ABSTRACT

*This chapter presents some theories that support central bank digital currency development and its usefulness. The theories provide useful explanations for the development and use of central bank digital currency in the economy. Some theories show that information about central bank digital currency, as well as the perceived usefulness and ease of use of central bank digital currency, is crucial for its success. Other theories show that central bank digital currency can facilitate the flow of funds to economic agebts, and enhance the functioning of the economic system, thereby contributing to economic growth. These theories are useful to economists, policymakers and researchers who are interested in how central bank digital currency affects economic activities.*

## INTRODUCTION

Academic research into central bank digital currency (CBDC) is growing. But existing studies have not used theories to explain central bank digital currency development or its usefulness. Existing academic research into central bank digital currency have not identified the relevant theories that support CBDC development or its usefulness. The reason for this is not far-fetched.

Some might think that '*we don't need a theory to explain* central bank digital currency *development or its usefulness*'. Others might think that '*building a theory to explain* central bank digital currency *development or usefulness is a waste of time*' or that '*a theory that explains the role of* central bank digital currency *in economic processes will not be relevant to practitioners and policymakers*'. Such opinions or conclusions might be wrong because theories play an important role in establishing a set of

DOI: 10.4018/978-1-6684-8397-8.ch004

principles to help us understand how central bank digital currency fits into existing economic processes and economic relationships.

Theories can help us understand who will benefit from central bank digital currency development and its use. Theories can also help us understand how economic agents might be affected by central bank digital currency development and use. Therefore, it is important to identify existing theories that can explain or support central bank digital currency development and use. Neglecting the role of theory in CBDC debates might create a disconnect between 'practical' economic policymaking and the monetary economics academic literature. Therefore, it is important to understand how existing theories support central bank digital currency development and its usefulness. Such understanding can help to create a synergy between central bank digital currency policymaking and the economic literature.

In this study, I present some theories that support central bank digital currency development or its usefulness. This study contributes to the CBDC literature by articulating how existing theories support central bank digital currency development and its usefulness in the economic system. Policymakers and academic economists can use these theories to provide believable explanations for central bank digital currency objectives and outcomes in the economy.

The remainder of the paper is organized as follows. Section 2 discusses the theories that support central bank digital currency development and its usefulness. Section 3 discuss the possibility of developing a central bank digital currency theory. Section 4 presents the future insights and future research direction. Section 5 presents the conclusion of the study.

## THE THEORIES

There are eight theories that support the development and use of a central bank digital currency. The theories are the Schumpeter finance and development theory, the innovation-growth model, the innovation diffusion theory, the technology acceptance model, the endogenous growth model, the theory of finance and growth, the dependency theory of development and the concerns-based innovation adoption theory. The theories are explained below.

### The Schumpeter Finance and Development Theory

The Schumpeter finance and development theory was developed by Joseph Schumpeter in 1911. The theory establishes a link between finance and development. Schumpeter (1911) states that the presence of uncertainty in an economy gives innovators an incentive to develop financial innovations and technological innovations that influence the level of economic development. The theory also states that the services provided by financial intermediaries – mobilizing savings, evaluating projects, managing risk, monitoring managers, and facilitating transactions – are essential for technological innovation and economic development (King and Levine, 1993). The implication of the theory for central bank digital currency is that the use of central bank digital currency would stimulate financial sector agents to deploy technological innovations and innovative financial services that are interoperable with the central bank digital currency in order to support financial intermediaries in their savings mobilization, project evaluation and risk management activities for greater economic development.

## The Innovation-Growth Model

The innovation-growth model was developed by Paul Romer in 1994. The theory states that economic forces influence the willingness of firms (including researchers and entrepreneurs) to produce new ideas and innovation (Romer, 1994). With the right economic conditions in place, firms, researchers and entrepreneurs will develop innovations that support economic activities and increase economic output (Rivera-Batiz and Romer, 1994). In other words, Romer (1994) states that innovation is the result of efforts by researchers and entrepreneurs who respond to economic incentives, and their innovative ideas lead to technological changes that contribute positively to economic growth in society. The implication of this theory is that innovation is significantly linked to economic growth.

This theory supports central bank digital currency development because the need to sustain a desired level of economic growth could provide incentives for innovators to develop new digital innovations, such as the central bank digital currency, that help to achieve a desired level of economic growth. The theory therefore supports central bank digital currency development because a central bank digital currency is a potential central bank innovation that could contribute to economic growth by facilitating the efficient flow of funds to consumption, production, investment and trade activities that contribute to economic growth.

## Innovation Diffusion Theory

The innovation diffusion theory was developed by Roger (2003). The theory describes the pattern and speed at which information about new innovations spread through a population (Roger, 2003; Wani and Ali, 2015). The theory explores the factors that influence an individual's interest in a new technology or innovation (Md Nor et al, 2010). The innovation diffusion theory identifies five factors that influence the adoption of any innovation. They are relative advantage, complexity, compatibility, trial-ability and observability (Md Nor et al, 2010). The theory further argues that information about new innovations are diffused or communicated through certain channels to members of a population (Roger, 2003), and the channel through which information about a new innovation is communicated can greatly influence people's interest in the innovation. And their response to information about the new innovation would give rise to early adopters, early majority adopters, late majority adopters and laggards (Roger, 2003).

The implication of the innovation diffusion theory for central bank digital currency development and its usefulness is that the communication channel through which people learn about the central bank digital currency plays an important role in influencing people's interest in central bank digital currency innovation. This means the central bank should carefully choose the channel of communication that is most appropriate to communicate information about the central bank digital currency.

## Technology Acceptance Model

The technology acceptance model was developed by Davis (1989). This theory has emerged as a useful theory to explain why people accept a technology or innovation, and why other people reject another technology or innovation.

The technology acceptance model states that only two factors influence an individual's willingness to accept a technology or innovation (Davis, 1989). The factors are: perceive ease of use and perceived usefulness of the technology or innovation (Davis, 1989; Lee et al, 2003). The theory argues that an individual who perceived a technology or innovation as too difficult to use or as a waste of time is unlikely to adopt the technology or innovation (Davis, 1989), while individuals who perceives the technology or innovation as easy to use, easy to learn, time-saving and valuable, will be more likely to accept and use the technology or innovation (Marangunić and Granić, 2015).

The implication of the technology acceptance model for the usefulness of central bank digital currency is that the perceived ease of use and the perceived usefulness of the central bank digital currency by citizens are significant determinants of whether the central bank digital currency will be accepted or rejected by the members of the population. Therefore, it is important for the central bank to embark on effective marketing or an information dissemination campaign to ensure that there is a positive perception about the ease of use and the usefulness of the central bank digital currency among members of the population.

## Endogenous Growth Model

The endogenous growth model states that economic growth is primarily the result of internal forces, not external forces (Aghion et al, 1998). This means that increases in economic output is caused by factors within the economic system such as new and better innovation, increase in knowledge, greater research and development (R&D) expenditure, higher investment in human capital by government and private firms, and better government policies that encourage entrepreneurship (Shaw, 1992; Howitt, 2010). All these internal factors work together to increase productivity and increase economic output towards economic growth (Palley, 1996).

The implication of the endogenous growth model for central bank digital currency is that the central bank digital currency may be viewed as an innovation that arises from within the economic system, thereby making it an endogenous determinant of economic growth. The central bank digital currency, as an endogenous determinant of growth, can also be viewed as a new and better innovation that increase productivity and increase economic output towards economic growth. The central bank digital currency, together with enabling government policies and significant research and development (R&D) spending, can further improve the contribution of the central bank digital currency to economic growth.

## Theory of Finance and Growth

The theory of finance and growth explains the role of the financial sector (and the payment system) in stimulating economic growth. The theory states that developing the financial sector to enable it ease financing conditions, and offer credit to deficit units, is the key to unlocking growth in an economy (Trew, 2006). Levine (2005) states that financial instruments, financial markets and financial institutions may arise to mitigate the effects of information and transaction costs (Levine, 2005). In doing so, financial arrangements will change the incentives and constraints facing economic agents (Levine, 2005). The change in incentives and constraints facing economic agents will influence saving rates, interest rates, investment decisions, technological innovation, and this will ultimately affect long-run growth rates (Levine, 2005).

The implication of the theory of finance and growth for central bank digital currency is that the central bank digital currency can be used to ease financing conditions by enhancing payments efficiency, and mitigating high transaction costs in the financial sector. As a result, the central bank digital currency can enhance credit allocation towards greater economic growth.

## The Dependency Theory of Development

The dependency theory of development emerged in the 1950s. The theory states that the development of society can be achieved through interdependencies among the various segments of society which includes interdependencies among the economic, social and political segments of society (Dos Santos, 1971; Marsh, 2014). The theory also states that, in order to create conditions of development within a country, it is necessary to (i) control the monetary exchange rate; (ii) place more governmental emphasis on fiscal policy; (iii) increase the role of government in national development; (vi) create a platform for investments; (v) increase the wages and salaries of workers to increase aggregate demand; (vi) provide adequate social services from the government to impoverished sectors in order to create conditions for those sectors to become more competitive; vii) and provide adequate coverage of social welfare from the government to impoverished people to improve their welfare (Dos Santos, 1971).

The implication of the theory for central bank digital currency development and use is that the central bank digital currency can be developed/designed and used to create efficient dependencies in society. For example, the central bank digital currency could be used to control the inflation rate. It can also be used to facilitate fiscal allocation by the fiscal authorities. It can also be used as a platform to enhance payments and the flow of funds to production and investment activities in the country. It can also be used to provide adequate economic stimulus to distressed businesses during economic downturns. It can also be used to provide adequate coverage of social welfare from the government to impoverished people to improve their welfare (Arat, 1988; Brown and Long, 2018; Gilman, 2018).

## The Concerns-Based Innovation Adoption Model

The concerns-based innovation adoption model was developed by Hall in 1975. The theory looks at innovation adoption from the perspective of those impacted by the adoption of the innovation and also from the perspective of those charged with implementing the subsequent change (Hall, 1975). The theory proposes that by addressing the concerns of adopters during the adoption process, the challenges they experience during the change process will be reduced if not eliminated.

The concerns-based innovation adoption model states that when people learn about a new innovation for the first time, the first set of questions they ask are self-oriented questions: What is it? and How will it affect me? When these questions are resolved, the next questions that emerge are task-oriented questions: How do I do it? How can I use this innovation efficiently? and Why is it taking so much time? Finally, when the self-oriented and task-oriented concerns are largely resolved, the implementers will ask questions that are impact-oriented: Is this change working for people? and Is there something that will work even better? (Hall and Hord, 1987).

There are six assumptions of the concerns-based innovation adoption model, namely, (i) change is a process, not an event; (ii) change is accomplished by individuals; (iii) change is a highly personal experience; (iv) change involves developmental growth; (v) change is best understood in operational terms, and (vi) the focus during implementation should be on individuals, innovation, and context (Straub, 2009). Based on these assumptions, there should be greater focus on the: stages of concern, innovation configuration mapping, and the levels of use, when implementing an innovation.

The implication of the concerns-based innovation adoption model for central bank digital currency is that a successful implementation of central bank digital currency will involve much more than providing staff with materials, resources, and training. It will also involve the human element — the people who are actually doing the work because each person involved in the central bank digital currency implementation process may respond to central bank digital currency adoption strategy with unique attitudes and beliefs.

## DEVELOPING A CENTRAL BANK DIGITAL CURRENCY THEORY

Scholars can use case studies on central bank digital currency to develop a central bank digital currency theory. Building a central bank digital currency theory from case studies is a research strategy that involves using one or more cases to create theoretical constructs and propositions from case-based or empirical evidence. Case studies are often descriptions of particular instances of a phenomenon that are based on a variety of data sources (Yin, 1984). Cases can be historical or recent accounts of central bank digital currency success in countries. Each case study on central bank digital currency can serve as a distinct experiment that stands on its own as an analytic unit, while multiple case studies will serve as discrete experiments that serve as replications, contrasts, and extensions to the existing or emerging theories. Building theories from central bank digital currency case studies is likely to become a popular and more relevant research strategy for future studies on the central bank digital currency. Although case studies have some problems such as the small sample size associated with case studies and the one-sided interviews that increase informant bias, these issues can be mitigated by careful choice of sample and sample size, and by conducting fair interviews that limit the informants bias.

## FUTURE INSIGHTS AND FUTURE RESEARCH DIRECTION

CBDC theories can explain current and future trends in addiction to internet-based technologies. CBDC theories can explain why people accept digital technology which when over-used could lead to digital addiction. The growing addiction in using internet-based technologies in the modern age makes it more likely that society will embrace CBDCs sooner or later. When CBDCs replace physical money, its positive features can improve our lives in almost every area. While digital addiction has some positives, it also has its downsides which should be considered. Some of the downsides include the unhealthy dependence on digital technologies and the alienation and exclusion of members of society who do not want to embrace digital technology or digital innovation. The implication is that people who do not want to use CBDC may be excluded from the financial system or may not be able to access CBDC-based financial products and services. CBDC theories can also be used to explain why some people may refuse to accept digital technology.

Future research studies can examine whether CBDC adoption can lead to digital addiction and the possible remedies. Future research studies can also examine the additional theories that could explain CBDC adoption and its usefulness.

## CONCLUSION

This paper presented some theories that support central bank digital currency development and its usefulness. The identified theories can be used in central bank digital currency research and policy debates. The purpose of this article has been to show that the central bank digital currency can be studied from a theoretical perspective. The theories presented in this paper may serve as a guide for what needs to be done to make the central bank digital currency become a potent tool to spur growth in an economy. Using these theories to explain the central bank digital currency will ensure that researchers are using the right theoretical constructs to explain the role of central bank digital currency in the economy.

A possible direction for future research is to develop a glossary of CBDC success stories across countries, and identify which theories have the highest explanatory power in explaining the success of CBDCs in these countries. Of course, many additional theories that explain CBDC development and its usefulness can be developed, and there is no limit to the number of theories or ideas that can be explored.

## REFERENCES

Aghion, P., Howitt, P., Howitt, P. W., Brant-Collett, M., & García-Peñalosa, C. (1998). *Endogenous growth theory*. MIT press.

Arat, Z. F. (1988). Democracy and economic development: Modernization theory revisited. *Comparative Politics*, *21*(1), 21–36. doi:10.2307/422069

Brown, U., & Long, G. (2018). Poverty and welfare. In *Social Welfare* (pp. 19–34). Routledge. doi:10.4324/9781315202686-3

Davis, F. D., Bagozzi, R. P., & Warshaw, P. R. (1989). User acceptance of computer technology: A comparison of two theoretical models. *Management Science*, *35*(8), 982–1003. doi:10.1287/mnsc.35.8.982

Gilman, N. (2018). Modernization theory never dies. *History of Political Economy*, *50*(S1), 133–151. doi:10.1215/00182702-7033896

Hall, G. E., & Hord, S. M. (1987). *Change in schools: Facilitating the process*. Suny Press.

Hall, G. E., Loucks, S. F., Rutherford, W. L., & Newlove, B. W. (1975). Levels of use of the innovation: A framework for analyzing innovation adoption. *Journal of Teacher Education*, *26*(1), 52–56. doi:10.1177/002248717502600114

Howitt, P. (2010). Endogenous growth theory. In *Economic growth* (pp. 68–73). Palgrave Macmillan.

King, R. G., & Levine, R. (1993). Finance and growth: Schumpeter might be right. *The Quarterly Journal of Economics*, *108*(3), 717–737. doi:10.2307/2118406

Lee, Y., Kozar, K. A., & Larsen, K. R. (2003). The technology acceptance model: Past, present, and future. *Communications of the Association for Information Systems*, *12*(1), 50. doi:10.17705/1CAIS.01250

Levine, R. (2005). Finance and growth: theory and evidence. Handbook of economic growth, 1, 865-934.

Marangunić, N., & Granić, A. (2015). Technology acceptance model: A literature review from 1986 to 2013. *Universal Access in the Information Society*, *14*(1), 81–95. doi:10.100710209-014-0348-1

Marsh, R. M. (2014). Modernization theory, then and now. *Comparative Sociology*, *13*(3), 261–283. doi:10.1163/15691330-12341311

Md Nor, K., Pearson, J. M., & Ahmad, A. (2010). Adoption of internet banking theory of the diffusion of innovation. *International Journal of Management Studies, 17*(1), 69–85. doi:10.32890/ijms.17.1.2010.9984

Palley, T. I. (1996). Growth theory in a Keynesian mode: Some Keynesian foundations for new endogenous growth theory. *Journal of Post Keynesian Economics, 19*(1), 113–135. doi:10.1080/01603477.1996.11490100

Rogers, E. M. (2003). *Diffusion of innovations* (5th ed.). Free Press.

Romer, P. M. (1994). The origins of endogenous growth. *The Journal of Economic Perspectives, 8*(1), 3–22. doi:10.1257/jep.8.1.3

Schumpeter, J. A. (1911). *The Theory of Economic Development.* Harvard University Press.

Shaw, G. K. (1992). Policy implications of endogenous growth theory. *Economic Journal (London), 102*(412), 611–621. doi:10.2307/2234298

Straub, E. T. (2009). Understanding technology adoption: Theory and future directions for informal learning. *Review of Educational Research, 79*(2), 625–649. doi:10.3102/0034654308325896

Trew, A. (2006). Finance and growth: A critical survey. *The Economic Record, 82*(259), 481–490. doi:10.1111/j.1475-4932.2006.00361.x

Wani, T. A., & Ali, S. W. (2015). Innovation diffusion theory. *Journal of general management research, 3*(2), 101-118.

Yin, R. K. (1984). *Case study research: Design and methods.* Sage.

## ADDITIONAL READINGS

Allen, F., Gu, X., & Jagtiani, J. (2022). Fintech, cryptocurrencies, and CBDC: Financial structural transformation in China. *Journal of International Money and Finance, 124*, 102625. doi:10.1016/j.jimonfin.2022.102625

Jiang, J. H. (2020). *CBDC adoption and usage: some insights from field and laboratory experiments (No. 2020-12).* Bank of Canada.

Khiaonarong, T., & Humphrey, D. (2019). Cash use across countries and the demand for central bank digital currency. *IMF Working Paper, 13*(1), 32–46. doi:10.5089/9781484399606.001

Liu, X., Wang, Q., Wu, G., & Zhang, C. (2022). Determinants of individuals' intentions to use central bank digital currency: Evidence from China. *Technology Analysis and Strategic Management*, 1–15. doi:10.1080/09537325.2022.2131517

Ngo, V. M., Van Nguyen, P., Nguyen, H. H., Tram, H. X. T., & Hoang, L. C. (2023). Governance and monetary policy impacts on public acceptance of CBDC adoption. *Research in International Business and Finance, 64*, 101865. doi:10.1016/j.ribaf.2022.101865

Oh, E. Y., & Zhang, S. (2022). Informal economy and central bank digital currency. *Economic Inquiry*, *60*(4), 1520–1539. doi:10.1111/ecin.13105

Ozili, P. K. (2022). Central bank digital currency research around the World: a review of literature. Journal of Money Laundering Control.

Söilen, K. S., & Benhayoun, L. (2021). Household acceptance of central bank digital currency: The role of institutional trust. *International Journal of Bank Marketing*, *40*(1), 172–196. doi:10.1108/IJBM-04-2021-0156

## KEY TERMS AND DEFINITIONS

**Central Bank Digital Currencies:** A digital equivalent of physical cash that is issued by the central bank.

**Model:** A representation of a system, or, of reality.

**Theory:** A supposition or a system of ideas intended to explain something, especially one based on general principles independent of the thing to be explained.

# Chapter 5
# Production and Consumption in the Relationship Between Digital Culture and New Communication Technologies

**Fırat Ata**
*Hatay Mustafa Kemal University, Turkey*

## ABSTRACT

*Digital culture is a concept that has gained attention due to the effectiveness of new communication technologies and new media in daily and social life. The structural link between digital culture and new communication technologies necessitates the transformation of concepts such as production and consumption and/or re-evaluation with additional expressions. Within the scope of this study, which focuses on the role of new communication technologies in digital culture, the dimensions of production and consumption are evaluated. According to the literature review carried out within the scope of the study, production and consumption processes can occur together in digital culture. At this point, users who are producers-consumers can also be producers of the content they consume by using the possibilities and features of new communication technologies in digital culture. The fact that production and consumption forms in new media environments directly or indirectly serve the capitalist order is another important piece of information reached within the scope of the study.*

## INTRODUCTION

The concept of culture, which encompasses material and spiritual values that a society produces and consumes has experienced a semantic expansion with digitalization (Akyüz, 2021, p. 139). Digital culture can serve as an indicator of all behaviors and processes in the process of using new media (Stapleton & Jaillant, 2022, p. 819). While traditional culture has formed over a rooted historical process, digital culture is still a new concept in terms of time. It is not easy to fully describe the cultural dimension in such

DOI: 10.4018/978-1-6684-8397-8.ch005

a new environment. This is because the process of general recognition required to determine whether a content, behavior, or element is part of digital culture is still very new (Smith, 2007, pp. 14-18).

One of the tools and/or fields that express the basic concepts and analyzes in the formation and shaping of digital culture is new communication technologies or new media (Bowker, 2008, p. 9; Shifman, 2013, p. 18). New communication technologies are related to the processes that enable the technical formation of new media (Başer, 2010). New media, on the other hand, is considered as a field/tool that is associated with connections and tools such as "internet, computer, mobile phone, tablet" and covers a wide range of areas such as "web sites, news sites, commercial sites, official institutions and organizations" (Törenli, 2005).

In addition to the many features such as interaction, hypertext, asynchrony, storage, archiving, speed, the concept of culture, like many other fields and concepts, emerges with a new dimension/transformation in new media which differs from traditional media with its digitalization feature (Manovich, 2001, p. 40; Flavian & Gurrea, 2016). Production processes such as "writing news, creating audio-visual content and making sales" have been added to the consumption processes of users such as "reading, watching, listening, using and buying." A new media user not only consumes the content presented to him/her, but also participates in the production processes by using new media fields and tools (Ruggiero, 2017). In this context, new media fields and tools can directly and/or indirectly affect the changing cultural life conditions due to reasons such as production-consumption balance and globalization (Akyüz, 2018, p. 120). Services in many areas such as trade, banking services, communication, health, education, media are offered digitally. This has led to the formation of a digital culture (Küçüktamer & Karakuyu, 2021, p. 71)

The digital culture in new media is multidimensional and one of these dimensions encompasses the relationships between production and consumption. In the relationship between traditional media and culture, the decisive points between the concepts of production-consumption and producer-consumer have not clearly stated yet (Bassett, 2013, pp. 323, 334). For example, while a journalist produces news, a reader consumes it. At this point, the relations of production and consumption have become apparent. Contrary to what has been stated, defining the relations of production and consumption in digital culture in new media becomes more complex. For example, the reader, who is the consumer of the news in the new media, can become a producer. Readers do not only comment on the news in an interactive environment, but they can also be directly or indirectly involved in the news content and thus in the news production process. In addition, readers, viewers and/or listeners can also produce news on personal portals, websites or social media networks/applications in the new media. This process in digital culture causes the production and consumption relations to be melted in a pot in some cases (Hansen et al., 2020).

In addition to technical classifications, the issue of capitalism-oriented problems is also present in the digital culture of new media, just as in the traditional version (Gere, 2019, pp. 19-20). In other words, the labor, product and/or service that emerges after the production processes has a dimension that serves large capital groups rather than individuals. This process, which is considered as cultural imperialism or cultural capitalism, shows that the production and consumption dimensions of digital culture require additional definitions and analysis after the new communication technologies (Başlar, 2013, p. 775). Anything that has the potential to generate capital in digital culture can be a part of the production process. For example, the content of a movie/series, a photograph of a famous singer, a report by a journalist, an ordinary post by a social media user can serve the production and consumption process in digital culture (Ritzer & Jurgenson, 2010, pp. 21-22).

This study, whose general framework is outlined, focuses on the role of new communication technologies in digital culture in terms of production and consumption. The study is important in terms of revealing the transformation of digital culture in new media forms, which is handled by researchers from different perspectives. In the theoretically structured study, four main titles are included. In the first part, the concept of digital culture is discussed. The second part introduces the new communication technologies from different perspectives, and the third part deals with the relationship between digital culture and new communication technologies. Production and consumption dimensions in digital culture, which is the focus of the study, are discussed in the fourth part. In this regard, the current transformation processes of the concepts of production and consumption are examined. The conclusion part of the study, which includes a general evaluation, is completed with suggestions related to the subject and an additional reading list that can be referred to for future studies.

## BACKROUND

### Digital Culture

The main feature that enables the formation of digital culture, which is considered as a new type of culture, is digitalization. The concept of digitalization refers to data that exists in different elements. Although it can be attributed to various systems such as numerical, linguistic, or similar, digital has become a concept that is used synonymously with computers and is used to describe the previously mentioned elements in addition to the current context. Although there is a close connection between computer technology and digital technologies, the term "digital" has gone beyond just referring to machines that categorize and sort data. Digital now refers to a world where virtual images are detailed, communication is instant, media is everywhere, and experiences are mostly shaped by global connections. Today, the concept of digital refers to cultural products arising from the ubiquity of virtual reality, digital effects, digital film and television, electronic music, computer games, multimedia, internet, wireless application protocol (WAP) and digital technology (Gere, 2019, p. 17).

Digitization, which refers to the digitization of cultural heritage and the digitization of heritage objects and services, produces three fundamental changes in the cultural process. First, technology has led to the creation of a digital heritage products. Digitization has resulted in the process of formalizing heritage information as an exchangeable commodity. Second, the consumer has gained a certain independence to acquire digital content that is no longer linked to the physical location of the producer. Thirdly, the widespread adoption of digital technology in every aspect of life has led to changes in consumer expectations, as they can now access digital heritage content at the right place and time and even participate in the production process (Navarrete, 2013, pp. 251-252).

According to Uzalac and Cvjeticanin, digital culture is a new and complex concept. Today's digital trends are increasingly intertwining with the world of culture and art that encompasses different aspects of the convergence of cultures, media, and information technologies, and affects new forms of communication. Information processing technologies and the internet, which are the basic dynamics of digital culture, have changed our relationship towards information and information society, intensifying the flow of cultural goods and services and leading to a new understanding of cultural creativity, adding a new dimension to these mutual relations (2008, p. 3).

The hyper-complex digital environment, which emerges as a new dimension, disrupts traditional linear approaches in order to understand the context in which business models are designed, and encompasses innovative interdisciplinary holistic models based on case studies of organizations and students

(Padua, 2021, pp. 1-6). As can be seen, digital culture, which expresses more than being technological, also includes organizational and communicative dimensions. In this respect, it can be said that digital culture can also shape a collective space for online communication, intercultural connections that support a shared democracy through the creation of cultural networks motivated by people and supported by technology (Snyder, 2005, p. 1).

In addition to the advantages of digital culture in daily and social life, there are also critical perspectives on the concept. Digital culture is a historical conditioned unexpected phenomenon whose various components first emerged as a response to the expansions of modern capitalism and then combined with the demands brought by the wars of the mid-twentieth century. Technology is only one of the resources that play a role in the development of digital culture. There are also sub-cultural formations such as techno-scientific debates about knowledge and information systems, avant-grade art, counterculture utopianism, critical theory and even punk. These different elements are the products of abstraction, coding, editing, virtualization and programming paradigms like computers. Digital culture is the product of complex and dialectical interactions between these elements (Gere, 2019, pp. 19-20). This dialectical culture industry is a story of corporate and counter-cultural social spheres, far from being the top-down domination of culture by corporate forces. More importantly, unlike the abstract macro narrative painted by critical theorists, the narrative of the digital culture industry is far from simple (Allen-Robertson, 2013, p. 5).

## New Communication Technologies

The use of the internet as a communication tool since the 1970s has initiated a new process called the digital communication age in the media. The transformation of the internet into a social media tool has paved the way for a global information mobility. As a result, electronic devices have developed rapidly, and online information has become digital. Since digital information is easy to access and share, it has created an environment appropriate for spreading news beyond boundaries and to the entire world (Akgül & Ayer, 2020, pp. 156). In other words, the internet, which is an important part of new communication technologies, is the name of combining computers or all computer networks in a decentralized structure. With the widespread use of the internet, it is observed that most of the concepts and practices in daily life are reshaped. This decentralized network enables "many-to-many" communication, rather than "one-to-many" communication, as is inherent in a leading tool of the digital age, such as television (Kergel, 2023, p. 1; Küçüktamer, 2017, p. 171).

Among the fields where new communication technologies are used are "online newspapers/magazines/books, downloadable music and videos, cinema, bloggers and podcasts." In addition to these, new or emerging technologies for indirect public communication include "wireless and mobile media, digital television and satellite radio, digital cameras, digital music players, and others," not just the internet and the Web. Furthermore, new communication technologies also encompass new media, which serves specialized audiences or communities, rather than mass audiences in the traditional sense, and is accessible online and through other digital distribution platforms (Pavlik, 2008, p. 8).

New communication technologies do not tend to be content that is ready to be consumed as a finite product by audiences as "standalone" things. Instead, digital media objects generally have as much in common with (telecom) conversations, media artifacts, or objects as they do with shared points. Therefore, when viewing traditional media content such as a movie, book, or painting, these objects have a limited "object-like" nature. Digital media contents are often in constant production, in constant dialogue and transformation with audiences and other digital products and technologies (Miller, 2020, p. 52).

The central role of mobile applications and software becomes visible in the processes of "expanding access, enhancing quality, and creating a whole greater than the sum of its parts that can support other revenue initiatives" (Paolini et al., 2013, p. 281). Like many cultural products, the access, usage, and importance of mobile media is determined by social stratification, wealth and income inequality, and established dynamics of inequality. Nonetheless, mobile media has entered the hands, pockets, wallets, bags, clothes, and lives of people from a wide range of societies, ages, cultures, and locations. Mobile media has evolved from a simple extension of a landline phone to a device that combines social and local media and has become an important and inevitable part of contemporary cultural practice (Goggin & Hjorth, 2014, p. 1).

New communication technologies have become so integral to society and organizations that it is difficult to imagine the world without them. "External environmental factors and internal socio-structural factors" can affect the development of digital culture. These two factors, located between new and existing digital cultural resources, may encourage new research focusing on their direct and interactive effects on organizational outcomes (Grover et al., 2022, p. 8). The use of new communication technologies to establish connections has contributions for society, economy, and individuals. Although the relationship between technological infrastructure and digital platform development and inequality is complex, policy makers emphasize that interventions have a direct and positive impact on the adoption and use of digital technologies and services (Mansell, 2017, p. 150).

In addition to what has been stated, when it comes to new communication technologies, firstly, the fact that inequalities in online participation are greater than those in offline participation (especially in discussions about the potential negative effects of digital technologies on cultural participation in the current socio-economic environment) are problematic. In this context, the quantity, diversity, and accessibility of cultural products can create opportunities for new forms of cultural fragmentation and exclusion, which exacerbates existing inequalities instead of improving them. Second, while the gap in household internet access closes, digital media is unequally distributed as a means of benefiting from cultural participation (online or offline) in the ability to use the internet. Third, new communication technologies confirm that the importance of socio-demographic variables continues in the process of cultural participation. In other words, "occupation, education, ethnicity, age and disability/being ill" can make it difficult to access new communication technologies and to involve users in digital culture (Mihelij, 2019, p. 1481).

## The Relationship Between Digital Culture and New Communication Technologies

Digital culture is at a historical transformation point with new content. Bits and bytes, which are the smallest file storage sizes in digital media, have replaced Johannes Guttenberg's ink, which has been the recording element of cultural heritage for many years, with the printing press (Stapleton & Jaillant, 2022, p. 819). Digital transformation does not only result directly from digital technology. For digital transformation to take root, digital technologies must be filled with social meaning. Since digital technologies were invented, many different things that can be done with these technologies have been understood over time. At the same time, we had to teach ourselves how to use these technologies, thinking that we can use these technologies in many different ways. From this mutual experience, current digital culture has emerged not as the natural expression or extension of these technologies, but as a social selection with consequences for the same technologies (Guy, 2019, p. 56). New communication technologies have been a major force of cultural innovation, from the virtualization of group networks and social identities to the digital convergence of tactile and audiovisual media. New communication technologies have become the symbol of user-centered content production and mentioned cultural transformation, from Wikipedia to YouTube and Open Access Source and applications. In addition to the aforementioned situation, digital culture also expresses the transformation of what it means to be creative in a vast and growing repository of media, data, computing power and communication possibilities (Bowker, 2008, p. 9).

One of the cornerstones of digital culture is that digital networks foster greater connectivity, collaboration, communication, community and participation. Facebook, Twitter, YouTube, blog, vlog cross-network or open source applications suggest the need for a community paradigm foundation (Gere, 2012, p. 1). In other words, social media applications such as YouTube, MySpace and Facebook reflect this latest participatory culture. They not only create virtual communities, but also enable viewers to become producers as well as buyers of the media. The Internet is also important because it allows fans of different cultural forms to create virtual communities that contribute to original understanding and even the content of their selected interests (Creeber & Martin, 2009, p. 19). The specified applications and environments are highly compatible with the way the culture is created by the users and exchangeable. At this point, it can be said that Youtube, Twitter, Facebook, Wikipedia and other similar applications and sites are based on a productive basis for users (Shifman, 2013, p. 18).

Artificial intelligence is one of the developments that allow the advancement of productive industries, which is possible with the use of new communication technologies. There are new socio-economic and communication technologies such as "virtual reality, augmented reality and blockchain" under this field that develop depending on this field. Artificial intelligence applications can be effectively utilized in production, sales, and consumption stages in productive industries such as video games, design, cinema, voice over, music, and culture-art. The development of virtual reality and/or augmented reality applications, and the advancements in technology have made it easier for productive industries to provide content and make the experience easier, leading to significant gains in terms of low cost. With the help of blockchain technology, access to digital works and applications such as books, music, culture-art, graphics, games, etc., that can be defined as products of productive industries has become easier (Söğüt, 2022, p. 14).

Bell, evaluates the relationship between new communication technologies and digital culture with the concept of cyber culture. According to Bell, "digital devices belonging to companies such as mp3 players or cell phone companies, as well as new medical imaging technologies, cyber-pets, digital animations, and all kinds of simulations" are among the fundamental tools of change and transformation in digital culture and cyber culture, which are frequently used interchangeably (2007).

New communication technologies are also determining factors in the field of heritage, which can be considered as one of the elements of digital culture, as well as in many other areas of society. New communication technologies are seen as important tools for increasing participation and diversity in culture and the arts. One of the most concerning aspects from a cultural perspective of the new communication technologies is the gap between those who have access to these technologies and those who do not. At this point, access to new communication technologies is associated with socio-economic factors such as "income, ethnic origin, age, gender, education, and geographical location" (Mihelij, 2019, p. 1465; Paolini et al., 2013, p. 272).

## Digital Culture and New Communication Technologies With Production and Consumption Dimensions

Production, which means creating concepts such as goods, services, and products for the continuity of social life, is undergoing a change in the value process. This process not only reproduces equivalent of its own value, but also transforms a surplus with a surplus value that can be more or less depending on the changing conditions. This process, which is defined as changing capital, shows that valuable concepts such as knowledge, products, objects, etc. go through value-generating processes in the production process (Marx, 2003, p. 191). Production, which is a new concept, has become crucial, especially for the sectors based on intangible labor, such as media technologies, Today, from social networks to content management systems, the exploitation of intangible labor is provided through production processes, and production plays an important role in defining the production environment through the new media and new economic system (Uzunoğlu, 2015, p. 181).

Consumption, which means the use of concepts such as products, services, and/or goods produced in the production process in accordance with certain needs or motivations, is emerging in a new form through the use of artificial intelligence applications that are growing along with new communication technologies, which are believed to deeply impact daily life and are among the external factors. With the notion that consumption has become a cultural phenomenon, it is believed that leisure time is shaped not by users' free choices but by manipulation. In this context, it is claimed that these forms of manipulation are carried out through the help of widely used internet-based intelligent applications and algorithms, aided by the electronic footprints collected from individuals, and that this creates a filter bubble effect (Gilanlioglu & Oze, 2020, p. 185). Consumption process in digital culture as in traditional culture can be analyzed with two basic dimensions. In the first dimension, it is considered as a signification and communication process based on a code in which consumption practices are registered and gain their meaning. In this dimension, consumption is a system of exchange and can be dealt with by structural analysis. In the second dimension, it is stated as the process of social classification and differentiation, in which objects/signs are arranged not only as meaningful differences within a code, but also as status values within a hierarchy (Baudrillard, 2016, p. 62). The shift from traditional consumption contexts to artificial intelligence and to the contexts based on internet of things has brought about a big change in the sense that the learning relationships are no longer only among actors (human) that learn by interacting with each other and using goods. Both types of contexts are supported by intelligent products that have structural cognitive connections and are capable of interacting with each other and with humans within a certain context (Grandinetti et al., 2022, p. 1).

The emergence of digital technologies has significantly changed human life and added new dimensions to our consumption behaviors. There is a conceptual framework that explains the mutual, repetitive, and dynamic relationship between digital consumption culture and digital culturalization, and highlights the three hereditary characteristics of digital consumption culture. These include "consumer empowerment, reciprocity between online and offline worlds, and differentiation of identities." The digital culturalization in the production and consumption process also highlights important concepts and views such as "digital integration, digital separation, and digital deprivation" in studying cultural forms in the digital age (Dey et al., 2020, p. 1).

Central formations with the new communication technologies have brought changes and transformations in the "sociological, cultural, and economic" fields. Lev Manovich associates the changes in communication technologies with social change, paralleling social and economic processes, while Dan

Schiller explains the new order brought by new media with the concept of "digital capitalism." Today, it is seen that new economic fields have emerged through the networks established with new media technologies, the Internet is effectively used by capital, and the capitalist mentality has spread to all areas of the virtual world (Başlar, 2013, p. 775).

According to Castells, the relationship between capitalist mode of production and the informational mode of development depends on adequate information regarding productivity, competitiveness, and long-term planning and investment in each sector. High-tech companies are dependent on financial resources to sustain their endless efforts towards innovation, productivity and competitiveness. The financial capital, which operates directly through financial institutions or indirectly through stock market dynamics, determines the fate of the high-tech industries. On the other hand, technology and knowledge are decisive tools for earning profits and acquiring market shares. Thus, even though industrial capital has its own specific operating styles, financial capital and high technology have become increasingly dependent on each other (2010, pp. 503-504).

In capitalist societies of the last two centuries, where production must be balanced with consumption, culture and communication tools have been used to impose consumption. In this sense, almost all activities of individuals are planned by capitalism. Capitalism continues its existence through digital capitalism as an economic system, while strategies that are profitable for the system are also kept alive and adapted to digitalization. In a world undergoing transformation through digitalization, the disappearance of time and space in communication results in social interaction, connectivity, and interactive participation, creating and transforming systems that are profitable. The philosophy of "production must be supported by consumption" that emerged in the first stages of the industrial revolution has encouraged mass society and the culture industries, leading to the formation of a consumption-centered structure/process (Gür Omay, 2022, pp. 42-43).

The concept of producer-consumer in digital culture appears with the dimensions of "control and exploitation" of capitalism. In particular, the trend towards free labor instead of paid labor and the provision of products for free is prevalent in social media applications, which have seen a significant increase in use with new communication technologies. The new producer-consumer that emerges in this form often performs free production but can consume for a fee. This situation raises the possibility of a capitalism in the form of producer-consumer (Ritzer & Jurgenson, 2010, p. 13). This formal transformation occurring in the process of production and consumption is explained through three different points. The first point is that capitalism has a large control over the producers and consumers within the digital structure. The second point is that producers and consumers are not aware that they are being exploited. The third point, at least, concerns the possibility of the emergence of a completely new economic form, especially on the Internet. Capitalism involves the exchange of money for goods and services, and profit is made in these exchanges. In many cases, there is almost no exchange of money between the users and owners of many websites (Ritzer & Jurgenson, 2010, pp. 21-22).

At this point, especially open-source software production and social media applications as Napster, Wikipedia, and YouTube have created millions of digital media communities that do not conform to the daily experience of sharp distinctions between production, distribution and consumption. These platforms criticize the traditional cultural production and consumption dimensions and emphasize the necessity of digital culture. This perspective has sharpened with a seemingly endless series of high-profile conflicts between new and old cultural intermediaries. Media companies versus YouTube, traditional encyclopedias versus Wikipedia, record companies versus Napster (or Grokster or iTunes), or publishers versus Google are just a few of them. These conflicts have highlighted the social and legal construction of digital culture in forms that are comparatively settled or slow moving for older technologies (Bowker, 2008, p. 10). According to Fuchs, the data generated by the use of Google services leads to a capitalist exploitation system. Producer-consumer activities in the new media environment, which creates such an exploitation system, serve the benefit of individuals and institutions different from those who produce and consume. This is just one example of the exploitation of users in digital culture. Capitalist consumption, in which new communication technologies play a significant role, appears as an extreme form of exploitation in which the producing consumers work entirely for free (2012, pp. 45-47).

In today's digital world, digital environments have become an environment that they have brought everyone together, from housewives to high school students, from businessmen to workers, and have made them equalized. For example, a person who is at home and not working, maybe who hasn't even received any education, can make very high amounts of money through Instagram. Digital environments trigger consumption day by day. This can be a source of income for some, but it also raises various questions and issues in the context of labor (Demirkaya & Koyuncu, 2021, p. 182). This new means of production and consumption is exactly what adds a lot of economic value to platforms while also raising any and all questions related to public costs. Some major technology companies can serve as examples of this causal relationship. For example, Google has intertwined intricately with Education Edition or Search. Apple's Health Kit and Research Kit are collector services that connect patients and health experts' data to Apple's infrastructure platforms. The acquisition of Whole Foods by Amazon or Google's 20% ownership in Uber can also be considered examples of mutual compatibility and, therefore, expansion in this process (Van Dijck et al., 2018, pp. 18-19).

Additionally, according to Manovich, the notion that every user in digital culture is a producer or that most users primarily consume content is a fallacy. In fact, only a small portion of users of the most popular social media sites (Flickr, YouTube, Wikipedia) contribute with their own content. Furthermore, there is a fundamental shift in culturally valued consumption as a phenomenon. The companies creating social media platforms have a direct interest in having as many users visit as possible to make money (by offering advertisements, selling user data to other companies, selling add-on services, etc.), leading to the users investing a significant portion of their lives into these platforms (2009, p. 320).

Some reference concepts are needed to evaluate the form and regulation processes taken by production and/or production relationships in digital culture. The first of these reference concepts is the "profile" category. In production within digital culture, the profile category represents the location or node point of data accumulation. An individual profile is considered very important in contemporary/digital culture. The second reference concept is "connection." Connection is established between people and things, either as a result of data collection and mining or by researching and scanning previously self-organized content. The third reference concept "metadata," ensures the organization of archives within the digital structure, classifies the content and makes it accessible. The fourth reference concept is "home gaming," which encourages people to generate data while having fun. The game is very important in understanding the new social data and the social life of these data and the methods that operate on this data (Beer & Burrows, 2013, pp. 50-51).

New communication technologies are characterized by complex dynamics between traditional media and the distribution of new content on the network, both in production and consumption. Products with information content do not have a set of fixed rules for producing a good film or a good entertainment program. Sometimes, conditional factors play a very important role in defining quality: if you are collecting news at the right time and place, you may get a valuable piece of information with very low production costs, maybe even just with a cell phone. Additionally, a one-dimensional approach does not fit everyone in new media content production. There are different contents with different cost structures, product conditions, and vertical chains (Gambaro, 2012, p. 50-53).

Over time, the advancements in information and communication technologies and their widespread use have also manifested themselves in the trade sector. The reality of "e-commerce," which presents itself with features such as ease of use, time and space savings, speed, reliability, and cost-effectiveness, is present today. There is a transformation in the way people interact with brands and companies, how they shop and purchase both online and offline. The digitalization of consumption has made competition even more intense in today's world. However, there have been changes in the contents and implementations of the facts as well. Consumption has almost become the purpose of life for people. Regardless of whether they are reading, working, traveling, or improving themselves, they are always in a constant consumption process. At the same time, they are exposed to serious information in terms of consumption (Opreana & Vinerean, 2015, p. 29; Demirkaya & Koyuncu, 2021, p. 191).

In addition to e-commerce, the production and consumption process of news is also one of the important topics between new communication technologies and digital culture. In situations where news production, consumption, and interpretation are directly related to online social interactions, the impact of the participant behavior on the trust in news media is often neglected. Furthermore, some alternative news platforms, especially social media and online news aggregators, fulfill multiple roles in terms of news consumption. In this regard, it is likely that some people who prefer alternative sources since they offer an alternative view, as well as some who have low confidence in the news media may prefer to use alternative sources because they provide fast access (Richard & Sora, 2017, p. 1294).

The abundance of news sources and the underlying expanded technological capabilities in digital culture means that in principle, anyone can participate. For example, politicians use social network sites to communicate their policies without obstruction, to clarify their positions if they feel they have been misreported or misrepresented by journalists, or even to resign. Ordinary citizens can start their own news stories on social networks or draw attention to topics that interest them (Jensen et al., 2016, p. 3). The changing forms of news production and consumption bring up a series of urgent questions. How and to what extent can citizens and those outside of institutionalized news media influence the form and content of news? How do changing.news consumption patterns and at least the more active role of users affect news production? How do "old" and "new" news platforms come together when people combine traditional news sources with interactive, participatory platforms for news production, distribution, and consumption? (Jensen et al., 2016, p. 2).

There are also studies focusing on automation of the production in the production process in digital culture. From this perspective, there is the view that automated teller machines (ATMs) are increasingly becoming more common in the material world that turns people into producer-consumers. Rather than relying on a paid worker (teller) to produce services, consumers become the providers of banking services that produce the same services simultaneously at ATMs (Ritzer, 2015, p. 412). According to Navarrete, the adoption of digital technologies in society has brought about a change in the demand and supply of cultural heritage. Digital cultural heritage (both goods and services) has become an object, consisting of two parts: representation (can be turned or be a proxy) and documentation (identification and contextualization). Digital products can be made through a digitalization process or can exist digitally. This expresses a change that can accommodate new objects (including layered and mixed media) in the production process, new production systems (assisted by consumers), and new forms of distribution (as information services) (2013, p. 265).

## FUTURE RESEARCH DIRECTIONS

In future studies on this study subject, the relationship between digital culture and new communication technologies can be discussed by including different key concepts in addition to the concepts of production and consumption. The relationship between digital culture and new communication technologies can be examined as a research subject in terms of economic as well as cultural, political and psychological factors. In this direction, multidimensional research can be carried out on the relationship between digital culture and new communication technologies, not with one science or discipline, but with more than one science/discipline.

## CONCLUSION

This study, which focuses on the role of new communication technologies in digital culture based on the dimensions of production and consumption, has yielded important findings. Firstly, digital culture has a different view from its traditional version. In other words, digital culture emerges as a result of digital technologies based on digitization. Therefore, many concepts and evaluations in the digital world are required to define and interpret digital culture. In this regard, it should be noted that digital culture is closely related to different concepts such as "technology, communication, media, social life, capitalism, information, production and consumption."

Within the scope of this study, the role of new communication technologies in digital culture has been highlighted. The literature review conducted showed that new communication technologies and new media are significant and central elements of digital culture. In fact, new communication technologies not only enable the formation of digital culture but also create areas where cultural capital is produced. Content that could be considered as a component of digital culture is produced and consumed in many internet-based environments such as social media, shopping sites, news sites, audio-visual content sites and official applications.

In the digital culture, where new communication technologies are the basis, the relations of production and consumption have appeared in multiple dimensions. First, the concepts of production/producer and consumption/consumer can be clearly categorized in traditional culture. This is not clearly demonstrated in digital culture. In other words, when it comes to digital culture, the concept of "producer-consumer," which includes both concepts, is included in the concepts of production and consumption. The concept of producer-consumer refers to the dimension of being the producer of the relevant product and service while consuming a content or service, while using new communication technologies in digital culture. Another dimension of production and consumption relations within the digital culture, where new communication technologies are fundamental, is related to the process of capitalism. The content produced in digital culture has a dimension that serves capitalist capital groups as well as the owner of the production. In fact, in some processes and situations, especially in the content produced in social media/network-based applications and platforms, companies or groups that have a capitalist structure, not producers, are in question.

Users involved in the production process in digital culture should have knowledge of the technical, economic and political structure of new communication technologies and new media. It should not be overlooked that production and consumption forms in digital culture are possible with new communication technologies. Users who know the structure of new communication technologies in line with the specified can have information about what kind of content can be produced on which platforms, how the produced content and/or services can be delivered to consumers, and how this content can be kept safe in the digital world. Users involved in the consumption process should also be familiar with the new communication technologies that enable the formation of digital culture from different perspectives and have knowledge about the "material and moral values/elements system" in the consumption process.

## REFERENCES


Akgül, B., & Ayer, Z. (2020). The change in the management structure of media institutions in the fourth industrial revolution (Industry 4.0) process. *Journal of Life Economics*, *7*(2), 151–160. doi:10.15637/jlecon.7.010

Akyüz, E. (2018). The role of university in the education of writers of children's literature: The model of Aarhus University. *International Journal of Languages'. Education and Teaching*, *6*(4), 113–121. doi:10.18298/ijlet.3203

Akyüz, E. (2021). Dijitalleşme bağlamında çocuk edebiyatı yapıtlarının taşıması gereken özellikler. [Characteristics of children's literature works in the context of digitalization] In O. Koksal (Ed.), *Dijital eğitim* [Digital education]. (pp. 139–151). Eğitim Publications.

Allen-Robertson, J. (2013). *Digital culture industry*. Palgrave Macmillan Publications. doi:10.1057/9781137033475

Başer, A. (2010). Yeni iletişim teknolojilerinin evriminde televizyonun yeri. [The place of television in the evolution of new communication technologies] In F. Aydoğan & A. Akyüz (Eds.), *İkinci medya çağında internet* [Internet in the second media age]. (pp. 36–60). Alfa Publishing.

Başlar, G. (2013). *Yeni medyanın gelişimi ve dijitalleşen kapitalizm* [Development in new media and digitalised capitalism]. Akademik Bilişim.

Bassett, C. (2013). Kültürel çalışmalar ve yeni medya. [Cultural studies and new media] In G. Hall & C. Birchall (Eds.), *Yeni kültürel çalışmalar: Kuramsal serüvenler* [New cultural studies: Theoretical adventures]. (KartalO., Trans.; pp. 323–350). Say Publishing.

Baudrillard, J. (2016). *Tüketim toplumu* [Consumer society]. (H. Deliceçaylı & F. Keskin, Trans.). Ayrıntı Publishing.

Beer, D., & Burrows, R. (2013). Popular culture, digital archives and the new social life of data. *Theory, Culture & Society*, *30*(4), 47–71. doi:10.1177/0263276413476542

Bell, D. (2007). *Cyberculture theorists: Manuel Castells and Donna Haraway*. Routledge Publishing. doi:10.4324/9780203357019

Bowker, G. (2008). *Structures of participation in digital culture*. Social Science Research Council Publications.

Bozkurt, G. (2016). *İnsan ve kültür* [People and culture]. Boyut Publishing.

Castells, M. (2010). *The rise of the network society*. Wiley Blackwell Publishing. doi:10.1002/9781444319514

Creeber, G., & Martin, R. (2009). *Digital culture: Understanding new media*. Open University Press.

Demirkaya, İ., & Koyuncu, E. (2021). Dijital kapitalizm, tüketim kültürü ve Y kuşağının değişen tüketim davranışları [Digital capitalism, consumption culture and changing consumption behaviours of generation Y]. *Intermedia. International Journal (Toronto, Ont.)*, *8*(15), 174–196. doi:10.21645/intermedia.2021.107

Dey, B. L., Yen, D., & Samuel, L. (2020). Digital consumer culture and digital acculturation. *International Journal of Information Management*, *51*, 1–6. doi:10.1016/j.ijinfomgt.2019.102057

Flavian, C., & Gurrea, R. (2016). Dijital gazeteleri seçmek- okuyucu amaçlarının ve kullanıcı deneyimlerinin etkisi [Choosing digital newspapers -the impact of reader intentions and user experiences] In H. Hülür & C. Yaşın (Eds.), Yeni medya kullanıcının yükselişi [The rise of the new media user] (pp. 417-438). Ütopya Publishing.

Fuchs, C. (2012). Google capitalism. *Journal for A Global Sustainable. TripleC*, *10*(1), 42–48. doi:10.31269/triplec.v10i1.304

Gambaro, M. (2012). Some economics of new media content production and consumption, and strategic ımplication for media companies. In M. Friedrichsen & W. Mühl-Benninghaus (Eds.), *Handbook of social media management* (pp. 49–58). Springer Publications. doi:10.1007/978-3-642-28897-5_4

Gere, C. (2008). *Dijital kültür* [Digital culture]. (A. Akın & N. Pembecioğlu, Trans.). Salon Publishing. doi:10.1177/1470412903002003014

Gere, C. (2019). *Community without community in digital culture*. Palgrave Macmillan Publications. doi:10.1057/9781137026675_12

Gilanlıoğlu, E., & Öze, N. (2020). Dijital tüketim kültürünün hegemonyası ve serbest zaman [Manipulation of digital consumption culture hegemony and leisure time]. *Yeni Medya Elektronik Dergisi*, *4*(3), 185–202. doi:10.17932/IAU.EJNM.25480200.2020/ejnm_v4i3004

Goggin, G., & Hjorth, L. (2014). *The routledge companion to mobile media*. Routledge Publications., doi:10.4324/9780203434833

Grandinetti, R., Bettiol, M., & Di Maria, E. (2022). Contexts of consumption and their evolution in the digital age: Beyond the service-dominant logic. *Administrative Sciences*, *12*(4), 121. doi:10.3390/admsci12040121

Grover, V., Tseng, S. H., & Pu, W. (2022). A theoretical perspective on organizational culture and digitalization. *Information & Management*, *59*(4), 1–13. doi:10.1016/j.im.2022.103639

Gür Omay, E. G. (2022). Dijitalleşme ekseninde tüketim kültürü. [Consumption culture on the axis of digitalization] In K. Çankaya (Ed.), *Medya ve tüketim I* [Media and consumption I]. (pp. 31–47). Eğitim Publishing.

Guy, J. S. (2019). Digital technology, digital culture and the metric/nonmetric distinction. *Technological Forecasting and Social Change*, *145*, 55–61. doi:10.1016/j.techfore.2019.05.005

Hansen, D., Shneiderman, B., Smith, M., & Himelboim, I. (2020). Social media: New technologies of collaboration. *Analyzing Social Media Networks with Node, XL*, 11–29. doi:10.1016/B978-0-12-817756-3.00002-9

Jensen, J. L., & Mortensen, M. (2016). Emerging patterns of news production and consumption across media. In J. L. Jensen, M. Mortensen, & J. Ormen (Eds.), *News across media: Production, distribution and consumption* (pp. 1–11). Routledge Publishing. doi:10.4324/9781315692456

Kergel, D. (2023). *Digital cultures*. Springer Publications. doi:10.1007/978-3-658-35250-9

Küçüktamer, T., & Karakuyu, A. (2021). Dijital dünyada okuryazarlık kavramı. [The concept of literacy in the digital world] In O. Koksal (Ed.), *Dijital eğitim* [Digital education]. (pp. 85–95). Eğitim Publications.

Küçüktamer, T., & Yardibi, N. (2017). Yapılandırmacı öğretim bağlamında bir örnek ders incelemesi: Coursera platformunda sanat ve etkinlik [An course examination in the context of constructivist learning: Art and activity through the platform of Coursera]. *International Journal of Innovative Research in Education, 4*(3), 170–178. doi:10.18844/ijire.v4i3.2645

Lister, M. (2013). *The photographic image in digital culture*. Routledge Publishing. doi:10.4324/9780203797563

Manovich, L. (2001). *The language of new media*. The MIT Publishing.

Manovich, L. (2009). The practice of everyday (media) life: From mass consumption to mass cultural production? *Critical Inquiry, 35*(2), 319–331. doi:10.1086/596645

Mansell, R. (2017). Inequality and digitally mediated communication: Divides, contradictions and consequences. *Javnost (Ljubljana), 24*(2), 146–161. doi:10.1080/13183222.2017.1287966

Marx, K. (2003). *Kapital* [Capital]. (A. Bilgi, Trans.). Eriş Publishing.

Mihelj, S., Leguina, A., & Downey, J. (2019). Culture is digital: Cultural participation, diversity and the digital divide. *New Media & Society, 21*(7), 1465–1485. doi:10.1177/1461444818822816

Miller, V. (2020). *Understanding digital culture*. Sage Publications.

Navarrete, T. (2013). Digital cultural heritage. In I. Rizzo & A. Mignosa (Eds.), *Handbook on the economics of cultural heritage* (pp. 251–272). Edward Elgar Publishing. doi:10.4337/9780857931009.00023

Opreana, A., & Vinerean, S. (2015). A new development in online marketing: Introducing digital inbound marketing. *Expert Journal of Marketing, 3*(1), 29–34.

Padua, D. (2021). *Digital cultural transformation: Building strategic mindsets via digital sociology*. Springer Publications. doi:10.1007/978-3-030-83803-4

Paolini, P., Silvers, M., & Proctor, N. (2013). Technologies for cultural heritage. In I. Rizzo & A. Mignosa (Eds.), *Handbook on the economics of cultural heritage* (pp. 273–289). Edward Elgar Publishing. doi:10.4337/9780857931009.00024

Pavlik, J. V. (2008). *Media in the digital age*. Columbia University Press.

Richard, F., & Sora, P. (2017). The impact of trust in the news media on online news consumption and participation. *Digital Journalism (Abingdon, England)*, *5*(10), 1281–1299. doi:10.1080/21670811.2017.1279979

Ritzer, G. (2015). Automating prosumption: The decline of the prosumer and the rise of the prosuming machines. *Journal of Consumer Culture*, *15*(3), 407–424. doi:10.1177/1469540514553717

Ritzer, G., & Jurgenson, N. (2010). Production, consumption, prosumption: The nature of capitalism in the age of the digital 'prosumer'. *Journal of Consumer Culture*, *10*(1), 13–36. doi:10.1177/1469540509354673

Ruggiero, T. E. (2017). Uses and gratifications theory in the 21st century. *ResearchGate*, *3*(1), 3–37. doi:10.4324/9781315679402-4

Shifman, L. (2013). *Memes in digital culture*. MIT Press. doi:10.7551/mitpress/9429.001.0001

Smith, P. (2007). *Kültürel kuram* [Cultural theory]. (S. Güzelsarı & İ. Gündoğdu, Trans.). Babil Publishing.

Snyder, K. (2005). The digital culture and communication: More than just classroom learning. *Seminar. Net, 1*(2), 1-9. . doi:10.7577/seminar.2529

Söğüt, Y. (2022). Üretken endüstrilerde kültürel ve dijital dönüşümlerin yansımaları üzerine: Medya ve tükctim kültürü. [On the reflections of cultural and digital transformations in productive ındustries: Media and consumer culture] In K. Çankaya (Ed.), *Medya ve tüketim I* [Media and consumption I]. (pp. 9–30). Eğitim Publishing.

Staplcton, L., & Jaillant, L. (2022). "Born digital" shedding light into the darkness of digital culture. *AI & Society*, *37*(3), 819–822. doi:10.100700146-021-01358-y

Törenli, N. (2005). *Yeni medya ve yeni iletişim ortamı* [New media and new communication environment]. Bilim ve Sanat Publishing.

Uzalac, A., & Cvjeticanin, B. (2008). *Digital culture: The changing dynamics*. Culturelink Publishing.

Uzunoğlu, S. (2015). Yeni medyada dijital emek sömürüsü: Tüketiciden Üreticiye yeni medya, yeni sömürü pratikleri [New media and new practices of exploitation: From consumer to prosumer]. *Intermedia International E-Journal*, *2*(1), 181–194.

Van Dijck, J., Poell, T., & De Waal, M. (2018). *The platform society: Public values in a connective world*. Oxford University Press., doi:10.1093/oso/9780190889760.001.0001

## ADDITIONAL READING

Blackman, L. (1998). Culture, technology and subjectivity. In J. Wood (Ed.), *The virtual embodied: Practices, theories and the new technologies* (pp. 132–147). Routledge Publications.

Coeckelbergh, M. (2007). *Imagination and principles: An essay on the role of imagination in moral reasoning*. Palgrave Macmillan Publishing. doi:10.1057/9780230589803

Degan, K. S. (2021). Communication and digital culture in present scenario. In P. K. Singh, Z. Polkowski, S. Tanwar, S. K. Pandey, G. Matei, & D. Pirvu (Eds.), *Innovations in information and communication technologies (IICT-2020)*. Springer Publications. doi:10.1007/978-3-030-66218-9_6

Hoyer, W. D., Kroschke, M., Schmitt, B., Kraume, K., & Shankar, V. (2020). Transforming the customer experience through new technologies. *Journal of Interactive Marketing*, *51*(1), 57–71. doi:10.1016/j.intmar.2020.04.001

Jenkins, H. (2006). *Convergence culture*. New York University Press.

Landsberg, A. (2004). *Prosthetic memory: The transformation of american remembrance in the age of mass culture*. Columbia University Press.

McNamara, K. (2011). The paparazzi industry and new media: The evolving production and consumption of celebrity news and gossip websites. *International Journal of Cultural Studies*, *14*(5), 515–530. doi:10.1177/1367877910394567

Quinton, S., Canhoto, A., Molinillo, S., Pera, R., & Budhathoki, T. (2018). Conceptualising a digital orientation: Antecedents of supporting SME performance in the digital economy. *Journal of Strategic Marketing*, *26*(5), 427–439. doi:10.1080/0965254X.2016.1258004

Schmidt, E., & Cohen, J. (2013). *The new digital age: Reshaping the future of people, nations and business*. John Murray Publishing.

Silver, D. (2004). Internet/cyberculture/digital culture/new media/fill in the blank studies. *New Media & Society*, *6*(1), 55–64. doi:10.1177/1461444804039915

Virta, L., & Raisanen, R. (2021). Three futures scenarios of policy instruments for sustainable textile production and consumption as portrayed in the finnish news media. *Sustainability (Basel)*, *13*(2), 594. doi:10.3390u13020594

## KEY TERMS AND DEFINITIONS

**Digital Capitalism:** Rather than the owner of the product produced within the digital culture, it is the fact that other ownership structures make a profit from the relevant product in material and/or moral terms.

**Digital Culture:** It is where digital technologies play a central role and refers to one of the important types of culture today.

**New Communication Technologies:** The Internet is the basic concept covering communication and computer technologies.

**New Media:** It refers to the tools and areas that can be used in the digital world with new communication technologies.

**Production and Consumption:** It is the process of making a product, service and/or idea ready for use and using it with some benefit/satisfaction motivations.

**Prosumer/ Pro-Consumer:** They are people who consume content in the digital world and can also be involved in the process of producing content in digital environments.

# Chapter 6
# Changing Society Order With Digitalization: Global Village Global Workers – Digital Nomads

**Eda Sezerer Albayrak**
*KTO Karatay University, Turkey*

## ABSTRACT

*Digital nomadism is defined as "the blending of tourism, leisure and professional activities to create a unique lifestyle based on remote work, global travel and multi-residential practices" (Mancinelli). Considering digital nomadism as a lifestyle, individuals need to be constantly on the move in order to maintain this lifestyle. In this case, lifestyle mobility can be mentioned at the intersection of travel, leisure time and migration. The relevant book chapter will address the issue of digital nomadism from a similar holistic perspective. For this purpose, developments in communication technologies and digitalization will be discussed in the first part, and the prominent features of digital nomadism as a lifestyle mobility will be mentioned in the second part, and finally, critical approaches to digital nomadism will be discussed and whether this lifestyle can be evaluated as a hedonic choice or a necessity.*

## INTRODUCTION

Today's experts state that the social structure has changed with the development of remote network communication, digital technologies, and the emergence of the information society. Physical space is no longer a barrier to communication and professional interaction. Digital nomads are portrayed as young professionals working in an online-only environment while leading a location-independent and often travel-based lifestyle, in which the boundaries between work, leisure and travel seem blurred. The virtual environment changes the social structure, people's lifestyles, values and interactions, and simultaneously creates the global information field that forms the basis of the information society.

DOI: 10.4018/978-1-6684-8397-8.ch006

Today, the virtual environment is a place where business, education and entertainment information is concentrated, public and private institutions, companies, libraries, etc. provides access to databases in almost every area of society from various information sources.

The number of organizations that put their employees in the "nomadic" mode of work and the number of free "nomads" is increasing rapidly. Social risks are an integral part of the mobile lifestyles and professional activities of nomads. It seems that digital nomads are constantly exposed to certain risks. As the rapid development of digital technologies and the formation of the information society make the nomadic lifestyle increasingly widespread, this scientific problem reveals the importance of it.

This book chapter aims to conceptualize the phenomenon of digital nomad by defining the concept of digital nomad. It also examines the motivations to adopt this lifestyle and how these are addressed in practice and how work, leisure and travel are interpreted. Digital nomads aim to create a holistic lifestyle characterized by extensive freedom, where both areas of life are equally enjoyable and do so through professional, spatial and personal freedom. Although this lifestyle is perceived as advantageous in a positive way, it brings with it personal challenges, which is also considered a different type of work.

## DIGITALIZATION AND NEW COMMUNICATION TECHNOLOGIES

The technology that has emerged from the past to the present has changed the sectoral activities by affecting the production methods and social life.

The first wave in technology is the transformation of humanity from gathering to farming. Regular settlements emerged. It has led to the formation of hierarchical structures and states. The second wave is the transition from agriculture to industry. Production, education, communication have been experienced on a massive scale. This process began with the use of steam engines in the 18th century. It started with the First Industrial Revolution (1760-1830).

Technological developments using electricity and internal combustion engines in mass production in the 20th century. It led to the Industrial Revolution. In the 1970s, a step was taken on a global scale to the digital age. In this period, especially computers taking their place in many areas and the development of communication network III. It started the Industrial Revolution. Developments in information, information and communication technologies since 2011 have led to the beginning of a new digital era in which the internet is used in production (Kagermann, Wahlsterand, & Helbig, 2013; Şahin and Yağcı, 2017). IV. This era, called the Industrial Revolution (Industry 4.0). It includes the co-integration of new production possibilities of internet, communication, automation, data collection and dissemination technologies. In addition, in all systems consisting of physical structures, internet and virtual applications are available (Banger, 2017).

With the postmodern period, great developments have been experienced in the technological field and these developments have also affected the production processes. Due to technological developments in production processes, brain power has replaced arm power and production has begun to be made without limits. The postmodern period, in which technological developments have emerged intensively, has increased and the fields of work that produce and share information have increased. It is a period of development. The emergence of the postmodern period, along with the trend from the modern period to the postmodern period, is related to the transition process from the Fordist mode of production, which represents two separate periods, in line with the capitalist process, to the post-Fordist mode of production. The concept of flexibility is one of the most important features of post-Fordism and this concept is not only in the field of production but also in the lives of individuals began to take shape. (Odabaşı, 2014, pp. 25-27). With flexible production models and technological developments, the priority in the production process has now passed to the concept of information. Knowledge has become the main power in the field of production, and thus, while the number of agricultural workers has decreased, it has been observed that the number of white-collar workers with technical knowledge has increased. (Lyotard, 2000, p.22)

With the development in internet technology, the third wave, the information age, is entered (Toffler, 1980, pp. 10-20). Digitalization refers to the conversion of data into binary digits so that it can be processed by computers (Gartner, 2020, p. 1). In addition, digitalization has provided new business models in distribution channels and customer relations (Osterwalder & Pigneur, 2010, pp. 20-30). Moreover, new technologies such as artificial intelligence have been developed (Yankın, 2018, p. 2).

Internet technology, on the other hand, is an international system that connects millions of computer networks around the world with a protocol and makes data communication possible thanks to the software developed (Lyytinen and King, 2002). Thanks to internet technology, users devices can stay connected to the World Wide Web (WEB-Network) continuously through virtual networks. Therefore, internet technology is in the infrastructure of most of the technologies used. Therefore, as internet technology develops, it can be seen that all businesses and the structure of the society are moving towards digitalization.

Internet users increased by 3.7 percent in the last 12 months, reaching 5.03 billion in July 2022. The annual increase of 178 million new users brought the global internet growth to 63.1 percent.

Social media users increased by 227 million last year, reaching 4.70 billion at the beginning of July 2022. Considering that there are approximately 6 billion mobile subscribers in the world today, it can be said that technological and digital developments touch every field and will continue to do so.

With the start of the Industrial Revolution IV, where digitalization is carried out intensively, new generation technologies such as robotics, analytics, artificial intelligence and cognitive technologies, nano technology, virtual (augmented) reality, robots, 3D printers, wearable technology and internet of things have taken their place in almost every sector. With technologies such as tablet computers, sensors, light robots, businesses have started to provide their services more economically (Topsakal, Yüzbaşıoğlu and Çuhadar, 2018). Indeed, industry 4.0. It is focused on digitalization and covers an integrated and high level of technology that is constantly evolving in the areas of speed, cost, compatibility and efficiency. Thanks to digitalization, a large number of digital devices that can quickly communicate with each other highlight a number of factors such as data processing (Soylu, 2018). With the rise of digitalization, competition and communication activities have become more palpable and visible (Mavnacıoğlu, 2022). Therefore, this emerging technology and digitalization developments started the era of digital evolution.

Digitalization, on the other hand, refers not only to data processing, but also to digital transformation and digital culture (Bloomberg, 2018). It should be thought of as the digitalization of a management, perception and process. This process has led to the development of productive businesses.

Thanks to digitalization, organizations are rapidly reaching the demands of users and redesigning their workflows. With Web 2.0 in the digital age, individuals no longer only consume online information, but also come to the point where it can be produced (Dunleavy & Margetts, 2010, p. 18). In the age of mass production, two-way communication with the internet has been changed from one-way communication. In particular, Web 2.0 enabled the development of platforms such as Wikis, blogs, and social networks. Thanks to Web 2.0's interactive communication in social media, information spreads at a great speed and across geography (Tapscott & Williams, 2006, p. 5-15).

Some thinkers who examine the social lives of individuals with technological developments emphasize that technological developments isolate individuals. David Harvey emphasizes that thanks to the technological developments in the fields of communication and transportation, the concepts of time and space have lost their meaning, that the communication processes have started to be done instantly, and thus the obstacles in front of globalization have been removed.

According to Harvey, who stated that individuals now enter a communication process mediated by technology, depending on the developments in communication processes, the habits and lives of individuals also change and a concept that can be defined as virtual culture emerges.

According to Harvey, the changes in the social lives of individuals lead individuals to loneliness, and individuals enter the process of alienation or loneliness over time. (Harvey, 1999, p.270).

According to Bauman, the emergence of mobile phones and social media poses a problem in terms of social distance of individuals. With the introduction of mobile phones and social media into the social life of individuals, the definition of the concept of social space has changed to a great extent, and the distinctions between spaces have begun to fade. (Bauman, 2011, p.40).

In today's society, which he considers as fluid modernity, individuals are no longer dependent on the degree and frequency of physical intimacy with each other in their communication processes. (Lyon and Bauman, 2013, p.46). In line with Bauman's point of view, social media brings individuals who are physically far away from each other closer, but it causes individuals who are close to each other to feel distant from each other. These technological developments in fluid modernity have begun to blur the face-to-face communication processes of individuals. (Bauman, 2011, p. 42).

Bauman believes that in this communication process dominated by keys and messages, real physical communication begins to lose its importance and underlines that individuals' face-to-face communication skills begin to decline day by day. According to Marcuse, who states that individuals do not have time to express themselves and socialize in the capitalist system, individuals have begun to meet their communication needs with communication tools. According to Jenkins, a participatory culture emerges with the convergence in media tools, and with this emerging participatory culture, individuals begin to lead a more active, social and nomadic life in digital environments. In parallel with the developments in digitalization and communication technologies, the developments in the internet also significantly affect the actions that individuals can continue through virtual environments.

As a result of the developments experienced, physical distances have disappeared with the disappearance of the limitations in the concept of space and everyone in the world has started to live in a global village with the definition of Marshall McLuhan. McLuhan emphasizes that the global village theory and developments in communication technologies unite individuals and as a result, the world will turn into a single consciousness.

Today, the global village is dominated by international companies. With the disappearance of space limitations, global companies have begun to be influential in every aspect of the lives of individuals living anywhere in the world, from their consumption habits to their way of thinking. The concept of "global village" underlines that the world has become a global village where similar senses are shared thanks to the developments in communication technologies. (Rigel et al., 2003, p.18).

The concept of global village is also very effective in the working lives of individuals. Individuals have started to look for ways to earn money with the freedoms they have created in their own fields by getting rid of the limitations of time and space, and thanks to the opportunities offered by the internet to individuals, they have succeeded in finding areas where they can both work and live their freedom as "digital nomads".

## DIGITAL NOMADS

The concept of digital nomadism, which was first introduced by Makimoto and Manners (1997) with the acceleration of internet usage, focused on what kind of changes the internet and new technologies cause in people's lives. It is predicted that there will be an increase in business life and leisure time, especially with the use of the internet. It has been stated that with this effect, employees will be able to work in environments where they can enjoy instead of staying in classic office environments (Thompson, 2019). Digital nomadism is among the new trends in lifestyle mobility. Digital nomadism is a new lifestyle mobility type that has emerged with the integration of mobile technologies into daily life and different work areas. It is also a transnational approach that is in stark contrast to the traditional sedentary lifestyle, home life and work environment. It can be predicted that the active lifestyles, family lives and working cultures of digital nomads will have profound effects on societies (Hannonen, 2020).

The rise of digital nomads began with the desire to escape the endless business competition of modern life. They accept that individuals have the opportunity to dream of living where and how they want. They build a structure that aims to make global travel without borders, flexibility in working hours, leaving the traditional office and working from anywhere in the world. Digital nomads emerged as an escape from the hustle and bustle of modern life and the 9-5 work requirement. (Nash, Jarrahi, Sutherland, Phillips, 2018, p. 2). Digital nomads are workers who work in the internet environment. Every place where there is internet and computer is the working environment of digital nomads. With the Internet offering individuals liberating spaces in terms of time and space, digital nomads do not need to be physically present at the workplace to run their business and are therefore spatially independent while working. (Thompson, 2018, p.3) This lifestyle offers its employees the opportunity to travel, flexibility in working hours, and escape from the accepted office environment. (Nash et al., 2018, p. 2)

According to Reichenberger (2018), digital nomads are "individuals who achieve location independence by conducting their work online, and transform this independence into mobility, not by constantly working in a designated personal office space, but by using the opportunity to work and travel simultaneously in a way that does not create permanent residence".

With the development of digital technology, global access to information infrastructures, more flexible working arrangements and business flexibility are provided (Dal Fiore, Mokhtarian, & Singer, 2014, p. 97; Freelancer, 2017, p. 1). As permanent travelers, digital nomads have abandoned the idea of a permanent home and adopted a location-independent way of working. While they are working in a cafe in Bali, Indonesia this month, they move to a co-working space in Berlin next month (Spinks, 2017, p. 1; Saiidi, 2017). The vast majority of digital nomads work in fields such as programmers, software developers, designers or content editors, blogging, graphic design, translation, digital marketing, podcast and youtube video production, and even financial and management consulting.

In addition to these job areas, jobs that are quite common for digital nomads include collaborating with companies in website construction, running their short-term business via online applications and store information over the cloud system, and informing the employer about the final product digitally.

Digital nomad research focuses on strategies developed by digital nomads to work and mobilize resources wherever they go (de Carvalhp, Ciolfi, & Gray, 2017). Due to their travel-based lifestyles, digital nomads prefer to exchange rather than own ownership in accessing resources (Hart, 2015, p. 2). Therefore, it is seen that they mostly use co-working areas or cafes instead of permanent office spaces. Digital nomads are in constant contact with customers and the community to run their business.

They have the role of both a traveler and an employee. Other employees who travel to another destination for business purposes other than digital nomads travel only to places determined by the workplace and their travel expenses are covered by the workplace. But digital nomads; they determine the place they will travel to, the duration of their stay and cover their own travel expenses. In short, digital nomads can travel according to their own preferences, regardless of workplace directives.

Perhaps the most striking aspect of the digital nomadic lifestyle is the constant movement, not only from country to country, but from workspace to workspace. Many digital nomads have started to gain freedom in the field of business by stepping out of the routine life with the lifestyle they have adopted. (Nash et al., 2018, p. 6). Those who run their business from home usually work in a specific place or at home. Digital nomads, on the other hand, continue their work by traveling both in the country and abroad, taking the situation of independent work even further. Digital nomads and home workers in terms of their lifestyles differs. While those who run their business from home often try to balance home and work, digital nomads rarely try to balance leisure and work, rarely raising children and work. (Thompson, 2018, p.4)

They choose the place where they will work not according to the job, but according to their entertainment and lifestyle expectations. For this reason, they usually prefer comfortable, warm, natural places where they can be very affordable and welcome. Digital nomads primarily prefer exotic destinations such as Mexico, Bangkok, Chiang Mai, Ubud and Phuket, Lisbon, Argentina to travel. The main reason why these places come first is that besides being exotic places to enjoy, living conditions are reasonable and access to the internet is seamless. Since digital nomads are individuals who can choose their own lifestyle, many of them prefer tropical places where hobbies such as surfing, mountaineering and skiing can be done. Some digital nomads spend their winters in the tropics and prefer northern Europe in the summer.

Those who research why Chiang Mai is a favorite place among digital nomads mention that this city offers many co-working spaces for digital nomads, as well as cafes serving healthy, local and international cuisine. These areas, which offer opportunities for both leisure and work, are important for work and productivity. Another strength of Chiang Mai is the large number of furnished studio apartments available for short or long term rentals. The prevalence of studio apartments and their frequent preference by digital nomads also necessitates the need for co-working spaces. (Green, 2020, 435-436)

In order for digital nomads to travel the world, there are programs such as Hacker Paradise, Digital Nomad Conference, where they communicate with each other about the regions they will travel to. Some digital nomads prefer to find travel companions to minimize their accommodation and travel expenses. (Thompson, 2018, p.3-6). One of the points that digital nomads consider when choosing the countries they will live in is the living expenses of the country they aim to live in.

The number of digital nomads in our country is too high to be underestimated. Istanbul, Bursa, Ankara, Izmir, Bodrum, Antalya, Alanya, Konya, Adana and Gaziantep are places preferred by digital nomads in our country. (Nomadlist, 2023)

By scoring and commenting on the places they go, digital nomads guide others and influence each other's choices. Digital nomads can arrange accommodation for themselves via Facebook pages and communicate with each other through NomadList and Slack applications. Through the forums, digital nomads offer each other suggestions about routes, strength of internet connection, living conditions, environments and activities where they can have fun. For example, a NomadList member shares how to arrange long-term and cheap accommodation on airbnb (Nash et al., 2018, p. 6) Digital nomads usually make their stays on airbnb.com, which is an example of the sharing economy. (Thompson, 2018, p.5)

## HEDONIC OR COMPULSORY? WHAT ABOUT CHALLENGES?

Digital nomadism is often considered as a lifestyle that individuals voluntarily choose in line with their tastes. Many people talk about the technological developments and digitalization experienced with the postmodern era, enabling individuals who live with pleasure-oriented life to go beyond the routine by creating spaces of freedom with the concept of flexibility in their work environment. Hedonistic individuals, who seek happiness by constantly trying to reach the new and give importance to living in the moment, can now both live the moment in a pleasant way and continue their working life by working in temporary and short-term jobs in their working life. It is stated that digital nomadism is associated with hedonism and individuals tend to this lifestyle with the motivation to enjoy their workspace. In addition, it is emphasized that the prominent aspect of the digital nomadic lifestyle is "accumulating experience and freedom". In short, the fact that digital nomads are constantly on the move and have adopted a lifestyle where they can discover new places by working is considered as a voluntary choice made by them in line with their own enthusiasm and pleasure (Reichenberger, 2018; KayaDeniz, 2019; Akın, 2021).

However, interpreting digital nomadism as merely a hedonistic pursuit or experience-gathering activity presents a limiting framework and leads to ignoring the impact of neoliberal conditions and precarious work in particular. Thompson states that while choosing places, digital nomads prefer places where they can make the most of their demographic conditions as well as their taste. (Thompson, 2019, p. 33).

The common feature of the countries in demand by digital nomads is that they stand out as countries with very low living costs for people coming from regions called the global north. Evaluating the flow of lifestyle migration along the north and south lines, Hayes summarizes the common point of life migration as the displacement of people from the "developed" countries of the global north to the "developing" countries of the global south (Hayes, 2015, p. 269). However, the mobility of digital nomads does not always occur along the north-south line. In the study by Nash et al., it is mentioned that some digital nomads have developed a seasonal travel style, such as spending the winter months in the tropics and returning to Northern Europe in the summer (Nash et al, 2018, p. 7).

One of the problems of digital nomads is the visa issue. The desire of digital nomads to travel the world is hindered by the visa problem. Visa-free entry and longer stay in foreign countries is possible when citizenship with strong passports. However, the visa regime for touristic purposes generally does not suit digital nomads. Other types of work visas are also costly.

When interviewed with a digital nomad, he expressed the difficulties he experienced during the visa process as follows:

"I lived in Costa Rica for 8 years. I was logging out and logging in every 3 months. To Mexico to Nicaragua, to Florida (to my family) I visited weekly. If I can't find the opportunity, go to the border of San Salvador, spend 1-2 hours and enter Costa Rica with a tourist visa. I did. I entered Europe between Schengen and non-Schengen countries. I made Bulgaria the center country. 3 months in Amsterdam, 3 months in Bulgaria, 3 months in Paris, 3 months in Bulgaria again. If you stay more than 183 days, you are considered to have resided. That's why I don't stay in one place for more than 183 days" (Akın, 2021).

There are fears of social security, income, loneliness and being stuck. They experience loneliness and social isolation away from their loved ones (Thompson, 2018). One of the other problems is mentioned as being deprived of social security rights. Those who work as digital nomads emphasize that they do not have unemployment and retirement insurance and this situation is not considered important when they are young, but they need a stable income as they get older. Another issue is the problems that occur as a result of the non-continuous income flow. Since it is not clear whether or when the next job will come, it is of course difficult for individuals to plan their income and make long-term investments and future plans. Another challenge mentioned in research is that people experience a feeling of being stuck. Individuals in their troubled days or when their energies are withdrawn, they are sick, etc. They talk about the fact that they do not have a house to seclude them in these days, and that running from one place to another gives a feeling of being stuck after a while. This feeling of being stuck, which is also contributed by the feeling of being neither on vacation nor at work, makes individuals think that they want to spend time in the place where they want to live (Akın, 2021). They are also far away from their families and the loved ones and they feel also lonely and homesick. Culture shock is another important item because they have to apply every regulations and cultural factors that they have been the country in and they continually change their places so they can feel identity complexity.

## FUTURE RESEARCH DIRECTIONS

In the digital nomadism market, which allows people to travel while working, new investments of tourism enterprises, accessibility and technological infrastructure developments will make significant contributions to attracting digital nomads, which is a new market, to touristic destinations. It is also important to promote the suitability of the existing technological infrastructure for the use of digital nomads in digital environments. In future studies, the research can be detailed methodologically by interviewing digital nomads.

## CONCLUSION

Technological developments in communication processes have enabled the emergence of a global village by eliminating the limitations of time and space, and thus, by removing the physical limitations in the working environment, it has also led to the emergence of digital nomads, who appear as the global workers of the global village. As internet technology develops around the world, the spread of remote working practices is accelerating. It can be predicted that the number of digital nomads will increase as they do business on the internet regardless of location. Conceptualized as a lifestyle where travel, work and leisure time are intertwined, digital nomadism is thought to be a prominent agenda throughout the world as a lifestyle mobility that finds the opportunity to travel to more places with the easy visa opportunities expected to be implemented. These people, who have the flexibility to work anywhere in the world thanks to internet technology, prioritize their own tastes and tastes when determining where they will work remotely. Digital nomadism is often considered as a lifestyle that individuals voluntarily choose in line with their tastes. However, the impact of social and economic factors, which are effective in the emergence of this lifestyle and contribute to its spread throughout the world, should not be ignored. This lifestyle is actually effective in the creation of a new market. While in the past, traditional nomads were seen as a threat to the modern state and its regulations, today many countries, including Iceland, Croatia, Dubai, Malta, are actively trying to attract remote-working people and digital nomads by providing new opportunities. It is thought that other countries, which see this spread and economic development potential in digital nomadism, will compete to attract more digital nomads with special visa applications.

However for this new market there has to be new regulations about some problems that they experience. Considering that it offers advantages such as flexible contracts and less responsibility towards employees for employers, it can be predicted that digital nomadism will continue to be promoted and supported more as a lifestyle. It is necessary to discuss the problems digital nomads have in exercising their legal rights as flexible workers and in terms of contracts with employers. In this way, it is thought that it will be possible to take measures to prevent loss of rights while this lifestyle becomes widespread. The other issue is visa procedure. When digital nomads work while traveling, they face legal uncertainty.

They often break the law by working while visiting the country on a tourist visa. As the digital nomad lifestyle increases, visa applications are changing. For digital nomads, all countries are required to make a special visa work for them. It is important to conduct studies investigating the relationship of digital nomads with the local economy and culture. Finally, as it can be discussed in all types of global mobility, it is thought that the lifestyles of digital nomads should be critically evaluated within the framework of sustainability, taking into account the environmental impact.

## REFERENCES

Akın, M. Ş. (2021). Dijital Göçebelik: Deneyim ve Özgürlük. *Sosyal Ekonomik Araştırmalar Dergisi, 21*(1), 41–52. doi:10.30976usead.799881

Banger, G. (2017). *Endüstri 4.0 ekstra*. Dorlion Yayınları.

Bauman, Z. (2011). Yaşam sanatı. (çev. Akın Sarı). İstanbul: Versus Kitap

Bloomberg. J. (2022, 12 19). Digitization, Digitalization, and Digital Transformation: Confuse Them at your Peril. *Forbes*. https://www.forbes.com/sites/jasonbloomberg/2018/04/29/digitization-digitalization

Dal Fiore, F., Mokhtarian, P. L., & Singer, M. E. (2014). Nomads at last? A set of perspectives on how mobile technology may affect travel. *Journal of Transport Geography*, *41*, 97–106. doi:10.1016/j.jtrangeo.2014.08.014

de Carvalhp, F. P., Ciolfi, L., & Gray, B. (2017). Detailing a Spectrum of Motivational Forces Shaping Nomadic Practices. *Conference on Computer Supported Cooperative Work and Social Computing*, (s. 962-977). 10.1145/2998181.2998313

Gartner. (2020). *Gartner Glossary*. Gartner. https://www.gartner.com/en/informationtechnology/

Green, P. (2020). *Disruptions of Self, Place and Mobility: Digital Nomads in Chiang* Mai, Thailand. *Mobilities, 15*(3), 431–445. doi:10.1080/17450101.2020.1723253

Hannonen, O. (2020). In search of a digital nomad: Defining the phenomenon. *Information Technology & Tourism*, *22*(3), 335–353. doi:10.100740558-020-00177-z

Hart, A. (2015). Living And Working İn Paradise: The Rise Of The 'Digital Nomad'. *The Telegraph.* http://www.telegraph.co.uk/news/features/11597145/Living-and-working-in-paradise the-rise-of-the-digital-nomad.html

Harvey, D. (1999). Postmodernliğin durumu. (çev.Sungur Savran). İstanbul: Metis Yayınları.

Kagermann, H., Wahlsterand, W., & Helbig, J. (2013). *Recommendations for implementing the strategic initiative industrie 4.0., final report of the industrie 4.0. working group.* DIN. https://www.din.de/blob/76902/e8cac883f42bf28536e7e8165993f1fd/recommendations for-implementing-industry-4-0-data.pdf in 13.01.2023.

KayaDeniz, A. (2019). Dijital çağın hedonist çalışanları: Dijital göçebeler. *IBAD Sosyal Bilimler Dergisi, 5*, 101-113.

Lyon, D., & Bauman, Z. (2013). Akışkan gözetim. (çev. ElçinYılmaz). İstanbul: Ayrıntı Yayınları.

Lyotard, J. F. (2000). Postmodern durum, bilgi üzerine bir rapor. (çev. Ahmet Çiğdem). Ankara: Vadi Yayınları.

Lyytinen, K., & King, J. L. (2002). Editorial: Around the cradle of the wireless revolution: the emergence and evolution of celiular telephony. *Telecommunications Policy, 26*(3-4), 97–100. doi:10.1016/S0308-5961(02)00002-2

Margetts, H., & Dunleavy, P. (2013). The second wave of digital-era governance: A quasi-paradigm for government on the Web. *Philosophical Transactions - Royal Society. Mathematical, Physical, and Engineering Sciences, 371*(1987), 20120382. doi:10.1098/rsta.2012.0382 PMID:23419851

Mavnacıoğlu, K. (2022). Dijital çağda pazarlama iletişimi etiği üzerine bir değerlendirme. *Ahi Evran Üniversitesi Enstitüsü Sosyal Bilimler Dergisi, 8*(1), 52–66. doi:10.31592/aeusbed.980897

Nash, C., Jarrahi, M. H., Sutherland, W., & Phillips, G. (2018). *Digital nomads beyond the buzzword: Defining digital nomadic work and use of digital technologies. Chowdhury, G., McLeod, J., Gillet, V. ve Willett, P. (Der.) Transforming Digital Worlds iConference.* Springer.

Odabaşı, Y. (2014). *Postmodern pazarlama.* MediaCat.

Osterwalder, A., & Pigneur, Y. (2010). *Business Model Generation: A Handbook for Visionaries, Game Changers, and Challengers.* Wiley.

Reichenberger, I. (2018). Digital nomads – a quest for holistic freedom in work and leisure. *Annals of Leisure Research, 21*(3), 364–380. doi:10.1080/11745398.2017.1358098

Rigel, N. Batuş, G. Yücedoğan & G., Çoban, B. (ed.). (2003). Kadife karanlık- 21. yüzyıl iletişim çağını aydınlatan kuramcılar. İstanbul: Su Yayınevi.

Şahin, N. & Yağcı, P. (2017). Endüstri 4.0 kavramında prosumer kavramının yiyecek içecek sektörü açısından değerlendirilmesi. *Journal of Recration and Tourism Research, 4*(Special Issue 1), 12-22.

Saiidi, U. (2017). *I tried living as a digital nomad for the day: CNBC Reports.* [Video]. Youtube. https://www.youtube.com/watch?v=zjf8Qxo_tXk&t=86s

Soylu, A. (2018). Endüstri 4.0 ve girişimcilikte yeni yaklaşımlar. *Pamukkale Üniversitesi Sosyal Bilimler Enstitüsü Dergisi*, (32), 43–57. doi:10.30794/pausbed.424955

Spinks, R. (2017). Meet the 'digital nomads' who travel the world in search of fast Wi-Fi. *The Guardian*. https://www.theguardian.com/cities/2015/jun/16/digital-nomads-travel-world-search-fast-wi-fi

Tapscott, D., & Willams, D. (2010, January/February). Innovating the 21st-Century University: It's Time! *Educase Review*, *45*(1), 16–29.

Thompson, B. Y. (2018). Digital nomads: Employment in the online gig economy. Glocalism: *Journal of Culture. Politics and Innovation*, *1*, 1–26.

Thompson, B. Y. (2019). The digital nomad lifestyle: (Remote) Work/Leisure balance, privilege and constructed community. *International Journal of the Sociology of Leisure*, *2*(1-2), 27–42. doi:10.100741978-018-00030-y

Toffler, A. (1980). *The Third Wave*. William Morrow.

Topsakal, Y., Yüzbaşıoğlu, N., & Çuhadar, M. (2018). Endüstri devrimleri ve turizm: Türkiye turizm 4.0 SWOT analizi ve geçiş süreci önerileri. *Süleyman Demirel Üniversitesi İktisadi ve İdari Bilimler Fakültesi Dergisi*, *23*, 1623–1638.

Yankın, F. B. (2018). Dijital Dönüşüm Sürecinde Çalışma Yaşamı. *Trakya Üniversitesi İktisadi ve İdari Bilimler Fakültesi E-Dergi*, *7*(2), 1–38.

## ADDITIONAL READING

Hermann, I., & Paris, C. M. (2020). Digital nomadism: The nexus of remote working and travel mobility. *Information. Information Technology & Tourism*, *22*(3), 329–333. doi:10.100740558-020-00188-w

Mancinelli, F. (2020). Digital nomads: Freedom, responsibility and the neoliberal order. *Information Technology & Tourism*, *22*(3), 417–437. doi:10.100740558-020-00174-2

Orel, M. (2019). Coworking environments and digital nomadism: Balancing work and leisure whilst on the move. *World Leisure Journal*, *61*(3), 215–227. doi:10.1080/16078055.2019.1639275

Orel, M. (2021). Life is better in Flip Flops. Digital nomads and their transformational travels to Thailand. *International Journal of Culture, Tourism and Hospitality Research*, *15*(1), 3–9. doi:10.1108/IJCTHR-12-2019-0229

Richter, S., & Richter, A. (2020). Richter, *A. Digital Nomads. Business & Information Systems Engineering*, *62*(1), 77–81. doi:10.100712599-019-00615-1

Spracklen, K. (2015). *Digital Leisure, The Internet and Popular Culture: Communities and Identities in a Digital Age*. Palgrave Macmillan. doi:10.1057/9781137405876

## KEY TERMS AND DEFINITIONS

**Digital Nomad:** The person who routinely changes his/her place (country, city) according to his/her job for maintaining lifestyle. They travel, work, and have leisure time also.

**Digitalization:** Using digital technologies to provide new revenue and value-producing opportunities.

**Hedonism:** Relishing in goods and pursuit of pleasure.

**Lifestyle Changings:** Changing people's ordinary lifestyles according to new technologies and scientific research.

# Chapter 7
# MetaStrategy of MetaCities:
## An Example of Ankara Municipality Project BLD 4.0

**Sevda Mutlu Akar**
https://orcid.org/0000-0003-1208-0258
*Bandirma Onyedi Eylul University, Turkey*

**Senem Nart**
*Bandirma Onyedi Eylul University, Turkey*

## ABSTRACT

*This study aims to analyze voter-municipality and virtual political communication within the scope of the BLD 4.0 project of the Ankara municipality, which is the first Turkish municipality to join the Metaverse world and to examine the voters' perceptions about the Metaverse world. The study evaluates the comments submitted to the official social media accounts of the Ankara municipality, which has declared it will participate in the Metaverse world. The results of the analysis conducted, the importance of digitalization in governance has emerged, and it has been found that there is awareness among citizens regarding the concepts of industry 4.0 and the Metaverse. In particular, it is understood that the perception of innovative leadership created by the digital municipalism approach creates trust in a political leader.*

## INTRODUCTION

The Internet is one of the most fundamental tools, enabling most of the world's population to access information and services, interact with each other, socialize, trade, and be entertained. Especially in recent years, the acceleration of the digitalization process and the integration of the digital and physical worlds has paved the way for the development and diversification of digital technologies. Spatial technologies such as Web 3.0, Virtual Reality (VR), and Augmented Reality (AR) have started to offer innovative digital products and services to individuals on the one hand, while on the other, they have helped organizations shape new business models (Mystakidis, 2022).

DOI: 10.4018/978-1-6684-8397-8.ch007

One of the most important factors accelerating the digitalization experience was the COVID-19 pandemic, which minimized the physical contact of individuals during this period. Due to this global pandemic, governments took many strict measures to prevent its spread and imposed curfews and travel restrictions. In this process, services in many areas of business life were either provided through hybrid working models or jobs were completely moved to digital platforms and directed to work from home. Individuals who work from home have shown more interest in computer games and online applications that allow them to visit cultural and historical cities online in their free time. As digital channels gained greater importance during the pandemic, this led to a heightened interest in the virtual-centered Metaverse. According to Hayrullahoğlu and Varol (2022, p. 246) and Sun et al. (2022, p. 6) the main interest was heightened when Facebook changed its name to Meta – the suffix of the Metaverse.

The term Metaverse consists of the words: "meta" and "verse," the former referring to "beyond" and the latter "universe" (Choi, 2022, p. 4; Park & Kim, 2022, p. 3; Sun et al., 2022, p. 7). The Metaverse refers to a three-dimensional virtual world inhabited by avatars created by real individuals (Kim, 2021). Avatars can perform various political, economic, social, and cultural activities in this virtual world (Park & Kim, 2022). We first heard about this technology during the COVID-19 pandemic, but it is a term we are familiar with from science fiction movies. In the literature, the Metaverse is known as a world of interconnected virtual communities and a new online digital space where users interact in a multidimensional way (STM ThinkTech, 2022, pp. 3–4). Accordingly, it can be argued that in the future, the Metaverse will replace the Internet. As the Metaverse has become more prominent, both the private sector and governments have started to direct their investments to adapt to this process. The Metaverse is considered an important step toward becoming a smart city as it can significantly impact public service delivery in the form of information, access to services, cultural activities, and economic opportunities (National League of Cities, 2022, p. 18).

Virtual cities in the Metaverse are called "Metacities." The first study that introduced the concept of a metacity to the literature was conducted by Wang et al. (2022), who state metacities are created by mapping real cities in the virtual world. Metaverse virtual cities are cities that run parallel to our real cities. In other words, all the elements in the real city exist as virtual elements in the virtual cities. Metacities are important because they promise to offer solutions to accelerate and improve the decision-making process on many fundamental issues, such as feasibility, efficiency, economy, communication, and security in real cities.

In Turkey, on January 5, 2022, Mansur Yavaş, the Mayor of Ankara Metropolitan Municipality, announced that Ankara Municipality was the 4th test city in the Metaverse after Los Angeles (USA), Bari (Italy), and Helsinki (Finland). With its BLD 4.0 project, Ankara Municipality has become one of the test cities of the Open AR Cloud Association, which develops standards for open and interoperable computing technologies to connect the physical and digital worlds of the Metaverse.

Therefore, Ankara Metropolitan Municipality, the first city from Turkey to enter the Metaverse universe, is a municipality worth examining. Ankara Municipality has taken an important step in achieving Turkey's goals for digitalization and technological transformation; accordingly, and its adaptation to technology needs to be better understood. Within this context, this study aims to analyze the effects of digitalization in the administration of Ankara Municipality within the scope of the BLD 4.0 V22 project through the voters and to investigate their perceptions regarding the Metaverse world. In general, the study seeks answers to the following questions:

(1) What are the perceptions of individuals in Turkey in general and specifically in Ankara for the Metaverse world?
(2) How does Ankara Municipality's BLD 4.0 V22 project affect voters' behaviors?
(3) Are individuals aware of Metaverse economic opportunities and smart city technology possibilities?
(4) Is there a perception of an innovative leader who follows digitalization and technological transformation in municipal governance in Turkey?

To the best of our knowledge, there is no study in the literature examining Metacities specific to Ankara. The study is expected to fill this gap in the literature and contribute to the metacity discussions in the world of Metaverse. The study was designed as follows: The first section provides the theoretical background and literature review. The second part includes methodology and findings. The study is completed with conclusions and policy recommendations.

## LITERATURE REVIEW: METAVERSE AND METACITIES

Although the term Metaverse came into our lives after the start of the COVID-19 pandemic, the term has been used in science fiction novels for the past 30 years. The term Metaverse first appeared in the 1992 science fiction novel *Snow Crash* by Neal Stephenson. In *Snow Crash*, the protagonist Hiro, a computer hacker, travels between Los Angeles and a virtual world known as the Metaverse. In the novel, the Metaverse represents a space-time extension and human-machine symbiosis (Collins, 2008, p. 52; Lee, 2021, p. 72; Kim, 2021, p. 141; Lee et al., 2021, p. 1; Kye et al., 2021, p. 1; Hayrullahoğlu & Varol, 2022, p. 246; Choi 2022, p. 4; Park & Kim, 2022, p. 3; Yang et al., 2022, p. 1; Sun et al., 2022, p. 5; Sun et al., 2022b, p. 1; Park & Kim, 2022b, p. 4211).

Since the Metaverse is still in its developmental stage, there is no clear consensus on its definition in the literature. For this reason, there are different definitions of the Metaverse. The first of these definitions is by Collins (2008) who asserts that the Metaverse is actually a terminal derived to describe a persistent and immersive 3D virtual environment in which everything from work to entertainment can be accessed by any user anywhere in the world. In other words, the Metaverse is a digital area that allows users to communicate and participate in interactive activities through a virtual world.

The literature includes studies that explain the Metaverse based on the derivation of the word (Choi, 2022, p. 4; Park & Kim, 2022, p. 3; Sun et al., 2022, p. 7; Park & Kim, 2022b, p. 4211; Morgan, 2022, p. 3). According to Park and Kim (2022b, p. 4211) Metaverse is a combination of the words "meta" and "universe" and refers to a three-dimensional virtual world in which avatars engage in political, economic, social, and cultural activities. Morgan (2022) reports that the Metaverse is a seamless fusion of physical and digital lives, creating a virtual community where all activities can take place. The key point of the Metaverse is that there is no single virtual world, but many worlds that are shaped to enable people to digitally deepen and extend their social interactions.

There are various studies in the literature that define the Metaverse based on its characteristics (Kye et al., 2021, p. 1; Kim, 2021, p. 141; Yang et al., 2022, p. 1; Lee, 2021, p. 72; NLC, 2022, p. 5; Mystakidis, 2022, p. 486; Jauhiainen et al. 2023, p. 1). According to Kye et al. (2021), the Metaverse refers to a virtual reality that exists beyond reality. The Metaverse describes the digitized world through digital media such as smartphones and the Internet as a new world. Kim (2021) considers the Metaverse as a kind of next-generation Internet and defines it as a digital world that exists beyond the physical world.

The most basic characteristics of a Metaverse are a three-dimensional (3D) virtual environment, the use of avatars, interoperability, continuity of entities, and synchronization. Hayrullahoğlu and Varol (2022) describe Metaverse as a collective virtual sharing platform. Moro-Visconti (2022) regards the Metaverse as a decentralized ecosystem and sees it as an evolution of the Internet that includes collaborative activities unleashed by technologies integrated into this ecosystem and exponentially increasing creativity.

According to Yang et al. (2022), the Metaverse is a digital world that seamlessly integrates the real world with the virtual world and allows avatars to be created, viewed, and engage in many activities such as entertainment, social networking, and commerce. Lee (2021) describes the Metaverse as an immersive 3D virtual environment, a true virtual artificial community where avatars act as the user's alter ego and interact with one another. Mystakidis (2022) regards the Metaverse as a post-reality universe that combines digital virtuality with physical reality in a perpetual and persistent multi-user environment. It is based on the convergence of technologies such as virtual reality (VR) and augmented reality (AR) that enable multisensory interaction with virtual environments, digital objects, and people. The Metaverse is, therefore, an interconnected social network on persistent multi-user platforms. It allows seamless and embodied user communication in real-time and dynamic interactions using digital artifacts.

Jauhiainen et al. (2023) describe the Metaverse as the next evolution of the Internet that merges the physical and digital worlds in a multi-user environment. Likewise, Mystakidis (2022), according to Jauhiainen et al. (2023), the Metaverse provides immersive real-time presence and interaction with digital objects and people in multisensory interactions in virtual environments, usually in three-dimensional (3D) spaces.

According to the National League of Cities (NLC) (2022), the Metaverse can be described as the next evolution of the Internet that focuses on the integration of physical and digital experiences. For some users, the Metaverse is an online space that aims to digitally recreate the real world. For others, it is experiences that have the potential to superimpose digital information on the physical world, using technologies such as 3D computing, virtual reality (VR), augmented reality (AR), and blockchain to create new and immersive virtual world experiences.

Metaverse was under development based on virtual reality before the COVID-19 pandemic. During the pandemic, it was re-imagined to meet the limitations of external activities and individual needs (Park & Kim, 2022, p. 3). As the COVID-19 pandemic progressed, the term Metaverse inspired tech giants such as Meta, Google, Microsoft, and Samsung. However, the event that increased the popularity of the term the most was on October 28, 2021, when Facebook changed its corporate name from Facebook to Meta with a prefix from Metaverse, and the company officially started a comprehensive transformation from a social media platform to the Metaverse ecosystem (Hayrullahoğlu & Varol, 2022, p. 246; Sun et al., 2022, p. 6).

Facebook is one of the leading social media companies, which includes Facebook Messenger, Watch, Portal, Instagram, WhatsApp, Oculus VR, Giphy, and Mapillary. Interest in the Metaverse increased after October 2021, when the company's name was changed. As seen in Figure 1, the volume of "Metaverse" worldwide searches on Google on a weekly basis in the last five years increased rapidly after this announcement. Since March 2022, however, interest in the term Metaverse has slowly started to decline. This was mainly due to the Metaverse being seen as a virtual land trading platform and the negative impact on the crypto market.

*Figure 1. Metaverse (21.01.2018–15.01.2023)*
*Source: Google Trends, 2022.*

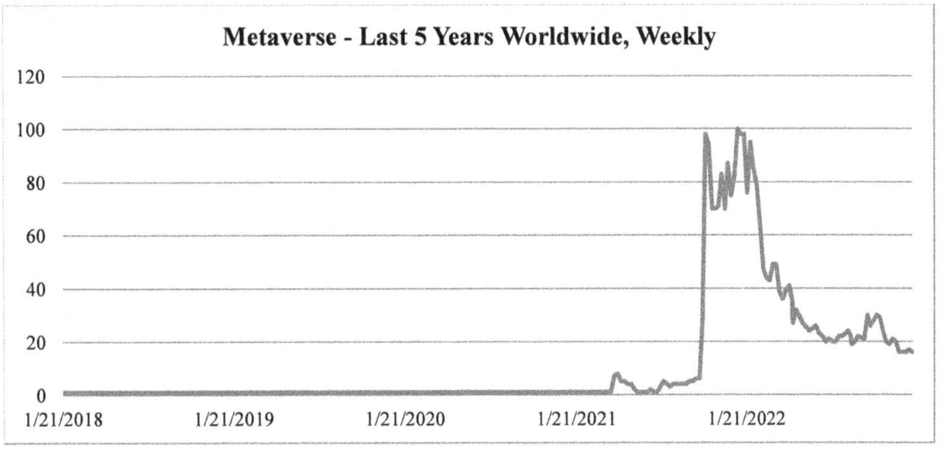


According to Sun et al. (2022), despite all these Google Trends searches, Metaverse has entered a phase of rapid development (see Table 1). Many companies started focusing on the Metaverse, especially in November 2021. Microsoft announced at the Ignite 2022 conference that it was officially entering the Metaverse and would be releasing Mesh12 for Microsoft Teams software to help with office work. NVIDIA released Omniverse13, a platform for creating interactive AI avatars. Again in 2022, Microsoft acquired Activision Blizzard, the world's largest game developer, and publisher, for $68.7 billion. These breakthroughs show that technological developments such as the Internet and social media will significantly affect all areas of life and that the Metaverse, with its unique features, will be used more widely and functionally in the future (Çelik et al., 2022, p. 383).

Any assessment regarding the potential market value of the Metaverse is considered science fiction because this fundamental concept is impossible to measure. However, the value of the meta database can be estimated. This estimation is important because investors are increasing their efforts to participate in the Metaverse market by anticipating potential returns on their expenditures. The Metaverse represents worlds where commercial exchanges are becoming increasingly important, along with the market capitalization of companies producing supporting technology. The market capitalization of companies operating in the Metaverse is expected to reach $800 billion by the middle of this decade and $2.5 trillion by 2030 (Moro-Visconti, 2022, p. 19).

From this economic perspective, this is an inevitable opportunity for municipalities that want to increase their market and brand value in the Metaverse. In the Metaverse, the virtual world and the physical world interact in a mutually value-enhancing way. Virtual cities, which have become an integral part of the Metaverse, are becoming an important asset for real cities and political decision-makers. Virtual cities in the Metaverse are called metacities. The concept of "metacity" was first introduced to the literature by Wang et al. (2022). Wang et al. (2022) describe Metacities as the mapping of real cities in virtual cyberspace. These virtual cities are those that can meet the definition of real cities and run parallel to real cities. The people, materials, organizations, scenarios, and other elements in real cities correspond to various virtual elements such as virtual people, virtual objects, virtual organizations and virtual scenarios in metacities.

*Table 1. Timeline of the metaverse*

| Year | Timeline of the Metaverse |
|---|---|
| 1992 | Snow Crash by Neal Stephenson |
| 1995 | CyberTown |
| 2002 | Digital twins |
| 2003 | Second Life |
| 2006 | Roblox |
| 2009 | Bitcoin and blockchain |
| 2010 | First prototype of the Oculus Rift VR headset |
| 2011 | Minecraft |
| 2012 | First known NFT |
| 2015 | Ethereum |
| 2016 | Pokémon Go |
| 2017 | Decentraland |
| 2018 | Axie Infinity |
| 2020 | First concerts in the Metaverse |
| 2021 | Facebook rebrands to Meta Inc. |
| 2022 | H&M store in the Metaverse |

Source: NLC (2022, p. 6).

Fei-Yue (2004) discusses parallel system methods for the management of complex systems such as cities. According to Fei-Yue, since real cities are typically complex systems that include societies and people, it is often difficult to build a sufficiently accurate mathematical model for them, and even it is almost impossible to build a model that can analytically predict their short-term behavior. Therefore, when studying such complex systems, the traditional "one-world" view that takes real cities as the only reference and standard no longer work, and a "multi-worlds" view needs to be adopted. From such a perspective, approaching real cities is no longer the standard when modeling real cities. The model is regarded as "reality" – a possible alternative form and mode of implementation of real cities. In other words, the complex systems of real cities are only one of the possible realities, and their behavior is "different" from the model; however, it is "equivalent" to the model. Metacities are consistent with real cities in terms of scale, behavior, and system characteristics. Therefore, the Metaverse is an effective tool for realizing Fei-Yue's (2004) "multi-world" vision (Wang et al., 2022, p. 1).

Once the definition of the Metaverse is fully understood and a consensus on the concept is established, the usefulness of the Metaverse in local governments will be better understood. However, local governments have already begun to explore how the Metaverse can contribute to cities, benefit municipal operations, and support community needs (NLC, 2022, p. 11). For example, the Seoul Metropolitan Government launched a virtual pilot of the platform, tentatively named "Metaverse Seoul," at Seoul City Hall in November 2022 for citizens to experience. Users can create an avatar and visit the lobby and the mayor's office, interact with other users, and even submit petitions in the 3D virtual space of Seoul City Hall as a mobile application. The municipality gathers feedback from citizens and identifies operational gaps using this application (Seoul Metropolitan Government, 2022). NLC (2022) reports that as the possibilities in the metadata store are endless, the Metaverse can help bring public services online. Citizens can access the metadata repository and submit their digital documents instead of having to go to the municipality building to file printed documents. This actually changes the hierarchy of institutional culture and allows society to reconsider the tools it uses to make its voice heard in urban spaces. In other words, the easy access of individuals (voters) to public officials in the Metaverse can strengthen the active participation of the local community in urban governance decisions (Hayrullahoğlu & Varol, 2022, p. 253).

Similarly, the STM ThinkTech report (2022) supports NLC (2022) and Hayrullahoğlu and Varol (2022). According to the STM ThinkTech report (2022), the Metaverse can also serve as a platform for political decision-makers to meet their voters by bringing important innovations to public services. Local and national executives can meet with the public in the Metaverse and get opinions on general issues. The Seoul Municipality aims to establish a virtual communication environment within the city's municipal boundaries using the "Metaverse Seoul" platform. The main objectives of the "Metaverse Seoul" platform, which will be created in three phases starting from 2022 and is expected to cost an estimated $2.8 billion, are as follows:

- Bringing city administrators and civilians together, enabling civilians to communicate their complaints and opinions directly, thereby increasing efficiency,
- Encouraging the participation of all civilians by organizing collective events virtually,
- Organizing virtual celebrations on New Year's days, festivals, and holidays,
- Meeting with people interested in investing in Seoul,
- Making it a platform where smart city technologies are developed,
- Informing the tourists who visit or want to visit the city, presenting the originals of the historical buildings that exist or no longer exist today to the tourists in the virtual environment,
- Providing better urban services to people with disabilities, the elderly, and those in need of care.

Innovations local governments used most in the digitalization of cities, besides the Metaverse, include the Internet of Things, augmented reality, and digital twin. Many cities use the Internet of Things (IoT) to gather data about physical space and how people move around the city. There are many potential applications of this technology. However, it is often used to monitor traffic patterns, service utilization, and environmental factors such as air quality, noise, and temperature. For example, the city of Pittsburgh has installed adaptive traffic signals on roads that change lights according to actual traffic in order to reduce commuting times and fuel consumption. The smart traffic system has reduced travel delays in Pittsburgh by about 20%. In addition, many cities are using augmented reality (AR) to support tourism and local economies. In New York, for example, The Buffalo Olmsted Parks Conservancy has developed a mobile app that allows visitors to scan signs in parks and get a historical view of the park wherever they have stopped. This feature allows visitors to interact with the park and enliven the local economy by attracting tourists to the parks (NLC, 2022, p. 11).

In addition, according to the NLC (2022), municipalities create digital twins to model how changes in the city's physical environment, such as traffic congestion, emissions, and sea level rise, will affect the city. A digital twin can be defined as a virtual model designed to accurately reflect an object or system. Lee et al. (2021) describe digital twins as large-scale and highly accurate digital models and entities replicated in virtual environments. Digital twins reflect the characteristics of physical counterparts of real cities, including object movement, temperature, and even function. Sun et al. (2022) suggest that digital twins be considered a fundamental part of the Metaverse. Using 3D technology, digital twins build a complete urban information model of the city, such as population, buildings, road traffic, infrastructure, lifelines, and other facilities, and obtain and detect the state of all these elements in real time by means of the Internet of Things. According to Ulubaş Hamurcu (2022) and Sun et al. (2022), the use of digital twins also has several benefits. Ulubaş Hamurcu asserts that policies developed by local governments can be tested quickly, and better and faster solutions to problems in cities can be found by using digital twins and virtual simulations. Similarly, according to Sun et al. (2022), the use of digital twins can promote economic development, allow effective management of human resources, and improve the ecological environment to enhance the overall quality of life of residents.

In Massachusetts, the Boston Planning and Development Agency (BPDA) designed a digital twin that maps the entire physical landscape of the city, from water and sewage systems to treetops. When there is a controversial development proposal in the municipality, the digital twin is used to evaluate the proposed project. For example, in BPDA, the shadows that a new building would cast on a popular park were analyzed using a digital twin, and as a result, the building plan that minimized the negative impact of the building on the park was preferred. Digital twins are a powerful tool in urban planning, allowing us to predict the impacts of new buildings, street changes, and land use decisions. Digital twins enable data-driven planning and help cities save money by predicting the future cost impacts of decisions made today. It is estimated that if U.S. cities use digital twins to improve the efficiency of energy, transportation, and infrastructure, cost savings of around $280 billion could be achieved (NLC, 2022, p. 11).

In short, local governments that create metacities using the Metaverse can achieve different benefits in many areas. Hayrullahoğlu and Varol (2022) state that there may be less mobility in urban areas due to virtual meetings, education, leisure activities, and shopping, thanks to the Metaverse. Considering that real estate is a scarce resource in the physical world, there may be a new opportunity for real estate investment, thereby allowing urban planners to be able to create utopian scenarios to make cities more livable in the future. According to Wang et al. (2022), the creation of metacities establishes a social interaction link between the virtual and reality. Thus, with this interaction and feedback between metacities and real cities, the effectiveness of various decisions in real cities and the improvement of the decisions taken can be achieved. In this way, the decision-making and operational efficiency of real cities can be greatly increased.

In addition to all these above-mentioned opportunities and benefits, it is also thought that municipalities can create new employment models in metacities. For example, individuals who will work in the virtual municipality building can be employed in the metacity. The avatars of employees in the virtual environment can speed up both the disruptions within the system and communication with citizens. Accordingly, many solutions can be offered for municipal activities, and efficiency and virtual communication can be increased. It can be argued that local governments (municipalities) will play an active role in urban planning practices and will speed up in the future using the Metaverse.

## METHODOLOGY AND FINDINGS

This study analyzed the Metaverse BLD 4.0 V22 project of Ankara Metropolitan Municipality, which was selected as the fourth city in the world after Los Angeles, Bari, and Helsinki by the Open AR Cloud Association, developing standards for the Metaverse. In addition, the study examined how users interpreted the posts made on Twitter and YouTube accounts by the BLD 4.0 V22 project of Ankara

Municipality. The study was prepared in a qualitative research design, a method helping to question and interpret the problem under investigation and to understand the form of the problem in its natural environment (Marshall & Rossman, 2014). The volume of raw data was reduced in the analysis process, and the essence of large amounts of data was analyzed through qualitative studies (Patton, 2014). The small pieces extracted play an important role in forming the general discourse. The qualitative method was based on certain details and qualities, focusing on showing the situation instead of understanding it. In the qualitative method, details and qualities are taken as bases, the data are described and interpreted in depth, and the perspectives of the people in the study are attempted to be understood (Eisner, 1998).

The present study is a case study. Creswell and Poth (2016) describes a case study as an approach where the researcher collects detailed and in-depth information about real life, a current bounded system (a situation), or multiple bounded systems (situations) over a period of time by using multiple sources of information (e.g., observations, interviews, audiovisual materials, and documents and reports). Bruns and Burgess (2016) emphasize the importance of social media research by arguing that social media data are in the quality of a shared social memory. They also argue that scientific research should be conducted on these platforms, which are social documentation tools, as social media has become one of the most fundamental communication channels for public communication. In the age of global communication, there is no other medium where billions of people can present their ideas, tastes, ambitions, tastes, and thoughts. No doubt, this power of social media does not mean that all voices will be heard equally; however, it is important for the visibility of some specific issues and themes.

In this context, the study data were obtained by using MAXQDA and retrieving 1,957 comments made for the BLD 4.0 V22 project of the mayor of Ankara Metropolitan Municipality on January 5, 2022, from his Twitter and YouTube accounts. Comments were screened in detail, and irrelevant comments were excluded from the analysis. In the final analysis, 1,592 comments were evaluated (Table 2).

*Table 2. The impact of the metaverse project on virtual political communication*

| Social Media | Views | Comments | Likes | Shares | Number of Subscribers |
|---|---|---|---|---|---|
| Twitter | 752.4 B | 523 | 26.1 B | 2,667 | 6.6 Mn |
| YouTube | 188 B | 1,434 | 20 B | N.A. | 67.4 B |

**Source:** YouTube (2022) and Twitter (2022)

It is possible to evaluate data analysis in qualitative research under six headings (Creswell & Creswell, 2017):

- Document identification and classification
- Identification of data
- Coding
- Classification of results
- Presentation of outputs
- Interpretation and inference.

The data obtained were analyzed using content analysis. The content analysis method creates generalization from qualitative to quantitative, which enables the structuring and classification of meanings that are important for revealing the common aspects of a large number of text contents (Weber, 1989). In this study, after the data were analyzed one by one, study results were formed based on categories in Table 3 (Merriam, 1998). Subsequently, the categories created based on the concepts extracted from the data were coded. Qualitative data analyses were performed using MAXQDA 2018 software; this program supports researchers in the case-based qualitative data analysis process (Kuckartz & Kuckartz, 2002). The data were sent to an independent researcher to receive feedback on the results for the purpose of the reliability of the study.

Users' comments on the digital project BLD 4.0 V22 on social media platforms play an important role in determining people's views on digitalization in governance and trust in the political leader. In this study, comments during the review period were analyzed both to determine the Metaverse and industry-4.0 perception of civilians and to evaluate the perspectives of these developments on local government[1]. The distribution of the categories and the number of coding numbers obtained as a result of the content analysis of the posts sent for the digital BLD 4.0 V22 project on the social media platforms Twitter and YouTube are presented in Table 3.

The frequency distribution of the categories determined for the BLD 4.0 V22 theme in line with the data obtained and the analyses is presented in Figure 2.

*Table 3. distribution of category-code numbers of sharing on Twitter and YouTube BLD 4.0 V22*

| Theme | Code Color | Categories | Code Number |
|---|---|---|---|
| BLD 4.0 V22 | ● | Trust in A Political Leader | 432 |
| | ● | Importance of Digitalization in the Management | 270 |
| | ● | Perception of Digital Municipality | 249 |
| | ● | Awareness of the Metaverse | 175 |
| | ● | Perception of Innovative Leadership | 168 |
| | ● | Perception of Industry-4.0 | 164 |
| | ● | Understand and Manage of Generation Z | 134 |

*Figure 2. Frequency graph of interaction information of BLD 4.0 V22*

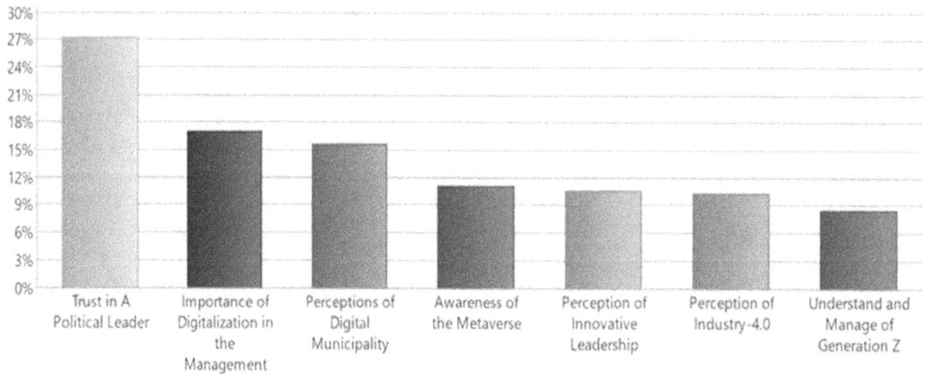

Figure 2 shows that users prioritized the main category of trust in a political leader (27.1%). The second main category is importance of digitalization in management (17.0%). The remaining main categories are perceptions of digital municipality (15.6%), awareness of the Metaverse (11.0%), perception of innovative leadership (10.6%), perception of industry-4.0 (10.3%), and understand and manage of generation Z (8.4%).

It can be argued that the posts about the project on social media platforms created a sense of trust in the leader among the commentators most. Again, it can be interpreted that the commentators care about the concepts of digitalization and digital municipality in the administration, and accordingly, an awareness of Metaverse and industry-4.0 technologies has developed. It can be argued that adaptation of these technologies creates a perception of innovative leadership, and although it represents the lowest number of coding, it can be argued that the category of understanding and managing of Generation Z, which is expressed as digital natives, should be addressed again at the point of creating the right digitalization policies.

*Figure 3. Frequency graph of interaction information of BLD 4.0 V22*

The code cloud above shows the most frequently repeated codes in the data obtained from the MAXQDA 2018 (Figure 3). The analysis of Figure 3 shows that, similar to the frequency distribution table, trust in a political leader is the most recurring code. The second most recurring code is the importance of digitalization in management, and the third most recurrent code is perceptions of a digital municipality.

Figure 4 shows the relationship between the codes. In the relationship graph, the strongest relationship of the BLD 4.0 V22 theme is between the codes' importance of digitalization in management and trust in a political leader. Accordingly, it can be assumed that digitalization in management may influence trust in a political leader. The next strongest relationship was between the importance of digitalization in management and perceptions of a digital municipality. In general terms, it can be understood that developing a digital strategy in management will also determine the perception of a digital municipality. The third level relationship occurred between the perception of industry-4.0 and the perceptions of the digital municipality codes and between the perceptions of innovative leadership and trust in political leader codes. Therefore, understanding industry-4.0 technologies and making investments in this direction will again strengthen the perception of a digital municipality. Moreover, it can be understood that the perception of innovative leadership will strengthen the sense of trust in a leader. Other relationships were considered low and shown with solid lines.

*Figure 4. Relationships among the codes*

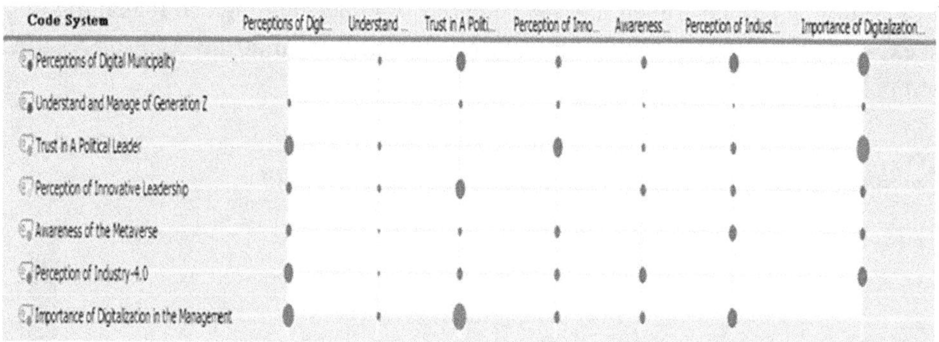


## FUTURE RESEARCH AND DIRECTIONS

Metaverse applications are still in the beginning and testing phase. Therefore, the BLD 4.0 V22 Metaverse project should be developed and planned in a way to follow the Metaverse practices of other municipalities globally, as Metaverse technology is not a development that one organization can manage alone. It is a very comprehensive application that includes many fields. Many more differentiated forms of Metaverse applications will be available and will start to have an impact in all fields in the near future. Any organization that can understand these developments in a timely manner and develops strategies accordingly will gain functionality. It will be beneficial for all stakeholders who want to adapt to the process by following the development of this new technology and evaluating the scientific world from different perspectives. Comparing the data obtained from different databases in future studies and sharing the results of the analysis on the Metaverse is also extremely important for the development of the field and for researchers so that they can see the current situation.

## CONCLUSION AND POLICY RECOMMENDATION

Adapting public services to digital technologies and reshaping public administration and policies on the axis of digital strategy provides opportunities for positive development in terms of quality, efficiency, access, and effectiveness in services. It is possible to introduce reforms in public administration by ensuring harmony between citizen demands and preferences and service requirements and possibilities offered by technology, especially in the digital age. Thanks to the developments in information and communication technologies, local government municipalities have benefited from "gov.tr. and Web 2.0" at the right time and have started to provide most of their services through the Internet. With the developments after Web 3.0, the needs of individuals or institutions have been transferred to artificial intelligence, and these needs have begun to be met much faster and more transparently. The Metaverse technology created by these developments, on the other hand, refers that municipalities creating virtual entities in the Metaverse, establishing their own worlds, and providing their citizens with the opportunity to participate in the processes using their virtual avatars.

The integration of municipalities and citizens takes place in a different interactive universe. Today, the main factor determining digital trends and shaping their use is the younger generations. Especially Generation Z, also referred to as "digital natives," who prefer services that are fully adapted to technology. The main users of the Metaverse are members of Generation Z. Since Generation Z grew up in a period when computers and mobile technologies had already greatly developed, this generation is much more active in the Metaverse. Thus, it is very important for public and private institutions, to adopt Metaverse technologies in order to develop the right service understanding for new generations.

There are few municipalities participating in the Metaverse universe around the world; however, the Ankara Metropolitan Municipality has become the first municipality in Turkey to introduce an application in this field. The Ankara Municipality aims to predetermine citizens' requests for virtual experiences and provide better public services through a metacity platform. Consequently, the Ankara Municipality has taken an important step in urban competitiveness as a metacity. In this study, the comments of social media users on the project within the scope of the Metaverse project BLD 4.0 V22 of the Ankara Metropolitan Municipality were examined within the framework of digitalization in public administration, trust in the leadership, virtual political communication, and the perspective to the Mayor. Through the results of the analysis conducted, the importance of digitalization in governance has emerged, and it has been found that there is an awareness among citizens regarding the concepts of industry-4.0 and the Metaverse. In particular, it is understood that the perception of innovative leadership created by the digital municipalism approach creates trust in a political leader. As stated by NLC (2022), Hayrullahoğlu and Varol (2022), STM ThinkTech (2022), Ulubaş Hamurcu (2022), Sun et al. (2022), and Wang et al. (2022), with this trust, the mayor and with Metacity Ankara Municipality can improve the effectiveness of various social, political, and economic decisions in Ankara. The analysis also showed that there was no sharing regarding virtual political communication, and the study concluded that, contrary to expectations, awareness of virtual political communication had not yet been realized at a sufficient level in society.

## REFERENCES

Bruns, A., & Burgess, J. (2016). Methodological innovation in precarious spaces: The case of Twitter. In *Digital methods for social science: An interdisciplinary guide to research innovation. (S. Ersöz Karakulakoğlu, Tr)* (pp. 17–33). Nobel Publication. doi:10.1057/9781137453662_2

Çelik, Z., Dülek, B., Aydın, I., & Saydan, R. (2022). Metaverse: Bibliometric Analysis, A Conceptual Model Proposal, and a Marketing-Oriented Approach. *Bingöl University Journal of Social Sciences Institute*, *24*, 383–394. doi:10.29029/busbed.1114777

Choi, H. Y. (2022). Working in the Metaverse: Does Telework in a Metaverse Office Have the Potential to Reduce Population Pressure in Megacities? Evidence from Young Adults in Seoul, South Korea. *Sustainability (Basel), 14*(3629), 1–17. doi:10.3390u14063629

Collins, C. (2008). Looking to the future: Higher education in the Metaverse. *EDUCAUSE Review, 43*(5), 51–63. https://er.educause.edu/-/media/files/article-downloads/erm0853.pdf

Creswell, J. W., & Creswell, J. D. (2017). *Research design: Qualitative, quantitative, and mixed methods approaches*. Sage publications.

Creswell, J. W., & Poth, C. N. (2016). *Research Design: Qualitative inquiry and research design: Choosing among five approaches. Sage Publications. (M. Bütün and S.B. Demir, Tr)*. Siyasal Publication.

Eisner, E. (1998). *The Enlightened Eye: Qualitative Inquiry and the Enhancement of Educational Practice*. Prentice-Simon and Schuster/A Viacom Company Hall.

Fei-Yue, F. (2004). Parallel system methods for management and control of complex systems. *Kongzhi yu Juece. Control and Decision, 19*(5), 485–489.

Hayrullahoğlu, G., & Varol, Ç. (2022). Urban Life and Urban Space in The Interaction of Unıverse and Metaverse. In E. Koçak, N. Kafadar, & O. Sevgul, (eds.) Design and Planning From Different Perspectives, (Ed.) Iksad Publication.

Jauhiainen, J. S., Krohn, C., & Junnila, J. (2023). Metaverse and Sustainability: Systematic Review of Scientific Publications until 2022 and Beyond. *Sustainability (Basel), 15*(346), 1–20. doi:10.3390u15010346

Kim, J. (2021). Advertising in the Metaverse: Research Agenda. *Journal of Interactive Advertising, 21*(3), 141–144. doi:10.1080/15252019.2021.2001273

Kuckartz, A. M., Kuckartz, U. (2012). *Qualitative Text Analysis*. MAXQDA, file:///C:/Users/lenovo/Downloads/Qualitative_Text_Analysis_with_MAXQDA.pdf, [Erişim Tarihi: 08.11.2020].

Kye, B., Han, N., Kim, E., Park, Y., & Jo, S. (2021). Educational applications of metaverse: Possibilities and limitations. *Journal of Educational Evaluation for Health Professions, 18*(32), 1–13. doi:10.3352/jeehp.2021.18.32 PMID:34897242

Lee, L. H., Braud, T., Zhou, P., Wang, L., Xu, D., Lin, Z., Kumar, A., Bermejo, C., & Hui, P. (2021). All one needs to know about metaverse: A complete survey on technological singularity, virtual ecosystem, and research agenda. *Journal of Latex Class Files, 14*(8), 1–66. doi:10.48550/arXiv.2110.05352

Lee, Y. J. (2021). A Study on Metaverse Hype for Sustainable Growth. *International Journal of Advanced Smart Convergence, 10*(3), 72–80. doi:10.7236/IJASC.2021.10.3.72

Marshall, C., & Rossman, G. B. (2014). *Designing Qualitative Research*. Sage.

Merriam, S. (1998). *Qualitative research and case study applications in education. Revised and expanded from case study research in education*. JB Printing.

Morgan, J. P. (2022). *Opportunities in the metaverse: How businesses can explore the metaverse and navigate the hype vs. reality,* 1-17. JP Morgan. https://www.jpmorgan.com/content/dam/jpm/treasury-services/documents/opportunities-in-the-metaverse.pdf

Moro-Visconti, R. (2022). From physical reality to the Metaverse: A Multilayer Network Valuation. *Journal of Metaverse*, *2*(1), 16–22. https://dergipark.org.tr/en/pub/jmv/issue/67967/1071950

Mystakidis, S. (2022). Metaverse. *Metaverse. Encyclopedia*, *2*(1), 486–497. doi:10.3390/encyclopedia2010031

National League of Cities. (2022). *The Future of Cities*. National League of Cities. https://www.nlc.org/resource/cities-and-themetaverse/#:~:text=The%20metaverse%20is%20the%20next,digitally%20recreate%20the%20real%20world

NLC. (2022). *The Future of Cities: Cities and the Metaverse*. NLC. https://www.nlc.org/wp-content/uploads/2022/04/CS-Cities-and-the-Metaverse_v4-Final-1.pdf

Park, S., & Kim, S. (2022). Identifying World Types to Deliver Gameful Experiences for Sustainable Learning in the Metaverse. *Sustainability (Basel)*, *14*(1361), 1–14. doi:10.3390u14031361

Park, S., & Kim, Y. (2022b). A Metaverse: Taxonomy, Components, Applications, and Open Challenges. *IEEE Access : Practical Innovations, Open Solutions*, *10*, 4209–4251. doi:10.1109/ACCESS.2021.3140175

Patton, M. Q. (2014). Qualitative Research & Evaluation Methods: Integrating Theory and Practice (M. Bütün ve S. B. Demir, Tr. Ed.), Ankara: Pegem Academy Publication.

Seoul Metropolitan Government. (2022, November 5). *Virtual Seoul City Hall via beta release of Metaverse Seoul*. SMG. https://english.seoul.go.kr/virtual-seoul-city-hall-via-beta-release-of-metaverse-seoul/ [21.01.2023]

STM ThinkTech. (2022). *Metaverse: Opportunities and Threats. Trend Analysis February*. STM. https://thinktech.stm.com.tr/tr/metaverse-firsatlar-ve-tehditler

Sun, J., Gan, W., & Chao, H. (2022). Metaverse: Survey, Applications, Security, and Opportunities. *arXiv:2210.07990*. https://doi.org//arXiv.2210.07990. doi:10.48550

Sun, J., Gan, W., & Chen, Z. (2022b). Big Data Meets Metaverse: A Survey. *arXiv:2210.16282*, 1-17. https://doi.org//arXiv.2210.16282 doi:10.48550

Ulubaş Hamurcu, A. (2022). The metaverse, online communities, and (real) urban space. *Urbani Izziv*, *33*(2), 73–81. doi:10.5379/urbani-izziv-en-2022-33-02-01

Wang, F., Qin, R., Wang, X., & Hu, B. (2022). MetaSocieties in Metaverse: MetaEconomics and MetaManagement for MetaEnterprises and MetaCities. *IEEE Transactions on Computational Social Systems*, *9*(1), 1–6. doi:10.1109/TCSS.2022.3145165

Weber, R. P. (1989). *Basic Content Analysis*. Sage.

Yang, Q., Zhao, Y., Huang, H., Xiong, Z., Kang, J., & Zheng, Z. (2022). Fusing blockchain and AI with metaverse: A survey. *IEEE Open Journal of the Computer Society*, IarXiv *preprint arXiv:2201.03201*, 1-15. https://doi.org//arXiv.2201.03201 doi:10.48550

## ADDITIONAL READING

Andrea, A. (2022). Metacity: città, Informatica e società. Impatti locali e globali da una prospettiva ecologica. *Catalogo dei prodotti della ricercar*, 1-302.

Joshi, L., & Narayan, J. P. (2022). Quantification of the Effects of an Urban Layer on Rayleigh Wave Characteristics and Development of a Meta-City. *Pure and Applied Geophysics*, *179*(9), 3253–3277. doi:10.100700024-022-03111-y

Moro Visconti, R. (2022). From physical reality to the Metaverse: A Multilayer Network Valuation. *Journal of Metaverse*, *2*(1), 16–22.

Polas, M. R., Ahamed, B., & Rana, M. M. (2023). Artificial Intelligence and Blockchain Technology in the 4.0 IR Metaverse Era: Implications, Opportunities, and Future Directions. In P. Lai (Ed.), *Strategies and Opportunities for Technology in the Metaverse World* (pp. 13–33). IGI Global. doi:10.4018/978-1-6684-5732-0.ch002

Ulubaş Hamurcu, A. (2022). The metaverse, online communities, and (real) urban space. *Urbani Izziv*, *33*(2), 73–81. doi:10.5379/urbani-izziv-en-2022-33-02-01

Vinod Kumar, T. M. (2022). International Collaborative Research: Smart Master Planning Case Studies of Domain Innovations and Conclusions of Cities. In T. M. Vinod Kumar (Ed.), *Smart Master Planning for Cities. Advances in 21st Century Human Settlements*. Springer. doi:10.1007/978-981-19-2386-9_9

Vishkaei, B. M. (2022). Metaverse: A New Platform for Circular Smart Cities. In P. De Giovanni (Ed.), *Cases on Circular Economy in Practice* (pp. 51–69). IGI Global. doi:10.4018/978-1-6684-5001-7.ch003

## KEY TERMS AND DEFINITIONS

**Ankara:** This is the capital of Turkey.

**Metacities:** These are virtual cities created in the Metaverse by using urban planning and mapping in parallel to real cities.

**MetaStrategy:** It is a plan that focuses on how a defined strategy is to be realized.

**Metaverse:** This is a combination of the words "meta" and "universe" and refers to a three-dimensional virtual world in which avatars engage in political, economic, social, and cultural activities.

**Municipality:** It is one of the local government structures authorized by the central government.

## ENDNOTE

1 In the study, the voter-municipality virtual political communication within the scope of Ankara Municipality's BLD 4.0 V22 project was also analyzed; however, it was observed that there were no posts or data on this relationship. Therefore, virtual political communication is not included in the frequency distribution and code cloud in the findings section.

# Chapter 8
# Technology Transfer Process in Brazil:
## An Overview of the National Context

**Luan Carlos Santos Silva**
https://orcid.org/0000-0002-8846-2511
*Federal University of Grande Dourados, Brazil*

**Carla Schwengber Ten Caten**
*Federal University of Rio Grande do Sul, Brazil*

## ABSTRACT

*The objective of this study is to analyze the technology transfer flow in Brazil from 2000 to 2014, considering the domestic and foreign markets, and also the activities carried out by universities and technological institutes from 1972 to 2015. From results, Brazil has been receiving technologies from major economic powers such as the United States, Germany, Japan, France, Italy, the United Kingdom, Switzerland, Canada, and Spain. The barriers regarding cooperation between university-industry are still present, currently there are 27.523 research groups distributed in all areas of knowledge, but only 0.31% develops activities related to technology transfer, and 58% do not establish any relationships with industry. Notwithstanding, the technology supply must depend on the technological diffusion process and the adoption of technology by the society through continuous learning, thereby enabling to increase the performance of services, processes, and products in the domestic market.*

## INTRODUCTION

Technology transfer is a crucial process in the development of a nation's economy, and it plays an important role in promoting innovation, generating employment, and fostering economic growth. In Brazil, technology transfer from universities to the industry is a crucial aspect that can drive the country's economy forward.

DOI: 10.4018/978-1-6684-8397-8.ch008

Questions concerning the technological and scientific innovation have been widely discussed by most researchers, since it brings benefits to both industries and universities. The process of production and implementation of knowledge by an organization is an important theme of literature on innovation, however only few works are focused on the commercialization of this kind of knowledge, a subject directly related to technology transfer.

Technology transfer is a mechanism by which the productive sector can conquer and maintain its competitiveness in the market, not been this only a result of technological advances, but result of an attitude in order to change and monitor the human, economic and social needs of today's world.

Thus, the interaction of research institutes and universities with industries facilitates the technology expansion in several areas of knowledge, enabling the growth of organizations and, consequently, producing greater national, regional and local economic development.

Relying on this line of thought, Debackere & Veugelers (2005) affirm that the development of a suitable structure for university-industry cooperation demands special attention on the interests of the university and, above all, the productive sector.

In addition, analyzing the interaction between these two segments, and understanding the advantages and limits of this process, is opportune by considering the importance of research for the socioeconomic development of society itself, and since industries play an important role in this context.

This cooperation also allows companies to obtain new knowledge and academic experiences. Companies are able to follow the rapid changes of new technologies and integrate new products into their portfolios (Malik et al. 2011; Philbin, 2008). Reciprocally, universities have access to different sources of funding and a better empirical understanding of current strategies and future ideas of companies (Veugelers & Cassiman, 2005; Malik et al., 2011).

Universities are a rich source of knowledge, innovation, and technology, and their research activities generate new ideas, methods, and technologies that can be used to solve a variety of problems. However, the commercialization of these ideas and technologies requires more than just scientific expertise; it requires a well-coordinated effort between universities and industry players.

The transfer of technology from universities to the industry is a process that enables the commercialization of research results, which can ultimately contribute to the development of new products and services, as well as the creation of new businesses. In Brazil, the importance of technology transfer is recognized, and the government has taken several steps to promote it.

One of the ways in which technology transfer is encouraged in Brazil is through the establishment of technology parks and incubators, which are designed to bring together researchers, entrepreneurs, and investors in a collaborative environment. These facilities provide a platform for the exchange of knowledge and ideas between universities and industry, facilitating the transfer of technology and fostering the development of new businesses.

Another important initiative is the creation of partnerships between universities and industry players. By collaborating on research projects, universities and companies can share resources, expertise, and technology, which can lead to the development of new products and services. These partnerships can also lead to the creation of spin-off companies, which are established to commercialize the technology developed by the university.

In addition to these initiatives, the Brazilian government has established several programs to promote technology transfer. For example, the Innovation Law, which was introduced in 2004, provides tax incentives for companies that invest in research and development. The Brazilian Agency for Industrial

Development (ABDI) also provides support for technology transfer by facilitating partnerships between universities and industry players.

Within this context, the objective of this work is to analyze the technology transfer flow in Brazil, by analyzing the internal and external context, from 2000 to 2014, the research was grounded on data collected at the National Institute of Industrial Property (INPI) and Central Bank of Brazil (BACEN). We also analyzed the activities related to technology transfer carried out by the technological institutes and universities from 1972 to 2015, based on information collected at the Research Groups Directory from the National Council for Scientific and Technological Development (CNPq).

## Technology Transfer in the Ambit University-Industry

Technology transfer has become a very effective mean to disseminate innovation. It is a competitive alternative for companies seeking not only the exploitation of internal resources for the use of new technologies, but to acquire new technologies from external partners, and also is the process of transferring knowledge, technology, and other intellectual property from a university to the industry. This process can lead to the development of new products and services, the creation of new businesses, and the promotion of economic growth. The university-industry environment is an important context for technology transfer, and there are several scientific concepts related to this area.

In the current context the technology transfer in the scope university-industry attracts considerable attention in the literature by the scientists involved in this area, being the scientific and technological institutions the agents of technology commercialization (e.g. offices of technology transfer), or in regarding to transferring modes, such as formal or informal (Edler et al., 2011).

The definition of technology transfer can be interpreted as a process of acquisition, development and use of technological knowledge by the individuals who generated it (Lima, 2004). However, it is understood as a process of implementation of new technologies developed for an environment that do not have the same technologies.

One important concept is the Triple Helix model, which was proposed by Etzkowitz (2003). This model describes the interdependent relationship between universities, industry, and government in promoting innovation and economic development. According to this model, the three entities work together in a mutually beneficial manner, with each contributing to the others' success. The university contributes knowledge, research, and education; the industry contributes resources, expertise, and funding; and the government provides policy support and infrastructure.

Another important concept is National Innovation Systems (Lundvall, 1992), which describes the networks of institutions, organizations, and individuals involved in the creation, diffusion, and use of new technologies and innovations. This concept emphasizes the importance of collaboration and knowledge-sharing among different actors in the innovation process, including universities, industry, and government.

Open innovation (Chesbrough, 2003) is another concept that is relevant to technology transfer in the university-industry environment. This concept refers to the use of external sources of innovation, such as collaborations with universities and other partners, to complement internal R&D efforts. Open innovation recognizes that no organization has a monopoly on good ideas, and that there is value in seeking out and leveraging external sources of knowledge and expertise.

In short, the concept is defined in different ways, in according to each research, but also in according to the purpose of the research. While the search for a single definition is useless, attention to definitions fosters some understanding of the differences between research traditions.

In research literature a lot concerning the development of technology transfer can be understood in terms of attempts to deal with thorny conceptual problems, there are different types of trends influencing research such as public policies and social changes which affect the technology transfer environment (Bozeman, 2000).

The stages of the process include six steps: selection of the technology to be used by the company, selection of suppliers, negotiation for acquisition, completion of the process, assimilation of technology transferred and implemented, adaptation and improvement (Deitos, 2002).

When transferring and implementing technologies to the productive sector, a thorough monitoring of all the steps is necessary to make everything happen as planned. To that end, support activities ensure the achievement of success (Bozarth, 2006).

People involved in this process must implement a methodology in a natural and direct way, observing points of control when monitoring (Romanenko et al., 2007).

Thus, cooperation between universities and the productive sector can help the search for new inventions that bring important stimulus to the development of innovations and technology transfer (Niedergassel & Leker, 2011).

In addition, it has been widely suggested that policy makers should support the conditions to stimulate innovation and promote industry interaction with universities (Davenport et al, 1998; Veugelers & Cassima, 2005). According to Fontana & Matt (2006) governments have noted how important the role of universities is, because they have acted as a provider of human capital and a center for new businesses and innovations.

In general, researchers at universities should see cooperation with industry as an organizational skill and develop ways to effectively do it (Malik et al., 2011).

In all types of cooperation, companies need to have a certain ability to absorb external knowledge in order to be a specialist in identifying and using transferred knowledge, for example being able to market new products (Cohen & Levinthal, 1990; Veugelers & Cassima, 2005; Fontana & Matt, 2006; Malik et al, 2011, Bishop et al., 2011).

Between this and that, technology transfer naturally appears as a strategic mechanism of cooperation for the use of industries and universities, and it is necessary that emerging countries guarantee its protection (Sun et al., 2010).

The technology transfer offices (TTOs) are an important institutional mechanism for facilitating technology transfer in the university-industry environment. TTOs are specialized units within universities that are responsible for managing the transfer of technology and intellectual property from the university to industry partners (Siegel et al., 2003). TTOs play an important role in identifying and protecting intellectual property, negotiating licensing agreements, and facilitating collaborations between researchers and industry partners.

Finally, the technology transfer is an important process that can promote innovation, economic growth, and the creation of new businesses. The university-industry environment is a critical context for technology transfer, and there are several scientific concepts related to this area, including the Triple Helix model, National Innovation Systems, open innovation, and technology transfer offices.

## Contract Endorsement Process of Technology Transfer in the Intellectual Property

As established by Law nº 5.648 from December 11, 1970, the National Institute of Intellectual Property (INPI) is responsible for registering acts or contracts that imply technology transfer in Brazil (Article 126).

The unique paragraph of the law emphasizes that the INPI will adopt measures aimed at accelerating and regulating technology transfer and establishing better conditions for negotiation and use of patents, also responsible for the pronouncement for the appropriateness of signature, ratification or denounce of conventions, treaties, and agreements on Intellectual Property.

As established by Brazilian Industrial Property Law nº 9279/96, there are the following types of technology transfer contracts: patent exploitation, industrial design, technology supply, provision of technical and scientific assistance service, use of trademarks and franchises.

The contracts can be formalized in three ways: (1) Assignment Contracts, which include the ownership transfer of intellectual property rights; (2) Licensing Contracts, which include licensing, and the use of the intellectual property rights, exclusively or not; (3) and Technology Transfer Contracts, which comprise the provision of information not protected by industrial property rights and technical assistance services.

The contracts related to the licensing of rights are: (EP) Patent Exploration; (EDI) Industrial Design Exploration; and (UTM) Use of Trademark. All these contracts refer to the explicit knowledge aroused from several researches of projects already executed, being contracts of assignment (transfer of title) and contracts of licensing of industrial property rights.

The contracts related to knowledge acquisition are: (PT) Provision of Technology, this type of contract aims at acquiring knowledge and techniques not covered by industrial property rights, intended for the production of industrial goods or services, having as object profile the codified knowledge in form of reports, manuals, drawings etc.

Technical and Scientific Assistance Services (SAT), this type of contract and/or invoices stipulate the conditions for obtaining services related to the techniques, planning and programming methods, as well as research, studies and projects destined to the execution or provision of specialized services, having as object profile the uncoded knowledge from human nature.

Already the Franchise Contract is intended to license trademarks (registration or order) and to exploit other industrial property rights, provide technical assistance services and the know-how necessary to achieve the business objective.

It is worth mentioning that there are several advantages in registering technology transfer contracts with the INPI, such as producing effects in relation to third parties, legitimizing payments abroad, and allowing the tax deduction of amounts paid.

Regarding the effects in relation to third parties, the license contracts must be registered in the INPI, according to Articles 62, 121 and 140 from the Intellectual Property Law/96, allowing the INPI to register contracts involving technology transfer, franchise agreements and similar, in order to produce effects with respect to third parties (INPI, article 211).

In concerning to legitimizing payments abroad, the Law nº 4131 from 1962 requires the application of foreign capital and remittances abroad, imposing the obligation to register contracts that involve remittances abroad in form of royalties and technical assistance.

And finally, the tax deduction which regulates the amounts paid as royalties for the exploitation or assignment of patents, or the use or assignment of trademarks, and also in the form of remuneration involving the technology transfer, only admitted from the endorsement of the respective contract in the INPI, having a maximum limit of 5% of net sales revenue.

It is worth noting that the importance of the registration of technology transfer contracts implies the generation of databases on the technology market, enabling the elaboration of studies and sector surveys, and subsidizing the formulation of technology transfer policy for Brazil.

## METHODOLOGICAL PROCEDURES

In order to understand the scenario of university-industry interaction, a comparative analysis at national level is presented, based on secondary data obtained through bibliographical and documentary research. From the point of view of objectives this research is characterized as exploratory and descriptive, being constituted as applied research, because it sought specific information on the object of study (Gil, 2007).

Concerning the technology transfer flow in Brazil the information was collected in three important bases:

The first information collection concerning the time period from 2000 to 2014, was carried out at the Directorate of Contracts, Geographical Indications and Registries (DICIG) from National Institute of Industrial Property (INPI), the survey was carried out on the number of endorsement certificates of technology transfer in according to the main sectors of activities of the assigning company, number of registration certificates from the assigning company (separated per Brazilian States), and number of endorsement certificates per contractual category, including the use of trademarks, exploitation of patents, technology supply, technical assistance services and franchises and also other categories.

The second information collection was carried out at the Central Bank of Brazil (BACEN) data was collected on remittances abroad by technology transfer from 2000 to 2014, into the categories: use of trademarks, exploitation of patents, technical assistance service and franchises.

The third part of research was held at the Research Groups Directory from the National Council for Scientific and Technological Development (CNPq) Brazil, soughing information concerning the technology transfer activities carried out by Brazilian universities and research centers during 1972 to 2015. Subsequently, the data obtained were tabulated in the program Microsoft Excel version 2007 in order to generate the graphics.

## ANALYSIS OF RESULTS

The information collected at INPI provided an overview of the technology transfer flow carried out in Brazil over the last decade.

Figure 1 presents the accumulated in Brazil over 15 years, in relation to the number of patents deposited and granted, as well as technology transfer contracts endorsements in all its categories (patent exploitation, industrial design exploitation, use of trademark, provision of technology, and provision of technical and scientific assistance services).

*Figure 1. Patents deposited and awarded versus technology transfer contracts registered*
**Source:** *Directory of Contracts, Geographical Indications Records from INPI, Brazil*

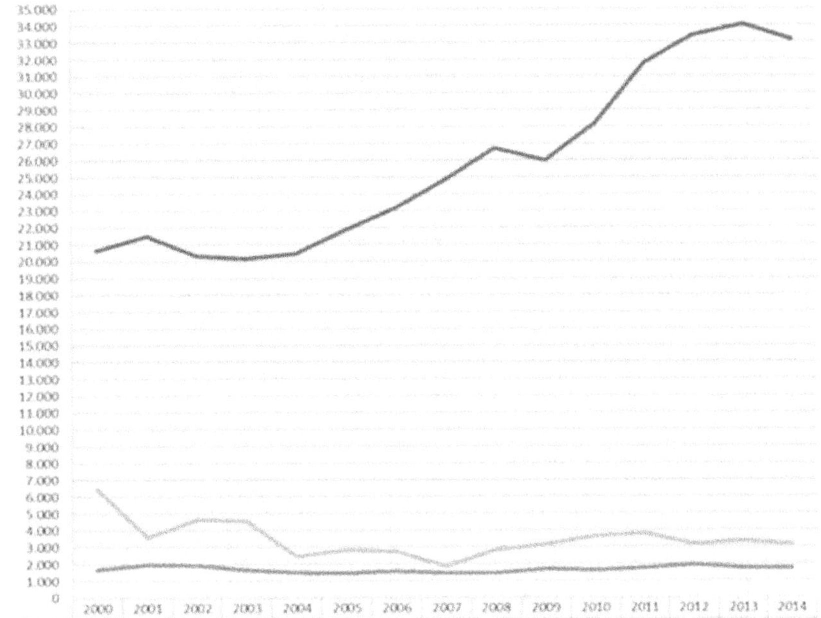


| | 2000 | 2001 | 2002 | 2003 | 2004 | 2005 | 2006 | 2007 | 2008 | 2009 | 2010 | 2011 | 2012 | 2013 | 2014 |
|---|---|---|---|---|---|---|---|---|---|---|---|---|---|---|---|
| Patents deposited | 20.639 | 21.474 | 20.317 | 20.169 | 20.430 | 21.850 | 23.144 | 24.841 | 26.681 | 25.967 | 28.141 | 31.767 | 33.395 | 34.050 | 33.182 |
| Patents granted | 6.434 | 3.573 | 4.654 | 4.567 | 2.432 | 2.803 | 2.742 | 1.840 | 2.815 | 3.144 | 3.609 | 3.799 | 3.130 | 3.325 | 3.122 |
| Contracts | 1.666 | 1.979 | 1.913 | 1.625 | 1.476 | 1.450 | 1.545 | 1.458 | 1.451 | 1.696 | 1.601 | 1.715 | 1.914 | 1.725 | 1.710 |

As can be seen in Figure 1, the number of patents deposited is higher than the number of patents granted. Comparing the data, the cumulative total indicates that only 14.28% of the patents deposited were actually granted. The number is still lower when compared to technologies transfer contracts recorded in all categories.

By contrasting the numbers of patents granted with the technology transfer contracts for patent exploitation (licensed patents), this numbers reduces even more. As shown in Table 1, over the last 15 years only 1.23% of the patents granted were licensed in the country. This directly reflects on the quality and innovation of technologies that are developed nationwide which do not meet the needs of the market.

Figure 2 shows the evolution of the last 15 years regarding the main suppliers of technology to Brazil. The United States always had the greatest cooperation in providing technology, followed by Germany. After the years of 2008 and 2009, the number of transfers increased, this period corresponds to the beginning of the economic crisis, and however, even affecting many countries in the world, Brazil still maintained a technological and financial balance.

It is worth mentioning that is important to Brazil to reach the technology transfer international market, in order to achieve its technological development through the participation of multinational companies.

International agreements are indispensable tools to make this activity feasible and effective, such as the Agreement on Trade-Related Aspects of Intellectual Property Rights (TRIPS), being considered the most important multilateral instrument for the globalization of intellectual property laws.

Figure 3 shows, the cumulative number of contracts registered from 2000 to 2014. As shown, the United States accounted for 27% of the total technology transactions flow.

*Table 1. Patents granted versus patents licensed*

| Year | Patents granted | Patents licensed | Percentage (%) |
|---|---|---|---|
| 2000 | 6.434 | 34 | 0.53 |
| 2001 | 3.573 | 39 | 1.09 |
| 2002 | 4.654 | 39 | 0.84 |
| 2003 | 4.567 | 39 | 0.85 |
| 2004 | 2.432 | 31 | 1.27 |
| 2005 | 2.803 | 53 | 1.89 |
| 2006 | 2.742 | 45 | 1.64 |
| 2007 | 1.840 | 46 | 2.50 |
| 2008 | 2.815 | 46 | 1.63 |
| 2009 | 3.144 | 40 | 1.27 |
| 2010 | 3.609 | 49 | 1.36 |
| 2011 | 3.799 | 57 | 1.50 |
| 2012 | 3.130 | 63 | 2.01 |
| 2013 | 3.325 | 26 | 0.78 |
| 2014 | 3.122 | 35 | 1.12 |
| Σ | 51.989 | 642 | - |

**Source:** Directory of Contracts, Geographical Indications Records from INPI, Brazil

*Figure 2. Main technology suppliers' countries to Brazil*
**Source:** *Directory of Contracts, Geographical Indications Records from INPI, Brazil*

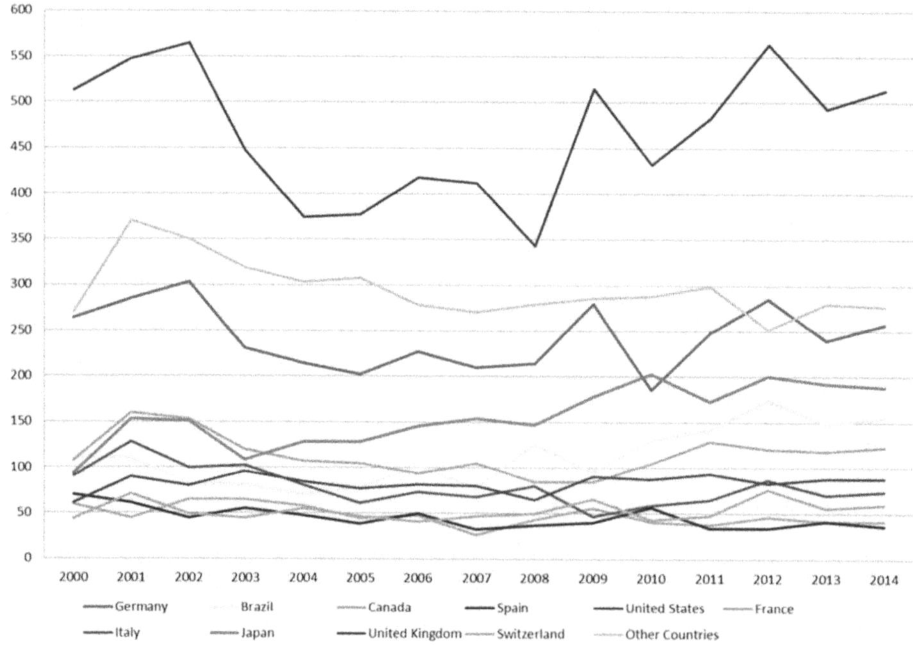

Regarding technology acquisition, Brazil had cooperation from major countries, being the United States, Germany, Japan, France, Italy, United Kingdom, Switzerland, Canada and Spain the most important ones, other countries correspond to 16% of the flow.

The development and acquisition of technology depends on the characteristics of companies, such as size (large companies), sector of activity (intensive activities in technology), positioning in the market (global markets), and the nature of capital (multinational corporations).

*Figure 3. Total number of technology transfer contracts made by the main technology suppliers' countries to Brazil*
**Source:** *Directory of Contracts, Geographical Indications Records from INPI, Brazil*

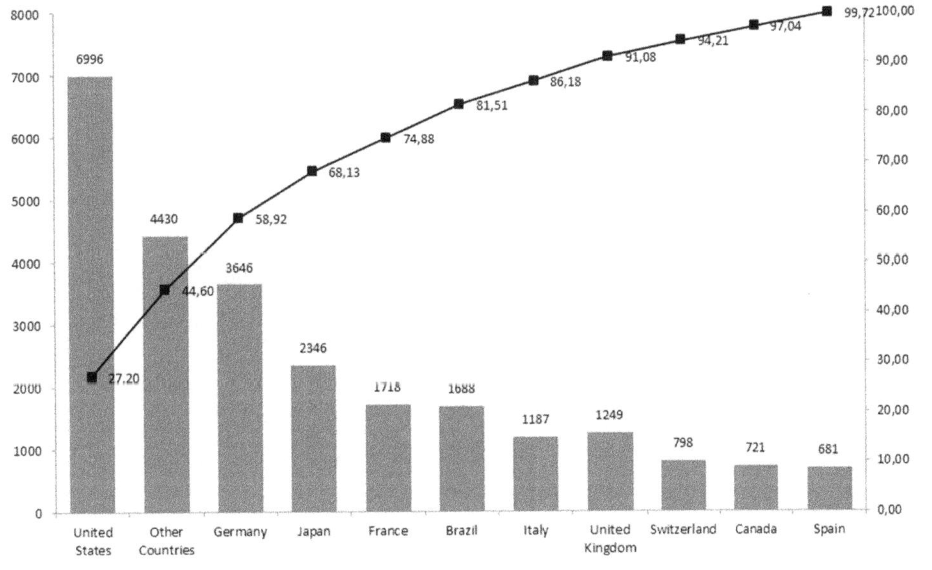


From 2000 to 2014, Brazil made technology shipments to other countries, the Figure 4 shows in details the categories: patent exploitation, use of brands, technology supply, technical assistance service, franchising and others, the information was collected from Central Bank of Brazil.

Contracts for the provision of technology (PT) were the most requested by other countries, these contracts aim at acquiring knowledge and techniques not covered by industrial property rights, intended for the production of industrial goods or services, being the knowledge encoded in the form of reports, manuals, drawings and others.

The technical assistance service (SAT) was the second most requested by other countries, the same refers to obtaining techniques, planning and programming methods, as well as research, studies and projects for the execution or provision of specialized services, derived from uncoded knowledge from tacit nature.

This fact is due to the high investment that Brazil has made in recent years in training programs for researchers established in other countries, from undergraduate, master's, doctoral and postdoctoral level, and also strategic alliances with developed nations.

One characteristic of the Brazilian Intellectual Property Law concerning technology export contracts (in which the transferring company is domiciled in Brazil and the assignee is foreign) is that the effects of the registration provided in the legislation do not apply to export contracts. The endorsement certificate may be required to recognize that the technology has national origin, thus these contracts are exempt from fee rates.

By comparing Figure 4 and Figure 2 an interesting fact is that over the last 15 years Brazil has transferred more technologies than it has imported, however the country still has a low index regarding patent exploitation.

*Figure 4. Technology transfer per category from Brazil to foreign countries*
**Source:** *Directory of Contracts, Geographical Indications Records from INPI, Brazil*

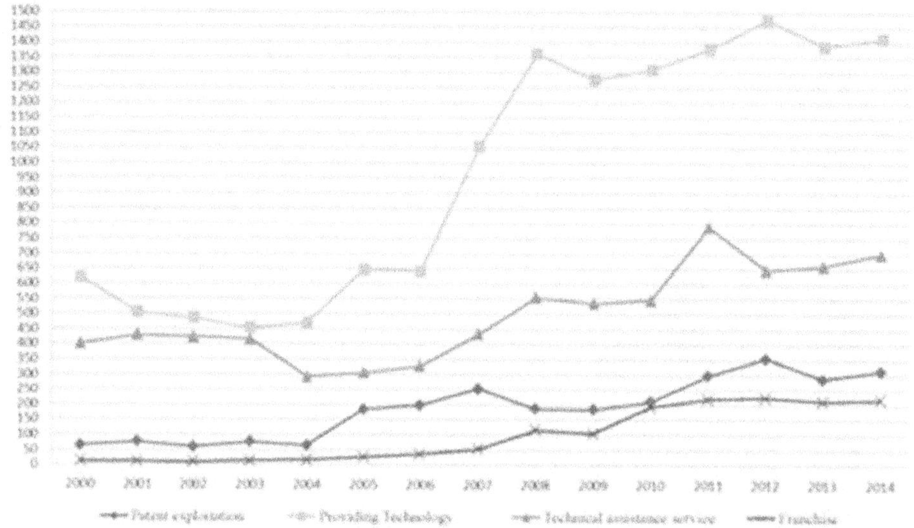

Figure 5 shows the technology transfer movements occurred in the Brazil per states. According to the results, the States with the greatest transfer potential are located in the Southeast and South regions. Currently, Brazil has 26 states and one federal district, but only 6 states from these two regions hold almost 90% of all movements. São Paulo, Rio de Janeiro, Minas Gerais, Paraná, Rio Grande do Sul and Santa Catarina. The State of São Paulo represents 43.58% of the share due to a high technological capacity, presence of large companies and strong research centers.

Table 2 shows in details a consolidated graphic concerning the transfer of technology requested by companies per industrial sector from 2000 to 2014.

The sectors of chemical manufacturing, automotive vehicle assembly, basic metallurgy, coal and coke, and petroleum refining, demands most part of technology transferred, reaching 8.087 contracts, and representing 37% of all operations. These sectors depend on high technology and invest in research and development (R&D).

*Figure 5. Technology transfer per state in Brazil*
**Source:** *Directory of Contracts, Geographical Indications Records from INPI, Brazil*

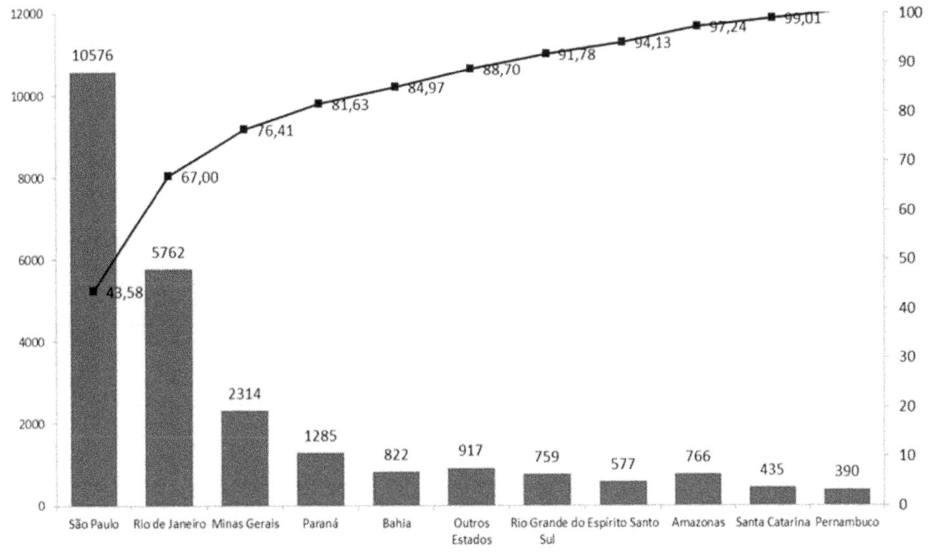


A considerable number of the multinationals that come to Brazil with the purpose to install factories belong to these sectors. Manufacturing sectors of rubber and plastic products, mineral and non-metallic products, and food and beverage products are sectors that also require high technology and R&D, because many of their products directly affect the planet's ecosystem, such as plastic packaging for food and beverages. However in Brazil these demanded least technology transfer contracts, having only 1.775 contracts, thus representing 8.1% of all transactions made.

The data presented below were collected from the Research Groups Directorates in Brazil, which belong to the National Council for Scientific and Technological Development (CNPq). The objective of collecting this data was to verify which groups are developing activities related to technology transfer in Brazil.

These directorates are the inventory of research groups in activity in Brazil. Their databases contain information on the constituent human resources of the groups, lines of research in progress, specialties of knowledge, sectors of activity involved, scientific, technological and artistic production of researchers and students that integrate the groups and the standards for the interaction with the productive sector. In most cases, these directorates are located in universities, or belong to higher education institutes, or scientific research institutes, technological institutes, R&D laboratories from state-owned or (ex) state-owned companies, and also in some non-governmental research organizations.

From results, it was verified that Brazil currently has 27.523 research groups distributed among all areas of knowledge, but only 86 groups develop activities related to technology transfer, representing only 0.31%.

Important information obtained from the directories is that the registered companies assist the development of applied research in universities and institutes. However, the 86 groups contain only 125 registered companies, and 58% of these groups do not establish any relationships with industry, even by working in some way with technology transfer.

*Table 2. Technology transfer sector per industrial in Brazil*

| Activity sector from assignee company | Contracts recorded |
|---|---|
| Manufacture of rubber and plastic products | 536 |
| Manufacture of non-metallic mineral products | 618 |
| Manufacture of food products and beverages | 621 |
| Manufacture of pulp, and paper products | 730 |
| Electricity, gas and hot water | 735 |
| Wholesale trade and intermediaries | 778 |
| Manufacture of metal product - exclusive machinery and equipment | 786 |
| Manufacture of electrical machinery, apparatus and equipment | 794 |
| Extraction of metallic minerals | 877 |
| Manufacture of machinery and equipment | 1046 |
| Business services | 1139 |
| Manufacture of coke, and petroleum refinement | 1910 |
| Basic metallurgy | 1976 |
| Manufacture and assembly of motor vehicles | 2099 |
| Manufacture of Chemical Products | 2102 |
| Other sectors | 5098 |
| Σ | 21.845 |

**Source:** Directory of Contracts, Geographical Indications Records from INPI, Brazil

These small percentages justify the low rate of participation of Brazilian universities and research institutes in partnership with industry, contributing with the technological deficit, which in 2013 represented US$ 93 billion, an increase of 11.5% in comparison to 2012 (Protec, 2014).

Among the 86 groups searched, there are 629 research lines registered, 1.175 researchers with master or doctoral level, 936 undergraduate students, or studying master's and/or doctorate degrees, and also 170 technicians who assist in administrative activities.

São Paulo is the Brazilian State that has more research groups recorded in the directorates that develop activities related to the transfer of technology, having 21 groups representing 24% of the sharing. The first group was created in this state in 1972, developing research related to poisons and toxins; this group belongs to an institute called National Commission of Nuclear Energy (CNEN).

Figure 6 shows the knowledge areas belonging to the 86 groups surveyed.

According to Figure 5 the most focused areas in developing technology transfer activities are Applied Social Sciences and Engineering, representing 59.30% of the sharing. However, areas such as Health Sciences and Biological Sciences require more cooperation with universities and institutes, since they develop applied research, but as can be seen these were the areas that least created activities related to technology transfer in Brazil, representing only 8.27%.

*Figure 6. Knowledge areas of the technology transfer research groups*
**Source:** *Research Groups Directories from Brazil*

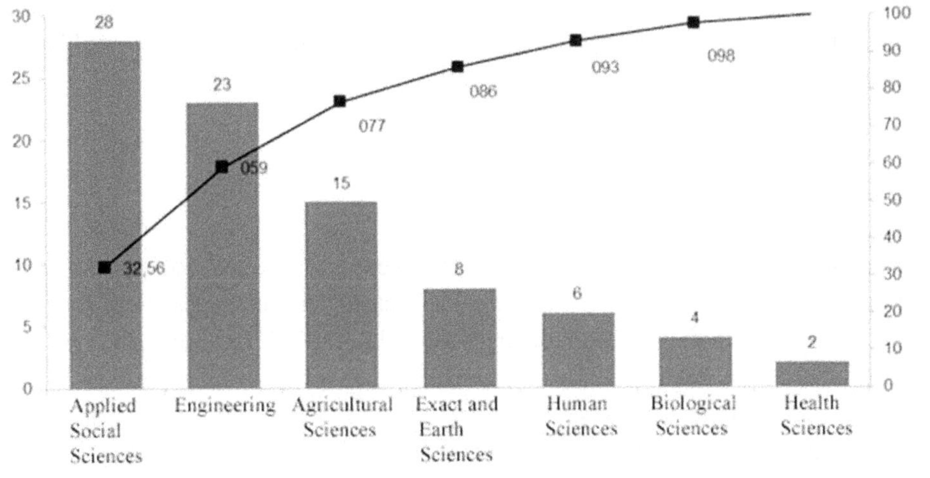


## FUTURE RESEARCH AND DIRECTIONS

Technology transfer is an important topic in Brazil, as the country is home to many innovative research institutions and companies. There are several emerging trends related to technology transfer that are likely to shape the future of this field in Brazil.

1- Increased collaboration between industry and academia: In recent years, there has been a growing emphasis on collaboration between universities and industry in Brazil. This trend is likely to continue, with more partnerships and joint ventures aimed at bringing new technologies to market.
2- Emphasis on intellectual property rights: As the importance of innovation and technology transfer grows, there is likely to be an increased emphasis on protecting intellectual property rights. This will involve developing better legal frameworks for patents and copyrights, as well as improving enforcement mechanisms.
3- Focus on startups: Startups are an important source of innovation and technology transfer in Brazil, and there is likely to be an increased focus on supporting and promoting these companies. This could involve government support for incubators and accelerators, as well as increased access to funding and other resources.
4- Expansion of international collaborations: Brazil is already involved in a number of international collaborations related to technology transfer, and this is likely to continue and expand in the future. This will involve partnerships with both developed and developing countries, as well as increased participation in international research networks.
5- Adoption of new technologies: Finally, the future of technology transfer in Brazil will be shaped by the adoption of new technologies, such as artificial intelligence, blockchain, and the Internet of Things. These technologies have the potential to transform many aspects of society, and will require new approaches to technology transfer and intellectual property management.

Overall, the future of technology transfer in Brazil looks bright, with a growing emphasis on collaboration, innovation, and international partnerships. However, there are still many challenges to overcome, including improving legal frameworks for intellectual property and addressing implementation issues related to proposed programs. Nevertheless, with the right focus and resources, Brazil has the potential to become a leader in technology transfer and innovation.

## CONCLUSION

It is known from international experience that the strengthening of the technology transfer structure involves the training of skilled workers to act in strategic sectors, and the necessity of incentives to carry out research in universities, institutes and industries related to the priority areas, in order to achieve the technological development of the country.

This research contributed in order to better understand the technology transfer flow in the national context concerning intellectual property, by identifying the main technology supplier's countries, the remittances abroad, and analyzing the practices related to these activities in universities and research institutes.

Brazil has been receiving technologies from major economic powers such as United States, Germany, Japan, France, Italy, the United Kingdom, Switzerland, Canada and Spain, having considerably increased its scenario even after the onset of the economic crisis in 2008, exporting more technology than importing over the last 15 years.

The domestic productive sector still needs more technology transfer, since its technological deficit in 2013 was US$ 93 billion.

The manufacturing sectors of chemical products, automotive assembly, basic metallurgy, coke and coal, petroleum refining, were the ones that most demanded technology, establishing more contracts. Sectors for the manufacturing of rubber and plastic products, mineral and non-metallic products, food products and beverages, that should focus more on sustainability aiming at reducing their environmental impact, were the ones that least acquired technology in this period.

The barriers between university-industry cooperation are still very present; this was verified through data obtained from 1972 to 2015 from the Research Groups Directories from CNPq. In fact, currently in Brazil there are 27.523 research groups distributed in all areas of knowledge, but only 86 groups carry out activities related to technology transfer, representing only 0.31% of the sharing. These 86 groups have only 125 registered companies, being that 58% do not establish relationships with industry.

In one hand the areas of knowledge Applied Social Sciences and Engineering are the ones that most develop activities aiming at establishing relations with the productive sector. In the other hand, areas such as Health Sciences and Biological Sciences that require much more cooperation with universities and institutes, does not present the same vision.

The technology transfer contracts registrations made by the National Institute of Intellectual Property (INPI) are important because generate a secure database on the technology market, allowing the elaboration of studies and sectoral research, and subsidizing the formulation of public policy to the area.

Traditionally, the internal market is responsible for the production of basic/applied scientific and technological knowledge. The diffusion of technology is influenced by nature, critical technologies and national security, by the maturity of technology, and also by consolidated processes.

Government, universities and institutes should create transfer mechanisms linked to the technology demand and characteristics of enterprises. Foreign-capital companies always undergo technology adaptation through articulation of innovative process with the parent company. State-owned companies (public law) are important producers of technology, having links with universities and institutes, and investments in research and development linked to State decisions. The national companies (mainly micro and small enterprises) import consolidated technologies, since they present low capacity for internal development of technology due having a limited interface with research institutes and universities.

The Brazilian government must reduce market failures, taking efforts concerning to reduce restrictions on appropriation of efforts for the technological development. By developing laws and regulations, such as intellectual property law, industrial property law, competition law, and tax law, besides developing public policies, scientific and technological policies, industrial policy, foreign trade policy, and technology transfer policy.

However, the technology supply should exceptionally depend from the process of technological diffusion, from technology adoption by society through continuous learning, and benchmarking of best existing techniques, thus enabling an increase in the performance of services, processes and products developed in partnership among industries, universities and technological centers.

The technology transfer is a critical process that can promote innovation, generate employment, and foster economic growth. In Brazil, the transfer of technology from universities to the industry is recognized as an important factor in driving the country's economy forward. Through the establishment of technology parks and incubators, the creation of partnerships, and the introduction of government programs, Brazil is well-positioned to leverage the potential of technology transfer to promote its economic development.

## REFERENCES


Bacen. (2015). *Dados sobre remessa de tecnologia ao exterior*. BC. http://www.bc.gov.br/

Bishop, K., Deste, P., & Neely, A. (2011). Gaining from interactions with universities: Multiple methods for nurturing absorptive capacity. *Research Policy*, *40*(1), 30–40. doi:10.1016/j.respol.2010.09.009

Bozarth, C. (2006). ERP implementation efforts at three firms: Integrating lessons from the SISP and IT-enabled change literature. *International Journal of Operations & Production Management*, *26*(11), 1223–1239. doi:10.1108/01443570610705836

Bozeman, B. (2000). Technology transfer and public policy: A review of research and theory. *Research Policy*, *29*(4-5), 627–655. doi:10.1016/S0048-7333(99)00093-1

Brasil. (1970). *Lei nº 5.648, de 11 de dezembro de 1970*. Presidência da República Casa Civil. http://www.planalto.gov.br/ccivil_03/leis/L5648.htm

Brasil. (1996). Lei de Propriedade Intelectual do Brasil nº 9.279, de 14 de maio de 1996. Plan Alto. http://www.planalto.gov.br/ccivil_03/leis/L9279.htm

Chesbrough, H. (2003). *Open innovation: The new imperative for creating and profiting from technology*. Harvard Business Press.

CNPq, Conselho Nacional de Desenvolvimento Científico e Tecnológico. (n.d.). *Diretório dos Grupos de Pesquisa no Brasil*. DGP. http://dgp.cnpq.br/buscaoperacional/

Cohen, W. M., & Levinthal, D. A. (1990). Absorptive capacity: A new perspective on learning and innovation. *Administrative Science Quarterly*, *35*(1), 128–152. doi:10.2307/2393553

Davenport, S., Davies, J., & Grimes, C. (1998). Collaborative research programmes: Building trust from difference. *Technovation*, *19*(1), 31–40. doi:10.1016/S0166-4972(98)00083-2

Debackere, K., & Veugelers, R. (2005). The role of academic technology transfer organizations in improving industry science. *Research Policy*, *34*(3), 321–342. doi:10.1016/j.respol.2004.12.003

Deitos, M. L. (2002). *A Gestão da Tecnologia em Pequenas e Médias Empresas*. Edunioeste.

Edler, J., Fier, H., & Grimpe, C. (2011). International scientist mobility and the locus of knowledge and technology transfer. *Research Policy*, *40*(6), 295–309. doi:10.1016/j.respol.2011.03.003

Edler, J., Krahmer, F. M., & Reger, G. (2002). Changes in the strategic management of technology: Results of a global benchmarking study. *R & D Management*, *32*(2), 149–164. doi:10.1111/1467-9310.00247

Etzkowitz, H. (2003). Innovation in innovation: The triple helix of university-industry-government relations. *Social Sciences Information. Information Sur les Sciences Sociales*, *42*(3), 293–337. doi:10.1177/05390184030423002

Fontana, R., Geuna, A., & Matt, M. (2006). Factors affecting university-industry R&D projects. *Research Policy*, *35*(2), 309–323. doi:10.1016/j.respol.2005.12.001

Gil, A. C. (2007). *Como elaborar projetos de pesquisa*. Atlas.

INPI, Instituto Nacional de Propriedade Intelectual. (n.d.). *Dados estatísticos sobre contratos de transferência de tecnologia*. INPI. http://www.inpi.gov.br/

Lima, I. A. (2004). *Estrutura de referência para a transferência de tecnologia no âmbito da cooperação universidade-empresa: Estudo de caso no CEFET-PR*. [Doctoral dissertation, Universidade Federal de Santa Catarina, Florianópolis].

Lundvall, B. Å. (1992). *National systems of innovation: Towards a theory of innovation and interactive learning*. Pinter Publishers.

Malik, K., Georgiou, L., & Grieve, B. (2011). Developing new technology platforms for new business models: Syngenta's partnership with the University of Manchester. *Research Technology Management*, *54*(1), 24–31. doi:10.1080/08956308.2011.11657670

Niedergassel, B., & Leker, J. (2011). Different dimensions of knowledge in cooperative R&D projects of university scientists. *Technovation*, *31*(4), 142–150. doi:10.1016/j.technovation.2010.10.005

Philbin, S. (2008). Process model for university-industry research collaboration. *European Journal of Innovation Management*, *11*(4), 488–521. doi:10.1108/14601060810911138

Protec. (2013). Monitor do Déficit Tecnológico em 2013. *Protec*. http://www.protec.org.br/

Romanenko, A., Santos, L. O., & Afonso, P. A. F. N. A. (2007). Application of agent technology concepts to the design of a fault-tolerant control system. *Control Engineering Practice*, *15*(4), 459–469. doi:10.1016/j.conengprac.2006.09.002

Siegel, D. S., Waldman, D. A., & Link, A. N. (2003). Assessing the impact of organizational practices on the relative productivity of university technology transfer offices: An exploratory study. *Research Policy*, *32*(1), 27–48. doi:10.1016/S0048-7333(01)00196-2

Sun, J., Debo, L. G., Kekre, S., & Xie, J. (2010). Component-based technology transfer in the presence of potential imitators. *Management Science*, *56*(3), 536–552. doi:10.1287/mnsc.1090.1111

Veugelers, R., & Cassiman, B. (2005). R&D cooperation between firms and universities. Some empirical evidence from Belgian manufacturing. *International Journal of Industrial Organization*, *23*(5-6), 355–379. doi:10.1016/j.ijindorg.2005.01.008

## ADDITIONAL READING

Arora, A., & Gambardella, A. (2010). Ideas for rent: An overview of markets for technology. *Industrial and Corporate Change*, *19*(3), 775–803. doi:10.1093/icc/dtq022

Autio, E., & Klofsten, M. (1998). A comparative study of technology transfer offices in Europe. *The Journal of Technology Transfer*, *23*(2), 109–123. doi:10.1023/A:1007906615672

Lockett, A., & Wright, M. (2005). Resources, capabilities, risk capital and the creation of university spin-out companies. *Research Policy*, *34*(7), 1043–1057. doi:10.1016/j.respol.2005.05.006

Mowery, D. C., & Sampat, B. N. (2005). Universities in national innovation systems. In Fagerberg, J., Mowery, D. C., & Nelson, R. R. (Eds.), The Oxford Handbook of Innovation (pp. 209-239). Oxford University Press.

Powers, J. B., McDougall, P. P., & Oviatt, B. M. (2009). Explorative and exploitative learning in new venture creation: A process model. *Entrepreneurship Theory and Practice*, *33*(2), 439–473. doi:10.1111/j.1540-6520.2009.00313.x

Rosenberg, N. (2004). Patenting and licensing of university inventions: Lessons from the history of research and development. *Industrial and Corporate Change*, *13*(3), 579–616. doi:10.1093/icc/dth023

Shane, S. (2004). *Academic entrepreneurship: University spinoffs and wealth creation*. Edward Elgar. doi:10.4337/9781843769828

Thursby, J. G., & Thursby, M. C. (2002). Who is selling the ivory tower? Sources of growth in university licensing. *Management Science*, *48*(1), 90–104. doi:10.1287/mnsc.48.1.90.14271

## KEY TERMS AND DEFINITIONS

**Industrial Property Law:** The legal framework in Brazil that governs the protection of intellectual property, including patents, trademarks, and industrial designs. The Industrial Property Law sets out the rules for obtaining and enforcing these rights.

**Intellectual Property (IP):** The legal rights granted to individuals or companies to protect their creations, such as inventions, artistic works, and designs. IP can be protected by patents, trademarks, copyrights, and trade secrets.

**Licensing:** The process of legally granting permission to use a product or technology to another party, typically in exchange for a fee or royalties. The license specifies the terms and conditions of use, including restrictions and limitations.

**Open Innovation:** A business model that involves collaboration and knowledge-sharing between individuals and organizations. Open innovation allows for external ideas and technology to be integrated into a company's products and services.

**Patent:** A form of IP protection that grants exclusive rights to an inventor or company for a certain period of time, typically 20 years. A patent prevents others from making, using, or selling the patented invention without permission.

**Public-Private Partnerships:** Collaborations between government agencies and private sector entities to achieve a common goal, such as the development and commercialization of new technologies. In Brazil, public-private partnerships have been used to support innovation and technology transfer in a variety of industries.

**Royalties:** Payments made to a patent holder, copyright owner, or trademark owner in exchange for the use of their intellectual property. Royalties are typically a percentage of sales or revenue generated from the IP.

**Spin-off:** A new company created by an existing organization to commercialize technology or other intellectual property. Spin-offs can occur when the existing organization is unable to fully develop or market the technology, or when a separate business opportunity is identified.

**Technology Transfer:** The process of moving technology or other intellectual property from one organization or individual to another. This can involve licensing, joint ventures, collaborations, or spin-offs, and is often done to commercialize the technology and bring it to market.

**Universities:** Institutions of higher education in Brazil that play an important role in technology transfer. Universities conduct research and development, file patents, and collaborate with industry and government to commercialize new technologies.

# Chapter 9
# Experience Design's Impact on Graphic Design

**İsmail Ergen**
*İstinye Üniveristesi, Turkey*

## ABSTRACT

*Even straightforward objects whose nature we believe we comprehend go through the design process. The task of design is to connect people and technology. Every advance in technology brings about new experiences and ways of life. In this chapter the authors explain how design alters the abilities, motivations, and expectations in daily life, and how graphic design reacts to this shift. If we want to anticipate the future, we need to look closely at the digital technologies that emerged recently and first analyze the transition how it occurred and how quickly it happened.*

## INTRODUCTION

Graphic design today occupies a position that goes far beyond the printing press. With the development of knowledge and technology, graphic design, where interdisciplinary works are generated frequently, continuously repositions and restructures. Additionally, it must react to human demands and experiences. If the history of Graphic Design is briefly addressed, it includes the drawings on the cave walls. Within the constraints of the design, the concern of passing the message to the other party by simplifying the current information in a certain format is addressed. Before Gutenberg's portable printing press, several woodcut works were produced, as is also known. However, Gutenberg's portable printing press also overlaps with the development of graphic design pieces, which is somewhat more contemporary (1450). With the advancement of technology, works in many formats have emerged because of the illustrative decoration of books printed with this technology and later the enrichment of page designs. One example is the usage of poster designs. The term "graphic design," which began to be used in the first quarter of the 20th century, opened the door for designers, who were previously known as painters or artists, to specialize further. The term "graphic design" today has many sub-categories. Examples include titles like interface design, book cover design, illustration design, character design for video games, environmental graphic design, motion graphic design, orientation design, infographic design, and interactive graphic

DOI: 10.4018/978-1-6684-8397-8.ch009

design. In this regard, it would be fair to state that graphic design, using the knowledge and technology that are updated and regenerated on a regular basis, generates new fields for itself. Depending on the technology developed, graphic designers have historically served as letter engravers, compositors, book illustrators, and artists who experiment with typographic materials. Graphic design always works with an ally, according to Niyaziolu (Niyaziolu, 2016). As a result, the technology, experience, and culture of the time immediately influence and form the designs. We now spend the majority of our waking hours staring at screens due to how quickly the world is becoming digital. As people's daily experiences have altered as a result of digitalization, professions have begun to transform in order to answer to these new needs, whether they like it or not. For graphic design, which has its roots in printing and printing, nothing has changed.

## EXPERIENCE DESIGN

One of life's most valuable tools is "experience." User experience design is a process that aims to give customers who use a product, service, or service relevant and meaningful experiences. Numerous topics are covered during this process, including branding, design, usability, features, and functionality. Examining users' behaviors, expectations, issues, and solutions to such issues is at the heart of user experience. To sum up, we notice that everything has a specific order when we visit a market. Fruits, vegetables, and dairy products can be found on either side. The consumer's entire shopping experience is determined by activities like the placement order set up in the market and the way the products of the week are displayed. In order for customers to travel to as many locations as possible, enjoy the experience, and shop more, this layout was created. The term "user experience" refers to what we experience when we transfer the concept of "customer" or "consumer experience" that you have in this physical context to the virtual environment. User experience is frequently referred to as UX. Early in the 1990s, cognitive scientist Donald Norman, while employed by Apple, coined the phrase. Norman coined the phrase "user experience" to refer to all the various components that affect how a user feels while interacting with a product, with a focus on the design, visuals, interface, and interaction but also including all other aspects of the user's experience with the product and service. Making the user's product experience as positive as possible is the goal of user experience design, to put it briefly. Getting visitors to a website that they are interested in; after that, from the home page to the product purchase, it attempts to make the process as simple and entertaining as possible and to offer a cohesive user experience. The goal of user experience design is to enhance the utility, usability, and effectiveness of the user's interaction with the product and service. Experience Strategy (ES), Interaction Design (ID), User Research (UR), and Information Architecture are the four key disciplines that make up the large umbrella term of user experience.

### Part of the UX

The experience strategy is the initial component of UX design. It involves developing a comprehensive business strategy that considers the requirements of the organization and the clientele. Interaction design is the second component. It examines user interaction with a system, accounting for all interactive components such links, page transitions, graphics, audio, and animations. The goal of interaction design is to produce simple designs that let users easily accomplish their goals. User research is the third component. To better understand the needs and objectives of the end user, UX designers carry out surveys, interviews, usability tests, and user persona creation at this stage. To create the greatest design, they gather both qualitative and quantitative data. Information architecture comes last. It is crucial to arrange data and material in a clear and understandable manner and to aid users in navigating a product. When deciding on the information architecture of any product, information architects take into account the relationships between various content types. Additionally, they pay special attention to the language utilized, making ensuring that it is convincing and coherent.

*Figure 1. What is UX*

## Difference of UX and UI

User interface design is referred to as UI (user interface). For example, everything on the screen of the phone you use is an interface design. The designer's choices are reflected in the positions, colors, and sizes of the icons. The visual design of websites, which includes all graphic components including images, buttons, lines, colors, page structures, and spaces, is the counterpart of interface design. Both user experience (UX) and user interface (UI) design aim to provide the greatest possible final product for users, yet there is a major difference between the two fields of study. User experience design, also known as UX, is an analytical process that covers all phases of product design, from user research and prototyping through marketing the finished product. The responsibility of UX designers is to balance the needs of the business or brand with those of the user. The goal of UI is to design the tangible and visible elements that users will interact with, whereas the goal of UX is to create a holistic experience. Both UI and UX designers collaborate well during the creation of a product, and both are crucial to its success. In brief, the UX designer concentrates on the overall functioning and flow of a website while consulting with product designers, analysts, users, and marketers along the way. It uses this method to identify the elements required to give website visitors a seamless browsing experience, then communicates the knowledge to the UI designer.

*Figure 2. UX and UI Differences*

The UI designer then decides on the aesthetics required to implement the solutions. It addresses concerns including image size, content organization, and word density. What is the most user-friendly website layout, for example? How much content should be displayed on the home page? Is the entire interface engaging and appealing to the eye?

### Principles of User Experience

The experience design process has its own steps, just like the application design steps. According to designer Peter Morville, there are seven fundamental concepts that encompass the user experience: is useful, readily available, dependable, appealing, approachable, and valuable.

## TECHNOLOGICAL IMPROVEMENT

It is important to remember that technology development and design requirements are closely related. The media and technology employed, along with how the design is used, influence the design's direction. This medium's impact on the message makes us think of McLuhan's adage, "The medium is the message," which states that "in every cultural age, the medium (the medium; the medium) through which the information is recorded and transmitted has played a decisive role in determining the character of that culture" (McLuhan, 2014).

Perhaps the comments of Gordon Moore, one of the founders of Intel, can be included to explain the development of technology: "For minimum component costs, complexity grows at a rate of about 2 units per year... Although it doesn't rise in the near future, this rate is anticipated to stay the same. I think a period this great can fit on a single plate (Demirel, 2015). The fact that the average processor technology will double every two years is one of the most crucial lessons we can take away from this situation. We can look at the brief historical image of processors against humans to better comprehend how this affects our life. Furthermore, given how information and technology have advanced since these remarks were spoken in the middle of the 1960s, it cannot be stated that they were untrue. The following quote from Ruacan both affirms Moore and demonstrates the strength of Technology is developing quickly, and as a result, design domains, diversity, and specialties are expanding as well. In the not-too-distant future, images will appear in front of us with the aid of lenses if we look deeper at this transformation process. A camera that will translate what we see with our eyes from the human brain to digital media is one of the most significant things I anticipate being created. The creation of smart glasses and their gradual onset of influence on daily life can be demonstrated as the concrete first steps in this. Technology is currently advancing at an uncontrollable rate, persuading people that life in the virtual world is far simpler, more enjoyable, and always sustainable, as opposed to encouraging people to experience of the life. Computers have ushered in the Second Machine Age, which will outpace all preceding eras, according to Brynjolfsson and McAfee (Brynjolfsson and Macafee, 2014). We are transitioning from machines that can do physical work to machines that can conduct cognitive work thanks to the technological advancements we are experiencing today. We already know that human behaviors are possible because of artificial intelligence because they can be replicated using algorithms. For instance, there is currently basic software available in online shops that can create your site design, banner, and logo for you.

*Figure 3. Evolution of the computer*

*Figure 4. Development of technology*

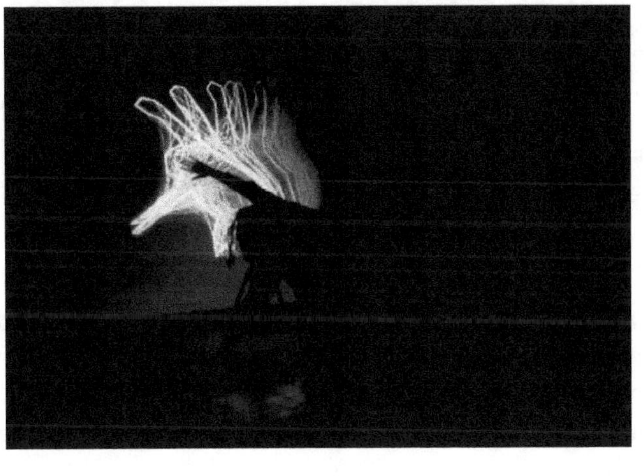

## VIRTUAL REALITY AND METAVERSE

Designers are being pushed further into augmented reality and virtual reality industries by the quick advancement of technology. It wouldn't be incorrect to argue that graphic design will increasingly focus on interactive and mobile design for both media. Motion design is a new phase in graphic design that was introduced by the initial stages of all these innovations. From one dimension to the moving one, the posters have changed. The sophistication of visuals and the development of interactive gadgets are both summarized by the stage that game ideas have reached. If technologically manufactured fictions combined with reality and imagination constitute virtual reality. By integrating emerging technology into educational settings, virtual learning environments aim to improve students' educational experiences. Alternative universes are only one of the many modern discoveries brought on by virtual reality. The "meta," or metaverse, is the most notable of these innovations; Facebook changed its name to it in order to gain more attention. The general definition of the term can be summed up as follows: to combine all the current digital world's components into one virtual environment in order to create a shared virtual communication area. This cosmos will be accessible to people via augmented virtual reality. The phrase "metaverse" has a very distinct history. Rather than technological companies, a novelist initially proposed this idea. In his book "Snow Crash," renowned author Neal Stephenson created a fictional version of the metaverse. According to this book, people use the avatars they choose to go about their daily lives in a virtual reality. With the film industry trying to address this issue, the idea of a commodity started to become more commonplace. The 2018 film Ready Player One serves as an illustration of this. Through the use of VR glasses, characters in this film were able to carry out all of their daily tasks in the made-up virtual world. (Fig. 5)

*Figure 5. Ready That What Player movie*

People began to purchase homes and land in the metaverse at that point and set up residence there. Even though this is the most cutting-edge technology, one cannot help but worry. The power of designers and creators will grow significantly as a result of these changes, but it will be increasingly crucial to consider what we generate with this power and what we sacrifice during the production and design process. Yuval Noah Harari, one of the most influential historians of our time in terms of spreading knowledge, said the following: summarize the connection between accountability and design: "21. In the twenty-first century, mankind will discover how to create plants, animals, and people the way we like, just as God did in the Bible... Being a god is not an easy role to play. Instead, then arguing that designers' responsibilities would grow, it will be more crucial for designers to understand their current obligations. Continuing with the dystopia scenario for designers, it is possible to replace many of the tasks they currently perform with cognitive machines by turning algorithms into instructors of new design. Few designers have the ability to educate machines and advance this profession by attempting to convert designs into digital data. With the ability to swiftly learn algorithms, they can create custom fonts, backgrounds, and images that represent the mood you're in that day and reflect it on your lenses. Designers may generate works for their own sake rather than that of their trade, much like craftsmen, or they may evolve into a new group that focuses on making unique, personal designs to cater to the demands of certain persons. Another benefit of these algorithms is the increase of hand-made typographic and artistic works.

*Figure 6. Metaverse*

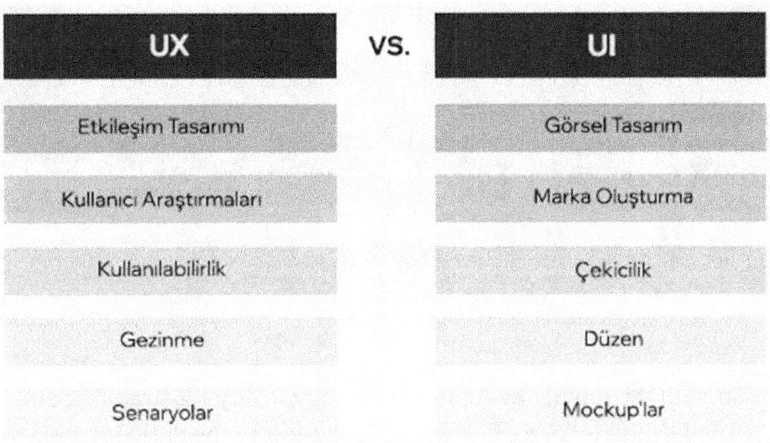


## NFT

Non Fungible Token is referred to as NFT. This definition can be translated into Turkish as "cash or a chip that cannot be swapped." NFT, a special kind of cryptographic token, cannot be traded for another token of the same kind because of its uniqueness. In this situation, it is simple to confirm the validity of a work of art that has been transmitted to NFT and copying of the work is avoided. The need for NFT, why? For generations, collectors have paid astronomical prices to buy and sell pieces of art. However, throughout the past ten years, several ways have been used to demonstrate the originality of the works. These methods include checking through records such as a list of previous buyers of the work or the sales letters that were included with it, or examining details like the age of the canvas, the kind of paints used, the brushstrokes, and the residue on the piece. These methods, meanwhile, are occasionally insufficient to demonstrate the work's originality. Forgery scams are popular in a market with millions of dollars. So much so that the most renowned museums in the world, including the Louvre and the Met, can purchase copies of original artwork. Even a Netflix documentary explored the swindle that targeted the US's Knoedler gallery. In the late 1990s, Knoedler, one of New York's oldest galleries, acquired nearly 60 forgeries. The gallery earned a total of $80 million from the sale of these paintings. NFT, on the other hand, provides artists with an alternative. The works are made available to everyone thanks to blockchain and its decentralized structure, while NFT protects the originality of the works. Despite appearing to have little to do with graphic design, they have a lot of relevance Digital art entered the process of change in a single day as a result of this method. When NFT is discussed, the designer and media artist Refik Anadol is the first person who comes to mind. The Machine Hallucinations - Nature Dreams: AI Data Sculpture 2021 1/1 NFT piece, which was posted on Anadol's OpenSea NFT platform, sold for 300,69420 ETH ($1,184,545.71) and generated a lot of buzz. Anadol is a designer who creates pieces that change with and incorporate new technology. One of the most effective instances of experience design that is constantly changing is the moving media work Alcazar's Dream that he created for Hope Alkazar.

*Figure 7. One of Refik Anadol's works*

In order to keep up with the rapidly evolving technology, many illustrators, painters, and designers, in addition to Refik Anadol, continue to transfer their creations to the digital realm. NFT exhibits began to rise steadily.

## REAL EXPERIENCE

Today, it is evident that galleries and museums also employ technology to their advantage. A video piece was presented in the most recent exhibition by Akbank. With the help of the project's sensors, it can recognize human movement and alter the video's color and shape in response. This piece, which was created using current technology and appears to have a straightforward mechanism, is referred to as an experience design. Only things that individuals live and feel directly shouldn't cross your mind while thinking about experience design. Experience design considers both biological sensations and technological developments.

*Figure 8. Akbank art, NFT exhibition*

*Figure 9. Akbank art, NFT exhibition*

Because of the UX and UI work he did when building the Google Art Culture website, he noticed that visitors needed to physically visit museums in order to use their materials. He began his well-liked virtual museum tour experiences as a result of this research. In this experience, you can go to the museum and see the piece of art you wish to see. (Fig. 10)

Once again, experience design may be seen in the portrait application developed by the Google Art and Culture site using artificial intelligence and producing noise in the world. This software compares the selfie you took with an artwork it has in its collection. This experience is made possible by the evolving technologies. (Figs 11 and 12)

The interval between inventions and new technologies is now quite small because of the quick development of information and technologies. Things that were once thought to be impossible are now even more improbable. Because of this, the designer needs continuously stay up to date, update, and improve his graphic design. The need to adapt to the digital age is critical because industries that do not advance technologically will perish. Instead of being a printed object, graphic design has increasingly become a screen experience. By visually assessing human requirements in all spheres of life, it has been a creative process that is successful in resolving a text or image and promoting communication.

*Figure 10. Google art and culture virtual tour*

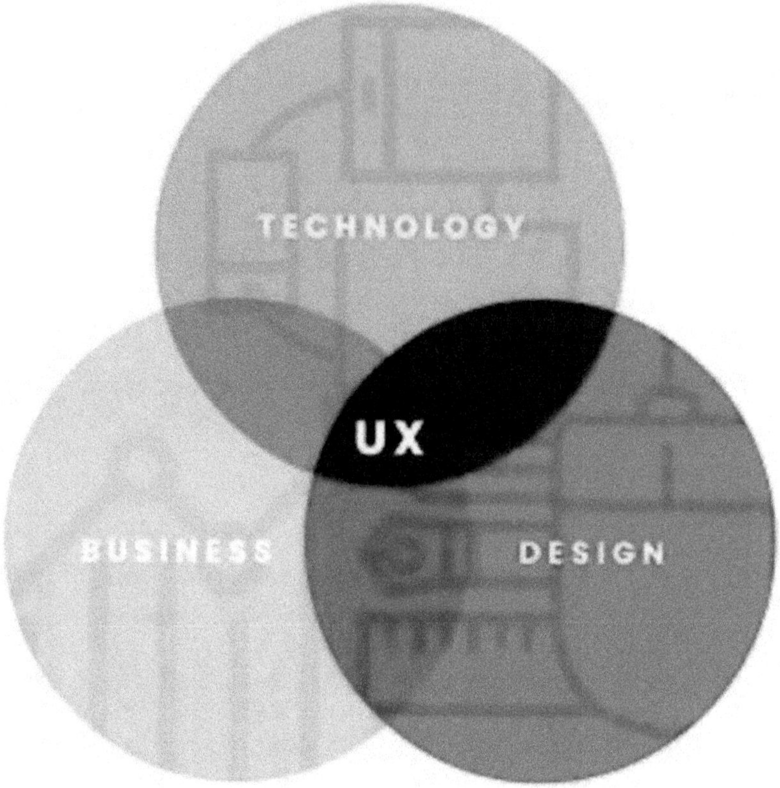


*Figure 11. Google art and culture portrait app*

*Figure 12. Google art and culture portrait app*

## FUTURE RESEARCH DIRECTONS

The concept of the metaverse refers to a virtual space where users can interact with each other through avatars, engage in various activities such as gaming, shopping, education, and socializing. It is essentially a convergence of virtual reality, augmented reality, and other immersive technologies that aim to create a seamless and interconnected virtual World.

The potential applications of the metaverse are vast and diverse, ranging from entertainment and gaming to education, healthcare, and even business. It has the potential to revolutionize how we work, learn, and socialize by providing a more immersive and engaging experience.

## CONCLUSION

By utilizing the comforts provided by technology, people can live easier lives and do so while spending more time looking and observing. It has been noted that displays come in a variety of sizes and are becoming more varied. Artificial intelligence is becoming more prevalent in the sector of creative business due to its ability to process data like that produced by human brain power. Artificial intelligence will undoubtedly develop to a level where it can digest information more efficiently than people in the future. It should be remembered that new technical solutions will inevitably result in new issues. In addition to the issues, innovations and fixes will also materialize. By offering a fresh experience and delivering the solutions users need when they click on a website, UX and UI design supports graphic design. Virtual reality has helped the metaverse movement by establishing a new view of reality by shifting the design from one dimension to numerous realities and by responding to the open call of evolving technology. NFT has released digital art from its restraints and maintained it. Digital media and computer technologies, which are useful for graphic design, have influenced designers and artists in modern life with the opportunities they have created and have managed to spread their use throughout the world with the effect and speed it has created. This is in addition to the technological developments experienced. Digital media technologies were first viewed merely as a tool for manufacturing, but with the advancements they have undergone, it is now obvious that they have evolved into a means for creating art in and of themselves. Every area of graphic design has been impacted by the works created using digital technology, and today's design products must start with these works to function. Technology has had an impact on design as well as on breaking old customs and replacing them with current technical practices. As a result of technology influences, design elements have become easier and more efficient than their traditional counterparts, enabling designers and artists to evoke the intended emotions and feelings more readily in their works and to develop new forms of expression. In numerous sectors, including design, the effects of technology advancements have impacted and changed people's lives. Digital technological advancements have led to the transformation of traditional aspects and brought about drastic changes in the field of illustration, one of the components of graphic design. The contemporary era's innovations have affected all illustration-based works, altered their modes of expression, and necessitated the adoption of new technological approaches. Digital media technologies, computers, and tablets as hardware, as well as two- and three-dimensional software packages were used to facilitate the development of computer-aided illustrations. Animation is a type of graphic design that has been similarly impacted by digital technology to illustration. Today's graphic design requires ongoing innovation around animation. With all these advancements, graphic design will continue to evolve, and these innovations and modifications will always raise the caliber of the output.

## REFERENCES

Adlassnig, K. P. (2002). Artificial-intelligence-augmented systems. Artificial Intelligence in Medicine, 24, 01-04. doi:10.1016/S0933-3657(01)00102-6

Bayrak, H. (2019a). Internet usage and social media statistics (January). *Dijilopedi.* https://dijilopedi.com/2019-internet-egitimi-ve-social-media-istatistikleri/

Bayrak, H. (2019b). Turkey internet usage and social media statistics (January). *Dijilopedi.* https://dijilopedi.com/2019-turkiye-internet-egitimim-ve-social-medya-istatistikleri/

Bilgiç It Academy. (2018). Big Data – What is Big Data? Bilgiç It Academy. https://www.bilginc.com/tr/egitim-haber/buyuk-veri-big-data-nedir

. Brynjolfsson, E. & MCafee, A. (2014). *The second machine age.* Turkish Airlines Publications.

Demirel, F. (2015). What is Moore's law? *Medium.* https://medium.com/turkce/ moore-yasası-moore-s-law-nedir-c31bee8da753

Documentary, D. W. (2018). *How cash is becoming a thing of the past.* DW (Deutsche Welle) Documentary. Video (00.28.00 – 00.32.25) https://www.youtube.com/watch?v=GbECT1J9bXg

Gutsche, J. (2018). Ai & the super future – future festival. *Trend Hunter.com.* https://www.youtube.com/watch?v=OzBJigTfGeE

Karaçeper, S. (2018). Innovations in digital technology and graphic design. *Journal of Istanbul Aydın University Faculty of Fine Arts*, *4*(8), 73–83.

KhanacademyTurkish. (2018). *Exponential growth and contraction (Mathematics) (Algebra).* [Video]. Youtube. https://www.youtube.com/watch?v=4uZX1s-vNhA

Kuzuloglu, S. (2018*). 21 lessons for the 21st century*: *Interview with Yuval Noah Harari.* Yucelbinici. http://yucelbinici.com/21-yuzyil-icin-21-ders/ Accessed on: 22.03.22

Lanier, J. (2018). How we need to remake the internet. TED. [Video]. Youtube. https:// www.youtube.com/watch?v=qQ-PUXPVlos

McLuhan, M. (2014). *The Gutenberg galaxy: the making of typographic man* (3rd ed.). Yapi Kredi Publications.

Newspaper, E. (2013). Cell phones are more powerful than the first craft to land on the Moon. *Aksam.* https://www.aksam.com.tr/teknoloji/cep-telefonlari-aya-inen-ilk-aractan-daha-guclu/haber-189320 Access Date: 05.03.22.

Niyazioglu, S. (2016). *Subjects in the history of graphic design in Turkey, Turkey Design Chronology, Essay, Graphics.* Istanbul Foundation for Culture and Arts. https://www.youtube.com/watch?v=AgnA32TAe3U

## ADDITIONAL READING

Ball, M. (July 19, 2022). *The Metaverse: And How It Will Revolutionize Everything.* Liverright..

Dionisio, J. D. N., III, W. G. B., & Gilbert, R. (2013). 3D virtual worlds and the metaverse: Status and future possibilities. *ACM Computing Surveys (CSUR), 45*(3), 1-38.

Duan, H., Li, J., Fan, S., Lin, Z., Wu, X., & Cai, W. (2021, October). Metaverse for social good: A university campus prototype. In *Proceedings of the 29th ACM international conference on multimedia* (pp. 153-161). ACM. 10.1145/3474085.3479238

Kemp, J., & Livingstone, D. (2006, August). Putting a Second Life "metaverse" skin on learning management systems. In *Proceedings of the Second Life education workshop at the Second Life community convention* (Vol. 20). CA, San Francisco: The University of Paisley.

Lee, L. H., Braud, T., Zhou, P., Wang, L., Xu, D., Lin, Z., & Hui, P. (2021). All one needs to know about metaverse: A complete survey on technological singularity, virtual ecosystem, and research agenda. *arXiv preprint arXiv:2110.05352.*

Mysticisms, S. (2022). Metaverse. *Encyclopedia, 2*(1), 486–497. doi:10.3390/encyclopedia2010031

Ning, H., Wang, H., Lin, Y., Wang, W., Dhelim, S., Farha, F., & Daneshmand, M. (2021). A Survey on Metaverse: The State-of-the-art, Technologies, Applications, and Challenges. *arXiv preprint arXiv:2111.09673.*

Stephenson, N. (1992). Snow Crash. Penguin Books Limited.

## KEY TERMS AND DEFINITIONS

**Augmented Reality:** Digitally created pictures are superimposed on the physical world in augmented reality (AR). Users can utilize a device, such as their tablet or cell phone, to add pictures and music to their actual environs.

**Avatar:** An avatar is a virtual representation of you in a computer-generated environment, such as the metaverse.

**Blockchain:** A blockchain is a platform that permits a distributed ledger of data that is updated and maintained by a network of computers rather than a single entity. Another name for a blockchain is distributed ledger technology (DLT). Cryptography is used by this distributed ledger to confirm, complete, and secure transactions.

**Extended reality:** The term "extended reality" (or "XR") refers to computer-generated settings that combine the actual and virtual worlds or provide consumers a fully virtual experience.

**Metaverse:** The term, has been used in different contexts and with different meanings over time, but it generally refers to a virtual world or universe that exists parallel to our physical world, where users can interact with each other and with digital objects in real-time.

**Virtual Reality:** Virtual reality, sometimes known as VR, is an immersive experience within a setting entirely produced by computer technology.

**Virtual World:** A virtual world is either a computer-rendered simulation of the real world or a completely original setting. Avatars enable for user engagement in virtual worlds that are designed to be inhabited (personified representations of the user within the digital environment).

**Web 3.0:** The Web 3.0 builds on ideas like decentralization, openness, data protection, and increased user utility. It is the progression of the current Web 2.0.

# Chapter 10
# The Impact of TikTok on the Viralization of the Entertainment Industry:
## The Netflix's Series Case

**Luísa Pinto Felício**
*ISCAP, Politécnico do Porto, Portugal*

**Paula Peres**
*GILT, ISCAP, Politécnico do Porto, Portugal*

## ABSTRACT

*The entertainment industry in the digital age is characterized by new technologies as well as a culture embedded in a context of new habits, particularly practiced by Generation Z. These factors result in the emergence of applications such as TikTok and Netflix. TikTok is an indispensable marketing tool and a social media characterized by the rapid viralization of content. The application stands out as a space for creativity and entertainment, where movies and series gain popularity, including content from the streaming platform Netflix. Thus, the impact of the social network in promoting entertainment will be further explored. This chapter synthesizes literature from the past decades to give readers insight into technologies such as streaming and VOD, Netflix's business model, the concept of fandom, and the social media marketing practiced by TikTok. Theory, research, and implications for a better understanding of TikTok's impact on the entertainment industry are outlined.*

## INTRODUCTION

The phenomenon of globalization and consequent technological revolution contributed to the formulation of the entertainment industry paradigm in the digital age. In this context Netflix stands out, giving autonomy to users through a unique and differentiated consumption method that has revolutionized the behavior and habits of entertainment consumers (Rossini and Renner, 2015). Thus, the streaming market

DOI: 10.4018/978-1-6684-8397-8.ch010

has been enjoying prominence through Netflix, as a distributor and producer of an extensive and diverse catalog of movies, documentaries, series, among other content for several generations of today's society.

In fact, due to the evidence of this increasingly digital society, there is a direct or indirect sharing on social media platforms of various entertainment-related content, particularly related to series. This type of content has been relatively prominent on the social media YouTube, Instagram and now also on TikTok. The search term "TikTok" yields more than 100,000 articles in Google Scholar, demonstrating that this is an area of study that has been gaining popularity. Thus, most of the present literature focuses on the social media as a marketing tool and promoter of entertainment.

This chapter introduces readers to the major changes in the entertainment industry post the emergence of Netflix and the influence of TikTok on the perception of the streaming platform's series, summarizing the literature from the past few decades. Finally, future directions to follow are identified, as well as a comprehensive research agenda that includes the potential of TikTok as a social media to integrate into companies' marketing strategies.

## CHAPTER OBJECTIVES

- Identify the major changes regarding the entertainment industry before and post the emergence of Netflix;
- Understand what are the habits and motivations of consumers to use the social media TikTok;
- Understand how TikTok has changed the perception of series on the streaming platform.

## ENTERTAINMENT INDUSTRY

Entertainment is a complex concept that comprises any action, activity, or event that is intended to entertain the interest of an audience (Acquaviva, 2019). Pinheiro (2017) points out that entertainment finds its motivation in five points: 1) psychological relaxation offered to the viewer; 2) break in daily life; 3) stimulation; 4) fun; 5) change of environment built as an escape from reality. It is precisely through the combination of these aspects that the entertainment industry later solidifies and seeks to provide a "unified and combined entertainment experience" (Pereira, 2015).

Azevedo (2016) believes that when the individual comes into contact with the image, be it through a television, computer or cell phone screen, a unique and identitary experience is created. Whether as producer or viewer, the use of the image mirrors social behavior and with each technological revolution the experimentation of content is changed and enhanced. In a current context the television industry is influenced by the effects of globalization and reflects an increasingly integrated business, governed by similar practices and principles, with interconnectivity through structural and institutional links between television systems (Waisbord, 2004). According to Alves (2018), there are several authors who consider that television integrates domestic culture and influences the mode of consumption of films, series, documentaries and videos, worldwide. However, we are witnessing the confrontation between television and new technologies from the moment online platforms appear that make it possible to watch audiovisual entertainment content.

Azevedo (2016), states that the internet emerged as a potential alternative for the dissemination of sound and image and "an aggregating tool for the dissemination of entertainment and information".

With the evolution of the digital environment in its relationship between interaction (how information is reproduced) and interactivity (information management from devices), the internet provides greater ease in the exchange of information. For Alves and Hamza (2018), a need for adaptability and emergence of companies that engage in new methods of creating, exploiting, developing, and distributing entertainment content has been brought about.

With a delivery of greater choice and new possibilities to audiences, streaming has brought television networks and technologies closer together, giving prominence to practices wrapped in distribution platforms (Faria, 2020).

*Table 1. Streaming technologies*

| Streaming Technologies | |
|---|---|
| Operation | Instantaneous digital transmission of audio and video content, through an Internet connection and with no download required (Coutinho, 2013). |
| | Sending and receiving multimedia content, compressed and in real time, over the network with the support of various programs (Castells, 2009); |
| Classification | Live streaming: there is a real-time signal reception and the viewer's behavior is that of watching television (Faria, 2020); |
| | Streaming video on demand technology: content is made available, with no download required, allowing video viewing simultaneously and in different locations (Azevedo, 2016). |
| Objective | Provide convenience - consumer watches a diversity of content available when and how they want (Silva & Dall'orto, 2017); |
| | Streaming video and audio across borders (Oliveira and Nobre, 2017); |
| Utilization | Live streaming of events or pre-recorded content (Alves, 2018). |

The revolution in the audiovisual market was largely advocated by VOD (video on demand) which is characterized by an "interactive multimedia system that operates over the Internet", where it is possible to select, order and receive remotely any kind of content offered by the service (Faria, 2020). The video on demand technology integrated in streaming services makes content available in a unicast format (only for one user), according to the user's entertainment content options (Topic, 2002). Another potential of the technology concerns the use of PVR commands (commands that enable the user to record, stop and restart the broadcast).

For the Higher Council of Cinema - CSC the VOD service is differentiated by its non-linearity and possibility of greater decision-making by the user in his particular management and organization of the programming. In fact, Rocha (2017) argues that it is precisely the factors presented by the CSC that are the main guarantors of the service's continued success and relevance.

According to Azevedo (2016) there are five types of video on demand:

1) Broadcast (No-VoD): first service to appear on the market and is the most common, being characterized by the static role of the participant, without control of the programs;
2) Pay-per-view (PPV): service where the viewer has to subscribe and pay to be able to watch certain specific programs;

3) Quasi video on demand (Q-VoD): service that allows a grouping by content and simplistic time control;
4) Near video on demand (N-VoD): service that allows foward and reverse functionalities, with discrete time interval simulation;
5) True video on demand (T-VoD): service where the viewer assumes total control over the programs he consumes, including foward, reverse, play, freeze random positioning functionalities. Azevedo (2016), mentions that this technology that allows viewer freedom also has the advantage of mobility, already mentioned above, and that makes it possible to watch content on smartphones and tablets, devices that typically do not have a large storage capacity.

*Table 2. VOD services*

| **Video on Demand Services** | |
|---|---|
| Operation | Use of broadband technology; |
| | Dissemination of content through different devices (television, tablet, smartphone, computer, etc); |
| | Optionally use pay TV signal devices. |
| Classification | OOT (Over the Top): Use of the Internet as the main channel for providing entertainment content; |
| | Cable VOD: access achieved through the set-up box, through cable operators. |
| Access | Subscription business models; |
| | Rental; |
| | Free access. |

In addition to these technologies, Pay TV services offer consumers live audiovisual content, but they are more expensive services. Precisely because of this factor, several authors consider that the number of customers of this service presents a decrease in face of more accessible options in the current market (Oliveira & Nobre, 2017). In this context marked by social, political, technical and economic transformations of the networked communication environment, content starts to circulate quickly, in an inexpensive and holistic way.

Marked by platform mobility, entertainment content becomes accessible through multiple screens and devices, allowing web user interactivity (Faria, 2020). Effectively, with the multivariate offer of mobile devices on the market, consumers are increasingly able to watch live audiovisual content wherever and whenever they want with the provision of mobile services, whether from their smartphones, tablets or other devices (Alves, 2018).

The digital era is thus marked by a change in consumer behavior that moves from a traditional fragile, flexible consumer image to a new dynamic of informed, involved, demanding consumer who seeks quick answers to their needs, becoming more difficult to deceive and persuade (Alves, 2018). The author even states that "if in the physical medium the consumer was demanding, in the digital medium he becomes a tyrant."

Camila Saccomori (2016) believes that online consumer behavior reflects a digital culture marked by the consumption of audiovisual content, verifying a behavior justified by control of time spent watching audiovisual content, variety of choice of available content, influence of opinions on social media and forums aimed at discussing opinions of movies and series. The impact of digital technology on the way television is consumed is a relevant study, in which Tay and Turner (2010) conclude the fusion of traditional media channels with new technologies.

Programming diversity is increasing and consumer behaviors tend to develop in consumption habits of streaming video platforms such as Netflix. These platforms offer more affordable subscription prices compared to cable or satellite television packages, enhancing a consumer decision based on an appealing cost-benefit analysis - since they are perceived as quality services at an affordable and fair price, taking into account the variety and attractiveness of the products offered (Crawford, 2016).

Alves and Hamza (2018), concluded that users of streaming services confirm that "technology provides fun, joy and entertainment, contributing to their pleasure and consequent intent to use the platforms" associated with the innovative service in the transmission of content. In fact, the authors present the relational variable that states that "the higher the performance expectation, the higher the usage intention".

Massarolo and Mesquita (2016), highlight that a characteristic practice of the new user profile of audiovisual technologies corresponds to binge watching (or marathon), meaning the act of watching programs, traditionally series or movies for hours at a time. Therefore, it is possible to affirm that the characterization of this profile mirrors with relative transparency the passion and integrity of users that contributes to the success of streaming platforms.

## NETFLIX

Founded in 1997 by Reed Hastings and Marc Randolph as a company that was only active in renting DVDs by mail in the United States, Netflix soon began to assert itself and improve its business model by creating a digital platform. Rocha (2017) argues that due to the constant and increasing evolution of the platform, a transformation of the homevideo industry was observed. In 1999, the platform launched a subscription model characterized by unlimited DVD rental for its subscribers for a monthly subscription. In 2000, the company developed a personalized system for recommending movies, based on an evaluation conducted by its members, and which in turn allowed a prediction of its subscribers' choices.

This algorithm technology put Netflix ahead of the competition, differentiating the company's business from other rental services. With the advances of the internet and the launch of the streaming service in 2007, the company made its content available through videos on demand, to devices with an internet connection, promoting greater reach of the service, offering more opportunities and visibility options to consumers. Because it was available from any Internet-connected device, in addition to personal computers Netflix began partnering with consumer electronics companies - such as Xbox, Playstation, Apple devices and Nintendo Wii. Growing notoriety has also allowed the company to establish contracts defining its successful business, having signed with audiovisual companies including: Paramount, Fox, Columbia, MGM and Warner.

The prevailing competitive paradigm is challenged by Netflix's business model. The platform's business is divided into three segments: 1) domestic streaming; 2) international streaming; 3) domestic DVD rental service (Cattley, 2020). The DVD segment is completely separate streaming business and has its own website, headquarters and management team. In this service, only available in the United States, subscribers can rent DVDs and Blu-rays online, opting for the two options provided - Standard or Premier - and receiving them at home (Cattley, 2020).

In the early years, the company was merely seen as a "vehicle" by television channels and movie studios, as Rocha (2017) recalls. However, the situation has changed since Netflix's first original productions, including the well-known series House of Cards in 2013. It was precisely from 2013 that the platform effectively began its investments towards acting in a vertically integrated way: 1) producing official and original content; 2) distributing content from TV channels and movie studios; 3) displaying exclusive content on the website.

In 2015 the company garnered 320 hours of original productions, including documentaries, films, children's programs and comedy specials. Rossini and Renner (2015), reinforce, however that Netflix does not act as a studio, the content displayed by the company being produced by entertainment companies that own the rights. What is known as original content is distinguished as exclusive, since only Netflix owns the distribution license, or by the fact that it is financially feasible content. In fact, when the company reached the scale that allowed the creation of original content, the business strategy became increasingly oriented towards in-house productions. Since 2015, the percentage of original content produced by Netflix has seen a percentage increase from 5% to 40% of the catalog.

Currently the company stands out for its VOD business, allowing niche content in the catalog through a search algorithm, with an easy-to-navigate interface and a recommendation mechanism based on customer preferences, history and behavior. Users have access to movies and series highlighted for them, through the aforementioned principle of personalized presentation and suggestion. Thus, there is no doubt that the streaming market has become popular with Netflix, revolutionizing the entertainment industry today (Cattley, 2020).

This principle of the popularity of the service with the company contradicts the previous dissatisfaction of consumers derived by their limited autonomy. For Noronha et al. (2018), companies' strategies are consolidated in the principle of relationship marketing, and it is common for platforms, in this case Netflix, to make an effort to build an almost "affective" relationship with consumers: "Netflix establishes, through the intense use of social media, an efficient communication channel with the customer, necessary to have the so-called relationship marketing". The streaming platform, has thus intensified a concept of fandom associated with content that arouses in its subscribers a "passion" built by the idea of "fan".

In order to aim for an acceptance of different audiences, the company seeks to create representativeness in its language, stories and characters. In terms of the representativeness of minority groups - a core issue in the "fan" community - in Netflix original content, in terms of analytics "because it is a cyberspace platform, Netflix is able to establish a greater bond with those who subscribe to its services" (Silva, 2019), and therefore, by creating its own content, the platform is able, in numbers, to capture what the majority of its audience expects from it.

Effectively, the company uses the online resource not only to position and sustain itself as a service, but also to create a bond with consumers and promote the concept of fandom. Within the entertainment industry, social media allows for a promotional and engagement approach, and the popular North American platform has not escaped the rule. Netflix's communication team is efficient in launching products and promotional videos, in addition it proceeded to create the Netflix persona, in order to establish an emotional connection with users (Noronha, et al., 2018).

It is then created what can be called a "fan persona", where the idea of disclosure has changed principle and a representation of identity similar to the key audience of the platform. Netflix in its social media, namely Twitter, uses a language and communication proper to the virtual world, discussing topics on current issues linked to the entertainment industry and content production.

Through the multiplicity of screens, Netflix practices a large-scale marketing, developing several strategies to disseminate content and seeking to turn the "fan" of a series into a "fan" of the company. The platform explores the concept of being present in the routine of its users, becoming increasingly essential in their daily lives and promoting the practice of worth of mouth. This principle combined with loyalty strategies contributes to the growth and success of the platform (Sabbag & Silva, 2022).

## TIKTOK

TikTok is a video making application developed on September 24, 2016, by Chinese technology company ByteDance. Created in a record time of 200 days, the digital platform was called Douyin and was dedicated exclusively to video editing. In 2017 the social media already had 100 million users, with a total of 1 billion daily video views (Faustino, 2021).

For Cares (2021), the success that the application acquired in the first year led to a decision by the Chinese company based on the internationalization of the business and purchase of an existing application that had more than 100 million young users, the Musical.ly application. It was precisely through this event, characterized by the merger of the companies, that the current name of the platform appears, officially affirming itself as the successful application: TikTok. In 2018, the platform experienced a sharp and exponential growth, achieving a milestone in the digital era: it reached a number of downloads that surpassed rival social media such as Facebook, Instagram and WhatsApp - something never seen in the emergence of any other recent app. The downloads took place not only in Asian countries, but also in the United States.

Currently considered one of the most successful Chinese social media applications in the world, attracting mainly young users to view and produce creative videos (Montag et al., 2021), the principle of the TikTok culture emerges that assumes as its main goal the mutual aid of users for rapid popularization, coupled with a consequent success in the act of making content go viral (Cares, 2021).

According to Yang, Zhao, and Ma (2019), TikTok corresponds to an application that is based on the promotion and development of creativity and personal values evidenced in the personality traits and tastes of young audiences, highlighting their desire to express themselves. Despite its recent debut - compared to other social media, such as Facebook, which was launched in 2004 -, TikTok stands out mainly by meeting the psychological needs of its users, related to social interaction and respect, and combined with effective online and offline promotion strategies (Ma, Feng, Feng & Wang, 2019).

TikTok was built on the pillar of interpersonal involvement, through the creation of content and interaction with the platform's characteristic personalized algorithm. This interaction happens repetitively and allows users to confront the content with various aspects of their personality (Bhandari & Bimo, 2020). In the research supported by Ma et al. (2019), the dominant factor that explains why consumers use TikTok, as well as the crucial perception of usefulness and social and entertainment values associated with the platform, is the users' level of satisfaction. In addition, the authors also point out that the audience has been won over, in large part, by the "short" feature of the social media - being a short video app -, because with the explosion and quantity of information in the digital age, the public's attention is increasingly restricted and fragmented, causing them to favor entertainment content that is short and enjoyable.

The number of video posts, accounts to follow and favorite videos is unlimited, and everything is created according to the user's will and intention. This innovative multiplicity of options and tools makes for a dynamic and uncomplicated use of the application, and this is one of the many advantages that attract so many users to TikTok (Anderson, 2020). In addition to this, "interesting content" is stated as an important reason for 92.1% of respondents in the study by Wang et al. (2019), which contributes to the growing and exponential popularization of the application.

TikTok's algorithm is verified as an effective mechanism in delivering content to a large number of users of the platform, reaching millions in a short interval of time (Cares, 2021). The TikTok application assumes as a resource the artificial intelligence of distribution and indication of videos, based on the algorithm practiced by the platform. This tool allows the user to receive content that is more in line with their interests, through the request for indication of areas of interest at the time of registration. TikTok is also able to suggest certain content, through the interactions performed by users.

*Table 3. Motives why consumers use TikTok*

| Authors | Motives |
|---|---|
| Anderson, K. E. (2020) | A multitude of options, shortcuts, and tools that contribute to a dynamic and uncomplicated use. |
| Bhandari, A., & Bimo, S. (2020) | Intrapersonal involvement. |
| Influencer Intelligence (2020) | Participation in challenges, dance videos, lip sync and humor. |
| | Search for an entertainment application that allows to escape from the harsh reality experienced globally in light of the events concerning the COVID-19 pandemic. |
| | Contextualize and visualize products while they are being used and reviewed. |
| Kumar, V. D., & Prabha, M. S. (2019) | Achieving a "minute of fame". |
| Launchmetrics (2020) | High potential to achieve virality. |
| Ma, L., Feng, J., Feng, Z., & Wang, L. (2019) | Satisfy psychological needs related to social interaction. |
| | By the feeling of satisfaction acquired by the perception of utility and the social values of entertainment. |
| | By the "short" characteristic - from short video app -; by favoring short and enjoyable entertainment content. |
| | To create and strengthen connections with others through the practice of interactive activities. |
| Montag, C., Yang, H., & Elhai, J. D. (2021) | For viewing and producing creative videos. |
| Omar, B., & Dequan, W. (2020) | Relax, entertain, and communicate/express publicly. |
| Palupi, N. D., Meifilina, A., & Harumike, Y. D. N. (2020) | Increased self-confidence. |
| Wang, Y., Gu, T., & Wang, S. (2019) | Increase online awareness and add value to their personal brand. |
| | To promote themselves among the community, in order to achieve more attention and recognition.. |
| | View interesting content. |
| | Keep up with music trends. |
| | Consuming information and knowledge, through useful tutorials for the user's daily life. |
| Yang, S., Zhao, Y., & Ma, Y. (2019) | By the desire to express themselves and to promote the development of their creativity and personal values. |
| | Aiming to achieve popularity through creative, different and beautiful content, in line with the trends seen on the social media. |

In this way, the platform closely monitors all user behaviors, such as the videos they have watched, for how long and the number of times they have watched the video, whether they have joined the content creator's profile and followed it, as well as when and where they watched the video. In this way, the TikTok team categorizes the multiple characteristics of the videos viewed, such as the interactions they have gotten, with the goal of finding content similar to the one that has become most popular and most liked by the user, creating a "For You" page tailored to the user's interests (Greenwald, 2021).

According to Montag et al. (2021), the captivating way in which the algorithm of the "For You" page is designed can result in a longer usage of TikTok than the user planned, causing the user to problematically use the social media, becoming more prone to develop addictive behavior towards TikTok. As the user explores his "For You" page, it is impossible to anticipate the videos that will appear, and a wide variety of content produced by all kinds of creators may appear: ordinary people, digital influencers, celebrities, brands, among others (Anderson, 2020). Coupled with the quality of the content, TikTok's algorithm has the power to put any publication in front of a larger audience and outside the creator's range of followers, allowing any user to go viral, resulting in a greater diversity of creators within the community (Influencer Intelligence, 2020).

The concept of going viral consists of making certain content viral, with a characteristically rapid and wide dissemination, via the Internet. The social media, TikTok is closely related to the phenomenon of making something viral, effectively, quickly and without associated costs. The platform thus stands out from the others, for its intrinsic ease in the dissemination of easily produced content (Smith, 2021).

## TIKTOK AS A PLATFORM FOR MARKETING AND PROMOTING ENTERTAINMENT

Understanding TikTok as a marketing tool is crucial, given the growing investment of companies in social media as vehicles to implement their strategies. The application is characterized by its efficiency and speed in generating engagement, in such a way that it potentiates possible sales of products and services. The social media, characterized by its entertainment content, has transformed the industry through highly interactive content that appeals to consumers' emotions (Cares, 2021).

TikTok is definitely a digital platform that marketers should pay attention to, however, it is necessary to design a unique strategy for the social media that is more appropriate to the type of content that characterizes it. The content designed for TikTok should not follow the aspirational, embellished and aesthetic model so evident in other social media such as Instagram and Facebook, but should be more focused on a more informal and authentic character. Thus, companies should take into account the language and type of content appropriate in the use of the TikTok platform, developing customized marketing tools for the type of audience characteristic of the application. Ferreira (2022), argues that the ideal is for organizations to develop videos sustained by a transparent storytelling that is faithful to the brand's values and, at the same time, has the power to entertain users.

TikTok is differentiated by its predominantly young audience. Due to the humorous content of the platform's videos, careful planning is necessary when the possibility of investing in the social media is raised. Faustino (2021) highlights a young or young/adult audience as a segment encompassed in the application, finding that 41% of users are between 16 and 24 years old and 66% are under 30 years old. Generation Z is the one associated with the rising social media and comprises the sociological definition for the generation of individuals born between the second half of the 1990s to the early 2010s. This generation possesses an understanding of technology and the Internet, consisting of young "digital natives" (Ceretta & Froemming, 2011). Due to this factor, the most prominent videos on the social media are, as a rule, related to trends, challenges, duets and reactions that make professional content management and keeping abreast of the trends of the moment necessary.

The exponential growth of TikTok led to an extension of the platform, through the creation and development of a specific segment for advertisers to promote their content through investment: TikTok Business. This creation consists of a current and innovative solution for companies willing to invest in a fast and effective way to reach audiences all over the world. Marketers have several formats available to advertise their products and services (Ferreira, 2022):

- In-Feed Video: auto-play ads, with audio and displayed on the For You Page;
- Brand Takeover: ads that last between three and five seconds and appear when the user opens the application;
- Top View: similar to Brand Takeover videos, with the difference that the content is auto-playing and lasts up to 60 seconds;
- Branded Hashtag Challenge: ads that focus on the target audience and promote their action through challenges, and can last up to six days;
- Branded Effects: ads that appear as filters, exclusive stickers and other content that encourage users to use them in their content.

The creation of TikTok Business boosted investment by companies linked to the entertainment industry. Thus, companies related to the production and distribution of content such as movies, series and documentaries, began to invest in creating brand awareness and promoting their services and content through TikTok. Netflix is an example that invested in the platform in order to make series known - namely Tribes of Europa, for which it developed a Branded Hashtag Challenge: #TribesChallenge. With this tool the company called on users to demonstrate loyalty to the four tribes depicted in the series in a creative way, through a Branded Effect.

In order to enhance the campaign, Netflix partnered with 10 famous German Tiktok creators to demonstrate how to participate in the challenge through different uses of creative clothing in scenarios inspired by the augmented tribes. This strategy generated a large reach, through the combined followers and inspiration for the content created by the users. To give the challenge even more prominence and exposure, the streaming company used a set of TopView and One Day Max In-Feed ads. Hashtags challenges register a high success rate and Netflix's case was no different as the campaign broke records, reaching 1.5 billion views that captivated the community to explore more about the series[1].

Jonathan Helfgot, Netflix's vice president of movie marketing, says that what the streamer sees with TikTok, probably more than with any platform, "is the need to appear first as a fan - and then as a marketer." TikTok users are looking for authenticity and creativity, a case in point being for Netflix's "The Gray Man" starring Ryan Gosling and Chris Evans, where Netflix recruited the directors of the action film - the Russo brothers - for a behind-the-scenes series on TikTok, targeted at the #filmtok community on the app. Jonathan Helfgot, applied a phrase from Kelli King, head of TikTok strategy for Netflix: "sprinkle chaos" to describe the streamer's approach to the short video app. He complements that one cannot outline something without proper customization to implement in the social media TikTok[2].

Thus, in the study developed by the author Cares (2021), the presence of the company Netflix on the platform has achieved its purpose, allowing a greater reach of possible audiences and user engagement with the streaming platform. The company relies on digital influencers and trends, betting on an effective combination of creative content to attract consumers. This way, there is a stimulus to the creation of an almost "affective" bond between the company and users, which precedes the viralization of content and, in turn, generates a growing number of active and loyal consumers.

## ENTERTAINMENT INDUSTRY DIGITALIZATION MODEL

The integrative literature review conducted allowed the construction of a conceptual model of the entertainment industry in the digital age, in order to establish relationships between concepts present in the research. Thus, the literature review was essential and indispensable in terms of consolidating data and information to build the necessary and contributive knowledge to the study of the impact of the digital era, namely the social media TikTok in the viralization of the Entertainment Industry, more specifically of series on the Netflix platform.

The searches carried out to structure the literature review were duly supported and performed in the B-on database (https://www.b-on.pt/), official websites and in institutional repositories, through the use of expressions such as: "Entertainment Industry", "Digital Age in the Entertainment Industry", "Netflix", "Social Media", "Social Media Marketing" and "TikTok". The scientific documents selected to substantiate this study were chosen taking into consideration the in-depth concepts and respective relationship between authors and publications in the areas of interest.

The information gathered allowed to conclude that globalization combined with a technological revolution marked by the use of the internet and web 2.0, inserted in a more interactive and collaborative scenario, have effectively brought about deep and exponential transformations in the entertainment industry. Companies linked to showbusiness recognize the need for dynamism and the idea of elitist television, built throughout the 20th century, undergoes adaptations with the emergence of global technological innovations, such as streaming platforms and VOD services. With the digitalization of content and reproduction through various internet media, the audiovisual industry has undergone an evolution characterized by changing relationships between: (1) markets; (2) producers; (3) audiences; (4) products.

It is in this context that Netflix asserts itself as a platform dedicated to the distribution and production of a comprehensive and varied catalog of movies, documentaries, series, among other content. The American company has acquired increasing success and recognition, establishing itself as a leader in the digital streaming market and segment and transforming the perceptions and habits of the entertainment consumer.

In fact, the availability of new technologies and tools contributed to verifiable changes related to contemporary consumer behavior, largely reflected in the accessibility, autonomy and convenience of platforms; time spent watching entertainment content; variety of choice of available content; influence of opinions on social media; forums for discussion of opinions of movies, documentaries, series, among others.

Thus, organizations seek to adapt their business models in order to meet the identified needs of the new consumer profile, increasingly demanding and informed. The technological capacity has thus revealed itself to be of extreme importance, since the individual creates the desire to comment, criticize, share, recommend and/or modify the contents, bringing to the technology and communication companies new business opportunities that facilitate new and improved possibilities to consumers. In order to face the challenges of the digital age, companies are exploring marketing applied to social media as a method of identifying consumers' main motivations and generating engagement, often resulting in fandoms associated with the audiovisual entertainment industry. Social media thus allows marketers to design strategies focused on the opportunity to reach new audiences.

TikTok, as an entertainment social media that promotes the creation and sharing of short videos based on a pillar of interpersonal engagement, thus enables, through its algorithm and operation, the delivery of content to a large number of users. With a record of growth and success proven by the number of downloads of the platform, TikTok privileges the provision of entertainment content that is short and enjoyable, which is verified as one of the main motivations of users for the consumption of the social media. The marketing practiced on the platform follows criteria related to authenticity and originality, leading to the association and investment of several companies in TikTok Business. Netflix already has a presence in the social media, for a possible viralization and popularity of its content, through the strategic use of the application as a space for creativity and entertainment.

In the model it is possible to conclude that the phenomenon of the digital revolution, focused on the entertainment industry, has enabled:

1) emergence of new technologies and platforms linked to content production and distribution: streaming and VOD;
2) emergence of a digital culture marked by new habits and characteristics of consumption and interaction: behaviors of entertainment consumers, importance of generation Z in the digital context and the concept of fandom;
3) popularity of applications, with the emergence of digital technologies and culture. Within the applications, TikTok (social media) and Netflix (streaming platform) stand out.

*Figure 1. Model of the digitalization of the entertainment industry*

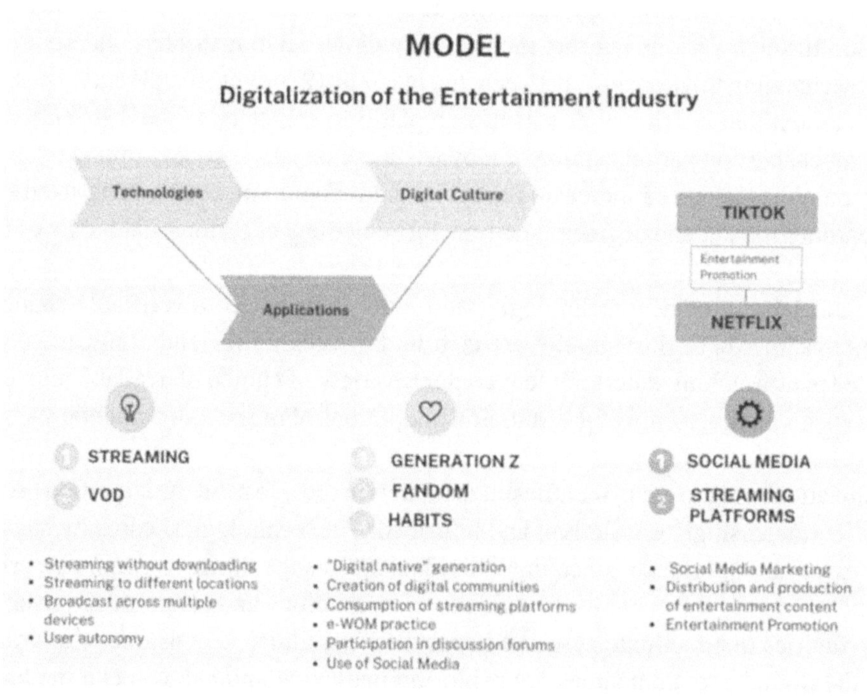

Thus, streaming technologies allow a live or pre-recorded transmission of audio and video, through Internet connection and without the need for downloading. The technologies thus provide convenience, security, and easy access to content, simultaneously and in different locations. Regarding video on demand technology, there is a use of broadband Internet with content broadcast through different devices (television, tablet, smartphone, computer) in an interactive multimedia system. In VOD services a differentiation is evident, characterized by non-linearity and a greater decision process for the user in his particular organization of programming. The popularization of technologies associated with new forms of distribution of entertainment content led to the affirmation of Netflix, as a paradigm in the consumption of movies, series, among others, and as a digital platform that offers dynamic content, through an algorithm that allows a personalized experience to consumers.

Digital culture is marked not only by new technologies and tools, but also by new habits of entertainment consumers. Consumers are largely composed of Generation Z, comprising a young-adult audience born between the 1990s and the year 2010. This generation is marked by its connection with technology and habits that characterize it as a "digital native":

- Consumption of entertainment from streaming platforms and VOD services;
- Participation in online discussion forums;
- Practice of e-WOM (electronic worth of mouth);
- Use of social meda as opinion-forming agents.

These practices lead to the emergence of fandoms, where physical or digital communities are formed with the sharing of common interests associated with entertainment culture - segmentation of fan groups according to their favorite movies, series, or actors. These communities acquire more and more prominence with the Internet and develop cultural products and more direct communications between fans, entertainment companies, and even between fans and actors, thanks to applications and platforms such as social media.

These characteristic applications of the digital age evolve into the contemporary concept of social media as highly interactive platforms that allow users to share, discuss, change, and co-create content. In this context comes the successful application TikTok, which allows, through its own algorithm and a set of tools, the creation and sharing of short videos inserted in an authentic and creative environment. In this way, the Chinese platform is linked to entertainment and its possible promotion, namely of the Netflix application.

## FUTURE DIRECTIONS

Over the past few years, there has been a proliferation of research studies that encompass TikTok as a social media on the rise. Several industries benefit from the platform, including not only entertainment, but also music and beauty, for example (Felizardo, 2021). However, the topic addressed is not yet widely explored and the main research priorities include the relationship between TikTok and the viralization of series on the Netflix platform. A theoretically grounded investigation is then needed, with comparison of results between studies, in order to discover verified and proven measures of analysis. For future work it would be interesting to delve deeper into the relationship of the social media with the entertainment industry in other dimensions. It could be explored an approach to the problem from the point of view of the producers and directors themselves, trying to understand to what extent they consider the social media as an asset for their productions.

## CONCLUSION

In the last few years, research has shown that the entertainment industry has been revolutionized by the emergence of the digital age. The paradigm with the emergence of new technologies, digital culture and applications has led to a transformation in the perception of entertainment consumption. TikTok is an application that promotes viralization through a perfectly developed algorithm. It becomes clear the importance of social media for the rise and promotion of entertainment and all the benefits it presents, namely when analyzing the motivations of the platform's consumers. Taking this into account, TikTok is seen as a strategic tool for companies like Netflix when promoting series. Thus, a holistic and theoretically grounded approach was necessary to understand how the social media changed the perception of the streaming platform's series.

## REFERENCES


Acquaviva, M. (2019). *Evolução das campanhas de comunicação na indústria do entretenimento: do cinema de rua às plataformas de streaming*. Universidade de São Paulo.

Alves, A. (2018). *O comportamento de consumo dos Millenials nas plataformas de video streaming e a prática do binge watching*. Instituto Superior de Contabilidade e Administração de Coimbra.

Alves, G., & Hamza, K. (2018). *Comportamento do consumidor de streaming de vídeo sob a ótica da extensão da teoria unificada de aceitação e uso da tecnologia*. UEM.

Anderson, K. E. (2020). Getting acquainted with social networks and apps: It's time to talk about TikTok. *Library Hi Tech News*, *37*(4), 7–12. doi:10.1108/LHTN-01-2020-0001

Azevedo, J. (2016). *A experiência televisiva: A Netflix e a cultura da receção audiovisual on demand no Brasil*.

Bhandari, A., & Bimo, S. (2020). *TikTok and the "algorithmized self": A new model of online interaction.* AoIR Selected Papers of Internet Research.

Cares, N. (2021). *O TikTok como instrumento de Marketing Digital: Estudo de caso @NetflixBrasil.* Universidade de Brasília.

Castells, M. (2009). *The Rise of the Network Society*.

Cattley, R. (2020). *Netflix – Um Novo Paradigma na Indústria de Entretenimento: Análise e Valuation.* Rio de Janeiro.

Ceretta, S. & Froemming, L. (2011). *Geração Z: Compreendendo os hábitos de consumo da geração emergente.* Revista eletrónica do Mestrado Profissional em Administração.

Coutinho, M. (2013). *Saiba mais sobre streaming, a tecnologia que se popularizou na web 2.0*. TechTudo.

Crawford, J. E. (2016). *Cutting the Cord—A Marketing Case: An Examination of Changing TV Viewership*. Atlantic Marketing Journal.

Faria, N. (2020). *A Indústria do Entretenimento e a expansão do streaming em meio a Pandemia*. Centro Universitário do Sul de Minas-UIS/MG.

Faustino, P. (2021). *TikTok Marketing - O guia completo para ter sucesso na rede social do momento.*

Felizardo, A. (2021). *Os vídeos virais e trends como estratégias de marketing de influência para as marcas de moda e beleza na rede social TikTok*. Universidade Beira Interior.

Ferreira, B. (2022). *TikTok Marketing em 2022: O Papel das Marcas no TikTok*. Bernardo Ferreira Marketing. https://bernardoferreiramarketing.pt/tiktok-marketing/

Greenwald, M. (2021). Audience, algorithm and virality: Why TikTok will continue to shape culture in 2021. *Forbes*.

Influencer Intelligence (2020). The state of influencer marketing in beauty. *Influencer Intelligence*.

Kumar, V. D., & Prabha, M. S. (2019). *Getting glued to TikTok: Undermining the psychology behind widespread inclination toward dub-mashed videos*. Archives of Mental Health.

Launchmetrics. (2020). *The state of influencer marketing 2020: Special focus on fashion, luxury and beauty industries*. Launchmetrics.

Ma, L., Feng, J., Feng, Z., & Wang, L. (2019). Research on user loyalty of short video app based on perceived value: Take TikTok as an example. *16th International Conference on Service Systems and Service Management*. IEEE. 10.1109/ICSSSM.2019.8887751

Massarolo, J., & Mesquita, D. (2016). *Vídeo sob Demanda: uma nova plataforma televisiva*. Compós.

Montag, C., Yang, H., & Elhai, J. D. (2021). On the psychology of TikTok use: A first glimpse from empirical findings. *Frontiers in Public Health*, *9*, 641673. doi:10.3389/fpubh.2021.641673 PMID:33816425

Noronha, I., Castellano, M., & Pinho, J. (2018). *"Netflix eu te amo!": o capital emocional no relacionamento entre a empresa de streaming e os consumidores-fãs*. Revista Fronteiras, Unisinos.

Oliveira, J., & Nobre, P. (2017). *Internet Video Streaming*.

Omar, B., & Dequan, W. (2020). Watch, share or create: The influence of personality traits and user motivation on TikTok mobile video usage. [Interactive Mobile Technologies.]. *International Journal (Toronto, Ont.)*, 100.

Palupi, N. D., Meifilina, A., & Harumike, Y. D. N. (2020). *The effect of using TikTok applications on self-confidance levels*. JOSAR.

Pereira, S. (2015). *A Produção televisiva na era da mudança e da concorrência*. Faculdade de Ciência Sociais e Humanas de Lisboa.

Pinheiro, G. (2017). *O mercado da produção de conteúdos para televisão: estudo do caso português*. Universidade Católica Portuguesa.

Rocha, D. (2017). *Vídeo por demanda: transformações e perspectivas para a tv na atualidade.*

Rossini, M., & Renner, A. (2015). *Nova cultura visual? Netflix e a mudança no processo de produção, distribuição e consumo do audiovisual.* Porto alegre.

Sabbag, D., & Silva, B. (2022). *Classificação de audiovisuais no catálogo da Netflix: transmídias, fandoms e nichos.* Obtido de Em Questão: https://www.researchgate.net/publication/361654832_Classificacao_de_audiovisuais_no_catalogo_da_Netflix_transmidias_fandoms_e_nichos

Saccomori, C. (2016). *Práticas de binge-watching na era digital: Novas experiências de consumo de seriados em maratonas no Netflix.*

Silva, M. Z., & Dall'orto, F. C. (2017). *O streaming e a sua influência sobre o audiovisual e o product placement.*

Silva, P. (2019). *Representações de minorias em séries da Netflix: estudo sobre o personagem Eric da série Sex Education.* Congresso de Ciências da Comunicação na região Centro-Oeste Goiânia.

Smith, B. (2021). How TikTok Reads Your Mind. *The New York Times.* https://www.nytimes.com/2021/12/05/business/media/tiktok-algorithm.html

Tay, J., & Turner, G. (2010). *Not the apocalypse: Television futures in the digital age.* International Journal of Digital Television.

Topic, M. (2002). *Streaming Media Demystified.*

Waisbord, S. (2004). *McTV: Understanding the Global Popularity of Television Formats.* SAGE Publications. doi:10.1177/1527476404268922

Wang, Y., Gu, T., & Wang, S. (2019). Causes and characteristics of short video platform Internet community taking the TikTok short video application as an example. *IEEE International Conference on Consumer Electronics.* IEEE. 10.1109/ICCE-TW46550.2019.8992021

Yang, S., Zhao, Y., & Ma, Y. (2019). Analysis of the reasons and development of short video application: Taking TikTok as an example. *9th International Conference on Information and Social Science.* IEEE.

## ADDITIONAL READING

Berthon, P. R., Pitt, L. F., Plangger, K., & Shapiro, D. (2012). Marketing meets Web 2.0, social media, and creative consumers: Implications for international marketing strategy. *Business Horizons, 55*(3), 261–271. doi:10.1016/j.bushor.2012.01.007

Gouveia, M. (2021). *Redes sociais: o que são, para que servem e como geri-las?* Obtido de MarcoGouveia. https://www.marcogouveia.pt/redes-sociais-o-que-sao/

Jenkins, H. (2015). *Invasores do texto: fãs e cultura participativa.* Marsupial.

Jenner, M. (2014). Is this TVIV? On Netflix, TVIII and binge-watching. *New Media & Society.*

Kantar, I. (2020). *Cinco maneiras em que o Coronavírus está mudando nossos hábitos de consumo de vídeo – e o significado disso para os anunciantes.*

Lima, B. I. (2020). *A história do TikTok.* Oficina da Net. https://www.oficinadanet.com.br/historiasdigitais/29943-a-historia-do-tiktok

Quesenberry, K. A. (2019). *Social media strategy: Marketing, advertising, and public relations in the consumer revolution* (2nd ed.). Rowman & Littlefield.

## KEY TERMS AND DEFINITIONS

**Entertainment Industry:** The entertainment industry is a branch that encompasses several spheres involving performing arts, namely film and television.

**Fandom:** Fandom is a term used for physical or digital communities that share common activities and interests.

**Generation Z:** Generation Z, commonly known as zoomers, comprises the generation of people born between the second half of the 1990s and the early 2010s.

**Globalization:** Globalization is a process of worldwide economic, political, cultural and digital expansion.

**Netflix:** Netflix is a streaming platform of American origin which allows members to watch television series and movies on a device connected to the Internet.

**Social Media:** Social media are digital platforms that enable a consumption, creation and sharing of content by its users.

**Streaming platforms:** Streaming platforms are platforms that allow for the transmission of audio and video without the need for downloading, through online access by the user.

**TikTok:** TikTok is a video making application developed on September 24, 2016, by Chinese technology company ByteDance.

**VOD services:** Video on Demand services are services that operate over broadband and on countless devices, allowing users greater freedom of choice regarding the audiovisual content to be consumed.

## ENDNOTES

1 Information available at https://www.tiktok.com/business/en/inspiration/netflix-317

2 Information available at https://variety.com/2022/digital/news/tiktok-marketing-culture-catalysts-dinner-netflix-paramount-1235379528/

# Chapter 11
# New Social Movements and Digital Activism

**İbrahim Toruk**
*Selçuk University, Turkey*

**Gülşah Sarı**
https://orcid.org/0000-0001-6590-6530
*Aksaray University, Turkey*

**Rengim Sine Nazlı**
https://orcid.org/0000-0001-9784-766X
*Bolu Abant Izzet Baysal University, Turkey*

## ABSTRACT

*The use of digital has shifted to a different format, especially with the prominence of interaction with Web 2.0-based social networking sites that developed after internet technology. These environments, which provide users with a platform independent of time and space, have transformed daily and professional life practices, and public spaces have been replaced by virtual communities. Historically, social movements based on class struggle have also been affected by this change. Although the use of media tools in social movements dates back to the 18th century, individuals can easily reach people who think like themselves and organize quickly through social media. Although digital activism, which is one of the trends of digital technology prevailing in the 21st century, has been exposed to criticism such as clicktivism, it has also become an effective force in the political arenas. In this study, changing social movements on the axis of digital technologies will be discussed in general terms to digital activism.*

## INTRODUCTION

Since the beginning of history, the type of communication has been shaped by the technology available in the era we live in. Just as smoke was a means of communication in the stone age, fire, which was instrumental in the formation of smoke, also functioned as a mechanism of rebellion. In this context, the

DOI: 10.4018/978-1-6684-8397-8.ch011

communication tools that dominate the age have determined the course of a movement that was initiated with the intention of creating the demanded change or resisting the change. Moreover, Innis (1950), who states that the development of civilizations is also related to the communication tools they have, emphasized the importance of communication in the collapse and rise of empires in his book called Empire and Communication. According to Innis, who deals with the effect link between communication technologies and social structure in a supra-individual context, the existing communication tools strongly affect the social organization and dominance occurs with the control of communication tools (Erdoğan & Alemdar, 2005: 139-140). On the axis of these thoughts, it is possible to associate the term social movements, which has been used since the 18th century, with the existing means of communication.

Human beings, who have been able to come together collectively since the invention of the printing press, have begun to theorize social movements against class differences with the effect of the concentration of capital in the hands of a certain group with industrialization. Social movements, in a sense, are the expression of the discontent experienced in the society and the needs to be met (Şentürk, 2006: 33). As a result of the use of new media and the development of its effects, a new generation of social movements has started to be mentioned as a result of the attention of social movements, which is a collective behavior.

## SOCIAL MOVEMENTS AND ACTIVISM

Saint-Simon first used the term social movements in France in the early eighteenth century, as a feature of new political forces opposed to the status quo to describe the social protest movements that emerged in his country and later elsewhere. Nowadays, it is a term that most commonly refers to groups and organizations that are outside the main body of the political system (Marshall, 1999: 746; Tilly 2008: 29-32) states that the social movements that emerged with the eighteenth century were carried out as interactive campaigns by overcoming individual initiatives, and discussed social movements as a process that unites three different areas in the context of identity and stance, which includes the necessity of the movement on the one hand, and the necessity of the movement on the other. In general, social movements can spread through modeling, cooperation and communication channels. John Markoff (1996: 45) explains this situation in its most general form as follows:

*"The social movements we know today began to sprout in England in the late 18th century and took root in Europe, North America and elsewhere in the 19th century. To understand why, we must consider many interrelated changes: strong government but weak king, people organized to claim government rights, political elites claiming to rule in the name of the people, developments in trade and transportation that connect people from far away, people living in the same places. new mass media and widespread literacy that combine it with a shared sense of action." (As cited in Tilly, 2008: 25)*

Social movements are a form of collective behavior in which action is taken to create a new lifestyle and a new model in society. In this respect, social movements, on the one hand, express social disturbances that are not satisfied with the flow of life, on the other hand, offer new solutions to solve them (Türkdoğan, 1997: 10). As the name suggests, social movements are wide-ranging organizations made up of various interest groups. Social movements include important social strata such as workers, women's groups, students, youth and intellectuals. These different interest groups of the society come together around a single complaint (Tilly, 2008: 13). Despite the diversity of definitions related to social movements, when we look at their general features, it is seen that the features that require individuals to take initiative and involve a joint action in order to eliminate social problems that directly concern a significant part of the society and affect the ordinary flow of daily life are at the forefront (Alpman, 2012: 21).

Tilly (2008: 16) explains social movements as the synthesis of three elements that came together after the 18th century and lists these elements as follows:

*"An ongoing, organized public initiative (campaign) making joint claims against the targeted authorities*

*2- The realization of various types of political action. These types of actions are: establishing special-purpose associations and unions, holding public rallies, official corteges, vigils, unions, demonstrations, petitioning, making statements to the media, and placarding (who calls the diverse group of initiatives the social movement repertoire)*

*3- Consistent public display of the principles of reasonableness, unity, number and loyalty to themselves and/or their constituents*

Social movements, which are seen to be based on class struggle, have emerged as a reaction against the social injustices experienced with industrialization in modern societiesIn the Western European countries that first experienced the industrialization process, social movements became identical with the workers' movements (Bottomore, 1997: 23). This process of group formation builds new solidarities. Once the consciousness for the need for solidarity is developed, it becomes impossible to tell whether the motives of the participants were altruistic or selfish. Because individual interest and collective interest are no longer in conflict, these interests are perceived as over. This process occurs not only in individuals, but also in groups, organizations and different segments. Thus, the formation of social movements becomes possible (Brecher et al., 2002: 43).

Although the new social movements emerged differently from the social movements of the past periods, they also showed themselves in a quality that included them (Sine, 2017: 97). The most common way of comparing old and new social movements, which are far from random coexistence by being defined as an organized community, are the forms of organization of the movements in question. However, Marta Fuentez and Andre Gunder Frank (1990: 29-41) explained the following features in both old and new social movements in 10 articles:

1. *"Although new social movements have some new features, they are not really new; 'classical' social movements are relatively new and perhaps transient.*
2. *Social movements show great diversity and variability, but they must mobilize individuals in line with a sense of morality and justice; they are common in their efforts to create a social force that will mobilize the society to survive against deprivation and to acquire identity.*
3. *The resilience and impact of social movements are cyclical; It depends on long political, economic and perhaps ideological cycles.*
4. *It is important to distinguish the class compositions of social movements in which they are mostly middle class in the West, popular-working class in the South, and both in the East.*

5. *There are different types of social movements. Social movements in general seek more autonomy rather than state power; Social movements seeking state power tend to deny themselves as social movements.*
6. *Although most social movements tend to be defensive and persistent rather than offensive, they are important drivers of social transformation.*
7. *In particular, social movements appear to be agents and redefiners of the "break" from contemporary capitalism and the "transition to socialism".*
8. *Some social movements are likely to enter into membership relations with other movements or to adapt more, to become open to alliance; some social movements are likely to clash and compete with others.*
9. *Since social movements, just like street theaters, write their scripts, if any, to the process themselves (tactics aside), it is out of the question (tactics aside) that agendas or strategies are decided by outsiders—intellectuals are not meant—it is even harmful.*
10. *Social movements will contribute to broadening, deepening and even redefining democracy in the transition from traditional state, political and economic democracy to civil society and civil democracy."*

Along with the existence of some criteria that put social movements into such a distinction, there are also opinions claiming that there is no break between the old and the new. However, the main point of the distinction is related to social structure and processes. The emergence of new social movements symbolizes the transformation between social movements and the political structure (Tiryaki, 2020: 40,42). Touraine (1988: 18), social actors now speak for themselves, their freedom; states that they want the right to be themselves without being crushed by power, violence and propaganda tools. The return of the "Actor" should be understood in a defensive spirit in this sense; It does not want individuals to dissolve themselves in a strong collective move, on the contrary, it is against the collectivity. The opposition of today's social actors is against the tools and discourses that prevent them from realizing their own projects, defining their goals, and entering into the conflicts, discussions and bargains they want. According to Touraine (1995: 282), the concept of social class is replaced by the concept of social movement. In these societies, the workers' movement has lost its "revolutionary subject" position, and has been replaced by "new social movements" created by new conflict grounds focusing on the production of cultural goods and the purposes of this production (As cited in Hasdemir & Coşkun, 2008: 138).

## AN OVERVIEW OF DIGITAL ACTIVISM

Today, developments in information and communication technologies have brought about more mobility and transparency of information and a different model change from the traditional model (Ersöz Karakulakoğlu, 2020: 59). In the last 30 years, globalization, the dominance of the free market, the ubiquity of communication and information technologies, and the development of techno-science have been clearly seen. (Gere, 2019: 16). "Digital technology enables the rapid spread of information through established networks while also reaching new participants" (O'Brien, 2021: 2).

The economic-political movement, which was started by the working class born with the industrial revolution and called the old social movements, has been moved to the digital environment with the development of the internet and technology and has started to continue as digital activism (Uysal, 2021:

45). “Digital activism is a phenomenon of rising political importance. With the advent of social media and online communication platforms, Internet mediated engagement has taken a centre stage in the way publics articulate views on controversial political issues” (Schlogl, 2022: 1). “The context of digital activism refers both to the digital technology that is used in a given activism campaign and to the economic, social, and political context in which such technology use occurs” (Joyce, 2010: 2). Digital activism is a networking organization. Therefore, while bringing the action that started locally to large masses, it increases the power of the action taken in a certain region to find solutions to problems such as environment, education, health, transportation, and combines it with those who struggle with similar problems anywhere in the world and carries the problem to the global level. (Uysal, 2021: 46, 47). “Civil society actors turn to digital means to address concerns and present claims that are significant to them in their context” (O’Brien, 2021: 2). Citizens’ interaction with political actors has changed both the way politics is done and the society itself, and issues such as the way of discussion on new possibilities for the citizen and participation in different democratic processes have gained importance (Ersöz Karakulakoğlu, 2020: 59). *“The public sphere is a field based on freedom of expression, where people can come together to share, present their opinions and criticize. Today, it creates a new public space that allows the formation of digital activism in digital media, where people can express themselves comfortably, have easy access, and can make their voices heard even between continents with a touch*”(Uysal, 2021: 46).

Joyce, on the other hand, states that technological infrastructure, social and political factors and economic factors are necessary for the formation of digital activism (As cited in Yetkin Cılızoğlu & Çetinkaya, 2018: 1947). Examples of digital activism are joining a campaign group on social networks, retweeting, creating a hashtag, or signing an online petition (Kırık et al., 2021: 304). Slativism, clicktivism, hacktivism are the most common types of digital activism. (Uysal, 2021: 47, 48).

## Slactivism

The term slactivism is increasingly used to describe the disconnect between awareness and action through the use of social media. (Glenn, 2015: 81). “Slactivism, a term first used by Dwight Ozard and Fred Clark at the Cornerstone Festival in 1995, means “supporting a digital action from where it stops” with its clearest definition.” (Yeğen, 2014: 90). According to Morozov, slativism describes activities that are easily performed with minimal effort and are considered more effective in making the participants feel good than in achieving the stated political goals (As cited in Scoric, 2012: 77). Goldsborough, (2011) and Landman, (2008) indicate that “Digital activism is all about reaching out, creating awareness, garnering support, and enabling asynchronous political discourse. Slacktivism is the belief that ‘liking’ a post on Facebook or changing one’s profile picture constitutes a form of activism” (As cited in Madison & Klang, 2020: 32).

An example of slactivism is Invisible Children’s attempt to raise awareness about Joseph Kony, the leader of the Lord’s Resistance Army in Central Africa, using social media and other forms of organization. Among the efforts to seize Kony and stop the use of children in war is the posting of Kony 2012 video on YouTube. With the video going viral, it also circulated on Facebook, enabling Invisible Children to gather more than 3.5 million supporters (Glenn, 2015: 82).

## Clicktivism

Clicktivism, which is derived from the word "click" which means click in English, is sometimes defined as slacktivism and sometimes as a micro-political action (Çil, 2021: 106; Bağ, 2020: 362). Halupka (2018: 131, 132) identifies clicktivism with seven features; "Situated Online", "An impulsive gesture", "Noncommittal", "Does not draw upon specialized knowledge", "Easily replicated", "Engages a political Object", "An action performed". With these features, clicktivism can easily be expressed as an impulsive and non-binding online political reaction that is repeated and does not require special knowledge (p. 132). "Clicktivism allows individuals to demonstrate which causes or SMOs they advocate in a remote, detached manner. Anyone may use this technology and they may use it anywhere, as long as they have a social media account, a computer, tablet, or smartphone, and internet access, therefore, it requires few digital resources" (George & Leidner, 2019: 7).

An example of clicktivism is Sleeping Giants. "Sleeping Giants is a novel activist campaign aimed at digital advertising that serves as an important provocation, both in the world of media activism and in the academic policy debates surrounding the appropriate relationship between journalism and advertising in the 21st century" (Braun et al, 2019: 69).

## Hacktivism

Hacktivism is the use of computer technology or programming systems to respond to a social problem (Demirkıran, 2013: 28). In order to raise awareness of a social problem, negativism in the digital world is hacktivism, but if these actions become harmful, cyber terrorism turns into actions and therefore there is a fine line between hacktivism and cyber terrorism (Uysal, 2021: 49).

The activities of the world-famous hacker group Anonymous can be given as an example of hacktivism. "Anonymous hacktivism emerged at the intersection of pranksterism, or "trolling," and reac-tion against institutional practices" (Goode, 2015: 76). Anonymous' public works were mostly done through blogs and these blogs did not include real person signatures (Aust & Ammann, 2018: 271).

# FUTURE RESEARCH AND DIRECTION

In this study, digital activism and its types are examined in the context of social movements. In future studies, its subtypes can be examined in the context of current activist movements with case studies.

# CONCLUSION

Undoubtedly, technology is the most fundamental force that enables humanity to progress. Although culture, which is a living organism, has the feature of transition between ages, it can vary according to the ages. Likewise, lifestyle and social practices are determined according to the technological characteristics of the age. With the functional use of new media, almost everything about life has begun to be experienced again and has been shaped to the extent that communication technologies allow. The world, which was a global village as McLuhan stated, is now surrounded by networks. Every individual living in the network society is in the position of an actor of a digital public space today. Every individual living in this society, from ordinary citizens to celebrities and politicians, interacted with each other on social platforms.

The most important feature of digital platforms, which has turned the traditional one-way line of communication into two-way, has been the interaction that made this situation possible. While the interaction enabled ordinary people to communicate easily with anyone they wish on social platforms, it also accelerated their organization. The structure of the new media, which accelerates the organization, has shifted the activists who are trying to create public opinion on a certain issue to the virtual environment. Individuals with a certain technological infrastructure can perform activist activities very quickly and effectively through social networks.

Internet activism, cyber activism, online activism, web activism, etc. The decentralized structure of digital activism, also called digital activism, allowed by new media, has had the power to create unity of opinion and action across the world by eliminating geographical borders. Numerous campaigns have been announced to internet users worldwide through digital activism. On the other hand, ordinary internet users have started to support activist movements through social networks in line with the issues they are sensitive to. There are optimistic, pessimistic and indecisive perspectives towards digital activism, which is still a new topic. Considering that internet technologies are changing rapidly, although it is not known how digital activism will take shape in the future, its structure that wants to achieve its purpose in the short term seems to be reaching its goal at the moment.

## REFERENCES

Alpman, P. S. (2012). Toplumsal Hareketler Tartışması İçin Kısa Bir Giriş. (Çevrimiçi). *Yurtvedunya.* http://www.yurtvedunya.net/Sayi3/4.pdf

Aust, S., & Ammann, T. (2018). *Dijital Diktatörlük: Kitlesel Gözetim, Verilerin Kötüye Kullanımı ve Siber Savaş*. Hece Yayınları ve Dergileri.

Bağ, S. (2020). Slaktivizm: Yeni Medya ve Siyasal Eylemin Dönüşümü. In H. Hülür & C. Yaşın (Eds.), *Yeni Medya, Toplum ve Siyasal İletişim* (pp. 350–368). Ütopya Yayınevi.

Bottomore, T. (1997). *Frankfurt Okulu* (A. Çiğdem, Trans.). Vadi Yayınları.

Braun, J. A., Coakley, J. D., & West, E. (2019). Activism, advertising, and far-right media: The case of sleeping giants. *Media and Communication*, *7*(4), 68–79. doi:10.17645/mac.v7i4.2280

Brecher, J., Costello, T., & Smith, B. (2002). *Aşağıdan Küreselleşme* (B. Kurt, Z. Kutluata, Ş. Özgün, & A. Yıldırım, Trans.). Aram.

Çil, S. (2021). Dijital Aktivizm. In A. Zinderen (Ed.), *Dijital Sosyoloji Çalışmaları* (pp. 93–121). Nobel Yayınevi.

Demirkan, P. (2013). Hacktivizm. In A. R. Keleş (Ed.), *Hack Kültürü ve Hacktivizm: Yeni bir Siyaset Biçimi* (pp. 27–33). Alternatif Bilişim.

Erdoğan, İ., & Alemdar, K. (2005). *Popüler Kültür ve İletişim (2. edition)*. Erk Yayınları.

Ersöz Karakulakoğlu, S. (2020). *Dijital Toplum: Kavram, Kuram ve Yöntem*. Ankara: Nobel yayınevi.

Fuentes, M., & Frank, A. G. (1990). *"Sivil hareketler üzerine on tez", Birikim Dergisi, 16.* Ağustos.

George, J. J., & Leidner, D. E. (2019). From clicktivism to hacktivism: Understanding digital activism. *Information and Organization, 29*(3), 100249. doi:10.1016/j.infoandorg.2019.04.001

Gere, C. (2019). *Dijital Kültür*, (Trans. Aydoğdu Akın). İstanbul: Salon yayınevi.

Glenn, C. L. (2015). Activism or "Slacktivism?": Digital media and organizing for social change. *Communication Teacher, 29*(2), 81–85. doi:10.1080/17404622.2014.1003310

Goode, L. (2015). Anonymous and the political ethos of hacktivism. *Popular Communication, 13*(1), 74–86. doi:10.1080/15405702.2014.978000

Halupka, M. (2018). The legitimisation of clicktivism. *Australian Journal of Political Science, 53*(1), 130–141. doi:10.1080/10361146.2017.1416586

Hasdemir, T. A., & Coşkun, M. K. (2008). Kamusal Alan Ve Toplumsal Hareketler. *Ankara Üniversitesi SBF Dergisi, 63*(01), 121–149. doi:10.1501/SBFder_0000002055

Innis, H. (1950). Empire and Communications. Oxford: Clarendon Press.

Joyce, M. C. (2010). *Digital activism decoded: The new mechanics of change*. IDEA.

Kırık, A., Çetinkaya, A., & Kurşun, A. (2021). Digital Activism in the Context of Social Movements: the Case of Change. Org. In E. K. Doru, S. Mengü, & E. Ulusoy (Eds.), *Digital Seige*. Istanbul University Press.

Madison, N., & Klang, M. (2020). The case for digital activism: Refuting the fallacies of slacktivism. *Journal of Digital Social Research, 2*(2), 28–47. doi:10.33621/jdsr.v2i2.25

Marshall, G. (1999). *Toplumsal Hareketler. Sosyoloji Sözlüğü* (A. Osman & K. Derya, Trans.). Bilim ve Sanat.

O'Brien, T. (2021) Digital activism and the state, Tapuya: Latin American Science. *Technology and Society, 4*(1). doi:10.1080/25729861.2021.1973291

Schlogl, L. (2022). *Digital Activism and the Global Middle Class: Generation Hashtag*. Routledge.

Şentürk, Ü. (2006). Küresel Yeni Sosyal Hareketler ve Savaş Karşıtlığı. *C. Ü. Sosyal Bilimler Dergisi, 30*(1), 31–46.

Sine, R. (2017). Alternatif Medya ve Haber. Konya: Literatürk.

Skoric, M. M. (2012). What is slack about slacktivism. *Methodological and conceptual issues in cyber activism research, 77*(7), 7-92.

Tilly, C. (2008). *Toplumsal Hareketler* (O. Düz, Trans.). Babil Yayınları.

Tiryaki, S. (2020). Toplumsal Hareketler ve Medya. Konya: Literatürk.

Touraine, A. (1988). *Return of the Actor*. University of Minnesota Press.

Touraine, A. (1995). *Modernliğin Eleştirisi* (H. Tufan, Trans.). Y.K.Y.

Türkdoğan, O. (1997). *Sosyal Hareketlerin Sosyolojisi*. Birleşik.

Uysal, Z. (2021). *Dijital medya ve toplum*. İstanbul: Cinius yayınları.

Yanık, C., & Öztürk, M. (2014). Toplumsal hareketlerin dönüşümü üzerine bir değerlendirme. *Mukaddime*, *5*(1), 45–63.

Yegen, C. (2014). Bir ijital aktivizm biçimi olarak slaktivizm: Change.org örneği. *Karadeniz Teknik Üniversitesi İletişim Araştırmaları Dergisi*, *4*(2), 84-108.

Yetkin Cılızoğlu, G., & Çetinkaya, A. (2018). Zaman ve mekandan bağımsız katılım; örgütlü yurttaştan dijital bireye: Change.org örneği. *Journal of Human Sciences*, *15*(4), 1944–1958. doi:10.14687/jhs.v15i4.5529

## ADDITIONAL READING

Della Porta, D., & Diani, M. (1999). Social movements. The SAGE Handbook of, 656.

Heberle, R. (1951). *Social movements*. Ardent Media.

Kaun, A., & Uldam, J. (2018). Digital activism: After the hype. *New Media & Society*, *20*(6), 2099–2106. doi:10.1177/1461444817731924

Mutsvairo, B. (2016). *Digital activism in the social media era*. Springer Nature. doi:10.1007/978-3-319-40949-8

Sivitanides, M., & Shah, V. (2011). The era of digital activism. In Conference for Information Systems Applied Research (Vol. 4, No. 1842, pp. 01-08). Semantic Scholar.

## KEY TERMS AND DEFINITIONS

**Internet:** A world-wide, continuously expanding communication network that consists of many computer systems linked together.

**New Communication Technologies:** The communication means for the simultaneous and multistrata interaction of the communication process that is based on the digital coding system.

**Social media:** Web-based developments that bring in sociality to the media that is developed by the integration of technology and communication.

**Social movement:** It is a set of collective actions that seek to accelerate, prevent or reverse social change.

**Technology:** All tools and the knowledge related to them that is developed by man to control and transform his material environment.

# Chapter 12
# Cyberbullying in Organizations

**Hasan Tutar**
*Bolu Abant İzzet Baysal University, Turkey*

**Gamze Ay**
*Eskişehir Osmangazi University, Turkey*

## ABSTRACT

*Cyberbullying in organizations refers to the use of technology, such as social media, email, instant messaging, or other digital platforms, to harass, intimidate, or humiliate someone in the workplace. Cyberbullying in organizations can have a significant impact on individuals and the workplace as a whole. It can lead to decreased morale, increased turnover, decreased productivity, and increased absenteeism. Cyberbullying can also have legal and financial consequences for both the victim and the organization. Organizations can take steps to prevent and address cyberbullying, such as establishing clear policies and procedures for online behavior, providing training to employees on appropriate digital communication, and responding quickly and effectively to reports of cyberbullying. By creating a culture of respect and accountability, organizations can work to prevent cyberbullying and promote a safe and supportive workplace for all employees.*

## INTRODUCTION

Cyberbullying in the workplace is harassment or bullying that occurs through digital channels, such as email, instant messaging, social media, or other online platforms. It involves using these digital channels to engage in behavior intended to harm, intimidate, or humiliate another person. Examples of cyberbullying in the workplace include; sending threatening or harassing messages to an individual or group through email or instant messaging, spreading rumors or making derogatory comments about a coworker on social media or other online forums, posting explicit or inappropriate material about a coworker online, using technology to stalk or monitor a coworker's activities, either online or offline, sending offensive or insulting emails or messages that are intended to cause distress or harm to a coworker. Cyberbullying in the workplace can significantly impact the victim's mental health and well-being, as

DOI: 10.4018/978-1-6684-8397-8.ch012

well as their job performance and productivity. It can also create a toxic work environment and damage the organization's reputation.

In the mutual relationship environment, one or more of the parties directly or indirectly to the physical, moral, moral, and spiritual integrity of the others; If he acts in a way that harms his symbolic and symbolic cultural values, there is violence there. Violence, which has always existed throughout the history of humanity, has emerged in new types in the information age. Wars, murders, and physical and psychological attacks have expanded with the possibilities of new media (Bayrak & Yengin, 2021; Michaud, 1986). The form of violence aimed at psychological, sexual, or economic attack in the digital environment is called digital violence. The possibilities offered by digital technology allow the uninterrupted practice of violence. This situation causes digital violence to enter human life as a new type of violence (Çelik, 2018; Barındık, 2018). The communication habit of the Internet, especially in social media environments, keeps people in a perception of freedom outside of social boundaries. Thus, all the possibilities of irregularity, evil, and rudeness in the chaotic world of human beings are transferred to the digital space. With the courage arising from invisibility in the digital environment, the individual can be unpredictable, unmeasured, and dangerous, unlike real social life.

The networks formed by the telecommunication network transform the world into a "network of interconnected relations," The individual who is watched, controlled, and monitored in the digital environment is increasingly isolated and alienated within this network. National structures face a communication spiral they cannot hold within the communication network. Today, states spy on individuals for "security" reasons, creating a kind of surveillance paranoia in societies. As a result of high-tech communication and transportation facilities, the possibility of surveillance is expanding in a wide range from individual-society and state-society relations to international relations. On a global scale, news and information are reprocessed and formatted, and a new type of information develops over events and news. Through this mechanism, the "perception of reality" is manipulated, and the "product" produced is packaged as news and presented to the consumption of all world societies (Bayrak, 2017; Paçacı, 2014; Ridings, Gefen & Arinze, 2002; Günüç, 2012). Some of them may contain various violent content.

Examples of cyberbullying in the workplace include sending threatening or harassing messages to an individual or group through email or instant messaging and spreading rumors or derogatory comments about a coworker on social media or other online forums, and posting explicit or inappropriate material about a coworker online and using technology to stalk or monitor a coworker's activities online or offline and sending offensive or insulting emails or messages intended to cause distress or harm to a coworker. Cyberbullying in the workplace can significantly impact the victim's mental health and well-being, as well as their job performance and productivity. It can also create a toxic work environment and damage the organization's reputation. Organizations can prevent cyberbullying in the workplace by establishing clear policies, providing education and training to employees, and taking swift action when cyberbullying is reported. Creating a culture of respect and inclusivity can also help to reduce the likelihood of cyberbullying and promote a positive work environment for all employees.

## Cyber/Virtual Bullying

Cyberbullying is a type of aggression where an imbalance of power is repeated and continued, mainly intended to harm and disturb. This power imbalance can be physical or psychological. Cyberbullying is an aggressive and bullying behavior that deliberately interferes with someone, that is, the act of the bully. With the increase in digital tools in recent years, bullying has gained a new dimension under "cyberbullying." It is an aggressive act of a person using digital technologies (Smith et al., 2008: 376). Cyberbullying is deliberate, designed bullying that aims to harm individuals or groups around individuals or groups through information and communication technologies. With the widespread use of communication tools such as the Internet and telephone, it is seen that peer bullying that occurs in physical environments has been carried over to virtual environments. Although these communication tools provide benefits in terms of quickly accessing information and accelerating interpersonal communication, the increase in use at a high rate and without supervision has led to the emergence of a type of bullying called cyberbullying (Campell, 2005; Sarak, 2012: 14). Cyberbullying is when an individual sends messages or engages in social aggression in an electronic environment to annoy other individuals. It is the intentionally hostile behavior of the individual to his/her environment for purposes such as cell phone, email, messaging, and scribbling on websites (Willard, 2007; Li, 2006).

Virtual or cyberbullying is a new form of crime that occurs due to deliberate and repetitive harm to the other person utilizing technological tools and the Internet (Ayas & Horzum, 2011). Cyberbullying is more common than physical bullying, as it is the behavior of technical harm done to individuals or private or legal entities through information and communication technologies (Arıcak, 2011; Kavuk, 2011). Individuals can easily do the behaviors they hesitate to do in real life by doing them in virtual environments because they are overlooked and will not be punished (Willard, 2007). The anonymity of the virtual environment encourages people to commit crimes by providing a kind of purification night. This situation can lead to the emergence of different forms of crime in virtual environments.

Although many distinctions are made, two types of cyberbullying can be mentioned. The first is electronic bullying, and the second is electronic communication bullying. Electronic bullying is aimed at harming others by obtaining passwords or sending contagious emails. On the other hand, the second type of electronic communication bullying includes behaviors such as constantly harassing individuals, mocking, calling them nicknames, trying to spread slander or gossip, and sending insulting messages (Arıcak et al., 2012: 103). When we look at the research, it is seen that cyberbullying includes many behaviors such as breaking passwords, sending viruses, publishing information and pictures that humiliate individuals on blogs, sending threatening messages, damaging someone else's relationships by impersonating them or opening discussions to humiliate people in virtual environments such as chat rooms (Çiftci, 2015; Willard, 2007). In addition, fighting online, slandering in the digital environment, existing under another identity, using others' information on the Internet without their permission, virtual exclusion, and virtual harassment are other forms of cyberbullying.

Exposure of an individual to more than one type of bullying in the virtual environment, intense cyber-harassment, or constant threats and aggressive behaviors may cause the individual to distrust the virtual environment. Although there are many types of cyberbullying, the most common form is online fighting and cyber harassment. Fighting online includes angry and harsh language discussions in virtual environments. Harming and cyber harassment includes intimidation by using offensive language, sending insulting messages, broadcasting in chat rooms with intimidating, threatening messages, taking different actions that will cause concern for the safety of the other person, or sending viruses. Slander, on the other hand, is to defame a person in virtual environments and to damage the prestige he has gained in his immediate environment. Obtaining someone else's identity can be exemplified as taking actions that may cause someone to lose their status by using their identity. Using another person's files or information without their permission is also among the types of bullying. This type includes sharing secrets or pictures that would embarrass the individual in virtual environments. In the type of cyber exclusion, it involves the deliberate exclusion of the individual from virtual environments. In addition, message bullying, picture and video bullying, phone call bullying, email bullying, and chat room bullying are other forms of cyberbullying.

Interaction in the virtual environment does not occur due to power imbalance as in traditional bullying. The uncertainty of power in virtual environments is a factor that facilitates bullying (Rigby, 2011; Çiftçi, 2015). Cyberbullying can be a response to being a victim face-to-face or online. This reactive aggression is targeted and deliberate. It can also be defined as intentional aggression, which differs from traditional bullying (Pellegrini & Bartini, 2000). This reactive aggression is an inappropriate way to counter victimization. At the same time, individuals who are exposed to traditional bullying can sometimes bully their peers who are weaker than themselves. For this reason, victims can use virtual environments to gain power and status (Çiftçi, 2015; Willard, 2007). The main reason for cyberbullying is the anonymity digital technology provides to people with high criminal potential.

## Cyberbullying in the Workplace

Communication created by advanced communication technologies reveals new social structures called "network society." In the network society, blurring emerges in the life cycle, production system, and hierarchies (Castells, 2004, 2005; Ergeç & Zateri, 2020). Definitions such as network, information, and digital society are based mainly on new interaction areas caused by technological developments. Their common feature is using technology as a communication tool in human actions (Çelik, 2018). The new developments in digital media characterize network societies as social media or new media.

In the new communication environments, while the storage and dissemination of information become more accessible, the concept of "cyber violence" has emerged simultaneously. Bullying in human relations includes malicious behaviors deliberately repeated by an individual or group and aims to harm others (Turan & Dilmen, 2016; Olweus, 2003). Cyberbullying arises from using digital communication tools (Anamur & Topsakal, 2019; Karaca et al., 2021). Bullying in almost every social group is encountered in the Internet environment. The spread of Internet use in all areas of life results in real-life dangers being seen on the Internet. Bullying in electronic environments is referred to as "electronic bullying" in the literature. They are given different names, such as "cyberbullying" or "electronic bullying" (Kowalski & Limber, 2007). The corruption of the completeness or authenticity of data or information is called a cyber-attack or a computer network attack. Besides subjecting a computing infrastructure to disruption, disabling, middle attacks made to remove information, control maliciously, or steal information in a controlled manner are considered cyber-attacks (Akçakanat et al., 2021; NIST, 2021).

In cyberbullying, there is power and control over human relations. The bully tries to gain power and control over the victim, whom he perceives as psychologically weak; however, unlike traditional bullying, in cyberbullying, the bully may be physically weaker than the victim (Strom & Strom, 2005; Belsey, 2004; Olweus, 2003). Cyberbullying is an unstable power and repetitive behavior that continues in the virtual environment. While the limits of what individuals can do are discussed, the risks of organized power in the virtual environment are constantly increasing (Ateş & Ateş, 2020). Cybercriminals benefit from the speed, anonymity, and the virtual world's exclusion from real-life laws (Dilmaç, 2020).

Content producers of the media, such as politicians, journalists, and artists, become more visible and have the opportunity to apply more asymmetrical power while producing content in the media. New forms of violence and bullying emerge in the blurred spaces between the media consumer and the content producer (Ergeç & Zateri, 2020; Thompson, 1995). Cyber or cyberbullying arises from the power asymmetry between those who control information and communication technologies and their unconscious consumers. Violence emerges as new media's symbolic and cultural dimension (Thompson, 1995; Couldry, 2002). Social networks are closely related to power in spreading ideology and keeping society under surveillance. The individual always tends to create a superior identity with the desire for power. The government, which uses surveillance technologies to keep track of the individual and obtain his information, can do this by applying asymmetrical power (Bakıroğlu, 2013).

Increased tolerance for violence is the first step in acknowledging the existence of violence. The normalization of violence on screens, the blurred distinction between virtuality and reality, and the rapid digitalization of society allow digital violence (Aksu & Işıklı, 2019). The new interaction possibilities offered by digital technologies, the use of social networks, and the possibility of being anonymous in online environments make cyberbullying a more significant problem day by day (Özmen, 2018).

Today, many institutions and organizations provide their services in a virtual environment. Considering that activities such as virtual hospitals, virtual classrooms, virtual universities, virtual schools, virtual conferences, virtual companies, and virtual municipalities are shown, all the problems experienced in natural environments continue in virtual environments (Günüç, 2012). Violence experienced in physical environments is transferred to virtual environments and turns into digital violence, creating cyberbullying in the workplace (Turan & Dilmen, 2016).

## Forms of Bullying in Virtual Organizations

The Internet environment has added a new dimension to crime types. Some people who use the opportunities offered by digital technology with bad intentions can produce new forms of crime in virtual environments. Attacks in the virtual environment can be made not only by people but also by companies, and this can cause damage to the entire society (Yalçın, 2003). Widespread use of computer and Internet technologies and, security vulnerabilities, malicious applications (computer hacking, etc.) can cause significant damage to institutions and organizations (Akçakanat et al., 2021). The malicious use of computer systems causes cyber-crimes (Tarter, 2017). The cybercrime economy, which had a size of three trillion dollars in 2015, will have increased to 6 trillion dollars by the end of 2021. The costs associated with cybercrime for organizations are enormous. Cybercrime costs include data damage and destruction, loss of productivity, theft of intellectual property, theft of personal and financial data, disruption to everyday workflow, damage to reputation, and more (Herjavec, 2020; Velioğlu, 2022). Today, one in five companies is trying to block their competitors online. In this competitive approach, called digital competition, cyber crimes are committed, from criticism of the competitor's goods or services to hacking the website. Cyber-attacks can be based not only on hackers who want to gain financial benefits but also on rival companies.

Cyberspace, where the demand for over-sharing is centralized, does not voluntarily involve users; it makes them both capital and partner of the personal data industry in which they participate as dependents. Personal data is constantly under threat (Bauman & Lyon, 2018). Because contrary to all marketing discourses, there is no such thing as "personal" in this transparent universe, and there never will be (Barrett-Maitland & Lynch, 2020). Everything that is shared flows into the memory of the virtual space in all its details, and large chunks of data are processed and marketed as identifying information outputs. There is no room for erasing and forgetting in digital memory. Every written word and every shared photo is always on the alert so that it can be used again when necessary. A simple keyboard touch is all it takes to disable one wherever the network reaches. Soon, a slight finger movement, a sudden thought, and perhaps even a reflex will narrow life to unidentified but real people (Demir & Özcan, 2021).

Once in the system, there are many possibilities for the attacker. Hackers are among the essential criminals of the virtual environment. In general, abuses such as unauthorized access to information, stealing user accounts, hacking into databases, changing, or stealing data in the system, accessing credit card accounts, harassment, and deception cause serious problems (Eriş, 2009). Worse, if the infiltrator is skilled enough, he can change the data without informing anyone of his existence and leave the system without being noticed. In such a case, no one will have any doubt about the integrity of the data hosted in the system, and the business in question will continue its daily operations with the data whose integrity has been corrupted (Hekim & Başıbüyük, 2013).

The most famous attack on the accessibility of information systems is the "DoS attack." Known as denial-of-service attacks. Such attacks are called Distributed DoS or DDoS attacks, which means Distributed Denial of Service Attacks, and are not easy to investigate. Because DDoS attacks are mainly carried out by malicious software called botnets (bot networks) written for this purpose. Software named botnet is installed on users' computers without being aware of it and only takes action once an instruction is received from the botnet administrator. An American hacker, in line with the demands of Internet advertising companies, downloaded and ran malicious code on the computers of more than 400,000 users and received over 100,000 dollars from these companies in return. The person in question carried out this action through botnet software installed on user computers (Wilson, 2008). As in the botnet example, malicious software is one of the most basic cyber-attack weapons. Using this software, a hacker can infiltrate a computer in another corner of the world and use that computer for cyber-attack purposes (Hekim & Başıbüyük, 2013).

Towards the end of 2013, criminal criminals launched a global attack targeting more than 100 banks worldwide. Nearly $1 billion was lost, called the 'Carbanak' attack. Along with the Carbanak attack, the cyber security methodology in the financial industry has also changed, and the cyber security activities focused on end-user security have revealed the importance of bank network security, such as ATM and money transfer systems, with this crisis. For this reason, in 2015, the Obama government signed the cyber security law. According to the law, financial institutions were allowed to share the cyber security shocks they experienced with the federal government (Johnson, 2016; Akçakanat et al., 2021).

The Stuxnet attack on Iran's nuclear facilities in June 2010 is also crucial in understanding that industrial control systems can be attacked even if they are protected. Another important example is the large-scale DDoS (Distributed Denial of Service) attack in the USA. The attack has been one of the most significant cyber-attacks on IoT devices. On October 21, 2016, it was stated that the attack targeting systems operated by Domain Name System provider Dyn was carried out through a botnet consisting of a large number of devices connected to the Internet, such as printers, IP cameras, home gateways and baby monitors infected with the Mirai malware.

Industry 4.0, the Internet of things (IoT), cloud computing, big data, cyber security, etc. made up with components. It is an industrial revolution. Especially with the increase in Internet speed, data is high-speed from business to business, from customer to business, and from business to customer (Velioglu, 2022). Industry 4.0 is a vision of intelligent factories built with innovative cyber-physical systems. This revolution's primary goals are accelerating production, increasing efficiency, and putting autonomous systems into operation by reducing the workforce. Internet technologies have confronted the practitioners of Industry 4.0 technologies with their unique security and privacy challenges as well as cyber security and data privacy issues (Gönen et al., 2021).

With Industry 4.0 Internet of things technology, many needs such as television, clock, electricity, heater, and water can be commanded over the Internet. Movements, sleep patterns, location information, etc. Devices that recognize much information in areas through their sensors can transmit this information to the devices they are connected to 24 hours a day. For example, thieves who enter the network system of a used smartwatch can quickly learn their usage habits at home and even when they leave the house with the help of location information, they can also commit physical theft based on the information learned in the virtual environment (Ateş & Ateş, 2020).

Dependence on computerized systems brings with it various cyber threats. Cybersecurity risks include the risk of a network data breach and the risk of harming the entire business through activities that rely on open digital connectivity and accessibility. As a result, learning how to deal with cybersecurity risks is critical for an organization (Akçakanat et al., 2021).

Cyberbullying is a form of harassment or intimidation that takes place online or through digital channels. While cyberbullying is commonly associated with children and teenagers, it can also occur in organizations in the public and private sectors. Cyberbullying in organizations can take many forms, including:

*Online harassment* involves sending abusive, threatening, or derogatory messages to an individual or group via email, social media, or other online platforms.

*Spreading rumors and gossip* can involve spreading false or malicious information about an individual, often through social media or online chat forums.

*Cyberstalking* involves using digital technologies to track and monitor an individual's activities, often with the intent of causing fear or distress.

*Doxing:* This involves publishing an individual's personal information online, such as their home address or phone number, without their consent.

*Posting inappropriate content:* This can involve sharing sexually explicit, racist, or other offensive material online, often with the intent of humiliating or degrading an individual.

Cyberbullying in organizations can have severe consequences for both the individual targeted and the organization as a whole. It can lead to decreased productivity, increased absenteeism, staff turnover, and damage to the organization's reputation. Additionally, cyberbullying can have significant mental health consequences for those targeted, including anxiety, depression, and post-traumatic stress disorder.

## Cyber Security Against Cyberbullying

Cyber security is the measures to protect a computer or computer system from unauthorized people or attacks, such as on the Internet (Merriam-Webster, 2021). Cybersecurity stems from cyber risks. The purpose of cybersecurity is to counter the risk of cybersecurity. Cybersecurity risk is the risk of digital systems being damaged by external attacks. Cyber-attacks are the essential element that creates a cyber security threat (Akçakanat et al., 2021). A cyber-attack is an attempt to disrupt, damage, or gain unauthorized access to a computer network, device, or system by using malicious code, techniques, or technologies. Cyber-attacks can come in many forms, including malware, phishing, ransomware, and denial of service attacks. Individuals or organized groups can carry out these attacks and target any individual, business, or government agency with an online presence. The goal of a cyber-attack can vary, but some common objectives include stealing sensitive information, disrupting services, stealing money or resources, or causing damage or destruction to a system. Cyber-attacks can have significant impacts, including financial losses, reputational damage, and even physical harm. Therefore, it is crucial to protect against cyber-attacks through security measures such as strong passwords, regular software updates, and security software.

It is necessary to protect personal data and ensure information security in the digital environment against cyber-attacks through mobile communication environments, social media accounts, emails, and websites (Paçacı, 2014).

In order to manage cyber security threats and breaches, it is necessary to take measures to detect, reduce and prevent them. Information Technologies gain importance in taking precautions against and managing these risks. One of the purposes of the Information Technologies audit is to ensure the compliance and confidentiality of information systems (Akçakanat et al., 2021). Protecting financial and other personal information, including information about customers and suppliers, is becoming increasingly important. According to recent reports on cybersecurity, more than 20% of companies experiencing security breaches experience a significant loss of revenue, reduction in customer numbers, and loss of business opportunities (Rosati et al., 2020).

The malicious use of the Internet causes the spread of cybercrime. Due to the anonymity feature provided by the Internet, it is often difficult or even impossible to identify the perpetrators. Therefore, cyberbullying cannot be prevented even though there are laws that make it a crime (Dilmaç, 2020). The measures to close or block the attacker's account are often ineffective. Facebook, YouTube, and Twitter use expert moderators in different languages to filter the content of attacks. These moderators control the content the accounts share regarding discrimination, violence, and hate speech. Censorship, content removal, moderator control, account blocking, and channel suspension cannot prevent digital violence (Özsungur, 2021). The violence of the virtual world is an extension of the violence in real life. For this reason, the intervention should not be made to virtual reality but to actual reality. The forces of mind, thoughts, and fantasy always filter reality. Since human is violent, their virtual world is also violent (Davies & Hoffman, 2002).

The perfection and enhancement of virtual reality is the conversion of any object or figure to a new image and presenting it to the user on the screen as if it were real (Çakır et al., 2015). People can act as if they are of the opposite sex in their sub-identities, change their age or appearance, and turn into a psychopath in their virtual life from very calm people in real life (Güdüm, 2016). With prolonged and frequent use of virtual and augmented reality systems (VR and AR (XR) systems), there is a risk that people will prioritize the virtual world over the real world. There is a risk of obtaining, using, and sharing personal data with third parties (Wassom, 2014; Madary & Metzinger, 2016; Slater et al., 2020).

## Consequences of Cyberbullying in the Workplace

Cyberbullying is not different from the practice of Workplace Bullying. Individuals who are exposed to cyberbullying are often also bullied face-to-face. The field of cyberbullying in the workplace is expanding day by day. This expansion's widespread use of digital tools is effective in remote working models (Privitera & Campbell, 2009; Oksanen et al., 2020). It has been stated that one out of every five people is exposed to bullying. In the same study, the rate of those exposed to cyberbullying at workplaces in Turkey was 11% (Microsoft, 2022). The emerging workplace cyberbullying phenomenon is accepted as an increasing and essential problem by employees and employers. (D'cruz & Noronha, 2013) Cyberbullying can take many forms of aggressive and threatening behavior in the workplace, such as sending offensive email messages, including insults, personal threats, intimidation, sexual harassment, or other verbal abuse. Hide rumors or unsolicited photos of colleagues on social media spread their shelves, generally in the form of social exclusion (Farley, Coyne, & D'Cruz, 2021; Baruch, 2005; Kowalski et al., 2018).

Cyberbullying can disrupt both the psychological and physical well-being of employees, and it is known that cyberbullying causes stress, mental strain, depression, and absenteeism. In addition, low self-esteem, poor self-confidence, self-hatred, sleep problems, anxiety, anger, depression, irritability, insecurity, doubt, bitterness, difficulty concentrating, chronic fatigue, and various physical problems, as well as suicidal thoughts are commonly reported (Hogh et al., 2011; Kowalski et al., 2018; Snyman & Loh, 2015; Farley et al., 2015). As a result of these psychosomatic disorders, the intention to quit and resign from work becomes more muscular, job satisfaction and performance decrease, and absenteeism increases. (Baruch, 2005; Coyne et al., 2017; Farley et al., 2015; Snyman & Loh, 2015). Studies have shown that bullying, which occurs physically, emotionally, and behaviorally, has a very high cost to the workplace (Nielsen & Einarsen, 2012; Farley et al., 2016). Cyberbullying is also one of the important reasons for the organizational exclusion of the individual.

## Measures To Be Taken Against Cyberbullying in the Workplace

With the beginning of the use of digital technologies, many "cybercrimes" have been created. Theft of bank data, email theft, infiltration of systems and data breaches, and viral attacks are primarily seen in the virtual world (Dilmaç, 2020). The greater the interaction with the cyber world and the prevalence of information technologies, the greater the cyber-attacks. Therefore, necessary measures must be taken to minimize these risks at the technical and organizational levels (Gönen et al., 2021). In addition to the measures to be taken at the organizational level, some measures should be taken against the cyber security risks that may come from the organization's managers, colleagues, and the organization itself. Organizations can take several steps to prevent cyberbullying, including:

*Establishing clear policies:* Organizations should have straightforward policies that prohibit cyberbullying and establish consequences for those who engage in it.

*Educating staff:* All staff should know what constitutes cyberbullying, how to recognize it, and what steps to take if they witness it.

*Encouraging reporting:* Staff should be encouraged to report any cyberbullying to management or HR.

*Investigating complaints:* Organizations should have a transparent process for investigating cyberbullying complaints and taking appropriate action.

*Providing support:* Organizations should support those targeted by cyberbullying, including access to counseling and other resources.

In summary, cyberbullying in organizations is a serious issue that can have significant consequences for both individuals and the organization. By taking proactive steps to prevent cyberbullying and providing support to those affected, organizations can create a safer and more productive workplace for all staff.

In addition to the steps outlined above, there are also several best practices that organizations can follow to help prevent cyberbullying. These include:

*Foster a culture of respect and inclusivity:* Organizations should prioritize creating a workplace culture built on respect and inclusivity, where all staff feels valued and supported.

*Encourage positive behavior:* Organizations can promote online behavior by highlighting positive interactions and recognizing staff who model respectful online conduct.

*Monitor online activity:* Organizations should monitor online activity to ensure that staff complies with company policies and identify any cyberbullying instances.

*Provide training and support:* Organizations should provide training and support to managers and HR staff to ensure that they are equipped to recognize and respond to instances of cyberbullying.

*Stay up to date with technology:* Cyberbullying tactics are constantly evolving, so organizations must stay up-to-date with the latest technologies and strategies for preventing cyberbullying.

By taking these steps, organizations can create a safe, respectful, and supportive workplace for all staff. This can increase job satisfaction, productivity, and overall organizational success. If an organization becomes aware of an instance of cyberbullying, several steps can be taken to address the situation. These steps include:

*Investigate the situation:* The organization should thoroughly investigate the situation to determine the facts and gather any evidence that may be available.

*Support the victim:* The organization should support the victim of cyberbullying, including access to counseling and other resources.

*Take appropriate action:* The organization should take appropriate action based on the investigation results. This may include disciplinary action against the individual who engaged in the cyberbullying, such as suspension or termination of employment.

*Communicate with staff:* The organization should communicate with staff about the situation and its actions to address it. This can help to reinforce the message that cyberbullying will not be tolerated in the workplace.

*Review policies and procedures:* The organization should review its policies and procedures related to cyberbullying to identify any areas that need to be updated or strengthened.

In summary, cyberbullying in organizations is a serious issue that requires a proactive and comprehensive approach to prevention and response. By fostering a culture of respect and inclusivity, providing education and support to staff, and taking appropriate action when cyberbullying occurs, organizations can create a safe, supportive, and productive workplace for all staff.

The extent of the interest in the Internet and digitalization has paved the way for the development and diversification of digital technologies. Spatial technologies such as Web 3.0, Virtual Reality (VR), and Augmented Reality (AR) have begun to provide innovative digital products and services. In terms of institutions, they have become the channels where new business models can be implemented (Mystakidis, 2022). While business models in organizations are mainly implemented with face-to-face interactions, today, many services can be done remotely in virtual environments (Atabay & Aytekin, 2022; Ripeanu et al., 2008). Shared business environments are increasing, regardless of being tied to a physical space. Organizations can offer their services to customers at any time with information technologies. New forms of crime and bullying are emerging in environments where the number of remote workers is increasing. Satellite centers (satellite offices), neighboring work centers, hybrid work, and mobile work are commonly mentioned as atypical work styles, which is a contemporary working method (Kurland & Bailey, 1999, 54; Tutar, 2007). In flexible work, the work does not have a specific time (overtime), and it is possible to do the work at any time or to postpone it. This flexibility, on the one hand, provides freedom of movement to the employees; on the other hand, it can create slack. This perception of idleness and extreme flexibility may lead to the emergence of new workplace crimes.

## CONCLUSION

In conclusion, cyberbullying in organizations is a serious issue that can have significant negative effects on both individuals and the organization. It can damage the mental health and well-being of employees, decrease productivity, and harm the organization's reputation. To prevent cyberbullying in the workplace, organizations should have clear policies and guidelines in place, provide training and education to employees, establish reporting mechanisms, and take appropriate action against perpetrators. It is also essential for organizations to foster a positive work culture that values respect, empathy, and inclusivity. By addressing cyberbullying in the workplace, organizations can create a safer and healthier work environment that benefits everyone. Furthermore, addressing cyberbullying in organizations requires a collective effort from all stakeholders, including employees, managers, and leadership. Employees should be aware of the impact of their online behavior and treat their colleagues with respect and empathy. Managers should provide support to employees who are experiencing cyberbullying and take appropriate measures to address the issue. Leadership should prioritize the well-being of employees and create a culture of transparency and accountability.

In today's digital age, cyberbullying is a growing concern for organizations. By recognizing the importance of addressing cyberbullying and taking proactive steps to prevent it, organizations can create a safer and more inclusive workplace for their employees. Ultimately, this can lead to a more positive work environment, increased productivity, and a stronger organization. It's important to note that cyberbullying can have serious legal and financial consequences for organizations, especially if they fail to take appropriate action. Lawsuits, loss of reputation, and loss of customers are just some of the potential consequences of not addressing cyberbullying in the workplace. Therefore, it's in the best interest of organizations to have a comprehensive anti-cyberbullying policy in place and to enforce it consistently. In conclusion, organizations have a responsibility to create a safe and inclusive work environment free from cyberbullying. By taking proactive steps to prevent cyberbullying and responding appropriately when it occurs, organizations can ensure that their employees feel valued, respected, and supported. This, in turn, can lead to a happier and more productive workforce, which benefits both the employees and the organization.

In conclusion, cyberbullying in organizations is a complex issue that requires a multifaceted approach to address. By implementing clear policies and guidelines, providing training and education for employees, promoting a positive workplace culture, and staying up to date on new forms of cyberbullying, organizations can create a safe and inclusive work environment that values and supports all employees. Additionally, it's important to recognize that cyberbullying can have legal implications for organizations. If an employee is being harassed or bullied online by a colleague, it can potentially lead to legal action against the organization if they do not take appropriate measures to address the situation. Therefore, organizations must ensure that they comply with local laws and regulations related to cyberbullying and harassment in the workplace. Finally, it's worth noting that addressing cyberbullying in organizations is not only the right thing to do, but it also makes good business sense. Creating a positive work environment can lead to increased employee morale, higher productivity, and improved organizational performance. On the other hand, allowing cyberbullying to persist can lead to decreased employee satisfaction, increased turnover, and damage to the organization's reputation. In conclusion, cyberbullying in organizations is a complex and evolving issue that requires a comprehensive approach to address. By implementing effective policies and practices, staying up-to-date on new forms of cyberbullying, addressing the unique challenges faced by different employee groups, ensuring legal compliance, and recognizing the business benefits of a positive work environment, organizations can create a safe and inclusive workplace that benefits everyone.

Organizations must also address the unique challenges faced by different employee groups, ensure legal compliance, and recognize the business benefits of creating a safe and inclusive work environment. By taking a comprehensive approach to address cyberbullying, organizations can create a work environment that values and supports all employees, leading to higher employee morale, increased productivity, and improved organizational performance. In conclusion, cyberbullying in organizations is a serious issue that can have negative impacts on individuals and the organization. It is a complex and evolving problem that requires a multifaceted approach to address. Organizations must prioritize the prevention and address of cyberbullying in the workplace, as it can have severe consequences, not just for the individuals involved, but also for the organization's reputation and productivity. Organizations should take responsibility and recognize the importance of creating a culture of respect, empathy, and inclusivity, while also acknowledging and addressing the evolving nature of cyberbullying in the workplace. By doing so, organizations can foster a positive work environment that benefits everyone.

## FUTURE RESEARCH DIRECTIONS

One area of research that would be valuable to explore is the effectiveness of current organizational policies and interventions to prevent and address cyberbullying. More specifically, studies could investigate whether the current policies and interventions are effective in reducing cyberbullying incidents and mitigating their impact on employees and the organization. Such studies could also explore the factors that contribute to the success or failure of these policies and interventions. Another area of research that could be explored is the role of leadership in addressing cyberbullying in organizations. Studies could examine the extent to which leadership values and practices influence the prevalence of cyberbullying in the workplace. Additionally, the research could investigate the impact of leadership interventions, such as training or coaching, on reducing cyberbullying and promoting a positive work environment. Specifically, studies could examine whether certain groups, such as minorities or women, are more vulnerable to cyberbullying in the workplace, and whether this vulnerability is related to broader issues of workplace discrimination and harassment. Such research could help organizations better understand the unique challenges faced by different employee groups and develop targeted interventions to address cyberbullying and promote diversity and inclusion. Overall, further research is needed to better understand the complex dynamics of cyberbullying in organizations and to identify effective strategies for preventing and addressing it. Additional research could also focus on the impact of cyberbullying on the mental health and well-being of employees. Another area of research that could be explored is the impact of cyberbullying on employee turnover and job satisfaction. While it is logical to assume that cyberbullying would lead to decreased job satisfaction and increased turnover, there is limited research on this topic. Further studies could examine the relationship between cyberbullying and employee retention, as well as the factors that mediate this relationship. Such research could help organizations understand the true costs of cyberbullying and develop targeted interventions to improve employee satisfaction and retention. Finally, future research could also explore the impact of cyberbullying on organizational culture and performance. Studies could examine the extent to which cyberbullying affects organizational climate, employee morale, and productivity. Additionally, the research could investigate the impact of organizational interventions, such as culture change initiatives or employee engagement programs, on reducing cyberbullying and improving organizational performance.

## REFERENCES


Akçakanat, Ö., Özdemir, O., & Mazak, M. (2021). İşletmelerde Siber Güvenlik Riskleri ve Bilgi Teknolojileri Denetimi: Bankaların Siber Güvenlik Uygulamalarının İncelenmesi. *Mehmet Akif Ersoy Üniversitesi Uygulamalı Bilimler Dergisi*, *5*(2), 246–270. doi:10.31200/makuubd.978263

Aksu, Z. U., & Işıklı, Ş. (2019). Teknolojik zehirlenme, semptomları ve teknolojik düzen. *ISophos: Uluslararası Bilişim. Teknoloji ve Felsefe Dergisi*, *2*(2), 57–87.

Anamur, D. D., & Topsakal, T. (2019). Herkesin herkesi gözetlediği toplum: siberuzamda alttan gözetimin farklı inşası olarak siber zorbalık. *İnönü Üniversitesi İletişim Fakültesi Elektronik Dergisi (İNİF E-Dergi)*, *4*(2), 37-58.

Arıcak, O. T. (2011). Siber zorbalık: Gençlerimizi bekleyen yeni tehlike. *Kariyer Penceresi*, *2*(6), 10–12.

Arıcak, O. T., Kınay, H., & Tanrıkulu, T. (2012). Siber zorbalık ölçeğinin ilk psikometrik bulguları. *Hasan Ali Yücel Eğitim Fakültesi Dergisi*, *17*(1), 101–114.

Atabay, E. S., & Aytekin, S. S. (2022). Metaverse: Örgüt kültürünün gelenekselden dijitale evrimi. *Uluslararası İktisadi ve İdari İncelemeler Dergisi*, (36), 21–36.

Ateş, E. C., & Ateş, A. P. (2020). Gençlik-dijital çağ ve suç youth-digital age and crime. *Gençlik ve Dijital Çağ*, *11*.

Ayas, T. & Horzum, M. B. (2013). Rehber öğretmenlerin sanal zorbalık fakındalık düzeyinin çeşitli değişkenlere göre incelenmesi. *Hacettepe Üniversitesi Eğitim Fakültesi Dergisi*, *28*(3), 195-205.

Bakıroğlu, C. T. (2013). Sosyalleşme ve kimlik inşası ekseninde sosyal paylaşım ağları. *Akademik Bilişim*, *13*, 2014.

Barındık, G. (2018). *Dijital şiddet nedir? Teknolojinin yarattığı yeni şiddet alanı.* Indigodergisi. https://indigodergisi.com/2018/11/dijital-siddet-nedir/.

Barrett-Maitland, N., & Lynch, J. (2020). Social media, ethics, and the privacy paradox. C. Kalloniatis & C. Travieso-Gonzales (Ed.), In Security and privacy from a legal, ethical, and technical perspective (p. 49-62). doi:10.5772/intechopen.90906

Baruch, Y. (2005). Bullying on the net: Adverse behaviour on e-mail and its impact. *Information & Management*, *42*(2), 361-371. https://doi.org/. im.2004.02.001. doi:10.1016/j

Bauman, Z., & Lyon, D. (2013). *Liquid surveillance: A conversation*. John Wiley & Sons.

Bayrak, T. (2017). Sosyal medyada dijital etik: Twitter'da şiddet içerikli iletilerin incelenmesi. *Yeni Medya Elektronik Dergisi*, *1*(1), 32–46. doi:10.17932/IAU.EJNM.m.25480200.2017.1/1.32-46

Bayrak, T., & Yengin, D. (2021). *Sanal dünyada yeni şiddet*. Der Yayınları.

Belsey, C. (2004). *Culture and the real: Theorizing cultural criticism*. Routledge. doi:10.4324/9780203001448

Çakır, R., Solak, E., & Tan, S. S. (2015). Artırılmış gerçeklik teknolojisi ile ingilizce kelime öğretiminin öğrenci performansına etkisi. *Gazi Eğitim Bilimleri Dergisi*, *1*(1), 45–58.

Campbell, M. A. (2005). Cyber bullying: An old problem in a new guise? *Australian Journal of Guidance & Counselling, 15*(1), 68–76. doi:10.1375/ajgc.15.1.68

Castells, M. (2004). *The network society: A cross-cultural perspective.* Edward Elgar Publishing, Incorporated., doi:10.4337/9781845421663

Castells, M. (2005). *Enformasyon çağı: Ekonomi, toplum ve kültür birinci cilt ağ toplumunun yükselişi* 1. Çev: Kılıç, E.) İstanbul Bilgi Üniversitesi Yayınları.

Çelik, E. (2018). İnternet ortamındaki şiddet sunumları ve yol açtığı sosyal travmalar. *Çağdaş Yönetim Bilimleri Dergisi, 5*(3), 280-296.

Çiftçi, H. (2015). Lise öğrencilerinin siber zorbalık eğilimlerinin facebook tutumu ile ilişkisinin incelenmesi. (Yüksek Lisans Tezi). Marmara Üniversitesi, İstanbul.

Couldry, N. (2002). *The place of media power: Pilgrims and witnesses of the media age.* Routledge. doi:10.4324/9780203007624

Coyne, I., Farley, S., Axtell, C., Sprigg, C., Best, L., & Kwok, O. (2017). Understanding the relationship between experiencing workplace cyberbullying, employee mental strain and job satisfaction: A dysempowerment approach. *International Journal of Human Resource Management, 28*(7), 945–972. doi:10.1080/09585192.2015.1116454

D'cruz, P., & Noronha, E. (2013). Navigating the extended reach: Target experiences of cyberbullying at work. *Information and Organization, 23*(4), 324–343. doi:10.1016/j.infoandorg.2013.09.001

Davies, T. N., & Hoffman, D. D. (2002). Reality check: Insights from cognitive science. *Topic, 1*(2), 102–105.

Demir, S. T., & Özcan, A. (2021). Sosyal medya ve linç kültürü: Sanal nedenler gerçek sonuçlar. *İletişim Kuram ve Araştırma Dergisi, 56*, 1-15. . doi:10.47998/ikad.957544

Dilmaç, J. A. (2020). Dijital ortamda sapkınlık: siber zorbalık, *Turkish Studies - Social, 15*(3), 1087-1099. . doi:10.29228/TurkishStudies.39895

Ergeç, N. E., & Zateri, İ. (2020). Toplumsal cinsiyet ve sosyal ağların şiddeti çoğaltan etkisi. *Çukurova Üniversitesi Sosyal Bilimler Enstitüsü Dergisi, 29*(1), 102-117.

Eriş, U. (2009). *Türkiye'de Kırıcı (Hacker) Kültürü.* Yayınlanmamış Doktora Tezi, Anadolu Üniversitesi Sosyal Bilimler Enstitüsü.

Farley, S., Coyne, I., Axtell, C., & Sprigg, C. (2016). Design, development, and validation of a workplace cyberbullying measure, the WCM. *Work and Stress, 30*(4), 293–317. doi:10.1080/02678373.2016.1255998

Farley, S., Coyne, I., & D'Cruz, P. (2021). Cyberbullying at Work: Understanding the Influence of Technology. In P. D'Cruz, E. Noronha, G. Notelaers, & C. Rayner (Eds.), *Concepts, Approaches and Methods. Handbooks of Workplace Bullying, Emotional Abuse and Harassment* (Vol. 1). Springer., doi:10.1007/978-981-13-0134-6_8

Farley, S., Coyne, I., Sprigg, C., Axtell, C., & Subramanian, G. (2015). Exploring the impact of workplace cyberbullying on trainee doctors. *Medical Education*, *49*(4), 436–443. doi:10.1111/medu.12666 PMID:25800304

Gönen, S., Yılmaz, E. N., Şanoğlu, S., Karacayılmaz, G., & Özbirinci, Ö. (2021). Endüstri 4.0'ın gelişim sürecinde unutulan bileşen: Siber güvenlik. *Düzce Üniversitesi Bilim ve Teknoloji Dergisi*, *9*(4), 1142–1158. doi:10.29130/dubited.905340

Güdüm, S. (2016). Sanal yaşamlar ve bilgisayar oyunlarında pazarlanan şiddet. *Journal of International Social Research*, *9*(42), 1986. doi:10.17719/jisr.20164216306

Günüç, S. (2012). *Sanal toplumda birlikte yaşama kültürü*. Anadolu Üniversitesi Paper. https://www.researchgate. net/publication/299431040

Hekim, H., & Başıbüyük, O. (2013). Siber suçlar ve Türkiye'nin siber güvenlik politikalari. *Uluslararası Güvenlik ve Terörizm Dergisi*, *4*(2), 135–158.

Hogh, A., Mikkelsen, E. G., & Hansen, A. M. (2011). Individual consequences of workplace bullying/mobbing (Chapter 4). In S. Einarsen, H. Hoel, D. Zapf, C. L. Cooper (Ed.) Bullying and harassment in the workplace: Developments in theory, research, and practice, 107, 128. doi:10.1201/EBK1439804896-7

Johnson, A. L. (2016). Cybersecurity for financial institutions: The integral role of information sharing in cyber-attack mitigation. *N.C. Banking Inst.*, *20*(1), 277–310.

Karaca, M., Mutlu, T., & Gencer, G. (2021). Siber mağduriyet: Kavramsal bir çalışma. *Anadolu Akademi Sosyal Bilimler Dergisi*, *3*(1), 177–191.

Kavuk, M. (2011). İlköğretim öğrencilerinin sanal zorba ve sanal kurban olma durumlarının incelenmesi. (Yayınlanmamış yüksek lisans tezi). Ankara Üniversitesi, Ankara.

Kowalski, R. M., & Limber, S. P. (2007). Electronic bullying among middle school students. *The Journal of Adolescent Health*, *41*(6), S22–S30. doi:10.1016/j.jadohealth.2007.08.017 PMID:18047942

Kowalski, R. M., Toth, A., & Morgan, M. (2018). Bullying and cyberbullying in adulthood and the workplace. *The Journal of Social Psychology*, *158*(1), 64–81. doi:10.1080/00224545.2017.1302402 PMID:28402201

Kurland, N. B., & Bailey, D. E. (1999). The advantages and challenges of working here, there, anywhere, and anytime. *Organizational Dynamics*, *28*(2), 53–68. doi:10.1016/S0090-2616(00)80016-9

Li, Q. (2006). Cyberbullying in schools: A Research of gender differences. *School Psychology International*, *27*(2), 157–170. doi:10.1177/0143034306064547

Madary, M., & Metzinger, T. (2016). Real virtuality: A code of ethical conduct recommendations for good scientific practice and the consumers of VR technology. *Frontiers in Robotics and AI*, *3*, 3. doi:10.3389/frobt.2016.00003

Michaud, Y. (1986). *Şiddet (Çev.: Cem Muhtaroğlu)*. Iletişim Yayınları.

Microsoft. (2022). *Civility, safety & interaction online: Turkey*. Microsoft. https://www.microsoft.com/en-us/digital-skills/digital-civility?activetab=dci_reports:primaryr4

Mystakidis, S. (2022). Metaverse. *Encyclopedia*, *2*(1), 486–497. doi:10.3390/encyclopedia2010031

Nielsen, M. B., & Einarsen, S. (2012). Outcomes of exposure to workplace bullying: A meta-analytic review. *Work and Stress*, *26*(4), 309–332. doi:10.1080/02678373.2012.734709

NIST. (2021). *Erişim tarihi*. NIST. https://csrc.nist.gov/glossary/term/cybersecurity

Oksanen, A., Oksa, R., Savela, N., Kaakinen, M., & Ellonen, N. (2020). Cyberbullying victimization at work: Social media identity bubble approach. *Computers in Human Behavior*, *109*, 106363. doi:10.1016/j.chb.2020.106363

Olweus, D. (2003). A profile of bullying at school. *Educational Leadership*, *60*(6), 12–17.

Özmen, Ş. Y. (2018). Dijital şiddet, siber zorbalık ve yeni medya okuryazarlığı üzerine bir değerlendirme. *Journal of International Social Research*, *11*(61), 958–966. doi:10.17719/jisr.2018.2989

Özsungur, F. (2021). Strategic social work management in digital violence against women. *Toplum ve Sosyal Hizmet*, *32*(2), 661–687. doi:10.33417/tsh.836215

Paçacı, İ. (2014). Elektronik iletişim çağı ve oluş (turul) makta olan yeni (!) toplum düzeni üzerinde küresel toplum mühendisliği etkisi. *Marmara İletişim Dergisi*, (21), 19–55. doi:10.17829/midr.20142110297

Pellegrini, A. D., & Bartini, M. (2000). A longitudinal study of bullying, victimization, and peer affiliation during the transition from primary school to middle school. *American Educational Research Journal*, *37*(3), 699–725. doi:10.3102/00028312037003699

Privitera, C., & Campbell, M. A. (2009). Cyberbullying: The new face of workplace bullying? *Cyberpsychology & Behavior*, *12*(4), 395–400. doi:10.1089/cpb.2009.0025 PMID:19594381

Ridings, C. M., Gefen, D., & Arinze, B. (2002). Some antecedents and effects of trust in virtual communities. *The Journal of Strategic Information Systems*, *11*(3-4), 271–295. doi:10.1016/S0963-8687(02)00021-5

Rigby, K. (2011). What can schools do about cases of bullying? *Pastoral Care in Education*, *29*(4), 273–285. doi:10.1080/02643944.2011.626068

Ripeanu, M., Singh, M. P., & Vazhkudai, S. S. (2008). Virtual organizations [guest editors' introduction]. *IEEE Internet Computing*, *12*(2), 10–12. doi:10.1109/MIC.2008.48

Rosati, P., Gogolin, F., & Lynn, T. (2020). Cyber-security incidents and audit quality. *European Accounting Review*, 1–28. doi:10.1080/09638180.2020.1856162

Sarak, Ö. (2012). Lise öğrencilerinde sanal zorbalık. (Yüksek Lisans Tezi), Haliç Üniversitesi, İstanbul.

Slater, M., Gonzalez-Liencres, C., Haggard, P., Vinkers, C., Gregory-Clarke, R., Jelley, S., Watson, Z., Breen, G., Schwarz, R., Steptoe, W., Szostak, D., Halan, S., Fox, D., & Silver, J. (2020). The ethics of realism in virtual and augmented reality. *Frontiers in Virtual Reality*, *1*, 1. doi:10.3389/frvir.2020.00001

Smith, P. K., Mahdavi, J., Carvalho, M., & Tippett, N. (2008). An investigation into cyberbullying, its forms, awareness and impact, and the relationship between age and gender in cyberbullying. (A Report to the Anti-Bullying Alliance). Family Studies, Goldsmiths College, University of London.

Snyman, R., & Loh, J. M. (2015). Cyberbullying at work: The mediating role of optimism between cyberbullying and job outcomes. *Computers in Human Behavior, 53*, 161–168. doi:10.1016/j.chb.2015.06.050

Strom, P. S., & Strom, R. D. (2005). When teens turn cyberbullies. *Education Digest, 71*(4), 35.

Tarter, A. (2017). Importance of cyber security. In P. Saskia Bayer, R. Karlovic, B. Akhgar, & G. Markarian (Eds.), *Community policing-A European perspective* (pp. 213–230). Springer., doi:10.1007/978-3-319-53396-4_15

Thompson, J. B. (1995). *The media and modernity: A social theory of the media.* Stanford University Press.

Turan, S. G., & Dilmen, N. E. (2016). Bilişim okuryazarlığı bağlamında siber şiddetin meşrulaştırılması. *Yeni Symposium,* 54(3), 25-29.

Tutar, H. (2007). Katı Olan Her "İş" Sanallaşıyor veya İşgörenin Artan Yalnızlığı Üzerine: Kuramsal Bir Yaklaşım. *ISGUC The Journal of Industrial Relations and Human Resources, 9*(2), 116–141.

Velioğlu, H. (2022). Endüstri 4.0 bağlamında siber güvenlik ile finansal tablolara ilişkin görüş oluşturma ve raporlama arasındaki ilişki. H. Şimşek, & M. Cihangir (Ed.) Değişim ve Geleceği Yönetmek. Holistence Publications.

Wassom, B. (2014). *Augmented Reality Law, Privacy, and Ethics: Law, Society, and Emerging AR Technologies.* Syngress., doi:10.1016/B978-0-12-800208-7.00003-X

Willard, N. (2007). *Cyberbullying and cyberthreats.* Research Press.

Wilson, C. (2008). *Botnets, cybercrime, and cyberterrorism: Vulnerabilities and policy issues for congress.* CRS Report for Congress.

Yalçın, C. (2003). Sosyolojik Bir Bakış Açısıyla İnternet. *Cumhuriyet Üniversitesi Edebiyat Fakültesi Sosyal Bilimler Dergisi, 27*(1), 77–89.

## ADDITIONAL READING

Chen, Q., Chan, K. L., Guo, S., Chen, M., Lo, C. K. M., & Ip, P. (2022). Effectiveness of digital health interventions in reducing bullying and cyberbullying: A meta-analysis. *Trauma, Violence & Abuse,* 15248380221082090. doi:10.1177/15248380221082090 PMID:35446724

Choi, Y. (2018). A study on the prevention of cyberbullying in workplaces. *International Journal of Technoethics, 9*(1), 18–26. doi:10.4018/IJT.2018010102

D'Cruz, D., & Noronha, E. (2013). Navigating the extended reach: Target experiences of cyberbullying at work. *Information and Organization, 23*(4), 324–343. doi:10.1016/j.infoandorg.2013.09.001

Forssell, R. (2016). Exploring cyberbullying and face-to-face bullying in working life–Prevalence, targets and expressions. *Computers in Human Behavior, 58*, 454–460. doi:10.1016/j.chb.2016.01.003

Gardner, D., O'Driscoll, M., Cooper-Thomas, H. D., Roche, M., Bentley, T., Catley, B., Teo, S., & Trenberth, L. (2016). Predictors of workplace bullying and cyber-bullying in New Zealand. *International Journal of Environmental Research and Public Health, 13*(5), 448–459. doi:10.3390/ijerph13050448 PMID:27128929

Keskin, H., Akgün, A. E., Ayar, H., & Kayman, Ş. S. (2016). Cyberbullying victimization, counterproductive work behaviours and emotional intelligence at workplace. *Procedia: Social and Behavioral Sciences, 235*, 281–287. doi:10.1016/j.sbspro.2016.11.031

Muhonen, T., Jönsson, S., & Bäckström, M. (2017). Consequences of cyberbullying behaviour in working life: The mediating roles of social support and social organisational climate. *International Journal of Workplace Health Management, 10*(5), 376–390. doi:10.1108/IJWHM-10-2016-0075 PMID:29721038

Vismara, M., Girone, N., Conti, D., Nicolini, G., & Dell'Osso, B. (2022). The current status of Cyberbullying research: A short review of the literature. *Current Opinion in Behavioral Sciences, 46*, 101152. doi:10.1016/j.cobeha.2022.101152

Vranjes, I., Baillien, E., Vandebosch, H., Erreygers, S., & De Witte, H. (2018). When workplace bullying goes online: Construction and validation of the Inventory of Cyberbullying Acts at Work (ICA-W). *European Journal of Work and Organizational Psychology, 27*(1), 28–39. doi:10.1080/1359432X.2017.1363185

Wang, Y. (2022). Understanding the role of social factors in cyberbullying at work. *Computers in Human Behavior, 134*, 107325. doi:10.1016/j.chb.2022.107325

Welsh, A., & Lavoie, J. A. (2012). Risky eBusiness: An examination of risk-taking, online disclosiveness, and cyberstalking victimization. *Cyberpsychology (Brno), 6*(1), 1–13. doi:10.5817/CP2012-1-4

Williams, M. L., Levi, M., Burnap, P., & Gundur, R. V. (2019). Under the corporate radar: Examining insider business cybercrime victimization through an application of routine activities theory. *Deviant Behavior, 40*(9), 1119–1131. doi:10.1080/01639625.2018.1461786

Zhang, S., Leidner, D., Cao, X., & Liu, N. (2022). Workplace cyberbullying: A criminological and routine activity perspective. *Journal of Information Technology, 37*(1), 51–79. doi:10.1177/02683962211027888

Zhang, S., & Leidner, D. E. (2018). From improper to acceptable: How perpetrators neutralize workplace bullying behaviors in the cyber world. *Information & Management, 55*(7), 850–865. doi:10.1016/j.im.2018.03.012

## KEY TERMS AND DEFINITIONS

**Cyber:** Including Internet and computer.

**Bullying:** In the environment of mutual relations, one's behavior that will cause financial and moral harm to the other.

**Cyberbullying:** Harassment or bullying that occurs through digital channels.

**Digital violence:** The form of violence in the digital environment for the purpose of psychological, sexual, or economic attack.

**Cyber-Crime:** Crime resulting from malicious use of the Internet.
**Network society:** new fields of interaction created by technological developments.
**Cyber security:** Society that uses technology as a means of communication in its actions.

# Chapter 13
# Life in the Digital World

**Tolga Karadas**
*Sivas Cumhuriyet University, Turkey*

**Tuncay Dilci**
*Sivas Cumhuriyet University, Turkey*

**Nuray Özge Sagbas**
*Ministry of National Education, Turkey*

## ABSTRACT

*For millions of years, mankind has made countless inventions and discoveries. These inventions are basically designed to facilitate humanity's life and serve humanity. So much so that at the cutting edge of technology, there are devices or virtual environments that can listen to people, talk to them, guide them, communicate with them, read, calculate, remember, remind, play, and do many other things on their behalf. Developments that have completely changed people's living habits have brought along many positive and negative developments. With the development of technology, the most widely used technological development is digital objects and virtual environments. Due to the existence of these objects and environments and the possibilities, diversity, and audiovisual richness they offer to people, many of them have deeply affected our perception of life and lifestyle. The basis of these effects is dependent on these devices and environments.*

## INTRODUCTION

For millions of years, mankind has made countless inventions and discoveries. These inventions are basically designed to facilitate humanity's life and serve humanity. So much so that at the cutting edge of technology, there are devices or virtual environments that can listen to people, talk to them, guide them, communicate with them, read, calculate, remember, remind, play and do many other things on their behalf. Developments that have completely changed people's living habits have brought along many positive and negative developments. With the development of technology, the most widely used technological development is digital objects and virtual environments. Due to the existence of these objects and environments and the possibilities, diversity, and audiovisual richness they offer to people, many of them

DOI: 10.4018/978-1-6684-8397-8.ch013

have deeply affected our perception of life and lifestyle. The basis of these effects is dependent on these devices and environments. Users become addicted to digital objects due to factors such as the aimless use of these digital objects and virtual environments, excessive time spent on games and social media, and the search for entertainment and communication. In the digital-dependent dimension, deviations are observed in people's perceptions, behaviors, and attitudes. In this context, it is necessary to take some precautions for the correct use of digital objects and virtual environments and to develop digital literacy skills. Individuals have a duty to ensure that digital objects and virtual environments do not negatively affect our health and are used in a healthy and conscious manner. Accordingly, in this part of the book, the concepts of technology, digitalization, digital literacy, digital addiction, digital obesity, digital detox, digital diet, and digital minimalism will be introduced. Awareness will be raised, and recommendations will be given for the healthy use of digital objects and virtual environments.

## THE CONCEPT OF TECHNOLOGY

The concept of technology covers all the products obtained as a result of the processing of information in order to increase the welfare of human life. The concept of technology, which is accepted as the 'Science of Craftsmanship', covers all the developments that penetrate every aspect of our lives. When it comes to technology, all kinds of tools ranging from tools produced to collect invisible dust falling on carpets in our homes to all kinds of materials that will help in the exploration of other planets by going outside the atmosphere are included in the scope. The common feature of all technologies is that they are first abstractly designed in the mind and then transferred to the material world. Anything that is first designed as an idea in the mind and then brought to life as a product and in a way to serve the purpose can be called technology. In relation to the subject, Batur and Uygun (2012) point out that the dictionary meaning of the concept of technology is the processing of information, the processing of raw information with the aim of providing better service to people, the development of the information obtained and the transformation of it into products.

"Man, who was expelled to Earth, is in search of a better life, which must be due to the knowledge of creation that he carries in the depths of his soul" (Günay & Çalık, 2019) . If we associate the life perceptions of human beings with Maslow's hierarchy of needs and consider all the needs such as shelter, nutrition, aesthetics, and sexuality in the journey of human beings to complete themselves by meeting their basic needs, we see that there is a need for a tool to meet each need. When we consider weapon technologies for hunting and survival, kitchen tools for cooking or storing food for nutrition, tools produced for situations that appeal to pleasure, tools produced/developed for aesthetic needs, and needs developing for communication, we reach the conclusion that the concept of technology is parallel to human history.

Productivity in revenue with the use of machines in agriculture, production diversity with the development of machines in industry, information products with printing technology and communication technologies with the development of communication technologies have increased revolutionarily. The development of the mechanical and machine industry with the industrial revolution that started in the West from the simple tools of primitive times has been the biggest turning point of technology. The mechanization that started with the industrial revolution has affected the whole of humanity. In this process, which has changed every area from people's lifestyles to their life goals, technology has evolved from serving humanity to using people in a capitalist sense. The need for raw materials and manpower for the operation of machines has continued to develop by exploiting people in different geographies, so to speak. The increase in mechanization and mechanization with the industrial revolution brought about many ideological perspectives. Gencer (2012) expresses this situation as follows: " Since western man could not bring things that were almost technical into human form, he began to mechanize man, to mechanize the natural".

Technology is perceived as a modernization today. Due to modernization and the capitalist order that has turned into a race for power, technology has ceased to be a tool and has become a goal for people. In order to look modern and powerful, technological devices, tools, and equipments are the desired goals to be reached and owned. In modern urbanization, houses designed with high technological equipment, motor vehicles with technological equipment, smart devices with technological equipment, etc. are the main technology products that are desired to be owned. The Internet technologies and digital technologies, which have entered every environment over time, are also indispensable parts of life.

## The Internet Technology

Internet technology originated with the US's ARPANET (Advanced Research Projects Agency Network) project to provide intelligence and faster transmission of information during wartime. The word itself means inter-network or network of networks. To establish Internet technology, the working group held its first meeting at the Stanford Research Institute in 1968. It was officially established in 1969 with four connections. The working principle of the Internet is based on the Transmission Control Protocol /Internet Protocol (TCP/IP). In a nutshell, the protocol working system IP transmits the data and TCP manages the flow and confirms the data.

TCP/IP is known as a model consisting of an application, transport, Internet, and link layers. TCP is the mechanism that enables the controlled transmission of data by communicating through an IP network. IP is the network system that carries sender/receiver information. We can think of it as addresses written on a letter. In short, it can be expressed as sender and receiver identities. The Internet initially focused on four main applications. These are the 'e-mail' system that allows sending and receiving electronic mail, the 'Remote Login' system that allows users to connect to a remote device and transfer data, the 'File Transfer' file transfer system that allows data to be transferred provided that there are valid accounts in two systems, and the 'Gopher' system, which is similar to the World Wide Web (www) system and older than www.

The biggest share in the development of the Internet technology from being used only for defense purposes to today's popular communication and information organ is the development of the World Wide Web (WWW) technology by Bernard Lee, a researcher working at the European Center for Nuclear Research (CERN - Europe pour la Recherche Nuclearie). WWW technology enables the creation and use of web pages that are different from each other and accessible to everyone. One of the most important contributions of Tim Bernard Lee to the development of Internet technology was the creation of the Hyper Text Markup Language (HTML). This enabled organizations and individuals to develop their own websites.

The Web system has gone through different phases since its inception. Each era of the web has its own characteristics of the Internet technologies. Today, when logging in to Internet Web sites and applications, using them, and generally dealing with information in digital media, we are not in an environment with a fixed structure and function; on the contrary, we are in the context of an environment that changes and evolves in line with technological developments and the needs of Internet users. At this point, we can explain the Web platform generations to date and those that are considered likely to occur in the near future as follows:

Web 1.0: This includes the first period after the discovery of the Internet. In the Web 1.0 period, there is one-way communication with the other computer. What is meant by one-way use is that the user connects to the opposite server and accesses the information on the web page. The Web 1.0 period was not as colorful and animated visually as it is used today. In this period, it was not possible to exchange any information, data, or messages over the network. The development of web technology was driven by the need for information and fast communication. Developments in mutual communication and information transfer led to the development of the next period for web technologies, the web 2.0 period.

Web 2.0: Tim O'Reilly is the first person to use the concept of Web 2.0 and activated the system that is open to interaction, where users can share, and is also one of the founders of 2.0 technology. Web 2.0 technology is an attempt to interpret the business revolution and the rules of this system by ensuring the systematic progress of the Internet. The basic rule to develop Web 2.0 technology is to build programs so that more people can use the network effects. Web 2.0 is the name given to advanced Internet technologies. Web 2.0 technology has ushered in a new era by enabling interaction, data transfers, visual richness, and mobility in a virtual environment. The most important factor in the development of Web 2.0 technology is the need to share information in a fast and interactive way. Web 2.0 has become the Internet technology that makes the transfer of information, saving it on the website and protecting it on the web, providing fast access to information and making web-human interaction even more effective. Web 2.0 technology is, in summary, the era of Internet technology in which Internet and human interaction, the interaction of people in the virtual environment, transfer of information, and file sharing are provided. With the development of Web 2.0 technology, tools such as social media networks and blog sites, where information and interaction increased, started to emerge in this period. In Web 2.0, needs such as electronic mail, mobile applications, and communication were met with the development of technologies such as XML, API, AJAX, RSS, blogs, etc.

Web 3.0: After the Web 2.0 period, when communication and interaction gained importance, it can be said that Web 3.0 technology is more individual-oriented. With the development of Artificial Intelligence technology and its integration into virtual environments, content has started to appear in virtual environments according to the interests and wishes of individuals. In the Web 3.0 era, access to information has become faster and easier compared to previous periods. With Web 3.0 technology, words have gained semantic importance. We can express this situation as semantic tags in web programming. In other words, with the development of Web 3.0 technology, the information on the web is not just words, but also the meanings of words have gained importance. By determining what the information shared on web pages means and what it is trying to tell, search engines will act according to the meaning of the content, according to the person. As a result of the development of this system, browsers will act according to people's previous search content, that is, if you try to access information by typing the same word on three different sites, you may get different results on each site. Because according to your previous searches and the sites you have visited, the search engine will semantically present the information that is most suitable for the user.

Web 4.0: Web 4.0 technology is the name given to the era of technology that is free from local disks and completely transferred to the virtual environment. Without waiting for the Web 3.0 era to spread over many years, the work of 4.0 technology accelerated before the entire technology has been discovered. In Web 4.0 Internet technology, Artificial Intelligence and Augmented Reality developments that offer virtual environments and the real world together come to the fore. This technological development is aimed to develop cloud systems known as data storage areas in virtual environments and to eliminate disks, which are physical storage areas. Today, we see that innovations continue in order to increase digitalization. An example of this is the 'EyeOS online operating system for 'Virtualization'. To use these technologies efficiently, it is important to have a fast Internet connection. Similarly, applications such as G.ho.st, Glide, YouOS, Goowy, DesktopTwo, and WebOS such as Google Docs & Spreads are used for storage and online sharing. These applications can be used by logging in directly from the Internet site without having to install a program on the computer to use them. Through these systems, it is possible to use many different applications such as media players, messaging-communication services, office programs, HTML compilers, file management, calendar and agenda applications, image editing, and e-mail programs through web browsers. The development of Web 4.0 technology and the opportunities it provides have also accelerated the digitalization process.

According to Chen (2021) 's web technology symptoms; the widespread use of information and communication technology has caused people to rapidly adapt to this development and search for information in the virtual environment, and it has become important to increase national competitiveness through technology. The availability of information in the virtual environment, its rapid accessibility, and the increase in the information population lead people to the economic information age. The rapid availability and individualization of information in the virtual environment have also led to a change in people's perceptions of learning. To look at this situation from the other side, accessing reliable information has gained importance. In addition, the search for information in the virtual environment has created the need to update the traditional understanding of education because individuals can access academic and practical information instantly. Learning models and life models have been affected by the development of information technologies. The rapid development of information technology and digitalization will reshape human learning perceptions and styles in the future as it has affected them today.

## DIGITALIZATION

Digitalization can be defined as accessing information and visuals that can be contacted in the virtual environment through any internet-connected computer, smartphone, tablet, etc. digital object, moving almost everything that exists inspired by the real world to virtual environments, and carrying out many transactions such as communication, workflow, commercial activities in virtual environments. The term digitalization is a general expression used to cover the transfer of society and economy to the virtual environment. Digitalization describes the era of the Internet, where information is easily accessible and creativity is more prominent, from the industrial era that developed with analog technologies to the era of digital technologies transferred to virtual environments and the development of digital business areas.

Using visual, auditory, and different methods to convey information tends to be more qualified and permanent through technological devices. Virtual environments contain extremely rich visuals in order to increase economic activities. The fact that it has very rich content in terms of visual and auditory media for the purpose of advertising, promotion, and interaction is effective in conveying information and attracting attention. Virtual environments serve as important tools to keep the presented content in mind. Especially in order to gain superiority in the competitive environment, businesses have to access and process information and present it to the customer in the fastest way. Üzmez and Büyükbeşe (2021) state that technological changes are the determining factors of competition in all sectors and that organizations that cannot provide technological development and change will lag behind their competitors in the market and will have to exit the market in the medium/long term. Technological changes have led to structural changes in all sectors and forced organizations into a restructuring process that requires continuity.

It has become inevitable and even indispensable to adapt to the digital era in order to respond to different needs and requirements. One of the most important elements that come to the fore in the digital era is access to information. Adapting to the period has almost completely changed the understanding of accessing information. The opportunity to access information quickly provided by virtual spaces has become indispensable for individuals. However, while trying to search for positive gains in virtual environments, the invisible or hidden effects of digitalization are reflected in real life. Digital devices and virtual environments were basically created for purposes such as fast access to information and communication, but the enrichment of their content over time negatively shapes individuals' living habits. Internet technology and digital objects, which basically emerged as a tool, are now the purpose. Zakharova et al. similarly state that digital environments have many negative effects on the behavior and consciousness of individuals. When scientific studies on the effects of the Internet and digital objects are examined, it is seen that there are more harms than benefits.

## Impacts of Digitalization

This phenomenon, which is a fact of our lives as digital life, has visibly influenced business areas, social life, lifestyles, education, production, and consumption. At the same time, we see that traditions and values are disappearing in societies under the influence of globalization and digitalization. The effects of digitalization on family environments are violence, miscommunication, ignoring, neglect, lack of cooperation and feeling of isolation, divorce, and similar problems. In individuals, there are negative effects on their lives such as irresponsibility, belief in making money in a short time, procrastination, laziness, pursuit of pleasure, passive affectivity, introversion, academic failure, insomnia, regression in thinking skills, regression in language development, decrease in creativity levels, mental effects such as forgetfulness, fear, physical pain or disorders, dizziness, deterioration of hand-eye coordination and many other effects.

It is possible to see even by careful observation that cyber siege and virtual terrorism practices are being carried out through subliminal messages or signals sent implicitly to the brains of societies in virtual environments. Monetary activities, pleasure culture, and consumption habits, which are the most valid concepts of life, enter the radar of the capital system and make feel their touch on life one by one with these sieges. Dilci, the president of the association for combating digital addiction and a digital addiction expert, summarizes this situation as follows: "In a world order where synthetic human models are experienced, humanity, whose human qualities have been taken away, whose emotions have been rasped, who has fallen into the lap of the consumerist and materialist trend as much as possible, has perhaps never been so impoverished in human terms in any period of history, never faced such spiritual hunger, never been so deeply internalized by the masked trap away from the sincerity of their relationships by moving away from real life."

## Effects of Digitalization on the Individual

The individual is both influencer and influenced by the digitalization process. The digitalization process includes gains that will make life easier and save time, transportation, and manpower. It is the process of transferring real life to the virtual environment. Conveniences such as being able to do banking transactions in minutes without going to a branch or shopping without going to a store are highly accepted by individuals. Applications such as fulfilling entertainment or hobby habits in virtual environments take life habits to different dimensions. The individual has become both the hero and the victim of this process. So, what is being the hero and victim of digitalization?

It is the individual, people, who are the heroes of the digitalization of communication, sharing of information, communication, and other conveniences in life. At the same time, people are the victims of digitalization in the sense that they are heavily affected by this digitalization and become addicted to it. The reason why people are characterized as victims is the effects of the perceptions created in social media on the individual. Another reason for being a victim is that individuals have difficulties about what and how to do without these devices, and even become unable to perform operations without devices. The biggest victims of the internet environment are those who do not experience a sense of success in the real world, do not feel a sense of belonging in the social environment, do not have a specific occupation, and seek what appeals to their tastes in the virtual environment. These are the victims who enter a vicious circle and become more and more dependent on virtual environments. They think that they satisfy themselves with the digital version of everything they cannot get in real life. Therefore, we can see the emergence of terms that are the digital version of almost everything in real life.

Different effects of digitalization on everyone are observed and scientifically stated. The most common effects on individuals are anxiety, stress, depression, communication disorders, asocial life, reluctance, violence, slang language, sleep disorders, inability to focus, aggressive attitudes, negative attitude towards rules, blunting of the imagination, nutritional disorders, social escape, loss of values, academic failure, inability to take responsibility, virtual theft. Although all of these effects may seem to be gathered in one sentence, each of them is a separate and bigger problem than the other.

## Effects of Digitalization on Society

In the reflection of the virtual world, which affects individuals mentally, spiritually, and physically so deeply, reflections will of course also be seen in societies. Commercial and material gains and ease of living are the most visible effects reflected in society. On the other hand, in the commercial sense, especially with the growth of e-commerce volume, workplaces and companies generate huge revenues through digitalization. The process of globalization, in which regional, national, and international businesses are integrated into vast interconnected global economic networks, has led to great strides in international trade. For businesses the Internet that is a major innovation has multiple meanings, and also multiple sources of income for companies. Long economic waves, also called Kondradiev waves, are related to inventions and technologies that change not only production processes but also the way of life.

Most of the things that people come into contact within the virtual environment end up becoming commercial activities. In this regard, it is possible to say that people experience negative teachings by encouraging people to the culture of consumption and rich lives. Behavioral changes and degeneration in ethical behavior in line with what is desired to be seen and owned in virtual environments bring great negative consequences to societies. People who practice their own professions with the idea that they can earn additional income in the virtual environment can appear as someone else in the virtual environment.

Among the positive effects of digitalization are innovations such as communication, information, communication, and data storage. It would be useful not to ignore the situations where it makes life more difficult with the innovations it provides to make life easier. Thanks to digitalization, it has become easier to reach what is beneficial and perhaps even easier to reach what is harmful. Therefore, it will be difficult to compensate for the reflection of easily accessible negative content on society. The more dangerous situation in this regard is that individuals who have intensive contact with virtual environments legitimize situations that are contrary to ethical values and reflect them in their lives. The entertainment industry's use of digital and virtual environments increases the risk of addiction more than ever.

Digital transformation has a great impact on shaping today's society. Rather than stating the positive and positive reflections of this transformation, it should be noted in terms of raising awareness that virtual environments and digital objects should remain only as tools. It should be noted that it is necessary to once again review the damaging and destructive effects of the values that form the identities of societies. It is possible to outline the effects of digitalization as alienating people from society, transforming the traditional structure -in a negative sense-, causing psycho-social problems, decreasing face-to-face communication, imposing the perception that violence can be applied to achieve success and money, content that attributes meanings to genders, perception of neo-orientalism, social depression.

In this context, it is important to increase digital literacy skills in order to protect against the destructive effects of digitalization. Accordingly, each individual, parents, and institutions have a duty on behalf of individual and public health to use virtual media consciously with the awareness of digital diet, digital detox, and digital minimalism.

## DIGITAL LITERACY SKILLS

Digital literacy is the set of knowledge, skills, and understanding that enable critical, creative, discerning, and safe practices when interacting with digital technologies in all aspects of life. Some people associate digital literacy with the functional skills of being able to use a computer or a particular software package effectively. But digital literacy is much more than accessing or using a computer. It is about comprehension, collaboration, staying safe, communicating effectively, cultural and social awareness, and being creative.

The demands of private and government institutions, the service sector and businesses from almost every field are to have online users. For citizens, using digital transactions is becoming a necessity rather than a choice. Digital literacy skills gain importance in order to prevent citizens from being disadvantaged in the networks created by the state. It is imperative to create a society where literacy skills are developed in order to reach the right information in cyber environments, not to be deprived of opportunities, not to be exposed to cyberbullying, to use Internet technologies correctly for their intended purpose, and to avoid damage.

It is necessary for people who are described as digitally literate to have an important life skill in order to internalize and increase the knowledge and skills they have learned. Digital literacy is more than just having technological knowledge. Digital literacy involves combining technology with basic knowledge skills and a wide range of ethical, social, and reflective practices that exist in daily life. For this reason, digital literacy, which means the ability to read digital life correctly, should not be limited to technology-related acquisitions in curricula in general. Digital literacy includes learning how to work a computer as well as having knowledge about computers, learning how to apply knowledge as well as theoretical learning about science. In general, digital literacy is about grasping the skills of using information technologies to acquire, internalize, analyze, synthesize, apply and apply information.

Literacy is traditionally defined as the development of listening, speaking, reading, writing, arithmetic, and thinking skills. The aim of providing individuals with these skills is to enable them to participate in society in an effective and meaningful way, to think actively, to solve problems, to produce products, and to raise learners. The acquisition and development of these skills are also necessary for the health of a digital society. However, these skills are only part of what is needed to achieve digital competence. This is because traditional literacy skills alone are not sufficient to guide the dynamism of society. In this respect, when aiming to develop the concept of digital literacy, it is necessary for individuals to acquire knowledge, skills, value, and attitude sets as a whole.

The concept of digital literacy includes several components. With these concepts, it is aimed to comprehend the information about the digital world and transform it into skills. Each of these components includes information that should be considered in its own field. The components of digital literacy are shown in Figure 1.

The e-safety component includes the ability to stay safe when using any website or application in virtual environments. Staying safe in the virtual environment includes the ability to understand the information that constitutes the correct use and appropriate content on a secure site. Protecting personal information includes the ability to have and apply the knowledge of how to prevent virtual theft. It is

*Figure 1. Components of digital literacy*

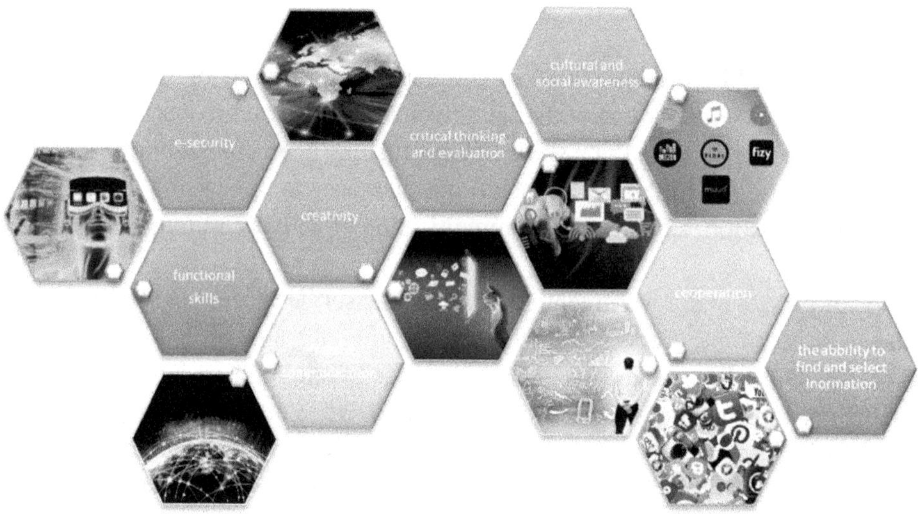


necessary for parents to have the necessary equipment for e-safety so that they can teach their children how to use it correctly. It is predicted that the inclusion of supportive practices in the curriculum in schools will increase the awareness of digital literacy.

The functional skills component includes having or learning technical knowledge about how to use digital objects and virtual environments. In other words, having this knowledge shows having a driver's license that shows competence in the use of virtual environments. Functional skills range from basic technical know-how, such as the use of word processors, browsers, e-mail, and other communication tools, to more advanced abilities and skills required to access and use emerging information resources such as search engines, online databases, and cloud computing systems. It covers the basic technical and content knowledge and application of all computer-based devices. It is an important detail to implement a curriculum in schools in which the use of computers will move from basic use to a more advanced dimension, where students will be able to recognize and use the technology in every aspect. The outcomes taught should also address students' critical and reflective thinking skills.

The creativity component represents the individual's ability to stimulate the imagination, think creatively, present information in different ways, and use technology to create original content. In addition to creating creative products, it also includes the issue of when and how digital technology can support creative thinking and the creative thinking process. Creative thinking in digital life is much more than having artistic talent. It is not only about producing creative content but also about presenting it to the relevant audience in a creative way. In the interaction period offered by Web 4.0 technology, there are unlimited possibilities in terms of visual, text, video, and design.

Communication is the desire to accurately convey the message, thoughts, and ideas to the receiver through the appropriate channel. The importance of digital literacy becomes more evident in the unlimited information presented in the virtual environment. The development of digital literacy skills is necessary to be able to perceive and interact with each message presented in the digital environment correctly. Digital literacy skills include having knowledge about the meaning of the interface of the application, the meaning of the video shared on social media, and being able to interpret this information with critical awareness.

The critical thinking and evaluation component includes the ability to reach conclusions by analyzing the answers to what, how, and why questions asked to digital content. Processing, transforming, analyzing, and synthesizing information or data, in other words, making the content meaningful and reaching a judgment by using reasoning skills to reflect the content of the component. A digitally literate person not only passively receives information or meaning but also questions, analyzes, evaluates, reshapes, and contributes to it. Questioning, matching, interpreting, and evaluating information, rather than passively accepting the information accessed or exposed to, reflects digital literacy.

The cultural and social awareness component reflects the cultures and cultural awareness of societies through the contents created by everyone sharing the digital environment and the interactions with these contents. Cultural and social awareness in digital life means recognizing the creation of content in the digital environment and the social, cultural, social, and historical influences that shape these formations. Cultural heritage shapes individuals' perspectives. Digital life cultural and social life awareness includes the ability to understand individuals' perspectives and to be aware of which digital media are created, how they are used, and how they affect individuals' perspectives.

The collaboration component of digital literacy is the development of the ability to work, create, share, understand, make sense of, and communicate with other digital users. The ability to work in a team is a part of not only human life but also virtual life. The development of this skill refers to the interaction with other people in the name of content creation and content interpretation, discussion, and interpretation.

Finally, the component of finding and selecting knowledge represents the ability to identify what kind of knowledge is needed, to question shared knowledge, and to know where and how to use knowledge. Along with knowledge itself, it is also necessary to question the source of knowledge. The development of skills to understand whether the information is stolen, relevant, valuable, and reliable represents this component. Digital environments present a myriad of information in different forms. Therefore, questioning this information, combining it, comprehending its reliability, and filtering it through critical interpretations involves the development of the ability to select information.

### Digital Literacy Competence Areas

Digital competence relates to the safe and critical use of digital objects and virtual spaces for professional, entertainment, research, and communication purposes. Digital literacy and competence include the basic knowledge of technology, the ability to manage the skills of using and interacting with technology, and the practices and evaluations for the management of content. In this context, digital literacy competency areas and skill classification are presented in Table 1.

## DIGITAL ADDICTION

Digital addiction refers to a harmful dependence on internet-based objects such as smartphones, computers, televisions, PlayStations, Xboxes, etc., and the opportunities offered through these objects. Some psychologists argue that addiction to digital objects and virtual media should be classified similarly to other substance abuse disorders. Symptoms similar to those seen in alcohol, tobacco, and other substance addicts are also seen in digital addicts. What distinguishes digital substance addiction from other substance addictions is that its causes and consequences are different. Studies show that there is a strong correlation between excessive use of digital media and mental health disorders such as depression and anxiety, mental and behavioral disorders, and physical deterioration in people who become addicted.

With the development of digital objects and the Internet technologies, the area of use has expanded, and these devices are always ready to touch us with their mobile features. The Internet and digital technologies have become a tool that has spread over a wide area rather than being used only in certain areas. In addition to the convenience provided by mobile technologies, the use of mobile technologies for entertainment purposes leads to addiction to using digital objects more than necessary. Being digitally addicted is not only spending too much time in these objects or virtual environments but also having difficulty in maintaining vital activities without these objects, exhibiting anxious, nervous, and aggressive attitudes in places where these objects are not present and where there is no internet connection. There is an inverse correlation between the time spent in digital and virtual spaces and real life. As the time spent in these areas increases, the time spent in work, family, and friendships decreases. The direct proportion between digital addiction and anxiety, stress, and depression shows that as the degree of addiction increases, the levels of mood disorders increase.

The use of technology in line with the individual's daily needs constitutes digital connectedness. Technological developments, together with the increase in interaction, appear as a deceptive fantasy and completely dazzle us. Daily activities and needs necessitate the use of the digitized world. For this reason, the individual is categorized as "digitally dependent" on using digital technology. Digital addiction is a behavioral technology addiction fueled by a sense of feeling incomplete. A dependent generation has emerged that does not have a social life outside the internet, feels lonely, differentiated, or asocial when away from mobile devices, closely follows all kinds of applications that occur or develop on the phone, and wants to be informed about all kinds of mobile innovations, meets with friends on social media and creates a new identity for itself on social media.

Every behavior that does not achieve satisfaction and success in real life, someone whose presence is desired to be felt, a sense of success, a search for entertainment, earning, learning desires and needs are all tried to be met in virtual environments, which is a great deception, form the basis of digital addiction.

Some of the symptoms of digital addiction as a behavioral disorder are as follows:

*Table 1. Digital literacy competency domains and skill classification*

| | |
|---|---|
| **Basic technology literacy** | • *Device technical information.*<br>• *Digital hardware information (mouse, keyboard).*<br>• *File and information management.*<br>• *Program and application management.*<br>• *Ability to communicate, email attachment management.*<br>• *Using browsers effectively.*<br>• *Ability to enter and navigate information in online applications.*<br>• *To solve basic problems, use ctrl/alt/delete.* |
| **Information and data literacy** | • *To be able to create and express the necessary information.*<br>• *Access to digital resources and information.*<br>• *To be able to evaluate resource-need matching.*<br>• *Control, organize and store digital content.*<br>• *Accessing, learning, questioning, and evaluating visual and auditory information other than written information.*<br>• *Effective communication management.*<br>• *Creating a personal website.* |
| **Communication and cooperation** | • *Communication, sharing, and interaction.*<br>• *Participate in social activities through digital technologies.*<br>• *Collaboration in digital spaces.*<br>• *Knowing, comprehending, and applying virtual ethics rules.*<br>• *Creating and protecting virtual identity and reputation.*<br>• *To be able to act with the awareness of cultural qualities in virtual communication and interaction.*<br>• *Preparing slides using PowerPoint, managing media, and presenting information.* |
| **Internet literacy skills** | • *Ability to choose appropriate content.*<br>• *Distinguish between irrelevant and redundant information.*<br>• *Problem-solving and project creation.*<br>• *Ability to conduct research, use the right communication channels, and use combinations for task management.*<br>• *Develop and manage virtual content.* |
| **Creating digital content** | • *To be able to have and apply the knowledge of the application of copyright and licenses.*<br>• *Integrate content with existing knowledge and new situations.*<br>• *Knowing how to give instructions in information systems.*<br>• *Developing, managing, and updating digital content.*<br>• *Integrating content into virtual environments.* |
| **Digital security** | • *To be able to protect device security, content security, personal information, and manage privacy in digital environments.*<br>• *Protecting physical, mental, and spiritual health, being aware of digital environments in socialization.*<br>• *Protect personal and family privacy.*<br>• *Adhere to virtual community ethics, protect the environment.*<br>• *Maintain health and well-being.*<br>• *Being aware of digital rights and responsibilities.*<br>• *Defining, being aware of, and protecting against cyberbullying.* |
| **Problem-solving** | • *Ability to determine the current situation, awareness of problem situations.*<br>• *Determining a solution for the solution of the identified problem and solving the problem.*<br>• *Use of digital tools for content and process management.*<br>• *Use digital and virtual tools creatively.*<br>• *Being aware of the level of digital competence.*<br>• *Keeping up with the digital transformation.* |

- Intense preoccupation with virtual games.
- Experiencing feelings of anxiety and deprivation, sadness, irritability, anxiety, or depression when not in play.
- Increased need to satisfy the urge to play with digital objects and reflection on the above feelings in behavior.
- Unsuccessful attempts to stop playing, aware that too much time is interfering with their daily responsibilities.
- Priority or preference for doing activities is virtual games/digital objects.
- Continuing contact/play despite being aware of the harms.
- Lying about playing time.
- Preferring to play to escape negative emotions, moods, or responsibilities.
- Loneliness.
- Keeping in touch on social media.
- Insomnia/Sleep disorders.
- Academic and social failure.

Some of the symptoms of digital addiction have been mentioned above. However, it is also important to understand the causes and consequences of digital addiction. In terms of digital literacy skills and for preventive purposes, it is necessary to understand these reasons, comprehend the information to prevent possible consequences, and ensure control in practice.

## Causes of Digital Addiction

As it is known, there are many means of entertainment and spending time on virtual media. These are easily accessible areas such as video calls, emojis, gifs, sticker-supported messaging areas, online/offline games, videos, and series/movies. There are many reasons why these spaces have become a center of attraction for almost every age group.

Ciris et al. stated that the reason why high school students become addicted to games is that they want to spend time in virtual games to get away from trouble. A clear understanding and resolution of the word "troubles" mentioned in this statement will help in preventing digital addiction. Since the post-20th century period, when individuality has become more prominent with the development of psychology, a simple homework assignment given in any lesson at school or going to the market to buy bread can be a problem for individuals, while domestic violence, anxiety about the future, asocial life, being in environments where one does not feel belonging, academic failure, economic situations, the desire to be liked, in short, everything that comes from outside, big and small, that needs to struggle in daily life can be perceived as a problem for individuals. Digital objects and social media tools seem to be a very easy escape ramp to get away from situations perceived as distress or daily responsibilities.

Analyzing the above-mentioned 'distress' situations in terms of deprivation, social, performance, impulsivity and self-perceptions will provide a better understanding. Individuals experiencing feelings of deprivation and social isolation may need digital objects and virtual environments for the following reasons:

- Controlling parental attitudes.
- Neglect, oppression, and violence.
- Lack of skills, activities, hobbies.
- Inconsistent and unhealthy relationships.
- Failure to discover oneself.
- Inability to manage emotions.
- Inability to reach love and attention satisfaction.
- Negative role model behaviors.
- Virtual dating to gain acceptance in the circle of friends.
- Peer bullying or pressure.
- Domestic violence, family miscommunication.
- Sense of isolation from society.
- Exclusion, belittlement, feeling of failure, ridicule.
- The desire to look different than you are.
- Not being at peace with oneself.
- Taking refuge in virtual filters.
- Wannabe behaviors.
- Exposure to comparison.
- Failure to manage perceptions of popular culture.

Individuals may want to continue their search in virtual environments for reasons that trigger feelings of deprivation. In addition, experiencing performance and productivity problems are other reasons for turning to digital media. These reasons can be summarized as follows:

- Following certain thoughts and people
- Inadequacy in verbal skills
- Playing too many virtual games
- Playing digital games and using apps instead of creative play
- Passive learning from screens instead of combining information into a product
- Inadequacy of activities to support creative thinking skills.
- Insufficient support for intellectual development
- Being a passive audience in virtual and digital content and being exposed to subliminal content
- Sedentary, passive lifestyle

Learning such behaviors causes deformations in the productivity of the individual. Therefore, an individual who cannot produce may prefer to search for digital objects or virtual environments with the desire to reach satisfaction. Impulsive reasons that lead individuals to digital addiction:

- Irregular living habits.
- Feelings of lack of emotional and social fulfillment.
- Living in a constant race, feeling overwhelmed by being goal-oriented.
- Lack of perception management and getting caught up in the content they are exposed to.

- Unconscious approaches to modern life criteria.
- Pursuing falsehoods that are known to be true.
- The inability to resist digital objects.
- A sense of ownership versus the popularity of digital objects.

The reasons for the self-perception dimension that lead individuals to digital addiction can be summarized as follows:

- Developing phobia against social life.
- Insecure environment understanding.
- Attempts to support ideas and beliefs developed by oneself.
- Desire to be listened to, liked/accepted.
- The desire to communicate, the desire to connect emotionally with people, even virtually.
- Anti-trauma experience.
- Feel a sense of belonging.
- Low self-perception.
- Inability to face the problems of daily life.
- Self-disapproval/perceiving oneself as inadequate.
- Irresponsible personality development.
- Anxiety state disorder.
- Exposure to sexual, emotional, and mental abuse.
- Feeling neglected.
- Communication needs.
- Exposure to physical or emotional violence.

## The Consequences of Digital Addiction

Possible consequences of digital addiction can be categorized under the headings of feelings of deprivation, social isolation, performance/productivity, impulsivity disorders, and problems in self-perception. Accordingly, the possible consequences of the feeling of deprivation can be stated as follows. Irritable behavior is observed in individual. These individuals generally display a restless attitude and have problems reaching the point of satisfaction. Anxiety, depression, and anxiety disorders are observed in individuals. Lack of focus and attention are among very wide seen consequences. These individuals generally appear to have a depressed mood. Digital-addicted individuals have a weakened sense of responsibility and self-regulation skills. Digital-addicted individuals tend to weaken their communication, friendship, and family relationships. As a result of the weakening of these relationships, they will have a problem with belonging and will want to fill the void in virtual environments where they will feel good again. Digitally addicted individuals face problems such as sleep disorders and physical pain that may cause postponement or disruption of responsibilities. Despite all the negative consequences, they are faced with the urge not to break away from virtual environments. They feel all the negative consequences and deprivation that an individual who is sleep deprived and exposed to consequences such as constipation would experience.

In the social isolation dimension, the negative consequences are usually related to poor communication with friends, work, school, and family. These individuals usually prefer to stay away from teamwork and focus on individual work. It is likely to result in negative character development with difficulty in expressing oneself, one's feelings, and thoughts. With the influence of social media and online popular characters, they may exhibit wannabe behaviors and fail to be themselves. The addict with social isolation problems may feel more comfortable communicating with strangers rather than his/her close circle. While being a digital addict creates a socially withdrawn individual who cannot express himself/herself, the inability to express himself/herself often leads to anger and violence. The addict, who feels incomplete, may also be in search of a spouse, a lover who will complete the aspects that they feel incomplete, and may also tend to establish faulty relationships. In the dimension of social isolation, we can say that people avoid confronting their problems. The individual who is uncomfortable with sociability prefers interaction instead of communication. Over time, he/she may become alienated from both his/her close environment and himself/herself, making all his/her relationships and the rest of his/her life difficult. Digitally addicted individuals who experience social deprivation live with expectations that they cannot express but nurture inside. As a result of these expectations not being met, anger, irritability, and alienation result. At the same time, these individuals often feel intense feelings of hatred and resentment.

Digital objects and Internet addiction have a number of negative consequences on the productivity/performance dimension of individuals. The most common and widespread effect is that digitally addicted individuals develop a reluctant attitude toward real-life habits and responsibilities. The working digitally addicted individual is reluctant to go to work and is in constant contact with his/her smartphone in the work environment, which means that this situation will create some negativities in the expected performance in the work environment. Another result seen in digitally addicted individuals is that they are weak in producing a new product or even generating ideas. The weakening of vocabulary in terms of communication results in a weakening in verbal production. They generally exhibit a lazy attitude. Digital addicts who cannot produce products themselves face internal problems such as criticizing others and feeling jealous. Their entrepreneurial skills are completely negatively affected and they gradually evolve towards burnout syndrome. The mental development of these individuals, such as their interpretation skills, inference skills, and ability to reach conclusions, are negatively affected. Digital-addicted individuals feel inadequate over time and want to completely withdraw from society and real life, they appear as individuals who are alienated from society and have a weakened sense of self.

Many negative consequences are seen in the impulsive disorder dimension, which causes deviations and behavioral disorders in the internal process of the individual, where perhaps the heaviest price of digital addiction is paid. Intolerant behaviors, interrupting others in group conversations, unnecessary insistence in line with their wishes, lack of anger control, inability to control reactions, and inability to postpone their wishes are the main impulsive disorders. Obsessive thoughts may be observed in digitally addicted individuals. Appearing restless and depressed moods are common moods. Inconsistencies and lies are seen in their speech. They cannot maintain self-control over the use of digital objects. No matter how much they use digital objects, they claim that they do not use them too much. They exhibit deviant behavioral tendencies in line with sexual impulses. It is seen that digital addicts cannot control their emotions and experience sadness, happiness, and anger at very extreme points. Digital addicts with impulsive disorders want to dominate everyone and everything. They may even resort to violence to get what they want. Narcissistic personality development is observed in digital addicts. They often exhibit violent and aggressive behavior.

Finally, it can be expressed that the negative personality developments of digital addiction towards self-perception as follows: A person with digital addiction wants to stay away from social life and be alone. Being in the internet environment is more important than being in the family environment and being with friends. For the digital addict, life is empty and meaningless. They are insensitive to society, people, and the environment. The only environment they want to be in when they feel in a difficult situation is virtual space. Digital-addicted individuals have a very weak sense of satisfaction. Social values and traditions are meaningless for individuals with a weakened sense of self-perception. The general mood of these individuals is tired, sluggish, stressed, and mood swings. Their moods can change very quickly. The personality development of digital addicts with a weak sense of self perception is passive and they often exhibit sensitive and fragile attitudes.

The results mentioned vary from person to person. While one or more consequences are seen in digital addicts, in individuals with an increased degree of addiction, this situation may cause more severe consequences. In order not to be exposed to even one of these consequences, it is necessary to ensure healthy family communication, to raise conscious individuals in the formation of a healthy society, and to increase the rate of digital literacy.

## DIGITAL OBESITY

The General Directorate of Public Health of the Ministry of Health of the Republic of Turkey identifies obesity as the most important health problem in developed and developing countries. As is known, obesity is a serious nutritional and health problem. It involves the disruption of the balance of fat and weight in the body, especially through excessive consumption of fast food and a sedentary lifestyle. Proper nutrition requires consuming sufficient and balanced amounts of nutrients that will enable people to grow, develop and live healthily for a long time. An obese candidate is a person who consumes much more energy to maintain this balance. Therefore, in case of excessive consumption of foods that are harmful to health, the problem of obesity arises, which will bring many health problems later.

Similar to physical obesity in real life, spending too much time in digital objects and virtual environments means that the individual is exposed to countless stimuli in digital objects and virtual environments. Over time, this leads to addiction, similar to body fat in physical obesity. Just as physical obesity disrupts the biological balance of individuals, digital obesity negatively affects the mental, spiritual and behavioral balance of individuals. "We have greatly increased the channels for the transmission of data and the regulatory frameworks that may require monitoring and/or retention of transmitted data. It is clear that digital obesity - the data explosion - is an urgent problem at both individual and organizational levels" .

Digital obesity encompasses all non-essential digital activities, such as spending too much time on social media, watching TV series/movies or videos in front of a screen all the time, and is a mental health problem like physical obesity. Digital obese people are also digital addicts. Just as treatment methods for physical obesity include a planned and balanced diet in terms of nutrition, activities that will ensure a balanced diet of the soul and mind should be carried out for digital obesity. Natural nutrition methods should be preferred by realizing that feeding the soul and mind in an artificial way is nothing but deteriorating health.

## DIGITAL DETOX

It is not possible to completely stay away from or not use the innovative digital objects and internet technologies that our age offers us, which are designed to make life easier. However, a digital detox is about conscious participation in digitalism by raising awareness of our relationship with internet technology and digital objects and actively rebuilding our role and control in this relationship. We can illustrate this with the example of healthy eating. Just as a person with a stomach disorder consumes certain foods and drinks in moderation, we need to control the digital environments that are good or harmful to us. The aim of digital detox is to minimize the effects of the Internet and digital objects on our lives without severing ties with them. Digital detox seems to be necessary to protect against the harmful effects that cause the degeneration of people and societies for life at the level of quality of life that people who eat regularly and exercise have.

Detoxing requires planning and stability both in terms of physical health and digital health. In this context, it is important to act strategically to take action. The strategies that can be applied in this regard are shown in table 2, which is based on Mirbabaie et al (2022) .

*Table 2. Examples of digital detox strategies covered by literature*

| Focus | Strategy |
|---|---|
| **Emotional-focused strategies (individual)** | Reflecting personal values and mindset<br>Emotion management<br>Mindfulness training |
| **Problem-focused strategies (individual)** | Non-use, withdrawal, and times-outs<br>Job Transition<br>Restricted social media use<br>Use of digital well-being applications<br>Switching to alternatives and offline behaviors<br>Segmentation of work and non-work |
| **Problem-based strategies (organized)** | Top-down regulation of usage behavior (e.g., shut down e-mail servers)<br>Organizational digital detox events<br>Training and support |

As indicated in Table 2, digital detox strategy practices were grouped under two dimensions: personal and organized; and three dimensions: affective-focused, problem-focused, and problem-based strategies. Awareness training, a reflection of personal values, and management of emotions were mentioned for affective-oriented strategies.

The more common reflection of personal values and personal ideas from affective-oriented strategies is in the real world, the less the need for the virtual world will be. Perhaps one of the biggest problems today is that people pretend to listen to each other or talk to each other. In order to overcome this, increasing real communication environments is indicated as a strategy for a digital detox. In addition to this, the topic of managing emotions covers situations in which individuals become emotionally withdrawn, and the effects of each emotion such as irritation, anger, depression, and happiness. Emotions have the biggest impact on how and in which direction our lives evolve. Being aware of and controlling them can help us control our relationship with digital life. Perhaps the most effective digital detox strategy is awareness training. Increasing the level of awareness will be one of the most important methods to use digital objects and virtual environments consciously, properly, and healthily.

Individual problem-oriented strategies are strategies aimed directly at eliminating the problem. In the case of a growing problem, this means stopping use until a normal and rational functional state is attained, and withdrawal from use. However, the strategy of switching to work according to the degree of the problem is a strategy that proposes to engage in real work and plans to move away from the internet by engaging in other work. Another strategy is social media restriction. This restriction can be provided directly by the individual, by someone else, or by digital well-being apps. Returning to alternative offline work is another individual strategy. Addicted individuals often try to get away from the Internet when their responsibilities are disrupted or when they feel inner discomfort, but they are not successful. To prevent relapse, alternative means of occupation may be more effective.

Finally, organizational problem-based strategies include more professional approaches. These strategies include the provision of education and support, organized digital detox events, and a thorough review and reorganization of user behaviors. Digital detox practices can be applied for interventive addiction dimensions or for preventive purposes. The underlying causes of digital addiction should be investigated to solve the problem. Addiction may involve processes that require pharmacotherapy and psychotherapy.

## DIGITAL DIET

Individuals who need a digital diet are naturally digitally obese. Digital obese people who use digital tools for personal, social, and educational purposes are disrupting their responsibilities in sleep, nutrition, social life, and business life and face a number of problems. They have to look for solutions by disrupting real-life requirements and communication breakdowns. The most well-known way of dieting is to eat in a planned way by regulating nutritional values according to the structure of the body. Diet is the act of balancing nutrients in the body. A digital diet is a process of balancing digital object usage habits according to the digital contact habits of the individual.

A person who eats a balanced diet and moves - assuming that he or she does not have a harmful substance addiction - can be characterized as healthy. On the contrary, if a person has an irregular diet and a sedentary lifestyle, health problems are inevitable. In the same way, digital contact habits bring vital problems with aimless use and require an emergency diet. Digital diet can be applied individually or with external support depending on the degree of addiction and usage habits. If the individual has willpower and can stop what is harmful to them, they will treat themselves, but if they cannot resist digital objects, treatment will be required at certain stages. It is very difficult for someone with a device in their pocket that is already connected to the internet to stop themselves. For this, the individual needs to set simple goals that they can achieve and stick to them. However, physical life and tasks should always be prioritized and face-to-face communication should be preferred.

Daniel Sieberg (2011), who brought the concept of digital diet to the agenda with his book of the same name, brought up how to live a balanced life between technology and life with the spread of the internet. Sieberg (2011) also sees dieting as a necessity by stating that the use of digital objects should not be avoided. Prof. Dr. Tuncay Dilci, with his book titled Digital Diet Time, has once again brought to the agenda that digital objects can be used to make life easier, but they should be carried out in a healthy way. Most of the results and suggestions in the research on similar topics support each other. Looking at the Internet usage statistics of research institutions, it is seen that the use of digital technology is very high worldwide. From this point of view, it can be concluded that there is not enough digital diet and the level of digital literacy is very low.

Living connected to digital objects and Internet technologies is an artificial life and a life full of temporary pleasures, far from real life. Naturally, it is imperative to turn to practices that should be done as digital minimalism, digital detox, or digital diet in order to experience real happiness in real life by staying away from being a victim of commercial ambitions and perception operations. The steps towards these are indicated in the conclusion and recommendation section.

## DIGITAL MINIMALISM

The idea of digital minimalism involves situations of controlling and filtering information flows from online communication. The trend of digital minimalism is gaining popularity in business and private life in the sense of using digital technologies effectively and correctly; certain forms of restriction for media presence and media consumption create new terminology for digital culture. Moreover, such digital disconnection creates certain digital behavioral practices and digital norms related to private and business interactions online.

Through digital assets, it becomes easier to connect with people, exchange information, share ideas, and get feedback. The media audience is also proactive with opportunities to choose the content and the amount of media information to be consumed. On the other hand, intense contact and increasing dependency on digital objects and virtual environments pose some problems both online and offline. In addition, information overload leads to a feeling of being overwhelmed, increased distraction, and some emotional problems.

There are many people who support minimalism in all areas of life. First of all, minimalism, which has gradually turned into a lifestyle by advocating the removal of unnecessary details from artistic painting and music, can represent digital health and well-being if it is transformed into a lifestyle for digital objects that surround every moment of our lives today. Digital minimalism as minimal digital contact, minimal social media use, Internet use at certain intervals as needed, and minimal digital communication should become widespread. Minimalism towards digital objects can start with choosing between two devices that serve the same function, but only the one that can do the job without being influenced by popular culture. Today, in developed and developing countries, smartphones, and smart tablets with internet connections mounted on vehicles, televisions, and computers in homes and workplaces are available in every environment. But the will of people is important in how and to what extent they use them. As much as it makes sense to make use of the functional conveniences they provide, it is equally important to use them consciously and minimally enough not to be dependent on them.

## FUTURE RESEARCH AND DIRECTIONS

As mentioned about the importance of developing digital literacy skills, digital literacy programs can be developed and implemented in pilot schools according to age groups. Before the training, a pre-test is applied for the individual's use of digital objects and virtual environments. At the end of the training, it can be observed whether there is a significant difference by applying a final test for people's use of digital objects and virtual environments. Continuous trainings aimed at raising awareness can be planned at workplaces and public education centers for adults. In order to minimize the effects of social platform perceptions that negatively affect the dynamism of society; digital minimalism, digital detox and digital diet applications can be applied planned by training centers with the development of digital literacy skills. According to the results obtained, the door to new studies is opened. It is important to implement these studies by professional trainers to keep individual and social mental health clean.

## CONCLUSION, SOLUTIONS, AND RECOMMENDATIONS

It is necessary to remember that the principle behind the transition from the machine revolution to the Internet age was "to mechanize humans after it became clear that it was impossible to humanize machines" and remind you how dangerous Internet addiction can be. Therefore, suggestions will be shared on how to combat addiction by nourishing the naturalness of human life, the soul, and the brain. Being human is much more than meeting the daily needs of nutrition, shelter, and safety. Being human is not only about meeting the need to eat, but also about nourishing one's thoughts and behaviors. Therefore, they will want to learn. We can see in almost every part of life that any information that is readily available for learning is worthless. Although the Internet seems to be a very easy way to learn, it also prepares the ground for false learning. Social media is the biggest example of this. The posts that artificial intelligence brings us according to their interests deeply affect our behavior. When viewed as areas where even academic, scientific, real, and useful information is distorted and reflected, the consequences of virtual learning and the harms of tacit or implicit information are heavy blows to humanity. Therefore, it should be everyone's primary duty not to fall into the traps of modern technology that harms us, our identity, our thoughts, and everything we have, and to join the mobilization to fight addiction.

In order to combat digital addiction, there are tasks starting from the individual to the highest authorities of the country. Individuals who lead a sufficiently social life are generally successful in human relations and act consciously about spending time with family, work, friends, and even themselves. However, there are solutions for people who have problems with the friendship and friendship they want, or for people who find themselves constantly on digital media for the reasons mentioned in the reasons for digital addiction section.

The strongest link in the fight against digital addiction is the individual himself/herself. By acting consciously about the use of computer and Internet technologies, they can compare the contributions of virtual spaces to themselves by making a comparison based on the question of whether being in virtual spaces is enough for success and satisfaction in order to meet the success and pleasure that should be taken in real life. It should be questioned how necessary it really is for individuals to be in virtual spaces by showing popular content that will enable individuals to be in virtual spaces and gathering them to the screen on similar but different platforms.

- The following activities are recommended to combat addiction due to withdrawal:
- If you are a parent, support your child's initiatives and let him/her do things on his/her own from the autonomy period, support him/her, and help him/her, but do not raise him/her as a ready-made person.
- Honor them by giving them small responsibilities where they can feel a sense of achievement.

- Avoid criticizing them for what they do and structure their communication channels correctly from an early age; listen, understand, explain and guide them, and teach them that they have to bear the consequences of their own decisions.
- Plan nuclear and extended family activities, increase the number of friends' visits and outside activities.
- Be the right role model for the correct and only necessary use of digital objects and Internet spaces.
- Be in control of correct communication in independent uses.
- Ensure that they take responsibility for their own self-care skills by being the right role model.
- Allow them to come together with their peers.
- Allow them to express themselves and make them feel that you understand them.
- Help them gain skills on how to manage their living habits.
- Help the individual to discover themselves outside the virtual space.

Suggestions for social life skills:

- Having digital life habits does not prevent you from making real friends.
- Virtual entertainment spaces will be an attractive obstacle for you to make steady progress in your career advancement and to work towards your goals. Virtual spaces are there to prevent you from succeeding and to take your most valuable time.
- Real friendships that are not acquired in real social life can never be filled by people in virtual environments. In virtual spaces, people can be like fairy tale heroes.
- Outside of school and work, take up a hobby that supports social life in one of the activities that will develop hand skills, artistic or sporting activities.
- Prefer activities that can be done in nature.
- Manually activate controlled and restricted internet connection of smartphones.
- Turn off notifications.
- Engage in self-development activities.
- Do not prioritize school, work, family, and friends. When setting your priorities, always leave virtual entertainment on the back burner.

Recommendations for performance and productivity improvement:

- The most important part of performance development is being active. Do not hesitate to express yourself and make your presence felt by making the right choices about the quality of time and every action taken.
- Do not spend so much time in front of the screen that your thinking skills, speaking skills, and idea-generation skills atrophy over time as a result of being passive in front of the screen.
- Ensure that they take part in activities where their language skills can develop and in environments where their thoughts can be expressed without judgment.

Suggestions for the impulsivity dimension:

- Behavioral therapy and cognitive therapy studies should be conducted.
- Consultations with parents and teachers should be organized.
- Treatment should be based on neuropsychological test results.
- Support their moral development and teach them spiritual values.
- Teach children to be conscious to avoid the feeling of making easy money.
- Build relationships based on mutual trust.
- Forbidding, rewarding, and punishing are not the right and sufficient methods; offer them alternative living habits.
- Take up a hobby or help children take up a hobby.
- Don't let mobile devices manipulate you, know that you are in control of them, and teach your children that these devices exist only to serve you

Suggestions for the self-perception dimension:

- Look for ways to spend time with people and groups instead of avoiding them.
- There may be environments where you will not be accepted, but there is always the right place for you.
- Create common interests together, even if you have nothing in common with other people.
- Identify what you can change and take action.
- Always face the mistakes you have made in the past.
- Listen to people who criticize you and listen to people who lift you up.
- Spend time with people who contribute to you and your life.
- Do not compare yourself with anyone, do not allow yourself to be compared.

We wish you to reach real-life satisfaction by discovering yourself instead of turning to virtual spaces with popular culture and pressure...

## REFERENCES

Batur, Z., & Uygun, K. (2012). Perception of two generations of a concept: Technology. *Usak University Journal of Social Sciences*, *5*(1), 74–88.

Chen, C. (2021). Effects of the application of WebQuest to technology education on business managements students' critical thinking psychology and operation capability. *Contemporary Educational Technology*, *13*(1), ep290. doi:10.30935/cedtech/9320

Ciris, V., Baskonus, T., Kartal, T., & Tasdemir, A. (2022). A study on digital game addictions of adolescents in the Covid-19 pandemic. [JESEH]. *Journal of Education in Science, Environment and Health*, *8*(2), 168–186. doi:10.55549/jeseh.01113707

Dilci, T. (2020). Dijitalim. Aralık, Ankara: Sonçağ Akademi

Dilci, T. (2021). Dijital Diyet Zamanı: Dijital Bağımlılık ve Başa Çıkma, Şubat, Ankara: Sonçağ Akademi.

Gencer, B. (2012). Medeniyet savaşında teknoloji. *Birey ve Toplum*, *2*(4), 7–26.

Gunay, D., & Calık, A. (2019, April). On concepts of innovation, invention, technology, and science. *Journal of University Research*, *2*(1), 1–11.

Karadas, T., & Aglar, C. (2022). Determination of Academic Problems Experienced at the Formal Education High School Level of the Turkish Education System According to the Opinions of Administrators, Teachers, and Students. *Conference: II. International Multidisciplinary Digital Life Congress.* doi:10.13140/RG.2.2.23099.28968

Kazaz, N., Dilci, T., & Karadas, T. (2022). Effects of digital media on education. iJET – Vol. 17(16). doi:10.3991/ijet.v17i16.32181

Martin, T. (2005). Fuzzy sets in the fight against digital obesity. *Fuzzy Sets and Systems*, *156*(3), 411–417. doi:10.1016/j.fss.2005.05.038

Mirbabaie, M., Stieglitz, S., & Marx, J. (2022). Digital detox. *Business & Information Systems Engineering*, *64*(2), 239–246. doi:10.100712599-022-00747-x

Özcan, M., & Keskin, B. (2020). Social transformation in the context of digitalization. *International Journal of Society Researchs*, *16*(29), 2216–2229. doi:10.26466/opus.775748

Payton, S., & Hague, C. (2010). *Digital Literacy in Practice. Case Studies of Primary and Secondary Clasrrooms.* Futurelab Innovation in Education. https://www.nfer.ac.uk/publications/FUTL06/FUTL06casestudies.pdf

Sieberg, D. (2011). *The Digital Diet: The 4-step plan to break your tech addiction and regain balance in your life*. Crown Publishing.

Skivko, M., Korneeva, E., & Kolmykova, M. (2019). Digital minimalism as a leading limitation of media communications in the heyday of digital culture. Advances in Social Science, Education and Humanities Research. In *6th International Conference on Social, economic, and academic leadership (ICSEAL-6-2019).* Research Gate.

Taşel, F. (2020). Dijitalleşmenin ticarete ve ekonomiye etkisi. *Beykoz Akademi*, *8*(2), 127–137. doi:10.14514/BYK.m.26515393.2020.8/2.127-137

Üzmez, S. S. ve Büyükbeşe, T. (2021). Dijitalleşme sürecinde bilgi yönetiminin işletmelerin teknoloji uyumuna etkileri. *BEYDER, 16*(2), 117-127. . doi:10.54860/beyder.1028117

Yengin, D. (2019). Teknoloji bağımlılığı olarak dijital bağımlılık. *The Turkish Online Journal of Design, Art and Communication – TOJDAC, 9*(2), 130-144.

Zakharova, V. A., Chernov, I. V., Nazarenko, T. I., Pavlov, P. V., Lyubchenko, V. S., & Kulikova, V. S. (2020). Social health and environmental behavior of students in the digital age. *Cypriot Journal of Educational Science.*, *15*(5), 1288–1294. doi:10.18844/cjes.v15i5.5167

## ADDITIONAL READING

Brabazon, T. (2012). Time for a digital detox? From information obesity to digital dieting. *Fast Capitalism*, *9*(1), 53–74. doi:10.32855/fcapital.201201.009

Brabazon, T. (2016). *Digital dieting: From information obesity to intellectual fitness*. Routledge. doi:10.4324/9781315577159

Dağıtmaç, M. (2019). Dijital Psikolojik Devrim. MOTTO, Üsküdar, İstanbul.

Dilci, T. (2020). *Dijitalim, Aralık*. Sonçağ Akademi.

Dilci, T. (2020). *Dijital Bağımlılıkla Mücadele Rehberi*. Dijital Yaşam Ar-Ge Eğitim ve Danışmanlık Merkezi.

*Dilci, Tuncay. Dijital Diyet Zamanı: Dijital Bağımlılık ve Başa Çıkma, Şubat*. (2021). Sonçağ Akademi.

Gültekin. (2022). *Mücahit. Algı Yönetimi ve Manipülasyon*. Pınar Yayınları.

Mathews, S. C., McShea, M. J., Hanley, C. L., Ravitz, A., Labrique, A. B., & Cohen, A. B. (2019). Digital health: A path to validation. *NPJ Digital Medicine*, *2*(1), 38. doi:10.103841746-019-0111-3 PMID:31304384

## KEY TERMS AND DEFINITIONS

**Digitalization:** The process of changing data into a digital form that can be easily read and processed by a computer.

**Digital Addiction:** the state of spending too much time in digital objects and virtual environments.

**Digital Diet:** Adopting a healthy digital diet involves spending time away from connected electronic devices and virtual environment.

**Digital Detox:** A digital detox is a period of time when a person voluntarily refrains from using digital devices such as smartphones, computers, and social media platforms.

**Digital Minimalism:** Using digital devices and social media platforms only in need. to use digital objects and virtual environments as little as possible.

# Chapter 14
# The Emerging Psychological Problem of the Digitalized World:
## Pathological Internet Use

**Eliz Volkan**
*Cyprus International University, Cyprus*

**Umut Çıvgın**
*Bursa Technical University, Turkey*

## ABSTRACT

*This chapter mainly aims to shed light on a rather overlooked phenomenon of pathological Internet use (PIU). Due to the rise of the technology, the global internet usage is almost inevitable, yet although it has many benefits, the dependency towards the internet usage (where it is specific or general) is an alarming psychological condition, especially for young adults and adolescents. The disorder and its related problems as well as treatment and intervention options that are evidence-based are reported. The results of treatment-outcome studies underlying the positive effects of CBT for PIU are presented. The necessity of more literature in the related field and the need for an official diagnosis for better understanding of etiology and treatment of PIU is underlined.*

## INTRODUCTION

Human beings adapt and learn their environment through various levels and types of stimulation. Through that, individuals activate their nervous systems and variety of synaptic communications occur that eventually led towards learning and memory formation (Carlson & Birkett, 2021). Stimulation therefore becomes necessary for healthy human development. However, it is shown that pretty much anything that can give you a stimulation, can also trigger adaptive processes when habitual stimulant turns into an obligatory stimulant for an individual (Alavi et al., 2012). Yet, that simple source of stimulation which is

DOI: 10.4018/978-1-6684-8397-8.ch014

needed for healthy development, can turn into a form of impulsive, sequential behavior through repetitive stimulation, hence can form the basis of what is known as an addiction.

Addiction in its simplest form is known to be the dependence on a substance or activity (Widyanto, & McMurran, 2004). It is crucially important to acknowledge the 'activity' part of the prior description as until very recently, it was not very common to conceptualize non-chemical addiction as a form of addiction (mostly because 'non-substance behavioral addiction' was not listed in any of the diagnostic tools like DSM-IV or ICD-10) (Ibid, 2004). However, recently it has been evident that in order to develop an addiction, one does not need to rely on a substance-based source, hence, as mentioned above, any form of activity that can create a stimulation, can in turn cause addiction (i.e.: gambling) (Alavi, et al., 2012). The main issue here is to differentiate between forms of addiction because in 'non-substance related addictions' in other words, behavioral addictions, the individual is known to be either addicted to the behavior, or to the feeling/emotion that one gets after the behavior is completed (Ibid, 2012). As this Chapter is mainly concerned, the non-substance-based addictions such as Internet addiction and the related psychopathologies of it have been loosely studied within the literature (Davis, 2001). Therefore, one of the aims of the current manuscript is to show the relevance of the Internet addictions (as seen by man clinicians (Ibid, 2001)), and to give a through description of both the notion at hand and the intervention methods related to it.

## PATHOLOGICAL INTERNET USE: ITS CAUSES AND PROBLEMS

Related to the previous indications, literature further points out that the behavioral addictions can be formed in two groups: passive (watching TV) or active (playing PlayStation) (Alavi, et al., 2012). Based on that, the main indicator of the addiction and the repetition of the behavior lies within the reinforcement. Regardless whether the behavior is passive or active, it needs to stimulate reinforcement mechanisms in an individual in order to be repeated. This further can be explained by brain-based learning mechanisms (mainly through dopamine and reward circuits of the brain) which will be focused on next, and the learning theories through reinforcement (Watson, 1913; Skinner, 1948).

Considering the importance of prior literature on addiction, the authors believe it is fundamental to also explain some basics of addiction. This is mainly because the neural mechanisms and neurocircuitry involving dopaminergic activation (as addictions are reward based) have often been studied through the lens of substance addictions. However, growing evidence suggests that behavioral addictions (like Pathological Internet Usage/Internet Addiction) are very similar to the substance addictions in terms of phenomenology, comorbidity, genetic contributions, neurobiological background and treatment modalities (incl. psychotherapy as well as psychopharmacological treatments which will further be mentioned) (Grant, Potenza, Weinstein, & Gorelick, 2010). Yet, based on a diagnostic perspective, according to DSM-5 (APA, 2013), the addiction term is associated mainly with substance use disorders (Koob, & Volkow, 2016). It is believed that, the former association was made as drug and other related substance addictions involve loss of control (impulsivity) when the intake is limited, even though the similar notion seems to be the case for the behavioral addictions (Grant, Potenza, Weinstein, & Gorelick, 2010). Moreover, behavioral addictions are further similar to substance-related addictions in terms of the anticipation of the stimulant, as well as the negative affect associated with it when the intake (or use/repetition) of the stimulant is prevented (Ibid, 2010). All in all, based on the recent review of Koob and Volkow (2016), addictions can be understood "as a three-stage, recurring cycle- binge/intoxication, withdrawal/negative affect, and preoccupation/anticipation (craving)- that worsens over time and involves neuroplastic changes in the brain reward, stress and executive function systems." Each of these stages are further associated with a brain region where basal ganglia, amygdala and prefrontal cortex, respectively, are the primary regions (Ibid, 2016). Although it is believed to be similar, related research for behavioral addictions in terms of the associated brain regions (as well as the neurotransmitter and neuromodulator changes) are also encouraged for the further research as the current empirical data is very limited and shows similarities only for gaming and online gaming (Kuss, 2013).

The source of the stimulation further can be versatile ranging from abusing drugs (substance use), to Internet usage. Although Internet has enormous number of advantages and can facilitate individuals' daily lives in many ways, growing number of studies show negative consequences as well, including Internet addiction (IA) (McNicol, & Thorsteinsson, 2017) or pathological Internet usage (PIU). Although both terms are widely used in the related research (hence included in the article) and considered to have the identical meanings (Li, et al., 2015), PIU will be used to explain the notion at hand further in this article as addiction often implies a 'physiological tendency' (Davis, 2001) whereas here the pathological use and/or abuse is the main concern. In its simplest form, PIU is conceptualized as extreme amount of desires or preoccupations that involves Internet and computer usage (Shaw, & Black, 2008). Although PIU (or Internet Addiction Disorder (IAD) in some studies (i.e.: Lozana-Blasco, Robres, & Sanchez, 2022)), is not officially recognized in DSM-5 (APA, 2013) or by WHO (2018) just yet, the known prevalence rates of PIU are reported to be more than 31% in men and over 21% in women (Xin, et al., 2018), hence it is believed and encouraged to be added as an official diagnosis urgently. Priorly, it was suggested PIU would be added to the new category of 'Substance Use and Addictive Disorders' in DSM-5 (APA, 2013) in order to acknowledge the similarities between the substance use disorders and the non-substance and/or behavioral addictions, yet only gambling disorder was the only non-substance addictive disorder added in the DSM-5 (APA, 2013). As PIU is a very well documented and studied form of behavioral addictions, it is suggested once again that the official addition of PIU can aid the diagnostic and treatment procedures both in the fields of clinical practice and research.

Although the exact cause(s) of PIU, like many other addictions is unknown (there are many theories around it based on genetics, biology and behavioral perspectives), it is mostly correlated with risk behaviors, especially in adolescent period (Durkee, et al., 2016) and it is often conceptualized as an impulse-control problem (Carli, et. al, 2013) as mentioned above. The main reason for this is because most of the research related to the area of PIU are correlational studies, hence they lack causation. The current Chapter therefore stresses the importance of carrying out different experimental methods and designs around the PIU to further establish a better understanding in PIU. Moreover, current studies further exhibit that PIU has significant associations with sex (men>women) and that it is more common within the young adults and adolescents (Poli, & Agrimi, 2012; Lozana-Blasco, Robres, & Sanchez, 2022). Additionally, Lozana-Blasco, Robres and Sanchez (2022) mentions the importance of the geographical impact of PIU as well in their meta-analysis, by indicating that Asian countries have the highest prevalence rates.

Here, it is further important to note that even though there are high prevalence rates mentioned above, there are researchers who believe that these numbers may have been exaggerated based on some problematic experimental designs (Grohol, 1999). Hence, one of the pioneer researchers in the field R. A. Davis, in his 2001 publication wanted to shed a light on the notion and distinguished PIU into two different forms: Specific Pathological Internet Use (sPIU) and Generalized Pathological Internet Use (gPIU). In its simplest form sPIU involves content-specific type of Internet usage where the individual is dependent on using Internet for specific purposes such as online-gaming, online stock market, etc. The gPIU on the other hand serves a more generalized purpose for the user and often involve general dependence on checking on e-mails for instance and it often occurs based on the lack of social contact (Davis, 2001). Table 1 below further shows the differences between the two distinct types of PIU.

*Table 1. Differences between sPIU and gPIU*

| Specific PIU (sPIU) | Generalized PIU (gPIU) |
|---|---|
| Dependence on specific function of Internet | Dependence on specific function of Internet |
| Independent of other sources of Internet | Dependent on multiple use of Internet |
| Content-specific | Multidimensional |
| Target specific | No objective |
| Virtual social life is not needed | Virtual social life is desired |

Although it is inevitable to deny the importance of digitalization in our generation, and that it will keep on better influencing individuals for various reasons, it is also fundamental to note the potential possible negative consequences of it as well, where PIU can be one of them. This almost daily increase in the digitalization of the world, will eventually cause a rapid increase in the Internet usage, hence a possible foundation for more PIU, whether it is sPIU or gPIU. In fact, it is further central to mention that considering various types of pathological internet usage (i.e.: Internet gaming, pornography) the way the researchers conceptualize, understand and formulate interventions about the PIU are also expected to differ as the source of the PIU will differ (Wölfling, & Dominick, 2022). So, better evaluation tools, more detailed studies, more awareness, specific intervention techniques as well as potential preventative techniques are encouraged to be studied within the field of PIU. Yet, even though the sources may be different, once an addiction and/or a form of dependence develops, it does have a similar pattern within the way human beings process it, hence it often becomes a health problem and needs to be treated. Therefore, the following chapters will focus on the treatment options and clinical understanding of PIU.

## TREATMENT MODALITIES OF PATHOLOGICAL INTERNET USE

Literature and field practices show that PIU can cause many negative physical, psychological and social dysfunctions (Chou, Condron, & Belland, 2005; Byeon, & Lee, 2007). Especially in the last 15 years, with the developing technology, it is understood that addiction to problematic internet use can also develop. Although diagnostic studies are conducted for some symptom clusters (such as gaming disorder), as stressed earlier on there is no definitive diagnostic classification yet for the PIU. In addition to the diagnostic factors, mental health disorders often coexist with other disorders. It is observed that in addition to the primary diagnosis, treatments are carried out with comorbidities or secondary diagnoses. Hence, it can be said that internet addiction can be a primary diagnosis as well as a co-morbid or secondary diagnosis that attracts attention in treatment (Pies, 2009). In the study conducted by Akın and İskender (2011), the PIU, depression, anxiety, and stress levels of 300 university students were examined. The results of the study revealed that PIU was highly positively associated with depression, anxiety, and stress. It is also stated that other psychological disorders that can be seen together with PIU may adversely affect the prognosis of PIU and in turn adversely affect treatment processes (Ko, Yen, Yen, Chen, & Chen, 2012).

For the diagnostic evaluation and treatment of PIU, it is necessary to differentiate the disorder well. Although there is no certainty regarding the diagnostic criteria, it is also necessary to consider how the purposes of using the Internet shape the disorder. For example, considering the prevalence of internet use in our lives, the internet can be used frequently in both business and personal time periods. Therefore, it is thought that it will be important to include it in the evaluations made for treatment in terms of masking the level of problematic internet use (Young, 2009) or increasing the level of PIU. At this point, the pattern to be considered in terms of evaluation is that the problematic internet use in the individual contains compulsive elements and points to a lack of impulse control. Such an evaluation will be important in terms of proper personalization of the treatment.

As PIU is a newly conceptualized disorder, evaluation and treatment methods are also new. Researchers mention that PIU can appear in many different ways. A recent frequency meta-analysis study showed that the worldwide prevalence of PIU is 7.02% (Pan, Chiu, & Lin, 2020). This prevalence rate is also very important, as it similar to the prevalence rate of another highly researched and official diagnosis of posttraumatic stress disorder (PTSD, prevalence rate is around 7-8%) (APA, 2013). Even this similarity in the prevalence rates alone can show the impact of the PIU and the need for more research and official diagnosis. Moreover, while Aboujaoude and his colleagues stated that PIU started to be seen frequently in America since 2006, they also stated that PIU can have different subcategories such as online sexual activities, online betting games, online games, online shopping, online dating, and instant messaging (Aboujaoude et al. al, 2006; Brand et al., 2022).

As a result, studies on PIU, which is defined and evaluated as a relatively new diagnostic pattern by the diagnostic systems (DSM and ICD), are continuing rapidly (APA, 2013; WHO, 2022). Although it is seen that PIU has many common features with impulse control and other addictions, it is thought that there are remarkable differences in both diagnostic evaluations and treatment processes of the above-mentioned features.

## Types of Treatments

The definition of the disorder further reveals the necessity of developing treatment methods. It is seen that experts working in the field of mental health have developed various treatment protocols. Considering the field applications and the literature, it is understood that these treatments can be psychopharmacological, psychotherapeutic and protocols that combine both methods (Dell'Osso, Hadley, Allen, Baker, Chaplin, & Hollander, 2008; Winkler, Dörsing, Rief, Shen, & Glombiewski, 2013). Therefore, the following parts will explain each of these proposed treatment methods respectively.

### Psychopharmacology

The study of the effects of drugs on mental, emotional and behavioral processes is called psychopharmacology (APA, n.d.). Psychopharmacology, which is a constantly evolving field, is frequently used in the symptomatic treatment of individuals and is sometimes seen as the first line of treatment for many mental disorders (Çetin, & Turgay, 2002; Ensari, Ceylan, Kilinç, & Edge, 2004). When psychopharmacological treatment tools are examined, it is observed that there is no specifically designed drug for the treatment of PIU just yet. However, many scientists in the field are currently working on projects involving drug trials in order to help the patients with PIU, and related case studies and anecdotal reports had been published accordingly.

Studies published so far suggest that substance abuse, gambling disorders and PIU may have a similar neurobiological structure as mentioned above (Charmadese, Leone, Walstra, Janiri, & Guglielmo, 2015). This remarkable neurobiological similarity is attributed to impairment in the reward system. In this system, which is examined on the basis of addiction, taking certain substances or performing certain behaviors cause a very intense and rapid sense of pleasure (complementary pleasure) resulting from the rapid increase of dopamine in the mesolimbic system (Di Chiara, & North, 1992). Therefore, addiction disrupts the normal activity of the dopaminergic cycle (mainly originating and terminating at the ascending mesocorticostriatal dopamine systems (Wise, 2009) and motivational priorities (individuals seek the substance over other needs, or play more online games, or spend more time on Internet over other necessities, etc.) are redefined. Moreover, researchers on the field also examined the brain images of individuals with addiction problems with neuroimaging systems including fMRI and similar techniques. Therefore, it is thought that PIU treatment may be similar to other addictions (Charmadese, Leone, Walstra, Janiri, & Guglielmo, 2015). Yet, even though propositions can be made, conclusions are yet to be drawn as the studies conducted so far have limitations due to both the number of samples and the methods used. Thus, evidence-based pharmacological treatments will be mentioned below, but more experimentation on the related topic is encouraged to better understand the topic.

When looking at psychopharmacological drugs, it is seen that antidepressants, opioid receptor antagonists and mood stabilizers are frequently used for addictions (Foddy, & Savulescu, 2006). This is mainly because previously mentioned phases of addiction (Koob, & Volkow, 2016), involve changes of the neurotransmitter systems involved in the neurocircuitry of addiction stages. For example, the intoxication phase is often associated with an increase in dopamine, whereas the withdrawal phase involves decrease in dopamine (Ibid, 2016). Therefore, the complex system of the neurocircuitry of the neurotransmitter/neuromodulator systems of the brain also changes the context of the applications of the related drugs. Although these drugs, which are often aimed at neurochemical regulation, and serve similar purposes in general, they still have some differences.

To illustrate further, antidepressants for instance are often used for mood disorders (i.e.: most commonly depression). Monoamine oxidase inhibitors (MAOIs), tricyclics, selective serotonin reuptake inhibitors (SSRIs), serotonin-norepinephrine reuptake inhibitors and melatonergic agents are derivatives of antidepressants. Treatments with these drugs, whose effects can be seen rather late, often involve long periods of application (Charmadese, Leone, Walstra, Janiri, & Guglielmo, 2015) yet controlled experimental studies revealed that antidepressants can have beneficial results in treating many forms of addictions. In addition, norepinephrine reuptake inhibitor has been reported to have effective results in smoking cessation (Hughes et al., 2007; Singh et al., 2023). The purpose of the use of antidepressants for PIU is to control the impulse of the SSRI and to reduce compulsive repetition (Grant et al., 2009). Antidepressants for PIU are seen as a group of drugs that provide short-term effects (Charmadese, Leone, Walstra, Janiri, & Guglielmo, 2015). Therefore, more research and controlled experimental trials are needed to further identify the effects of antidepressants on addictions. As it is mentioned above, researchers generally base the treatment mechanism of PIU on impulse control (Bernardi & Pallanti, 2009). Hence, most of the studies can show that PIU decreases with the control of impulsivity. Another group of drugs, in addition to the antidepressants that can be used in the treatment of PIU are Opioid receptor antagonists. These can reduce behavioral cycles by inhibiting dopamine release in the nucleus accumbens and ventral pallidum. Although studies in the related areas are few, it is seen that this group of agents can also be used in treatment (Charmadese, Leone, Walstra, Janiri, & Guglielmo, 2015).

Another type of drug that is frequently used in substance use disorders specifically tackle on mechanisms of Opioid Receptor Antagonists. The most frequently heard ingredients in this group are Naltrexone and Nalmefen (Huang, Li, & Tao, 2010). This group blocks the effects of opioids and alleviates the craving for substances that need to be used (Charmadese, Leone, Walstra, Janiri, & Guglielmo, 2015). The abuse of the active ingredients of the drugs in this group, like the active ingredients in other drugs, is very low. The fact that it does not have strong side effects in terms of side effects can cause it to be used frequently in addiction treatment. Since the mechanism and treatment methods of PIU are developing, researchers generally base the treatment mechanism of PIU on impulse control (Bernardi, & Pallanti, 2009). Most of the studies can show that PIU decreases with the control of impulsivity. Opioid receptor antagonists can reduce behavioral cycles by inhibiting dopamine release in the nucleus accumbens and ventral pallidum. Although studies in this sense are few, it is seen that this group of agents can also be used in treatment (Charmadese, Leone, Walstra, Janiri, & Guglielmo, 2015). Similar to the effects of other active substances, it is understood that Mood Stabilizers (MS) can be used in reducing impulsive behavior for PIU. MS which is generally used for mood disorders, is used to prevent impulsive activity in mood disorders (Di Nicola et al., 2010). Although it is not frequently used in the psychopharmacological treatment of PIU, studies are needed in this area of research.

Antipsychotics include drugs that act on the neurotransmitter systems of dopaminergic and serotonergic pathways (Seeman, 2004). This group of pharmacological drugs is used against the psychotic effects of diseases such as schizophrenia or bipolar disorder (Scherk & Falkai, 2006). Olanzapine, an antipsychotic, appears to be used to control impulsivity in some specific phobias and personality disorders (Barnett, Kramer, Casat, Connor, & Davidson, 2002; Stoffers-Winterling, Storebø, & Lieb, 2020). In this sense, it is understood that there is a positive attitude towards the use of antipsychotics in PIU. However, it is stated that it is necessary to test this with placebo-controlled studies (Charmadese, Leone, Walstra, Janiri, & Guglielmo, 2015).

In a review study, it was examined how various pharmacological factors differ in pathological internet use and other secondary psychological disorders. The results obtained are shared in Table 2. Although the number of participants in the studies examined is relatively small, obtained results can show that treatment agents such as Escitalopram, Bupropion, Naltrexon seem promising in reducing the level of pathological internet disruption (Lukawski, Rusek, & Czuczwar, 2019).

As a result, if pathological internet use is not seen as a secondary diagnosis of another disorder, drugs used as mood stabilizers can be preferred in the treatment of PIU. In addition, if there are depressive symptoms accompanying Internet addiction, another widely used pharmacological intervention involves antidepressants (Arısoy, 2009). On the other hand, the drug "naltrexone" is used as a different psychopharmacological method in virtual addictions (gambling, virtual sex, etc.). It is understood that the aim here is to reduce the frequency of behavior by creating an effect on the reward center in the brain, as used in other addictions (Blum et al., 2000).

*Table 2. Summary of Lukawski and collegues' (2019) study**

| Treatment | Patients | Comorbid disorder | Outcomes |
|---|---|---|---|
| Escitalopram | PIU, Internet gambling addicts | Major depressive disorder (MDD) | Reduction in time spent online, reduction online gambling drive, improvement in MDD |
| Bupropion | Internet gaming addicts | MDD | Reduction in time spent online, decrease in craving for online gaming, improvements in MDD |
| Quetiapine (in combination with citalopram) | Internet addict | No comorbid diagnosis | Reduction in time spent online |
| Naltrexone | Internet sex addict | Obsessive-compulsive disorder (OCD) | Remission from OCD and improvements in depressive symptoms |
| Methyphenidate | Internet gaming addicts | ADHD | Reduction in internet use, improvements in ADHD |

* Łukawski, K., Rusek, M., & Czuczwar, S. J. (2019). Can pharmacotherapy play a role in treating internet addiction disorder? *Expert Opinion on Pharmacotherapy*, *20*(11), 1299-1301.

## Psychotherapy

In addition to psychopharmacological treatments, the psychotherapeutic treatments are frequently used for PIU and related disorders (Wölfling, & Dominick, 2022). When the psychotherapeutic treatments examined, it is seen that classical cognitive behavioral therapy (CBT), group application protocols of CBT, acceptance and commitment therapy (ACT), and positive psychotherapy practices often be used (Khazaei, Khazaei, & Ghanbari, 2017; Twohig, & Crosby, 2010; Winkler, Dörsing, Rief, Shen, & Glombiewski, 2013). When the literature is examined, it is seen that CBT is an evidnece-based treatment method for addictions (Dutra et al., 2008). According to Davis (2001) there are negative cognitions in PIU, as in depression, and accordingly, excessive internet use may occur to compensate for failed areas in life. Thus, it is stated that PIU will be perceived as a rewarding behavior for individuals and may be a problematic strategy for coping with negative emotions. From this point of view, the fact that cognitions and behaviors that develop problem behaviors are at the forefront makes CBT more remarkable in comparison to other psychotherapy methods among the appropriate treatment options.

It is seen that CBT content and techniques are generally used more frequently in changing and diversifying treatment methods (Davis, 2001; Zhong, Tao, Zu, Sha, & Yang, 2009; Du, Jiang, & Vance, A, 2010) for PIU. With CBT, it is aimed to realize the dysfunctional thoughts and beliefs of the person regarding the PIU and to restructure them. The situations that trigger the pathological Internet use, excessive use, and the definition and evaluation of emotional states together with the excessive use are also important for cognitive behavioral formulation (Davis, 2001). Davis (2001) theoretically conceptualized pathological internet use as follows (see Figure 1).

When related literature is examined, one particular name; K. S. Young (1998) is noted, who further can be considered as one the pioneers of the field as he developed an effective treatment protocol using the CBT model (Young, 2007). Within this protocol several topics are mentioned, which are; defining and structuring the problem, self-observation of the client/patient and keeping an internet monitoring chart, working on time management, defining and evaluating offline activities, and relapse prevention studies respectively. It is argued that catastrophizing thinking style can dominate in this therapy protocol and this will increase compulsive internet use to escape from real or perceived problems (Young, 1998). Subsequent studies have shown that in addition to catastrophizing, overgeneralization, negative core beliefs, and other maladaptive cognitions can also increase compulsive internet use (Caplan, 2002; Davis, 2001). Negative core beliefs further may lead to using the Internet to overcome perceived inadequacies. On the other hand, it is also stated that anonymity that individuals receive while using the internet also motivates individuals more, hence plays a fundamental role in increasing the internet usage.

*Figure 1. The cognitive-behavioral model PIU*
*(Davis, 2001)*

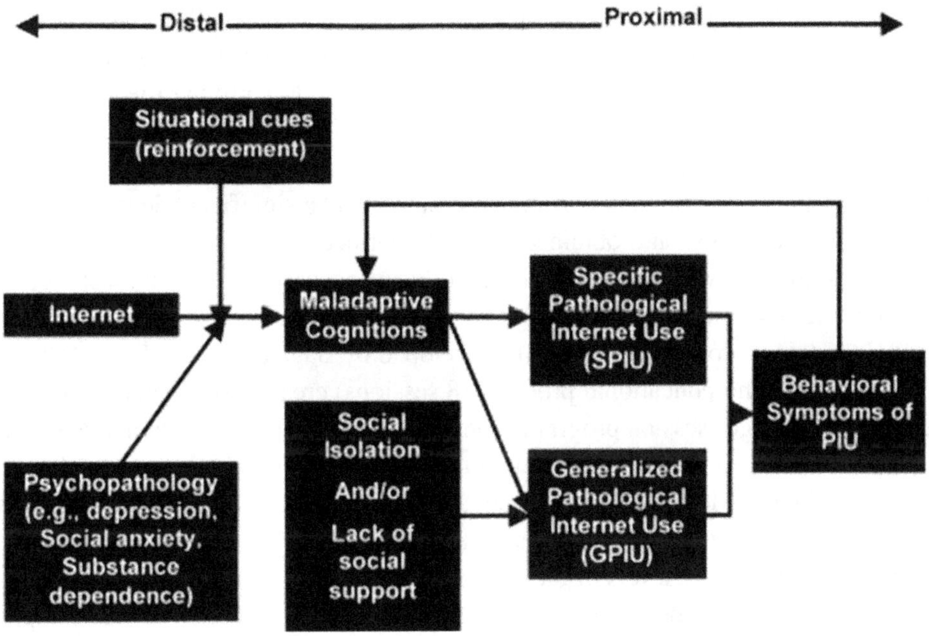


Studies emphasize that the cognition contents in the PIU are important in terms of guiding the treatment. For example, Young (2009) states that individuals' cognitions in PIU can be focused on two directions. These are "on-line" life cognitions on the internet and "off-line" content cognitions in real life. It will be important for an effective treatment to examine the cognitions of people who experience this disorder and to differentiate the contents of the direction of their cognitive distortions. In particular, good and personalized structuring of "off-line" times can also increase the individual's motivation for treatment. In connection with the part, Young (2009) draws much attention to the social aspect specific to this disorder, stating that excessive internet use reveals that individuals neglect their routine work and/or life responsibilities. It is also stated that being discreet about being online, being socially isolated, and privacy can be at a high level while roaming online. Therefore, it is thought that it will be important to include such titles in the therapy formulation in order to personalize the therapy.

It is known that CBT has many different protocols and it has been presented in the literature that CBT is combined with many different techniques. Some examples of this are also being tested for the PIU. The content of PIU can be diversified such as online shopping, online pornography, online gaming, etc. Park and colleagues (2016) combined CBT with a vastly recognized and relatively new phenomenon of virtual reality applications for the treatment of addictions related to online gaming (Park et al., 2016). In this experimentally designed study, some of the participants were used as a CBT group, some as a virtual reality (VR) (with CBT) group and some as a control group. The results show that there are significant decreases in internet addiction levels in the other two groups compared to the control group. Hence, the results indicated the effects of CBT based therapies, as well as the effectivity of VR. Here the authors believe it is important to note that VR can be specifically helpful in the treatment of internet related addictions considering it is also technology related and hence may increase the familiarity and aid in the treatment process for the individuals. Yet, not many studies involve this technique as a form of treatment, hence the authors believe it is significant to suggest the need for more versatile and technology-based treatments (such as VR) for the future. Another study by Du and colleagues (2010) tested a different CBT PIU protocol which was designed for adolescents. This protocol, called "Multimodal school-based CBT", consisted observation of behaviors on the Internet, emotional discrimination techniques and psychoeducational sessions for teachers. This protocol was given to a group of teachers selected in the study. Later, researchers asked the teachers to apply this protocol they learned to the students. Analyzes were carried out by taking measurements before and after the application. After the analysis, it was determined that the participants who took part in this protocol had a significant decrease in their harmful behaviors regarding internet use and obtained a significant decrease in the designated time spent for online games. In addition, it was observed that the intervention effects were long-lasting as they lasted for 6 months after the first intervention (Du, Jiang, & Vance, 2010).

Another PIU treatment protocol was recently developed by Bağatarhan and Siyez (2022). This protocol is a CBT-based psycho-educational program (8 sessions) created to prevent problematic internet use. The purpose of this eight-session program is designed both to prevent problematic internet use and to improve the relationship of the individuals with their parents. The effectiveness of the program was tested with the experimental design [2 (experimental and control groups) × 3 (pretest–posttest—follow-up test) split-plot quasi-experimental design], and it was reported that there were significant decreases in the problematic internet usage levels of the participants who took the training program.

In addition to CBT, new treatment protocols have also emerged over the years. For example, "Positive Psychology Intervention for Pathological Internet Use", which has its origins in positive psychology, can be a good example (Khazaei, Khazaei, & Ghanbari, 2017). The previously mentioned intervention program created by Khazaei and colleagues (2017) aims to treat PIU by taking a rather contrary stance to CBT, as it mostly focusses on increasing positive affect and social communication for individuals with PIU on the basis of positive psychology. In addition to developing new tools to treat PIU, some intervention programs are being developed to prevent the occurrence of it, hence these are specifically important as they aid in the prevention. Therefore, protective and preventive protocols, especially designed for adolescents (such as CBT-based psycho-educational program), include the goals of preventing future pathological internet use and acquiring better time management skills (Bağatarhan & Siyez, 2022).

Considering the treatment of PIU with psychotherapy, it is noteworthy that there is a constantly updated literature. In addition to being a frequently used psychotherapy method, CBT is also seen to be used as a hybrid with other methods (virtual reality, positive psychology, etc.). It is also observed that the effectiveness rates of CBT are remarkable in terms of the effectiveness of the treatment methods that will be mentioned in the next section. As a result, it is understood that psychotherapy is a treatment method that can make significant differences in terms of regulating behaviors, recreating/changing the thought content, and maintaining the well-being of individuals with PIU.

## EFFECTIVENESS OF TREATMENTS

As the PIU is still shown to be an emerging disorder, the related research on the diagnosis, evaluation and treatment on PIU are still ongoing. During the development of psychopharmacological and psychological treatments, as described, effectiveness studies show important implications for the use of treatments. While experimental designs with placebo groups, case studies and reports are preferred in psychopharmacological studies; Randomized controlled experimental designs, single-subject experimental studies and case studies have been used to determine the effectiveness of different psychotherapy modalities. In a review study examining the effectiveness of PIU treatment methods, it was stated that the use of pharmacological and psychological treatments together caused a significant decrease in the severity of PIU, time spent online, and depression and anxiety symptoms related to PIU (Winkler, Dörsing, Rief, Shen, & Glombiewski, 2013).

There are remarkable findings in some of the effectiveness studies conducted within the scope of pharmacological treatments. Medications containing escitalopram (Dell'Osso et al., 2008), bupropion, and methylphenidate (Han et al., 2010) are shown to cause observable reductions in the symptoms of PIU. Nevertheless, there are studies showing that the effectiveness levels of psychotherapies applied together with pharmacological treatments are higher (Kim, Han, Lee, & Renshaw, 2012). Another result of the study by Kim and colleagues was that the "CBT + bupropion group" and "treatment groups receiving only bupropion" were compared and the results indicated that there was no difference between the two groups in terms of the reduction of the PIU symptoms (Kim et al, 2012). Therefore, it is anticipated that the efficacy of treatment methods may show inconsistent results and that more controlled experimental studies should be conducted in the future.

When the effectiveness of psychotherapies is examined alone, it can be said that CBT is the most evidence based? treatment method that can reduce the symptoms of PIU, although different results are encountered. In the study of Wölfling and Dominick (2022), it was reported that CBT-based treatment protocols provide reductions in PIU symptoms and time spent on the internet usage. The results of Wölfling and Dominick's (2022) study are also remarkable. Another study, a therapy protocol called "Telemedicine" was created and the effectiveness of a tele-psychotherapy protocol that can be applied to both PIU patients and their relatives was tested (Bottel et al., 2023). It has been stated that this protocol, which is seen as an effective tool, can be a useful tool both in reaching people in rural areas and in terms of local health practices.

In summary, there appears to be conflicting results regarding the effectiveness of treatment protocols. It can be understood that it is more recommended to use pharmacological therapies together with psychotherapies. In addition, it can also be said that there is a need to use different methodologies to test different modalities regarding the effectiveness of treatment methods.

## CONCLUSION

As a result, the psychological health of individuals is negatively affected and dysfunctional behaviors emerge through digitalization and problematic use of internet in an increasingly digitalized world. PIU is one of these negative consequences. In a nutshell, PIU is characterized by excessive internet usage with severe preoccupations and urges about the internet usage in various forms, which in turn results in some form of impairment in the individuals' mental health (Shaw, & Black, 2008). Studies show that

PIU can appear in various forms (gaming disorder, porn addiction, online shopping, etc.). In addition, epidemiological studies indicate that PIU is more common in males and in the Asian continent as a region. Although pathological internet use has not been determined as a diagnosis yet, PIU criteria and its symptoms are rapidly changing. Both psychopharmacological and psychotherapeutic interventions are shown to have an effect on reducing PIU related symptoms and therefore helps with the coping for the individual, thus research still continues for new developments for both forms of treatment.

There is no clear prescription for the pharmacological treatment of pathological internet use. Medications used for mood disorders or psychotic disorders are usually recommended for PIU. In addition, based on the studies the authors have covered to prepare this manuscript, it is seen that CBT protocols stand out as the main source of psychotherapeutic intervention for PIU and that their effectiveness is sufficient (REF). On the other hand, various studies have shown that CBT protocols are enriched with other modalities such as positive psychotherapy and virtual reality in order to enhance the effect of intervention. Hence, the treatment methods for PIU can be used interchangeably or together. In studies examining some hybrid treatment methods, it can be said that psychopharmacology and psychotherapy methods are used together. Researchers recommend using the two methods together for a higher overall functioning and better level of psychological well-being.

## FUTURE RESEARCH AND DIRECTIONS

While the scientific knowledge is still developing concerning PIU in terms of its diagnosis, evaluation and intervention, it is thought that it will be fundamental to examine the effectiveness of different treatment approaches towards PIU. Moreover, in the study of Young (2009), in which the effectiveness of the CBT protocol for PIU was assessed, results indicated that the intensity of the Internet usage of the participants has significantly decreased. In the recent years, more evidence further showed that CBT-based interventions provide promising results for the effective treatment of PIU (Du, Jiang, & Vance, 2010; Bağatarhan, & Siyez, 2022). In addition, it is stated that conducting follow-up studies with different time intervals in order to compare the durations for the effect of the developed treatments can also indicate important results which literature can vastly benefit.

Another important note is that most of the studies mentioned above implied that often individuals do not have PIU on its own, and that PIU may occur secondary to another already established disorder or there may be other accompanying psychological disorders. Hence, there is a need for more evidence-based research examining comorbid conditions.

All in all, we believe it is inevitable to deny the importance and the significance of the emerging psychopathology of PIU. Therefore, more research is definitely needed in order to better understand the etiology, development, diagnostic criteria, prognosis and of course the intervention methods for PIU. Moreover, the treatment-outcome research on effective treatment protocols is also encouraged to better identify how to help individuals with OIU effectively. It is also considered important to make intervention related samples culturally sensitive. In addition, it is believed that it would be more suitable to benefit from the newest tools and more technological advances such as brain imaging techniques, in the related field of research. These advanced methods are thought to be particularly important as the proposed intervention for PIU often involves pharmacological treatment as well as psychotherapy (either combined or separately). Therefore, understanding the brain regions involved, the neurocircuitry and the neurochemical changes of the brain, is believed to further shed a light on many unknown features of PIU.

## REFERENCES


Aboujaoude, E., Koran, L. M., Gamel, N., Large, M. D., & Serpe, R. T. (2006). Potential markers for problematic internet use: A telephone survey of 2, 513 adults CNS spectrum. *CNS Spectrums*, *11*(10), 750–755. doi:10.1017/S1092852900014875 PMID:17008818

Akın, A., & İskender, M. (2011). Internet addiction and depression, anxiety and stress. *International Online Journal of Educational Sciences*, *3*(1), 138–148.

Alavi, S. S. (2012). Behavioral addiction versus substance addiction. Correspondence of psychiatric and psychological views. *International Journal of Preventive Medicine*, *4*, 290–294. PMID:22624087

American Psychiatric Association. (2013). *DSM-5 – Diagnostic and statistical manual of mental disorders: DSM-5* (5th ed.). American Psychiatric Association.

American Psychological Association. (n.d.). Psychopharmacology. In *APA dictionary of psychology*. APA. https://dictionary.apa.org/psychopharmacology

Arısoy, Ö. (2009). İnternet bağımlılığı ve tedavisi. *Psikiyatride Güncel Yaklasimlar*, *1*(1), 55–67.

Bağatarhan, T., & Siyez, D. M. (2022). The Effectiveness of a Cognitive-Behavioral Prevention Program for Internet Addiction. *Journal of Rational-Emotive & Cognitive-Behavior Therapy*, *40*(4), 1–26. doi:10.100710942-021-00439-7

Barnett, S. D., Kramer, M. L., Casat, C. D., Connor, K. M., & Davidson, J. R. (2002). Efficacy of olanzapine in social anxiety disorder: A pilot study. *Journal of Psychopharmacology (Oxford, England)*, *16*(4), 365–368. doi:10.1177/026988110201600412 PMID:12503837

Bernardi, S., & Pallanti, S. (2009). Internet addiction: A descriptive clinical study focusing on comorbidities and dissociative symptoms. *Comprehensive Psychiatry*, *50*(6), 510–516. doi:10.1016/j.comppsych.2008.11.011 PMID:19840588

Blum, K., Braverman, E. R., Holder, J. M., Lubar, J. F., Monastra, V. J., Miller, D., Lubar, J.O., Chen, T.J.H., & Comings, D. E. (2000). The reward deficiency syndrome: A biogenetic model for the diagnosis and treatment of impulsive, addictive and compulsive behaviors. *Journal of psychoactive drugs*, *32*(sup1), 1-112.

Bottel, L., Te Wildt, B. T., Brand, M., Pape, M., Herpertz, S., & Dieris-Hirche, J. (2023). Telemedicine as bridge to the offline world for person affected with problematic internet use or internet use disorder and concerned significant others. *Digital Health*, *9*, 20552076221144185. doi:10.1177/20552076221144185 PMID:36636726

Brand, M., Rumpf, H. J., Demetrovics, Z., Müller, A., Stark, R., King, D. L., Goudriaan, A. E., Mann, K., Trotzke, P., Fineberg, N. A., Chamberlain, S. R., Kraus, S. W., Wegmann, E., Billieux, J. Ë., & Potenza, M. N. (2020). Which conditions should be considered as disorders in the International Classification of Diseases (ICD-11) designation of "other specified disorders due to addictive behaviors"? *Journal of Behavioral Addictions*, *11*(2), 150–159. doi:10.1556/2006.2020.00035 PMID:32634114

Byeon, Y. S., & Lee, H. S. (2007). The effects of internet addiction on mental health among adolescents. *Journal of Korean Academy of Community Health Nursing*, *18*(3), 460–468.

Camardese, G., Leone, B., Walstra, C., Janiri, L., & Guglielmo, R. (2015). Pharmacological treatment of Internet addiction. In *Internet addiction* (pp. 151–165). Springer. doi:10.1007/978-3-319-07242-5_10

Caplan, S. E. (2002). Problematic internet use and psychosocial wellbeing: Development of a theory-based cognitive-behavioral measurement instrument. *Computers in Human Behavior*, *18*(5), 553–575. doi:10.1016/S0747-5632(02)00004-3

Carli, V., Durkee, T., Wasserman, D., Hadlaczky, G., Despalins, R., Kramarz, E., Wasserman, C., Sarchiapone, M., Hoven, C. W., Brunner, R., & Kaess, M. (2013). The Association between Pathological Internet Use and Comorbid Psychopathology: A Systematic Review. *Psychopathology*, *46*(1), 1–13. doi:10.1159/000337971 PMID:22854219

Carlson, N. R., & Birkett, M. A. (2021). *Physiology of Behavior*. Pearson Publications.

Çetin, M., & Turgay, A. (2002). Modern Psikofarmakolojinin Ellinci Yılında Klorpromazinden Günümüze Antipsikotik Tedavinin Dünü Bugünü. *Klinik Psikofarmakoloji Bülteni*, *12*, 211–226.

Chou, C., Condron, L., & Belland, J. C. (2005). A review of the research on Internet addiction. *Educational Psychology Review*, *17*(4), 363–388. doi:10.100710648-005-8138-1

Davis, R. A. (2001). A cognitive-behavioral model of pathological Internet use. *Computers in Human Behavior*, *17*(2), 187–195. doi:10.1016/S0747-5632(00)00041-8

Dell'Osso, B., Hadley, S., Allen, A., Baker, B., Chaplin, W. F., & Hollander, E. (2008). Escitalopram in the treatment of impulsive-compulsive internet usage disorder: An open-label trial followed by a double-blind discontinuation phase. *The Journal of Clinical Psychiatry*, *69*(3), 452–456. doi:10.4088/JCP.v69n0316 PMID:18312057

Di Chiara, G., & North, R. A. (1992). Neurobiology of opiate abuse. *Trends in Pharmacological Sciences*, *13*, 185–193. doi:10.1016/0165-6147(92)90062-B PMID:1604711

Du, Y. S., Jiang, W., & Vance, A. (2010). Longer term effect of randomized, controlled group cognitive behavioural therapy for Internet addiction in adolescent students in Shanghai. *The Australian and New Zealand Journal of Psychiatry*, *44*(2), 129–134. doi:10.3109/00048670903282725 PMID:20113301

Du, Y. S., Jiang, W., & Vance, A. (2010). Longer term effect of randomized, controlled group cognitive behavioural therapy for Internet addiction in adolescent students in Shanghai. *The Australian and New Zealand Journal of Psychiatry*, *44*(2), 129–134. doi:10.3109/00048670903282725 PMID:20113301

Durkee, T., Carli, V., Floderus, B., Wasserman, C., Sarchiapone, M., Apter, A., Balazs, J. A., Bobes, J., Brunner, R., Corcoran, P., Cosman, D., Haring, C., Hoven, C. W., Kaess, M., Kahn, J. P., Nemes, B., Postuvan, V., Saiz, P. A., Värnik, P., & Wasserman, D. (2016). Pathological Internet Use and Risk-Behaviors among European Adolescents. *International Journal of Environmental Research and Public Health*, *13*(3), 294. doi:10.3390/ijerph13030294 PMID:27005644

Dutra, L., Stathopoulou, G., Basden, S. L., Leyro, T. M., Powers, M. B., & Otto, M. W. (2008). A meta-analytic review of psychosocial interventions for substance use disorders. *The American Journal of Psychiatry, 165*(2), 179–187. doi:10.1176/appi.ajp.2007.06111851 PMID:18198270

Ensari, H., Ceylan, M. E., Kilinç, E., & Kenar, J. (2004). Türk'ye'deki Ruh Hastalıkları Hastanelerindeki Psikofarmakolojik Tedavilerin Kalite Yönünden Değerlendirilmesi. *Klinik Psikofarmakoloji Bulteni, 14*(2), 68–78.

Foddy, B., & Savulescu, J. (2006). Addiction and autonomy: Can addicted people consent to the prescription of their drug of addiction? *Bioethics, 20*(1), 1–15. doi:10.1111/j.1467-8519.2006.00470.x PMID:16680876

Grant, J. E., Kim, S. W., & Odlaug, B. L. (2009). A double-blind, placebo-controlled study of the opiate antagonist, naltrexone, in the treatment of kleptomania. *Biological Psychiatry, 65*(7), 600–606. doi:10.1016/j.biopsych.2008.11.022 PMID:19217077

Grant, J. E., Potenza, M. N., Weinstein, A., & Gorelick, D. A. (2010). Introduction to behavioral addictions. *The American Journal of Drug and Alcohol Abuse, 36*(5), 233–241. doi:10.3109/00952990.2010.491884 PMID:20560821

Han, D. H., Hwang, J. W., & Renshaw, P. F. (2011). Bupropion sustained release treatment decreases craving for video games and cue-induced brain activity in patients with Internet video game addiction. *Experimental and Clinical Psychopharmacology, 18*(4), 297–304. doi:10.1037/a0020023 PMID:20695685

Huang, X. Q., Li, M. C., & Tao, R. (2010). Treatment of internet addiction. *Current Psychiatry Reports, 12*(5), 462–470. doi:10.100711920-010-0147-1 PMID:20697848

Hughes, J. R., Stead, L. F., & Lancaster, T. (2007). Antidepressants for smoking cessation [published correction appears in Cochrane Database Syst Rev. 2014; 1: CD000031]. *Cochrane Database of Systematic Reviews*, 1. PMID:17253443

Khazaei, F., Khazaei, O., & Ghanbari-H, B. (2017). Positive psychology interventions for internet addiction treatment. *Computers in Human Behavior, 72*, 304–311. doi:10.1016/j.chb.2017.02.065

Kim, S. M., Han, D. H., Lee, Y. S., & Renshaw, P. F. (2012). Combined cognitive behavioral therapy and bupropion for the treatment of problematic on-line game play in adolescents with major depressive disorder. *Computers in Human Behavior, 28*(5), 1954–1959. doi:10.1016/j.chb.2012.05.015

Ko, C. H., Liu, G. C., Hsiao, S., Yen, J. Y., Yang, M. J., Lin, W. C., Yen, C.-F., & Chen, C. S. (2009). Brain activities associated with gaming urge of online gaming addiction. *Journal of Psychiatric Research, 43*(7), 739–747. doi:10.1016/j.jpsychires.2008.09.012 PMID:18996542

Ko, C. H., Yen, J. Y., Yen, C. F., Chen, C. S., & Chen, C. C. (2012). The association between Internet addiction and psychiatric disorder: A review of the literature. *European Psychiatry, 27*(1), 1–8. doi:10.1016/j.eurpsy.2010.04.011 PMID:22153731

Koob, G. F., & Volkow, N. D. (2016). Neurobiology of addiction: A neurocircuitry analysis. *The Lancet. Psychiatry, 3*(8), 760–773. doi:10.1016/S2215-0366(16)00104-8 PMID:27475769

Li, W., O'Brien, J. E., Snyder, S. M., & Howard, M. (2015). Characteristics of internet addiction/pathological internet use in u.s. university students: A qualitative-method investigation. *PLoS One*, *10*(2), e0117372. doi:10.1371/journal.pone.0117372 PMID:25647224

Lozano-Blasco, R., Robres, A. Q., & Sanchez, A. S. (2022). Internet addiction in young adults: A meta-analysis and systematic review. *Computers in Human Behavior*, *130*, 107201. doi:10.1016/j.chb.2022.107201

Łukawski, K., Rusek, M., & Czuczwar, S. J. (2019). Can pharmacotherapy play a role in treating internet addiction disorder? *Expert Opinion on Pharmacotherapy*, *20*(11), 1299–1301. doi:10.1080/14656566.2019.1612366 PMID:31058549

McNichol, M. L., & Thorsteinsson, E. B. (2017). Internet addiction, psychological distress, and coping responses among adolescents and adults. *Cyberpsychology, Behavior, and Social Networking*, *20*(5), 296–304. doi:10.1089/cyber.2016.0669 PMID:28414517

Pan, Y. C., Chiu, Y. C., & Lin, Y. H. (2020). Systematic review and meta-analysis of epidemiology of internet addiction. *Neuroscience and Biobehavioral Reviews*, *118*, 612–622. doi:10.1016/j.neubiorev.2020.08.013 PMID:32853626

Park, S. Y., Kim, S. M., Roh, S., Soh, M. A., Lee, S. H., Kim, H., Lee, Y. S., & Han, D. H. (2016). The effects of a virtual reality treatment program for online gaming addiction. *Computer Methods and Programs in Biomedicine*, *129*, 99–108. doi:10.1016/j.cmpb.2016.01.015 PMID:26860055

Pies, R. (2009). Should DSM-V designate "internet addiction"a mental disorder? *Psychiatry*, *6*, 31–37. PMID:19724746

Poli, R., & Agrimi, E. (2012). Internet addiction disorder: Prevalence in an Italian student population. *Nordic Journal of Psychiatry*, *66*(1), 55–59. doi:10.3109/08039488.2011.605169 PMID:21859396

Scherk, H., & Falkai, P. (2006). Effects of antipsychotics on brain structure. *Current Opinion in Psychiatry*, *19*(2), 145–150. doi:10.1097/01.yco.0000214339.06507.d8 PMID:16612194

Seeman, P. (2004). Atypical antipsychotics: Mechanism of action. *Focus (San Francisco, Calif.)*, *47*(1), 27–58. PMID:11873706

Shaw, M., & Black, D. W. (2008). Internet addiction. *CNS Drugs*, *22*(5), 353–365. doi:10.2165/00023210-200822050-00001 PMID:18399706

Shaw, M., & Black, D. W. (2008). Internet addiction: Definition, assessment, epidemiology and clinical management. *CNS Drugs*, *22*(5), 353–365. doi:10.2165/00023210-200822050-00001 PMID:18399706

Singh, R., Gupta, R., Grover, T., Ambekar, A., Jain, R., Vaswani, M., Mishra, A., & Sharma, A. (2023). Role of the Serotonin and GABAA Receptor Gene Polymorphisms in patients with Alcohol Dependence. *Asian Journal of Psychiatry*, *80*, 103326. doi:10.1016/j.ajp.2022.103326 PMID:36463616

Skinner, B. F. (1948). Superstition' in the pigeon. *Journal of Experimental Psychology*, *38*(2), 168–172. doi:10.1037/h0055873 PMID:18913665

Stoffers-Winterling, J., Storebø, O. J., & Lieb, K. (2020). Pharmacotherapy for borderline personality disorder: An update of published, unpublished and ongoing studies. *Current Psychiatry Reports*, *22*(8), 1–10. doi:10.100711920-020-01164-1 PMID:32504127

Twohig, M. P., & Crosby, J. M. (2010). Acceptance and commitment therapy as a treatment for problematic internet pornography viewing. *Behavior Therapy*, *41*(3), 285–295. doi:10.1016/j.beth.2009.06.002 PMID:20569778

Watson, J. B. (1913). Psychology as behaviourist views it. *Psychological Review*, *20*(2), 158–177. doi:10.1037/h0074428

WHO. (2018). *Public health implications of excessive use of the Internet and other communication and gaming platforms*. WHO. https://www.who.int/news/item/13-09-2018-public-health-implications-of-excessive-use-of-the-internet-and-other-communication-and-gaming-platforms

Widyanto, L., & McMurran, M. (2004). The Psychometric properties of the internet addiction test. *Cyberpsychology & Behavior*, *7*(4), 443–450. doi:10.1089/cpb.2004.7.443 PMID:15331031

Winkler, A., Dörsing, B., Rief, W., Shen, Y., & Glombiewski, J. A. (2013). Treatment of internet addiction: A meta-analysis. *Clinical Psychology Review*, *33*(2), 317–329. doi:10.1016/j.cpr.2012.12.005 PMID:23354007

Wise, R. A. (2009). Roles for nigrostriatal-not just mesocorticolimbic-dopamine in reward and addiction. *Trends in Neurosciences*, *32*(10), 517–524. doi:10.1016/j.tins.2009.06.004 PMID:19758714

Wölfling, K., & Dominick, N. (2022). Using cognitive behavioral therapy as the select treatment approach for problematic Internet usage. *Current Opinion in Behavioral Sciences*, *45*, 101–121. doi:10.1016/j.cobeha.2022.101121

Wölfling, K., & Dominick, N. (2022). Using cognitive behavioral therapy as the select treatment approach for problematic Internet usage. *Current Opinion in Behavioral Sciences*, *45*, 101121. doi:10.1016/j.cobeha.2022.101121

World Health Organization. (2022). *ICD-11 for Mortality and Morbidity Statistics*. WHO. https://icd.who.int/browse11/l-m/en

Young, K. (2009). Internet addiction: Diagnosis and treatment considerations. *Journal of Contemporary Psychotherapy*, *39*(4), 241–246. doi:10.100710879-009-9120-x

Young, K. S. (1998). *Caught in the net: How to recognize the signs of internet addiction—and a winning strategy for recovery*. John Wiley & Sons.

Young, K. S. (2007). Cognitive behavior therapy with Internet addicts: Treatment outcomes and implications. *Cyberpsychology & Behavior*, *10*(5), 671–679. doi:10.1089/cpb.2007.9971 PMID:17927535

Yüksel, N., Soygür, H., Tural, Ü., & Demet, M. M. (2010). *Temel psikofarmakoloji*. Türkiye Psikiyatri Derneği Yayınları.

Zhong, X., Tao, R., Zu, S., Sha, S., & Yang, F. (2009). Effect of group psychological intervention in adolescents on Internet addiction. *Journal of Capital Medical University*, *30*, 494–499.

## ADDITIONAL READING

Eşkisu, M., Boysan, M., & Çam, Z. (2023). A Mixture Modeling of the Predictors of Internet Addiction: Cognition and Dissociation. *Psychological Reports*, 00332941221149180. PMID:36596295

Haghighatfard, A., Ghaderi, A. H., Mostajabi, P., Kashfi, S. S., Shahrani, M., Mehrasa, M., & Alizadenik, A. (2023). The first genome-wide association study of internet addiction; Revealed substantial shared risk factors with neurodevelopmental psychiatric disorders. *Research in Developmental Disabilities*, *133*, 104393. doi:10.1016/j.ridd.2022.104393 PMID:36566681

Lukose, E. (2023). Optimizing Patient Care in Psychiatry–Behavioral Addictions. In *Handbook on Optimizing Patient Care in Psychiatry* (pp. 169–179). Routledge.

Shek, D. T., Chai, W., Dou, D., Zhu, X., Chan, C. H., Zhou, K., Chu, C. K. M., Chu, K.-Y., & Sun, P. C. (2023). Internet Addiction Amongst University Students Under COVID-19: Prevalence and Correlates. *Asian Journal on Addictions*, *1*(1), 26–26. doi:10.58896/aja.v1i1.2

Sun, Y. (2023). The role of family on internet addiction: A model analysis of co-parenting effect. *Cogent Social Sciences*, *9*(1), 2163530. doi:10.1080/23311886.2022.2163530

## KEY TERMS AND DEFINITONS

**Cognitive and Behavioural Therapy:** It is a talk therapy that can help you manage your problems by changing and regulating the way you think and act.

**Pathological Internet Use:** It is a disorder that is characterized by poorly controlled urges and behaviours in relation to excessive Internet usage which often results in impaired mental well-being.

**Psychopharmacology:** It is the field of science that creates the structure of drugs used in the field of mental health, uses them, and examines their effects on individuals.

**Psychotherapy:** It is a treatment method through speech communication, which includes procedures aimed at solving emotional and behavioral problems of individuals, improving and protecting their mental health.

# Chapter 15
# The Concept of Addiction and Its Causes

**Yunus Emre Bulut**
https://orcid.org/0000-0003-1501-2525
*Gülhane School of Medicine, University of Health Sciences, Turkey*

## ABSTRACT

*Addiction can be briefly defined as the inability to stop using or control a substance or behavior. This concept can be used for many substances such as cigarettes, alcohol, drugs, as well as behavioral addictions such as eating, gaming, sex, gambling, computer and smartphone usage, television watching, internet and social media usage, digital game shopping, etc. Among these addictions, we can collectively consider computer, smartphone, television, internet, social media, and digital game addictions as "technological addictions." The concept of technology addiction entered our lives after the 2000s, when the internet and technological tools became widespread. In this chapter, the concept of addiction and the causes of addiction are defined in general, followed by the concept of behavioral addiction and its causes. And finally, the concept of technology addiction and its causes are explained with the support of the literature. In addition, the equivalents of these definitions in the relevant diagnostic guidelines and ICD diagnosis codes are mentioned.*

## INTRODUCTION

In our century, addiction is a serious public health problem that causes excessive mortality, morbidity and economic losses (Bickel et al., 2017). While society has not yet been able to find a complete solution to its struggle with substance addiction, the increasing use of technology in all areas of life by individuals of all age groups brings to mind the question of whether "internet addiction is the new epidemic of this century". (Christakis, 2010).

Restrictive measures such as curfews imposed to prevent the spread of disease during pandemia have made it necessary for individuals to do almost all their personal and social activities from home. This has led to an increase in the amount of time individuals spend online (smartphones, computers, gaming devices). It is now observed that parents turn their children's use of technology into a means of

DOI: 10.4018/978-1-6684-8397-8.ch015

rewarding them, protecting them from the dangers of the outside, distracting them when they are left alone at home, curbing active children; they tolerate and even encourage the use of technology so that they do not make noise or do household chores comfortably (Mitchell, 2021; Yıldız and Kanak, 2021) .

In addition, it can be said that individuals are more inclined to behaviors that carry the risk of technology addiction such as surfing the internet, watching TV series, movies and videos, playing games and using social media in order to reduce the anxiety they experience in their changing social lives (Körpe & Küçük, 2021).

Accurately defining the concepts and sub-headings related to addiction, whether substance or behavioral, will be important in terms of developing algorithms for research on the causes of addiction and its treatment.

## THE CONCEPT OF ADDICTION

### What is Addiction?

Addiction is briefly defined as the inability to stop or control the use of a substance or behavior. More broadly, addiction is a treatable, chronic medical condition that involves complex interactions between genes, the environment and the individual's life experiences, characterized by continued substance use or compulsive actions despite knowledge of harmful consequences (Rastegar & Fingerhood, 2020). For a long time, addiction was only used to refer to the uncontrollable habit of smoking, drinking alcohol or using other drugs.

More recently, the concept of addiction has expanded to include behaviors such as gambling, as well as ordinary and necessary activities such as exercise, eating, gaming, sex, computers, smartphones, television, internet, social media, digital gaming, shopping, etc. Among these addictions, computer, smartphone, television, internet, social media and digital game addictions can be collectively considered as "technological addictions". Technology addiction can be defined as increasingly frequent and obsessive technology-related behaviors despite the negative consequences of technology on the user (Sherer & Levounis, 2022).

### Symptoms of Addiction

Signs and symptoms of addiction can vary from one type of addiction to another, but some common addiction symptoms usually include Inability to stop using, changes in emotional state, changes in appetite and sleep, continuing to use despite negative consequences, denying addiction, engaging in risky behaviors, substance-seeking behavior, legal and financial problems, losing interest in other things that used to be pleasurable, putting the substance or behavior ahead of other areas of life, including family, work and other responsibilities, concealment, using increasing amounts; taking more of the substance than intended, and withdrawal symptoms.

Within these defining characteristics of addiction, there are two aspects common to all addictions:

1. Addictive behavior is dysfunctional.
2. Addictive behavior is continuous/permanent.

Addictive behavior, which initially appears to be a problem-solving behavior, causes different problems for both the individual and those around him/her over time. Therefore, instead of helping the person cope with situations or overcome problems, addictive behavior becomes dysfunctional in the person's life. When people are addicted, they will continue to engage in the addictive behavior despite the dysfunction it causes. Therefore, it is important to remember that while occasional use may cause different kinds of problems, it is not an addiction, addiction is characterized by frequent use, and use is continuous.

An important confusion here is the distinction between addiction and abuse. When people become "addicted" to a substance or behavior, it means that they experience tolerance and withdrawal symptoms. In other words, the sine qua non of addiction are tolerance and withdrawal symptoms. Tolerance means that the body adapts to the presence of the substance/behavior and the person takes more and more of the substance to produce the same effects, i.e. increased use. Withdrawal is defined as the sudden reduction or cessation of use and the appearance of certain physical and psychological symptoms (NIDA, 2018).

## Diagnosis of Addiction

Current guidelines in the Diagnostic and Statistical Manual of Mental Disorders-5 (DSM-5) indicate that most psychoactive substances, including drugs, have the potential to be addictive, but the term addiction is not recognized as an official diagnosis in DSM-5. Instead, a generic term such as "substance use disorders" is preferred. Although the diagnostic criteria differ for each substance, the DSM-5 defines these disorders as a problematic pattern of use of intoxicating substances that leads to significant impairment and distress (APA, 2013). The different substance use disorders included in the DSM-5 are: Alcohol-related disorders, Caffeine-related disorders, Cannabis-related disorders, Hallucinogen-related disorders, Opioid-related disorders, Sedative, hypnotic or anxiolytic-related disorders, Stimulant-related disorders, Tobacco-related disorders.

Substance use disorders cover a wide range of problems resulting from substance use. These are:

1. Taking larger amounts each time or for longer than they should
2. Wanting to reduce or stop using, but not being able to do so
3. Spending a lot of time acquiring, using or getting rid of
4. The desire to use it continuously
5. Not being able to do what you need to do at work, home or school because of its use
6. Continue to use even if it causes problems in relationships
7. giving up important social, professional or recreational activities due to use
8. Repeated use even if it endangers the person
9. Continuing to use when you know you have a physical or psychological problem that it may cause or worsen
10. Needing more of a substance to achieve the desired effect (tolerance)
11. Development of withdrawal symptoms that can be relieved by taking more substances

The 11 criteria outlined in the DSM-5 can be grouped into four main categories: physical dependence, risky use, social problems and impaired control.

The DSM-5 also defines two types of behavioral addiction: Gambling disorder and Internet gaming disorder. Gambling disorder is the only non-substance-related disorder proposed in the DSM-5 among substance-related and addictive disorders. However, there are other behavioral disorders that show some similarities to substance use disorders and gambling disorder, including compulsive internet gaming, for which there is a substantial literature. Internet gaming disorder is of significant public health importance. Research shows that Internet Gaming Disorder (commonly referred to as Internet use disorder, Internet addiction, gaming addiction) deserves to be an independent disease. There is still debate, even in reference guidelines, about whether many other behavioral addictions are "true" addictions.

At the time the DSM-5 was first published in 2013, there was insufficient evidence to determine whether Internet gaming disorder was a specific mental disorder or whether there were any criteria for classifying it. However, in the section recommending conditions for further research, Internet gaming disorder was recognized along with caffeine use disorder and other conditions. The DSM-5 states that gaming should cause "significant impairment or distress" in various aspects of a person's life. This proposed condition is limited to gaming and does not include general internet use, online gambling or problems with social media or smartphone use. Suggested symptoms of internet gaming disorder include:

1. Constant preoccupation with the game
2. Withdrawal symptoms (sadness, anxiety, irritability) when play is taken away or not possible
3. Tolerance, the need to spend more time playing to satisfy the urge
4. Inability to reduce play, unsuccessful attempts to quit
5. Abandonment of other activities, loss of interest in previously enjoyed activities due to gaming
6. Keep playing despite the problems
7. Deceiving family members or others about the time spent playing
8. Playing games to relieve negative moods such as guilt or hopelessness
9. Risk of jeopardizing or losing a job or relationship due to gaming

According to the proposed criteria, a diagnosis of internet gaming disorder requires experiencing five or more of these symptoms within one year. The condition can involve gaming on the internet or any electronic device, but most people who develop clinically significant gaming problems primarily play on the internet.

## CAUSES OF ADDICTION

There are many theories about the causes of addiction, both about the use and abuse of legal and illegal psychoactive substances and the compulsive use of a behavior. Biological, psychological, social and cultural elements all play a role in the highly complex causal process that results in addiction, and these theories weight all these factors differently. In fact, all of these outcomes reflect the fact that there is no single pathway to addiction and that no single factor alone makes addiction a foregone conclusion. Addiction cannot occur without exposure to agents, but this is not the determining factor. Addiction is not a property of the substance taken or the activity performed.

Research shows that what makes the sensation caused by a substance or behavior so appealing has more to do with what is or is not happening in a person's life. Among the many factors that have been shown to influence the development of an addiction are feelings/thoughts about oneself, quality of family relationships, social ties, community characteristics, employment status, stress response and coping skills, history of physical or emotional pain, personality traits and physiological reactions to events. Each seems to exert some degree of influence, although no one factor is dominant.

It is still not clear what exactly causes addiction, as risk factors vary from person to person. Scientific research shows that if a person has more risk factors for addiction, they may have a higher chance of abusing substances or developing an addiction. There are many risk factors for addiction, from individual factors such as stress tolerance and personality structure to social factors such as friendships, education and job opportunities. However, what can mean addiction for everyone is the emotional and physical attraction of a substance at a particular moment in a person's life.

## Genetic Factors

The science of genetics studies how and why certain characteristics are passed on from parents to children. Some research suggests that genes may be moderately to highly responsible for a person's risk of addiction, meaning that addiction is considered moderately to highly heritable, but the degree of genetic influence seems to lose importance over time. For example, environmental factors such as family and social relationships are more strongly linked to alcohol and nicotine use during adolescence than later in life. However, no single gene, or even a group of genes, has been found for addiction. Especially for people who have first-degree relatives (parents, children, siblings) who struggle with addiction, genetics can play an important role in addiction.

In addition, there are a number of personality traits, each partly genetically influenced, that contribute to addiction risk. These include impulsivity, frustration tolerance and sensitivity to rejection. Impulsivity is thought to play the strongest role in the early stages of addiction, driving the motivation to seek substances.

## Biological Factors

Biology contributes to addiction beyond genes. How the body metabolizes or breaks down and eliminates addictive substances such as drugs or alcohol depends largely on the presence of various enzymes, and these can vary significantly between individuals and even between ethnic groups.

For example, research shows that far eastern countries have unique variations of certain alcohol metabolizing enzymes not found in other populations that discourage alcohol consumption and alcoholism because they act quickly. Biological factors such as the enzyme profile can influence the amount of alcohol people drink, the pleasantness of the experience, the harmful effects on the body and the development of disease.

## Environmental Factors

There are many factors beyond genes and biology that influence addiction. One of the most important is the family environment and early onset experiences. Family interactions, parenting style and control abilities all play a role in the development of coping skills and predisposition to mental health problems. Studies have linked authoritarian or neglectful parenting, domestic violence and divorce with an increased likelihood of substance use problems later in life. Growing up with strong ties to a family, a faith tradition and a culture is known to be protective against addiction. Children of parents who use drugs and alcohol and are involved in criminal activity are at risk of substance abuse. Parents may willingly or unwillingly introduce children to drugs and model negative behaviors.

A person's social environment, the people they interact with and are exposed to, and where they live can also influence whether they develop addiction (NIDA, 2014). Friends are important in the lives of adolescents. Peers play a huge role in predisposing to addiction, especially among adolescents and young adults; it is well known that most people first use drugs during adolescence. For example, abuse of prescription drugs is highest among young adults between the ages of 18 and 25 (NIDA, 2020). Alcohol is the most commonly abused substance among adolescents in the United States. The availability of drugs at home and/or school can provide additional opportunities for children to experiment and possibly develop an addiction. Community attitudes and influence can also be an environmental factor for addiction. For example, in communities where substance use is normalized, individuals are more likely to become addicted. Low academic achievement is another environmental factor for substance use (NIDA, 2003).

Although environmental factors can put children at risk of addiction, protective factors can minimize the risk of addiction. Children who grow up and develop good parental support, positive relationships, a sense of community, and anti-drug policies at school can be protected from some risk factors for self-control and addiction (NIDA, 2014).

### Childhood Traumas

Both positive and negative childhood experiences can have a significant impact on a person's physical and mental health. Adverse childhood experiences can lead to stressful, traumatic events that can lead to physical and emotional difficulties and even substance use disorders (Khoury et al., 2010). Traumatic childhood experiences can be summarized as physical and/or sexual abuse, parental separation or divorce, verbal abuse, physical or emotional neglect, witnessing domestic violence, having a family member with a mental illness, having a family member in prison, having a family member addicted to drugs or alcohol. Adverse childhood experiences such as trauma, especially when combined with an unpredictable and chaotic childhood, constitute a risk factor for many types of maladaptive behaviors and poor health outcomes. Studies show that having multiple adverse childhood experiences puts children at risk for poor school performance, unemployment, and high-risk health behaviors, including smoking and drug use (Substance Abuse and Mental Health Services Administration, 2021).

## BEHAVIORAL ADDICTIONS AND THEIR CAUSES

When certain behaviors are repeated, they can lead to persistent behaviors as a result of decreased control over the behavior, even though the negative consequences are known, as is the case with substance use. Decreased control is a basic defining concept of substance use disorder or addiction. This similarity has given rise to the concept of non-substance or "behavioral" addictions, that is, as a focus of syndromes similar to substance addiction. The concept of behavioral addiction has some scientific and clinical value, but is still controversial (Potenza, 2006).

Some behavioral addictions are recognized to have similarities with substance addictions. The DSM-IV-TR established formal diagnostic criteria for many of these disorders (e.g., pathological gambling, kleptomania) and classified them as impulse control disorders, a category separate from substance use disorders. Other behaviors such as compulsive buying, pathological skin picking, sexual addiction (non-paraphilic hypersexuality), excessive tanning, computer/video game playing and internet addiction were considered for inclusion in the DSM, but only internet gaming disorder found a place in DSM 5. Which behaviors should be included as behavioral addictions is still open to debate (Holden, 2010).

Internet gaming disorder was included in Section III of the DSM-5 as a condition that needs further study, and in the ICD-11, it was included in the "Disorders due to substance use or addictive behaviours" section (APA, 2013; WHO, 2018, Arnoud, 2021). A careful review of the existing literature by 66 researchers from 25 countries at a series of annual expert meetings on the public health implications of behavioral addictions held under the auspices of the World Health Organization since 2014 concluded that gaming disorder is an independent behavioral disorder and that a significant proportion of the general population suffers from the condition and shows functional impairment (Rumpt et al., 2018). Although a number of behavioral addictions were suggested for inclusion, the working group concluded that further research is needed before internet use disorder, smartphone use disorder, sex addiction, exercise addiction and shopping addiction are included (WHO, 2018).

Besides gambling and gaming, the evidence for other behavioral addictions is more limited. Many studies use a concept of "Internet addiction" that encompasses activities such as gaming, social networking, pornography viewing or online purchasing/shopping. Although the term Internet addiction is relatively non-specific and therefore has conceptual problems, it can refer to a range of common and problematic behaviors, and research on the topic is growing rapidly (Baggio et al., 2018).

The main characteristic of behavioral addictions lies in the individual's inability to resist motives, urges or temptations. The main characteristics found in individuals with a behavioral addiction:

- Attention seeking (the activity becomes highly valued and takes precedence over other activities),
- Mood change (the emotional response to the behavior; this may take the form of an adrenaline rush when engaging in the behavior, or it may lead to a decrease in the form of a depressed state).
- Tolerance (the need for increasing amounts of behavior to achieve the desired level of mood change),
- Withdrawal symptoms (unpleasant feelings or physiological withdrawal symptoms when reducing or stopping activity),
- Conflict (conflict with other activities or people due to behavior) and
- Repetition (a relatively high rate of returning to the initial behavior) (Griffiths, 2005).

Although some behavioral addictions (e.g., compulsive shopping, sexual addiction, smartphone addiction) appear to be more typical of middle-aged and even older adults, many of these behavioral disorders have been shown to occur during childhood and/or adolescence. The consequences and problems associated with a behavioral addiction may be more severe in adulthood, but for children and adolescents, the emerging problems associated with a behavioral addiction may be more common (Derevensky et al., 2018).

The best model to explain behavioral addiction is the biopsychosocial model (Rosenberg & Feder, 2014). This model is defined as the interaction of the following factors:

- Biological (i.e., genetic predispositions, the resulting effects of addiction in the brain),
- Psychological (i.e. emotional, behavioral and cognitive factors) and
- Sociocultural (influences of one's family, friends and wider culture).

This model has been widely accepted in the field of chemical dependency and in the emerging field of behavioral addiction (Donovan & Marlatt, 2005, Rosenberg & Feder, 2014).

It is still unclear why some people develop compulsive or addictive tendencies, although there are different social, biological and psychological factors that make some people more vulnerable to these behaviors. Those with a family history of addiction or mental illness, those who have experienced childhood trauma, abuse or neglect are generally thought to be at higher risk for addiction. There is a high rate of comorbidity between mental illness and addictive disorders, so those with an existing diagnosis are likely to be at higher risk. Those with existing substance use disorders are also more likely to develop behavioral addictions (Potenza, 2006).

Patterns of behavior and personal choices also influence a person's risk of behavioral addiction. To develop a behavioral addiction, they usually need to have engaged in the behavior on multiple occasions and multiple times. Those who do this often and for a long time are also more likely to develop an addiction. Also, those who use the behavior as a way of coping with stress or other difficult emotions are more likely to develop problematic patterns and addictions. Certain personality traits can also increase a person's risk of developing a behavioral addiction. Research on drug, alcohol and behavioral addictions shows that people who are more impulsive and prone to risk-taking are more likely to develop addictions (Potenza 2006). Across all behavioral addictions, youth and young adults are overrepresented, suggesting that young people are particularly vulnerable (Grant et al., 2010).

## TECHNOLOGY ADDICTION AND ITS CAUSES

Technology is increasingly used in every aspect of human life. As devices such as computers, internet, smartphones, smartwatches, smart bracelets and smartphones have become an important part of daily life, technology is being used intensively.

Intensive use of technology is associated with problematic or pathological consumption. With the effect of the pandemic announced in 2020, the increase in the time spent by individuals of all age groups with technological devices, especially online (smartphones, computers, game playing tools), has brought the concept of technology addiction to the forefront. In this context, "can technology be an addiction?" is one of the frequently discussed issues in the literature (Griffiths, 2004). Recent studies emphasize that individuals with internet addiction, social media addiction, digital game addiction and smartphone addiction show similar symptoms to individuals with other behavioral or chemical addictions (Griffiths & Szabo, 2014).

Internet addiction, social media addiction and smartphone addiction are not classified as a disorder in the guidelines. However, in DSM-5, digital game addiction is recognized as "internet gaming disorder". In the literature, there are many studies addressing internet addiction, social media addiction and smartphone addiction as behavioral addictions (Shapira et al., 2003; Griffiths, 2004; Kuss & Griffiths, 2011; Griffiths, 2013; Lin et al., 2014; Van den Eijnden et al., 2016).

A common definition can be made for the concepts of internet addiction, social media addiction, digital game addiction and smartphone addiction: Technology addiction. In fact, in addition to these, TV addiction (Kubey R and Csikszentmihalyi 2002), phubbing (when people are buried in their smartphones and not interested in what is next to them) (Karadag et al., 2016), online pornography addiction (Owens et al., 2012), online shopping addiction (Dittmar et al., 2007) and online sex addiction (Grubbs et al., 2020) are considered within the scope of technological addictions in the literature. Excessive use, insatiable desire to use, neglecting needs due to excessive use, disruption of family and social relationships due to excessive use, using as a means of escape from negative emotions and stress, trying to give up and trying to reduce use, being nervous and anxious when it cannot be used, deceiving others about the duration and amount of use generally define technology addiction (Savcı & Aysan, 2017).

Technological addictions are associated with biopsychosocial problems such as depression, impulsivity, loneliness, impaired sleep quality, impaired self-esteem, and decreased academic performance. Therefore, research emphasizes the association of problematic technology use with mental illnesses and disorders such as depression, attention deficit hyperactivity disorder, anxiety, eating disorders, anger, panic attacks, social phobia, personality disorders and sleep disorders (Ikiz et al., 2015; Samaha & Hawi, 2016).

There are certain risk factors for technology addiction. These risk factors are:

- Young age: The earlier the problematic technology use starts, the higher the likelihood of addiction (Ögel, 2012).
- Male gender: It has been found that male users have higher addiction levels than female users (Morahan-Martin & Schumacher, 2000).
- Presence of another psychopathology: It has been found that those with impulse control disorder or substance addiction problems tend to use technology more excessively and pathologically. It has been stated that risky technology use can be seen especially in the presence of attention deficit-hyperactivity disorder, social phobia and depression in the young age group (Arısoy, 2009).
- Disorder in social and family relationships: It is stated that children who are not taken care of, who cannot find a healthy and safe environment within the family or who experience conflict within the family, who have experienced loss, who have few friends, who do not have sincere relations with their relatives, who are unsuccessful at school may use technology as a means of escape and that these children are the ones who suffer the most from the negative effects of computer games and the internet (Kelleci, 2008). It is observed that parents reward their children's use of technology, protect them from the dangers of the outside, distract them when they are left alone at home, turn them into a means of restraining active children; they turn a blind eye to the use of technology in order to prevent them from making noise or to do housework comfortably, and even encourage the use of technology. Failure to establish a secure attachment pattern during infancy, inadequate family relationships, inadequate attention and love, not spending enough quality time with the family, inconsistent behaviors within the family and unbalanced role distribution within the family are considered among the risk factors for technology addiction for adolescents.
- Peer relationships: Adolescents may see the widespread use of technology as a coping mechanism. A strong correlation was found between technology addiction and feelings of loneliness. In addition, peer pressure, lack of perceived social support, shyness and social anxiety levels are also triggers for technology addiction. In a study, hedonistic motivation, peer commitment and trust were found to be the causes of social media addiction (Nasr & Rached, 2021).

Since the scope of technology addiction is quite wide, the factors that cause technology addiction are also quite wide. In particular, developments in information technologies are the main problem that leads to the emergence of technology addictions (Chen et al., 2021). General factors that cause technology addiction are personality, personality traits, mood and environmental factors (Kuem and Ray., 2022). In addition, neighborhood relationships and past activities (busy weekends), low emotional intelligence (Hamissi et al., 2013), harsh working conditions (Li et al., 2017), anxiety for social acceptance (Seo &

Ray, 2019), and a wide range of other reasons seem to affect technology addiction. In this respect, it can be said that technology addiction is affected by many factors from macro to micro. Considering all factors, it is possible to say that personality traits and relationships with the environment are among the main causes of technology addiction.

The findings of the studies reveal that the causes of technology addiction are mostly based on psychological factors. This situation shows that it is important to question the psychological background of technology addicts in detail, as in other addictions. Factors affecting technology addiction are not only related to personality and psychological processes. It is also seen that environmental factors are also important. The use of technology is increasing day by day. This naturally leads to an increase in technology addictions. In this context, more research, information and treatment programs for addicts will be needed more frequently in the near future (Uslu, 2022).

## SOLUTIONS AND RECOMMENDATIONS

The definition of addiction has been clearly defined in the past, but today there is no consensus on the sub-headings of this concept. It is still controversial which of the many sub-types of addiction, such as gambling, digital gaming, shopping, sex, eating and exercise addiction, should be considered behavioral addictions. The term "addiction" is not included as a diagnosis in the DSM-5, a diagnostic guide for clinicians. Instead, a general term such as "substance use disorders" is used. The only 2 behavioral addictions that can be included in the guide are "gambling disorder" and "Internet gaming disorder". The term addiction, with all its subtypes, should be treated as a separate section in diagnostic guidelines.

The same is true for technology addiction. Although there are many subtypes of technology addiction such as internet, social media, computer, smartphone, screen, television, etc., it is only referred to simply as "internet gaming disorder" in DSM-5. It is clear that the definition in the guide does not cover all of the disorders. DSM-5 should be revised and technology-related addiction types should be included.

## FUTURE RESEARCH DIRECTIONS

The concept of addiction, which is an important public health problem, seems to be more popular for researchers in the coming period. However, although it is known that addiction is a problem caused by a combination of biological, social and environmental reasons, the factors leading to addiction should be investigated more deeply. In particular, the genetic aspect of addiction, which has not yet been clarified and not even a single gene or gene group has been found yet, should be tried to be elucidated.

## CONCLUSION

The concept of addiction, which has become one of the most important public health problems, was until recently used only for smoking, alcohol and other drugs. Today, however, it is used for a wide range of addictions such as gambling, exercise, eating, gaming, sex, computers, smartphones, television, internet, social media, digital gaming and shopping.

Both substance addiction in the traditional meaning and the newly added technology-related addictions are defined as a chronic medical condition that involves complex interactions between genes, environment and the individual's life experiences, characterized by continued use or compulsive actions despite the knowledge of harmful consequences.

Cultural, psychological, biological, personal, social and situational factors are thought to play a role in the development of addiction through a complex mechanism. In addition, technology is increasingly used in all areas of life. With the pandemic affecting the whole world, especially technology addiction has made a significant impact. The increase in the time spent with technological devices by individuals of all age groups has been found to be associated with technology addiction. Parents' wrong attitudes towards their children and family problems can also be a triggering factor for technology addiction. The widespread use of technology by adolescents as a coping mechanism for problems, feelings of loneliness, peer pressure, shyness and social anxiety may trigger technology addiction. In addition, technology addiction may be associated with some mental illnesses and disorders.

## REFERENCES

American Psychiatric Association (APA). (2013). *Diagnostic and Statistical Manual of Mental Disorders (DSM-5)*. American Psychiatric Publishing.

Arısoy, Ö. (2009). İnternet bağımlılığı ve tedavisi. *Psikiyatride Güncel Yaklasimlar, 1*(1), 55–67.

Arnaud, N., & Thomasius, R. (2021). Störungen durch Substanzgebrauch und abhängige Verhaltensweisen in der ICD-11 [Disorders due to substance use or addictive behaviours in the ICD-11]. *Zeitschrift für Kinder- und Jugendpsychiatrie und Psychotherapie, 49*(6), 486–493. doi:10.1024/1422-4917/a000748 PMID:32795136

Baggio, S., Starcevic, V., Studer, J., Simon, O., Gainsbury, S. M., & Gmel, G. (2018). Technology-mediated addictive behaviors constitute a Spectrum of related yet distinct conditions: A network perspective. *Psychology of Addictive Behaviors, 32*(6), 594. doi:10.1037/adb0000405 PMID:30211582

Bickel, W. K., Mellis, A. M., Snider, S. E., Athamnch, L. N., Stein, J. S., & Pope, D. A. (2018). 21st century neurobehavioral theories of decision making in addiction: Review and evaluation. Pharmacology Biochemistry and Behavior, *164*(February 2017), 4–21. doi:10.1016/j.pbb.2017.09.009

Chen, C., Zhang, K. Z., Gong, X., Lee, M. K., & Wang, Y. Y. (2021). Preventing relapse to information technology addiction through weakening reinforcement: A self-regulation perspective. *Information & Management, 58*(5), 103485. doi:10.1016/j.im.2021.103485

Christakis, D. A. (2010). Internet addiction: A 21st century epidemic? *BMC Medicine, 8*(1), 61. doi:10.1186/1741-7015-8-61 PMID:20955578

Derevensky, J. L., Hayman, V., & Lynette Gilbeau. (2019). Behavioral Addictions. *Pediatric Clinics of North America, 66*(6), 1163–1182. doi:10.1016/j.pcl.2019.08.008 PMID:31679605

Dittmar, H., Long, K., & Bond, R. (2007). When a better self is only a button click away: Associations between materialistic values, emotional and identity-related buying motives, and compulsive buying tendency online. *Journal of Social and Clinical Psychology, 26*(3), 34–361. doi:10.1521/jscp.2007.26.3.334

Donovan, D. M., & Marlatt, G. A. (Eds.). (2005). *Assessment of addictive behaviors* (2nd ed.). The Guilford Press.

Grant, J. E., Potenza, M. N., Weinstein, A., & Gorelick, D. A. (2010). Introduction to behavioral addictions. *The American Journal of Drug and Alcohol Abuse, 36*(5), 233–241. doi:10.3109/00952990.2010.491884 PMID:20560821

Griffiths, M. (2000). Does internet and computer "addiction" exist? Some case study evidence. *Cyberpsychology & Behavior, 3*(2), 211–218. doi:10.1089/109493100316067

Griffiths, M. (2005). A 'components' model of addiction within a biopsychosocial framework. *Journal of Substance Use, 10*(4), 191–197. doi:10.1080/14659890500114359

Griffiths, M. D., & Szabo, A. (2014). Is excessive online usage a function of medium or activity? An empirical pilot study. *Journal of Behavioral Addictions, 3*(1), 74–77. doi:10.1556/JBA.2.2013.016 PMID:25215216

Grubbs, J. B., Hoagland, K. C., Lee, B. N., Grant, J. T., Davison, P., Reid, R. C., & Kraus, S. W. (2020). Sexual addiction 25 years on: A systematic and methodological review of empirical literature and an agenda for future research. *Clinical Psychology Review, 82*, 101925. doi:10.1016/j.cpr.2020.101925 PMID:33038740

Hamissi, J., Babaie, M., Hosseini, M., & Babaie, F. (2013). The relationship between emotional intelligence and technology addiction among university students. *International Journal of Collaborative Research on Internal Medicine & Public Health, 5*(5), 310–319.

Holden, C. (2010). Psychiatry. Behavioral addictions debut in proposed DSM-V. *Science, 327*(5968), 935. doi:10.1126cience.327.5968.935 PMID:20167757

Ikiz, F. E., Savci, M., Asici, E., & Yoruk, C. (2015). Investigation of relationship between problematic internet use and psychological symptoms of university students. *International Journal of Human Sciences, 12*(2), 688–702. doi:10.14687/ijhs.v12i2.3336

Karadag, E, Tosuntas, SB, Erzen, E, Duru, P, & Bostan, N, Mizrak- Sahin B, Culha I, & Babadag, B. (2016). The virtual world's current addiction: Phubbing. Addicta. *The Turkish Journal on Addiction, 3*, 223–269.

Kelleci, M. (2008). The effects of internet use, cell phones and computer games on mental health of children and adolescents. *Turk Silahli Kuvvetleri Koruyucu Hekimlik Bulteni, 7*(3), 253.

Khoury, L., Tang, Y. L., Bradley, B., Cubells, J. F., & Ressler, K. J. (2010). Substance use, childhood traumatic experience, and Posttraumatic Stress Disorder in an urban civilian population. *Depression and Anxiety, 27*(12), 1077–1086. doi:10.1002/da.20751 PMID:21049532

Körpe, G. & Küçük, L. (2021). Covid-19 Döneminde Hemşirelik Öğrencilerinde Teknoloji Bağımlılığı. *İstanbul Gelişim Üniversitesi Sağlık Bilimleri Dergisi, 15*, 581-592. doi:10.38079/igusabder.981591

Kubey, R., & Csikszentmihalyi, M. (2002). Television addiction is no mere metaphor. *Scientific American, 286*(2), 74–80. doi:10.1038cientificamerican0202-74 PMID:11828703

Kuem, J., & Ray, S. (2022). Personality antecedents and consequences of internet addiction vis-à-vis Internet habit: A theory and an empirical investigation. *Information Systems Frontiers*, *24*(2), 579–594. doi:10.100710796-021-10110-2

Kuss, D. J., & Griffiths, M. D. (2011). Online social networking and addictiona review of the psychological literature. *International Journal of Environmental Research and Public Health*, *8*(9), 3528–3552. doi:10.3390/ijerph8093528 PMID:22016701

Li, Q., Guo, X., & Bai, X. (2017). Weekdays or weekends: Exploring the impacts of microblog posting patterns on gratification and addiction. *Information & Management*, *54*(5), 613–624. doi:10.1016/j.im.2016.12.004

Lin, Y. H., Chang, L. R., Lee, Y. H., Tseng, H. W., Kuo, T. B., & Chen, S. H. (2014). Development and validation of the Smartphone Addiction Inventory (SPAI). *PLoS One*, *9*(6), e98312. doi:10.1371/journal.pone.0098312 PMID:24896252

Mitchell, A. M. (2012). Overview of Special Topic Issue: Addiction and Technology. *Journal of Addictions Nursing*, *32*(3), 177–179. doi:10.1097/JAN.0000000000000421 PMID:34473445

Morahan-Martin, J., & Schumacher, P. (2000). Incidence and correlates of pathological Internet use among college students. *Computers in Human Behavior*, *16*(1), 13–29. doi:10.1016/S0747-5632(99)00049-7

Nasr, H. E., & Rached, K. S. B. (2021). The psychological and behavioural antecedents of Facebook addiction. *Academy of Entrepreneurship Journal*, *27*, 1–14.

National Institute on Drug Abuse. (2003). *Preventing drug use among children and adolescents: A research-based guide for parents, educators, and community leaders*. NIDA.

National Institute on Drug Abuse. (2014). Drugs, brains, and behavior: The science of addiction. *NIH Pub No.14, 5605*. NIDA.

National Institute on Drug Abuse. (2019). *Genetics and Epigenetics of Addiction Drug Facts*. NIDA.

National Institute on Drug Abuse. (2020). Drug Misuse and Addiction: What is addiction? Owens EW, Behun RJ, Manning JC, Reid RC. (2012). The impact of internet pornography on adolescents: a review of the research. *Sexual Addiction & Compulsivity*, *19*(1-2), 99–122.

Ögel, K. (2012). *İnternet bağımlılığı: İnternetin psikolojisini anlamak ve bağımlılıkla başa çıkmak*. Türkiye İş Bankası Kültür Yayınları.

Potenza, M. N. (2006). Should addictive disorders include non-substance-related conditions? *Addiction (Abingdon, England)*, *101*(Suppl 1), 142–151. doi:10.1111/j.1360-0443.2006.01591.x PMID:16930171

Rastegar, D., & Fingerhood, M. I. (Eds.). (2020). *The American society of addiction medicine handbook of addiction medicine*. Oxford University Press. doi:10.1093/med/9780197506172.001.0001

Rosenberg, K., & Feder, L. (2014). *An introduction to behavioral addictions. Behavioral addictions: criteria, evidence and treatment*. Elsevier.

Rumpf HJ, Achab S, Billieux J, Bowden-Jones H, Carragher N, Demetrovics Z. (2018). Including gaming disorder in the ICD-11: the need to do so from a clinical and public health perspective. *J Behav Addict. 7*(3), 556-561. doi:10.1556/2006.7.2018.59

Samaha, M., & Hawi, N. S. (2016). Relationships among smartphone addiction, stress, academic performance, and satisfaction with life. *Computers in Human Behavior, 57*, 321–325. doi:10.1016/j.chb.2015.12.045

Savci, M., & Aysan, F. (2017). Technological addictions and social connectedness: Predictor effect of internet addiction, social media addiction, digital game addiction and smartphone addiction on social connectedness. *Dusunen Adam : Bakirkoy Ruh Ve Sinir Hastaliklari Hastanesi Yayin Organi, 30*(3), 202–216. doi:10.5350/DAJPN2017300304

Seo, D., & Ray, S. (2019). Habit and addiction in the use of social networking sites: Their nature, antecedents, and consequences. *Computers in Human Behavior, 99*, 109–125. doi:10.1016/j.chb.2019.05.018

Shapira, N. A., Lessig, M. C., Goldsmith, T. D., Szabo, S. T., Lazoritz, M., Gold, M. S., & Stein, D. J. (2003). Problematic internet use: Proposed classification and diagnostic criteria. *Depression and Anxiety, 17*(4), 207–216. doi:10.1002/da.10094 PMID:12820176

Sherer, J., & Levounis, P. (2022). Technological Addictions. *Current Psychiatry Reports, 24*(9), 399–406. doi:10.100711920-022-01351-2 PMID:35792965

Uslu, O. (2022). Causes and consequences of technology addiction: A review of information systems and information technology studies. *International Journal of Social Sciences and Education Research, 8*(3), 299–306. doi:10.24289/ijsser.1131136

Van den Eijnden, R. J. J. M., Lemmens, J. S., & Valkenburg, P. M. (2016). The Social Media Disorder Scale. *Computers in Human Behavior, 61*, 478–487. doi:10.1016/j.chb.2016.03.038

World Health Organization. (2023). ICD-11 for mortality and morbidity statistics (Version: 01/2023). *06 Mental, behavioural or neurodevelopmental disorders*. ICD. https://icd.who.int/browse11/l-m/en

Yıldız, İ., & Kanak, M. (2021). Children's Digital Technology Usage and Parental Approaches: A Cross Sectional Study. *TJFMPC, 15*(2), 306–314. doi:10.21763/tjfmpc.797346

## KEY TERMS AND DEFINITIONS

**Addiction:** A treatable, chronic medical condition that involves complex interactions between genes, the environment and the individual's life experiences, characterized by continued substance use or compulsive actions despite knowledge of harmful consequences.

**Behavioral addictions:** Behavior-based addictions that cannot be linked to a physical substance. These include addictions to games, computers, television, gambling, etc. and technological addictions with human-machine interaction.

**Technology Addiction:** Excessive use of technology, insatiable desire to use technology, neglecting one's own needs due to excessive use, disruption of family and social relationships due to excessive use, using technology as a means of escape from negative emotions and stress, trying to give up and reduce use, being tense and anxious when it cannot be used, deceiving others about the duration and amount of use generally define technology addiction.

**Tolerance:** It is the body's adaptation to the presence of the substance/behavior and the person's taking more and more of the substance or increasing use to produce the same effects.

**Withdrawal:** The sudden reduction or cessation of use and the appearance of certain physical and psychological symptoms.

# Chapter 16
# Digital Addiction and Its Reflections on the Individual and Society

**Hülya Şirin**
https://orcid.org/0000-0001-8489-5005
*Gulhane School of Medicine, University of Health Sciences, Turkey*

**Gamze Ketrez**
*Gulhane School of Medicine, University of Health Sciences, Turkey*

## ABSTRACT

*Digital technologies greatly affect many aspects of our lives and make life easier in every way. Nowadays, more than half of the world's population uses digital technology. Continuous and excessive use of digital technological tools or applications can lead to digital addiction. Presently, digital addiction is considered as a behavioral addiction, although there seems to be a lack of consensus on its definition. Effects of digital addiction on individuals are physical, mental, cognitive, behavioral, etc. Also, digital addiction, characterized by excessive and compulsive use of digital technologies, can have significant effects on society. Those are social, economic, legal and ethical, educational, cultural and societal norms, healthcare, environmental, privacy, security, and mental health, impacts. From a public health perspective, the priority is to prevent the prevalence of digital addiction. Effective programs in prevention and treatment should include a multi-sectoral and interdisciplinary approach and be methodologically strong, evidence-based programs.*

## INTRODUCTION

Post-industrial societies have emerged with the realization of production by digital technologies. For this reason, the current era is also called the digital age (Yengin, 2019). The digital technologies used in this era were introduced into individuals' lives with the development of the computer in the 1940s and the discovery of the internet in the 1970s. (Çakır, 2005). The spread of digital devices like computers,

DOI: 10.4018/978-1-6684-8397-8.ch016

internet, smartphones and tablets in areas such as access to information, communication, education, health, socialization and entertainment has created digital culture (Biricik, 2022). Digital technologies greatly affect many aspects of our lives and make life easier in every way (Joseph & Joy-Telu Hamiliton-Ekeke, 2016). As digital technologies facilitate life more and more, are easy to access and are present in almost every field (such as education, health, communication, socialization, entertainment), their use is constantly increasing. According to the Digital 2022 Global Overview Report published in partnership with We Are Social and Hootsuite, more than half of the world's population is a digital technology user. Of the approximately 7.9 billion people worldwide, 67.1% use mobile phones, 62.5% use the internet and 58.4% use social media. The number of internet users has more than doubled in the last 10 years. It is also estimated that the number of internet users will continue to grow at an average rate of 4.8% per year until 2030 (We Are Social and Hootsuite, 2022).

As of January 2023, there are 5.16 billion internet users worldwide, equivalent to 64.4% of the world population. Among the regions of the world that use the internet the most, Northern Europe ranks first in terms of population in 2023. In Ireland, Norway, Saudi Arabia and the United Arab Emirates, 99% of the population used the internet as of January. North Korea ranks last worldwide (Statista, 2023b).

Digital technologies occupy a large share of time for people all over the world. The Digital 2022 Global Overview Report states that the daily internet usage time in the world is about 7 hours. So, if a person sleeps on average 7 to 8 hours a day, they spend more than 40% of their waking time online. The report also states that a person with internet access spends an average of 2.5 hours on social media every day (We Are Social and Hootsuite, 2022). According to Statista 2023 data, the average daily social media usage of internet users worldwide increased from 90 minutes in 2012 to 147 minutes in 2022 (Statista, 2023a). In a study conducted in the US, it was reported that participants looked at their phones 80 times a day (Deloitte, 2018).

The use of digital technologies has increased today compared to the period before the COVID-19 pandemic. During the pandemic, more people have spent more time using the internet, social media and mobile than ever before. The fact that the number of people using the internet worldwide increased from 4.3 billion in 2020 to 4.9 billion in 2022 with an increase of 12% during the pandemic period is an indicator of this (We Are Social and Hootsuite, 2022). The prevalence of internet use among women worldwide is 63% and 69% among men by 2022 (Statista, 2023b).

Young people appear to be the group that uses digital technology the most. Global internet use is higher among individuals aged 15 to 24 in all regions by 2022. Young people in Europe represent the most significant frequency of use at 98%. The world average of this prevalence among young people is 75% (Statista, 2023b).

The United Nations International Children's Emergency Fund (UNICEF) report on the use of digital technologies by children states that children under the age of 18 constitute approximately 30% of all internet users worldwide. It is also stated that internet use is shifting towards early childhood (UNICEF, 2017).

While the frequency of internet use in low-income countries is 26%, it is reported that 92% of the population in high-income countries use the internet (Statista, 2023b).

Increasing access to the internet leads to an increase in the use of digital devices. It is stated that the use of digital devices may have harms as well as benefits (Joseph & Joy-Telu Hamiliton-Ekeke, 2016). In this context, there is a possibility that increased frequency of use may lead to addiction (Christakis, 2019).

Digital addiction (DA) has emerged as an important area of research in recent years due to its increasing prevalence (Cemiloglu et al., 2022). Addiction is defined as an individual's excessive use of a substance despite being harmed, or the inability to continue, give up or control a behavior. Although substance addiction comes to mind when it comes to addiction, behavioral addictions such as gambling, overeating, sex, playing computer games, etc., which exhibit the characteristics of substance seeking without being addicted to a substance, are also discussed today (Griffiths, 1996). Addiction manifests itself in various ways such as preoccupation, tolerance, lack of control, withdrawal, mood change, conflict, lies, overuse and loss of interest (Lee et al., 2017). Continuous and excessive use of digital technological tools (such as computers, smartphones) or applications (such as social media, digital games) can lead to digital addiction (Christakis, 2019). Concerns about the increasing risks of digital addiction during the pandemic period have also been raised (Király et al., 2020). In order to prevent and treat the problems caused by digital addiction, it is urgently needed to systematically identify the prevalence characteristics and influencing factors (Meng et al., 2022). Presently, DA is considered as a behavioral addiction, although there seems to be a lack of consensus on its definition (Cemiloglu et al., 2022; Joseph & Joy-Telu Hamiliton-Ekeke, 2016).

Digital dependent individuals are those who do not have a social life outside the internet, feel lonely, alienated or asocial when they are away from digital devices, follow all kinds of applications and want to be informed about innovations, keep their social media accounts active, meet their friends on social media, disconnect from real life, feel excluded by society, and create a new identity for themselves on social media (Yengin, 2019).

The concept of digital addiction, which is tried to be evaluated in the category of behavioral addictions, first emerged when Goldberg and Young introduced the term "internet addiction" in 1996 (K. S. Young, 1998). Although there is not yet any diagnostic criteria for digital technology addiction, digital gaming addiction is considered as Internet Gaming Disorder in The Diagnostic and Statistical Manual of Mental Disorders (DSM-5) published by the American Psychiatric Association (APA) in 2013 (American Psychiatric Association, 2013). Furthermore, the World Health Organization (WHO) officially defined online gaming and gambling addiction as a disease in the International Classification of Diseases (ICD)-11 in 2018 (World Health Organization (WHO), 2022).

Digital addiction is an umbrella term that includes subtypes such as internet addiction, the much-discussed gaming addiction, smartphone addiction and social media addiction (Christakis, 2019). According to the studies, the prevalence of digital technology addiction and its different subtypes varies due to different diagnostic criteria and sample sizes. There is not yet a comprehensive study on the prevalence characteristics of digital addiction and its different subtypes in the general population worldwide and a corresponding prevalence rate. Therefore, in a meta-analysis of studies on the prevalence of digital addiction and its subtypes in general populations, which examined studies conducted on a total of approximately two million people from 64 countries, the prevalence rates of the subtypes of digital addiction are given separately. These rates vary between 6.04% and 26.9% (Meng et al., 2022). Epidemiologic studies have shown that the prevalence of different subtypes of digital addiction ranges from 0.5% to 84%, with large differences in the subtypes of digital media, diagnostic tools and methodological quality, and bias due to small sample size, single population, non-random sampling (Alhassan et al., 2018). Digital addiction can be categorized according to digital domains as in Table 1 (Singh & Singh, 2019).

Although digital addictions are divided into different subtypes such as internet, gaming and social media, they all mean the same thing: the person loses control over digital devices. Symptoms such as prominence, mood changes, tolerance, withdrawal symptoms and relapse, which are seen in behavioral addiction, are also seen in digital addictions (Griffiths, 1996). In addition, many studies have shown that digital addiction has many negative effects on human health and public health; it causes significant impairments in health, work and other social functions and significant problems in personal, family and social welfare (Bell et al., 2015; Dahl & Bergmark, 2020). Digital addiction manifests itself in both physical and emotional symptoms (Singh & Singh, 2019).

*Table 1. Classification of digital addictions according to digital domains*

| Digital Devices | Digital Platforms | Digital Media |
|---|---|---|
| Computer | YouTube | Video games |
| Smartphone | Facebook | Computer games |
| Tablet | Twitter | Internet |
| | Instagram | Online media |
| | | Online shopping |

# REFLECTIONS OF DIGITAL ADDICTION ON THE INDIVIDUAL AND SOCIETY

## Effects of Digital Addiction on Individuals

**Physical health effects:** Excessive use of digital devices can lead to various physical health issues, such as musculoskeletal problems (e.g., neck pain, back pain, eye strain), sleep disturbances, and sedentary behavior. Prolonged sitting and poor posture while using digital devices can result in musculoskeletal discomfort and pain (Straker et al., 2018). Sleep disturbances, such as difficulty falling asleep, staying asleep, or poor sleep quality, have been associated with excessive screen time and digital device use, particularly before bedtime (Hale & Guan, 2015). Additionally, prolonged sedentary behavior while engaging in digital activities can contribute to a sedentary lifestyle, which is associated with various health risks, including obesity, cardiovascular disease, and diabetes (Matthews et al., 2007).

**Mental health effects:** Digital addictions can also have negative impacts on mental health. Excessive use of digital devices has been linked to increased risk of developing mental health issues such as depression, anxiety, stress, and loneliness. Studies have found that heavy social media use and online gaming can lead to symptoms of depression, anxiety, and stress, as well as decreased well-being and life satisfaction (Kross et al., 2013; Lemola et al., 2015). Additionally, excessive use of digital devices can contribute to social isolation and loneliness, as individuals may prioritize online interactions over face-to-face interactions, leading to decreased social connections and increased feelings of loneliness (Primack et al., 2017).

**Cognitive health effects:** Digital addictions can also impact cognitive health. Excessive use of digital devices, particularly for entertainment purposes, can lead to decreased cognitive functioning, such as reduced attention span, impaired concentration, and decreased academic or work performance. Studies have shown that heavy digital media use, including social media, video games, and online browsing, can lead to decreased attention span, lower academic performance, and reduced cognitive control (Gentile et al., 2012; Rideout et al., 2010). Digital addictions may also contribute to multitasking behavior, which can negatively impact cognitive performance and productivity (Ophir et al., 2009).

**Behavioral health effects:** Digital addictions can also affect behavior, leading to issues such as cyberbullying, online harassment, and compulsive online shopping or gambling. Excessive use of digital devices, particularly in the form of social media, online gaming, or online shopping/gambling, can lead to addictive behaviors and impulsive decision-making. Cyberbullying and online harassment can also lead to psychological distress, emotional trauma, and negative impacts on mental health (Hinduja & Patchin, 2022; Kowalski et al., 2014).

## Effects of Digital Addiction on Society

Digital addiction, characterized by excessive and compulsive use of digital technologies, can have significant effects on society.

**Social impacts:** Digital addiction can have significant social impacts on society. Excessive use of digital technologies can lead to decreased face-to-face interactions, reduced social skills, and increased social isolation, which can contribute to a breakdown in interpersonal relationships and social cohesion (Elhai et al., 2017; Kraut et al., 1998). Moreover, the proliferation of online echo chambers and filter bubbles can lead to social polarization, reinforcing existing beliefs and contributing to societal divisions (Sunstein C.R., 2017). Digital addiction may also contribute to the spread of misinformation, cyberbullying, online harassment, and other negative social behaviors, which can have detrimental effects on individuals and communities (Kardefelt-Winther, 2014).

**Economic impacts:** Digital addiction can also have economic effects on society. Excessive use of digital technologies can result in decreased productivity, increased absenteeism, and decreased work performance, leading to economic losses for individuals and organizations (Leung, 2007). For instance, decreased productivity due to excessive technology use at work, impaired academic performance due to online distractions, and increased healthcare costs associated with technology-related health issues can all impact the economy (Andreassen et al., 2017). Moreover, the economic costs associated with treating digital addiction-related physical health problems and mental health issues, such as depression, anxiety, and sleep disorders, can also have a significant impact on society (Roberts et al., 2014; Ryan et al., 2006). Additionally, digital addiction may contribute to excessive spending on online shopping, online gambling, and other online activities, leading to financial strain for individuals and their families (Chóliz, 2010).

**Mental Health impacts:** Digital addiction can also have significant effects on mental health at the societal level. Excessive use of digital technologies, such as social media, online gaming, and online gambling, has been associated with increased rates of anxiety, depression, sleep disturbances, and other mental health issues (Turel et al., 2016; Twenge et al., 2018). The widespread use of digital technologies and the normalization of excessive technology use can also contribute to the perception of constant connectivity, leading to increased stress and burnout in society (Wilmer et al., 2017). Moreover, the constant need for validation and comparison on social media can negatively impact self-esteem and body image, contributing to mental health concerns and affecting societal perceptions of beauty and worth (Perloff, 2014).

**Legal and Ethical impacts:** Digital addiction can also raise legal and ethical concerns in society. Issues such as online harassment, cyberstalking, cybercrime, and intellectual property violations can arise due to excessive use of digital technologies (K. Young, 2009). For instance, issues related to privacy, data security, cyberbullying, online harassment, and digital misinformation can all have significant societal implications (Kuss et al., 2013). Digital addiction can also impact legal frameworks and regulations related to digital technologies, such as the need for regulatory measures to address addictive features in digital platforms and applications.

**Educational impacts:** Digital addiction can impact education at various levels. Excessive use of digital technologies, such as social media and online gaming, can lead to decreased academic performance, reduced focus and attention, and impaired learning outcomes (Rosen et al., 2013). Moreover, digital addiction can contribute to online plagiarism, cheating, and academic dishonesty, posing ethical challenges in educational settings (Bouhnik & Deshen, 2014).

**Cultural and societal norms:** Digital addiction can shape cultural and societal norms around technology use. The pervasive use of digital technologies can influence social norms and behaviors related to communication, social interactions, leisure activities, and information consumption (Mustafaoğlu et al., 2018). The normalization of excessive technology use and the constant need to be connected can impact social norms, expectations, and behaviors related to technology use (L. H. Shaw & Gant, 2002). This can result in a society that is overly reliant on digital technologies for communication, entertainment, and information, leading to potential loss of traditional social interactions and cultural practices.

**Healthcare impacts:** Digital addiction can also have healthcare implications for society. Excessive use of digital technologies, such as smartphones and computers, can lead to physical health issues such as musculoskeletal problems, eye strain, and sleep disturbances (Wu et al., 2013). Additionally, the increased use of social media and online platforms for seeking health information and support can impact healthcare practices, including patient-doctor communication, health information accuracy, and privacy concerns (Ventola C.L., 2014).

**Environmental impacts:** Digital addiction can also have environmental impacts. The production, use, and disposal of digital technologies can contribute to environmental pollution, energy consumption, and electronic waste, which can have detrimental effects on the environment and society (Hilty et al., 2006). Digital addiction can also have environmental impacts. The extensive use of digital technologies, including electronic devices and data centers, contributes to energy consumption, electronic waste, and carbon emissions, which can have adverse effects on the environment and contribute to climate change (Belkhir & Elmeligi, 2018). The increasing demand for digital technologies and the constant need for upgrades and replacements can contribute to a culture of consumerism and environmental degradation.

**Privacy and security impacts:** Digital addiction can also impact privacy and security in society. The constant sharing of personal information on social media and other online platforms can lead to privacy breaches and identity theft, exposing individuals and society to security risks (Dinev & Hart, 2004). Moreover, the spread of misinformation, fake news, and cyberbullying on digital platforms can have negative societal consequences, including social polarization and erosion of trust (Vosoughi et al., 2018).

## PREVENTION AND INTERVENTION STRATEGIES FOR DIGITAL ADDICTION

It is observed that concepts such as digital competence, digital well-being, digital literacy, digital minimalism and digital detox are used in studies aimed at preventing digital addictions. A brief overview of these concepts; Digital competence and digital literacy is the possession of the knowledge, cognitive, cognitive, motor, sociological and emotional skills, awareness and attitudes necessary for the informed, safe, critical and effective use of digital tools (Eshet-alkalai, 2004; Tso et al., 2022).

Digital wellbeing is seen as a way to maintain individual's mental and physical health in an environment of intensive use of digital technologies. It is an intervention in which digital technology is used to take control of the habits of use of digital technologies and to develop healthier habits, prioritizing the level of self-control that an individual can demonstrate over the use of digital devices (Thomas et al., 2022).

Digital minimalism, which also includes terms such as digital detox and digital diet, is the determination of digital activities that are beneficial for individuals, adjusting their online time and ensuring that they spend the rest of their time away from digital spaces (Biricik, 2022). In other words, it is a restriction of digital consumption.

In a US study, 65% of respondents agreed that a "digital detox" was important for mental health, but only 28% practiced it (American Psychological Association, 2017). Given the applicability of these measures, the APA offers seven recommendations to help use technology in healthy ways. These include not using the phone behind the wheel, not using the phone for alarms late at night and in the morning, muting all but the really needed notifications, letting people know when the phone is going offline, using social media wisely, staying away from the phone in face-to-face situations, and setting aside quiet time to recharge (American Psychological Association, 2017).

In a study examining recommended anti-digital addiction measures in the last decade, it was shown that, in general, the recommended measures were effective in reducing the addictive use of digital technologies (Cemiloglu et al., 2022). Considering these measures, what really needs to be done is to draw the framework of the use of digital technologies, which is the first step on the road to addiction (Dinç, 2015). Especially for young people and children born in the digital age, when it is not possible to live away from technological devices, clearly defining how they should be used and gaining correct and healthy usage habits from an early age will ensure that they both benefit from technology as much as possible and protect them from the harms of digital technologies.

Education and awareness programs aimed at promoting healthy digital habits, responsible technology use, and awareness of the risks and consequences of digital addiction can be effective in preventing and reducing digital addiction (Li et al., 2014). These programs can be targeted towards various age groups, including children, adolescents, and adults, and can be implemented in schools, workplaces, and community settings.

Parents play a crucial role in preventing digital addiction in their children. Setting clear rules and boundaries for screen time, monitoring online activities, and engaging in open communication about digital technology use can help prevent the development of unhealthy digital habits (Wang et al., 2019). Parental involvement and guidance can also support early intervention when signs of digital addiction emerge.

Cognitive-behavioral therapies, such as cognitive-behavioral therapy for Internet addiction (CBT-IA), can be effective in treating digital addiction by addressing underlying cognitive and behavioral patterns associated with excessive technology use (K. S. Young, 2007). CBT-IA focuses on cognitive restructuring, skills training, and relapse prevention strategies to help individuals develop healthier digital habits.

Mindfulness-based interventions, such as mindfulness-based cognitive therapy (MBCT) and mindfulness-based relapse prevention (MBRP), can also be effective in preventing and treating digital addiction. These interventions help individuals develop mindful awareness of their digital technology use, regulate their behaviors, and cope with cravings and triggers associated with digital addiction (Woods & Scott, 2016).

Technological solutions, such as apps and tools that promote responsible technology use, screen time tracking, and digital well-being, can also aid in preventing and reducing digital addiction. These tools can provide individuals with feedback, reminders, and support to manage their digital habits effectively (Elhai et al., 2017).

A multi-disciplinary approach involving collaboration among various stakeholders, including mental health professionals, educators, policymakers, technology developers, and parents, can be effective in addressing digital addiction comprehensively. This approach can involve a combination of education, prevention, intervention, policy, and technological solutions to address digital addiction from multiple angles (Hawi & Samaha, 2017). By integrating perspectives from different fields, a multi-disciplinary approach can provide a more holistic and comprehensive approach to preventing and intervening in digital addiction.

Family and social support can play a crucial role in preventing and addressing digital addiction. Creating a supportive and nurturing environment at home and in the community, where individuals can have healthy social interactions, engage in offline activities, and find meaningful connections, can help prevent the development of excessive reliance on digital technology (M. Shaw & Black, 2008).

Governmental policies and regulations can also be effective in preventing and reducing digital addiction. These can include regulations on advertising and marketing practices of digital technology companies, guidelines for responsible technology use in educational and workplace settings, and policies promoting digital literacy and healthy technology habits. Governments can regulate the advertising and marketing practices of digital technology companies to mitigate the potential negative impacts of digital addiction. For example, regulations can be implemented to restrict or control the targeting of digital advertisements to vulnerable populations, such as children and adolescents (Livingstone et al., 2011). Also, governments can establish guidelines for responsible technology use in educational and workplace settings to promote healthy technology habits. For example, guidelines can include recommendations on appropriate screen time limits, digital detox practices, and strategies for managing technology-related stress (Hill et al., 2016). Governments can implement policies that promote digital literacy skills among individuals of all ages, which can help them develop critical thinking and digital citizenship skills necessary for responsible and healthy technology use. Digital literacy programs can include education and training on topics such as online safety, digital etiquette, and media literacy (Fraillon et al., 2014). Health and safety regulations: Governments can implement health and safety regulations related to digital technology use, such as ergonomics standards for devices, warnings on potential health risks, and regulations on blue light emission from screens. These regulations can help mitigate the negative impacts of prolonged and excessive digital technology use on physical health and well-being.

## FUTURE RESEARCH DIRECTIONS

Although the concept of digital addiction is a controversial issue in terms of determining and measuring its frequency, it is accepted as a worldwide problem. It is also worrying that its negative effects on human health are quite high. From a public health perspective, the priority is to prevent the prevalence of digital addiction. Studies indicate that effective programs in prevention and treatment should include a multi-sectoral and interdisciplinary approach and be methodologically strong, evidence-based programs (Throuvala et al., 2019).

## CONCLUSION

In conclusion, digital addiction can have significant impacts on individuals and society as a whole. Excessive and compulsive use of digital technology can lead to a range of negative consequences, including physical health issues, mental health disorders, strained relationships, decreased productivity, and impaired social skills. It can also contribute to societal problems, such as increased cyberbullying, privacy concerns, and the erosion of face-to-face communication and social interactions.

At the individual level, digital addiction can result in a decline in overall well-being and quality of life. Physical health problems, such as sedentary behavior, sleep disturbances, and eye strain, can arise from prolonged and excessive use of digital devices. Mental health issues, such as depression, anxiety, and addiction disorders, can also be exacerbated by digital addiction. Additionally, strained relationships with family, friends, and colleagues can occur as a result of excessive technology use, leading to social isolation and a diminished support system.

On a societal level, digital addiction can contribute to broader societal issues. Cyberbullying, harassment, and online conflicts can arise from excessive use of social media and other digital platforms, leading to negative impacts on mental health and well-being. Privacy concerns, such as data breaches and identity theft, can also arise as a result of excessive sharing of personal information online. Moreover, the erosion of face-to-face communication and social interactions due to excessive reliance on digital technology can have detrimental effects on social cohesion, empathy, and communication skills in society.

It is important to recognize and address the factors that contribute to digital addiction, both at the individual and societal levels. Developing healthy digital habits, setting boundaries on technology use, improving coping skills, and promoting digital literacy and responsible technology use can help mitigate the negative impacts of digital addiction. Additionally, creating supportive environments that prioritize physical and mental well-being, healthy relationships, and balanced technology use can also play a crucial role in addressing the issue of digital addiction and its reflection on individuals and society.

In conclusion, although digital addiction seems to be a new concept and a controversial issue, it is an important public health problem of today and the future. There is a need to raise awareness and conduct more studies on this issue.

## ACKNOWLEDGMENT

This research received no specific grant from any funding agency in the public, commercial, or not-for-profit sectors.

## REFERENCES

Alhassan, A. A., Alqadhib, E. M., Taha, N. W., Alahmari, R. A., Salam, M., & Almutairi, A. F. (2018). The relationship between addiction to smartphone usage and depression among adults: A cross sectional study. *BMC Psychiatry*, *18*(1), 148. doi:10.118612888-018-1745-4 PMID:29801442

American Psychiatric Association. (2013). *Diagnostic and Statistical Manual of Mental Disorders* (5th ed.). American Psychiatric Association.

American Psychological Association. (2017). *Connected and content: Managing healthy technology use*. APA. Https://www.Apa.Org/Topics/Social-Media-Internet/Healthy-Technology-Use

Andreassen, C. S., Pallesen, S., & Griffiths, M. D. (2017). The relationship between addictive use of social media, narcissism, and self-esteem: Findings from a large national survey. *Addictive Behaviors*, *64*, 287–293. doi:10.1016/j.addbeh.2016.03.006 PMID:27072491

Belkhir, L., & Elmeligi, A. (2018). Assessing ICT global emissions footprint: Trends to 2040 & recommendations. *Journal of Cleaner Production*, *177*, 448–463. doi:10.1016/j.jclepro.2017.12.239

Bell, V., Bishop, D. V. M., & Przybylski, A. K. (2015). The debate over digital technology and young people. *BMJ (Clinical Research Ed.)*, h3064. doi:10.1136/bmj.h3064 PMID:26268481

Biricik, Z. (2022). Digital Addictions and Digital Minimalism as A Road to Escape from Digital Addictions. *The Turkish Online Journal of Design Art and Communication*, *12*(3), 897–912. doi:10.7456/11203100/022

Bouhnik, D., & Deshen, M. (2014). WhatsApp Goes to School: Mobile Instant Messaging between Teachers and Students. *Journal of Information Technology Education*, *13*, 217–231. http://www.jite.org/documents/Vol13/JITEv13ResearchP217-231Bouhnik0601.pdf. doi:10.28945/2051

Çakır, H. (2005). Internet as a Communication Language. *Erciyes University Journal of Social Sciences Institute*, *1*(19), 71–96.

Cemiloglu, D., Almourad, M. B., McAlaney, J., & Ali, R. (2022). Combatting digital addiction: Current approaches and future directions. *Technology in Society*, *68*, 101832. doi:10.1016/j.techsoc.2021.101832

Chóliz, M. (2010). Mobile phone addiction: A point of issue. *Addiction (Abingdon, England)*, *105*(2), 373–374. doi:10.1111/j.1360-0443.2009.02854.x PMID:20078493

Christakis, D. A. (2019). The Challenges of Defining and Studying "Digital Addiction" in Children. *Journal of the American Medical Association*, *321*(23), 2277. doi:10.1001/jama.2019.4690 PMID:31095260

Dahl, D., & Bergmark, K. H. (2020). Persistence in Problematic Internet Use—A Systematic Review and Meta-Analysis. In *Frontiers in Sociology* (Vol. 5). Frontiers Media S.A. doi:10.3389/fsoc.2020.00030

Deloitte. (2018). *Global Mobile Consumer Survey*. Deloitte. Https://www2.Deloitte.Com/Content/Dam/Deloitte/Us/Documents/Technology-Media-Telecommunications/Us-Tmt-Global-Mobile-Consumer-Survey-Exec-Summary-2018.Pdf

Dinç, M. (2015). Technology Addiction and Youth. *Journal of Youth Research*, *3*(3), 31–65.

Dinev, T., & Hart, P. (2004). Internet privacy concerns and their antecedents -measurement validity and a regression model. *Behaviour & Information Technology*, *23*(6), 413–422. doi:10.1080/01449290410001715723

Elhai, J. D., Dvorak, R. D., Levine, J. C., & Hall, B. J. (2017). Problematic smartphone use: A conceptual overview and systematic review of relations with anxiety and depression psychopathology. *Journal of Affective Disorders*, *207*, 251–259. doi:10.1016/j.jad.2016.08.030 PMID:27736736

Eshet-alkalai, Y. (2004). Digital Literacy: A Conceptual Framework for Survival Skills in the Digital Era. *Journal of Educational Multimedia and Hypermedia*, *13*(1), 93–106.

Fraillon, J., Ainley, J., Schulz, W., Friedman, T., & Gebhardt, E. (2014). Preparing for Life in a Digital Age. *Preparing for Life in a Digital Age*.

Gentile, D. A., Swing, E. L., Guan Lim, C., & Khoo, A. (2012). Video game playing, attention problems, and impulsiveness: Evidence of bidirectional causality. *Psychology of Popular Media Culture, 1*(1), 62–70. doi:10.1037/a0026969

Griffiths, M. (1996). Behavioural addiction: An issue for everybody? *Employee Counselling Today: The Journal of Workplace Learning, 8*(3), 19–25. doi:10.1108/13665629610116872

Hale, L., & Guan, S. (2015). Screen time and sleep among school-aged children and adolescents: A systematic literature review. *Sleep Medicine Reviews, 21*, 50–58. doi:10.1016/j.smrv.2014.07.007 PMID:25193149

Hawi, N. S., & Samaha, M. (2017). The Relations Among Social Media Addiction, Self-Esteem, and Life Satisfaction in University Students. *Social Science Computer Review, 35*(5), 576–586. doi:10.1177/0894439316660340

Hill, D., Ameenuddin, N., Chassiakos, Y. R., Cross, C., Radesky, J., Hutchinson, J., Boyd, R., Mendelson, R., Moreno, M. A., Smith, J., & Swanson, W. S. (2016). Media and young minds. *Pediatrics, 138*(5). PMID:27940793

Hilty, L. M., Arnfalk, P., Erdmann, L., Goodman, J., Lehmann, M., & Wäger, P. A. (2006). The relevance of information and communication technologies for environmental sustainability - A prospective simulation study. *Environmental Modelling & Software, 21*(11), 1618–1629. doi:10.1016/j.envsoft.2006.05.007

Hinduja, S., & Patchin, J. W. (2022). Bullying and Cyberbullying Offending Among US Youth: The Influence of Six Parenting Dimensions. *Journal of Child and Family Studies, 31*(5), 1454–1473. doi:10.100710826-021-02208-7

Joseph, R. (2016). A Review of Digital Addiction: A Call for Safety Education. *Journal of Education and e-learning Research, 3*(1), 17–22. doi:10.20448/journal.509/2016.3.1/509.1.17.22

Kardefelt-Winther, D. (2014). A conceptual and methodological critique of internet addiction research: Towards a model of compensatory internet use. *Computers in Human Behavior, 31*(1), 351–354. doi:10.1016/j.chb.2013.10.059

Király, O., Potenza, M. N., Stein, D. J., King, D. L., Hodgins, D. C., Saunders, J. B., Griffiths, M. D., Gjoneska, B., Billieux, J., Brand, M., Abbott, M. W., Chamberlain, S. R., Corazza, O., Burkauskas, J., Sales, C. M. D., Montag, C., Lochner, C., Grünblatt, E., Wegmann, E., & Demetrovics, Z. (2020). Preventing problematic internet use during the COVID-19 pandemic: Consensus guidance. *Comprehensive Psychiatry, 100*, 100. doi:10.1016/j.comppsych.2020.152180 PMID:32422427

Kowalski, R. M., Giumetti, G. W., Schroeder, A. N., & Lattanner, M. R. (2014). Bullying in the digital age: A critical review and meta-analysis of cyberbullying research among youth. *Psychological Bulletin, 140*(4), 1073–1137. doi:10.1037/a0035618 PMID:24512111

Kraut, R., Patterson, M., Lundmark, V., Kiesler, S., Mukophadhyay, T., & Scherlis, W. (1998). Internet paradox. A social technology that reduces social involvement and psychological well-being? *The American Psychologist, 53*(9), 1017–1031. doi:10.1037/0003-066X.53.9.1017 PMID:9841579

Kross, E., Verduyn, P., Demiralp, E., Park, J., Lee, D. S., Lin, N., Shablack, H., Jonides, J., & Ybarra, O. (2013). Facebook Use Predicts Declines in Subjective Well-Being in Young Adults. *PLoS One*, *8*(8), 69841. doi:10.1371/journal.pone.0069841 PMID:23967061

Kuss, D. J., Griffiths, M. D., & Binder, J. F. (2013). Internet addiction in students: Prevalence and risk factors. *Computers in Human Behavior*, *29*(3), 959–966. doi:10.1016/j.chb.2012.12.024

Lee, H., Kim, J. W., & Choi, T. Y. (2017). Risk factors for smartphone addiction in Korean adolescents: Smartphone use patterns. *Journal of Korean Medical Science*, *32*(10), 1674–1679. doi:10.3346/jkms.2017.32.10.1674 PMID:28875613

Lemola, S., Perkinson-Gloor, N., Brand, S., Dewald-Kaufmann, J. F., & Grob, A. (2015). Adolescents' electronic media use at night, sleep disturbance, and depressive symptoms in the smartphone age. *Journal of Youth and Adolescence*, *44*(2), 405–418. doi:10.100710964-014-0176-x PMID:25204836

Leung, L. (2007). Stressful life events, motives for Internet use, and social support among digital kids. *Cyberpsychology & Behavior*, *10*(2), 204–214. doi:10.1089/cpb.2006.9967 PMID:17474837

Li, W., Garland, E. L., & Howard, M. O. (2014). Family factors in Internet addiction among Chinese youth: A review of English- and Chinese-language studies. *Computers in Human Behavior*, *31*(1), 393–411. doi:10.1016/j.chb.2013.11.004

Livingstone, S., Haddon, L., Görzig, A., & Ólafsson, K. (2011). *Risks and safety on the internet: the perspective of European children: full findings and policy implications from the EU Kids Online survey of 9-16 year olds and their parents in 25 countries*. LSE.

Matthews, C. E., Jurj, A. L., Shu, X. O., Li, H. L., Yang, G., Li, Q., Gao, Y. T., & Zheng, W. (2007). Influence of exercise, walking, cycling, and overall nonexercise physical activity on mortality in Chinese women. *American Journal of Epidemiology*, *165*(12), 1343–1350. doi:10.1093/aje/kwm088 PMID:17478434

Meng, S.-Q., Cheng, J.-L., Li, Y.-Y., Yang, X.-Q., Zheng, J.-W., Chang, X.-W., Shi, Y., Chen, Y., Lu, L., Sun, Y., Bao, Y.-P., & Shi, J. (2022). Global prevalence of digital addiction in general population: A systematic review and meta-analysis. *Clinical Psychology Review*, *92*, 102128. doi:10.1016/j.cpr.2022.102128 PMID:35150965

Mustafaoğlu, R., Zirek, E., Yasacı, Z., & Özdinçler, A. R. (2018). Negative Health Effects of the Use of Digital Technology on The Development of Children. *Addicta: The Turkish Journal on Addictions*, *5*, 227–247. doi:10.15805/addicta.2018.5.2.0051

Ophir, E., Nass, C., & Wagner, A. D. (2009). Cognitive control in media multitaskers. *Proceedings of the National Academy of Sciences of the United States of America*, *106*(37), 15583–15587. doi:10.1073/pnas.0903620106 PMID:19706386

Perloff, R. M. (2014). Social Media Effects on Young Women's Body Image Concerns: Theoretical Perspectives and an Agenda for Research. *Sex Roles*, *71*(11–12), 363–377. doi:10.100711199-014-0384-6

Primack, B. A., Shensa, A., Sidani, J. E., Whaite, E. O., Lin, L., Rosen, D., Colditz, J. B., Radovic, A., & Miller, E. (2017). Social Media Use and Perceived Social Isolation Among Young Adults in the U.S. *American Journal of Preventive Medicine, 53*(1), 1–8. doi:10.1016/j.amepre.2017.01.010 PMID:28279545

Rideout, V. J., Ulla, M. A., Foehr, G., & Roberts, D. F. (2010). *A Kaiser Family Foundation Study GENERATION M 2 Media in the Lives of 8-to 18-Year-Olds*. Kaiser Family Foundation.

Roberts, J. A., Yaya, L. H. P., & Manolis, C. (2014). The invisible addiction: Cell-phone activities and addiction among male and female college students. *Journal of Behavioral Addictions, 3*(4), 254–265. doi:10.1556/JBA.3.2014.015 PMID:25595966

Rosen, L. D., Mark Carrier, L., & Cheever, N. A. (2013). Facebook and texting made me do it: Media-induced task-switching while studying. *Computers in Human Behavior, 29*(3), 948–958. doi:10.1016/j.chb.2012.12.001

Ryan, R. M., Rigby, C. S., & Przybylski, A. (2006). The motivational pull of video games: A self-determination theory approach. *Motivation and Emotion, 30*(4), 347–363. doi:10.100711031-006-9051-8

Shaw, L. H., & Gant, L. M. (2002). In defense of the internet: The relationship between Internet communication and depression, loneliness, self-esteem, and perceived social support. *Cyberpsychology & Behavior, 5*(2), 157–171. doi:10.1089/109493102753770552 PMID:12025883

Shaw, M., & Black, D. W. (2008). Internet addiction: Definition, assessment, epidemiology and clinical management. *CNS Drugs, 22*(5), 353–365. doi:10.2165/00023210-200822050-00001 PMID:18399706

Singh, A. K., & Singh, P. K. (2019). Digital Addiction: a conceptual overview. *Library Philosophy and Practice (e-Journal)*. https://digitalcommons.unl.edu/libphilprac/3538

Statista. (2023a). *Average daily time spent on social media worldwide 2012-2022*. Statista. Https://Www.Statista.Com/Statistics/433871/Daily-Social-Media-Usage-Worldwide/

Statista. (2023b). *Worldwide digital population 2023*. Https://Www.Statista.Com/Statistics/617136/Digital-Population-Worldwide

Straker, L., Harris, C., Joosten, J., & Howie, E. K. (2018). Mobile technology dominates school children's IT use in an advantaged school community and is associated with musculoskeletal and visual symptoms. *Ergonomics, 61*(5), 658–669. doi:10.1080/00140139.2017.1401671 PMID:29103354

Sunstein, C. R. (2017). *Divided democracy in the age of social media*. Princeton University Press. doi:10.1515/9781400884711

Thomas, N. M., Choudhari, S. G., Gaidhane, A. M., & Quazi Syed, Z. (2022). 'Digital Wellbeing': The Need of the Hour in Today's Digitalized and Technology Driven World! *Cureus*. doi:10.7759/cureus.27743 PMID:36106276

Throuvala, M. A., Griffiths, M. D., Rennoldson, M., & Kuss, D. J. (2019). School-based Prevention for Adolescent Internet Addiction: Prevention is the Key. A Systematic Literature Review. *Current Neuropharmacology, 17*(6), 507–525. doi:10.2174/1570159X16666180813153806 PMID:30101714

Tso, W. W. Y., Reichert, F., Law, N., Fu, K. W., De La Torre, J., Rao, N., Leung, L. K., Wang, Y.-L., Wong, W. H. S., & Ip, P. (2022). Digital competence as a protective factor against gaming addiction in children and adolescents: A cross-sectional study in Hong Kong. *The Lancet Regional Health. Western Pacific*, *20*, 100382. doi:10.1016/j.lanwpc.2022.100382 PMID:35967602

Turel, O., Romashkin, A., & Morrison, K. M. (2016). Health Outcomes of Information System Use Lifestyles among Adolescents: Videogame Addiction, Sleep Curtailment and Cardio-Metabolic Deficiencies. *PLoS One*, *11*(5), e0154764. doi:10.1371/journal.pone.0154764 PMID:27149512

Twenge, J. M., Joiner, T. E., Rogers, M. L., & Martin, G. N. (2018). Increases in Depressive Symptoms, Suicide-Related Outcomes, and Suicide Rates Among U.S. Adolescents After 2010 and Links to Increased New Media Screen Time. *Clinical Psychological Science*, *6*(1), 3–17. doi:10.1177/2167702617723376

UNICEF. (2017). *The State of The World's Children 2017 Children in a Digital World*. UNICEF.

Ventola, C. L. (2014). Social Media and Health Care Professionals: Benefits, Risks, and Best Practices. *P&T*, *39*(7), 492–520. PMID:25083128

Vosoughi, S., Roy, D., & Aral, S. (2018). The spread of true and false news online. *Science*, *359*(6380), 1146–1151. doi:10.1126cience.aap9559 PMID:29590045

Wang, F., Lu, J., Lin, L., & Zhou, X. (2019). Mental health and risk behaviors of children in rural China with different patterns of parental migration: A cross-sectional study. *Child and Adolescent Psychiatry and Mental Health*, *13*(1), 1–9. doi:10.118613034-019-0298-8 PMID:31649750

We Are Social and Hootsuite. (2022). *Digital 2022 Global Overview Report*. Data Portal. Https://Datareportal.Com/Reports/Digital-2022-Global-Overview-Report. 2022.

Wilmer, H. H., Sherman, L. E., & Chein, J. M. (2017). Smartphones and Cognition: A Review of Research Exploring the Links between Mobile Technology Habits and Cognitive Functioning. *Frontiers in Psychology*, *8*(APR), 605. doi:10.3389/fpsyg.2017.00605 PMID:28487665

Woods, H. C., & Scott, H. (2016). #Sleepyteens: Social media use in adolescence is associated with poor sleep quality, anxiety, depression and low self-esteem. *Journal of Adolescence*, *51*(1), 41–49. doi:10.1016/j.adolescence.2016.05.008 PMID:27294324

World Health Organization (WHO). (2022). *Gaming disorder*. WHO. Https://Www.Who.Int/Standards/Classifications/Frequently-Asked-Questions/Gaming-Disorder

Wu, A. M. S., Cheung, V. I., Ku, L., & Hung, E. P. W. (2013). *Psychological risk factors of addiction to social networking sites among Chinese smartphone users*.

Yengin, D. (2019). Digital Addiction as Technology Addiction. *Turkish Online Journal of Design Art and Communication*, *9*(2), 130–144. doi:10.7456/10902100/007

Young, K. S. (1998). Internet Addiction: The Emergence of a New Clinical Disorder. *Cyberpsychology & Behavior*, *1*(3), 237–244. doi:10.1089/cpb.1998.1.237

Young, K. S. (2007). Cognitive behavior therapy with Internet addicts: Treatment outcomes and implications. *Cyberpsychology & Behavior*, *10*(5), 671–679. doi:10.1089/cpb.2007.9971 PMID:17927535

Young, K. S. (2009). Internet addiction: Diagnosis and treatment considerations. *Journal of Contemporary Psychotherapy, 39*(4), 241–246. doi:10.100710879-009-9120-x

## ADDITIONAL READING

American Psychological Association. (2017). *Connected and content: Managing healthy technology use*. APA. Https://Www.Apa.Org/Topics/Social-Media-Internet/Healthy-Technology-Use

Dinç, M. (2015). Technology Addiction and Youth. *Journal of Youth Research, 3*(3), 31–65.

Fraillon, J., Ainley, J., Schulz, W., Friedman, T., & Gebhardt, E. (2014). Preparing for Life in a Digital Age. *Preparing for Life in a Digital Age.*

Statista. (2023b). *Worldwide digital population 2023.* Statista. Https://Www.Statista.Com/Statistics/617136/Digital-Population-Worldwide/

UNICEF. (2017). *The State of The World's Children 2017 Children in a Digital World.* UNICEF.

We Are Social and Hootsuite. (2022). *Digital 2022 Global Overview Report.* Data Reportal. Https://Datareportal.Com/Reports/Digital-2022-Global-Overview-Report. 2022.

## KEY TERMS AND DEFINITIONS

**Addiction:** Addiction is defined as an individual's excessive use of a substance despite being harmed, or the inability to continue, give up or control a behavior.

**Digital addiction:** Digital addiction is identified as functionally equivalent to all addictions, characterized by the compulsive, habitual, and uncontrolled use of digital devices and an excessively repeated engagement in a particular online behavior.

# Chapter 17
# Internet Addiction and Self-Esteem Amid the COVID-19 Pandemic:
## A Preliminary Study in Junior High School Students

**Thanos Touloupis**
*Hellenic Open University, Greece*

**Antonia Armaou**
*Hellenic Open University, Greece*

**Aikaterini Vasiou**
*Hellenic Open University, Greece*

## ABSTRACT

*Considering excessive internet use by early and middle adolescents during the COVID-19 pandemic, the present chapter describes an original preliminary study of junior high school students' internet addiction during the pandemic period, while also examining the role of self-esteem. Overall, 235 students (60.4% girls) of the three grades of schools in Attica (Greece) completed a self-report questionnaire, which included scales on internet addiction and self-esteem. Above average/normal and excessive/addictive internet use and indicative behaviors (e.g., lack of control) seemed to concern students, especially girls. Self-esteem proved to be a statistically significant negative predictor of the students' internet addiction. The findings contribute not only theoretically but also practically, highlighting the necessity of implementing school awareness-prevention actions to strengthen early and middle adolescents' social-emotional skills and safe internet use.*

DOI: 10.4018/978-1-6684-8397-8.ch017

## INTRODUCTION

The present study investigated internet addiction among junior high school students during the period of the COVID-19 pandemic, while also examining the predictive role of self-esteem. Over the last two decades, the penetration of the internet into our daily lives for entertainment, information and transactions has justified the labeling of the new generation as "digital natives" (Scolari, 2019). However, the multiple benefits that are offered by the internet, and especially the social media platforms (e.g., Facebook, Instagram, Twitter), can easily lead to risky online behaviors, such as internet addiction. Internet addiction is reflected in an individual's daily, long, and forced use of the internet, which negatively affects their social, psychological, and professional life (Wartberg et al., 2019). Even though internet addiction is not considered to be a clinical entity (American Psychiatric Association, 2013), it shares symptoms that are indicative of pathological gambling, such as withdrawal, neglect of social life, and denial of the addictive situation (Griffiths, 1995). According to Young's (1998) internationally used Internet Addiction Test, internet users are categorized based on their time spent online into those who use the internet below average/normal limits, within average/normal limits, above average/normal limits, and excessively/addictively.

The risk of excessive/addictive internet use seems to be more pronounced during the period between early and middle adolescence (i.e., 12-15 years old), due to its accompanying developmental characteristics. Specifically, during this period adolescents tend to manifest behaviors such as lack of boundaries, experimentation, need for acceptance, pursuit of new experiences, and identity research to a greater extent when compared to late adolescents and emerging adults (i.e., 17 years old and on), whose social-emotional and sexual development gradually stabilizes (Berk, 2015; Slater & Bremner, 2017). As a result, between the ages of 12-15, individuals are considered to be more prone to use the internet to meet their developmental needs (e.g., joining online groups, dating through social networks, online gaming), often developing maladaptive patterns of online behaviors (Blakemore, 2019) such as excessive/addictive internet use. Although internet addiction has frequently been investigated in the period of adolescence, most related studies focus on late adolescents (17 years old and on) or a mixed age sample of students between 12-19 years old, which results in an unclear picture of the extent of this phenomenon among early/middle adolescents (e.g., Aydm & San, 2011; Feng et al., 2019; Gunuc & Dogan, 2013; Lam et al., 2009; Li et al., 2019; Peng et al., 2019; Shek & Yu, 2016; Touloupis & Teli, 2021). Only a limited number of studies have focused exclusively on the vulnerable period between early and middle adolescence (12-15 years old) (Avar et al., 2017; Chung et al., 2019; Tamarit et al., 2021). However, these studies have mainly investigated internet addiction in relation to the adolescent's personal and environmental factors, and do not focus on the epidemiological aspect of the phenomenon. Therefore, further investigation of the extent of early and middle adolescents' excessive/addictive internet use is needed.

The literature highlights that intrapersonal social-emotional characteristics, such as self-esteem, can play a significant and negative predictive role in the manifestation of online addictive behaviors. According to Rosenberg (1989), self-esteem (i.e., an individual's global evaluative self-perspective) is significantly influenced by their interaction with important others, and the acceptance or rejection that they receive from them. Considering the important role of peers during the vulnerable period of adolescence (Berk, 2015; Slater & Bremner, 2017), it could be stated that: adolescents with a sense of low self-esteem trying to experience peer support and acceptance (Bastiaensens et al., 2019) are likely to be prone to spend many hours not only in face to face but also in online peer interaction (e.g., through social platforms, chat rooms, video games) (Hamilton et al., 2022; Odgers et al., 2020), probably ending up in excessive/addictive internet use. The predictive role of self-esteem in internet addiction has frequently been investigated in late adolescents and young adults (Angulo et al., 2021; Aydm & San, 2011; Bahrainian et al., 2014; Bozoglan et al., 2013; Peng et al., 2019; Shi et al., 2017; van Dijk et al., 2021; Yao et al., 2014; Zhang et al., 2015), while only a few studies have confirmed this predictive relationship for the vulnerable age group of students between early and middle adolescence (Chen et al., 2020; Lin et al., 2018). In addition, findings from cross-cultural studies do not mention an interaction between self-esteem and internet addiction (e.g., Sariyska et al., 2014). Consequently, questions arise about the pattern of this predictive relationship generally, and more specifically for the group of early and middle adolescents. Therefore, future studies could support the evidence-based necessity of timely implementation of school prevention actions regarding the enhancement of students' social-emotional skills (e.g., self-esteem), and subsequently their prudent internet use.

A discussion of adolescents' online risk behaviors (e.g., internet addiction) and their social-emotional characteristics (e.g., self-esteem) should consider the broader ecological context of these variables. According to Bronfenbrenner's (1989) ecological theory, an individual's behavior and skills are affected by a multilevel interaction of people and facts, from microsystem (e.g., family, friends) to macrosystem (e.g., social circumstances, governmental rules, laws). The latter was especially reflected in the recent unprecedented period of the COVID-19 pandemic. The restrictions that were imposed by governments worldwide during the pandemic period (macrosystem level), and the resulting limited face-to-face interactions with relatives and friends (microsystem) (Knox et al., 2022), appear to have negatively affected adolescents, both behaviorally and social-emotionally. Specifically, during and after the period of the lockdowns, the circumstances of the pandemic highlighted the internet as the most dominant means of communication and learning among youths, and especially adolescents (e.g., Fernandes et al., 2020). In addition, the unstable emotional state (e.g., low self-esteem) of many young people has been reported during the pandemic period (Vall-Roqué et al., 2021). Therefore, it could be likely that the period during the COVID-19 pandemic (amid and/or after the lockdown), such as the period when the present study was conducted, may act as fertile ground for making youths emotionally vulnerable and subsequently prone to problematic internet use. Considering that only one study confirms the predictive role of (14–19-year-old) adolescents' self-esteem in their internet addiction during the pandemic period (Stefani et al., 2021), there is a clear need to further investigate this issue, especially in the current period.

Finally, most studies related to internet addiction examine gender differences among adolescents. International findings conclude that boys, due to their over-engagement with online games (Griffiths, 1995; Leonhardt & Overå, 2021), are more prone to excessive/addictive internet use, developing indicative behaviors (e.g., neglect of social life), when compared to girls (Bayractar & Gün, 2007; Heo et al., 2014; Shek & Yu, 2016; Tsitsika et al., 2009). However, recent studies during the period of the COVID-19 pandemic seem to reflect a very different picture. They either mention that girls appear to be more addicted to the internet and smart phones (Davey et al., 2020: Effatpanah et al., 2020), or find that there are no statistically significant gender-based differences because males are more addicted to online games while females are more addicted to social media (Su et al., 2020; Günaydin, 2021). Therefore, it seems that the previous gender-based profile of addicted internet users probably began to change after the outbreak of the COVID-19 pandemic. However, further studies are necessary to clarify whether this is just an echo of the pandemic or if it is an emerging gender-based reality of adolescent internet users. The latter could inform us about possible gender-based at-risk student groups for excessive/addictive internet use.

Considering this literature review, the aim of the present study was to investigate internet addiction among junior high school students[1] during the period of the COVID-19 pandemic, while also examining the predictive role of self-esteem. Specifically, the research goals of this study were to investigate:

(a) The extent of internet addiction and the manifestation of indicative behaviors.
(b) The predictive relationship between self-esteem, and internet addiction and its indicative behaviors.
(c) The effect of the student's gender on their internet addiction and its indicative behaviors.

According to the related literature, the following hypotheses were developed:

**Hypothesis 1:** Students make excessive/addictive internet use, manifesting indicative behaviors (e.g., neglect of social life) (Feng et al., 2019; Lam et al., 2009; Li et al., 2019; Peng et al., 2019; Shek & Yu, 2016).
**Hypothesis 2:** Self-esteem negatively predicts internet addiction and its indicative behaviors (Chen et al., 2020; Lin et al., 2018).
**Hypothesis 3:** Male students make excessive/addictive internet use and manifest indicative behaviors to a greater extent when compared to their female peers (Bayractar & Gün, 2007; Heo et al., 2014; Shek & Yu, 2016).

## METHOD

### Sample

Overall, 235 junior high school students (93 boys, 142 girls) participated in the study from two school units of Attica, which is the largest Prefecture in Greece. The students attended the 1st (38%), 2nd (28%) and 3rd grade (34%) of junior high schools. Students' ages ranged from 12 to 15 years (*Mean* = 13.1, *SD* = .97). Since the pilot study did not indicate the necessity of modifying the questionnaire, the pilot sample (*N* = 73) was incorporated into the new sample resulting in the total sample of 235 students.

### Measures

The self-report questionnaire included initial demographic/personal questions (gender, age, class study) as well as the following two main parts:

*Internet Addiction Test*: Students' internet addiction was measured through the Greek version (using the back-and-forth translation method) of the Internet Addiction Test (IAT; Young, 1998), which has been previously used in Greek early and middle adolescents with satisfactory psychometric properties (from $a = .65$ to $a = .88$) (Touloupis & Athanasiades, 2014; Touloupis & Teli, 2021). This test includes 22 questions which reflect four behaviors indicative of internet addiction: (a) Salience (e.g., "How often do you fear that life without the Internet would be boring, empty, and joyless?"), (b) Lack of control (e.g., "How often do you find that you stay on-line longer than you intended?"), (c) Neglecting schoolwork (e.g., "How often does your job performance or productivity suffer because of the Internet?"), and (d) Neglecting social life (e.g., "How often do you choose to spend more time on-line over going out with others?"). Students were asked to respond on a 6-point Likert-type scale (from 0 = *Does not apply* to 5

= *Always*). According to Young (1998), the total score of each respondent is obtained from the sum of the answers given to the 22 questions, which ranges from 0 to 110 points. Students according to their score are classified into the following four levels of internet use: "below average/normal use" (0-21 points), "within average-normal use" (22-43 points), "above average/normal use" (44-76 points), and "excessive/addictive use" (77-110 points).

*Self-esteem Scale*: Students' self-esteem was examined through the Greek version (using the back-and-forth translation method) (Kokkiades & Kourkoutas, 2016) of Rosenberg's "Self-esteem Scale" (Rosenberg, 1989), which has satisfactory psychometric properties ($a = .75$). The scale includes 10 proposals/statements (e.g., "I take a positive attitude toward myself") reflecting a unidimensional structure ("Self-esteem"), which concerns the way individuals feel about themselves. The proposals/statements are answered on a five-point Likert scale (from 1 = *Strongly disagree* to 5 = *Strongly agree*).

## Procedure

Upon the approval for the study by the Institute of Educational Policy of the Greek Ministry of Education, the data collection took place in the classroom settings in the presence of the researchers and the students' teachers, after the end of lockdown in Greece but still amid the period of the COVID-19 pandemic (November-December 2021). Initially, the researchers obtained permission from the school administration to conduct the study, and then the consent form signed by the students' parents/guardians was secured. Before completing the questionnaire, both in the pilot and in the main phase of the study, the students were informed by the researchers about the purpose, anonymity and voluntary nature of the study and they were asked if they make internet use (within/away from home), to ensure their suitability of the sample for the purpose of the study. All the students mentioned they make internet use. Completing the questionnaire lasted approximately 15-20 minutes. Undoubtedly, all the prescribed rules of ethics were observed.

## Methods of Analyses

Statistical analyses were performed using the SPSS software package (V.28.0). To test the psychometric properties of "Internet Addiction Test" and "Self-esteem Scale", the principal component analysis method was used, as well as the internal reliability test through the Cronbach's alpha index. Descriptive statistics were used to depict the extent of internet addiction and its indicative behaviors (Hypothesis 1). Pearson correlation analysis (Pearson *r*) was applied to investigate the binary relationships among the variables involved. The predictive role of self-esteem in internet addiction (and its indicative behaviors) was examined through simple linear regressions (Hypothesis 2). Finally, multivariate analysis of variance (MANOVA) was applied to investigate gender effect on internet addiction (and its indicative behaviors) (Hypothesis 3).

## RESULTS

### Psychometric Properties

Regarding the "Internet Addiction Test", a principal component analysis was applied using the Varimax-type rotation (KMO = .863, Bartlett Chi-square = 1873.464, $p < .001$). In accordance with the proposed structure, four factors emerged with an eigenvalue > 1.0 and significant interpretive value (Table 1): Factor 1 = *Salience*, explaining 42.6% of the total variance; Factor 2 = *Lack of control*, explaining 8.3% of the total variance; Factor 3 = *Neglecting schoolwork*, explaining 5.4% of the total variance; and Factor 4 = *Neglecting social life*, explaining 5.1% of the total variance. The internal consistency indexes for the four factors were: $\alpha = .81$ (Factor 1), $\alpha = .82$ (Factor 2), $\alpha = .73$ (Factor 3), and $a = .68$ (Factor 4).

*Table 1. Principal component analysis of the internet addiction test*

| Questions | F1 | F2 | F3 | F4 |
|---|---|---|---|---|
| 1. How often do you find that you stay on-line longer than you intended? | .711 | | | |
| 5. How often do others in your life complain to you about the amount of time you spend on-line? | .654 | | | |
| 7. How often do you check your email/social media before something else that you need to do? | .556 | | | |
| 11. How often do you block out disturbing thoughts about your life with soothing thoughts of the Internet? | .612 | | | |
| 12. How often do you find yourself anticipating when you will go on-line again? | .803 | | | |
| 13. How often do you fear that life without the Internet would be boring, empty, and joyless? | .552 | | | |
| 16. How often do you feel preoccupied with the Internet when off-line, or fantasize about being on-line? | .628 | | | |
| 17. How often do you find yourself saying "just a few more minutes" when on-line? | .520 | | | |
| 22. How often do you feel depressed, moody, or nervous when you are off-line, which goes away once you are back on-line? | .659 | | | |
| 9. How often do you try to spend less time online but failing? | | .793 | | |
| 10. How often, when others ask you about what you do online, do you find yourself lying or hiding the truth? | | .897 | | |
| 14. How often do you snap, yell, or act annoyed if someone bothers you while you are on-line? | | .767 | | |
| 15. How often do you lose sleep due to late-night logins? | | .778 | | |
| 18. How often do you try to hide how long you've been on-line? | | .773 | | |
| 19. How often do you try to cut down the amount of time you spend on-line and fail? | | .602 | | |
| 20. How often do you try to hide how long you've been on-line? | | .573 | | |
| 2. How often do you neglect household chores to spend more time on-line? | | | .518 | |
| 6. How often do your grades or schoolwork suffers because of the amount of time you spend on-line? | | | .681 | |
| 8. How often does your school performance or productivity suffer because of the Internet? | | | .865 | |
| 3. How often do you prefer the excitement of the Internet to intimacy with your partner/? | | | | .564 |
| 4. How often do you form new relationships with fellow on-line users? | | | | .503 |
| 21.How often do you choose to spend more time online than going out with others? | | | | .840 |

*Note 1*: **F1**: Factor "Salience", **F2**: Factor "Lack of control", **F3**: Factor "Neglecting schoolwork", **F4**: Factor "Neglecting social life".
*Note 2*: All the above standardized loadings of the factors are statistically significant ($p < .05$).

Accordingly, regarding the "Self-esteem Scale", a principal component analysis was applied using the Varimax-type rotation (KMO = .879, Bartlett Chi-square = 752.686, $p < .001$). In accordance with the proposed structure, one factor emerged with an eigenvalue > 1.0 and significant interpretive value (Table 2): Factor 1 = *Self-esteem*, explaining 55.01% of the total variance. The internal consistency index for the factor was $\alpha = .83$.

*Table 2. Principal component analysis of the self-esteem scale*

| Proposals/Statements | F1 |
|---|---|
| 5. I don't have much to be proud of. (R) | .809 |
| 6. I have a positive self-attitude. | .757 |
| 7. Overall, I am satisfied with myself. | .709 |
| 3. All I can think about is that I'm a failure. (R) | .659 |
| 1.I feel I'm not a person of worth, at least on an equal plane with others. (R) | .750 |
| 9. I feel useless at times. (R) | .751 |
| 10. Sometimes, I think I am not good at all. (R) | .739 |
| 4. I can do things as well as others. | .792 |
| 2. I think as a person I have some good qualities. | .714 |
| 8. I think I should have more respect for myself. (R) | .807 |

*Note 1*: **F1**: Factor "Self-esteem".
*Note 2*: All the above standardized loadings of the factors are statistically significant ($p < .05$).
*Note 3*: (R) means reversed scored item.

## Descriptive Findings

Regarding the students' internet use, according to Young' s (1998) criteria, it was found that 5.53% of them used the internet below average/normal limits, 31.91% used it within average/normal limits, 56.17% used it above average/normal limits, while 6.39% made excessive/addictive internet use. Also, Table 3 informs about the Means and standard deviations of students' behaviors indicative of internet addiction (factors of internet addiction) as well as of their self-esteem. Based on the 5-point Likert type response system of the two scales, it seems that only perceiving internet as salience in students' daily life is slightly above average, while their self-esteem ranges above average.

*Table 3. Means and Standard deviations (S.D.) of the factors (behaviors indicative) of internet addiction and self-esteem*

| | Mean | S.D. |
|---|---|---|
| Salience | 2.60 | .93 |
| Lack of control | 2.02 | .98 |
| Neglecting schoolwork | 2.03 | 1.13 |
| Neglecting social life | 1.38 | 1.12 |
| Self-esteem | 3.11 | .55 |

## Correlations Among the Variables

Table 4 reflects the correlations among the variables involved (4 levels of internet use, 4 factors/behaviors indicative of internet addiction, self-esteem). It seems that there are positive correlations among the factors (behaviors indicative) of internet addiction (from $r = .151$ to $r = .634$, $p < .01$). Also, there are both positive and negative correlations among the levels of internet use (from $r = -.089$ to $r = .638$, $p < .01$), as well as between these levels of internet use, on the one hand, and the factors (behaviors indicative) of internet addiction, on the other hand (from $r = .202$ to $r = -.893$, $p < .01$). Finally, self-esteem was correlated both negatively and positively with the levels of internet use (from $r = .132$ to $r = -.275$, $p < .01$), and negatively with the factors (behaviors indicative) of internet addiction (from $r = -.271$ to $r = -.321$, $p < .01$).

*Table 4. Correlations among variables*

| | 1 | 2 | 3 | 4 | 5 | 6 | 7 | 8 | 9 |
|---|---|---|---|---|---|---|---|---|---|
| 1. Salience | - | | | | | | | | |
| 2. Lack of control | .634** | - | | | | | | | |
| 3. Neglecting schoolwork | .558** | .518** | - | | | | | | |
| 4. Neglecting social life | .355** | .151** | .169** | - | | | | | |
| 5. Below average/normal internet use | -.893* | | | | - | | | | |
| 6. Within average/normal internet use | -.714** | | | -.364** | .117** | - | | | |
| 7. Above average/normal internet use | .796** | .632** | .472** | .202** | -.215** | -.438** | - | | |
| 8. Excessive/addictive internet use | .699** | .557** | .441** | | -.389** | -.453** | .638** | - | |
| 9. Self-esteem | -.293** | -.271** | -.321** | | | .132** | -.213** | -.275** | - |

*Note 1*: ** $p < .01$.
*Note 2*: No statistically significant correlations ($p > .05$) were omitted.

## Predictive Relationship Between Self-Esteem and Internet Addiction

Based on Table 5, self-esteem seemed to negatively predict the three factors (behaviors indicative) of internet addiction (salience, lack of control, neglecting schoolwork) as well as the above average/normal and the excessive/addictive internet use.

## Gender Effect on Internet Addiction

The results showed that there is a statistically significant gender effect on the levels of internet use, Pillai's trace = .045, $F(4, 231) = 8.89$, $p = .002$, partial $\eta^2 = .88$, and specifically on average/normal $F(1, 233) = 4.32$, $p = .009$, $\eta^2 = .81$, above average/normal, $F(1, 233) = 5.41$, $p = .008$, $\eta^2 = .58$, and excessive/addictive internet use, $F(1, 233) = 5.98$, $p = .005$, $\eta^2 = .55$. Furthermore, there was a statistically significant gender effect on the factors (behaviors indicative) of internet addiction, Pillai's trace = .039, $F(4, 231) = 3.59$, $p = .007$, partial $\eta^2 = .82$, and specifically on lack of control, $F(1, 233) = 5.02$, $p =$

.026, $\eta^2 = .59$. All the above cases (average/normal / above average/normal / excessive/addictive internet use, lack of control) seemed to concern girls to a greater extent compared to boys (Table 6).

*Table 5. Self-esteem as predictor of internet addiction (and its indicative behaviors)*

| | | Predictor | $R^2$ | *Beta* | *t* | *p* |
|---|---|---|---|---|---|---|
| Factors of internet addiction | Salience | Self-esteem | .184 | - .466 | -5.479 | < .001 |
| | Lack of control | Self-esteem | .174 | - .271 | -2.039 | < .001 |
| | Neglecting schoolwork | Self-esteem | .189 | - .228 | -3.077 | < .001 |
| Levels of internet use | Above average/normal | Self-esteem | .145 | - .112 | -3.073 | < .001 |
| | Excessive/addictive | Self-esteem | .175 | - .293 | -5.385 | < .001 |

*Table 6. Gender differences in internet addiction (and its indicative behaviors)*

| | | Gender | *Mean* | *S.D.* |
|---|---|---|---|---|
| Factor of internet addiction | Lack of control | Boys | 2.07 | .78 |
| | | Girls | 2.31 | 1.05 |
| Levels of internet use | Within average/normal | Boys | 2.19 | .93 |
| | | Girls | 2.51 | 1.09 |
| | Above average/normal | Boys | 2.05 | .89 |
| | | Girls | 2.49 | 1.12 |
| | Excessive/addictive | Boys | 2.11 | 1.01 |
| | | Girls | 2.53 | 1.44 |

S.D.: Standard Deviation

## DISCUSSION

The present study aimed to investigate internet addiction among junior high school students during the period of the COVID-19 pandemic, while also examining the predictive role of self-esteem. According to the students' self-reports and Young's (1998) criteria of internet addiction, almost one-third (31.9%) seemed to be within average/normal internet users. However, more than half of the students (approximately 56.2%) mentioned they have above average/normal internet use, a stage before addicted online behaviors, while a significant part of them (approximately 6.5%) were categorized as excessive/addictive internet users. The students also seemed to perceive the internet as an important and integral part of their everyday life (salience). This behavior is indicative of their risky internet use (above average/normal, excessive/addictive). These results confirm Hypothesis 1 and related studies, which report middle and late adolescents' excessive/addictive internet use (Feng et al., 2019; Lam et al., 2009; Li et al., 2019; Peng et al., 2019; Shek & Yu, 2016).

The fact that the present study was carried out immediately after the end of lockdown in Greece probably explains to some extent the low percentage of excessive/addictive internet users because the participating adolescents are likely to have gradually started to return to most of their face-to-face daily habits and activities. A related study amid the period of the lockdown may have revealed higher percentages of excessive/addictive internet use among 12–15-year-old adolescents (as the participating students), as similar studies have revealed for older adolescents (Diotaiuti et al., 2022; Siste et al., 2021). Accordingly, the participating students' gradual return to school life during the period of the present study may have brought them closer to school duties, social life with friends, and a more disciplined time allocation, justifying to some extent why neglecting schoolwork, neglecting social life, and lack of control were not highlighted as the most dominant behaviors indicative of adolescent internet addiction, despite the fact that to some extent these students may still consider the internet as an important daily occupation (salience).

Given the younger age group of the participating adolescents, as well as the slower rates of technological penetration in the daily life of Greek youths when compared to other countries (Internet World Stats, 2016), the percentages of above average/normal and excessive/addictive internet use in the present study could be considered to be at least awakening, generally reflecting young people's risky internet use worldwide in the aftermath of the COVID-19 pandemic (Dong et al., 2020). In this context, the present findings highlight that school prevention actions regarding adolescents' prudent internet use should be intensified during and after unstable periods of crisis, such as the pandemic period.

This study also showed that the student's self-esteem negatively predicts their risky internet use (above average/normal, excessive/addictive) and indicative behaviors, such as salience, lack of control, and neglecting schoolwork. This finding confirms Hypothesis 2 and is in line with limited studies conducted on early and/or middle adolescents before and after the period of the pandemic period (Chen et al., 2020; Lin et al., 2018; Stefani et al., 2021). In the case of the participating students, it seems that their self-reported above average sense of self-esteem could act as a protective factor that led to their low percentage of excessive/addictive internet use. Generally, it is implied that the pattern of the negative predictive relationship between self-esteem and internet addiction is observed not only in late adolescence and emerging adulthood (e.g., Aydm & San, 2011; Bahrainian et al., 2014; Bozoglan et al., 2013; Shi et al., 2017; Zhang et al., 2015) but also for early and middle adolescents, whose more intense psycho-emotional rearrangements (e.g., need for peer acceptance, identity research) probably make the internet an escape for them (Berk, 2015; Slater & Bremner, 2017). This significant predictive relationship could be associated with prevention actions that are aimed at strengthening early adolescents' social-emotional skills (e.g., self-esteem) and their safe online behaviors, which have been applied to schools during the period of the COVID-19 pandemic (Blažević & Klein, 2022; Khairi et al., 2022; Touloupis & Athanasiades, 2022). Nevertheless, a related longitudinal study could reach firmer conclusions regarding the stability of the predictive relationship between self-esteem and internet addiction before and after the pandemic period.

Finally, it was found that female adolescents seemed to have risky internet use (above average/normal, excessive/addictive) and developed indicative behaviors (lack of control) to a greater extent than their male peers. This finding does not confirm Hypothesis 3 and is in contrast with studies that report male over-representation in internet addiction (Bayractar & Gün, 2007; Heo et al., 2014; Shek & Yu, 2016; Touloupis & Athanasiades, 2014). However, it is in line with recent findings amid the COVID-19 pandemic of female higher internet addiction (Davey et al., 2020; Effatpanah et al., 2020; Smahel et al., 2020). Regarding the latter, it could be stated that girls developmentally tend to enter adolescence earlier than boys from a biological and psychological perspective, and consequently their desire for experimentation, social interaction, and acquaintance (especially with the opposite sex) is usually more intense (Berk, 2015; Slater & Bremner, 2017). Therefore, during the pandemic period, these female psychological and behavioral characteristics were likely to have been channeled into a virtual environment (e.g., through social media platforms), which resulted in prolonged internet use (above average/normal, excessive/addictive), and subsequently in a greater lack of control than their male peers. Undoubtedly, future related studies could explore this emerging gender-based profile of excessive/addicted internet use in adolescence in more detail.

Undoubtedly, the findings of the present study should be interpreted with caution, due to specific limitations, such as the geographically limited sample, the possibly socially acceptable responses, the restriction to the quantitative methodology, as well as the cross-sectional research design. Nevertheless, the findings of the present study contribute on both a theoretical and an applied level. First, they enrich the international and especially Greek literature of internet addiction among early and middle adolescents amid the pandemic period, as well as the intrapersonal emotional characteristics (e.g., self-esteem) that could act protectively against risky internet use. The findings could also inform the school community (i.e., teachers, parents, and school psychologists and counselors), especially in junior high school education, to plan and intensify prevention actions that aim to convey a safe online behavior from the vulnerable period of early adolescence during and after unstable periods of crisis, such as the pandemic period. Finally, in the context of these actions, experiential activities should be integrated to enhance the adolescent's social-emotional skills (e.g., self-esteem), and subsequently their prudent internet use (Jolliffe & Farrington, 2006; Touloupis & Athanasiades, 2022).

## FUTURE RESEARCH DIRECTIONS

Within the general scope of the book "Perspectives on Society and Technology Addiction" and the more specific framework of the present chapter, future research directions emerge in this field. For example, future related studies could be conducted on a more geographically and numerically representative sample to strengthen the generalizability of the present results regarding junior high school students' internet addiction and the role of self-esteem. Furthermore, complimentary semi-structured interviews with adolescents could better capture the characteristics of their emotional state and their internet use, possibly reflecting more qualitative aspects of the issue studied. Additionally, extending the study to other age groups of students, such as elementary school students, late adolescents, and university students (emerging adults), through a longitudinal research design would allow safer casual relationships to be established between the variables involved during different developmental stages. The latter makes sense considering the limited number of studies that mention a reverse direction of the relationship between the variables involved, namely the predictive role of excessive internet use in self-esteem (Naseri et al., 2015; Stieger & Burger, 2010). Also, a longitudinal study that will cover the period immediately after (such as the current period) and years after the pandemic period and examine the effect of the COVID-19 through related variables (e.g., fear of COVID-19) could lead to safer conclusions regarding the longitudinal effect of social and hygienic circumstances on students' pattern of internet use and the role of their emotional state (e.g., self-esteem).

## CONCLUSION

Overall, the present chapter implies that in the aftermath of the COVID-19 pandemic the phenomenon of internet addiction seems to concern, not only late adolescents and young adults, but also younger age groups such as junior high school students. Furthermore, the relatively high levels of students' self-esteem seemed to constitute a protective filter against risky internet use (excessive/addictive, above average/normal) and the development of indicative behaviors (e.g., lack of control). Finally, in contrast to most of the previous findings, the present study reveals a different gender-based profile of excessive/ addictive internet users in early/middle adolescence, as the risky internet use and its indicative behaviors concerned mainly female students.

## REFERENCES

American Educational Research Association. (2013). *Prevention of bullying in schools, colleges, and universities. Research report and recommendations*. AERA.

Angulo, P. G., Mendoza, J. S., Contreras, E. C., Martínez, J. U. C., Hernández, C. B. E., & Hernández, M. E. C. (2021). The meaning of life as a mediator between self-esteem and Internet addiction in adolescents. *Enfermería Global*, *20*(4), 519–531. doi:10.1177/17456916211014189

Ayar, D., Bektas, M., Bektas, I., Kudubes, A. A., Ok, Y. S., Altan, S. S., & Celik, I. (2017). The effect of adolescents' internet addiction on smartphone addiction. *Journal of Addictions Nursing*, *28*(4), 210–214. doi:10.1097/JAN.0000000000000196 PMID:29200048

Aydm, B., & San, S. V. (2011). Internet addiction among adolescents: The role of self-esteem. *Procedia: Social and Behavioral Sciences*, *15*, 3500–3505. doi:10.1016/j.sbspro.2011.04.325

Bahrainian, S. A., Alizadeh, K. H., Raeisoon, M. R., Gorji, O. H., & Khazaee, A. (2014). Relationship of Internet addiction with self-esteem and depression in university students. *Journal of Preventive Medicine and Hygiene*, *55*(3), 86–89. PMID:25902574

Bastiaensens, S., Van Cleemput, K., Vandebosch, H., Poels, K., DeSmet, A., & De Bourdeaudhuij, I. (2019). "Were You Cyberbullied? Let Me Help You." Studying Adolescents' Online Peer Support of Cyberbullying Victims Using Thematic Analysis of Online Support Group Fora. In H. Vandebosch & L. Green (Eds.), *Narratives in Research and Interventions on Cyberbullying among Young People* (pp. 95–112). Springer. doi:10.1007/978-3-030-04960-7_7

Bayraktar, F., & Gün, Z. (2007). Incidence and Correlates of Internet Usage Among Adolescents in North Cyprus. *Cyberpsychology & Behavior*, *10*(2), 191–197. doi:10.1089/cpb.2006.9969 PMID:17474835

Berk, L. (2015). *Child development*. Pearson Higher Education AU.

Blakemore, S. J. (2019). Adolescence and mental health. *Lancet*, *393*(10185), 2030–2031. doi:10.1016/S0140-6736(19)31013-X PMID:31106741

Blažević, I., & Klein, N. (2022). Digital Media and Internet Safety Among Primary School Students During the Covid-19 Pandemic. *Journal of Elementary Education, 15*(2), 127–144. doi:10.18690/rei.15.2.127-144.2022

Bozoglan, B., Demirer, V., & Sahin, I. (2013). Loneliness, self-esteem, and life satisfaction as predictors of Internet addiction: A cross-sectional study among Turkish university students. *Scandinavian Journal of Psychology, 54*(4), 313–319. doi:10.1111jop.12049 PMID:23577670

Bronfenbrenner, U. (1989). Ecological systems theory. In R. Vasta (Ed.), *Annals of child development* (Vol. 6, pp. 187–249). JAI Press.

Chen, H. C., Wang, J. Y., Lin, Y. L., & Yang, S. Y. (2020). Association of internet addiction with family functionality, depression, self-efficacy and self-esteem among early adolescents. *International Journal of Environmental Research and Public Health, 17*(23), 8820. doi:10.3390/ijerph17238820 PMID:33260988

Chung, S., Lee, J., & Lee, H. K. (2019). Personal factors, internet characteristics, and environmental factors contributing to adolescent internet addiction: A public health perspective. *International Journal of Environmental Research and Public Health, 16*(23), 4635. doi:10.3390/ijerph16234635 PMID:31766527

Davey, A., Nasser, K., & Davey, S. (2020). Gender differential for smart phone addiction and its predictors among adolescents: Assessing relationship with self-control via sem approach. *Journal of Indian Association for Child and Adolescent Mental Health, 16*(3), 80–101. doi:10.1177/0973134220200305

Diotaiuti, P., Girelli, L., Mancone, S., Corrado, S., Valente, G., & Cavicchiolo, E. (2022). Impulsivity and depressive brooding in internet addiction: A study with a sample of Italian adolescents during COVID-19 lockdown. *Frontiers in Psychiatry, 13*, 941313. doi:10.3389/fpsyt.2022.941313 PMID:35898621

Dong, H., Yang, F., Lu, X., & Hao, W. (2020). Internet addiction and related psychological factors among children and adolescents in China during the coronavirus disease 2019 (COVID-19) epidemic. *Frontiers in Psychiatry, 11*, 751. doi:10.3389/fpsyt.2020.00751 PMID:32982806

Effatpanah, M., Moharrami, M., Damavandi, G. R., Aminikhah, M., Nezhad, M. H., Khatami, F., Arjmand, T., Tarighatnia, H., & Yekaninejad, M. S. (2020). Association of internet addiction with emotional and behavioral characteristics of adolescents. *Iranian Journal of Psychiatry, 15*(1), 55–56. doi:10.18502/ijps.v15i1.2440 PMID:32377215

Feng, Y., Ma, Y., & Zhong, Q. (2019). The relationship between adolescents' stress and internet addiction: A mediated-moderation model. *Frontiers in Psychology, 10*, 2248. doi:10.3389/fpsyg.2019.02248 PMID:31636590

Fernandes, B., Biswas, U. N., Mansukhani, R. T., Casarín, A. V., & Essau, C. A. (2020). The impact of COVID-19 lockdown on internet use and escapism in adolescents. *Revista de psicología clínica con niños y adolescentes, 7*(3), 59-65.

Griffiths, M. D. (1995). Technological addictions. *Clinical Psychology Forum, 76*, 14-19.

Günaydin, H. D. (2021). Personality Traits, Gender, Frequency of Internet Use as Predictors of Turkish Teenagers' Internet Addiction. *Turkish Online Journal of Educational Technology-TOJET, 20*(4), 44–52.

Gunuc, S., & Dogan, A. (2013). The relationships between Turkish adolescents' Internet addiction, their perceived social support and family activities. *Computers in Human Behavior, 29*(6), 2197–2207. doi:10.1016/j.chb.2013.04.011

Hamilton, J. L., Nesi, J., & Choukas-Bradley, S. (2022). Reexamining social media and socioemotional well-being among adolescents through the lens of the COVID-19 pandemic: A theoretical review and directions for future research. *Perspectives on Psychological Science, 17*(3), 662–679. doi:10.1177/17456916211014189 PMID:34756118

Heo, J., Oh, J., Subramanian, S. V., Kim, Y., & Kawachi, I. (2014). Addictive Internet use among Korean adolescents: A national survey. *PLoS One, 9*(2), e87819. doi:10.1371/journal.pone.0087819 PMID:24505318

Internet World Stats. (2016). *Database for worldwide Internet statistics.* Internet World Stats. http:www.internetworldstats.com/Europa.htm

Jolliffe, D., & Farrington, D. (2006). Examining the relationship between low empathy and bullying. *Aggressive Behavior, 32*(6), 540–550. doi:10.1002/ab.20154

Khairi, A. K., Li, W., Yeo, S. H., Tong, Y. S., Nazri, M., Rahman, B. A., & Motevalli, S. (2022). The Importance of Emotional Competence in Preventing Cyberbullying: The Role of Family as Moderator. *International Journal of Academic Research in Business & Social Sciences, 12*(4), 262–278. doi:10.6007/IJARBSS/v12-i4/13062

Knox, L., Karantzas, G. C., Romano, D., Feeney, J. A., & Simpson, J. A. (2022). One Year On: What we have learned about the psychological effects of Covid-19 social restrictions–a meta-analysis. *Current Opinion in Psychology, 101315*, 101315. doi:10.1016/j.copsyc.2022.101315 PMID:35398753

Kokkiades, M., & Kourkoutas, I. (2016). School bullying/victimization, self-esteem and emotional difficulties in children with and without SEN [in Greek]. *Scientific Annals of the Pedagogical Department of Preschool Education of the University of Ioannina, 9*, 88–128.

Lam, L. T., Peng, Z. W., Mai, J. C., & Jing, J. (2009). Factors associated with Internet addiction among adolescents. *Cyberpsychology & Behavior, 12*(5), 551–555. doi:10.1089/cpb.2009.0036 PMID:19619039

Leonhardt, M., & Overå, S. (2021). Are there differences in video gaming and use of social media among boys and girls?-A mixed methods approach. *International Journal of Environmental Research and Public Health, 18*(11), 6085. doi:10.3390/ijerph18116085 PMID:34200039

Li, G., Hou, G., Yang, D., Jian, H., & Wang, W. (2019). Relationship between anxiety, depression, sex, obesity, and internet addiction in Chinese adolescents: A short-term longitudinal study. *Addictive Behaviors, 90*, 421–427. doi:10.1016/j.addbeh.2018.12.009 PMID:30553156

Lin, M. P., Wu, J. Y. W., You, J., Chang, K. M., Hu, W. H., & Xu, S. (2018). Association between online and offline social support and internet addiction in a representative sample of senior high school students in Taiwan: The mediating role of self-esteem. *Computers in Human Behavior, 84*, 1–7. doi:10.1016/j.chb.2018.02.007

Naseri, L., Mohamadi, J., Sayehmiri, K., & Azizpoor, Y. (2015). Perceived social support, self-esteem, and internet addiction among students of Al-Zahra University, Tehran, Iran. *Iranian Journal of Psychiatry and Behavioral Sciences*, *9*(3), e421. doi:10.17795/ijpbs-421 PMID:26576175

Odgers, C. L., Schueller, S. M., & Ito, M. (2020). Screen time, social media use, and adolescent development. *Annual Review of Developmental Psychology*, *2*(1), 485–502. doi:10.1146/annurev-devpsych-121318-084815

Peng, W., Li, D., Li, D., Jia, J., Wang, Y., & Sun, W. (2019). School disconnectedness and Adolescent Internet Addiction: Mediation by self-esteem and moderation by emotional intelligence. *Computers in Human Behavior*, *98*, 111–121. doi:10.1016/j.chb.2019.04.011

Rosenberg, M. (1989). *Society and the adolescent self-image*. Wesleyan University Press.

Sariyska, R., Reuter, M., Bey, K., Sha, P., Li, M., Chen, Y. F., Liu, W.-Y., Zhu, Y.-K., Li, C.-B., Suárez-Rivillas, A., Feldmann, M., Hellmann, M., Keiper, J., Markett, S., Young, S. K., & Montag, C. (2014). Self-esteem, personality and internet addiction: A cross-cultural comparison study. *Personality and Individual Differences*, *61*, 28–33. doi:10.1016/j.paid.2014.01.001

Scolari, C. A. (2019). Beyond the myth of the "digital native" Adolescents, collaborative cultures and transmedia skills. *Nordic Journal of Digital Literacy*, *14*(3-4), 164–174. doi:10.18261/issn.1891-943x-2019-03-04-06

Shek, D. T., & Yu, L. (2016). Adolescent internet addiction in Hong Kong: Prevalence, change, and correlates. *Journal of Pediatric and Adolescent Gynecology*, *29*(1), S22–S30. doi:10.1016/j.jpag.2015.10.005 PMID:26461526

Shi, X., Wang, J., & Zou, H. (2017). Family functioning and Internet addiction among Chinese adolescents: The mediating roles of self-esteem and loneliness. *Computers in Human Behavior*, *76*, 201–210. doi:10.1016/j.chb.2017.07.028

Siste, K., Hanafi, E., Sen, L. T., Murtani, B. J., Christian, H., Limawan, A. P., Siswidiani, L. P., & Adrian. (2021). Implications of COVID-19 and lockdown on internet addiction among adolescents: Data from a developing country. *Frontiers in Psychiatry*, *12*, 665675. doi:10.3389/fpsyt.2021.665675 PMID:34054619

Slater, A., & Bremner, J. G. (2017). *An introduction to developmental psychology*. Wiley.

Smahel, D., Machackova, H., Mascheroni, G., Dedkova, L., Staksrud, E., Ólafsson, K., Livingstone, S., & Hasebrink, U. (2020). *EU Kids Online 2020: Survey results from 19 countries*. EU Kids Online 2020. http://hdl.handle.net/20.500.12162/5299

Stefani, S., & Tiatri, S. (2021, August). How Adolescent's Self-Esteem Affects Internet Addiction Tendency During COVID-19 Pandemic in Takengon, Central Aceh. In *International Conference on Economics, Business, Social, and Humanities (ICEBSH 2021)* (pp. 951-957). Atlantis Press. 10.2991/assehr.k.210805.150

Stieger, S., & Burger, C. (2010). Implicit and explicit self-esteem in the context of internet addiction. *Cyberpsychology, Behavior, and Social Networking*, *13*(6), 681–688. doi:10.1089/cyber.2009.0426 PMID:21142993

Su, W., Han, X., Yu, H., Wu, Y., & Potenza, M. N. (2020). Do men become addicted to internet gaming and women to social media? A meta-analysis examining gender-related differences in specific internet addiction. *Computers in Human Behavior, 113*, 106480. doi:10.1016/j.chb.2020.106480

Tamarit, A., Schoeps, K., Peris-Hernández, M., & Montoya-Castilla, I. (2021). The impact of adolescent internet addiction on sexual online victimization: The mediating effects of sexting and body self-esteem. *International Journal of Environmental Research and Public Health, 18*(8), 4226. doi:10.3390/ijerph18084226 PMID:33923552

Touloupis, T., & Athanasiades, C. (2014). The Risky Use of New Technology among Elementary School Students: Internet Addiction and Cyberbullying [in Greek]. *Hellenic Journal of Psychology, 11*, 83–110.

Touloupis, T., & Athanasiades, C. (2022). Evaluation of a cyberbullying prevention program in elementary schools: The role of self-esteem enhancement. *Frontiers in Psychology (section: Positive Psychology), 13*, 980091. doi:10.3389/fpsyg.2022.980091

Touloupis, T., & Teli, A. (2021). Internet Addiction among Adolescents: The Role of Social Self-Efficacy and General Locus of Control. In J. J. Jaworski (Ed.), *Advances in Sociology Research* (Vol. 36, pp. 81–112). Nova Science Publishers. doi:10.52305/GPAQ8046

Tsitsika, A., Critselis, E., Kormas, G., Konstantoulaki, E., Constantopoulos, A., & Kafetzis, D. (2009). Adolescent pornographic internet site use: A multivariate regression analysis of the predictive factors of use and psychosocial implications. *Cyberpsychology & Behavior, 12*(5), 545–550. doi:10.1089/cpb.2008.0346 PMID:19772438

Vall-Roqué, H., Andrés, A., & Saldaña, C. (2021). The impact of COVID-19 lockdown on social network sites use, body image disturbances and self-esteem among adolescent and young women. *Progress in Neuro-Psychopharmacology & Biological Psychiatry, 110*, 110293. doi:10.1016/j.pnpbp.2021.110293 PMID:33662532

van Dijk, R., van der Valk, I. E., Vossen, H. G., Branje, S., & Deković, M. (2021). Problematic internet use in adolescents from divorced families: The role of family factors and adolescents' self-esteem. *International Journal of Environmental Research and Public Health, 18*(7), 3385. doi:10.3390/ijerph18073385 PMID:33805855

Wartberg, L., Kriston, L., Zieglmeier, M., Lincoln, T., & Kammerl, R. (2019). A longitudinal study on psychosocial causes and consequences of Internet gaming disorder in adolescence. *Psychological Medicine, 49*(2), 287–294. doi:10.1017/S003329171800082X PMID:29622057

Yao, M. Z., He, J., Ko, D. M., & Pang, K. (2014). The influence of personality, parental behaviors, and self-esteem on Internet addiction: A study of Chinese college students. *Cyberpsychology, Behavior, and Social Networking, 17*(2), 104–110. doi:10.1089/cyber.2012.0710 PMID:24003966

Young, K. (1998). *Caught in the net: How to recognize the signs of internet addiction and a winning strategy for recovery*. John Wiley & Sons.

Zhang, Y., Mei, S., Li, L., Chai, J., Li, J., & Du, H. (2015). The relationship between impulsivity and internet addiction in Chinese college students: A moderated mediation analysis of meaning in life and self-esteem. *PLoS One, 10*(7), e0131597. doi:10.1371/journal.pone.0131597 PMID:26171860

## ADDITIONAL READING


Adiele, I., & Olatokun, W. (2014). Prevalence and determinants of Internet addiction among adolescents. *Computers in Human Behavior*, *31*, 100–110. doi:10.1016/j.chb.2013.10.028

Chi, X., Hong, X., & Chen, X. (2020). Profiles and sociodemographic correlates of Internet addiction in early adolescents in southern China. *Addictive Behaviors*, *106*, 106385. doi:10.1016/j.addbeh.2020.106385 PMID:32187574

Fumero, A., Marrero, R. J., Voltes, D., & Penate, W. (2018). Personal and social factors involved in internet addiction among adolescents: A meta-analysis. *Computers in Human Behavior*, *86*, 387–400. doi:10.1016/j.chb.2018.05.005

Goswami, V., & Singh, D. R. (2016). İnternet addiction among adolescents: A review of the research. *International Journal of Indian Psychology*, *3*(3), 37–44.

Lin, M. P. (2020). Prevalence of internet addiction during the COVID-19 outbreak and its risk factors among junior high school students in Taiwan. *International Journal of Environmental Research and Public Health*, *17*(22), 8547. doi:10.3390/ijerph17228547 PMID:33218018

Mak, K. K., Lai, C. M., Watanabe, H., Kim, D. I., Bahar, N., Ramos, M., Young, S. K., Roger, C. M., Cho, N.-R. A., & Cheng, C. (2014). Epidemiology of internet behaviors and addiction among adolescents in six Asian countries. *Cyberpsychology, Behavior, and Social Networking*, *17*(11), 720–728. doi:10.1089/cyber.2014.0139 PMID:25405785

Malinauskas, R., & Malinauskiene, V. (2019). A meta-analysis of psychological interventions for Internet/smartphone addiction among adolescents. *Journal of Behavioral Addictions*, *8*(4), 613–624. doi:10.1556/2006.8.2019.72 PMID:31891316

Ozturk, F. O., & Ayaz-Alkaya, S. (2021). Internet addiction and psychosocial problems among adolescents during the COVID-19 pandemic: A cross-sectional study. *Archives of Psychiatric Nursing*, *35*(6), 595–601. doi:10.1016/j.apnu.2021.08.007 PMID:34861951

Sarıalioğlu, A., Atay, T., & Arıkan, D. (2022). Determining the relationship between loneliness and internet addiction among adolescents during the covid-19 pandemic in Turkey. *Journal of Pediatric Nursing*, *63*, 117–124. doi:10.1016/j.pedn.2021.11.011 PMID:34801327

Tsitsika, A., Critselis, E., Louizou, A., Janikian, M., Freskou, A., Marangou, E., Kormas, G., & Kafetzis, D. A. (2011). Determinants of Internet addiction among adolescents: A case-control study. *TheScientificWorldJournal*, *11*, 866–874. doi:10.1100/tsw.2011.85 PMID:21516283


## KEY TERMS AND DEFINITIONS

**Addiction:** A neuropsychological disorder which is reflected in a persistent urge to engage in certain behaviors.

**Adolescence:** The transitional phase of growth and development between childhood and adulthood.

**COVID-19 pandemic:** The ongoing global pandemic of coronavirus disease 2019 (COVID-19) caused by severe acute respiratory syndrome coronavirus 2.

**Internet addiction:** A risky online behavior that interferes with and causes stress in individuals' personal, school, and/or work life.

**Junior High Schools:** An educational stage between primary and secondary school, which usually includes the seventh, eighth, and ninth grades.

**Preliminary Study:** An initial exploration of an issue related to a proposed literature review.

**Self-esteem:** A belief about how we value and perceive ourselves.

## ENDNOTE

1 In Greece junior high schools correspond to the age of 12-15 years (Ministry of Education, n.d.).

# Chapter 18
# Health Impacts of Internet Gaming Addiction

**Seçil Özkan**
*Gazi University, Turkey*

**Enis Taha Özkan**
*Gazi University, Turkey*

## ABSTRACT

*The frequency of internet gaming addiction varies between 1-15% in the world. There are some demographic factors, psychosocial factors, and game-related factors in the etiology of gaming addiction. In demographic factors, male gender, adolescent age group, separation of parents, high income, and being a student are seen as risks. Psychosocial factors include low social cohesion, aggressive behavior, anxiety or depression, low academic performance, attention problems, low life satisfaction, problems in family / friend relationships, and low self-esteem. Internet gaming addiction has many health effects, physiological, psychological, and social problems. In addition to determining the diagnostic criteria for gaming addiction, there is a need for national and international studies that will guide protection and intervention efforts, especially for at-risk youth. As a result of these studies, effective and effective evidence-based public health intervention programs should be developed.*

## INTRODUCTION

Playing games has been a behavioral form of humanity since ancient times (Onur, 1992). In various sources, games are defined as "entertaining activity/sport or equipment used for this purpose, especially performed by children" and "activity that a person does for entertainment or pleasure" (TLI., 2019 &, lexio,2019 &, University C., 2019). When behaviors reach the addiction dimension, they threaten human health. According to the definition of ASAM (American Society of Addiction Medicine), addiction is defined as "a primary chronic disease of brain reward, motivation, memory, and related circuitry dysfunction that leads to characteristic biological, social, and spiritual manifestations, and an individual's pathological pursuit of reward or relief through substance use or other behaviors that disrupts personal

DOI: 10.4018/978-1-6684-8397-8.ch018

functioning" (Medicine ASoA.,2011). In ICD 11 (International Classification of Diseases), disorders arising from addictive behaviors are defined as "clinically significant syndromes associated with disruption in personal functioning that develops as a result of repetitive rewarding behaviors other than the use of addictive substances" (WHO.,2019). With the advances in technology and the widespread use of computers and the internet, the concept of digital games has become part of everyday life. The concept of digital games has made it necessary to define the concept of "game addiction" as a diagnosis due to the time individuals spend playing games with technological devices and the physical, psychological, and social problems they experience as a result. According to DSM 5 (The Diagnostic and Statistical Manual of Mental Disorders), internet gaming disorder is defined as "persistent and recurrent use of the internet to engage in games, often with other players, leading to clinically significant impairment or distress" over a period of 12 months (Association AP., 2013).

## EPIDEMIOLOGY OF INTERNET GAME ADDICTION

Many definitions have been developed regarding the problematic use of digital technologies for gaming or non-gaming purposes. There are definitions that do not directly examine gaming behavior, such as "internet addiction, technology addiction, pathological technology use, pathological internet use, computer addiction, screen addiction, smartphone addiction, cyber-relationship addiction," and definitions that particularly focus on gaming behavior, such as "internet gaming addiction, pathological game playing, addiction to video games and online role-playing games, excessive gaming, gaming disorder."(Paulus FW. Et al., 2018).

The DSM's definition of gaming addiction is defined as "internet gaming addiction." Internet gaming addiction was first defined with diagnostic criteria in DSM-V. According to DSM-V, individuals who meet five or more of the following nine diagnostic criteria within a 12-month period are recognized as internet gaming addicts:

1. Engaging in internet gaming activities (such as internet being the dominant activity during the day, thinking about the previous game played, and contemplating the next gaming stage.)
2. Experiencing withdrawal symptoms when away from internet gaming (these symptoms can typically be interpreted as irritability, anxiety, and sadness, but there are no physical pharmacological withdrawal symptoms.)
3. Tolerance (an increasing need for time to play internet games)
4. Inability to control participation in internet gaming
5. Due to internet gaming losing interest in previous hobbies and activities other than internet games
6. Continuing to play excessive internet games despite being aware of psychosocial problems
7. Lying to family members and treatment providers about internet gaming time
8. Using internet games to escape from negative moods or to relax (such as feelings of helplessness, guilt, anxiety, etc.)
9. Losing or endangering significant relationships, profession, education, or career opportunities due to participation in internet games(Association AP., 2013).

In ICD-11, the diagnosis code "gaming disorder" is used instead of the definition of internet gaming addiction. According to this diagnosis, gaming addiction is a persistent or recurrent gaming ("digital game" or "video game") behavior that can be demonstrated online or offline characterized by the following criteria:

1. Lack of control over gaming behavior (such as initiation, frequency, intensity, duration, termination, and context)
2. Giving priority to gaming over other areas of life and daily activities
3. Continuing or increasing gaming despite the emergence of negative consequences.

The behavior pattern is severe enough to cause significant problems in personal, familial, social, educational, occupational, and other important areas. The gaming behavior pattern can be continuous or episodic and repetitive. A minimum of 12 months is required for diagnosis, but if all diagnostic criteria are met and symptoms are severe, shorter periods may be considered.

The ICD has divided game addiction, as defined in this way, into three subgroups: "Game Addiction, Primarily Online," "Game Addiction, Primarily Offline," and "Game Addiction, Unspecified" (WHO.,2019).

There are many studies on internet game addiction in different countries, with varying frequencies reported. The use of different diagnostic criteria and different populations studied can be cited as the most important reason for this situation.

A meta-analysis conducted by Fam to examine the prevalence of internet game addiction showed that the prevalence ranged from 0.6% (Spain, AICA-S) to 19.9% (England, DSM III). The average prevalence in the study pool was found to be 4.6% (Evren C., et al.,2018).

In a systematic review conducted by Festl et al., the term "problematic computer use" was used, and the prevalence values ranged from 0.6% (Norway, Gaming Addiction Scale) to 46% (Taiwan, Online Games Addiction Scale for Adolescents in Taiwan) (Festl R., et al.,2013).

Another systematic review conducted by Paulus et al. showed that the prevalence of internet game addiction ranged from 0.6% (Norway, Gaming Addiction Scale) to 50% (South Korea, IAII and IAD), with internet game addiction being particularly common in East Asian countries. The median prevalence was calculated to be 5.5% (Paulus FW. Et al., 2018).

## ETIOLOGY AND RISK FACTORS

### Demographic Factors

There are many studies on the etiology and risk groups of gaming addiction. Studies examining demographic risk factors for gaming addiction have shown that being male (ages 12-24), being in the adolescent age group (especially individuals aged 16-21, which includes late adolescents) (Paulus FW.et al., 2018., & Mannikko N., 2015 & Mentzoni RA., et al. 2011 & Fam JY.,2018 & Bargeron AH, Hormes JM.,2017), having divorced or separated parents (WHO.,2019 & Muller KW., et al. 2015), having a high socioeconomic status (Toker S, Baturay MH.,2016 & Çavuş S, et al.,2016 &, Horzum MB.,2011), currently being a student (Mannikko N.,et al.2015), smoking (Kasper D., et al.1999 & Desai RA., et al.2010), having a low maternal education level (Inan A.,2010 & Şahin C, et al.,2012), and having a low level of physical activity and exercise (Mihara S., et al,2017 & Henchoz Y.,et al.,2016) are effective in gaming addiction.

## Gaming-Related Factors

Studies examining the effective factors related to gaming addiction have shown that playing online games, especially MMORPGs (Paulus FW., et al.,2018 & Muller KW., et al.,2015 & Wang C-W.,et al., 2014 & Toker S., et al., 2016 &, Mannikko N., et al., 2015 & Mentzoni RA.,et al., 2011 & Mihara S., et al.,2017), starting to play games at an early age (Ko C-H., et al.,2005), identifying oneself as a "gamer" (Bargeron AH.,et al.,2017), having internet access at home (Horzum MB., 2011), owning a personal computer at home (Horzum MB., 2011, Şahin C., et al.,2012), and having a high weekly average gaming time (Wang C-W.,et al.,2014 & Mannikko N., et al., 2015 & Mihara S., et al.,2017 & Bargeron AH., et al., 2017) are effective in gaming addiction.

## Psychosocial Factors

Studies examining psychosocial factors related to gaming addiction have shown that having low self-esteem and self-worth (Gentile DA., et al.,2011 & Mannikko N., et al., 2015 & Mihara S., et al.,2017 & Gentile D.,2009 & Lemos IL., et al.,2016), having low satisfaction with daily life (Festl R., et al.,2013 & Mentzoni RA., et al., 2011 & Mihara S., et al.,2017 & Bargeron AH.,et al., 2017 & Ko C-H., et al., 2005), having antisocial behavior and anger control problems (Festl R., et al.,2013 & Wartberg L.,et al.,2017 & Mihara S., et al.,2017 & Desai RA., et al., 2010), having emotional stress and depression (Wartberg L.,et al.,2017 & Mannikko N., et al., 2015 & Mentzoni RA.,et al., 2011 & Mihara S., et al.,2017 & Bargeron AH.,et al., 2017 & Kasper D.,et al.,1999), having attention deficit and hyperactivity disorder (Wartberg L.,et al.,2017 & Mihara S., et al.,2017), having a neurotic personality type (Müller KW., et al.,2014), having a reckless personality type (Müller KW., et al.,2014), having an introverted personality type (Mihara S., et al.,2017 & Müller KW., et al.,2014), having low social conformity (Paulus FW., et al., 2018 & Gentile DA., et al., 2011), having impulsive behavior (Bargeron AH.,et al., 2017 & Gentile DA., et al., 2011), having lower academic performance (Paulus FW., et al., 2018 & Wang C-W.,et al.,2014 & Mihara S., et al.,2017), and having poor family harmony (Paulus FW., et al., 2018 & Wang C-W.,et al.,2014 & Mihara S., et al.,2017) are effective in gaming addiction.

# HEALTH EFFECTS

## Effects on Physical Health

The effect of game addiction on physical health has been evaluated in many studies with various aspects. In multiple studies, it was found that game addiction leads to some changes in the autonomic nervous system and plasma catecholamine responses and levels (Kim K., et al.,2015 & Coyne SM., et al.,2015 & Mannikko N., et al., 2017 & Kim N., et al.,2016). In a study conducted in Switzerland, game addiction was associated with low physical activity (Henchoz Y.,et al.,2016). There are many studies that associate game addiction with sleep problems (Mannikko N., et al., 2017 & Kim N., et al.,2016 & Henchoz Y.,et al.,2016 & Allison SE., et al., 2006 & Dworak M., et al.,2007 & Kuss DJ., et al.,2012 & Achab S.,et al.,2011 & Rehbein F., et al., 2010). Sleep problems, including reduced sleep duration and quality, are frequently encountered, especially among those who play MMORPGs (Lam LT.,2014). A study conducted in China found a positive relationship between game addiction and seizures (Chuang YC.,2006).

There is also a study that associates internet game addiction with enuresis, encopresis, tendosynovitis, obesity, and calluses (Weinstein AM.,2010 & D Griffiths M., et al.,2012).

## Effects on Mental Health

Messias et al. stated that individuals who play games for more than 5 hours a day are at a higher risk of sadness, suicidal ideation, and planning. Rehbein et al. also associate game addiction with suicide (Rehbein F., et al.,2010 & Messias E., et al.,2011). The relationship between game addiction and psychiatric disorders such as depression and anxiety has been reported (Muller KW., et al.,2015 & Mannikko N.,et al., 2017 & Lehenbauer-Baum M., et al.,2015 & Kim NR., et al., 2016 & Lemos IL., et al., 2016 & Bouna-Pyrrou P., et al., 2015 & Andreassen CS.,et al., 2016). Somatization disorders have also been associated with game addiction in several studies (Muller KW., et al.,2015 & Mannikko N.,et al., 2017 & Kim NR., et al., 2016). Attention deficit, hyperactivity, concentration problems, and increased impulsivity have also been associated with game addiction in many studies (Muller KW., et al., 2015 & Gentile DA., et al., 2011 & Mannikko N.,et al., 2017 & Kuss DJ., et al.,2012 & Kim NR., et al.,2016 & Andreassen CS.,et al., 2016 & Batthyany D., et al.,2009 & Baer S.,et al.,2012 & Walther B., et al.,2012 & Chan PA., et el.,2006). Obsessive-compulsive disorder is another mental health problem associated with game addiction (Mannikko N.,et al., 2017 & Kim NR., et al.,2016 & Andreassen CS.,et al., 2016 & Vukosavljevic-Gvozden T.,et al.,2015 & Starcevic V., et al.,2011). Additionally, game addiction is associated with low quality of life and low life satisfaction (Mentzoni RA., et al.,2011 & Festl R., et al.,2013 & Mannikko N.,et al., 2017 & Lehenbauer-Baum M., et al.,2015 & Montag C., et al., 2012 & Lemmens JS., et al., 2015), aggressive behavior (Kuss DJ., et al.,.,2012 & Chan PA., et al.,2006 & Chiu S-I., et al.,2004), and decreased self-esteem (Festl R.,et al., 2013 & Mannikko N.,et al., 2017 & Lemmens JS., et al., 2015 & Pápay O., et al., 2013).

## Effects on Social Health

It has been shown that there is a negative relationship between pathological gaming behavior and self-esteem and self-confidence. Professional and academic problems such as poor grades and financial problems may also arise (Toker S., et al.,2016). The relationship between game addiction and low academic achievement, in particular, is highlighted in many studies (Kuss DJ., et al.,2012 & Rehbein F.,et al.,2010 & Chiu S-I.,et al.,2004 & Koric MM.,et al.,2009 & Jeong EJ., et al.,2011). The aspect of game addiction leading to problems in social adaptation to school is also shown in the literature (Mannikko N.,et al., 2017 & Rehbein F., et al., 2013). Game addiction can lead to psychosocial consequences and mental health problems that affect free time, work, education, family life, social life, psychosocial well-being, social adaptation, and self-esteem (Toker S., et al.,2016 & D Griffiths M., et al.,2012 & Sublette VA., et al.,2012 & Lemmens JS., et al.,2011 & Chou C.,et al.,2005). There are many studies that indicate that game addiction particularly has a negative impact on family relationships, family harmony, and parent-child attachment (Wang C-W., et al.,2014 & Kim K.,et al., 2015 & Mannikko N.,et al., 2017 & Jeong EJ.,et al.,2011 & Rikkers W., et al.,2016).

Additionally, gaming addiction is also associated with loneliness (Mannikko N.,et al., 2017 & Kim NR.,et al.,2016 & Lemmens JS., et al.,2011 & Van Rooij AJ.,et al.,2011), shyness, social phobia, and difficulty in interpersonal relationships (Muller KW., et al.,2015 & Festl R., et al.,2013 & Mannikko

N.,et al., 2017 & Lehenbauer-Baum M., et al.,2015 & Baer S.,et al.,2012 & Rikkers W.,et al.,2016 & Peng W, Liu M.,2010 & Kim EJ.,et al.,2008).

## PROTECTION AND TREATMENT

When evaluating the studies related to prevention and intervention of game addiction, 3 groups are considered for intervention. Measures related to the general population evaluated within the scope of primary prevention, studies conducted in target groups that include both primary prevention and early assessment as secondary prevention, and treatment and interventions that include tertiary prevention for individuals identified with game addiction are considered in this context.

Universal protection strategies that target the entire population are evaluated under 5 headings:

a. Activities Related to Education: Digital literacy courses to increase target-oriented internet use, activities that encourage healthy internet and computer usage times, physical activity and other healthy lifestyle behaviors
b. Prohibitive Measures: Measures such as mandatory shutdown of online game service providers during certain hours of the day
c. Limitations with Technological Criteria: Parental filters/locks, time-limiting settings on gaming platforms, systems that alert users when they exceed the allowed playtime
d. Social Awareness Measures: Campaigns that promote national days without internet usage, providing information on basic symptoms and referral centers related to internet game addiction
e. Accessibility Reduction Activities: Reducing the number of owned devices, removing gaming devices from the bedroom, etc.

Activities that address risky groups, as well as strategies targeting the entire population, are also important. These are evaluated under 3 headings.

1. Regular Screening Activities: Epidemiological surveillance studies typically targeting schools and universities
2. Mental Health Screenings: Monitoring and evaluating situations such as emotional stress that increase the risk of game addiction with healthcare professionals
3. School-Based Educational Programs: Educational programs that focus on healthy use of the internet and technology, promoting non-gaming hobbies and physical activity

Protection strategies that address society and risky groups alone are not sufficient. Ensuring early treatment and protection from possible sequelae is also an important part of protection strategies for individuals who have been diagnosed with internet game addiction. Strategies addressed in this context are examined under 4 headings.

a. Creation of Support Groups
b. Outpatient Mental Health Services: Effective treatment of diseases such as depression and anxiety that contribute to or are involved in the etiology of game addiction

c. Psychosocial Rehabilitation: Rehabilitation programs that focus on socialization and alternative areas of interest, including digital detoxification
d. Mental Education: Educational programs that aim to provide detailed information about symptoms and explain strategies that minimize the harms of game addiction (Pediatrics AAO.,2011 & Xu Z.,et al.,2012 & King DL, Delfabbro PH.,2017).

There are multiple studies in the literature regarding game addiction treatment. Treatments are grouped into pharmacotherapy, cognitive-behavioral therapy-based psychotherapy, and other approaches (Zajac K., et al.,2017).

There are studies examining the effects of bupropion, methylphenidate, bupropion-escitalopram combination, and atomoxetine/methylphenidate in pharmacotherapy, and it has been found that these treatments significantly reduce gaming time (Han DH, Renshaw PF.,2012 & Han DH., et al.,2011 & Song J., et al.,2016 & Han DH., et al.,2009 & Park JH., et al.,2016). When studies including cognitive behavioral therapy as another fundamental treatment approach were examined, it was observed that gaming time was also shortened with this treatment approach (Kim SM, .,et al.,2012 & Park SY.,et al.,2016 & Zhang J-T., et al.,2016 & Li H, Wang S.,2013).

Regarding other intervention studies on the subject, applied treatments include family therapy, self-discovery camp, eclectic psychotherapy approach, and education approach in MMORPG games. Significant decreases in gaming time have been observed in all of these other methods (Han DH.,et al.,2012 & Pallesen S.,et al.,2015 & Kim PW., et al.,2013 & Sakuma H., et al., 2017).

## CONCLUSION AND RECOMMENDATIONS

Considering the frequency and consequences of Internet gaming addiction, it emerges as an important public health issue. Symptoms such as vision problems, hearing problems, musculoskeletal problems, sleep and fatigue are commonly seen in gaming addicts. In addition, obesity is also a significant consequence of gaming addiction. Especially the frequent occurrence of these symptoms and health outcomes among young people emphasizes the importance of taking action on this issue. Investigating the prevalence of digital gaming addiction worldwide by age and mapping the risk is important for future interventions. In addition, conducting social awareness campaigns regarding gaming addiction will be an important intervention.

In studies examining family relationships, being an only child, parental separation, and defining family relationships as poor are identified as risk factors. Especially young individuals are significantly affected by the family environment and intra-family relationships. Individuals who are only children and in a more sensitive position in terms of a bad family environment, poor family relationships, and social communication are particularly at risk, and individuals in this situation are the target group for intervention and protection efforts. Similarly, feeling unhappy and having low life satisfaction also pose an important risk for individuals under the subheading of avoiding negative emotions associated with game addiction. Organizing parent attitude and communication-related training for parents to communicate healthily with their children, especially raising awareness among parents about safe digital game playing in healthy life centers and working in collaboration with families, is important.

When healthy lifestyle behaviors are considered as a whole, they appear in many points in the etiology of addiction. Firstly, physical inactivity, as well as smoking, alcohol consumption, and unbalanced and irregular nutrition, are identified as important risk factors for internet gaming addiction. It is also noteworthy that the most common reason for playing games among game addicts is pleasure and spending time. Therefore, directing young people towards more positive activities rather than prohibition and making physical activity a positive leisure activity and lifestyle can be the main starting point for protection and interventions in this regard.

Risks related to the game being played, in addition to individual risk factors, are also present in game addiction. Risks such as online games and preference for MMORPG games while playing fall into this category. Typically, in these types of games, a social environment is created for mutual communication with other players, and game-addicted individuals are usually those whose family-friend relationships are weak and whose self-confidence and respect have decreased. These factors should be evaluated together in the etiology, in addition to considering the fact that these types of games show continuity in content and trigger reward mechanisms. In this context, providing media literacy education in schools can contribute to the development of correct internet use and proper game-playing behaviors for individuals.

## REFERENCES

Achab, S., Nicolier, M., Mauny, F., Monnin, J., Trojak, B., Vandel, P., Sechter, D., Gorwood, P., & Haffen, E. (2011). Massively multiplayer online role-playing games: Comparing characteristics of addict vs non-addict online recruited gamers in a French adult population. *BMC Psychiatry*, *11*(1), 144. doi:10.1186/1471-244X-11-144 PMID:21871089

Allison, S. E., von Wahlde, L., Shockley, T., & Gabbard, G. O. (2006). The development of the self in the era of the internet and role-playing fantasy games. *The American Journal of Psychiatry*, *163*(3), 381–385. doi:10.1176/appi.ajp.163.3.381 PMID:16513856

Andreassen, C. S., Billieux, J., Griffiths, M. D., Kuss, D. J., Demetrovics, Z., Mazzoni, E., & Pallesen, S. (2016). The relationship between addictive use of social media and video games and symptoms of psychiatric disorders: A large-scale cross-sectional study. *Psychology of Addictive Behaviors*, *30*(2), 252–262. doi:10.1037/adb0000160 PMID:26999354

APA. (2013). *Diagnostic and statistical manual of mental disorders (DSM-5®)*. American Psychiatric Pub. doi:10.1176/appi.books.9780890425596

Baer, S., Saran, K., & Green, D. A. (2012, October). Computer/gaming station use in youth: Correlations among use, addiction and functional impairment. *Paediatrics & Child Health*, *17*(8), 427–431. doi:10.1093/pch/17.8.427 PMID:24082802

Bargeron, A. H., & Hormes, J. M. (2017). Psychosocial correlates of internet gaming disorder: Psychopathology, life satisfaction, and impulsivity. *Computers in Human Behavior*, *68*, 388–394. doi:10.1016/j.chb.2016.11.029

Batthyany, D., Müller, K. W., Benker, F., & Woelfling, K. (2009). Computer game playing: Clinical characteristics of dependence and abuse among adolescents. *Wiener Klinische Wochenschrift*, *121*(15-16), 502–509. PMID:19787320

Beard, C. L., Haas, A. L., Wickham, R. E., & Stavropoulos, V. (2017). Age of Initiation and Internet Gaming Disorder: The Role of Self-Esteem. *Cyberpsychology, Behavior, and Social Networking*, *20*(6), 397–401. doi:10.1089/cyber.2017.0011 PMID:28622030

Bouna-Pyrrou, P., Mühle, C., Kornhuber, J., & Lenz, B. (2015). Internet gaming disorder, social network disorder and laterality: Handedness relates to pathological use of social networks. *Journal of Neural Transmission (Vienna, Austria)*, *122*(8), 1187–1196. doi:10.100700702-014-1361-5 PMID:25576300

Çakır, Ö., Ayas, T., & Horzum, M. B. (2011). An investigation of university students' internet and game addiction with respect to several variables. Ankara University. *Journal of Faculty of Educational Sciences.*, *44*(2), 95–117.

Çavuş S, Ayhan B, Tuncer M. (2016), Computer games and addiction: A field study on university students. *Communication Theory and Research Journal, 43.*

Chan, P. A., & Rabinowitz, T. (2006). A cross-sectional analysis of video games and attention deficit hyperactivity disorder symptoms in adolescents. *Annals of General Psychiatry*, *5*(1), 16. doi:10.1186/1744-859X-5-16 PMID:17059614

Chiu, S.-I., Lee, J.-Z., & Huang, D.-H. (2004). Video game addiction in children and teenagers in Taiwan. *Cyberpsychology & Behavior*, *7*(5), 571–581. doi:10.1089/cpb.2004.7.571 PMID:15667052

Chou, C., Condron, L., & Belland, J. C. (2005). A review of the research on Internet addiction. *Educational Psychology Review*, *17*(4), 363–388. doi:10.100710648-005-8138-1

Chuang, Y. C. (2006). Massively multiplayer online role-playing game-induced seizures: A neglected health problem in Internet addiction. *Cyberpsychology & Behavior*, *9*(4), 451–456. doi:10.1089/cpb.2006.9.451 PMID:16901249

Coyne, S. M., Dyer, W. J., Densley, R., Money, N. M., Day, R. D., & Harper, J. M. (2015). Physiological indicators of pathologic video game use in adolescence. *The Journal of Adolescent Health*, *56*(3), 307–313. doi:10.1016/j.jadohealth.2014.10.271 PMID:25586229

Griffiths, M., Kuss, D., & King, D. (2012). Video game addiction: Past, present and future. *Current Psychiatry Reviews*, *8*(4), 308–318. doi:10.2174/157340012803520414

Desai, R. A., Krishnan-Sarin, S., Cavallo, D., & Potenza, M. N. (2010). Video-gaming among high school students: Health correlates, gender differences, and problematic gaming. *Pediatrics*, *126*(6), e1414–e24. doi:10.1542/peds.2009-2706 PMID:21078729

Dworak, M., Schierl, T., Bruns, T., & Struder, H. K. (2007). Impact of singular excessive computer game and television exposure on sleep patterns and memory performance of school-aged children. *Pediatrics*, *120*(5), 978–985. doi:10.1542/peds.2007-0476 PMID:17974734

Evren, C., Dalbudak, E., Topcu, M., Kutlu, N., Evren, B., & Pontes, H. M. (2018). Psychometric validation of the Turkish nine-item internet gaming disorder scale–short form (IGDS9-SF). *Psychiatry Research*, *265*, 349–354. doi:10.1016/j.psychres.2018.05.002 PMID:29793049

Fam, J. Y. (2018). Prevalence of internet gaming disorder in adolescents: A meta-analysis across three decades. *Scandinavian Journal of Psychology*, *59*(5), 524–531. doi:10.1111jop.12459 PMID:30004118

Festl, R., Scharkow, M., & Quandt, T. (2013). Problematic computer game use among adolescents, younger and older adults. *Addiction (Abingdon, England)*, *108*(3), 592–599. doi:10.1111/add.12016 PMID:23078146

Gentile, D. (2009). Pathological video-game use among youth ages 8 to 18: A national study. *Psychological Science*, *20*(5), 594–602. doi:10.1111/j.1467-9280.2009.02340.x PMID:19476590

Gentile, D. A., Choo, H., Liau, A., Sim, T., Li, D., Fung, D., & Khoo, A. (2011). Pathological video game use among youths: A two-year longitudinal study. *Pediatrics*, *127*(2), e319–e29. doi:10.1542/peds.2010-1353 PMID:21242221

Gentile, D. A., Choo, H., Liau, A., Sim, T., Li, D., Fung, D., & Khoo, A. (2011). Pathological video game use among youths: A two-year longitudinal study. *Pediatrics*, *127*(2), e319–e29. doi:10.1542/peds.2010-1353 PMID:21242221

Han, D.H., Hwang, J.W., & Renshaw, P.F. (2011). *Bupropion sustained release treatment decreases craving for video games and cue-induced brain activity in patients with Internet video game addiction.*

Han, D. H., Kim, S. M., Lee, Y. S., & Renshaw, P. F. (2012). The effect of family therapy on the changes in the severity of on-line game play and brain activity in adolescents with on-line game addiction. *Psychiatry Research: Neuroimaging*, *202*(2), 126–131. doi:10.1016/j.pscychresns.2012.02.011 PMID:22698763

Han, D. H., Lee, Y. S., Na, C., Ahn, J. Y., Chung, U. S., Daniels, M. A., Haws, C. A., & Renshaw, P. F. (2009). The effect of methylphenidate on Internet video game play in children with attention-deficit/hyperactivity disorder. *Comprehensive Psychiatry*, *50*(3), 251–256. doi:10.1016/j.comppsych.2008.08.011 PMID:19374970

Han, D. H., & Renshaw, P. F. (2012). Bupropion in the treatment of problematic online game play in patients with major depressive disorder. *Journal of Psychopharmacology (Oxford, England)*, *26*(5), 689–696. doi:10.1177/0269881111400647 PMID:21447539

Henchoz, Y., Studer, J., Deline, S., N'Goran, A. A., Baggio, S., & Gmel, G. (2016). Video Gaming Disorder and Sport and Exercise in Emerging Adulthood: A Longitudinal Study. *Behavioral Medicine (Washington, D.C.)*, *42*(2), 105–111. doi:10.1080/08964289.2014.965127 PMID:25258243

Horzum, M. B. (2011). Examination of elementary school students' computer game addiction levels according to various variables. *Education in Science*, *36*(159).

Inan, A. (2010).Internet addiction in secondary and high school students. Erzurum: Atatürk University.

Jeong, E. J., & Kim, D. H. (2011). Social activities, self-efficacy, game attitudes, and game addiction. *Cyberpsychology, Behavior, and Social Networking*, *14*(4), 213–221. doi:10.1089/cyber.2009.0289 PMID:21067285

Kasper, D., Welsh, S., & Chambliss, C. (1999). *Educating Students about the Risks of Excessive Videogame Usage.* ERIC. https://files.eric.ed.gov/fulltext/ED426315.pdf

Kim, E. J., Namkoong, K., Ku, T., & Kim, S. J. (2008). The relationship between online game addiction and aggression, self-control and narcissistic personality traits. *European Psychiatry*, *23*(3), 212–218. doi:10.1016/j.eurpsy.2007.10.010 PMID:18166402

Kim, K., & Kim, K. (2015). Internet game addiction, parental attachment, and parenting of adolescents in South Korea. *Journal of Child & Adolescent Substance Abuse*, *24*(6), 366–371. doi:10.1080/1067828X.2013.872063

Kim, N., Hughes, T. L., Park, C. G., Quinn, L., & Kong, I. D. (2016). Resting-State Peripheral Catecholamine and Anxiety Levels in Korean Male Adolescents with Internet Game Addiction. *Cyberpsychology, Behavior, and Social Networking*, *19*(3), 202–208. doi:10.1089/cyber.2015.0411 PMID:26849530

Kim, N. R., Hwang, S. S.-H., Choi, J.-S., Kim, D.-J., Demetrovics, Z., Király, O., Nagygyörgy, K., Griffiths, M. D., Hyun, S. Y., Youn, H. C., & Choi, S.-W. (2016). Characteristics and psychiatric symptoms of Internet gaming disorder among adults using self-reported DSM-5 criteria. *Psychiatry Investigation*, *13*(1), 58. doi:10.4306/pi.2016.13.1.58 PMID:26766947

Kim, P. W., Kim, S. Y., Shim, M., Im, C.-H., & Shon, Y.-M. (2013). The influence of an educational course on language expression and treatment of gaming addiction for massive multiplayer online role-playing game (MMORPG) players. *Computers & Education*, *63*, 208–217. doi:10.1016/j.compedu.2012.12.008

Kim, S. M., Han, D. H., Lee, Y. S., & Renshaw, P. F. (2012). Combined cognitive behavioral therapy and bupropion for the treatment of problematic on-line game play in adolescents with major depressive disorder. *Computers in Human Behavior*, *28*(5), 1954–1959. doi:10.1016/j.chb.2012.05.015

King, D. L., & Delfabbro, P. H. (2017). Prevention and policy related to Internet gaming disorder. *Current Addiction Reports*, *4*(3), 284–292. doi:10.100740429-017-0157-8

Ko, C.-H., Yen, J.-Y., Chen, C.-C., Chen, S.-H., & Yen, C.-F. (2005). Gender differences and related factors affecting online gaming addiction among Taiwanese adolescents. *The Journal of Nervous and Mental Disease*, *193*(4), 273–277. doi:10.1097/01.nmd.0000158373.85150.57 PMID:15805824

Koric, M. M., Teo, L. L. C., & Neo, R. L. (2009). Children and video games: Addiction, engagement, and scholastic achievement. *Cyberpsychology & Behavior*, *12*(5), 567–572. doi:10.1089/cpb.2009.0079 PMID:19624263

Kuss, D. J., & Griffiths, M. D. (2012). Internet gaming addiction: A systematic review of empirical research. *International Journal of Mental Health and Addiction*, *10*(2), 278–296. doi:10.100711469-011-9318-5

Lam, L. T. (2014). Internet gaming addiction, problematic use of the internet, and sleep problems: A systematic review. *Current Psychiatry Reports*, *16*(4), 444. doi:10.100711920-014-0444-1 PMID:24619594

Lehenbauer-Baum, M., Klaps, A., Kovacovsky, Z., Witzmann, K., Zahlbruckner, R., & Stetina, B. U. (2015). Addiction and engagement: An explorative study toward classification criteria for internet gaming disorder. *Cyberpsychology, Behavior, and Social Networking*, *18*(6), 343–349. doi:10.1089/cyber.2015.0063 PMID:26075922

Lemmens, J. S., Valkenburg, P. M., & Gentile, D. A. (2015). The Internet gaming disorder scale. *Psychological Assessment*, *27*(2), 567–582. doi:10.1037/pas0000062 PMID:25558970

Lemmens, J. S., Valkenburg, P. M., & Peter, J. (2011). Psychosocial causes and consequences of pathological gaming. *Computers in Human Behavior*, *27*(1), 144–152. doi:10.1016/j.chb.2010.07.015

Lemos, I. L., Cardoso, A., & Sougey, E. B. (2016). Cross-cultural adaptation and evaluation of the psychometric properties of the Brazilian version of the Video Game Addiction Test. *Computers in Human Behavior*, *55*, 207–213. doi:10.1016/j.chb.2015.09.019

Lexico. (2019) *Game: Definition of Game by Lexico* Lexico. https://www.lexico.com/en/definition/game.

Li, H., & Wang, S. (2013). The role of cognitive distortion in online game addiction among Chinese adolescents. *Children and Youth Services Review*, *35*(9), 1468–1475. doi:10.1016/j.childyouth.2013.05.021

Lopez-Fernandez, O., Honrubia-Serrano, M. L., Baguley, T., & Griffiths, M. D. (2014). Pathological video game playing in Spanish and British adolescents: Towards the exploration of Internet Gaming Disorder symptomatology. *Computers in Human Behavior*, *41*, 304–312. doi:10.1016/j.chb.2014.10.011

Mannikko, N., Billieux, J., & Kaariainen, M. (2015). Problematic digital gaming behavior and its relation to the psychological, social and physical health of Finnish adolescents and young adults. *Journal of Behavioral Addictions*, *4*(4), 281–288. doi:10.1556/2006.4.2015.040 PMID:26690623

Mannikko, N., Ruotsalainen, H., Miettunen, J., Pontes, H. M., & Kaariainen, M. (2017). Problematic gaming behaviour and health-related outcomes: A systematic review and meta-analysis. *Journal of Health Psychology*, 1359105317740414. PMID:29192524

Medicine ASoA. (2011). *Public policy statement: Definition of addiction*. American Society of Addiction Medicine Chevy Chase.

Mentzoni, R. A., Brunborg, G. S., Molde, H., Myrseth, H., Skouverøe, K. J. M., Hetland, J., & Pallesen, S. (2011). Problematic video game use: Estimated prevalence and associations with mental and physical health. *Cyberpsychology, Behavior, and Social Networking*, *14*(10), 591–596. doi:10.1089/cyber.2010.0260 PMID:21342010

Messias, E., Castro, J., Saini, A., Usman, M., & Peeples, D. (2011). Sadness, suicide, and their association with video game and internet overuse among teens: Results from the youth risk behavior survey 2007 and 2009. *Suicide & Life-Threatening Behavior*, *41*(3), 307–315. doi:10.1111/j.1943-278X.2011.00030.x PMID:21463355

Mihara, S., & Higuchi, S. (2017). Cross-sectional and longitudinal epidemiological studies of Internet gaming disorder: A systematic review of the literature. *Psychiatry and Clinical Neurosciences*, *71*(7), 425–444. doi:10.1111/pcn.12532 PMID:28436212

Montag, C., Flierl, M., Markett, S., Walter, N., Jurkiewicz, M., & Reuter, M. (2012). Internet addiction and personality in first-person-shooter video gamers. *Journal of Media Psychology*.

Müller, K. W., Beutel, M., Egloff, B., & Wölfling, K. (2014). Investigating risk factors for internet gaming disorder: A comparison of patients with addictive gaming, pathological gamblers and healthy controls regarding the big five personality traits. *European Addiction Research*, *20*(3), 129–136. doi:10.1159/000355832 PMID:24247280

Muller, K. W., Janikian, M., Dreier, M., Wolfling, K., Beutel, M. E., Tzavara, C., Richardson, C., & Tsitsika, A. (2015). Regular gaming behavior and internet gaming disorder in European adolescents: Results from a cross-national representative survey of prevalence, predictors, and psychopathological correlates. *European Child & Adolescent Psychiatry*, *24*(5), 565–574. doi:10.100700787-014-0611-2 PMID:25189795

Onur, B. (1992). *Oyuncaklı Dünya - Toplumsal Tarih Üzerine Eğlenceli Bir Deneme* [Toy World - An Entertaining Essay on Social History]. V Yayınları.

Pallesen, S., Lorvik, I. M., Bu, E. H., & Molde, H. (2015). An exploratory study investigating the effects of a treatment manual for video game addiction. *Psychological Reports*, *117*(2), 490–495. doi:10.2466/02.PR0.117c14z9 PMID:26340051

Pápay, O., Urbán, R., Griffiths, M. D., Nagygyörgy, K., Farkas, J., Kökönyei, G., Felvinczi, K., Oláh, A., Elekes, Z., & Demetrovics, Z. (2013). Psychometric properties of the problematic online gaming questionnaire short-form and prevalence of problematic online gaming in a national sample of adolescents. *Cyberpsychology, Behavior, and Social Networking*, *16*(5), 340–348. doi:10.1089/cyber.2012.0484 PMID:23621688

Park, J. H., Lee, Y. S., Sohn, J. H., & Han, D. H. (2016). Effectiveness of atomoxetine and methylphenidate for problematic online gaming in adolescents with attention deficit hyperactivity disorder. *Human Psychopharmacology*, *31*(6), 427–432. doi:10.1002/hup.2559 PMID:27859666

Park, S. Y., Kim, S. M., Roh, S., Soh, M.-A., Lee, S. H., Kim, H., Lee, Y. S., & Han, D. H. (2016). The effects of a virtual reality treatment program for online gaming addiction. *Computer Methods and Programs in Biomedicine*, *129*, 99–108. doi:10.1016/j.cmpb.2016.01.015 PMID:26860055

Paulus, F. W., Ohmann, S., Von Gontard, A., & Popow, C. (2018). Internet gaming disorder in children and adolescents: A systematic review. *Developmental Medicine and Child Neurology*, *60*(7), 645–659. doi:10.1111/dmcn.13754 PMID:29633243

Pediatrics, A. A. O. (2011). Media use by children younger than 2 years. Council on communications and media. *Pediatrics*, *128*(5), 6.

Peng, W., & Liu, M. (2010). Online gaming dependency: A preliminary study in China. *Cyberpsychology, Behavior, and Social Networking*, *13*(3), 329–333. doi:10.1089/cyber.2009.0082 PMID:20557254

Rehbein, F., & Baier, D. (2013). Family-, media-, and school-related risk factors of video game addiction. *Journal of Media Psychology*, *25*(3), 118–128. doi:10.1027/1864-1105/a000093

Rehbein, F., Kleimann, M., & Mossle, T. (2010). Prevalence and risk factors of video game dependency in adolescence: Results of a German nationwide survey. *Cyberpsychology, Behavior, and Social Networking*, *13*(3), 269–277. doi:10.1089/cyber.2009.0227 PMID:20557246

Rehbein, F., Kliem, S., Baier, D., Mossle, T., & Petry, N. M. (2015). Prevalence of Internet gaming disorder in German adolescents: Diagnostic contribution of the nine DSM-5 criteria in a state-wide representative sample. *Addiction (Abingdon, England)*, *110*(5), 842–851. doi:10.1111/add.12849 PMID:25598040

Rikkers, W., Lawrence, D., Hafekost, J., & Zubrick, S. R. (2016). Internet use and electronic gaming by children and adolescents with emotional and behavioural problems in Australia–results from the second Child and Adolescent Survey of Mental Health and Wellbeing. *BMC Public Health, 16*(1), 399. doi:10.118612889-016-3058-1 PMID:27178325

Şahin C. & Tuğrul VM. (2012). Examination of computer game addiction levels of primary school students. *Zeitschrift für die Welt der Türken [Journal of World of Turks,] 4*(3), 115-30.

Sakuma, H., Mihara, S., Nakayama, H., Miura, K., Kitayuguchi, T., Maezono, M., Hashimoto, T., & Higuchi, S. (2017). Treatment with the self-discovery camp (SDiC) improves internet gaming disorder. *Addictive Behaviors, 64*, 357–362. doi:10.1016/j.addbeh.2016.06.013 PMID:27321966

Song, J., Park, J. H., Han, D. H., Roh, S., Son, J. H., Choi, T. Y., Lee, H., Kim, T. H., & Lee, Y. S. (2016). Comparative study of the effects of bupropion and escitalopram on I nternet gaming disorder. *Psychiatry and Clinical Neurosciences, 70*(11), 527–535. doi:10.1111/pcn.12429 PMID:27487975

Starcevic, V., Berle, D., Porter, G., & Fenech, P. (2011). Problem video game use and dimensions of psychopathology. *International Journal of Mental Health and Addiction, 9*(3), 248–256. doi:10.100711469-010-9282-5

Strittmatter, E., Kaess, M., Parzer, P., Fischer, G., Carli, V., Hoven, C. W., Wasserman, C., Sarchiapone, M., Durkee, T., Apter, A., Bobes, J., Brunner, R., Cosman, D., Sisask, M., Värnik, P., & Wasserman, D. (2015). Pathological Internet use among adolescents: Comparing gamers and non-gamers. *Psychiatry Research, 228*(1), 128–135. doi:10.1016/j.psychres.2015.04.029 PMID:25959265

Sublette, V. A., & Mullan, B. (2012). Consequences of play: A systematic review of the effects of online gaming. *International Journal of Mental Health and Addiction, 10*(1), 3–23. doi:10.100711469-010-9304-3

Toker, S., & Baturay, M. H. (2016). Antecedents And Consequences Of Game Addiction. *Computers in Human Behavior, 55*, 668–679. doi:10.1016/j.chb.2015.10.002

Turkish Language Institution. (2019) *OYUN.* Turkish Language Institution. https://sozluk.gov.tr/.

Van Rooij, A.J., Schoenmakers, T.M., Vermulst, A.A., Van Den Eijnden, R.J., & Van De Mheen, D. (2011). Online video game addiction: identification of addicted adolescent gamers. *Addiction, 106*(1), 205-12.

Vukosavljevic-Gvozden, T., Filipovic, S., & Opacic, G. (2015). The mediating role of symptoms of psychopathology between irrational beliefs and internet gaming addiction. *Journal of Rational-Emotive & Cognitive-Behavior Therapy, 33*(4), 387–405. doi:10.100710942-015-0218-7

Walther, B., Morgenstern, M., & Hanewinkel, R. (2012). Co-occurrence of addictive behaviours: Personality factors related to substance use, gambling and computer gaming. *European Addiction Research, 18*(4), 167–174. doi:10.1159/000335662 PMID:22398819

Wang, C.-W., Chan, C. L., Mak, K.-K., Ho, S.-Y., Wong, P. W., & Ho, R. T. (2014). Prevalence and correlates of video and internet gaming addiction among Hong Kong adolescents: A pilot study. *TheScientificWorldJournal, 2014*, 2014. doi:10.1155/2014/874648 PMID:25032242

Wartberg, L., Kriston, L., Kramer, M., Schwedler, A., Lincoln, T. M., & Kammerl, R. (2017). Internet gaming disorder in early adolescence: Associations with parental and adolescent mental health. *European Psychiatry*, *43*, 14–18. doi:10.1016/j.eurpsy.2016.12.013 PMID:28365463

Weinstein, A. M. (2010). Computer and video game addiction—A comparison between game users and non-game users. *The American Journal of Drug and Alcohol Abuse*, *36*(5), 268–276. doi:10.3109/00952990.2010.491879 PMID:20545602

WHO. (2019). *ICD-11 - Disorders due to addictive behaviours 2019*. WHO. https://icd.who.int/browse11/l-m/en#/http%3a%2f%2fid.who.int%2ficd%2fentity%2f499894965. (accessed 30.12.2020)

WHO. (2019). *ICD-11 - Gaming disorder*. WHO. https://icd.who.int/browse11/l-m/en#/http%3a%2f%2fid.who.int%2ficd%2fentity%2f1448597234

Xu, Z., Turel, O., & Yuan, Y. (2012). Online game addiction among adolescents: Motivation and prevention factors. *European Journal of Information Systems*, *21*(3), 321–340. doi:10.1057/ejis.2011.56

Zajac, K., Ginley, M. K., Chang, R., & Petry, N. M. (2017). Treatments for Internet gaming disorder and Internet addiction: A systematic review. *Psychology of Addictive Behaviors*, *31*(8), 979–994. doi:10.1037/adb0000315 PMID:28921996

Zhang, J.-T., Yao, Y.-W., Potenza, M. N., Xia, C.-C., Lan, J., Liu, L., Wang, L.-J., Liu, B., Ma, S.-S., & Fang, X.-Y. (2016). Effects of craving behavioral intervention on neural substrates of cue-induced craving in Internet gaming disorder. *NeuroImage. Clinical*, *12*, 591–599. doi:10.1016/j.nicl.2016.09.004 PMID:27699148

## ADDITIONAL READING

Darvesh. (2020). Exploring the prevalence of gaming disorder and Internet gaming disorder: a rapid scoping review. Springer. , https://link.springer.com/content/pdf/10.1186/s13643-020-01329-2.pdf doi:10.1186/s13643-020-01329-2

## KEY TERMS AND DEFINITIONS

**Gaming disorder:** A condition recognized by the World Health Organization (WHO) as a mental health disorder in which an individual has a pattern of persistent or recurrent gaming behavior, either online or offline, that becomes so extensive and severe that it impairs an individual's personal, family, social, educational, occupational or other important areas of functioning.

**ICD-11 (International Classification of Diseases, Eleventh Revision):** A global health classification system developed by the World Health Organization (WHO).

**MMORPGs (Massively Multiplayer Online Role-Playing Games):** A type of online video game where a large number of players can simultaneously interact with each other in a virtual world. Players create their own character, which they control as they explore the game world, interact with other players, and complete quests or missions.

# Chapter 19
# Digital Game Addiction and Children

**Mustafa Ersoy**
*Sivas Cumhuriyet University, Turkey*

**Ahmet Furkan Şahbaz**
*Independent Researcher, Turkey*

## ABSTRACT

*This study examines the topic of digital game addiction and children. The study addresses the effects of digital games on children, addiction symptoms, and the impact of addiction on children's social, academic, and psychological development. According to the results of the research, symptoms of digital game addiction include excessive time spent playing games, loss of control, preoccupation with games, developing tolerance, neglecting social and academic responsibilities, and experiencing physical health problems such as sleep disorders and eye strain. Digital game addiction can negatively impact children's social skills, academic performance, and psychological well-being, thus reducing their quality of life. Therefore, it is recommended for parents and teachers to limit children's use of digital games and encourage them to engage in other activities. Parents and teachers should monitor children's use of digital games, recognize addiction symptoms, and take necessary precautions.*

## INTRODUCTION

Digital games are one of the most popular entertainment tools for children today. However, these games can also pose a significant threat to children. In particular, the increasing prevalence of digital game addiction in recent years has had a negative impact on many children's physical and psychological health. Children's sleep patterns, eating habits, and social relationships can also be affected by digital game addiction. Therefore, the issue of digital game addiction is a topic that needs to be closely monitored by both parents and the digital gaming industry. This part will address the issue of digital game addiction and children and provide information on studies conducted in this area, risk factors, protective factors, and treatment methods.

DOI: 10.4018/978-1-6684-8397-8.ch019

## Game

Games are an activity played to improve communication among people, develop the ability to follow rules, enhance personal skills, and increase knowledge accumulation. Games are often played using different factors such as skill or luck, and sometimes involve a situation of winning or losing. Games are enjoyable for all age groups and include various activities. This activity is fun and enjoyable, allowing us to take a break from daily life and enjoy doing something different. Playing games is not only a fun hobby, but also a social activity (Kuss & Griffiths, 2012). Game is a versatile tool that contributes to the social, mental, and biological development of children. It is particularly beneficial to their development during primary school and pre-school periods. Games contribute to children's sociocultural and psychological development, while also helping to develop communication, language, and sharing skills. Additionally, games help to develop important skills such as decision-making, problem-solving, and environmental awareness (Yalçın & Bertiz, 2019).

Game is the most natural learning environment that prepares children for their lives. During play, children learn by experimenting on their own, develop their potential abilities, effortlessly gain many skills, and escape from the pressures of adults and the outside world. Games are played during childhood, and as children age, the frequency of games decreases, their variety changes, and their characteristics disappear. However, the effect of play on children's physical, cognitive, psychological, social, and language development is of great importance that nothing else can replace (İnce & Işır, 2016). Although games are often preferred to meet children's sensory, cognitive, and psychological needs, they can also negatively affect their mental climate.

In the past, games that were played with friends in physical environments such as playgrounds and streets have become digitized and particularly popular among young people who closely follow technology, following the impact of computers and the internet on every aspect of life. These games have become part of popular culture due to the influence of technological advancements.

## Digital Game

Digital games have evolved over time to go beyond the classic definition of games, and can now be played alone or against others, either online or offline, with humans or artificial intelligence. These games have emerged as a product of human-machine interaction and have become the most intense virtual environment in individuals' daily internet use.

Kirriemuir (2002) stated that there are various types of digital games. These types include games played with input devices such as gamepads connected to a television console, games accessible via satellite or digital subscription systems played on a television, games played on a personal computer or Macintosh, arcade-style games known as game cabinets, games played on portable devices such as Gameboy, and finally, games played on electronic devices such as cell phones or handheld computers. These games can be classified as browser games, massively multiplayer online role-playing games, real-life simulation games, online shooters, and 3D games. Within the game, players often socialize through conversation and messaging, and can collaborate to achieve game-related goals. Virtual personalities are represented by avatars and play roles. Simulation games offer an environment in which virtually anything that can be done in real life can be done in a virtual metaverse. These games simulate real life activities and allow for activities that could be carried out in a second life to be conducted virtually (Kuss & Griffiths, 2012).

## Motivation Sources of Digital Games

As stated by Tekkurşun-Demir and Bozkurt (2019), factors such as seeking diversion, entertainment, social maladjustment/isolation, challenge, escaping from the real world, and fulfilling desires in the virtual world can influence individuals' attitudes and approaches towards digital games. Due to their rapidly increasing popularity and the fact that a large portion of users spend their time playing these games, digital games have the potential to shape individuals' behaviors.

Digital games are an activity with addiction potential due to their content, design, graphics, and overall experience. This potential can increase based on individuals' motivations and prolonged engagement with the games. Children, in particular, may spend excessive amounts of time playing digital games due to their fast-paced and enjoyable nature. However, some games may have inappropriate content or contain violence, which can affect children's psychological and behavioral health.

According to Carlisle (2017), there are three main motivational factors for online gaming: achievement, socialization, and escapism. Some research suggests that motivation sources for digital games, such as coping with negative emotions, stress, fear and escapism, virtual friendship/relationships, entertainment, playfulness and loyalty, empowerment, mastery, control, recognition, completion, excitement and challenge, curiosity and obligation, particularly maladaptive coping, socialization, and personal satisfaction, serve as risk factors in the development of digital game addiction (Kuss & Griffiths, 2012).

These motivations not only contribute to providing the best gaming experience and making players want to keep playing the games, but also influence their preferences and help them choose from among different games. As digital games have become more widespread, research has begun to focus on their negative effects. A significant portion of this research is related to gaming addiction.

## Digital Game Addictıon

The concept of addiction was first used in the 19th century in the context of the definition and treatment of alcohol addiction. Later, in the mid-20th century, the definition of addiction was expanded in the psychiatric field to include drug addiction and other behavioral addictions. In the 21st century, understanding and defining technological addictions such as digital game addiction, internet addiction, and smartphone addiction have become prominent. The development of the addiction concept has continually evolved through the identification and examination of psychological, sociological, and biological factors (Nathan, Conrad & Skinstad, 2016).

Addiction can be defined as a pathological disorder in a person's body or behavior caused by certain foods, pharmaceutical toxins, or specific ideas and objects that lead to the loss of rational thinking ability (Lemmens et al., 2011; Seay and Kraut, 2007; Shaw and Black, 2008). Digital games, which are generally played online, can be defined as internet addiction according to some views and can arise due to factors such as family relationships, psychological, and social factors (Bhagat et al., 2020).

Internet addiction is a broad concept that arises as a result of many activities performed on the internet causing psychological addiction. These activities include research, learning, social network usage, gambling, shopping, and computer gaming. Four terms are used to describe inappropriate patterns of internet use: Internet addiction, Internet addiction disorder, Internet pathological use, and Internet dependency. It has been found that children are more likely to become addicted to computer games due to better and more appealing sound and visual effects, which they experience while playing on various gaming platforms and handheld devices. Computer game addiction involves excessive computer use both online and offline and is a part of the compulsive-impulsive spectrum disorder. Computer game addiction includes four unhealthy characteristics such as excessive use, withdrawal, tolerance, and negative consequences (Warburton, 2021).

Digital game addiction is coded as "Gaming Disorder" in the 11th edition of the International Classification of Diseases by the World Health Organization (6C51). This disorder is defined as the individual's loss of control over gaming, prioritizing gaming over daily activities and other interests, and continuing to game despite experiencing negative consequences in personal, family, social, educational, occupational, or other important areas of life (World Health Organization, April 2019).

Digital game addiction is considered a psychological disorder by experts who work on digital addiction (American Psychiatric Association, 2013). Digital game addiction is a condition that arises when individuals play digital games continuously or excessively, either unwillingly or uncontrollably (Kuss & Griffiths, 2012a). The causes of addiction can be explained by external reasons (staying within the system or enhancing virtual experiences) or internal reasons (time management, fear of losing one's surroundings, fear of exclusion, fear of missing out on the agenda). Addiction is a combination of certain conditions reduced to the necessities of communication, interaction, and culture.

## Reasons for Digital Game Addiction

The internet has become a vital tool used for many different purposes in the modern world. However, the internet also has addictive potential. Internet addiction occurs when individuals cannot control the amount of time they spend online and when this behavior affects their normal lives. Among individuals with internet addiction, digital gaming is observed to be one of the most commonly preferred activities. Digital games are one of the most addictive activities on the internet. The addictive features of these games can help individuals escape from their real-life problems and trigger addiction formation.

Internet addiction and digital game addiction are closely related and fall under the category of behavioral addictions. Studies by Günüç (2015) have shown a strong correlation between internet addiction and digital game addiction. This relationship indicates that individuals' addiction to digital games is also associated with internet use. Digital game addiction has similar causes to other addictions.

The causes of digital game addiction are diverse and depend on many factors. These include the environment in which children live, parental attitudes, children's personality traits, social interactions, psychological and emotional problems, and others. Failure or lack of success in children's environment and activities may lead to digital game addiction. When children experience difficulties in their daily lives, they try to relieve themselves by immersing themselves in the world of games. In addition, since children may not have developed many different skills to cope with various problems, digital games may become an easy way for them to escape and solve their problems.

Parents' attitudes can also contribute to digital game addiction. If parents do not set boundaries while allowing their children to play games, children can spend a significant amount of their time playing games. In addition, if parents do not show enough attention to their children, children may feel lonely, which can lead them to escape into the gaming world. During adolescence, when the influence of parents decreases and the importance of the peer group increases, online games can be used as a coping strategy for stress, which can negatively affect their psychosocial development. It has been reported that problematic gamers have a higher frequency of playing games to reduce negative emotions such as anger and disappointment. Therefore, it is suggested that adolescents who excessively play online games may not develop healthy coping strategies for stress and their psychosocial development may be significantly affected. If this addiction is left untreated, problems such as depression, anxiety, and somatization may arise (Kuss & Griffiths, 2012b).

Children's personality traits can influence their susceptibility to digital game addiction. For example, when children have lower self-esteem, they may put more effort into being successful in the gaming world. Additionally, when children have a competitive nature, digital games can fulfill their need for competition.

Social interactions can also lead to digital game addiction. Children connect to the internet to play games with their friends, and when they receive invitations to play, they feel drawn into the world of gaming.

Psychological and emotional problems can also lead to digital game addiction. Children may turn to the gaming world to cope with issues such as depression, anxiety, loneliness, or stress. These problems can increase the tendency to start playing games and lead children to spend more time playing games.

As Horzum (2011) pointed out, playing computer games at an addictive level can lead students to be unable to quit playing, neglect their responsibilities, and prefer playing games over other activities. It is important to consider the danger that the virtual world of gaming can become a child's reality over time. Spending more time in front of the screen with increasing pleasure can lead to increased addictive behavior. Addiction is a multidimensional concept, and psychologists study not only its cognitive, mental, and physiological aspects, but also its social aspects. Internet tools can be defined as virtual spaces where communicative and sensory inferences can be made, and can lead to an increase in asocial behavior in individuals and their relationships with themselves and others.

The symptoms and negative effects of digital game addiction are similar to those of internet addiction. For instance, both types of addiction can affect individuals' normal lives, cause problems in family and friend relationships, and negatively impact work performance. Studies conducted by Kim, Jeong, and Zhong (2010) reveal that the symptoms and negative effects of internet addiction and digital game addiction are similarly expressed.

Research on internet gaming addiction appears to have findings that can be interpreted as a relationship between various personality traits that can be grouped under core characteristics such as introversion, neuroticism, and impulsivity, and digital gaming addiction. Additionally, the structural characteristics of digital games can also lead players to be at risk of developing addiction. Positive reinforcement can lead to the continuity of the game. Game features such as rare in-game elements, watching cutscenes, and adult content can cause addicted players to enjoy the game more. Additionally, addicted players have been observed to take pride in their avatars and aspire to be like their virtual characters. As a result, digital games appear to have a higher potential for addiction than games that do not contain these structures, such as offline games. Excessive online gaming has also been associated with significantly reduced slow wave sleep, decreased verbal memory performance, and delayed onset of long-term sleep (Kuss & Griffiths, 2012).

## Biological Factors

Digital game addiction can be associated with biological causes and factors such as the release of regulatory substances with pleasurable effects in the brain, habit formation, and increased cravings. In addition, genetic predisposition, stress, social or psychological problems, unmet needs, and many other factors can contribute to the development of this addiction type. Biological factors such as increased dopamine levels, genetic factors, structural brain differences, and an individual's mental state can play a significant role in the development of digital game addiction. However, other factors such as age, gender, social and cultural factors can also affect addiction risk. Therefore, many factors that cause digital game addiction can interact together to increase a person's susceptibility to this type of addiction.

Biological causes and factors of digital game addiction include genetic factors, brain structure and function, neurotransmitter levels, and behavioral-cognitive factors. For example, some studies have shown that the brains of individuals with digital game addiction become more active in certain regions and that these regions are different from normal brains. In addition, the enjoyment and increase of certain neurotransmitter levels during the use of digital games can also lead to the development of digital game addiction. Personal and behavioral factors, especially factors such as stress, depression, social isolation, and low self-esteem, can increase the risk of digital game addiction. The effects of biological factors on the brain and nervous system are important. Playing digital games increases the levels of neurotransmitters such as dopamine, norepinephrine, and serotonin that increase pleasure and enjoyment in certain regions of the brain. This increase can make playing the game more pleasurable and addictive. In addition, genetic and biological predisposition can also cause digital game addiction to develop (Stevens, King, Dorstyn, & Delfabbro, 2019).

Another biological factor is the effect of brain structure on experiences and persistence of playing digital games. The brain of a person who constantly plays games prioritizes playing games and continuing to play. As a result, the motivation and desire required for playing games increase, which can lead to the development of digital game addiction (Green, Bavelier, 2012).

## Psychological Factors

Game addiction refers to the negative consequences and unhealthy behaviors resulting from compulsive or excessive use of computer games (Jeong & Kim, 2011). Different terms have been used for this issue, such as "problematic game use" (Seay & Kraut, 2007), "pathological video game playing" (Choo et al., 2010), "internet gaming addiction" (Kuss & Griffiths, 2012), "internet gaming disorder" (APA, 2013), and "game addiction" (Lemmens, Valkenburg, & Peter, 2009). The American Psychiatric Association has suggested conducting further research to determine whether game addiction should be recognized as a pathological disorder (APA, 2013). Game addiction or Internet Gaming Disorder (IGD) has been included as an additional research condition in section III of the DSM-5 (APA, 2013).

Scientists have evaluated gaming addiction as a multidimensional concept. For example, Griffiths (1998) measured gaming addiction by using symptoms such as salience, conflict, and withdrawal. Similarly, Young (1996, 1998) created the Internet Addiction Test (IAT) by identifying symptoms of internet gaming addiction. Widyanto and McMurran (2004) proposed a gaming addiction scale consisting of six dimensions, including salience, excessive use, neglect of work, expectancy, lack of self-control, and neglect of social life, by adapting the IAT. Liu and Peng (2009) suggested multidimensional scales including cognitive and behavioral factors, such as lack of control, neglect of work, and social problems. In this study, digital game addiction was defined using the six dimensions proposed by Widyanto and McMurran (2004).

## The Relationship Between Loneliness and Game Addiction

Loneliness is an expression of a distressing emotion that arises from the absence of companionship, and is strongly associated with digital games as a psychological characteristic (Peplau and Perlman, 1982).

Previous studies have shown that loneliness may precede gaming addiction and may also be associated with aggression and depression (Kim, LaRose, and Peng, 2009; Mentzoni et al., 2011). While the relationship between social isolation and loneliness is generally accepted, individuals can also feel lonely among others. Therefore, the qualitative aspects of social relationships may be more closely related to loneliness (Hawkley, Thisted, and Cacioppo, 2009). Some previous studies have shown a positive relationship between pathological gaming and loneliness. For example, a cross-sectional study by Kim et al. (2009) showed that pathological gaming and loneliness were interrelated. Lemmens et al. (2011) demonstrated that loneliness and low social competence could be important predictors of pathological gaming, but loneliness was the strongest predictor.

Individuals having psychological problems such as loneliness may lack social skills and have low social competence in real life (Caplan, 2003). This may lead them to prefer online games to fulfill their unmet needs or to escape from negative moods (Caplan, 2003). At the same time, they may exhibit maladaptive cognitive distortions about themselves and the world or have a tendency to display their abilities both online and offline (Davis, 2001). Therefore, they are likely to perceive the online environment as a safer place (Caplan, 2003). As a result, lonely and emotionally sensitive individuals may immerse themselves deeply in digital games. Consequently, lonely individuals may prefer to play computer games in a virtual environment instead of communicating face-to-face with people in the real world (Liu and Peng, 2009). This situation leads to the assumption of a positive relationship between loneliness and digital game addiction.

## The Relationship Between Depression and Game Addiction

Depression is a significant psychological condition that has been linked to online gaming addiction or problematic Internet use (J. Kim et al., 2009). According to the National Institute of Mental Health (NIMH, 2015), depression includes symptoms such as persistent sadness, anxiety, pessimism, emptiness, hopelessness, or feelings of guilt.

There is a lot of research on the relationship between depression and online game addiction (Seay & Kraut, 2007). Davis (2001) proposed a cognitive-behavioral model of problematic Internet use, suggesting that excessive time spent online could lead to problematic behaviors. In Davis's model, there may be "maladaptive cognitive distortions" in both online and offline realms regarding oneself and the world. Based on Davis's model, Caplan (2003) suggested that depressed individuals may have difficulty initiating and maintaining face-to-face communication, making computer environments attractive. The likelihood of lonely and depressed individuals having low social competence may be explained by the idea that online interpersonal interactions and relationships are safer, more effective, and more comfortable than face-to-face social activities (Caplan, 2003).

Previous studies provide evidence that depression may be positively related to digital game addiction. Individuals with depression may use digital games as a way to escape from negative emotions. Individuals who experience social difficulties may prefer digital games and other online social interactions due to negative beliefs about their social skills, which may lead to excessive and compulsive digital game use and addiction. Thus, it is assumed that depression may be positively related to digital game addiction.

## The Relationship Between Aggression and Game Addiction

One of the most discussed psychological variables related to game addiction is aggression, depression, and loneliness. Previous studies (Griffiths 2000, Kim et al. 2008, Lemmens et al. 2011, Mehroof &Griffiths 2010) acknowledge aggression as a significant predictor of problematic gaming. Aggressive individuals are prone to excessive digital game play, leading to a tendency to engage in digital games, including video games. Two different explanations exist for this. According to one view, players can choose certain media forms because they fit pre-existing aggressive traits; this means that seeking out a specific type of game is an active process (Ferguson, 2011). Another explanation is that repeated aggressive behavior and excessive or addictive game playing can be caused by obtaining high scores for game violence (Mehroof &Griffiths, 2010). In this process, aggressive behaviors can become goal-oriented.

Previous research has repeatedly highlighted the connections between aggression and game addiction. These include: (1) the aggression trait being associated with higher scores on online game addiction (Griffiths, 2000; E.J. Kim et al., 2008; Lemmens et al., 2011; Mehroof & Griffiths, 2010); (2) aggressive behavior may promote the development of online game addiction (Mehroof & Griffiths, 2010); (3) the preference for violent games is strongly linked with excessive gaming (Griffiths et al., 2004); (4) adolescent male gamers prefer violent video games (Lemmens et al., 2011); and (5) aggressive children are drawn to violent games (Griffiths, 2000).

### Social and Cultural Factors

Digital game addiction is a problem that negatively affects an individual's social life and interpersonal relationships. While game addicts seek refuge in games to escape real-life problems, they actually experience more loneliness, depression, and aggressiveness. Additionally, game addicts feel misunderstood and excluded by their surroundings, which further leads them to play more games. The social and cultural factors of digital game addiction also include variables such as family structure, friend group, education level, income level, gender, and age (Uzunoğlu, 2021).

It is stated that urbanization has increased the demand for computer games for children due to the lack of safe play areas. In addition, factors such as the socioeconomic status of students' families, their mothers' educational level, and the presence of a game console/computer at home also influence the level of addiction to computer games. These factors are mentioned as social and cultural factors that should be taken into account in identifying students who are prone to digital game addiction and in prevention studies. (Muslu &Aygün, 2020).

Research shows that students from higher socio-economic backgrounds are more at risk for digital game addiction, and there is a relationship between gender and digital game addiction. Male students are at a higher risk for digital game addiction than female students. This can lead to social anxiety and hinder healthy communication during an important period of adolescence and can also be associated with obesity. Therefore, it is important for parents and teachers to raise awareness and help young people control their digital game use and maintain a healthy lifestyle (Bilginer, Karadeniz, & Arslan, 2021).

## Symptoms of Digital Game Addiction

The pathological gambling criteria in DSM (APA, 2013) are generally accepted for evaluating digital game addiction. Griffiths, a prominent researcher, defined digital game addiction with 7 criteria inspired by pathological gambling diagnosis criteria (Griffiths &Davies, 2005).

### Clarity

Games play a significant role in players' lives, with a dominant presence in their brains (intense mental focus), emotions (strong desire), and behavior (excessive use). Players' minds are usually preoccupied with games, and they often daydream while playing. They ignore responsibilities, tasks, projects, assignments, or social activities like school or work and miss deadlines, focusing on games that have become the center of their lives. As addiction progresses, players show less interest in other hobbies or social relationships/activities and prefer only to play digital games.

### Tolerance

Players aim to maintain the feeling they experience while playing games by extending the time they spend in games. There is a positive relationship between the time spent on games and digital game addiction (Gentile, 2009; Rideout et al., 2010). Another study showed that the time spent on games can accelerate the addiction process and support the development of its symptoms (Ögel, 2012; Van Rooij et al., 2011); however, it should not be considered as only a single diagnostic criterion. For example, even if two players spend the same amount of time playing games, addiction symptoms may be different for each player (Ögel, 2012). Therefore, excessive time spent on games by a player cannot be assumed as game addiction unless it is supported by other diagnostic criteria.

### Withdrawal

It is defined as the unpleasant physical and emotional reactions that occur when addicted gamers cannot play games. They have an excessive need to play games and may experience negative emotions such as anger, anxiety, isolation, and depression when they are unable to play. They may become angry and prone to violent reactions towards factors that prevent them from playing their games. The feeling of alienation may also become permanent.

### Mood Modification

It is defined as the impact of games on players' emotional experiences. While playing games, players may feel excitement or relaxation. Games can be used as a way to avoid problems or negative emotions (such as sadness, guilt, unhappiness, depression, and anxiety) and to try to enjoy playing. However, if overwhelming problems persist or increase, the frequency and duration of game playing may increase.

## Relapse

Players struggle to control their gaming behavior and have difficulty giving up their games. If the duration of their gameplay is restricted, players may re-elevate the level of their addiction and have difficulty controlling it. Children can become angry or aggressive as a result of restrictions.

## Conflict

Players experience conflicts with themselves or people in their environment (work, school, or social circle). These conflicts can involve lying, deception, or physical or verbal aggression. For example, they may disregard personal hygiene routines, eating, sleeping, or bathing to continue playing their games. They may also lie to their family and friends about their gaming habits.

## Problems

The desire to play games can lead to problems such as job loss, academic failure, loss of scholarships, breakups, divorces, and neglect of personal hygiene. Despite the negative consequences of playing games, players continue their extensive gaming experiences (Griffiths & Davies, 2005).

## Physical Symptoms

The increasing use of digital games and their becoming an indispensable part of children's daily lives can lead not only to positive but also negative effects (Rosen, Lim, Felt, et al., 2014). The literature indicates that digital games containing violence are associated with mental and psychological problems such as loneliness, depression, anxiety, aggression, violent tendencies, and attention deficit (Wack & Tantleff-Dunn, 2019). However, some studies have shown that children who spend excessive time with digital games experience problems such as decreased academic achievement, irregular and insufficient sleep patterns, low physical activity, obesity, and musculoskeletal system problems. The latest review published by the Journal of Addiction reports that inappropriate use of technological devices by children in terms of time, frequency, and position can lead to health risks such as developmental problems, musculoskeletal system problems, physical inactivity, obesity, and sleep quality (Ballard, Gray, Reilly& Noggle, 2009).

## Emotional Symptoms

Digital game addiction is a serious problem that can affect people of all ages. It can manifest itself through emotional symptoms such as depression, anxiety, and irritability. If left untreated for too long, these symptoms can have a negative impact on an individual's physical and mental health.

Depression is one of the most common emotional symptoms associated with digital game addiction; it often leads to feelings of hopelessness or worthlessness (Yalçın, 2019). Those who suffer from this condition may withdraw from their friends and family or find themselves completely isolated due to their obsession with gaming (Çelebı, 2020). Additionally, they may have difficulty sleeping or concentrating on tasks outside of gaming activities, which can lead to other problems such as low academic performance among children or job loss among affected adults.

Anxiety is another common symptom experienced by digital game addicts; they may feel overwhelmed when faced with real-life responsibilities because they have been focused on playing video games instead of engaging in more productive pursuits such as school assignments, work projects, etc. This creates situations that further lead to isolation, resulting in loneliness and only intensifying the cycle. Additionally, individuals struggling with digital game addiction are prone to sudden outbursts of anger caused by the disappointment of not achieving goals in the virtual worlds that have no real consequences for failure (Özdemir &Akar, 2021).

In conclusion, digital game addiction should be taken seriously as it carries many potential psychological risks such as depression, anxiety, and irritability that should be addressed before any lasting damage occurs. If you suspect that a loved one may be suffering from this condition, seeking professional help early on can greatly increase the chances of successful recovery.

## Social and Educational Symptoms

The most common social symptom associated with digital game addiction is the tendency for individuals suffering from this disorder to withdraw from their friends or family members, as they spend more time playing video games instead of building meaningful relationships outside of game activities. This can lead to feelings of loneliness or isolation, which if left untreated, can result in further mental health problems such as depression or anxiety disorders. Additionally, individuals affected by this condition may neglect important responsibilities such as going out with friends or attending school due to being engrossed in video games; thus, leading them down a path towards weaker academic performance than expected given their individual abilities and talents prior to the onset of the addiction-prone behavior pattern (Kuss, Griffiths, Karila, & Billieux, 2014).

Lastly, there are also physical symptoms directly associated with excessive gaming, such as potential eye strain caused by staring at a screen for long hours without breaks in between sessions. In severe cases, these physical problems can worsen and even lead to sleep deprivation, which can further exacerbate other health problems related to the addiction itself, such as headaches or migraines. All of these factors coming together highlight that digital game addiction is a serious issue that should not be taken lightly, as the long-term effects of its impact on individuals' lives can result in permanent damage if left untreated or completely ignored (Aziz, Nordin, Abdulkadir, & Salih, 2021).

## Long-Term Results

Digital game addiction is a growing problem in today's world, and its long-term consequences can be much more serious than most people think. From physical health issues to mental and emotional anxieties, digital game addiction can have a negative impact on a person's life if left unchecked.

The physical effects of digital game addiction include sleep deprivation, inadequate nutrition due to unhealthy eating habits while playing, headaches caused by prolonged screen time, and even obesity or carpal tunnel syndrome caused by prolonged poor posture or hand positions while playing games (Gentile& Douglas, 2009). In addition to these physical ailments, there are also psychological concerns related to long-term game play, such as depression and anxiety due to social isolation caused by spending excessive hours online instead of participating in real-world activities or interacting face-to-face with others, academic performance declines because the addicted person has difficulty focusing on anything other than their favorite video games, increased aggression towards both virtual opponents and real people in their environment, financial difficulties due to spending too much money on new games or related equipment, and relationship problems because the addicted person may prioritize their game obsession over family time (Griffiths & Mark, 2008).

The best way for someone who suspects they may have a problem is to seek professional help before it spirals out of control - especially now that therapy sessions aimed at treating video game addictions are more available than ever, so there is no excuse to ignore this issue if you think it may negatively affect your quality of life in the long run. Taking proactive steps now will ensure that the negative effects do not become permanent fixtures in the future, but attempting to address them becomes a much more difficult task in the early stages than it would have been earlier (King& Daniel, 2007).

## Consequences of Digital Game Addiction

Digital game addiction can have a negative impact on a child's social interactions and academic achievement, leading to physical, behavioral, emotional, or social disorders.

Individuals may play games to cope with issues such as stress, social exclusion, and depression. These games can be repeated in an uncontrolled manner, and other tasks may be neglected. This addiction can negatively affect personal, social, and work life over time, and can lead to health problems. Like other addictions, digital game addiction involves uncontrolled and repeated use. People enjoy playing these games and constantly repeat them. Addictive games can neglect other important tasks and disrupt relationships. These similarities show that digital game addiction is no different from other addictions and needs to be treated as a serious problem. Individuals need to be aware of this and intervene in a timely manner (Kanat, 2019). People with game addiction struggle with control skills and play games for long periods of time on a daily basis. If they cannot continue to play games, they become uncomfortable and restless and sacrifice other social activities for games. Children addicted to computer games isolate themselves like other addicts and use computer games as a way to escape from real-world pressures.

The uncontrolled use of digital games has caused digital game addiction to be equivalent to drug addiction in severity. Game addiction negatively affects individuals' mental, psychological, and social areas. In terms of mental concepts, it can manifest in individuals who have difficulty in practical thinking, response difficulty (Zhou, Yuan &Yao, 2012), attention deficit (Gentile, 2009), repetition of the same responses, hyperactivity, and restlessness problems. Additionally, game addiction also negatively affects a person's social relationships and community activities. The individual feels compelled to continue playing games and sacrifices other social activities for games. Furthermore, prolonged game playing can also have a negative impact on physical health. Physical problems such as fatigue, eye strain, sleep disorders, and lack of regular physical exercise may arise.

The use of digital games has been associated with enhanced cognitive performance in areas such as memory recall and spatial reasoning. This is due to the fact that many modern video games contain puzzles or challenges that require strategic thinking to progress through levels or successfully complete objectives - something that strengthens mental sharpness over time with regular gameplay sessions. While there are benefits to playing video games in certain age groups, such as improving hand-eye coordination or problem-solving skills, prolonged excessive use can lead to negative outcomes such as sleep deprivation, difficulty communicating with family and friends due to a lack of face-to-face interaction, weak self-control resulting in impulsiveness when making decisions outside of the virtual world, increased levels of aggression stemming from disappointment in losing or not reaching goals, and decreased concentration leading to generally lower grades in school (Gentile &Gentile, 2008).

## Diagnosis and Treatment of Digital Game Addiction

The American Psychiatric Association has developed a nine-item criteria to identify digital game addiction. These include the interaction between mind and game, tolerance (the need to play more on the internet), withdrawal symptoms (irritability, anxiety, and sadness), continuity (failure to stop or reduce playing), displacement (preferring online games to hobbies and entertainment activities), continued excessive use despite known harms, lying (giving deceptive information to others about internet playing time), escape (using online games to escape negative effects), and conflict/loss (loss of opportunities related to work, education, or career) (APA, 2013).

Diagnosis of addiction can be made using various methods such as clinical interviews and personality tests (King & Delfabbro, 2018). Treatment approaches may include individual therapy, family therapy, pharmacological treatment, behavioral or cognitive therapy, parent education, and preventive methods such as setting limits for gaming (King & Delfabbro, 2018).

The criteria for identifying digital game addiction are as follows:

- Uncontrolled game usage: exceeding the limits set for playing games and being unable to quit playing games.
- Allocating time to play games: tendency to neglect other priorities in order to continue playing games.
- Using games to relieve stress: tendency to use playing games as a way to relax.
- Anxiety to continue playing games: anxiety about not being able to stop playing games.
- Disruption of social relationships: tendency to neglect social relationships in order to play games.
- Disruption of personal life: tendency to neglect other priorities and personal life in order to play games.

These criteria are used to determine the presence of problems arising from continuing to play games and to identify the presence of digital game addiction (Irmak &Erdoğan, 2016).

## Treating Digital Gaming Addiction

The treatment of digital game addiction should be taken very seriously by experts. It is important to raise awareness among children and adolescents about digital game addiction and to educate families on this issue. In this way, children can learn to use digital games in a healthy way. Parents can implement a range of strategies to limit their children's game play and encourage them to engage in healthy activities.

Understanding how to approach and treat digital gaming addiction is important as it can have serious consequences for those affected. Psychosocial interventions and medication-based treatments can be used to treat digital gaming addiction depending on the severity of an individual's symptoms. Psychosocial interventions are designed to identify triggers, develop coping mechanisms, improve relationships, learn problem-solving skills, and gain insight into behavioral patterns. Cognitive Behavioral Therapy (CBT) is a type of psychotherapy used in the treatment of digital gaming addiction, which helps to change negative thought patterns. Medication-based treatments can also be effective and may sometimes require hospitalization. However, with proper diagnosis and treatment strategies, a hopeful future is possible.

Clinical treatment approaches and preventive measures can be used in the treatment of digital game addiction.

## Clinical Treatment Approaches

Cognitive-behavioral therapy (CBT) offers strategies for individuals to identify unhealthy behaviors associated with gaming addiction and replace them with healthier ones. Additionally, it teaches patients to recognize triggers that lead to addictive behavior so they can avoid or manage them better in the future. When used in conjunction with other therapies, such as family counseling or group sessions that focus on specific topics related to gaming habits like self-control or communication skills, CBT has been shown to be effective in treating video game addiction (Stevens, King, Dorstyn, & Delfabbro, 2019).

Motivational interviewing (MI) focuses on helping individuals find their intrinsic motivations rather than relying on external rewards, such as successes within games. This technique provides therapists and counselors with more insight into the thought processes related to addiction and offers practical advice that patients can benefit from throughout their recovery journey. (Burke, Arkowitz, & Menchola, 2013).

Clinical treatments are important tools to help individuals experiencing digital game addiction. Since each person's situation is unique, treatment plans should always be tailored to the individual. Cognitive-behavioral therapy, motivational interviewing, family counseling, or other techniques provide experts with the opportunity to create personalized treatment plans for each patient. These treatments provide significant support to individuals struggling with digital game addiction.

## Preventive Approaches

One of the primary preventive approaches for digital game addiction is for parents to manage their children's gaming habits. By limiting their children's playing time and developing alternative interests, parents can reduce their children's interest in games. Additionally, it is important for parents to monitor their children's gaming habits and seek professional help if their children have problems related to gaming (Stevens, Delfabbro, & King, 2021).

Another way to prevent digital game addiction is to raise awareness. Being conscious of the emotional and physical effects of playing games and playing them in a mindful way to avoid the negative consequences can reduce the risk of addiction. Additionally, lifestyle changes can also be helpful. Healthy habits such as exercising, maintaining a healthy diet, and getting enough sleep can reduce the risk of game addiction (Lee &Morgan, 2018).

In conclusion, digital gaming addiction is a problem that many people face, and there are treatment options available to combat it. It is important to use personalized approaches tailored to each patient's individual situation to create the most effective treatment plan. Additionally, clinical treatment approaches and preventative measures are also important approaches to preventing digital gaming addiction.

# Future Research and Directions

It is suggested a few ideas for future research on digital game addiction and children. Firstly, more research is needed to gather data on how much time children spend on digital games, what types of games they play, how much pleasure they derive from games, and how addicted they are to games. Secondly, it is important for parents to be educated about the harms of digital games and how to use games responsibly, so that they can better communicate these risks to their children. Thirdly, new methods need to be developed for treating children who are addicted to digital games. Lastly, the digital game industry should take more responsibility for ensuring that children are able to interact with digital games in a healthy way by offering age-appropriate games, restricting violent or sexual content, and being transparent about data collection in games. These suggestions can provide a roadmap for future research on digital game addiction and children.

## CONCLUSION AND RECOMMENDATIONS

Digital game addiction is a growing concern in today's society. With the rise of online gaming and mobile games, more and more children are becoming addicted to these digital games. This addiction can have serious consequences on an individual's mental health, physical health, and social life. It can lead to depression, anxiety, obesity, and even isolation from friends and family. The addictive nature of these games makes it difficult for individuals to stop playing even when they know it's harmful to their well-being. It's important for individuals to recognize the signs of digital game addiction and seek help if needed before it becomes too late.

As technology advances, it's no surprise that students are becoming increasingly addicted to digital games. It's important for teachers to recognize this issue and take action. The first step is to educate students on the negative effects of excessive game time, such as poor academic performance and social isolation. Teachers can also incorporate interactive games into their lessons, creating a balance between traditional learning methods and technology. Additionally, setting clear boundaries for technology use in the classroom can help limit distractions during instruction time. Lastly, teachers can encourage healthy habits outside of school by promoting physical activity and face-to-face social interactions with peers.

Digital game addiction has become a major concern for parents in today's world. Parents should take preventive measures to ensure that their children do not get addicted to digital games. They can set time limits on the usage of electronic devices and encourage their children to engage in outdoor activities or other hobbies. It is also essential for parents to monitor their children's gaming habits and talk to them about the negative effects of excessive gaming. Setting boundaries and enforcing rules around digital gameplay can help prevent addiction. Families can also seek professional help if they suspect that their child is struggling with addiction.

## REFERENCES

American Psychiatric Association. (2013). *Diagnostic and Statistical Manual of Mental Disorders* (5th ed.). American Psychiatric Publishing.

Aziz, N., Nordin, M. J., Abdulkadir, S. J., & Salih, M. M. M. (2021). Digital addiction: Systematic review of computer game addiction impact on adolescent physical health. *Electronics (Basel)*, *10*(9), 996. doi:10.3390/electronics10090996

Ballard, M., Gray, M., Reilly, J., & Noggle, M. (2009). Correlates of video game screen time among males: Body mass, physical activity, and other media use. *Eating Behaviors*, *10*(3), 161–167. doi:10.1016/j.eatbeh.2009.05.001 PMID:19665099

Bhagat, S., Jeong, E. J., & Kim, D. J. (2020). The Role of Individuals Need for Online Social Interactions and Interpersonal Incompetence in Digital Game Addiction. *International Journal of Human-Computer Interaction*, *36*(5), 449–463. doi:10.1080/10447318.2019.1654696

Bilginer, Ç., Karadeniz, S., & Arslan, E. (2021). Digital gaming among adolescents in clinical settings: Do we underestimate this issue? *Entertainment Computing*, *36*, 100392. doi:10.1016/j.entcom.2020.100392

Burke, B. L., Arkowitz, H., & Menchola, M. (2003). The efficacy of motivational interviewing: A meta-analysis of controlled clinical trials. *Journal of Consulting and Clinical Psychology*, *71*(5), 843–861. doi:10.1037/0022-006X.71.5.843 PMID:14516234

Caplan, S. E. (2003). Preference for Online Social Interaction: A Theory of Problematic Internet Use and Psychosocial Well-Being. *Communication Research*, *30*(6), 625–648. doi:10.1177/0093650203257842

Carlisle, K. L. (2017). *Personality, motivation, and Internet gaming disorder: Understanding the addiction*. Old Dominion University.

Çelebi, E. (2020). Dijital Oyun ve Bağımlılık. *Yeni Medya Elektronik Dergisi.*, *16*(1), 241–256.

Choo, H., Gentile, D., Sim, T., Li, D. D., Khoo, A., & Liau, A. (2010). Pathological video gaming among Singaporean youth. *Annals of the Academy of Medicine*, *39*(11), 822–829. PMID:21165520

Davis, R. A. (2001). A cognitive-behavioral model of pathological Internet use. *Computers in Human Behavior*, *17*(2), 187–195. doi:10.1016/S0747-5632(00)00041-8

Dünya Sağlık Örgütü. (2019). *ICD-11 for Mortality and Morbidity Statistics*. WHO. https://icd.who.int/browse11/l-m/en#/http%3a%2f%2fid.who.int%2ficd%2fentity%2f1448597234

Ferguson, C. J. (2011). Video games and youth violence: A prospective analysis in adolescents. *Journal of Youth and Adolescence*, *40*(4), 377–391. doi:10.100710964-010-9610-x PMID:21161351

Gentile, D. A. (2009). Pathological video-game use among youth ages 8 to 18: A national study. *Psychological Science*, *20*(5), 594–602. doi:10.1111/j.1467-9280.2009.02340.x PMID:19476590

Gentile, D. A., & Gentile, J. R. (2008). Violent video games as exemplary teachers: A conceptual analysis. *Journal of Youth and Adolescence*, *37*(2), 127–141. doi:10.100710964-007-9206-2

Green, C. S., & Bavelier, D. (2012). Learning, attentional control, and action video games. *Current Biology*, *22*(6), R197–R206. doi:10.1016/j.cub.2012.02.012 PMID:22440805

Griffiths, M. (1998). Internet addiction: Does it really exist? In J. Gackenbach (Ed.), *Psychology and the Internet: Intrapersonal, Interpersonal, and Transpersonal Implications* (pp. 61–75). Academic Press.

Griffiths, M. D. (2000). Internet addiction—Time to be taken seriously? *Addiction Research*, *8*(5), 413–418. doi:10.3109/16066350009005587

Griffiths, M. D., & Davies, M. N. O. (2005). Videogame addiction: Does it exist? In J. Goldstein & J. Raessens (Eds.), *Handbook of Computer Game Studies* (pp. 359–368). MIT Press.

Griffiths, M. D., Kuss, D. J., & King, D. L. (2012). Video game addiction: Past, present and future. *Current Psychiatry Reviews*, *8*(4), 308–318. doi:10.2174/157340012803520414

Günüç, S. (2015). Relationships and associations between video game and internet addictions: Is tolerance a symptom seen in all conditions? *Computers in Human Behavior*, *49*, 517–525. doi:10.1016/j.chb.2015.03.063

Hawkley, L. C., Thisted, R. A., & Cacioppo, J. T. (2009). Loneliness predicts reduced physical activity: Cross-sectional and longitudinal analyses. *Health Psychology*, *28*(3), 354–363. doi:10.1037/a0014400 PMID:19450042

Horzum, M. B. (2011). Investigation of elementary school students' computer game addiction levels according to various variables. *Eğitim ve Bilim*, *36*(159), 328–338.

İnce, M. & Işır, Ö. (2016). A workshop of art-based application through game-supported education. *İnönü Üniversitesi Uluslararası Sosyal Bilimler Dergisi*, *5*(1), 225-236.

Irmak, A. Y., & Erdogan, S. (2016). Digital game addiction among adolescents and young adults: A current overview. *Turkish Journal of Psychiatry*, *27*(2), 1–10.

Jeong, S. H., & Kim, S. T. (2011). Reviews of science for science librarians: Genome-wide association studies (GWAS). *Science & Technology Libraries*, *30*(3), 229–243. doi:10.1080/0194262X.2011.595315

Kanat, S. (2019). The relationship between digital game addiction, communication skills, and loneliness perception levels of university students. *International Education Studies*, *12*(11), 80–93. doi:10.5539/ies.v12n11p80

Kim, D. H., Jeong, E. J., & Zhong, H. (2010). Preventive role of parents in adolescent problematic internet game use in Korea. *Korean Journal of Sociology*, *44*(6), 111–133.

Kim, J., LaRose, R., & Peng, W. (2009). Loneliness as the Cause and the Effect of Problematic Internet Use: The Relationship between Internet Use and Psychological Well-Being. *Cyberpsychology & Behavior*, *12*(4), 541–455. doi:10.1089/cpb.2008.0327 PMID:19514821

Kirriemuir, J. (2002, February). Video gaming, education and digital learning technologies. *D-Lib Magazine : the Magazine of the Digital Library Forum*, *8*(2). doi:10.1045/february2002-kirriemuir

Kuss, D. J., & Griffiths, M. D. (2012). Internet gaming addiction: A systematic review of empirical research. *International Journal of Mental Health and Addiction*, *10*(2), 278–296. doi:10.100711469-011-9318-5

Kuss, D. J., & Griffiths, M. D. (2012). Online gaming addiction: The role of sensation seeking, self-esteem, neuroticism, aggression, state anxiety, and trait anxiety. *Cyberpsychology, Behavior, and Social Networking*, *15*(8), 481–487. doi:10.1089/cyber.2011.0324

Kuss, D. J., & Griffiths, M. D. (2012). Problematic video game use: A comprehensive review. *International Journal of Mental Health and Addiction*, *10*(2), 349–371.

Kuss, D. J., & Griffiths, M. D. (2012a). Online gaming addiction in children and adolescents: A review of empirical research. *Journal of Behavioral Addictions*, *1*(1), 3–22 doi:10.1556/JBA.1.2012.1.1 PMID:26166826

Kuss, D. J., & Griffiths, M. D. (2012b). Adolescent online gaming addiction. *Education for Health, 30*(1), 15–17.

Kuss, D. J., Griffiths, M. D., Karila, L., & Billieux, J. (2014). Internet addiction: A systematic review of epidemiological research for the last decade. *Current Pharmaceutical Design, 20*(25), 4026–4052. doi:10.2174/13816128113199990617 PMID:24001297

Lee, G. L., & Morgan, H. (2018). Understanding children's attraction toward digital games and preventing their gaming addiction. *US-China Education Review A., 8*(1), 11–17.

Lemmens, J. S., Valkenburg, P. M., & Peter, J. (2011). Psychosocial causes and consequences of pathological gaming. *Computers in Human Behavior, 27*(1), 144–152. doi:10.1016/j.chb.2010.07.015

Liu, M., & Peng, W. (2009). Cognitive and psychological predictors of the negative outcomes associated with playing MMOGs (massively multiplayer online games). *Computers in Human Behavior, 25*(6), 1306–1311. doi:10.1016/j.chb.2009.06.002

Mehroof, M., & Griffiths, M. D. (2010). Online gaming addiction: The role of sensation seeking, self-control, neuroticism, aggression, state anxiety, and trait anxiety. *Cyberpsychology, Behavior, and Social Networking, 13*(3), 313–316. doi:10.1089/cyber.2009.0229 PMID:20557251

Mentzoni, R. A., Brunborg, G. S., Molde, H., Myrseth, H., Skouverøe, K. J. M., Hetland, J., & Pallesen, S. (2011). Problematic video game use: Estimated prevalence and associations with mental and physical health. *Cyberpsychology, Behavior, and Social Networking, 14*(10), 591–596. doi:10.1089/cyber.2010.0260 PMID:21342010

Muslu, G. K., & Aygun, O. (2020). An analysis of computer game addiction in primary school children and its affecting factors. *Journal of Addictions Nursing, 31*(1), 30–38. doi:10.1097/JAN.0000000000000322 PMID:32132422

Nathan, P. E., Conrad, M., & Skinstad, A. H. (2016). History of the Concept of Addiction. *Annual Review of Clinical Psychology, 12*(1), 29–51. doi:10.1146/annurev-clinpsy-021815-093546 PMID:26565120

National Institute of Mental Health. (2015). *What Is Depression?* NIH. https://www.nimh.nih.gov/health/topics/depression/index.shtml

Ögel K. (2012). *İnternet Bağımlılığı, İnternetin Psikolojisini Anlamak ve Bağımlılıkla Başa Çıkmak*, 47-60. Türkiye İş Bankası Kültür Yayınları.

Özdemir, M.,& Akar, F. (2018). Ergenlerde İnternette Amaçsız Gezinme ile Dijital Oyun Bağımlılığı Arasındaki İlişkinin Anksiyete ve Sosyal Kaygı Açısından İncelenmesi. *İnsan ve Toplum Bilimleri Araştırmaları Dergisi, 7*(4), 3123-3136.

Peplau, L. A., & Perlman, D. (1982). Perspectives on loneliness. In L. A. Peplau & D. Perlman (Eds.), *Loneliness: A sourcebook of current theory, research and therapy* (pp. 1–18). Wiley New York.

Rideout, V. J., Foehr, U. G., & Roberts, D. F. (2010). Generation M2: Media in the lives of 8- to 18- year olds. Kaiser Family Foundation. KFF. https://www.kff.org/entmedia/entmedia012010nr.com

Rosen, L. D., Lim, A., Felt, J., Carrier, L. M., Cheever, N. A., Lara-Ruiz, J. M., Mendoza, J. S., & Rokkum, J. (2014). Media and technology use predicts ill-being among children, preteens, and teenagers independent of the negative health impacts of exercise and eating habits. *Computers in Human Behavior, 35*, 364–375. doi:10.1016/j.chb.2014.01.036 PMID:25717216

Seay, A. F., & Kraut, R. E. (2007). Project massive: Self-regulation and problematic use of online gaming. In *Proceedings of the SIGCHI Conference on Human Factors in Computing Systems*. ACM. 10.1145/1240624.1240749

Shaw, M., & Black, D. W. (2008). Internet addiction: Definition, assessment, epidemiology and clinical management. *CNS Drugs, 22*(3), 53–65. doi:10.2165/00023210-200822050-00001 PMID:18399706

Stevens, M. W., Delfabbro, P. H., & King, D. L. (2021). Prevention approaches to problem gaming: A large-scale qualitative investigation. *Computers in Human Behavior, 115*, 106611. doi:10.1016/j.chb.2020.106611

Stevens, M. W., King, D. L., Dorstyn, D., & Delfabbro, P. H. (2019). Cognitive-behavioral therapy for Internet gaming disorder: A systematic review and meta-analysis. *Clinical Psychology & Psychotherapy, 26*(2), 191–203. doi:10.1002/cpp.2341 PMID:30341981

Tekkurşun-Demir, G., & Mutlu-Bozkurt, T. (2019). Digital Game Playing Attitude Scale (DGPAS): Validity and reliability study. Sportif Bakış. *Spor ve Eğitim Bilimleri Dergisi, 6*(1), 1–18. doi:10.33468bsebd.79

Uzunoğlu, A. (2021). Digital games and addiction. *Yeni Medya, 2021*(11), 116–131.

Van Rooij, A. J., Schoenmakers, T. M., Vermulst, A. A., Van Den Eijnden, R. J., & Van De Mheen, D. (2011). Online video game addiction: Identification of addicted adolescent gamers. *Addiction (Abingdon, England), 106*(1), 205–212. doi:10.1111/j.1360-0443.2010.03104.x PMID:20840209

Wack, E., & Tantleff-Dunn, S. (2009). Relationships between electronic game play, obesity, and psychosocial functioning in young men. *Cyberpsychology & Behavior, 12*(2), 241–244. doi:10.1089/cpb.2008.0151 PMID:19006465

Warburton, W. A. (2021). Should internet addiction and gaming addiction be categorized as disorders. In Masters of media: Controversies and solutions (pp. 43-58). Macquarie University.

Widyanto, L., & McMurran, M. (2004). The psychometric properties of the internet addiction test. *Cyberpsychology & Behavior, 7*(4), 443–450. doi:10.1089/cpb.2004.7.443 PMID:15331031

Yalcin, S., & Bertiz, Y. (2019). Qualitative study on the effects of game addiction on university students. Science, Education [SEAT Journal]. *Art and Technology Journal, 3*(1), 27–34.

Young, K. S. (1996, August). *Internet addiction: The emergence of a new clinical disorder.* Paper presented at the American Psychological Association, Toronto, Canada.

Young, K. S. (1998). *Caught in the net: How to recognize the signs of internet addiction—and a winning strategy for recovery*. John Wiley & Sons.

Zhou, Z., Yuan, G., & Yao, J. (2012). Cognitive bases toward internet game-related pictures and executive deficits in individuals with an internet game addiction. *PLoS One*, *7*(11), 1–9. doi:10.1371/journal.pone.0048961 PMID:23155434

## ADDITIONAL READING

Blades, M., Blumberg, F. C., & Oates, C. (1890). Children and Digital Games. *Zeitschrift für Psychologie mit Zeitschrift für Angewandte Psychologie*, *221*(2), 2013.

Christakis, D. A. (2019). The challenges of defining and studying "digital addiction" in children. *Journal of the American Medical Association*, *321*(23), 2277–2278. doi:10.1001/jama.2019.4690 PMID:31095260

Hazar, Z. (2018). *Çağın vebası dijital oyun bağımlılığı ve başa çıkma yöntemleri*. Gazi Kitabevi.

Nielsen, R. K., & Kardefelt-Winther, D. (2018). Helping parents make sense of video game addiction. *Video game influences on aggression, cognition, and attention*, 59-69.

Salerno, L. (2015). Video Game Addiction: A Parent's Guide to Freeing Your Child from the Grip of Video Game Addiction. Createspace Publishing Platform.

## KEY TERMS AND DEFINITIONS

**Children:** Individuals up to the age of adolescence.
**Digital Games:** Interactive entertainment programs played on electronic devices.
**Game Addiction:** A behavioral disorder characterized by excessive dependence on playing games.
**Health Effects:** Refers to the effects of digital games on children's health.
**Treatment Methods:** Refers to the methods used to treat game addiction.

# Chapter 20
# A SWOT Analysis of Gender Creations From Digital Games to Metaverse

**Mustafa Eren Akpınar**
https://orcid.org/0000-0002-3917-3203
*Independent Researcher, Turkey*

## ABSTRACT

*In today's digital age, digital games point to an extremely important structure in terms of the audiences they appeal to, and the concept of metaverse, which has experienced a great increase in the speed of development in recent years, is also an area that affects digital games. Therefore, within the scope of this study, the process of digital games becoming metaverse in the near future is discussed. However, the study does not address only these two issues. Within the scope of this chapter, virtual gender creations that can be created in the context of the metaverse, together with the participation of digital games in the metaverse universe, are also examined with SWOT analysis. In addition, attention is drawn to the situations that may arise in terms of the fact that these developing technological structures can be reconfigured with virtual or meta-avatars that can be created. For this reason, within the scope of the study, it has been tried to be explained by examining how gender creations from digital games to meta-universe can affect the current situation.*

## INTRODUCTION

Considering today's conditions, it is observed that each of the changes experienced by technology has become more visible on human life. When we look at the main reason for this, the fact that technology is a constantly developing structure can be given as an example. Because almost every technological development is tried to be integrated into the daily life of humanity, and this gives rise to the assumption that each technological movement is important for humanity. However, in this case, it is necessary to mention the existence of a few minor points.

DOI: 10.4018/978-1-6684-8397-8.ch020

The concepts of digital games and metaverse have emerged as a frequently discussed and discussed topic both in the academic community and in the sectoral structure, especially in recent years. Because, thanks to the many opportunities opened by the developing technologies, humanity has undergone great changes and continues to undergo these changes. Among these changes, the most important developments in terms of communication sciences are the innovations brought by digitalization.

Among the innovations brought by digitalization in today's structure, the concepts of digital games, metaverse and gender creation are among the most popular topics. The main reason for the popularity of these concepts can be explained as the contribution of new generation technology studies in recent years to the development of digital games and metaverse concepts. At the same time, the fact that gender creation and equality issues have a very serious agenda in the society has contributed greatly to the popularization of another topic of our study, gender creation.

For this reason, within the scope of the study, not only the concepts of digital games and metaverse, but also the concept of gender creation is included, and the opportunities and threats that the digital game and meta world can create in terms of gender creation, which is a social issue, are examined with SWOT analysis. Thus, this chapter study both touches on the concepts of digital games and metaverse as a result of developing technologies and shows the feature of being an interdisciplinary study by focusing on the concept of gender creation in the light of these developments.

## CONCEPT OF DIGITAL GAMING

In order to understand digital games or digital games, it is first necessary to divide the concept into two and explain each word in itself. Because the concept of digital game is a concept that is formed by the combination of the words digital and game. Therefore, first of all, it is necessary to explain what digital signifies. It indicates the continuity of codes with digital, analog indicators (Chandler and Munday 2018: 92). According to another definition to support this view, the concept of digital is explained as a structure that covers the process of electronic processing of data (Bozkurt, et al. 2021: 36), not electronic devices in general. In this respect, it is not wrong to define digital as the electronification or digitization of traditional systems.

Another concept that should be mentioned after understanding what digital is the concept of game. Because, in order to understand the digital game, first of all, it is necessary to know what the concepts of digital and game are. The concept of game can generally be expressed as a form of entertainment that children or individuals perform depending on a certain rule or independently (Samur 2016: 2). In addition, it is possible to explain the concept of game as a structure or verb that can be expressed as irrational rather than mechanical (Tekerek 2006: 47) that emerged as a result of the need to enjoy human nature. From this perspective, it is possible to explain the game as an action with or without rules coming from the human mind.

When we look at the concept of digital game, it would not be wrong to see it as a roof structure that combines digital and game in general terms. Because, as the name suggests, digital game emerges as a field that is formed as a result of the combination of the above-mentioned concept of game with the concept of digital and is frequently examined by different disciplines (Karahisar 2013: 108). At the same time, it is possible to define the concept of digital game as a new generation interaction model or digital processes that offer an alternative view to the perception of physical game (Ilgaz Büyükbaykal and Abay Cansabuncu 2020: 3) that occur with new communication technologies. In addition to the definition made by Ilgaz Büyükbaykal and Abay Cansabuncu, Marsh et al. defines digital games as a process of creative development (Marsh, et al. 2016: 244) that takes place alongside traditional games. In the light of this definition, it can be assumed that digital games are actually the continuation of traditional games or that they are an advanced version of traditional game activities.

## SIMULATION THEORY AND META UNIVERSE (METAVERSE)

With the effect of the digitalization process and the development of virtual technologies, there are also openings in existing realities. The most important of these openings is undoubtedly the concept of metaverse, which is a concept that has been discussed and researched frequently in recent years, or in other words, the concept of meta-universe. Because, as the simulation theory put forward by Jean Baudrillard says, apart from the reality we live in, other appearances, called simulacrum, as expressed in the ATILF and Petit Robert Dictionary, have occurred (Baudrillard 2020: 7). When we look at the concept of metaverse, it can be stated that it is actually a platform, a reality that supports Baudrillard's speech. For this reason, in order to understand the meta-universe, it is necessary to talk about the simulation theory first.

Considering the emergence of the simulation theory, it can be stated as an important step that Western civilizations, which are considered among the developed societies, think about the existing reality (Yıldıran Önk 2009: 202). Because, in this way, the relationship between existing reality and truth could be thought about and the theory could be tested with productions (Karaduman and Aciyan 2020: 455) about whether there really a simulation universe like is "The Matrix". In addition to this test, Baudrillard also explains Einstein's simulation theory with the concept of relativity and connects the dimensions consisting of different polarizations to the Einsteinian fourth dimension concept. As a result of this context, he underlines that many fields such as politics, media and psychology, where bilateral polarizations have ended, have moved to the simulation universe (Baudrillard 2020: 56). In today's world, with the transition of these many fields to the simulation universe, new changes are experienced and as a result of these changes, many fields actually experience a reality reflection or in other words, a process of simulating the truth, as Baudrillard suggests. In this simulated process, the concept of metaverse has had a privileged position in terms of creating its own reality and has become a concept that needs to be discussed and defined.

Metaverse, or in other words, the concept of meta-universe can be expressed as the post-reality universe (Mystakidis 2022: 486) that integrates the perception of physical reality with digitalized virtuality and recreates or recreates it. In addition, another three-dimensional world (Suzuki, et al. 2020: 2129) can be defined for the metaverse, which users in the real or accepted world can reach through their avatars. However, it is not very accurate to define the concept of meta-universe or metaverse only as a three-dimensional world. Because there are four basic progresses that need to be achieved in order to make the transition to the meta-universe. These four basic conditions can be explained as having an immersive reality, ubiquity of access and identity, compliance with the principle of interoperability and scaling in the process (Dionisio, Burns III and Gilbert 2013: 1). In the light of these definitions, it should be underlined that reaching the meta-universe is not as easy as it seems, and that some basic principles need to be developed first. However, it should be mentioned that these four basic conditions or principles have begun to be met in today's developing structure and that it has a growing market dominance day by day. In this process of domination, it should be mentioned that the most affected sectors are the digital game sector and that digital games are gradually starting to merge with meta-universes as well as virtual worlds.

## AN OVERVIEW OF THE CONCEPT OF GENDER (SEX) CREATION

In order to understand the concept of sex creation, it is necessary to first look at what the concept of sex is. Because the concept of sex creation generally means the re-creation or fictionalization of existing sex. For this reason, first of all, it is essential to know what is meant by sex. The notion of sex has different definitions in today's conditions. The main reason for this is that although the concept of sex pointed to a single point until recently, it is necessary to talk about two different concepts (Akpınar 2021: 115) as biological sex and gender in today's conditions. Sex, in general, can be expressed as a feature that is determined by the time people are born, that is, by their creation (Türk Dil Kurumu (Turkish Language Institution) 2011: 468). At the same time, sex is explained as a concept that determines the social category of the individual from the very first years (Vatandaş 2007: 29). Due to the fact that sex individuals have turned into a social category from the first years and women have a disadvantaged position in the patriarchal system, Butler uses the phrase "biology is destiny" when describing sex, and in fact, gender is built within culture, therefore, although sex is a biologically irreversible one. Although it is thought of as a thing, he says that sex is not fixed with gender (Butler 2014: 50). In this respect, while it is possible to explain the term sex as being born as a woman or a man, it is possible to see the term gender as a term integrated with society and culture (Saraç 2013: 27). At this point, it is necessary to mention the gender creation.

Gender creation emerges as a concept that can be expressed as a re-creation or fictionalization of an existing gender in general terms. In fact, this concept can be expressed as allowing people or individuals to redefine or recreate themselves in the sex they are in or with a gender other than the sex they are in. Because, regardless of whether the individual is born as a man or a woman, the fact that the future is open and not all structures are born with the same living conditions (Elsrud 2006: 183) is known, and it is possible to provide the created gender, especially avatars in virtual worlds, meta universes or digital games.

## PURPOSE AND METHOD OF RESEARCH

This research chapter aims to shed light on the changes that may occur based on gender creation as a result of the intertwining of digital games, which are a product of today's developing technologies, with the meta universe. For this reason, the method followed during the chapter study is the SWOT analysis method. SWOT analysis is a method that examines the strengths, weaknesses, opportunities and threats of a situation in general terms (Çoban and Karakaya 2010: 347). Because of this, it has been accepted as the most appropriate method for examining the situations that gender creations can create in meta-universes and has been constructed as one of the cornerstones of the chapter.

## FINDINGS AND EVALUATION OF THE RESEARCH

In order to evaluate the findings of the research, the situations created by the transition from digital games to the metaverse and the situations created by the independent creation of genders in the metaverse world were examined with SWOT analysis.

## GENDER CREATIONS FROM DIGITAL GAMES TO METAVERSE STRENGTHS, WEAKNESSES, OPPORTUNITIES, AND THREATS

SWOT analysis is a very effective structure for analyzing the strengths, weaknesses, opportunities and threats that this situation or event can create when it comes to an event or situation. For this reason, two SWOT analyzes were conducted within the scope of this study. One of these analyzes is the transition of digital games to the meta-universe and the other is the possibilities of gender creations in the meta-universe. For this reason, analysis was carried out by preparing two different tables.

*Table 1. SWOT analysis of the metaverse transition of digital games*

| Strengths | Weaknesses | Opportunities | Threats |
|---|---|---|---|
| Thanks to the transition of digital games to the meta-universe, or in other words, to the metaverse, the most powerful aspect is undoubtedly the opportunity to enter into a closer relationship with reality. Because the 2D environments offered by digital games have become 3D with the metaverse and have acquired a different reality plane outside the existing reality. For this reason, it can be expressed as a great strength that there will be an increase in the number of users, or in other words, the number of players, with the transition of digital games to the metaverse. | With the transition of digital games to the meta-universe, the weakest aspect can be explained as the changes in habits. Because users or players who are accustomed to the 2D management offered by digital games or the ease of management provided on the screen will have to encounter a situation outside of the structure they are used to when transitioning to the meta universe, and this may cause the attitude of users or players towards digital games to develop negatively. | With the transition of digital games to the meta-universe, many opportunities have occurred. At the beginning of these opportunities, the people who participate in the position of spectator in digital games, together with the metaverse, have a more experiential and deeper structure can be given as an example. Users or players can have the feeling of being in the game by evaluating these opportunities positively. Thus, players or users can have a more passionate experience and have the chance to seize this opportunity. | With the transition of digital games to the meta universe, many threats emerge. The most important among these threats is the threats that the metaverse world can create on the psychology of the human, that is, the user or the player. In short, these threats are the destruction of the perception of reality that may occur as a result of the user or the player getting too caught up in the digital game in the metaverse. Because each individual or person has the possibility of coming to a level that does not perceive the difference between reality and metaverse. In this case, it may cause them to face a psychological threat. |

**Reference:** Prepared by the chapter author.

In Table 1 above, various situations that may arise as a result of the merger of digital games with the metaverse are analyzed. As a result of these analyzes, as a result of the fusion of digital games with the metaverse, there is no perception that everything can go very well or everything can go very badly, but as in every situation and event, with the transformation of digital games into metaverse, individuals pay more attention to themselves and evaluate the meta universe in all its forms is considered necessary.

In Table 2 above, various positive and negative situations that gender creations can cause in meta-universes are analyzed. As a result of these analyzes, it has been determined that there are many good and bad aspects of being able to create gender in the metaverse. Considering this determination, it can be stated that the metaverse world is still full of unknowns and deficits. For this reason, it is considered as one of the best suggestions that all users who will enter the metaverse world should pay attention to these points and approach them cautiously. Because, while sharing a new experience full of obscurities and gaps, it is thought that one should first prepare oneself. Thus, it has been concluded that the problems that users may encounter in the metaverse world can be solved more easily.

*Table 2. SWOT analysis on gender creations in the meta-universe*

| Strengths | Weaknesses | Opportunities | Threats |
|---|---|---|---|
| The most important strength at the point of making gender creations in meta universes is undoubtedly the ability of individuals to produce themselves with the gender they want. Because, in general, in the metaverse world, people can access with the avatars they create, not as the person they are. For this reason, if people have a gender statement different from their current gender, then they can enter the meta universes with an avatar with the gender in their statement. This can cause individuals to feel better and reconstruct their existence. | The weakest aspect in terms of making gender creations in meta universes is actually related to the strong side. Because individuals can create avatars in a gender other than their existing gender and can affect their existence thanks to this avatar. However, this situation may cause uncertainty about the real identities of people or individuals by creating a situation where other users are not sure who the person they encounter is. For this reason, being able to create gender in the metaverse world can be expressed as both a strength and a weakness. | The creation of gender in meta-universes undoubtedly brings with it a tremendous opportunity. At this opportunity, it enables people to produce a new body for themselves when they are not actually in the body they feel. Moreover, how the body in the meta universe will look and will be left to the user's decision, in this case, the person will be able to edit not only his gender, but also many other parameters such as his hair, image, weight and height when creating his own metaverse avatar and profile. In this case, it allows the person or individual to create their own idea and construct themselves as someone they want to be. | The biggest threat to the creation of gender in meta-universes is actually the fact that people and individuals can construct themselves as a much different and more independent person than the person they exist. Because, in order to provide access to the metaverse, people, users or individuals must first create their own avatars. However, since there is no avatar restriction in the metaverse, the profiles created by malicious users can create a serious threat by causing a very serious confusion in the metaverse. |

**Reference:** Prepared by the chapter author.

## FUTURE RESEARCH DIRECTIONS

All the issues discussed in this book section are among the issues that have been frequently considered and discussed recently in many interdisciplinary fields such as communication sciences, computer sciences, social and human sciences. Because the process of continuous development of technology and integrating academic spelling with this speed is located in an essential position both in a national and international sense. In this respect, it is thought that each subject mentioned within the scope of this study is a basic source for the subjects that will be frequently mentioned not only in a field but also in many fields of science. In particular, the fact that the study has a structure that includes several titles increases the value of the study and is one of the first studies in this sense.

For this reason, it is believed that the book section can make significant contributions to the field both for the present and the future and will be one of the pioneering sources. In this context, it is thought that a few suggestions should be made. At the beginning of these suggestions, there are several suggestions to be made in terms of being a very innovative issue and being slow in terms of spread. Because it is not easy to access sufficient data for future studies, as the issue is a new issue. In order to prevent this, it is recommended that future studies be examined by detailed content analysis of the contents of some games from the focus group, questionnaire and subject framework. In this way, the subject can be examined more in depth and in the field. In addition, the tables related to strengths, weaknesses, opportunities and threats mentioned in the book section may be confirmed or falsified. This will contribute to the provision and development of scientific criticism and scientific knowledge. In this respect, it is believed that this study is both a source for the literature and a pioneering position for scientific development and accumulation.

## CONCLUSION AND RECOMMENDATIONS

Thanks to today's developing technologies and changing user experiences, many new generation technologies have been integrated into our lives and many independent variables have occurred with this integration process. However, as a result of the unity of the independent variables with the integration systems over time, different perspectives have developed and everything that used to be independent has begun to be seen as a whole. For exactly this reason, it was necessary to conduct this chapter study. In particular, the concepts of digital games and metaverse, which have come to a very important stage in the field of communication sciences in recent years, have been examined in this study and have gained the feature of being an interdisciplinary study by combining them with the concept of gender creations, which has a great social importance.

With this chapter study, many concepts have been re-evaluated and integrated with other concepts and explained. At this point, the concept of digital game was first mentioned. As it is known, digital games have emerged as an important research topic not only in the field of communication sciences but also in many other disciplines in recent years. Because the integration of digitalization into all human life and its constant change cause the concept of game to be affected at this point. As a result of this influence, the digitalization process has gained a great importance in the game industry and has reproduced the digital game industry as it is known today. At the same time, it has become inevitable for digitalization to reproduce and change the concept of game, resulting in different concepts. This concept, on the other hand, is the concept of metaverse, which is a frequent subject of research especially in recent years.

The concept of metaverse appears as a concept created by people in recent years, and with the emergence of this concept, humanity has gained a creative perspective. Because a virtual three-dimensional world has been created by simulating the 3D reality universe in which humanity lives. As a result of this creation process, humanity has made a serious progress and made a great leap forward. In this respect, the concept of metaverse is another pillar of this study, and the opportunities and threats it creates, along with its strengths and weaknesses, are detailed. As a result of this elaboration, it is concluded that the concept of metaverse points to a new formation yet and therefore has not reached a perfect threshold yet. One of the biggest reasons for reaching this conclusion is undoubtedly the reality that meta universes have many vulnerabilities.

The concept that constitutes another pillar of the research and carries the study to a more interdisciplinary perspective has been gender creations. Gender creations are a concept that has been actively involved in almost every process of humanity, but has gained a more theoretical framework, especially in the last twenty or thirty years, and it has actually emerged as a notion examined from the framework of sex-gender. For this reason, when talking about gender creations, the notions of biological sex and gender were examined and evaluated. As a result of this evaluation, it has been concluded that gender creations have a much different angle, especially with the metaverse, and have a much more independent and easier plane. However, with the SWOT analysis made in the study, it has been seen that this convenience can also be manipulated by some malicious segments of the society. Because of this, it is thought that it is necessary to suggest that users in the metaverse world should be more conscious and cautious.

Some of the inferences and results obtained in the research are briefly summarized above. However, since the suggestions made in the above paragraphs are thought to be insufficient, the suggestions in this paragraph are a little more diversified. As a result of the information obtained from the research, it is thought that although digital games, meta-universes and gender creations are concepts that seem independent from each other, they are actually intertwined and complementary or explaining each other.

However, when the current situation is analyzed, it is thought that these three concepts are not sufficiently detailed and understood in terms of academic, sectoral and social meanings. Therefore, considering that many questions are still open and not fully answered, it is recommended that users, individuals or players be more careful when interacting with these concepts and sectors, act more planned and manage the necessary verification processes when necessary. In this way, both these new concepts and sectoral processes will be overcome more easily and people will be able to act with more confident steps.

## REFERENCES

Akpınar, M. E. (2021). Analysis of Advertisements from Different Sectors in Turkey within the Context of Gender Equality. Communication and Technology Congress – CTC 2021, Bologna. doi:10.17932/CTCSPC.21/ctc21.010

Baudrillard, J. (2020). Simülakrlar ve Simülasyon. Ankara: Doğu Batı Yayınları.

Bozkurt, A., Hamutoğlu, N. B., Kaban, A. L., Taşçı, G., & Aykul, M. (2021). Dijital bilgi çağı: Dijital toplum, dijital dönüşüm, dijital eğitim ve dijital yeterlilikler. *Açıköğretim Uygulamaları ve Araştırmaları Dergisi*, *7*(2), 35–63. doi:10.51948/auad.911584

Butler, J. (2014). Cinsiyet Belası Feminizm ve Kimliğin Altüst Edilmesi. İstanbul: Metis Yayınları.

Chandler, D., & Munday, R. (2018). *Medya ve İletişim Sözlüğü* (B. Taşdemir, Trans.). İletişim Yayınları.

Çoban, B., & Karayaka, Y. E. (2010). Geleceği Planlamada Stratejik Yönetim ve SWOT Analizi: Kavramsal Yaklaşımlar. *e-Journal of New World Sciences Academy Social Sciences, 5*(4), 342-352.

Dionisio, J. D. N., III, W. G. B., & Gilbert, R. (2013). 3D Virtual Worlds and the Metaverse: Current Status and Future Possibilities. *ACM Computing Surveys 45*(3), 1-38.

Elsrud, T. (2006). Gender Creation in Travelling, or the Art of Transforming an Adventuress. Tourism, Consumption & Resperesentation. In K. Meethan, A. Anderson, & S. Miles (Eds.), (pp. 178–195). CABI Publisher.

Ilgaz Büyükbaykal, C., & Abay Cansabuncu, İ. (2020). Türkiye'de Yeni Medya Ortamı ve Dijital Oyun Olgusu. *Yeni Medya Elektronik Dergisi*, *4*(1), 1–9.

Karaduman, M., & Aciyan, E. P. (2020). Baudrillard'ın Simülasyon Kuramı Bağlamında Dijital Oyunlar ve Bağımlılık Üzerine Bir Değerlendirme. *Trakya Üniversitesi Sosyal Bilimler Dergisi*, *22*(1), 453–472. doi:10.26468/trakyasobed.550935

Karahisar, T. (2013). *Türkiye'de Dijital Oyun Sektörünün Durumu. Sanat Tasarım ve Manipülasyon*, 107- 114. Sakarya: Sakarya Üniversitesi Güzel Sanatlar Fakültesi Yayınları.

Marsh, J., Plowman, L., Yamada-Rice, D., Bishop, J., & Scott, F. (2016). Digital Play: A New Classification. *Early Years Journal of International Research and Development*, *36*(3), 242–253. doi:10.1080/09575146.2016.1167675

Mystakidis, S. (2022). Metaverse. *Encyclopedia*, *2*(1), 486–497. doi:10.3390/encyclopedia2010031

Samur, Y. (2016). *Dijital Oyun Tasarımı*. Pusula Yayınları.

Saraç, S. (2013). Toplumsal Cinsiyet. In L. Gültekin, G. Güneş, C. Ertung, & A. Şimşek (Eds.), Toplumsal Cinsiyet ve Yansımaları, (pp. 27–32). Atılım Üniversitesi Yayınları.

Suzuki, S. N., Kanematsu, H., Barry, D. M., Ogawa, N., Yajima, K., Nakahira, K. T., Shirai, T., Kawaguchi, M., Kobayashi, T., & Yoshitake, M. (2020). Virtual Experiments in Metaverse and their Applications to Collaborative Projects: The Framework and Its Significance. *Procedia Computer Science*, *176*, 2125–2132. doi:10.1016/j.procs.2020.09.249

Tekerek, N. (2006). Oyun Kavramı'ndan Drama'ya Drama'dan Dramatik Eğitim'e. *Tiyatro Araştırmaları Dergisi*, *22*(22), 47–73.

Türk Dil Kurumu. (2011). *Türkçe Sözlük. 11b*. Türk Dil Kurumu Yayınları.

Vatandaş, C. (2007). Toplumsal Cinsiyet ve Cinsiyet Rollerinin Algılanışı. *Sosyoloji Konferansları*, (35), 29–56.

Yıldıran, Ö. Ü. (2009). Baudrillard Perspektifinden Bir Kitle İletişim ve Sanat Aracı Olarak Simülasyon Evreninde Televizyon. *Selçuk İletişim Dergisi*, *5*(4), 201–218.

## ADDITIONAL READING

Averbek, G. S., and Türkyılmaz, C. A. (2022). Sanal Evrende Markaların Geleceği: Yeni İnternet Dünyası Metaverse Ve Marka Uygulamaları. *Sosyal Bilimlerde Multidisipliner Çalışmalar Teori, Uygulama ve Analizler*, 99.

Bayraktar, E., and Kaleli, F. (2007). Sanal Gerçeklik Ve Uygulama Alanları. *Akademik Bilişim*, *1*(6).

Greengard, S. (2019). *Virtual Reality*. Mit Press. doi:10.7551/mitpress/11836.001.0001

Lee, L. H., Braud, T., Zhou, P., Wang, L., Xu, D., Lin, Z., & Hui, P. (2021). All One Needs To Know About Metaverse: A Complete Survey On Technological Singularity, Virtual Ecosystem, And Research Agenda. arXiv preprint arXiv:2110.05352.

Maurice, L., & Bibring, T. (Eds.). (2022). *Gender, Creation Myths and Their Reception in Western Civilization: Prometheus, Pandora, Adam and Eve*. Bloomsbury Publishing. doi:10.5040/9781350212855

Mustafa, A. (2020). Sanal Dünya Sarmalında Gençlik. *Avrasya Sosyal ve Ekonomi Araştırmaları Dergisi*, *7*(9), 199–209.

Savcı, M., & Aysan, F. (2017). Teknolojik Bağımlılıklar Ve Sosyal Bağlılık: İnternet Bağımlılığı, Sosyal Medya Bağımlılığı, Dijital Oyun Bağımlılığı Ve Akıllı Telefon Bağımlılığının Sosyal Bağlılığı Yordayıcı Etkisi. *Dusunen Adam : Bakirkoy Ruh Ve Sinir Hastaliklari Hastanesi Yayin Organi*, *30*(3), 202–216.

Zheng, J. M., Chan, K. W., & Gibson, I. (1998). Virtual Reality. *IEEE Potentials*, *17*(2), 20–23. doi:10.1109/45.666641 PMID:9699075

## KEY TERMS AND DEFINITIONS

**Digital Game:** In general, it can be expressed as games designed using digital technologies and developing with digital developments.

**Gender Creation:** Within the scope of this study, this concept can be expressed as a kind of gender statement that is produced or recreated in addition to the male or female genders assigned to individuals at birth.

**Metaverse:** In other words, it can be expressed as a kind of neo-universe, which is called the meta-universe and is obtained by reproducing the existing reality in virtual or digital environments.

**Simulation Theory:** It appears as a concept attributed to the French scientist Baudrillard. This theory, which is similar to Plato's cave analogy with the discourses it produces, basically states that the universe we live in is actually a reflection of the truth. In this context, it can be expressed as a concept that contains the reproduction of reality.

**SWOT Analysis:** This analysis, which is frequently used by companies, examines the strengths, weaknesses, opportunities, and threats of a situation in detail. In this respect, we can express SWOT Analysis as a comparative method or a method that provides multiple perspectives.

**Virtual Reality:** It is an expression that can be used to express all the developments such as the metaverse resulting from digitalization. This expression in general can be expressed as an abstract and concrete reality as a result of the virtualization of the existing reality.

**Virtually Created Avatar:** It has occurred as a result of the great development of digital technologies and the development of virtual universes, or in other words, technologies called metaverse (meta-universe, neo-universe). It can be expressed as a virtual-reflection, virtual-creation figure that people using this technology use to show their virtual existence.

# Chapter 21
# Digital Game Addiction:
## Research About Children and Adolescents

**Inês Relva**
https://orcid.org/0000-0003-3718-8142
*Department of Education and Psychology, University of Trás-os-Montes and Alto Douro, Portugal*

**Ana Paula Monteiro**
*Department of Education and Psychology, University of Trás-os-Montes and Alto Douro, Portugal & Researcher at Centre for Research and Intervention in Education (CIIE), Portugal*

**Bárbara Costa**
*Gabinete Psicologia Porto, Portugal*

**Margarida Simões**
*Department of Education and Psychology, University of Trás-os-Montes and Alto Douro, Portugal & Researcher at Centre for Research and Intervention in Education (CIIE), Portugal*

## ABSTRACT

*The internet and the use of digital technologies are more and more generalized for everyday tasks such as school activities—communication but also entertainment. Its use is cross-sectional at various ages, starting earlier and earlier. Thus, this chapter aims to clarify the meaning of digital game addiction and its implication to the child/adolescent life, namely on the family functioning but also other areas. Risk and protector factors will be explored regarding digital game addiction. Positive outcomes that have been considered important in the use of digital games will be explored motives as well for digital gaming. Research in area has shown that parents have difficulties in management of child behavior because they also have difficulties themselves to stop their behaviors, so warning signs of the presence of digital game addiction will also be explored to help parents recognize this problem. Some measures will be presented. Finally, preventive and intervention strategies will be presented at the family level. Some empirically validated intervention strategies stand out.*

DOI: 10.4018/978-1-6684-8397-8.ch021

## INTRODUCTION

Our children and adolescents are what some author called as "generation cord" (Patrão, 2017). This generation "it is one that cannot disconnect from technologies and develop a mixed socialization (virtual and face to face)" (Patrão, 2017; p. 200). They have born already in the time of internet, so they don't know what it is to live without the internet in their lives. This fact it is related with how children and adolescents occupy their leisure time. Know the play assume different characteristics.

## BACKGROUD

### Definition

Before we define internet gaming addiction it is important to clarify the features of video games. According to Granic et al. (2014) when comparing with other media (e.g., television) video games imply an interaction. These videogames are developed "for players to actively engage with their systems and for these systems to, in turn, react to players' agentive behaviors" (p.67).

Internet gaming addiction (IGA) has been defined by DSM 5 as "a pattern of excessive and prolonged Internet gaming that results in a cluster of cognitive and behavioral symptoms, including progressive loss of control over gaming, tolerance, and withdrawal symptoms, analogous to the symptoms of substance use disorders" (American Psychiatric Association, 2013, p. 796).

More recently the 11th Revision of the International Classification of Diseases (ICD-11; 2018) argued that gaming disorder:

*"is characterised by a pattern of persistent or recurrent gaming behaviour ('digital gaming' or 'video-gaming'), which may be online (i.e., over the internet) or offline, manifested by: 1. impaired control over gaming (e.g., onset, frequency, intensity, duration, termination, context); 2. increasing priority given to gaming to the extent that gaming takes precedence over other life interests and daily activities; and 3. continuation or escalation of gaming despite the occurrence of negative consequences. The pattern of gaming behaviour may be continuous or episodic and recurrent. The pattern of gaming behaviour results in marked distress or significant impairment in personal, family, social, educational, occupational, or other important areas of functioning. The gaming behaviour and other features are normally evident over a period of at least 12 months in order for a diagnosis to be assigned, although the required duration may be shortened if all diagnostic requirements are met and symptoms are severe".*

Although gaming disorder may be online or offline, we will focus in this last one. According with a recent systematic review conducted by Paulus et al. (2018) we can find several terms and concepts for "describing the pathological use of computer technology: IGD, Internet addiction, technology-based addiction, pathological technology use, pathological video gaming, pathological Inter-net use, computer addiction, screen addiction, addictions to video games and online role-playing games, game overuse, video game addiction, smartphone addiction, cyber-relationship addiction, net compulsions, information overload, excessive, problem, dependent, pathological, and addicted gamers" (p. 646). However, and according with Gentile et al. (2017) IGD does not required that individuals exhibit symptoms of addiction solely with online video games, it can occur in both. Problematic use can occur in both offline and online settings. Another problematic use of digital gaming is the Multiplayer Online Role-Playing Game (MMORPG) dependency, impulse by the networked online game. This kind of game seems to be more attractive video games when compared with others king of online games (Billieux et al., 2015).

Although the distinction of game addiction from Internet addiction, the results from a meta-analysis conducted by Koo and Jung-Hye (2014) suggest psychological factors may be similar for both game addiction and Internet addiction. For classifying IGD, Paulus et al. (2018) suggest that the "the recommendation is to differentiate between high engagement, addiction, gaming enthusiasm, and problems related to excessive gaming" (p. 647).

## RISK AND PROTECTOR FACTORS

### Risk Factors

Although a recent phenomenon, the research already allows the identification of several risk factors in different areas of the lives of children and adolescents related to digital gaming addiction, according with Kuss and Grifiths (2012) the groups that are more vulnerable and susceptible of be addicted of digital games. André et al. (2022) in a recent study conducted with 144 children and adolescents aged 8–18 years from child and adolescent psychiatry in Sweden found a significantly association between ADHD and over consumption of video games.

Additionally, most of the participants reported the negligent of other activities, the difficulty in talk with parents about over games, the lack of parental supervision and the unsatisfactory results in school (Wong & Lam, 2016). In fact, family function and the way parents lead with internet use can have an impact on gaming by children and adolescents. A recent study conducted by Zhou and Xing (2021) with 617 college students found that 247 of them were addicted to online games and 179 of them were male. The study intends to explore the relationship between online game addiction, self-control ability and family function. The results suggests that "self-control and family function had a significant predictive effect on online game addiction" (p. 917). Similar results were found by Yayman and Bilgin (2020) in their study with 762 Turkish high school students where a positive association was found between both social media and game addiction and unhealthy family functions.

Regarding gender the results indicate that males are more propense to play online games when compared to females (Griffiths et al. 2004; Ko et al., 2005. Also, adolescents that present both lower self-esteem daily life satisfaction (Ko et al., 2005), engage more easily in online games. A more concerning issue it is the fact that children or adolescents are spending more time on screen-based activities (e.g., playing games online) there less time to spend in other activities healthier (Yu & Baxter, 2016). Regarding the MMORPG a study conducted with young players (aged from 10 to 24 years, all males) and having at least one month of experience in MMORPG playing, Son et al. (2013) found that when compared with non-players, players presented higher mental health risk, and here as also a negative association between such mental status and the level of self-control. Age it is also related with MMORPG. The results of Hussain et al. 2012 study suggest that as gamers get older, play frequency decreases. As showed by Billieux et al. (2015) the development and maintenance of MMORPG addiction it is associated with some specific structural characteristics of the games, with psychological factors (e.g., impulsivity traits) and neurobiological features. Regarding preschool children, the literature is scarce. In Covid 19 pandemic, with lockdown there was a generalized increased on the internet use across all ages, inclusive in preschool children. However, this digital game addiction in children seems to negatively affect both social and emotional development (Şenol et al., 2023).

With technological advancement, video and online games are increasingly attractive and challenging with eye-catching graphics, realistic images, realistic characters, and highly sophisticated gaming systems. Although great attention has been paid to the negative consequences of the online game (exposure to violence and desensitization to violent stimuli, increased obesity, and the risks of addiction), these may have educational, social, and therapeutic benefits (Paulus et al., 2017).

Granic et al. (2014) in a theoretical article present several benefits of play game online and underline how the use of gaming can beneficiate the mental health. The authors suggest a "more balanced perspective", focus not only on the consequences of the online gaming but also the benefits for playing the games. The authors present the results of several research focusing on four domains: cognitive, motivational, emotional, and social benefits. In fact, the research conducted in turn of digital game point several benefits that this activity can have in life experiences. Regarding the cognitive level, it suggests that video games improve attention/concentration capacity, promote impulsivity control, problem-solving capacity, information processing speed and mental flexibility. At an emotional level, the use of video games helps regulate players' emotions and moods.). At the social level, they promote the development of social skills, such as cooperation, interpersonal communication, socialization, the development of new friendships and the strengthening of existing ones. Self-confidence is another of the dimensions that video games can promote, as the effectiveness of strategies used to overcome obstacles to level up increases self-confidence to progress in the game (Granic et al., 2014). These skills are transferred to other activities and contexts of your daily life (Granic et al., 2014).

In educational settings, individuals have experimented with different digital game formats and educators see the potential benefits of using games to engage students in learning. Also, learning appears to take place at several levels during a therapeutic board game, specifically: (i) the psychoeducational or skill-element level, where players practice the social and emotional skills embedded in the game; (ii) the interactional level, where these skills are used with each other during the game; (iii), the mediated level, where facilitators enhance learning with strategies such as modelling, scripts, or hinting at solutions (Hromek & Roffey, 2009). In turn, Paulus et al. (2017) state that the use of video games provides benefits in terms of attention processes and integration between sensory and motor areas, improving selective and peripheral visual attention while optimizing dexterity in visual tasks.

Recently Tso et al. (2022) with a sample of 1956 students (690 primary and 1266 secondary) find out that digital competence is associated with less gaming addiction and can contribute to the risks of gaming addiction and cyberbullying. The study of Wong and Lam (2016) already mentioned, although the identification of risk factors for game addiction, it was signalled several benefits from being playing online. The authors underline the "fun and satisfaction, fostering social support and teamwork, meeting new friends and becoming sociable, boosting cognitive techniques and intellectual agility, improved responsiveness and quick thinking" (p. 1).

Video games can also bring a set of benefits in the elderly population. In a systematic review of the literature on digital videogames for older adults, Hall et al. (2019) found that, in the studies analyzed, significant mental health positive outcomes, such as cognitive improvement, were reported in multiple digital video game interventions, which used measures such as working memory, focused attention, fluid intelligence, scales for dementia, scales for depression, information processing, enjoyment of physical exercise, and balance confidence to assess cognitive improvement.. Overall, the reviewed studies found positive effects of game play on mental health status.

In addition to the discussion between the benefits and harms of digital games, another subject that has received great attention in the literature is the motives for playing, specifically, because they play people and because they dedicate so much time and effort to the same activity and the same digital game. To Billieux et al. (2013), gaming motivations are behaviour specific factors that drive people to start and continue with gaming, and investigative these different motives is important in understanding gaming behaviour (Demetrovics et al. 2011).

The gaming motivation model from Yee (2006) laid a solid foundation for subsequent research on the large variety of gaming motivation styles. To this end, 3000 players participated, and identified the existence of ten distributed motivations on three related factors: achievement (such as advancement, accumulate resources mechanics, and competition), social (such as socializing, relationships, and teamwork) and immersion (such as discovery, role-playing, personalization and escapism).

Resulting from this model Yee et al. (2012) developed the *Motivation Scale for Online Games*, is composed of 12 items distributed in three dimensions, relative to the motivations to play: achievement (e.g., *Improve your character as much as possible*), Social (e.g., *Grouping with other players*) and immersion (e.g., *Feeling immersed in the world*). Participants are asked to indicate the degree of importance that each behavior has when you're playing online games, using the response scale of the Likert type, five points, ranging from 1 (no important) to 5 (very important).

Demetrovics et al. (2011) suggest that online games represent new ways of satisfying basic human needs within the conditions of modern society. The authors identified seven motivational dimensions for online gaming: social (motivation related to the pleasure of meeting people, being with other people and playing with other people), escape (motivation related to escaping from reality, particularly problems of the real life) competition (characterize motives of competing with and defeating others in order to feel a sense of achievement), skill development (motivation to play is in order to improve coordination, concentration, or other skills), coping (motivation to play is in channeling and coping with distress and aggression and improving mood), fantasy (refers to the motive of stepping out of one's usual identity, trying new identities in a different fantasy world, and trying things that one cannot do in real life) and recreation (recreational and relaxing aspects of online gaming). To evaluate these motives Demetrovics et al. (2011) developed the *Motives for Online Gaming Questionnaire* (MOGQ). The MOGQ is composed of 27 items classified on a 5-point scale, from 1- "never" to 5 -" always". Scores range from 27 to 135 and higher scores suggest high game motivation. The internal consistency of the subscale is satisfactory, with Cronbach's alphas ranging from α .79 to α .91 (Demetrovics et al., 2011).

In 2003, Bartle presented the first motivational approach regarding gaming based on observing Multi-User Dungeon players. Bartle (2003) proposed that motives are associated with four different playing styles, specifically: achievers are motivated by realizing the aims set up by the game; explorers are interested in the structure of the virtual world, and the exploration and conquest of mysterious scenes and possibilities; socializers are motivated by building relationships and role playing, and "killers" use the virtual environment for disturbing and irritating other players. Bartle's proposal has not been empirically tested.

It should be noted that, in the systematic review of the literature on motivations of playing digital games, Cheah et al. (2019) found that, in the studies analyzed, that escapism increased play is related with poorer psychological wellbeing, specifically, where there is greater player motivation for immersion and escapism, which points towards a negative association between using games to escape from real-life problems and poor mental health.

## Consequences

In 2016 qualitative research was conducted by Wong and Lam with the aim to explore adolescent gaming behavior and addiction at the Internet cafe but also explore perceived thought an interview benefits and harms associated with that activity. The sample was composed by 13 male high school students with ages ranged between 12 and 15 years old. According with the authors "most of the interviewees experienced physical discomforts and health problems (e.g., dry eyes, blurred vision, dizziness, finger and waist strain, back pain, and feeling exhausted, anxious, irritable or depressed) because of extended period of gaming" (p. 14). A study conducted by Milani et al. (2017) in Italy with 612 participants, with ages between 9 and 19 years found that both children and adolescents with IGD reported "worse quality of interpersonal relations, worse coping strategies, and some developmental adaptation issues, which are anxiety/depression, withdrawal, social problems, thought problems, attention problems, aggressive behavior, internalization, and externalization". Another effect, it seems to be low academic performance (Wright, 2011).

In small children, digital game addiction can negatively affect their social and emotional development (Şenol et al., 2023).

## Warning Signs of Digital Game Addiction

Considering the implications that this issue has on family functioning, which have already been explored, it is important that parents are aware of their children's behaviour and supervise their use of technology. Nowadays, it has become difficult not to use technology to deal with any issue in our daily lives. Furthermore, it serves the great purpose of entertaining, and this is where digital games play a very important role. Even for parents, engagement in digital games becomes very attractive as there is a specific market to attract different age groups. Since they themselves have difficulty monitoring their behaviour regarding this issue, it becomes more complicated to set limits for their children regarding the use of technology. The warning signs that will be presented should also be signalled to the parents themselves so that they can monitor their own behaviour, reduce the likelihood of becoming addicted and act as a role model for their children.

Compared to television, online and digital devices may be more difficult for parents to manage because they are more technologically complex. Also, market innovations present parents with the need to constantly update and adapt their habits. As parents themselves become less familiar with some digital devices or services, they may feel outmanoeuvred by their often-savvy children. Third, as digital devices become more personalized and portable, traditional media sharing or monitoring strategies are less available or effective (Haddon & Vincent, 2014; Mascheroni & Ólafsson, 2014).

Warning signs that parents need to recognize are related to:

1) Preoccupation with gaming like excessive thoughts about games when not playing (Cerniglia et al., 2019; Guerada, 2021; King et al., 2020; Young, 2009), instead of worrying about the work that needs to be completed for class, or going to school, as the child becomes completely focused on playing the game. Being online and playing the game becomes their main priority (Young, 2009). This can decrease school performance as they start to miss deadlines.

2) Lying and hiding gaming use. Some children spend days and nights online. They do not eat, sleep, or take a shower because of the game (Cerniglia et al., 2019; Guerada, 2021; King et al., 2020; Young, 2009). They can also be distraught from house duties that were once established.
3) As the addiction progress grows, children can also start choosing games over socializing, isolating themselves from social groups or family (Young, 2009).
4) Because of their addiction, players may defend their need to play the game and become angry when they are forced to do without. Players who do not have access to the game feel a sense of loss. This feeling can become so strong that they become irritable, anxious, or depressed when they are forced to give up (Cerniglia et al., 2019; Guerada, 2021; King et al., 2020; Young, 2009).
5) There are also physical symptoms to watch out for, such as migraines due to excessive concentration or eye strain, fatigue, and carpal tunnel syndrome due to excessive computer use. When a child shows any of these signs, parents need to be very alert and seek professional help.

## Measures of the Game Addiction

To evaluate the presence of these signs it is possible to use different measures, although the lack of "consensus regarding which rating scales should be used for diagnosing disordered gaming and different scales are used both in research and in clinical practice" (André et al., 2022; p. 1). Some noteworthy measures include:

### Digital Addiction Scale for Children (DASC)

This scale is a 25-item self-report instrument that was developed based on nine diagnostic DSM-5 (APA, 2015) criteria and mapped onto Griffiths (2005) six core addiction criteria (preoccupation, tolerance, withdrawal, mood modification, conflict, and relapse) (e.g., "I argue with my parents when they ask me to stop using my device"). Added to those were three additional criteria (i.e., problems, deception, and displacement). These are answered on a five-point scale (1 = never, 2 = rarely, 3 = sometimes, 4 = often, and 5 = always). The criterion problems refer to life necessities that could become uncontrollable due to digital addiction, such as sleep, disagreement with parents, money management, and school performance. The criterion deception refers to children lying to their parents about how much time they spend on their digital devices and what they do there. Displacement refers to parents feeling disconnected from their children, which leads to impairment of the family unit. The DASC produced excellent internal consistency reliability ($\alpha = .94$) (Hawi et al., 2019).

### Game Addiction Scale for Adolescents (GASA)

It is one of one of the most frequently used questionnaire to evaluate game addiction in adolescents and developed by Lemmens et al. (2009). GASA was theoretically based on the seven of the DSM-5 criteria for pathological gambling: salience, tolerance, mood modification, withdrawal, relapse, conflicts, and problems (APA, 2015). The seven-item GASA applies to gaming behaviour in the last six months (e.g., "Have you thought all day long about playing a game?") answered on a five-point scale: 1 = never, 2 = rarely, 3 = sometimes, 4 = often, 5 = very often and should be considered endorsed when rated 3 or higher. The model showed an acceptable fit (CFI = 0.973; RMSEA = 0.065) (André et al., 2022).

## Gaming Disorder Symptom Questionnaire (GDSQ)

The GDSQ was developed by Zhang et al. (2022) based on the diagnostic guidelines of ICD-11 for Gaming Disorder. It contains 24 items where the subjects were asked to respond about the frequency of the event or situation described in the items within the last 12 months on a five-point Likert scale (0 = never, 1 = less than monthly, 2 = monthly, 3 = weekly, and 4 = almost daily) (e.g., "Once I start playing the game, it is hard to stop"). The results showed an overall good fit to the data. This model showed an acceptable fit ($\chi^2 = 1{,}219.11$ ($p < 0.001$); CFI = 0.958; TLI = 0.951; RMSEA = 0.038) (Zhang et al., 2022).

## Assessment of Internet and Computer Addiction Scale-Gaming (AICA-Sgaming)

The AICA-S is based on the criteria of loss of control, tolerance, withdrawal, continued use despite negative consequences, loss of interest, emotion regulation, jeopardizing perspectives, and craving. It contains 16 items being used for clinical and epidemiological research (e.g., "How often do you play to avoid negative feelings such as boredom and grief?"). The items are in a 5-step-likert-scale. It presented good internal consistency ($\alpha = .86$) (Wölfling et al., 2010). This scale is noteworthy because it is regularly used to assess patients in an outpatient behavioural addiction treatment clinic. This makes the scale different from other measurement instruments that have typically been used only in random samples of university students or online gamblers (King et al., 2020).

## Prevention and Intervention

Gaming addiction is a social problem with consequences at different areas of children and adolescent lives. Intervention should have a multi context perspective: home, school, and community. Tso et al. (2022) suggest the existence of training program for teachers were the risks related with increased screen time but also give teachers knowledge to identify students with or at risk of developing gaming addiction but also cyberbullying.

Preventing digital gaming addiction is an important goal, and identifying the risks that contribute to digital gaming addiction is essential to instituting preventive measures (Meng et al., 2022). A study was conducted in four elementary school located in different regions of Hong Kong with a sample of 248 students aged 7 to 13 years old. This study aimed to evaluate the effectiveness of the Wise IT-use (WIT evidence-based) prevention program, which aimed to contribute to an increase in students' awareness of internet gaming disorder and consequent risky behaviors (Aziz et al., 2021; Chau et al., 2019; Li et al., 2021; Meng et al., 2022). Evaluation of the program reveals that it ameliorates the risks of implementing digital gaming-related pathologies, as well as, promoting students' well-being over time (Chau et al., 2019).

According to Brown (2011) access and time spent playing games tend to be risk factors for Internet gaming disorder, pediatricians should recommend parents that their children should not have media in their rooms, as well as limit the daily contact time with games (between one and two hours). In other words, pediatricians should help parents set rules and limits for their children, and adult supervision is key (Brown et al., 2015). Gentile et al. (2014) conducted a longitudinal study that showed that limiting the amount and content of media is a strong protector for children.

In 2016, the Wong and Lam investigation in Hong Kong, already mentioned, indicate that prevention programs should be implemented at three different levels, namely primary, secondary, and tertiary prevention. Primary prevention should promote psychoeducational sessions exploring the risks, harms and signs of addiction associated with gambling; assertiveness training (showing that loyalty to the group is not broken by the fact that the adolescent does not gamble); in cybercafés warning messages regarding gambling addiction should be displayed. Secondary prevention should be directed solely and exclusively at the young people most vulnerable to gambling addiction. Tertiary prevention is aimed at addictive and problem gamblers who will follow gambling addiction treatment programs where symptoms, emotional distress and physical harm will be treated. The types of gamblers mentioned used gaming as a means of easing negative emotions (Gentile et al. 2011; Hussain and Griffiths, 2009) and dealing with everyday problems (Griffiths, 2008; Li et al. 2011). In this sense, it is also essential to equip parents with skills to monitor their children's internet use, both inside and outside the home environment (Wong & Lam., 2016).

In the study by Kuss and Griffiths (2012a), the classification of children and adolescents who are potentially vulnerable to online gaming addiction is of great importance for the initiation of preventive actions. By better understanding and in a more comprehensive way the gambling addiction, risk variables and protective factors applied to mental health can be better targeted. These preventive efforts can include psychoeducation, information, and tools to develop healthy ways to deal with daily stressors. These should be applied as early as possible so that more children and adolescents are protected from the dangers of online gaming addiction. On the other hand, the same authors argue that understanding online gaming addiction as a mental disorder allows a better classification within the mental health area and, on the other hand, a better performance of psychotherapeutic and/or psychopharmacological treatments, which will allow a better prognosis of this psychopathology (Kuss & Griffiths, 2012a).

Hidaayah et al. (2022) conducted a systematic literature review with the purpose of describing the preventive management of parenting in children and adolescents at risk of gambling addiction. The game over intervention (GOI) programs stand out among the parenting preventions presented, where 3 distinct thematic areas are developed, namely: parental monitoring, parental care, and psychoeducation, created to enhance autonomy, involvement, and competence (Hidaayah et al., 2022; Li et al., 2019). Parental monitoring is conducted through a parent-child dialogue about the benefits and harms of internet games, which ones can or cannot be played, and contact time with them. Parental care regarding displays of affection and the ability to empathize with their children's suffering, creating moments of fun activities for the whole family. Finally, the psychoeducation performed between parents and children where expectations and rewards related to alternative activities are explored and discussed.

Lee and Morgan (2018) conducted a study in Korea where it was highlighted that parents' demand for expert advice proves to be very important in preventing and combating online gaming addiction. This growing trend by children and adolescents should be controlled by parents and close adults through supervision and guidance on computer use (when to use, where to use, how many minutes per day, location of the computer in one's home) (Kaya et al. 2022), adult interest in the youth's own online activity, encouraging youth and adolescents to participate in varied activities and healthy experiences, and finally, parental explanation of the concept of online game violence and addiction is critical in understanding youth to distinguish between the benefits and harms thereby promoting positive social behavior and achieving desired outcomes (Lee & Morgan, 2018).

Another study recently conducted by Kaya and Pazarcıkc (2023) aimed to analyze digital gaming addiction in adolescents and the relationship with its underlying factors, with parental support being considered a key factor in preventing digital gaming addiction in adolescents (Juthamanee & Gunawan,

2021). In this sense, it is particularly important to create programs to help in the education of children and teach youngsters good practices in the correct use of digital technologies, warn about the risks of digital games, and help create appropriate restrictions on time and content. These programs not only create more interaction between parents and children, but also help parents with concrete examples of how to approach the correct use of digital games by their children. Programs like these can be implemented in child education centers, health clinics, and even on digital platforms with the help of specialized professionals such as psychiatric or pediatric nurses. On the other hand, they can also be implemented at the school level towards the prevention and reduction of online gaming addiction, which in this framework count on the help of nurses (Kaya & Pazarcıkc, 2023).

Also, Choo et al. (2015) in a longitudinal study with 2,974 primary and secondary school students in Singapore, ascertained the main effects of parent-child closeness and parental restriction of children's video games on children and adolescents with pathological video game symptoms over time. The results of the study reinforce the relevance of working on the close parent-child relationship as a preventive measure in the pathological development of gaming addiction in children and adolescents. In this sense, when the school psychologist or other professionals notice that students begin to exhibit psychopathological symptoms associated with gaming it is advised that the students' relationship with their parents be assessed and worked on to strengthen the bond between them (Choo et al., 2015).

Finally, digital games are engaging for all ages, but we are seeing an exponential increase in children and adolescents, especially those who started digital games before the age of six who are at higher risk of addiction than others (Cemiloglu et al., 2022; Karayaÿiz & Aygun, 2020), which needs to be curbed regardless of the family preventive measures presented, be they at the primary, secondary, and tertiary prevention level. Wood and Neal (2016) argue that habit modification over time is unlikely to be achieved by only one intervention at the prevention level but through interventions undertaken constantly throughout the life course (Paglia & Room, 1999).

Wang and Lam (2006) regarding the intervention on gaming they considered that home gaming seems to be more safer comparing with internet café gaming taking in count that parents can have a biggest supervision and intervention (e.g., parental control of gaming duration and frequency). In fact, parents have an important role since gaming occurs at home and it is difficult for teacher identified this behavior. Parents should be raised of the consequences that excessive exposure to digital devices have in health of adolescents (Tso et al., 2022). Community intervention it is also important. Patrão (2019) suggest a promotion of the management of the online healthier behavior since the child first years.

## FUTURE RESEARCH DIRECTIONS

Future studies should explore more deeply the relationship between family function and internet use by children and adolescents. As already seen, a negative family function, predicted the gaming addiction in both children and adolescent. It is important to explore if the way parents use internet also have a negative impact in this disorder.

## CONCLUSION

Digital game addiction it is a social problem with negative consequences for children and adolescents related with the excessive play of games online. problem related to the negative use of new media. Digital game addiction it is related with consequences at several areas of the individual (e.g., mental health, academic results, relationship with others).

Parents, teachers, school and community should be aware of these consequences in order to provide management of a healthier behavior not only online but also offline.

## ACKNOWLEDGMENT

National funds support Inês Relva work through the FCT—Portuguese Foundation for Science and Technology under the project the Scientific Employment Stimulus - Institutional Call – CEECINST/00127/2018. This work was partially supported by national funds, through FCT - Foundation for Science and Technology, IP, within the scope of the strategic program of CIIE - Center for Research and Intervention in Education at the University of Porto [ref. UIDB/00167/2020; UIDP/00167/2020].

## REFERENCES

American Psychiatric Association. (2013). *Diagnostic and statistical manual of mental disorders* (5th ed.). American Psychiatric Publishing.

André, F., Munck, I., Håkansson, A., & Claesdotter-Knutsson, E. (2022). Game Addiction Scale for Adolescents: Psychometric analyses of gaming behavior, gender differences and ADHD. *Frontiers in Psychiatry*, *13*, 791254. doi:10.3389/fpsyt.2022.791254 PMID:35356720

Aziz, N., Nordin, M. J., Abdulkadir, S. J., & Salih, M. M. M. (2021). Digital addiction: Systematic review of computer game addiction impact on adolescent physical health. *Electronics (Basel)*, *10*(9), 1–18. doi:10.3390/electronics10090996

Bartle, R. (2003). *Designing virtual worlds*. New Riders.

Billieux, J., Deleuze, J., Griffiths, M. D., & Kuss, D. J. (2015). Internet gaming addiction: The case of massively multiplayer online role-playing games. In N. el-Guebaly, (Eds.), *Textbook of addiction treatment: International perspectives* (pp. 1515–1525). Springer-Verla. doi:10.1007/978-88-470-5322-9_105

Billieux, J., Van der Linden, M., Achab, S., Khazaal, Y., Paraskevopoulos, L., Zullino, D., & Thorens, G. (2013). Why do you play World of Warcraft? An in-depth exploration of self-reported motivations to play online and in-game behaviours in the virtual world of Azeroth. *Computers in Human Behavior*, *29*(1), 103–109. doi:10.1016/j.chb.2012.07.021

Brown, A. (2011). Media use by children younger than 2 years. *Pediatrics*, *128*(5), 1040–1047. doi:10.1542/peds.2011-1753 PMID:22007002

Brown, A., Shifrin, D. L., & Hill, D. L. (2015). Beyond 'turn it off': How to advise families on media use. *AAP News*, *36*(10), 54. doi:10.1542/aapnews.20153610-54

Cemiloglu, D., Almourad, M. B., McAlaney, J., & Ali, R. (2022). Combatting digital addiction: Current approaches and future directions. *Technology in Society*, *68*, 1–11. doi:10.1016/j.techsoc.2021.101832

Chau, C. L., Tsui, Y. Y. Y., & Cheng, C. (2019). Gamification for internet gaming disorder prevention: Evaluation of a Wise IT-Use (WIT) Program for Hong Kong primary students. *Frontiers in Psychology*, *10*, 1–13. doi:10.3389/fpsyg.2019.02468 PMID:31736842

Cheah, I., Shimul, A. S., & Phau, I. (2022). Motivations of playing digital games: A review and research agenda. *Psychology and Marketing*, *39*(5), 937–950. doi:10.1002/mar.21631

Choo, H., Sim, T., Liau, A. K., Gentile, D. A., & Khoo, A. (2015). Parental influences on pathological symptoms of video-gaming among children and adolescents: A prospective study. *Journal of Child and Family Studies*, *24*(5), 1429–1441. doi:10.100710826-014-9949-9

Gentile, D. (2009). Pathological video-game use among youth ages 8 to 18: A national study. *Psychological Science*, *20*(5), 594–602. doi:10.1111/j.1467-9280.2009.02340.x PMID:19476590

Gentile, D. A., Bailey, K., Bavelier, D., Brockmyer, J. F., Cash, H., Coyne, S. M., Doan, A., Grant, D. S., Green, C. S., Griffiths, M., Markle, T., Petry, N. M., Prot, S., Rae, C. D., Rehbein, F., Rich, M., Sullivan, D., Woolley, E., & Young, K. (2017). Internet Gaming Disorder in Children and Adolescents. *Pediatrics*, *140*(Suppl 2), S81–S85. doi:10.1542/peds.2016-1758H PMID:29093038

Gentile, D. A., Choo, H., Liau, A., Sim, T., Li, D., Fung, D., & Khoo, A. (2011). Pathological video game use among youths: A two-year longitudinal study. *Pediatrics*, *127*(2), 319–329. doi:10.1542/peds.2010-1353 PMID:21242221

Gentile, D. A., Reimer, R. A., Nathanson, A. I., Walsh, D. A., & Eisenmann, J. C. (2014). Protective effects of parental monitoring of children's media use: A prospective study. *JAMA Pediatrics*, *168*(5), 479–484. doi:10.1001/jamapediatrics.2014.146 PMID:24686493

Granic, I., Lobel, A., & Engels, R. (2014). The benefits of playing video games. *The American Psychologist*, *69*(1), 66–78. doi:10.1037/a0034857 PMID:24295515

Griffiths, M. (2005). A 'components' model of addiction within a biopsychosocial framework. *Journal of Substance Use*, *10*(4), 191–197. doi:10.1080/14659890500114359

Griffiths, M. D. (2008). Video game addiction: Further thoughts and observations. *International Journal of Mental Health and Addiction*, *6*(2), 182–185. doi:10.100711469-007-9128-y

Guerada, K. (2021). Impact of online games on children's mental health. *Journal La Medihealthico*, *2*(1), 13–19. doi:10.37899/journallamedihealtico.v2i1.281

Haddon, L., & Vincent, J. (2014). *European children and their carers' understanding of use, risks and safety issues relating to convergent mobile media*. Educatt.

Hawi, N. S., Samaha, M., & Griffiths, M. D. (2019). The Digital Addiction Scale for Children: Development and validation. *Cyberpsychology, Behavior, and Social Networking*, *22*(12), 771–778. doi:10.1089/cyber.2019.0132 PMID:31755742

Hidaayah, N., Yunitasari, E., Kusnanto, K., Nihayati, H. E., Santy, W. H., Putri, R. A., & Rahman, F. S. (2022). Parenting in the Prevention of Internet Gaming Addiction. *Open Access Macedonian Journal of Medical Sciences, 10*(G), 731-738. doi:10.3889/oamjms.2022.7980

Hromek, R., & Roffey, S. (2009). Promoting social and emotional learning with games: "It's fun and we learn things". *Simulation & Gaming*, *40*(5), 626–644. doi:10.1177/1046878109333793

Hussain, Z., & Griffiths, M. D. (2009b). The attitudes, feelings, and experiences of online gamers: A qualitative analysis. *Cyberpsychology & Behavior*, *12*(6), 747–753. doi:10.1089/cpb.2009.0059 PMID:19788376

ICD11. (2018). *Gaming disorder*. ICD. https://icd.who.int/browse11/l-m/en#http%3A%2F%2Fid.who.int%2Ficd%2Fentity%2F1448597234.

Juthamanee, S., & Gunawan, J. (2021). Factors related to internet and game addiction among adolescents: A scoping review. *Belitung Nursing Journal*, *7*(2), 62–71. doi:10.33546/bnj.1097

Karayağiz Muslu, G., & Aygun, O. (2020). An analysis of computer game addiction in primary school children and its affecting factors. *Journal of Addictions Nursing*, *31*(1), 30–38. doi:10.1097/JAN.0000000000000322 PMID:32132422

Kaya, A., Karatas¸, N., Gürcan, M., & Isler Dalgıç, A. (2022). A grounded theory study to explore the digital gameplay experiences of adolescents at risk of addiction in Turkey. *Journal of Pediatric Nursing, 63*, e36–e43. https://doi.org/. pedn.2021.10.019 doi:10.1016/j

Kaya, A., & Pazarcıkcı, F. (2023). Structural equation modeling analysis of risk factors for digital game addiction in adolescents: A web-based study. *Archives of Psychiatric Nursing*, *43*, 22–28. doi:10.1016/j.apnu.2022.12.031 PMID:37032011

King, D. L., & Delfabbro, P. H. (2020). Video game addiction. In A. E. Cecilia & H. D. Paul (Eds.), *Adolescent addiction: Epidemiology, assessment, and treatment* (pp. 335–341). Academic Press. doi:10.1016/B978-0-12-818626-8.00007-4

Ko, C. H., Yen, J. Y., Chen, C. C., Chen, S. H., & Yen, C. F. (2005). Gender differences and related factors affecting online gaming addiction among Taiwanese adolescents. *The Journal of Nervous and Mental Disease*, *193*(4), 273–277. doi:10.1097/01.nmd.0000158373.85150.57 PMID:15805824

Koo, H. J., & Kwon, J. H. (2014). Risk and protective factors of internet addiction: A meta-analysis of empirical studies in Korea. *Yonsei Medical Journal*, *55*(6), 1691–1711. doi:10.3349/ymj.2014.55.6.1691 PMID:25323910

Kuss, D. J., & Griffiths, M. D. (2012a). Online gaming addiction in children and adolescents: A review of empirical research. *Journal of Behavioral Addictions*, *1*(1), 3–22. doi:10.1556/JBA.1.2012.1.1 PMID:26166826

Lee, G., & Morgan, H. (2018). Understanding children's attraction toward digital games and preventing their gaming addiction. *US-China Education Review, 8*(1), 11–17. doi:10.17265/2161-623X/2018.01.002

Lemmens, J. S., Valkenburg, P. M., & Peter, J. (2009). Development and validation of a Game Addiction Scale for Adolescents. *Media Psychology, 12*(1), 77–95. doi:10.1080/15213260802669458

Li, A. Y. L., Chau, C. L., & Cheng, C. (2019). Development and validation of a parent-based program for preventing gaming disorder: The game over intervention. *International Journal of Environmental Research and Public Health, 16*(11), 1–47. doi:10.3390/ijerph16111984 PMID:31167457

Li, D., Liau, A., & Khoo, A. (2011). Examining the influence of actual-ideal self-discrepancies, depression and escapism on pathological gaming among massively multiplayer online adolescent gamers. *CybePsychology, Behavior and Social. Cyberpsychology, Behavior, and Social Networking, 14*(9), 535–539. doi:10.1089/cyber.2010.0463 PMID:21332374

Li, Y. Y., Sun, Y., Meng, S. Q., Bao, Y. P., Cheng, J. L., Chang, X. W., Ran, M. S., Sun, Y. K., Kosten, T., Strang, J., Lu, L., & Shi, J. (2021). Internet addiction increases in the general population during COVID-19: Evidence from China. *The American Journal on Addictions, 30*(4), 389–397. doi:10.1111/ajad.13156 PMID:33738888

Mascheroni, G., & Ólafsson, K. (2014). *Net children go mobile: Risks and opportunities* (2nd ed.). Educatt.

Meng, S., Cheng, J. L., Li, Y. Y., Yang, X. Q., Zheng, J. W., Chang, X. W., Shi, Y., Chen, Y., Lu, L., Sun, Y., Bao, Y. P., & Shi, J. (2022). Global prevalence of digital addiction in general population: A systematic review and meta-analysis. *Clinical Psychology Review, 92*, 102128. doi:10.1016/j.cpr.2022.102128 PMID:35150965

Milani, L., La Torre, G., Fiore, M., Grumi, S., Gentile, D. A., Ferrante, M., Miccoli, S., & Blasio, P. (2018). Internet gaming addiction in adolescence: Risk factors and maladjustment correlates. *International Journal of Mental Health and Addiction, 16*(4), 888–904. doi:10.100711469-017-9750-2

Paglia, A., & Room, R. (1999). Preventing substance use problems among youth: A literature review and recommendations. *The Journal of Primary Prevention, 20*(1), 3–50. doi:10.1023/A:1021302302085

Patrão, I. (2019). A importância da autorregulação do comportamento online nas crianças da geração cordão. In R. Brito & P. Dias (Coords.), Crianças, famílias e tecnologias. Que desafios? Que caminhos? (pp. 184-197). Centro Interdisciplinar de Estudos Educacionais. doi:10.34629/ipl.eselx.cap.livros.025

Paulus, F. W., Ohmann, S., von Gontard, A., & Popow, C. (2018). Internet gaming disorder in children and adolescents: A systematic review. *Developmental Medicine and Child Neurology, 60*(7), 645–659. doi:10.1111/dmcn.13754 PMID:29633243

Şenol, Y., Şenol, F. B., & Can Yaşar, M. (2023). (2023). Digital game addiction of preschool children in the Covid-19 pandemic: Social emotional development and parental guidance. *Current Psychology (New Brunswick, N.J.)*. doi:10.100712144-023-04323-8 PMID:36819754

Son, D. T., Yasuoka, J., Poudel, K. C., Otsuka, K., & Jimba, M. (2013). Massively multiplayer online role-playing games (MMORPG): Association between its addiction, self-control and mental disorders among young people in Vietnam. *The International Journal of Social Psychiatry*, *59*(6), 570–577. doi:10.1177/0020764012445861 PMID:22718852

Tso, W., Reichert, F., Law, N., King, F., Torre, J., Rao, N., Leung, L., Wang, Y.-L., Wong, W., & Ip, P. (2022). Digital competence as a protective factor against gaming addiction in children and adolescents: A cross-sectional study in Hong Kong. *The Lancet Regional Health. Western Pacific*, *20*, 100382. doi:10.1016/j.lanwpc.2022.100382 PMID:35967602

Wölfling, K., Müller, K. W., & Beutel, M. (2010). Reliability and validity of the Scale for the Assessment of Pathological Computer-Gaming (AICA-S). *Psychotherapie, Psychosomatik, Medizinische Psychologie*, 1–16. doi:10.1055-0030-1263145 PMID:20878599

Wong, I. L. K., & Lam, M. P. (2016). Gaming behavior and addiction among Hong Kong adolescents. *Asian Journal of Gambling Issues and Public Health*, *6*(1), 6. doi:10.118640405-016-0016-x PMID:27630813

Wood, W., & Neal, D. T. (2016). Healthy through habit: Interventions for initiating & maintaining health behavior change. *Behavioral Science & Policy*, *2*(1), 71–83. doi:10.1353/bsp.2016.0008

Wright, J. (2011). The effects of video game play on academic performance. *Modern Psychological Studies, 17*(1), 37-44. https://scholar.utc.edu/mps/vol17/iss1/6

Yayman, E., & Bilgin, O. (2020). Relationship between social media addiction, game addiction and family functions. *International Journal of Evaluation and Research in Education, 9*, 979-986. doi:10.11591/ijere.v9i4.20680

Yee, N. (2006). Motivations for play in online games. *Cyberpsychology & Behavior*, *9*(6), 772–775. doi:10.1089/cpb.2006.9.772 PMID:17201605

Yee, N., Ducheneaut, N., & Nelson, L. (2012). Online gaming motivations scale: Development and validation. In *Proceedings of the SIGCHI Conference on Human Factors in Computing Systems*, Austin, TX. 10.1145/2207676.2208681

Young, K. (2009). Understanding online gaming addiction and treatment issues for adolescents. *The American Journal of Family Therapy*, *37*(5), 355–372. doi:10.1080/01926180902942191

Yu, M., & Baxter, J. (2016). Australian children's screen time and participation in extracurricular activities. In *LSAC Annual Statistical Report 2015* (pp. 99–125). Australian Institute of Family Studies.

Zhang, L., Luo, T., Hao, W., Cao, Y., Yuan, M., & Liao, Y. (2022). Gaming Disorder Symptom Questionnaire: The development and validation of a screening tool for ICD-11 gaming disorder in adolescents. *Frontiers in Psychiatry*, *13*, 1–12. doi:10.3389/fpsyt.2022.848157 PMID:35401279

Zhou, X. H., & Xing, J. (2021). The relationship between college students' online game addiction, family function and self-control. *Health*, *13*(9), 910–919. doi:10.4236/health.2021.139070

## ADDITIONAL READING

Clark, N., & Scott, P. S. (2009). *Game addiction: The experience and the effects*. McFarland.

Deliyannis, I. (2020). *Game design and intelligent interaction*. IntechOpen. doi:10.5772/intechopen.77403

Görgülü, Z., & Özer, A. (2023). Conditional role of parental controlling mediation on the relationship between escape, daily game time, and gaming disorder. *Current Psychology*, 1-9. doi:10.100712144-023-04557-6

Larrieu, M., Billieux, J., & Decamps, G. (2022). Problematic gaming and quality of life in online competitive videogame players: Identification of motivational profiles. *Addictive Behaviors*, *107363*, 107363. doi:10.1016/j.addbeh.2022.107363 PMID:35689906

Whitton, N. (2014). *Digital games and learning: Research and theory*. Routledge. doi:10.4324/9780203095935

Xu, Z., Turel, O., & Yuan, Y. (2012). Online game addiction among adolescents: Motivation and prevention factors. *European Journal of Information Systems*, *21*(3), 321–340. doi:10.1057/ejis.2011.56

## KEY TERMS AND DEFINITIONS

**Digital game addiction:** Excessive use of internet in digital game.
**Warning signs:** Indicators that something is wrong.
**Prevention:** Preventing something wrong from happening.
**Intervention:** Action to improve or reduce something.

# Chapter 22
# A Study on the Digital Game Addiction Tendency of Generation Z Individuals

**Özgün Arda Kuş**
*Independent Researcher, Turkey*

**Betül Başer**
*Independent Researcher, Turkey*

## ABSTRACT

*We are living in an age in which technological developments are stunning. Each change facilitates the lives of humans and introduces innovation. Individuals can complete most of their work independently of time and space thanks to smart devices and internet access. Although these technological developments are built to facilitate our lives, spending too much of our time on these devices also has a dangerous aspect. Continuously spending time on social media via these smart devices, or having the opportunity to play downloaded games all the time, lays the foundation of new behavioural addictions of our age. This study investigates the digital game tendency of Generation Z individuals who were born with this technology and have a good command of this technology by in-depth interview method. The target number of participants for the in-depth interviews considering gender equality is 18 participants. This study aims both to measure the digital game addiction tendency of Generation Z individuals and to synthesise opinions regarding addiction.*

## INTRODUCTION

Since generations live in similar social structures, each generation has a unique experience specific to their period. Therefore, it is possible to say that individuals have similar characteristics to the generation they belong to and live in (Kupperscmidt, 2000, p. 66). There are many different classifications in the literature. One of the reasons for this is the different political, cultural, economic, social and technological

DOI: 10.4018/978-1-6684-8397-8.ch022

events in each country. While selecting the generation classification adopted in this study, the appropriate generation classification was preferred considering the social structure in Turkey. Altuntuğ, (2006, p. 205-206) divides the generations into 5 groups. This classification includes the Silent Generation, Baby Boomer Generation, Generation X, Generation Y and Generation Z. The sample of this study consist of university student Generation Z individuals.

Today, with the development of technology, traditional games are replaced by games played in digital environments. Digital games include computer games, mobile games, arcade games and console games. In this context, digital games include the digital, modularity and interactivity characteristics of new communication environments. With these features, the game creates a personal communication environment that can be incorporated into the act of playing (Binark & Bayraktutan-Sütcü 2020, p. 43). If the individual is able to control the duration of play while exhibiting digital gameplay behaviour, does not neglect the responsibilities or is not disconnected from the real world, this situation is considered normal. However, if the individual has become unable to control the time of play, has developed a tolerance to digital gameplay, or is deprived when playing behaviour isn't present and has moved away from real life, it is possible to talk about a behavioural addiction developed against digital game playing behaviour. This study aimed to reveal the consequences of Generation Z individuals for digital game addiction. The research data was collected through face-to-face in-depth interviews with 18 Generation Z university students via the structured form.

## THEORY OF GENERATION AND THE TERM GENERATION

The theory of generation is used to define the identities of the groups. In various study fields such as marketing, psychology, mass communication and management sciences, the classification of the term generation is associated with the fact that individuals were born in a certain year range. In other words, the theory of generational theory refers to the fact that individuals born in a given year range adopt similar behaviours, lifestyles, and social values because they were born at the same age (Chen, 2010, p. 132). While these individuals show similar behaviors and beliefs to that generation group due to certain behaviour and belief types, they show differences from different generation groups. It is possible to express that the generations will be formed according to the characteristics of the period they are in, and their behaviour will be affected, and these characteristics will differ from other generations. The historical development of the theory of generation expressed by Karl Mannheim, Strauss and Howe that emerged from different regions around the world will be explained below.

Sociologist Karl Mannheim was the first scientist to conduct comprehensive and systematic research in the field of management related to generations using social science research methods. In his "Problem of Generations" work, he described generations from a sociological perspective (Jeager, 1985, p. 278). This study was published in 1928, but it was not popularized until the 1950s when the text was translated into the English language. Mannheim's work looked at historical groups that had clear and detectable distinctions rather than revealing the "sociology of ages". (Pilcher, 1994, p. 483).

Mannheim describes the existence of generations by five characteristics of society (1952, p. 290-292):

- New people must be constantly added to society.
- In the following stages, individuals who exist in society must disappear.
- Individuals must participate in a designated part of the process.

- There must be a reason for the transfer of cultural and historical heritage to future generations.
- The transition from generation to generation should be an uninterrupted process.

According to Strauss and Howe (1997, p. 57), the theory of generations occurs cyclically all over the world, and once it has started, it regenerates itself. On average, a generation lasts no more than 15-20 years, and this cycle lasts 80-90 years and returns to the beginning.

Strauss and Howe express that generations are formed by successive periods and express these periods as follows: The first cycle (period of ascension), the second cycle (period of awakening), the third cycle (period of dissolution), the fourth cycle (period of crisis) (1997, p. 250-254).

According to Strauss and Howe's perspective, there are four archetypes, each of which reflects the characteristics of a generation. Four successive generations express their archetype in this way. These are the generation of the artist, the generation of the prophet, the nomadic generation, and the heroic generation (1997, p. 50-59)

The theory of generation is used to express a community of individuals who are exposed to similar political and social events starting from the years of their birth, who have similar beliefs and social values in their characters and who show similar character traits. These individuals have similar ideas regarding the political events that occurred in society during their lifetime, events such as war and famine as well as the changing economic situation (Lamm & Meeks, 2019, p. 615). The theory of generation is based on the assumption that individuals living in the same period exhibit similar characteristics since they exist in similar social conditions.

Alwin, (2002, p. 645-646) considers it necessary to explain and present three questions to explain and define the concept of generation. These three problems are as follows:

- First, it must consist of individuals born in the same period.
- Second, the position of the individual in the family in which the individual was born should be known.
- Third, the individual must be able to identify himself/herself as a member of any group or be seen as a member of a group by his/her environment.

Generations are made up of individuals born in the same years in a certain date range. In addition to the time between one generation and the other, this term is used for explaining the age and cultural differences between the parents and children (Lotfi, Kabiri & Ghasemlou, 2013, p. 94).

According to Hung, Gu, and Yim (2007, p. 840), the term generation consists of individuals born and living in similar time periods, witnessing, and experiencing similar social, political and cultural events that shape their lives.

Altuntuğ (2012, p. 204) specified that generations are used to express the community of individuals who were born in the same period, who were influenced by the social, economic, political, and cultural events of the period in which they took part and the values that dominated the period.

The generations are affected by the social structure they are in and affect society with their emotions and thoughts. Although there are many definitions of the term generation, there is no single common definition for this term. When the common phrases in the definitions are considered, a generation consists of individuals born in the same period, who are affected by the political, historical, economic, and technological conditions of the society in which they are involved. It is possible to say that the reason why each generation has different value judgments within itself is that they lived in different social conditions and witnessed different events.

Although the years in which individuals are born are considered when classifying generations, various scientists emphasize that generations are influenced by the social events of the period rather than by age. According to Strauss and Howe, there are different characteristics to explain the concept of generation beyond the years in which individuals are born (Reeves & Oh, 2014, p. 821). These characteristics are classified as the perception of belonging, common beliefs, and behaviours, and being in the same place in history. Strauss and Howe suggested that these characteristics are more important than the birth years of an individual. When the literature is examined, various generation classifications can be seen. When these variables are taken into consideration, the period in which individuals are born and the social variables that occur during this period are effective. It can be seen that the names and years of birth for the generation around the world and in our country are different. The classification of the generation selected in accordance with the study is given in Table 1.

*Table 1. Generation classification to be used*

| | |
|---|---|
| Silent Generation | (1922- 1945) |
| Baby Boomer Generation | (1946- 1964) |
| Generation X | (1965- 1979) |
| Generation Y | (1980- 1999) |
| Generation Z | (2000-) |

**Source:** (Altuntuğ, 2012, p. 205-206).

This study will focus on Generation Z and therefore, it is necessary to provide information about the periods in which they were born to understand the characteristics of the generation. This generation, which was born in 2000, is also called the digital nomads (iGen), code generation, internet generation, new millennium generation and crystal generation (Adıgüzel, Batur & Ekşili, 2014, p. 174; Senbir, 2004, p. 29). The general characteristics of Generation Z can be summarized as follows (Ünal, 2017, p. 26).

- Quality education is very important to them.
- They care about their freedom, and they have high self-confidence.
- They communicate with friends through social networks.
- They are dissatisfied with information because they grew up in the age of technology.
- They are innately consumers.

The most important feature of this generation is that they were born in a world dominated by technology (Demirdöğmez, Küçükoğlu & Taş, 2017, p. 1033). Since Generation X is born into an environment surrounded by technology, they are intertwined with technology in every field. Speed is the most important concept that defines this generation. This generation makes use of the Internet and computer technologies and often uses iPads, tablet computers, and smartphones (Ünal, 2017, p. 22). They desire communication to be at high speed since they are used to speed. Therefore, they use platforms that allow messaging instead of sending an email (Arthur, 2016, p. 8). Individuals who were born in technology and lived an intertwined life actively use technology in their daily lives and sometimes turn themselves into addicts. The social consequences of this technological addiction are also noteworthy. This generation prefers to socialize using the internet in their homes instead of socializing in public spaces, such as previous generations. With their technological capabilities, they can do their work without leaving the home through communication tools such as computers or phones and without the need to communicate face-to-face (Patranabis, 2012, p. 97). Technology has become a part of this generation's identity.

## DIGITAL GAMING CONCEPT

Technological developments have brought innovations to many areas of our lives. While these innovations have been beneficial for humanity in various fields, they have also profoundly influenced habits. One of these affected concepts is the game concept. A game is a competitive activity that is played for entertainment purposes one-to-one or in groups fundamentally based on having a good time. Throughout human history, the game was always there. The adventure of playing games that started with bones has always existed with various means parallel to the development of humanity.

A turning point in which technological developments have changed the habits in our lives is also reflected in the game concept. Digitized tools incorporated a new type of game based on entertainment into our lives and the concept of digital gaming has been born. According to Frasca (2001, p. 168), digital gaming is a free-time evaluation activity software on digital software that can be used physically by one or more people, either alone (against artificial intelligence) or via a mutual (with a friend/acquaintance) online network, installed on game tools. Digital games today with the necessary software and hardware conditions provide the individual with access to the experience of playing games independent of time and space. Consoles and smart mobile phones are the technological tools that are instrumental to this experience. One of the most important features of digital games is that it allows games to be played in communities on the internet. Thus, players can be a part of a challenge, both individually and in teams, simultaneously against real opponents or with allies.

Since the mid-1980s, Digital Games are defined as video games, computer games and electronic games (Kerr, 2006, p. 3). The definition commonly used in Turkey is computer games. However, since the mid-2000s, the conceptualization of digital games has also been adopted (Binark & Bayraktutan-Sütcü 2008, p. 42). Mutlu Binark and Günseli Bayraktutan Sütcü examined the new game environments under the title of "Digital Game" in their books titled "Digital Game as a Product of the Culture Industry". The definition of digital gaming is as follows: "Digital gaming as an individual means of communication differs from traditional gaming by incorporating new communication environment features into gaming" (2008, p. 45). Although digital games include the "interaction, modularity, digitality, virtuality and variability" characteristics of new communication mediums, all these characteristics are considered as a personal communication medium including the game playing performance (Binark & Bayraktutan-Sütcü, 2008, p. 43). Digital games are cultural, economic, and technological artefacts that can be considered in various ways. Digital games, which have taken place in many fields from education to culture, politics to trade, have become an increasingly interesting area with the rapid progress of digitalization (Sezen, 2011, p. 145).

Digital games are becoming the most time-consuming activity today. According to the Newzoo Global Games Market (2022) report, there are 3 billion people playing digital games worldwide, a 5.3% increase in the number of people playing digital games compared to the previous year (2021).

## A TECHNOLOGICAL ADDICTION: DIGITAL GAMING ADDICTION

The increase in digital games, the increase in the number of devices for gaming and the spread of the internet transformed 37.5% of the world's population into digital game players. Within the routine of everyday life, it is accepted that playing a certain level of digital games is considered normal, and even has positive contributions to the individual such as emotional relaxation. (Green & Bavelier, p. 2003) In addition to entertaining the individual, it contributes to problem-solving and decision-making skills as well as body coordination.

However, the fact that the individual is extremely absorbed in the digital game world that the individual is away from everyday life has introduced a new concept of behavioural addiction into the literature. Digital games, which were previously played on offline-based and limited platforms, have reached an accessible position at any time through constantly evolving technologies and in this case have strengthened the bond between the individual and the game (Kuş, 2021). As this link becomes stronger, the digital game addiction concept was first stated in 2019 as the World Health Organization (WHO) classified this addiction as a technology-based behavioural addiction. Instead of digital game addiction, the literature adopts terms such as excessive use of games, game-playing disease, game addiction, obsessive-compulsive game-playing behaviour, pathological or problematic game play behaviour or game-playing behaviour.

According to ICD 11, gaming addiction is considered in 3 dimensions. These are "6C51.0[1] Online Game Addiction", "6C51.1[1] Offline game Addiction" and "6C51.Z[1] Unspecified Game Addiction". The diagnostic criteria of these addictions are common, and disease is coded according to the way the game is played. According to ICD 11, to diagnose an individual with a gaming addiction, the following criteria must be observed in the individual:

- *"A persistent pattern of gaming behaviour ('digital gaming' or 'video-gaming'), which may be predominantly online (i.e., over the internet or similar electronic networks) or offline, manifested by all of the following:*
- *Impaired control over gaming behaviour (e.g., onset, frequency, intensity, duration, termination, context).*
- *Increasing priority given to gaming behaviour to the extent that gaming takes precedence over other life interests and daily activities; and*
- *Continuation or escalation of gaming behaviour despite negative consequences (e.g., family conflict due to gaming behaviour, poor scholastic performance, negative impact on health).*
- *The pattern of gaming behaviour may be continuous or episodic and recurrent but is manifested over an extended period of time (e.g., 12 months).*
- *The gaming behaviour is not better accounted for by another mental disorder (e.g., Manic Episode) and is not due to the effects of a substance or medication.*
- *The pattern of gaming behaviour results in significant distress or impairment in personal, family, social, educational, occupational, or other important areas of functioning."* (ICD 11, 2022)

According to the American Psychiatric Association's latest 5th version of the Diagnostic and Statistical Manual of Mental Disorders (DSMV), 5 of the following 9 criteria must be observed in the individual in the last 12 months for this individual to be diagnosed with gaming addiction:

- *"Constant mental preoccupation with games*
- *Withdrawal symptoms when games are not accessible (weakness, nerve, anxiety, earthquake, etc.)*
- *Develop a tolerance to play and display an increased amount of play behaviour.*
- *Trying to regulate gameplay behaviour and constant failure.*
- *Being unable to stay away from playing despite the damage and negative effects of social life.*
- *Reduced interest in real life due to excessive gaming behaviour and activities that were previously enjoyable are no longer meaningful and unpleasant.*
- *When there is a change in mood or stress, turn to play behaviour to get rid of this mood.*
- *Lying to family members and those around them to play more games.*
- *Negative, tedious consequences due to dependence on games in close relationships, academic life, or business responsibilities."* (Amerikan Psikiyatri Birliği, 2014)

Although the concept of digital game addiction has been debated for nearly 30 years, there is still no consensus on both the clarity of the concept and the diagnostic criteria. Apart from the APA and WHO, numerous researchers conducted research on the subject and different diagnostic criteria were determined. In particular, Grifiths' work made significant contributions to the literature.

There are various scales developed related to game addiction, differing according to the age group. These scales do not include a scale developed by the World Health Organization or the American Psychiatric Association. No consensus has yet been reached on the use of scales.

Games are a safe harbour since they allow people to move away from the real world and have freedom. Individuals can take on the character they want in the virtual space of the game and can realize their fantasies to the extent that the structure of the game allows. With these features, games allow people to relax and have fun by removing problems and problems in the real world for a while. The difference between addiction and gaming behaviour is determined by frequency, immersion in the world of the game, and long-term distance from real life. If the individual is able to control the duration of play while exhibiting digital gameplay behaviours, does not neglect his responsibilities or is not disconnected from the real world, this situation is considered normal. However, if the individual has become unable to control the time of play, has developed a tolerance to digital gameplay, or is deprived when he does not exhibit the behaviour of playing and has moved away from real life, there is a behavioural addiction to digital gameplay behaviour that develops here. Digital games already have elements intended to make users dependent in terms of their design and structure, and the pleasure created by the act of playing games on the person causes the cognitive structure to change because it affects the reward system of the brain. (Yeşilay, 2022, p. 33) Considering that all addictions are a brain disease and related to dopamine in the brain, the fact that pleasure from digital games directly raises dopamine levels is the key to causing addiction.

## TOPIC AND PURPOSE OF THE STUDY

Although developing new technologies make our lives easier by bringing innovations to many areas of our lives, these technological developments can also have negative effects. One of these negative effects is digital game addiction. In the light of developing and changing technological developments, digital games can now be played without the condition of space and time. In addition, the realism of games is increasing, and the digital game industry is gaining momentum every day. The aim of this study is to reveal the results of the digital game addiction levels of students at Ondokuz Mayıs University in Samsun, Turkey.

## METHOD, LIMITATIONS, SAMPLE, AND DATA MEASUREMENT SCALES

The target audience of the research consists of individuals who were born after 2000 (including 2000), continue their education at Ondokuz Mayıs University in Samsun, Turkey, and play digital games. Within the scope of the study, other age groups, generation Z individuals who were not educated at Ondokuz Mayıs University were excluded from this study.

The data of the research, the short form of the scale called "Game Addiction Scale for Adolescents" developed by Lemmens et al. (2009), consisting of 7 questions, was structured in accordance with qualitative analysis and made suitable for in-depth interviews. In-depth interview method: in line with a predetermined purpose, it is explained as a mutually realized qualitative research method based on the principle of asking questions and getting answers in return. According to a different definition, an "in-depth interview" is explained as a communication process carried out by at least one of two people in line with a pre-prepared plan. The research was applied face-to-face to 18 participants, who were randomly selected among the students who were in the specified age range among the students continuing their education at Samsun Ondokuz Mayıs University. A question about gender was not asked to the participants. All the information given by the participants to the questions was recorded in writing. A total of 12 questions were asked to each participant, and apart from the "Game Addiction Scale for Adolescents" integrated among these questions, the participants were asked about their age, for what purpose they primarily play digital games, from which platform they prefer to play games, and the average time they spend playing digital games per day.

The research has several limitations in order to be suitable for its purpose. Due to the limitations of the research being conducted at Samsun Ondokuz Mayıs University, the student ID cards of the participants were checked, and their birth dates were confirmed due to the generation Z limitation. In addition, the interviews with the participants who did not play digital games were terminated. Individuals outside the limitations were not included in the study.

The study was carried out in line with the following questions:

1. What is your date of birth? Please specify.
2. Do you play digital games on any platform (Mobile Phone, Computer, Tablet, Console, etc.)?

*** Please take your last 6 months as a basis when answering the following questions.

3. Have you ever wanted to play a digital game all day long? If so, please specify the reason and frequency.
4. Has there been a significant increase in the time you spend playing digital games? If so, what do you think is the reason for this increase?
5. Have you ever played digital games to escape from everyday life? If so, how often did this occur?
6. Have people close to you (such as family members or friends) failed to reduce your digital gaming time? Despite all the suggestions, did you continue to play games with the same frequency?

7. Have you ever felt bad when you weren't playing digital games? If so, how often did this happen to you?
8. Have you had argument with people close to you (such as family members or friends) about the time you spend in the game? If so, what are the most frequently used words in these arguments and how often do these arguments take place?
9. Have you neglected other important activities (such as school, work, sports) to play games? If so, how often has this happened to you?
10. What is the main purpose of your game play? (Getting away from people, spending time, enjoying, socializing, competing, etc.) Please explain.
11. On which platform (mobile phone, PC, tablet, console) do you play digital games the most? Why do we choose this platform?
12. On average, how much time do you spend playing digital games during the day? In what time period of the day can you spare time for gaming?

## FINDINGS AND ANALYSIS

According to the results of face-to-face interviews with 18 participants, 12 participants (66.7%) were identified as digital game addicts. In order to diagnose addiction, the results of the quantitative evaluation created by Lemmens et al. (2009) were adapted to the qualitative research method. Polythetic evaluation criteria were used to diagnose the individual as a digital game addict. While all criteria must be met for personality disorders with monothetic criteria, different symptom variances for the same personality disorder are allowed for polythetic personality disorders. In order to diagnose all disorders after DSM III, it was decided that the polythetic diagnostic criteria would be sufficient and accepted as the cut-off point. The rate of 66.7% constitutes a very high rate for digital game addiction. Since the study has never been applied qualitatively in the literature, there is no data to compare.

Digital game addicted individuals in the sample selected from the members of the generation Z at Ondokuz Mayıs University, 58.3% of them stated that they play digital games via computer and 41.7% of them play with smart mobile phones. Another factor to consider is that those who play digital games on a tablet or console are not addicted to digital games. However, due to the small sample size, it is not possible for us to conclude that those who play digital games on a tablet or console are not game addicts. Most of the digital game addicted participants who stated that they played games on the computer stated that the screen size of the computers was important to them. Participant number 12 said the following about this situation: "*I mostly play games on a laptop. It is easy to carry with me, and the screen is wider than the phone,*". The thing that people who are addicted to digital games and play games on their smart mobile phones mostly express is that the phones are easily portable. Participant number 5 said the following about this issue: "*I play on my mobile phone. It is convenient to carry anywhere. At the same time, being small is also an advantage*".

In the question directed to the digital game addicted individuals in the sample, to reveal the primary reasons for playing digital games; 7 people (58.3%) spend leisure time, 2 people (16.7%) enjoy, 1 person (8.3%) socialize, 1 person (8.3%) escape from reality, 1 person (8.3%) stated that they play digital games to forget anxiety and panic attacks. Participant number 5 expressed that his/her primary purpose is to spend time with the following words "*Very ideal for leisure time*". Participant number 10 states that he/she plays games for the purpose of socialization with the following words: "*I can say very clearly that the main purpose of playing games is to socialize. I play games with all my close friends who have similar game tastes, especially with my friends whom I do not have the chance to spend time with physically, both to have fun together and to have the pleasure of chatting while having fun.*" Participant number 11, who shared the words "*Getting away from anxiety and panic attacks*", stated that behind the experience of playing digital games is getting rid of mental problems.

Considering the daily time spent playing digital games, the average of all participants is approximately 4 hours. For individuals addicted to digital games, the average time spent on daily gaming is approximately 5 and a half hours. In the study, there are participants who can be described as digital game addicts who play games for 14 hours a day.

## FUTURE RESEARCH AND DIRECTIONS

In this study, the digital game addiction disposition of the individuals in generation Z was considered. Today, all generations became a part of the digital world in addition to generation Z. The difference between them is that while the generation Z is born in a world surrounded by technology, other generations adapted to the advancing technology. Therefore, the future studies might investigate the intergeneration digital game addiction.

## CONCLUSION AND DISCUSSION

Although it is not the case for every technological development, most technological developments can bring negative features that can sometimes be dangerous as much as they add to our lives. Among these negative features, there are many problems such as financial losses, physical or mental disorders, unnecessary waste of time, and an increase in the number of asocial individuals. Digital game addiction is a behavioural addiction that increases in parallel with the development of technology. As seen in the research, although it is sometimes played to enjoy and pass time, it can also be played because of getting away from people and escape from reality. Each generation has some unique features. When we look at the generation X, the risk of digital game addiction is calculated to be less because of their weaker technological predispositions. However, this situation becomes different for generation Y and generation Z. The reason why the generation Z is preferred in this study is that they were born in a time period when all technological developments gained momentum and they had an extreme command of technological tools.

The main purpose of this study is to show that quantitative addiction scales are only intended to reveal the addiction level of the individual but do not question the underlying causes in the addiction situation. When the study is conducted with in-depth interviews, which is a qualitative research method, the addicted individuals have the chance to access information such as why they play digital games, on which platform they play, how much time they spend on digital games. In the treatment phase of the individual, a more effective treatment planning can be made in the light of the information in question. In this way, the recovery of the individual from the addiction in question can both be accelerated, and programming can be made for a permanent state of well-being. Regarding behavioural addictions, qualitative studies rather than quantitative studies will contribute to the treatment process, and it is necessary to increase qualitative studies in this direction.

## REFERENCES


Adıgüzel, O., Batur, H. Z., & Ekşili, N. (2014). The Changing Face of Generations and the New Working Style Emerged with Generation Y: Mobile Collars [Kuşakların Değişen Yüzü ve Y kuşağı İle Ortaya Çıkan Yeni Çalışma Tarzı: Mobil Yakalılar]. *Süleyman Demirel Üniversitesi Sosyal Bilimler Enstitüsü Dergisi*, *1*(19), 165–182.

Altuntuğ, N. (2012). Consumption Phenomenon from Generation to Generation and Consumer Profile of the Future [Kuşaktan Kuşağa Tüketim Olgusu ve Geleceğin Tüketici Profili]. *Organizasyon ve Yönetim Bilimleri Dergisi*, *4*(1), 203–212.

Alwin, D. F. (2002). Generations X, Y And Z: Are They Changing America, *American Sociological Association. Contexts*, *42*(1), 42–51. doi:10.1525/ctx.2002.1.4.42

Amerikan Psikiyatri Birliği. (2014). *Diagnostic and Statistical Manual of Mental Disorders* [Mental Bozuklukların Tanısal ve Sayımsal El Kitabı]. Hekimler Yayın Birliği.

Arthur, R. (2016). Generation Z: 10 StatsFrom SXSW YouNeedToKnow. *Forbes/Tech.* https://www.forbes.com/sites/rachelarthur/2016/03/16/generationz/#4d22f7a52.

Binark, M., & Bayraktutan-Sütçü, G. (2008). *Digital Game as a Culture Industry* [Kültür Endüstrisi Olarak Dijital Oyun]. Kalkedon Yayıncılık.

Chen, H. (2010). *Advertising and generational identity: A theoretical model.* Conference- American Academy of Advertising CD-ROM–Edition, Minneapolis, MN.

Demirdöğmez, M., Küçükoğlu, M., & Taş, H. Y. (2017). Possible Effects on Working Life of Generation Z, Our Future [Geleceğimiz Olan Z Kuşağının Çalışma Hayatına Muhtemel Etkileri]. *Uluslararası Toplum Araştırmaları Dergisi*, *7*(13), 1033–1046.

Frasca, G. (2001). Rethinking Agency and İmmersion: Video Games as A Means of Consciousness-Raising. *Digital Creativity (Exeter)*, *12*(3), 167–174. doi:10.1076/digc.12.3.167.3225

Green, S. C., & Bavelier, D. (2003). Action Video Game Modifies Visual Selective Attention. *Nature*, *423*(6939), 534–537. doi:10.1038/nature01647 PMID:12774121

Hung, K. H., Gu, F. F., & Yim, C. K. B. (2007). A social institutional approach to identifying generation cohorts in China with a comparison with American consumers. *Journal of International Business Studies*, *38*(5), 836–853. doi:10.1057/palgrave.jibs.8400288

ICD 11. (2022). 6C51 Gaming disorder. *ICD-11 for Mortality and Morbidity Statistics*. ICD. https://icd.who.int/browse11/lm/en#/http%3a%2f%2fid.who.int%2ficd%2fentity%2f1448597234. (12.20.2022).

Jaeger, H. (1985). Generations in History: Reflections on a Controversial Concept. *History and Theory*, *24*(3), 273-292.

Kerr, A. (2006). *The Business and Culture of Digital Games, Gamework/Gameplay*. Sage Publications. doi:10.4135/9781446211410

Kupperschmidt, B. R. (2000). Multigeneration Employees: Strategies for Effective Management. *The Health Care Manager*, *19*(1), 65–76. doi:10.1097/00126450-200019010-00011 PMID:11183655

Kuş, Ö. A. (2021). Games in the Context of Addiction and Digitization; Investigation of Generation Y on the Axis of Digital Game Addiction within the Scope of Istanbul Province. [Bağımlılık ve Dijitalleşme Bağlamında Oyunlar; İstanbul İli Kapsamında, Y Kuşağı'nın Dijital Oyun Bağımlılığı Ekseninde İncelenmesi] In Ö. A. Kuş & Ö. Uğurlu Akbaş (Eds.), *Digital Version of Games* [Oyunların Dijital Hali]. (pp. 13–44). Urzeni.

Lamm, E., & Meeks, M. D. (2009). Workplace Fun: The Moderating Effects of Generational Differences. *Employee Relations*, *31*(6), 613–631. doi:10.1108/01425450910991767

Lemmens, J. S., Valkenburg, P. M., & Peter, J. (2009). Development and Validation of a Game Addiction Scale for Adolescents. *Media Psychology*, *12*(1), 77–95. doi:10.1080/15213260802669458

Lotfi, A., Kabiri, S., & Ghasemlou, H. (2013). Change of Values and Intergenerational Conflict: The Case of Iran Khoy City [Değerler Değişimi ve Kuşaklararası Çatışma: İran Khoy Kenti Örneği]. *Eskişehir Osmangazi Üniversitesi Sosyal Bilimler Dergisi*, *14*(2), 93–113.

Mannheim, K. (1952). The Problem of Generations. In P. Kecskemeti (Ed.), *Essays on the Sociology of Knowledge* (pp. 276–320). Routledge and Kegan Paul.

Newzoo. (2022). Newzoo Global Games Market Report 2022. *Newzoo.* https://newzoo.com/insights/trend-reports/newzoo-global-games-market-report-2022-free-version

Patranabis, I. C. (2012). The Future of Workforce Management: Perspectives and Way Ahead. In R. K. Mishra, S. Sarkar, & P. Singh (Eds.), Today's HR for a Sustainable Tomorrow, Allied Publishers.

Pilcher, J. (1994). Mannheim's Sociology of Generations: An Undervalued Legacy. *The British Journal of Sociology*, *45*(3), 481–495. doi:10.2307/591659

Reeves, T. C., & Oh, E. (2014). Generational Difference sand the Integration of Technology in Learning, Instruction, and Performance. In J. M. Spector. (Eds.), Handbook of Research on Educational Communications and Technology (pp. 819-828). New York: Springer Science+Business Media.

Senbir, S. (2004). *"The Last Man"? Thoughts on Generation Z and Beyond* ["Son İnsan" mı? Z Kuşağı ve Sonrasına Dair Düşünceler]. Okyan Us Yayınları.

Sezen, T. İ. (2011). Understanding Digital Games: Digital Games from Game, Narrative, Software and Platform Perspectives. [Dijital Oyunları Anlamak: Oyun, Anlatı, Yazılım ve Platform Perspektiflerinden Dijital Oyunlar] In G. T. Ünal & U. Batı (Eds.), *Digital Games: "Live in Your World Play in Ours"* [Dijital Oyunlar: "Kendi Dünyanda Yaşa Bizimkinde Oyna"]. (pp. 119–148). İstanbul Derin Yayınları.

Strauss, W., & Howe, N. (1997). *The Fourth Turning: What the Cycles of History Tell Us About America's Next Rendezvous with Destiny*. Broadway Books.

Ünal, M. (2017). *Management of Generations Y and Z* [Y ve Z Kuşaklarının Yönetimi]. Beta Basım Yayım Dağıtım A.Ş.

Yeşilay. (2022). *Technology addiction* [Teknoloji Bağımlılığı]. Yeşilay Yayınları.

## ADDITIONAL READING

Bernard, S. (2005). *The Grasshopper: Games, Life and Utopia*. Broadview Press.

Berne, E. (1976). *Games People Play* [Hayat Denen Oyun]. (S. Sargut, Trans.). Altın Kitaplar Yayınevi.

Caillois, R. (2001). *Man, Play and Games*. (M. Barash, Trans.). University of Illinois Press.

Fink, E. (2010). *Spiel als Weltsymbol* [Bir Dünya Sembolü Olarak Oyun]. (N. Aça, Trans.). Dost Kitabevi.

Yengin, D. (2012). *Violence in Digital Games* [Dijital Oyunlarda Şiddet]. Beta Yayınları.

## KEY TERMS AND DEFINITIONS

**Addiction:** It is the state of being attached to any event, material, object or behaviour to exclude other activities of life or to physically, mentally or socially damage others.

**Digital Game:** Digital games include the "interactivity, modularity, digitality, virtuality and changeability" features of the new communication environments and considered as a personal communication environment including all these features to the act of game playing.

**Game:** Game can be defined as an event with general rules and certain purpose yet enabling frivolous individuals of the society to contact with each other that is unreal with the feeling of real.

**Generation:** It consists of individuals who are born on the same years within the certain period.

## ENDNOTE

1 ICD 11 disease classification code

# Chapter 23
# A Field Research on Digital Playing Tendencies and Addiction of High School Students

**Süleyman Türkoğlu**
*Istanbul University, Turkey*

**Hülya Semiz Türkoğlu**
*Istanbul University, Turkey*

## ABSTRACT

*All the needs for education, social relations, social activities, and personal development are now being provided through digital resources. Based on the fact that studies on digital game addiction are not at the desired level, the main purpose of the study is to investigate the factors affecting digital game addiction in high school students and the relationship between digital game addiction, which has become a growing problem, and mindfulness concepts. According to the results of the survey applied to 181 high school students studying in Istanbul Esenyurt, the general and all sub-dimensions of the Digital Game Addiction Scale do not differ significantly according to gender, grade level and school success. The answer to the question 'I prefer playing games to spend time with my friends physically,' 3.24, 'I discuss the time I spend in the game with people close to me,' is 2.99, 'I postpone my sleep time to reach my goal in the game,' with an average of 2.93. reveals the result that he is addicted to digital games as an indicator of addiction.*

## INTRODUCTION

The continuous advancement of technology and the increase in digitalization increase the importance of individuals' virtualization and digital addiction levels day by day. Virtualization and digital addiction draw attention as an important agenda topic in many developed or developing countries in the world. At

DOI: 10.4018/978-1-6684-8397-8.ch023

this point, the virtualization of individuals causes the virtualization of society over time, and the society creates the impulse of virtualization.

With the development of technology, there is a great transformation in the world.

In parallel with the rapid development of technology, digital media tools such as mobile phones, tablets, computers, and televisions, which have entered almost every home, have become an integral part of life. So much so that some people cannot do without digital media tools. This situation has revealed the concept of digital addiction today (Montag & Walla, 2016).

It has been revealed by more and more researchers that digital addiction affects the emotions and personality traits of individuals. Individuals who interact intensively with technological tools begin to decrease the importance they attach to interaction and bonding with other individuals and to break away from social life.

With the widespread use of digital media tools, it has become possible to access computer games or digital games easily from almost any environment.

However, since digital games are prepared to attract everyone's attention, not only children or young people, but also adults may become addicted to these games.

"Digital game addiction"; It can be defined as the inability of individuals to stop playing games for a long time, to identify the game with real life, to become unable to fulfill their basic responsibilities due to playing games, to prefer playing games to other activities, to make sacrifices from their social relationships or not to give up digital games despite having to sleep deprivation (Gürcan, 2007). Ozhan & Uslu, 2008). In this context, it is seen that computer games, which have become so important and effective in the lives of children, young people and adults, cause digital game addiction.

Games always have an important place in people's lives. In the past, games such as hide-and-seek, hopscotch, and hopscotch have been legendary games for those who play these games. With the development of technology, such games have been replaced by games on the computer and atari, and because of these games, people have begun to spend less time with their friends. Nowadays, studies on digital game addiction have begun to be carried out due to the fact that even young children have mobile phones in their hands, computers, tablets or game consoles are in almost every home, and the interest in these is increasing day by day (Köksal, 2015, p. 27).

It is possible to say that children who follow technology closely today show intense sympathy for digital games and digital games have become one of the popular culture concepts among young people.

Griffiths (2009) determined seven criteria to determine the child's digital game addictions. These seven items are; "Does he play games almost every day?", "Does he play video games for long periods of time?", "Does he play games for excitement and enthusiasm?", "Does he feel restless, uncomfortable, and unstable when he does not play?", "Does he have a social life to play? and does he sacrifice his sportive activities?", "Does he prefer to play games instead of doing his homework?", "He tries to reduce the time he plays, but does not succeed?" is If the child answers yes to at least four or more of these seven items, he/she said that he/she has problematic playing behavior (Act. Hazar, 2016, pp. 82-83).

By negatively affecting the physical and psychological development and social lives of children and young people, digital games cause problems such as sleep disorders, excretion problems, deterioration in eating habits, deterioration in social life and human relations (Nazlıgül et al., 2018, p. 13).

The age range in which the effect of internet and game addiction is seen is not limited to 'digital native' and 'digital immigrant' or Y and Z generations. So much so that the symptoms of internet and game addiction are also seen in preschool and primary school children (Bilgin, 2015). The fact that children in this age group are in a critical developmental period can cause permanent behavioral problems in children with symptoms of addiction. For this reason, the importance of early intervention and preventive services in secondary school students has a remarkable place in addiction studies. In this sense, determining the variables that cause and increase addiction is a critical step in preventive studies, especially for preschool and primary school children.

In the preparation of protective and preventive studies on digital game addiction and in determining the possible risk and protective factors related to this addiction area, multidimensional studies that include variables such as school, family, friends and expert staff are needed (Kneer, Rieger, & Ivory, 2014). In fact, the risk factors of internet and digital game addiction are sometimes related to environmental factors such as social support (Esen & Siyez, 2011), and sometimes to internal factors such as self-esteem (Hazar, 2019) or psychological resilience (Ağır, 2018). is happening. This proves to us the versatility of the risk factors of this type of addiction. Studies on internet or game addiction in the past years also confirm the versatility of the risk and protective factors of this type of addiction.

The fact that the use of these internet and digital games among the young population is becoming more widespread in younger age groups has necessitated some precautions to be taken. In Turkey, serious steps have been taken in recent years in the treatment of internet addiction resulting from uncontrolled internet use. The Internet Addiction Polyclinic, which was opened within the body of Ankara Polatlı Duatepe State Hospital (Ministry of Health [SB], 2019), offers remedial services that internet addicts need.

It is a behavioral addiction fueled by the feeling of incompleteness as a result of careless, impulsive and excessive contact with the latest technology and digital devices, including addictions such as social network addiction and online/offline game addictions (Yengin, 2019).

The aim of this study is to review the remarkable studies on internet and game addiction in the literature in the past years and the variables whose effects were examined in those studies and to examine digital game addiction in terms of some variables in high school students.

Considering that digital game addiction has become one of the most important problems of our time, this study aimed to determine the level of digital game addiction and the factors associated with digital game addiction in high school students.

The problem sentence of the research is "What is the level of digital game addiction of high school students?" is in the form.

In the study, high school students were selected between childhood and adulthood, a period in which intense exam stress is experienced and families have high expectations for choosing a good profession and for gaining the right to university.

Quantitative research method will be used in the study and questionnaire technique was used as a data collection tool. There are some limitations arising from the universe, the sample and the scales used in the research. High school students studying in Esenyurt, which is the most populous district of Istanbul, which is the research universe, were selected.

## DIGITAL GAME CONCEPT

Today, people play every game they played in the streets, parks and playgrounds such as coffee houses, in their own homes, workplaces and places such as cafes. Games such as online shopping have had their share of the virtual world and have begun to be played from the virtual world. Now, instead of playing in parks, streets and playgrounds, individuals play games on devices such as phones, computers, tablets and playstations.

Since the beginning of history, humanity has discovered many things and made different inventions. Every new invention has brought about a change in human life. One of the areas that has undergone change is games. With the development of information technologies, the games that we know and are used to have started to differentiate and become digitalized by moving away from the traditional. The word 'digital' means "electronic display of data on a screen" (TDK, 2019). Face-to-face games with friends are now being played in front of a screen. These types of games have been given many names such as electronic games, computer games, console games, online games, but the concept of "digital game" meets the features and types expressed by all these concepts (Binark & Bayraktutan-Sütçü, 2008). From this point of view, the concept of 'digital game' was preferred in this study.

When defining digital game, it is necessary to distinguish between traditional game and digital game. Traditional and digital games; They are similar to each other in terms of definition and main constructive qualities. These game concepts differ from each other in terms of their basic elements, the place to play the games, the number of players, the materials used during the game, the game type and content.

Traditional games are games in which bodily activities are prioritized and the people playing the game freely adapt the game according to themselves by determining the rules, place, time, number of players and the most important game tools and equipment. According to Postman, the child plays with the aim of having fun by using the tools he finds around him. Creativity, interpersonal communication and organizing the game are important in traditional games. In this context, traditional games are extremely beneficial for the physical, cognitive and social development of individuals (Hazar et al., 2017a, p. 180).

Digital games are "monitor, mouse, keyboard or joystick etc. It can be defined as a set of systems with rules and purposes, in which interfaces interact with computer programs (Hazar, 2016, p. 62).

Digital games, which are considered as games that can be played by individuals of all ages, are played in digital environments, unlike traditional games. Digital games are generally defined as games played on technological devices such as computers, smart phones, game consoles, tablets. Kirriemuir (2002) stated that concepts such as "digital games", "computer games" and "video games" are often used interchangeably.

Usually, adolescents get away from real life and immerse themselves in the world of dreams because of digital games. Being predictable and repeatable is among the greatest joys of the digital world. Everyone can experience development and success as the hero of their own story (Chatfield, 2013: 121).

The age of technology, which promises eternity and consists of virtual networks, becomes the tools of the concepts of violence and pleasure in the game. Computer and computer-based games create a new living space in the space of instant and eternity by enabling the audience to be perceived as seemingly online. Today, digital games are rapidly diversified and released to the market due to the production of ever-increasing doses of content, the strengthening of technological infrastructures, the presentation of content that surrounds human life, and the increase in consumption. Although it has the potential to negatively affect mental and physical health among the numerous games in the digital game industry, it has developed from computers to televisions in order to keep this industry alive and spreads over a wide area (Çavuş et al., 2016: 266).

PwC (PricewaterhouseCoopers), which examines the gaming, entertainment and media industry from many perspectives, has published the "Global Entertainment and Media Outlook Perspectives" report. The report, which collects, analyzes and questions the data and forecasts of the global entertainment and media industry, includes valuable predictions for Turkey until 2026. The research conducted by PwC included the opinions of many experts.

Although the extreme growth phase experienced due to the pandemic has been left behind, some experts state that such explosions are a good step for healthy growth. With the contribution of this effect, the digital games sector has been among the sectors experiencing the most significant growth. According to the report: Total video games revenue (excluding esports) in 2021 reached $214.2 billion and will rise to $321.1 billion in 2026, at a CAGR of 8.4%. It is expected that 75.58% of this revenue ($242.7 billion) will be made up of casual (extremely simple, games that anyone can play with a single tap, with short chapters and tasks).

*Figure 1. 2021 is the latest available data; 2022-2026 values are forecast*
*Source: PwC's Global Entertainment & Media Outlook 2022-2026, Omdia*

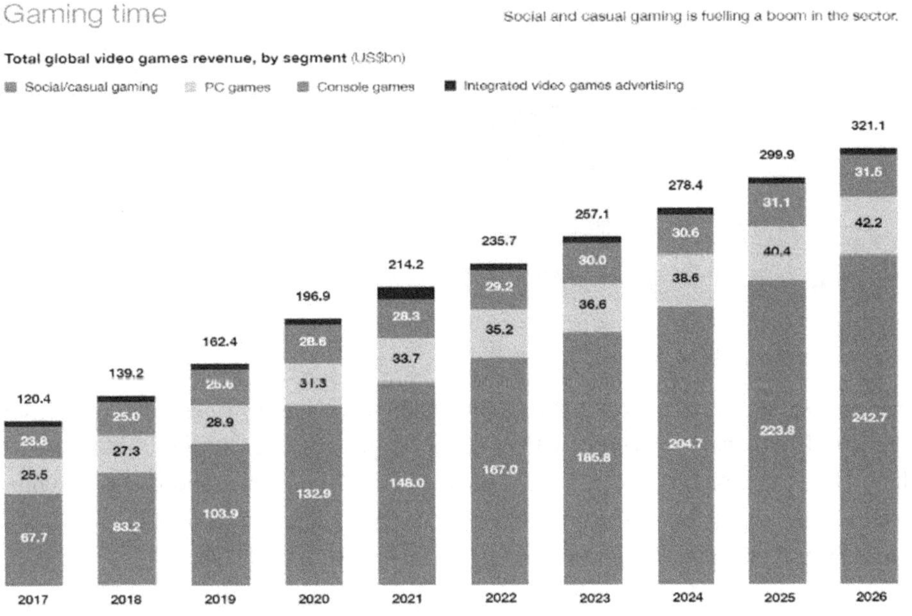


According to the report, although growth is predicted in most of the crowded but less wealthy countries, it is stated that Turkey will be the fastest growing video games market with a compound growth rate of 24.1% between 2021 and 2026. Turkey is followed by Pakistan (21.9%) and India (18.3%), respectively.

In the research conducted by PwC, which included the opinions of many experts, it is also predicted that Turkey will be the fastest growing country in terms of consumer income with a rate of 14.2% in the period from 2021 to 2026. This rate covers not only the gaming industry but the entire entertainment industry, but the biggest share comes from games. Argentina and India follow Turkey in terms of consumer income in the research.

Turkey is currently the country that receives the most investments in terms of gaming investments in Europe. In the first 6 months of 2022, Turkish gaming startups received an investment of 333 million dollars, making Turkey the first in Europe in this regard. Our country is followed by England with 158 million dollars and Norway with 60 million dollars in the ranking of the countries that receive the most investment in the gaming sector in Europe.

*Figure 2. 2021 is the latest available data; 2022-2026 values are forecast*
*Source: PwC's Global Entertainment & Media Outlook 2022-2026, Omdia*

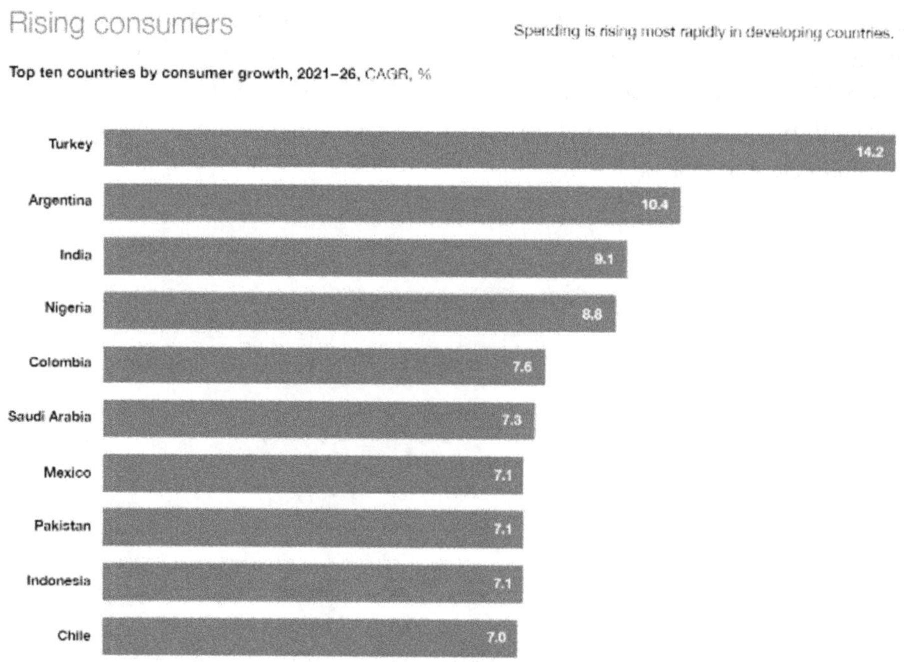


The remainder of the report covers many topics such as advertising, the metaverse, and the music industry. The report, which was written with a focus on growth rates in the entertainment and media sector, predicted that the next break will be experienced with Metaverse, and it was emphasized that the digital games industry opened the way to Metaverse experiences. The report also included Citibank's estimate that the Metaverse economy could be worth $13 trillion by 2030.

## DIGITAL GAME HISTORY

Looking at the history of digital games, the first game prototype is "Tennis for Two", which was developed by William Higinbotham in 1958 to entertain the visitors of Brokhaven National Laboratory and played on an analog computer (Kirriemuir, 2006). This was followed by the game "Spacewar" developed by Steven Russell in 1962. The aim of the game is to shoot down rival ships and it is designed to develop military technologies (Binark & Bayraktutan-Sütçü, 2008; Kirriemuir, 2006). Later, this process continued with the first generation console games "Computer Space", which went on sale in 1971, and "Pong", which was released in 1972. These games are all American made. In 1978, the Japanese game "Space Invaders" was released (Ankara Development Agency, 2016).

There was a commercial boom with Pong. Digital games started to become widespread after Atari, which can be considered a pioneer in this field, first developed console games that can be played using coins in arcades, and then released games that can be played by connecting to home televisions.

The development of digital games continued with the creation of better quality images and animations, the addition of sound effects, and the transfer of games from arcades to personal computers. As information technology continues to evolve, the hardware and software of digital games continue to change.

When we look at the history of digital games in Turkey, it is seen that the journey that started with arcade halls continues with internet cafes and personal computers (Akbulut, 2013).

Our country met with digital games in 1980. People living in this period had a craze for watching videos, color televisions and playing arcade. During this period, many people became addicted as arcade halls were opened in many cities. In the following years, the differentiation of game consoles, the emergence of personal computers and the spread of game devices with much more affordable prices increased addiction. With the spread of computers, "internet cafes" emerged in the 1990s.

## DIGITAL ADDICTION

In order to understand digital game addiction, first of all, the concept of 'addiction' should be emphasized. Addiction is defined as "a picture that occurs when a substance is taken outside of its purpose and as a result of tolerance to that substance, taken in increasing amounts, continued use despite causing problems in the person's life, and withdrawal symptoms occur when the substance intake is reduced or stopped" (Uğurlu, Şengül & Şengül)., 2012).

One of the most important factors in the emergence of addiction is the constant change and development of technology. The individual, who gets used to and uses every emerging technology, quickly adopts the next technology and incorporates it into his life. The possibilities offered by technology and the virtual world it creates include elements that are not found in the real world, making individuals dependent on technology.

Since the concept of addiction is a multidimensional concept, it can be met with many other definitions in the relevant literature. However, 21 points about the concept that are agreed upon is that addiction manifests itself as a type of relationship. Because the concept of addiction is generally considered as a special situation that occurs after a relationship with a certain situation or object and is seen as a result of behaviors related to each other (Young, 1999). In other words, addiction; It can be defined as the temporary feeling of well-being of individuals as a result of using a certain substance, product and/or service for a long time.

Digital Addiction Because people cannot resist the urges due to the pleasure and reward mechanisms in their brains; are addicted to tobacco, alcohol, drugs or gambling and have to endure the negative consequences of these addictions. The rapid advances in technology, which makes the present age a modern age, have enabled intensive technological tools to enter daily life at the same speed.

Daily needs and activities in the digitalized world require individuals to be digitally connected. However, this dependency has risen above the expected level due to the dazzling aspects of technology and has begun to evolve into digital dependency (Yengin, 2019). So much so that people have become unable to lift their heads from smart phones, which are the products of high technology, from the moment they wake up to the moment they go back to sleep. This situation prevents people from staying in the moment during the day to have a nice conversation, a beautiful view or a problem solving. Because instead of staying in the moment and enjoying the moment, people usually spend their days by sharing the photos of the scenery they see and the videos of the moment they live on social media or by following the shared ones. Digital tools, which have become an indispensable element of human life, facilitate people's lives by allowing many jobs and transactions to be done quickly and comfortably, especially thanks to internet access. However, these devices have brought with them some problems that people have to deal with, as well as the comfort they provide. One of these problems is the problem of digital addiction, which can be considered as the excessive use of digital media tools fueled by the feeling of incompleteness (Yengin, 2019).

Dependence; It is defined as a state of uncontrollable desire that negatively affects the physical, social, mental and spiritual health of the person as a result of a habit formed against a certain activity or substance use, which also causes negative effects on the economic situation (Griffiths, 2000). Addictions are classified as substance and behavioral addictions. Under the heading of substance abuse, alcohol, cigarettes, drugs, etc. while dependencies are involved; Under the title of behavioral addiction, there are addiction types such as gambling, extreme sports, spending too much time with technological tools. Behavioral addiction; It is defined as a type of addiction in which there is no addiction to any substance, but the problems seen in substance addiction are observed, which occurs with frequent repetition of the habit, in which the individual continues to continue the behavior despite being aware of the negative impact (Günüç & Kayri, 2010). Behavioral addictions are discussed in six stages (Griffiths, 2000). These are: "attention", "mood change", "tolerance", "withdrawal symptom", "conflict" and "relapse". Attracting attention; The behavior of the individual takes place at a point that is most important and of vital importance in his life. In mood change; Since the individual feels the obvious emotional changes and effects of his behaviors on himself, he wants to control the situation he lives in while continuing the activity. In tolerance, the individual feels obliged to increase the activity in order to achieve the pleasure of the first activity. In deprivation, since the individual cannot reach the same pleasure, he may experience negative situations such as trembling and sweating. In conflict, when the individual cannot engage in addictive behavior, he may experience conflicts with his environment as well as internal conflicts. In relapse, even if the individual manages to take control of the addictive behavior, there is a possibility that the addictive behavior will come back due to withdrawal. Digital addiction, which is considered as one of the behavioral addictions, can be summarized as the inability of individuals to control themselves against using digital tools and applications despite feeling negative emotions as a result of the integration of mass media with technology. Digital addiction internet addiction, social network addiction, game addiction, etc. it also includes dependencies (Jiang et al., 2015).

Digital addiction can be defined as the beginning of being harmed by the negative effects of this interaction as a result of being in constant interaction with technology (Arısoy, 2009). Digital addiction, which has started to be at the center of many people's lives today and is accepted to directly affect the dynamics of daily life, causes many problems in the social and psychological lives of individuals. Because individuals who are constantly interacting with technological tools begin to ignore being in relationship and interaction with other individuals, and thus bring alienation.

Cell phone, social media, internet etc. Digital media tools such as these are not necessarily such that they can be completely excluded from life, especially as of today. However, this situation causes digital addiction in cases where the use of digital media tools is not properly managed, and it can cause problems because people do not know how to balance between using these digital media tools and not being digitally dependent.

## DIGITAL GAMING ADDICTION

The issue of addiction to technology is actually different from classical addiction situations. In addiction, people become addicted to drugs, but in technology, there is an addiction to the information, entertainment and personal connections offered by these technologies rather than direct substance/object dependence, in other words, addiction to computers, smartphones, video consoles or tablets. When we evaluate it in terms of technology, here; As a result of the use of technology, which manifests itself as an excessive, severe and continuous addiction, people become slaves of this technology.

Games always have an important place in people's lives. In the past, games such as hide-and-seek, hopscotch, and hopscotch have been legendary games for those who play these games. With the development of technology, such games have been replaced by games on the computer and atari, and because of these games, people have begun to spend less time with their friends. Nowadays, studies on digital game addiction have begun to be carried out due to the fact that even small children have mobile phones in their hands, computers, tablets or game consoles are in almost every home, and the interest in these is increasing day by day.

In the simplest way, games played in front of a screen and through a control device are defined as digital games (Sağlam & Topsümer, 2019). Defines digital games as "games that are programmed with various technologies and provide user input with a visual environment". When we look at digital games in terms of the basic features of the game, it can be said that they are not much different from traditional games. Features such as the fact that the game is a voluntary action, that it is a fun free time activity rather than a task, and that it offers a free environment are also valid for digital games. However, the game tools used differ in terms of elements such as the form and content of the game (Binark & Bayraktutan-Sütçü, 2008)

With the widespread use of digital media tools, it has become possible to access computer games or digital games easily from almost any environment. However, since digital games are prepared to attract everyone's attention, not only children or young people, but also adults may become addicted to these games. "Digital game addiction"; It can be defined as the inability of individuals to stop playing games for a long time, to identify the game with real life, to become unable to fulfill their basic responsibilities due to playing games, to prefer playing games to other activities, to make sacrifices from their social relationships or not to give up digital games despite having to sleep deprivation (Gürcan, 2007). Ozhan & Uslu, 2008).

It is seen that the motivations of the players are effective in bringing digital games to the level of addiction in individuals. Competition and interaction elements form the basis of motivations that attract individuals to play these games. In other motivational elements that ensure the continuation of the started games; coping, escape, skill development, fantasy, socialization, recreation. It can be stated that all of these processes are generally found in multiplayer online games (Banyai, Griffiths, Kiraly, & Demetrovics, 2018).

In this context, it is seen that computer games, which have become so important and effective in the lives of children, young people and adults, cause digital game addiction. In line with having such a wide range of influence, digital game addiction; Attention Deficit Hyperactivity Disorder (ADHD) can cause some problems such as depression, obesity, feeling of loneliness, increased anxiety and anxiety, social adaptation problem and social isolation and atrophy of communication skills (Şahin & Tuğrul, 2012). It is stated that the number of individuals with digital game addiction is increasing with the increasing scope of developing technologies and digital media tools. Because now individuals; They can easily access digital games not only through computers, tablets or game consoles, but also via smart phones. The fact that the digital game industry is a constantly growing industry also brings with it the support of digital game addiction. Because the increase in the supply of digital games causes an increase in the demand for digital games and this demand can turn into addiction after a while. According to Horzum, Ayas & Çakır (2008), the following factors are at the root of the demand for digital games turning into digital game addiction after a while;

- Individuals; They may prefer digital games on the basis of their desire to spend their free time, to get away from stress and to relax, but this may turn into addiction after a while.
- Individuals may prefer digital games because they think they can't find anything better to do and have fun, but this can turn into addiction after a while.
- Individuals; They may prefer digital games to get away from the negative conditions they are in, to get rid of them or to break their ties with real life for a while, but this situation can turn into addiction after a while.
- Individuals may prefer digital games with the desire to communicate with different characters, albeit virtual, and to exist in imaginary environments, but this may turn into addiction after a while.
- Individuals may prefer digital games because they do not want to think about anything else by focusing their minds only on these games for a while, but this can turn into addiction after a while. It is stated that online games played over the Internet can also cause digital game addiction due to the fictions they contain. These games, which are especially violent, are described as strategic games and attract the attention of individuals in the 12-18 age group, require individuals to make emotional judgments and this can bring emotional attachment to the games (Charlton & Danforth, 2007). However, in line with the fact that digital games constantly arouse the desire of individuals to win or to be the first, and social life does not contain such dynamics, it may be the case that it causes alienation from social life and harms social relations. In line with the competition reaching its peak, the degree of addiction may increase and digital games can be seen by individuals as an inseparable part of life.

Digital game addiction is generally seen in the Z generation. Before talking about the Z generation, it is necessary to include the generation classification (Metin and Kızıldağ, 2017, p.345) 1. Silent Generation: Those born in 1925-1945 and are also referred to as adults, traditionalists and veterans in some sources. The grandparents of our age who saw the first years of the Republic constitute this generation. This generation, which consists of a small part of the world's population, has witnessed many political, economic and social upheavals in history. 2. Baby Boom: It is defined as the generation born between 1946-1964. The biggest reason why it is called Baby Boom or Explosion Belt is II. The rapid increase in birth rates after World War II. This generation has witnessed many political, economic, social and technological advances. It has attracted attention especially as the first generation to use television effectively in communication. 3. Generation X: This generation, born in 1964-1979, is referred to as the Haylaz Generation, the MTV generation, a generation that constantly questions "Why Me", the Bumerang Generation (Çetin and Karalar, 2016: 160). The fact that the Baby Boom generation lived a prosperous life with the post-war development policies paved the way for economic and political problems. These economic policies implemented with the understanding of the social state; Over time, the state's power to meet the welfare costs has not been left, and due to the economic problems brought about by the oil crisis in the 70s, it has caused the members of the X generation to grow up in a turbulent period.

In a sense, the comfortable life bill of the baby boom generation has been cut to the X generation. 4. Generation Y: It is considered as those born between 1980-1999. According to the data obtained from other sources, the 80 generation is named as the Millennial Generation, the Future Generation. According to TUIK data, Generation Y constitutes a large part of Turkey's population, such as 35% (TUIK, 2017). The most distinctive feature that distinguishes the Y generation from other generations is their commitment to technology and their intertwining with technology both in business and social life. 5. Generation Z: This generation, born between 2000 and 2020, is also called the crystal generation. In the age of the Internet and in technology, the crystal generation differs from other generations by using new communication technologies such as computers, smart phones, Ipads, mobile phones, MP3 players to perform multiple tasks faster and at the same time. Digital game addiction is mostly seen in adolescents. There are two main reasons for this. The first of these is the abilities of the Z generation, which has individuals born after 2000, growing in parallel with the age of communication and information technologies. Since the individuals in the Z generation are more interested in technology, they can get used to the speed of information and time more quickly. For individuals in Generation Z, "Technology is their need. These people do not know the world without devices such as phones and computers, and these people see technology as a natural way of life. In addition, the inclination of these people to technology, their unconscious and uncontrolled use; It can cause individuals to become addicted". The second reason why digital game addiction is more common in adolescents is that the decision-making skills of individuals in adolescence have not yet fully developed. In addition, in this period, individuals can give more importance to their friends when necessary. Adolescents' interactions with their friends on digital games can also cause game addiction.

Internet gaming disorder was included in the 5th issue of the Diagnosis and Statistical Manual of Mental Disorders (DSM-5) in 2013 by the American Psychiatric Association (APA). DSM-5 defines IOOD (Internet gaming disorder) as "extreme and prolonged periods of cognitive and behavioral symptoms, including progressive loss of control, tolerance development, and withdrawal symptoms similar to substance use disorder observed in the last 12 months. Internet gaming behavior" (APA, 2013, p. 796). In order to understand whether individuals have IOBD, 9 criteria were determined. These;

- Mind being busy with games all the time
- Showing withdrawal symptoms when not playing games
- Increasing game play time
- Failure in efforts to control urges to play
- Loss of interest in hobbies
- Continuing to play despite the impact of psychosocial problems
- Not telling or lying about playing time
- Turning to games to avoid negative emotions
- Endangering duties and responsibilities by playing games. At least 5 of these symptoms must have been seen in the last 12 months.

The World Health Organization (Who, 2018) defined the concept of "Gaming Disorder" both online and offline in the 11th edition of the "International Classification of Diseases" (ICD) handbook published in June 2018. diagnosed and recognized as a disease. Digital or video game playing disorder; It has been defined as "a behavioral pattern characterized by the deterioration of the individual's ability to control playing, the increasingly displacing of the individual's other interests and daily activities, continuing to play despite negative consequences, and an increase in playing games" (Who, 2018).

The extraordinary and impressive environment offered by digital games draws individuals away from the real world and allows them to connect to virtual screens, imprisoning them in this world. When he returns to the real world, faced with an ordinary and boring environment, the individual feels the lack of what the virtual world has to offer him mentally and psychologically and is impatient to reunite with technological devices as soon as possible. When individuals leave these devices for a long time, they begin to experience the type of addiction we call deprivation and become depressed and unhappy individuals.

## A FIELD RESEARCH ON DIGITAL PLAYING TENDENCIES AND ADDICTION OF HIGH SCHOOL STUDENTS

Today, adolescents who follow technology closely show intense sympathy for digital games, and digital games are rapidly becoming one of the popular culture concepts among adolescents and young people. As a healthy lifestyle, it is accepted that it is normal to play digital games without going too far, and even this type of digital game play provides positive contributions such as pleasure and emotional relaxation. On the other hand, if the person cannot control the playing time and desire and causes significant changes in his behavior and social life, addiction can be mentioned (Young, 2009, p. 356). As a matter of fact, Lemmens et al. (2009, p. 77) defined digital game addiction as the obsessive use of digital games (computer and video games) by individuals, and this way they cannot control their excessive use, causing social and emotional problems.

It is known that digital game addiction has both sociological and psychological consequences. It affects not only the individual himself, but also his family and society. Increased gaming behavior may lead to deterioration of physical and psychological health, increased insensitivity and tendency to violence, increased crime rates, academic failure, and school dropouts. From this point of view, digital game addiction can be seen as a public health problem that also concerns areas such as education, economy, security and law in the social dimension. In the light of all this information, it is necessary to examine the relationship between digital game addiction, which has become a growing problem among secondary school students, the most frequently mentioned problem by families and teachers, and can cause different health problems, to understand the situation and to make preventive and remedial interventions in this direction.

In this context, with our study titled "A Field Study on Digital Game Playing Tendencies and Addiction of High School Students", it is important for the literature and guidance programs to be prepared in schools to examine the relationship between digital game addiction and mindfulness of high school students in adolescence, which is a transition period that brings with it adaptation problems. is considered.

## UNIVERSE AND SAMPLE OF THE RESEARCH

The universe includes all the individuals and objects to be observed in order to obtain information in a research. In other words, it can be said that the research unit or units that are explained or described, can be defined. The universe is the source provider of data in a research. The size of the universe of studies differs from each other. Sometimes the universe can be very comprehensive, and sometimes the research universe is realistically complete when the research subject covers all individuals and objects. As a result, the subject of this research universe is not entered as a whole, but it can be handled as a representative.

It consists of 181 high school students studying in Istanbul Esenyurt district. However, considering the possible shortcomings, 200 students participated in the survey. These students were excluded from the study due to the incomplete filling of the data collection tools by 19 students.

## OBJECTIVE AND METHOD

Digital addiction, which is considered as one of the most important addictions of individuals as of today, is seen as a problem especially seen in young individuals, but it can also become a great danger for individuals of middle age and above. In this context, digitally addicted individuals, whose numbers are increasing day by day, are considered among the fastest spreading addictions around the world.

The main purpose of this study is to investigate the relationship between digital game addiction, which has become a growing problem for individuals in adolescence, which is a transitional period, and mindfulness concepts. In addition, the level of digital game addiction, which is the dependent variable of the study, was determined by gender, class, number of siblings, family status, education level of parents, school success, income level, having a separate room, having a chronic illness, experiencing negative life events, adequate social support. The sub-purpose of the study is to examine whether it differs according to the digital tools owned or not.

The main purpose of the research is in the context of Examining the Digital Addictions of High School Students; Determining the digital addiction levels of high school students within the scope of "Game Dimension" and examining them in the context of different variables.

Questionnaire method was used as data collection tool in the research. The survey consists of 2 main parts. In the first part, there are questions about the sociodemographic characteristics of the students, while in the second part there are questions to determine the levels of digital game addiction.

## DATA COLLECTION AND ANALYSIS

The survey study was applied to high school students between November 1 and December 5, 2022. Descriptive statistical analysis methods were used in the data analysis of the study, which was carried out with a total of 181 participants. Data analysis was obtained through the SPSS 16 package program.

In the analysis, the acceptance point for factor loading values was determined as 0.30. In the study, the validity and reliability of the scale were carried out by designing the students' "A Field Study on Digital Game Playing Tendencies of High School Students and Addiction" in accordance with the five-point Likert type model (Tavşancıl, 2014, p. 36). In determining this reliability, the Cronbach Alpha reliability coefficient was examined and found to be 0.79.

## FINDINGS

Table 1 shows the gender distribution of the students participating in the research. Of the 181 students who participated in the study, 92 were female and 89 were male students.

*Table 1. Gender distribution of the students participating in the research*

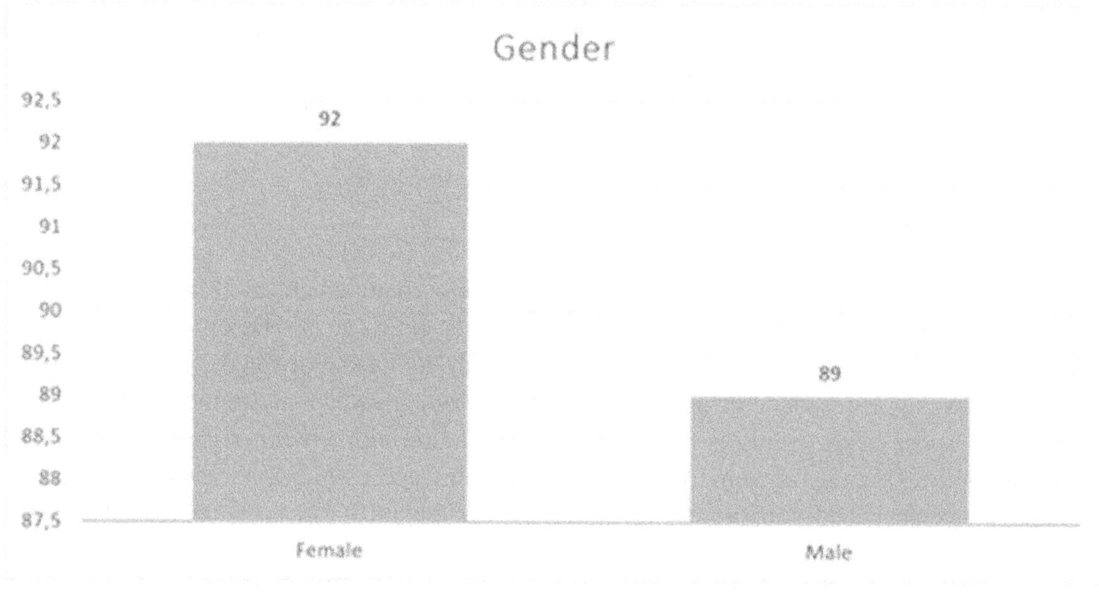


*Table 2. Grade levels of the students participating in the research*

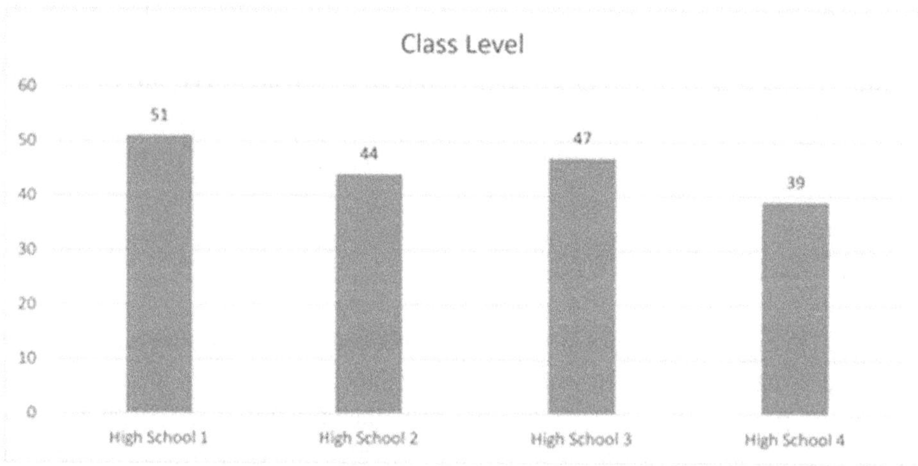


Table 2 shows the grade levels of the students participating in the research. Of the 181 students who participated in the research, 51 were 1st grade high school students, 47 3rd grade high school students, 44 2nd grade high school students, and 39 high school 4th grade students.

In Table 3, what is the educational status of Father, one of the parents of 181 students who participated in the research? 98 of them answered "High School Graduate", 62 of them "High School - University Graduate", 19 of them "Primary School Banana" and 2 of them "Graduate of Postgraduate Education (Master's / Doctorate)". "Secondary School Graduate" and "Not Reader-Writer" answers were not given.

*Table 3. Educational status of the fathers of the students participating in the study*

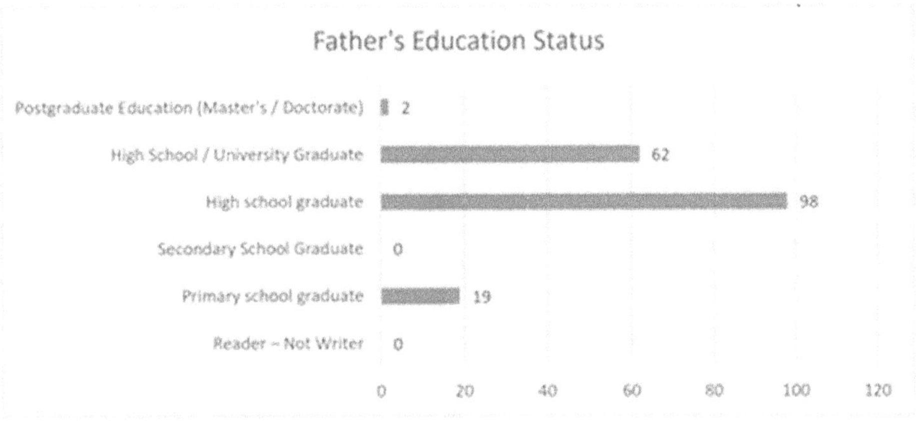


*Table 4. Educational status of the mothers of the students participating in the research*

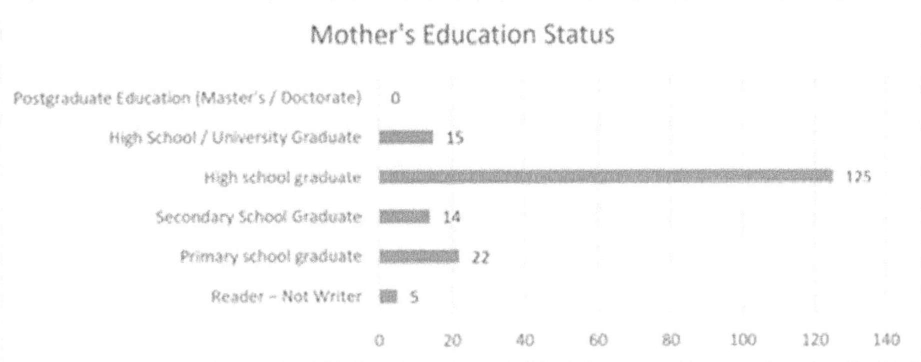


In Table 4, what is the educational status of Anne, one of the parents of 181 students who participated in the research? 125 of them answered the question "High School Graduate", 22 "Primary School Banana", 15 "High School - University Graduate", 14 "Middle School Graduate", 5 "Irritable". No response was given as "Graduate of Postgraduate Education (Master's / Doctorate)".

How do you evaluate your school success in Table 5 129 of the 181 students who participated in the research gave the answer "Average", 21 "Good", 12 "Bad", 10 "Very Bad", and 9 "Very Good".

In Table 6, the question was asked whether the students owned any of the digital game tools such as computers, tablets, and mobile phones, 141 of them had a "Mobile Phone", 24 of them had a "Tablet", and 13 of them had a "Computer"., and 3 of them did not have any of these tools.

*Table 5. Answers to "How do you evaluate your school success?" by the students participating in the research*

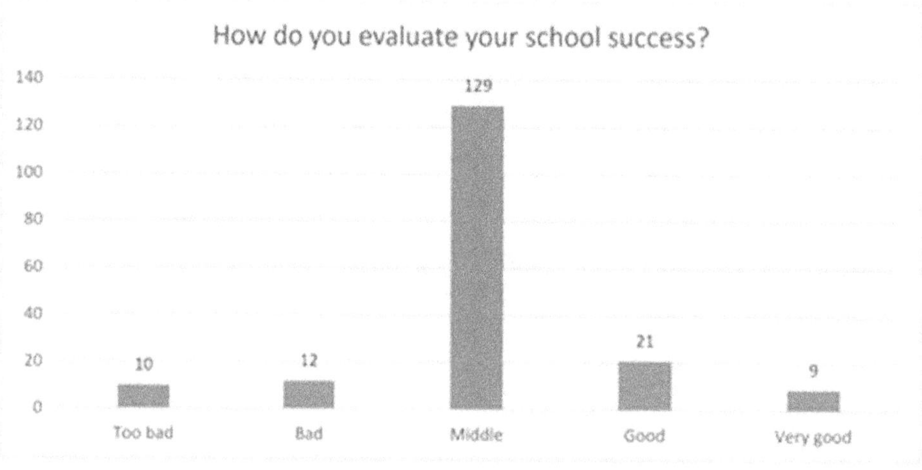


*Table 6. Answers to "Which of the following digital game tools do you have?"*

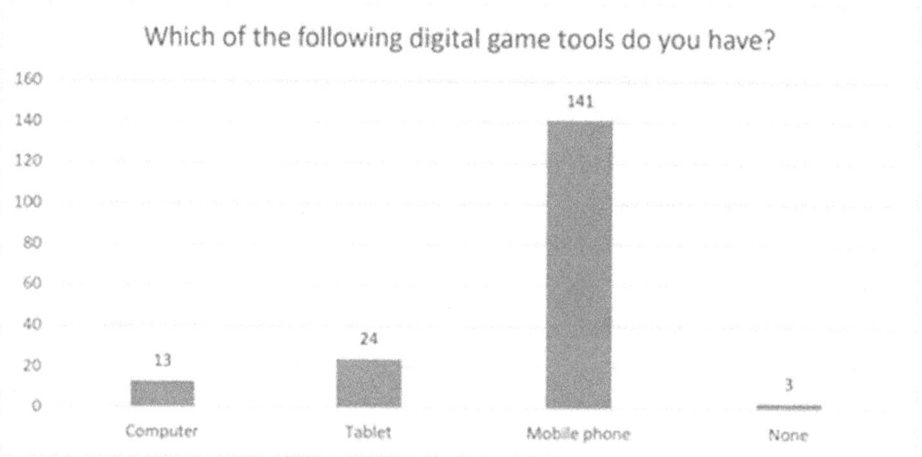


In Table 7, 114 answered "Medium", 42 "Low", and 25 "High" to the question of their families' income levels.

Do you have a room of your own directed to the students in Table 7 It is seen that 126 of them answered "No" and 55 of them "Yes" to the question.

When the survey study was evaluated, the students who participated in the research said, "I don't feel alone when I play." "3.86" to the question, "It is very important for me to be successful in the game." "3.75" to the question, "I play games to get away from the stress of daily life." "3.56" to the question, "I prefer playing games to spending time with my friends physically." It seems that they answered the question of **"Strongly Agree"** with an average of "3.24".

*Table 7. Answers to "How do you evaluate the income level of your family?"*

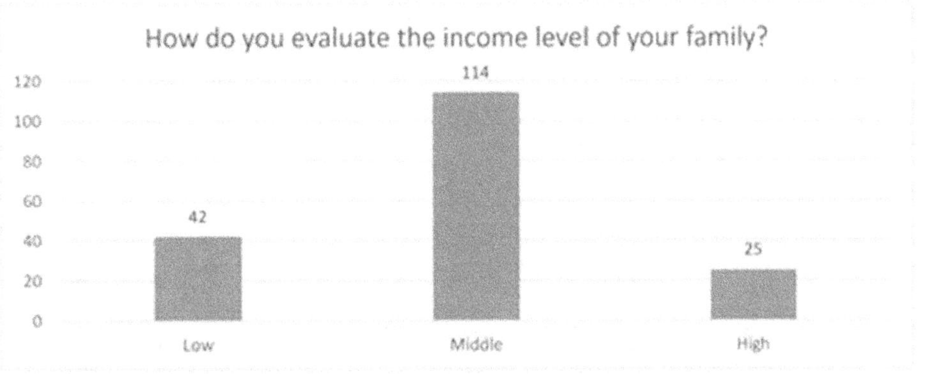


*Table 8. "Do you have a room of your own?"*

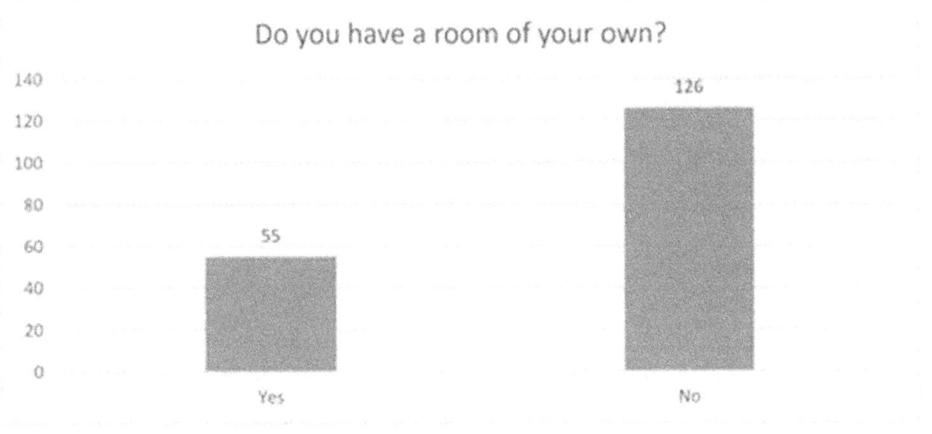


In Table 9, the students stated, "I discuss the time I spend in the game with the people close to me (such as family members, friends)." "2.99" to his question, "I postpone my bedtime to reach my goal in the game." "2.93" to the question, "Have you thought of playing a computer game all day?" "2.91" to the question, "I would like to play and finish the newly released games before my friends." "2.87" to his question, "I am increasing the time I spend for the game." "2.84" to the question, "I feel bad when you can't play." It is stated that they answered the question "2.81" to the question "I usually eat my meal in front of the computer" and **"I agree"** with an average of "2.77" to the question.

In addition, in the table, the students stated, "I neglect other important activities (such as school, work, sports) for playing games." and "I spend less time physically with my friends because I play digital games." It is seen that they gave the answer **"I am undecided"** with an average of "2.26" to their questions.

*Table 9. Digital game behavior orientations of students. In the evaluation made using a 5-point Likert scale, it was coded as Strongly Disagree 0, Disagree 1, Undecided 2, Agree 3 and Strongly Agree 4.*

| | | Average | Standard Deviation |
|---|---|---|---|
| 1 | Have you thought about playing a video game all day long? | 2.91 | 0.63 |
| 2 | I'm gradually increasing the time I spend on the game. | 2.84 | 0.55 |
| 3 | I play games to get away from the stress of daily life. | 3.56 | 0.19 |
| 4 | I feel bad when you can't play games. | 2.81 | 0.21 |
| 5 | I discuss with people close to me (such as family members, friends) about the time I spend in the game. | 2.99 | 0.78 |
| 6 | I neglect other important activities (such as school, work, sports) to play games. | 2.26 | 0.33 |
| 7 | I would like to play and finish the new games before my friends. | 2.87 | 0.78 |
| 8 | Being successful in the game is very important to me. | 3.75 | 0.09 |
| 9 | I don't feel alone when I play games. | 3.86 | 0.11 |
| 10 | I postpone my bedtime to reach my goal in the game. | 2.93 | 0.43 |
| 11 | I spend less time physically with my friends because I play digital games. | 2.26 | 1.01 |
| 12 | I prefer playing games to spending time with my friends physically. | 3.24 | 0.73 |
| 13 | I usually eat my meal at the computer. | 2.77 | 0.94 |

## RESULT

Digital tools and applications within the scope of digital media have become an integral part of daily life as of today. In this context, both in terms of prevalence and duration of use, digital media tools can cause some negative effects on all individuals in general and on children and young people in particular. It is important to eliminate the negative effects of these tools and practices, which have an impact on our lives if they are used correctly, especially on children and young people, in terms of eliminating some physical and social problems.

Along with the developing and advancing technology day by day, the way individuals have fun, receive news, communicate and socialize has also changed. Especially the Z generation youth and children have started to spend almost their entire lives in front of virtual screens thanks to technological devices such as phones, tablets and computers. The Internet has both positive and negative sides, and these negative aspects are often not noticed by many. Internet and technology used outside the control of parents lead to many negative consequences. After the development of technology and the internet, new concepts have emerged, some of which are; It can be exemplified as computer addiction, internet addiction and game addiction. Although game addiction is very high especially for young and child users, it is possible to see game addiction symptoms in adults as well. When internet addiction is considered, it can be said that one of the most obvious factors triggering this is digital game addiction. Internet addiction and digital game addiction often progress in parallel with each other. In this sense, there is a strong relationship between internet addiction and digital game addiction, which are in the category of behavioral addictions.

There is a need for multidimensional studies that include variables such as school, family, friends and expert staff in the preparation of protective and preventive studies on digital game addiction and in determining the possible risk and protective factors related to this addiction area. In fact, the risk factors of internet and digital game addiction are sometimes related to environmental factors such as social support, and sometimes to internal factors such as self-esteem or psychological resilience. This proves to us the versatility of the risk factors of this type of addiction. Studies on internet or game addiction in the past years also confirm the versatility of the risk and protective factors of this type of addiction.

The students stated, "I don't feel alone when I play games.", "I prefer playing games to spending time with my friends physically." and "Have you thought of playing a video game all day?" Answering the question "Strongly Agree" and "Agree" with a high average results in the result that they see digital tools and digital games as a friend and feel like they are spending time with a human being. It is a fact that choosing a virtual game or a digital tool as a friend instead of a real friend will push them away from society and become lonely. As a result, it is inevitable that individuals who are asocial and unable to keep up with the society are formed.

Students say, "I discuss the time I spend in the game with people close to me (such as family members, friends)." The answers given to the question **"I agree"** show that children who play digital games for long periods of time take harsh attitudes towards people who will restrict them about the games they play. This can cause children to exhibit aggressive behavior towards their parents and their environment.

"I want to play and finish new games before my friends.", "I feel bad when I can't play games.", "I postpone my bedtime to reach my goal in the game." and "I am increasing the time I spend playing the game." **"I agree"** answers to their questions show that students spend time and effort to play digital games and this situation is increasing gradually. Therefore, it is thought that they spend their time in front of digital tools that they would spend on traveling, having fun and learning new things, and this situation is inconvenient in terms of both physical and mental health.

It is a fact that the answer of **"I agree"** given to the question "I usually eat my meal in front of the computer" and the fact that students eat at the computer and turn it into a habit is an unhealthy situation and will lead to some nutritional disorders.

It consists of 200 high school students studying in Istanbul Esenyurt district. However, considering the possible shortcomings, 181 students participated in the survey. These students were excluded from the study due to the incomplete filling of the data collection tools by 19 students.

Considering the findings of our study; The Educational Status of the Mothers of the students participating in the research has 125 high school education, and the Educational Status of the Fathers has 98 high school education. Which of the digital game tools do you have? The result obtained from the answers given to the question is the mobile phone with 141.

How do you evaluate the income level of your family?" The answers given to the question were 114, including that they were at a moderate level. "Do you have a room of your own?" It is seen that 126 of them answered "No" to the question. When we look at the digital game behavior orientations of the students, the first rank is "3.86" and "I don't feel alone when I play games." It turns out that they chose their question.

In addition, according to the results of the research, the general and all sub-dimensions of the Digital Game Addiction Scale do not differ significantly according to gender, grade level and school success.

Again, the answer to the question "I prefer playing games to spending time with my friends physically.", "3.24", "I discuss the time I spend in the game with the people close to me (such as family members, friends).", "2.99" The answer to the question "I postpone my sleep time to reach my goal in the game", "2.93", "I gradually increase the time I spend on the game", the answer to the question "2.84" reveals the result that the average children are addicted to digital games as an indicator of digital addiction.

## FUTURE RESEARCH DIRECTIONS

This study has been prepared to include high school students. The extent and cause of digital game addiction can be investigated for students studying in primary and secondary education, and then a comparison can be made. Within the scope of this study, gender, family income, school, class, etc. Digital game addiction was investigated on the variables. A digital game addiction can be examined with different variables. This research is limited to the Esenyurt district of Istanbul province. Digital game addiction research can be done and compared in different provinces and districts. The effects of digital game addiction can be investigated. Conferences can be organized for parents on digital game addiction and social media use in schools. This type of research can be done for every school and guidance services in schools can take action within the scope of the results.

All segments of society should be made aware of digital tools and applications. The society should be made aware that digital tools and applications are not only a means of leisure, games and entertainment, but can also be used for the purpose of obtaining information and helping lessons. In schools, students, teachers and parents should be informed about digital addiction and their awareness should be raised. Educational authorities should measure the digital addiction levels of students and expert support should be provided to students with high addiction levels. Courses that teach the necessary behaviors for the conscious use of digital tools and applications at all levels of education should be offered or included in the curricula of related courses.

In addition, education support should be given to young people on digital games, which started with digital addiction and turned into negativities such as game addiction. The digital game industry is one of the fastest growing industries with the contribution of dynamic and creative young people. In order to meet the need for trained/competent manpower in order to get a significant share in international markets, our children and youth at all levels, starting from primary school, should receive a good education and all kinds of technical/technological support should be provided. Considering Turkey's young population potential, we need to take quick steps knowing that we are in a very privileged position to develop competence in this regard.

## REFERENCES

Ağır, M. (2018). *Ergenlerde psikolojik sağlamlık, okul tükenmişliği ve internet bağımlılığı üzerine.*

Akbulut, Y. (2013). Çocuk ve ergenlerde bilgisayar kullanımının gelişimsel sonuçları. *Trakya Üniversitesi Eğitim Fakültesi Dergisi*, *3*(2), 53–68.

Arısoy, Ö. (2009). İnternet bağımlılığı ve tedavisi. Psikiyatride Güncel Yaklaşımlar Dergisi, *1*(1), 55-67. https://core.ac.uk/download/pdf/26663761.pdf

Banyai, F., Griffiths, M. D., Kiraly, O., & Demetrovics, Z. (2018). The psychology of esports: A systematic literature review. *Journal of Gambling Studies*, *35*(2), 351–364. doi:10.100710899-018-9763-1 PMID:29508260

BİNARK. (2008). Mutlu ve Günseli Bayraktutan-Sütcü Kültür Endüstrisi Ürünü Olarak Dijital Oyun.

Çavuş, S., & Ayhan, B. ve Tuncer, M. (2016). Bilgisayar Oyunları ve Bağımlılık: Üniversite Öğrencileri Üzerine Bir Alan Araştırması. İletişim Kuram ve Araştırma Dergisi. Gazi Üniversitesi. *Sayı, 43*, 266.

Çetin, C. ve Karalar, S. (2016). X, Y ve Z Kuşağı Öğrencilerin Çok Yönlü Ve Sınırsız Kariyer Algıları Üzerine Bir Araştırma. *Yönetim Bilimleri Dergisi, 14*(28), 157–197.

Charlton, J. P., & Danforth, I. D. W. (2007). Distinguishing addiction and high engagement in the context of online game playing. *Computers in Human Behavior, 23*(3), 1531–1548. doi:10.1016/j.chb.2005.07.002

Chatfield, T. (2013). Dijital Çağa Nasıl Uyum Sağlarız. (Çev. ve Haz.: L. Konca), İstanbul.

Esen, E., & Siyez, D. M. (2011). An Investigation of Psycho-Social Variables in Predicting Internet Addiction Among Adolescents. *Türk Psikolojik Danışma ve Rehberlik Dergisi, 4*(36), 127–138.

Griffiths, M. (2000). Does ınternet and computer "addiction" exist? Some case study evidence. *Cyberpsychology & Behavior, 3*(2), 211–219. doi:10.1089/109493100316067

Griffiths, M. D. (2008). *Internet and Video-Game Addiction. Adolescent Addiction: Epidemiology, Assessment and Treatment*. Academic Press.

Gülbetekin, E., Güven, E., & Tuncel, O. (2021). Adolesanların Dijital Oyun Bağımlılığı ile Fiziksel Aktivite Tutum ve Davranışlarını Etkileyen Faktörler. *Bağimlik Dergisi, 22*(2), 148–160. doi:10.51982/bagimli.866578

Günüç, S. & ve Kayri, M. (2010). *Türkiye'de internet bağımlılık profili ve internet bağımlılık ölçeğinin geliştirilmesi: Geçerlik güvenirlik çalışması.* Hacettepe Üniversitesi Eğitim Fakültesi Dergisi, (39), 220-232. https://dergipark.org.tr/tr/pub/hunefd/issue/7799/102177 adresinden erişilmiştir.

Gürcan, A., & Özhan, S., & ve Uslu, R. (2008). Dijital oyunlar ve çocuklar üzerindeki etkileri. Ankara: T.C. Başbakanlık Aile ve Sosyal Araştırmalar Genel Müdürlüğü

Hazar, Z., & ve Hazar, M. (2019). Üniversite Öğrencileri İçin Dijital Oyun Bağımlılığı Ölçeği (Uyarlama Çalışması). *Journal of Sport Sciences Researches, 4*(2).

Hazar, Z., Hazar, M., Hazar, M., & Hazar, M. (2017). Digital Game Addiction Scale for Children Çocuklar İçin Dijital Oyun Bağımlılığı Ölçeği. *International Journal of Human Sciences, 14*(1), 203–216. doi:10.14687/jhs.v14i1.4387

Horzum, M. B., Ayas, T., & Çakır, Ö. B. (2008). Çocuklar için bilgisayar oyun bağımlılığı. *Türk Psikolojik Danışma ve Rehberlik Dergisi, 30*, 76–88.

Jiang, J., Phalp, K. T., & Ali, R. (2015). *Digital addiction: Gamification for precautionary and recovery requirements.* Bourne Mouth. http://eprints.bournemouth.ac.uk/21887/1/04-Posters.pdf

Kirriemuir, J. (2002). Video gaming, education and digital learning technologies. *The Magazine Of Digital Library Research, 8*(2).

Kneer, J., Rieger, D., Ivory, J. D., & Ferguson, C. (2014). Awareness of risk factors for digital game addiction: Interviewing players and counselors. *International Journal of Mental Health and Addiction, 12*(5), 585–599. doi:10.100711469-014-9489-y

Lemmens, J. S., Valkenburg, P. M., & Peter, J. (2009). Development and Validation of A Game Addiction Scale For Adolescents. *Media Psychology, 12*(1), 77–95. doi:10.1080/15213260802669458

Metin, S., & Kızıldağ, D. (2017). Kuşakların Kariyer Beklentilerinin Farklılaşması: Otomotiv Sektöründe Bir Araştırma. *Mustafa Kemal Üniversitesi Sosyal Bilimler Enstitüsü Dergisi, 14*(40), 340–363.

Nazlıgül, Denizci, M., Baş, S., Akyüz, Z. & Yorulmaz, O. (2018). İnternette oyun oynama bozukluğu ve tedavi yaklaşımları: Sistematik bir gözden geçirme. Addicta. *The Turkish Journal on Addictions, 5*, 13–35.

Sağlam, M., & Topsümer, F. (2019). Dijital oyunlar ve öznel iyi oluş ilişkisi: Muğla Sıtkı Koçman Üniversitesi örneği. *Humanities Sciences, 4*(2), 31–50.

Şahin, C. ve Tuğrul, V. M. (2012). İlköğretim öğrencilerinin bilgisayar oyunu bağımlılık düzeylerinin incelenmesi. *Journal of World of Turks, 4*(3), 115–130.

Tavşancıl, E. (2014). *Tutumların ölçülmesi ve SPSS ile veri analizi*. Nobel Yayın Dağıtım.

Uğurlu, T. T., Şengül, C., & Şengül, C. (2012). Bağımlılık Psikofarmakolojisi. *Psikiyatride Güncel Yaklasimlar, 4*(1), 37–50. doi:10.5455/cap.20120403

Yengin, D. (2019). Teknoloji bağımlılığı olarak dijital bağımlılık. The Turkish Online Journal of Design, Art and Communication. *TOJDAC, 9*(2), 130-144. doi:10.7456/10902100/007

Young, K. S. (1999). Internet addiction: Evaluation and treatment. *Student BMJ, 7*, 351–352.

Young, K. S. (2009). Understanding Online Gaming Addiction and Treatment İssues For Adolescents. *The American Journal of Family Therapy, 37*(5), 355–372. doi:10.1080/01926180902942191

## ADDITIONAL READING

Allcott, H., & Gentzkow, M., & ve Song, L. (2021). Digital addiction (No. w28936). National Bureau of Economic Research.

Baş, M., Tarakçı, E., & İnci, A. Ramazan (2022). Dijitalleşme, İstanbul: Efe Akademik Yayıncılık, Çetin, E. Tanımlar ve temel kavramlar, Eğitsel dijital oyunlar. Ankara, Pegem Akademi.

Basu, R. (2019). Impact of Digital Detox on Individual Performance of the Employees. *Int. J. Res. Anal. Rev, 6*(2), 378–381.

Feindel, H. (2019). *İnternet Bağımlılığı, (Çev. Atilla Dirim)*. İletişim Yayınları.

Newport, C. (2019). *Dijital Minimalizm (C. Mavituna çev.)*. Metropolis Yayıncılık.

Sayar, K., & Benli, S. (2020). *Dijital çocuk*. Kapı Yayınları.

Yalcin, S., & Bertiz, Y. (2019). Qualitative Study on the Effects of Game Addiction on University Students. *Sci Educ Art Technol J., 3*(1), 27–34.

## KEY TERMS AND DEFINITION

**Addiction:** Desire for an entity or object cannot stop oneself even though it negatively affects one's life.

**Digital Addiction:** It is a behavioral disorder that occurs as a result of excessive attachment to virtual reality on mobile devices. The factors that make the individual addicted have changed over time. The continuous development of technology has revealed the concept of "digital dependent individual".

**Digital Communication:** It is the structure that allow people to communicate and exchange data with each other through computers, people with machines via computers, and machines directly with machines over networks.

**Digital Game Addiction:** It is excessive and extremely prolonged digital game playing behavior. Progressive loss of control, increased play time, and various withdrawal symptoms are typical for excessive gaming. People can be irritable and reactive in a situation that prevents them from playing games. Digital game addiction can cause inability to concentrate, sleep and nutrition problems, academic, familial and social problems, eye diseases, inactivity and accordingly obesity and various diseases affecting the skeletal-muscular system.

**Digital Game:** It is the display of the result that occurs as a result of the interaction of the player with their devices, through the screen display system. Therefore, in the past, digital games; Also called video games or computer games.

**Digital Loneliness:** In digital loneliness, which is defined as the new form of loneliness, while individuals try to take more part in digital environments and socialize in the digital world in order to avoid their emotional loneliness, the probability of their socialization in real life to be damaged more increases and digital loneliness can be defined as a growing social problem. The fact that individuals feel inadequate, and unhappiness is both a matter of depression and means peace for them.

**Leisure management:** Leisure management is the process of planning, organizing, directing, coordinating, and controlling the leisure time activities of individuals.

**Netlessphobia:** Netlessphobia is one of the 3 psychological disorders caused by the digital age. Although there is not enough information in the literature yet, it is quite common especially in the Z generation. In addition to this disease, which is also known as the fear of being without the Internet, nomophobia and fomo diseases are also seen. For those who meet the digital age later, namely digital immigrants, the internet means freedom.

# Chapter 24
# Digital Game Addiction and Children

**Shilpa Elza Sebastian**
*CHRIST University (Deemed), India*

**Derik George**
*CHRIST University (Deemed), India*

**S. Girish**
*CHRIST University (Deemed), India*

## ABSTRACT

*Nowadays the usage of digital games has increased a lot. Console games, PC games, and online games are all examples of digital games. Aside from these, it has been observed that digital games are also played with portable technologies such as mobile phones and tablets. Children's play equipment, play habits, and play perceptions have all changed as a result of these changes. As a result, digital games have a significant influence on children. This chapter focuses on the effects of digital games on children and how children became addicted to digital games. It also discusses how to avoid overusing digital games. It also explains the meaning of digital games and discusses their history and future.*

## INTRODUCTION

Technology is an essential part of everyone's life, and it has changed everyone's perspective on many issues. As technology advanced, it paved the way for many other technological aspects, such as YouTube, digital or online games, and so on. In this chapter, we will discuss digital game addiction and children. There are numerous resources available on the Internet. We can get as much information as we want with just one click. The Internet has created a new playground where anyone, regardless of where they are, can meet at any time. It has paved the way for online games, to which we are addicted, particularly children. There is a question here. Are children truly addicted to digital games? If so, what are the reasons?

DOI: 10.4018/978-1-6684-8397-8.ch024

Before we get to that, let's define digital games. A digital game is played using digital technology. It is a form of electronic stimulation that can be both educational and entertaining. Any type of electronic game is considered a digital game. A game is a type of entertainment that includes competitive or role-playing elements. It allows humans and technology to interact. We now understand what digital games are. The following section discusses the distinction between physical and online games. If we're talking about differences, there are many to discuss. In physical games, we must be physically present on the field or in the stadium where we compete, whereas in online games, participants can be anywhere and compete with each other. Which is the best practice? In my opinion. Physical games are always preferable because they promote more interaction between people. But, as we all know, humans go around doing simple things. So, half of the population is addicted to digital games, which are easily accessible if we have a smartphone or a laptop. According to various studies, digital games play an important role in the lives of everyone, particularly children.

## HISTORY OF DIGITAL GAMES

Gaming has grown from a technological oddity at a science fair in the 1950s to one of the world's most profitable entertainment industries. Dr. Edward Uhler Condon unveiled the first known example of a game machine at the New York World's Fair in 1940. The game, based on the ancient mathematical game of Nim, was played by approximately 50,000 people during its six-month run, with the computer reportedly winning more than 90% of the games (Chikhani, 2015).

The practice of playing games online is not new. It has been around since the earliest indoor sports, only taking different forms. Digital gaming has developed over time into a stand-alone sector with tremendous creative and employment potential. In terms of their historical development (1940–1960), video games have their roots in attempts to create artificial intelligence. Video games have advanced alongside hardware and software developments from the earliest ENIAC computer to the potent microprocessors of today. It is challenging to identify the first video game ever made because of this. Any number of long-forgotten puzzles, arcade and card games, and/or military sims could be competitors for the title of first video game. However, the first widely played commercial video game was Nimrod, which appeared in 1951. At the same time, William Higinbotham's pioneering "Tennis for Two" (1958) and IBM's well-known "Checkers game programme" (the 1950s) became well-known. (*A Brief History of Digital Gaming*, 2014).

Next is the Nascent stage (1960 - 1990), Steve Russell, an MIT employee, created 'Spacewar,' the game that is widely regarded as the first widely available and influential computer game, in 1960. In 1972, Nolan Bushnell founded Atari, Inc. and took the first steps towards commercializing the digital gaming industry. Soon after, Atari released the widely popular 'Pong' game. In 1983, the video game market crashed, bankrupting several companies in the United States that produced home computers and video game consoles. Between 1978 and 1990, the arcade industry was at its peak. Taito's 'Space Invaders' was such a success that it inspired a slew of video game companies to enter the market. During this formative period, evergreen computer and arcade games such as 'Pac-Man' and 'Donkey Kong' were introduced (*A Brief History of Digital Gaming*, 2014).

At last, the recovery of the video game market during The Golden Years (1990–2010) led to the emergence of new players in the sector. The "Super NES," Nintendo's next-generation platform, was released in 1990. Sega responded with its own 'Sonic the Hedgehog' using similar 16-bit technology.

From 1991 onwards, PC gaming gained popularity. First-person shooter online multiplayer possibilities were invented by Id Software's 1996 release of "Quake." Its 64-bit device, the Nintendo 64, debuted in 1996. During this time, Sony Corporation, with the help of the well-known PlayStation, started to rule the market. In 2002, Nintendo revealed the GameCube, the company's flagship product. The GameCube utilised 80mm mini-DVD discs with 1.4GB of data each, which is more than 200 times the size of the largest N64 cartridge ROM. Microsoft simultaneously joined the bandwagon with the now-famous Xbox. Mobile phones also rose to prominence as console devices during this time (*A Brief History of Digital Gaming*, 2014).

## FUTURE OF ONLINE GAMING

The digital gaming market has grown dramatically in recent years as a result of the quick development of internet, mobile, and other downloadable games for hardware consoles. Approximately $63 billion of the overall market for digital media is made up of the digital gaming industry. The sector is expected to expand in the upcoming years, according to emerging trends such game live streaming and e-Sports competitions. Mobile games dominate the digital gaming market, which should come as no surprise given that 60% of people worldwide own a smart device and that nearly 50% spend more than 5 hours every day using one. The worldwide market for mobile games hit $40 billion in 2017, which is still more than the whole market for console games sold online and for download. In addition, by the end of 2022, mobile gaming is predicted to grow by 27% (*The Future of Digital Gaming - ADK INSIGHTS Inspiration*, n.d.).

It seems as though the video game industry has a bright future. New monetization methods are taking off, consumer demand is rising, and technology is developing swiftly. Over the next five years, worldwide game income may rise by more than 50%, according to Bain's study. In addition, gamers are significantly more prevalent than other consumers in the metaverse, a collection of virtual worlds. The gaming industry's growth is being accelerated by the high level of involvement of younger players (13 to 17 years old), who play video games more than any other media, such as social, music, and television, by a margin of almost 40%. More time will be spent playing augmented and virtual reality games, watching e-sports, and spending more time in virtual worlds by younger players than slightly older gamers (18-34 years old). They feel more at ease in virtual environments, and nearly half of them would rather play a game with their friends than meet in person (Christofferson et al., 2022).

Nowadays, the gaming industry is rapidly expanding. Children are more addicted to digital games than adults. What will happen to the younger generation if they become severely addicted to it? Will this situation be resolved, or will it continue?

## TRENDS IN DIGITAL GAMES

While people have long enjoyed sports and adventure video games from the comfort of their homes, we can now participate in activities beyond lone or couch play through scheduled events with competitors around the world thanks to online accessibility. Video games have advanced significantly from their early, pixelated era and are today immensely popular with thousands of real-time players. Visual advancements and other elements are closely tied to technological advancements that allow for the deployment of more resource-intensive processes (Neal, 2023).

People's preference for mobile gaming has been influenced by technological advancements like immersive technologies (AR, VR, MR). The enormous increase in 3D game production, on the other hand, is primarily due to the popularity of streaming video games (Guide, n.d.). In the modern period, many different trends are evolving. These are:

- AR and VR:

Virtual and physical elements are combined in augmented reality (AR). This technology is appropriate for both desktops and mobile devices. The capability it provides to reflect digital elements in the physical world is what distinguishes it. A computer-generated simulation is virtual reality. This implies that reality or an alternate world is graphically constructed. The user can get completely immersed in the digital environment with the right hardware (*Augmented Reality (AR) Vs Virtual Reality (VR) | The Difference Explained*, 2022).

- Cross - Platform Gaming Trends:

Software that works with many operating systems is referred to as cross-platform. The terms "cross-platform" and "cross-play" must be familiar to anyone who participates in the gaming community. It alludes to programmes and games that work with different operating systems. This feature aids users in bridging the gaps between various systems, such as those of game consoles, laptops, mobile devices, and others. Users should make sure they are using software with cross-platform functionality for a variety of reasons. File compatibility is the most crucial factor to take into account while utilizing software. If one operating system only accepts a certain file format, you might want to convert it into a format that is supported by a number of operating systems (*Explained: What Is Cross-Platform Gaming and How Is It Useful for Gamers*, 2022).

- Competitive Multiplayer Mobile Gaming:

Participants directly compete with one another in "Player Versus Player" games, as well as maybe with characters that the computer is controlling. Teams of players may be formed. Fighting games, sports games, racing games, party games, puzzle games, and any other online game often offer a single-player (or co-op) "main game" option as well. (*Competitive Multiplayer*, n.d.). There are various types of competitive multiplayer mobile games like Clash Royale, Team fight tactics, etc.

- Fitness Gaming:

Exergaming, often known as fitness gaming, is more than just a fad. Technology has evolved in such a way that the fun of gaming is now combined with the practical requirement to exercise for maintaining and enhancing health. Fitness equipment creators, however, had broader goals in mind than having people peddle virtual bicycles and hop around on mats in a repetitive manner for an eternity. I came to the conclusion that in order to be fully engaged, both gamers and fitness fanatics needed attainable objectives, challenges, and hurdles to accomplish. The need for choice and control, however, increased along with the technology in fitness games. A one-size-fits-all manufacturing model was no longer used to create fitness games. Exercise and videogames were customized to each user's preferences, providing them the freedom to choose the routes that work best for them while maintaining an intuitive interface (McFerren, 2012).

- Esports:

Electronic sports, or "esports," is a term for competition involving video games. Esports are frequently planned, multiplayer video game contests between professional players, either individually or in teams. Despite the fact that organised competitions have long been a feature of the video game culture, until the late 2000s, the majority of these were primarily between amateur players. Since then, professional gamers' participation and live streaming of these events have experienced a significant increase in popularity. By the 2010s, esports had a substantial impact on the video game business. A number of game companies were actively involved in designing and supporting tournaments and other events (Stout, n.d.).

- Metaverse Gaming:

The term "metaverse" refers to a shared, persistent, immersive, three-dimensional virtual environment that combines the physical and digital worlds and allows users to interact in real time while shopping, working, playing, and hanging out (Koss, n.d.). An enormously large-scale and interoperable network of real-time rendered 3D virtual worlds that an almost infinite number of users can experience simultaneously and persistently with a consistent sense of presence and continuity of data, including identity, history, entitlements, objects, communications, and payments (Ball, 2022).

These are the few video game trends that are expected to grow in popularity over the next several years.

## DIGITAL GAMES AND CHILDREN

Various research has found that playing video games offers several advantages for kids, even the youngest ones. Digital gaming of a certain kind can enhance education and foster digital skills. Digital games can also help preschoolers and adolescents raise "executive function," including impulse control and working memory. In spite of the fact that they are no less significant, several additional advantages of digital play are much less frequently highlighted as justifications for playing games online. Children can interact with their families, friends, and peers through digital play. Growing data also shows that playing video games on a computer or other digital device can bring children and their families joy and comfort, especially during trying times (Scott, 2022).

Spending time playing with children or talking to them about the digital games they enjoy can promote their social and emotional growth and help them acquire skills. Young children's play and creativity in particular are supported by digital games that promote parental involvement, according to research. It has been demonstrated that different game design features enable a variety of play styles and beneficial consequences for kids. Five digital games dominate the list that we can play along with the children (Scott, 2022). They are as follows:

## Just Dance Series (Ubisoft):

This game is primarily beneficial for physical activity. This game can be played with both friends and family. Just Dance is a platform where players can learn and perform various dance moves and routines by watching screen demonstrations. It is available on several platforms. The primary goal of this game is to get children moving. It also encourages kids to spend more time with their families and friends. Another important aspect is that it assists children in maintaining their attention skills. In kids mode, this is primarily for children aged 10 or younger (Scott, 2022).

## Little Red Coding Club (Twinkl):

This game improves computational thinking skills and also aids in critical thinking. It is an exploratory game. This game is intended primarily for children aged 4 to 8. This game is available for both Apple and Android devices. Children use basic coding skills and knowledge to get Little Red Riding Hood and other familiar fairytale characters to Grandma's house safely by guiding them through an immersive 3D forest. According to recent research, young children learn how to create and debug simple algorithms fast because to Little Red Coding Club's usage of augmented reality technology (Scott, 2022).

## Animal Crossing: New Horizons (Nintendo)

This game promotes relaxation and is a social activity. This game is appropriate for children aged 3 and up. More people are becoming aware of how social growth can be aided by digital games. Animal Crossing: New Horizons, a game that was popular during the pandemic, lets kids progressively create a fanciful island paradise with a fully customisable avatar and a variety of odd neighbours. By visiting other kids' islands, children may interact safely online thanks to Nintendo's safety safeguards. The popularity of video games among kids encourages social connection through online and offline fan communities (Scott, 2022).

## Minecraft (Mojang Studios)/LEGO Worlds (Warner Bros.):

This game promotes creativity. It is both an open-ended game and a social play. This game is primarily intended for children aged 7 and up. Minecraft and LEGO Worlds are open-ended construction games with numerous ways to play and few or no fixed goals. The open-ended games and creativity have been related (Scott, 2022).

## Dora and Friends (Nickelodeon):

This game is good for representation and it helps in multimodal story creation. The game is mainly for children aged 5 and above. Players can build own characters in Dora and Friends, select music, photos, and backgrounds, and record their voices before mixing various scenarios to produce a story. The components in this combination referred to as multimodal story creation, and it helps children develop their literacy skills. Children can play as characters who look like them in Dora and Friends. Because digital play has the potential to help children develop their identities, having characters who are similar to them is critical. Even if the children's media sector clearly needs to do more, games that merely let kids design or play as characters that resemble them are a good place to start (Scott, 2022).

Digital games are used differently and have varied meanings in different households, even if the five games mentioned above contain design aspects that support a variety of benefits for kids. A digital game does not need to be well designed or instructive to provide enjoyable and meaningful play experiences for kids and their families (Scott, 2022).

The games listed above are primarily for small children aged 4 to 10. These are not dangerous games. Even if the children become addicted, it will not harm them. However, many other digital games are extremely dangerous to play. They, too, can end their lives. The blue whale was one of the most well-known and dangerous games. These games were primarily enjoyed by young children and teenagers aged 18 and up. Children used to believe everything that happened in the game and live in it.

Children were willing to go to any length to play these types of digital games. They, too, were not afraid to fight or even kill their loved ones. They were also prepared to commit suicide. Why did these actions take place on the part of children? Is it because the parents have given their children too much freedom? This demonstrates that digital games have both positive and negative aspects.

## DIGITAL GAME ADDICTION

Computers and world wide web have made life easier in many ways but at the same time, these tools are widely used for gaming and other entertainment activities. In simple terms, digital games are those games that are played with the assistance of computers or any other electronic device. The development of new technologies and the lack of safe places for children to play in cities due to rapid urbanization leads to the replacement of digital games with conventional games. (Irmak & Erdogan, 2015). This eventually will lead to gaming addiction, particularly among children.

Digital gaming addiction is a situation when you lose control over your gaming habits and leads to negative consequences in many aspects of your life including relationships and self-care. Gaming addiction is being engaged in gaming constantly in mind and playing games for a very long time neglecting all the day-to-day activities. (Altun & Atasoy, 2018).According to American Psychiatric Association, gaming addiction was considered an Internet Gaming Disorder. (Irmak & Erdogan, 2015).In recent years the number of people seeking treatments in Psychiatric clinics for problems caused by digital games has increased. This also increased the demand for family support. The current trend suggests that medical professionals including psychiatrists, pediatricians, and people who are focusing on social issues will be witnessing an increase in demand for treatment for digital gaming addiction. (Irmak & Erdogan, 2015). If a person is not able to control his desire to be engaged in digital gaming then it should be considered an issue.

Video games similarly affect the brain just as any other drugs. Digital games trigger the release of dopamine, which would reinforce human behavior and because of this playing these video games can lead to addictive behavior among people. Neurotransmitter and hormone, dopamine has both functions. This hormone promotes happiness. Your happiness depends on it in a big way. They have a close connection to our brain's reward system. We will therefore be more receptive to incentives the more dopamine our bodies produce. For example, Battlegrounds Mobile India was one of the most awaited games in the past year. Given that PUBG's predecessor in India had 50 million active users, pre-registrations in the Google play store were surging. The number of kills that a person is earning in PUBG will increase his dopamine level and that is one of the reasons why these youngsters are playing it day and night. (Why Do We Play PUBG Day-Night? What Are Its Psychological Underpinnings? 2021)

One of the other reasons for digital gaming addiction is variable schedule reward. There is an experiment that was done by B.F Skinner. This test was easy to conduct. Skinner's boxes A and B, which he built separately, were made by him. Box A. The box was stuffed with a rat or a bird. Rats can acquire food from the food dispenser by pulling a lever. When the rat pulls the lever in box A, it always receives food; however, in box B, the food is only delivered randomly. The rat in box B will pull the lever so often checking when it will be provided with food. This experiment is relevant to digital game addiction. If you are having success, the algorithm of the game will automatically place you with a high-level player, which will make it much harder for you to finish the mission or reach the objective. The opposite will happen if you are going on a losing streak. This algorithm will ensure that the rewards are unpredictable which will motivate you to play the game over and over again and this can lead to addiction. (Why Do We Play PUBG Day-Night? What Are Its Psychological Underpinnings? 2021)

There are certain mis-consumptions related to digital gaming addiction. Firstly, it is very important to understand that the amount of time spent playing a game does not indicate an addiction. Someone might be spending a lot of time playing a game just because he/she enjoys playing that game. A person can spend a lot of time playing a game and still stop it without any difficulty. On the other hand, a person is said to be addicted to digital games when they cannot stop playing a game even if they know they should stop it. A person is said to be addicted when he starts to show certain withdrawal symptoms. They are aware that video game is tempting them to neglect their parents, friends, and their social life.

Digital games are not just for entertainment. They can act as a useful ground for collecting scientific data as well as for entertainment purposes. Sea Hero Quest, for instance, is a smartphone game. The game serves as an experiment in this virtual lab. Players are given a task to memorize a map and navigate a virtual fishing boat through the waterways and visit a set of buoys. Researchers at the University College London used the information to study how spatial navigation skills differ around the world (Irvine et al., 2019).

People often think that gaming disorder and gaming addiction are just the same. But gaming addiction and gaming disorder cannot be equated. According to the reports of the World Health Organization, gaming disorder cannot be considered just the same as gaming addiction. Gaming disorder does not satisfy any of the criteria such as withdrawal symptoms and tolerance issues by WHO to be considered an addiction.

People have concerns over whether these digital games are good or bad for the children. Some of them argue that this entirely depends on the content of the game. Many parents are complaining about the disinterest of children to learn and their desire to spend time playing games. This shows that computer games are quite powerful in motivating children and their interest to play them over and over again (Altun & Atasoy, 2018).

Social gaming involves playing games along with others. It can be either competitive or co-operative. In co-operative games the, two or more players play the video game on the same team with same goals. In competitive games, two or more players play against each other in a competitive manner (Halbrook, O'Donnell, & Msetf, 2019). There are two explanations for digital gaming addiction, either games operate on the same reward centers in the brain as drugs or those who are getting addicted to games are weak, unintelligent or actively pursue an addictive state (Elliott, Ream, & McGinsky, 2012).

## FACTORS ATTRACTING CHILDREN TO DIGITAL GAMING (WHY ARE YOUNG PEOPLE BECOMING INTERESTED IN ONLINE GAMING?)

Young children and teenagers aged 18 to 25 are becoming increasingly interested in online gaming. People are playing online games like PUBG, Battleground Mobile India (BGMI), Free Fire, and others. According to surveys conducted by private companies, before the first lockdown, approximately 21.5 million children and adolescents were drawn to online games, but after two years, approximately 51.5 million children and adolescents are playing online games for 5 to 12 hours per day (Jakhar, 2022).

In India, the Central Government should also work on ways to attract young people and children to physical games rather than online video games or video games, so that they can improve their mental and physical health. In China, the government has introduced rules and regulations for gaming companies stating that " Companies should prepare a software that allows children and youngsters to play digital games not more than 3 hours in a week". China did this so that children and teenagers who spend a lot of time in front of digital games or playing online games can spend their time with their parents or on their studies (Jakhar, 2022).

India should adopt this rule and regulation so that people who are drawn to gaming can improve their skills as well as their mental and physical health. It will also help to keep children and adolescents healthy. India is rapidly becoming the world's largest digital gaming market. Only the organizations profit from this. The Indian government, on the other hand, should put a stop to this as soon as possible (Jakhar, 2022).

Various examples show digital games are very dangerous as mentioned above. One of them is, there was news showing that in the first week of June, a 16-year-old boy shot his mother dead and kept her body in the same game he was playing for two days, while also threatening his younger sister. This occurred as a result of his mother prohibiting him from playing online games. So he gunned her down (Jakhar, 2022). He killed his mother and threatened his younger sister because his mother would not allow him to use the phone or play digital games. We can see from the preceding example that digital games are not only entertaining, but also dangerous to human lives. In this scenario, a question arises: if children become enraged and murder their parents, how can their future be bright?

## POSITIVE AND NEGATIVE IMPACTS OF DIGITAL GAMES

Digital games can have both positive and negative impacts on a person's behavior. Video games can create new chances to learn new behaviors and skills. It can also help people to develop pre-existing skills and behaviors. These changes can widely affect a teenager or an adolescent. The effect of video games varies from person to person depending upon how the content is displayed and interpreted in player's mind (Quwaider, Alabed, & Duwairi, 2019)

One of the studies says that digital game addiction can lead to anxiety, depression & over controlled behaviors also can lead to externalized issues like aggressive and hyperactive behaviors. The popularity of Massively Multiplayer Online Role-Playing Games led to some problems like anxiety and withdrawal. In many of the Massively Multiplayer Online Role Playing Games, people can choose virtual characters which are close to their real-life personalities. Reincarnation of some of these virtual characters can be reflected on the player's real personality in real life and this can lead to violence among the players, especially among adolescent people. For example, playing as a violent character in a game can increase the violent behavior among children (Quwaider, Alabed, & Duwairi, 2019).

The video game addiction can lead to internal behavior issues like depression and conduct issues. Also, the negative things that a person experiences in a video game will have close relationships with certain real-life issues. The violent video games can lead to certain external behavioral issues like aggressive behavior. The study also shows that people are trying to fulfill their real-life needs by accomplishing their needs in the game which is not a good sign (Quwaider, Alabed, & Duwairi, 2019).

One of the major negative effects of digital games is less sleep or poor sleep Hygiene. If you sleep for very less time then it will eventually lead to other issues. You won't be able to be focused in your day-to-day activities which will adversely affect your performance in various areas of life. Playing games during late nights particularly your gaming partners are from different time zones (Adair, n.d.)

Sometimes excessive gaming can lead to poor diet and dehydration. Dehydration can lead to various health issues like headaches. Poor diet will lead to muscle loss. If this poor diet continues for a longer period of time, it can lead to more severe health issues like cancer, bowel syndrome. You might forget to eat your meals three times a day and drink at least 2-3 liters of water because of your excessive gaming habits (Adair, n.d.)

Excessive gaming can lead to health issues like obesity and heart problems. Playing digital games excessively can lead to less physical activities and that can further lead to weight gain, muscle loss etc. Sitting in front of a device for the whole day can lead to chronic headaches and neck problems. Even though studies show that digital games are less likely to get affected with obesity, there are chances that players might get affected with issues like obesity. Obesity can lead to heart related problems. Studies show that 1% of all gamers will suffer from obesity (Adair, n.d.)

Playing digital games excessively can lead to suicidal thoughts. Individuals can experience suicidal tendencies while going through gaming addiction. Sometimes individuals start to play digital games due to depression and bullying but it can later lead to withdrawal from life. This can later lead to suicides (Adair, n.d.)

Excessive gaming can lead to low self-esteem which can lead to problems like social anxiety. Studies show that there is a direct relationship between computer games addiction and anxiety, depression (Zamani, Chashmi, & Hedayati, 2009). Playing digital games might lead to gender stereotyping because there are a smaller number of female characters in games and these characters have restricted roles. This might lead to stereotyped behaviors among women and men. This can lead to problems regarding gender identity (Boyle, Connolly, & Hainey, 2011).

In a digital game a child moves within the boundaries set by the people who are giving to the players. A child who is addicted to digital is less likely to play face-to-face games. A child might have little interaction with the external environment. It may prevent a child from using his or her ability to comprehend and feel what those around them are feeling. This might affect a child's communication with his peers and their parents as well. Studies have found that children who are playing digital games for a long period of time will have consequences related to all aspects of life like communication, health and psychological wellbeing. Some studies stated that people who are playing digital games for a long period of time might find it difficult to stop it. They cannot identify the difference between real life and virtual games. The possibilities of depression and the children who are addicted to digital games are more prone to smoking and substance abuse in the later stages of their life. Digital games are associated with accomplishing different goals and children might even harm themselves to complete those tasks.

Games like 'blue whale' and 'Momo' are examples for this type of game. Furthermore, looking at the screen for a long period of time might lead to watering of eyes and visual disturbances (Aydemir, 2022)

People are concentrating more on the cons of digital gaming, such as social withdrawal. However, playing digital games has some advantages. The controlled use of digital games can lead children's areas of development (Aydemir, 2022). Digital games will increase a person's cognitive abilities particularly their visuospatial skills and concentration. Visuospatial skills refer to a person's ability to recognize and remember objects. This is one of the main advantages of playing digital games required for every student or professional (Adair, n.d.)

Digital gaming can improve one's logic and problem-solving abilities, according to certain Australian and Chinese researchers. To complete various game objectives, many games need a significant amount of preparation, reasoning, and planning. Additionally, it advances the growth of the parts of the brain involved in problem-solving (Adair, n.d.).

According to researchers, playing digital games allows a person to make more quick and accurate decisions which can improve your decision-making skills. Studies also found that if you are playing action games, you will be able to make more accurate and quicker decisions over those who are playing other types of games (Adair, n.d.)

Some video games will promote teamwork. Nowadays video games require a lot of cooperation between team members to achieve desired goals. For example, PUBG required gamers to play as a team and achieve the goals. According to a research by Brigham Young University, teams that engaged in video game play for 45 minutes outperformed teams that participated in other team-building exercises by up to 20%. Teamwork is a much-required skill in today's job market. In addition to these benefits, digital games help us to improve our multi-tasking ability. Digital games will help us to complete different tasks at the same time. Many games require its players to complete multiple tasks at the same time. For example, while playing PUBG, you have to control your character at the same time you are required to communicate through microphones with your teammates.

Some studies have also found that playing digital games will lead to mental development of a child. Some of the games will stimulate the mental skills and help the child to concentrate for a long period of time (Aydemir, 2022).Digital games will help to reduce the problems of hyperactivity like impatience among children. It also teaches children how to persist in a condition (Aydemir, 2022).

A child's creativity, motor, and sensory skills will all advance with the use of digital games. Additionally, attention focus and eye-hand coordination would improve as a result. It would increase a child's self-confidence and ability to cope up with real world problems. Digital games have a positive impact on education also. Children are more motivated and interested in learning when they are drawn to a challenging subject while learning it. Children who were introduced to the digital games at early ages find it very easy to learn literacy skills, reading and language skills. Digital games also allow a child to repeat and reinforce the concepts that they have previously learned. Studies have shown that the use of digital games as a tool to teach the lessons will increase the interest to learn among the children. Studies also found out that digital games used in classrooms are effective in science education. (Aydemir, 2022)

When digital games are played moderately, it can give you a positive as well as beneficial experience. The positive impacts of video games can be studied by identifying motivation to play digital games. Digital games have advantages if you play them for fun and entertainment, but if you use them as a way to avoid dealing with problems in real life, they can cause a lot of problems. Playing digital games has both positive and adverse effects on the quality of our lives. So, it is very important to be aware of these issues and keep them in balance. (Adair, n.d.)

Digital helps the players to achieve their needs of competence and autonomy and this competence and autonomy will increase their intrinsic motivation. Computer games can be effective learning tool for learners and it has a potential for to be applied in the educational field (Reid, 2012). Social gaming has a positive impact on psychological aspects of wellbeing of a person. It is even more true for cooperative games because it leads to higher level of positive interaction which will lead higher level of enjoyment and lower levels of aggression (Halbrook, O'Donnell, & Msetf, 2019).

An important aspect of self-identity is membership of social groups Playing games was considered as a valued activity among children peer group. Video games were considered as a very important aspect in a child's life, especially for boys. Video games were considered as a positive thing both in terms of learning and entertainment (Bassiouni & Hackley, 2016). Studies shows that people use to get very anxious during the pandemic and video games always helped with as they give something else focus. And video games have been a source of stress relief during the pandemic (Barr & Copeland-Stewart, 2021).

Studies have found that playing violent video games has both long term and short-term effect on aggression including intensity aggressive thoughts, effects, behavior and delinquency. In short-term, effects of video game violence on aggression are partly driven by in game rewarding for violent behavior (Lavoie, Main, King, & King, 2021). Studies found that symptoms of internet gaming disorder are positively correlated with symptoms of depression anxiety etc. Although symptoms of internet gaming disorder and symptoms of psychopathology co-occur there is no explanation for that (Hygen, et al., 2020).

## CHALLENGES FACED BY CHILDREN DUE TO DIGITAL GAME ADDICTION

Children are facing a lot of challenges due to digital gaming addiction. This includes physical issues like anxiety and depression. Computers play an important role in a child's life. Children are introduced to computers at a very young age. It is a known fact that problematic internet and computer usage is one of the major issues among children of different age groups. (Karaca, Karakoc, Gurkan, Onan, & Barlas, 2020). During the pandemic children especially teens use computers and other electronic gadgets widely to play video games. It is because the kids were restricted from going outside their home and they had nothing to do, they might have found video games very entertaining and engaging.

Playing video games are normal part of a teenager's life but it can be issue if a child starts to play video games excessively. If they are playing it beyond a limit, then it can affect a child's day to day activities. There are small number of kids who are having hard time with gaming addiction. Many researchers are trying to learn more about this issue. During a six-year study, they found that 10% of adolescents are facing the issue of unhealthy gaming. The study also identified that these kids have some attributes in common. (McCarthy, 2020)

- The children who have unhealthy gaming conditions tend to be boys more often.
- In order to play video games, they neglect their work, sleep, exercise, and relationships with friends and family.
- They could struggle with anger, shyness, depression, or anxiety.

There are some symptoms to identify unhealthy gaming among children:

- They might feel obsessed with gaming and they feel sad and irritable when the game is taken away from them.
- Wanting more and more gaming and unable to quit gaming.
- Use games as a relief for their real-life problems

In addition to these, there are some other challenges faced by children due to digital gaming addiction. Children are using passive games as health promotion material, as inactiveness among children is increasing. Game play might have an influence on cognitive, social and health behavior. Some content in a digital game like alcohol, tobacco using promoting content or content that promotes unrealistic expectation are connected to changes in sexual behavior, substance use and body image (Parisod, 2014). Nowadays children are also facing challenges like webcam hacking, Malwares, hidden fees etc. Webcams have been a hacking target since they were introduced. At first webcams were separated from the devices but now laptops and tablets are introduced with inbuilt webcams, which made hacking a regular event. Any connected recording device can be attacked by attackers and used to exploit children. Trojan virus may modify a legitimate app in google play store and insert unwanted contents in digital games. So parents have to make sure that they read all the terms and conditions before installing a digital game. In addition to this there are dangerous online games which are working on a 'freemium' basis, which means a certain part of the game is available for free but to enjoy the entire version they have to pay a certain amount. These types of dangerous games are very popular now. Their main targets are children. Some online predators try to send inappropriate chats to children. They can even send webcam chats or can arrange video calls which can lead to sexual exploitation. They do so by becoming a child's teammate or defender and after completing a difficult level or exploring a new level, they create a bond with the child and get into their private space (Internet Safety for Kids: Top 7 Online Gaming Dangers, n.d.)

There are a lot of steps which can be taken to prevent unhealthy gaming habits among children. Firstly, the parents can use a media plan tool to control children's media diet. Parents have to make sure that digital gaming is not preventing their children from doing their day to day activities like doing homework, exercise and sleep. Secondly, parents have to be mindful about their children's electronic devices usage and what apps they are downloading. Parents have to make sure that their children are aware of the dangers of online and other digital games. Parents should try to keep the gaming in common areas but this is not usually possible as teens are more likely to play games inside their rooms. This makes it very difficult to keep a track on children's mobile usage. Parents should try to play games along with their children and set a good example to their children. This helps the parents to keep an eye on their screen time and try to reduce it. Parents should try to engage their children in real-world games. This would encourage them to connect with other people and this would help them to learn a lot. Parents should encourage their kids to play with toys. Parents should ask their children whether they require any help. Most children did not become addicted but when gaming goes beyond a certain limit and it starts to affect your daily life then it will be an issue and the child should seek help (McCarthy, 2020).

One of the studies shows that feeling alone increases the addiction to technological devices or addiction to technological devices will increase the loneliness. But a licensed athlete will feel less lonely because sports will increase socialization among the children. This will reduce loneliness among them (EKİNCI, KARAALI, PARÇALI, SUNER, & SATILMIŞ, 2021).

## METHODS TO OVERCOME THE OVERUSE OF DIGITAL GAMES

In the twenty-first century, half of the young population is addicted solely to online digital games. It is difficult to get them out of this digital world because they place more importance on the digital world than on their own lives. Regardless of how busy they are, they will find time to play online games. It's not just playing online games; everything has changed now that they can play in groups online.

In this section, we will discuss the methods that can be used to educate children about the dangers of excessive use of digital games and also how to get rid of these games. At first, we will see what dangers online games have.

- Digital games have the potential to take our lives (suicidal thoughts)
- It will force us to take the lives of others
- Young people will become connected to people they have never met. As a result, they are vulnerable to grooming and other forms of online abuse
- It may have an impact on students' studies
- Gaming on a regular basis can be harmful to one's health
- It can lead to obesity and heart problems
- It can have a negative psychological or emotional impact
- It will cause you to lose concentration, resulting in poor concentration
- Addiction to digital or online games may cause children to become aggressive.
- It will have an impact on the children's sleep

These are some of the things that can happen if a person becomes addicted to digital or online games. Let us now look at the methods for overcoming this addiction to online games.

The first step is to acknowledge that you have a problem if you think you are experiencing the impacts or symptoms of a gaming addiction. You will recover control of your life even though beating a gaming addiction requires time and dedication. If you removed the bad impacts of gaming from your life, think of all the opportunities and improvements that might arise (Adair, n.d.).

- If you're looking for motivation, check out a few examples of cases where players have successfully stopped playing games (Adair, n.d.).
- Take a short online quiz to determine whether you have a gaming addiction or are suffering from the negative effects of video games (Adair, n.d.).
- If you need a step-by-step guide to quitting video games, there is a company called Respawn that offers a thorough manual for gamers. Reclaim, a step-by-step manual for supporting your loved one to cut down the negative aspects of gaming, is available for families (Adair, n.d.).
- Working with a therapist or coach can supplement Respawn and Reclaim if you want more personalized attention. Working with a therapist or coach can help you overcome your gaming addiction and reduce the negative effects it has on your physical and mental health (Adair, n.d.).
- For those who desire to stop playing video games or develop better gaming habits, Game Quitters is a resource, community, and advocacy group. We work in conjunction with parents, players, instructors, and experts from all around the world to advance research and offer evidence-based programmes focused at preventing and treating gaming disorders (Adair, n.d.).

- An online gaming community for seasoned players is accessible through Game Quitters. Gamers from over the world can discuss their issues on their community forum and in their hundreds of free films (Adair, n.d.).

If we are addicted to online games, these are some of the ways we can break free from them. Some of the online platforms that will assist one in getting rid of digital games are Respawn, Game Quitters, and so on. Many other platforms, such as these, can assist young people, as well as adults, in overcoming their addiction to digital games.

## SUGGESTIONS

We all now understand what digital games are and the effects they have on children. As this paper primarily focuses on digital game addiction and children, I have a few suggestions. We know that the character of children is changing day by day. Why is this happening? Digital games, in some ways, play a significant role in this. Children used to play outside before the invention of digital games. They had many friends around their house, and the children were healthier than they are now. What is the reason for this? This is primarily because parents valued outdoor games more than indoor games back then. They used to make children leave the house. But what is going on right now? The situation has completely changed. Parents use mobile phones or other gadgets to feed their children, and they also provide them with other games, particularly video games. In my opinion, it is preferable to use the traditional method of outdoor games to help children both mentally and physically. That doesn't mean children can't play digital games; they can, but only those that aren't harmful to them.

Children may fall behind in technology and fail to acquire essential digital skills if video games are removed from their daily life. Instead of forbidding kids from playing video games, we should teach them how to use them properly and consciously. The adoption of digital games will therefore aid in the development of kids. However, certain digital games could be hazardous to kids because of their content. Therefore, it is crucial that families identify and assess potentially dangerous games (Aydemir, 2022).

Digital games can help children develop when they are played in a controlled environment. When played for an extended period of time, they can lead to addiction. It's important to limit the amount of time kids spend playing video games on the computer. As a result, relevant state institutions and organizations should place greater emphasis on the subject, and educators and parents should learn more about it or increase their knowledge base. In a same vein, youth should be educated about the issue and given follow-up care (Aydemir, 2022).

The government should also make many changes, such as establishing time limits for children to play digital games. It will turn off automatically after the time limit has expired. From a political standpoint, this is also best practice. So, create an environment in which children can play games in a way that does not have a negative impact on them, but rather a space in which they can enjoy themselves freely.

## CONCLUSION

This chapter mainly focused on digital games and their impact on children. Digital games had both a negative and positive impact on children, particularly on children. Today you cannot eliminate digital games from a child's life which can lead to a lack of digital skills among children (Aydemir, 2022). So they should be trained on how to use it in a controlled manner. There are digital games that can lead to a child's overall development. On the other hand, we have digital games which are harmful to children. So, it is the duty of their parents to keep an eye on their media usage. When digital games are played in a controlled manner, it supports children's overall growth but when it is played for a long period of time, then it becomes an addiction. Digital games can also be used as a health promotion tool. However, these professionals who consider digital games as a tool for health promotion should also consider the harmful side of digital games. They should suggest ways in which children can come out of digital game addiction. Parents should keep an eye on their children's usage of digital gadgets. They should make sure that their children are aware of the harmful effects of digital gaming. Children should be encouraged to take part in outdoor activities and mingle with their friends. This will also improve communication and social skills. It also helps the children to build their social network. The outdoor games will also help a child to be healthy. This chapter will help people, especially parents to understand the harmful effects of digital games on their children and some ways through which you can try to reduce the impact of these issues. This chapter might be useful for educational institutions to identify the problems faced by students due to digital gaming addiction and take initiatives to counter this issue.

This chapter also discusses the benefits of digital games. For example, the book claims that digital games help children develop attention skills and that some digital games help children develop arithmetic skills. However, along with these positive effects, there are some drawbacks, such as children becoming addicted and affecting their studies, children's concentration, and so on. One of the most serious disadvantages is that it can harm people's health because they are constantly seated in front of a screen. This chapter also discusses how to avoid the overuse of digital games. Experts recommend a variety of applications that have emerged from the world of digital games. They also recommend a number of books that can assist children and others. These books are very interesting and can help them get out of the digital world.

## REFERENCES

*A brief history of digital gaming*. (2014, November 14). MAAC. https://www.maacindia.com/blog/a-brief-history-of-digital-gaming

Adair, C. (n.d.). *11 Positive Effects of Video Games*. Game Quitters. https://gamequitters.com/positive-effects-of-video-games/

Adair, C. (n.d.). *The Negative Effects of Video Games - 12 Symptoms*. Game Quitters. https://gamequitters.com/negative-effects-of-video-games/

Altun, M., & Atasoy, M. (2018). Investigation Of Digital Game Addiction Of Children Between 9-11 Age Groups: Kirşehir Sample. *International Journal of Eurasia Social Sciences*, 1740-1757.

*Augmented Reality (AR) vs Virtual Reality (VR): The difference explained*. (2022, April 12). TeamViewer. https://www.teamviewer.com/en/augmented-reality-ar-vs-virtual-reality-vr/

Aydemir, F. (2022). Digital games and their effects on children. *Adiyaman üniversitesi sosyal bilimler enstitüsü dergisi*, 40-69.

Ball, M. (2022). *The Metaverse: And How It Will Revolutionize Everything*. Liveright. doi:10.15358/9783800669400

Barr, M., & Copeland-Stewart, A. (2021). Playing Video Games During the COVID-19 Pandemic and Effects on Players' Well-Being. *Games and Culture*, *17*(1), 122–139. doi:10.1177/15554120211017036

Bassiouni, D. H., & Hackley, C. (2016). Video games and young children's evolving sense of identity: A qualitative study. *Young Consumers*, *17*(2), 127–142. doi:10.1108/YC-08-2015-00551

Boyle, E., Connolly, T. M., & Hainey, T. (2011). The role of psychology in understanding the impact of computer games. *Entertainment Computing*, *2*(2), 69–74. doi:10.1016/j.entcom.2010.12.002

Chikhani, R. (2015, October 31). *The History Of Gaming: An Evolving Community*. TechCrunch. https://techcrunch.com/2015/10/31/the-history-of-gaming-an-evolving-community/

Christofferson, A., & James, A. O'Brien, A., & Rowland, T. (2022, October 12). *Level Up: The Future of Video Games Is Bright*. Bain & Company. https://www.bain.com/insights/level-up-the-future-of-video-games-is-bright/

*Competitive Multiplayer*. (n.d.). TV Tropes. https://tvtropes.org/pmwiki/pmwiki.php/Main/CompetitiveMultiplayer

Ekinci, N. E., Karaali, E., Parçali, B., Suner, A., & Satilmiş, S. E. (2021). COVID-19 Pandemic. *Loneliness and Digital Game Addiction.*, *15*(7), 2175–2179.

Elliott, L., Ream, G., & McGinsky, E. (2012). Video Game Addiction: User Perspectives. In Critical Perspectives on Addiction (pp. 225-243).

*Explained: What is cross-platform gaming and how is it useful for gamers*. (2022, March 3). Times of India. https://timesofindia.indiatimes.com/gadgets-news/explained-what-is-cross-platform-gaming-and-how-is-it-useful-for-gamers/articleshow/89974015.cms

Guide, S. (n.d.). *Gaming Trends 2023 - Top 10 Trends that Will Rule Industry*. EDIIIE. https://www.ediiie.com/blog/gaming-trends/

Halbrook, Y. J., O'Donnell, A. T., & Msetfi, R. M. (2019). When and How Video Games Can Be Good: A Review of the Positive Effects of Video Games on Well-Being. *Perspectives on Psychological Science*, *14*(6), 1096–1104. doi:10.1177/1745691619863807 PMID:31672105

Hygen, B. W., Skalicka, V., Stenseng, F., Belsky, J., Steinsbekk, S., & Wichstrøm, L. (2020). The co-occurrence between symptoms of internet gaming disorder and psychiatric disorders in childhood and adolescence: Prospective relations or common causes? *Journal of Child Psychology and Psychiatry, and Allied Disciplines*, *61*(8), 890–898. doi:10.1111/jcpp.13289 PMID:32623728

*Internet Safety for Kids: Top 7 Online Gaming Dangers*. (n.d.). Kaspersky. https://usa.kaspersky.com/resource-center/threats/top-7-online-gaming-dangers-facing-kids

Irmak, A. Y., & Erdogan, S. (2015). Digital Game Addiction Among Adolescents and Young Adults: A Current Overview. *Turkish Journal of Psychiatry*.

Irvine, L., Melaugh, J., Etchells, P., Collins, S., & Tse, D. (2019, April 6). Five damaging myths about video games – let's shoot 'em up. *The Guardian.* https://www.theguardian.com/games/2019/apr/06/five-damaging-myths-about-video-games-lets-shoot-em-up

Jakhar, A. (2022, June 9). *Why Are Children Getting Attracted To Online Gaming?* Youth Ki Awaaz. https://www.youthkiawaaz.com/2022/06/why-children-are-getting-attracted-towards-online-gaming/

Karaca, S., Karakoc, A., Gurkan, O. C., Onan, N., & Barlas, G. U. (2020). Investigation of the Online Game Addiction Level, Sociodemographic Characteristics and Social Anxiety as Risk Factors for Online Game Addiction in Middle School Students. *Community Mental Health Journal, 56*(5), 830–838. doi:10.100710597-019-00544-z PMID:31907803

Koss, H. (n.d.). *What Is the Metaverse? Examples and Definition.* Built In. https://builtin.com/media-gaming/what-is-metaverse

Lavoie, R., Main, K., King, C., & King, D. (2021). Virtual experience, real consequences: The potential negative emotional consequences of virtual reality gameplay. *Virtual Reality (Waltham Cross), 25*(1), 69–81. doi:10.100710055-020-00440-y

Lieberman, D., Fisk, M., & Biely, E. (n.d.). *Digital games for young children ages three to six: From research to design.* Taylor & Francis Group. https://www.tandfonline.com/doi/abs/10.1080/07380560903360178

McCarthy, C. (2020, October 28). *Unhealthy Video Gaming: What Parents Can Do to Prevent It.* Healthy Children. https://www.healthychildren.org/English/family-life/Media/Pages/Unhealthy-Video-Gaming.aspx

McFerren, D. (2012, January 26). *Fitness Gaming: Two Words. One Meaning.* Nexersys. https://nexersys.com/fitness-gaming-two-words-one-meaning/

Neal, S. (2023, February 3). 5 trends that will shape the gaming sector in 2023. *Times of India.* https://timesofindia.indiatimes.com/blogs/voices/5-trends-that-will-shape-the-gaming-sector-in-2023/

Parisod, H. (2014). The advantages and limitations of digital games in children's health promotion. *Finnish Journal of eHealth and eWelfare, 6*(4).

Quwaider, M., Alabed, A., & Duwairi, R. (2019). The Impact of Video Games on the Players Behaviors: A Survey. *Procedia Computer Science, 151*, 575–582. doi:10.1016/j.procs.2019.04.077

Reid, G. (2012). Motivation in video games: A literature review. *The Computer Games Journal, 1*(2), 70–81. doi:10.1007/BF03395967

Scott, F. (2022, May 23). *Five digital games to help your child's development. The Conversation.* https://theconversation.com/five-digital-games-to-help-your-childs-development-183483

Stout, A. (n.d.). Esports. *Wikipedia.* https://en.wikipedia.org/wiki/Esports

*The future of digital gaming - ADK INSIGHTS Inspiration.* (n.d.). ADK Insights. https://adk-insights.com/the-future-of-digital-gaming/

*Why we play PUBG day-night? What are its psychological underpinnings?* (2021, June 19). Times of India. https://timesofindia.indiatimes.com/readersblog/nothing-important/why-we-play-pubg-day-night-what-are-its-psychological-underpinnings-33843/

Zamani, E., Chashmi, M., & Hedayati, N. (2009). Effect of Addiction to Computer Games on Physical and Mental Health of Female and Male Students of Guidance School in City of Isfahan. *Addiction & Health*, *1*(2), 98–104. PMID:24494091

## KEY TERMS AND DEFINITIONS

**Children:** A young human being below the age of puberty or below the legal age of majority.

**Cybernated:** The automatic control of a process or operation (as in manufacturing) by means of computers.

**Figurative Game:** Any figure of speech — a statement or phrase not intended to be understood literally.

**Inclination:** A person's natural tendency or urge to act or feel in a particular way; a disposition.

**Indoor Games:** Indoor games and sports are a variety of structured forms of play or competitive physical activity, typically carried out either in the home or in specially constructed indoor.

**Outdoor Games:** Sports or athletic games typically performed in the open, including physical exertion.

**Pedagogy:** The method and practice of teaching, especially as an academic subject or theoretical concept.

# Chapter 25
# Investigating Social Media Addiction in the Context of Digital Storytelling

**Veysel Çakmak**
*Aksaray University, Turkey*

## ABSTRACT

*Being easy to access and share, social media platforms cause people to spend most of their time in these places. Individuals share pictures, music, and video content in these places; they follow the content shared by others as well. Such appeals of social media lead individuals to become addicted to social media. In this study, social media addiction was evaluated on the basis of the platform, the addicted environment, and the characteristics of the user. In addition, the study is explained with examples, especially on the Instagram platform, through digital storytelling.*

## INTRODUCTION

Human beings have experienced oral culture and written culture from past to present, and today they live digital culture with communication technologies. Individuals living in digital culture can easily reach other people through communication technologies, share what they do, follow other users' posts, and get synchronized with other people in many fields of education, culture and economy. In addition, the use of social media, together with participatory, interactive, personal and mass sharing, has become a place of interest and being a compulsory activity for individuals. Due to the fact that social media is a place of attraction and has become a necessity, individuals have become constantly using social media.

When considered in an individual and social context, the addiction typology has three sub-Dimensions (DeFleur and Ball-Rokeach, 1989, as cited: Işık and at all, 2022, p. 102). The first dimesion is interpretation. Interpretation is learning the requirements of spiritual, physical and social existence. In addition, it is the ability to understand and interpret the social environment in which one lives. Another dimension, adaptability, is the ability to decide how to meet vital needs. It is also to get clues and symptoms on how to act in a new situation. Play and entertainment which is the final dimension, is deciding what to

DOI: 10.4018/978-1-6684-8397-8.ch025

do when one is alone. In the entertainment dimension, examples of planning events with family, friend groups, going to the movies and concerts can be given.

According to most researchers, social media addiction is a type of internet addiction. However, when the available information is analysed, social media addiction should be examined under an independent context. Social media addiction can be defined as "prolonged preoccupation with social media with an uncontrollable motivation to access or use social media, spending so much time and effort on social media that it affects other priority areas" (Demirkol & Harmancı, 2021, p. 62).

Social media addiction has three pillars. The first of them is the characteristics of the addicted substance, the second is the effect of the environment in which the addicted person lives, and the third is the personality characteristics (Tarhan & Nurmedov, 2011, p. 43). The study is conducted within the scope of this information. First of all, social media, Instagram and digital storytelling that the user becomes connected are evaluated. Secondly, the society and culture in which individuals live today will be investigated. In addition, the effect of popular culture is discussed in this context .

## THE PLATFORM ADDICTION AND OBJECT

Technological tools have many features. The most important of these features is how they affect human life. These effects are not innocent and technology will definitely find the power to connect people to itself. From another point of view, technology is an extension of human beings. Questioning technology in human life, where the technique is decisive, McLuhan stated that people need technology and this need has reached an irreversible turning point (Yengin, 2019, p. 136).

Along with Web 2.0 technology, individuals use Facebook, Twitter and Instagram platforms effectively. These platforms, which were used due to their popularity at the beginning, are being used in many areas such as education, culture, health and economy over time. In recent years, it has become a necessity for everyone to benefit these technologies.

It is essential to deal with the basic characteristics of internet addiction and, accordingly, social media addiction. According to Tarhan and Nurmedov (2011, p. 74), the main features of internet addiction are as follows;

- The internet is used every day of the week and 24 hours a day.
- Instagram usage status is also accessible wherever internet is available
- Internet home, workplace, etc. available everywhere.
- Also it can be used anywhere on Instagram.
- Even on mobile lines, internet packages vary according to social media usage.
- Users receive internet packages according to their social media usage status.

It is fascinating.

It is confirmatory.

It has been determined that the social media usage purposes of the youth are entertainment, communication, agenda tracking, messaging and leisure activities (Çömlekçi & Başol, 2019, p. 183). According to studies, it is obvious that many studies are associated with social media.

Tümer et al. examined the studies on social media addiction in the last five years (2022, p.29). They found a positive and significant relationship between social media addiction and anxiety, depression, negative self, somatization and hostility. However, it has been determined that there is a high correlation between fear of missing out (FoMO) and social media addiction (Zıvdır & Karakul, 2023, p. 1064). According to the research conducted on 5176 internet users in Turkey, social media addiction rised as age decreased, but there was a slight increase in retirees. At the age of fourteen, during the pupilage, addiction was found to be high, and with the start of business life at the age of twenties and with the increase in occupation, addiction was found to be high again. However, addiction was found to be almost non-existent between the ages of 30-40. It can be said that addiction decreases as the age increases, but in the 60s, which is the retirement age, the addiction score was found to be slightly higher. The most used social media application was 90% Instagram, 57% Facebook, 47% Twitter, 2% Reddit, 1% Tinder (Uslu, 2021,p. 385). In the study conducted by Özkan et al., (2020, p. 399) they found that smartphone and internet addiction positively affect the dimensions of social integration and emotional attachment.

The characteristics of social media networks lead individuals to reach a central role in the life of society, pull them into a spiral, that is, make them live or accept a different addiction. Social media addiction of the individual occurs within the framework of "freedom of the subject", "alternative media", "culture of democracy" and "psychological satisfaction", which are the main areas of social media (Babacan, 2016 p. 10-17; Kuşçalı, 2019, p. 107).

Photolurking is another characteristic of social media. As Olcay stated; "Photolurking" is a combination of the word "photo", which is the equivalent of the English word "photo", and the word "lurking", which means "sneaking". The platform where photolurking behavior is most likely to be seen is Instagram. Because image sharing and monitoring activity is most common in the Instagram. Therefore, the user only intends to access the platform for a few minutes, but they experience various problems such as headaches and dizziness due to staring at the screen for a long time. Waste of time, feeling of regret, starting to create an identity, activity of following and being followed, postponing responsibilities instead of doing them, looking at images until late at night, fear of missing something if the pictures are not looked at, and feeling like desolation are indicators of photolurking (Olcay, 2018, p. 9-97). These behaviors lead individuals become addicted to social media.

## Addictive Substance: Creating and Tracking Digital Storytelling

One of the most important components of addiction is the substance two which hat the person is addicted. In this study, the substance that the person is addicted to is creating a story in virtual environments, following the created stories and navigating the platform.

Storytelling is one of the most important communication instruments of oral culture. It has been used frequently in the past and still continues to be used. The storytelling has a plot, and the aesthetic of the flow is engaging. Culture consisting of spoken language is considered as "primary oral culture" in communication. The "oral" qualities of tools such as telephone, radio and television constitute the "secondary oral culture" (Ong, 2018, p. 24).

The traditional concept and structure of storytelling has changed with the emergence of images and photography. After the 19th century, the emergence of image-oriented societies as well as the palpable impact of the image on people's lives and its ability to satisfy needs rapidly increased the demand for the image. The invention of the image changed the conventions of storytelling. The development of video applications with platforms in photography, cinema, television and the internet transformed the structure of storytelling. The fact that everyone has a story and people need to listen and look at them made images even more attractive (Çokluk & Okmen, 2020, p. 1118).

The emergence of new communication technologies and their use by the masses also affected literature and language. These technologies, also called social media, have inevitably caught the attention of writers and poets failing to have their works published or who were not able to reach out to as many readers as they wished, even if they were accepted. Social media, which offers different opportunities for writers and poets, caused changes in the field of language and literature with its unique understanding of language and literature. Social media broke and changed the link between traditional text-language-literature and the reader (Avcı & Topçu, 2021, p. 22). At this point, with new communication technologies, story writing, story creation and storytelling was transformed in terms of language and literature in recent years and manifested itself as "digital storytelling".

Stories, which are as old as human history, carry cultural heritage and values from the past to the present. Stories are transmitted by word of mouth and form a collective consciousness as a form of communication. It is one of the most important bridges connecting the past to the present. The transformation in many areas driven by the rapid advances in technology caused stories to change and transform. The development of new media technologies transformed storytelling into digital storytelling (Sunal, Furuncu Kutluhan, & Bağdatlı Kalkan, 2022, p. 226).

*Table 1. Differences between traditional and digital storytelling*

| Traditional Storytelling | Digital Storytelling |
|---|---|
| The most important organ is the ear | The most important organ is the eye |
| It is important to keep things in memory | There is no need for memorizing things, creativity is important |
| The number of narrators is few and limited | Narrators are many, being a narrator is easy |
| The number of listeners is very limited | The number of listeners is unlimited, global |
| There are places involved such as cafes and village houses | No space limitations, there are studios and virtual studios |
| No technical knowledge and equipment required | Requires technical knowledge, equipment and current technology |
| Instant interaction can happen | Interaction can also happen after the story is told and published |
| Social, economic and ideological concerns are not the primary element of story-telling | Social, economic and ideological concerns are at the forefront and there may even be an agenda. |

Reference:(Çokluk & Okmen, 2020, p. 1128).

The popularity of digital stories among social media users causes the emergence of certain negative behaviors. Although there are so many of them, the most important of these is digital addiction.

Almost everyone uses gadgets such as television, computers, smartphones and tablets. The prevalence of the Internet in both personal and commercial affairs made it an indispensable technology for people. While the concept of addiction was first known as a disease related to substances such as drugs, alcohol and cigarettes, in recent years it has led to the formation of internet addiction or social media addiction. This is because when internet users do not have access to the internet, they also experience withdrawal symptoms. In other words, it is the inability to quit a substance or the emergence of uncontrolled use behavior (Sağbaş, 2022, p. 18).

With social media stories, people both share their own lives and follow the stories of others showing a performance intended to engage users with an expectation to be appreciated. The main purpose of the performance on stage is to tell one's own story (Tokgöz, 2017, p. 266). According to Goffman, people appear on the stage with performances that identify with them. Thus, the actors who appear on the stage wait and perform in order to reveal their selves in all areas of their lives and to win the appreciation of other people (Kırık & Yazıcı, 2017, p. 97).

The fact that storytelling is audio, visual and instantaneous on social media, as well as the ability to post comments under the content created, has greatly increased its appeal. The fact that people want to broadcast social activities to create stories and that everyone wants to look at each other's different stories has led to the emergence of digital story addiction.

Three important features are required to create new communication environments. First of all, user-oriented content should be produced and there should be an interaction between the content and the target audience. Content that receives users' interest, likes and comments are the most important functions of new media. Secondly, the contents on digital platforms should be produced concise, short and understandable. At the same time, it is necessary to immediately return the messages sent. Third, it is of great importance to support the narratives with visuals such as photographs or videos (Ökmen & Çokluk, 2021, p. 196; Aktan, 2018, p. 408)

Digital stories are constructed using five basic components: media, communication, movement, relationship, and context. The first benefit of media is its rich content, which combines graphics, text, sound, animation, photos, and images with multimedia options. These instruments in digital contexts assist oral culture's narrative power to grow. The second component of the digital story, movement, shows that the content is active and under your control. Relationship is a tool used by narrators to add to or alter interactions with previously presented stories. On the other hand, context can be defined as the links to the story that is located on the website and that displays the contents of the same story presented in various formats. Thanks to the context, the sharing of the digital story and its interaction with other users can be easier. The final element of digital storytelling is communication. Communication is the most important element that provides interaction between the narrator and the other user via chat, forum, e-mail or SMS. In addition, each tool used in the narration strengthens communication within the framework of creating a message. In digital storytelling, the users explore their own knowledge in an interactive setting while attempting to create it in a way that makes sense within a flow. Digital storytelling is the process of presenting information, education, entertainment, etc., with multimedia applications such as pictures, graphics, animation, music, text, photography, together with the storyteller's own voice in the narration (İnceelli, 2005, p. 141).

Other significant aspects in the creation of addictive behaviour of a person include the incorporation of text, visuality, music, and other elements in digital storytelling, as well as the process of constant engagement.

As the existing social media platforms do not assert professionalism, having the required tools is not necessary to develop digital storytelling. Actually, the amateurishness of digital storytelling is what gives it its strength. (Şimşek, 2018, p.14).

The amateurish content production of today's social media contributes to the natural appearance of life. People utilize social media more frequently as a result of this circumstance. Also, the great number of views and the admiration of the user-generated natural material are seen as rewards. In addition, the interaction initiated by the creation of the digital story causes the creation of new and different stories with the messaging located under or next to the content. Although social media platforms and the digital stories created on these platforms were initially used for wonder, discovery and experimentation, it has turned into a necessity and even an addiction over time.

## DEPENDENT ENVIRONMENT

The environment in which a person lives is another aspect that contributes to addiction. Individuals are constantly growing their use of social media in today's environment, where digital culture is intense, both due to necessity as well as due to influence of popular culture.

Those who grew up with popular culture in the world of mass communication can not imagine a life without popular culture. Thus, social media tools allow them to enjoy the lifestyle they want. How will you know where a fire broke out, a robbery took place, who was killed, and how many lives the traffic monster stole when you get home from work? How will you find out who won and lost the football game, what celebrities and wealthy people say about movies, sports, and fashion? Popular culture, mass culture, arabesque, lush music, newspaper, radio, cinema, television, games, ambitions, excitements, likes and dislikes (fashion) are efforts and manipulations to preserve the status quo within the framework of mass commercial concerns. In addition, popular culture not only popularize certain goods, uses and activities, but also popularise certain worldviews and thoughts. Especially magazines, novels and magazines for women are seen to be helpful towards ideology (Erdoğan & Alemdar, 2005, p. 99; Kuşcalı, 2019, p. 20).

Many behaviors appear as a result of heavy social media use. One of them is the "Selfie move". People share their photos and show them to everyone. The "selfie" movement has become a popular culture activity for the user, who is instantly satisfied with the likes of these posts. Nonetheless, social media has provided a great forum for fan culture and celebrity culture. Especially young people have become an element of popular culture by quickly adapting to these platforms. In addition, having fun by playing games in social media applications has reached the level of addiction. The symbols and images used in the games include the characteristics of the global market (Karamduman, 2017, p. 23). After snapping selfies at various events, it is unavoidable to share the digital story content that's been made on digital networks.Investigating the concept of storytelling in social media, Kırık and Yazıcı (2017, p. 90-96) examined Instagram through different groups. In storytelling and sharing, the newlyweds highlighted tools such as baby items, clothes, and toys. They offer a good mother performance to their followers. Airplanes, cars and bicycles were shared as vehicles in the group of people who travel a lot. The cities and countries visited by the participants were shared. Tools such as jewelry, clothes, shopping places, brand labels were shared and presented by the shopping group. The show-off group, on the other hand, presented their identities by sharing tools such as jewellery, clothes, shopping venues, luxury restaurants, houses, exhibitions, cars and phones. The group, which showed itself, shared floors such as home, gym, seaside, hairdresser, and tools such as smile with glasses, sports equipment, skin care products. The wealthy group, on the other hand, shared tools such as car keys, earrings, bracelets, sunglasses, sports cars, wardrobes, and ostentatious places, luxury stores, and night venues. Therefore, people in different groups have used storytelling for different purposes. This is an indication that storytelling includes people from all groups.

Social media addiction is the use of technology in line with one's needs. People are captivated by advances in technology and manipulated by them just like a wizard. With the technological transformation, the passive user has become active and interactive. Everyone is attempting to be visible as society shifts toward one of demonstration. The show is to make sense of the visible events by combining the differences. Visuality used with communication tools has made everything ordinary, as Postman Da Debord said. Given the deluge of demonstrations and digital settings, it has become vital for the individual to consume and create content in this context. The transfer of all activities and needs to digital makes it mandatory for people to use digital. For this reason, people use digital technology and become social media addicts (Yengin, 2019, p. 142).

## PERSONAL CHARACTERISTICS AND ADDICTION

Personality qualities are another factor in social media addiction. People spend hours on social media platforms for activities including learning about new technologies, performing, connecting, and just being alone. Technological dependency develops with persistent use.

There are certain criteria for the emergence of behavioral addiction. Accordingly, social network addiction:

- - Excessive involvement with social networks (directive motive),
- Use of social media to reduce negative emotions (mood regulation),
- increased use of social networks (tolerance, craving) to enjoy again.
- Experiencing distress when not in use (deficiency),
- Waiving other obligations for the use of social networks and experiencing problems in important living areas (conflict, loss of functionality),
- Attempts to control social network usage (repetition, loss of control) fail (Demirkol & Harmancı, 2021, p. 66; Can, Koçer, & Toprak, 2021, p. 340).

Researchers have tried to measure the relationship between an individual's personality and social media addiction. The relationship between the sub-dimensions of the five-factor personality ("adaptation", "neuroticism", "responsibility", "openness to development" and "extraversion", and the sub-dimension of social media addiction "repetition", "busy", "mood change", "conflict"") was examined. The investigation revealed that the sub-factors of social media addiction, such as repetition, preoccupation, conflict, mood changes, and personality, were unaffected by the compatibility factor. Yet, it has been found that people with responsibility, openness, and neurotic personality traits are more likely to develop social media addiction. (Mutlu, 2021, p. 141).

Examining media addiction within the framework of uses and gratifications, Ayhan and Çavuş (2014, p. 49) stressed that user behaviors can change as media exposure time increases. The authors stated that with the use and satisfaction of individuals in the media, the level of satisfaction and habits evolve into addiction.

The creation of a digital identity is one of the most significant aspects of digital culture. A person's or group's self-identification and positioning on digital platforms is known as their "digital identity."

Thereby, Internet users frequently share communication content such as pictures, video, text and audio that defines themselves in digital environments (Çakmak, 2020, p. 23).

When we examine the underlying reasons of social media addiction, we find that loneliness is high on the list. When people are lonely, they resort to social media for solace. In addition, there may be reasons such as the fear of missing out, the inability to use free time well, and social phobia (Çelik, 2022).

The increase in the use of social media, being alone in the society, socialization efforts and efforts to create a digital identity are some of the steps that make the individual dependent on social media.

Those who are connected to computers or the internet spend a lot of time using this technology in their daily lives, and these individuals exhibit addictive tendencies. The person's activities on the internet and computer gradually increase. Therefore, this activity becomes the center of one's life. The communication of the person with the environment develops and is organized according to the internet usage activities of other people. Addiction and habit arise. Internet use is not the same as being affected by an external chemical substance that changes consciousness, but it does involve internal chemicals that are connected to behaviors like sexual stimulation, gambling, and gaming. Internet leads to identity change. This gives rise to a distinctive enthusiasm (Tarhan & Nurmedov, 2011, p. 70).

The study found that the degree of narcissism has a statistically significant and advantageous impact on the risk variables for social media addiction. This effect applies to all dimensions of narcissism: exposure, superiority, entitlement, exploitation, authority, and self-sufficiency (Yüksel Avcılar & Atalar, 2019, p. 1397).

Internet addiction has been found to be positively correlated with fomo, cognitive disfunction and hyperactivity disorder, and neurotic personality characteristics. However, Internet addiction was found an inverse relationship between life satisfaction, self-esteem and sense of responsibility (Çınar & Mutlu, 2019, p. 140). In the study, It was shown that teenagers often have a high level of psychologically fundamental needs. In addition, it has been found that there is a positive way and significant relationship between the Instagram addiction of adolescents and their basic psychological needs. It was also determined that the adolescents participating in the study spent a lot of time in front of the screen. It has been revealed that adolescents mostly use Whatsapp and Instagram applications (Üstündüğ A., 2022, p.19).

Via social media platforms, people who fear rejection or unpopularity in face-to-face interactions can engage with a huge audience. In addition, the social media tool where disorder and comfort are found wins the admiration of many people with torn socks, greasy hair, and ketchup on the side of the lips. Therefore, likability in the digital environment reinforces the dependence on the virtual environment while escaping from the real environment (Hazar, 2011, p. 162). According to the research conducted by Kırcaburun and Griffiths (2018, p. 166), they revealed that self-liking is negatively related to Instagram addiction and daily internet use is positively related to Instagram addiction.

## FUTURE RESEARCH AND DIRECTIONS

In this study, social media addiction was examined within the framework of digital storytelling and Instagram use. In future studies, it is recommended to investigate social media addiction within the framework of different social media platforms. In addition, social media addiction was evaluated in the context of the addicted material, the environment and personality traits in this study. In today's world, where technological tools direct human life, it is recommended to examine social media addiction through different theories.

## CONCLUSION

The object of addiction, the surroundings, and personality factors are the main topics of this study on social media addiction. It has been determined that people frequently enter Instagram, where visuality is at the forefront, and they engage in digital storytelling as an addicted object. With the help of digital media and popular culture, people utilize social media to broadcast all of their everyday activities and to keep up with previously shared content. Users present themselves utilizing digital storytelling methods.

With the influence of the individual's personality traits, the social media user continues as an addicted avatar on social media platforms that they initially spend their free time on and then enter compulsorily.

Işık et al., according to DeFleur and Ball-Rokeach's addiction typology, concluded that there is a "social understanding" type dependency relationship in the use of Instagram by young people (2022, p. 111). People watch videos, play games and access the contents of different communication tools in order to understand life and the environment they live in, to listen, to get information and to have fun. Aside from the conventional communication channels that are appealing to a broad audience, people can move, select, and engage in conversation more readily within the confines of their interests. They are followed by others, criticized, admired and nurturing the sense of personal satisfaction as well as providing motivation by continuing their actions here. The results of the research prove that the use of Instagram by young people develops "understanding, play and orientation" type addiction relationships (Işık ve Others, 2022, p. 113).

In order to become conscious of and prevent social media addiction, it is necessary to learn social media literacy first. This literacy can be focused on topics such as digital storytelling, playing digital games, following social media statuses, taking selfies. In addition, social media users need to be aware of digital diseases.

## REFERENCES

Aktan, E. (2018). Üniversite Öğrencilerinin Sosyal Medya Bağımlılık Düzeylerinin Çeşitli Değişkeneler Göre İncelenmesi. *Erciyes İletişim Dergisi*, 405-421.

Avcı, N., & Topçu, D. (2021). Sosyal Medya, Dil ve Edebiyat. *Birey ve Toplum Sosyal Bilimler Dergisi*, 5-26.

Ayhan, B., & Çavuş, S. (2014). İzleyici Araştırmalarında Değişim; Kullanımlar ve Doyumlardan Bağımlılığa. *Selçuk İletişim*, 32-60.

Babacan, M. E. (2016). Sosyal Medya Kullanım Alanları ve Bağımlılık İlişkisi. *Addicta: The Turkish Journal on Addictions*, 7-28.

Bal, E. (202). Sosyal Medyada Mahremiyet ve Paylaşım Kültürü. In M. Akdağ (Ed.), *Dijital Kültür ve Sosyal Medya* (pp. 122–142). Atatürk Üniversitesi Açıköğretim Fakültesi Yayını.

Bütüner, R., Bütüner, N., & Bütüner, M. (2022). Ergenlerde Sosyal Medya Bağımlılığı Konusunda Son Beş Yılda Yapılmış Çalışmaların İncelenmesi. *Journal of Information Systems and Management Research*, 17-34.

Çakmak, V. (2020). Dijital Kültür ve Kimliğin İnşası. In M. Akdağ (Ed.), *Dijital Kültür ve Sosyal Medya* (pp. 20–38). Erzurum Üniversitesi Açıköğretim Fakültesi Yayını.

Can, E. N., Koçer, M., & Toprak, H. H. (2021). Tüketicilerin Netflix Kullanımları Üzerine Bir Araştırma. *Erciyes Akademi*, 323-344.

Çelik, C. (2022, 8 5). *İnternet ve Sosyal Medya Bağımlılığı*. Celik. cemilcelik.com.tr: https://www.cemilcelik.com.tr/internet-ve-sosyal-medya-bagimliligi/

Çınar, Ç., & Mutlu, E. (2019). İnternet Bağımlılığının Benlik Saygısı, Dikkat, Gelişmeleri Kaçırma Korkusu, Yaşam Doyumu ve Kişilik Özellikleri ile İlişkisi. *Bağımlılık Dergisi/Journal of Dependence*, 133-142.

Çokluk, N., & Okmen, Y. E. (2020). Sözlü Kültürden Dijital Kültüre Hikaye Anlatımı: Youtuberlar Üzerine Kültürel Bir Çözümleme. *Selçuk İletişim Dergisi*, 1114-1148.

Çömlekçi, M. F., & Başol, O. (2019). Gençlerin Sosyal Medya Kullanım Amaçları ile Sosyal Medya Bağımlılığı. *Celal Bayar Üniversitesi Sosyal Bilimler Dergisi*, 173-188.

Demirkol, G., & Harmancı, P. (2021). *Davranışsal Bağımlılıklar-Bağımlılıktan Bağımsızlığa Doğru*. İksad Publications.

Erdoğan, İ., & Alemdar, K. (2005). *Popüler Kültür ve İletişim*. Pozitif Matbaacılık.

Hazar, M. (2011). Sosyal Medya Bağımlılığı: Bir Alan Çalışması. *İletişim Kuram ve Araştırma Dergisi*, 151-175.

İnceelli, A. (2005). Dijital Hikaye Anlatımın Bileşenleri. *The Turkish Online Journal of Educational Technology*, 132–142.

Işık, U., Kalem, M., Aliyeva, F., & Ülker, M. (2022). Medya Bağımlılığı Teorisi Doğrultusunda Instagram: Üniversite Öğrencileri Üzerine Bir Araştırma. *ANkara Hacı Bayram Veli Üniversitesi*, 97-116.

Karaduman, N. (2017). Popüler Kültürün Oluşmasında ve Aktarılmasında Sosyal Medyanın Rolü. *Erciyes Üniversitesi Sosyal Bilimler Enstitüsü Dergisi*, 7-27.

Kırcaburun, K., & Griffiths, M. D. (2018). Instagram Addiction and the Big Five of Personality: The Mediating of Self-Liking. *Journal of Behavioral Addictions*, *7*(1), 158–170. doi:10.1556/2006.7.2018.15 PMID:29461086

Kırık, A. M., & Yazıcı, N. (2017). Instagram Örneği Üzerinden Sosyal Medyada Hikaye Anlatıcılığı. *Erciyes İletişim Dergisi*, 82-99.

Koçyiğit, M., & Koçyiğit, A. (2018). Değişen ve Gelişen Dijital İletişim: Yazılabilir Web Teknolojisi (Web 2.0). In V. Çakmak & S. Çavuş (Eds.), *Dijital Kültür ve İletişim* (pp. 19–49). LİTERATÜRK.

Küngerü, A. (2016). Bir İfade Aracı Olarak Dijital Öykü Anlatımı. *Abant Kültürel Araştırmalar Dergisi*, 33-46.

Kuşcalı, A. (2019). İslami İlimler Fakültesi Öğrencilerinin Sosyal Medya Kullanım Motivasyonlarının İncelenmesi. *Simetrik İletişim Araştırmaları Dergisi*, 100-110.

Mutlu, T. (2021). *Sosyal Medya Bağımlılığı ve Kişilik İlişkisi: Sosyal Medya Üzerinden Bir Uyguama.* Sakarya: Sakarya Üniversitesi Sosyal Bilimler Enstitüsü / Yayımlanmamış Yüksek Lisans Tezi.

Ökmen, Y. E., & Çokluk, N. (2021). Ben de Artık Bir Hikaye Anlatıcısıyım: Hikaye Anlatımında Dijital Olanaklar Açısından Yotuber "Fly with Haifa" Üzerine Bir İnceleme. *Etkileşim*, 190-215.

Olcay, S. (2018). Sosyalleşmenin Dijitalleşmesi Olarak Sosyaleşmesi Olarak Sosyal Medya ve Resimler Arasında Kaybolma Bozukluğu: Photolurking. *e-Journal of New Media/Yeni Medya Elektronik Dergi*, 90-104.

Ong, V. (2018). *Sözlü ve Yazılı Kültür*. Metis Yayınları.

Özkan, O., Özer, Ö., & Özmen, S. (2020). Akıllı Telefon Bağımlılığı, İnternet Bağımlılığı ve Sosyal Medya Kullanımının İncelenmesi: Sağlık Yönetimi Öğrencilerinde Bir Uygulama. *The Academic Elegance*, 391-405.

Sağbaş, Ö. F. (2022). *İlkokul Öğrencilerinin Youtube'u Eğtiim amaçlı Kullanma Durumları, Ebeveynlerin Demoğrafik Özellikleri ve İnternet Bağımlılığı Arasındaki ilişki.* Ispart: Süleyman Demirel üniversitesi, Eğitim Bilimleri Enstitüsü (Yayınlanmamış Yüksek Lisans Tezi).

Şimşek, B. (2018). *Dijital Hikaye Anlatımı*. Alternatif Bilişim Derneği.

Sunal, G., Furuncu Kutluhan, D., & Bağdatlı Kalkan, S. (2022). Geleneksel ve Dijital Hikaye Anlatıcılığı Arasındaki Farkın Covid 19 Pandemi Sürecinde Maske Kullanımına ilişkin Bir Video Filmi Üzerinden İncelenmesi. *e-Journal of New Media/Yeni Medya elektronik Dergi*, 221-228.

Tarhan, N., & Nurmedov, S. (2011). *Bağımlılık*. Timaş Yayınları.

Tokgöz, C. (2017). Kimlik ve Bellek Ekseninde Sosyal Medya Anlatıları. *Intermedia. International Journal (Toronto, Ont.)*, 255–268.

Uslu, M. (2021). Türkiye'de Sosyal Medya Bağımlılığı ve Kullanımı Araştırması. *Turkish Academic Research Review*, 370-396.

Üstündağ, A. (2022). Çocukların Sosyal Medya, Akıllı Telefon ve Oyun Bağımlılığı Arasındaki İlişkinin İncelenmesi. *Bağımlılık Dergisi*, 316-326.

Üstündağ, A. (2022). Ergenlerin Instagram Bağımlılık Düzeyleri ile Psikolojik İhtiyaçları Arasındaki İlişki. *Bağımlılık Dergisi*, 8-21.

Yengin, D. (2019). Teknoloji Bağımlılığı Olarak Dijital Bağımlılık. *The Turkish Online Journal Of Design, Art and Communication- TOJDAC*, 130-144.

Yüksel Avcılar, M., & Atalar, S. (2019). Narsistik Kişilik Özelliklerinin Sosyal Medya Bağımlılık Düzeyi ve Gösterişçi Tüketim Eğilimleri Üzerine Etkisinin Tespiti. *Opus, Uluslararası Toplum Araştırmaları Dergisi*, 1373-1407.

Zıvdır, P., & Karakul, A. (2023). Üniversite Öğrencilerinin Sosyal Medya Bağımlılığı Düzeyleri ve FOMO İlişkisi. *İnönü Üniversitesi Sağlık Hizmetleri Meslek Yüksekokulu Dergisi*, 1054-1067.

## ADDITIONAL READING

Crowley, D. & Heyer, P. (2007). Communication in History, / Technology-Culture-Society. Pearson Education Inc.

Twenge, J. (2014), Generation Me. Atria Books.

Twenge, J. (2017). *I-Gen*. Atria Books.

## KEY TERMS AND DEFINITIONS

**Digital Storytelling:** Creating a plot in digital environments, especially on social media platforms such as Facebook, Instagram, Whatsapp, by using communication equipment.

**Addiction:** Loss of control over a substance, object or behavior (action) that a person uses.

**Digital Culture:** It is the application of the behaviors that individuals perform in their daily lives in digital environments.

**Social Media Addiction:** Although the person does not want to use social media, it is the use and inability to maintain his existence without it.

**Instagram:** It is a social media platform that works using Web 2.0 infrastructure and focuses on visual communication.

**Social Media Criticism:** It is a critical view that examines the negative aspects of social media on human life.

# Chapter 26
# The Interaction of Social Media Addiction and Communication Anxiety During the COVID-19 Period:
## The Case of Individuals Over 65 in Konya Province

**Özge Akcaoğlu Erdem**
*Bolu Abant İzzet Baysal University, Turkey*

**Ahmet Tuncay Erdem**
*Bolu Abant İzzet Baysal University, Turkey*

## ABSTRACT

*While it is known that the COVID-19 epidemic has adversely affected many countries in the world, the stress and anxiety experienced by elderly individuals, especially during pandemic periods, has been more than that of younger individuals. The avoidance of the disease, especially by individuals over the age of 65, has prevented these individuals from communicating face-to-face with other people. In this context, the main purpose of the research is to determine the effect of communication concerns of individuals over the age of 65 on social media addiction. The research question was determined as "Does the communication anxiety seen in individuals over the age of 65 have an effect on social media addiction during the COVID-19 process?" In order to answer the research question, a study was conducted on the population of individuals over the age of 65 living in Konya. 423 individuals who use social media actively participated in the research. As a result of the research, it was determined that communication anxiety strengthens social media addiction behavior.*

DOI: 10.4018/978-1-6684-8397-8.ch026

## INTRODUCTION

People live in society. It is known that the most basic communication occurs within the family because the individuals who make up society are brought up in the family environment. Communication within the family is also seen as the most religious education. It is known that the lack of communication is the basis of the conflicts and disagreements experienced by individuals in societies formed by families. Societies are prosperous with the spread of healthy communication to society, starting from the family. Family members then continue their education by establishing friendships with their external environment and then continue their lives with business friendship relations. In this context, bilateral relations are of great importance for the lives of individuals. Individuals meet their physical needs through their relationships with their external environment. On the other hand, in addition to their physical needs, individuals should also meet their psychological needs. Especially as Masluw explains in the hierarchy of needs pyramid, after the physiological needs of the individuals that make up the society are satisfied, individuals want their security needs to be met, and after these needs are met, they wait for their needs for love and socialization to come. Since the socialization and communication needs of individuals, who are social beings, are the most basic needs, it is vital to meet these needs.

Individuals living in societies live collectively in interaction with each other in order to maintain their lives. This does not mean that individuals only come together. It is used in the sense that individuals should live in a society by establishing relationships. Because individuals are expected to have this whole cultural, economic, and social relation at the point of meeting their needs from the most basic to the most complex, in this framework, society can be characterized as a complex set of relations rather than a numerical community. The most basic tool in establishing the interactions between individuals is communication. For this reason, individuals are in constant communication with each other, and communication is an activity that requires individuals to live in society. Establishing and maintaining these relations can only be achieved through communication activities. Although communication is the sharing of feelings and thoughts with other people, it contributes to the development of societies by ensuring that individuals exist in society. On the other hand, it will be possible for the individual to gain sufficient communication skills in establishing healthy human relations by recognizing their self. Individuals will live peacefully in society by continuing to interact with others. For this reason, communicating and acquiring communication skills are considered indispensable obligations for society.

Today, information and communication technologies are used intensively, and individuals have become more dependent on these networks by using information networks and are trying to use technology as a facilitator for their work. Communicating over the Internet has become an indispensable part of the modern age. People can communicate through emails, messaging apps, social media, and other online communication tools. With communication, individuals convey their emotions, such as anger, anxiety, fear, happiness, and joy, to others. These emotional behaviors occur through interaction and communication between individuals and are vital for individuals to live in society and share with others. In this context, it has become more difficult for the individuals who make up society to socialize during the COVID-19 pandemic. The compulsory isolation experienced by individuals during the pandemic has created an obstacle to the need for socialization, which Maslow also stated in the hierarchy of needs. During the pandemic, the problems of individuals not being able to socialize played a leading role in the occurrence of psychological and physical problems. Individuals who cannot fulfill their socialization needs will experience societal problems and take on a negative mood. In other words, with COVID-19, individuals may face negative emotional states such as anxiety, dissatisfaction, and dissatisfaction. However, individuals with problems in socialization will lead a more solitary life and become more distant from society. Individuals in such a negative mood will try to meet their online socialization needs. Individuals using the Internet will try to relieve their loneliness on the screen or the phone. The main reason for this is that individuals will socialize through social media in an environment of loneliness, where they feel healthier without exposure to the COVID-19 virus. Especially in the pandemic process, the use of social media by individuals aged 65 and over, who may experience the most problems from the diseases that may be possible, is more common in this period.

In the study, the research was carried out considering the possibility of individuals in society being dependent on social media to meet their communication and socialization needs due to the difficulties they experience in communicating with the people around them during the COVID-19 pandemic period. It has become inevitable for individuals who have become lonely during the pandemic to meet their socialization and communication needs with different methods. In this context, the research problem is the idea that these individuals use social media and become addicted due to the lack of communication and socialization during the COVID-19 period. In this direction, it aims to determine that individuals over the age of 65, who suffer more from compulsory isolation during the pandemic, experience social media addiction and that this addiction is due to direct communication anxiety. The study's primary purpose is to determine the effect of communication concerns of individuals over the age of 65 on their social media addictions during the COVID-19 period. In this direction, the research's main question was, "Is the reason for social media addiction communication anxiety?" To answer the research question, the population and sample for individuals aged 65 and over were determined. In this context, the purpose of selecting individuals aged 65 and over is that they experience more communication concerns because they are more affected by compulsory isolation, and their limited range of movement affects these individuals more. In this direction, they tend to determine that social media addiction is caused by communication anxiety, based on the idea that individuals over 65 get used to social media and use these platforms more.

## CONCEPTUAL FRAMEWORK

### Communication

Communication is a Latin word derived from the word communication. Community or community life, which informs individuals about changes and developments related to objects, phenomena, and events in a specific environment, transfers their knowledge to each other regarding these findings and is formed by individuals who have similar experiences in the face of the same objects, problems and phenomena, and who have similar feelings and express them to each other. The statements of judgment, attitude, emotion, and thought carried out within the body are defined as communication (Öksüzoğulları, 2013; Karademir and Aytekin, 2022; Douglas and Sutton, 2023; Schlosser, 2023). Communication, images, writings, words, movements, etc., can be transmitted between groups, individuals, and societies of thoughts, feelings, or information. It is described as a mutual information transfer process with tools.

Successful and effective communication starts with listening well to the other person. With careful listening, the messages sent by the receiver can be understood effectively and accurately, and it also makes communication effective (Öksüzoğulları, 2013: 21). For effective communication, it is crucial to know the communication processes and act according to these processes. Communication items; Source (sender, transmitter), Message (message), Channel (communication medium), Receiver-target (the party to which the message is intended), Feedback (return, feedback) (Gönen, 2015: 7; Freelon and Wells, 2020; Schlosser, 2023)). On the other hand, as the first step in the communication process, there is a need for the person or persons who initiate the communication. This person or persons is called the "Donor". The person or persons who will receive the message sent by the sender are also called "Recipients". The vehicle that carries the message from the transmitter to the receiver is the "Carrier". The recipient takes action when they receive the message. The elements that inform the quality and quantity of this action are also called "Feedback" (Başaran, 1996: 64). To be able to communicate effectively, it is essential to be motivated and knowledgeable; however, for these two to turn into appropriate action, individuals must also have skills (Spitzberg, 1983).

## Communication Anxiety

Although communication anxiety is defined as the tension, anxiety, and fear that a person feels during the communication process that he/she plans to establish or establishes, individuals have difficulties during communication due to this situation. On the other hand, individuals cannot be sure of the messages they receive or transmit, and as a result, the effectiveness and success of communication decrease. Although this situation is also described as communication anxiety, communication anxiety expresses a negative situation that should be prevented (Çakmak and Aktan, 2016: 20). Societies develop by being strengthened effectively with communication, and the fact that communication is widespread, the environments created by communication and the needs of individuals are taken into account, and the situation that their needs cannot be met with lack of communication makes communication a source of anxiety in individuals, and this negative situation necessitates the investigation of communication anxiety (McCroskey et al., 1976:377). According to some individuals, although communication anxiety is not seen as a serious problem that threatens the lives of individuals, it is considered one of the most researched communication problems because it negatively affects the quality of life of individuals and limits the choice of individuals who feel anxiety. In addition, it continues to be one of the subjects of great interest to researchers who conduct research in the field of communication today (McCroskey et al., 1976; McCroskey et al., 1982; Burgoon and Hale, 1983).

Along with the developing information technologies, the exposure of individuals to a lot of information and information causes communication anxiety in individuals. However, today, excessive information overload causes communication anxiety and the anxiety created by the ever-widening gap in the flow of information that individuals understand and think they should understand. It is the anxiety of deprivation caused by the communication of individuals with other people in society or the possible communication. Communication anxiety also expresses the sadness of not being able to participate in communication cognitively (Mutlu, 2012: 153-156). McCroskey has a similar definition of communication anxiety; it expresses reluctance or silence to communicate and states that these two expressions are synonymous. Communication anxiety differs from other structures because it causes fear and anxiety (McCroskey, 1977: 79). On the other hand, communication anxiety refers to a family consisting of situations such as shyness, unwillingness to communicate, silence, and stage fright (Allen and Bourhis, 1996: 215).

Communication anxiety is also defined as "social anxiety". However, social anxiety covers a broader area of human behavior (Matsuoka and Rahimi, 2011: 899). Communication anxiety is a broad-based fear or anxiety about the communicative act carried out by many individuals. These people expect negative emotions and results from communication and avoid communication if possible or suffer from various anxiety-type feelings when forced to communicate (McCroskey et al., 1976: 376). People with high communication anxiety often avoid communication in order not to experience this anxiety and fear. This does not mean that a person with high communication anxiety will never communicate. That is, individuals with high communication anxiety prefer to communicate less than those with low (McCroskey, 1977: 79). Communication anxiety is an individual's emotional response to the communication process or the other party. Students who experience such anxiety become tense and uncomfortable in the classroom and have little enthusiasm for communicating with their peers or teachers. Because of this anxiety, they may hesitate to talk, forget what they want to say, or make mistakes while speaking (Geçer and Gümüş, 2010: 3008). An individual who has never experienced communication anxiety is a rare individual.

Similarly, although such people exist, it is a relatively rare individual who experiences anxiety in all communication situations. Except for these rare individuals, even people with very high-attribute communication anxiety find some situations in which they are comfortable communicating. The most common of these situations is communication with close friends. Close friends produce less anxiety and anxiety because less anxious individuals can be close friends. In contrast, more threatening individuals are avoided (McCroskey, 1984: 20). In particular, people with high communication anxiety are more likely to avoid or withdraw from communicative contact when the option is available. It is crucial to distinguish communication anxiety from the constructs of silence and shyness. Silence relates to people who communicate ineffectively because they do not have adequate communication skills. Shyness is seen as a tendency to speak less than average, which may be caused by high communication anxiety, reticence, or other causal factors. People with high communication anxiety may be reticent or shy. However, many people who are reticent and shy may not experience high communication anxiety (McCroskey et al., 1983: 213-214).

## Social Media Addiction

Although social media is defined as the environment in which individuals in society socialize and socialize to communicate with each other, social media can also be defined as a communication environment in which the whole of the content determines the blogs created by the users of this platform and the issues that shape the society are shaped (Şeker, 2018). Social media is also described as platforms where people constantly meet with their external environment, reach the information they want to research about the subjects they are curious about, stay up-to-date, and create a suitable environment for the rest of their lives (Demir and Kumcagiz, 2019). The most basic feature that makes social media different from other internet platforms is that it is personal and can be used by individuals of all ages. However, everyone uses social media differently, and while some use social media to become lonely, others use it to meet new people and relieve their loneliness (Aksoy, 2020).

Social media addiction is a term used when the individual spends a lot of time on social media, this time is increasing, and the time spent on social media negatively affects the other functions of the person in daily life (Durar, 2018). The advancement of science and technology day by day has taken humanity one step further. However, individuals desire more to be happy and to be satisfied with the life they live in. In addition, instead of being dependent on technology while using the blessings it brings, it will be healthier to make life easier by using it appropriately and correctly. It is thought that these will be done through social support (Marengo et al., 2022; Lin et al., 2023; Saputri and Yumarni, 2023). Social support channels are family, friends, and a special person. Determining which of these channels affects the individual's happiness, life satisfaction, and social media addiction is important. In this way, the social support channels of individuals will be improved, and the relevant variables will be changed positively. In this respect, this study is thought to help those working with positive psychology and social media addiction (Parlak Sert and Başkale, 2022; Laçin Doğan et al., 2023: 16; Matsuzaka et al., 2023). Social media addiction is being extremely fond of social media platforms and the desire to be constantly in these environments, and this situation affects the person's daily life (Andreassen and Hetland, 2014).

## METHOD

### Population and Sample of the Research

The research population consists of individuals aged 65 and over living in Konya. Since the research universe could not be determined precisely, it was aimed to reach 400 samples in the research. In the sample selection process from the population, male individuals over 65 living in Konya were determined, and 423 non-random individuals were selected as the sample from the population. The universe of the study could not be determined as an integer; in this case, it was determined that 387 samples represented the universe with a 5% margin of error according to Balcı (2001: 95)'s universe sampling table. In addition, when it is desired to determine a sample with a 5% error (95% confidence) in the research, it is sufficient to select a minimum of 383 data from the sample in case the universe consists of 100,000 units, and if the sample consists of 1,000,000 units or more (Cohen et al., 2007; Tutar and Erdem, 2020). In this context, obtaining 423 pieces of data is considered sufficient.

### Research Model, Scales, and Data Collection Technique

The research used a field research method, and a questionnaire form was created in line with the information obtained from the literature. The questionnaire consists of three parts; questions about communication anxiety, social media addiction, and demographic characteristics are included. The first of the scales used in the research is the "Communication Anxiety Scale"; It was developed by McCroskey (1982) and consisted of 24 expressions. This scale was adapted to Turkish by Çakmak (2018). The social media addiction scale, the second research scale, was developed by Tutgun-Ünal and Deniz (2016) and consisted of 41 statements. The research model is given below.

*Figure 1. Research model*

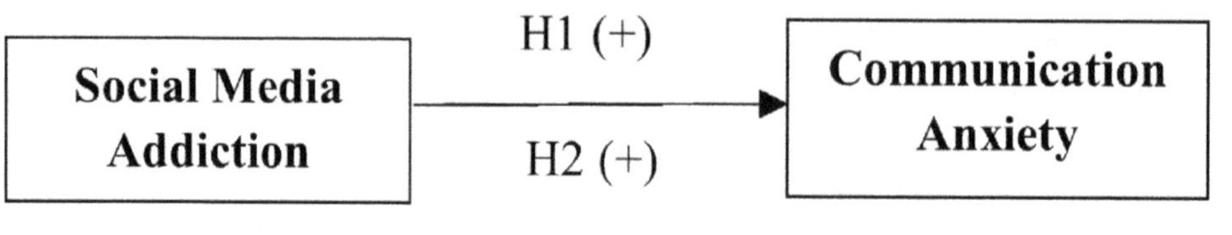

## Research Hypotheses

The hypotheses to be tested in the research are stated below;

H1: There is a positive relationship between social media addiction and communication anxiety perception.
H2: Communication anxiety affects social media addiction positively and significantly.

# FINDINGS

## Demographic Findings

Demographic data obtained from the research data are shown in Table 1.

*Table 1. Demographic findings*

| Gender | Frequency (n) | Percentage (%) | Marital Status | Frequency (n) | Percentage (%) |
|---|---|---|---|---|---|
| Female | 175 | 41,37 | Married | 356 | 84,16 |
| Male | 248 | 58,62 | Single | 67 | 15,84 |
| **Level of Education** | **Frequency (n)** | **Percentage (%)** | **Age** | **Frequency (n)** | **Percentage (%)** |
| Elementary Education | 113 | 26,71 | 65 | 319 | 75,41 |
| Associate Degree | 182 | 43,03 | 66-70 | 71 | 16,79 |
| License | 103 | 24,35 | 71-75 | 24 | 5,67 |
| Graduate | 25 | 5,91 | 76-above | 9 | 2,13 |

Within the scope of the research, it was determined that 58% of the participants were male, and approximately 42% were female. While 84% of the participants in the study are married individuals, 15% are single individuals. Considering their educational status, it was determined that the participants were generally high school graduates, and this rate was 43%. Other educational backgrounds of the participants were determined as 26% primary school, 24% undergraduate, and 5% graduate. Finally, when the age levels of the participants were examined, it was determined that 75% of the individuals were 65 years old, while 16% were 66-70 years old, 5% were 71-75 years old, and 2% were 76 years old and over.

## Validity and Reliability Analysis of Research Questionnaire Statements

Within the scope of the research, factor analysis was applied to the questionnaire statements. Table 2 shows the factor analysis expressions for communication anxiety.

As seen in Table 2, the answers given to the statements regarding the communication anxiety scale were subjected to factor analysis. The Kaiser-Meyer-Olkin coefficient, which shows the suitability of the data set for factor analysis, was determined as 0.957. The Bartlett value was determined to be significant (P=0.00), and the question set was suitable for factor analysis. There are 24 statements related to the communication anxiety scale. As a result of the analysis, only one factor was determined. Factors with eigenvalues of 1 and above were taken into account, and it was seen that there was one dimension. It is seen that this dimension takes 9,712 eigenvalues and explains 64,431% of the total variance. The second scale considered within the scope of the research is the social media addiction scale, and the factor analysis and factor loads related to this scale are given in Table 3.

*Table 2. Communication anxiety factor loads*

| Communication Anxiety Expressions | | Factor Loads |
|---|---|---|
| I am afraid to express myself in meetings. | | ,855 |
| I feel very nervous when chatting with someone I just met. | | ,852 |
| I don't like to participate in group discussions. | | ,849 |
| I usually feel comfortable participating in group discussions. | | ,838 |
| Being in a group discussion with new people makes me nervous and irritable. | | ,830 |
| I am relaxed and calm when participating in group discussions. | | ,825 |
| I am usually calm and relaxed during dialogue | | ,814 |
| I feel quite comfortable in dialogue with someone I have just met. | | ,810 |
| I am usually nervous when I have to attend a meeting | | ,807 |
| For the most part, I am calm and relaxed when attending meetings. | | ,801 |
| I am very calm and relaxed when invited to a meeting to express an idea | | ,820 |
| Communicating in meetings often bothers me | | ,817 |
| I get nervous and irritable when participating in group discussions | | ,798 |
| I like to be involved in group discussions. | | ,797 |
| I am very comfortable answering questions in a meeting | | ,786 |
| I am not afraid to express myself clearly in dialogues | | ,781 |
| I am usually irritable and nervous during dialogue | | ,776 |
| I'm afraid to express myself openly in dialogues | | ,612 |
| I'm not afraid/shy to make a speech | | ,602 |
| I feel very tense and tight in parts of my body when giving a speech | | ,592 |
| I feel comfortable giving a speech | | ,543 |
| When I'm speaking, I get confused and my thoughts are jumbled | | ,521 |
| I can speak confidently | | ,513 |
| I get so anxious when giving a speech that I forget facts that I actually know. | | ,505 |
| **Eigenvalue** | | 9,712 |
| **Explained Variance** | | 64,431 |
| **Total Variance** | | 64,431 |
| **Kaiser-Meyer-Olkin (KMO) sample adequacy measure** | | ,957 |
| **Bartlett Test** | **Chi-Square** | 5115,209 |
| | **df** | 107 |
| | **Sig.** | ,000 |

*Table 3. Social media addiction factor loads*

| Social Media Addiction Expressions | Factor Loads |
|---|---|
| Social media is the best place I take refuge when I'm overwhelmed by my problems. | ,901 |
| As long as I use social media, I forget everything. | ,896 |
| When I don't use social media for a while, the thought of using social media keeps my mind busy. | ,832 |
| I think my life would be boring, empty and tasteless without social media. | ,831 |
| When I'm not connected to the internet, I think about social media intensively. | ,829 |
| Because of social media, I give less priority to my hobbies, leisure and recreational activities. | ,821 |
| It happens that I spend more time on social media than I think. | ,811 |
| Every time I decide to disconnect from social media, I say to myself "just a few more minutes". | ,809 |
| I cannot give up using social media for a long time. | ,802 |
| It happens that I use social media more than I planned. | ,799 |
| When using social media, I cannot understand how time passes. | ,782 |
| I spend long periods of time on social media-related actions (games, chats, looking at photos, etc.). | ,780 |
| I use social media to forget about my personal problems. | ,697 |
| When I feel alone, I spend time on social media. | ,697 |
| I prefer to surf social media to get rid of negative thoughts in my life. | ,682 |
| I think a lot about what's been going on social media recently. | ,665 |
| There are times when I try to stop the use of social media and fail. | ,660 |
| If I have a job to do, I check social media beforehand. | ,660 |
| I have an intense desire to control social media use. | ,659 |
| I make fruitless efforts to quit using social media. | ,591 |
| I make fruitless efforts to control social media use. | ,588 |
| I try to reduce the time I spend on social media, I fail. | ,582 |
| I use social media more even though it has a negative impact on my job/work. | ,580 |
| The use of social media causes me to have problems in my relationships with people who are important to me. | ,579 |
| My use of social media creates problems in my life. | ,578 |
| I prefer spending time on social media to going out with my friends. | ,574 |
| People criticize me for the amount of time I spend on social media. | ,571 |
| I find myself trying to hide how long I've been surfing social media. | ,570 |
| There are times when I forget to eat because of social media. | ,561 |
| Because of the use of social media, I spend less time on my personal care. | ,554 |
| There are changes/disorders in my sleep pattern due to the use of social media. | ,552 |
| I wonder what's going on on social media. | ,550 |
| There are times when I neglect my spouse or family members because of social media. | ,549 |
| Sometimes I neglect my friends because of social media. | ,544 |
| Due to social media, I cannot finish the activities I started on time. | ,540 |
| I neglect school or work-related work to spend more time on social media. | ,539 |
| I prefer spending time on social media to spending time with my friends. | ,536 |

*continues on following page*

*Table 3. Continued*

| Social Media Addiction Expressions | | Factor Loads |
|---|---|---|
| My school work or work is interrupted because of the time I spend on social media. | | ,532 |
| My productivity decreases because of social media. | | ,523 |
| I sometimes experience physical problems (back, headache, eye pain, etc.) due to social media use. | | ,512 |
| The more things I have to do, the more my desire to use social media increases. | | ,505 |
| **Eigenvalue** | | 12,992 |
| **Explained Variance** | | 75,912 |
| **Total Variance** | | 75,912 |
| **Kaiser-Meyer-Olkin (KMO) sample adequacy measure** | | ,913 |
| **Bartlett Test** | **Chi-Square** | 6619,981 |
| | **df** | 198 |
| | **Sig.** | ,000 |

As seen in Table 3, the answers given to the statements about the social media addiction scale were subjected to factor analysis. The Kaiser-Meyer-Olkin coefficient, which shows the suitability of the data set for factor analysis, was determined as 0.913. The Bartlett value was determined to be significant (P=0.00), and the question set was suitable for factor analysis. There are 41 statements related to the social media addiction scale. As a result of the analysis, only one factor was determined. Factors with eigenvalues of 1 and above were taken into account, and it was seen that there was one dimension. It is seen that this dimension takes 12,992 eigenvalues and explains 75,912% of the total variance. According to these results, it is seen that all the questions within the scope of the research are valid. After this stage, reliability analysis was applied to the scale expressions. The mean, standard deviation, and Cronbach's alpha values for the communication anxiety and social media addiction scales are shown in Table 4.

*Table 4. Reliability of variables and frequency mean*

| Scales | Mean Frekans | Standard Deviation | Alpha (α) | Number of Questions (n) |
|---|---|---|---|---|
| Social Media Addiction | 3,26 | 0,960 | 0,88 | 24 |
| Communication Anxiety | 3,14 | 0,991 | 0,85 | 41 |

According to the model designed in the research, reliability analysis was applied to the scales of social media addiction, the independent variable, and communication anxiety, the dependent variable. As seen in Table 4, the alpha (Cronbach alpha) coefficient in the scales was determined as 0.85 for communication anxiety and 0.88 for social media addiction, and these results show that the research data is highly reliable.

## Research Hypothesis Analysis

The correlation values for testing the first hypothesis in the study are given in Table 5.

*Table 5. Analysis results for social media addiction and communication anxiety correlation values*

| | | Social Media Addiction |
|---|---|---|
| **Communication Anxiety** | Pearson Correlation<br>Sig. (2-tailed) | , 629**<br>,000 |

**Correlation is significant at the 0.01 level (2-tailed).
*Correlation is significant at the 0.05 level (2-tailed).

Table 3 shows the correlation relationship between the scales. Looking at the results of the correlation analysis, It is seen that there is a positive and significant relationship between communication anxiety and social media addiction (r=-0.629; p<0.01). In other words, a positive 62% relationship was found between communication anxiety and social media addiction. In this context, the H1 hypothesis of the research was accepted.

The results of the regression analysis performed to determine the effect of communication anxiety on social media addiction are summarized in Table 6.

*Table 6. Analysis results for social media addiction and communication anxiety regression values*

| | | Sig. | Beta | t |
|---|---|---|---|---|
| | | ,000 | | 5,724 |
| Social Media Addiction | | ,000 | 0,525 | 1,252 |
| R | | ,011 | | |
| R2 | | ,270 | | |
| Adjusted R2 | | ,291 | | |
| Standard error | | ,066 | | |
| F Value | 41,671 | | | |
| Durbin-Watson | 2,414 | | | |

When the regression analysis results in Table 6 are examined, it can be stated that the model as a whole is significant F(2,414)= 41,671; p<0.05. It has been determined that communication anxiety (p= 0.525) positively affects social media addiction, and it can be said that 29.2% of the change in social media addiction is explained by independent variables (Adjusted R2 = 0.292). The H2 hypothesis is accepted.

## FUTURE RESEARCH AND DIRECTIONS

It can be said that researchers who want to do research in the future can come to different results with different samples. It is also recommended that researchers who wish to conduct research in the future collect data from individuals in different age groups and conduct exploratory research with in-depth interviews with individuals using the qualitative research method. Researchers can also conduct blended research using quantitative and qualitative research methods. On the other hand, a reanalysis by adding different mediator or regulatory variables to the variables in the research model can also be within the scope of the recommendation. Finally, it is recommended to conduct research by relating the concepts of social media addiction and communication anxiety to digital addiction, life satisfaction, job satisfaction, future anxiety, happiness at work, social intelligence, and emotional intelligence, which are other behavioral sciences.

## CONCLUSION

Maslow states in his hierarchy of needs that socialization is the most critical need of a person after physiological and safety needs. In this context, the most fundamental reason why Maslow stated the need to love, be loved, and socialize as needed in the 3rd step is that people are social beings and that people who are social beings should interact with others. Since human existence, before communicating with other people, the most basic communication is established with the mother in the family. On the other hand, people establish the education they receive from their family through communication. As communication is the most basic need, individuals who make up society should be in contact with others in their private and business lives. This communication need requires other communication skills and communication efforts. The primary purpose of all the essential components that facilitate communication efforts is to ensure that the messages produced by individuals reach the opposite channel, that is, the receiver, accurately.

On the other hand, considering that the most critical tool in the development and development of communication is information communication technologies, it is inevitable for all individuals to use information communication technologies today. Since our age is the information age, the use of information technologies is becoming increasingly common, both at the level of companies and the state and at the level of individual communication. In this framework, individual communication transforms into community communication and becomes communication between countries.

With the support of today's communication with digital tools, individuals and institutions have become more prone to communication. Especially the development of individual communication has led to the widespread use of social media platforms. With social media, individuals can easily communicate with all members of society, including other institutions or organizations, and have the opportunity to convey their messages correctly. With social media platforms, individuals can quickly transfer their messages to the other party, that is, to the receiver, wherever and whenever they want. In addition to the message, individuals can also find the opportunity to send other sharing materials such as pictures, files, and photos as they wish.

On the other hand, with the continuous development of information and communication technologies, communication opportunities are constantly developing. However, communication, which has been adversely affected by the crises and problems occurring in the world, has become increasingly digital. Economic crises, wars, and diseases in recent years have negatively affected traditional verbal communication and made it more digital. In particular, the pandemic epidemic, which is described as COVID-19, has negatively affected the verbal communication of individuals with each other, causing individuals to become unable to communicate with each other. Individuals who cannot communicate have become more unhappy in societies and cannot enjoy life. This situation negatively affected the quality of life of individuals and caused people to become lonely.

Within the scope of the research, people who cannot communicate due to the COVID-19 pandemic disease, which negatively affects society, and who try to overcome this deprivation in digital environments are subject. Although it is known that the communication opportunities of all individuals in society are limited during the pandemic period, individuals aged 65 and over were more affected by this restriction. It has been observed that these individuals have been virtually isolated by completely restricting their freedom to go out. In Turkey and other countries, individuals aged 65 and over have been banned from leaving their homes, especially in the early stages of the pandemic. Thus, people aged 65 and over experienced extreme miscommunication. In other words, individuals aged 65 and over who cannot go out and communicate with other people around them are seen as the individuals most affected by the COVID-19 pandemic. Many negative situations, such as anxiety, not being able to enjoy life, anxiety, and unhappiness, have been observed in these individuals who have to stay at home.

Although it is seen that lack of communication turns into anxiety in individuals aged 65 and over, these individuals have become more use of digital communication tools because they cannot communicate face to face. Individuals using digital tools had to learn to communicate, and others had to learn to use social media opportunities for meetings and correspondence. Despite their attractive functions, social media platforms also bring many problems. These individuals, who used keys and simple phones before, have started to use smart devices with more complex algorithms with the pandemic. These individuals, who have become more dependent on digital technology, have used more widespread technological communication tools and become addicted to social media. According to the findings obtained from the analysis of the data collected within the scope of the research, it was determined that communication anxiety had a positive and significant effect on social media addiction ($p<0.05$). At the same time, a significant positive relationship ($p<0.01$) between communication anxiety and social media addiction has been determined. In other words, it has been determined that communication anxiety strengthens social media addiction. Studies have shown that social media addiction causes a decrease in social relations (Müller et al., 2016), sleep problems (Wolniczak et al., 2013), low life satisfaction (Błachnio et al., 2017), and similar problems. One of these problems concerns communication activity, which is vital for people (Abd Rahman, 2014). For example, problems such as decreased communication and prevention of face-to-face interaction may occur. These problems become more critical, especially in professions such as nursing, where communication is essential (Açıkgöz et al., 2019). Nursing focuses on serving the needs of the human being as a biopsychosocial being. Although it is seen in the relevant literature that social media addiction affects many factors negatively, it shows that the findings obtained within the scope of the research also overlap with the literature. On the other hand, it has been observed that these individuals, who commonly use push-button phones, have started to be exposed to more technology by switching to smartphones. It has been observed that this situation causes both social media addiction and technology addiction in elderly individuals.

Cases like the collection of research data only from Konya (Turkey), the sample obtained only from persons aged 65 and over, and the use of only quantitative research methods in the research show the research limitations. The fact that the term social media addiction is only associated with one term, namely communication anxiety, can also be shown to be a limitation of the research.

## REFERENCES


Abd Rahman, S. H. (2014). Can't live without my FB, LoL: The influence of social networking sites on the communication skills of TESL students. *Procedia: Social and Behavioral Sciences*, *134*, 213–219. doi:10.1016/j.sbspro.2014.04.241

Açıkgöz, A., Ezen, M., Emir, B., & Özkaraman, A. (2019). Effect of social media dependence of nursing students on communication skills. *Kocaeli Medical Journal*, *8*(1), 130–140. doi:10.5505/ktd.2019.04934

Aksoy, S. (2020). *Üniversite Öğrencilerinde Sosyal Medya Bağımlılığının, Sosyal Kaygı ve Kişisel İyi Oluş İle Arasındaki İlişkinin İncelenmesi.* Yüksek Lisans Tezi, Üsküdar Üniversitesi Sosyal Bilimler Enstitüsü, Allen, M. and Bourhis, J. (1996). The relationship of communication apprehension to communication behavior: A meta-analysis. *Communication Quarterly*, *44*(2), 214–226.

Andreassen, C., & Hetland, J. (2014). i Pallesen, S.(2014). *Social network site addiction–an overview. Current Pharmaceutical Design*, *20*(25), 4053–4061. doi:10.2174/13816128113199990616 PMID:24001298

Balcı, A. (2001). *Sosyal bilimlerde araştırma. Yöntem, Teknik ve İlkeler*. PegemA Yayınları.

Başaran, İ. E. (1996). *Eğitim yönetimi (5. baskı)*. Yargıcı Matbaası.

Błachnio, A., Przepiorka, A., Senol-Durak, E., Durak, M., & Sherstyuk, L. (2017). The role of personality traits in Facebook and Internet addictions: A study on Polish, Turkish, and Ukrainian samples. *Computers in Human Behavior*, *68*, 269–275. doi:10.1016/j.chb.2016.11.037

Burgoon, J. K. and Hale, J. L. (1983). *A research note on the dimensions of communication reticence.*

Çakmak, V. (2018). *İletişim Kaygisi Ve Sosyal Medya*. Eğitim Yayınevi.

Çakmak, V. and Aktan, E. (2016). Öğrencilerin İletişim Kaygısı, Muziplik/Takılma ve Okul Başarısı Arasındaki İlişkinin İncelenmesi. *İletişim Kuram ve Araştırma Dergisi*(42).

Cohen, L., Manion, L., & Morrison, K. (2007). *Research methods in education, 6.* Routledge. doi:10.4324/9780203029053

Demir, Y., & Kumcağiz, H. (2019). Üniversite öğrencilerinin sosyal medya bağımlılığının farklı değişkenler açısından incelenmesi. *Türk Psikolojik Danışma ve Rehberlik Dergisi*, *9*(52), 23–42.

Douglas, K. M., & Sutton, R. M. (2023). What are conspiracy theories? A definitional approach to their correlates, consequences, and communication. *Annual Review of Psychology*, *74*(1), 271–298. doi:10.1146/annurev-psych-032420-031329 PMID:36170672

Durar, E. (2018). Üniversite öğrencilerinde sosyal medya bağımlılığının depresyon ve sosyal fobi ile ilişkisi. Sağlık Bilimleri Enstitüsü, Freelon, D. and Wells, C. (2020). Disinformation as political communication, (Vol. 37, pp. 145-156). Taylor & Francis.

Geçer, A. K., & Gümüş, A. E. (2010). Prediction of public and private university students' communication apprehension with lecturers. *Procedia: Social and Behavioral Sciences, 2*(2), 3008–3014. doi:10.1016/j.sbspro.2010.03.456

Gönen, M. (2015). *Akdeniz Üniversitesi Beden Eğitimi ve Spor Yüksekokulu öğrencilerinin iletişim beceri düzeyleri ile atılganlık düzeylerinin incelenmesi.*

Karademir, F., & Aytekin, Ç. (2022). İşitme Kayıplı Ebeveynlerin Çocukları (CODA): Ebeveynleri ile Sözlü İletişim Yoksunluğunun Dil ve Sosyal-Duygusal Gelişime Etkisine Genel Bir Bakış. *Gelişim ve Psikoloji Dergisi, 3*(6), 167–183. doi:10.51503/gpd.1062798

Laçin Doğan, B. G., Yilmaz, Y., & İşgör, İ. Y. (2023). Sosyal Desteğin Mutluluk, Yaşam Doyumu Ve Sosyal Medya Bağimliliği Üzerindeki Etkisinin Araştirilmasi. [IJOESS]. *Social Sciences, 14*(51), 13–26.

Lin, S., Longobardi, C., Gastaldi, F. G. M., & Fabris, M. A. (2023). Social Media Addiction and Aggressive Behaviors in Early Adolescents: The Mediating Role of Nighttime Social Media Use and Sleep Quality. *The Journal of Early Adolescence*, 02724316231160142. doi:10.1177/02724316231160142

Marengo, D., Fabris, M. A., Longobardi, C., & Settanni, M. (2022). Smartphone and social media use contributed to individual tendencies towards social media addiction in Italian adolescents during the COVID-19 pandemic. *Addictive Behaviors, 126*, 107204. doi:10.1016/j.addbeh.2021.107204 PMID:34875508

Matsuoka, R., & Rahimi, A. (2011). The positive effect of conference participation on reducing L2 communication apprehension. *Procedia Computer Science, 3*, 898–907. doi:10.1016/j.procs.2010.12.147

Matsuzaka, S., Avery, L. R., & Stanton, A. G. (2023). Black Women's Social Media Use Integration and Social Media Addiction. *Social Media + Society, 9*(1), 20563051221148977. doi:10.1177/20563051221148977

McCroskey, J., Richmond, V., Berger, B., & Baldwin, H. (1983). How to make a good thing worse: A comparison of approaches to helping students overcome communication apprehension. *Communication, 12*(1), 213–219.

McCroskey, J. C. (1977). Oral communication apprehension: A summary of recent theory and research. *Human Communication Research, 4*(1), 78–96. doi:10.1111/j.1468-2958.1977.tb00599.x

McCroskey, J. C. (1982). An introduction to rhetorical communication, (4 b.). Englewood Cliffs: Prentice Hall, Routledge.

McCroskey, J. C. (1984). The communication apprehension perspective. *Avoiding communication: Shyness, reticence, and communication apprehension*, 13-38.

McCroskey, J. C., Daly, J. A., & Sorensen, G. (1976). Personality correlates of communication apprehension: A research note. *Human Communication Research, 2*(4), 376–380. doi:10.1111/j.1468-2958.1976.tb00498.x

McCroskey, J. C., Simpson, T. J., & Richmond, V. P. (1982). Biological sex and communication apprehension. *Communication Quarterly, 30*(2), 129–133. doi:10.1080/01463378209369439

Müller, K. W., Dreier, M., Beutel, M. E., Duven, E., Giralt, S., & Wölfling, K. (2016). A hidden type of internet addiction? Intense and addictive use of social networking sites in adolescents. *Computers in Human Behavior, 55*, 172–177. doi:10.1016/j.chb.2015.09.007

Mutlu, E. (2012). *İletişim Sözlüğü, Sofos Yayınları*. Baskı.

Öksüzoğulları, H. (2013). *4-6 yaş grubu çocuğu olan ebeveynlerin çocuklarıyla iletişimlerinin çeşitli değişkenler açısından incelenmesi*. Mehmet Akif Ersoy Üniversitesi Eğitim Bilimleri Enstitüsü.

Saputri, R. A. M., & Yumarni, T. (2023). Social media addiction and mental health among university students during the COVID-19 pandemic in Indonesia. *International Journal of Mental Health and Addiction, 21*(1), 96–110. doi:10.100711469-021-00582-3 PMID:34230820

Schlosser, R. W. (2023). *The efficacy of augmentative and alternative communication*. Brill.

Şeker, V. T. (2018). Sosyal medya bağımlılığı ile depresyon ve anksiyete arasındaki ilişki. Sosyal Bilimler Enstitüsü, Tutar, H. and Erdem, A. T. (2020). *Örnekleriyle bilimsel araştırma yöntemleri ve SPSS uygulamaları*. Seçkin Yayıncılık, *1*.

Spitzberg, B. H. (1983). Communication competence as knowledge, skill, and impression. *Communication Education, 32*(3), 323–329. doi:10.1080/03634528309378550

Tutgun-Ünal, A., & Deniz, L. (2016). Üniversite öğrencilerinin sosyal medya bağımlılığının incelenmesi. *Route Educational and Social Science Journal, 3*(2), 155–181. doi:10.17121/ressjournal.488

Wolniczak, I., Cáceres-DelAguila, J. A., Palma-Ardiles, G., Arroyo, K. J., Solís-Visscher, R., Paredes-Yauri, S., Mego-Aquije, K., & Bernabe-Ortiz, A. (2013). Association between Facebook dependence and poor sleep quality: A study in a sample of undergraduate students in Peru. *PLoS One, 8*(3), e59087. doi:10.1371/journal.pone.0059087 PMID:23554978

## ADDITIONAL READING

Freiling, I., Krause, N. M., Scheufele, D. A., & Brossard, D. (2023). Believing and sharing misinformation, fact-checks, and accurate information on social media: The role of anxiety during COVID-19. *New Media & Society, 25*(1), 141–162. doi:10.1177/14614448211011451 PMID:36620434

Stone, L. B., & Veksler, A. E. (2022). Stop talking about it already! Co-ruminating and social media focused on COVID-19 was associated with heightened state anxiety, depressive symptoms, and perceived changes in health anxiety during Spring 2020. *BMC Psychology, 10*(1), 22. doi:10.118640359-022-00734-7 PMID:35130965

Wong, F. H. C., Leung, D. K. Y., Wong, E. L. Y., Liu, T., Lu, S., Chan, O. F., Wong, G. H. Y., & Lum, T. Y. S. (2022). The moderating role of community capacity for age-friendly communication in mitigating anxiety of older adults during the COVID-19 infodemic: Cross-sectional survey. *JMIR Infodemiology, 2*(1), e33029. doi:10.2196/33029 PMID:35257090

## KEY TERMS AND DEFINITIONS

**Addiction:** Addiction continuing to take a substance although it causes mental, physical, or social problems, not responding to the desire to quit, and the desire to take the substance cannot be stopped. For many years, it has been thought that the problem of addiction is a moral problem, that it arises as a result of a lack of will, and even that it is a result of personality weakness.

**Age:** It is each of the phases of existence, such as childhood, youth, old age, or time, which has passed since birth and is measured in years.

**Anxiety:** Anxiety is the response to an uncertain, potentially dangerous stimulus, while fear is the response to a "concrete danger". Sensation about future events with uncertain outcomes but believed to have negative results.

**Communication Anxiety:** Communication anxiety is a human quality characterized by fear or anxiety that arises in some communication efforts with other people.

**COVID-19:** The Novel Coronavirus Disease (COVID-19) is a virus that was first identified on January 13, 2020, as a result of research conducted in a group of patients who developed respiratory symptoms (fever, cough, shortness of breath) in Wuhan Province, China, in late December.

**Social Media:** Social media is an interactive communication platform that users search for, use, and produce content on the internet. With the introduction of Web 2.0 from the traditional media, it is media communication that provides access from one-way content sharing to two-way content exchange.

# Chapter 27
# How Adolescents Use Social Media to Navigate Their Mental Health:
## Examining Reddit's "/r/teenagers" Community

**Mohid Khan**
*Polygence Research Academy, USA*

**Ian Scott Stark**
*Texas Tech University, USA*

## ABSTRACT

*Research on the negative impact of social media on mental health is extensive and well-documented. However, in this process, relatively little attention has been paid to social media communities oriented around mental health. This study aimed to address this gap by using uses and gratifications theory to analyze the posts and comments related to mental health, anxiety, depression, and self-esteem in the "/r/teenagers" community on Reddit. The results revealed that many users in these communities turn to social media to identify with others and seek advice, while a smaller percentage uses social media for entertainment and escapism. An even smaller minority of users leverage social media platforms to educate others. By exploring the motivations and reasons behind social media use in mental health communities, this study provides valuable insights into the potential benefits and drawbacks of social media use in this context, as well as avenues for future research and intervention.*

DOI: 10.4018/978-1-6684-8397-8.ch027

## INTRODUCTION

The COVID-19 pandemic has led to a significant increase in screen time, particularly among adolescents. Among twelve and thirteen-year-olds, this number has doubled since the pandemic, with an average of 7.7 hours of non-school-related screen time a day (Fitzpatrick et al., 2020). As more educational resources, social interactions, and commercial transactions are moving online, the trend of increased screen time is showing no signs of slowing down. One specific area of screen time that has seen significant growth is social media (Moreno et al., 2009). Social media platforms provide free and accessible ways for users to connect with others around the world. They have transformed the way people communicate and share information (Rosen et al., 2013), but they also raise concerns about their impact on adolescent mental health (Twenge & Campbell, 2018). As the rates of adolescent depression continue to rise, it is essential to explore how young people use social media to navigate their mental health. It is also critical to examine the safety and reliability of mental health communities on social media, as these groups can provide vital support for those who may be struggling (Andreassen et al., 2017). Nonetheless, the humorous use of social media by young people for addressing mental health issues cannot be ignored, and more research is needed to understand this phenomenon (Wang et al., 2020).

Mental health is a crucial aspect of an individual's overall well-being, encompassing emotional, social, and physiological dimensions. Mental health issues can be caused by a range of factors such as genetic predispositions and traumatic experiences, leading to the development of a wide range of disorders, including depression, anxiety, schizophrenia, and many others (American Psychiatric Association, 2013). While numerous studies have been conducted to examine the relationship between screen time, social media, and adolescent mental health, the findings are still inconclusive (Twenge et al., 2018). Some studies suggest that social media usage can lead to lower self-esteem and increased anxiety levels (Kross et al., 2013), while others propose that screen time can promote cognitive growth and enhance extracurricular involvement (Canadian Paediatric Society, 2017). Although the results are not definitive, it is clear that excessive screen time has the potential to harm adolescent mental health. Therefore, it is crucial to continue exploring the relationship between screen time and mental health, to better understand how to promote positive mental health outcomes for young people.

Limiting screen time among adolescents is a complex issue, and it is important to consider how young people are coping with the mental health issues that arise from screen use. In recent years, economic recession and family breakdown have made it increasingly challenging for adolescents to access professional support for their mental health (Blum et al., 2000; Mojtabai, 2010). As a result, many young people have turned to social media platforms, which offer a sense of community and a place to seek help, regardless of geographic location or financial constraints. These online communities provide an accessible space for young people to share their experiences and connect with others who may be facing similar challenges. However, it is crucial to recognize the limitations of these platforms in providing effective support for mental health issues. While online communities can offer valuable emotional support, they are not a substitute for professional therapy or treatment. Therefore, it is necessary to explore how to best leverage social media and other digital tools to support young people's mental health and ensure that they have access to the resources and care they need.

To that effect, this study involved collecting data from the "/r/teenagers" community on Reddit, where young people discuss a wide range of topics, including mental health. Specifically, the study focused on posts related to four major mental health issues: "mental health," "anxiety," "depression," and "self-esteem." The collected data was transferred to a spreadsheet and categorized according to uses and gratifications theory (Keum et al, 2022). Using Reddit was essential in this study, as the platform is a popular social media site that enables users to communicate openly about their lives and issues (Xi et al., 2018). Moreover, the platform provides users with anonymity, which allows for more candid and honest conversations about sensitive topics such as mental health. With over 2.9 million members in the "/r/teenagers" community, the study was able to access a substantial amount of data. However, it is important to note that the sample obtained from Reddit is not necessarily representative of the wider adolescent population, and as such, the findings must be interpreted with caution. Nonetheless, this study provides valuable insights into the ways young people use social media to discuss and seek support for their mental health issues, and these insights can inform the development of effective digital interventions and support resources.

## LITERATURE REVIEW

Social media has become an integral part of everyday life, with millions of people around the world using these platforms to connect with others, share information, and stay informed about current events. While social media has revolutionized communication and made it easier than ever to stay connected, it has also brought about a range of new challenges and concerns. In this section, we will detail the contemporary understanding of social media use - its positive affordances, negative side effects, and theoretical framework - in order to shed light on this complex and rapidly evolving topic. We will examine the latest research on social media use, explore its impact on mental and physical health, and consider the implications of these findings for individuals, communities, and society as a whole. By taking a comprehensive and multidisciplinary approach, we hope to provide a deeper understanding of social media use and its effects, as well as identify areas for future research and potential interventions.

### Positive Affordances

One of the positive affordances of social media use is the ability to connect with others and form online communities. This can be especially important for individuals who are isolated or who live in areas where there is limited access to mental health resources. Social media provides a platform for individuals to connect with others who have similar experiences and to seek support from a supportive community. Studies have found that social media platforms can be particularly effective in connecting individuals with mental health conditions to supportive communities. For example, in a study of individuals with depression, anxiety, and other mental health disorders, participants reported using social media to find a sense of belonging and support from others who were experiencing similar issues (Naslund et al., 2019). Additionally, online communities formed on social media platforms can be especially important for individuals who may not have access to mental health resources in their local area (Shensa et al., 2017). The support and connection found in online communities can help to reduce feelings of isolation and improve overall well-being, as well as provide an avenue for peer support and self-help (Grieve et al., 2013).

Another positive aspect of social media use is the ability to access information and resources related to mental health. Social media provides a wealth of information and resources related to mental health, including articles, videos, and support groups. The accessibility of this information is particularly beneficial for individuals who may not have access to traditional mental health resources, or for whom the process of seeking help is too heavily stigmatized (Clement et al., 2015). Additionally, social media platforms can provide information in a variety of formats, such as infographics and videos, that can make the information more accessible and engaging (Chen & Wang, 2021). Social media also provides opportunities for mental health professionals to share their expertise and provide guidance to individuals seeking support (Välimäki et al., 2016).

Social media can also serve as a powerful tool for individuals to express themselves and advocate for mental health awareness. Social media platforms provide a space for individuals to share their personal experiences and stories related to mental health, which can help to reduce the stigma surrounding mental health issues. Additionally, social media can be used to raise awareness about mental health issues and promote mental health resources and services. For example, in a study of individuals with depression, participants reported using social media to share information and resources related to mental health, and to encourage others to seek help (Gowen et al., 2012). Through social media, individuals can use their voices to promote change and create a community that supports mental health advocacy.

## Negative Side Effects

Social media addiction is a growing concern in today's society, and it has been shown to have adverse effects on both mental and physical health (Lin et al., 2016). Individuals who struggle with social media addiction have been shown to experience increased levels of anxiety, depression, and loneliness, as well as a decreased quality of sleep (Andreassen et al., 2017). Moreover, excessive social media use has been linked to physical health problems such as headaches, neck and back pain, and obesity (Kuss & Griffiths, 2017). The addictive behavior is characterized by a strong desire to constantly check social media, leading to feelings of withdrawal and discomfort when not engaged with it (Ryan et al., 2014). This behavior is reinforced by the platforms, which use techniques such as notifications, instant gratification, and endless scrolling to keep users hooked. While social media platforms were originally designed to keep people connected, the addictive nature of these platforms can be harmful, leading to reduced productivity and overall quality of life (Kuss & Griffiths, 2017). Therefore, it is crucial to understand the risks associated with social media use and develop effective interventions to mitigate the negative effects of social media addiction on individuals and society as a whole.

People have an inherent tendency to compare themselves to others, particularly on social media platforms, which can lead to increased feelings of envy, and low self-esteem, and ultimately contribute to social media addiction (Chou & Edge, 2012). The pressure to present a perfect image on social media, driven by the desire to create a certain perception in the minds of others, can lead to further negative effects, including anxiety and depression (Lin et al., 2016). Additionally, the fear of missing out (FOMO) is a significant factor in social media addiction, as individuals feel compelled to constantly check social media for fear of missing out on important events or news (Andreassen et al., 2017). Finally, the rise of influencer culture, where individuals can make a living by promoting products or services on social media platforms, may also contribute to the addictive nature of social media (Falgoust et al., 2022). Altogether, many individuals may feel pressured to maintain a high level of engagement on social media to increase their visibility, or the visibility of others, further fueling the addiction.

## Theoretical Framework

The relationship between social media, addiction, and mental health is complex and requires further research to fully understand. One framework that can help to better understand the motivations and outcomes of social media use is uses and gratification theory (Keum et al, 2022). One of the key concepts of uses and gratifications theory is the idea that individuals use media to fulfill specific needs and desires. Unlike many other theories, it assumes focuses on the user, not the media itself, proposing that the media use is motivated (i.e. people have a purpose to use that form of media), which includes, but is not limited to seeking information, support, escaping from the demands of daily life. Additionally, the media will satisfy their expectations, the use of media was driven by an individual's choice, and the media competes with other forms of communication to fulfill desires (i.e. people would rather use mobile forms of communication such as FaceTime rather than in-person interactions), and that the media does not exert control over the users.

Uses and gratifications theory can be applied to understand media use in a variety of contexts. In the context of mental health, uses and gratification theory can be applied to understand why individuals use social media to discuss their experiences and seek support. For example, one might apply the theory to understand the motivations for using online support groups for mental health. Are these platforms' users there for support, to seek information about mental health, or perhaps simply as a coping mechanism to escape from their daily lives? That, indeed, is the question this chapter seeks to answer.

Specifically, adolescents are a group that is at a higher risk for mental health issues, and social media provides a platform for them to connect with others and seek support. However, while social media has the potential to support mental health, the motivations and outcomes of social media use for mental health among adolescents are not well understood. Thus, there is a critical need for research that examines the specific ways in which adolescents use social media to fulfill their mental health needs. This study aims to fill this gap by using uses and gratifications theory to analyze the posts and comments in the mental health communities of the /r/teenagers subreddit.

## METHODS

The data for this study was collected from the subreddit "r/teenagers" on the social media platform Reddit. This platform was chosen as a data source due to its large community of over 2.9 million members who can discuss a variety of topics, including personal experiences and mental health issues. Reddit's anonymous nature allows users to feel comfortable sharing personal information and opinions. Furthermore, Reddit provides access to a diverse range of individuals who may be hard to reach through traditional research methods, allowing for a broader sample space. Using a platform like Reddit increases the accuracy and generalizability of the study's findings.

### Data Collection Protocol

To collect the data for this study, a systematic approach was taken. First, a search was conducted by typing "mental health" into the search bar of the "/r/teenagers" subreddit on Reddit. The search was then sorted by "Top" and limited to posts from the past year to ensure the most relevant and up-to-date data was collected. The top twenty posts were selected to provide a representative sample of the most popular and engaging content related to mental health on the platform. Next, the comments were sorted by "Best," taking into account the comments with the highest upvote-to-downvote ratio, which indicates a positive consensus among the community. The first five comments in each post were then collected, providing a more comprehensive understanding of the attitudes and opinions of the community toward mental health topics.

To obtain more specific information, the previous steps were repeated using the search terms "depression," "anxiety," and "self-esteem," which are all major areas within mental health that adolescents, in particular, tend to struggle with. This allowed for a more in-depth analysis of the data, providing a comprehensive understanding of the issues most relevant to the target population. The use of these specific search terms allowed for a more nuanced view of mental health issues affecting adolescents, which can be used to develop targeted interventions and support services.

## Content Analysis Protocol

The data collected was then subject to content analysis based on the uses-and-gratification model. The application of uses and gratifications theory in this study is essential for gaining a more comprehensive understanding of the motivations and outcomes of social media use among adolescents. This theoretical framework offers a valuable lens for examining why individuals use media and the specific needs and desires they seek to satisfy. Through its use in this study, we aim to gain insight into the reasons why adolescents use /r/teenagers to discuss their mental health challenges and the outcomes they hope to achieve through such interactions. To that effect, the following five categories of uses and gratifications were identified:

1. **Information seeking:** the desire to be informed or educated about a topic related to mental health
2. **Social identification:** the need to identify with characters or situations related to mental health in the media environment
3. **Entertainment:** the desire for simple enjoyment and distraction from mental health issues
4. **Social interaction and support:** the desire to connect with others and enhance social relationships related to mental health
5. **Coping:** the need to escape from the stresses of daily life related to mental health.

To categorize each post, the following questions were used:

1. **Information seeking:** Does the post or comment ask questions to learn more about mental health topics, or seek and/or provide advice related to mental health?
2. **Social identification:** Does the post or comment relate to or identify with mental health issues or individuals experiencing them?
3. **Entertainment:** Is the post or comment completely irrelevant to the given mental health topic, or does it include jokes and memes related to mental health issues?
4. **Social interaction and support**: Does the post or comment share personal experiences related to mental health, or seek and/or provide support for others?
5. **Coping:** Does the post or comment describe stressful situations related to mental health, or seek and/or provide emotional release or catharsis?

The keywords used to identify each category are as follows:

1. **Information seeking:** advice, help, how to, questions
2. **Social identification:** relate, identify, empathize, connect
3. **Entertainment:** memes, jokes, humor
4. **Social interaction and support:** share, support, listen, feedback
5. **Coping:** vent, rant, stressed, overwhelmed

After collecting the data from Reddit, it was entered into Google Sheets, where each table contained the text of the post or comment and the corresponding URL to allow for replication of the study. The data was analyzed using formulas to identify trends and recurring themes based on the categories derived from uses and gratifications theory. It is worth noting that some of the twenty total posts that were included in the study had fewer than five comments, with some having only one or two, despite receiving a high number of upvotes. While this may limit the overall sample size, the available data was still sufficient for identifying key themes and trends in adolescent social media use related to mental health.

## RESULTS

This section presents the results of the content analysis on a tag-by-tag basis.

### Mental Health

The category of mental health was chosen as a broad topic to provide a general understanding of how teenagers use social media to cope with their mental health. It was hypothesized that the majority of posts would fall into the "4" category (users identifying with others in the environment) or the "5" category (users seeking to escape their daily stresses). This is because, according to common stereotypes, stressed individuals are expected to seek community support or vent about their problems to gain advice from others. As expected, the data analysis showed similar results, with 55% of users posting to identify with others and 30% posting to escape their daily stresses. A small proportion of users (10%) posted to give or receive advice, while 5% of posts were for simple entertainment purposes. The precise distribution is included in **Table 1** below:

*Table 1. Mental health posts*

| "MENTAL HEALTH" - POSTS | | | |
|---|---|---|---|
| CODE | CATEGORY | *n* | % |
| 1 | Information seeking | 1 | 5 |
| 2 | Social identification | 1 | 5 |
| 3 | Entertainment | 1 | 5 |
| 4 | Social interaction and support | 11 | 55 |
| 5 | Coping | 6 | 30 |

The hypothesis for the comments was that they would mostly fall under the "4" and "2" categories, with users either providing valuable advice or identifying with the original post to create a sense of community. The data showed some similarities to the hypothesis, with 52% of the 100 analyzed comments falling under the "4" category, and 15% falling under the "2" category. However, the data also revealed an unexpected result, with 25% of the comments categorized under "3" (simple entertainment). Moreover, the comments only matched their original post in 36% of the cases on average. The precise distribution is included in **Table 2** below:

*Table 2. Mental health comments*

| "MENTAL HEALTH" - COMMENTS | | | |
|---|---|---|---|
| CODE | CATEGORY | *n* | % |
| 1 | Information seeking | 0 | 0 |
| 2 | Social identification | 15 | 15 |
| 3 | Entertainment | 29 | 29 |
| 4 | Social interaction and support | 52 | 52 |
| 5 | Coping | 4 | 4 |

The analysis of both posts and comments showed that 52% of users utilized social media to identify with others in the community or environment, making it the most prevalent category. Perhaps unsurprisingly, 25% of users used humor as a coping mechanism, while 13% provided advice to others. Only a small percentage of users (8%) used social media to escape daily stresses, and an even smaller percentage (less than 1%) posted to educate or provide information. The precise distribution is included in **Table 3** below:

*Table 3. Mental health aggregate*

| "MENTAL HEALTH" - AGGREGATE | | | |
|---|---|---|---|
| CODE | CATEGORY | *n* | % |
| 1 | Information seeking | 1 | 0.8 |
| 2 | Social identification | 16 | 13.3 |
| 3 | Entertainment | 30 | 25 |
| 4 | Social interaction and support | 63 | 52.5 |
| 5 | Coping | 10 | 8.3 |

## Anxiety

Anxiety is a prevalent mental health issue among adolescents, which can have a significant impact on their daily lives. It was hypothesized that most of the posts related to anxiety would fall under the "5" category, as people often seek to escape their daily stresses, or the "2" category, where users may offer advice or share coping strategies. The data showed some alignment with these predictions, as 30% of the posts were written to give advice, and 15% to escape daily stresses. Surprisingly, 25% of the posts were for entertainment purposes, while 25% were written to identify with others. The precise distribution is included in **Table 4** below:

*Table 4. Anxiety posts*

| "ANXIETY" - POSTS | | | |
|---|---|---|---|
| CODE | CATEGORY | *n* | % |
| 1 | Information seeking | 1 | 5 |
| 2 | Social identification | 6 | 30 |
| 3 | Entertainment | 5 | 25 |
| 4 | Social interaction and support | 5 | 25 |
| 5 | Coping | 3 | 15 |

It was expected that the comments collected would mostly fall under the "4" or "2" categories, with users either identifying with others or offering advice. The analysis showed that almost half of the comments (49%) fell into the "4" category, demonstrating that users sympathized with others by identifying with them. However, surprisingly, over 40% of the comments were categorized as "3", indicating that users made unrelated jokes or comments. Only a small proportion of the comments (6%) provided advice. On average, the comments matched their original post in 46% of cases. The precise distribution is included in **Table 5** below:

*Table 5. Anxiety comments*

| "ANXIETY" - COMMENTS | | | |
|---|---|---|---|
| CODE | CATEGORY | *n* | % |
| 1 | Information seeking | 1 | 1.1 |
| 2 | Social identification | 6 | 6.3 |
| 3 | Entertainment | 41 | 43.2 |
| 4 | Social interaction and support | 47 | 49.5 |
| 5 | Coping | 0 | 0 |

Looking at the data as a whole, the results showed that 42% of the data (including both posts and comments) fell under the "4" category, while 40% were categorized under the "3" category. The remaining 17% of the data were divided among categories "1", "2", and "5". The precise distribution is included in **Table 6** below:

*Table 6. Anxiety aggregate*

| "ANXIETY" - AGGREGATE | | | |
|---|---|---|---|
| **CODE** | **CATEGORY** | *n* | % |
| 1 | Information seeking | 2 | 1.7 |
| 2 | Social identification | 12 | 10.4 |
| 3 | Entertainment | 46 | 40 |
| 4 | Social interaction and support | 52 | 45.2 |
| 5 | Coping | 3 | 2.6 |

## Depression

Depression, a common mental disorder characterized by persistent feelings of sadness and hopelessness, was used as a sub-category to explore how teenagers use social media to cope with their mental health. Given that depression is a prevalent issue, with serious implications for mental health, it was hypothesized that many posts would fall under the "5" category, where users seek to escape daily stresses, or the "2" category, where users provide strategies for coping with negative emotions. The data supported these predictions, with 45% of the collected posts categorized as "5" and only 10% as "2". Notably, many posts (25%) were written to identify with others in the community. In contrast to anxiety, far fewer posts (15%) fell under the "3" category. The precise distribution is included in **Table 7** below:

*Table 7. Depression posts*

| "DEPRESSION" - POSTS | | | |
|---|---|---|---|
| **CODE** | **CATEGORY** | *n* | % |
| 1 | Information seeking | 1 | 5 |
| 2 | Social identification | 2 | 10 |
| 3 | Entertainment | 3 | 15 |
| 4 | Social interaction and support | 5 | 25 |
| 5 | Coping | 9 | 45 |

The comments for depression were expected to fall mainly under the "4" and "2" categories, with users providing support and empathy or giving the advice to cope with the situation. As predicted, a majority of the comments (60%) were categorized under "4", where users sympathized with others by identifying with them. However, there were also a significant number of comments under "3" (23%), where users made jokes or comments unrelated to the original post. Fewer comments provided advice, with only 14% of comments falling under the "2" category, but it was still a higher percentage than that of anxiety. On average, 44% of the comments matched their original post. The precise distribution is included in **Table 8** below:

*Table 8. Depression comments*

| "DEPRESSION" - COMMENTS | | | |
|---|---|---|---|
| CODE | CATEGORY | *n* | % |
| 1 | Information seeking | 2 | 2 |
| 2 | Social identification | 14 | 14 |
| 3 | Entertainment | 23 | 23 |
| 4 | Social interaction and support | 60 | 60 |
| 5 | Coping | 1 | 1 |

The collected data from all categories showed that the majority of the posts and comments (54%) were under the "4" category, where users identified with others in their environment. On the other hand, the lowest percentage (21%) belonged to the "3" category, which focused on providing entertainment. Categories "1", "2", and "5" accounted for the remaining 24.1% of the data. The precise distribution is included in **Table 9** below:

*Table 9. Depression aggregate*

| "DEPRESSION" - AGGREGATE | | | |
|---|---|---|---|
| CODE | CATEGORY | *n* | % |
| 1 | Information seeking | 3 | 2.5 |
| 2 | Social identification | 16 | 13.3 |
| 3 | Entertainment | 26 | 21.7 |
| 4 | Social interaction and support | 65 | 54.2 |
| 5 | Coping | 10 | 8.3 |

## Self-Esteem

The topic of self-esteem was included to understand how teenagers use social media to cope with their self-confidence. Though it is not a mental disorder in itself, low self-esteem is a major contributing factor to various mental health disorders such as depression and anxiety. Cyberbullying, which is becoming increasingly prevalent, is a significant cause of low self-esteem among adolescents. Self-esteem is a belief that someone has about themselves, which can be influenced by societal comments. Therefore, it was hypothesized that the majority of the posts would fall into the "5" category, as users would vent their issues, or the "2" category, where users who have overcome low self-esteem issues would advise others. The data collected supported the hypothesis to some extent, with 25% of posts being in the "2" category, and ten out of twenty (50%) being in the "4" category. Surprisingly, a small proportion of posts (10%) were categorized as "5", with more posts (15%) being classified as "3". The precise distribution is included in **Table 10** below:

*Table 10. Self-esteem posts*

| "SELF-ESTEEM" - POSTS | | | |
|---|---|---|---|
| **CODE** | **CATEGORY** | *n* | % |
| 1 | Information seeking | 0 | 0 |
| 2 | Social identification | 5 | 25 |
| 3 | Entertainment | 3 | 15 |
| 4 | Social interaction and support | 10 | 50 |
| 5 | Coping | 2 | 10 |

The expectation was that comments would mostly fall into the "4" or "2" categories, with users either identifying with the original post or giving advice to those with low self-esteem. The results showed that 64% of comments were classified as "4", indicating users identified with the post by either agreeing or disagreeing with it. However, a considerable number of comments were categorized as "3" for simple entertainment. As with the previous categories, there were few comments providing advice (9%). The remaining comments (11%) fell into the subcategories of being informed, giving advice, and escaping from daily stresses. On average, 65% of comments matched their original post, a considerably larger percentage compared to the other categories. The precise distribution is included in **Table 11** below:

*Table 11. Self-esteem comments*

| "SELF-ESTEEM" - COMMENTS | | | |
|---|---|---|---|
| **CODE** | **CATEGORY** | *n* | % |
| 1 | Information seeking | 1 | 1.1 |
| 2 | Social identification | 9 | 9.7 |
| 3 | Entertainment | 22 | 23.7 |
| 4 | Social interaction and support | 60 | 64.5 |
| 5 | Coping | 1 | 1.1 |

The majority of data points (61%) in the self-esteem category fell under the "4" category, with users either identifying with the original post or expressing their opinions on it. The proportion of data points in the "3" category was 22%, which was consistent with the data points in the anxiety category. Categories "1", "2", and "5" made up the remaining 16% of the data. The precise distribution is included in **Table 12** below:

*Table 12. Self-esteem aggregate*

| "SELF-ESTEEM" - AGGREGATE | | | |
|---|---|---|---|
| **CODE** | **CATEGORY** | *n* | % |
| 1 | Information seeking | 1 | 0.9 |
| 2 | Social identification | 14 | 12.4 |
| 3 | Entertainment | 25 | 22.1 |
| 4 | Social interaction and support | 70 | 61.9 |
| 5 | Coping | 3 | 2.7 |

# DISCUSSION

## Practical Recommendations

This section of the chapter will focus on the key findings of the study and the implications that they hold for readers. The results of the study can be used to provide recommendations on how to use social media to manage mental health issues. While these recommendations are not intended to be prescriptive, they can serve as useful guidelines for readers to consider.

### Practical Recommendation #1: Share Your Troubles With Others, Especially in Online Communities, as it Can Have a Positive Impact on Your Mental Health

This recommendation is supported by the data collected in the study, which showed that at least 55% of the comments fell into the "1", "2", or "4" categories, indicating that users were providing support or advice to others. In fact, closer to 60% or 70% of the comments were positive responses. These results suggest that sharing one's feelings with others in online communities can be an effective way to manage stress and cope with mental health issues. Online platforms like Reddit provide dissociative anonymity that allows for disinhibition, emotional engagement, and feedback without fear of judgment, making them an excellent source of support. This option can be especially useful for those who are unable to access professional help or cannot afford to pay for it. By sharing one's feelings with others in online communities, individuals can find a sense of community and support, which can positively impact their mental health.

To implement this recommendation, individuals feeling stressed or struggling with mental health should consider joining online communities that offer support. While meeting with a psychologist or trusted individual may be preferable in certain cases, online communities provide a diverse range of opinions and experiences that can be beneficial, particularly when access to other resources is limited. Although some people view online communities as inappropriate or even detrimental, the data shows that these concerns may be unfounded. Less than 10% of the comments collected under serious posts (categories "4" and "5") were written for entertainment purposes, indicating that these communities can be a source of meaningful support. It's important to remember that every community, whether online or not, may have negative elements, and to approach these communities with an open mind and willingness to engage with others.

## Practical Recommendation #2: Be Clear About the Seriousness of Your Situation When Sharing Personal Experiences With Others Online to avoid Misunderstandings

Many people are hesitant to share their struggles on online communities because they fear being ridiculed. Although the data collected in this study showed that only a small minority of comments under serious posts were written for entertainment, it's still important to be clear about the gravity of the situation to prevent any misunderstanding. When sharing personal experiences, try to be as specific and honest as possible. Even from the vantage point of a researcher collecting data for this study, it can be challenging to determine the purpose of certain posts when they are ambiguous. Being transparent can help create a safer and more supportive environment. While this won't eliminate all cyberbullying, it can significantly reduce the number of misunderstandings and inappropriate responses.

To implement this recommendation, individuals should take their time to compose a well-thought-out post that outlines their situation and clearly conveys the severity of their struggle. Use descriptive language to help others understand the situation, but avoid oversharing personal information that could be used against you. It's also important to choose the right platform and community to share your post with. Do some research to find online communities that are known for being supportive and respectful. Additionally, consider asking a trusted friend or family member to review your post before sharing it to ensure it's clear and not easily misinterpreted. By being clear about the seriousness of your situation and carefully choosing the platform and community to share it with, you can minimize the risk of misunderstandings and find the support and advice you need.

## Practical Recommendation #3: Participate Actively in Online Communities and Provide Advice to Others

Many people may feel hesitant to share their problems in online mental health communities, fearing potential bullying. However, they still seek help from others to address their issues. By offering advice, whether random or not, users can provide insights on how to solve problems and make the community more welcoming. For instance, in a post published in 2022, a 20-year-old boy shared advice on how to improve one's life, covering topics such as enhancing social skills and the importance of education. The comments on his post were overwhelmingly positive, with users expressing gratitude for his advice and sharing their own success stories. Participating in online communities by offering guidance to others can be a fulfilling and rewarding experience for both the giver and the receiver.

To implement this recommendation, users can start by regularly browsing online mental health communities and looking for posts where they can offer advice based on their own experiences. When writing advice, it's important to be respectful and considerate, offering constructive and actionable solutions rather than criticizing or invalidating the original post. Users can also start their own threads, inviting others to share their experiences and offering support and guidance. Engaging in conversation with others by replying to comments and asking follow-up questions can also foster a sense of community and make the experience more meaningful. By actively participating in online mental health communities, users can make a positive impact on others and help create a more supportive environment for everyone.

## Limitations and Future Research

This study provides valuable insights into how adolescents use Reddit to manage their mental health, but there is still much to be explored. Future studies could build upon this approach by applying the same search queries and uses and gratifications model to different social media platforms such as Twitter, Facebook, and Instagram. As social media continues to evolve and become more sophisticated, it is critical to analyze the potential harms and benefits that may arise from different platforms. By conducting more extensive research, we can continue to develop a comprehensive understanding of how social media impacts mental health management among adolescents. That being said, it's important to note that while this study's approach is efficient, it also has its limitations, and additional research using other methods is still needed to gain a deeper understanding of the relationship between social media use and mental health.

One important limitation of using the teenager's subreddit on Reddit to assess adolescents' mental health is the potential for selection bias. Adolescents who are experiencing mental health issues may be more likely to seek out support on this subreddit, while those who are not struggling may be less likely to participate. This can result in a non-representative sample that may not accurately reflect the broader adolescent population. Therefore, caution must be exercised when generalizing the findings from this study to the larger population of adolescents. Additionally, it is important to acknowledge that using online data to assess mental health concerns may have limitations as it does not allow for clinical assessment or diagnosis, and may not capture the full complexity of individuals' experiences.

Self-report bias is another limitation of using the teenagers subreddit on Reddit to assess the mental health of adolescents. Adolescents who participate in the subreddit may not disclose their experiences truthfully, and this may lead to a distorted view of their mental health. Additionally, the anonymity of the platform may encourage adolescents to be more candid than they would be in person or on other social media platforms. However, this could also lead to individuals exaggerating or minimizing their experiences, which could skew the data collected. Moreover, some posts/comments may be vague or ambiguous, making the categorization process challenging and potentially leading to inaccurate assessments of the prevalence and severity of mental health issues among adolescents on the subreddit. Therefore, it is essential to interpret the findings with caution and recognize the limitations of using self-reported data.

Additionally, while the anonymity of Reddit can facilitate open and honest communication, it can also limit the verifiability of the data collected. Without personal identification, it is difficult to validate factors such as a poster's age, life status, or other specific details that may be relevant to their mental health. Although the assumption is that most participants are being genuine, there is a possibility that some responses may not accurately reflect their true experiences. However, given the large sample size, it is reasonable to assume that any inaccurate responses would be outweighed by the overall findings.

Finally, there are some limitations to uses-and-gratifications theory that must be acknowledged. While Reddit is a widely used platform in well-developed countries, it may not be accessible to all individuals, potentially excluding a significant portion of the population from the study. Additionally, the theory does not account for how media messages can influence user behavior, such as persuading them to use one form of media over another. This means that other factors, such as advertising, can play a significant role in shaping how individuals use social media and what outcomes they seek to attain. Therefore, it is important to consider additional frameworks and theories that can complement uses-and-gratifications theory to gain a more complete understanding of the impact of social media on mental health.

## CONCLUSION

Overall, this research highlights the potential of uses and gratifications theory to gain insight into the variety of purposes for which adolescents use social media such as Reddit. The theory suggests that media use is motivated by various factors, and this study reveals that many of these motives are positive, such as the desire to help others. However, it is important to note that a portion of users, at least 20%, utilize Reddit for simple entertainment purposes – sometimes at the expense of the prior group(s). Understanding these different motives for using social media is crucial in developing effective strategies to promote positive mental health behaviors and reduce potential negative outcomes associated with excessive screen time.

### Declaration of Conflicting Interests

The author(s) declared no potential conflicts of interest concerning the research, authorship, and/or publication of this article.

## REFERENCES

American Psychiatric Association. (2013). *Diagnostic and statistical manual of mental disorders* (5th ed.). APA.

Blum, R. W., Beuhring, T., Shew, M. L., Bearinger, L. H., Sieving, R. E., & Resnick, M. D. (2000). The effects of race/ethnicity, income, and family structure on adolescent risk behaviors. *American Journal of Public Health, 90*(12), 1879–1884. doi:10.2105/AJPH.90.12.1879 PMID:11111260

Chen, J., & Wang, Y. (2021). Social media use for health purposes: Systematic review. *Journal of Medical Internet Research, 23*(5), e17917. doi:10.2196/17917 PMID:33978589

Chou, H. T., & Edge, N. (2012). "They are happier and having better lives than I am": The impact of using Facebook on perceptions of others' lives. *Cyberpsychology, Behavior, and Social Networking, 15*(2), 117–121. doi:10.1089/cyber.2011.0324 PMID:22165917

Clement, S., Schauman, O., Graham, T., Maggioni, F., Evans-Lacko, S., Bezborodovs, N., Morgan, C., Rüsch, N., Brown, J. S., & Thornicroft, G. (2015). What is the impact of mental health-related stigma on help-seeking? A systematic review of quantitative and qualitative studies. *Psychological Medicine, 45*(1), 11–27. doi:10.1017/S0033291714000129 PMID:24569086

Creswell, J. W. (2009). *Research design: qualitative, quantitative, and mixed methods approaches* (3rd ed.). Sage Publications.

Falgoust, G., Winterlind, E., Moon, P., Parker, A., Zinzow, H., & Chalil Madathil, K. (2022). Applying the uses and gratifications theory to identify motivational factors behind young adult's participation in viral social media challenges on TikTok. *Human Factors in Healthcare, 2*, 2. doi:10.1016/j.hfh.2022.100014

Fitzpatrick, K. M., Harris, C., & Drawve, G. (2020). How bad is it? Suicidality in the middle of the COVID-19 pandemic. *Suicide & Life-Threatening Behavior, 50*(6), 1241–1249. doi:10.1111ltb.12655 PMID:32589799

Gowen, K., Deschaine, M., Gruttadara, D., & Markey, D. (2012). Young adults with mental health conditions and social networking websites: Seeking tools to build community. *Psychiatric Rehabilitation Journal, 35*(3), 245–250. doi:10.2975/35.3.2012.245.250 PMID:22246123

Grieve, R., Indian, M., Witteveen, K., Tolan, G. A., & Marrington, J. (2013). Face-to-face or Facebook: Can social connectedness be derived online? *Computers in Human Behavior, 29*(3), 604–609. doi:10.1016/j.chb.2012.11.017

Keum, B. T., Wang, Y. W., Callaway, J., Abebe, I., Cruz, T., & O'Connor, S. (2022). Benefits and harms of social media use: A latent profile analysis of emerging adults. *Current Psychology (New Brunswick, N.J.)*, 1–13. doi:10.100712144-022-03473-5 PMID:35891891

Kross, E., Verduyn, P., Demiralp, E., Park, J., Lee, D. S., Lin, N., Shablack, H., Jonides, J., & Ybarra, O. (2013). Facebook use predicts declines in subjective well-being in young adults. *PLoS One, 8*(8), e69841. doi:10.1371/journal.pone.0069841 PMID:23967061

Kuss, D. J., & Griffiths, M. D. (2017). Social networking sites and addiction: Ten lessons learned. *International Journal of Environmental Research and Public Health, 14*(3), 311. doi:10.3390/ijerph14030311 PMID:28304359

Lin, L. Y., Sidani, J. E., Shensa, A., Radovic, A., Miller, E., Colditz, J. B., Hoffman, B. L., Giles, L. M., & Primack, B. A. (2016). Association between social media use and depression among U.S. young adults. *Depression and Anxiety, 33*(4), 323–331. doi:10.1002/da.22466 PMID:26783723

Mojtabai, R. (2010). Mental illness stigma and willingness to seek mental health care in the European Union. *Social Psychiatry and Psychiatric Epidemiology, 45*(7), 705–712. doi:10.100700127-009-0109-2 PMID:19680588

Moreno, M. A., Parks, M. R., Zimmerman, F. J., Brito, T. E., & Christakis, D. A. (2009). Display of health risk behaviors on MySpace by adolescents: Prevalence and associations. *Archives of Pediatrics & Adolescent Medicine, 163*(1), 27–34. doi:10.1001/archpediatrics.2008.528 PMID:19124700

Naslund, J. A., Aschbrenner, K. A., McHugo, G. J., Unützer, J., Marsch, L. A., & Bartels, S. J. (2019). Exploring opportunities to support mental health care using social media: A survey of social media users with mental illness. *Early Intervention in Psychiatry, 13*(3), 405–413. doi:10.1111/eip.12496 PMID:29052947

Ponti, M., Bélanger, S., Grimes, R., Heard, J., Johnson, M., Moreau, E., Norris, M., Shaw, A., Stanwick, R., Van Lankveld, J., & Williams, R.Canadian Paediatric Society. (2017). Screen time and young children: Promoting health and development in a digital world. *Paediatrics & Child Health, 22*(8), 461–477. doi:10.1093/pch/pxx123 PMID:29601064

Rosen, L. D., Whaling, K., Carrier, L. M., Cheever, N. A., & Rokkum, J. (2013). The media and technology usage and attitudes Scale: An empirical investigation. *Computers in Human Behavior, 29*(6), 2501–2511. doi:10.1016/j.chb.2013.06.006 PMID:25722534

Ryan, T., Chester, A., Reece, J., & Xenos, S. (2014). The uses and abuses of Facebook: A review of Facebook addiction. *Journal of Behavioral Addictions*, *3*(3), 133–148. doi:10.1556/JBA.3.2014.016 PMID:25317337

Schou Andreassen, C., Billieux, J., Griffiths, M. D., Kuss, D. J., Demetrovics, Z., Mazzoni, E., & Pallesen, S. (2016). The relationship between addictive use of social media and video games and symptoms of psychiatric disorders: A large-scale cross-sectional study. *Psychology of Addictive Behaviors*, *30*(2), 252–262. doi:10.1037/adb0000160 PMID:26999354

Shensa, A., Escobar-Viera, C. G., Sidani, J. E., Bowman, N. D., Marshal, M. P., & Primack, B. A. (2017). Problematic social media use and depressive symptoms among U.S. young adults: A nationally-representative study. *Social Science & Medicine*, *182*, 150–157. doi:10.1016/j.socscimed.2017.03.061 PMID:28446367

Twenge, J. M., & Campbell, W. K. (2018). Associations between screen time and lower psychological well-being among children and adolescents: Evidence from a population-based study. *Preventive Medicine Reports*, *12*, 271–283. doi:10.1016/j.pmedr.2018.10.003 PMID:30406005

Twenge, J. M., Martin, G. N., & Campbell, W. K. (2018). Decreases in psychological well-being among American adolescents after 2012 and links to screen time during the rise of smartphone technology. *Emotion (Washington, D.C.)*, *18*(6), 765–780. doi:10.1037/emo0000403 PMID:29355336

Välimäki, M., Athanasopoulou, C., Lahti, M., & Adams, C. E. (2016). Effectiveness of social media interventions for people with schizophrenia: A systematic review and meta-analysis. *Journal of Medical Internet Research*, *18*(4), e92. doi:10.2196/jmir.5385 PMID:27105939

Wang, C., Pan, R., Wan, X., Tan, Y., Xu, L., Ho, C. S., & Ho, R. C. (2020). Immediate psychological responses and associated factors during the initial stage of the 2019 coronavirus disease (COVID-19) epidemic among the general population in China. *International Journal of Environmental Research and Public Health*, *17*(5), 1729. doi:10.3390/ijerph17051729 PMID:32155789

Xie, J., Liu, X., & Dajun Zeng, D. (2018). Mining e-cigarette adverse events in social media using Bi-LSTM recurrent neural network with word embedding representation. *Journal of the American Medical Informatics Association : JAMIA*, *25*(1), 72–80. doi:10.1093/jamia/ocx045 PMID:28505280

## ADDITIONAL READING

Brinkman, L., & Francot, R. (2022). Developing a resilient sexual and gender minority identity online: The importance of social media for youth before coming out. In D. Woodman (Ed.), *LGBT communities*. IntechOpen.

Brough, M., Ikin, A., & Literat, I. (2021). “Good social media”?: Underrepresented youth perspectives on the ethical and equitable design of social media platforms. In S. Gennaro & B. Miller (Eds.), *Young people and social media: Contemporary children’s digital culture*. Vernon Press.

Chatterjee, J. S., Pasricha, R., Mitra, R., & Frank, L. B. (2021). Challenging the forcefield: Crafting entertainment-education transmedia campaigns. In L. B. Frank & P. Falzone (Eds.), *Entertainment-education behind the scenes: Case studies for theory and practice*. Palgrave Macmillan. doi:10.1007/978-3-030-63614-2_16

Niezgoda, B. C. (2021). Lonely typers at midnight: Investigating the quandaries of millennial illness through digital ethnography of reddit. In S. Sekalala & B. C. Niezgoda (Eds.), *Global perspectives on health communication in the age of social media*. IGI Global.

Popoola, O., Olagundoye, O., & Alugo, M. (2020). Social media and suicide. In V. V. Kalinin, C. Hocaoglu, & S. Mohamed (Eds.), *Anxiety disorders*. IntechOpen.

Stark, I. (2021). Response: "You dropped your butter" – Laughing the pain away: The cathartic value of relief humor in health communication. In M. K. Cundall & S. Kelly (Eds.), *Cases on applied and therapeutic humor*. IGI Global. doi:10.4018/978-1-7998-4528-7.ch002

Thelandersson, F. (2022). Social media sadness: Sad girl culture and radical ways of feeling bad. In F. Thelandersson (Ed.), 21st century media and female mental health: Profitable vulnerability and sad girl culture. Palgrave Macmillan.

Trindade, L. V. P. (2020). Race joking, social media and the legal landscape. In L. Z. P. Trindade (Ed.), *No laughing matter: Race joking and resistance in Brazilian social media*. Vernon Press.

## KEY TERMS AND DEFINITIONS

**Anxiety:** A mental health disorder characterized by persistent and excessive worry or fear about everyday situations, which can interfere with daily activities and relationships.

**Depression:** A mental disorder characterized by persistent feelings of sadness, hopelessness, and a lack of interest in activities that were once enjoyable.

**Mental Health:** The state of a person's psychological and emotional well-being, encompassing factors such as mood, behavior, and cognitive functions.

**Self-Esteem:** The overall evaluation of one's worth or value as a person, based on their beliefs and perceptions about themselves.

**Social Media Addiction:** The excessive and compulsive use of social media platforms such as Facebook, Twitter, and Instagram, to the point where it interferes with daily life activities.

**Social Media:** Online platforms that allow people to create, share, and exchange information and content with others around the world.

**Uses and Gratifications Theory:** A theoretical framework that explains how individuals use media to satisfy their needs and desires, such as information seeking, entertainment, socialization, and personal identity formation.

# Chapter 28
# Social Media Addiction and Fear of Missing Out

**Ana Paula Monteiro**
*Department of Education and Psychology, University of Trás-os-Montes and Alto Douro, Portugal & Researcher at Centre for Research and Intervention in Education (CIIE), Portugal*

**Cláudio J. S. Cardoso**
*Department of Education and Psychology, University of Trás-os-Montes and Alto Douro, Portugal*

**Sílvia Andrade**
*Department of Education and Psychology, University of Trás-os-Montes and Alto Douro, Portugal*

**Inês Relva**
https://orcid.org/0000-0003-3718-8142
*Department of Education and Psychology, University of Trás-os-Montes and Alto Douro, Portugal*

**Margarida Simões**
*Department of Education and Psychology, University of Trás-os-Montes and Alto Douro, Portugal & Researcher at Centre for Research and Intervention in Education (CIIE), Portugal*

## ABSTRACT

*Social networks are part of daily life, and their use has been growing exponentially. Despite its potential, research has shown that social networks can be enhancers of addition. Psychological well-being can be called into question by the restlessness of the subject caused by the dependence on wanting to be online, particularly in social networks that gives rise to the term FoMO (fear of missing out), explaining the desire to remain online continuously. This chapter characterizes addiction to social networks and its relationship with FoMO. The concept of FoMO is discussed and explanatory theories. Some measures will be presented. Individual, intrafamilial, and extrafamilial characteristics associated with fear of missing out will be analyzed. The consequences of FoMO in different areas of the individual's life are presented. Some strategies for managing digital technologies to minimize this symptomatology will be discussed.*

DOI: 10.4018/978-1-6684-8397-8.ch028

## INTRODUCTION

In modern day society, social networking sites (SNSs) are becoming more and more popular, giving users the chance to be connected with the whole world (Chai et al., 2019; Su & Chan, 2017; Tanhan et al., 2022). Therefore, SNSs like Instagram or Facebook have gained huge popularity in the latest years (Chai et al., 2019). Helping its growing is the fact that internet and smart phones are becoming more popular around the world (Tanha et al., 2022). Smart phones are devices that can access the digital world in a matter of seconds, receiving updates at any moment (Tanha et al., 2022).

More than half of world´s population is now using the internet, according to Tanhan et al. (2022). In the year 2020 the average time spent on smart phones per day in Turkey was four hours, and, in general population, the average time on social media was very close to three hours (Tanhan et al., 2022).

The digital world, in particular social media, is enhancing curiosity into people, giving them the chance to share with the others their personal information (Tanhan et al., 2022). However, in social media only tends to appear the content that people publish, therefore, if someone is unhappy, they may not share such information regarding to that effect (Tanhan et al., 2022). That seems to be the reason why social media is so important these days. Because it exists this idealization of the way others are living that simply isn´t real. So, the information that users are seeing is generally made to present their lives in a much more glorified world they´re living at. The continuing use of social media to communicate and socialize with their peers may give a contribute to the increase of a phenomenon called fear of missing out (FoMO) (Casale & Fioravanti, 2020).

Some research suggests that it exists a positive correlation between SNS stress and FoMO, which enhances the role that social media has in modern day lifestyle (Beyens et al., 2016; Bloemen & De Coninck, 2020). Individuals who have a higher FoMO are likely to use internet intensively as well as social media (Elhai et al., 2016; Sapadin, 2015). Therefore, these individuals put themselves at greater vulnerability. This emerging phenomenon can cause depression, increase anxiety, stress, risk of psychopathology and technology addiction, as well as having a significant impact in the psychological well-being of an individual (O'Connell, 2020; Rozgonjuk et al., 2021).

This chapter aims to bring new information about social media addiction and the fear of missing out. In this way, the aim was to explore the relationship between addiction to social networks and FOMO, to analyse the concept of Fear of Missing Out, presented by the different types and explanatory theories, and to make known the main negative effects for the individual. Individual, intrafamilial and extrafamilial characteristics associated with the Fear of Missing Out will be analysed. As well as, expose the consequences of the Fear of Missing in the different areas of the individual's life. Finally, some digital technology management strategies will be addressed to minimize this symptomatology, thus aiming at the search for specialized help.

## BACKGROUD

### Social Media Addiction

In today´s world it is undeniable the variety of places we can visit online (Costa et al., 2018). Thus, one of the biggest changes that appeared in the last decade was the development of social media. This online platform allows you to communicate efficiently and at a fast rate with pretty much anyone anywhere around the globe (Chambers, 2013). The word "friendship" has now a different meaning, because it may be used in a context of a friend from social media, who we may not even know for sure if it´s real or not. Which brings new implications to modern times, namely, since it's suggested by Chambers (2013, p. 1), digital communication is now modifying "experiences of intimacy, friendship and identity through new forms of social interaction".

Terms like problematic social media use, Social Media Addiction (SMA) or compulsive social media use may appear on the scientific literature and used as a reference to the same concept, which is the addictive use of these platforms (Marino et al., 2018), though the term most used seems to be SMA (Sun & Zhang, 2021). Scientific investigations still haven´t come with an agreeable definition for this concept, but it seems to be a generalized idea that this use can be compared with problematic use of internet and online gaming, suggesting that users may feel compelled to use social media constantly, showing preoccupation in moments where they simply can´t use it.

Caplan (2010) propose that people who have poor social skills may feel compelled to use the internet. This author empathises the role of digital world in a way that allows people who don´t feel comfortable in areas like intersubjectivity, to compensate their social life in the online world. Caplan (2010) argues that this online world, including social media, may yet be preferred to the "real world", and, in line this investigator, other authors propose that shyness can be linked to social media use (Leung et al., 2017). Because it opens to its users a more controlled environment where they may feel more comfortable in it.

The prevalence of SMA is yet to be clarified, though, a meta-analysis study from Cheng et al. (2021) cross-cultural comparisons revealed the pooled prevalence estimate from 26% to 36%. Other study (Costa et al., 2018), who used Social Media Disorder Scale-Short Form (SMDS-SF) (Eijnden et al., 2016) to measure SMA showed on a European sample prevalence's from 24%, which corroborates the findings from the first study. The same study also demonstrated that social media users who had some form of addiction refused to believe they were compromising their interpersonal relationships.

Cheng et al. (2021), in a meta-analysis study, concluded there were two principal perspectives that could demonstrate the role of environmental factors helping the development of SMA. First, it can be argued that individuals who have unmet psycho-social needs, like need for relatedness, are more vulnerable to use social media in order to achieve some sort of compensation, which, therefore could lead to an addictive use. On the other hand, because there´s a massive usage of the internet in today´s era, namely social media, individuals may feel compelled to use these platforms simply do to the growing of social media in their culture and peers. Ending up feeling that its use is inevitable and almost mandatory to stay social.

Therefore, the excessive use of social networks can be partially explained by the concept of Fear of Missing Out (FoMO), given that individuals with high levels of FOMO may feel compelled to frequently check their social networks to keep constantly updated and connected with others (Moore & Craciun, 2021; Oberst et al., 2017;).

## Fear of Missing Out (FoMO): Characterization and Types

Chai et al. (2019, p. 87) defines FoMO as a "pervasive apprehension that others might be having rewarding experiences from which one is absent". According with Tanhan et al. (2022), the word fear is a reference to the anxiety that someone may feel by having to do something that, in reality, is not needed. Following this idea, Oxford Dictionary (2018) expresses FoMO as a form of anxiety about missing interesting activities on social media. Tanhan et al. (2022) also defines FoMO as the sum of negative and persistent feelings given the assumption and perception that the others have a much better life than the individual at self. These authors argue that it may exist a desire linked to the obligation of having continuously new information posted online. In line with this, the scientific literature suggests that FoMO can be characterized by a desire and will of being connected with the other´s activities (Przybylski et al., 2013; Rozgonjuk et al., 2021).

Interestingly, though FoMO can be linked to the context of digital media and, therefore, the online world, the actual behaviour that is being measured refers only to offline world, or in other words, the real-life world (Casale & Fioravanti, 2020; Przybylski et al., 2013). This term was firstly used by Dan Herman, who was studying the effects of consumption in marketing products (Herman, 2000). In line with this author, when consumers felt that they could not purchase a certain item, they would fear the risk of missing out the opportunity. This happened since there was a various number of products consumers could pick, not all of them desirable, therefore, individuals started having the need to rush and buy that specific product. Two decades after, we can argue that social media can be used as a tool that shows what´s more desirable or not to the audience. Aligned with the massive spreading of social media users, it seems easy to conclude that this platform may have a huge influence in masses, including younger generations.

Mazlum and Atalay (2022, p. 21) stated that the "desire to be socially connected, and to be a part of satisfying experiences is a basic human need present from infancy and is not limited to social media use". Following this perspective, FoMO appears to be the overall fear of just missing out on something, fearing the possibility of not knowing that a certain event is occurring (Wegmann et al., 2017). From a rational perspective, we can say that most of our actions are indeed rational, therefore, we think carefully about the cost and benefit of our choices (Mazlum & Atalay, 2022). So, it can be argued that we try to make the best choice, and to take the highest benefit from it (Mazlum & Atalay, 2022). Even though we do this, Mazlum and Atalay (2022) make an interesting point, because we can make the best rational choice and then think about it and regret it. So, these authors suggest that, even if we think we did the best choice by doing something that makes us happier, we may yet feel curiosity about our other options and therefore feel FoMO.

Contributing to this point is the increasing number of social media applications, which, linked to an intensive use, allow its users to be permanently close with digital world, where we can see new content at any moment, allowing users to share it with their friends and followers (Tanhan et al., 2022). These platforms also enhance the way people live their lives, and, as said earlier, people don´t often share their unhappy moments publicly. Therefore, users will end up paying extra attention to the people who get more likes and followers, comparing themselves to them. Other authors are in line with this thought, since it is known that neuroticism is positively associated with FoMO (Rozgonjuk et al., 2021).

According to Przybylski et al. (2013)_FoMO integrates a cognitive dimension and a behavioral dimension. The cognitive dimension concerns the apprehension that others are having rewarding experiences from which one is absent, which can generate worry and rumination. And, the behavioral dimension results from the persistent desire to stay connected with people on your social network. This behavioral dimension can manifest itself actively (persistent behavior of checking what occurs online to maintain social connections and avoid being left out in rewarding experiences) or reactive (compulsion to respond through notifications related to social networks received throughout the day (to which there is a compulsion to respond).

The literature has suggested that individuals who experience FoMO present a set of symptoms described by Metz (2019) such as: constantly checking mobile devices even when in the company of friends, browsing and actively sharing on social networks, questioning people about what to do and where to go, accepting invitations to all parties and events, for "fear of being left out or feeling excluded" and engaging in rumors. Emotions such as the feeling of emptiness, depression, restlessness or nervousness arise in case the individual cannot access social networks (Gil et al., 2015; Przybylsji et al., 2013).

As already mentioned, o fear of missing out is not a new phenomenon, nor is it exclusive to social networks, however, several studies indicate that high levels of FoMO are associated with greater use and involvement in these networks (Buglass et al., 2017; Oberst et al., 2017; Tandon et al., 2022). The fact that people can now be chronically reminded of events in which they are losing acts as a potentiating factor for this type of anxiety (Riordan et al., 2020).

Alutaybi et al. (2020) characterized different types of FOMO, of which we highlight: FoMO when others do not interact as expected (results from the fear of losing the ability to be popular and interesting); FoMO when it is not possible to interact or connect as desired (it stems from the fear of losing information due to the large volume; from the fear of losing the ability to interact in different social networks; from the fear of losing information temporarily available; from the fear of losing a timely interaction and from the fear of not being able to maintain followers and the fear of losing information/events); FoMO when having/feeling the need to engage in continuous interactions (without time) (it is provoked by fear of losing popularity, fear of missing an important opportunity; fear of losing a sense of belonging and fear of losing what happens in the lives of others) and FoMO when an online meeting/event is expected (emerges from the fear of missing the opportunity to attend the meeting/event, fear of losing the feeling of belonging and the fear of losing the ability to be popular).

## THEORETICAL PERSPECTIVES

### Theory of Social Comparison and FoMO

The Theory of Social Comparison, developed by Festinger (1954), is based on the fact that the subjects compare themselves to other individuals whenever they are confronted with questions: how others are, what they can or cannot do, and what they can or cannot conquer. Consequently, individuals more unsure about some aspects of their lives and with feelings of inadequacy have an increased concern about the behaviour of others and are more likely to engage in social comparations in online interactions (Lee, 2014; Reer et al., 2019; Servidio et al., 2021). Studies indicate that individuals with high levels of guidance for social comparison are positively associated with higher levels of FoMO (Servidio et al., 2021; Reer et al., 2019). FoMO involves a social comparison between the individual's experiences versus those of others, thus resulting in feelings of envy, because other individuals are considered to be doing better or having more rewarding social and personal experiences (Przybylski et al., 2013; Reer et al., 2019). Thus, the individual feels the need to constantly check his smartphone as it allows quick access to information and the pages/accounts of his social networks (Coskun & Muslu, 2019; Elhai et al., 2020a; Przybylski et al.,2013; Tanhan et al., 2022). The underlying reason for this behaviour stems from the need to obtain social approval and acceptance and to satisfy this need, individuals are constantly in virtual environments in order not to lose the actions of others (Tanhan et al., 2022).

In fact, in the study conducted by Reer et al (2019) with a sample of 1929 German internet users between the age of 14 and 39, the authors found that loneliness, depression and anxiety are positively related to social media engagement. And, FoMO and social comparison orientation jointly mediate the connection between well-being and social media engagement, that is, decreases in well-being are associated with increases in FoMO and social comparison orientation, which in turn positively predict social media engagement.

A variable to consider in the use of social networks and FoMO is the concept of self-presentation. Individuals can use social networks as a way to communicate with a large audience, as a way to promote themselves and their achievements, and/or as a way to keep track of what others do. In fact, some individuals have an excessive concern about how others see them on social networks and are very careful with the images and content they post seeking to convey an ideal and socially desired image (Kim & Tussyadiah, 2013; Zhu & Xiong, 2022). The search for this ideal self-presentation and the consequent social comparison can also lead to the appreciation that others are more interesting and live a more attractive life, which in turn is related to the fear of missing out (Reer et al., 2019; Zhu & Xiong, 2022).

## Self-Determination Theory and FoMO

Self-determination theory (Deci & Ryan, 1985; Ryan & Deci, 2000) has been used to explain what drives the FoMO. Self-determination theory is a motivational theory that is based on the relational perspective and explains the individual behavior oriented to the satisfaction of three needs, namely the need for autonomy, need for competence and need for relationship (Deci & Ryan, 1985; Ryan & Deci, 2000). The theory of self-determination suggests that people need to achieve these three needs to achieve their psychological growth. This theory differentiates two forms of motivation: extrinsic and intrinsic motivation, these forms of intrinsic and extrinsic motivation form a continuum, ranging from lack of motivation (*amotivation*), through various levels of extrinsic motivation, to reaching intrinsic motivation (Deci & Ryan, 1985).

Thus, based on the theory of self-determination, low levels of satisfaction basic psychological needs could influence the involvement in social networks either directly or indirectly. In the first case, individuals with low levels of their needs would use digital media more because they are perceived as a means to be in contact with others, a tool to develop their social competence and a good possibility to deepen ties. Indirectly, the low level of needs can lead individuals to be more sensitive to FoMO, which in turn would serve as a mediator for greater involvement in social networks (Przybylski et al., 2013). In fact, the results of the study by Przybylski et al. (2013) indicated that individuals who presented less satisfaction with basic psychological needs of competence, autonomy and relationship had higher levels of FoMO.

In turn, the investigation of Masur et al. (2014) suggests that the daily satisfaction of the needs of autonomy, competence, and relationship independently predicts various reasons for using Facebook, which in turn have been associated with higher or lower levels of Facebook addiction. And, the results of the study by Reinecke et al. (2014) revealed that the social pressure to use Facebook was negatively related to feelings of autonomy, however, the involvement with this social network was positively related to the satisfaction of the needs of competence and relationship.

Additionally, social networks offer various opportunities to satisfy basic human needs and allow their users to obtain important gratifications (Masur et al., 2014; Reinecke et al., 2014). On the other hand, seeking these gratifications can lead to excessive use of social networks (Masur et al. 2014; Reinecke et al., 2014) and also increase the anxiety of remaining continuously online that can result from Fear of Missing Out (Dempsey et al., 2019; Przybylski et al., 2013).

## Fear of Missing Out Evaluation

Fear of Missing Out has been evaluated predominantly through the *Fear of Missing Out scale* (FoMOs) developed by Przybylski et al. (2013). FoMOs is a scale consisting of ten items that assess the fear of "being left out" used is a 5-point *Likert* scale ranging from 1 (does not apply to me) to 5 (applies very much to me). The score ranges from 10 to 15 points. The higher the total score, the greater the concern or apprehension present (Przybylski et al., 2013). Regarding the psychometric properties of the instrument, in particular internal consistency, in the original study of scale development, Cronbach's alpha value was .90, and a unifactorial solution was obtained.

FoMOs has been adapted in several countries such as Turkey (Can & Satici, 2019; Gökler et al., 2016), Spain (Gil et al., 2015), Arabia (Al-Menayes, 2016), Germany (Wegmann et al., 2017) and Italy (Casale & Fioravanti, 2020). Despite the existence of discrepancies found in the adaptation studies at the level of the dimensionality of the scale, the internal consistency values found were adequate.

Another proposal to evaluate FoMO is the *Scale of Assessment of FOMO* developed by Abel et al. (2016). The scale consists of 10 items (Likert type, with seven response options) organized into three dimensions, namely, sense of self (five items that assess an individual's perception of himself), social interaction (three items that assess an individual's feelings when interacting with others, their shyness issues and comfort level in talking to other members of a group) and social anxiety (two items that assess anxiety caused by the use of social media). Internal consistency values, evaluated with Cronbach's alpha in the three subscales, were equal to or higher than .70.

Riordan et al. (2018) developed the *Fear of Missing Out Short Form* (FoMOsf) consisting of only one FoMOsf item. According to the authors, FoMOsf provides a valid and reliable method of measuring FoMO and allows overcoming some of the limitations associated with longer measures in certain research contexts (Riordan et al., 2018).

Finally, it is worth mentioning the *Online Fear of Missing Out Inventory* (ON-FoMO) by Sette et al. (2020) consisting of 20 items, distributed in four dimensions, namely the need for belonging (referring to the need to form and maintain stable relationships, need for popularity (refers to the dependence of online approval by peers), anxiety (evaluates the symptoms of abstinence and anxiety that an individual with FoMO tends to present when the use of the internet or smartphone is not available) and addition (referring to the protrusion and evaluates professional problems, academic or relational lived because of the excessive use of social networks). The values of internal consistency, evaluated with Cronbach's alpha in the subscales ranged between .73 and .85. The alpha value for the total scale was .92. According to Sette et al. (2020), the instrument can be applied to a wide variety of population groups, and may be especially useful in clinical contexts with individuals who have symptoms of addiction to social networks such as anxiety, abstinence and loss of control.

## Characteristics Associated With Fear of Missing Out

In the literature review carried out, it was found that there are few investigations dedicated to the relationship between Fear of Missing Out and sociodemographic variables, namely age and gender. Most investigations dedicated to the study of these sociodemographic variables attribute secondary importance to the relationship between Fear of Missing Out and problematic use of digital technology (Elhai et al., 2021; Stead & Bibby, 2017). It should be noted that, in some investigations, Fear of Missing Out was associated with younger ages and gender differences were found, with females achieving higher scores (Bloemen & De Coninck, 2020; Elhai et al., 2018; Rozgonjuk et al., 2021; Stead & Bibby, 2017). In other investigations, these gender differences were not found (e.g., Beyens et al., 2016; Casale et al., 2018).

Przybylski et al. (2013) investigated the behaviour and the emotional side linked to FoMO in a sample of young adults and concluded that it is associated with more depressive mood states and lower levels of satisfaction with life. FoMO has also been associated with greater social isolation, anxiety and depression, worse sleep quality, tiredness, stress and feelings of inferiority relative to others having a more interesting reality than the individual himself (Baker et al., 2016; Milyavskaya et al., 2018; Rajan et al., 2022). This construct is also revealed as a strategy for self-regulation and satisfaction of psychological needs, such as competence, autonomy and connection (Alt, 2015; Beyens et al., 2016). The psychological traits, states and factors that are present when someone uses Social Media are key aspects to help understand this phenomenon (Abel et al., 2016).

According to the literature (e.g., Rozgonjuk et al., 2021; Savitri et al., 2021) some personality traits are related to the experience of Fear of Missing Out. Studies carried out (Alt & Boniel-Nissim, 2018; Blackwell et al., 2017; Rozgonjuk et al., 2021) report that the personality trait Neuroticism is positively associated with Fear of Missing Out. The neurotic personality is characterized by showing less affection and more anxiety, as individuals who experience Fear of Missing Out share the same feelings regarding the loss of rewarding experiences (Judge et al., 1999; Przybylski et al., 2013).

In the relationship between FoMO and personality traits, studies indicate that there is a positive relationship with Agreeableness, (Hamutoglu et al., 2020; Hidayati et al., 2021) and that Extroversion and Openness to Experience do not relate to Fear of Missing Out (Rozgonjuk et al., 2021; Stead & Bibby, 2017). As for Conscientiousness, Wegmann et al. (2017) found a negative relationship with FoMO, explaining these authors that individuals with less self-discipline, and who have difficulty focusing on tasks, spend more time online.

There are still few investigations dedicated to the study of the relationship between the role of the family, namely that of parents, and the use of the internet and Social Networks by children (Notten, 2013) and even fewer that study the family characteristics that contribute to the FoMO (Alt & Boniel-Nissim, 2018a). However, it is mentioned in the literature that parents play an important role in relation to the use of social networks by their children, and there may be a relationship between some family and parental characteristics with the use and dependence of these online platforms in adolescents (Alt & Boniel-Nissim, 2018a; Durak, 2018; López et al., 2015; Vaala & Bleakley, 2015).

With regard to family structure, the literature reports that adolescents who live with only one parent (single-parent regime) use social networks more frequently and to manifest risky behaviour in relation to these platforms (e.g., disclosing personal information to individuals who do not know) compared to adolescents living with both parents (two-parent families) (Notten, 2013). This can be explained by increased stress, financial problems, and the lesser amount of time teenagers spend with their parents in separated families (Notten, 2013). In the study carried out by Wu et al. (2018), in which the type of family in which young people were inserted was related to the problematic use of the internet, it was found that orphaned adolescents or those who live with only one of the parents were those who were more likely to develop use problematic or excessive use of the internet, compared to young people who live with both parents. The study by Jablonska and Lindberg (2007) also found that single parenthood is related to risky behaviour in adolescence, this is explained by the fact that there is less parental control over their children.

Adolescents from single-parent families report having more social support compared to two-parent families (Riggio, 2004). A possible explanation is the fact that young people adapt to less availability on the part of their parents, thus resorting more to social support outside their family nucleus. Through Social Networks, teenagers from single-parent families can connect with other young people in order to obtain support outside the family, which demonstrates that they are more independent and, therefore, are not as vulnerable to the development of Fear of Missing Out, compared to young people from two-parent families (Bloemen & Coninck, 2020).

The study by Alt and Boniel-Nissim (2018a) involved 270 young people and adolescents, aged between 13 and 18 years old, and investigated the relationship between parent-child communication and the children's level of internet addiction and FoMO. Results indicated that positive parental communication (e.g., listening to children to understand how they feel and what they think) is associated with lower levels of FoMO and internet addiction in children (Alt & Boniel-Nissim, 2018a). Therefore, the higher the level of communication (perceived support), the lower the Fear of Missing Out experienced by the individual (Alt & Boniel-Nissim, 2018; Bloemen & Coninck, 2020).

In the study by Chang et al. (2015), which aimed to analyse the relationship between parent-child attachment and internet addiction, the authors found that a strong attachment to parents was negatively correlated with problematic internet use in adolescents. In addition, a parent-child relationship based on trust and communication are protective factors against the development of Fear of Missing Out. A possible explanation for this fact is that when adolescents have problems with their parents, they resort to peer relationships in order to escape conflicts (López et al., 2015).

Ko et al. (2015), through a longitudinal study, investigated family conflict, where they found that adolescents who live with only one parent, who often experience conflicts in their relationship with their parents, or who witness frequent conflicts within their family, have a greater predisposition to develop addiction to online platforms. Since, parental conflict proved to be the predictor with more weight in the development of addiction (Ko et al., 2015).

A study carried out in China concluded that adolescents who indicate having a more intrusive parenting style, with high levels of control and who perceive less affection are those who tend to suffer more from internet addiction, which in turn can result in Fear of Missing Out. Thus, parental behaviour can be a risk factor for the development of online addictions in children (Xiuqin et al., 2010).

## Consequences of Fear of Missing Out

FoMO have been associated with several negative consequences in different life areas of the individuals independently of the age.

Recently, Barry et al. (2017) found that FoMO may lead to the development of internalized problems. Symptoms as anxiety (Elhai et al., 2016; Ibrahim et al., 2022), increasing dissatisfaction with life (Stead & Bibby, 2017), diminished emotional well-being (Stead & Bibby, 2017), alienation from the social environment (Köseliören et al., 2022), less mindful attention (Baker et al., 2016) depression (Baker et al., 2016; Ibrahim et al., 2022), and loneliness (Alt & Boniel-Nissim, 2018) have been reported from individuals that also present FoMO. Recent studies have associated FoMO with the presence of physical symptoms (e.g., Baker et al., 2016) insomnia (Köseliören et al., 2022) sleep duration (Milyavskaya et al., 2018) and sleep disturbances (Scott & Woods, 2018). Citko and Owsieniuk (2020) conducted a study in

Poland with 1,060 participants with 15 or older aged and the results showed that one fifth of respondents with FoMO presents somatic symptoms: as nausea, dizziness, abdominal pain or increased sweating.

Regarding impulsivity and FoMO association the studies are scarce. One of the studies that explored this issue was carried out by Li et al. (2020) and found that those respondents that present high levels of FoMO were more likely to present impulsivity and spend more time gaming. In fact, rash impulsivity, but also reward seeking and FoMO, near a sample of six hundred and twelve young drivers age aged between 17 and 24 years, were all significant predictors of sending texting while driving (Brown et al., 2021) with the risks that can have on driving.

In 2015, Riordan et al., with a sample of 432 students, aged ranged between 18-25 years, found that FoMO was associated with "an increased incidence of negative alcohol-related consequences" (p. 4) but also with both risk taking and social consequences. The authors argue that those students that exhibit more fear of missing out were in risky when they drank alcohol, and according with Mckee et al. (2022) more depressant stimulant, cannabis, and hallucinogen use. Casale and Fioravanti (2020) also describe an association between FoMO and alcohol use habits.

With a sample of 159 university students (*M*age=18) Milyavskaya et al. (2018) intend to explore FoMO experiences. The authors found that FoMO experiences were associated with an increased negative affect, fatigue, greater stress, as well sleep problems and physical symptoms. In another sample Milyavskaya et al. (2018) with the aim to explore their moment experiences, the participants report more distraction and more difficulties to focus on what they were doing. Additionally, and regarding the distraction attention and learning disengagement, Al-Furaih and Al-Awidi (2021) investigate their relationship with FoMO with 2084 undergraduate students in University in Kuwait. The authors found a positive association between these variables and defends that "might be related to the students' use of their smartphones during lectures to avoid missing anything on social media applications" (p. 2365) independently of being enrolled in humanities or scientific colleges. More recently, in with aim to deeper explored the attention factor, Matias et al. (2021) with a sample of twenty-nine college students ($M = 20$ years old) in a laboratory setting found that under attention-demanding conditions FoMO it is a predictor of attentional capture by social reward distractors.

Another study recently conducted by McKee et al. (2022) in USA with 472 college students found that FoMO predicts the occurrence of several maladaptive behaviours such alcohol use, academic misconduct, and illegal behaviour (e.g., stealing, physical fighting…). The results also suggested that higher rates of FoMO was associated with plagiarism and cheating.

Regarding the research of impact of FoMO in the work field stills scarce. In a study conducted by Tandon et al. (2021) with a sample of 312 participants in USA, where the aim was to explore relationships between exhibitionism and voyeurism and FoMO, as well as psychological and behavioural outcome. The authors found a positive association between FoMO and work outcomes, namely work performance decrement and procrastination.

Since the fear of missing out it is related with "the concern of people not knowing or missing news, developments, and information in daily life" (Köseliören et al., 2022; p. 354) when this fear increase there is a high probability of the excessive duration of social media use via smartphone (Coskun & Muslu, 2019) namely social media use addiction (Yali et al., 2021). Additionally, in a study conducted in Indonesia, with a total of 259 participants Rahardjo and Mulyani (2020) found that FoMO affect Instagram addiction.

Regarding problematic use of internet and FoMO, Baker et al. (2016) found that FoMO was positively associated with the time spent on social media. As well Talwar et al. (2019) found that FoMO affected fake news sharing and could encourage gossip-sharing on social media.

Regarding the above results, and although the research it is recent, more studies need to be done, lamely longitudinal ones. However, there is no doubt of the risks that the fear of missing out can have on individuals' life.

## Prevention Strategies

FoMO is considered a social and educational challenge, Stošiÿ and Stošiÿ (2015) alert to the importance of young people using modern electronic devices, without any critical spirit about the post and against their use, which may lead to the use of them impulsively and the adoption of addictive behaviors that may significantly interfere in different areas of life (school, family, work, university), harming their psychological, social and family well-being. In this sense, we will present some studies which aimed essentially to point out some preventive and remediate measures to combat the phenomenon in question.

Modzelewski (2020) conducted a study in Poland with a sample of 500 Internet users indicating that 17.6% of respondents showed strong evidence of FoMO with greater intensity in females and at ages under 35. In this investigation are also presented some recommendations of psychopedagogical prevention carried out by educators and psychologists directed to young people and young adults. The recommendations presented are as follows:

- Create during the day periods of time without phone use and simultaneously check the time spent with it and the number of unlocks performed, this verification is possible through the inclusion of special applications teaching digital balance;
- Involvement of different therapies, such as those that defend and teach to live as best as possible the present moment, Acceptance and Commitment Therapy (ACT) and mindfulness. Develop a posture of gratitude before life (e.g., make a list of things where we feel grateful) (Modzelewski, 2020).

In addition, Citko and Owsieniuk (2020) taking into account the results of the above mentioned research point out as a possible measure to be adopted, implement a pilot project to prevent cyberdiseases for young people aged between 15 and 18 years, which consisted of a joint work between family doctors and clinical psychologists. Family doctors, being closer to the community (where they live), are the "first gateway" to primary health care (Citko & Owsieniuk, 2020). The benefits of collaboration between the family doctor and a clinical psychologist include access to psychologists for the community in general, consequent reduction of social stigma and intervention of a psychologist in the initial phase of the threat, not losing the trail of patients, as usually occurs in psychological practice (Solano et al., 2009).

Another recent study emerged in Korea with a sample of 260 adolescents aged 12-15 years for the purpose of evaluating the mediating roles of self-esteem and the FoMO on the influence of parental support on adolescents' Problematic Smartphone Use (PSU) (Kim, 2022). According to the results of the study and aiming at reducing the risk of PSU, Kim (2022) recommends 3 main lines of action:

1st) Parents' support emerges as a protective factor for the PSU of young people. Thus, it creates the need to establish a family program to support parents in order to promote increasingly strong bonds and increase the self-esteem of their children. These results are corroborated by a previous study (Ho, 2021) that showed that young people who experience insecure family relationships feel more loneliness and for this reason interact more with other people on social networks;

2nd) It is proven that high levels of self-esteem protect the PSU of young people, requiring them to integrate programs to promote self-esteem;

3rd) Constituting the FoMO a risk factor for the PSU it is crucial to mitigate this fear by preventing THE, training educators and school nurses in counseling. The relationship between fear of missing out and problematic smartphone use is consistent with other studies that have proven this relationship. (Coco et al., 2020 ; Fang et al., 2020 ; Wolniewicz et al., 2018 ; Yuan et al., 2021). Young people with FoMO seek to reduce their negative emotions by focusing on the experiences of others and may increase the PSU (Elhai et al., 2020b; Yuan et al.,2021;). Geng et al. (2021) and Elhai et al. (2020b) mention that FoMO is affected by other psychological factors, and there is a need to use other approaches to restore their psychological well-being. Geng et al. (2021) in a study conducted in China, in a sample of 1,447 Young Chinese with an average age of 16.15 years, analyzed different variables such as parents' perception of phubbing, loneliness, FOMO and PSU and based on the results point to some preventive strategies. The results show that perceived parental Phubbing is a high-risk factor for the loneliness of young people, FoMO and PSU. Thus, it is suggested by the authors the implementation of family intervention programs with the objective of reducing parental phubbing, making the family environment more supportive, proposing a more open communication between parents and children, discussing the advantages and disadvantages of the use of the Internet (Sela et al., 2019), avoiding, by parents, the verification of smartphones (Liu et al., 2020), to train the social (e.g., face-to-face communication) and cognitive skills of young people in order to establish adjusted relationships with others (e.g., family, peers) by altering negative schemes or beliefs about themselves and others (Ho, 20219) and satisfying their social needs (Geng et al., 2021) and Beyens et al. (2016). Regarding the relevance of reducing FoMO and PSU, Fang et al. (2020) also propose that professionals explore with young people the negative consequences of FoMO.

## FUTURE RESEARCH DIRECTIONS

Taking into account the literature review carried out and the fact that research dedicated to exploring the intrafamilial and extrafamilial variables in FoMO is still scarce, future studies should focus on the analysis of these two variables. It is also important to analyze the impact that FoMO can have on the sleep of adolescents and young people, due to the need to be constantly online. It would also be relevant to develop qualitative studies on *Fear of Missing Out* in order to understand the behaviors and feelings of individuals resulting from the persistent desire to stay connected with people in social networks.

## CONCLUSION

FOMO is a new social problem related to the negative use of social networks, being considered as a driver of engagement and addiction to these online platforms. As a result of the increased anxiety present in the FoMO experience, there is a decrease in psychological well-being and a greater dependence on social networks, which translates into several negative consequences for the individuals who experience it. It is important to view FoMO as a social and educational challenge, making individuals aware that the impulsive, uncritical and addictive use of electronic devices can lead to habits that are difficult to break and impair psychological well-being and academic, social and personal functioning.

## ACKNOWLEDGMENT

National funds support Inês Relva work through the FCT—Portuguese Foundation for Science and Technology under the project the Scientific Employment Stimulus - Institutional Call – CEECINST/00127/2018. This work was partially supported by national funds, through FCT - Foundation for Science and Technology, IP, within the scope of the strategic program of CIIE - Center for Research and Intervention in Education at the University of Porto [ref. UIDB/00167/2020; UIDP/00167/2020].

## REFERENCES

Abel, J. P., Buff, C. L., & Burr, S. A. (2016). Social Media and the Fear of Missing Out: Scale Development and Assessment. [JBER]. *Journal of Business & Economics Research, 14*(1), 33–44. doi:10.19030/jber.v14i1.9554

Al-Furaih, S. A. A., & Al-Awidi, H. M. (2021). Fear of missing out (FoMO) among undergraduate students in relation to attention distraction and learning disengagement in lectures. *Education and Information Technologies, 26*(2), 2355–2373. doi:10.100710639-020-10361-7

Al-Menayes, J. (2016). The Fear of Missing Out Scale: Validation of the Arabic version and correlation with social media addiction. *International Journal of Applied Psychology, 6*(2), 41–46.

Alt, D. (2015). College students' academic motivation, media engagement and fear of missing out. *Computers in Human Behavior, 49*, 111–119. doi:10.1016/j.chb.2015.02.057

Alt, D., & Boniel-Nissim, M. (2018a). Parent–adolescent communication and problematic internet use: The mediating role of Fear of Missing Out (FoMO). *Journal of Family Issues, 39*(13), 3391–3409. doi:10.1177/0192513X18783493

Alt, D., & Boniel-Nissim, M. (2018b). Links between adolescents' deep and surface learning approaches, problematic internet use, and fear of missing out (FoMO). *Internet Interventions : the Application of Information Technology in Mental and Behavioural Health, 13*, 30–39. doi:10.1016/j.invent.2018.05.002 PMID:30206516

Alutaybi, A., Al-Thani, D., McAlaney, J., & Ali, R. (2020). Combating fear of missing out (FoMO) on Social Media: The FoMO-R Method. *International Journal of Environmental Research and Public Health, 17*(17), 6128. doi:10.3390/ijerph17176128 PMID:32842553

Baker, Z. G., Krieger, H., & LeRoy, A. S. (2016). Fear of missing out: Relationships with depression, mindfulness, and physical symptoms. *Translational Issues in Psychological Science*, *2*(3), 275–282. doi:10.1037/tps0000075

Beyens, I., Frison, E., & Eggermont, S. (2016). “I don’t want to miss a thing”: Adolescents’ fear of missing out and its relationship to adolescents’ social needs, Facebook use, and Facebook related stress. *Computers in Human Behavior*, *64*, 1–8. doi:10.1016/j.chb.2016.05.083

Blackwell, D., Leaman, C., Tramposch, R., Osborne, C., & Liss, M. (2017). Extraversion, neuroticism, attachment style and fear of missing out as predictors of social media use and addiction. *Personality and Individual Differences*, *116*, 69–72. doi:10.1016/j.paid.2017.04.039

Bloemen, N., & De Coninck, D. (2020). Social media and fear of missing out in adolescents: The role of family characteristics. *Social Media + Society*, *6*(4), 2056305120965517. doi:10.1177/2056305120965517

Brown, P., George, A. M., & Rickwood, D. J. (2021). Rash impulsivity, reward seeking and fear of missing out as predictors of texting while driving: Indirect effects via mobile phone involvement. *Personality and Individual Differences*, *171*, 171. doi:10.1016/j.paid.2020.110492

Buglass, S. L., Binder, J. F., Betts, L. R., & Underwood, J. D. (2017). Motivators of online vulnerability: The impact of social network site use and FOMO. *Computers in Human Behavior*, *66*, 248–255. doi:10.1016/j.chb.2016.09.055

Can, G., & Satici, S. A. (2019). Adaptation of fear of missing out scale (FoMOs): Turkish version validity and reliability study. *Psicologia: Reflexão e Crítica*, *32*(1), 32. doi:10.118641155-019-0117-4 PMID:32026206

Caplan, S. E. (2010). Theory and measurement of generalized problematic Internet use: A twostep approach. *Computers in Human Behavior*, *26*(5), 1089–1097. doi:10.1016/j.chb.2010.03.012

Casale, S., & Fioravanti, G. (2020). Factor structure and psychometric properties of the Italian version of the Fear of Missing Out Scale in emerging adults and adolescents. *Addictive Behaviors*, *102*, 106179. doi:10.1016/j.addbeh.2019.106179 PMID:31704432

Casale, S., Rugai, L., & Fioravanti, G. (2018). Exploring the role of positive metacognitions in explaining the association between the fear of missing out and social media addiction. *Addictive Behaviors*, *85*, 83–87. doi:10.1016/j.addbeh.2018.05.020 PMID:29864680

Chai, H. Y., Niu, G. F., Lian, S. L., Chu, X. W., Liu, S., & Sun, X. J. (2019). Why social network site use fails to promote well-being? The roles of social overload and fear of missing out. *Computers in Human Behavior*, *100*, 85–92. doi:10.1016/j.chb.2019.05.005

Chambers, D. (2013). *Social media and personal relationships: Online intimacies and networked friendship*. Springer. doi:10.1057/9781137314444

Chang, F. C., Chiu, C. H., Miao, N. F., Chen, P. H., Lee, C. M., Chiang, J. T., & Pan, Y. C. (2015). The relationship between parental mediation and Internet addiction among adolescents, and the association with cyberbullying and depression. *Comprehensive Psychiatry*, *57*, 21–28. doi:10.1016/j.comppsych.2014.11.013 PMID:25487108

Cheng, C., Lau, Y. C., Chan, L., & Luk, J. W. (2021). Prevalence of social media addiction across 32 nations: Meta-analysis with subgroup analysis of classification schemes and cultural values. *Addictive Behaviors, 117*, 106845. doi:10.1016/j.addbeh.2021.106845 PMID:33550200

Citko, A., & Owsieniuk, I. (2020). Epidemiology and the consequences of fear of missing out (FoMO). The role of general practitioners in early diagnosis, treatment and prevention of FoMO in teenagers and young adults. *Pediatria i Medycyna Rodzinna, 16*(1), 70–76. doi:10.15557/PiMR.2020.0012

Coco, G. L., Salerno, L., Franchina, V., Latona, A., & Giordano, C. (2020). Examining bi-directionality between fear of missing out and problematic smartphone use. A two-wave panel study among adolescents. *Addictive Behaviors, 106*, 106360. doi:10.1016/j.addbeh.2020.106360 PMID:32135397

Coskun, S., & Muslu, G. K. (2019). Investigation of problematic mobile phones use and fear of missing out (FoMO) level in adolescents. *Community Mental Health Journal, 55*(6), 1004–1014. doi:10.100710597-019-00422-8 PMID:31209716

Costa, M., Matos, A., & Costa, J. (2018). Social Media Disorder Scale–Short Form (SMDS-SF): Estudo de algumas propriedades psicométricas em jovens adultos portugueses. *Revista Portuguesa de Enfermagem de Saúde Mental, 6*, 65–70. doi:10.19131/rpesm.0216

Deci, E. L., & Ryan, R. M. (1985). *Intrinsic motivation and self-determination in human behaviour.* Plenum. doi:10.1007/978-1-4899-2271-7

Dempsey, A. E., O'Brien, K. D., Tiamiyu, M. F., & Elhai, J. D. (2019). Fear of missing out (FoMO) and rumination mediate relations between social anxiety and problematic Facebook use. *Addictive Behaviors Reports, 9*, 100150. doi:10.1016/j.abrep.2018.100150 PMID:31193746

Durak, H. Y. (2018). Investigation of nomophobia and smartphone addiction predictors among adolescents in Turkey: Demographic variables and academic performance. *The Social Science Journal, 56*(4), 492–517. doi:10.1016/j.soscij.2018.09.003

Elhai, J. D., Gallinari, E. F., Rozgonjuk, D., & Yang, H. (2020a). Depression, anxiety and fear of missing out as correlates of social, non-social and problematic smartphone use. *Addictive Behaviors, 105*, 106335. doi:10.1016/j.addbeh.2020.106335 PMID:32062337

Elhai, J. D., Levine, J. C., Alghraibeh, A. M., Alafnan, A. A., Aldraiweesh, A. A., & Hall, B. J. (2018). Fear of missing out: Testing relationships with negative affectivity, online social engagement, and problematic smartphone use. *Computers in Human Behavior, 89*, 289–298. doi:10.1016/j.chb.2018.08.020

Elhai, J. D., Levine, J. C., Dvorak, R. D., & Hall, B. J. (2016). Fear of missing out, need for touch, anxiety and depression are related to problematic smartphone use. *Computers in Human Behavior, 63*, 509–516. doi:10.1016/j.chb.2016.05.079

Elhai, J. D., Yang, H., Fang, J., Bai, X., & Hall, B. J. (2020b). Depression and anxiety symptoms are related to problematic smartphone use severity in Chinese young adults: Fear of missing out as a mediator. *Addictive Behaviors, 101*, 105962. doi:10.1016/j.addbeh.2019.04.020 PMID:31030950

Elhai, J. D., Yang, H., & Montag, C. (2021). Fear of missing out (FOMO): Overview, theoretical underpinnings, and literature review on relations with severity of negative affectivity and problematic technology use. *The British Journal of Psychiatry*, *43*(2), 203–209. doi:10.1590/1516-4446-2020-0870 PMID:32401865

Ellis, P. D. (2010). *The essential guide to effect sizes: Statistical power, meta-analysis, and the interpretation of research results*. Cambridge university press. doi:10.1017/CBO9780511761676

Fang, J., Wang, X., Wen, Z., & Zhou, J. (2020). Fear of missing out and problematic social media use as mediators between emotional support from social media and phubbing behavior. *Addictive Behaviors*, *107*, 106430. doi:10.1016/j.addbeh.2020.106430 PMID:32289745

Festinger, L. (1954). A theory of social comparison processes. *Human Relations*, *7*(2), 117–140. doi:10.1177/001872675400700202

Geng, J., Lei, L., Ouyang, M., Nie, J., & Wang, P. (2021). The influence of perceived parental phubbing on adolescents' problematic smartphone use: A two-wave multiple mediation model.*Addictive Behaviors*, *121*, 106995. doi:10.1016/j.addbeh.2021.106995 PMID:34090204

Gökler, M. E., Aydin, R., Ünal, E., & Metintaş, S. (2016). Determining validity and reliability of Turkish version of fear of missing out scale. *Anadolu Psikiyatri Dergisi*, *17*(1), 53–59. doi:10.5455/apd.195843

Hamutoglu, N. B., Topal, M., & Gezgin, D. M. (2020). Investigating Direct and Indirect Effects of Social Media Addiction, Social Media Usage and Personality Traits on FOMO. *International Journal of Progressive Education*, *16*(2), 248–261. doi:10.29329/ijpe.2020.241.17

Herman, D. (2000). Introducing short-term brands: A new branding tool for a new consumer reality. *Journal of Brand Management*, *7*(5), 330–340. doi:10.1057/bm.2000.23

Hidayati, N., Syaf, A., & Hartati, R. (2021). Fear of Missing Out ditinjau dari Big Five Personality. *Psychopolytan: Jurnal Psikologi*, *4*(2), 77–83. doi:10.36341/psi.v4i2.1392

Ho, T. T. Q. (2021). Facebook addiction and depression: Loneliness as a moderator and poor sleep quality as a mediator. *Telematics and Informatics*, *61*, 101617. doi:10.1016/j.tele.2021.101617

Ibrahim, S. A., Dahlan, A., Pauzi, N. W., & Vetrayan, J. (2022). Fear of missing out (FoMO) and its relation with depression and anxiety among university students. *Environment-Behaviour Proceedings Journal*, *7*(20), 233–238. doi:10.21834/ebpj.v7i20.3358

Jablonska, B., & Lindberg, L. (2007). Risk behaviors, victimization and mental distress among adolescents in different family structures. *Social Psychiatry and Psychiatric Epidemiology*, *42*(8), 656–663. doi:10.100700127-007-0210-3 PMID:17522746

Jérémy, M., Jean-Charles, Q., Michèle, C., Alice, N., Marie, I., & Laetitia, S. (2021). Fear of missing out predicts distraction by social reward signals displayed on a smartphone in difficult driving situations. *Frontiers in Psychology*, 12. PMID:34335405

Judge, T. A., Higgins, C. A., Thoresen, C. J., & Barrick, M. R. (1999). The Big Five personality traits, general mental ability, and career success across the life span. *Personnel Psychology*, *52*(3), 621–652. doi:10.1111/j.1744-6570.1999.tb00174.x

Kim, J., & Tussyadiah, I. P. (2013). Social networking and social support in tourism experience: The moderating role of online self-presentation strategies. *Journal of Travel & Tourism Marketing*, *30*(1-2), 78–92. doi:10.1080/10548408.2013.751220

Kim, J. H. (2022). Parental support and problematic smartphone use: A serial mediating model of self-esteem and fear of missing out. *International Journal of Environmental Research and Public Health*, *19*(13), 7657. doi:10.3390/ijerph19137657 PMID:35805315

Ko, C. H., Wang, P. W., Liu, T. L., Yen, C. F., Chen, C. S., & Yen, J. Y. (2015). Bidirectional associations between family factors and Internet addiction among adolescents in a prospective investigation. *Psychiatry and Clinical Neurosciences*, *69*(4), 192–200. doi:10.1111/pcn.12204 PMID:24836367

Köseliören, M., & Çakır, C., & ve Beşikci, S. (2022). The effect of fear of death in the elderly creating FoMO on the perception of health news published on social media. *Intermedia International e-Journal*, *9*(17), 324-340. doi:10.56133/intermedia.1180852

Kuss, D. J., & Griffiths, M. D. (2011). Online social networking and addiction: A review of the psychological literature. *International Journal of Environmental Research and Public Health*, *8*(9), 3528–3552. doi:10.3390/ijerph8093528 PMID:22016701

Lee, S. Y. (2014). How do people compare themselves with others on social network sites?: The case of Facebook. *Computers in Human Behavior*, *32*, 253–260. doi:10.1016/j.chb.2013.12.009

Leung, L., Liang, J., & Zhang, Y. (2017). Media addiction. The International Encyclopedia of Media Effects, 1-14.

Li, L., Griffiths, M. D., Niu, Z., & Mei, S. (2020). Fear of missing out (FoMO) and gaming disorder among Chinese university students: Impulsivity and game time as mediators. *Issues in Mental Health Nursing*, *41*(12), 1104–1113. doi:10.1080/01612840.2020.1774018 PMID:32634040

Liu, Q., Wu, J., Zhou, Z., & Wang, W. (2020). Parental technoference and smartphone addiction in Chinese adolescents: The mediating role of social sensitivity and loneliness. *Children and Youth Services Review*, *118*, 105434. doi:10.1016/j.childyouth.2020.105434

López, M. C. L. A., Gutierrez, J. C. S., & Jiménez, A. G. (2015). Problematic internet use among Spanish adolescents: The predictive role of internet preference and family relationships. *European Journal of Communication*, *30*(4), 470–485. doi:10.1177/0267323115586725

Marino, C., Gini, G., Vieno, A., & Spada, M. M. (2018). The associations between problematic Facebook use, psychological distress and well-being among adolescents and young adults: A systematic review and meta-analysis. *Journal of Affective Disorders*, *226*, 274–281. doi:10.1016/j.jad.2017.10.007 PMID:29024900

Masur, P. K., Reinecke, L., Ziegele, M., & Quiring, O. (2014). The interplay of intrinsic need satisfaction and Facebook specific motives in explaining addictive behavior on Facebook. *Computers in Human Behavior*, *39*, 376–386. doi:10.1016/j.chb.2014.05.047

Mazlum, M., & Atalay, A. (2022). Developing the fear of missing out (FoMO) scale for university students: The validity and reliability study. *Journal of Pedagogical Research*, *6*(4), 4. doi:10.33902/JPR.202215485

McKee, P. C., Budnick, C. J., Walters, K. S., & Antonios, I. (2022). College student Fear of Missing Out (FoMO) and maladaptive behavior: Traditional statistical modeling and predictive analysis using machine learning. *PLoS One*, *17*(10), e0274698. doi:10.1371/journal.pone.0274698 PMID:36197889

Metz, J. (2019). Fomo and regret for non-doings. *Social Theory and Practice*, *45*(3), 451–470. doi:10.5840octheorpract201992767

Milyavskaya, M., Saffran, M., Hope, N., & Koestner, R. (2018). Fear of missing out: Prevalence, dynamics, and consequences of experiencing FOMO. *Motivation and Emotion*, *42*(5), 725–737. doi:10.100711031-018-9683-5

Modzelewski, P. (2020). Fomo (fear of missing out) – an educational and behavioral problem in times of new communication forms. *Konteksty Pedagogiczne*, *14*(1), 215–232.

Moore, K., & Craciun, G. (2021). Fear of missing out and personality as predictors of social networking sites usage: The Instagram case. *Psychological Reports*, *124*(4), 1761–1787. doi:10.1177/0033294120936184 PMID:32659168

Notten, N. (2013). Risicogedrag en het wereldwijde web: De invloed van gezin en samenleving op het online risicogedrag van adolescenten vanuit een Europees perspectief. *Mens en Maatschappij*, *88*(4), 350–374. doi:10.5117/MEM2013.4.NOTT

O'Connell, C. (2020). How FOMO (Fear of Missing Out), the Smartphone, and Social Media May Be Affecting University Students in the Middle East. *North American Journal of Psychology*, *22*(1).

Oberst, U., Wegmann, E., Stodt, B., Brand, M., & Chamarro, A. (2017). Negative consequences from heavy social networking in adolescents: The mediating role of fear of missing out. *Journal of Adolescence*, *55*(1), 51–60. doi:10.1016/j.adolescence.2016.12.008 PMID:28033503

Oxford Dictionary. (2018) FOMO. *Oxford Dictionary.* Oxford Press. https://en.oxforddictionaries.com/definition/fomo

Przybylski, A. K., Murayama, K., DeHaan, C. R., & Gladwell, V. (2013). Motivational, emotional, and behavioral correlates of fear of missing out. *Computers in Human Behavior*, *29*(4), 1841–1848. doi:10.1016/j.chb.2013.02.014

Rahardjo, W., & Mulyani, I. (2020). Instagram addiction in teenagers: The role of type D personality, self-esteem, and fear of missing out. *Psikohumaniora: Jurnal Penelitian Psikologi*, *5*(1), 29–44. doi:10.21580/pjpp.v5i1.4916

Rajan, B., Jose, L. G., & Sundar, T. (2022). Are You Hooked to the 'Gram'? Exploring the Correlation between Loneliness, the Fear of Missing Out, and Instagram Usage among Young Indians. *Palabra Clave (La Plata)*, *25*(2), e2525.

Reinecke, L., Vorderer, P., & Knop, K. (2014). Entertainment 2.0? The role of intrinsic and extrinsic need satisfaction for the enjoyment of facebook use. *Journal of Communication*, *64*(3), 417–438. doi:10.1111/jcom.12099

Riggio, H. R. (2004). Parental marital conflict and divorce, parent child relationships, social support, and relationship anxiety in young adulthood. *Personal Relationships*, *11*(1), 99–114. doi:10.1111/j.1475-6811.2004.00073.x

Riordan, B. C., Cody, L., Flett, J. A., Conner, T. S., Hunter, J., & Scarf, D. (2020). The development of a single item FoMO (fear of missing out) scale. *Current Psychology (New Brunswick, N.J.)*, *39*(4), 1215–1220. doi:10.100712144-018-9824-8

Riordan, B. C., Flett, J. A. M., Hunter, J. A., Scarf, D., & Conner, T. S. (2015). Fear of missing Out (FoMO): The relationship between FoMO, alcohol use, and alcohol-related consequences in college students. *Journal of Psychiatry and Brain Functions*, *2*(9), 1–7. doi:10.7243/2055-3447-2-9

Rozgonjuk, D., Sindermann, C., Elhai, J. D., & Montag, C. (2021). Individual differences in Fear of Missing Out (FoMO): Age, gender, and the Big Five personality trait domains, facets, and items. *Personality and Individual Differences*, *171*, 110546. doi:10.1016/j.paid.2020.110546

Ryan, R. M., & Deci, E. L. (2000). Self-determination theory and the facilitation of intrinsic motivation, social development, and well-being. *The American Psychologist*, *55*(1), 68–78. doi:10.1037/0003-066X.55.1.68 PMID:11392867

Savitri, I., Wicaksono, A. S., & Fastari, C. (2021). The effect of big five personality on fear of missing out. *Journal Universitas Muhammadiyah Gresik*, *1*(2), 956–964. doi:10.30587/umgeshic.v1i2.3499

Sela, Y., Zach, M., Amichay-Hamburger, Y., Mishali, M., & Omer, H. (2019). Family environment and problematic internet use among adolescents: The mediating roles of depression and fear of missing out. *Computers in Human Behavior*, *106*, 106226. doi:10.1016/j.chb.2019.106226

Sette, C. P., Lima, N. R., Queluz, F. N., Ferrari, B. L., & Hauck, N. (2020). The online fear of missing out inventory (ON-FoMO): Development and validation of a new tool. *Journal of Technology in Behavioral Science*, *5*(1), 20–29. doi:10.100741347-019-00110-0

Solano, L., Pirrotta, E., Ingravalle, V., & Fayella, P. (2009). The family physician and the psychologist in the office together: A response to fragmentation. *Mental Health in Family Medicine*, *6*(2), 91–98. PMID:22477897

Stead, H., & Bibby, P. A. (2017). Personality, fear of missing out and problematic internet use and their relationship to subjective well-being. *Computers in Human Behavior*, *76*, 1–17. doi:10.1016/j.chb.2017.08.016

Stošić, L., & Stošić, I. (2015). Perceptions of teachers regarding the implementation of the internet in education. *Computers in Human Behavior*, *53*, 462–468. doi:10.1016/j.chb.2015.07.027

Su, C. C., & Chan, N. K. (2017). Predicting social capital on Facebook: The implications of use intensity, perceived content desirability, and Facebook-enabled communication practices. *Computers in Human Behavior*, *72*, 259–268. doi:10.1016/j.chb.2017.02.058

Sun, Y., & Zhang, Y. (2021). A review of theories and models applied in studies of social media addiction and implications for future research. *Addictive Behaviors, 114*, 106699. doi:10.1016/j.addbeh.2020.106699 PMID:33268185

Talwar, S., Dhir, A., Kaur, P., Zafar, N., & Alrasheedy, M. (2019). Why do people share fake news? Associations between the dark side of social media use and fake news sharing behavior. *Journal of Retailing and Consumer Services, 51*, 72–82. doi:10.1016/j.jretconser.2019.05.026

Tandon, A., Dhir, A., Islam, N., Talwar, S., & Mäntymäki, M. (2021). Psychological and behavioral outcomes of social media-induced fear of missing out at the workplace. *Journal of Business Research, 136*, 186–197. doi:10.1016/j.jbusres.2021.07.036

Tandon, A., Dhir, A., Talwar, S., Kaur, P., & Mäntymäki, M. (2022). Social media induced fear of missing out (FoMO) and phubbing: Behavioural, relational and psychological outcomes. *Technological Forecasting and Social Change, 174*, 121149. doi:10.1016/j.techfore.2021.121149

Tanhan, F., Özok, H. İ., & Tayiz, V. (2022). Fear of missing out (FoMO): A current review. *Psikiyatride Güncel Yaklasimlar, 14*(1), 74–85. doi:10.18863/pgy.942431

Vaala, S. E., & Bleakley, A. (2015). Monitoring, mediating, and modelling: Parental influence on adolescent computer and internet use in the United States. *Journal of Children and Media, 9*(1), 40–57. doi:10.1080/17482798.2015.997103

Wegmann, E., Oberst, U., Stodt, B., & Brand, M. (2017). Online-specific fear of missing out and Internet-use expectancies contribute to symptoms of Internet-communication disorder. *Addictive Behaviors Reports, 5*, 33–42. doi:10.1016/j.abrep.2017.04.001 PMID:29450225

Wolniewicz, C. A., Tiamiyu, M. F., Weeks, J. W., & Elhai, J. D. (2018). Problematic smartphone use and relations with negative affect, fear of missing out, and fear of negative and positive evaluation. *Psychiatry Research, 262*, 618–623. doi:10.1016/j.psychres.2017.09.058 PMID:28982630

Wu, A. M. S., Lau, J. T. F., Cheng, K. M., Law, R. W., Tse, V. W. S., & Lau, M. M. C. (2018). Direct and interaction effects of co-existing familial risk factors and protective factors associated with internet addiction among Chinese students in Hong Kong. *The Journal of Early Adolescence, 38*(4), 1–22. doi:10.1177/0272431616671826

Xiuqin, H., Huimin, Z., Mengchen, L., Jinan, W., Ying, Z., & Ran, T. (2010). Mental health, personality, and parental rearing styles of adolescents with Internet addiction disorder. *Cyberpsychology, Behavior, and Social Networking, 13*(4), 401–406. doi:10.1089/cyber.2009.0222 PMID:20712498

Yali, Z., Sen, L., & Guoliang, Y. (2021). The relationship between social media use and fear of missing out: A meta-analysis. *Acta Psychologica Sinica, 53*(3), 273–290.

Yuan, G., Elhai, J. D., & Hall, B. J. (2021). The influence of depressive symptoms and fear of missing out on severity of problematic smartphone use and internet gaming disorder among Chinese young adults: A three-wave mediation model. *Addictive Behaviors, 112*, 106648. doi:10.1016/j.addbeh.2020.106648 PMID:32977268

Zhu, X., & Xiong, Z. (2022). Exploring association between social media addiction, fear of missing out, and self-presentation online among university students: A cross-sectional study. *Frontiers in Psychiatry*, *13*(13), 896762. doi:10.3389/fpsyt.2022.896762 PMID:35633794

## ADDITIONAL READING

Aygul, T. A., & Akbay, S. E. (2019). Smartphone addiction, fear of missing out, and perceived competence as predictors of social media addiction of adolescents. *European Journal of Educational Research*, *8*(2), 559–566. doi:10.12973/eu-jer.8.2.559

Barry, C. T., & Wong, M. Y. (2020). Fear of missing out (FoMO): A generational phenomenon or an individual difference? *Journal of Social and Personal Relationships*, *37*(12), 2952–2966. doi:10.1177/0265407520945394

Dhir, A., Yossatorn, Y., Kaur, P., & Chen, S. (2018). Online social media fatigue and psychological wellbeing—A study of compulsive use, fear of missing out, fatigue, anxiety and depression. *International Journal of Information Management*, *40*, 141–152. doi:10.1016/j.ijinfomgt.2018.01.012

McGinnis, P. J. (2020). *Fear of missing out: Practical decision-making in a world of overwhelming choice*. Sourcebooks, Inc.

Rodriguez, B. L. (2022). *30-Day Sobriety Challenge: Take a Break from Social Drinking and Create New Habits*. Rockridge Press.

Soriano Sánchez, J. G. (2022). Factores psicológicos y consecuencias del Síndrome Fear of Missing Out. [R]. *Revista de Psicología y Educación*, *17*(1), 69–78. doi:10.23923/rpye2022.01.217

## KEY TERMS AND DEFINITIONS

**Fear of Missing Out:** An intense concern or anxiety that others may be having rewarding experiences from which one is absent.

**Social Media Addiction:** Addictive or compulsive social media.

**Symptoms:** Signs or indications that an individual may suffer from FoMO.

**Problematic Smartphone Use:** A form of psychological or behavioral dependence on cell phones.

**Prevalence:** This refers to the number of cases of involvement in social media addiction found in an investigation.

# Chapter 29
# Negative Impacts of Technology and Digital Diseases

**Selahattin Çavuş**
*Aksaray University, Turkey*

## ABSTRACT

*Computers, the internet, and other smart devices have become indispensable in daily life. These tools make life easier in communication, access to information, time management, transportation, and many more. Unfortunately, not all the consequences of technology on people and society are advantageous and constructive. When misused, technological tools can have a harmful impact on lifestyle. The proliferation of new media has brought forth several issues, including the emergence of various addictions, cyberbullying, and privacy violations. The problems caused by digitalization are not limited to these. New types of diseases are emerging due to technological tools. These diseases cause or trigger more serious health problems. These disorders are usually caused by uncontrolled and unconscious use or the nature of technological devices. This study aims to examine disorders such as nomophobia, social media depression, phantom vibration syndrome, and cybersickness. The study focuses particularly on the causes of digital diseases, as well as their effects and preventative measures.*

## INTRODUCTION

There is hardly a time when electronic tools are not utilized to control private and business life. Computers, the internet, and other smart devices have become indispensable in daily life. These tools make life easier in communication, access to information, time management, transportation, and many more. Unfortunately, not all the consequences of technology on people and society are advantageous and constructive. When misused, technological tools can have a negative impact on lifestyle. Due to its social and psychological impacts, communication technologies are among the key research subjects of communication scholars. The proliferation of new media has brought forth several issues, including the emergence of various addictions, cyberbullying, and privacy violations. The problems caused by digitalization are not limited to these. New types of diseases are emerging due to technological tools. These diseases cause or trigger more serious health problems.

DOI: 10.4018/978-1-6684-8397-8.ch029

The study aims to draw the framework of digital diseases that arise with the negative effects of digitalization. Technology-related disorders that result in more severe diseases are seen today, in addition to illnesses that have a negative impact on physical and mental health. These disorders are usually caused by uncontrolled and unconscious use. However, some of digital diseases are caused by the nature of technological devices. In this direction, this study aims to examine disorders such as nomophobia, social media depression, phantom vibration syndrome, and cybersickness. The study focuses particularly on the causes of digital diseases, as well as their effects and preventative measures.

## DIGITAL SOCIETY

Throughout history, there have been turning points in the transformation of societies. After the transition from a hunter-gatherer culture to an agricultural society, the way of organization and welfare of humanity increased rapidly, and the lifestyle changed completely. The same situation was experienced in the transition from an agricultural society to an industrial society. The industrialization of the engine, the invention of the steam engine; brought industry-technology integration to the top with electricity and the internet. Oswald Spengler called the post-industrial era the Age of Machine Techniques, and McLuhan called it the Gutenberg Age. The term postindustrial society was coined by Daniel Bell. While Jose Ortega Gasset called the post-industrial era as the 3-stage age of technology, Walter Ong called it Electronic Culture, Toffler (2008) the Third Wave, and Castells (2008) the Information Age. Due to the development of information and communication technologies, this period has been called the Electronic Communication Age (Postman, 2006, 34).

Computer and internet technologies take over the leverage role of the post-industrial era. With the spread of these technologies, production, and consumption patterns are changing. It can be said that digital technologies affect every moment of human life. The use of technological tools in education, health, marketing, media and tourism, and many other fields, especially in the defense industry and production industry, is increasing and redesigning the sectors completely. Digital technologies, on the other hand, are mostly described as a part of the computer revolution that took place after the Second World War. Military research has a great role in the development of computers and the Internet. Studies carried out during the 1960s and 1970s formed the backbone of today's network structure. Internet technologies, whose prevalence has increased rapidly after the millennium, have become the most important and decisive carriers of digitalization.

Internet and internet-based technologies completely encompass daily life. The internet, which differs from the manipulative character of one-way media such as newspapers, radio, and television, completely changes the structure and profile of its participants, thanks to its features such as simultaneity and immediacy. The interactive structure called new media has transformed human-machine interaction into human-human interaction. This structure is called Web 2.0 or social media as it is known (Çavuş, 2018, 285).

Social media and other digital tools that promote engagement and community modify behaviors, needs, and different modes of communication in addition to feelings and thoughts. The unique position assigned to social media by the Internet, which can fulfill the functions of all mass media such as newspapers, magazines, radio, and television, makes it necessary to address the effects of this technology on society in all its dimensions. The Internet and social media encompass every area from daily routines to professional business life. Therefore, these technologies change the way of thinking, doing business, and leisure activities. The direction and severity of change intensify the debates on whether the effects of technological tools and practices are positive or negative. It can be said that there are two dominant views in this field: Techno-optimists and techno-pessimists…

## Techno-Optimism

Many technological advancements have been made in the fields of artificial intelligence, media, finance, education, and defense. Each of these developments results in technologies that can be applied over several years. It appears that new technology is simplifying people's daily life. The development of communication and transportation facilities has accelerated globalization. This situation has improved both the interaction within the society and the tendency of acculturation between societies. The development of communication has also accelerated the flow of information. The facilitation of access to information has affected the developments in the field of education. Every invention continues to improve living standards. For this reason, techno-optimism focuses on the continuity of technological development and what it offers to humanity, explaining progress and development with the idea that "everything goes well".

The foundation of techno-optimism is the conviction that technology will advance steadily and improve society. Technology, in the opinion of Danaher (2022), has a key role in the prevailing of good over evil. Danaher contends that technology is essential for good to prevail, defining it as "a set of instruments that humans utilize to solve problems and achieve goals." Techno-optimism promotes the idea that good will prevail over evil rather than that everything will always turn out for the best. Postman (2006, 14) makes the argument that it is incorrect to read the impacts of technology from only one perspective. Technophiles, as defined by Postman, are techno-optimists who obsess over technology as though they were in love. According to technophiles, technology is something pure and spotless.

## Techno-Pessimism

Techno-pessimism is based on the idea that even though technological advancements make people's life simpler, they will ultimately lead to more serious issues. Postman (2006, 14), who refers to techno-pessimists as one-eyed soothsayers, states that techno-pessimists' goals tend to speak only of the negative aspects of technology. Techno-pessimists dislike emphasizing the advantages of technological advancements and the opportunities they create. Still, Postman emphasizes that it is important to thoroughly consider what technology has gained and lost to draw conclusions about it.

Königs (2022), who disagrees with Danaher's assertion that techno-optimism is superior, asserts that it is unreasonable to believe that technology will upset the balance between good and evil. Applying superiority to specific technologies as opposed to the technology may make more sense. Someone optimistic about AI, for instance, need not think that these innovations will help ensure that good prevails over evil. Future technological developments and their effects on society are difficult to foresee.

Beyond the theoretical and philosophical debates, it is clear that technological tools cause psychological and physical issues. For instance, communication technologies' surveillance capabilities have a negative impact on both social privacy and personal privacy. Digital technologies are used in the information society for information production, distribution, and preservation. Due to the growth of social media, the protection of personal data has grown to be a significant issue. Academic research is increasingly focusing on strategies for addressing privacy violations and legal requirements for the security of personal data (Romansky, 2014).

Digital addictions are yet another issue brought on by digitalization. There are many addictions caused by digital technologies. Just a few of them include addiction to the internet, social media, digital games, tablets, and TV. A study conducted in 31 countries in 2014 found that 6% of people worldwide suffer from Internet addiction (Cheng & Li, 2014). The Middle East has the highest prevalence of addiction. The regions of Northern and Western Europe with the lowest rates of internet addiction. However, research has shown that internet addiction is more common than average in the Far East, which is rapidly developing. For instance, in regional nations like China, South Korea, and Taiwan, the prevalence of internet addiction is 30%.

Video game addiction is widespread in kids and teenagers. According to studies, playing games for 12 to 14 hours is addictive. Online games can lead to addiction to digital games. Studies have shown that certain games exhibit the effects of gambling. According to a study conducted in 2016, 21.4 percent of university students are at risk of game addiction. The situation is worse for male students. Male students are exposed to the negative effects of violent games such as action-adventure, strategy, and online games. More surprisingly, the level of addiction also rises as mothers' income and education levels rise (Çavuş et al., 2016). One percent of the participants in a different study to gauge the extent of high school students' game addictions were found to be addicted. 28.5% of the students participating in the research are in the risk group (Ayhan & Çavuş, 2015).

In recent years, specific studies on digital addiction have been conducted. Researchers are particularly interested in addictions brought on by platforms like Instagram, Facebook, and Tiktok in addition to research on social media addiction. For instance, it was discovered in a 2015 study that prolonged use of Facebook leads to addiction in users. According to the study, 2.9 percent of the participants have a Facebook addiction. 43.2% of the participants are at risk of Facebook addiction (Tiryaki, 2015, 246). The fact that almost half of the participants face the threat of addiction is worrisome. Emotional issues are arguably the most significant side effect of social media addiction. People's feelings of worthlessness and helplessness hurt all aspects of life. Addiction causes performance issues in both the workplace and the classroom. One of the issues brought on by addiction is the drop in workplace productivity. In addition, relationship problems also occur with addiction. Physical disorders represent the most advanced stages of addiction (Tiryaki & Karakuş, 2019, 148). Another study conducted in 2015 focused on the problematic internet use of university students. In the study based on information obesity, it was measured whether university students use the internet and social media healthily. It was determined that the students in the sample group tended to use the internet problematically. There is a significant relationship between problematic internet usage and gender. Men are more problematic internet users than women. The study also evaluated that problematic internet use may cause information obesity (Eşitti, 2015).

Cyberbullying is another risk associated with digital technologies. Cyberbullying is defined as intentionally and repeatedly harming someone through computers, mobile phones, and similar technological devices (Hinduja & Patchin, 2010, 208). As a result, cyberbullying constitutes a new dimension of traditional bullying that has been shaped by technology. When cyberbullying studies are examined, victimization and cyberbullying behaviors develop at the same time as social media. In the study examining the cyberbullying and victimization behaviors of university students in 2017, it was determined that the students were below the risky level in terms of bullying and exposure to such behaviors in the virtual environment. However, there are gender-specific differences in victimization and cyberbullying behaviors. Male students are more likely than female students to use the internet to bully others. However, compared to male students, female students are more likely to become cyber victims. It has also been shown among the results that students who have just started university are more exposed to cyberbullying. The most important source of discomfort for students is instant messages (Çavuş & Ayhan, 2017).

## TYPES OF DIGITAL DISEASES

The drawbacks of digital technologies are not limited to digital addictions, privacy violations and cyberbullying behaviors. Physical and psychological issues are more prevalent due to the unrestrained use of computers, smartphones, tablets, and other smart devices. Major among these problems are nomophobia, social media depression, imaginary vibration syndrome and cybersickness. The causes, effects, and discussions of the four disorders mentioned above are covered in this study section.

### Nomophobia

Nomophobia is the shortened form for "no mobile phobia." Nomophobia is defined as the involuntary fear that a person experiences when he/she cannot reach his/her mobile device (Betoncu & Ozdamli, 2019, 599). In daily life, the amount of time a person spends with smart devices such as mobile phones are increasing. The prevalence of mobile phone, internet, and social media use has surpassed 95%, particularly among children and young adults. As a result, constant communication has an impact on how people live their daily lives. The state of fear or anxiety that occurs when smartphone use is stopped, even for a short time, is associated with the development of nomophobia.

Thanks to communication technologies, people interact with each other every hour of the day. The usage time of smart devices at home, work or school is increasing. Young people, who use technology the most, access the phone hundreds of times a day. Classrooms and locations outside of school hours are examples of places with phone access. According to studies, prohibiting the use of mobile devices during class time makes students more anxious and may even cause nomophobia (Rosen et al., 2016, 54).

Nomophobia is associated with the withdrawal symptom that occurs in the development of internet addiction. Nomophobics are concerned about missing their social media posts and experiences on social media platforms. Technical difficulties can also lead to worry or anxiety developing. For example, empty battery phones and network problems make nomophobic individuals more nervous. For this reason, the person wants to carry his/her phone with his/her at all hours of the day. It has been reported that Covid-19 increases addiction, which leads to nomophobia (Lai et al, 2022). According to a study involving university students in 2022, the level of nomophobia differs significantly according to gender, daily use of smartphones and the number of daily checks. It was observed that social media addiction significantly predicted the level of fear of nomophobia (Çırak & Dost, 2022).

### Social Media Depression

Usenet, the first network system that enables communication, was created in 1979. The first social media platform in today's sense is Open Diary. Open Diary was created in 1998. MySpace and Facebook became one of the first and most significant examples of social media in the following few years. YouTube, Instagram, Twitter, Twich, Tiktok are among the other social media platforms with the most users in the world. WhatsApp, one of the messaging applications, is also widely used. Facebook has close to 3 billion users. YouTube alone accounts for 25 percent of global mobile mobility (Çavuş, 2022, 11-12).

Research shows that the use of social media, especially among children and young people, continues to increase rapidly. The rate of social media use among young people has exceeded 95 percent (Auxier & Anderson, 2021).

Social media usage purposes include motivations such as information, entertainment, education, and socialization-identity acquisition (Çavuş, 2022). In addition, it can be mentioned about usage purposes such as self-aggrandizement or playing. However, the idealized identities in the social media environment show people differently than they are, and a new reality is built in virtual environments. This situation eventually leads the person to compare herself to others and make excuses for her deficiencies. Thus, physiological, and psychological problems arise in users. The relationship between social media and depression is one of the main topics of interest to researchers recently.

Depression is a disease of unhappiness and listlessness that causes people to feel sad and pessimistic. Depression is reportedly a common illness that makes it challenging to go about daily tasks and rituals. People who are depressed have trouble focusing, getting distracted, and making decisions. Anyone who is depressed does not feel well, either physically or mentally. In fact, many chronic diseases occur during the depression (Mete, 2008, 4).

According to studies, social media addiction and depression levels are significantly correlated. In a study conducted on university students during the Covid-19 pandemic, it was shown that the depression levels of university students during the pandemic period were a predictor of their social media addictions. University students' social media addictions rise along with their depression levels. In the study, it was reported that there were students with moderate and few severe depression symptoms. In addition, daily internet use has a significant relationship with social media addiction and depression levels (Dikmen, 2021).

In another study conducted in the same year, the relationship between adults' social media use and depression and social anxiety levels was examined. It has been reported that there is a significant relationship between social media addiction and the depression scores of the participants. The story of anxiety is higher in people who use social media more. Additionally, a significant relationship exists between social media addiction and time spent on social media (Özkapı, 2021).

## Phantom Vibration Syndrome

Technological tools, in McLuhan's words, are extensions that shape people's perceptions. Long use of technology in daily life results in some physical issues as well as psychological dysfunctions. For example, the mobile phone's incoming calls and message notifications can be detected through ringtones and vibrations. Even when there is no call, imaginary ringtones and imaginary vibrations that create the feeling of receiving a call or message can be experienced. Imaginary vibration syndrome occurs with such illusions.

Research on phantom vibration syndrome, described by Robert D. Jones in 2003, has been increasing in recent years. In a 2016 study, the phenomenon of calling or feeling like a vibration was characterized as a signal detection problem. In a study focusing on problems in interpersonal relationships, it was reported that phantom vibration syndrome is more common in those with attachment anxiety. This situation, which is reported to be psychological, increases the probability of experiencing phantom vibration syndrome as the expectation of calls or messages increases (Kruger & Djerf, 2016).

In 2014, a study was designed to determine the prevalence of newly reported disorders, like phantom vibration syndrome, phantom ringing syndrome, nomophobia, and possible risk for sleep disorders and infertility among medical students. It was reported that the frequency of phantom vibration syndrome ona daily, weekly, rarely and never observed basis was 19%, 18%, 56%, and 7% respectively. Overall 93% of students felt Phantom Vibration Syndrome but in different frequencies. The majority of the students (70%) kept their mobile phones in their trousers' pockets. Around 10% of students kept their mobile phones in their upper pockets while 6% of students preferred to attach their mobile phones to their belts. Only 14% of students answered that they kept their mobile phones in places other than those mentioned above. Around 59% of students woke up from sleep upon hearing a mobile phone ringtone. The percentage of students using mobile phones before sleeping was found to be very high. According to this, Mobile phone usage is contributing a major role in increasing psychological stress and related problems among medical students (Alam, et. al, 2014).

Shatrughan and Pareek (2017) reported that the frequent use and dependency on cell phone lead to phantom vibration syndrome. According to the research, people are affected with phantom vibration syndrome at the global level and its prevalence rate is too high. Phantom Vibration Syndrome is a tactile hallucination that occurs due to psychological or neurological damage. Persistent phantom vibration syndrome may lead to burnout syndrome.

## Cybersickness

Cybersickness is directly related to exposure to virtual environments. This term, developed by McCauley and Sharkey, was derived from research on driving simulators. This condition, called simulator sickness, refers to motion sickness that occurs in military flight simulators and various simulators. Motion sickness, on the other hand, refers to the syndromes seen in carsickness, or seasickness. Motion sickness, which was thought to be seen in land, air or sea voyages in the early periods, was later observed to be experienced in virtual environments, augmented reality platforms and 3D cinemas (Algül, et, al. 2019, 11).

Although motion sickness and cybersickness are technically two separate diseases, the result is the same. For example, in a boat, nausea occurs due to the body moving up and down. In the interior cabin, this situation often occurs even when the eyes do not see the movement. Situation changes when you go up on the deck and focus on the horizon. Eyes and emotions in sync set things right again. Cybersickness is not caused by an actual motion, such as sea or motion sickness. It is only the perception of motion that triggers the symptoms (Pietrangelo, 2023).

Cybersickness is caused by software and hardware. Helmets and virtual reality technologies are among the factors that cause this disease. Since the early days of virtual reality technologies, cybersickness has been observed. Initially, this disease was considered as motion sickness. It is manifested by a combination of symptoms such as nausea, fatigue, headache, straining, postural instability, and vomiting. 20-80 percent of virtual reality users report experiencing cybersickness at least once (Chandra, Jamiy, & Reza, 2022).

There are various factors that affect the disease caused by the use of virtual reality. In the studies, findings were obtained about whether virtual reality elements cause disease and trigger symptoms. The severity of the symptoms was tried to be measured in the questionnaires for the users of virtual reality helmets and apparatus. In addition, age and gender factor, individual characteristics factor, experience factor, screen type factor, field of view factor and exposure to virtual environment factors were examined in the studies. As a result, it has been found that these factors can cause disease (Algül, et.al, 2019, 20-24).

There are ways to deal with cybersickness. You can start by trying to reduce screen time first. In addition, articles can be read and printed to get away from the computer and phone. Another way to protect yourself from this disease is to increase movement during the hours of screen exposure. It's good to take a break from time to time. Well-planning after hours will also help one's productivity. Apart from all these, utilities can be used to control screen time. Proper use of virtual reality helmets will also help limit the occurrence of symptoms (Miller, 2023).

## FUTURE RESEARCH DIRECTIONS

Every new technological tool, application, and service that enters our lives changes our way of living in both positive and negative ways. Particularly, the use of the internet, communication, accessibility, and constant connectivity not only cause new diseases but also cause old ones to surface. Many new diseases such as cyberchondria, which means the diagnosis of disease on the Internet, photolurking, which means secretly looking at a photo, and stalking, which is defined as spying on someone or someone, are growing more and more prevalent. These diseases are studied by researchers in communication, psychology and various branches of medicine. It is crucial that communication scholars focus on this area given the revolutionary changes that communication technology have undergone. In this direction, it would be beneficial to diversify the studies in the field in an interdisciplinary way and to deal with the studies with original methods, models and approaches belonging to different disciplines. Researchers should also focus on other issues (addiction, cyberbullying, virtual socialization, surveillance) that degrade interpersonal communication and obstruct healthy communication.

## CONCLUSION AND RECOMMENDATIONS

In this study, only some of the digital diseases, which are increasing in types and social effects, are mentioned. Digital technologies, which are used for countless purposes, not only change lifestyles, but also negatively affect the quality of life. In fact, these technologies can be the precursors of defined diseases or syndromes. These tools, which people keep close even after hours, disrupt the perception of free time and rest. People are constantly exposed to notifications due to the phone standing at their bedside during sleep hours, and laptop computers and tablets occupying the trunk of their car on vacation. Due to the misuse of digital technologies, notifications become triggers of psychological and physiological diseases over time. Digital addictions are the most common type of digital diseases. There are numerous studies on characteristic types such as digital game addiction, computer and internet addiction, and social media addiction.

In recent years, there has been an increase in disease complaints such as Nomophobia, Social Media Depression, Phantom Vibration Syndrome, and Cybersickness. The main factor triggering these diseases is uncontrolled and unconscious use. For example, staying away from mobile phones causes anxiety, fear, and stress in users. Nomophobia is associated with the withdrawal symptom that occurs in the development of internet addiction. Nomophobics are afraid of missing out on experiences on social media platforms. It has been reported that the time users spend on social media is related to their depression and social anxiety levels. Physiological and psychological depression caused by social media paves the way for many chronic diseases. Image, sound, vibration, and many other features of technological devices cause perception disorders and illusions. Phantom Vibration Syndrome and Cybersickness are prime examples of this. Hearing unreal sounds, and feeling fake movements, is a trick played by technological devices on the brain. The psychiatric effects of these illusions are becoming more and more common.

There are ways to protect yourself from digital diseases. As stated in the study, it can be started by trying to reduce screen time as much as possible. Even if it is not possible to remove technological devices from our lives, measures should be taken to increase the control over these devices. Spending time on sports and cultural activities will help limit screen exposure. It is important to plan work hours and leisure activities well. Steps should be taken to prevent the technology-oriented planning of houses. The usage recommendations for devices that seem indispensable for daily life should not be ignored. In addition, if necessary, software and applications that helps correct use can be used. On the other hand, if it is felt that problematic use cannot be prevented, professional help should not be avoided.

## REFERENCES

Alam, M., Qureshi, M. S., Sarwat, A., Haque, Z., Masroor, M. S., Makki, M. A., & Aslam, S. (2014). Prevalence of Phantom Vibration Syndrome and Phantom Ringing Syndrome (Ringxiety): Risk of Sleep Disorders and Infertility among Medical Students. *International Journal of Advanced Research, 2*(12), 688–693.

Algül, A., Yengin, D., Karadağ, G. H., Övür, A., & Bayrak, T. (2019). Sanal Gerçeklik Hastalığı. In G. H. Karadağ (Ed.), *Dijital Hastalıklar* (pp. 9–54). Der Yayınları.

Auxier, B., & Anderson, M. (April 2021). *Social Media Use in 2021.* Pew Research Center.

Ayhan, B., & Çavuş, S. (2015). Online Game Addiction Among High School Students. In C. Daba-Buzoianu, H. Arslan, & M. A. Icbay (Eds.), *Contextual Approaches in Communication* (pp. 85–93). Peter Lang.

Beck, U. (2019). *Risk Toplumu (3* (B. Doğan & K. Özdoğan Eds. & Trans.). İthaki Yayınları.

Betoncu, O., & Ozdamli, F. (2019). The Disease of 21st Century: Digital Disease. *TEM Journal, 8*(2), 598–603.

Castells, M. (2008). *Enformasyon Çağı: Ekonomi, Toplum ve Kültür Ağ Toplumunun Yükselişi (Birinci Cilt) (2* (E. Kılıç Ed. & Trans.). İstanbul Bilgi Üniversitesi Yayınları.

Çavuş, S. (2018). Dijital Çağda Gazeteciliğin Dönüşümü ve Transmedyal Haber Üretimi. In E. Aktan (Ed.), *Transmedya Hikayeciliği* (pp. 279–298). Literatürk Yayınları.

Çavuş, S. (2022). Üniversite öğrencilerinin sosyal medya kullanımları üzerine bir alan araştırması: Aksaray Üniversitesi örneği. *İNİF E- Dergi, 7*(2), pp. 9-25.

Çavuş, S., & Ayhan, B. (2017). Cyberbullying and Victimization Experiences of University Students. In H. Arslan, M. A. İcbay, & C. Ruggiero (Eds.), *Communication and Media Researches* (pp. 159–168). E-BWN.

Çavuş, S., Ayhan, B., & Tuncer, M. (2016). *Bilgisayar Oyunları ve Bağımlılık: Üniversite Öğrencileri Üzerine Bir Alan Araştırması.* İletişim Kuram ve Araştırma Dergisi.

Chandra, A. N., Jamiy, F. E., & Reza, H. (2022). A Systematic Survey on Cybersickness in Virtual Environments. *Computers, 11*(51), 1–15.

Cheng, C., & Li, A. Y. (2014). Internet Addiction Prevalence and Quality of (Real) Life: A Meta-Analysis of 31 Nations Across Seven World Regions. *Cyberpsychology, Behavior, and Social Networking*, *7*(12), 755–760. doi:10.1089/cyber.2014.0317 PMID:25489876

Çırak, M., & Dost, M. T. (2022). Nomophobia in University Students: The Roles of Digital Addiction, Social Connectedness, and Life Satisfaction. *Turkish Psychological Counseling and Guidance Journal*, *64*, 35–52.

Danaher, J. (2022). Techno-optimism: An Analysis, an Evaluation and a Modest Defence. *Philosophy & Technology*, *54*(2), 1–29. doi:10.100713347-022-00550-2

Dikmen, M. (2021). COVID-19 Pandemisinde Üniversite Öğrencilerinin Depresyon Düzeyleri ile Sosyal Medya Bağımlılıkları Arasındaki İlişki: Bir Yapısal Eşitlik Modeli. *Bağimlik Dergisi*, *22*(1), 20–30. doi:10.51982/bagimli.790750

Eşitti, Ş. (2015). Bilgi çağında problemli internet kullanımı ve enformasyon obezitesi: Problemli internet kullanımı ölçeğinin üniversite öğrencilerine uygulanması. *İstanbul Üniversitesi İletişim Fakültesi Dergisi,* (49), 75-97.

Hinduja, S., & Patchin, J. W. (2010). Bullying, Cyberbullying, and Suicide. *Archives of Suicide Research*, *14*(3), 206–221. doi:10.1080/13811118.2010.494133 PMID:20658375

Königs, P. (2022). What is Techno-Optimism? *Philosophy & Technology*, *35*(63).

Kruger, D. J., & Djerf, J. M. (2016). High Ringxiety: Attachment Anxiety Predicts Experiences of Phantom Cell Phone Ringing. *Cyberpsychology, Behavior, and Social Networking*, *19*(1), 56–60. doi:10.1089/cyber.2015.0406 PMID:26701188

Lai, S. A., Pang, K. Y., Siau, C. S., Chan, C. M., Tan, Y. K., Ooi, P. B., & Ho, M. C. (2022, June 2). Social support as a mediator in the relationship between perceived stress and nomophobia: An Investigation among Malaysian university students during the COVID-19 pandemic. *Nature Public Health Emergency Collection*, 1-8.

Mete, H. E. (2008). Kronik Hastalık ve Depresyon. *Klinik Psikiyatri*, *11*(3), 3–18.

Miller, E. (2023, February 1). *Cybersickness: what is it, symptoms, and treatment.* Ro. https://ro.co/health-guide/cybersickness/

Özkapı, M. (2021). *Yetişkinlerde sosyal medya kullanımının depresyon ve sosyal kaygı düzeyleri ile ilişkisi*. Yayınlanmamış Yüksek Lisans Tezi.

Pietrangelo, A. (2023, February 1). *All About Cybersickness*. Healthline. https://www.healthline.com/health/cybersickness

Postman, N. (2006). *Teknopoli Yeni Dünya Düzeni (2* (M. E. Yılmaz Ed. & Trans.). Paradigma Yayınları.

Romansky, R. (2014). *Digital Privacy in the Network World. Proceedings of the International Conference on Information Technologies (InfoTech-2014)*, Bulgaria.

Rosen, L. M., Carrier, L., Miller, A., Rokkum, J., & Ruiz, A. (2016). Sleeping with technology: Cognitive, affective, and technology usage predictors of sleep problems among college students. *Sleep Health*, *2*(1), 49–56. doi:10.1016/j.sleh.2015.11.003 PMID:29073453

Shatrughan, P., & Pareek, S. (2017). Phantom Vibration Syndrome: An Emerging Phenomenon. *Asian J. Nursing Edu. and Research*, *7*(4), 1–2.

Tiryaki, S. (2015). *Sosyal Medya ve Facebook Bağımlılığı*. Literatürk Yayınları.

Tiryaki, S., & Karakuş, M. (2019). Sosyal Medya Bağımlılığı. In T. Livberber & S. Tiryaki (Eds.), *Sosyal Medya Çalışmaları* (pp. 133–154). Literatürk Yayınları.

Toffler, A. (2008). *Üçüncü Dalga* (S. Yeniçeri, Trans.). Koridor Yayıncılık.

## ADDITIONAL READING

Esen. R. & Yengin. D. (2021). Yeni medya bağımlılığında photolurking sonucu ortaya çıkan dijital şiddet üzerine bir inceleme. *E-Journal of new media, 5*(2), 156-171.

Ayhan, B., & Çavuş, S. (2015). Online game addiction among high school students In Daba-Buzoianu C. Arslan H. Icbay M. A. (eds.), Contextual Approaches in Communication (pp. 85-93). Frankfurt: Peterlang.

## KEY TERMS AND DEFINITIONS

**Anxiety:** A reaction that is excessively fearful of an event or situation that is perceived to be dangerous, as shown by a troubling inner restlessness

**Communication Technologies:** All equipment and programs used to process information.

**Digitalization:** The process of transferring data to digital media so that a computer can read and process it.

**Information Age:** The post-modern period in which computer technologies allow easy access to information.

**Symptom:** A disease sign that causes body functions to be abnormal and noticed by the patient.

**Virtual Reality:** Combining real world and fictional world through technological tools.

**Web 2.0:** The word used to describe second generation internet services.

# Chapter 30
# I Am Online; Therefore, I Am!
## Digital Obesity From a Sociological Perspective

**Nuriye Çelik**
https://orcid.org/0000-0001-6368-1956
*Sinop University, Turkey*

## ABSTRACT

*The digitalization of data has profoundly affected every aspect of our lives: how we communicate and socialize, how we work, learn, and participate in politics and the economy. Digital sociology is concerned with all these new social fields. Digital obesity, which is overconsuming digital information, is a disease of the postmodern individual. Therefore, living in a digital society is a form of communication and membership in a virtual society in the postmodern era. New forms of sociality have been created as a result of this connection. The purpose of this study is to contribute to the literature on digital obesity, to sociologically explain digital obesity, and to shed light on the situation in Turkey. To categorize digital obesity in Turkey, the number of followers on Instagram, Facebook, YouTube, and Twitter will be reviewed and, to demonstrate the interest areas in Turkey, Twitter trending topics, Google, and YouTube trends will be examined for thirty days. This data was obtained from the Boomsocial website, and the Maxqda analysis program will be used to create the images.*

## INTRODUCTION

In the digital world, people interact with each other regardless of time or place. Social actors in this world have gained visibility and, to some extent, online presence. A new social way of life was created by consuming Big Data and remaining permanently online. The digital world has shaped much of modern life, creating a new social group known as online communities. Online communities enable people with similar education, culture, and taste to connect quickly, but they don't know who lives nearby. Communication technologies have modified the meaning and content of social interaction between people. "An online community is a group of people who interact in a virtual environment, and they have a purpose,

DOI: 10.4018/978-1-6684-8397-8.ch030

are supported by technology, and are guided by norms and policies" (Preece et al., 2003). Technology companies and social influencers decide what online communities should do, how they should act, and what their policies should be. As a result, this virtual world does not serve as a free zone or provide a pathway out of the real world. Therefore, why do people prefer the virtual world over the real world, and why do they feel a sense of belonging there?

Virtual life creates an online community as an alternative to real life, but society also continues its sociological relations internally. Online societies create representation processes as in real life, depending on how individuals present themselves. An individual is represented by what he ought to look like, what he ought to consume, what he ought to love, and what he ought not to love. It was about winning more followers or likes, which replaces acceptance and appreciation. Creating the most engaging speech, image, or action is important to enhance popularity. Consequently, a reciprocal relationship is created: being more online, and being more beloved. In this virtual field area, making political criticisms, watching a video of a popular make-up product, communicating via e-mail, working online, and catching the instant flow with all the tools of the new media have become a basic way of life. The establishment of a virtual network around them and being online has become a sign of being alive. The digital world which infiltrates in this way at every moment of life is inevitably the field of study of sociology. Because sociology tries to analyze society, it also needs to analyze and challenge the online version of society.

Digital obesity refers to consumption forms and amounts. In addition to the concept of a society of the spectacle, it is necessary to consider the sociological position of the individual who consumes excessively. Today, the spectacle itself is becoming a dependency, a digital dependency. With this quote from Ludwig Feuerbach, The Essence of Christianity, Debord reveals the most popular wish of postmodern society (Debord, 2020):

*"But for the present age, which prefers the sign to the thing signified, the copy to the original, representation to reality, appearance to essence, ... the truth is considered profane, and only illusion is sacred. Sacredness is held to be enhanced in proportion as truth decreases and illusion increases so that the highest degree of illusion comes to be seen as the highest degree of sacredness.''*

It is now a new social form of life to always be online and to create the highest degree of illusion. When individuals consume a lot of data and spend every minute online, they are stuck in a cycle of consuming. Online life, which also affects the individual's daily life, affects the relationship between the individual and society, and that change is a study area in sociology. Although there are remarkable studies in the literature under the subtitle of digital sociology, it is insufficient for the issue of digital obesity. Digital obesity is a new type of disease of virtual life, a new type of society, and it needs to be examined.

In this study, the concept of digital obesity, which is examined under digital sociology, is discussed. Using digital sociology as a tool, one can explore, analyze, and explain the impact, development, and use of technologies on social worlds, social institutions, and ideas of self and embodiment (Lupton, 2015). Digital obesity is a concept that requires an understanding of how individuals interact with the online world. The charm of virtual life is only visible from a sociological perspective. There are several reasons for this, including trying to escape from the pains and problems in the real world. A person who has attained enlightenment has a lot of responsibilities. However, in the postmodern era, all humanity learned by living is that an individual is not always a rationalist and does not always need the whole truth. The consequences of wars and grand narratives have forced society to consider modernism and reality's structure. Individuals in postmodernism question whether they still wish to reach reality. By giving the right to speak and think for themselves to the closest representatives of the reality they create, perhaps they gave up on this never-ending search for modern humans (Çelik, 2021). To understand the digital obesity environment, it is necessary to figure out these sociological concepts, such as the postmodern era, post-truth, identity representation, and society-individual interaction. In this study, all these terms will be explained first, and then the digital obesity concept will be defined.

The purpose of this study is to contribute to the literature on digital obesity, to sociologically explain digital obesity, and to shed light on the situation in Turkey. The first step in this process will be to look at the causes and consequences of digital obesity to the extent that they relate to the sociology of virtual society. The study will use data from Turkey to show how metadata is consumed and how virtual lives are transformed. To categorize digital obesity in Turkey, the number of followers on Instagram, Facebook, YouTube, and Twitter will be reviewed and, to demonstrate the interest areas in Turkey, Twitter trending topics, Google and YouTube trends will be examined for thirty days between 30 November and 30 December. By using this method, it is possible to determine which type of content they consumed and loved most. These data were obtained from the Boomsocial website and the Maxqda analysis program will be used to create the images.

## BACKGROUND

Understanding and analyzing social changes is the task of social sciences. Sociology studies social changes primarily as one of its main fields. Through social theories, these issues are analyzed in the social sciences.

*"Tasks of the (critical) social theory include to point out and make people aware of unrealized potentials of society, to point out possibilities of action in contemporary society, to ask new and different questions about the present order of society" (Fuchs, 2014, p. 71).*

Therefore, social theories study the changes in socialization and everyday life. In contemporary sociology, digital social life plays a significant role due to its impact on society as a whole. Digital society has found its way into the literature in a variety of fields, including health, education, art, and politics (Özel Sağlamtimur, 2010; Özlem, 2015; Turan & Avcı, 2018; Büyükgöze & Dereli, 2019; Gürel & Nazlı, 2019; Karoğlu et al., 2020; Köksal, 2021). Because of the digital revolution, there are also significant changes in the political sphere. The digital space allows young people to participate in democratic debates. A substantial amount of literature has been written to show the importance of the new media tools for participation in the democratic process within the digital society, especially among the younger generation (Loader, 2007; Loader, 2007a; Bennett, 2008; Dahlgren, 2011; Leerdam, 2014; Collin, 2015; Edwards, 2015). As a result, the digital society has significantly impacted areas such as democratic participation, virtual public spaces, and access to authority. However, some studies argue that there are gatekeepers in both traditional and new media tools that determine what a user knows at the beginning of an information source (Çelik, 2022).

A social mechanism created by the digital society contributes to the reproduction of digital obesity. There is a lack of adequate literature on digital obesity, and social scientists, especially sociologists, haven't shown the necessary interest in this issue. There are, however, some studies examining the relationship between media and digital obesity the impact it had on students during the pandemic period, and its health effects on children (Aktaş, 2021; Bayrak & Cihan, 2021; Akkuş, 2022; Baltaş, 2023). However, digital addiction can also lead to digital obesity. Digital addiction is examined under titles such as internet addiction, social addiction, and video game addiction (Savcı & Aysan, 2017; Eryilmaz & Çukurluöz, 2018; Ertemel & Aydın, 2018; Christakis, 2019; Arslan, 2020; Arslan, 2020a; Almourad et al., 2020; Altınok, 2021; Allcott et al., 2022; Cemiloglu et al., 2022). A closer look at the relationship of digital society with media becomes more important when considering digital obesity and new media tools as addictions. The new media has created an interaction between the user and the content that presents on new media tools. As a result, active users can produce and edit content and influence the content of others by posting comments on their videos, tweets, or photos. Thus, the domain of new media becomes wider and more active than traditional media tools.

Digital obesity has become an integral part of everyday life in a digital society. So, social sciences such as sociology need to study this field to figure out how digitalization is changing society. Literature on this field is inadequate. This study aims to analyze digital obesity in Turkey through a sociological perspective and examine digital content consumption during December based on Boomsocial data. At this point, it is necessary to explain the point of view to be used in sociological analysis. A postmodern social theory will be used to analyze digital obesity. Using this theory is justified because, in a postmodern society, all socialization processes are transferred to the digital field, since the digital world is a part of the postmodern world. Baudrillard explains that societies change from modernity to postmodernity through three stages: early modernity, which began during the Renaissance and culminated in the Industrial Revolution; modernity, which followed the industrial revolution until the second world war; and postmodernity is the era following World War II until the present day (Sarup, 2014). In contrast to historians like Arnold Toynbee who see the postmodern era as occurring in the 1870s, social scientists view the postmodern era as a period of social change that took place between 1960 and 1970, and these changes have affected many fields, including art, philosophy, and history (Pakulski, 2009, p. 251).

*"The prefix "post" indicates both the historical transcendence (passing of a threshold, transcending modernity) and the tentative nature of theoretical formulations, uncertainty as to the direction of change beyond the fact that we are no longer living in modern society. It implies a sociohistorical discontinuity, a redirection of change, an ending of a distinctive (modern) period with its specific social forms and cultural outlooks"(Pakulski, 2009, p.252).*

Postmodernism refers to a state of culture which shapes mostly by media through imitating reality. During this imitation process, reality lost its meaningful root and emerges a new but unreal thing. Therefore, media creates images, ideas, lifestyles, moral rules, and social interactions by imitating. At the end of this process, the postmodern society, according to Baudrillard, as an imitator, gathers more value from the imitation than from the original and creates a simulation of the world. In the premodern era, there were painters and artist which represent reality under the effect of religion, the Christianity, and they exhibited the right way of living, praying et al. In the modern era television, photo, filming, and radio arose, and this representation become much more powerful. But besides the decreased effect of religion, some new concepts arose, such as consuming as a result of capitalism, and communism (Kellner, 2006). It is obvious the powerful connection between culture and media. That connection transformed into a place that promotes and sells new lifestyles, ways of thinking, and ideal types in the postmodern era, and it will be the focus of the article.

## THE FOCUS OF THE ARTICLE

"*You can do whatever you like with my image,*
*my music, remix it, re-release it, whatever...*
*just never make me boring.*"
Freddie Mercury

Postmodernity represents a mode of thinking and intellectual movement that criticizes enlightenment norms. It is broadly defined as a kind of skepticism that criticizes grand narratives such as objectivity, rationality, and historical progress and caused radical changes in both cultural and political activities since 1970. As a result of these radical changes, our perception of time and space has been transformed (Harvey, 2020), as well as our cultural values and social lives. For example, the forms of socialization affected and changed individual and social relations in the pre-modern, modern, and postmodern periods and even these nomenclatures were given by observing as a result of these social changes. Therefore, no society has experienced the same changes in the same order with a progressive approach, and every social change has arisen in its socio-cultural circumstances. When distinctive features are taken into account, however, it is possible to observe that in modern society the acceptance of the individual and discussion of the quality of the individual has begun. For example, "according to anthropological and sociological folklore, in traditional societies, one's identity was fixed, solid, and stable" (Kellner, 2003). On the other hand, "in premodern societies, identity was unproblematical and not subject to reflection or discussion. Individuals did not undergo identity crises, or radically modify their identity" (Kellner, 2003). Individuals have acquired their identity through their roles in their groups. Individuals began to form, construct, and change their identities throughout the modern period. "Thus, in modernity, the problem of identity consisted in how we constitute, perceive, interpret, and present ourselves to ourselves and others" (Kellner, 2003). To figure out how an individual presents herself/himself to others, it is necessary to take into account both the interpretation of the other person and the presentation itself. Similar to the forms of socialization, these forms of presentation have been adapted for the digital age.

To understand the postmodern individual, it is important to understand how individual represents themself in the postmodern period and how they re-produce their culture in the new media. A new form of socialization has been created in the online community (Fuchs, 2014), where individuals feel a connection to their own identity. The individual uses the new media on the one hand as political channels (Leerdam, 2014) and on the other as a virtual public space (Van Dijck & Poell, 2015), as well as a form of commodification (Taylor & Kent, 2010; Fuchs, 2014). Using these patterns of usage exposes the individual to a more diverse range of information. However, unlike modernism, the postmodern individual is open to ready-made thoughts that the digital field provides him instead of seeking the truth. Digital fields, which flow continuously and vary, are also effective in constructing an individual's identity. In the postmodern society, identity has also changed, and a fluid form has emerged.

*"It is thus claimed that in postmodern culture, the subject has disintegrated into a flux of euphoric intensifies, fragmented and disconnected and that the decentered postmodern self no longer experiences anxiety (with hysteria becoming the typical postmodern psychic malady) and no longer possesses the depth, substantiality, and coherency that was the ideal and sometimes achievement of the modern self," (Kellner, 2003).*

As a result of non-continuous representational relations, culture has been transformed, produced, sold, imitated, and idealized and has become commodified in the postmodern period. The tweets we read daily, the Instagram posts we see, and the videos we watch have become a part of our cultural structure beyond just content, product, or advertisement. Thus, culture has become an object of consumption that is reproduced, consumed, and changed daily. Additionally, "everywhere socialization is measured by the exposure to media messages. Whoever is underexposed to the media is desocialized or virtually asocial" (Baudrillard, 1994). About the transformation of culture, Baudrillard has made some observations (Baudrillard, 1994): The necessity of referencing the previous cultural codes in every new cultural production, the indistinctness of hyperreality, and meaning implosion. Pre-modern, modern, and postmodern societies can exchange images and meanings by referencing the previous cultural codes. As a result, society is capable of producing copies of copies. The separation of culture from objective reality has led to it becoming an object of consumption and a part of everyday life. The nature of society has evolved from the pre-modern period, when the real was copied, to the modern period, when it could best be mimicked using photography and the camera, to the postmodern period, where the replica was replicated and so created the simulation of the simulation. All kinds of images produced by social media or film companies place the indicators in our minds, that is, the imitation of imitation as reality.

The indistinctness of reality created the field of hyperreality. Examples of this can be seen in Turkey: people learn about the Ottoman Empire from television series, or the other is Ertuğrul Gazi's sculpture created by the metropolitan municipality using an actor's image from the television series in which he starred (image 1). In the same way, people who watch historical television series with swords in their hands (image 2) or who learn about women's ideal appearances, the use of make-up, and whom to marry from reality shows and TV series (image 3) are examples of new forms of culture that replace reality. How archetypes of femininity and masculinity are infused into daily life, how we accept them naturally, and how they are re-interpreted in these productions are all examples of hyperreality.

*Figure 1. The bust of Ertuğrul Gazi [1]*
*Resource: NTV, 2020.*

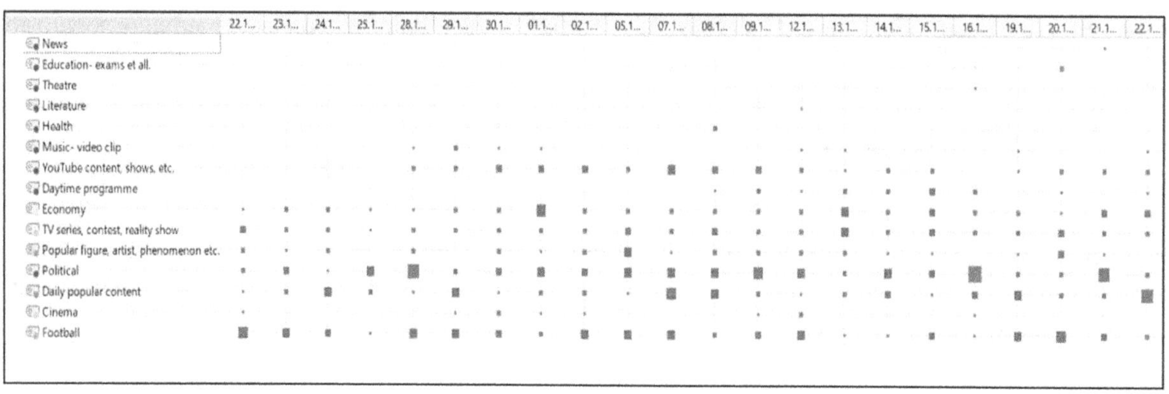

*Figure 2. The historical TV series watcher*

*Figure 3. Historical TV series*
*Resource: Habertürk Video, 2018. Resource: Hürriyet Video, 2017.*

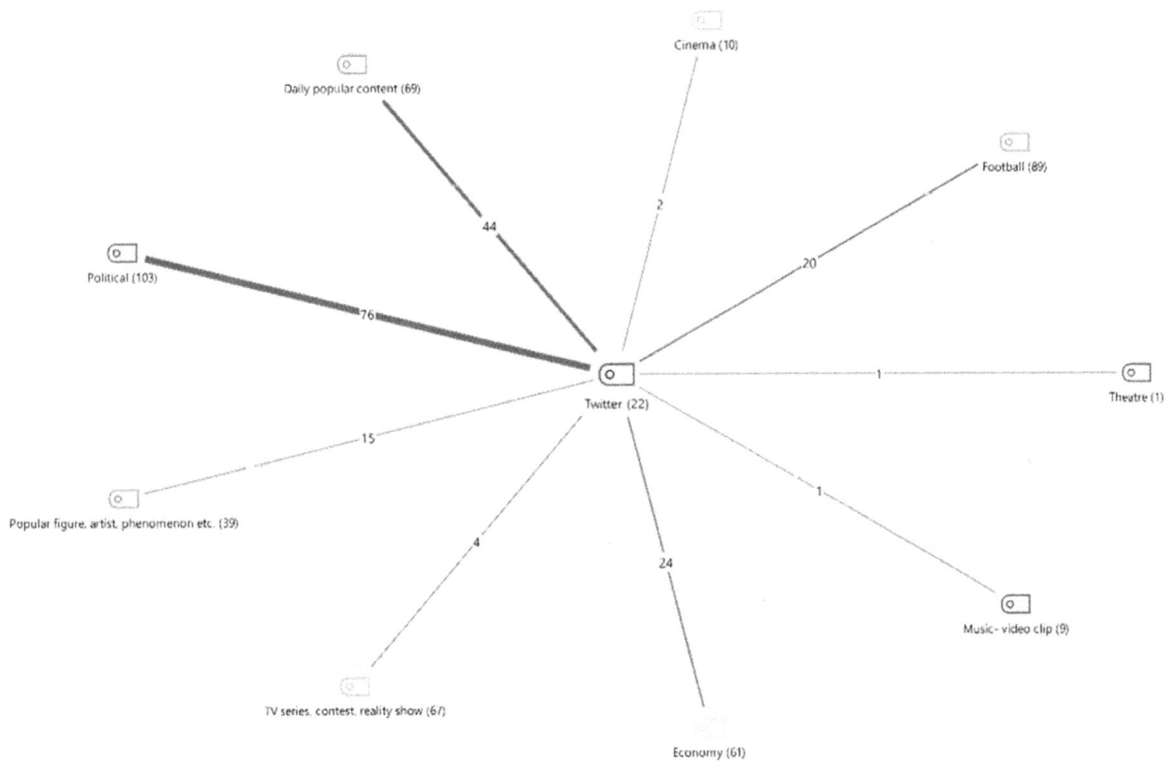

*Figure 4. The reality show "Kısmetse Olur"* [2]
*Resource: Kanal D, 2023.*

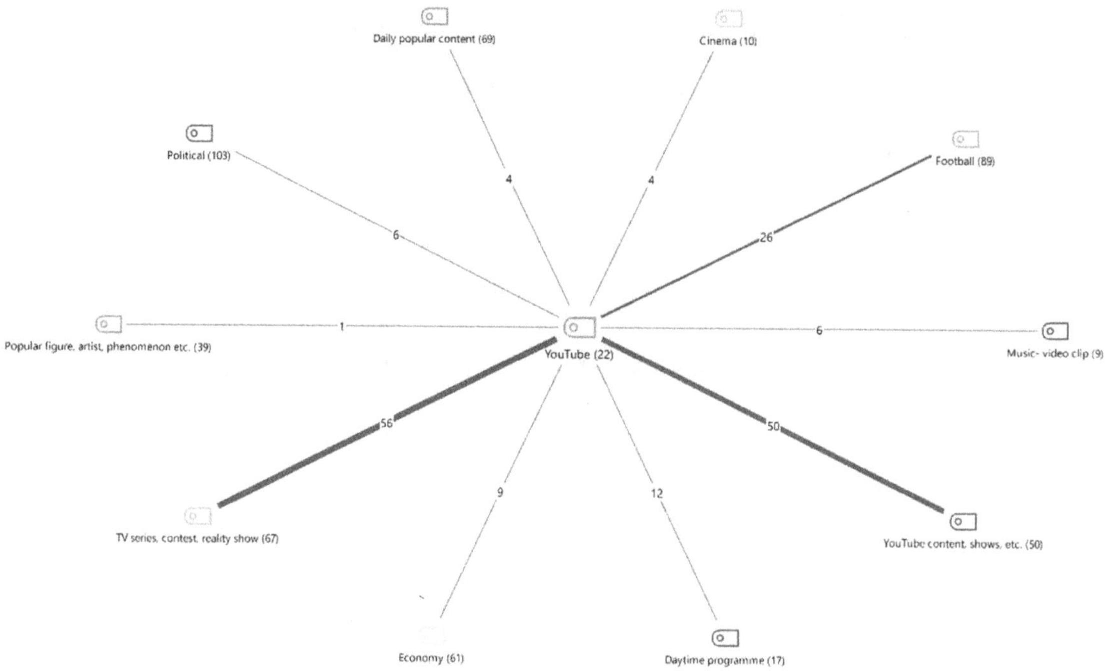


The hyperreality which is produced from reality has its own rules. In this social space, it is important to be more admired and more visible to be accepted, and being known is equivalent to being appreciated regardless of the quality of the content. Moreover, this digital space is not only produced in the virtual space, such as the game The Second Life, but also it changes the daily lives of both users and content producers and redefines social rules. Thus, social life is produced digitally and consumed in daily space. The content and amount of consumption lead us to the concept of digital obesity. Baudrillard's other observation is about the meaning of implosion. According to him, the problem of finding the truth arises among individuals who have faced too much contradictory information that copied and reproduced facts (Baudrillard, 1994; Çelik, 2021; Çelik, 2022). This analysis summarizes the postmodern individual's perspective on the social and digital realm: for the individual level, the reality of knowledge has lost its value in daily life, and anything presented as enjoyable is considered valid. So one of the sources of digital obesity was reached at this point: the changes in the way they obtain information and how content is presented increase digital data consumption. Therefore, digital obesity corresponds to the daily consumption pattern of a postmodern individual living in a digital society. Digital obesity, which is defined as excessive digital data consumption, can spread to every moment of daily life. This is the result of the digital society. The condition of receiving too much dispersed and unconnected information, content, and notifications in the digital environment can adversely affect a person's mental, physical, and spiritual well-being. When individuals consume too much digital media content, they become addicted to it and desire to consume more. Before digital content became a part of our daily lives, society didn't even realize how essential it would be. Baltaş (2023) considers as a sign of digital obesity many daily actions, such as looking at the phone at a red light in traffic, looking at the phone when the focus is away from oneself, and going to the toilet by phone. Similarly, the fear of being away from the phone and ego surfing are among the symptoms that Baltaş considers digital obesity. People are surrounded by continuous information through new media tools during the digital era. Social media is the most effective and fastest communication network among these tools, and it transforms the social with the interaction networks it provides. Digital society is the socialization form of the postmodern era. When we look at the effect of time spent in the digital space on daily life, it can be observed that digital obesity is not just about stockpiling useless digital data but also about being social, making fun, and being online all the time. Persistent desire to be online has become a part of the individual's social life. Moreover, this online community whispers to the individual how to live with a set of norms and rules. The feeling of fear that the individual feels when he cannot be online shakes their belief in this virtual community. Digital obesity affects the relationship between reality and individuals who maintain an important part of their life in the virtual space. But let's add that in the postmodern era, reality has no equivalent meaning as in modernism. On the contrary, the relative reality of postmodernism allows a form of socialization suitable for the virtual society. At this stage, to look at the sociological factors that cause digital obesity, a sample digital data consumption pattern will be analyzed.

## The Sample Analysis of Digital Content Consumption

Using Twitter, YouTube, and Google trending data over a month, this study will analyze how people consume digital data as they increasingly live in the digital world. Based on BoomSocial bulletins, these data were analyzed using Maxqda2022. As shown in the graph below, the generated codes were distributed over one month as follows:

*Figure 5. Codes used in data analysis*

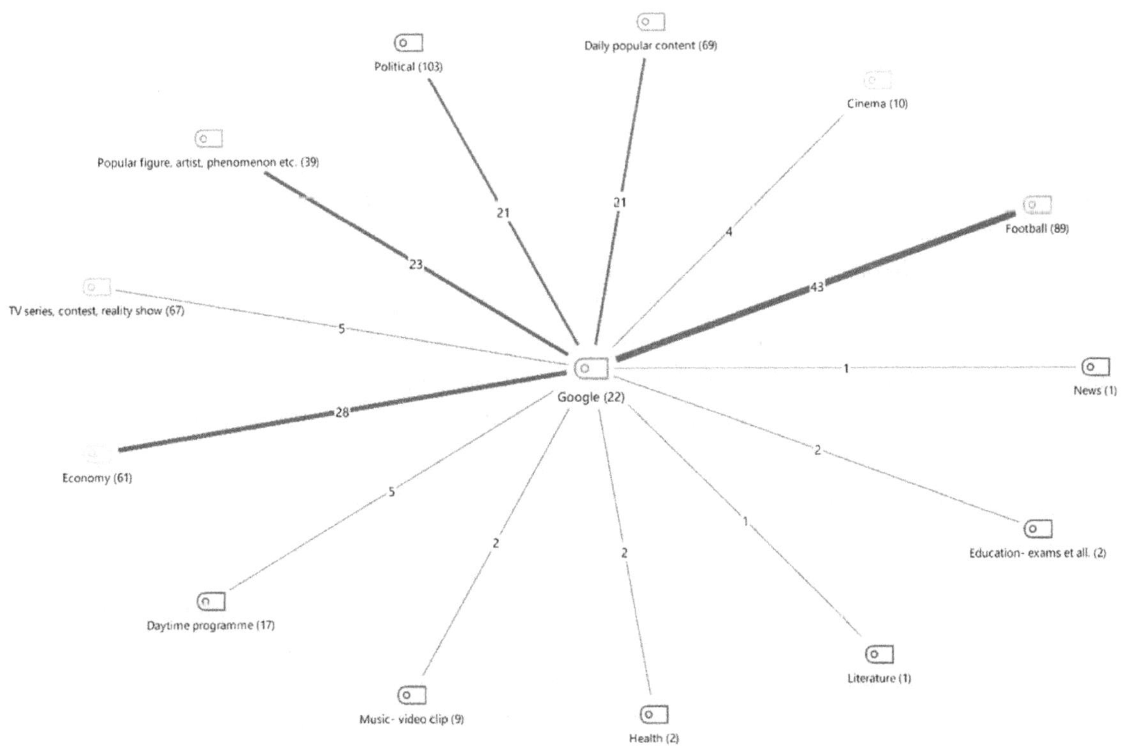

Using the codes specified in the table above, it was analyzed the top ten titles searched on Google, watched on YouTube, and trended on Twitter each day in the monthly newsletter. Following is a word cloud indicating the frequency of use of these codes:

*Figure 6. Word cloud of codes*

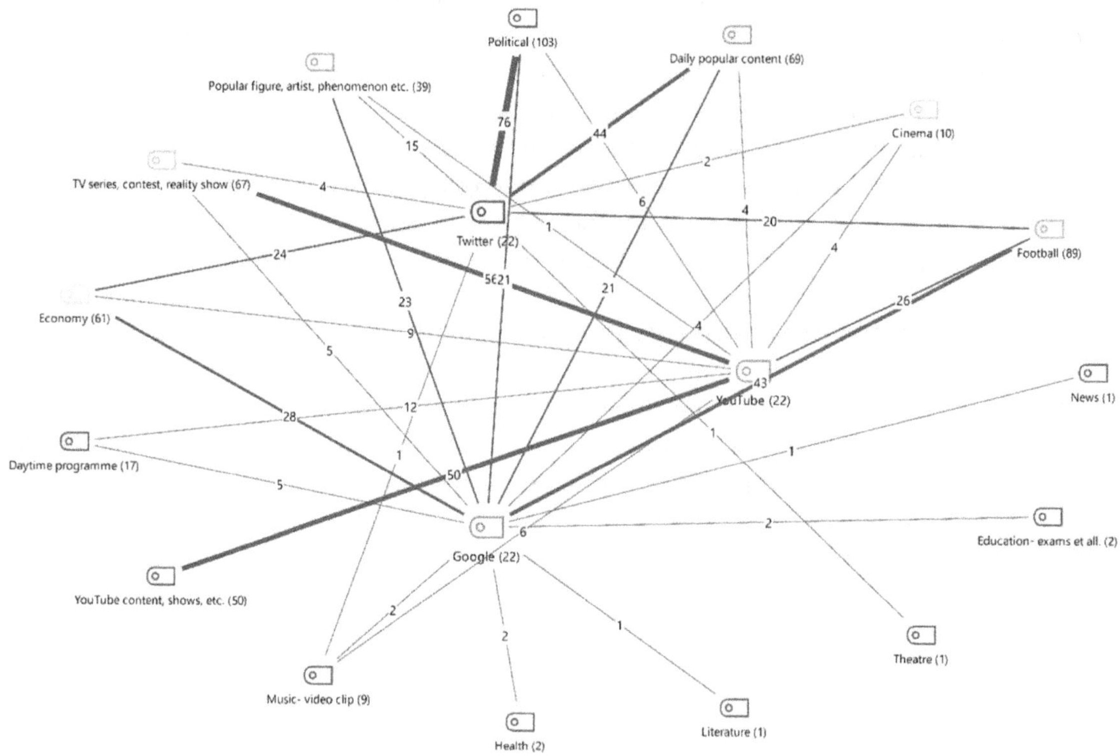


The most searched titles are concentrated in the economy, TV series, and policy codes. There are different concentrations on each platform.

Many studies (Colleoni et all., 2014; Bruns & Highfield, 2015) have shown that Twitter is a virtual public space where political discussions take place. By using their digital representations, individuals participate in democratic debates and follow the statements of political figures and news sources. Thus, it can be seen that the individual consumes political digital data in the virtual space. Earthquake discussions and femicides are the most common daily popular content, while the general subjects mostly consist of justice debates such as the İsmailağa community and child bride debates, and also the demands for amnesty are voiced in this digital space. Therefore, it can be observed the concept of Twitter justice has emerged (Dursun & Yıldız, 2020; Okray, 2020).

Rewatching television series on YouTube essentially illustrates the shift from traditional mass media to new media. It is for this reason that television shows produce data from their content on social media at the same time as their TV series, so they can attract the attention of their followers on Twitter and YouTube (Akınerdem, 2012; Kazaz & Özkent, 2016; Kırık & Domaç, 2014; Ünür, 2016). As a result, mass media are being challenged by new media tools, but it can be observed that they are not fighting, but rather collaborating. Further, YouTube's most requested content is competitions, vlogs, and makeup videos, which are entertainment oriented. Additionally, there is content that needs to be added here is both YouTube content and a YouTube program, which is the new media version of mass media policy debates and primarily targets young people (Mevzular Açık Mikrofon series on BaBaLa TV YouTube channel). In terms of the political impact of new media tools, it is seen that this content contributes to the inclusion of younger people in politics and reduces the power distance between leaders and voters to zero.

Due to the 2022 World Cup coincident with the analyzed period, the football title stands out in Google searches. The economy is the next title, with a focus on the negative economic situation in the country and early retirement. There is no way to separate social and periodic contexts from trending topics in all forms of digital media. Google searches, however, include actors from popular daily events.

When the relationship between the codes in Google, Twitter, and YouTube trends is examined, it is seen that economy, politics, and football can be common codes. However, as a result of the characteristics of all three digital realms, it is observed that Twitter concentrates on politics, and YouTube on television series, music, and its content. It is clear that Google changes according to daily popularity, especially football, and is an intermediary channel that accesses other platforms. These results will be discussed in detail under the solutions and recommendations title.

## SOLUTIONS AND RECOMMENDATIONS

By examining Twitter, YouTube, and Google trending data over a month, it is possible to see the origins of digital obesity. Firstly, the path of consumption forms changes depending on the purpose and content of the digital media used. For example, the virtual public space offered by Twitter replaces the indirect forms of government in existing democratic systems, power distances, and contact that the governed cannot establish with the rulers. Thus, in countries such as Turkey, where the independence of mass media is discussed, alternative public spaces are becoming an inevitable part of daily life. Therefore, these digital channels, as the only area that provides political awareness, constitute one of the sources of digital obesity. Similarly, watching TV series on YouTube is a result of the transformation of traditional media, and it ultimately attracts the individual to the digital realm which is driven by algorithms, and this is another source of digital obesity. Thus, this analysis provides a sociological explanation of the origins of digital obesity. Digital obesity cannot be analyzed independently of social context, which is the most important finding. Digital obesity is observed in which societies, generations, and age ranges, and in what economic, cultural, and political contexts? Without answering these questions, it is impossible to understand digital obesity. Nevertheless, many lectures need to be organized on the use of digital data, as well as more studies regarding digital obesity and sociological analyses of the postmodern individual. It is, however, possible to create a level of consciousness about the effects of consumed data. In the end, staying away from digital life seems impossible.

## FUTURE RESEARCH DIRECTIONS

Foremost, there are not enough sociological studies on digital obesity in the literature, so it is worth noting that we look at the consumed digital content superficially. Therefore, more studies should be researched about digital obesity. It is possible to compare digital assets among societies with different cultural structures and consumption patterns to analyze digital obesity. In addition, qualitative research methods and direct consumption patterns of individuals can be used to analyze the resources that contribute to digital obesity in Turkey. Thence, the sociological dimension of the concept can be revealed, and preventative training and measures can be taken based on the nature of the content consumed.

## CONCLUSION

*We live in a world where*
*there is more and more information*
*and less and less meaning.*
Jean Baudrillard, Simulacra and Simulation (1994)

One of the main fields of sociology is the study of the social structure change. Any form of social change, from premodern society to modern society and from there to the postmodern era, is studied by sociology. Digital social structures are one of the contemporary counterparts of these change processes. In the historical process, political events, religion, geographical conditions, and communication technologies had an impact on social life. Communication technology is largely responsible for the emergence of digital society. Digital data has penetrated every aspect of our daily lives, affecting everything from receiving news to continuing work. It also influences consumer preferences, social relations with the environment, and consumption patterns. On the other hand, individuals who interact with digital data can spend time in the digital space as an entertainment activity. It is therefore possible to observe in the digital field an imitation of all aspects of daily life. But the imitation here emerges through a reproduction process rather than a copy of the original. In other words, the reproduced products have a postmodern origin. While sociology examines social changes also deals with postmodern social theory. Let's add that there are social scientists who think that the postmodern era is a continuation of the modern era, or it is an improved or a bad version. In this study, it is argued that the postmodern era differs markedly from the modern era given social thinking, criticism, rejection of meta-narratives, and the method of deconstruction. Starting with art, postmodern thought, which rejects all meta-narratives, has necessitated the re-definition of reality and meaning. In this era where reproduced copies create a hyperreality, representations have become more important than reality, including cultural elements. That's exactly why digital society becomes valuable in terms of understanding and explaining the existence of the individual in a virtual social space.

Digital obesity occurs as a result of the over-consumption of the lifestyle created by the virtual society in the postmodern era. It is the actors' images that have taken the place of historical figures. Ideal male and female role images are produced and marketed in daytime programs. Besides that, the nature of digital data consumed maintains the connection with cultural codes. As postmodern societal developments do not follow the same patterns in every society, neither does the digital era follow the same patterns in every society. On the other hand, digital society affects the life of every individual inevitably nowadays. Digital life, which stands out as the socialization form of the postmodern society, is shaped by the digital data we consume. In this study, digital society tried to be analyzed through postmodern social theory. The field of contemporary sociology is inevitably affected by digital society. Because a new kind of society is being rebuilt every day by virtual communities.

Digital obesity is a diagnosis of a kind of lifestyle in which an individual consumes more digital data than needed, stocks up on data, never has time to look back, and tries to be online always because of fear of missing out. It is explained in postmodern social theory that the digital field that infiltrates every moment of everyday life, how changes and transforms individuals' perception of reality. Reality depends on the quality of the presentation rather than the content. The presentation style has cultural features. The cultural characteristics of the audience to be influenced determine the presentation, and the commodification of culture occurs in this production process. Thus, the sociological roots of digital obesity emerged: social, economic, and cultural conditions. Over a month, let's examine how much and what kind of digital data was consumed. Data obtained from BoomSocial bulletins were used in this study. Accordingly, the most consumed data such as trending searches on Google, trend topics on Twitter, and popular videos on YouTube constitute the exemplary content of digital obesity. Political discussions are most common on Twitter because political powers mostly share information from here. Users can share videos and images but, the original format of this digital realm is based on sharing texts with word restrictions. Thus, the nature of digital data on Twitter changes depending on the political situation of the country and the events. According to analysis, YouTube is the most popular platform for watching television series and YouTube videos. There has been a change due to the new media replacing mass media, and it can serve users in a way that includes all content, such as news, music, and entertainment. The position of the individual in the new media, which has evolved from the passive viewer role to the active content producer, has expanded the digital space and contributed to digital data being a part of daily life. Google, in the role of a seeker providing access to other digital spaces, has been discussed in the analysis as a realm where daily trending topics are researched. It is seen that the economy title is effective in trend searches such as social housing projects, discussion of the minimum wage, early retirement discussions, stock market, and foreign exchange, especially with the effect of the negative economic situation.

Considering all these data, this study claims that it is not enough to explain digital obesity only with concepts such as individual loneliness, alienation, and social media addiction. While it is accepted that these concepts make an important contribution when analyzing digital data consumption, it has been observed that data consumption in the virtual space is also affected by existing social structures, just as social factors affect what we consume in real life. Consumption as an economic behavior is related to status representation and identity (Çelik, 2013). The data consumed in the digital field has a structure that is affected by social conditions. Therefore, looking at data consumption sociologically makes it easier to understand the sociological structure that causes digital obesity. The digital society exists in a form of communication produced by the postmodern era. This form of communication contains significant differences from the modern period. Foremost, the individual who is exposed to heaps of unrelated content every day represents themselves in the digital field where they spend a significant part of their life. This representation takes place in the virtual public space created by the individual with their virtual identity. Therefore, the content of excessively consumed digital data in this virtual space is not independent of the social ties of the identity represented. However, the amount of consumption is increasing in parallel with the size of daily life consumed in the digital space.

As a result, in the sociological dimension of digital obesity, the following should be looked at:

- nature of digital data consumed,
- a type of digital field used,

- the sociological, political, and economic agenda of the era in which digital obesity is measured or analyzed.

However, it is clear that digital obesity studies conducted at a certain sample level, such as intergenerational studies, are also fed by sociological factors. Like it is also included in the literature studies mentioned under the title of the background of the study, for example, when examining the effect of internet addiction on generation z, it is not possible to analyze without looking at the sociological differences of this generation from the previous generation. It should be included in the analysis the generation, gender, education level, and even the political preference of consumers experiencing digital obesity. The expressions in the 2018 Konda electorate clusters report can be an example of this situation (Uncu, 2018): The report states that 36% of voters of a political party have never accessed the internet and, in Turkey's 2017 general electoral average, the rate of those who never use the internet is 29%. Therefore, this group, which is not in the digital space, in terms of policymakers and other voters in the digital space can make significant differences. Similarly, the filtering rule that influencers have to obey in Norway also affects digital data consumption. Accordingly, influencers have to show the filter applications they use in the post they share (Grant, 2021). Although this decision is a step taken to prevent the loss of reality caused by digital data consumption, it makes visible the blurred region between content producers' own identities and the identities they represent on social media. Laws like this or extraordinary events in the current period are also can affect the consumption of digital data. Data sources of digital obesity are a result of the digital society that shapes the daily life of the postmodern era. For this reason, without analyzing the postmodern individual who exists in the digital space, it is not possible to explain why they consume digital data excessively.

## REFERENCES

Akınerdem, F. (2012). Yerli Dizi Anlatıları ve İzleyici Katılımı: Uçurum Dizisini Ekşi sözlük ve Twitter'la Birlikte İzlemek. *Folklor/Edebiyat, 18*(72), 77-90.

Akkuş, T. (2022). Dijital Minimalizm: Ekran Bağımlılığı ve Teknoloji Yorgunluğu Sarmalından Kurtulmak İçin Bir Yol Haritası. *Trt Akademi*, *7*(14), 366–371. doi:10.37679/trta.1064029

Aktaş, F. (2021). *Pandemi Sürecinde İlköğretim Öğrencilerinin Dijital Bağımlılığına İlişkin Öğretmen Görüşleri.* Pamukkale University.

Allcott, H., Gentzkow, M., & Song, L. (2022). Digital Addiction. *The American Economic Review, 112*(7), 2424–2463. doi:10.1257/aer.20210867

Almourad, M. B., Mcalaney, J., Skinner, T., Pleya, M., & Ali, R. (2020). Defining Digital Addiction: Key Features from The Literature. *Psihologija (Beograd)*, *53*(3), 237–253. doi:10.2298/PSI191029017A

Altınok, M. (2021). Lise Öğrencilerinin Dijital Bağımlılık ve Yaşam Doyumunun İncelenmesi. *Türk Eğitim Bilimleri Dergisi*, *19*(1), 262–291. doi:10.37217/tebd.689774

Arslan, A. (2020a). Ortaöğretim Öğrencilerinin Dijital Bağımlılık Düzeyleri ve Şiddet Eğilimlerinin Belirlenmesi. *Journal of Computer and Education Research*, *8*(15), 86–113. doi:10.18009/jcer.652390

Arslan, A. (2020b). Üniversite Öğrencilerinin Dijital Bağımlılık Düzeylerinin Çeşitli Değişkenler Açısından İncelenmesi. *International E-Journal of Educational Studies*, *4*(7), 27–41. doi:10.31458/iejes.600483

Baltaş, A. (2023). *Dijital Obezite* [Blog]. Acarbaltas.com. https://www.acarbaltas.com/dijital-obezite/

Baudrillard, J. (1994). *Simulacra and simulation*. University of Michigan Press.

Bayrak, T., & Cihan, B. (2021). Yeni Medyada Bağımlılık Sonucu Gelişen Dijital Obezite Olgusu Üzerine Bir İnceleme: Netflix Türkiye Örneği. *E-Journal of New Media–Ejnm, 5*(1).

Bennett, W. L. (2008). *Changing Citizenship in The Digital Age*. Macarthur Foundation Digital Media and Learning Initiative.

Bruns, A., & Highfield, T. (2015). Is Habermas on Twitter? Social Media and the Public Sphere. In The Routledge Companion to social media and Politics (pp. 56-73). Routledge Publications.

Büyükgöze, S., & Dereli, E. (2019). Toplum 5.0 ve Dijital Sağlık. *VI. International Scientific and Professional Studies Congress-Science and Health, 7*(10).

Çelik, N. (2013). Thorstein Veblen'in Gösterişçi Tüketim Yaklaşımı: Niğde Üniversitesi İdari Personeli Örneği. *Erciyes University Journal of Social Sciences Institute*, *1*(34), 171–203.

Çelik, N. (2022). Yeni Medyada Bilginin Üretimi ve Paylaşımı Sorunsalı. In F. Ayaz & B. Taşdelen (Eds.), *Bir Yaşam Alanı Olarak Dijital Medya* (1st ed., pp. 55–72). Eğitim Publications.

Cemiloglu, D., Almourad, M. B., Mcalaney, J., & Ali, R. (2022). Combatting Digital Addiction: Current Approaches and Future Directions. *Technology in Society*, *68*, 101832. doi:10.1016/j.techsoc.2021.101832

Christakis, D. A. (2019). The Challenges of Defining and Studying Digital Addiction in Children. *Journal of the American Medical Association*, *321*(23), 2277–2278. doi:10.1001/jama.2019.4690 PMID:31095260

Colleoni, E., Rozza, A., & Arvidsson, A. (2014). Echo Chamber or Public Sphere? Predicting Political Orientation and Measuring Political Homophily in Twitter Using Big Data. *Journal of Communication*, *64*(2), 317–332. doi:10.1111/jcom.12084

Collin, P. (2015). *Young citizens and political participation in a digital society: addressing the democratic disconnect*. Springer. doi:10.1057/9781137348838

Dahlgren, P. (2011). Young Citizens and Political Participation: Online Media and Civic Cultures. *Taiwan Journal of Democracy*, *7*(2).

Debord, G. (2020). *The Society of the spectacle* (D. Nicholson-Smith, Trans.). Zone Books. doi:10.2307/j.ctv1453m69

Dursun, O., & Yıldız, F. (2020). Kamu Adaletinin Büyük Veri Aracılığı ile İnşası: Şule Çet Davası Üzerine Bir Twitter Analizi. *Connectist: Istanbul University Journal of Communication Sciences*, *58*, 291–328. doi:10.26650/CONNECTIST2020-0009

Edwards, K. (2015). Young citizens and political participation in a digital society. *Information Communication and Society*, *18*(12), 1470–1472. doi:10.1080/1369118X.2015.1062037

Ertemel, A. V., & Aydın, G. (2018). Dijital Ekonomide Teknoloji Bağımlılığı ve Çözüm Önerileri. *Addicta-The Turkish Journal on Addictions*, *5*(4), 665–690. doi:10.15805/addicta.2018.5.4.0038

Eryilmaz, S., & Çukurluöz, Ö. (2018). Lise öğrencilerinin dijital bağimliliklarinin incelenmesi: Ankara ili, Çankaya ilçesi örneği. *Electronic Journal of Social Sciences*, *17*(67), 889–912.

Fuchs, C. (2014). *Social media: a critical introduction*. Sage Publications. doi:10.4135/9781446270066

Grant. (2021, July 6). Influencers React to Norway Photo Edit Law: "Welcome Honesty" or a "Shortcut"? *BBC News*. https://www.bbc.com/news/newsbeat-57721080

Gürel, E., & Nazlı, A. (2019). Dijital Aktivizm: Change. org Kampanyaları Üzerine Bir Analiz. *Anadolu University Journal of Social Sciences*, *19*(4), 187–206. doi:10.18037/ausbd.668642

Habertürk. (2018, 21 April). 'Diriliş Ertuğrul' Dizisini Kılıç ve Baltayla İzlerken Adeta Kendilerinden Geçtiler. [Video]. *Habertürk*. https://www.haberturk.com/video/eglence/izle/dirilis-ertugrul-dizisini-kilic-ve-baltayla-izlerken-adeta-kendilerinden-gectiler/477066

Harvey, D. (2020). The Condition of Postmodernity. In *The New Social Theory Reader* (pp. 235–242). Routledge. doi:10.4324/9781003060963-38

Hürriyet. (2017, 9 June). Elinde Kılıcıyla Diriliş Ertuğrul İzleyen Dede! *Hürriyet*. https://www.hurriyet.com.tr/video/elinde-kiliciyla-dirilis-ertugrul-izleyen-dede-40484794

Kanal D. (2023). *Kısmetse Olur Programme*. Kanal D. https://www.kanald.com.tr/kismetse-olur

Karoğlu, A. K., Kübra, B. A. L., & Çimşir, E. (2020). Toplum 5.0 Sürecinde Türkiye'de Eğitimde Dijital Dönüşüm. *Journal of University Studies*, *3*(3), 147–158.

Kazaz, M., & Özkent, Y. (2016). Televizyon Dizileriyle Eş Zamanlı Olarak Twitter Kullanımı: İletişim Fakültesi Öğrencileri Üzerine Bir Araştırma. *Selçuk Communication*, *9*(2), 205–224.

Kellner, D. (2003). *Media culture: cultural studies, identity, and politics between the modern and the post-modern*. Routledge. doi:10.4324/9780203205808

Kellner, D. (2006). Jean Baudrillard After Modernity: Provocations on a Provocateur and Challenger. *International Journal of Baudrillard Studies*, *3*(1), 1–32.

Kırık, A. M., & Domaç, A. (2014). Sosyal Medya Üzerinde Televizyon Reyting Ölçümlerinin Analizi: Twitter Örneği. *Journal of Academic Social Research*, *5*, 414–430.

Köksal, T. (2021). Dijital Dünya'da 'Suretsiz Toplum'. *Journal of Atatürk University Institute of Social Sciences*, *25*(3), 1249–1259.

Leerdam, H. (2014). Young Citizens and Political Participation in a Digital Society: Addressing the Democratic Disconnect. *Politics, Culture, And Socialization*, *5*(2), 224–228. doi:10.3224/pcs.v5i2.20822

Loader, B. D. (2007a). Introduction: Young Citizens in The Digital Age: Disaffected or Displaced? In Young Citizens in the Digital Age (pp. 15-32). Routledge.

Loader, B. D. (2007b). *Young citizens in the digital age*. Routledge London. doi:10.4324/9780203946725

Lupton, D. (2015). *Digital sociology*. Routledge, Taylor & Francis Group.

NTV. (2020) Tartışılan "Ertuğrul Gazi" Büstü Kaldırıldı, İki Müdür Görevden Alındı (Diriliş Ertuğrul'daki Engin Altan Düzyatan'a Benzetilmişti). *NTV*. https://www.ntv.com.tr/turkiye/tartisilan-ertugrul-gazi-bustu-kaldirildi-iki-mudur-gorevden-alindi-dirilis-ertugruldaki-engin-altan-duzyatana-benzetilmisti,VxLp2oLHNUSvhjQDj8iR0Q

Okray, Z. (2020). "Şule Çet İçin Adalet": Bir Twitter Etiketi Üzerine İçerik Analizi. *Kadin/Woman 2000, 21*(2).

Özel Sağlamtimur, Z. (2010). Dijital Sanat. *Anadolu University Journal of Social Sciences, 10*(3), 213–238.

Özlem, A. (2015). Dijital Yaşamın Dijital Özneleri: Herkes ya da Hiç Kimse. *Uşak University Journal of Social Sciences, 8*(1), 249–266.

Pakulski, J. (2009). Postmodern Social Theory. In B. S. Turner (Ed.), *The New Blackwell Companion to Social Theory* (pp. 251–280). Blackwell Publishing Ltd. doi:10.1002/9781444304992.ch13

Preece, J., Maloney-Krichmar, D., & Abras, C. (2003). History of Online Communities. In K. Christensen & D. Levinson (Eds.), *Encyclopedia of Community: From Village To Virtual World* (pp. 1023–1027). Sage Publications Sage.

Sarup, M. (2014). Post-yapısalcılık ve postmodernizm (A. Güçlü, Trans., 2. Edit.). Pharmakon Publications.

Savcı, M., & Aysan, F. (2017). Teknolojik Bağımlılıklar ve Sosyal Bağlılık: İnternet Bağımlılığı, Sosyal Medya Bağımlılığı, Dijital Oyun Bağımlılığı ve Akıllı Telefon Bağımlılığının Sosyal Bağlılığı Yordayıcı Etkisi. *Dusunen Adam : Bakirkoy Ruh Ve Sinir Hastaliklari Hastanesi Yayin Organi, 30*(3), 202–216.

Taylor, M., & Kent, M. L. (2010). Anticipatory Socialization in the use of social media in Public Relations: A Content Analysis of Prsa's Public Relations Tactics. *Public Relations Review, 36*(3), 207–214. doi:10.1016/j.pubrev.2010.04.012

Turan, S., & Avcı, E. K. (2018). 2018 Sosyal Bilgiler Öğretim Programı'nın Dijital Vatandaşlık Bağlamında İncelenmesi. *Journal of Education and New Approaches, 1*(1), 28–38.

Uncu, B. A. (2018). Konda (2018) Seçmen Kümeleri: Ak Parti Seçmeni. *Konda*. https://konda.com.tr/uploads/konda-secmenkumeleri-akparti-secmenleri-mayis2018-f3848f8d2137abf61eb8f9d2a-b392e27a01c13f29fc7a5334ee3cc1336fd753c.pdf

Ünür, E. (2016). Geleneksel Medya'nın Sosyal Medyayı Nasıl Kullandığına İlişkin Bir İnceleme: Dizilerin Twitter Kullanımı. *Turkish Journal of Social Research, 20*(1), 153–170.

Van Dijck, J., & Poell, T. (2015). Social Media and The Transformation of Public Space. *Social Media + Society, 1*(2), 1–5. doi:10.1177/2056305115622482

## ADDITIONAL READING

Baudrillard, J. (1998). *The Consumer Society*. Sage.

Beck, U. (1992). *Risk Society*. Sage.

Fukuyama, F. (1999). *The Great Disruption*. The Free Press.

## KEY TERMS AND DEFINITIONS

**Digital society:** By transferring sociological analyses to the digital field and analyzing digital life according to sociological theories, it offers a new and questioning perspective on sociological thought.

**Digital obesity:** The condition of receiving too much dispersed and unconnected information, content, and notifications in the digital environment can define as the source of digital obesity, which is defined as excessive digital data consumption.

**New media:** New media is any form of media delivered digitally, such as newspaper articles, blogs, music, and podcasts. Blogs, Email, music and television streaming services, and social media networks are just a few examples of new media.

**Postmodern social theory:** It is a sociological approach that analyses the social and cultural features of the postmodern era and, through the questioning of modernism, extends sociological inquiry into new fields.

## ENDNOTES

1 The bust of Ertuğrul Gazi, exhibitions in the city square by the Ordu Metropolitan Municipality, surprised those who saw it. This bust was the same Engin Altan Düzyatan, who plays Ertuğrul Gazi in a TV series. After criticism, the bust was removed by the municipality.

2 It is a reality show that aired on the national channel and aimed at the marriage with each other of nine women and nine men who came together at the studio. Their YouTube channel has these promotional statements: "How to behave in a relationship? What are the wrongs we know right?" This program demonstrates the ideal men and women stereotypes in this postmodern era, and thus they reproduce the ideal images regardless of the real ones.

# Chapter 31
# An Intergenerational Comparison Within the Framework of Digital Minimalism

**Arzu Kizbaz**
*Istinye University, Turkey*

## ABSTRACT

*Mankind is by nature a social being, and therefore wants to be able to look face to face, to chat, to see and feel while looking. Not being able to communicate face-to-face—only communicating through social media—is not enough, and this situation creates new problems by multiplying the deficiencies. Minimalism is a space of liberation. Self-sufficiency is a must for renewing and producing itself. Harari describes those who cannot transform in this digital age as 'global superfluous.' To transform is to adapt to digital, but not to get lost in digital. Digital minimalism proposes to filter information with the philosophy of 'less is more.' In this philosophy, balance is essential. This study will analyze the approaches of X, Y, and Z generations to digital minimalism by in-depth interview technique. In this context, in the digitalizing universe, the concepts of loneliness, liberation, socialization and self-sufficiency will be traced.*

*"Conversation enriches the understanding, but solitude is the school of genius."* ~ Cal Newport

## INTRODUCTION

'Communication is to a relationship what breathing is to maintaining life' Virginia Satir points out the importance of communication in life with this quote.

Communication plays an essential role in our daily lives and influences the way we interact and share information with others. Over the years, communication has evolved significantly, and the 21st century has seen a significant shift in the way we communicate. The advancement of technology and the rise of social media have changed the communication dynamics in unprecedented ways.

DOI: 10.4018/978-1-6684-8397-8.ch031

One significant aspect that has influenced communication dynamics in the 21st century is technology's advancement. Technological innovation has revolutionized the way people communicate and interact with one another. The proliferation of mobile telephony and the Internet has shifted communication towards digital platforms. Today, people can easily communicate with anyone, anywhere in the world, at any time. Communication is no longer limited to verbal or face-to-face interaction but is taking place through digital platforms such as WhatsApp, Facebook Messenger, Skype, and Zoom, to mention a few.

In his book *The Interpersonal Communication*, Joseph A. Devito addresses the dwindling importance of face-to-face communication in these words:

'You can communicate power much as you communicate any other message. Here we can consider how you can communicate power through speaking, nonverbal communication, and listening'. (DeVito A. Joseph, 2007) But social media changed the way of communication.

Moreover, the rise of social media has transformed the way we communicate in the 21st century. Social media platforms such as Facebook, Twitter, and Instagram have become the primary means of social interaction. People can connect with friends, family, and even strangers on social media platforms, share information, and express their opinions. Social media has also become a platform for information dissemination, and people rely on it for news updates and information sharing. Social media has also provided businesses with a new platform to reach their potential customers and interact with them.

Another significant aspect of the changing communication dynamics in the 21st century is the emergence of new communication methods. Today, we have a wide range of communication methods such as video conferencing, instant messaging, SMS, email, and others that have changed the way we communicate. Video conferencing has revolutionized the way companies hold meetings and interact with clients, reducing the need for physical meetings. Also, instant messaging services such as WhatsApp and Facebook Messenger have become the go-to method for quick and informal chats.

The 21st century has seen a significant shift in communication dynamics that has been largely driven by technological advancement. Digital platforms and new communication methods have provided people with new ways of interacting and communicating with each other. Social media has also played a significant role in transforming the way we communicate and share information. Communication is likely to continue evolving in the coming years, and it is our responsibility to adapt and leverage these platforms to foster better communication and improve our relationships.

In the digital age, losing attention and not being able to focus is one of the most important problems. The examples given by Goleman and Kahneman are remarkable:

*'Focusing in the midst of a mess is indicative of selective attention, a neural capacity to focus on a single goal, ignoring a flood of stun stimuli, each in its own right'.(Goleman, 2013)*

Daniel Kahneman describes what he calls the primary allocation of attention as follows: '*Imagine being behind the wheel of a car that unexpectedly starts slipping over a massive oil leak. You will see that it reacts to danger before you are fully conscious'.*

The fact that the digital age affects communication styles to such an extent reflects the quality of communication and causes some losses such as attention and focus. In this study, it will be traced how the X, Y, Z generation has achieved this harmony in this digital age and what kind of digital transformation they have undergone.

## Social Media as a Means of Communication

Social media has revolutionized the way we communicate with each other. We no longer have to rely on traditional mediums such as letters and phone calls to stay in touch with friends and family. Social media platforms like Facebook, Twitter, Instagram and WhatsApp have made it incredibly easy to connect with people from all over the world in real-time. The power of social media is such that it has become a dominant means of communication, allowing individuals and organizations to connect with their audiences instantly.

One of the biggest advantages of social media as a means of communication is its ability to reach a large and diverse audience at a very low cost. With billions of users active on social media platforms, it has become an excellent tool for businesses to connect with their customers, promote their brand and increase their reach. Similarly, social media has become a platform for individuals to share their creative work and connect with like-minded individuals with similar interests. Social media also helps in spreading information and awareness about various issues and events, allowing people to stay informed and updated about the world around them. Overall, social media's impact on communication is unparalleled and will continue to shape the way we interact and engage with each other. Face-to-face communication has numerous benefits.

In this period of dependence on social media, we can list these benefits as follows: (Valueprop; 2023)

*"-Easier to convince people.*

*When you're conversing with someone who disagrees with you, communication over text or email can be cumbersome and ineffective. You may not have their full attention, or they may just be skimming over the words you've written.*

*-Stronger Connections. Better non-verbal understanding*

*It's not just about talking. There's another important dimension of communication: body language. Non-verbal cues can tell you a lot about a person, and that's information that you can't get over email, over the phone, or even over video chat. So, don't be full facial on your next Zoom call - let people see your arms and hands - you know, let them feel they're having a meeting not just a phone call with video.*

*-Quicker and more effective*

*Whether we're talking with our own team or communicating with a client or investor, email can cause more problems than it solves. Problem-solving is done better face-to-face.*

*-More team participation*

*Getting your team all in one room can be a hassle, but it's worth it. People are more engaged and more collaborative in face-to-face settings. This seems especially true for millennials, the generation most known for being tech-reliant."*

The power of face to face communication in interaction is undeniable. The ability to persuade a person is related to a good tone of voice, gesture, body posture. In a communication process, body language takes precedence over words and creates an effect. For this reason, face to face communication should be preferred in processes that require persuasion, problem solving, creativity.

Social media addiction is unfortunately an ongoing problem in all generations. While addiction causes the problem to be ignored, the problems caused by addiction continue to increase.

Social Media Effects on Communication can be summarized as: (UOPeople, 2023)

Information Overload

The most important competency in the digital age is to be able to filter information.

-Young People Read News

On social media, people share interesting news they read, and people follow various news sources.

-Getting the Full Picture

To see the full picture both adults and young people prefer social media.

-Boredom in Conversation

People are becoming sad when they have real in person conversations.

-Reactions to Non-Verbal, Emotional, and Social Cues

In-person reactions to non-verbal, emotional, or social cues are changing in that people don't need to respond to these types of communication when they are online.

-Self Expression, Sense of Urgency

People are always enxious if they haven't heard back from a family member. No one has to wait for longer than a few hours.

-Need to share

Sharing is psychologically challenging.

-How We Value Ourselves

There is a feeling of needing to paint a positive and 'fun' version of one's own life.

-Inside Perspective of Afar

Especially on Instagram, users are able to see what others are doing around the World.

-Broadcasting Live

Broadcasting live started as a fun, innocent idea to share life's moments, but it's transformed to become a large part of political movements, sharing some dark aspects of today's society.

-Personalized Digital Messages

Both Instagram and Snapchat have popularized the highly personalized message. It's a problem for people to make themselves look different, but the time they spend on it is a bigger problem.

Social media has become a part of life with its negative and positive effects, but the formula to benefit from social media is to find balance in this area as in everything.

We Are Social and Meltwater, a world leader in social and media intelligence, have released their latest annual report on social media and digital trends worldwide, Digital 2023: The analyses in the report raised important findings:"(Adjust Brand, 2023)

-Digital 2023 shows that globally, a typical internet user has reduced their average daily internet usage by 20 minutes in the past twelve months to 6 hours and 37 minutes, which equates to a reduction of about 5 percent compared to the previous year. .

-The report also shows that social platforms are increasingly demanding a share of search activity around the world. Those between the ages of 16 and 34 now visit a social network more than using a search engine when searching for information about brands, and half of the world's social media users say that they actively visit social platforms to learn more about brands and see their content.

The report also includes the following information (Adjust Brand, 2023)

*"There are 5.16 billion internet and 4.76 billion social media users in the world. The average daily duration of mobile use has increased by seven minutes per day over the past year, and the typical Android user now spends more than five hours a day using their smartphone. Computers account for more than half of the time people in North America and Europe spend using the internet.*

*Cryptocurrency ownership is in decline: The share of internet users who own at least one type of digital currency fell three percent between July and October. TikTok tops the list of global social media platforms when it comes to time spent per user on Android devices, followed by YouTube and Facebook ".*

Although the time spent on social media is 5 hours or more, the decrease of 20 minutes in the last twelve months is also an important indicator in the context of minimalism.

## Life in the Focus of Social Media and Generational Differences

Social media platforms have become an indispensable part of our lives, and with their ever-growing popularity, their positive and negative effects on different generations have become more evident.

The Generation X has seen the birth and rise of various social media platforms like Facebook, Twitter, and LinkedIn, among others. These platforms have helped them stay connected with their friends, family members, and former colleagues. Social media has enabled the X generation to network more efficiently, which can lead to better job opportunities, work collaborations, and partnerships. The X generation has also faced the detrimental consequences of social media on their lives.The X generation witnessed the birth of cyberbullying, fake news, and online harassment, which can significantly affect their mental health and well-being.

The Generation Y is known for being digital natives as they grew up with the internet and social media. Social media has enabled them to become informed on news and current events, and it has also helped them stay connected with their friends and family members who live far away. Y generation has leveraged social media to build their personal brands and online presence, leading to better job opportunities, collaborations, and partnerships. The Y generation has also been adversely affected by social media. Social media addiction has had a significant impact on their mental health and well-being.

The Generation Z is the newest generation to use social media platforms, and they have been able to leverage social media to express themselves creatively. Social media has enabled them to showcase their artistic talents, photography skills, and unique personalities. Z generation has also been able to learn from social media platforms like Instagram, YouTube, and Pinterest, which can help them develop new skills and interests. The Z generation has also been affected by the negative consequences of social media. Social media addiction can lead to a lack of sleep and distract them from focusing on their academic or personal lives.

## Minimalism and Digital Minimalism in the Digital Age

Minimalism has taken the world by storm over the past few years. As a movement, it advocates living with less, focusing on simplicity, and decluttering one's possessions. However, in today's digital era, minimalism has taken on a new form: digital minimalism. This minimalist lifestyle focuses on decluttering digital spaces, limiting the use of technology and social media, and being mindful about our digital consumption.

Minimalism is a lifestyle that promotes reducing clutter and focusing on the essentials. With the rapid advancement of technology, minimalism has become increasingly relevant in the digital age. Many people find themselves overwhelmed with the amount of digital clutter in their lives, including emails, social media notifications, and digital files. This overload of information can lead to stress, anxiety, and decreased productivity. Minimalism in the digital age, therefore, involves decluttering and simplifying one's digital life to achieve a sense of calm and order.

Adopting minimalism in the digital age involves conscious consumption of technology. This includes managing digital subscriptions, organizing files, and limiting time spent on social media. It also involves choosing digital tools and platforms that align with one's values and priorities. For example, using a digital planner instead of a paper planner or choosing an e-reader instead of physical books can reduce physical clutter and promote minimalism. Ultimately, by embracing minimalist practices in the digital age, one can achieve a sense of simplicity, peace, and focus in their digital life.

In the digital age, creativity has become an essential skill that can be used to enhance productivity and innovation in personal and professional life. Creative professionals are in high demand, as they bring new ideas and innovation to the table while using technology to achieve their goals.

Staying creative in the digital age can also be achieved with the following suggestions:

- Practice mind mapping as Tony Buzan suggesting: Mind mapping is a technique that helps to brainstorm and organize ideas in a visual manner. It is a useful tool for approaching complex problems, as it opens up the thought process to generate innovative ideas.
- Collaborate with others: Collaborating with others can lead to creative breakthroughs. When working with others, there is an opportunity to share knowledge, brainstorm ideas, and work through problems, which can lead to innovative solutions.

Use technology to your advantage: There are numerous software tools and applications that can assist in enhancing creativity, such as graphic design, photography, and video editing software.

Take risks: Taking risks is a crucial part of developing creativity. As Sinan Canan suggesting by stepping outside of your comfort zone (Canan S, 2020) and trying new things, you open up the possibility of finding innovative ideas that have yet to be discovered.

Keep learning: Learning new skills and exploring different areas can lead to more creative insights. Taking courses, reading books, and attending workshops can provide different perspectives that can generate new ideas, skills, and techniques.

Set goals: Setting goals is a great way to develop creativity. By setting specific, achievable goals, you can motivate yourself to explore, learn, and create new things.

Overall, developing creativity in the digital age requires an open mind, persistence, and a willingness to take risks. With these tips in mind, you can cultivate your creativity to achieve better productivity, innovation, and success in your personal and professional life.

Creativity is a skill that is blinded by digitalization, but it is also a skill that gains meaning with attention and focus. It is a feature that needs to be protected and developed in the digital age.

## Sustainability and Digital Minimalism

Sustainability can be called the ability to be permanent. (Vikipedia,2023)

The term sustainability has become synonymous with environmental conservation in recent times. Sustainability refers to the concept of meeting the needs of the present without compromising the ability of future generations to meet their own needs. One aspect of sustainability that has gained significant traction in the digital age is digital sustainability. The concept of digital sustainability seeks to reconcile the rapid growth of technology with sustainability concerns and the finite resources of planet earth. On the other hand, digital minimalism advocates for the intentional and mindful use of technology to optimize one's well-being and reduce the negative impacts associated with tech addiction.

Digital minimalism is an approach that prioritizes the essential and eliminates the excess by using technology for specific purposes and avoiding the clamor of digital noise. By utilizing only what is necessary, digital minimalism reduces the common consequences of constant distraction and addictive habits, such as digital pollution or poor mental health. Digital minimalism also connects to sustainability principles because it reduces the excess, especially through the reduction of e-waste.

E-waste is electronic waste that results from the disposal or abandonment of electronic devices, and it is a significant contributor to pollution. E-waste is generated when electronic devices are replaced, and the old devices discarded or ends up in landfills. As technology continues to evolve, and people shift to the latest gadgets, e-waste continues to pile up. However, digital minimalism advocates for digitally purposed purchases that align with the sustainable practice of reducing, reusing, and recycling. It advocates keeping electronics for longer before replacing them, and recycling them when no longer in use, hence contributing to the sustainability concept.

Sustainability also intersects with digital minimalism in other ways, such as reducing energy consumption. Digital minimalism as an approach has the potential to reduce energy consumption used on digital devices. By minimizing screen time and adopting eco-friendly practices such as turning off unused devices or shifting to renewable energy, individuals can contribute to a sustainable future.

Sustainability and digital minimalism intersect in various ways. Digital minimalism contributes to sustainability principles by reducing e-waste while sustainable principles ensure that digital minimalism accounts for environmental concerns. Therefore, by adopting digital minimalism practices, people can facilitate a more sustainable future. Individuals also have the power to use technology mindfully, be aware of its impact, and adopt eco-friendly practices that contribute to sustainable living.

## Digital Transformation

Digital transformation is a necessity, but the contributions of face-to-face communication are undeniable. To put it briefly:

- Provides the opportunity to establish trust and build stronger relationships.
- Allows for more effective and clear communication, as nonverbal cues can be easily observed and interpreted.
  - Minimizes uncertainty and promotes better understanding.
  - Facilitates problem-solving and conflict resolution in a more collaborative manner.
- Helps to convey empathy and establish personal connections.
  - Promotes active listening and better feedback.

Allows for the exchange of ideas and sharing of knowledge in real-time.

- Helps to identify and address any misunderstandings or concerns.
- Provides immediate clarification and quick resolution to any arising issues.
- Enhances the overall quality of communication and work productivity.

*"Digital transformation is the integration of digital technology into all areas of a business, fundamentally changing how you operate and deliver value to customers. It's also a cultural change that requires organizations to continually challenge the status quo, experiment, and get comfortable with failure. This reimagining of business in the digital age is digital transformation ". (Yadav, A, 2023)*

Harari, author of Homo sapiens, who describes those who cannot transform in the digital age as global superfluous, lists his predictions for the future as follows: (Harari, 2023)

'-The rise of data belief

According to Harari, as problems become solvable with technology, people will turn to the belief in data and begin to believe in the power of data.

-The disappearance of the human will

Data will be trusted in a world governed by the power of professional-level data.

- Immortality

The human lifespan in 100 years

-The problem of unemployment

Another effect of developing technology is on people's income distribution

- Emotional Intelligence

Emotions are biochemical algorithms that are vital for humans. This means that emotions can also be developed by people. In this way, machine intelligence will be able to understand and empathize with human emotions'.

Ultimately, Harari believes that the transformation needed will require a fundamental shift in the way we think about ourselves and our relationship to the world around us. This will require a willingness to challenge our assumptions, adopt new perspectives, and work together towards a shared vision of a more sustainable and equitable future.

Once an overview is made to achieve a successful and valuable digital transformation,

Inspired by Acungil (2018), the suggestions for transformation are listed below.

- Define the strategic objectives: Clearly define the goals and objectives and make sure they align with the business strategy. Identify the areas you want to transform, and why.
- Assess your current state: Evaluate your organization's current digital capabilities, including technology, people, and processes. Identify the gaps between your current and desired state.
- Develop a digital transformation roadmap: Develop a comprehensive roadmap that outlines the steps, priority areas, timelines, and milestones for your transformation journey
- Invest in the right technology: Invest in the right technology that aligns with your strategic objectives, addresses the identified gaps, and is scalable and adaptable.
    - Develop a culture of innovation: Foster a culture of innovation that encourages experimentation, risk-taking, and continuous learning. Empower employees to innovate and embrace change.
- Build digital skills: Train employees and develop their digital skills to support the transformation process. Digital skills are essential to achieving a successful transformation.
- Embrace data-driven decision-making: Integrate data into your decision-making processes. Use data analytics to make informed decisions, identify new opportunities, and optimize your operations.
- Engage with your customers: Engage with your customers and involve them in your transformation process. Listen to their feedback and use it to improve your products and services.

Changes and transformations need to proceed more moderately and long-term, not in an all-or-nothing manner. Because these processes require harmony and adaptation. As with any change, uncertainty and insecurity arise in the process of change. In the digital age, it is essential to look at these uncertainties more moderately, to try, to be mistaken, but never to be left out. Being out of the system hinders progress as well as isolation, which means that being outside the system in the digital age is becoming isolated. For this reason, it should be essential to change and transform, to adapt and not to ignore the benefits of digital.

This study aims to determine how 3 different generations in the age of digital transformation explain digital through concepts and how they make sense of the concept of minimalism in this transformation, while determining the points where generations separate and unite.

## Purpose of the Research

In this research, which is carried out in order to reveal whether the 3 generations, X, Y, Z, who are trapped in social media tools in the 21st century, are aware of their surroundings, for what purpose they use social media and whether they are establishing a balance in their lives, the aim is to reveal the perspectives of these three generations on digital minimalism.

## The Universe and the Scope of the Research

The universe of the research consists of 24 people who are defined as digital natives and digital immigrants, that is, 24 people who are X, Y, Z generations.

Within the scope of the qualitative research, each of them was interviewed face-to-face with university graduates, 12 boys and 12 girls X, Y, Z generations with the in-depth interview method and the structured questions were asked.

The universe of the research consists of the mass described as digital natives and digital immigrants.

Marc Prensky describes digital natives and digital immigrants in the following sentences: (Prensky, 2001: 1)

'What should we call these "new" students of today? Some refer to them as the N-[for Net]-gen or D-[for digital]-gen. But the most useful designation I have found for them is Digital Natives. Our students today are all "native speakers" of the digital language of computers, video games and the Internet. What should we call these "new" students of today? Some refer to them as the N-[for Net]-gen or D-[for digital]-gen. But the most useful designation I have found for them is Digital Natives. Our students today are all "native speakers" of the digital language of computers, video games and the Internet.

## The Methodology of the Research

The research will be carried out with the in-depth interview technique from qualitative research methods. In the research referred to, in-depth interview technique was used and a semi-structured questionnaire was used.

The main feature of a structured conversation is that the questions to be directed to the participant are ordered in a standardized way and in a certain order. In structured interviews, categories of answers to questions may have been established or open-ended questions may have been used without flexibility. In this respect, structured interviews are seen as the data collection technique closest to the quantitative method (Punch, 2005).

The questions posed to generations X, Y, Z are as follows.

1. Can you describe what digital minimalism means to you in one word?
2. How has digital minimalism impacted your daily routine or lifestyle?
3. How has digital minimalism helped or hindered your mental and emotional well-being?
4. Do you feel like digital minimalism has improved your ability to focus and be productive?
5. How has digital minimalism impacted your social life and relationships?
6. Do you think digital minimalism is more beneficial to one generation over another?
7. Do you think digital minimalism is a fad or a long-term trend?

8. How has digital minimalism impacted your consumption habits ?
9. Have you noticed any differences in how X, Y, and Z generations approach digital minimalism?
10. Do you think digital minimalism can be applied in a moderate way? Or is it an all or nothing approach?

The questions listed above were asked to the X, Y, Z Generations who were interviewed in depth and the findings obtained from the answers were analizyed.

## Findings

In general, minimalism is a concept that has grown in popularity over the past few years, and it has influenced people of all ages. However, there are some differences in the way the X, Y, and Z generations interpret minimalism.

The X generation, born between the mid-1960s and the early-1980s, was raised during a time of consumerism and materialism. While they tend to appreciate the idea of minimalism, they may struggle to put it into practice due to their tendency to hold onto sentimental items and the notion of collecting possessions as a status symbol.

In line with the questions asked, the answers of X, Y, Z generations to the questions were analyzed and visualized as follows on the basis of concept.,

*Table 1. Responses and analysis of Generation X on a conceptual basis*

| Answers | Generation X |
|---|---|
| 1 | Optimization, Self-Control, Calmness, Comfort |
| 2 | Time, Area |
| 3 | Self Knowledge, Focus |
| 4 | Focus, Productive |
| 5 | Contributed |
| 6 | Necessary for Generation X, Y,Z |
| 7 | Long term Trend |
| 8 | Rational consumer, environmentalist |
| 9 | X - Conscious<br>Y – Dilemma<br>Z - They don't care |
| 10 | Can be applied in moderation |

According to the table on a conceptual basis, it is revealed that Generation X attaches importance to time management, focus and productivity, but Generation X states that digital mininalism leads them to consume less. Although digital minimalism is trend for generation X, it is only possible to apply digital minimalism in moderation.

The Y generation, born between the early-1980s and the late-1990s, have had minimalism thrust upon them to a greater degree. Growing up in a world where overconsumption and materialism are seen as negatives, they tend to be more open to the idea of minimalism. Many young adults in this generation are gravitating towards tiny homes, minimalistic design, and simple living.

*Table 2. Responses and analysis of Generation Y on a conceptual basis*

| Answers | Generation Y |
|---|---|
| 1 | Serenity, Time, Comfort, Self-Control, Calmness |
| 2 | Focus, Sticking to routines |
| 3 | Stay in the moment, Stay stable, Calmness, Focus |
| 4 | Focus |
| 5 | Become a better listener, New Media Literacy |
| 6 | Necessary for Generation X, Y,Z |
| 7 | Long term Trend, Lifestyle, Fashionable |
| 8 | Did not effect |
| 9 | X - Minimal<br>Y – Not sure<br>Z -Resilient |
| 10 | Can be applied in moderation |

According to the table, Generation Y focus on serenity, time and self-control, and express that they are good listeners with digital minimalism. They see digital minimalism as a trend and lifestyle and emphasize that it is essential for everyone. They also believe that it will only succeed if it is applied in a moderate way.

The Generation Z, born between the late-1990s and the late-2000s, are coming of age at a time when environmental concerns are urgent, and minimalism is seen as an important part of sustainability. Many people in this generation prioritize experiences over possessions and are comfortable living in small spaces. Overall, while each generation may approach minimalism differently, it is clear that the idea has gained momentum and influence across all generations.

According to the table Generation Z defines minimalism as a concept as win win, simplicity, relaxation, benefit. Generation X and Y state that all generations need minimalism, while Generation Z believes that only they need minimalism.

The impact of digital media on focus, productivity, social life, digital obesity, self-control, and happiness has been a topic of much discussion and debate in recent years.

The data obtained as a result of the research can be summarized as follows:

1. Focus and Productivity: Digital media can often be a distraction, leading to decreased focus and productivity. For example, spending too much time scrolling through social media feeds or checking emails can take away valuable time that could be used for more productive activities.
2. Social Life: Digital media can have both positive and negative effects on an individual's social life. On one hand, it can provide a platform for connecting with friends and family, and even building

new relationships. However, excessive use of digital media can also lead to social isolation, as individuals may prioritize their screens over face-to-face interactions.

3. Digital Obesity: Spending too much time sitting in front of screens can lead to increased weight gain and decreased physical activity, also known as "digital obesity."
4. Self-Control: Digital media can also negatively impact an individual's self-control. For example, using social media or online shopping can lead to impulsive behavior, leading to financial and personal problems.
5. Happiness: The impact of digital media on happiness is complex and varies for each individual. On one hand, it can provide entertainment and connection with others.

*Table 3. Responses and analysis of Generation Z on a conceptual basis*

| Answers | Generation Z |
|---|---|
| 1 | Benefit, Relaxation, Order, Win-Win, Simplicity, Decrease, |
| 2 | Stay in the moment, Hobbies, Focus, Turning to hobbies |
| 3 | Being strong, Enabled mental and emotional well being |
| 4 | Productive, Project-oriented |
| 5 | Value, Quality time, Meaningful social life, Avoid misunderstanding |
| 6 | Necessary for Generation Z |
| 7 | Long term Trend |
| 8 | Consumption awareness |
| 9 | X - Close<br>Y – Conscious<br>Z -Distant |
| 10 | Can be applied in moderation |

Overall, the effect of digital media on an individual's focus, productivity, social life, digital obesity, self-control, and happiness depends on how it is used and to what extent. It is important to strike a balance between the benefits and potential negative impacts related to digital media use.

## Future Research and Directions

The most important skill in the 21st century will be the ability to filter information and time management.. In order for this generation, which is addicted to social media, to get rid of this addiction and to realize the digital transfomation effectiely, it is necesarry to realize this addiction and take precautions. Generations in that have lost many of their abilities with digitalization are in danger of losing their creativity and human abilities. In the future skills not professions will be at the forefront. Therefore by developing and specializing skills, it will be possible to exist in the digital age. The 21st century will be the world of digital transformationers. Those who can use both traditional and digital will come to the fore. Those who manage their time well by filtering information and who bring their creativity to the fore will make a difference and become preferred employees. Therefore future research must follow the trail of time management, minimalism, sustainability and staying creative in the digital world.

## CONCLUSION

"Where we want to be cautious . . . is when the sound of a voice or a cup of coffee with a friend is replaced with 'likes' on a post." Holly Shakya, summed up the changing dynamic in communication in a very meaningful way.

Humans are social beings by nature. They need face-to-face communication, and social media should not replace face-to-face communication, no matter what. 1

As a result of the research, the elements that converged at one point in three generations have been focus, time management, quality time and the moderate transition to digital minimalism.

Digital minimalism is a philosophy that encourages individuals to be more intentional with their use of technology, to eliminate distractions and focus on what's truly important. This can be done by reducing the amount of time spent on social media and other digital distractions and instead prioritizing offline activities that bring joy and meaning to their lives.

Time management is the process of organizing, planning, and prioritizing tasks and activities to make the most efficient use of time. This can help individuals maximize productivity and reduce stress and anxiety caused by feeling overwhelmed or stretched thin.

In combination, digital minimalism and time management can be powerful tools to help individuals achieve their goals and find balance in their lives. By setting clear priorities and minimizing distractions, individuals can reduce unnecessary stress and increase their focus and productivity, which can ultimately lead to greater success and happiness.

Digital minimalism is a term that refers to the practice of reducing the dependence on technology and digital devices in the daily life. This philosophy is based on the idea that too much technology can actually hinder the ability to live a fulfilling and well-rounded life.

One of the biggest challenges with modern technology is the constant distraction it creates. The individuals are always checking their phones, checking their email, and browsing social media websites. This constant need to be connected to technology can prevent them from fully experiencing the world around them and engaging in meaningful, face-to-face interactions with other people.

Spending quality time with the loved ones is one of the most important things that the individuals can do in life. It's crucial for their mental and emotional well-being, and can help them feel more connected and fulfilled in their relationships.

However, spending quality time with others can be difficult in today's digital age. With so many distractions constantly vying for their attention, it's easy to get caught up in checking their phones, scrolling through social media feeds, and watching videos online. This can make it difficult to truly engage with them and build meaningful connections.

To combat this, digital minimalism encourages the individuals to be intentional with their use of technology. This might involve setting limits on how much time they spend browsing social media, turning off their phones during meals or other important events, or even taking extended breaks from technology altogether.

By reducing their dependence on technology, the individuals can free up more time to spend with loved ones and engage in meaningful activities that bring them joy and fulfillment. Whether it's going for a hike in nature, having a picnic in the park, or simply having a conversation with a friend, spending quality time is an essential part of living a happy and healthy life.

In the digital age, the most important problem of the generations that receive countless stimuli from their environment has been determined as attention and inability to focus. These problems are followed by the inability to manage time, to live in the moment, to control oneself and one's consumption habits.

The common opinion of all 3 generations is that the all-or-nothing approach to digital minimalism will not be successful in the transition process. On the contrary, generations who see digital minimalism as a long-term trend, a way of life, agree that a moderate transition is sustainable and will create change.

The findings obtained as a result of the research indicate the necessity of a long-term process for a sustainable change. Suggestions for steps that can be taken to make a difference and be effective in change can be summarized as follows.

-Set a specific goal for reducing your time spent on social media.
Use the screen time feature on your phone to track your usage.
Make a plan to check social media only during specific times of the day
Start by reducing your usage by 10-15 minutes a day
Replace social media time with other activities like reading, exercising or spending time with friends.
Turn off notifications for social media apps.
Use social media only when necessary, like for work or messaging friends.
Use a website blocker to limit access to social media sites
. Set a time limit for how long you can spend on each social media app.
Create a list of things you enjoy doing that don't involve social media.
Identify triggers that make you turn to social media, and find ways to address those triggers.
Consider taking a social media detox for a week or more.
Try a different type of app or platform, like meditation or language learning apps.
Unfollow accounts that make you feel negative or unhappy.
Limit your social media use during specific events, like dinner with family or time with friends.

-Ask a friend or family member to hold you accountable for reducing social media usage. Use social media less often on weekends or holidays.
Practice mindfulness techniques to become more present and less reliant on social media.
Set achievable goals for how often you want to use social media each week
Experiment with limiting your use of one social media app at a time.
Create rules for when you can and cannot use social media, like before bedtime or during meals.

It is possible to apply the recommendations listed above to create a change and transformation in the axis of digital minimalism, but as with any decision, the importance of the first step leading to that decision cannot be denied.

Let Cal Newport have the final word, on this article, which is the first step for digital minimalism, as he said very clearly: 'Leisure Lesson #1: Prioritize demanding activity over passive consumption'.

## REFERENCES

Aayushi, Y. (2023). The Wisdom of Digital Transformation. *Raamaya*. http://raamayatechnologies.com/blog/technology/the-wisdom-of-digital-transformation

Acungil, M. (2018). Dijtal Dönüşümi. Tuti Kitap Adjust Brand. https://www.adjustbrand.com/arastirmalar/we-are-social-dijital-2023-raporunu-yayinladi/

Buzan, T. (2020). *Zihin Haritalama*. Olimpos Yayınları.

Canan, S. (2020). *Sınırları Aşmak*. Tuti Kitap.

Car, N. (2020). *The Shallows: What the Internet is Doing to Our Brains*. W.W. Norton.

DeVito, A. J. (2007). *The Interpersonal Book*. Pearson Education.

Goleman, D. (2013). *Odak, Filiz Deniztekin*. Varlık Yayınları.

Harari, J. N. (2023). Harariden Insanligin Gelecegine Dair 5 Ongoru. *Digital Age*. https://digitalage.com.tr/harariden-insanligin-gelecegine-dair-5-ongoru/

Kahneman, D. (2017). *Hızlı ve Yavaş Düşünme, Osman Ç. Deniztekin, Filiz N. Deniztekin*. Varlık Yayınları.

Kaku, M. (2015). *The Future of the Mind: The Scientific Quset to Understand, Enhamce and Empower the Mind*. Anchor Publishing.

Newport, C. (2016). *Deep Work: Rules for Focused Success in a Distracted World*. Grand Central Publishing.

Prensky, M. (2001). Digital Natives, Digital Immigrants. On the Horizon, 9(5). MCB University Press.

Valueprop. (2023). *5 Benefits of Face to Face Communication*. Value Prop. https://www.valueprop.com/blog/5-benefits-face-face-communication in 20.2.2023

Westerman Gonnet, D., & Mcafee, A. (2014). *Leading Digital*. HBR.

## KEY TERMS AND DEFINITIONS

**Social Media Addiction:** Not being able to live without social media.
**Minimalism:** To be able to use less efficiently.
**Time Management:** To be able to live without procrastination.
**Digital Transformation:** To be able to manage a digitally adaptable process.
**Digital Minimalism:** Being able to filter information.

# Compilation of References


Çakır, Ö., Ayas, T., & Horzum, M. B. (2011). An investigation of university students' internet and game addiction with respect to several variables. Ankara University. *Journal of Faculty of Educational Sciences.*, *44*(2), 95–117.

*A brief history of digital gaming*. (2014, November 14). MAAC. https://www.maacindia.com/blog/a-brief-history-of-digital-gaming

Aayushi, Y. (2023). The Wisdom of Digital Transformation. *Raamaya.* http://raamayatechnologies.com/blog/technology/the-wisdom-of-digital-transformation

Abd Rahman, S. H. (2014). Can't live without my FB, LoL: The influence of social networking sites on the communication skills of TESL students. *Procedia: Social and Behavioral Sciences*, *134*, 213–219. doi:10.1016/j.sbspro.2014.04.241

Abel, J. P., Buff, C. L., & Burr, S. A. (2016). Social Media and the Fear of Missing Out: Scale Development and Assessment. [JBER]. *Journal of Business & Economics Research*, *14*(1), 33–44. doi:10.19030/jber.v14i1.9554

Aboudi, S. E. L., & Khanchaoui, I. (2021). Exploring the impact of inflation and external debt on economic growth in Morocco: An empirical investigation with an ARDL approach. *Asian Economic and Financial Review*, *11*(11), 894–907. doi:10.18488/journal.aefr.2021.1111.894.907

Aboujaoude, E., Koran, L. M., Gamel, N., Large, M. D., & Serpe, R. T. (2006). Potential markers for problematic internet use: A telephone survey of 2, 513 adults CNS spectrum. *CNS Spectrums*, *11*(10), 750–755. doi:10.1017/S1092852900014875 PMID:17008818

Abubakr, M., Abbas, A. T., Tomaz, I., Soliman, M. S., Luqman, M., & Hegab, H. (2020). Sustainable and smart manufacturing: An integrated approach. *Sustainability (Basel)*, *12*(6), 2280. doi:10.3390u12062280

Achab, S., Nicolier, M., Mauny, F., Monnin, J., Trojak, B., Vandel, P., Sechter, D., Gorwood, P., & Haffen, E. (2011). Massively multiplayer online role-playing games: Comparing characteristics of addict vs non-addict online recruited gamers in a French adult population. *BMC Psychiatry*, *11*(1), 144. doi:10.1186/1471-244X-11-144 PMID:21871089

Açıkgöz, A., Ezen, M., Emir, B., & Özkaraman, A. (2019). Effect of social media dependence of nursing students on communication skills. *Kocaeli Medical Journal*, *8*(1), 130–140. doi:10.5505/ktd.2019.04934

Acquaviva, M. (2019). *Evolução das campanhas de comunicação na indústria do entretenimento: do cinema de rua às plataformas de streaming*. Universidade de São Paulo.

Acungil, M. (2018). Dijtal Dönüşümi. Tuti Kitap Adjust Brand. https://www.adjustbrand.com/arastirmalar/we-are-social-dijital-2023-raporunu-yayinladi/

Adair, C. (n.d.). *11 Positive Effects of Video Games*. Game Quitters. https://gamequitters.com/positive-effects-of-video-games/

Adair, C. (n.d.). *The Negative Effects of Video Games - 12 Symptoms*. Game Quitters. https://gamequitters.com/negative-effects-of-video-games/

Adel, A. (2022). Future of industry 5.0 in society: Human-centric solutions, challenges and prospective research areas. *Journal of Cloud Computing (Heidelberg, Germany)*, *11*(1), 1–15. doi:10.118613677-022-00314-5 PMID:36101900

Adıgüzel, O., Batur, H. Z., & Ekşili, N. (2014). The Changing Face of Generations and the New Working Style Emerged with Generation Y: Mobile Collars [Kuşakların Değişen Yüzü ve Y kuşağı İle Ortaya Çıkan Yeni Çalışma Tarzı: Mobil Yakalılar]. *Süleyman Demirel Üniversitesi Sosyal Bilimler Enstitüsü Dergisi*, *1*(19), 165–182.

Adlassnig, K. P. (2002). Artificial-intelligence-augmented systems. Artificial Intelligence in Medicine, 24, 01-04. doi:10.1016/S0933-3657(01)00102-6

Aghion, P., Howitt, P., Howitt, P. W., Brant-Collett, M., & García-Peñalosa, C. (1998). *Endogenous growth theory*. MIT press.

Ağır, M. (2018). *Ergenlerde psikolojik sağlamlık, okul tükenmişliği ve internet bağımlılığı üzerine.*

Ahmedov, I. (2020). The impact of digital economy on international trade. *European Journal of Business and Management Research*, *5*(4), 1–7. doi:10.24018/ejbmr.2020.5.4.389

Akbulut, Y. (2013). Çocuk ve ergenlerde bilgisayar kullanımının gelişimsel sonuçları. *Trakya Üniversitesi Eğitim Fakültesi Dergisi*, *3*(2), 53–68.

Akçakanat, Ö., Özdemir, O., & Mazak, M. (2021). İşletmelerde Siber Güvenlik Riskleri ve Bilgi Teknolojileri Denetimi: Bankaların Siber Güvenlik Uygulamalarının İncelenmesi. *Mehmet Akif Ersoy Üniversitesi Uygulamalı Bilimler Dergisi*, *5*(2), 246–270. doi:10.31200/makuubd.978263

Akgül, B., & Ayer, Z. (2020). The change in the management structure of media institutions in the fourth industrial revolution (Industry 4.0) process. *Journal of Life Economics*, *7*(2), 151–160. doi:10.15637/jlecon.7.010

Akın, A., & İskender, M. (2011). Internet addiction and depression, anxiety and stress. *International Online Journal of Educational Sciences*, *3*(1), 138–148.

Akınerdem, F. (2012). Yerli Dizi Anlatıları ve İzleyici Katılımı: Uçurum Dizisini Ekşi sözlük ve Twitter'la Birlikte İzlemek. *Folklor/Edebiyat, 18*(72), 77-90.

Akın, M. Ş. (2021). Dijital Göçebelik: Deneyim ve Özgürlük. *Sosyal Ekonomik Araştırmalar Dergisi*, *21*(1), 41–52. doi:10.30976usead.799881

Akkuş, T. (2022). Dijital Minimalizm: Ekran Bağımlılığı ve Teknoloji Yorgunluğu Sarmalından Kurtulmak İçin Bir Yol Haritası. *Trt Akademi*, *7*(14), 366–371. doi:10.37679/trta.1064029

Akpınar, M. E. (2021). Analysis of Advertisements from Different Sectors in Turkey within the Context of Gender Equality. Communication and Technology Congress – CTC 2021, Bologna. doi:10.17932/CTCSPC.21/ctc21.010

Aksentijevic, N. K., Ježic, Z., & Zaninovic, P. A. (2021). The effects of information and communication technology (ICT) use on human development – A macroeconomic approach. *Economics*, *9*(128), 1–12.

Aksoy, S. (2020). *Üniversite Öğrencilerinde Sosyal Medya Bağımlılığının, Sosyal Kaygı ve Kişisel İyi Oluş İle Arasındaki İlişkinin İncelenmesi.* Yüksek Lisans Tezi, Üsküdar Üniversitesi Sosyal Bilimler Enstitüsü, Allen, M. and Bourhis, J. (1996). The relationship of communication apprehension to communication behavior: A meta-analysis. *Communication Quarterly*, *44*(2), 214–226.

Aksu, Z. U., & Işıklı, Ş. (2019). Teknolojik zehirlenme, semptomları ve teknolojik düzen. *ISophos: Uluslararası Bilişim. Teknoloji ve Felsefe Dergisi, 2*(2), 57–87.

Aktan, E. (2018). Üniversite Öğrencilerinin Sosyal Medya Bağımlılık Düzeylerinin Çeşitli Değişkeneler Göre İncelenmesi. *Erciyes İletişim Dergisi*, 405-421.

Aktaş, F. (2021). *Pandemi Sürecinde İlköğretim Öğrencilerinin Dijital Bağımlılığına İlişkin Öğretmen Görüşleri.* Pamukkale University.

Akyüz, E. (2018). The role of university in the education of writers of children's literature: The model of Aarhus University. *International Journal of Languages'. Education and Teaching, 6*(4), 113–121. doi:10.18298/ijlet.3203

Akyüz, E. (2021). Dijitalleşme bağlamında çocuk edebiyatı yapıtlarının taşıması gereken özellikler. [Characteristics of children's literature works in the context of digitalization] In O. Koksal (Ed.), *Dijital eğitim* [Digital education]. (pp. 139–151). Eğitim Publications.

Alam, M., Qureshi, M. S., Sarwat, A., Haque, Z., Masroor, M. S., Makki, M. A., & Aslam, S. (2014). Prevalence of Phantom Vibration Syndrome and Phantom Ringing Syndrome (Ringxiety): Risk of Sleep Disorders and Infertility among Medical Students. *International Journal of Advanced Research, 2*(12), 688–693.

Alavi, S. S. (2012). Behavioral addiction versus substance addiction. Correspondence of psychiatric and psychological views. *International Journal of Preventive Medicine, 4*, 290–294. PMID:22624087

Aleksandrova, A., Truntsevsky, Y., & Polutova, M. (2022). Digitalization and its impact on economic growth. *Revista de Economia Política, 42*(2), 424–441. doi:10.1590/0101-31572022-3306

Al-Furaih, S. A. A., & Al-Awidi, H. M. (2021). Fear of missing out (FoMO) among undergraduate students in relation to attention distraction and learning disengagement in lectures. *Education and Information Technologies, 26*(2), 2355–2373. doi:10.100710639-020-10361-7

Algül, A., Yengin, D., Karadağ, G. H., Övür, A., & Bayrak, T. (2019). Sanal Gerçeklik Hastalığı. In G. H. Karadağ (Ed.), *Dijital Hastalıklar* (pp. 9–54). Der Yayınları.

Alhashem, M., Moraes, C., & Szmigin, I. T. (2020). Use and social value in peer-to-peer prosumption communities. *European Journal of Marketing*, 1–55.

Alhassan, A. A., Alqadhib, E. M., Taha, N. W., Alahmari, R. A., Salam, M., & Almutairi, A. F. (2018). The relationship between addiction to smartphone usage and depression among adults: A cross sectional study. *BMC Psychiatry, 18*(1), 148. doi:10.118612888-018-1745-4 PMID:29801442

Ali, M. A., Alam, K., & Taylor, B. (2019). Incorporating affordability, efficiency, and quality in the ICT development index: Implications for index building and ICT policymaking. *The Information Society, 36*(2), 71–96.

Allcott, H., Gentzkow, M., & Song, L. (2022). Digital Addiction. *The American Economic Review, 112*(7), 2424–2463. doi:10.1257/aer.20210867

Allen-Robertson, J. (2013). *Digital culture industry.* Palgrave Macmillan Publications. doi:10.1057/9781137033475

Allison, S. E., von Wahlde, L., Shockley, T., & Gabbard, G. O. (2006). The development of the self in the era of the internet and role-playing fantasy games. *The American Journal of Psychiatry, 163*(3), 381–385. doi:10.1176/appi.ajp.163.3.381 PMID:16513856

Al-Menayes, J. (2016). The Fear of Missing Out Scale: Validation of the Arabic version and correlation with social media addiction. *International Journal of Applied Psychology, 6*(2), 41–46.

Almourad, M. B., Mcalaney, J., Skinner, T., Pleya, M., & Ali, R. (2020). Defining Digital Addiction: Key Features from The Literature. *Psihologija (Beograd), 53*(3), 237–253. doi:10.2298/PSI191029017A

Alpman, P. S. (2012). Toplumsal Hareketler Tartışması İçin Kısa Bir Giriş. (Çevrimiçi). *Yurtvedunya.* http://www.yurtvedunya.net/Sayi3/4.pdf

Alt, D. (2015). College students' academic motivation, media engagement and fear of missing out. *Computers in Human Behavior, 49*, 111–119. doi:10.1016/j.chb.2015.02.057

Alt, D., & Boniel-Nissim, M. (2018a). Parent–adolescent communication and problematic internet use: The mediating role of Fear of Missing Out (FoMO). *Journal of Family Issues, 39*(13), 3391–3409. doi:10.1177/0192513X18783493

Alt, D., & Boniel-Nissim, M. (2018b). Links between adolescents' deep and surface learning approaches, problematic internet use, and fear of missing out (FoMO). *Internet Interventions : the Application of Information Technology in Mental and Behavioural Health, 13*, 30–39. doi:10.1016/j.invent.2018.05.002 PMID:30206516

Altınok, M. (2021). Lise Öğrencilerinin Dijital Bağımlılık ve Yaşam Doyumunun İncelenmesi. *Türk Eğitim Bilimleri Dergisi, 19*(1), 262–291. doi:10.37217/tebd.689774

Altun, M., & Atasoy, M. (2018). Investigation Of Digital Game Addiction Of Children Between 9-11 Age Groups: Kirşehir Sample. *International Journal of Eurasia Social Sciences*, 1740-1757.

Altuntuğ, N. (2012). Consumption Phenomenon from Generation to Generation and Consumer Profile of the Future [Kuşaktan Kuşağa Tüketim Olgusu ve Geleceğin Tüketici Profili]. *Organizasyon ve Yönetim Bilimleri Dergisi, 4*(1), 203–212.

Alutaybi, A., Al-Thani, D., McAlaney, J., & Ali, R. (2020). Combating fear of missing out (FoMO) on Social Media: The FoMO-R Method. *International Journal of Environmental Research and Public Health, 17*(17), 6128. doi:10.3390/ijerph17176128 PMID:32842553

Alves, A. (2018). *O comportamento de consumo dos Millenials nas plataformas de video streaming e a prática do binge watching*. Instituto Superior de Contabilidade e Administração de Coimbra.

Alves, G., & Hamza, K. (2018). *Comportamento do consumidor de streaming de vídeo sob a ótica da extensão da teoria unificada de aceitação e uso da tecnologia*. UEM.

Alwin, D. F. (2002). Generations X, Y And Z: Are They Changing America, *American Sociological Association. Contexts, 42*(1), 42–51. doi:10.1525/ctx.2002.1.4.42

Aly, H. (2020). Digital transformation, development and productivity in developing countries: Is artificial intelligence a cure or a blessing? *Review of Economics and Political Science, 7*(4), 1–19.

American Educational Research Association. (2013). *Prevention of bullying in schools, colleges, and universities. Research report and recommendations*. AERA.

American Psychiatric Association (APA). (2013). *Diagnostic and Statistical Manual of Mental Disorders (DSM-5)*. American Psychiatric Publishing.

American Psychiatric Association. (2013). *Diagnostic and Statistical Manual of Mental Disorders* (5th ed.). American Psychiatric Association.

American Psychiatric Association. (2013). *Diagnostic and statistical manual of mental disorders* (5th ed.). American Psychiatric Publishing.

American Psychiatric Association. (2013). *DSM-5 – Diagnostic and statistical manual of mental disorders: DSM-5* (5th ed.). American Psychiatric Association.

American Psychological Association. (2017). *Connected and content: Managing healthy technology use*. APA. Https://www.Apa.Org/Topics/Social-Media-Internet/Healthy-Technology-Use

American Psychological Association. (n.d.). Psychopharmacology. In *APA dictionary of psychology*. APA. https://dictionary.apa.org/psychopharmacology

Anamur, D. D., & Topsakal, T. (2019). Herkesin herkesi gözetlediği toplum: siberuzamda alttan gözetimin farklı inşası olarak siber zorbalık. *İnönü Üniversitesi İletişim Fakültesi Elektronik Dergisi (İNİF E-Dergi), 4*(2), 37-58.

Anderson, K. E. (2020). Getting acquainted with social networks and apps: It's time to talk about TikTok. *Library Hi Tech News, 37*(4), 7–12. doi:10.1108/LHTN-01-2020-0001

Andreassen, C. S., Billieux, J., Griffiths, M. D., Kuss, D. J., Demetrovics, Z., Mazzoni, E., & Pallesen, S. (2016). The relationship between addictive use of social media and video games and symptoms of psychiatric disorders: A large-scale cross-sectional study. *Psychology of Addictive Behaviors, 30*(2), 252–262. doi:10.1037/adb0000160 PMID:26999354

Andreassen, C. S., Pallesen, S., & Griffiths, M. D. (2017). The relationship between addictive use of social media, narcissism, and self-esteem: Findings from a large national survey. *Addictive Behaviors, 64*, 287–293. doi:10.1016/j.addbeh.2016.03.006 PMID:27072491

Andreassen, C., & Hetland, J. (2014). i Pallesen, S.(2014). *Social network site addiction–an overview. Current Pharmaceutical Design, 20*(25), 4053–4061. doi:10.2174/13816128113199990616 PMID:24001298

André, F., Munck, I., Håkansson, A., & Claesdotter-Knutsson, E. (2022). Game Addiction Scale for Adolescents: Psychometric analyses of gaming behavior, gender differences and ADHD. *Frontiers in Psychiatry, 13*, 791254. doi:10.3389/fpsyt.2022.791254 PMID:35356720

Angulo, P. G., Mendoza, J. S., Contreras, E. C., Martínez, J. U. C., Hernández, C. B. E., & Hernández, M. E. C. (2021). The meaning of life as a mediator between self-esteem and Internet addiction in adolescents. *Enfermería Global, 20*(4), 519–531. doi:10.1177/17456916211014189

APA. (2013). *Diagnostic and statistical manual of mental disorders (DSM-5®)*. American Psychiatric Pub. doi:10.1176/appi.books.9780890425596

Appiah-Otoo, I., & Song, N. (2021). The impact of ICT on economic growth-comparing rich and poor countries. *Telecommunications Policy, 45*(2), 1–15. doi:10.1016/j.telpol.2020.102082

Arabi, A. M. K., & Allah, B. A. W. (2017). The impact of information and communication technology (ICT) development on economic growth in Sudan: An application of ARDL bounds testing approach. *Archives of Business Research, 5*(3), 155–165.

Arat, Z. F. (1988). Democracy and economic development: Modernization theory revisited. *Comparative Politics, 21*(1), 21–36. doi:10.2307/422069

Arıcak, O. T. (2011). Siber zorbalık: Gençlerimizi bekleyen yeni tehlike. *Kariyer Penceresi, 2*(6), 10–12.

Arıcak, O. T., Kınay, H., & Tanrıkulu, T. (2012). Siber zorbalık ölçeğinin ilk psikometrik bulguları. *Hasan Ali Yücel Eğitim Fakültesi Dergisi, 17*(1), 101–114.

Arısoy, Ö. (2009). İnternet bağımlılığı ve tedavisi. Psikiyatride Güncel Yaklaşımlar Dergisi, *1*(1), 55-67. https://core.ac.uk/download/pdf/26663761.pdf

Arısoy, Ö. (2009). İnternet bağımlılığı ve tedavisi. *Psikiyatride Güncel Yaklasimlar, 1*(1), 55–67.

Arnaud, N., & Thomasius, R. (2021). Störungen durch Substanzgebrauch und abhängige Verhaltensweisen in der ICD-11 [Disorders due to substance use or addictive behaviours in the ICD-11]. *Zeitschrift für Kinder- und Jugendpsychiatrie und Psychotherapie, 49*(6), 486–493. doi:10.1024/1422-4917/a000748 PMID:32795136

Arslan, A. (2020a). Ortaöğretim Öğrencilerinin Dijital Bağımlılık Düzeyleri ve Şiddet Eğilimlerinin Belirlenmesi. *Journal of Computer and Education Research, 8*(15), 86–113. doi:10.18009/jcer.652390

Arslan, A. (2020b). Üniversite Öğrencilerinin Dijital Bağımlılık Düzeylerinin Çeşitli Değişkenler Açısından İncelenmesi. *International E-Journal of Educational Studies, 4*(7), 27–41. doi:10.31458/iejes.600483

Arthur, R. (2016). Generation Z: 10 StatsFrom SXSW YouNeedToKnow. *Forbes/Tech.* https://www.forbes.com/sites/rachelarthur/2016/03/16/generationz/#4d22f7a52.

Ashraf, S. N., & Singh, A. K. (2022). Implications of appropriate technology and farm inputs in the agricultural sector of Gujarat: Empirical analysis based on primary data. *Agricultural Economics Research Review, 35*(2), 59–77. doi:10.5958/0974-0279.2022.00031.3

Aslam, F., Aimin, W., Li, M., & Ur Rehman, K. (2020). Innovation in the era of IoT and industry 5.0: Absolute innovation management (AIM) framework. *Information (Basel), 11*(2), 124. doi:10.3390/info11020124

Atabay, E. S., & Aytekin, S. S. (2022). Metaverse: Örgüt kültürünün gelenekselden dijitale evrimi. *Uluslararası İktisadi ve İdari İncelemeler Dergisi*, (36), 21–36.

Ateş, E. C., & Ateş, A. P. (2020). Gençlik-dijital çağ ve suç youth-digital age and crime. *Gençlik ve Dijital Çağ, 11.*

*Augmented Reality (AR) vs Virtual Reality (VR): The difference explained.* (2022, April 12). TeamViewer. https://www.teamviewer.com/en/augmented-reality-ar-vs-virtual-reality-vr/

Aust, S., & Ammann, T. (2018). *Dijital Diktatörlük: Kitlesel Gözetim, Verilerin Kötüye Kullanımı ve Siber Savaş*. Hece Yayınları ve Dergileri.

Auxier, B., & Anderson, M. (April 2021). *Social Media Use in 2021.* Pew Research Center.

Avcı, N., & Topçu, D. (2021). Sosyal Medya, Dil ve Edebiyat. *Birey ve Toplum Sosyal Bilimler Dergisi*, 5-26.

Ayar, D., Bektas, M., Bektas, I., Kudubes, A. A., Ok, Y. S., Altan, S. S., & Celik, I. (2017). The effect of adolescents' internet addiction on smartphone addiction. *Journal of Addictions Nursing, 28*(4), 210–214. doi:10.1097/JAN.0000000000000196 PMID:29200048

Ayas, T. & Horzum, M. B. (2013). Rehber öğretmenlerin sanal zorbalık fakındalık düzeyinin çeşitli değişkenlere göre incelenmesi. *Hacettepe Üniversitesi Eğitim Fakültesi Dergisi, 28*(3), 195-205.

Aydemir, F. (2022). Digital games and their effects on children. *Adiyaman üniversitesi sosyal bilimler enstitüsü dergisi*, 40-69.

Aydm, B., & San, S. V. (2011). Internet addiction among adolescents: The role of self-esteem. *Procedia: Social and Behavioral Sciences, 15*, 3500–3505. doi:10.1016/j.sbspro.2011.04.325

Ayhan, B., & Çavuş, S. (2014). İzleyici Araştırmalarında Değişim; Kullanımlar ve Doyumlardan Bağımlılığa. *Selçuk İletişim*, 32-60.

Ayhan, B., & Çavuş, S. (2015). Online Game Addiction Among High School Students. In C. Daba-Buzoianu, H. Arslan, & M. A. Icbay (Eds.), *Contextual Approaches in Communication* (pp. 85–93). Peter Lang.

Azevedo, J. (2016). *A experiência televisiva: A Netflix e a cultura da receção audiovisual on demand no Brasil.*

Aziz, N., Nordin, M. J., Abdulkadir, S. J., & Salih, M. M. M. (2021). Digital addiction: Systematic review of computer game addiction impact on adolescent physical health. *Electronics (Basel), 10*(9), 996. doi:10.3390/electronics10090996

Babacan, M. E. (2016). Sosyal Medya Kullanım Alanları ve Bağımlılık İlişkisi. *Addicta: The Turkish Journal on Addictions*, 7-28.

Bacen. (2015). *Dados sobre remessa de tecnologia ao exterior.* BC. http://www.bc.gov.br/

Baer, S., Saran, K., & Green, D. A. (2012, October). Computer/gaming station use in youth: Correlations among use, addiction and functional impairment. *Paediatrics & Child Health, 17*(8), 427–431. doi:10.1093/pch/17.8.427 PMID:24082802

Bağatarhan, T., & Siyez, D. M. (2022). The Effectiveness of a Cognitive-Behavioral Prevention Program for Internet Addiction. *Journal of Rational-Emotive & Cognitive-Behavior Therapy, 40*(4), 1–26. doi:10.100710942-021-00439-7

Baggio, S., Starcevic, V., Studer, J., Simon, O., Gainsbury, S. M., & Gmel, G. (2018). Technology-mediated addictive behaviors constitute a Spectrum of related yet distinct conditions: A network perspective. *Psychology of Addictive Behaviors, 32*(6), 594. doi:10.1037/adb0000405 PMID:30211582

Bağ, S. (2020). Slaktivizm: Yeni Medya ve Siyasal Eylemin Dönüşümü. In H. Hülür & C. Yaşın (Eds.), *Yeni Medya, Toplum ve Siyasal İletişim* (pp. 350–368). Ütopya Yayınevi.

Bahrainian, S. A., Alizadeh, K. H., Raeisoon, M. R., Gorji, O. H., & Khazaee, A. (2014). Relationship of Internet addiction with self-esteem and depression in university students. *Journal of Preventive Medicine and Hygiene, 55*(3), 86–89. PMID:25902574

Bakari, S. (2022). *The impact of digitalization and patent on economic growth in Romania.* MPRA Paper No. 114259.

Baker, Z. G., Krieger, H., & LeRoy, A. S. (2016). Fear of missing out: Relationships with depression, mindfulness, and physical symptoms. *Translational Issues in Psychological Science, 2*(3), 275–282. doi:10.1037/tps0000075

Bakıroğlu, C. T. (2013). Sosyalleşme ve kimlik inşası ekseninde sosyal paylaşım ağları. *Akademik Bilişim, 13*, 2014.

Balcı, A. (2001). *Sosyal bilimlerde araştırma. Yöntem, Teknik ve İlkeler.* PegemA Yayınları.

Bal, E. (202). Sosyal Medyada Mahremiyet ve Paylaşım Kültürü. In M. Akdağ (Ed.), *Dijital Kültür ve Sosyal Medya* (pp. 122 142). Atatürk Üniversitesi Açıköğretim Fakültesi Yayını.

Ballard, M., Gray, M., Reilly, J., & Noggle, M. (2009). Correlates of video game screen time among males: Body mass, physical activity, and other media use. *Eating Behaviors, 10*(3), 161–167. doi:10.1016/j.eatbeh.2009.05.001 PMID:19665099

Ball, M. (2022). *The Metaverse: And How It Will Revolutionize Everything.* Liveright. doi:10.15358/9783800669400

Balsmeier, B., & Woerter, M. (2019). Is this time different? How digitalization influences job creation and destruction. *Research Policy, 48*(8), 1–1. doi:10.1016/j.respol.2019.03.010

Baltaş, A. (2023). *Dijital Obezite* [Blog]. Acarbaltas.com. https://www.acarbaltas.com/dijital-obezite/

Banger, G. (2017). *Endüstri 4.0 ekstra.* Dorlion Yayınları.

Banyai, F., Griffiths, M. D., Kiraly, O., & Demetrovics, Z. (2018). The psychology of esports: A systematic literature review. *Journal of Gambling Studies, 35*(2), 351–364. doi:10.100710899-018-9763-1 PMID:29508260

Bargeron, A. H., & Hormes, J. M. (2017). Psychosocial correlates of internet gaming disorder: Psychopathology, life satisfaction, and impulsivity. *Computers in Human Behavior, 68*, 388–394. doi:10.1016/j.chb.2016.11.029

Barındık, G. (2018). *Dijital şiddet nedir? Teknolojinin yarattığı yeni şiddet alanı.* Indigodergisi. https://indigodergisi.com/2018/11/dijital-siddet-nedir/.

Barnett, S. D., Kramer, M. L., Casat, C. D., Connor, K. M., & Davidson, J. R. (2002). Efficacy of olanzapine in social anxiety disorder: A pilot study. *Journal of Psychopharmacology (Oxford, England), 16*(4), 365–368. doi:10.1177/026988110201600412 PMID:12503837

Barocas, S., & Selbst, A. D. (2016). Big Data's Disparate Impact. *SSRN.* doi:10.2139srn.2477899

Barrett-Maitland, N., & Lynch, J. (2020). Social media, ethics, and the privacy paradox. C. Kalloniatis & C. Travieso-Gonzales (Ed.), In Security and privacy from a legal, ethical, and technical perspective (p. 49-62). doi:10.5772/intechopen.90906

Barr, M., & Copeland-Stewart, A. (2021). Playing Video Games During the COVID-19 Pandemic and Effects on Players' Well-Being. *Games and Culture, 17*(1), 122–139. doi:10.1177/15554120211017036

Bartle, R. (2003). *Designing virtual worlds.* New Riders.

Bartosik-Purgat, M., & Bednarz, J. (2021). The usage of new media tools in prosumer activities–a corporate perspective. *Technology Analysis and Strategic Management, 33*(4), 453–464. doi:10.1080/09537325.2020.1820475

Bartosik-Purgat, M., & Mińska-Struzik, E. (2022). Social media and mobile tools in consumers' decisions of Polish consumers. In M. Bartosik-Purgat & F. Nela (Eds.), *European Consumers in the Digital Era* (pp. 129–144). Routledge. doi:10.4324/9781003263685-11

Baruch, Y. (2005). Bullying on the net: Adverse behaviour on e-mail and its impact. *Information & Management, 42*(2), 361-371. https://doi.org/. im.2004.02.001. doi:10.1016/j

Başaran, İ. E. (1996). *Eğitim yönetimi (5. baskı).* Yargıcı Matbaası.

Başer, A. (2010). Yeni iletişim teknolojilerinin evriminde televizyonun yeri. [The place of television in the evolution of new communication technologies] In F. Aydoğan & A. Akyüz (Eds.), *İkinci medya çağında internet* [Internet in the second media age]. (pp. 36–60). Alfa Publishing.

Başlar, G. (2013). *Yeni medyanın gelişimi ve dijitalleşen kapitalizm* [Development in new media and digitalised capitalism]. Akademik Bilişim.

Bassett, C. (2013). Kültürel çalışmalar ve yeni medya. [Cultural studies and new media] In G. Hall & C. Birchall (Eds.), *Yeni kültürel çalışmalar: Kuramsal serüvenler* [New cultural studies: Theoretical adventures]. (KartalO., Trans.; pp. 323–350). Say Publishing.

Bassiouni, D. H., & Hackley, C. (2016). Video games and young children's evolving sense of identity: A qualitative study. *Young Consumers, 17*(2), 127–142. doi:10.1108/YC-08-2015-00551

Bastiaensens, S., Van Cleemput, K., Vandebosch, H., Poels, K., DeSmet, A., & De Bourdeaudhuij, I. (2019). "Were You Cyberbullied? Let Me Help You." Studying Adolescents' Online Peer Support of Cyberbullying Victims Using Thematic Analysis of Online Support Group Fora. In H. Vandebosch & L. Green (Eds.), *Narratives in Research and Interventions on Cyberbullying among Young People* (pp. 95–112). Springer. doi:10.1007/978-3-030-04960-7_7

Batthyany, D., Müller, K. W., Benker, F., & Woelfling, K. (2009). Computer game playing: Clinical characteristics of dependence and abuse among adolescents. *Wiener Klinische Wochenschrift, 121*(15-16), 502–509. PMID:19787320

Batur, Z., & Uygun, K. (2012). Perception of two generations of a concept: Technology. *Usak University Journal of Social Sciences, 5*(1), 74–88.

Baudrillard, J. (2020). Simülakrlar ve Simülasyon. Ankara: Doğu Batı Yayınları.

Baudrillard, J. (1994). *Simulacra and simulation*. University of Michigan Press.

Baudrillard, J. (2016). *Tüketim toplumu* [Consumer society]. (H. Deliceçaylı & F. Keskin, Trans.). Ayrıntı Publishing.

Bauman, Z. (2011). Yaşam sanatı. (çev. Akın Sarı). İstanbul: Versus Kitap

Bauman, Z., & Lyon, D. (2013). *Liquid surveillance: A conversation*. John Wiley & Sons.

Bayrak, H. (2019a). Internet usage and social media statistics (January). *Dijilopedi*. https://dijilopedi.com/2019-internet-egitimi-ve-social-media-istatistikleri/

Bayrak, H. (2019b). Turkey internet usage and social media statistics (January). *Dijilopedi*. https://dijilopedi.com/2019-turkiye-internet-egitimim-ve-social-medya-istatistikleri/

Bayrak, T., & Cihan, B. (2021). Yeni Medyada Bağımlılık Sonucu Gelişen Dijital Obezite Olgusu Üzerine Bir İnceleme: Netflix Türkiye Örneği. *E-Journal of New Media–Ejnm, 5*(1).

Bayrak, T. (2017). Sosyal medyada dijital etik: Twitter'da şiddet içerikli iletilerin incelenmesi. *Yeni Medya Elektronik Dergisi, 1*(1), 32–46. doi:10.17932/IAU.EJNM.m.25480200.2017.1/1.32-46

Bayrak, T., & Yengin, D. (2021). *Sanal dünyada yeni şiddet*. Der Yayınları.

Bayraktar, F., & Gün, Z. (2007). Incidence and Correlates of Internet Usage Among Adolescents in North Cyprus. *Cyberpsychology & Behavior, 10*(2), 191–197. doi:10.1089/cpb.2006.9969 PMID:17474835

Beard, C. L., Haas, A. L., Wickham, R. E., & Stavropoulos, V. (2017). Age of Initiation and Internet Gaming Disorder: The Role of Self Esteem. *Cyberpsychology, Behavior, and Social Networking, 20*(6), 397–401. doi:10.1089/cyber.2017.0011 PMID:28622030

Beck, U. (2019). *Risk Toplumu (3* (B. Doğan & K. Özdoğan Eds. & Trans.). İthaki Yayınları.

Bednarz, J. (2022). Who is a consumer in the digital era? Still a consumer or a prosumer? In M. Bartosik- Purgat and F. Nela (Ed.), European Consumers in the Digital Era (pp. 27-42). Routledge.

Beer, D., & Burrows, R. (2013). Popular culture, digital archives and the new social life of data. *Theory, Culture & Society, 30*(4), 47–71. doi:10.1177/0263276413476542

Belkhir, L., & Elmeligi, A. (2018). Assessing ICT global emissions footprint: Trends to 2040 & recommendations. *Journal of Cleaner Production, 177*, 448–463. doi:10.1016/j.jclepro.2017.12.239

Bell, D. (2007). *Cyberculture theorists: Manuel Castells and Donna Haraway*. Routledge Publishing. doi:10.4324/9780203357019

Bell, V., Bishop, D. V. M., & Przybylski, A. K. (2015). The debate over digital technology and young people. *BMJ (Clinical Research Ed.)*, h3064. doi:10.1136/bmj.h3064 PMID:26268481

Belsey, C. (2004). *Culture and the real: Theorizing cultural criticism*. Routledge. doi:10.4324/9780203001448

Benjamin, B., & Woerter, M. (2019). Is this time different? How digitalization influences job creation and destruction. *Research Policy, 48*(8), 1–10.

Bennett, W. L. (2008). *Changing Citizenship in The Digital Age*. Macarthur Foundation Digital Media and Learning Initiative.

Berk, L. (2015). *Child development*. Pearson Higher Education AU.

Bernardi, S., & Pallanti, S. (2009). Internet addiction: A descriptive clinical study focusing on comorbidities and dissociative symptoms. *Comprehensive Psychiatry*, *50*(6), 510–516. doi:10.1016/j.comppsych.2008.11.011 PMID:19840588

Betoncu, O., & Ozdamli, F. (2019). The Disease of 21st Century: Digital Disease. *TEM Journal*, *8*(2), 598–603.

Beyens, I., Frison, E., & Eggermont, S. (2016). "I don't want to miss a thing": Adolescents' fear of missing out and its relationship to adolescents' social needs, Facebook use, and Facebook related stress. *Computers in Human Behavior*, *64*, 1–8. doi:10.1016/j.chb.2016.05.083

Bhagat, S., Jeong, E. J., & Kim, D. J. (2020). The Role of Individuals Need for Online Social Interactions and Interpersonal Incompetence in Digital Game Addiction. *International Journal of Human-Computer Interaction*, *36*(5), 449–463. doi:10.1080/10447318.2019.1654696

Bhandari, A., & Bimo, S. (2020). *TikTok and the "algorithmized self": A new model of online interaction*. AoIR Selected Papers of Internet Research.

Bickel, W. K., Mellis, A. M., Snider, S. E., Athamneh, L. N., Stein, J. S., & Pope, D. A. (2018). 21st century neurobehavioral theories of decision making in addiction: Review and evaluation. Pharmacology Biochemistry and Behavior, *164*(February 2017), 4–21. doi:10.1016/j.pbb.2017.09.009

Bilgiç It Academy. (2018). Big Data – What is Big Data? Bilgiç It Academy. https://www.bilginc.com/tr/egitim-haber/buyuk-veri-big-data-nedir

Bilginer, Ç., Karadeniz, S., & Arslan, E. (2021). Digital gaming among adolescents in clinical settings: Do we underestimate this issue? *Entertainment Computing*, *36*, 100392. doi:10.1016/j.entcom.2020.100392

Billieux, J., Deleuze, J., Griffiths, M. D., & Kuss, D. J. (2015). Internet gaming addiction: The case of massively multiplayer online role-playing games. In N. el-Guebaly, (Eds.), *Textbook of addiction treatment: International perspectives* (pp. 1515–1525). Springer-Verla. doi:10.1007/978-88-470-5322-9_105

Billieux, J., Van der Linden, M., Achab, S., Khazaal, Y., Paraskevopoulos, L., Zullino, D., & Thorens, G. (2013). Why do you play World of Warcraft? An in-depth exploration of self-reported motivations to play online and in-game behaviours in the virtual world of Azeroth. *Computers in Human Behavior*, *29*(1), 103–109. doi:10.1016/j.chb.2012.07.021

Billon, M., Lera-Lopez, F., & Marco, R. (2010). Differences in digitalization levels: A multivariate analysis studying the global digital divide. *Review of World Economics*, *146*(1), 39–73. doi:10.100710290-009-0045-y

BİNARK. (2008). Mutlu ve Günseli Bayraktutan-Sütcü Kültür Endüstrisi Ürünü Olarak Dijital Oyun.

Binark, M., & Bayraktutan-Sütçü, G. (2008). *Digital Game as a Culture Industry* [Kültür Endüstrisi Olarak Dijital Oyun]. Kalkedon Yayıncılık.

Biricik, Z. (2022). Digital Addictions and Digital Minimalism as A Road to Escape from Digital Addictions. *The Turkish Online Journal of Design Art and Communication*, *12*(3), 897–912. doi:10.7456/11203100/022

Bishop, K., Deste, P., & Neely, A. (2011). Gaining from interactions with universities: Multiple methods for nurturing absorptive capacity. *Research Policy*, *40*(1), 30–40. doi:10.1016/j.respol.2010.09.009

Błachnio, A., Przepiorka, A., Senol-Durak, E., Durak, M., & Sherstyuk, L. (2017). The role of personality traits in Facebook and Internet addictions: A study on Polish, Turkish, and Ukrainian samples. *Computers in Human Behavior*, *68*, 269–275. doi:10.1016/j.chb.2016.11.037

Blackwell, D., Leaman, C., Tramposch, R., Osborne, C., & Liss, M. (2017). Extraversion, neuroticism, attachment style and fear of missing out as predictors of social media use and addiction. *Personality and Individual Differences, 116*, 69–72. doi:10.1016/j.paid.2017.04.039

Blakemore, S. J. (2019). Adolescence and mental health. *Lancet, 393*(10185), 2030–2031. doi:10.1016/S0140-6736(19)31013-X PMID:31106741

Blažević, I., & Klein, N. (2022). Digital Media and Internet Safety Among Primary School Students During the Covid-19 Pandemic. *Journal of Elementary Education, 15*(2), 127–144. doi:10.18690/rei.15.2.127-144.2022

Bloemen, N., & De Coninck, D. (2020). Social media and fear of missing out in adolescents: The role of family characteristics. *Social Media + Society, 6*(4), 2056305120965517. doi:10.1177/2056305120965517

Bloomberg. J. (2022, 12 19). Digitization, Digitalization, and Digital Transformation: Confuse Them at your Peril. *Forbes*. https://www.forbes.com/sites/jasonbloomberg/2018/04/29/digitization-digitalization

Blum, K., Braverman, E. R., Holder, J. M., Lubar, J. F., Monastra, V. J., Miller, D., Lubar, J.O., Chen, T.J.H., & Comings, D. E. (2000). The reward deficiency syndrome: A biogenetic model for the diagnosis and treatment of impulsive, addictive and compulsive behaviors. *Journal of psychoactive drugs, 32*(sup1), 1-112.

Blum, R. W., Beuhring, T., Shew, M. L., Bearinger, L. H., Sieving, R. E., & Resnick, M. D. (2000). The effects of race/ethnicity, income, and family structure on adolescent risk behaviors. *American Journal of Public Health, 90*(12), 1879–1884. doi:10.2105/AJPH.90.12.1879 PMID:11111260

Bobrowicz-Campos, E., & Matos, A. P. (2022). Ageing and Health in the Digital Society: Challenges and Opportunities. In I. Management Association (Ed.), Research Anthology on Supporting Healthy Aging in a Digital Society (pp. 1-17). IGI Global. doi:10.4018/978-1-6684-5295-0.ch001

Bottel, L., Te Wildt, B. T., Brand, M., Pape, M., Herpertz, S., & Dieris-Hirche, J. (2023). Telemedicine as bridge to the offline world for person affected with problematic internet use or internet use disorder and concerned significant others. *Digital Health, 9*, 20552076221144185. doi:10.1177/20552076221144185 PMID:36636726

Bottomore, T. (1997). *Frankfurt Okulu* (A. Çiğdem, Trans.). Vadi Yayınları.

Bougheas, S., Demetriades, P. O., & Mamuneas, T. P. (2000). Infrastructure, specialization, and economic growth. *The Canadian Journal of Economics. Revue Canadienne d'Economique, 33*(1), 506–522. doi:10.1111/0008-4085.00026

Bouhnik, D., & Deshen, M. (2014). WhatsApp Goes to School: Mobile Instant Messaging between Teachers and Students. *Journal of Information Technology Education, 13*, 217–231. http://www.jite.org/documents/Vol13/JITEv13ResearchP217-231Bouhnik0601.pdf. doi:10.28945/2051

Bouna-Pyrrou, P., Mühle, C., Kornhuber, J., & Lenz, B. (2015). Internet gaming disorder, social network disorder and laterality: Handedness relates to pathological use of social networks. *Journal of Neural Transmission (Vienna, Austria), 122*(8), 1187–1196. doi:10.100700702-014-1361-5 PMID:25576300

Bowker, G. (2008). *Structures of participation in digital culture*. Social Science Research Council Publications.

Boyle, E., Connolly, T. M., & Hainey, T. (2011). The role of psychology in understanding the impact of computer games. *Entertainment Computing, 2*(2), 69–74. doi:10.1016/j.entcom.2010.12.002

Bozarth, C. (2006). ERP implementation efforts at three firms: Integrating lessons from the SISP and IT-enabled change literature. *International Journal of Operations & Production Management, 26*(11), 1223–1239. doi:10.1108/01443570610705836

Bozeman, B. (2000). Technology transfer and public policy: A review of research and theory. *Research Policy, 29*(4-5), 627–655. doi:10.1016/S0048-7333(99)00093-1

Bozkurt, A., Hamutoğlu, N. B., Kaban, A. L., Taşçı, G., & Aykul, M. (2021). Dijital bilgi çağı: Dijital toplum, dijital dönüşüm, dijital eğitim ve dijital yeterlilikler. *Açıköğretim Uygulamaları ve Araştırmaları Dergisi, 7*(2), 35–63. doi:10.51948/auad.911584

Bozkurt, G. (2016). *İnsan ve kültür* [People and culture]. Boyut Publishing.

Bozoglan, B., Demirer, V., & Sahin, I. (2013). Loneliness, self-esteem, and life satisfaction as predictors of Internet addiction: A cross-sectional study among Turkish university students. *Scandinavian Journal of Psychology, 54*(4), 313–319. doi:10.1111jop.12049 PMID:23577670

Brand, M., Rumpf, H. J., Demetrovics, Z., Müller, A., Stark, R., King, D. L., Goudriaan, A. E., Mann, K., Trotzke, P., Fineberg, N. A., Chamberlain, S. R., Kraus, S. W., Wegmann, E., Billieux, J. Ë., & Potenza, M. N. (2020). Which conditions should be considered as disorders in the International Classification of Diseases (ICD-11) designation of "other specified disorders due to addictive behaviors"? *Journal of Behavioral Addictions, 11*(2), 150–159. doi:10.1556/2006.2020.00035 PMID:32634114

Brasil. (1970). *Lei nº 5.648, de 11 de dezembro de 1970.* Presidência da República Casa Civil. http://www.planalto.gov.br/ccivil_03/leis/L5648.htm

Brasil. (1996). Lei de Propriedade Intelectual do Brasil nº 9.279, de 14 de maio de 1996. Plan Alto. http://www.planalto.gov.br/ccivil_03/leis/L9279.htm

Braun, J. A., Coakley, J. D., & West, E. (2019). Activism, advertising, and far-right media: The case of sleeping giants. *Media and Communication, 7*(4), 68–79. doi:10.17645/mac.v7i4.2280

Brecher, J., Costello, T., & Smith, B. (2002). *Aşağıdan Küreselleşme* (B. Kurt, Z. Kutluata, Ş. Özgün, & A. Yıldırım, Trans.). Aram.

Breque, M., De Nul, L., & Petridis, A. (2021). *Industry 5.0: towards a sustainable, human-centric and resilient European industry.* European Commission, Directorate-General for Research and Innovation.

Bronfenbrenner, U. (1989). Ecological systems theory. In R. Vasta (Ed.), *Annals of child development* (Vol. 6, pp. 187–249). JAI Press.

Brown, A. (2011). Media use by children younger than 2 years. *Pediatrics, 128*(5), 1040–1047. doi:10.1542/peds.2011-1753 PMID:22007002

Brown, A., Shifrin, D. L., & Hill, D. L. (2015). Beyond 'turn it off': How to advise families on media use. *AAP News, 36*(10), 54. doi:10.1542/aapnews.20153610-54

Brown, P., George, A. M., & Rickwood, D. J. (2021). Rash impulsivity, reward seeking and fear of missing out as predictors of texting while driving: Indirect effects via mobile phone involvement. *Personality and Individual Differences, 171*, 171. doi:10.1016/j.paid.2020.110492

Brown, U., & Long, G. (2018). Poverty and welfare. In *Social Welfare* (pp. 19–34). Routledge. doi:10.4324/9781315202686-3

Bruns, A., & Highfield, T. (2015). Is Habermas on Twitter? Social Media and the Public Sphere. In The Routledge Companion to social media and Politics (pp. 56-73). Routledge Publications.

Bruns, A. (2019). Filter bubble. *Internet Policy Review, 8*(4). doi:10.14763/2019.4.1426

Bruns, A., & Burgess, J. (2016). Methodological innovation in precarious spaces: The case of Twitter. In *Digital methods for social science: An interdisciplinary guide to research innovation. (S. Ersöz Karakulakoğlu, Tr)* (pp. 17–33). Nobel Publication. doi:10.1057/9781137453662_2

Buglass, S. L., Binder, J. F., Betts, L. R., & Underwood, J. D. (2017). Motivators of online vulnerability: The impact of social network site use and FOMO. *Computers in Human Behavior, 66*, 248–255. doi:10.1016/j.chb.2016.09.055

Burgoon, J. K. and Hale, J. L. (1983). *A research note on the dimensions of communication reticence.*

Burke, B. L., Arkowitz, H., & Menchola, M. (2003). The efficacy of motivational interviewing: A meta-analysis of controlled clinical trials. *Journal of Consulting and Clinical Psychology, 71*(5), 843–861. doi:10.1037/0022-006X.71.5.843 PMID:14516234

Butler, J. (2014). Cinsiyet Belası Feminizm ve Kimliğin Altüst Edilmesi. İstanbul: Metis Yayınları.

Bütüner, R., Bütüner, N., & Bütüner, M. (2022). Ergenlerde Sosyal Medya Bağımlılığı Konusunda Son Beş Yılda Yapılmış Çalışmaların İncelenmesi. *Journal of Information Systems and Management Research*, 17-34.

Büyükgöze, S., & Dereli, E. (2019). Toplum 5.0 ve Dijital Sağlık. *VI. International Scientific and Professional Studies Congress-Science and Health, 7*(10).

Buzan, T. (2020). *Zihin Haritalama.* Olimpos Yayınları.

Byeon, Y. S., & Lee, H. S. (2007). The effects of internet addiction on mental health among adolescents. *Journal of Korean Academy of Community Health Nursing, 18*(3), 460–468.

Çakır, H. (2005). Internet as a Communication Language. *Erciyes University Journal of Social Sciences Institute, 1*(19), 71–96.

Çakır, R., Solak, E., & Tan, S. S. (2015). Artırılmış gerçeklik teknolojisi ile ingilizce kelime öğretiminin öğrenci performansına etkisi. *Gazi Eğitim Bilimleri Dergisi, 1*(1), 45–58.

Çakmak, V. and Aktan, E. (2016). Öğrencilerin İletişim Kaygısı, Muziplik/Takılma ve Okul Başarısı Arasındaki İlişkinin İncelenmesi. *İletişim Kuram ve Araştırma Dergisi*(42).

Çakmak, V. (2018). *İletişim Kaygisi Ve Sosyal Medya.* Eğitim Yayınevi.

Çakmak, V. (2020). Dijital Kültür ve Kimliğin İnşası. In M. Akdağ (Ed.), *Dijital Kültür ve Sosyal Medya* (pp. 20–38). Erzurum Üniversitesi Açıköğretim Fakültesi Yayını.

Calvo-Porral, C., & Pesqueira-Sanchez, R. (2020). Generational differences in technology behaviour: Comparing millennials and Generation X. *Kybernetes, 49*(11), 2755–2772. doi:10.1108/K-09-2019-0598

Camardese, G., Leone, B., Walstra, C., Janiri, L., & Guglielmo, R. (2015). Pharmacological treatment of Internet addiction. In *Internet addiction* (pp. 151–165). Springer. doi:10.1007/978-3-319-07242-5_10

Campbell, M. A. (2005). Cyber bullying: An old problem in a new guise? *Australian Journal of Guidance & Counselling, 15*(1), 68–76. doi:10.1375/ajgc.15.1.68

Can, E. N., Koçer, M., & Toprak, H. H. (2021). Tüketicilerin Netflix Kullanımları Üzerine Bir Araştırma. *Erciyes Akademi*, 323-344.

Canan, S. (2020). *Sınırları Aşmak.* Tuti Kitap.

Can, G., & Satici, S. A. (2019). Adaptation of fear of missing out scale (FoMOs): Turkish version validity and reliability study. *Psicologia: Reflexão e Crítica, 32*(1), 32. doi:10.118641155-019-0117-4 PMID:32026206

Caplan, S. E. (2002). Problematic internet use and psychosocial wellbeing: Development of a theory-based cognitive-behavioral measurement instrument. *Computers in Human Behavior, 18*(5), 553–575. doi:10.1016/S0747-5632(02)00004-3

Caplan, S. E. (2003). Preference for Online Social Interaction: A Theory of Problematic Internet Use and Psychosocial Well-Being. *Communication Research, 30*(6), 625–648. doi:10.1177/0093650203257842

Caplan, S. E. (2010). Theory and measurement of generalized problematic Internet use: A twostep approach. *Computers in Human Behavior, 26*(5), 1089–1097. doi:10.1016/j.chb.2010.03.012

Carbo-Valverde, S. (2017). The impact on digitalization on banking and financial stability. *Journal of Financial Management. Markets and Institutions, 5*(1), 133–140.

Cares, N. (2021). *O TikTok como instrumento de Marketing Digital: Estudo de caso @NetflixBrasil*. Universidade de Brasília.

Carlisle, K. L. (2017). *Personality, motivation, and Internet gaming disorder: Understanding the addiction*. Old Dominion University.

Carli, V., Durkee, T., Wasserman, D., Hadlaczky, G., Despalins, R., Kramarz, E., Wasserman, C., Sarchiapone, M., Hoven, C. W., Brunner, R., & Kaess, M. (2013). The Association between Pathological Internet Use and Comorbid Psychopathology: A Systematic Review. *Psychopathology, 46*(1), 1–13. doi:10.1159/000337971 PMID:22854219

Carlson, N. R., & Birkett, M. A. (2021). *Physiology of Behavior*. Pearson Publications.

Car, N. (2020). *The Shallows: What the Internet is Doing to Our Brains*. W.W. Norton.

Casale, S., & Fioravanti, G. (2020). Factor structure and psychometric properties of the Italian version of the Fear of Missing Out Scale in emerging adults and adolescents. *Addictive Behaviors, 102*, 106179. doi:10.1016/j.addbeh.2019.106179 PMID:31704432

Casale, S., Rugai, L., & Fioravanti, G. (2018). Exploring the role of positive metacognitions in explaining the association between the fear of missing out and social media addiction. *Addictive Behaviors, 85*, 83–87. doi:10.1016/j.addbeh.2018.05.020 PMID:29864680

Castells, M. (2005). *Enformasyon çağı: Ekonomi, toplum ve kültür birinci cilt ağ toplumunun yükselişi* 1. Çev: Kılıç, E.) İstanbul Bilgi Üniversitesi Yayınları.

Castells, M. (2009). *The Rise of the Network Society*.

Castells, M. (2004). *The network society: A cross-cultural perspective*. Edward Elgar Publishing, Incorporated., doi:10.4337/9781845421663

Castells, M. (2008). *Enformasyon Çağı: Ekonomi, Toplum ve Kültür Ağ Toplumunun Yükselişi (Birinci Cilt) (2* (E. Kılıç Ed. & Trans.). İstanbul Bilgi Üniversitesi Yayınları.

Castells, M. (2010). *The rise of the network society*. Wiley Blackwell Publishing. doi:10.1002/9781444319514

Cattley, R. (2020). *Netflix – Um Novo Paradigma na Indústria de Entretenimento: Análise e Valuation*. Rio de Janeiro.

Çavuş S, Ayhan B, Tuncer M. (2016), Computer games and addiction: A field study on university students. *Communication Theory and Research Journal, 43*.

Çavuş, S. (2022). Üniversite öğrencilerinin sosyal medya kullanımları üzerine bir alan araştırması: Aksaray Üniversitesi örneği. *İNİF E- Dergi, 7*(2), pp. 9-25.

Çavuş, S. (2018). Dijital Çağda Gazeteciliğin Dönüşümü ve Transmedyal Haber Üretimi. In E. Aktan (Ed.), *Transmedya Hikayeciliği* (pp. 279–298). Literatürk Yayınları.

Çavuş, S., & Ayhan, B. (2017). Cyberbullying and Victimization Experiences of University Students. In H. Arslan, M. A. İcbay, & C. Ruggiero (Eds.), *Communication and Media Researches* (pp. 159–168). E-BWN.

Çavuş, S., & Ayhan, B. ve Tuncer, M. (2016). Bilgisayar Oyunları ve Bağımlılık: Üniversite Öğrencileri Üzerine Bir Alan Araştırması. İletişim Kuram ve Araştırma Dergisi. Gazi Üniversitesi. *Sayı, 43*, 266.

Çavuş, S., Ayhan, B., & Tuncer, M. (2016). *Bilgisayar Oyunları ve Bağımlılık: Üniversite Öğrencileri Üzerine Bir Alan Araştırması*. İletişim Kuram ve Araştırma Dergisi.

Çelebi, E. (2020). Dijital Oyun ve Bağımlılık. *Yeni Medya Elektronik Dergisi.*, *16*(1), 241–256.

Çelik, C. (2022, 8 5). *İnternet ve Sosyal Medya Bağımlılığı*. Celik. cemilcelik.com.tr: https://www.cemilcelik.com.tr/internet-ve-sosyal-medya-bagimliligi/

Çelik, E. (2018). İnternet ortamındaki şiddet sunumları ve yol açtığı sosyal travmalar. *Çağdaş Yönetim Bilimleri Dergisi, 5*(3), 280-296.

Çelik, N. (2013). Thorstein Veblen'in Gösterişçi Tüketim Yaklaşımı: Niğde Üniversitesi İdari Personeli Örneği. *Erciyes University Journal of Social Sciences Institute, 1*(34), 171–203.

Çelik, N. (2022). Yeni Medyada Bilginin Üretimi ve Paylaşımı Sorunsalı. In F. Ayaz & B. Taşdelen (Eds.), *Bir Yaşam Alanı Olarak Dijital Medya* (1st ed., pp. 55–72). Eğitim Publications.

Çelik, Z., Dülek, B., Aydın, I., & Saydan, R. (2022). Metaverse: Bibliometric Analysis, A Conceptual Model Proposal, and a Marketing-Oriented Approach. *Bingöl University Journal of Social Sciences Institute, 24*, 383–394. doi:10.29029/busbed.1114777

Cemiloglu, D., Almourad, M. B., McAlaney, J., & Ali, R. (2022). Combatting digital addiction: Current approaches and future directions. *Technology in Society, 6*, 101832. doi:10.1016/j.techsoc.2021.101832

Ceretta, S. & Froemming, L. (2011). *Geração Z: Compreendendo os hábitos de consumo da geração emergente.* Revista eletrónica do Mestrado Profissional em Administração.

Çetin, C. ve Karalar, S. (2016). X, Y ve Z Kuşağı Öğrencilerin Çok Yönlü Ve Sınırsız Kariyer Algıları Üzerine Bir Araştırma. *Yönetim Bilimleri Dergisi, 14*(28), 157–197.

Çetin, M., & Turgay, A. (2002). Modern Psikofarmakolojinin Ellinci Yılında Klorpromazinden Günümüze Antipsikotik Tedavinin Dünü Bugünü. *Klinik Psikofarmakoloji Bülteni, 12*, 211–226.

Chai, H. Y., Niu, G. F., Lian, S. L., Chu, X. W., Liu, S., & Sun, X. J. (2019). Why social network site use fails to promote well-being? The roles of social overload and fear of missing out. *Computers in Human Behavior, 100*, 85–92. doi:10.1016/j.chb.2019.05.005

Chambers, D. (2013). *Social media and personal relationships: Online intimacies and networked friendship*. Springer. doi:10.1057/9781137314444

Chandler, D., & Munday, R. (2018). *Medya ve İletişim Sözlüğü* (B. Taşdemir, Trans.). İletişim Yayınları.

Chandra, A. N., Jamiy, F. E., & Reza, H. (2022). A Systematic Survey on Cybersickness in Virtual Environments. *Computers, 11*(51), 1–15.

Chang, F. C., Chiu, C. H., Miao, N. F., Chen, P. H., Lee, C. M., Chiang, J. T., & Pan, Y. C. (2015). The relationship between parental mediation and Internet addiction among adolescents, and the association with cyberbullying and depression. *Comprehensive Psychiatry*, *57*, 21–28. doi:10.1016/j.comppsych.2014.11.013 PMID:25487108

Chan, P. A., & Rabinowitz, T. (2006). A cross-sectional analysis of video games and attention deficit hyperactivity disorder symptoms in adolescents. *Annals of General Psychiatry*, *5*(1), 16. doi:10.1186/1744-859X-5-16 PMID:17059614

Charlton, J. P., & Danforth, I. D. W. (2007). Distinguishing addiction and high engagement in the context of online game playing. *Computers in Human Behavior*, *23*(3), 1531–1548. doi:10.1016/j.chb.2005.07.002

Chatfield, T. (2013). Dijital Çağa Nasıl Uyum Sağlarız. (Çev. ve Haz.: L. Konca), İstanbul.

Chau, C. L., Tsui, Y. Y. Y., & Cheng, C. (2019). Gamification for internet gaming disorder prevention: Evaluation of a Wise IT-Use (WIT) Program for Hong Kong primary students. *Frontiers in Psychology*, *10*, 1–13. doi:10.3389/fpsyg.2019.02468 PMID:31736842

Chayko, M. (2020). *Superconnected: The Internet, Digital Media, and Techno-Social Life.* SAGE Publications, Inc.

Cheah, I., Shimul, A. S., & Phau, I. (2022). Motivations of playing digital games: A review and research agenda. *Psychology and Marketing*, *39*(5), 937–950. doi:10.1002/mar.21631

Chen, H. (2010). *Advertising and generational identity: A theoretical model.* Conference- American Academy of Advertising CD-ROM–Edition, Minneapolis, MN.

Chen, C. (2021). Effects of the application of WebQuest to technology education on business managements students' critical thinking psychology and operation capability. *Contemporary Educational Technology*, *13*(1), ep290. doi:10.30935/cedtech/9320

Chen, C., Zhang, K. Z., Gong, X., Lee, M. K., & Wang, Y. Y. (2021). Preventing relapse to information technology addiction through weakening reinforcement: A self-regulation perspective. *Information & Management*, *58*(5), 103485. doi:10.1016/j.im.2021.103485

Cheng, C., Lau, Y. C., Chan, L., & Luk, J. W. (2021). Prevalence of social media addiction across 32 nations: Meta-analysis with subgroup analysis of classification schemes and cultural values. *Addictive Behaviors*, *117*, 106845. doi:10.1016/j.addbeh.2021.106845 PMID:33550200

Cheng, C., & Li, A. Y. (2014). Internet Addiction Prevalence and Quality of (Real) Life: A Meta-Analysis of 31 Nations Across Seven World Regions. *Cyberpsychology, Behavior, and Social Networking*, *7*(12), 755–760. doi:10.1089/cyber.2014.0317 PMID:25489876

Chen, H. C., Wang, J. Y., Lin, Y. L., & Yang, S. Y. (2020). Association of internet addiction with family functionality, depression, self-efficacy and self-esteem among early adolescents. *International Journal of Environmental Research and Public Health*, *17*(23), 8820. doi:10.3390/ijerph17238820 PMID:33260988

Chen, J., & Wang, Y. (2021). Social media use for health purposes: Systematic review. *Journal of Medical Internet Research*, *23*(5), e17917. doi:10.2196/17917 PMID:33978589

Chesbrough, H. (2003). *Open innovation: The new imperative for creating and profiting from technology*. Harvard Business Press.

Chikhani, R. (2015, October 31). *The History Of Gaming: An Evolving Community.* TechCrunch. https://techcrunch.com/2015/10/31/the-history-of-gaming-an-evolving-community/

Chiu, S.-I., Lee, J.-Z., & Huang, D.-H. (2004). Video game addiction in children and teenagers in Taiwan. *Cyberpsychology & Behavior*, *7*(5), 571–581. doi:10.1089/cpb.2004.7.571 PMID:15667052

Choi, H. Y. (2022). Working in the Metaverse: Does Telework in a Metaverse Office Have the Potential to Reduce Population Pressure in Megacities? Evidence from Young Adults in Seoul, South Korea. *Sustainability (Basel)*, *14*(3629), 1–17. doi:10.3390u14063629

Chóliz, M. (2010). Mobile phone addiction: A point of issue. *Addiction (Abingdon, England)*, *105*(2), 373–374. doi:10.1111/j.1360-0443.2009.02854.x PMID:20078493

Choo, H., Gentile, D., Sim, T., Li, D. D., Khoo, A., & Liau, A. (2010). Pathological video gaming among Singaporean youth. *Annals of the Academy of Medicine*, *39*(11), 822–829. PMID:21165520

Choo, H., Sim, T., Liau, A. K., Gentile, D. A., & Khoo, A. (2015). Parental influences on pathological symptoms of video-gaming among children and adolescents: A prospective study. *Journal of Child and Family Studies*, *24*(5), 1429–1441. doi:10.100710826-014-9949-9

Chou, C., Condron, L., & Belland, J. C. (2005). A review of the research on Internet addiction. *Educational Psychology Review*, *17*(4), 363–388. doi:10.100710648-005-8138-1

Christakis, D. A. (2010). Internet addiction: A 21st century epidemic? *BMC Medicine*, *8*(1), 61. doi:10.1186/1741-7015-8-61 PMID:20955578

Christakis, D. A. (2019). The Challenges of Defining and Studying "Digital Addiction" in Children. *Journal of the American Medical Association*, *321*(23), 2277. doi:10.1001/jama.2019.4690 PMID:31095260

Christofferson, A., & James, A. O'Brien, A., & Rowland, T. (2022, October 12). *Level Up: The Future of Video Games Is Bright*. Bain & Company. https://www.bain.com/insights/level-up-the-future-of-video-games-is-bright/

Chuang, Y. C. (2006). Massively multiplayer online role-playing game-induced seizures: A neglected health problem in Internet addiction. *Cyberpsychology & Behavior*, *9*(4), 451–456. doi:10.1089/cpb.2006.9.451 PMID:16901249

Chung, S., Lee, J., & Lee, H. K. (2019). Personal factors, internet characteristics, and environmental factors contributing to adolescent internet addiction: A public health perspective. *International Journal of Environmental Research and Public Health*, *16*(23), 4635. doi:10.3390/ijerph16234635 PMID:31766527

Çiftçi, H. (2015). Lise öğrencilerinin siber zorbalık eğilimlerinin facebook tutumu ile ilişkisinin incelenmesi. (Yüksek Lisans Tezi). Marmara Üniversitesi, İstanbul.

Çil, S. (2021). Dijital Aktivizm. In A. Zinderen (Ed.), *Dijital Sosyoloji Çalışmaları* (pp. 93–121). Nobel Yayınevi.

Çınar, Ç., & Mutlu, E. (2019). İnternet Bağımlılığının Benlik Saygısı, Dikkat, Gelişmeleri Kaçırma Korkusu, Yaşam Doyumu ve Kişilik Özellikleri ile İlişkisi. *Bağımlılık Dergisi/Journal of Dependence*, 133-142.

Cioffi, R., Travaglioni, M., Piscitelli, G., Petrillo, A., & Parmentola, A. (2020). Smart manufacturing systems and applied industrial technologies for a sustainable industry: A systematic literature review. *Applied Sciences (Basel, Switzerland)*, *10*(8), 2897. doi:10.3390/app10082897

Çırak, M., & Dost, M. T. (2022). Nomophobia in University Students: The Roles of Digital Addiction, Social Connectedness, and Life Satisfaction. *Turkish Psychological Counseling and Guidance Journal*, *64*, 35–52.

Ciris, V., Baskonus, T., Kartal, T., & Tasdemir, A. (2022). A study on digital game addictions of adolescents in the Covid-19 pandemic. [JESEH]. *Journal of Education in Science, Environment and Health*, *8*(2), 168–186. doi:10.55549/jeseh.01113707

Citko, A., & Owsieniuk, I. (2020). Epidemiology and the consequences of fear of missing out (FoMO). The role of general practitioners in early diagnosis, treatment and prevention of FoMO in teenagers and young adults. *Pediatria i Medycyna Rodzinna, 16*(1), 70–76. doi:10.15557/PiMR.2020.0012

Clement, S., Schauman, O., Graham, T., Maggioni, F., Evans-Lacko, S., Bezborodovs, N., Morgan, C., Rüsch, N., Brown, J. S., & Thornicroft, G. (2015). What is the impact of mental health-related stigma on help-seeking? A systematic review of quantitative and qualitative studies. *Psychological Medicine, 45*(1), 11–27. doi:10.1017/S0033291714000129 PMID:24569086

CNPq, Conselho Nacional de Desenvolvimento Científico e Tecnológico. (n.d.). *Diretório dos Grupos de Pesquisa no Brasil*. DGP. http://dgp.cnpq.br/buscaoperacional/

Çoban, B., & Karayaka, Y. E. (2010). Geleceği Planlamada Stratejik Yönetim ve SWOT Analizi: Kavramsal Yaklaşımlar. *e-Journal of New World Sciences Academy Social Sciences, 5*(4), 342-352.

Cochoy, F., Hagberg, J., McIntyre, M. P., & Sörum, N. (Eds.). (2017). *Digitalising consumption: How devices shape consumer culture*. Taylor & Francis. doi:10.4324/9781315647883

Coco, G. L., Salerno, L., Franchina, V., Latona, A., & Giordano, C. (2020). Examining bi-directionality between fear of missing out and problematic smartphone use. A two-wave panel study among adolescents. *Addictive Behaviors, 106*, 106360. doi:10.1016/j.addbeh.2020.106360 PMID:32135397

Cohen, L., Manion, L., & Morrison, K. (2007). *Research methods in education, 6*. Routledge. doi:10.4324/9780203029053

Cohen, W. M., & Levinthal, D. A. (1990). Absorptive capacity: A new perspective on learning and innovation. *Administrative Science Quarterly, 35*(1), 128–152. doi:10.2307/2393553

Çokluk, N., & Okmen, Y. E. (2020). Sözlü Kültürden Dijital Kültüre Hikaye Anlatımı: Youtuberlar Üzerine Kültürel Bir Çözümleme. *Selçuk İletişim Dergisi*, 1114-1148.

Colleoni, E., Rozza, A., & Arvidsson, A. (2014). Echo Chamber or Public Sphere? Predicting Political Orientation and Measuring Political Homophily in Twitter Using Big Data. *Journal of Communication, 64*(2), 317–332. doi:10.1111/jcom.12084

Collin, P. (2015). *Young citizens and political participation in a digital society: addressing the democratic disconnect*. Springer. doi:10.1057/9781137348838

Collins, C. (2008). Looking to the future: Higher education in the Metaverse. *EDUCAUSE Review, 43*(5), 51–63. https://er.educause.edu/-/media/files/article-downloads/erm0853.pdf

Çömlekçi, M. F., & Başol, O. (2019). Gençlerin Sosyal Medya Kullanım Amaçları ile Sosyal Medya Bağımlılığı. *Celal Bayar Üniversitesi Sosyal Bilimler Dergisi*, 173-188.

*Competitive Multiplayer*. (n.d.). TV Tropes. https://tvtropes.org/pmwiki/pmwiki.php/Main/CompetitiveMultiplayer

Coskun, S., & Muslu, G. K. (2019). Investigation of problematic mobile phones use and fear of missing out (FoMO) level in adolescents. *Community Mental Health Journal, 55*(6), 1004–1014. doi:10.100710597-019-00422-8 PMID:31209716

Costa, M., Matos, A., & Costa, J. (2018). Social Media Disorder Scale–Short Form (SMDS-SF): Estudo de algumas propriedades psicométricas em jovens adultos portugueses. *Revista Portuguesa de Enfermagem de Saúde Mental, 6*, 65–70. doi:10.19131/rpesm.0216

Couldry, N. (2002). *The place of media power: Pilgrims and witnesses of the media age*. Routledge. doi:10.4324/9780203007624

Coutinho, M. (2013). *Saiba mais sobre streaming, a tecnologia que se popularizou na web 2.0.* TechTudo.

Coyne, I., Farley, S., Axtell, C., Sprigg, C., Best, L., & Kwok, O. (2017). Understanding the relationship between experiencing workplace cyberbullying, employee mental strain and job satisfaction: A dysempowerment approach. *International Journal of Human Resource Management, 28*(7), 945–972. doi:10.1080/09585192.2015.1116454

Coyne, S. M., Dyer, W. J., Densley, R., Money, N. M., Day, R. D., & Harper, J. M. (2015). Physiological indicators of pathologic video game use in adolescence. *The Journal of Adolescent Health, 56*(3), 307–313. doi:10.1016/j.jadohealth.2014.10.271 PMID:25586229

Crawford, J. E. (2016). *Cutting the Cord—A Marketing Case: An Examination of Changing TV Viewership.* Atlantic Marketing Journal.

Creeber, G., & Martin, R. (2009). *Digital culture: Understanding new media.* Open University Press.

Creswell, J. W. (2009). *Research design: qualitative, quantitative, and mixed methods approaches* (3rd ed.). Sage Publications.

Creswell, J. W., & Creswell, J. D. (2017). *Research design: Qualitative, quantitative, and mixed methods approaches.* Sage publications.

Creswell, J. W., & Poth, C. N. (2016). *Research Design: Qualitative inquiry and research design: Choosing among five approaches. Sage Publications. (M. Bütün and S.B. Demir, Tr).* Siyasal Publication.

D'cruz, P., & Noronha, E. (2013). Navigating the extended reach: Target experiences of cyberbullying at work. *Information and Organization, 23*(4), 324–343. doi:10.1016/j.infoandorg.2013.09.001

Dahl, D., & Bergmark, K. H. (2020). Persistence in Problematic Internet Use—A Systematic Review and Meta-Analysis. In *Frontiers in Sociology* (Vol. 5). Frontiers Media S.A. doi:10.3389/fsoc.2020.00030

Dahlgren, P. (2011). Young Citizens and Political Participation: Online Media and Civic Cultures. *Taiwan Journal of Democracy, 7*(2).

Dahlman, C., Mealy, S., & Wermelinger, M. (2016). Harnessing the digital economy developing countries. *OECD Development Centre, Working Paper No. 334.* OECD Publishing, Paris.

Dal Fiore, F., Mokhtarian, P. L., & Singer, M. E. (2014). Nomads at last? A set of perspectives on how mobile technology may affect travel. *Journal of Transport Geography, 41*, 97–106. doi:10.1016/j.jtrangeo.2014.08.014

Danaher, J. (2022). Techno-optimism: An Analysis, an Evaluation and a Modest Defence. *Philosophy & Technology, 54*(2), 1–29. doi:10.100713347-022-00550-2

Das, S. (2021). A systematic study of integrated marketing communication and content management system for millennial consumers. In *Innovations in digital branding and content marketing* (pp. 91–112). IGI Global. doi:10.4018/978-1-7998-4420-4.ch005

Davenport, S., Davies, J., & Grimes, C. (1998). Collaborative research programmes: Building trust from difference. *Technovation, 19*(1), 31–40. doi:10.1016/S0166-4972(98)00083-2

Davey, A., Nasser, K., & Davey, S. (2020). Gender differential for smart phone addiction and its predictors among adolescents: Assessing relationship with self-control via sem approach. *Journal of Indian Association for Child and Adolescent Mental Health, 16*(3), 80–101. doi:10.1177/0973134220200305

Davies, T. N., & Hoffman, D. D. (2002). Reality check: Insights from cognitive science. *Topic, 1*(2), 102–105.

Davis, F. D., Bagozzi, R. P., & Warshaw, P. R. (1989). User acceptance of computer technology: A comparison of two theoretical models. *Management Science*, *35*(8), 982–1003. doi:10.1287/mnsc.35.8.982

Davis, R. A. (2001). A cognitive-behavioral model of pathological Internet use. *Computers in Human Behavior*, *17*(2), 187–195. doi:10.1016/S0747-5632(00)00041-8

de Carvalhp, F. P., Ciolfi, L., & Gray, B. (2017). Detailing a Spectrum of Motivational Forces Shaping Nomadic Practices. *Conference on Computer Supported Cooperative Work and Social Computing*, (s. 962-977). 10.1145/2998181.2998313

De Felice, F., Travaglioni, M., & Petrillo, A. (2021). Innovation trajectories for a society 5.0. *Data*, *6*(11), 115. doi:10.3390/data6110115

De Hoyos Guevara, A. J., Terra, D. M., Portes, J. H., da Silva, J. L. A., & Magalhães, K. E. (2020). A Ranking of countries concerning progress towards a society 5.0. *Journal on Innovation and Sustainability RISUS*, *11*(4), 188–199. doi:10.23925/2179-3565.2020v11i4p188-199

De Pablos, P. O. (2021). Preface: Intellectual capital, efficiency and organisational performance: some lessons. *Int. J. Learning and Intellectual Capital*, *18*(3), 219.

Debackere, K., & Veugelers, R. (2005). The role of academic technology transfer organizations in improving industry science. *Research Policy*, *34*(3), 321–342. doi:10.1016/j.respol.2004.12.003

Debord, G. (2020). *The Society of the spectacle* (D. Nicholson-Smith, Trans.). Zone Books. doi:10.2307/j.ctv1453m69

Deci, E. L., & Ryan, R. M. (1985). *Intrinsic motivation and self-determination in human behaviour*. Plenum. doi:10.1007/978-1-4899-2271-7

Deguchi, A., Hirai, C., Matsuoka, H., Nakano, T., Oshima, K., Tai, M., & Tani, S. (2020). What is society 5.0. *Society*, *5*, 1–23.

Deitos, M. L. (2002). *A Gestão da Tecnologia em Pequenas e Médias Empresas*. Edunioeste.

Dell'Osso, B., Hadley, S., Allen, A., Baker, B., Chaplin, W. F., & Hollander, E. (2008). Escitalopram in the treatment of impulsive-compulsive internet usage disorder: An open-label trial followed by a double-blind discontinuation phase. *The Journal of Clinical Psychiatry*, *69*(3), 452–456. doi:10.4088/JCP.v69n0316 PMID:18312057

Deloitte. (2018). *Global Mobile Consumer Survey*. Deloitte. Https://www2.Deloitte.Com/Content/Dam/Deloitte/Us/Documents/Technology-Media-Telecommunications/Us-Tmt-Global-Mobile-Consumer-Survey-Exec-Summary-2018.Pdf

Demir, S. T., & Özcan, A. (2021). Sosyal medya ve linç kültürü: Sanal nedenler gerçek sonuçlar. *İletişim Kuram ve Araştırma Dergisi*, *56*, 1-15. . doi:10.47998/ikad.957544

Demirdöğmez, M., Küçükoğlu, M., & Taş, H. Y. (2017). Possible Effects on Working Life of Generation Z, Our Future [Geleceğimiz Olan Z Kuşağının Çalışma Hayatına Muhtemel Etkileri]. *Uluslararası Toplum Araştırmaları Dergisi*, *7*(13), 1033–1046.

Demirel, F. (2015). What is Moore's law? *Medium.* https://medium.com/turkce/ moore-yasası-moore-s-law-nedir-c31bee8da753

Demir, K. A., Döven, G., & Sezen, B. (2019). Industry 5.0 and human-robot co-working. *Procedia Computer Science*, *158*, 688–695. doi:10.1016/j.procs.2019.09.104

Demirkan, P. (2013). Hacktivizm. In A. R. Keleş (Ed.), *Hack Kültürü ve Hacktivizm: Yeni bir Siyaset Biçimi* (pp. 27–33). Alternatif Bilişim.

Demirkaya, İ., & Koyuncu, E. (2021). Dijital kapitalizm, tüketim kültürü ve Y kuşağının değişen tüketim davranışları [Digital capitalism, consumption culture and changing consumption behaviours of generation Y]. *Intermedia. International Journal (Toronto, Ont.)*, *8*(15), 174–196. doi:10.21645/intermedia.2021.107

Demirkol, G., & Harmancı, P. (2021). *Davranışsal Bağımlılıklar-Bağımlılıktan Bağımsızlığa Doğru*. İksad Publications.

Demir, Y., & Kumcağiz, H. (2019). Üniversite öğrencilerinin sosyal medya bağımlılığının farklı değişkenler açısından incelenmesi. *Türk Psikolojik Danışma ve Rehberlik Dergisi*, *9*(52), 23–42.

Dempsey, A. E., O'Brien, K. D., Tiamiyu, M. F., & Elhai, J. D. (2019). Fear of missing out (FoMO) and rumination mediate relations between social anxiety and problematic Facebook use. *Addictive Behaviors Reports*, *9*, 100150. doi:10.1016/j.abrep.2018.100150 PMID:31193746

Derevensky, J. L., Hayman, V., & Lynette Gilbeau. (2019). Behavioral Addictions. *Pediatric Clinics of North America*, *66*(6), 1163–1182. doi:10.1016/j.pcl.2019.08.008 PMID:31679605

Desai, R. A., Krishnan-Sarin, S., Cavallo, D., & Potenza, M. N. (2010). Video-gaming among high school students: Health correlates, gender differences, and problematic gaming. *Pediatrics*, *126*(6), e1414–e24. doi:10.1542/peds.2009-2706 PMID:21078729

DeVito, A. J. (2007). *The Interpersonal Book*. Pearson Education.

Dev, K., Tsang, K. F., & Rodríguez, J. M. C. (2022). Guest Editorial: The era of industry 5.0—Technologies from no recognisable hm interface to hearty touch personal products. *IEEE Transactions on Industrial Informatics*, *18*(8), 5432–5434. doi:10.1109/TII.2022.3153833

Dewi, H. P. (2021, June). Determination of green marketing strategies through marketing communication in the business world in the society 5.0 era. In *18th International Symposium on Management (INSYMA 2021)* (pp. 181-187). Atlantis Press. 10.2991/aebmr.k.210628.030

Dey, B. L., Yen, D., & Samuel, L. (2020). Digital consumer culture and digital acculturation. *International Journal of Information Management*, *51*, 1–6. doi:10.1016/j.ijinfomgt.2019.102057

Di Chiara, G., & North, R. A. (1992). Neurobiology of opiate abuse. *Trends in Pharmacological Sciences*, *13*, 185–193. doi:10.1016/0165-6147(92)90062-B PMID:1604711

Di Sacco, A., Hardwick, K. A., Blakesley, D., Brancalion, P. H. S., Breman, E., Cecilio Rebola, L., Chomba, S., Dixon, K., Elliott, S., Ruyonga, G., Shaw, K., Smith, P., Smith, R. J., & Antonelli, A. (2021). Ten golden rules for reforestation to optimize carbon sequestration, biodiversity recovery and livelihood benefits. *Global Change Biology*, *27*(7), 1328–1348. doi:10.1111/gcb.15498 PMID:33494123

Dikmen, M. (2021). COVID-19 Pandemisinde Üniversite Öğrencilerinin Depresyon Düzeyleri ile Sosyal Medya Bağımlılıkları Arasındaki İlişki: Bir Yapısal Eşitlik Modeli. *Bağimlik Dergisi*, *22*(1), 20–30. doi:10.51982/bagimli.790750

Dilci, T. (2020). Dijitalim. Aralık, Ankara: Sonçağ Akademi

Dilci, T. (2021). Dijital Diyet Zamanı: Dijital Bağımlılık ve Başa Çıkma, Şubat, Ankara: Sonçağ Akademi.

Dilmaç, J. A. (2020). Dijital ortamda sapkınlık: siber zorbalık, *Turkish Studies - Social, 15*(3), 1087- 1099. . doi:10.29228/TurkishStudies.39895

Dinç, M. (2015). Technology Addiction and Youth. *Journal of Youth Research*, *3*(3), 31–65.

Dinev, T., & Hart, P. (2004). Internet privacy concerns and their antecedents -measurement validity and a regression model. *Behaviour & Information Technology*, *23*(6), 413–422. doi:10.1080/01449290410001715723

Dionisio, J. D. N., III, W. G. B., & Gilbert, R. (2013). 3D Virtual Worlds and the Metaverse: Current Status and Future Possibilities. *ACM Computing Surveys 45*(3), 1-38.

Diotaiuti, P., Girelli, L., Mancone, S., Corrado, S., Valente, G., & Cavicchiolo, E. (2022). Impulsivity and depressive brooding in internet addiction: A study with a sample of Italian adolescents during COVID-19 lockdown. *Frontiers in Psychiatry, 13*, 941313. doi:10.3389/fpsyt.2022.941313 PMID:35898621

Dittmar, H., Long, K., & Bond, R. (2007). When a better self is only a button click away: Associations between materialistic values, emotional and identity-related buying motives, and compulsive buying tendency online. *Journal of Social and Clinical Psychology, 26*(3), 34–361. doi:10.1521/jscp.2007.26.3.334

Dobrota, M., Jeremic, V., & Markovik, A. (2012). A new perspective of the ICT development index. *Information Development, 28*(4), 271–280. doi:10.1177/0266666912446497

Documentary, D. W. (2018). *How cash is becoming a thing of the past.* DW (Deutsche Welle) Documentary. Video (00.28.00 – 00.32.25) https://www.youtube.com/watch?v=GbECT1J9bXg

Dong, H., Yang, F., Lu, X., & Hao, W. (2020). Internet addiction and related psychological factors among children and adolescents in China during the coronavirus disease 2019 (COVID-19) epidemic. *Frontiers in Psychiatry, 11*, 751. doi:10.3389/fpsyt.2020.00751 PMID:32982806

Donovan, D. M., & Marlatt, G. A. (Eds.). (2005). *Assessment of addictive behaviors* (2nd ed.). The Guilford Press.

Douglas, K. M., & Sutton, R. M. (2023). What are conspiracy theories? A definitional approach to their correlates, consequences, and communication. *Annual Review of Psychology, 74*(1), 271–298. doi:10.1146/annurev-psych-032420-031329 PMID:36170672

Dulong de Rosnay, M., & Stalder, F. (2020). Digital commons. *Internet Policy Review, 9*(4). doi:10.14763/2020.4.1530

Dünya Sağlık Örgütü. (2019). *ICD-11 for Mortality and Morbidity Statistics.* WHO. https://icd.who.int/browse11/l-m/en#/http%3a%2f%2fid.who.int%2ficd%2fentity%2f1448597234

Durak, H. Y. (2018). Investigation of nomophobia and smartphone addiction predictors among adolescents in Turkey: Demographic variables and academic performance. *The Social Science Journal, 56*(4), 492–517. doi:10.1016/j.soscij.2018.09.003

Durar, E. (2018). Üniversite öğrencilerinde sosyal medya bağımlılığının depresyon ve sosyal fobi ile ilişkisi. Sağlık Bilimleri Enstitüsü, Freelon, D. and Wells, C. (2020). Disinformation as political communication, (Vol. 37, pp. 145-156). Taylor & Francis.

Durkee, T., Carli, V., Floderus, B., Wasserman, C., Sarchiapone, M., Apter, A., Balazs, J. A., Bobes, J., Brunner, R., Corcoran, P., Cosman, D., Haring, C., Hoven, C. W., Kaess, M., Kahn, J. P., Nemes, B., Postuvan, V., Saiz, P. A., Värnik, P., & Wasserman, D. (2016). Pathological Internet Use and Risk-Behaviors among European Adolescents. *International Journal of Environmental Research and Public Health, 13*(3), 294. doi:10.3390/ijerph13030294 PMID:27005644

Durmaz, A., & Kitapcı, H. (2021). Revisiting customer involved value chains under the conceptual light of industry 5.0. *Proceedings On Engineering, 3*(2), 201–210.

Dursun, O., & Yıldız, F. (2020). Kamu Adaletinin Büyük Veri Aracılığı ile İnşası: Şule Çet Davası Üzerine Bir Twitter Analizi. *Connectist: Istanbul University Journal of Communication Sciences, 58*, 291–328. doi:10.26650/CONNECTIST2020-0009

Dutra, L., Stathopoulou, G., Basden, S. L., Leyro, T. M., Powers, M. B., & Otto, M. W. (2008). A meta-analytic review of psychosocial interventions for substance use disorders. *The American Journal of Psychiatry*, *165*(2), 179–187. doi:10.1176/appi.ajp.2007.06111851 PMID:18198270

Dutta, A. (2001). Telecommunications and economic activity: An analysis of Granger causality. *Journal of Management Information Systems*, *17*(4), 71–95. doi:10.1080/07421222.2001.11045658

Du, Y. S., Jiang, W., & Vance, A. (2010). Longer term effect of randomized, controlled group cognitive behavioural therapy for Internet addiction in adolescent students in Shanghai. *The Australian and New Zealand Journal of Psychiatry*, *44*(2), 129–134. doi:10.3109/00048670903282725 PMID:20113301

Dworak, M., Schierl, T., Bruns, T., & Struder, H. K. (2007). Impact of singular excessive computer game and television exposure on sleep patterns and memory performance of school-aged children. *Pediatrics*, *120*(5), 978–985. doi:10.1542/peds.2007-0476 PMID:17974734

Edler, J., Fier, H., & Grimpe, C. (2011). International scientist mobility and the locus of knowledge and technology transfer. *Research Policy*, *40*(6), 295–309. doi:10.1016/j.respol.2011.03.003

Edler, J., Krahmer, F. M., & Reger, G. (2002). Changes in the strategic management of technology: Results of a global benchmarking study. *R & D Management*, *32*(2), 149–164. doi:10.1111/1467-9310.00247

Edwards, K. (2015). Young citizens and political participation in a digital society. *Information Communication and Society*, *18*(12), 1470–1472. doi:10.1080/1369118X.2015.1062037

Effatpanah, M., Moharrami, M., Damavandi, G. R., Aminikhah, M., Nezhad, M. H., Khatami, F., Arjmand, T., Tarighatnia, H., & Yekaninejad, M. S. (2020). Association of internet addiction with emotional and behavioral characteristics of adolescents. *Iranian Journal of Psychiatry*, *15*(1), 55–56. doi:10.18502/ijps.v15i1.2440 PMID:32377215

Eisner, E. (1998). *The Enlightened Eye: Qualitative Inquiry and the Enhancement of Educational Practice*. Prentice-Simon and Schuster/A Viacom Company Hall.

Ekinci, N. E., Karaali, E., Parçali, B., Suner, A., & Satilmiş, S. E. (2021). COVID-19 Pandemic. *Loneliness and Digital Game Addiction.*, *15*(7), 2175–2179.

Elangovan, U. (2022). *Industry 5.0: The future of the industrial economy*. CRC Press.

Elhai, J. D., Dvorak, R. D., Levine, J. C., & Hall, B. J. (2017). Problematic smartphone use: A conceptual overview and systematic review of relations with anxiety and depression psychopathology. *Journal of Affective Disorders*, *207*, 251–259. doi:10.1016/j.jad.2016.08.030 PMID:27736736

Elhai, J. D., Gallinari, E. F., Rozgonjuk, D., & Yang, H. (2020a). Depression, anxiety and fear of missing out as correlates of social, non-social and problematic smartphone use. *Addictive Behaviors*, *105*, 106335. doi:10.1016/j.addbeh.2020.106335 PMID:32062337

Elhai, J. D., Levine, J. C., Alghraibeh, A. M., Alafnan, A. A., Aldraiweesh, A. A., & Hall, B. J. (2018). Fear of missing out: Testing relationships with negative affectivity, online social engagement, and problematic smartphone use. *Computers in Human Behavior*, *89*, 289–298. doi:10.1016/j.chb.2018.08.020

Elhai, J. D., Levine, J. C., Dvorak, R. D., & Hall, B. J. (2016). Fear of missing out, need for touch, anxiety and depression are related to problematic smartphone use. *Computers in Human Behavior*, *63*, 509–516. doi:10.1016/j.chb.2016.05.079

Elhai, J. D., Yang, H., Fang, J., Bai, X., & Hall, B. J. (2020b). Depression and anxiety symptoms are related to problematic smartphone use severity in Chinese young adults: Fear of missing out as a mediator. *Addictive Behaviors*, *101*, 105962. doi:10.1016/j.addbeh.2019.04.020 PMID:31030950

Elhai, J. D., Yang, H., & Montag, C. (2021). Fear of missing out (FOMO): Overview, theoretical underpinnings, and literature review on relations with severity of negative affectivity and problematic technology use. *The British Journal of Psychiatry*, *43*(2), 203–209. doi:10.1590/1516-4446-2020-0870 PMID:32401865

Elliott, L., Ream, G., & McGinsky, E. (2012). Video Game Addiction: User Perspectives. In Critical Perspectives on Addiction (pp. 225-243).

Ellis, P. D. (2010). *The essential guide to effect sizes: Statistical power, meta-analysis, and the interpretation of research results*. Cambridge university press. doi:10.1017/CBO9780511761676

ElMaraghy, H., Monostori, L., Schuh, G., & ElMaraghy, W. (2021). Evolution and future of manufacturing systems. *CIRP Annals*, *70*(2), 635–658. doi:10.1016/j.cirp.2021.05.008

Elsrud, T. (2006). Gender Creation in Travelling, or the Art of Transforming an Adventuress. Tourism, Consumption & Resperesentation. In K. Meethan, A. Anderson, & S. Miles (Eds.), (pp. 178–195). CABI Publisher.

Ensari, H., Ceylan, M. E., Kilinç, E., & Kenar, J. (2004). Türk'ye'deki Ruh Hastalıkları Hastanelerindeki Psikofarmakolojik Tedavilerin Kalite Yönünden Değerlendirilmesi. *Klinik Psikofarmakoloji Bulteni*, *14*(2), 68–78.

Erdoğan, İ., & Alemdar, K. (2005). *Popüler Kültür ve İletişim (2. edition)*. Erk Yayınları.

Erdoğan, İ., & Alemdar, K. (2005). *Popüler Kültür ve İletişim*. Pozitif Matbaacılık.

Ergeç, N. E., & Zateri, İ. (2020). Toplumsal cinsiyet ve sosyal ağların şiddeti çoğaltan etkisi. *Çukurova Üniversitesi Sosyal Bilimler Enstitüsü Dergisi*, *29*(1), 102-117.

Eriş, U. (2009). *Türkiye'de Kırıcı (Hacker) Kültürü*. Yayınlanmamış Doktora Tezi, Anadolu Üniversitesi Sosyal Bilimler Enstitüsü.

Ersöz Karakulakoğlu, S. (2020). *Dijital Toplum: Kavram, Kuram ve Yöntem*. Ankara: Nobel yayınevi.

Ertemel, A. V., & Aydın, G. (2018). Dijital Ekonomide Teknoloji Bağımlılığı ve Çözüm Önerileri. *Addicta-The Turkish Journal on Addictions*, *5*(4), 665–690. doi:10.15805/addicta.2018.5.4.0038

Eryilmaz, S., & Çukurluöz, Ö. (2018). Lise öğrencilerinin dijital bağimliliklarinin incelenmesi: Ankara ili, Çankaya ilçesi örneği. *Electronic Journal of Social Sciences*, *17*(67), 889–912.

Esen, E., & Siyez, D. M. (2011). An Investigation of Psycho-Social Variables in Predicting Internet Addiction Among Adolescents. *Türk Psikolojik Danışma ve Rehberlik Dergisi*, *4*(36), 127–138.

Eshet-alkalai, Y. (2004). Digital Literacy: A Conceptual Framework for Survival Skills in the Digital Era. *Journal of Educational Multimedia and Hypermedia*, *13*(1), 93–106.

Eşitti, Ş. (2015). Bilgi çağında problemli internet kullanımı ve enformasyon obezitesi: Problemli internet kullanımı ölçeğinin üniversite öğrencilerine uygulanması. *İstanbul Üniversitesi İletişim Fakültesi Dergisi*, (49), 75-97.

Etzkowitz, H. (2003). Innovation in innovation: The triple helix of university-industry-government relations. *Social Sciences Information. Information Sur les Sciences Sociales*, *42*(3), 293–337. doi:10.1177/05390184030423002

European Commission. (2022). *Research and Innovation*. EC. https://research-and-innovation.ec.europa.eu/research-area/industrial-research-and-innovation/industry-50_en

European Economic and Social Committee. (2017). *The future evolution of civil society in the European Union by 2030*. EU Press.

Evangelista, R., Guerrieri, P., & Meliciani, V. (2014). The economic impact of digital technologies in Europe. *Economics of Innovation and New Technology*, *23*(8), 802–824. doi:10.1080/10438599.2014.918438

Evren, C., Dalbudak, E., Topcu, M., Kutlu, N., Evren, B., & Pontes, H. M. (2018). Psychometric validation of the Turkish nine-item internet gaming disorder scale–short form (IGDS9-SF). *Psychiatry Research*, *265*, 349–354. doi:10.1016/j.psychres.2018.05.002 PMID:29793049

*Explained: What is cross-platform gaming and how is it useful for gamers*. (2022, March 3). Times of India. https://timesofindia.indiatimes.com/gadgets-news/explained-what-is-cross-platform-gaming-and-how-is-it-useful-for-gamers/articleshow/89974015.cms

Falgoust, G., Winterlind, E., Moon, P., Parker, A., Zinzow, H., & Chalil Madathil, K. (2022). Applying the uses and gratifications theory to identify motivational factors behind young adult's participation in viral social media challenges on TikTok. *Human Factors in Healthcare*, *2*, 2. doi:10.1016/j.hfh.2022.100014

Fam, J. Y. (2018). Prevalence of internet gaming disorder in adolescents: A meta-analysis across three decades. *Scandinavian Journal of Psychology*, *59*(5), 524–531. doi:10.1111jop.12459 PMID:30004118

Fang, J., Wang, X., Wen, Z., & Zhou, J. (2020). Fear of missing out and problematic social media use as mediators between emotional support from social media and phubbing behavior. *Addictive Behaviors*, *107*, 106430. doi:10.1016/j.addbeh.2020.106430 PMID:32289745

Fanibhare, V., Sarkar, N. I., & Al-Anbuky, A. (2021). A survey of the tactile Internet: Design issues and challenges, applications, and future directions. *Electronics (Basel)*, *10*(17), 2171. doi:10.3390/electronics10172171

Farhadi, M., Ismail, R., & Fooladi, M. (2012). Information and communication technology use and economic growth. *PLoS One*, *7*(11), e48903. doi:10.1371/journal.pone.0048903 PMID:23152817

Faria, N. (2020). *A Indústria do Entretenimento e a expansão do streaming em meio a Pandemia*. Centro Universitário do Sul de Minas-UIS/MG.

Farley, S., Coyne, I., Axtell, C., & Sprigg, C. (2016). Design, development, and validation of a workplace cyberbullying measure, the WCM. *Work and Stress*, *30*(4), 293–317. doi:10.1080/02678373.2016.1255998

Farley, S., Coyne, I., & D'Cruz, P. (2021). Cyberbullying at Work: Understanding the Influence of Technology. In P. D'Cruz, E. Noronha, G. Notelaers, & C. Rayner (Eds.), *Concepts, Approaches and Methods. Handbooks of Workplace Bullying, Emotional Abuse and Harassment* (Vol. 1). Springer., doi:10.1007/978-981-13-0134-6_8

Farley, S., Coyne, I., Sprigg, C., Axtell, C., & Subramanian, G. (2015). Exploring the impact of workplace cyberbullying on trainee doctors. *Medical Education*, *49*(4), 436–443. doi:10.1111/medu.12666 PMID:25800304

Faustino, P. (2021). *TikTok Marketing - O guia completo para ter sucesso na rede social do momento.*

Fei-Yue, F. (2004). Parallel system methods for management and control of complex systems. *Kongzhi yu Juece. Control and Decision*, *19*(5), 485–489.

Felizardo, A. (2021). *Os vídeos virais e trends como estratégias de marketing de influência para as marcas de moda e beleza na rede social TikTok*. Universidade Beira Interior.

Feng, Y., Ma, Y., & Zhong, Q. (2019). The relationship between adolescents' stress and internet addiction: A mediated-moderation model. *Frontiers in Psychology*, *10*, 2248. doi:10.3389/fpsyg.2019.02248 PMID:31636590

Ferguson, C. J. (2011). Video games and youth violence: A prospective analysis in adolescents. *Journal of Youth and Adolescence*, *40*(4), 377–391. doi:10.100710964-010-9610-x PMID:21161351

Fernandes, B., Biswas, U. N., Mansukhani, R. T., Casarín, A. V., & Essau, C. A. (2020). The impact of COVID-19 lockdown on internet use and escapism in adolescents. *Revista de psicología clínica con niños y adolescentes, 7*(3), 59-65.

Ferreira, B. (2022). *TikTok Marketing em 2022: O Papel das Marcas no TikTok.* Bernardo Ferreira Marketing. https://bernardoferreiramarketing.pt/tiktok-marketing/

Ferreira, C. M., & Serpa, S. (2018). Society 5.0 and social development. *Management and Organizational Studies, 5*(4), 26–31. doi:10.5430/mos.v5n4p26

Festinger, L. (1954). A theory of social comparison processes. *Human Relations, 7*(2), 117–140. doi:10.1177/001872675400700202

Festl, R., Scharkow, M., & Quandt, T. (2013). Problematic computer game use among adolescents, younger and older adults. *Addiction (Abingdon, England), 108*(3), 592–599. doi:10.1111/add.12016 PMID:23078146

Fitzpatrick, K. M., Harris, C., & Drawve, G. (2020). How bad is it? Suicidality in the middle of the COVID-19 pandemic. *Suicide & Life-Threatening Behavior, 50*(6), 1241–1249. doi:10.1111ltb.12655 PMID:32589799

Flavian, C., & Gurrea, R. (2016). Dijital gazeteleri seçmek- okuyucu amaçlarının ve kullanıcı deneyimlerinin etkisi [Choosing digital newspapers -the impact of reader intentions and user experiences] In H. Hülür & C. Yaşın (Eds.), Yeni medya kullanıcının yükselişi [The rise of the new media user] (pp. 417-438). Ütopya Publishing.

Floridi, L. (Ed.). (2015). *The Onlife Manifesto Being Human in a Hyperconnected Era.* Springer Open Press.

Foddy, B., & Savulescu, J. (2006). Addiction and autonomy: Can addicted people consent to the prescription of their drug of addiction? *Bioethics, 20*(1), 1–15. doi:10.1111/j.1467-8519.2006.00470.x PMID:16680876

Fontana, R., Geuna, A., & Matt, M. (2006). Factors affecting university-industry R&D projects. *Research Policy, 35*(2), 309–323. doi:10.1016/j.respol.2005.12.001

Fraillon, J., Ainley, J., Schulz, W., Friedman, T., & Gebhardt, E. (2014). Preparing for Life in a Digital Age. *Preparing for Life in a Digital Age.*

Frank, A. G., Dalenogare, L. S., & Ayala, N. F. (2019). Industry 4.0 technologies: Implementation patterns in manufacturing companies. *International Journal of Production Economics, 210*, 15–26. doi:10.1016/j.ijpe.2019.01.004

Frasca, G. (2001). Rethinking Agency and İmmersion: Video Games as A Means of Consciousness-Raising. *Digital Creativity (Exeter), 12*(3), 167–174. doi:10.1076/digc.12.3.167.3225

Fuchs, C. (2012). Google capitalism. *Journal for A Global Sustainable. TripleC, 10*(1), 42–48. doi:10.31269/triplec.v10i1.304

Fuchs, C. (2014). *Social media: a critical introduction.* Sage Publications. doi:10.4135/9781446270066

Fuentes, M., & Frank, A. G. (1990). *"Sivil hareketler üzerine on tez", Birikim Dergisi, 16.* Ağustos.

Fujii, T., Guo, T., & Kamoshida, A. (2018, August). A consideration of service strategy of Japanese electric manufacturers to realise super smart society (Society 5.0). In *International Conference on Knowledge Management in Organisations* (pp. 634-645). Springer, Cham.

Fukuda, K. (2020). Science, technology and innovation ecosystem transformation toward society 5.0. *International Journal of Production Economics, 220*, 107460. doi:10.1016/j.ijpe.2019.07.033

Fukuyama, M. (2018). Society 5.0: Aiming for a new human-centred society. *Japan Spotlight, 27*(5), 47–50.

Gambaro, M. (2012). Some economics of new media content production and consumption, and strategic ımplication for media companies. In M. Friedrichsen & W. Mühl-Benninghaus (Eds.), *Handbook of social media management* (pp. 49–58). Springer Publications. doi:10.1007/978-3-642-28897-5_4

Gartner. (2020). *Gartner Glossary*. Gartner. https://www.gartner.com/en/informationtechnology/

Geçer, A. K., & Gümüş, A. E. (2010). Prediction of public and private university students' communication apprehension with lecturers. *Procedia: Social and Behavioral Sciences*, *2*(2), 3008–3014. doi:10.1016/j.sbspro.2010.03.456

Gencer, B. (2012). Medeniyet savaşında teknoloji. *Birey ve Toplum*, *2*(4), 7–26.

Geng, J., Lei, L., Ouyang, M., Nie, J., & Wang, P. (2021). The influence of perceived parental phubbing on adolescents' problematic smartphone use: A two-wave multiple mediation model. *Addictive Behaviors*, *121*, 106995. doi:10.1016/j.addbeh.2021.106995 PMID:34090204

Gentile, D. (2009). Pathological video-game use among youth ages 8 to 18: A national study. *Psychological Science*, *20*(5), 594–602. doi:10.1111/j.1467-9280.2009.02340.x PMID:19476590

Gentile, D. A., Bailey, K., Bavelier, D., Brockmyer, J. F., Cash, H., Coyne, S. M., Doan, A., Grant, D. S., Green, C. S., Griffiths, M., Markle, T., Petry, N. M., Prot, S., Rae, C. D., Rehbein, F., Rich, M., Sullivan, D., Woolley, E., & Young, K. (2017). Internet Gaming Disorder in Children and Adolescents. *Pediatrics*, *140*(Suppl 2), S81–S85. doi:10.1542/peds.2016-1758H PMID:29093038

Gentile, D. A., Choo, H., Liau, A., Sim, T., Li, D., Fung, D., & Khoo, A. (2011). Pathological video game use among youths: A two-year longitudinal study. *Pediatrics*, *127*(2), e319–e29. doi:10.1542/peds.2010-1353 PMID:21242221

Gentile, D. A., & Gentile, J. R. (2008). Violent video games as exemplary teachers: A conceptual analysis. *Journal of Youth and Adolescence*, *37*(2), 127–141. doi:10.100710964-007-9206-2

Gentile, D. A., Reimer, R. A., Nathanson, A. I., Walsh, D. A., & Eisenmann, J. C. (2014). Protective effects of parental monitoring of children's media use: A prospective study. *JAMA Pediatrics*, *168*(5), 479–484. doi:10.1001/jamapediatrics.2014.146 PMID:24686493

Gentile, D. A., Swing, E. L., Guan Lim, C., & Khoo, A. (2012). Video game playing, attention problems, and impulsiveness: Evidence of bidirectional causality. *Psychology of Popular Media Culture*, *1*(1), 62–70. doi:10.1037/a0026969

George, J. J., & Leidner, D. E. (2019). From clicktivism to hacktivism: Understanding digital activism. *Information and Organization*, *29*(3), 100249. doi:10.1016/j.infoandorg.2019.04.001

Gere, C. (2019). *Dijital Kültür*, (Trans. Aydoğdu Akın). İstanbul: Salon yayınevi.

Gere, C. (2008). *Dijital kültür* [Digital culture]. (A. Akın & N. Pembecioğlu, Trans.). Salon Publishing. doi:10.1177/1470412903002003014

Gere, C. (2019). *Community without community in digital culture*. Palgrave Macmillan Publications. doi:10.1057/9781137026675_12

Gerpott, T. J., & Ahmadi, N. (2015). Composite indices for the evaluation of a country's information technology development level: Extension of the IDI of the ITU. *Technological Forecasting and Social Change*, *98*(1), 174–185. doi:10.1016/j.techfore.2015.03.012

Ghobakhloo, M., Iranmanesh, M., Mubarak, M. F., Mubarık, M., Rejeb, A., & Nilashi, M. (2022). Identifying industry 5.0 contributions to sustainable development: A strategy roadmap for delivering sustainability values. *Sustainable Production and Consumption*, *33*, 716–737. doi:10.1016/j.spc.2022.08.003

Gil, A. C. (2007). *Como elaborar projetos de pesquisa*. Atlas.

Gilanlıoğlu, E., & Öze, N. (2020). Dijital tüketim kültürünün hegemonyası ve serbest zaman [Manipulation of digital consumption culture hegemony and leisure time]. *Yeni Medya Elektronik Dergisi, 4*(3), 185–202. doi:10.17932/IAU.EJNM.25480200.2020/ejnm_v4i3004

Gill, S. S., Tuli, S., Xu, M., Singh, I., Singh, K. V., Lindsay, D., Tuli, S., Smirnova, D., Singh, M., Jain, U., Pervaiz, H., Sehgal, B., Kaila, S. S., Misra, S., Aslanpour, M. S., Mehta, H., Stankovski, V., & Garraghan, P. (2019). Transformative effects of IoT, blockchain and artificial intelligence on cloud computing: Evolution, vision, trends and open challenges. *Internet of Things, 8*, 100118. doi:10.1016/j.iot.2019.100118

Gilman, N. (2018). Modernization theory never dies. *History of Political Economy, 50*(S1), 133–151. doi:10.1215/00182702-7033896

Gladden, M. E. (2019). Who will be the members of Society 5.0? Towards an anthropology of technologically posthumanized future societies. *Social Sciences (Basel, Switzerland), 8*(5), 148. doi:10.3390ocsci8050148

Glenn, C. L. (2015). Activism or "Slacktivism?": Digital media and organizing for social change. *Communication Teacher, 29*(2), 81–85. doi:10.1080/17404622.2014.1003310

Goggin, G., & Hjorth, L. (2014). *The routledge companion to mobile media*. Routledge Publications., doi:10.4324/9780203434833

Gökler, M. E., Aydin, R., Ünal, E., & Metintaş, S. (2016). Determining validity and reliability of Turkish version of fear of missing out scale. *Anadolu Psikiyatri Dergisi, 17*(1), 53–59. doi:10.5455/apd.195843

Goldsmith, J., & Wu, T. (2006). *Who Controls the Internet?: Illusions of a Borderless World,* 175. Faculty Books. https://scholarship.law.columbia.edu/books/175

Goleman, D. (2013). *Odak, Filiz Deniztekin*. Varlık Yayınları.

Gönen, M. (2015). *Akdeniz Üniversitesi Beden Eğitimi ve Spor Yüksekokulu öğrencilerinin iletişim beceri düzeyleri ile atılganlık düzeylerinin incelenmesi.*

Gönen, S., Yılmaz, E. N., Şanoğlu, S., Karacayılmaz, G., & Özbirinci, Ö. (2021). Endüstri 4.0'ın gelişim sürecinde unutulan bileşen: Siber güvenlik. *Düzce Üniversitesi Bilim ve Teknoloji Dergisi, 9*(4), 1142–1158. doi:10.29130/dubited.905340

Goode, L. (2015). Anonymous and the political ethos of hacktivism. *Popular Communication, 13*(1), 74–86. doi:10.1080/15405702.2014.978000

Gowen, K., Deschaine, M., Gruttadara, D., & Markey, D. (2012). Young adults with mental health conditions and social networking websites: Seeking tools to build community. *Psychiatric Rehabilitation Journal, 35*(3), 245–250. doi:10.2975/35.3.2012.245.250 PMID:22246123

Grabowska, S., Saniuk, S., & Gajdzik, B. (2022). Industry 5.0: Improving humanisation and sustainability of Industry 4.0. *Scientometrics, 127*(6), 1–28. doi:10.100711192-022-04370-1 PMID:35502439

Grandinetti, R., Bettiol, M., & Di Maria, E. (2022). Contexts of consumption and their evolution in the digital age: Beyond the service-dominant logic. *Administrative Sciences, 12*(4), 121. doi:10.3390/admsci12040121

Granic, I., Lobel, A., & Engels, R. (2014). The benefits of playing video games. *The American Psychologist, 69*(1), 66–78. doi:10.1037/a0034857 PMID:24295515

Grant. (2021, July 6). Influencers React to Norway Photo Edit Law: "Welcome Honesty" or a "Shortcut"? *BBC News*. https://www.bbc.com/news/newsbeat-57721080

Grant, J. E., Kim, S. W., & Odlaug, B. L. (2009). A double-blind, placebo-controlled study of the opiate antagonist, naltrexone, in the treatment of kleptomania. *Biological Psychiatry*, *65*(7), 600–606. doi:10.1016/j.biopsych.2008.11.022 PMID:19217077

Grant, J. E., Potenza, M. N., Weinstein, A., & Gorelick, D. A. (2010). Introduction to behavioral addictions. *The American Journal of Drug and Alcohol Abuse*, *36*(5), 233–241. doi:10.3109/00952990.2010.491884 PMID:20560821

Green, C. S., & Bavelier, D. (2012). Learning, attentional control, and action video games. *Current Biology*, *22*(6), R197–R206. doi:10.1016/j.cub.2012.02.012 PMID:22440805

Green, P. (2020). *Disruptions of Self, Place and Mobility: Digital Nomads in Chiang* Mai, Thailand. *Mobilities*, *15*(3), 431–445. doi:10.1080/17450101.2020.1723253

Green, S. C., & Bavelier, D. (2003). Action Video Game Modifies Visual Selective Attention. *Nature*, *423*(6939), 534–537. doi:10.1038/nature01647 PMID:12774121

Greenwald, M. (2021). Audience, algorithm and virality: Why TikTok will continue to shape culture in 2021. *Forbes*.

Grewal, D., Hulland, J., Kopalle, P. K., & Karahanna, E. (2020). The future of technology and marketing: A multidisciplinary perspective. *Journal of the Academy of Marketing Science*, *48*(1), 1–8. doi:10.100711747-019-00711-4

Grieve, R., Indian, M., Witteveen, K., Tolan, G. A., & Marrington, J. (2013). Face-to-face or Facebook: Can social connectedness be derived online? *Computers in Human Behavior*, *29*(3), 604–609. doi:10.1016/j.chb.2012.11.017

Griffiths, M. D. (1995). Technological addictions. *Clinical Psychology Forum, 76*, 14-19.

Griffiths, M., Kuss, D., & King, D. (2012). Video game addiction: Past, present and future. *Current Psychiatry Reviews*, *8*(4), 308–318. doi:10.2174/157340012803520414

Griffiths, M. (1996). Behavioural addiction: An issue for everybody? *Employee Counselling Today: The Journal of Workplace Learning*, *8*(3), 19–25. doi:10.1108/13665629610116872

Griffiths, M. (1998). Internet addiction: Does it really exist? In J. Gackenbach (Ed.), *Psychology and the Internet: Intrapersonal, Interpersonal, and Transpersonal Implications* (pp. 61–75). Academic Press.

Griffiths, M. (2000). Does internet and computer "addiction" exist? Some case study evidence. *Cyberpsychology & Behavior*, *3*(2), 211–218. doi:10.1089/109493100316067

Griffiths, M. (2005). A 'components' model of addiction within a biopsychosocial framework. *Journal of Substance Use*, *10*(4), 191–197. doi:10.1080/14659890500114359

Griffiths, M. D. (2000). Internet addiction—Time to be taken seriously? *Addiction Research*, *8*(5), 413–418. doi:10.3109/16066350009005587

Griffiths, M. D. (2008). *Internet and Video-Game Addiction. Adolescent Addiction: Epidemiology, Assessment and Treatment*. Academic Press.

Griffiths, M. D. (2008). Video game addiction: Further thoughts and observations. *International Journal of Mental Health and Addiction*, *6*(2), 182–185. doi:10.100711469-007-9128-y

Griffiths, M. D., & Davies, M. N. O. (2005). Videogame addiction: Does it exist? In J. Goldstein & J. Raessens (Eds.), *Handbook of Computer Game Studies* (pp. 359–368). MIT Press.

Griffiths, M. D., & Szabo, A. (2014). Is excessive online usage a function of medium or activity? An empirical pilot study. *Journal of Behavioral Addictions*, *3*(1), 74–77. doi:10.1556/JBA.2.2013.016 PMID:25215216

Grover, V., Tseng, S. H., & Pu, W. (2022). A theoretical perspective on organizational culture and digitalization. *Information & Management*, *59*(4), 1–13. doi:10.1016/j.im.2022.103639

Grubbs, J. B., Hoagland, K. C., Lee, B. N., Grant, J. T., Davison, P., Reid, R. C., & Kraus, S. W. (2020). Sexual addiction 25 years on: A systematic and methodological review of empirical literature and an agenda for future research. *Clinical Psychology Review*, *82*, 101925. doi:10.1016/j.cpr.2020.101925 PMID:33038740

Güdüm, S. (2016). Sanal yaşamlar ve bilgisayar oyunlarında pazarlanan şiddet. *Journal of International Social Research*, *9*(42), 1986. doi:10.17719/jisr.20164216306

Guerada, K. (2021). Impact of online games on children's mental health. *Journal La Medihealthico*, *2*(1), 13–19. doi:10.37899/journallamedihealtico.v2i1.281

Guide, S. (n.d.). *Gaming Trends 2023 - Top 10 Trends that Will Rule Industry*. EDIIIE. https://www.ediiie.com/blog/gaming-trends/

Gülbetekin, E., Güven, E., & Tuncel, O. (2021). Adolesanların Dijital Oyun Bağımlılığı ile Fiziksel Aktivite Tutum ve Davranışlarını Etkileyen Faktörler. *Bağimlik Dergisi*, *22*(2), 148–160. doi:10.51982/bagimli.866578

Gunay, D., & Calık, A. (2019, April). On concepts of innovation, invention, technology, and science. *Journal of University Research*, *2*(1), 1–11.

Günaydin, H. D. (2021). Personality Traits, Gender, Frequency of Internet Use as Predictors of Turkish Teenagers' Internet Addiction. *Turkish Online Journal of Educational Technology-TOJET*, *20*(4), 44–52.

Günüç, S. & ve Kayri, M. (2010). *Türkiye'de internet bağımlılık profili ve internet bağımlılık ölçeğinin geliştirilmesi: Geçerlik güvenirlik çalışması.* Hacettepe Üniversitesi Eğitim Fakültesi Dergisi, (39), 220-232. https://dergipark.org.tr/tr/pub/hunefd/issue/7799/102177 adresinden erişilmiştir.

Günüç, S. (2012). *Sanal toplumda birlikte yaşama kültürü.* Anadolu Üniversitesi Paper. https://www. researchgate. net/publication/299431040

Günüç, S. (2015). Relationships and associations between video game and internet addictions: Is tolerance a symptom seen in all conditions? *Computers in Human Behavior*, *49*, 517–525. doi:10.1016/j.chb.2015.03.063

Gunuc, S., & Dogan, A. (2013). The relationships between Turkish adolescents' Internet addiction, their perceived social support and family activities. *Computers in Human Behavior*, *29*(6), 2197–2207. doi:10.1016/j.chb.2013.04.011

Gür Omay, E. G. (2022). Dijitalleşme ekseninde tüketim kültürü. [Consumption culture on the axis of digitalization] In K. Çankaya (Ed.), *Medya ve tüketim I* [Media and consumption I]. (pp. 31–47). Eğitim Publishing.

Gürcan, A., & Özhan, S., & ve Uslu, R. (2008). Dijital oyunlar ve çocuklar üzerindeki etkileri. Ankara: T.C. Başbakanlık Aile ve Sosyal Araştırmalar Genel Müdürlüğü

Gürel, E., & Nazlı, A. (2019). Dijital Aktivizm: Change. org Kampanyaları Üzerine Bir Analiz. *Anadolu University Journal of Social Sciences*, *19*(4), 187–206. doi:10.18037/ausbd.668642

Gutsche, J. (2018). Ai & the super future – future festival. *Trend Hunter.com*. https://www.youtube.com/watch?v=OzBJigTfGeE

Guy, J. S. (2019). Digital technology, digital culture and the metric/nonmetric distinction. *Technological Forecasting and Social Change*, *145*, 55–61. doi:10.1016/j.techfore.2019.05.005

Habermas, J. (2003). *The Future of Human Nature*. Polity Press.

Habertürk. (2018, 21 April). 'Diriliş Ertuğrul' Dizisini Kılıç ve Baltayla İzlerken Adeta Kendilerinden Geçtiler. [Video]. *Habertürk.* https://www.haberturk.com/video/eglence/izle/dirilis-ertugrul-dizisini-kilic-ve-baltayla-izlerken-adeta-kendilerinden-gectiler/477066

Habibi, F., & Zabardast, M. A. (2020). Digitalization, education and economic growth: A comparative analysis of Middle East and OECD countries. *Technology in Society*, *63*(101370), 101370. doi:10.1016/j.techsoc.2020.101370

Haddon, L., & Vincent, J. (2014). *European children and their carers' understanding of use, risks and safety issues relating to convergent mobile media*. Educatt.

Haidi, H. (2023). A Digital Ethnographic Account of a Digital Islamic Society During COVID-19: An Islamic Governance Perspective. In M. Anshari, A. Razzaq, M. Fithriyah, & A. Kamal (Eds.), *Digital Psychology's Impact on Business and Society* (pp. 150–178). IGI Global. doi:10.4018/978-1-6684-6108-2.ch007

Halbrook, Y. J., O'Donnell, A. T., & Msetfi, R. M. (2019). When and How Video Games Can Be Good: A Review of the Positive Effects of Video Games on Well-Being. *Perspectives on Psychological Science*, *14*(6), 1096–1104. doi:10.1177/1745691619863807 PMID:31672105

Hale, L., & Guan, S. (2015). Screen time and sleep among school-aged children and adolescents: A systematic literature review. *Sleep Medicine Reviews*, *21*, 50–58. doi:10.1016/j.smrv.2014.07.007 PMID:25193149

Hall, G. E., & Hord, S. M. (1987). *Change in schools: Facilitating the process*. Suny Press.

Hall, G. E., Loucks, S. F., Rutherford, W. L., & Newlove, B. W. (1975). Levels of use of the innovation: A framework for analyzing innovation adoption. *Journal of Teacher Education*, *26*(1), 52–56. doi:10.1177/002248717502600114

Halupka, M. (2018). The legitimisation of clicktivism. *Australian Journal of Political Science*, *53*(1), 130–141. doi:10.1080/10361146.2017.1416586

Hamissi, J., Babaie, M., Hosseini, M., & Babaie, F. (2013). The relationship between emotional intelligence and technology addiction among university students. *International Journal of Collaborative Research on Internal Medicine & Public Health*, *5*(5), 310–319.

Hamutoglu, N. B., Topal, M., & Gezgin, D. M. (2020). Investigating Direct and Indirect Effects of Social Media Addiction, Social Media Usage and Personality Traits on FOMO. *International Journal of Progressive Education*, *16*(2), 248–261. doi:10.29329/ijpe.2020.241.17

Han, D.H., Hwang, J.W., & Renshaw, P.F. (2011). *Bupropion sustained release treatment decreases craving for video games and cue-induced brain activity in patients with Internet video game addiction.*

Han, C., Wang, H., Hahn, A., Fisher, C., Kandrik, M., Fasolt, V., Morrison, D., Lee, A., Debruine, L., & Jones, B. (2017). Cultural differences in preferences for facial coloration. *Evolution and Human Behavior*, *39*(2), 154–159. doi:10.1016/j.evolhumbehav.2017.11.005

Han, D. H., Hwang, J. W., & Renshaw, P. F. (2011). Bupropion sustained release treatment decreases craving for video games and cue-induced brain activity in patients with Internet video game addiction. *Experimental and Clinical Psychopharmacology*, *18*(4), 297–304. doi:10.1037/a0020023 PMID:20695685

Han, D. H., Kim, S. M., Lee, Y. S., & Renshaw, P. F. (2012). The effect of family therapy on the changes in the severity of on-line game play and brain activity in adolescents with on-line game addiction. *Psychiatry Research: Neuroimaging*, *202*(2), 126–131. doi:10.1016/j.pscychresns.2012.02.011 PMID:22698763

Han, D. H., Lee, Y. S., Na, C., Ahn, J. Y., Chung, U. S., Daniels, M. A., Haws, C. A., & Renshaw, P. F. (2009). The effect of methylphenidate on Internet video game play in children with attention-deficit/hyperactivity disorder. *Comprehensive Psychiatry*, *50*(3), 251–256. doi:10.1016/j.comppsych.2008.08.011 PMID:19374970

Han, D. H., & Renshaw, P. F. (2012). Bupropion in the treatment of problematic online game play in patients with major depressive disorder. *Journal of Psychopharmacology (Oxford, England)*, *26*(5), 689–696. doi:10.1177/0269881111400647 PMID:21447539

Hannonen, O. (2020). In search of a digital nomad: Defining the phenomenon. *Information Technology & Tourism*, *22*(3), 335–353. doi:10.100740558-020-00177-z

Hansen, D., Shneiderman, B., Smith, M., & Himelboim, I. (2020). Social media: New technologies of collaboration. *Analyzing Social Media Networks with Node, XL*, 11–29. doi:10.1016/B978-0-12-817756-3.00002-9

Harari, J. N. (2023). Harariden Insanligin Gelecegine Dair 5 Ongoru. *Digital Age.* https://digitalage.com.tr/harariden-insanligin-gelecegine-dair-5-ongoru/

Hart, A. (2015). Living And Working İn Paradise: The Rise Of The 'Digital Nomad'. *The Telegraph.* http://www.telegraph.co.uk/news/features/11597145/Living-and-working-in-paradise the-rise-of-the-digital-nomad.html

Harvey, D. (1999). Postmodernliğin durumu. (çev.Sungur Savran). İstanbul: Metis Yayınları.

Harvey, D. (2020). The Condition of Postmodernity. In *The New Social Theory Reader* (pp. 235–242). Routledge. doi:10.4324/9781003060963-38

Hasdemir, T. A., & Coşkun, M. K. (2008). Kamusal Alan Ve Toplumsal Hareketler. *Ankara Üniversitesi SBF Dergisi*, *63*(01), 121–149. doi:10.1501/SBFder_0000002055

Hawi, N. S., & Samaha, M. (2017). The Relations Among Social Media Addiction, Self-Esteem, and Life Satisfaction in University Students. *Social Science Computer Review*, *35*(5), 576–586. doi:10.1177/0894439316660340

Hawi, N. S., Samaha, M., & Griffiths, M. D. (2019). The Digital Addiction Scale for Children: Development and validation. *Cyberpsychology, Behavior, and Social Networking*, *22*(12), 771–778. doi:10.1089/cyber.2019.0132 PMID:31755742

Hawkley, L. C., Thisted, R. A., & Cacioppo, J. T. (2009). Loneliness predicts reduced physical activity: Cross-sectional and longitudinal analyses. *Health Psychology*, *28*(3), 354–363. doi:10.1037/a0014400 PMID:19450042

Hayrullahoğlu, G., & Varol, Ç. (2022). Urban Life and Urban Space in The Interaction of Unıverse and Metaverse. In E. Koçak, N. Kafadar, & O. Sevgul, (eds.) Design and Planning From Different Perspectives, (Ed.) Iksad Publication.

Hazar, M. (2011). Sosyal Medya Bağımlılığı: Bir Alan Çalışması. *İletişim Kuram ve Araştırma Dergisi*, 151-175.

Hazar, Z., & ve Hazar, M. (2019). Üniversite Öğrencileri İçin Dijital Oyun Bağımlılığı Ölçeği (Uyarlama Çalışması). *Journal of Sport Sciences Researches, 4*(2).

Hazar, Z., Hazar, M., Hazar, M., & Hazar, M. (2017). Digital Game Addiction Scale for Children Çocuklar İçin Dijital Oyun Bağımlılığı Ölçeği. *International Journal of Human Sciences*, *14*(1), 203–216. doi:10.14687/jhs.v14i1.4387

Hekim, H., & Başıbüyük, O. (2013). Siber suçlar ve Türkiye'nin siber güvenlik politikalari. *Uluslararası Güvenlik ve Terörizm Dergisi*, *4*(2), 135–158.

Henchoz, Y., Studer, J., Deline, S., N'Goran, A. A., Baggio, S., & Gmel, G. (2016). Video Gaming Disorder and Sport and Exercise in Emerging Adulthood: A Longitudinal Study. *Behavioral Medicine (Washington, D.C.)*, *42*(2), 105–111. doi:10.1080/08964289.2014.965127 PMID:25258243

Heo, J., Oh, J., Subramanian, S. V., Kim, Y., & Kawachi, I. (2014). Addictive Internet use among Korean adolescents: A national survey. *PLoS One*, *9*(2), e87819. doi:10.1371/journal.pone.0087819 PMID:24505318

Herman, D. (2000). Introducing short-term brands: A new branding tool for a new consumer reality. *Journal of Brand Management*, *7*(5), 330–340. doi:10.1057/bm.2000.23

Hernandez, K., Faith, B., Martín, P. P., & Ramalingam, B. (2016). The impact of digital technology on economic growth and productivity, and its implications for employment and equality: An evidence review. *Evidence Report No. 207.* Institute of Development Studies, England.

Hidaayah, N., Yunitasari, E., Kusnanto, K., Nihayati, H. E., Santy, W. H., Putri, R. A., & Rahman, F. S. (2022). Parenting in the Prevention of Internet Gaming Addiction. *Open Access Macedonian Journal of Medical Sciences, 10*(G), 731-738. doi:10.3889/oamjms.2022.7980

Hidayati, N., Syaf, A., & Hartati, R. (2021). Fear of Missing Out ditinjau dari Big Five Personality. *Psychopolytan: Jurnal Psikologi*, *4*(2), 77–83. doi:10.36341/psi.v4i2.1392

Hill, D., Ameenuddin, N., Chassiakos, Y. R., Cross, C., Radesky, J., Hutchinson, J., Boyd, R., Mendelson, R., Moreno, M. A., Smith, J., & Swanson, W. S. (2016). Media and young minds. *Pediatrics*, *138*(5). PMID:27940793

Hilty, L. M., Arnfalk, P., Erdmann, L., Goodman, J., Lehmann, M., & Wäger, P. A. (2006). The relevance of information and communication technologies for environmental sustainability - A prospective simulation study. *Environmental Modelling & Software*, *21*(11), 1618–1629. doi:10.1016/j.envsoft.2006.05.007

Hinduja, S., & Patchin, J. W. (2010). Bullying, Cyberbullying, and Suicide. *Archives of Suicide Research*, *14*(3), 206–221. doi:10.1080/13811118.2010.494133 PMID:20658375

Hinduja, S., & Patchin, J. W. (2022). Bullying and Cyberbullying Offending Among US Youth: The Influence of Six Parenting Dimensions. *Journal of Child and Family Studies*, *31*(5), 1454–1473. doi:10.100710826-021-02208-7

Hogh, A., Mikkelsen, E. G., & Hansen, A. M. (2011). Individual consequences of workplace bullying/mobbing (Chapter 4). In S. Einarsen, H. Hoel, D. Zapf, C. L. Cooper (Ed.) Bullying and harassment in the workplace: Developments in theory, research, and practice, 107, 128. doi:10.1201/EBK1439804896-7

Holden, C. (2010). Psychiatry. Behavioral addictions debut in proposed DSM-V. *Science*, *327*(5968), 935. doi:10.1126cience.327.5968.935 PMID:20167757

Holroyd, C. (2022). Technological innovation and building a 'super smart'society: Japan's vision of society 5.0. *Journal of Asian Public Policy*, *15*(1), 18–31. doi:10.1080/17516234.2020.1749340

Horzum, M. B. (2011). Examination of elementary school students' computer game addiction levels according to various variables. *Education in Science*, *36*(159).

Horzum, M. B. (2011). Investigation of elementary school students' computer game addiction levels according to various variables. *Eğitim ve Bilim*, *36*(159), 328–338.

Horzum, M. B., Ayas, T., & Çakır, Ö. B. (2008). Çocuklar için bilgisayar oyun bağımlılığı. *Türk Psikolojik Danışma ve Rehberlik Dergisi*, *30*, 76–88.

Ho, T. T. Q. (2021). Facebook addiction and depression: Loneliness as a moderator and poor sleep quality as a mediator. *Telematics and Informatics*, *61*, 101617. doi:10.1016/j.tele.2021.101617

Howitt, P. (2010). Endogenous growth theory. In *Economic growth* (pp. 68–73). Palgrave Macmillan.

Hromek, R., & Roffey, S. (2009). Promoting social and emotional learning with games: "It's fun and we learn things". *Simulation & Gaming*, *40*(5), 626–644. doi:10.1177/1046878109333793

Huang, S., Wang, B., Li, X., Zheng, P., Mourtzis, D., & Wang, L. (2022). Industry 5.0 and Society 5.0—Comparison, complementation and co-evolution. *Journal of Manufacturing Systems*, *64*, 424–428. doi:10.1016/j.jmsy.2022.07.010

Huang, X. Q., Li, M. C., & Tao, R. (2010). Treatment of internet addiction. *Current Psychiatry Reports*, *12*(5), 462–470. doi:10.100711920-010-0147-1 PMID:20697848

Hughes, J. R., Stead, L. F., & Lancaster, T. (2007). Antidepressants for smoking cessation [published correction appears in Cochrane Database Syst Rev. 2014; 1: CD000031]. *Cochrane Database of Systematic Reviews*, 1. PMID:17253443

Hung, K. H., Gu, F. F., & Yim, C. K. B. (2007). A social institutional approach to identifying generation cohorts in China with a comparison with American consumers. *Journal of International Business Studies*, *38*(5), 836–853. doi:10.1057/palgrave.jibs.8400288

Hürriyet. (2017, 9 June). Elinde Kılıcıyla Diriliş Ertuğrul İzleyen Dede! *Hürriyet*. https://www.hurriyet.com.tr/video/elinde-kiliciyla-dirilis-ertugrul-izleyen-dede-40484794

Hu, S. J. (2013). Evolving paradigms of manufacturing: From mass production to mass customisation and personalisation. *Procedia CIRP*, *7*, 3–8. doi:10.1016/j.procir.2013.05.002

Hussain, Z., & Griffiths, M. D. (2009b). The attitudes, feelings, and experiences of online gamers: A qualitative analysis. *Cyberpsychology & Behavior*, *12*(6), 747–753. doi:10.1089/cpb.2009.0059 PMID:19788376

Hygen, B. W., Skalicka, V., Stenseng, F., Belsky, J., Steinsbekk, S., & Wichstrøm, L. (2020). The co-occurrence between symptoms of internet gaming disorder and psychiatric disorders in childhood and adolescence: Prospective relations or common causes? *Journal of Child Psychology and Psychiatry, and Allied Disciplines*, *61*(8), 890–898. doi:10.1111/jcpp.13289 PMID:32623728

Ibrahim, S. A., Dahlan, A., Pauzi, N. W., & Vetrayan, J. (2022). Fear of missing out (FoMO) and its relation with depression and anxiety among university students. *Environment-Behaviour Proceedings Journal*, *7*(20), 233–238. doi:10.21834/ebpj.v7i20.3358

ICD 11. (2022). 6C51 Gaming disorder. *ICD-11 for Mortality and Morbidity Statistics*. ICD. https://icd.who.int/browse11/lm/en#/http%3a%2f%2fid.who.int%2ficd%2fentity%2f1448597234. (12.20.2022).

ICD11. (2018). *Gaming disorder*. ICD. https://icd.who.int/browse11/l-m/en#http%3A%2F%2Fid.who.int%2Ficd%2Fentity%2F1448597234.

Ikiz, F. E., Savci, M., Asici, E., & Yoruk, C. (2015). Investigation of relationship between problematic internet use and psychological symptoms of university students. *International Journal of Human Sciences*, *12*(2), 688–702. doi:10.14687/ijhs.v12i2.3336

Ilgaz Büyükbaykal, C., & Abay Cansabuncu, İ. (2020). Türkiye'de Yeni Medya Ortamı ve Dijital Oyun Olgusu. *Yeni Medya Elektronik Dergisi*, *4*(1), 1–9.

Inan, A. (2010).Internet addiction in secondary and high school students. Erzurum: Atatürk University.

İnce, M. & Işır, Ö. (2016). A workshop of art-based application through game-supported education. *İnönü Üniversitesi Uluslararası Sosyal Bilimler Dergisi*, *5*(1), 225-236.

İnceelli, A. (2005). Dijital Hikaye Anlatımın Bileşenleri. *The Turkish Online Journal of Educational Technology*, 132–142.

Influencer Intelligence (2020). The state of influencer marketing in beauty. *Influencer Intelligence*.

Innis, H. (1950). Empire and Communications. Oxford: Clarendon Press.

INPI, Instituto Nacional de Propriedade Intelectual. (n.d.). *Dados estatísticos sobre contratos de transferência de tecnologia.* INPI. http://www.inpi.gov.br/

*Internet Safety for Kids: Top 7 Online Gaming Dangers.* (n.d.). Kaspersky. https://usa.kaspersky.com/resource-center/threats/top-7-online-gaming-dangers-facing-kids

Internet World Stats. (2016). *Database for worldwide Internet statistics.* Internet World Stats. http:www.internetworldstats.com/Europa.htm

Ipek, I. (2020). Understanding consumer behaviour in technology-mediated spaces. In *Digital Transformation in Business and Society* (pp. 169–189). Palgrave Macmillan. doi:10.1007/978-3-030-08277-2_11

Irmak, A. Y., & Erdogan, S. (2015). Digital Game Addiction Among Adolescents and Young Adults: A Current Overview. *Turkish Journal of Psychiatry.*

Irmak, A. Y., & Erdogan, S. (2016). Digital game addiction among adolescents and young adults: A current overview. *Turkish Journal of Psychiatry, 27*(2), 1–10.

Irtyshcheva, I., Stehnei, M., Popadynets, N., Bogatyrev, K., Boiko, Y., Kramarenko, I., Senkevich, O., Hryshyna, N., Kozak, I., & Ishchenko, O. (2021). The effect of digital technology development on economic growth. *International Journal of Data and Network Science, 5*(1), 25–36. doi:10.5267/j.ijdns.2020.11.006

Irvine, L., Melaugh, J., Etchells, P., Collins, S., & Tse, D. (2019, April 6). Five damaging myths about video games – let's shoot 'em up. *The Guardian.* https://www.theguardian.com/games/2019/apr/06/five-damaging-myths-about-video-games-lets-shoot-em-up

Işık, U., Kalem, M., Aliyeva, F., & Ülker, M. (2022). Medya Bağımlılığı Teorisi Doğrultusunda Instagram: Üniversite Öğrencileri Üzerine Bir Araştırma. *ANkara Hacı Bayram Veli Üniversitesi*, 97-116.

Jablonska, B., & Lindberg, L. (2007). Risk behaviors, victimization and mental distress among adolescents in different family structures. *Social Psychiatry and Psychiatric Epidemiology, 42*(8), 656–663. doi:10.100700127-007-0210-3 PMID:17522746

Jacobsen, K. F. L. (2003). Telecommunications-a means to economic growth in developing countries? *CMI Report*, (13).

Jaeger, H. (1985). Generations in History: Reflections on a Controversial Concept. *History and Theory, 24*(3), 273-292.

Jakhar, A. (2022, June 9). *Why Are Children Getting Attracted To Online Gaming?* Youth Ki Awaaz. https://www.youthkiawaaz.com/2022/06/why-children-are-getting-attracted-towards-online-gaming/

Jauhiainen, J. S., Krohn, C., & Junnila, J. (2023). Metaverse and Sustainability: Systematic Review of Scientific Publications until 2022 and Beyond. *Sustainability (Basel), 15*(346), 1–20. doi:10.3390u15010346

Javaid, M., & Haleem, A. (2020). Critical components of Industry 5.0 towards a successful adoption in thefield of manufacturing. *Journal of Industrial Integration and Management, 5*(03), 327–348. doi:10.1142/S2424862220500141

Jensen, J. L., & Mortensen, M. (2016). Emerging patterns of news production and consumption across media. In J. L. Jensen, M. Mortensen, & J. Ormen (Eds.), *News across media: Production, distribution and consumption* (pp. 1–11). Routledge Publishing. doi:10.4324/9781315692456

Jeong, E. J., & Kim, D. H. (2011). Social activities, self-efficacy, game attitudes, and game addiction. *Cyberpsychology, Behavior, and Social Networking, 14*(4), 213–221. doi:10.1089/cyber.2009.0289 PMID:21067285

Jeong, S. H., & Kim, S. T. (2011). Reviews of science for science librarians: Genome-wide association studies (GWAS). *Science & Technology Libraries*, *30*(3), 229–243. doi:10.1080/0194262X.2011.595315

Jérémy, M., Jean-Charles, Q., Michèle, C., Alice, N., Marie, I., & Laetitia, S. (2021). Fear of missing out predicts distraction by social reward signals displayed on a smartphone in difficult driving situations. *Frontiers in Psychology*, 12. PMID:34335405

Jiang, J., Phalp, K. T., & Ali, R. (2015). *Digital addiction: Gamification for precautionary and recovery requirements.* Bourne Mouth. http://eprints.bournemouth.ac.uk/21887/1/04-Posters.pdf

Jiménez-Zarco, A. I., Rospigliosi, A., Martínez-Ruiz, M. P., & Izquierdo-Yusta, A. (2019). Marketing 4.0: Enhancing consumer-brand engagement through big data analysis. In Web Services: Concepts, Methodologies, Tools, and Applications (pp. 2172-2195). IGI Global.

Jio, S., & Sun, Q. (2021). Digital economic development and its impact on economic growth in China: Research based on the perspective of sustainability. *Sustainability (Basel)*, *13*(10245), 1–18. doi:10.3390u131810245

Johnson, A. L. (2016). Cybersecurity for financial institutions: The integral role of information sharing in cyber-attack mitigation. *N.C. Banking Inst.*, *20*(1), 277–310.

Jolliffe, D., & Farrington, D. (2006). Examining the relationship between low empathy and bullying. *Aggressive Behavior*, *32*(6), 540–550. doi:10.1002/ab.20154

Joseph, R. (2016). A Review of Digital Addiction: A Call for Safety Education. *Journal of Education and e-learning Research*, *3*(1), 17–22. doi:10.20448/journal.509/2016.3.1/509.1.17.22

Joyce, M. C. (2010). *Digital activism decoded: The new mechanics of change*. IDEA.

Judge, T. A., Higgins, C. A., Thoresen, C. J., & Barrick, M. R. (1999). The Big Five personality traits, general mental ability, and career success across the life span. *Personnel Psychology*, *52*(3), 621–652. doi:10.1111/j.1744-6570.1999.tb00174.x

Just, N., & Latzer, M. (2017). Governance by Algorithms: Reality Construction by Algorithmic Selection on the Internet. *Media, Culture & Society*, *39*(2), 238-258. , https://ssrn.com/abstract=3871903 doi:10.1177/0163443716643157

Juthamanee, S., & Gunawan, J. (2021). Factors related to internet and game addiction among adolescents: A scoping review. *Belitung Nursing Journal*, *7*(2), 62–71. doi:10.33546/bnj.1097

Jyoti, B., & Singh, A. K. (2020). Characteristics and determinants of new start-ups in Gujarat, India. *Entrepreneurship Review*, *1*(2), 1–25. doi:10.38157/entrepreneurship-review.v1i2.154

Kagermann, H., Wahlsterand, W., & Helbig, J. (2013). *Recommendations for implementing the strategic initiative industrie 4.0., final report of the industrie 4.0. working group.* DIN. https://www.din.de/blob/76902/e8cac883f42b-f28536e7e8165993f1fd/recommendations for-implementing-industry-4-0-data.pdf in 13.01.2023.

Kahneman, D. (2017). *Hızlı ve Yavaş Düşünme, Osman Ç. Deniztekin, Filiz N. Deniztekin*. Varlık Yayınları.

Kaku, M. (2015). *The Future of the Mind: The Scientific Quset to Understand, Enhamce and Empower the Mind*. Anchor Publishing.

Kanal D. (2023). *Kısmetse Olur Programme.* Kanal D. https://www.kanald.com.tr/kismetse-olur

Kanat, S. (2019). The relationship between digital game addiction, communication skills, and loneliness perception levels of university students. *International Education Studies*, *12*(11), 80–93. doi:10.5539/ies.v12n11p80

Karaca, M., Mutlu, T., & Gencer, G. (2021). Siber mağduriyet: Kavramsal bir çalışma. *Anadolu Akademi Sosyal Bilimler Dergisi*, *3*(1), 177–191.

Karaca, S., Karakoc, A., Gurkan, O. C., Onan, N., & Barlas, G. U. (2020). Investigation of the Online Game Addiction Level, Sociodemographic Characteristics and Social Anxiety as Risk Factors for Online Game Addiction in Middle School Students. *Community Mental Health Journal*, *56*(5), 830–838. doi:10.100710597-019-00544-z PMID:31907803

Karaçeper, S. (2018). Innovations in digital technology and graphic design. *Journal of Istanbul Aydın University Faculty of Fine Arts*, *4*(8), 73–83.

Karadag, E, Tosuntas, SB, Erzen, E, Duru, P, & Bostan, N, Mizrak- Sahin B, Culha I, & Babadag, B. (2016). The virtual world's current addiction: Phubbing. Addicta. *The Turkish Journal on Addiction*, *3*, 223–269.

Karadas, T., & Aglar, C. (2022). Determination of Academic Problems Experienced at the Formal Education High School Level of the Turkish Education System According to the Opinions of Administrators, Teachers, and Students. *Conference: II. International Multidisciplinary Digital Life Congress.* doi:10.13140/RG.2.2.23099.28968

Karademir, F., & Aytekin, Ç. (2022). İşitme Kayıplı Ebeveynlerin Çocukları (CODA): Ebeveynleri ile Sözlü İletişim Yoksunluğunun Dil ve Sosyal-Duygusal Gelişime Etkisine Genel Bir Bakış. *Gelişim ve Psikoloji Dergisi*, *3*(6), 167–183. doi:10.51503/gpd.1062798

Karaduman, N. (2017). Popüler Kültürün Oluşmasında ve Aktarılmasında Sosyal Medyanın Rolü. *Erciyes Üniversitesi Sosyal Bilimler Enstitüsü Dergisi*, 7-27.

Karaduman, M., & Aciyan, E. P. (2020). Baudrillard'ın Simülasyon Kuramı Bağlamında Dijital Oyunlar ve Bağımlılık Üzerine Bir Değerlendirme. *Trakya Üniversitesi Sosyal Bilimler Dergisi*, *22*(1), 453–472. doi:10.26468/trakyasobed.550935

Karahisar, T. (2013). *Turkiye'de Dijital Oyun Sektörünün Durumu. Sanat Tasarım ve Manipülasyon*, 107- 114. Sakarya: Sakarya Üniversitesi Güzel Sanatlar Fakültesi Yayınları.

Kardefelt-Winther, D. (2014). A conceptual and methodological critique of internet addiction research: Towards a model of compensatory internet use. *Computers in Human Behavior*, *31*(1), 351–354. doi:10.1016/j.chb.2013.10.059

Karoğlu, A. K., Kübra, B. A. L., & Çimşir, E. (2020). Toplum 5.0 Sürecinde Türkiye'de Eğitimde Dijital Dönüşüm. *Journal of University Studies*, *3*(3), 147–158.

Kartajaya, H., Setiawan, I., & Kotler, P. (2021). *Marketing 5.0: Technology for humanity*. John Wiley & Sons.

Kasper, D., Welsh, S., & Chambliss, C. (1999). *Educating Students about the Risks of Excessive Videogame Usage*. ERIC. https://files.eric.ed.gov/fulltext/ED426315.pdf

Katzenbach, C., & Bächle, T. C. (2019). Defining concepts of the digital society. *Internet Policy Review*, *8*(4). doi:10.14763/2019.4.1430

Katz, R., Koutroumpis, P., & Martin Callorda, F. (2014). Using a digitization index to measure the economic and social impact of digital agendas. *Info*, *16*(1), 32–44. doi:10.1108/info-10-2013-0051

Kavuk, M. (2011). İlköğretim öğrencilerinin sanal zorba ve sanal kurban olma durumlarının incelenmesi. (Yayınlanmamış yüksek lisans tezi). Ankara Üniversitesi, Ankara.

Kaya, A., & Pazarcıkcı, F. (2023). Structural equation modeling analysis of risk factors for digital game addiction in adolescents: A web-based study. *Archives of Psychiatric Nursing*, *43*, 22–28. doi:10.1016/j.apnu.2022.12.031 PMID:37032011

KayaDeniz, A. (2019). Dijital çağın hedonist çalışanları: Dijital göçebeler. *IBAD Sosyal Bilimler Dergisi*, *5*, 101-113.

Kazaz, N., Dilci, T., & Karadas, T. (2022). Effects of digital media on education. iJET – Vol. 17(16). doi:10.3991/ijet.v17i16.32181

Kazaz, M., & Özkent, Y. (2016). Televizyon Dizileriyle Eş Zamanlı Olarak Twitter Kullanımı: İletişim Fakültesi Öğrencileri Üzerine Bir Araştırma. *Selçuk Communication, 9*(2), 205–224.

Keidanren. (2022). Digital Transformation—Opening up the Future through Co-creation of Values. *Keidanren.* https://www.keidanren.or.jp/en/policy/2020/038.html

Kelleci, M. (2008). The effects of internet use, cell phones and computer games on mental health of children and adolescents. *Turk Silahli Kuvvetleri Koruyucu Hekimlik Bulteni, 7*(3), 253.

Kellner, D. (2003). *Media culture: cultural studies, identity, and politics between the modern and the post-modern.* Routledge. doi:10.4324/9780203205808

Kellner, D. (2006). Jean Baudrillard After Modernity: Provocations on a Provocateur and Challenger. *International Journal of Baudrillard Studies, 3*(1), 1–32.

Kergel, D. (2023). *Digital cultures.* Springer Publications. doi:10.1007/978-3-658-35250-9

Kerr, A. (2006). *The Business and Culture of Digital Games, Gamework/Gameplay.* Sage Publications. doi:10.4135/9781446211410

Keum, B. T., Wang, Y. W., Callaway, J., Abebe, I., Cruz, T., & O'Connor, S. (2022). Benefits and harms of social media use: A latent profile analysis of emerging adults. *Current Psychology (New Brunswick, N.J.),* 1–13. doi:10.100712144-022-03473-5 PMID:35891891

Khairi, A. K., Li, W., Yeo, S. H., Tong, Y. S., Nazri, M., Rahman, B. A., & Motevalli, S. (2022). The Importance of Emotional Competence in Preventing Cyberbullying: The Role of Family as Moderator. *International Journal of Academic Research in Business & Social Sciences, 12*(4), 262–278. doi:10.6007/IJARBSS/v12-i4/13062

KhanacademyTurkish. (2018). *Exponential growth and contraction (Mathematics) (Algebra).* [Video]. Youtube. https://www.youtube.com/watch?v=4uZX1s-vNhA

Khazaei, F., Khazaei, O., & Ghanbari-H, B. (2017). Positive psychology interventions for internet addiction treatment. *Computers in Human Behavior, 72,* 304–311. doi:10.1016/j.chb.2017.02.065

Khoury, L., Tang, Y. L., Bradley, B., Cubells, J. F., & Ressler, K. J. (2010). Substance use, childhood traumatic experience, and Posttraumatic Stress Disorder in an urban civilian population. *Depression and Anxiety, 27*(12), 1077–1086. doi:10.1002/da.20751 PMID:21049532

Kim, D. H., Jeong, E. J., & Zhong, H. (2010). Preventive role of parents in adolescent problematic internet game use in Korea. *Korean Journal of Sociology, 44*(6), 111–133.

Kim, E. J., Namkoong, K., Ku, T., & Kim, S. J. (2008). The relationship between online game addiction and aggression, self-control and narcissistic personality traits. *European Psychiatry, 23*(3), 212–218. doi:10.1016/j.eurpsy.2007.10.010 PMID:18166402

Kim, J. (2021). Advertising in the Metaverse: Research Agenda. *Journal of Interactive Advertising, 21*(3), 141–144. doi:10.1080/15252019.2021.2001273

Kim, J. H. (2022). Parental support and problematic smartphone use: A serial mediating model of self-esteem and fear of missing out. *International Journal of Environmental Research and Public Health, 19*(13), 7657. doi:10.3390/ijerph19137657 PMID:35805315

Kim, J., LaRose, R., & Peng, W. (2009). Loneliness as the Cause and the Effect of Problematic Internet Use: The Relationship between Internet Use and Psychological Well-Being. *Cyberpsychology & Behavior*, *12*(4), 541–455. doi:10.1089/cpb.2008.0327 PMID:19514821

Kim, J., & Tussyadiah, I. P. (2013). Social networking and social support in tourism experience: The moderating role of online self-presentation strategies. *Journal of Travel & Tourism Marketing*, *30*(1-2), 78–92. doi:10.1080/10548408.2013.751220

Kim, K., & Kim, K. (2015). Internet game addiction, parental attachment, and parenting of adolescents in South Korea. *Journal of Child & Adolescent Substance Abuse*, *24*(6), 366–371. doi:10.1080/1067828X.2013.872063

Kim, N. R., Hwang, S. S.-H., Choi, J.-S., Kim, D.-J., Demetrovics, Z., Király, O., Nagygyörgy, K., Griffiths, M. D., Hyun, S. Y., Youn, H. C., & Choi, S.-W. (2016). Characteristics and psychiatric symptoms of Internet gaming disorder among adults using self-reported DSM-5 criteria. *Psychiatry Investigation*, *13*(1), 58. doi:10.4306/pi.2016.13.1.58 PMID:26766947

Kim, N., Hughes, T. L., Park, C. G., Quinn, L., & Kong, I. D. (2016). Resting-State Peripheral Catecholamine and Anxiety Levels in Korean Male Adolescents with Internet Game Addiction. *Cyberpsychology, Behavior, and Social Networking*, *19*(3), 202–208. doi:10.1089/cyber.2015.0411 PMID:26849530

Kim, P. W., Kim, S. Y., Shim, M., Im, C.-H., & Shon, Y.-M. (2013). The influence of an educational course on language expression and treatment of gaming addiction for massive multiplayer online role-playing game (MMORPG) players. *Computers & Education*, *63*, 208–217. doi:10.1016/j.compedu.2012.12.008

Kim, S. M., Han, D. H., Lee, Y. S., & Renshaw, P. F. (2012). Combined cognitive behavioral therapy and bupropion for the treatment of problematic on-line game play in adolescents with major depressive disorder. *Computers in Human Behavior*, *28*(5), 1954–1959. doi:10.1016/j.chb.2012.05.015

King, D. L., & Delfabbro, P. H. (2017). Prevention and policy related to Internet gaming disorder. *Current Addiction Reports*, *4*(3), 284–292. doi:10.100740429-017-0157-8

King, D. L., & Delfabbro, P. H. (2020). Video game addiction. In A. E. Cecilia & H. D. Paul (Eds.), *Adolescent addiction: Epidemiology, assessment, and treatment* (pp. 335–341). Academic Press. doi:10.1016/B978-0-12-818626-8.00007-4

King, R. G., & Levine, R. (1993). Finance and growth: Schumpeter might be right. *The Quarterly Journal of Economics*, *108*(3), 717–737. doi:10.2307/2118406

Király, O., Potenza, M. N., Stein, D. J., King, D. L., Hodgins, D. C., Saunders, J. B., Griffiths, M. D., Gjoneska, B., Billieux, J., Brand, M., Abbott, M. W., Chamberlain, S. R., Corazza, O., Burkauskas, J., Sales, C. M. D., Montag, C., Lochner, C., Grünblatt, E., Wegmann, E., & Demetrovics, Z. (2020). Preventing problematic internet use during the COVID-19 pandemic: Consensus guidance. *Comprehensive Psychiatry*, *100*, 100. doi:10.1016/j.comppsych.2020.152180 PMID:32422427

Kırcaburun, K., & Griffiths, M. D. (2018). Instagram Addiction and the Big Five of Personality: The Mediating of Self-Liking. *Journal of Behavioral Addictions*, *7*(1), 158–170. doi:10.1556/2006.7.2018.15 PMID:29461086

Kırık, A. M., & Yazıcı, N. (2017). Instagram Örneği Üzerinden Sosyal Medyada Hikaye Anlatıcılığı. *Erciyes İletişim Dergisi*, 82-99.

Kırık, A. M., & Domaç, A. (2014). Sosyal Medya Üzerinde Televizyon Reyting Ölçümlerinin Analizi: Twitter Örneği. *Journal of Academic Social Research*, *5*, 414–430.

Kırık, A., Çetinkaya, A., & Kurşun, A. (2021). Digital Activism in the Context of Social Movements: the Case of Change. Org. In E. K. Doru, S. Mengü, & E. Ulusoy (Eds.), *Digital Seige*. Istanbul University Press.

Kirriemuir, J. (2002). Video gaming, education and digital learning technologies. *The Magazine Of Digital Library Research, 8*(2).

Kirriemuir, J. (2002, February). Video gaming, education and digital learning technologies. *D-Lib Magazine : the Magazine of the Digital Library Forum*, *8*(2). doi:10.1045/february2002-kirriemuir

Kneer, J., Rieger, D., Ivory, J. D., & Ferguson, C. (2014). Awareness of risk factors for digital game addiction: Interviewing players and counselors. *International Journal of Mental Health and Addiction*, *12*(5), 585–599. doi:10.100711469-014-9489-y

Knox, L., Karantzas, G. C., Romano, D., Feeney, J. A., & Simpson, J. A. (2022). One Year On: What we have learned about the psychological effects of Covid-19 social restrictions–a meta-analysis. *Current Opinion in Psychology*, *101315*, 101315. doi:10.1016/j.copsyc.2022.101315 PMID:35398753

Ko, C. H., Liu, G. C., Hsiao, S., Yen, J. Y., Yang, M. J., Lin, W. C., Yen, C.-F., & Chen, C. S. (2009). Brain activities associated with gaming urge of online gaming addiction. *Journal of Psychiatric Research*, *43*(7), 739–747. doi:10.1016/j.jpsychires.2008.09.012 PMID:18996542

Ko, C. H., Wang, P. W., Liu, T. L., Yen, C. F., Chen, C. S., & Yen, J. Y. (2015). Bidirectional associations between family factors and Internet addiction among adolescents in a prospective investigation. *Psychiatry and Clinical Neurosciences*, *69*(4), 192–200. doi:10.1111/pcn.12204 PMID:24836367

Ko, C. H., Yen, J. Y., Yen, C. F., Chen, C. S., & Chen, C. C. (2012). The association between Internet addiction and psychiatric disorder: A review of the literature. *European Psychiatry*, *27*(1), 1–8. doi:10.1016/j.eurpsy.2010.04.011 PMID:22153731

Ko, C.-H., Yen, J.-Y., Chen, C.-C., Chen, S.-H., & Yen, C.-F. (2005). Gender differences and related factors affecting online gaming addiction among Taiwanese adolescents. *The Journal of Nervous and Mental Disease*, *193*(4), 273–277. doi:10.1097/01.nmd.0000158373.85150.57 PMID:15805824

Koçyiğit, M., & Koçyiğit, A. (2018). Değişen ve Gelişen Dijital İletişim: Yazılabilir Web Teknolojisi (Web 2.0). In V. Çakmak & S. Çavuş (Eds.), *Dijital Kültür ve İletişim* (pp. 19–49). LİTERATÜRK.

Kökcü, M. (2021). Global Transformation of the Public Sphere in the Digital World: From Public to Silent Sphere? *Academia Letters. Article*, *3018*. doi:10.20935/AL3018

Kokkiades, M., & Kourkoutas, I. (2016). School bullying/victimization, self-esteem and emotional difficulties in children with and without SEN [in Greek]. *Scientific Annals of the Pedagogical Department of Preschool Education of the University of Ioannina*, *9*, 88–128.

Köksal, T. (2021). Dijital Dünya'da 'Suretsiz Toplum'. *Journal of Atatürk University Institute of Social Sciences*, *25*(3), 1249–1259.

Konhäusner, P., Shang, B., & Dabija, D. C. (2021). Application of the 4Es in online crowdfunding platforms: A comparative perspective of Germany and China. *Journal of Risk and Financial Management*, *14*(2), 49. doi:10.3390/jrfm14020049

Königs, P. (2022). What is Techno-Optimism? *Philosophy & Technology*, *35*(63).

Koob, G. F., & Volkow, N. D. (2016). Neurobiology of addiction: A neurocircuitry analysis. *The Lancet. Psychiatry*, *3*(8), 760–773. doi:10.1016/S2215-0366(16)00104-8 PMID:27475769

Koo, H. J., & Kwon, J. H. (2014). Risk and protective factors of internet addiction: A meta-analysis of empirical studies in Korea. *Yonsei Medical Journal*, *55*(6), 1691–1711. doi:10.3349/ymj.2014.55.6.1691 PMID:25323910

Koric, M. M., Teo, L. L. C., & Neo, R. L. (2009). Children and video games: Addiction, engagement, and scholastic achievement. *Cyberpsychology & Behavior*, *12*(5), 567–572. doi:10.1089/cpb.2009.0079 PMID:19624263

Körpe, G. & Küçük, L. (2021). Covid-19 Döneminde Hemşirelik Öğrencilerinde Teknoloji Bağımlılığı. *İstanbul Gelişim Üniversitesi Sağlık Bilimleri Dergisi, 15*, 581-592. doi:10.38079/igusabder.981591

Köseliören, M., & Çakır, C., & ve Beşikci, S. (2022). The effect of fear of death in the elderly creating FoMO on the perception of health news published on social media. *Intermedia International e-Journal*, *9*(17), 324-340. doi:10.56133/intermedia.1180852

Koss, H. (n.d.). *What Is the Metaverse? Examples and Definition.* Built In. https://builtin.com/media-gaming/what-is-metaverse

Kotler, P., & Keller, K. L. (2012). *Marketing management* (14th ed.). Pearson Education.

Koutroumpis, P. (2009). The economic impact of broadband on growth: A simultaneous approach. *Telecommunications Policy*, *33*(9), 471–485. doi:10.1016/j.telpol.2009.07.004

Kowalski, R. M., Giumetti, G. W., Schroeder, A. N., & Lattanner, M. R. (2014). Bullying in the digital age: A critical review and meta-analysis of cyberbullying research among youth. *Psychological Bulletin*, *140*(4), 1073–1137. doi:10.1037/a0035618 PMID:24512111

Kowalski, R. M., & Limber, S. P. (2007). Electronic bullying among middle school students. *The Journal of Adolescent Health*, *41*(6), S22–S30. doi:10.1016/j.jadohealth.2007.08.017 PMID:18047942

Kowalski, R. M., Toth, A., & Morgan, M. (2018). Bullying and cyberbullying in adulthood and the workplace. *The Journal of Social Psychology*, *158*(1), 64–81. doi:10.1080/00224545.2017.1302402 PMID:28402201

Kraut, R., Patterson, M., Lundmark, V., Kiesler, S., Mukophadhyay, T., & Scherlis, W. (1998). Internet paradox. A social technology that reduces social involvement and psychological well-being? *The American Psychologist*, *53*(9), 1017–1031. doi:10.1037/0003-066X.53.9.1017 PMID:9841579

Krishnan, U. (2021). The Industry 4.0 and its associated technologies. *Journal of Emerging Technologies*, *1*(1), 1–10. doi:10.57040/jet.v1i1.24

Kross, E., Verduyn, P., Demiralp, E., Park, J., Lee, D. S., Lin, N., Shablack, H., Jonides, J., & Ybarra, O. (2013). Facebook Use Predicts Declines in Subjective Well-Being in Young Adults. *PLoS One*, *8*(8), 69841. doi:10.1371/journal.pone.0069841 PMID:23967061

Kruger, D. J., & Djerf, J. M. (2016). High Ringxiety: Attachment Anxiety Predicts Experiences of Phantom Cell Phone Ringing. *Cyberpsychology, Behavior, and Social Networking*, *19*(1), 56–60. doi:10.1089/cyber.2015.0406 PMID:26701188

Kubey, R., & Csikszentmihalyi, M. (2002). Television addiction is no mere metaphor. *Scientific American*, *286*(2), 74–80. doi:10.1038cientificamerican0202-74 PMID:11828703

Kuckartz, A. M., Kuckartz, U. (2012). *Qualitative Text Analysis*. MAXQDA, file:///C:/Users/lenovo/Downloads/Qualitative_Text_Analysis_with_MAXQDA.pdf, [Erişim Tarihi: 08.11.2020].

Küçüktamer, T., & Karakuyu, A. (2021). Dijital dünyada okuryazarlık kavramı. [The concept of literacy in the digital world] In O. Koksal (Ed.), *Dijital eğitim* [Digital education]. (pp. 85–95). Eğitim Publications.

Küçüktamer, T., & Yardibi, N. (2017). Yapılandırmacı öğretim bağlamında bir örnek ders incelemesi: Coursera platformunda sanat ve etkinlik [An course examination in the context of constructivist learning: Art and activity through the platform of Coursera]. *International Journal of Innovative Research in Education, 4*(3), 170–178. doi:10.18844/ijire.v4i3.2645

Kuem, J., & Ray, S. (2022). Personality antecedents and consequences of internet addiction vis-à-vis Internet habit: A theory and an empirical investigation. *Information Systems Frontiers, 24*(2), 579–594. doi:10.100710796-021-10110-2

Kumar, V. D., & Prabha, M. S. (2019). *Getting glued to TikTok: Undermining the psychology behind widespread inclination toward dub-mashed videos.* Archives of Mental Health.

Kumar, A., Ahmad, M. M., & Sharma, P. (2015). Carbon emission and global food security: A cross country analysis. *PENCIL Publication of Agricultural Sciences, 2*(1), 7–24.

Kumar, A., Ahmad, M. M., & Sharma, P. (2017). Influence of climatic and non-climatic factors on sustainable food security in India: A statistical investigation. *International Journal of Sustainable Agricultural Management and Informatics, 3*(1), 1–30. doi:10.1504/IJSAMI.2017.082917

Küngerü, A. (2016). Bir İfade Aracı Olarak Dijital Öykü Anlatımı. *Abant Kültürel Araştırmalar Dergisi*, 33-46.

Kupperschmidt, B. R. (2000). Multigeneration Employees: Strategies for Effective Management. *The Health Care Manager, 19*(1), 65–76. doi:10.1097/00126450-200019010-00011 PMID:11183655

Kurland, N. B., & Bailey, D. E. (1999). The advantages and challenges of working here, there, anywhere, and anytime. *Organizational Dynamics, 28*(2), 53–68. doi:10.1016/S0090-2616(00)80016-9

Kuşcalı, A. (2019). İslami İlimler Fakültesi Öğrencilerinin Sosyal Medya Kullanım Motivasyonlarının İncelenmesi. *Simetrik İletişim Araştırmaları Dergisi*, 100-110.

Kuş, Ö. A. (2021). Games in the Context of Addiction and Digitization; Investigation of Generation Y on the Axis of Digital Game Addiction within the Scope of Istanbul Province. [Bağımlılık ve Dijitalleşme Bağlamında Oyunlar; İstanbul İli Kapsamında, Y Kuşağı'nın Dijital Oyun Bağımlılığı Ekseninde İncelenmesi] In Ö. A. Kuş & Ö. Uğurlu Akbaş (Eds.), *Digital Version of Games* [Oyunların Dijital Hali]. (pp. 13–44). Urzeni.

Kuss, D. J., & Griffiths, M. D. (2011). Online social networking and addictiona review of the psychological literature. *International Journal of Environmental Research and Public Health, 8*(9), 3528–3552. doi:10.3390/ijerph8093528 PMID:22016701

Kuss, D. J., & Griffiths, M. D. (2012). Internet gaming addiction: A systematic review of empirical research. *International Journal of Mental Health and Addiction, 10*(2), 278–296. doi:10.100711469-011-9318-5

Kuss, D. J., & Griffiths, M. D. (2012). Online gaming addiction: The role of sensation seeking, self-esteem, neuroticism, aggression, state anxiety, and trait anxiety. *Cyberpsychology, Behavior, and Social Networking, 15*(8), 481–487. doi:10.1089/cyber.2011.0324

Kuss, D. J., & Griffiths, M. D. (2012). Problematic video game use: A comprehensive review. *International Journal of Mental Health and Addiction, 10*(2), 349–371.

Kuss, D. J., & Griffiths, M. D. (2012a). Online gaming addiction in children and adolescents: A review of empirical research. *Journal of Behavioral Addictions, 1*(1), 3–22 doi:10.1556/JBA.1.2012.1.1 PMID:26166826

Kuss, D. J., & Griffiths, M. D. (2012b). Adolescent online gaming addiction. *Education for Health, 30*(1), 15–17.

Kuss, D. J., & Griffiths, M. D. (2017). Social networking sites and addiction: Ten lessons learned. *International Journal of Environmental Research and Public Health, 14*(3), 311. doi:10.3390/ijerph14030311 PMID:28304359

Kuss, D. J., Griffiths, M. D., & Binder, J. F. (2013). Internet addiction in students: Prevalence and risk factors. *Computers in Human Behavior, 29*(3), 959–966. doi:10.1016/j.chb.2012.12.024

Kuss, D. J., Griffiths, M. D., Karila, L., & Billieux, J. (2014). Internet addiction: A systematic review of epidemiological research for the last decade. *Current Pharmaceutical Design, 20*(25), 4026–4052. doi:10.2174/13816128113199990617 PMID:24001297

Kutsuri, G. N., Kamberdieva, S. S., Dedegkaev, V. K. H., Sopoeva, I. A., & Shelkunova, T. G. (2019). Impact of digitalization on improvement of economy, IT and internet of business. *Journal of Physics: Conference Series, 1399*(3), 1–6. doi:10.1088/1742-6596/1399/3/033008

Kuzuloglu, S. (2018*). 21 lessons for the 21st century: Interview with Yuval Noah Harari.* Yucelbinici. http://yucelbinici.com/21-yuzyil-icin-21-ders/ Accessed on: 22.03.22

Kye, B., Han, N., Kim, E., Park, Y., & Jo, S. (2021). Educational applications of metaverse: Possibilities and limitations. *Journal of Educational Evaluation for Health Professions, 18*(32), 1–13. doi:10.3352/jeehp.2021.18.32 PMID:34897242

Laçin Doğan, B. G., Yilmaz, Y., & İşgör, İ. Y. (2023). Sosyal Desteğin Mutluluk, Yaşam Doyumu Ve Sosyal Medya Bağimliliği Üzerindeki Etkisinin Araştirilmasi. [IJOESS]. *Social Sciences, 14*(51), 13–26.

Lahlou, S. (2008). Identity, social status, privacy and face-keeping in digital society. *Social Sciences Information. Information Sur les Sciences Sociales, 47*(3), 299–330. doi:10.1177/0539018408092575

Lai, S. A., Pang, K. Y., Siau, C. S., Chan, C. M., Tan, Y. K., Ooi, P. B., & Ho, M. C. (2022, June 2). Social support as a mediator in the relationship between perceived stress and nomophobia: An Investigation among Malaysian university students during the COVID-19 pandemic. *Nature Public Health Emergency Collection*, 1-8.

Lam, L. T. (2014). Internet gaming addiction, problematic use of the internet, and sleep problems: A systematic review. *Current Psychiatry Reports, 16*(4), 444. doi:10.100711920-014-0444-1 PMID:24619594

Lam, L. T., Peng, Z. W., Mai, J. C., & Jing, J. (2009). Factors associated with Internet addiction among adolescents. *Cyberpsychology & Behavior, 12*(5), 551–555. doi:10.1089/cpb.2009.0036 PMID:19619039

Lamm, E., & Meeks, M. D. (2009). Workplace Fun: The Moderating Effects of Generational Differences. *Employee Relations, 31*(6), 613–631. doi:10.1108/01425450910991767

Lanier, J. (2018). How we need to remake the internet. TED. [Video]. Youtube. https:// www.youtube.com/watch?v=qQ-PUXPVlos

Launchmetrics. (2020). *The state of influencer marketing 2020: Special focus on fashion, luxury and beauty industries.* Launchmetrics.

Lavoie, R., Main, K., King, C., & King, D. (2021). Virtual experience, real consequences: The potential negative emotional consequences of virtual reality gameplay. *Virtual Reality (Waltham Cross), 25*(1), 69–81. doi:10.100710055-020-00440-y

Lee, G. L., & Morgan, H. (2018). Understanding children's attraction toward digital games and preventing their gaming addiction. *US-China Education Review A., 8*(1), 11–17.

Lee, G., & Morgan, H. (2018). Understanding children's attraction toward digital games and preventing their gaming addiction. *US-China Education Review, 8*(1), 11–17. doi:10.17265/2161-623X/2018.01.002

Lee, H., Kim, J. W., & Choi, T. Y. (2017). Risk factors for smartphone addiction in Korean adolescents: Smartphone use patterns. *Journal of Korean Medical Science, 32*(10), 1674–1679. doi:10.3346/jkms.2017.32.10.1674 PMID:28875613

Lee, J. D., & See, K. A. (2004). Trust in Automation: Designing for Appropriate Reliance. *Human Factors*, *46*(1), 50–80. doi:10.1518/hfes.46.1.50.30392 PMID:15151155

Lee, L. H., Braud, T., Zhou, P., Wang, L., Xu, D., Lin, Z., Kumar, A., Bermejo, C., & Hui, P. (2021). All one needs to know about metaverse: A complete survey on technological singularity, virtual ecosystem, and research agenda. *Journal of Latex Class Files*, *14*(8), 1–66. doi:10.48550/arXiv.2110.05352

Leerdam, H. (2014). Young Citizens and Political Participation in a Digital Society: Addressing the Democratic Disconnect. *Politics, Culture, And Socialization*, *5*(2), 224–228. doi:10.3224/pcs.v5i2.20822

Lee, S. M., & Lee, D. (2020). Untact: A new customer service strategy in the digital age. *Service Business*, *14*(1), 1–22. doi:10.100711628-019-00408-2

Lee, S. Y. (2014). How do people compare themselves with others on social network sites?: The case of Facebook. *Computers in Human Behavior*, *32*, 253–260. doi:10.1016/j.chb.2013.12.009

Lee, Y. J. (2021). A Study on Metaverse Hype for Sustainable Growth. *International Journal of Advanced Smart Convergence*, *10*(3), 72–80. doi:10.7236/IJASC.2021.10.3.72

Lee, Y., Kozar, K. A., & Larsen, K. R. (2003). The technology acceptance model: Past, present, and future. *Communications of the Association for Information Systems*, *12*(1), 50. doi:10.17705/1CAIS.01250

Lehenbauer-Baum, M., Klaps, A., Kovacovsky, Z., Witzmann, K., Zahlbruckner, R., & Stetina, B. U. (2015). Addiction and engagement: An explorative study toward classification criteria for internet gaming disorder. *Cyberpsychology, Behavior, and Social Networking*, *18*(6), 343–349. doi:10.1089/cyber.2015.0063 PMID:26075922

Lemmens, J. S., Valkenburg, P. M., & Gentile, D. A. (2015). The Internet gaming disorder scale. *Psychological Assessment*, *27*(2), 567–582. doi:10.1037/pas0000062 PMID:25558970

Lemmens, J. S., Valkenburg, P. M., & Peter, J. (2009). Development and validation of a Game Addiction Scale for Adolescents. *Media Psychology*, *12*(1), 77–95. doi:10.1080/15213260802669458

Lemmens, J. S., Valkenburg, P. M., & Peter, J. (2011). Psychosocial causes and consequences of pathological gaming. *Computers in Human Behavior*, *27*(1), 144–152. doi:10.1016/j.chb.2010.07.015

Lemola, S., Perkinson-Gloor, N., Brand, S., Dewald-Kaufmann, J. F., & Grob, A. (2015). Adolescents' electronic media use at night, sleep disturbance, and depressive symptoms in the smartphone age. *Journal of Youth and Adolescence*, *44*(2), 405–418. doi:10.100710964-014-0176-x PMID:25204836

Lemos, I. L., Cardoso, A., & Sougey, E. B. (2016). Cross-cultural adaptation and evaluation of the psychometric properties of the Brazilian version of the Video Game Addiction Test. *Computers in Human Behavior*, *55*, 207–213. doi:10.1016/j.chb.2015.09.019

Leng, J., Sha, W., Wang, B., Zheng, P., Zhuang, C., Liu, Q., Wuest, T., Mourtzis, D., & Wang, L. (2022). Industry 5.0: Prospect and retrospect. *Journal of Manufacturing Systems*, *65*, 279–295. doi:10.1016/j.jmsy.2022.09.017

Leonhardt, M., & Overå, S. (2021). Are there differences in video gaming and use of social media among boys and girls?-A mixed methods approach. *International Journal of Environmental Research and Public Health*, *18*(11), 6085. doi:10.3390/ijerph18116085 PMID:34200039

Leung, L., Liang, J., & Zhang, Y. (2017). Media addiction. The International Encyclopedia of Media Effects, 1-14.

Leung, L. (2007). Stressful life events, motives for Internet use, and social support among digital kids. *Cyberpsychology & Behavior*, *10*(2), 204–214. doi:10.1089/cpb.2006.9967 PMID:17474837

Levine, R. (2005). Finance and growth: theory and evidence. Handbook of economic growth, 1, 865-934.

Lexico. (2019) *Game: Definition of Game by Lexico* Lexico. https://www.lexico.com/en/definition/game.

Li, R., & Gospodarik, C. G. (2021). The impact of digital economy on economic growth based on pearson correlation test analysis. In: J. Jansen, B., Liang, H., Ye, J. (eds) *International Conference on Cognitive based Information Processing and Applications (CIPA 2021), Lecture Notes on Data Engineering and Communications Technologies,* 85. Springer, Singapore.

Li, A. Y. L., Chau, C. L., & Cheng, C. (2019). Development and validation of a parent-based program for preventing gaming disorder: The game over intervention. *International Journal of Environmental Research and Public Health, 16*(11), 1–47. doi:10.3390/ijerph16111984 PMID:31167457

Li, D., Liau, A., & Khoo, A. (2011). Examining the influence of actual-ideal self-discrepancies, depression and escapism on pathological gaming among massively multiplayer online adolescent gamers. *CybePsychology, Behavior and Social. Cyberpsychology, Behavior, and Social Networking, 14*(9), 535–539. doi:10.1089/cyber.2010.0463 PMID:21332374

Lieberman, D., Fisk, M., & Biely, E. (n.d.). *Digital games for young children ages three to six: From research to design.* Taylor & Francis Group. https://www.tandfonline.com/doi/abs/10.1080/07380560903360178

Li, G., Hou, G., Yang, D., Jian, H., & Wang, W. (2019). Relationship between anxiety, depression, sex, obesity, and internet addiction in Chinese adolescents: A short-term longitudinal study. *Addictive Behaviors, 90*, 421–427. doi:10.1016/j.addbeh.2018.12.009 PMID:30553156

Li, H., & Wang, S. (2013). The role of cognitive distortion in online game addiction among Chinese adolescents. *Children and Youth Services Review, 35*(9), 1468–1475. doi:10.1016/j.childyouth.2013.05.021

Li, L., Griffiths, M. D., Niu, Z., & Mei, S. (2020). Fear of missing out (FoMO) and gaming disorder among Chinese university students: Impulsivity and game time as mediators. *Issues in Mental Health Nursing, 41*(12), 1104–1113. doi:10.1080/01612840.2020.1774018 PMID:32634040

Lima, I. A. (2004). *Estrutura de referência para a transferência de tecnologia no âmbito da cooperação universidade-empresa: Estudo de caso no CEFET-PR.* [Doctoral dissertation, Universidade Federal de Santa Catarina, Florianópolis].

Lin, L. Y., Sidani, J. E., Shensa, A., Radovic, A., Miller, E., Colditz, J. B., Hoffman, B. L., Giles, L. M., & Primack, B. A. (2016). Association between social media use and depression among U.S. young adults. *Depression and Anxiety, 33*(4), 323–331. doi:10.1002/da.22466 PMID:26783723

Lin, M. P., Wu, J. Y. W., You, J., Chang, K. M., Hu, W. H., & Xu, S. (2018). Association between online and offline social support and internet addiction in a representative sample of senior high school students in Taiwan: The mediating role of self-esteem. *Computers in Human Behavior, 84*, 1–7. doi:10.1016/j.chb.2018.02.007

Lin, S., Longobardi, C., Gastaldi, F. G. M., & Fabris, M. A. (2023). Social Media Addiction and Aggressive Behaviors in Early Adolescents: The Mediating Role of Nighttime Social Media Use and Sleep Quality. *The Journal of Early Adolescence*, 02724316231160142. doi:10.1177/02724316231160142

Lin, Y. H., Chang, L. R., Lee, Y. H., Tseng, H. W., Kuo, T. B., & Chen, S. H. (2014). Development and validation of the Smartphone Addiction Inventory (SPAI). *PLoS One, 9*(6), e98312. doi:10.1371/journal.pone.0098312 PMID:24896252

Li, Q. (2006). Cyberbullying in schools: A Research of gender differences. *School Psychology International, 27*(2), 157–170. doi:10.1177/0143034306064547

Li, Q., Guo, X., & Bai, X. (2017). Weekdays or weekends: Exploring the impacts of microblog posting patterns on gratification and addiction. *Information & Management, 54*(5), 613–624. doi:10.1016/j.im.2016.12.004

Lister, M. (2013). *The photographic image in digital culture*. Routledge Publishing. doi:10.4324/9780203797563

Liu, M., & Peng, W. (2009). Cognitive and psychological predictors of the negative outcomes associated with playing MMOGs (massively multiplayer online games). *Computers in Human Behavior*, *25*(6), 1306–1311. doi:10.1016/j.chb.2009.06.002

Liu, Q., Wu, J., Zhou, Z., & Wang, W. (2020). Parental technoference and smartphone addiction in Chinese adolescents: The mediating role of social sensitivity and loneliness. *Children and Youth Services Review*, *118*, 105434. doi:10.1016/j.childyouth.2020.105434

Livingstone, S., Haddon, L., Görzig, A., & Ólafsson, K. (2011). *Risks and safety on the internet: the perspective of European children: full findings and policy implications from the EU Kids Online survey of 9-16 year olds and their parents in 25 countries*. LSE.

Li, W., Garland, E. L., & Howard, M. O. (2014). Family factors in Internet addiction among Chinese youth: A review of English- and Chinese-language studies. *Computers in Human Behavior*, *31*(1), 393–411. doi:10.1016/j.chb.2013.11.004

Li, W., O'Brien, J. E., Snyder, S. M., & Howard, M. (2015). Characteristics of internet addiction/pathological internet use in u.s. university students: A qualitative-method investigation. *PLoS One*, *10*(2), e0117372. doi:10.1371/journal.pone.0117372 PMID:25647224

Li, Y. Y., Sun, Y., Meng, S. Q., Bao, Y. P., Cheng, J. L., Chang, X. W., Ran, M. S., Sun, Y. K., Kosten, T., Strang, J., Lu, L., & Shi, J. (2021). Internet addiction increases in the general population during COVID-19: Evidence from China. *The American Journal on Addictions*, *30*(4), 389–397. doi:10.1111/ajad.13156 PMID:33738888

Loader, B. D. (2007a). Introduction: Young Citizens in The Digital Age: Disaffected or Displaced? In Young Citizens in the Digital Age (pp. 15-32). Routledge.

Loader, B. D. (2007b). *Young citizens in the digital age*. Routledge London. doi:10.4324/9780203946725

Longo, F., Padovano, A., & Umbrello, S. (2020). Value-oriented and ethical technology engineering in industry 5.0: A human-centric perspective for the design of the factory of the future. *Applied Sciences (Basel, Switzerland)*, *10*(12), 4182. doi:10.3390/app10124182

Lopez-Fernandez, O., Honrubia-Serrano, M. L., Baguley, T., & Griffiths, M. D. (2014). Pathological video game playing in Spanish and British adolescents: Towards the exploration of Internet Gaming Disorder symptomatology. *Computers in Human Behavior*, *41*, 304–312. doi:10.1016/j.chb.2014.10.011

López, M. C. L. A., Gutierrez, J. C. S., & Jiménez, A. G. (2015). Problematic internet use among Spanish adolescents: The predictive role of internet preference and family relationships. *European Journal of Communication*, *30*(4), 470–485. doi:10.1177/0267323115586725

Lotfi, A., Kabiri, S., & Ghasemlou, H. (2013). Change of Values and Intergenerational Conflict: The Case of Iran Khoy City [Değerler Değişimi ve Kuşaklararası Çatışma: İran Khoy Kenti Örneği]. *Eskişehir Osmangazi Üniversitesi Sosyal Bilimler Dergisi*, *14*(2), 93–113.

Lozano-Blasco, R., Robres, A. Q., & Sanchez, A. S. (2022). Internet addiction in young adults: A meta-analysis and systematic review. *Computers in Human Behavior*, *130*, 107201. doi:10.1016/j.chb.2022.107201

Łukawski, K., Rusek, M., & Czuczwar, S. J. (2019). Can pharmacotherapy play a role in treating internet addiction disorder? *Expert Opinion on Pharmacotherapy*, *20*(11), 1299–1301. doi:10.1080/14656566.2019.1612366 PMID:31058549

Lundvall, B. Å. (1992). *National systems of innovation: Towards a theory of innovation and interactive learning*. Pinter Publishers.

Lupton, D. (2015). *Digital sociology*. Routledge, Taylor & Francis Group.

Lu, Y., Adrados, J. S., Chand, S. S., & Wang, L. (2021). Humans are not machines-anthropocentric human-machine symbiosis for ultra-flexible smart manufacturing. *Engineering (Beijing)*, *7*(6), 734–737. doi:10.1016/j.eng.2020.09.018

Lyon, D., & Bauman, Z. (2013). Akışkan gözetim. (çev. ElçinYılmaz). İstanbul: Ayrıntı Yayınları.

Lyotard, J. F. (2000). Postmodern durum, bilgi üzerine bir rapor. (çev. Ahmet Çiğdem). Ankara: Vadi Yayınları.

Lyytinen, K., & King, J. L. (2002). Editorial: Around the cradle of the wireless revolution: the emergence and evolution of celiular telephony. *Telecommunications Policy*, *26*(3-4), 97–100. doi:10.1016/S0308-5961(02)00002-2

Madary, M., & Metzinger, T. (2016). Real virtuality: A code of ethical conduct recommendations for good scientific practice and the consumers of VR technology. *Frontiers in Robotics and AI*, *3*, 3. doi:10.3389/frobt.2016.00003

Maddikunta, P. K. R., Pham, Q. V., Prabadevi, B., Deepa, N., Dev, K., Gadekallu, T. R., & Liyanage, M. (2022). Industry 5.0: A survey on enabling technologies and potential applications. *Journal of Industrial Information Integration*, *26*, 100257. doi:10.1016/j.jii.2021.100257

Madison, N., & Klang, M. (2020). The case for digital activism: Refuting the fallacies of slacktivism. *Journal of Digital Social Research*, *2*(2), 28–47. doi:10.33621/jdsr.v2i2.25

Magomedov, I. A., Murzaev, H. A., & Bagov, A. M. (2020). The role of digital technologies in economic development. *IOP Conference Series. Materials Science and Engineering*, *862*(052071), 1–4. doi:10.1088/1757-899X/862/5/052071

Ma, L., Feng, J., Feng, Z., & Wang, L. (2019). Research on user loyalty of short video app based on perceived value: Take TikTok as an example. *16th International Conference on Service Systems and Service Management*. IEEE. 10.1109/ICSSSM.2019.8887751

Malik, R., & Trivedi, S. (2022). Big data analytics in predicting consumer behaviour. *Big Data: A Road Map for Successful Digital Marketing*, 9.

Malik, K., Georgiou, L., & Grieve, B. (2011). Developing new technology platforms for new business models: Syngenta's partnership with the University of Manchester. *Research Technology Management*, *54*(1), 24–31. doi:10.1080/08956308.2011.11657670

Mamasioulas, A., Mourtzis, D., & Chryssolouris, G. (2020). A manufacturing innovation overview: Concepts, models and metrics. *International Journal of Computer Integrated Manufacturing*, *33*(8), 769–791. doi:10.1080/0951192X.2020.1780317

Mannheim, K. (1952). The Problem of Generations. In P. Kecskemeti (Ed.), *Essays on the Sociology of Knowledge* (pp. 276–320). Routledge and Kegan Paul.

Mannikko, N., Billieux, J., & Kaariainen, M. (2015). Problematic digital gaming behavior and its relation to the psychological, social and physical health of Finnish adolescents and young adults. *Journal of Behavioral Addictions*, *4*(4), 281–288. doi:10.1556/2006.4.2015.040 PMID:26690623

Mannikko, N., Ruotsalainen, H., Miettunen, J., Pontes, H. M., & Kaariainen, M. (2017). Problematic gaming behaviour and health-related outcomes: A systematic review and meta-analysis. *Journal of Health Psychology*, 1359105317740414. PMID:29192524

Manovich, L. (2001). *The language of new media*. The MIT Publishing.

Manovich, L. (2009). The practice of everyday (media) life: From mass consumption to mass cultural production? *Critical Inquiry*, *35*(2), 319–331. doi:10.1086/596645

Mansell, R. (2017). Inequality and digitally mediated communication: Divides, contradictions and consequences. *Javnost (Ljubljana)*, *24*(2), 146–161. doi:10.1080/13183222.2017.1287966

Marangunić, N., & Granić, A. (2015). Technology acceptance model: A literature review from 1986 to 2013. *Universal Access in the Information Society*, *14*(1), 81–95. doi:10.100710209-014-0348-1

Marengo, D., Fabris, M. A., Longobardi, C., & Settanni, M. (2022). Smartphone and social media use contributed to individual tendencies towards social media addiction in Italian adolescents during the COVID-19 pandemic. *Addictive Behaviors*, *126*, 107204. doi:10.1016/j.addbeh.2021.107204 PMID:34875508

Margetts, H., & Dunleavy, P. (2013). The second wave of digital-era governance: A quasi-paradigm for government on the Web. *Philosophical Transactions - Royal Society. Mathematical, Physical, and Engineering Sciences*, *371*(1987), 20120382. doi:10.1098/rsta.2012.0382 PMID:23419851

Marino, C., Gini, G., Vieno, A., & Spada, M. M. (2018). The associations between problematic Facebook use, psychological distress and well-being among adolescents and young adults: A systematic review and meta-analysis. *Journal of Affective Disorders*, *226*, 274–281. doi:10.1016/j.jad.2017.10.007 PMID:29024900

Marshall, C., & Rossman, G. B. (2014). *Designing Qualitative Research*. Sage.

Marshall, G. (1999). *Toplumsal Hareketler. Sosyoloji Sözlüğü* (A. Osman & K. Derya, Trans.). Bilim ve Sanat.

Marsh, J., Plowman, L., Yamada-Rice, D., Bishop, J., & Scott, F. (2016). Digital Play: A New Classification. *Early Years Journal of International Research and Development*, *36*(3), 242–253. doi:10.1080/09575146.2016.1167675

Marsh, R. M. (2014). Modernization theory, then and now. *Comparative Sociology*, *13*(3), 261–283. doi:10.1163/15691330-12341311

Martin, T. (2005). Fuzzy sets in the fight against digital obesity. *Fuzzy Sets and Systems*, *156*(3), 411–417. doi:10.1016/j.fss.2005.05.038

Marx, K. (2003). *Kapital* [Capital]. (A. Bilgi, Trans.). Eriş Publishing.

Mascheroni, G., & Ólafsson, K. (2014). *Net children go mobile: Risks and opportunities* (2nd ed.). Educatt.

Massarolo, J., & Mesquita, D. (2016). *Vídeo sob Demanda: uma nova plataforma televisiva*. Compós.

Masur, P. K., Reinecke, L., Ziegele, M., & Quiring, O. (2014). The interplay of intrinsic need satisfaction and Facebook specific motives in explaining addictive behavior on Facebook. *Computers in Human Behavior*, *39*, 376–386. doi:10.1016/j.chb.2014.05.047

Matarazzo, M., Penco, L., Profumo, G., & Quaglia, R. (2021). Digital transformation and customer value creation in made in Italy SMEs: A dynamic capabilities perspective. *Journal of Business Research*, *123*, 642–656. doi:10.1016/j.jbusres.2020.10.033

Matsuoka, R., & Rahimi, A. (2011). The positive effect of conference participation on reducing L2 communication apprehension. *Procedia Computer Science*, *3*, 898–907. doi:10.1016/j.procs.2010.12.147

Matsuzaka, S., Avery, L. R., & Stanton, A. G. (2023). Black Women's Social Media Use Integration and Social Media Addiction. *Social Media + Society*, *9*(1), 20563051221148977. doi:10.1177/20563051221148977

Matthews, C. E., Jurj, A. L., Shu, X. O., Li, H. L., Yang, G., Li, Q., Gao, Y. T., & Zheng, W. (2007). Influence of exercise, walking, cycling, and overall nonexercise physical activity on mortality in Chinese women. *American Journal of Epidemiology*, *165*(12), 1343–1350. doi:10.1093/aje/kwm088 PMID:17478434

Matzner, T., & Ochs, C. (2019). Privacy. *Internet Policy Review*, *8*(4). doi:10.14763/2019.4.1427

Mavnacıoğlu, K. (2022). Dijital çağda pazarlama iletişimi etiği üzerine bir değerlendirme. *Ahi Evran Üniversitesi Enstitüsü Sosyal Bilimler Dergisi*, *8*(1), 52–66. doi:10.31592/aeusbed.980897

Mavrodieva, A. V., & Shaw, R. (2020). Disaster and climate change issues in Japan's Society 5.0—A discussion. *Sustainability (Basel)*, *12*(5), 1893. doi:10.3390u12051893

Mazlum, M., & Atalay, A. (2022). Developing the fear of missing out (FoMO) scale for university students: The validity and reliability study. *Journal of Pedagogical Research*, *6*(4), 4. doi:10.33902/JPR.202215485

McCarthy, C. (2020, October 28). *Unhealthy Video Gaming: What Parents Can Do to Prevent It*. Healthy Children. https://www.healthychildren.org/English/family-life/Media/Pages/Unhealthy-Video-Gaming.aspx

McCroskey, J. C. (1982). An introduction to rhetorical communication, (4 b.). Englewood Cliffs: Prentice Hall, Routledge.

McCroskey, J. C. (1984). The communication apprehension perspective. *Avoiding communication: Shyness, reticence, and communication apprehension*, 13-38.

McCroskey, J. C. (1977). Oral communication apprehension: A summary of recent theory and research. *Human Communication Research*, *4*(1), 78–96. doi:10.1111/j.1468-2958.1977.tb00599.x

McCroskey, J. C., Daly, J. A., & Sorensen, G. (1976). Personality correlates of communication apprehension: A research note. *Human Communication Research*, *2*(4), 376–380. doi:10.1111/j.1468-2958.1976.tb00498.x

McCroskey, J. C., Simpson, T. J., & Richmond, V. P. (1982). Biological sex and communication apprehension. *Communication Quarterly*, *30*(2), 129–133. doi:10.1080/01463378209369439

McCroskey, J., Richmond, V., Berger, B., & Baldwin, H. (1983). How to make a good thing worse: A comparison of approaches to helping students overcome communication apprehension. *Communication*, *12*(1), 213–219.

McFerren, D. (2012, January 26). *Fitness Gaming: Two Words. One Meaning*. Nexersys. https://nexersys.com/fitness-gaming-two-words-one-meaning/

McIntyre, D. P., & Srinivasan, A. (2017). Networks, platforms, and strategy: Emerging views and next steps. *Strategic Management Journal*, *38*(1), 141–160. doi:10.1002mj.2596

McKee, P. C., Budnick, C. J., Walters, K. S., & Antonios, I. (2022). College student Fear of Missing Out (FoMO) and maladaptive behavior: Traditional statistical modeling and predictive analysis using machine learning. *PLoS One*, *17*(10), e0274698. doi:10.1371/journal.pone.0274698 PMID:36197889

McLuhan, H. M., McLuhan, M., & Nevitt, B. (1972). *Take today: The executive as dropout*. Longman Canada.

McLuhan, M. (2014). *The Gutenberg galaxy: the making of typographic man* (3rd ed.). Yapi Kredi Publications.

McNichol, M. L., & Thorsteinsson, E. B. (2017). Internet addiction, psychological distress, and coping responses among adolescents and adults. *Cyberpsychology, Behavior, and Social Networking*, *20*(5), 296–304. doi:10.1089/cyber.2016.0669 PMID:28414517

Md Nor, K., Pearson, J. M., & Ahmad, A. (2010). Adoption of internet banking theory of the diffusion of innovation. *International Journal of Management Studies*, *17*(1), 69–85. doi:10.32890/ijms.17.1.2010.9984

Medicine ASoA. (2011). *Public policy statement: Definition of addiction*. American Society of Addiction Medicine Chevy Chase.

Medina-Borja, A. (2017). Smart human-centred service systems of the future. *Future Services & Societal Systems in Society*, *5*, 235–239.

Mehroof, M., & Griffiths, M. D. (2010). Online gaming addiction: The role of sensation seeking, self-control, neuroticism, aggression, state anxiety, and trait anxiety. *Cyberpsychology, Behavior, and Social Networking*, *13*(3), 313–316. doi:10.1089/cyber.2009.0229 PMID:20557251

Mejias, U. A., & Couldry, N. (2019). Datafication. *Internet Policy Review*, *8*(4). doi:10.14763/2019.4.1428

Meng, S.-Q., Cheng, J.-L., Li, Y.-Y., Yang, X.-Q., Zheng, J.-W., Chang, X.-W., Shi, Y., Chen, Y., Lu, L., Sun, Y., Bao, Y.-P., & Shi, J. (2022). Global prevalence of digital addiction in general population: A systematic review and meta-analysis. *Clinical Psychology Review*, *92*, 102128. doi:10.1016/j.cpr.2022.102128 PMID:35150965

Mentsiev, A. U., Engel, M. V., Tsamaev, A. M., Abubakarov, M. V., & Yushaeva, R. S. E. (2020). The concept of digitalization and its impact on the modern economy. *Advances in the Economics. Business and Management Research*, *128*(1), 2960–2964.

Mentzoni, R. A., Brunborg, G. S., Molde, H., Myrseth, H., Skouverøe, K. J. M., Hetland, J., & Pallesen, S. (2011). Problematic video game use: Estimated prevalence and associations with mental and physical health. *Cyberpsychology, Behavior, and Social Networking*, *14*(10), 591–596. doi:10.1089/cyber.2010.0260 PMID:21342010

Merriam, S. (1998). *Qualitative research and case study applications in education. Revised and expanded from case study research in education*. JB Printing.

Messias, E., Castro, J., Saini, A., Usman, M., & Peeples, D. (2011). Sadness, suicide, and their association with video game and internet overuse among teens: Results from the youth risk behavior survey 2007 and 2009. *Suicide & Life-Threatening Behavior*, *41*(3), 307–315. doi:10.1111/j.1943-278X.2011.00030.x PMID:21463355

Mete, H. E. (2008). Kronik Hastalık ve Depresyon. *Klinik Psikiyatri*, *11*(3), 3–18.

Metin, S., & Kızıldağ, D. (2017). Kuşakların Kariyer Beklentilerinin Farklılaşması: Otomotiv Sektöründe Bir Araştırma. *Mustafa Kemal Üniversitesi Sosyal Bilimler Enstitüsü Dergisi*, *14*(40), 340–363.

Metz, J. (2019). Fomo and regret for non-doings. *Social Theory and Practice*, *45*(3), 451–470. doi:10.5840octheorpract201992767

Michaud, Y. (1986). *Şiddet (Çev.: Cem Muhtaroğlu)*. İletişim Yayınları.

Microsoft. (2022). *Civility, safety & interaction online: Turkey*. Microsoft. https://www.microsoft.com/en-us/digital-skills/digital-civility?activetab=dci_reports:primaryr4

Mihara, S., & Higuchi, S. (2017). Cross-sectional and longitudinal epidemiological studies of Internet gaming disorder: A systematic review of the literature. *Psychiatry and Clinical Neurosciences*, *71*(7), 425–444. doi:10.1111/pcn.12532 PMID:28436212

Mihelj, S., Leguina, A., & Downey, J. (2019). Culture is digital: Cultural participation, diversity and the digital divide. *New Media & Society*, *21*(7), 1465–1485. doi:10.1177/1461444818822816

Milani, L., La Torre, G., Fiore, M., Grumi, S., Gentile, D. A., Ferrante, M., Miccoli, S., & Blasio, P. (2018). Internet gaming addiction in adolescence: Risk factors and maladjustment correlates. *International Journal of Mental Health and Addiction*, *16*(4), 888–904. doi:10.100711469-017-9750-2

Miller, E. (2023, February 1). *Cybersickness: what is it, symptoms, and treatment*. Ro. https://ro.co/health-guide/cyber-sickness/

Miller, V. (2020). *Understanding digital culture*. Sage Publications.

Milyavskaya, M., Saffran, M., Hope, N., & Koestner, R. (2018). Fear of missing out: Prevalence, dynamics, and consequences of experiencing FOMO. *Motivation and Emotion*, *42*(5), 725–737. doi:10.100711031-018-9683-5

Minges, M. (2015). Exploring the relationship between broadband and economic growth. *Background Paper, World Development Report 2016*. Digital Dividends.

Mirbabaie, M., Stieglitz, S., & Marx, J. (2022). Digital detox. *Business & Information Systems Engineering*, *64*(2), 239–246. doi:10.100712599-022-00747-x

Mitchell, A. M. (2012). Overview of Special Topic Issue: Addiction and Technology. *Journal of Addictions Nursing*, *32*(3), 177–179. doi:10.1097/JAN.0000000000000421 PMID:34473445

Modzelewski, P. (2020). Fomo (fear of missing out) – an educational and behavioral problem in times of new communication forms. *Konteksty Pedagogiczne*, *14*(1), 215–232.

Mojtabai, R. (2010). Mental illness stigma and willingness to seek mental health care in the European Union. *Social Psychiatry and Psychiatric Epidemiology*, *45*(7), 705–712. doi:10.100700127-009-0109-2 PMID:19680588

Mondejar, M. E., Avtar, R., Diaz, H. L. B., Dubey, R. K., Esteban, J., Gómez-Morales, A., Hallam, B., Mbungu, N. T., Okolo, C. C., Prasad, K. A., She, Q., & Garcia-Segura, S. (2021). Digitalization to achieve sustainable development goals: Steps towards a smart green planet. *The Science of the Total Environment*, *794*(148539), 1–20. doi:10.1016/j.scitotenv.2021.148539 PMID:34323742

Montag, C., Flierl, M., Markett, S., Walter, N., Jurkiewicz, M., & Reuter, M. (2012). Internet addiction and personality in first-person-shooter video gamers. *Journal of Media Psychology*.

Montag, C., Yang, H., & Elhai, J. D. (2021). On the psychology of TikTok use: A first glimpse from empirical findings. *Frontiers in Public Health*, *9*, 641673. doi:10.3389/fpubh.2021.641673 PMID:33816425

Moore, K., & Craciun, G. (2021). Fear of missing out and personality as predictors of social networking sites usage: The Instagram case. *Psychological Reports*, *124*(4), 1761–1787. doi:10.1177/0033294120936184 PMID:32659168

Morahan-Martin, J., & Schumacher, P. (2000). Incidence and correlates of pathological Internet use among college students. *Computers in Human Behavior*, *16*(1), 13–29. doi:10.1016/S0747-5632(99)00049-7

Moreno, M. A., Parks, M. R., Zimmerman, F. J., Brito, T. E., & Christakis, D. A. (2009). Display of health risk behaviors on MySpace by adolescents: Prevalence and associations. *Archives of Pediatrics & Adolescent Medicine*, *163*(1), 27–34. doi:10.1001/archpediatrics.2008.528 PMID:19124700

Morgan, J. P. (2022). *Opportunities in the metaverse: How businesses can explore the metaverse and navigate the hype vs. reality,* 1-17. JP Morgan. https://www.jpmorgan.com/content/dam/jpm/treasury-services/documents/opportunities-in-the-metaverse.pdf

Moro-Visconti, R. (2022). From physical reality to the Metaverse: A Multilayer Network Valuation. *Journal of Metaverse*, *2*(1), 16–22. https://dergipark.org.tr/en/pub/jmv/issue/67967/1071950

Mourtzis, D. (2016). Challenges and future perspectives for the life cycle of manufacturing networks in the mass customisation era. *Logistics Research*, *9*(1), 1–20. doi:10.100712159-015-0129-0

Mourtzis, D. (2018). Development of skills and competences in manufacturing towards Education 4.0: A teaching factory approach. In *International Conference on the Industry 4.0 model for Advanced Manufacturing* (pp. 194-210). Springer, Cham. 10.1007/978-3-319-89563-5_15

Mourtzis, D., Angelopoulos, J., & Panopoulos, N. (2022). A literature review of the challenges and opportunities of the transition from industry 4.0 to society 5.0. *Energies*, *15*(17), 6276. doi:10.3390/en15176276

Müller, J. (2020). Enabling technologies for industry 5.0-results of a workshop with europe's technology leaders. *Europea*. https://op. europa. eu/en/publication-detail/-/publication/8e5de100-2a1c-11eb-9d7e-01aa75ed71a1/language-en.

Müller, K. W., Beutel, M., Egloff, B., & Wölfling, K. (2014). Investigating risk factors for internet gaming disorder: A comparison of patients with addictive gaming, pathological gamblers and healthy controls regarding the big five personality traits. *European Addiction Research*, *20*(3), 129–136. doi:10.1159/000355832 PMID:24247280

Müller, K. W., Dreier, M., Beutel, M. E., Duven, E., Giralt, S., & Wölfling, K. (2016). A hidden type of internet addiction? Intense and addictive use of social networking sites in adolescents. *Computers in Human Behavior*, *55*, 172–177. doi:10.1016/j.chb.2015.09.007

Muller, K. W., Janikian, M., Dreier, M., Wolfling, K., Beutel, M. E., Tzavara, C., Richardson, C., & Tsitsika, A. (2015). Regular gaming behavior and internet gaming disorder in European adolescents: Results from a cross-national representative survey of prevalence, predictors, and psychopathological correlates. *European Child & Adolescent Psychiatry*, *24*(5), 565–574. doi:10.100700787-014-0611-2 PMID:25189795

Muslu, G. K., & Aygun, O. (2020). An analysis of computer game addiction in primary school children and its affecting factors. *Journal of Addictions Nursing*, *31*(1), 30–38. doi:10.1097/JAN.0000000000000322 PMID:32132422

Mustafaoğlu, R., Zirek, E., Yasacı, Z., & Özdinçler, A. R. (2018). Negative Health Effects of the Use of Digital Technology on The Development of Children. *Addicta: The Turkish Journal on Addictions*, *5*, 227–247. doi:10.15805/addicta.2018.5.2.0051

Mutlu, T. (2021). *Sosyal Medya Bağımlılığı ve Kişilik İlişkisi: Sosyal Medya Üzerinden Bir Uyguama*. Sakarya: Sakarya Üniversitesi Sosyal Bilimler Enstitüsü / Yayımlanmamış Yüksek Lisans Tezi.

Mutlu, E. (2012). *İletişim Sözlüğü, Sofos Yayınları*. Baskı.

Myovella, G., Karacuka, M., & Haucap, J. (2020). Digitalization and economic growth: A comparative analysis of Sub-Saharan Africa and OECD economies. *Telecommunication Policy*, *44*(2).

Mystakidis, S. (2022). Metaverse. *Metaverse. Encyclopedia*, *2*(1), 486–497. doi:10.3390/encyclopedia2010031

Nahavandi, S. (2019). Industry 5.0-A human-centric solution. *Sustainability (Basel)*, *11*(16), 4371. doi:10.3390u11164371

Nakanishi, H. (2022) Modern society has reached its limits. society 5.0 will liberate us. *We Forum*. https://www.weforum.org/agenda/2019/01/modern-society-has-reached-its-limits-society-5-0-will-liberate-us/

Narvaez Rojas, C., Alomia Peñafiel, G. A., Loaiza Buitrago, D. F., & Tavera Romero, C. A. (2021). Society 5.0: A japanese concept for a super-intelligent society. *Sustainability (Basel)*, *13*(12), 6567. doi:10.3390u13126567

Naseri, L., Mohamadi, J., Sayehmiri, K., & Azizpoor, Y. (2015). Perceived social support, self-esteem, and internet addiction among students of Al-Zahra University, Tehran, Iran. *Iranian Journal of Psychiatry and Behavioral Sciences*, *9*(3), e421. doi:10.17795/ijpbs-421 PMID:26576175

Nash, C., Jarrahi, M. H., Sutherland, W., & Phillips, G. (2018). *Digital nomads beyond the buzzword: Defining digital nomadic work and use of digital technologies. Chowdhury, G., McLeod, J., Gillet, V. ve Willett, P. (Der.) Transforming Digital Worlds iConference*. Springer.

Naslund, J. A., Aschbrenner, K. A., McHugo, G. J., Unützer, J., Marsch, L. A., & Bartels, S. J. (2019). Exploring opportunities to support mental health care using social media: A survey of social media users with mental illness. *Early Intervention in Psychiatry*, *13*(3), 405–413. doi:10.1111/eip.12496 PMID:29052947

Nasr, H. E., & Rached, K. S. B. (2021). The psychological and behavioural antecedents of Facebook addiction. *Academy of Entrepreneurship Journal*, *27*, 1–14.

Nathan, P. E., Conrad, M., & Skinstad, A. H. (2016). History of the Concept of Addiction. *Annual Review of Clinical Psychology*, *12*(1), 29–51. doi:10.1146/annurev-clinpsy-021815-093546 PMID:26565120

National Institute of Mental Health. (2015). *What Is Depression?* NIH. https://www.nimh.nih.gov/health/topics/depression/index.shtml

National Institute on Drug Abuse. (2003). *Preventing drug use among children and adolescents: A research-based guide for parents, educators, and community leaders*. NIDA.

National Institute on Drug Abuse. (2014). Drugs, brains, and behavior: The science of addiction. *NIH Pub No.14, 5605*. NIDA.

National Institute on Drug Abuse. (2019). *Genetics and Epigenetics of Addiction Drug Facts*. NIDA.

National Institute on Drug Abuse. (2020). Drug Misuse and Addiction: What is addiction? Owens EW, Behun RJ, Manning JC, Reid RC. (2012). The impact of internet pornography on adolescents: a review of the research. *Sexual Addiction & Compulsivity*, *19*(1-2), 99–122.

National League of Cities. (2022). *The Future of Cities*. National League of Cities. https://www.nlc.org/resource/cities-and-themetaverse/#:~:text=The%20metaverse%20is%20the%20next,digitally%20recreate%20the%20real%20world

Navarrete, T. (2013). Digital cultural heritage. In I. Rizzo & A. Mignosa (Eds.), *Handbook on the economics of cultural heritage* (pp. 251–272). Edward Elgar Publishing. doi:10.4337/9780857931009.00023

Nazlıgül, Denizci, M., Baş, S., Akyüz, Z. & Yorulmaz, O. (2018). İnternette oyun oynama bozukluğu ve tedavi yaklaşımları: Sistematik bir gözden geçirme. Addicta. *The Turkish Journal on Addictions*, *5*, 13–35.

Neal, S. (2023, February 3). 5 trends that will shape the gaming sector in 2023. *Times of India*. https://timesofindia.indiatimes.com/blogs/voices/5-trends-that-will-shape-the-gaming-sector-in-2023/

Newport, C. (2016). *Deep Work: Rules for Focused Success in a Distracted World*. Grand Central Publishing.

Newspaper, E. (2013). Cell phones are more powerful than the first craft to land on the Moon. *Aksam*. https://www.aksam.com.tr/teknoloji/cep-telefonlari-aya-inen-ilk-aractan-daha-guclu/haber-189320 Access Date: 05.03.22.

Newzoo. (2022). Newzoo Global Games Market Report 2022. *Newzoo*. https://newzoo.com/insights/trend-reports/newzoo-global-games-market-report-2022-free-version

Nguyen, V. B. (2021). The digitalization – economic growth relationship in developing countries and the role of governance. *Scientific Annals of Economics and Business*, *68*(4), 481–493. doi:10.47743aeb-2021-0028

Nhamo, G., Nhemachena, C., & Nhamo, S. (2020). Using ICT indicators to measure readiness of countries to implement industry 4.0 and the SDGs. Environmental Economics and Policy Studies, Springer. *Environmental Economics and Policy Studies*, *22*(2), 315–337. doi:10.100710018-019-00259-1

Niedergassel, B., & Leker, J. (2011). Different dimensions of knowledge in cooperative R&D projects of university scientists. *Technovation*, *31*(4), 142–150. doi:10.1016/j.technovation.2010.10.005

Nielsen, M. B., & Einarsen, S. (2012). Outcomes of exposure to workplace bullying: A meta-analytic review. *Work and Stress*, *26*(4), 309–332. doi:10.1080/02678373.2012.734709

NIST. (2021). *Erişim tarihi*. NIST. https://csrc.nist.gov/glossary/term/cybersecurity

Niyazioglu, S. (2016). *Subjects in the history of graphic design in Turkey, Turkey Design Chronology, Essay, Graphics*. Istanbul Foundation for Culture and Arts. https://www.youtube.com/watch?v=AgnA32TAe3U

NLC. (2022). *The Future of Cities: Cities and the Metaverse*. NLC. https://www.nlc.org/wp-content/uploads/2022/04/CS-Cities-and-the-Metaverse_v4-Final-1.pdf

Noronha, I., Castellano, M., & Pinho, J. (2018). *"Netflix eu te amo!": o capital emocional no relacionamento entre a empresa de streaming e os consumidores-fãs*. Revista Fronteiras, Unisinos.

Notten, N. (2013). Risicogedrag en het wereldwijde web: De invloed van gezin en samenleving op het online risicogedrag van adolescenten vanuit een Europees perspectief. *Mens en Maatschappij*, *88*(4), 350–374. doi:10.5117/MEM2013.4.NOTT

NTV. (2020) Tartışılan "Ertuğrul Gazi" Büstü Kaldırıldı, İki Müdür Görevden Alındı (Diriliş Ertuğrul'daki Engin Altan Düzyatan'a Benzetilmişti). *NTV*. https://www.ntv.com.tr/turkiye/tartisilan-ertugrul-gazi-bustu-kaldirildi-iki-mudur-gorevden-alindi-dirilis-ertugruldaki-engin-altan-duzyatana-benzetilmisti,VxLp2oLHNUSvhjQDj8iR0Q

O'Brien, T. (2021) Digital activism and the state, Tapuya: Latin American Science. *Technology and Society*, *4*(1). doi:10.1080/25729861.2021.1973291

O'Connell, C. (2020). How FOMO (Fear of Missing Out), the Smartphone, and Social Media May Be Affecting University Students in the Middle East. *North American Journal of Psychology*, *22*(1).

Oberst, U., Wegmann, E., Stodt, B., Brand, M., & Chamarro, A. (2017). Negative consequences from heavy social networking in adolescents: The mediating role of fear of missing out. *Journal of Adolescence*, *55*(1), 51–60. doi:10.1016/j.adolescence.2016.12.008 PMID:28033503

Odabaşı, Y. (2014). *Postmodern pazarlama*. MediaCat.

Odgers, C. L., Schueller, S. M., & Ito, M. (2020). Screen time, social media use, and adolescent development. *Annual Review of Developmental Psychology*, *2*(1), 485–502. doi:10.1146/annurev-devpsych-121318-084815

Ögel K. (2012). *İnternet Bağımlılığı, İnternetin Psikolojisini Anlamak ve Bağımlılıkla Başa Çıkmak*, 47-60. Türkiye İş Bankası Kültür Yayınları.

Ögel, K. (2012). *İnternet bağımlılığı: İnternetin psikolojisini anlamak ve bağımlılıkla başa çıkmak*. Türkiye İş Bankası Kültür Yayınları.

Ökmen, Y. E., & Çokluk, N. (2021). Ben de Artık Bir Hikaye Anlatıcısıyım: Hikaye Anlatımında Dijital Olanaklar Açısından Yotuber "Fly with Haifa" Üzerine Bir İnceleme. *Etkileşim*, 190-215.

Okray, Z. (2020). "Şule Çet İçin Adalet": Bir Twitter Etiketi Üzerine İçerik Analizi. *Kadin/Woman 2000, 21*(2).

Oksanen, A., Oksa, R., Savela, N., Kaakinen, M., & Ellonen, N. (2020). Cyberbullying victimization at work: Social media identity bubble approach. *Computers in Human Behavior*, *109*, 106363. doi:10.1016/j.chb.2020.106363

Öksüzoğulları, H. (2013). *4-6 yaş grubu çocuğu olan ebeveynlerin çocuklarıyla iletişimlerinin çeşitli değişkenler açısından incelenmesi.* Mehmet Akif Ersoy Üniversitesi Eğitim Bilimleri Enstitüsü.

Olcay, S. (2018). Sosyalleşmenin Dijitalleşmesi Olarak Sosyaleşmesi Olarak Sosyal Medya ve Resimler Arasında Kaybolma Bozukluğu: Photolurking. *e-Journal of New Media/Yeni Medya Elektronik Dergi*, 90-104.

Oliveira, J., & Nobre, P. (2017). *Internet Video Streaming*.

Olweus, D. (2003). A profile of bullying at school. *Educational Leadership*, *60*(6), 12–17.

Omar, B., & Dequan, W. (2020). Watch, share or create: The influence of personality traits and user motivation on TikTok mobile video usage. [Interactive Mobile Technologies.]. *International Journal (Toronto, Ont.)*, 100.

Ong, V. (2018). *Sözlü ve Yazılı Kültür*. Metis Yayınları.

Onur, B. (1992). *Oyuncaklı Dünya - Toplumsal Tarih Üzerine Eğlenceli Bir Deneme* [Toy World - An Entertaining Essay on Social History]. V Yayınları.

Ophir, E., Nass, C., & Wagner, A. D. (2009). Cognitive control in media multitaskers. *Proceedings of the National Academy of Sciences of the United States of America*, *106*(37), 15583–15587. doi:10.1073/pnas.0903620106 PMID:19706386

Opreana, A., & Vinerean, S. (2015). A new development in online marketing: Introducing digital inbound marketing. *Expert Journal of Marketing*, *3*(1), 29–34.

Osterwalder, A., & Pigneur, Y. (2010). *Business Model Generation: A Handbook for Visionaries, Game Changers, and Challengers*. Wiley.

Oxford Dictionary. (2018) FOMO. *Oxford Dictionary*. Oxford Press. https://en.oxforddictionaries.com/ definition/fomo

Özcan, M., & Keskin, B. (2020). Social transformation in the context of digitalization. *International Journal of Society Researchs*, *16*(29), 2216–2229. doi:10.26466/opus.775748

Özdemir, M.,& Akar, F. (2018). Ergenlerde İnternette Amaçsız Gezinme ile Dijital Oyun Bağımlılığı Arasındaki İlişkinin Anksiyete ve Sosyal Kaygı Açısından İncelenmesi. *İnsan ve Toplum Bilimleri Araştırmaları Dergisi, 7*(4), 3123-3136.

Özel Sağlamtimur, Z. (2010). Dijital Sanat. *Anadolu University Journal of Social Sciences*, *10*(3), 213–238.

Özkan, O., Özer, Ö., & Özmen, S. (2020). Akıllı Telefon Bağımlılığı, İnternet Bağımlılığı ve Sosyal Medya Kullanımının İncelenmesi: Sağlık Yönetimi Öğrencilerinde Bir Uygulama. *The Academic Elegance*, 391-405.

Özkapı, M. (2021). *Yetişkinlerde sosyal medya kullanımının depresyon ve sosyal kaygı düzeyleri ile ilişkisi*. Yayınlanmamış Yüksek Lisans Tezi.

Özlem, A. (2015). Dijital Yaşamın Dijital Özneleri: Herkes ya da Hiç Kimse. *Uşak University Journal of Social Sciences*, *8*(1), 249–266.

Özmen, Ş. Y. (2018). Dijital şiddet, siber zorbalık ve yeni medya okuryazarlığı üzerine bir değerlendirme. *Journal of International Social Research*, *11*(61), 958–966. doi:10.17719/jisr.2018.2989

Özsoy, S., Ergüzel, O. Ş., Ersoy, A. Y., & Saygılı, M. (2022). The impact of digitalization on export of high technology products: A panel data approach. *The Journal of International Trade & Economic Development*, *31*(2), 277–298. doi:10.1080/09638199.2021.1965645

Özsungur, F. (2021). Strategic social work management in digital violence against women. *Toplum ve Sosyal Hizmet*, *32*(2), 661–687. doi:10.33417/tsh.836215

Paçacı, İ. (2014). Elektronik iletişim çağı ve oluş (turul) makta olan yeni (!) toplum düzeni üzerinde küresel toplum mühendisliği etkisi. *Marmara İletişim Dergisi*, (21), 19–55. doi:10.17829/midr.20142110297

Padua, D. (2021). *Digital cultural transformation: Building strategic mindsets via digital sociology*. Springer Publications. doi:10.1007/978-3-030-83803-4

Paglia, A., & Room, R. (1999). Preventing substance use problems among youth: A literature review and recommendations. *The Journal of Primary Prevention*, *20*(1), 3–50. doi:10.1023/A:1021302302085

Pakulski, J. (2009). Postmodern Social Theory. In B. S. Turner (Ed.), *The New Blackwell Companion to Social Theory* (pp. 251–280). Blackwell Publishing Ltd. doi:10.1002/9781444304992.ch13

Pallesen, S., Lorvik, I. M., Bu, E. H., & Molde, H. (2015). An exploratory study investigating the effects of a treatment manual for video game addiction. *Psychological Reports*, *117*(2), 490–495. doi:10.2466/02.PR0.117c14z9 PMID:26340051

Palley, T. I. (1996). Growth theory in a Keynesian mode: Some Keynesian foundations for new endogenous growth theory. *Journal of Post Keynesian Economics*, *19*(1), 113–135. doi:10.1080/01603477.1996.11490100

Palupi, N. D., Meifilina, A., & Harumike, Y. D. N. (2020). *The effect of using TikTok applications on self-confidance levels*. JOSAR.

Pamudyarini, R. A. (2021). The effect of innovation and consumer behaviour towards sustainable fashion in the era of society 5.0 students of fsr ikj product design. *International Journal of Multicultural and Multireligious Understanding*, *8*(2), 394–402. doi:10.18415/ijmmu.v8i2.2353

Pan, Y. C., Chiu, Y. C., & Lin, Y. H. (2020). Systematic review and meta-analysis of epidemiology of internet addiction. *Neuroscience and Biobehavioral Reviews*, *118*, 612–622. doi:10.1016/j.neubiorev.2020.08.013 PMID:32853626

Paolini, P., Silvers, M., & Proctor, N. (2013). Technologies for cultural heritage. In I. Rizzo & A. Mignosa (Eds.), *Handbook on the economics of cultural heritage* (pp. 273–289). Edward Elgar Publishing. doi:10.4337/9780857931009.00024

Pápay, O., Urbán, R., Griffiths, M. D., Nagygyörgy, K., Farkas, J., Kökönyei, G., Felvinczi, K., Oláh, A., Elekes, Z., & Demetrovics, Z. (2013). Psychometric properties of the problematic online gaming questionnaire short-form and prevalence of problematic online gaming in a national sample of adolescents. *Cyberpsychology, Behavior, and Social Networking*, *16*(5), 340–348. doi:10.1089/cyber.2012.0484 PMID:23621688

Parasuraman, R., & Manzey, D. H. (2010). Complacency and bias in human use of automation: An attentional integration. *Human Factors*, *52*(3), 381–410. doi:10.1177/0018720810376055 PMID:21077562

Parisod, H. (2014). The advantages and limitations of digital games in children's health promotion. *Finnish Journal of eHealth and eWelfare, 6*(4).

Park, J. H., Lee, Y. S., Sohn, J. H., & Han, D. H. (2016). Effectiveness of atomoxetine and methylphenidate for problematic online gaming in adolescents with attention deficit hyperactivity disorder. *Human Psychopharmacology*, *31*(6), 427–432. doi:10.1002/hup.2559 PMID:27859666

Park, S. Y., Kim, S. M., Roh, S., Soh, M. A., Lee, S. H., Kim, H., Lee, Y. S., & Han, D. H. (2016). The effects of a virtual reality treatment program for online gaming addiction. *Computer Methods and Programs in Biomedicine*, *129*, 99–108. doi:10.1016/j.cmpb.2016.01.015 PMID:26860055

Park, S., & Kim, S. (2022). Identifying World Types to Deliver Gameful Experiences for Sustainable Learning in the Metaverse. *Sustainability (Basel)*, *14*(1361), 1–14. doi:10.3390u14031361

Park, S., & Kim, Y. (2022b). A Metaverse: Taxonomy, Components, Applications, and Open Challenges. *IEEE Access : Practical Innovations, Open Solutions*, *10*, 4209–4251. doi:10.1109/ACCESS.2021.3140175

Patranabis, I. C. (2012). The Future of Workforce Management: Perspectives and Way Ahead. In R. K. Mishra, S. Sarkar, & P. Singh (Eds.), Today's HR for a Sustainable Tomorrow, Allied Publishers.

Patrão, I. (2019). A importância da autorregulação do comportamento online nas crianças da geração cordão. In R. Brito & P. Dias (Coords.), Crianças, famílias e tecnologias. Que desafios? Que caminhos? (pp. 184-197). Centro Interdisciplinar de Estudos Educacionais. doi:10.34629/ipl.eselx.cap.livros.025

Patton, M. Q. (2014). Qualitative Research & Evaluation Methods: Integrating Theory and Practice (M. Bütün ve S. B. Demir, Tr. Ed.), Ankara: Pegem Academy Publication.

Paulus, F. W., Ohmann, S., Von Gontard, A., & Popow, C. (2018). Internet gaming disorder in children and adolescents: A systematic review. *Developmental Medicine and Child Neurology*, *60*(7), 645–659. doi:10.1111/dmcn.13754 PMID:29633243

Pavlik, J. V. (2008). *Media in the digital age*. Columbia University Press.

Payton, S., & Hague, C. (2010). *Digital Literacy in Practice. Case Studies of Primary and Secondary Clasrrooms*. Futurelab Innovation in Education. https://www.nfer.ac.uk/publications/FUTL06/FUTL06casestudies.pdf

Pediatrics, A. A. O. (2011). Media use by children younger than 2 years. Council on communications and media. *Pediatrics*, *128*(5), 6.

Peeters, M. M., van Diggelen, J., Van Den Bosch, K., Bronkhorst, A., Neerincx, M. A., Schraagen, J. M., & Raaijmakers, S. (2021). Hybrid collective intelligence in a human–AI society. *AI & Society*, *36*(1), 217–238. doi:10.100700146-020-01005-y

Pellegrini, A. D., & Bartini, M. (2000). A longitudinal study of bullying, victimization, and peer affiliation during the transition from primary school to middle school. *American Educational Research Journal*, *37*(3), 699–725. doi:10.3102/00028312037003699

Peng, W., Li, D., Li, D., Jia, J., Wang, Y., & Sun, W. (2019). School disconnectedness and Adolescent Internet Addiction: Mediation by self-esteem and moderation by emotional intelligence. *Computers in Human Behavior*, *98*, 111–121. doi:10.1016/j.chb.2019.04.011

Peng, W., & Liu, M. (2010). Online gaming dependency: A preliminary study in China. *Cyberpsychology, Behavior, and Social Networking*, *13*(3), 329–333. doi:10.1089/cyber.2009.0082 PMID:20557254

Peplau, L. A., & Perlman, D. (1982). Perspectives on loneliness. In L. A. Peplau & D. Perlman (Eds.), *Loneliness: A sourcebook of current theory, research and therapy* (pp. 1–18). Wiley New York.

Pereira, S. (2015). *A Produção televisiva na era da mudança e da concorrência*. Faculdade de Ciência Sociais e Humanas de Lisboa.

Perloff, R. M. (2014). Social Media Effects on Young Women's Body Image Concerns: Theoretical Perspectives and an Agenda for Research. *Sex Roles*, *71*(11–12), 363–377. doi:10.100711199-014-0384-6

Peter, J. P., Olson, J. C., & Grunert, K. G. (1999). *Consumer behaviour and marketing strategy*. McGraw-hill.

Philbin, S. (2008). Process model for university-industry research collaboration. *European Journal of Innovation Management*, *11*(4), 488–521. doi:10.1108/14601060810911138

Pies, R. (2009). Should DSM-V designate "internet addiction"a mental disorder? *Psychiatry*, *6*, 31–37. PMID:19724746

Pietrangelo, A. (2023, February 1). *All About Cybersickness*. Healthline. https://www.healthline.com/health/cybersickness

Pilcher, J. (1994). Mannheim's Sociology of Generations: An Undervalued Legacy. *The British Journal of Sociology*, *45*(3), 481–495. doi:10.2307/591659

Pinheiro, G. (2017). *O mercado da produção de conteúdos para televisão: estudo do caso português*. Universidade Católica Portuguesa.

Plantin, J. C., Lagoze, C., Edwards, P. N., & Sandvig, C. (2018). Infrastructure studies meet platform studies in the age of Google and Facebook. *New Media & Society*, *20*(1), 293–310. doi:10.1177/1461444816661553

Poell, T., Nieborg, D., & van Dijck, J. (2019). Platformisation. *Internet Policy Review*, *8*(4). doi:10.14763/2019.4.1425

Poli, R., & Agrimi, E. (2012). Internet addiction disorder: Prevalence in an Italian student population. *Nordic Journal of Psychiatry*, *66*(1), 55–59. doi:10.3109/08039488.2011.605169 PMID:21859396

Ponti, M., Bélanger, S., Grimes, R., Heard, J., Johnson, M., Moreau, E., Norris, M., Shaw, A., Stanwick, R., Van Lankveld, J., & Williams, R.Canadian Paediatric Society. (2017). Screen time and young children: Promoting health and development in a digital world. *Paediatrics & Child Health*, *22*(8), 461–477. doi:10.1093/pch/pxx123 PMID:29601064

Postman, N. (2006). *Teknopoli Yeni Dünya Düzeni (2* (M. E. Yılmaz Ed. & Trans.). Paradigma Yayınları.

Potenza, M. N. (2006). Should addictive disorders include non-substance-related conditions? *Addiction (Abingdon, England)*, *101*(Suppl 1), 142–151. doi:10.1111/j.1360-0443.2006.01591.x PMID:16930171

Preece, J., Maloney-Krichmar, D., & Abras, C. (2003). History of Online Communities. In K. Christensen & D. Levinson (Eds.), *Encyclopedia of Community: From Village To Virtual World* (pp. 1023–1027). Sage Publications Sage.

Prensky, M. (2001). Digital Natives, Digital Immigrants. On the Horizon, 9(5). MCB University Press.

Primack, B. A., Shensa, A., Sidani, J. E., Whaite, E. O., Lin, L., Rosen, D., Colditz, J. B., Radovic, A., & Miller, E. (2017). Social Media Use and Perceived Social Isolation Among Young Adults in the U.S. *American Journal of Preventive Medicine*, *53*(1), 1–8. doi:10.1016/j.amepre.2017.01.010 PMID:28279545

Privitera, C., & Campbell, M. A. (2009). Cyberbullying: The new face of workplace bullying? *Cyberpsychology & Behavior*, *12*(4), 395–400. doi:10.1089/cpb.2009.0025 PMID:19594381

Protec. (2013). Monitor do Déficit Tecnológico em 2013. *Protec.* http://www.protec.org.br/

Przybylski, A. K., Murayama, K., DeHaan, C. R., & Gladwell, V. (2013). Motivational, emotional, and behavioral correlates of fear of missing out. *Computers in Human Behavior*, *29*(4), 1841–1848. doi:10.1016/j.chb.2013.02.014

Qiang, C. Z. W. 2009. Telecommunications and Economic Growth. Banque mondiale, Washington D.C.

Quwaider, M., Alabed, A., & Duwairi, R. (2019). The Impact of Video Games on the Players Behaviors: A Survey. *Procedia Computer Science*, *151*, 575–582. doi:10.1016/j.procs.2019.04.077

Raeskyesa, D. G. S., & Lukas, E. N. (2019). Does digitalization increase economic growth? Evidence from ASEAN8 countries. *Jurnal Ekonomi Indonesia*, *8*(2), 267–278. doi:10.52813/jei.v8i2.33

Rahardjo, W., & Mulyani, I. (2020). Instagram addiction in teenagers: The role of type D personality, self-esteem, and fear of missing out. *Psikohumaniora: Jurnal Penelitian Psikologi*, *5*(1), 29–44. doi:10.21580/pjpp.v5i1.4916

Rajan, B., Jose, L. G., & Sundar, T. (2022). Are You Hooked to the 'Gram'? Exploring the Correlation between Loneliness, the Fear of Missing Out, and Instagram Usage among Young Indians. *Palabra Clave (La Plata)*, *25*(2), e2525.

Rascão, J. P. (2021). The Value of Economic Information in the Digital Society. [JTA]. *Journal of Technological Advancements*, *1*(1), 1–33. doi:10.4018/JTA.20210101.oa3

Rastegar, D., & Fingerhood, M. I. (Eds.). (2020). *The American society of addiction medicine handbook of addiction medicine*. Oxford University Press. doi:10.1093/med/9780197506172.001.0001

Rath, B. N., & Hermawan, D. (2019). Do information and communication technologies foster economic growth in Indonesia? *Bulletin of Monetary Economics and Banking*, *22*(1), 103–122. doi:10.21098/bemp.v22i1.1041

Reeves, T. C., & Oh, E. (2014). Generational Difference sand the Integration of Technology in Learning, Instruction, and Performance. In J. M. Spector. (Eds.), Handbook of Research on Educational Communications and Technology (pp. 819-828). New York: Springer Science+Business Media.

Rehbein, F., & Baier, D. (2013). Family-, media-, and school-related risk factors of video game addiction. *Journal of Media Psychology*, *25*(3), 118–128. doi:10.1027/1864-1105/a000093

Rehbein, F., Kleimann, M., & Mossle, T. (2010). Prevalence and risk factors of video game dependency in adolescence: Results of a German nationwide survey. *Cyberpsychology, Behavior, and Social Networking*, *13*(3), 269–277. doi:10.1089/cyber.2009.0227 PMID:20557246

Rehbein, F., Kliem, S., Baier, D., Mossle, T., & Petry, N. M. (2015). Prevalence of Internet gaming disorder in German adolescents: Diagnostic contribution of the nine DSM-5 criteria in a state-wide representative sample. *Addiction (Abingdon, England)*, *110*(5), 842–851. doi:10.1111/add.12849 PMID:25598040

Reichenberger, I. (2018). Digital nomads – a quest for holistic freedom in work and leisure. *Annals of Leisure Research*, *21*(3), 364–380. doi:10.1080/11745398.2017.1358098

Reid, G. (2012). Motivation in video games: A literature review. *The Computer Games Journal*, *1*(2), 70–81. doi:10.1007/BF03395967

Reinecke, L., Vorderer, P., & Knop, K. (2014). Entertainment 2.0? The role of intrinsic and extrinsic need satisfaction for the enjoyment of facebook use. *Journal of Communication*, *64*(3), 417–438. doi:10.1111/jcom.12099

Rekha, G., Rajamani, K., & Resmi, G. (2021). Digital financial inclusion, economic freedom, financial development, and growth: Implications from panel data analysis. *ADBI Working Paper 1244*. Tokyo: Asian Development Bank Institute.

Richard, F., & Sora, P. (2017). The impact of trust in the news media on online news consumption and participation. *Digital Journalism (Abingdon, England)*, *5*(10), 1281–1299. doi:10.1080/21670811.2017.1279979

Rideout, V. J., Foehr, U. G., & Roberts, D. F. (2010). Generation M2: Media in the lives of 8- to 18- year olds. Kaiser Family Foundation. KFF. https://www.kff.org/entmedia/entmedia012010nr.com

Rideout, V. J., Ulla, M. A., Foehr, G., & Roberts, D. F. (2010). *A Kaiser Family Foundation Study GENERATION M 2 Media in the Lives of 8-to 18-Year-Olds*. Kaiser Family Foundation.

Ridings, C. M., Gefen, D., & Arinze, B. (2002). Some antecedents and effects of trust in virtual communities. *The Journal of Strategic Information Systems*, *11*(3-4), 271–295. doi:10.1016/S0963-8687(02)00021-5

Rigby, K. (2011). What can schools do about cases of bullying? *Pastoral Care in Education*, *29*(4), 273–285. doi:10.1080/02643944.2011.626068

Rigel, N. Batuş, G. Yücedoğan & G., Çoban, B. (ed.). (2003). Kadife karanlık- 21. yüzyıl iletişim çağını aydınlatan kuramcılar. İstanbul: Su Yayınevi.

Riggio, H. R. (2004). Parental marital conflict and divorce, parent child relationships, social support, and relationship anxiety in young adulthood. *Personal Relationships*, *11*(1), 99–114. doi:10.1111/j.1475-6811.2004.00073.x

Rikkers, W., Lawrence, D., Hafekost, J., & Zubrick, S. R. (2016). Internet use and electronic gaming by children and adolescents with emotional and behavioural problems in Australia–results from the second Child and Adolescent Survey of Mental Health and Wellbeing. *BMC Public Health*, *16*(1), 399. doi:10.118612889-016-3058-1 PMID:27178325

Riordan, B. C., Cody, L., Flett, J. A., Conner, T. S., Hunter, J., & Scarf, D. (2020). The development of a single item FoMO (fear of missing out) scale. *Current Psychology (New Brunswick, N.J.)*, *39*(4), 1215–1220. doi:10.100712144-018-9824-8

Riordan, B. C., Flett, J. A. M., Hunter, J. A., Scarf, D., & Conner, T. S. (2015). Fear of missing Out (FoMO): The relationship between FoMO, alcohol use, and alcohol-related consequences in college students. *Journal of Psychiatry and Brain Functions*, *2*(9), 1–7. doi:10.7243/2055-3447-2-9

Ripeanu, M., Singh, M. P., & Vazhkudai, S. S. (2008). Virtual organizations [guest editors' introduction]. *IEEE Internet Computing*, *12*(2), 10–12. doi:10.1109/MIC.2008.48

Ritzer, G. (2015). Automating prosumption: The decline of the prosumer and the rise of the prosuming machines. *Journal of Consumer Culture*, *15*(3), 407–424. doi:10.1177/1469540514553717

Ritzer, G., & Jurgenson, N. (2010). Production, consumption, prosumption: The nature of capitalism in the age of the digital 'prosumer'. *Journal of Consumer Culture*, *10*(1), 13–36. doi:10.1177/1469540509354673

Roberts, J. A., Yaya, L. H. P., & Manolis, C. (2014). The invisible addiction: Cell-phone activities and addiction among male and female college students. *Journal of Behavioral Addictions*, *3*(4), 254–265. doi:10.1556/JBA.3.2014.015 PMID:25595966

Roblek, V., Meško, M., Bach, M. P., Thorpe, O., & Šprajc, P. (2020). The interaction between Internet, sustainable development, and the emergence of society 5.0. *Data*, *5*(3), 80. doi:10.3390/data5030080

Rocha, D. (2017). *Vídeo por demanda: transformações e perspectivas para a tv na atualidade.*

Rodríguez-Molina, J., Martínez-Núñez, M., Martínez, J. F., & Pérez-Aguiar, W. (2014). Business models in the smart grid: Challenges, opportunities and proposals for prosumer profitability. *Energies*, *7*(9), 6142–6171. doi:10.3390/en7096142

Rogers, E. M. (2003). *Diffusion of innovations* (5th ed.). Free Press.

Romanenko, A., Santos, L. O., & Afonso, P. A. F. N. A. (2007). Application of agent technology concepts to the design of a fault-tolerant control system. *Control Engineering Practice*, *15*(4), 459–469. doi:10.1016/j.conengprac.2006.09.002

Romansky, R. (2014). *Digital Privacy in the Network World. Proceedings of the International Conference on Information Technologies (InfoTech-2014)*, Bulgaria.

Romer, P. M. (1994). The origins of endogenous growth. *The Journal of Economic Perspectives*, *8*(1), 3–22. doi:10.1257/jep.8.1.3

Ronit, K. (2021). Business and consumer policy. In *Handbook of Business and Public Policy*. Edward Elgar Publishing. doi:10.4337/9781788979122.00014

Rosati, P., Gogolin, F., & Lynn, T. (2020). Cyber-security incidents and audit quality. *European Accounting Review*, 1–28. doi:10.1080/09638180.2020.1856162

Rosemann, M., Becker, J., & Chasin, F. (2021). City 5.0. *Business & Information Systems Engineering*, *63*(1), 71–77. doi:10.100712599-020-00674-9

Rosenberg, K., & Feder, L. (2014). *An introduction to behavioral addictions. Behavioral addictions: criteria, evidence and treatment*. Elsevier.

Rosenberg, M. (1989). *Society and the adolescent self-image*. Wesleyan University Press.

Rosen, L. D., Lim, A., Felt, J., Carrier, L. M., Cheever, N. A., Lara-Ruiz, J. M., Mendoza, J. S., & Rokkum, J. (2014). Media and technology use predicts ill-being among children, preteens, and teenagers independent of the negative health impacts of exercise and eating habits. *Computers in Human Behavior*, *35*, 364–375. doi:10.1016/j.chb.2014.01.036 PMID:25717216

Rosen, L. D., Mark Carrier, L., & Cheever, N. A. (2013). Facebook and texting made me do it: Media-induced task-switching while studying. *Computers in Human Behavior*, *29*(3), 948–958. doi:10.1016/j.chb.2012.12.001

Rosen, L. D., Whaling, K., Carrier, L. M., Cheever, N. A., & Rokkum, J. (2013). The media and technology usage and attitudes Scale: An empirical investigation. *Computers in Human Behavior*, *29*(6), 2501–2511. doi:10.1016/j.chb.2013.06.006 PMID:25722534

Rosen, L. M., Carrier, L., Miller, A., Rokkum, J., & Ruiz, A. (2016). Sleeping with technology: Cognitive, affective, and technology usage predictors of sleep problems among college students. *Sleep Health*, *2*(1), 49–56. doi:10.1016/j.sleh.2015.11.003 PMID:29073453

Rossini, M., & Renner, A. (2015). *Nova cultura visual? Netflix e a mudança no processo de produção, distribuição e consumo do audiovisual.* Porto alegre.

Rozgonjuk, D., Sindermann, C., Elhai, J. D., & Montag, C. (2021). Individual differences in Fear of Missing Out (FoMO): Age, gender, and the Big Five personality trait domains, facets, and items. *Personality and Individual Differences*, *171*, 110546. doi:10.1016/j.paid.2020.110546

Ruggiero, T. E. (2017). Uses and gratifications theory in the 21st century. *ResearchGate*, *3*(1), 3–37. doi:10.4324/9781315679402-4

Rumpf HJ, Achab S, Billieux J, Bowden-Jones H, Carragher N, Demetrovics Z. (2018). Including gaming disorder in the ICD-11: the need to do so from a clinical and public health perspective. *J Behav Addict*, *7*(3), 556-561. doi:10.1556/2006.7.2018.59

Rüßmann, M., Lorenz, M., Gerbert, P., Waldner, M., Justus, J., Engel, P., & Harnisch, M. (2015). Industry 4.0: The future of productivity and growth in manufacturing industries. *Boston consulting group, 9*(1), 54-89.

Ryan, R. M., & Deci, E. L. (2000). Self-determination theory and the facilitation of intrinsic motivation, social development, and well-being. *The American Psychologist*, *55*(1), 68–78. doi:10.1037/0003-066X.55.1.68 PMID:11392867

Ryan, R. M., Rigby, C. S., & Przybylski, A. (2006). The motivational pull of video games: A self-determination theory approach. *Motivation and Emotion*, *30*(4), 347–363. doi:10.100711031-006-9051-8

Ryan, T., Chester, A., Reece, J., & Xenos, S. (2014). The uses and abuses of Facebook: A review of Facebook addiction. *Journal of Behavioral Addictions*, *3*(3), 133–148. doi:10.1556/JBA.3.2014.016 PMID:25317337

Sabbag, D., & Silva, B. (2022). *Classificação de audiovisuais no catálogo da Netflix: transmídias, fandoms e nichos.* Obtido de Em Questão: https://www.researchgate.net/publication/361654832_Classificacao_de_audiovisuais_no_catalogo_da_Netflix_transmidias_fandoms_e_nichos

Saccomori, C. (2016). *Práticas de binge-watching na era digital: Novas experiências de consumo de seriados em maratonas no Netflix.*

Sağbaş, Ö. F. (2022). *İlkokul Öğrencilerinin Youtube'u Eğtiim amaçlı Kullanma Durumları, Ebeveynlerin Demoğrafik Özellikleri ve İnternet Bağımlılığı Arasındaki ilişki.* Ispart: Süleyman Demirel üniversitesi, Eğitim Bilimleri Enstitüsü (Yayınlanmamış Yüksek Lisans Tezi).

Sağlam, M., & Topsümer, F. (2019). Dijital oyunlar ve öznel iyi oluş ilişkisi: Muğla Sıtkı Koçman Üniversitesi örneği. *Humanities Sciences*, *4*(2), 31–50.

Şahin C. & Tuğrul VM. (2012). Examination of computer game addiction levels of primary school students. *Zeitschrift für die Welt der Türken [Journal of World of Turks,]* *4*(3), 115-30.

Şahin, N. & Yağcı, P. (2017). Endüstri 4.0 kavramında prosumer kavramının yiyecek içecek sektörü açısından değerlendirilmesi. *Journal of Recration and Tourism Research, 4*(Special Issue 1), 12-22.

Şahin, C. ve Tuğrul, V. M. (2012). İlköğretim öğrencilerinin bilgisayar oyunu bağımlılık düzeylerinin incelenmesi. *Journal of World of Turks*, *4*(3), 115–130.

Sahoo, D., Nayak, S., & Behera, J. (2021). Digitalization and economic performance of two fast-growing asian economies: India and the People's Republic of China. *ADBI Working Paper 1243*. Tokyo: Asian Development Bank Institute.

Saiidi, U. (2017). *I tried living as a digital nomad for the day: CNBC Reports*. [Video]. Youtube. https://www.youtube.com/watch?v=zjf8Qxo_tXk&t=86s

Sakuma, H., Mihara, S., Nakayama, H., Miura, K., Kitayuguchi, T., Maezono, M., Hashimoto, T., & Higuchi, S. (2017). Treatment with the self-discovery camp (SDiC) improves internet gaming disorder. *Addictive Behaviors*, *64*, 357–362. doi:10.1016/j.addbeh.2016.06.013 PMID:27321966

Salgues, B. (2018). *Society 5.0: Industry of the Future, Technologies, Methods and Tools*. John Wiley & Sons. doi:10.1002/9781119507314

Samaha, M., & Hawi, N. S. (2016). Relationships among smartphone addiction, stress, academic performance, and satisfaction with life. *Computers in Human Behavior*, *57*, 321–325. doi:10.1016/j.chb.2015.12.045

Samur, Y. (2016). *Dijital Oyun Tasarımı*. Pusula Yayınları.

Saniuk, S., Grabowska, S., & Straka, M. (2022). Identification of social and economic expectations: Contextual reasons for the transformation process of industry 4.0 into the industry 5.0 concept. *Sustainability (Basel)*, *14*(3), 1391. doi:10.3390u14031391

Sanwal, R. (2022). How new age technologies are used to identify consumer behaviour and its change during and after a pandemic. In *Handbook of Research on Innovative Management Using AI in Industry 5.0* (pp. 279–290). IGI Global. doi:10.4018/978-1-7998-8497-2.ch020

Saputri, R. A. M., & Yumarni, T. (2023). Social media addiction and mental health among university students during the COVID-19 pandemic in Indonesia. *International Journal of Mental Health and Addiction*, *21*(1), 96–110. doi:10.100711469-021-00582-3 PMID:34230820

Saraç, S. (2013). Toplumsal Cinsiyet. In L. Gültekin, G. Güneş, C. Ertung, & A. Şimşek (Eds.), Toplumsal Cinsiyet ve Yansımaları, (pp. 27–32). Atılım Üniversitesi Yayınları.

Sarak, Ö. (2012). Lise öğrencilerinde sanal zorbalık. (Yüksek Lisans Tezi), Haliç Üniversitesi, İstanbul.

Sariyska, R., Reuter, M., Bey, K., Sha, P., Li, M., Chen, Y. F., Liu, W.-Y., Zhu, Y.-K., Li, C.-B., Suárez-Rivillas, A., Feldmann, M., Hellmann, M., Keiper, J., Markett, S., Young, S. K., & Montag, C. (2014). Self-esteem, personality and internet addiction: A cross-cultural comparison study. *Personality and Individual Differences*, *61*, 28–33. doi:10.1016/j.paid.2014.01.001

Sarup, M. (2014). Post-yapısalcılık ve postmodernizm (A. Güçlü, Trans., 2. Edit.). Pharmakon Publications.

Savci, M., & Aysan, F. (2017). Technological addictions and social connectedness: Predictor effect of internet addiction, social media addiction, digital game addiction and smartphone addiction on social connectedness. *Dusunen Adam : Bakirkoy Ruh Ve Sinir Hastaliklari Hastanesi Yayin Organi, 30*(3), 202–216. doi:10.5350/DAJPN2017300304

Savcı, M., & Aysan, F. (2017). Teknolojik Bağımlılıklar ve Sosyal Bağlılık: İnternet Bağımlılığı, Sosyal Medya Bağımlılığı, Dijital Oyun Bağımlılığı ve Akıllı Telefon Bağımlılığının Sosyal Bağlılığı Yordayıcı Etkisi. *Dusunen Adam : Bakirkoy Ruh Ve Sinir Hastaliklari Hastanesi Yayin Organi, 30*(3), 202–216.

Savitri, I., Wicaksono, A. S., & Fastari, C. (2021). The effect of big five personality on fear of missing out. *Journal Universitas Muhammadiyah Gresik, 1*(2), 956–964. doi:10.30587/umgeshic.v1i2.3499

Scherk, H., & Falkai, P. (2006). Effects of antipsychotics on brain structure. *Current Opinion in Psychiatry, 19*(2), 145–150. doi:10.1097/01.yco.0000214339.06507.d8 PMID:16612194

Schlogl, L. (2022). *Digital Activism and the Global Middle Class: Generation Hashtag*. Routledge.

Schlosser, R. W. (2023). *The efficacy of augmentative and alternative communication*. Brill.

Schmidt, F. A. (2017). *Digital labour markets in the platform*. The Friedrich-Ebert-Stiftung.

Schumpeter, J. A. (1911). *The Theory of Economic Development*. Harvard University Press.

Scolari, C. A. (2019). Beyond the myth of the "digital native" Adolescents, collaborative cultures and transmedia skills. *Nordic Journal of Digital Literacy, 14*(3-4), 164–174. doi:10.18261/issn.1891-943x-2019-03-04-06

Scott, F. (2022, May 23). *Five digital games to help your child's development. The Conversation*. https://theconversation.com/five-digital-games-to-help-your-childs-development-183483

Seay, A. F., & Kraut, R. E. (2007). Project massive: Self-regulation and problematic use of online gaming. In *Proceedings of the SIGCHI Conference on Human Factors in Computing Systems*. ACM. 10.1145/1240624.1240749

Seeman, P. (2004). Atypical antipsychotics: Mechanism of action. *Focus (San Francisco, Calif.), 47*(1), 27–58. PMID:11873706

Şeker, V. T. (2018). Sosyal medya bağımlılığı ile depresyon ve anksiyete arasındaki ilişki. Sosyal Bilimler Enstitüsü, Tutar, H. and Erdem, A. T. (2020). *Örnekleriyle bilimsel araştırma yöntemleri ve SPSS uygulamaları*. Seçkin Yayıncılık, *1*.

Sela, Y., Zach, M., Amichay-Hamburger, Y., Mishali, M., & Omer, H. (2019). Family environment and problematic internet use among adolescents: The mediating roles of depression and fear of missing out. *Computers in Human Behavior, 106*, 106226. doi:10.1016/j.chb.2019.106226

Senbir, S. (2004). *"The Last Man"? Thoughts on Generation Z and Beyond* ["Son İnsan" mı? Z Kuşağı ve Sonrasına Dair Düşünceler]. Okyan Us Yayınları.

Sennett, R. (2003). *The Fall of Public Man*. Penguin Books Ltd.

Şenol, Y., Şenol, F. B., & Can Yaşar, M. (2023). (2023). Digital game addiction of preschool children in the Covid-19 pandemic: Social emotional development and parental guidance. *Current Psychology (New Brunswick, N.J.)*. doi:10.100712144-023-04323-8 PMID:36819754

Şentürk, Ü. (2006). Küresel Yeni Sosyal Hareketler ve Savaş Karşıtlığı. *C. Ü. Sosyal Bilimler Dergisi, 30*(1), 31–46.

Seo, D., & Ray, S. (2019). Habit and addiction in the use of social networking sites: Their nature, antecedents, and consequences. *Computers in Human Behavior, 99*, 109–125. doi:10.1016/j.chb.2019.05.018

Seoul Metropolitan Government. (2022, November 5). *Virtual Seoul City Hall via beta release of Metaverse Seoul.* SMG. https://english.seoul.go.kr/virtual-seoul-city-hall-via-beta-release-of-metaverse-seoul/ [21.01.2023]

Sepasgozar, S. M., Hawken, S., Sargolzaei, S., & Foroozanfa, M. (2019). Implementing citizen centric technology in developing smart cities: A model for predicting the acceptance of urban technologies. *Technological Forecasting and Social Change*, *142*, 105–116. doi:10.1016/j.techfore.2018.09.012

Serpa, S., & Ferreira, C. M. (2019). Society 5.0 and sustainability digital innovations: A social process. *Journal of Organizational Culture. Communications and Conflict*, (2), 1–14.

Sette, C. P., Lima, N. R., Queluz, F. N., Ferrari, B. L., & Hauck, N. (2020). The online fear of missing out inventory (ON-FoMO): Development and validation of a new tool. *Journal of Technology in Behavioral Science*, *5*(1), 20–29. doi:10.100741347-019-00110-0

Sezen, T. İ. (2011). Understanding Digital Games: Digital Games from Game, Narrative, Software and Platform Perspectives. [Dijital Oyunları Anlamak: Oyun, Anlatı, Yazılım ve Platform Perspektiflerinden Dijital Oyunlar] In G. T. Ünal & U. Batı (Eds.), *Digital Games: "Live in Your World Play in Ours"* [Dijital Oyunlar: "Kendi Dünyanda Yaşa Bizimkinde Oyna"]. (pp. 119–148). İstanbul Derin Yayınları.

Sezgin, A. A. (2018). Selfies: New Visual Culture of New Digital Society. In S. Hai-Jew (Ed.), *IGI Global.*, doi:10.4018/978-1-5225-3373-3.ch004

Shapira, N. A., Lessig, M. C., Goldsmith, T. D., Szabo, S. T., Lazoritz, M., Gold, M. S., & Stein, D. J. (2003). Problematic internet use: Proposed classification and diagnostic criteria. *Depression and Anxiety*, *17*(4), 207–216. doi:10.1002/da.10094 PMID:12820176

Sharma, P., & Singh, A. K. (2017). Association of state-wise food security index with climatic factors in India: Evidence from state-wise panel data. *Journal of Global Agriculture and Ecology*, *6*(3), 196–205.

Shatrughan, P., & Pareek, S. (2017). Phantom Vibration Syndrome: An Emerging Phenomenon. *Asian J. Nursing Edu. and Research*, *7*(4), 1–2.

Shaw, G. K. (1992). Policy implications of endogenous growth theory. *Economic Journal (London)*, *102*(412), 611–621. doi:10.2307/2234298

Shaw, L. H., & Gant, L. M. (2002). In defense of the internet: The relationship between Internet communication and depression, loneliness, self-esteem, and perceived social support. *Cyberpsychology & Behavior*, *5*(2), 157–171. doi:10.1089/109493102753770552 PMID:12025883

Shaw, M., & Black, D. W. (2008). Internet addiction. *CNS Drugs*, *22*(5), 353–365. doi:10.2165/00023210-200822050-00001 PMID:18399706

Shayo, E. H., Kivuyo, S., Seeley, J., Bukenya, D., Karoli, P., Mfinanga, S. G., Jaffar, S., & van Hout, M. C. (2022). The acceptability of integrated healthcare services for HIV and non-communicable diseases: Experiences from patients and healthcare workers in Tanzania. *BMC Health Services Research*, *22*(1), 655. doi:10.118612913-022-08065-4 PMID:35578274

Shek, D. T., & Yu, L. (2016). Adolescent internet addiction in Hong Kong: Prevalence, change, and correlates. *Journal of Pediatric and Adolescent Gynecology*, *29*(1), S22–S30. doi:10.1016/j.jpag.2015.10.005 PMID:26461526

Shensa, A., Escobar-Viera, C. G., Sidani, J. E., Bowman, N. D., Marshal, M. P., & Primack, B. A. (2017). Problematic social media use and depressive symptoms among U.S. young adults: A nationally-representative study. *Social Science & Medicine*, *182*, 150–157. doi:10.1016/j.socscimed.2017.03.061 PMID:28446367

Sherer, J., & Levounis, P. (2022). Technological Addictions. *Current Psychiatry Reports*, *24*(9), 399–406. doi:10.100711920-022-01351-2 PMID:35792965

Shifman, L. (2013). *Memes in digital culture*. MIT Press. doi:10.7551/mitpress/9429.001.0001

Shiroishi, Y., Uchiyama, K., & Suzuki, N. (2018). Society 5.0: For human security and well-being. *Computer*, *51*(7), 91–95. doi:10.1109/MC.2018.3011041

Shiroishi, Y., Uchiyama, K., & Suzuki, N. (2019). Better actions for society 5.0: Using AI for evidence-based policy making that keeps humans in the loop. *Computer*, *52*(11), 73–78. doi:10.1109/MC.2019.2934592

Shi, X., Wang, J., & Zou, H. (2017). Family functioning and Internet addiction among Chinese adolescents: The mediating roles of self-esteem and loneliness. *Computers in Human Behavior*, *76*, 201–210. doi:10.1016/j.chb.2017.07.028

Sieberg, D. (2011). *The Digital Diet: The 4-step plan to break your tech addiction and regain balance in your life*. Crown Publishing.

Siegel, D. S., Waldman, D. A., & Link, A. N. (2003). Assessing the impact of organizational practices on the relative productivity of university technology transfer offices: An exploratory study. *Research Policy*, *32*(1), 27–48. doi:10.1016/S0048-7333(01)00196-2

Silva, M. Z., & Dall'orto, F. C. (2017). *O streaming e a sua influência sobre o audiovisual e o product placement.*

Silva, P. (2019). *Representações de minorias em séries da Netflix: estudo sobre o personagem Eric da série Sex Education*. Congresso de Ciências da Comunicação na região Centro-Oeste Goiânia.

Şimşek, B. (2018). *Dijital Hikaye Anlatımı*. Alternatif Bilişim Derneği.

Sine, R. (2017). Alternatif Medya ve Haber. Konya: Literatürk.

Singh, A. K., & Singh, P. K. (2019). Digital Addiction: a conceptual overview. *Library Philosophy and Practice (e-Journal)*. https://digitalcommons.unl.edu/libphilprac/3538

Singh, A. K. (2020). Technology transfer and commercialization models and policies in India, USA, China and Malaysia: A conceptual review. *Asian Journal of Sociological Research*, *3*(1), 19–45.

Singh, A. K., & Ashraf, S. N. (2020). Association of entrepreneurship ecosystem with economic growth in selected countries: An empirical exploration. *Journal of Entrepreneurship. Business Economics (Cleveland, Ohio)*, *8*(2), 36–92.

Singh, A. K., Ashraf, S. N., & Arya, A. (2019b). Estimating factors affecting technical efficiency in Indian manufacturing sector. *Eurasian Journal of Business and Economics*, *12*(24), 65–86. doi:10.17015/ejbe.2019.024.04

Singh, A. K., Ashraf, S. N., & Sharma, S. K. (2023). Farmer's perception on climatic factors and social-economic characteristics in the agricultural sector of Gujarat. *Research on World Agricultural Economy*, *4*(1), 36–53. doi:10.36956/rwae.v4i1.788

Singh, A. K., Issac, J., & Narayanan, K. G. S. (2019a). Measurement of environmental sustainability index and its association with socio-economic indicators in Asian economies: An empirical investigation. *International Journal of Environment and Sustainable Development*, *18*(1), 57–100. doi:10.1504/IJESD.2019.098641

Singh, A. K., Jyoti, B., Kumar, S., & Lenka, S. K. (2021). Assessment of global sustainable development, environmental sustainability, economic development and social development index in selected economies. *International Journal of Sustainable Development and Planning*, *16*(1), 123–138. doi:10.18280/ijsdp.160113

Singh, A. K., & Kumar, S. (2022a). Exploring the impact of sustainable and environmental sustainability development on social-economic, science and technological development in selected countries: A country-wise panel data analysis. *Society & Sustainability*, *4*(1), 55–83. doi:10.38157s.v4i1.405

Singh, A. K., & Kumar, S. (2022b). Factors influencing entrepreneurship ecosystem and economic development: Evidence from cross-sectional country-wise imbalanced panel data analysis. *The IUP Journal of Entrepreneurship Development*, *19*(3), 24–47.

Singh, A. K., & Kumar, S. (2022c). Expert's perception on technology transfer and commercialization, and intellectual property rights in India: Evidence from selected research organizations. *Journal of Management, Economics, and Industrial Organization*, *6*(1), 1–33. doi:10.31039/jomeino.2022.6.1.1

Singh, A. K., Kumar, S., & Jyoti, B. (2022a). Does sustainable livelihood security have a relationship with climatic and geographical factors? evidence from a state-wise panel data investigation in India. *The IUP Journal of Applied Economics*, *21*(1), 7–35.

Singh, A. K., Kumar, S., Sharma, A. K., & Sinha, S. (2022b). Does green entrepreneurship have an association with sustainable development and its components? Evidence from country-wise panel data investigation. In M. Magd, D. Singh, D. Spicer, & R. T. Syed (Eds.), *International Perspectives on Value Creation and Sustainability Through Social Entrepreneurship*. IGI Global. doi:10.4018/978-1-6684-4666-9.ch008

Singh, A. K., Sharma, S. K., & Lenka, S. K. (2023a). Causality between green entrepreneurship and sustainable development: A cross country analysis using ARDL model. *The IUP Journal of Applied Economics*, *22*(1), 1–34.

Singh, A. K., & Singh, B. (2020). Implications of intellectual property protection, and science and technological development in the manufacturing sector in selected economies. *Journal of Advocacy. Research in Education*, *7*(1), 16–35.

Singh, A. K., Singh, B. J., & Negi, V. (2020). Does sustainable development have causal relationship with environmental development? Evidence from country wise panel data analysis. *International Journal of Technology Management & Sustainable Development*, *19*(2), 147–171. doi:10.1386/tmsd_00020_1

Singh, R., Gupta, R., Grover, T., Ambekar, A., Jain, R., Vaswani, M., Mishra, A., & Sharma, A. (2023). Role of the Serotonin and GABAA Receptor Gene Polymorphisms in patients with Alcohol Dependence. *Asian Journal of Psychiatry*, *80*, 103326. doi:10.1016/j.ajp.2022.103326 PMID:36463616

Siste, K., Hanafi, E., Sen, L. T., Murtani, B. J., Christian, H., Limawan, A. P., Siswidiani, L. P., & Adrian. (2021). Implications of COVID-19 and lockdown on internet addiction among adolescents: Data from a developing country. *Frontiers in Psychiatry*, *12*, 665675. doi:10.3389/fpsyt.2021.665675 PMID:34054619

Skinner, B. F. (1948). Superstition' in the pigeon. *Journal of Experimental Psychology*, *38*(2), 168–172. doi:10.1037/h0055873 PMID:18913665

Skivko, M., Korneeva, E., & Kolmykova, M. (2019). Digital minimalism as a leading limitation of media communications in the heyday of digital culture. Advances in Social Science, Education and Humanities Research. In *6th International Conference on Social, economic, and academic leadership (ICSEAL-6-2019)*. Research Gate.

Skoric, M. M. (2012). What is slack about slacktivism. *Methodological and conceptual issues in cyber activism research*, *77*(7), 7-92.

Slater, A., & Bremner, J. G. (2017). *An introduction to developmental psychology*. Wiley.

Slater, M., Gonzalez-Liencres, C., Haggard, P., Vinkers, C., Gregory-Clarke, R., Jelley, S., Watson, Z., Breen, G., Schwarz, R., Steptoe, W., Szostak, D., Halan, S., Fox, D., & Silver, J. (2020). The ethics of realism in virtual and augmented reality. *Frontiers in Virtual Reality, 1*, 1. doi:10.3389/frvir.2020.00001

Smahel, D., Machackova, H., Mascheroni, G., Dedkova, L., Staksrud, E., Ólafsson, K., Livingstone, S., & Hasebrink, U. (2020). *EU Kids Online 2020: Survey results from 19 countries.* EU Kids Online 2020. http://hdl.handle.net/20.500.12162/5299

Smith, B. (2021). How TikTok Reads Your Mind. *The New York Times*. https://www.nytimes.com/2021/12/05/business/media/tiktok-algorithm.html

Smith, P. K., Mahdavi, J., Carvalho, M., & Tippett, N. (2008). An investigation into cyberbullying, its forms, awareness and impact, and the relationship between age and gender in cyberbullying. (A Report to the Anti-Bullying Alliance). Family Studies, Goldsmiths College, University of London.

Smith, P. (2007). *Kültürel kuram* [Cultural theory]. (S. Güzelsarı & İ. Gündoğdu, Trans.). Babil Publishing.

Snyder, K. (2005). The digital culture and communication: More than just classroom learning. *Seminar.Net, 1*(2), 1-9. . doi:10.7577/seminar.2529

Snyman, R., & Loh, J. M. (2015). Cyberbullying at work: The mediating role of optimism between cyberbullying and job outcomes. *Computers in Human Behavior, 53*, 161–168. doi:10.1016/j.chb.2015.06.050

Söğüt, Y. (2022). Üretken endüstrilerde kültürel ve dijital dönüşümlerin yansımaları üzerine: Medya ve tüketim kültürü. [On the reflections of cultural and digital transformations in productive ındustries: Media and consumer culture] In K. Çankaya (Ed.), *Medya ve tüketim I* [Media and consumption I]. (pp. 9–30). Eğitim Publishing.

Solano, L., Pirrotta, E., Ingravalle, V., & Fayella, P. (2009). The family physician and the psychologist in the office together: A response to fragmentation. *Mental Health in Family Medicine, 6*(2), 91–98. PMID:22477897

Solomon, E. M., & van Klyton, A. (2020). The impact of digital technology usage on economic growth in Africa. *Utilities Policy, 67*(101104), 1–12. doi:10.1016/j.jup.2020.101104 PMID:32904493

Son, D. T., Yasuoka, J., Poudel, K. C., Otsuka, K., & Jimba, M. (2013). Massively multiplayer online role-playing games (MMORPG): Association between its addiction, self-control and mental disorders among young people in Vietnam. *The International Journal of Social Psychiatry, 59*(6), 570–577. doi:10.1177/0020764012445861 PMID:22718852

Song, J., Park, J. H., Han, D. H., Roh, S., Son, J. H., Choi, T. Y., Lee, H., Kim, T. H., & Lee, Y. S. (2016). Comparative study of the effects of bupropion and escitalopram on I nternet gaming disorder. *Psychiatry and Clinical Neurosciences, 70*(11), 527–535. doi:10.1111/pcn.12429 PMID:27487975

Soylu, A. (2018). Endüstri 4.0 ve girişimcilikte yeni yaklaşımlar. *Pamukkale Üniversitesi Sosyal Bilimler Enstitüsü Dergisi*, (32), 43–57. doi:10.30794/pausbed.424955

Spinks, R. (2017). Meet the 'digital nomads' who travel the world in search of fast Wi-Fi. *The Guardian*. https://www.theguardian.com/cities/2015/jun/16/digital-nomads-travel-world-search-fast-wi-fi

Spitzberg, B. H. (1983). Communication competence as knowledge, skill, and impression. *Communication Education, 32*(3), 323–329. doi:10.1080/03634528309378550

Stapleton, L., & Jaillant, L. (2022). "Born digital" shedding light into the darkness of digital culture. *AI & Society, 37*(3), 819–822. doi:10.100700146-021-01358-y

Starcevic, V., Berle, D., Porter, G., & Fenech, P. (2011). Problem video game use and dimensions of psychopathology. *International Journal of Mental Health and Addiction*, *9*(3), 248–256. doi:10.100711469-010-9282-5

Statista. (2023a). *Average daily time spent on social media worldwide 2012-2022*. Statista. Https://Www.Statista.Com/Statistics/433871/Daily-Social-Media-Usage-Worldwide/

Statista. (2023b). *Worldwide digital population 2023*. Https://Www.Statista.Com/Statistics/617136/Digital-Population-Worldwide

Stead, H., & Bibby, P. A. (2017). Personality, fear of missing out and problematic internet use and their relationship to subjective well-being. *Computers in Human Behavior*, *76*, 1–17. doi:10.1016/j.chb.2017.08.016

Stefani, S., & Tiatri, S. (2021, August). How Adolescent's Self-Esteem Affects Internet Addiction Tendency During COVID-19 Pandemic in Takengon, Central Aceh. In *International Conference on Economics, Business, Social, and Humanities (ICEBSH 2021)* (pp. 951-957). Atlantis Press. 10.2991/assehr.k.210805.150

Stevens, M. W., Delfabbro, P. H., & King, D. L. (2021). Prevention approaches to problem gaming: A large-scale qualitative investigation. *Computers in Human Behavior*, *115*, 106611. doi:10.1016/j.chb.2020.106611

Stevens, M. W., King, D. L., Dorstyn, D., & Delfabbro, P. H. (2019). Cognitive-behavioral therapy for Internet gaming disorder: A systematic review and meta-analysis. *Clinical Psychology & Psychotherapy*, *26*(2), 191–203. doi:10.1002/cpp.2341 PMID:30341981

Stieger, S., & Burger, C. (2010). Implicit and explicit self-esteem in the context of internet addiction. *Cyberpsychology, Behavior, and Social Networking*, *13*(6), 681–688. doi:10.1089/cyber.2009.0426 PMID:21142993

STM ThinkTech. (2022). *Metaverse: Opportunities and Threats. Trend Analysis February*. STM. https://thinktech.stm.com.tr/tr/metaverse-firsatlar-ve-tehditler

Stoffers-Winterling, J., Storebø, O. J., & Lieb, K. (2020). Pharmacotherapy for borderline personality disorder: An update of published, unpublished and ongoing studies. *Current Psychiatry Reports*, *22*(8), 1–10. doi:10.100711920-020-01164-1 PMID:32504127

Stošić, L., & Stošić, I. (2015). Perceptions of teachers regarding the implementation of the internet in education. *Computers in Human Behavior*, *53*, 462–468. doi:10.1016/j.chb.2015.07.027

Stout, A. (n.d.). Esports. *Wikipedia*. https://en.wikipedia.org/wiki/Esports

Straker, L., Harris, C., Joosten, J., & Howie, E. K. (2018). Mobile technology dominates school children's IT use in an advantaged school community and is associated with musculoskeletal and visual symptoms. *Ergonomics*, *61*(5), 658–669. doi:10.1080/00140139.2017.1401671 PMID:29103354

Straub, E. T. (2009). Understanding technology adoption: Theory and future directions for informal learning. *Review of Educational Research*, *79*(2), 625–649. doi:10.3102/0034654308325896

Strauss, W., & Howe, N. (1997). *The Fourth Turning: What the Cycles of History Tell Us About America's Next Rendezvous with Destiny*. Broadway Books.

Strittmatter, E., Kaess, M., Parzer, P., Fischer, G., Carli, V., Hoven, C. W., Wasserman, C., Sarchiapone, M., Durkee, T., Apter, A., Bobes, J., Brunner, R., Cosman, D., Sisask, M., Värnik, P., & Wasserman, D. (2015). Pathological Internet use among adolescents: Comparing gamers and non-gamers. *Psychiatry Research*, *228*(1), 128–135. doi:10.1016/j.psychres.2015.04.029 PMID:25959265

Strom, P. S., & Strom, R. D. (2005). When teens turn cyberbullies. *Education Digest*, *71*(4), 35.

Sublette, V. A., & Mullan, B. (2012). Consequences of play: A systematic review of the effects of online gaming. *International Journal of Mental Health and Addiction, 10*(1), 3–23. doi:10.100711469-010-9304-3

Su, C. C., & Chan, N. K. (2017). Predicting social capital on Facebook: The implications of use intensity, perceived content desirability, and Facebook-enabled communication practices. *Computers in Human Behavior, 72*, 259–268. doi:10.1016/j.chb.2017.02.058

Sun, J., Gan, W., & Chao, H. (2022). Metaverse: Survey, Applications, Security, and Opportunities. *arXiv:2210.07990*. https://doi.org//arXiv.2210.07990. doi:10.48550

Sunal, G., Furuncu Kutluhan, D., & Bağdatlı Kalkan, S. (2022). Geleneksel ve Dijital Hikaye Anlatıcılığı Arasındaki Farkın Covid 19 Pandemi Sürecinde Maske Kullanımına ilişkin Bir Video Filmi Üzerinden İncelenmesi. *e-Journal of New Media/Yeni Medya elektronik Dergi*, 221-228.

Sun, J., Debo, L. G., Kekre, S., & Xie, J. (2010). Component-based technology transfer in the presence of potential imitators. *Management Science, 56*(3), 536–552. doi:10.1287/mnsc.1090.1111

Sunstein, C. R. (2017). *Divided democracy in the age of social media*. Princeton University Press. doi:10.1515/9781400884711

Sun, Y., & Zhang, Y. (2021). A review of theories and models applied in studies of social media addiction and implications for future research. *Addictive Behaviors, 114*, 106699. doi:10.1016/j.addbeh.2020.106699 PMID:33268185

Su, W., Han, X., Yu, H., Wu, Y., & Potenza, M. N. (2020). Do men become addicted to internet gaming and women to social media? A meta-analysis examining gender-related differences in specific internet addiction. *Computers in Human Behavior, 113*, 106480. doi:10.1016/j.chb.2020.106480

Suzuki, S. N., Kanematsu, H., Barry, D. M., Ogawa, N., Yajima, K., Nakahira, K. T., Shirai, T., Kawaguchi, M., Kobayashi, T., & Yoshitake, M. (2020). Virtual Experiments in Metaverse and their Applications to Collaborative Projects: The Framework and Its Significance. *Procedia Computer Science, 176*, 2125–2132. doi:10.1016/j.procs.2020.09.249

Syed, M. H. (2021). Digitalisation to society 5.0: the new paradigm. In *A Step Towards Society 5.0* (pp. 1–10). CRC Press. doi:10.1201/9781003138037-1

Talwar, S., Dhir, A., Kaur, P., Zafar, N., & Alrasheedy, M. (2019). Why do people share fake news? Associations between the dark side of social media use and fake news sharing behavior. *Journal of Retailing and Consumer Services, 51*, 72–82. doi:10.1016/j.jretconser.2019.05.026

Tamarit, A., Schoeps, K., Peris-Hernández, M., & Montoya-Castilla, I. (2021). The impact of adolescent internet addiction on sexual online victimization: The mediating effects of sexting and body self-esteem. *International Journal of Environmental Research and Public Health, 18*(8), 4226. doi:10.3390/ijerph18084226 PMID:33923552

Tandon, A., Dhir, A., Islam, N., Talwar, S., & Mäntymäki, M. (2021). Psychological and behavioral outcomes of social media-induced fear of missing out at the workplace. *Journal of Business Research, 136*, 186–197. doi:10.1016/j.jbusres.2021.07.036

Tandon, A., Dhir, A., Talwar, S., Kaur, P., & Mäntymäki, M. (2022). Social media induced fear of missing out (FoMO) and phubbing: Behavioural, relational and psychological outcomes. *Technological Forecasting and Social Change, 174*, 121149. doi:10.1016/j.techfore.2021.121149

Tanhan, F., Özok, H. İ., & Tayiz, V. (2022). Fear of missing out (FoMO): A current review. *Psikiyatride Güncel Yaklasimlar, 14*(1), 74–85. doi:10.18863/pgy.942431

Tanwar, S., Popat, A., Bhattacharya, P., Gupta, R., & Kumar, N. (2022). A taxonomy of energy optimisation techniques for smart cities: Architecture and future directions. *Expert Systems: International Journal of Knowledge Engineering and Neural Networks*, *39*(5), e12703. doi:10.1111/exsy.12703

Tapscott, D., & Willams, D. (2010, January/February). Innovating the 21st-Century University: It's Time! *Educase Review*, *45*(1), 16–29.

Tarhan, N., & Nurmedov, S. (2011). *Bağımlılık*. Timaş Yayınları.

Tarter, A. (2017). Importance of cyber security. In P. Saskia Bayer, R. Karlovic, B. Akhgar, & G. Markarian (Eds.), *Community policing-A European perspective* (pp. 213–230). Springer., doi:10.1007/978-3-319-53396-4_15

Taşel, F. (2020). Dijitalleşmenin ticarete ve ekonomiye etkisi. *Beykoz Akademi*, *8*(2), 127–137. doi:10.14514/BYK.m.26515393.2020.8/2.127-137

Tavşancıl, E. (2014). *Tutumların ölçülmesi ve SPSS ile veri analizi*. Nobel Yayın Dağıtım.

Tay, J., & Turner, G. (2010). *Not the apocalypse: Television futures in the digital age*. International Journal of Digital Television.

Taylor, M., & Kent, M. L. (2010). Anticipatory Socialization in the use of social media in Public Relations: A Content Analysis of Prsa's Public Relations Tactics. *Public Relations Review*, *36*(3), 207–214. doi:10.1016/j.pubrev.2010.04.012

Tekerek, N. (2006). Oyun Kavramı'ndan Drama'ya Drama'dan Dramatik Eğitim'e. *Tiyatro Araştırmaları Dergisi*, *22*(22), 47–73.

Tekkurşun-Demir, G., & Mutlu-Bozkurt, T. (2019). Digital Game Playing Attitude Scale (DGPAS): Validity and reliability study. Sportif Bakış. *Spor ve Eğitim Bilimleri Dergisi*, *6*(1), 1–18. doi:10.33468bsebd.79

*The future of digital gaming - ADK INSIGHTS Inspiration*. (n.d.). ADK Insights. https://adk-insights.com/the-future-of-digital-gaming/

Thomas, N. M., Choudhari, S. G., Gaidhane, A. M., & Quazi Syed, Z. (2022). 'Digital Wellbeing': The Need of the Hour in Today's Digitalized and Technology Driven World! *Cureus*. doi:10.7759/cureus.27743 PMID:36106276

Thompson, B. Y. (2018). Digital nomads: Employment in the online gig economy. Glocalism: *Journal of Culture. Politics and Innovation*, *1*, 1–26.

Thompson, B. Y. (2019). The digital nomad lifestyle: (Remote) Work/Leisure balance, privilege and constructed community. *International Journal of the Sociology of Leisure*, *2*(1-2), 27–42. doi:10.100741978-018-00030-y

Thompson, J. B. (1995). *The media and modernity: A social theory of the media*. Stanford University Press.

Throuvala, M. A., Griffiths, M. D., Rennoldson, M., & Kuss, D. J. (2019). School-based Prevention for Adolescent Internet Addiction: Prevention is the Key. A Systematic Literature Review. *Current Neuropharmacology*, *17*(6), 507–525. doi:10.2174/1570159X16666180813153806 PMID:30101714

Tilly, C. (2008). *Toplumsal Hareketler* (O. Düz, Trans.). Babil Yayınları.

Tiryaki, S. (2020). Toplumsal Hareketler ve Medya. Konya: Literatürk.

Tiryaki, S. (2015). *Sosyal Medya ve Facebook Bağımlılığı*. Literatürk Yayınları.

Tiryaki, S., & Karakuş, M. (2019). Sosyal Medya Bağımlılığı. In T. Livberber & S. Tiryaki (Eds.), *Sosyal Medya Çalışmaları* (pp. 133–154). Literatürk Yayınları.

Tiutiunyk, I., Drabek, J., Antoniuk, N., Navickas, V., & Rubanov, P. (2021). The impact of digital transformation on macroeconomic stability: Evidence from EU countries. *Journal of International Students*, *14*(3), 220–234. doi:10.14254/2071-8330.2021/14-3/14

Tiwari, S., Bahuguna, P. C., & Walker, J. (2022). Industry 5.0: A Macro perspective Approach. In Handbook of Research on Innovative Management Using AI in Industry 5.0 (pp. 59-73). IGI Global.

Tkaczyk, J. (2016). Digital consumer: Trends and challenges. *The impact of the digital world on management and marketing*, 353-367.

Toffler, A. (1981). *The Third Wave*. Bantam Books.

Toffler, A. (2008). *Üçüncü Dalga* (S. Yeniçeri, Trans.). Koridor Yayıncılık.

Toker, S., & Baturay, M. H. (2016). Antecedents And Consequences Of Game Addiction. *Computers in Human Behavior*, *55*, 668–679. doi:10.1016/j.chb.2015.10.002

Tokgöz, C. (2017). Kimlik ve Bellek Ekseninde Sosyal Medya Anlatıları. *Intermedia. International Journal (Toronto, Ont.)*, 255–268.

Topic, M. (2002). *Streaming Media Demystified.*

Topsakal, Y., Yüzbaşıoğlu, N., & Çuhadar, M. (2018). Endüstri devrimleri ve turizm: Türkiye turizm 4.0 SWOT analizi ve geçiş süreci önerileri. *Süleyman Demirel Üniversitesi İktisadi ve İdari Bilimler Fakültesi Dergisi*, *23*, 1623–1638.

Törenli, N. (2005). *Yeni medya ve yeni iletişim ortamı* [New media and new communication environment]. Bilim ve Sanat Publishing.

Touloupis, T., & Athanasiades, C. (2022). Evaluation of a cyberbullying prevention program in elementary schools: The role of self-esteem enhancement. *Frontiers in Psychology (section: Positive Psychology)*, *13*, 980091. doi:10.3389/fpsyg.2022.980091

Touloupis, T., & Athanasiades, C. (2014). The Risky Use of New Technology among Elementary School Students: Internet Addiction and Cyberbullying [in Greek]. *Hellenic Journal of Psychology*, *11*, 83–110.

Touloupis, T., & Teli, A. (2021). Internet Addiction among Adolescents: The Role of Social Self-Efficacy and General Locus of Control. In J. J. Jaworski (Ed.), *Advances in Sociology Research* (Vol. 36, pp. 81–112). Nova Science Publishers. doi:10.52305/GPAQ8046

Touraine, A. (1988). *Return of the Actor*. University of Minnesota Press.

Touraine, A. (1995). *Modernliğin Eleştirisi* (H. Tufan, Trans.). Y.K.Y.

Trew, A. (2006). Finance and growth: A critical survey. *The Economic Record*, *82*(259), 481–490. doi:10.1111/j.1475-4932.2006.00361.x

Tsitsika, A., Critselis, E., Kormas, G., Konstantoulaki, E., Constantopoulos, A., & Kafetzis, D. (2009). Adolescent pornographic internet site use: A multivariate regression analysis of the predictive factors of use and psychosocial implications. *Cyberpsychology & Behavior*, *12*(5), 545–550. doi:10.1089/cpb.2008.0346 PMID:19772438

Tso, W. W. Y., Reichert, F., Law, N., Fu, K. W., De La Torre, J., Rao, N., Leung, L. K., Wang, Y.-L., Wong, W. H. S., & Ip, P. (2022). Digital competence as a protective factor against gaming addiction in children and adolescents: A cross-sectional study in Hong Kong. *The Lancet Regional Health. Western Pacific*, *20*, 100382. doi:10.1016/j.lanwpc.2022.100382 PMID:35967602

Turan, S. G., & Dilmen, N. E. (2016). Bilişim okuryazarlığı bağlamında siber şiddetin meşrulaştırılması. *Yeni Symposium,* 54(3), 25-29.

Turan, S., & Avcı, E. K. (2018). 2018 Sosyal Bilgiler Öğretim Programı'nın Dijital Vatandaşlık Bağlamında İncelenmesi. *Journal of Education and New Approaches*, *1*(1), 28–38.

Turel, O., Romashkin, A., & Morrison, K. M. (2016). Health Outcomes of Information System Use Lifestyles among Adolescents: Videogame Addiction, Sleep Curtailment and Cardio-Metabolic Deficiencies. *PLoS One*, *11*(5), e0154764. doi:10.1371/journal.pone.0154764 PMID:27149512

Türk Dil Kurumu. (2011). *Türkçe Sözlük. 11b.* Türk Dil Kurumu Yayınları.

Türkdoğan, O. (1997). *Sosyal Hareketlerin Sosyolojisi.* Birleşik.

Turkish Language Institution. (2019) *OYUN.* Turkish Language Institution. https://sozluk.gov.tr/.

Tutar, H. (2007). Katı Olan Her "İş" Sanallaşıyor veya İşgörenin Artan Yalnızlığı Üzerine: Kuramsal Bir Yaklaşım. *ISGUC The Journal of Industrial Relations and Human Resources*, *9*(2), 116–141.

Tutgun-Ünal, A., & Deniz, L. (2016). Üniversite öğrencilerinin sosyal medya bağımlılığının incelenmesi. *Route Educational and Social Science Journal*, *3*(2), 155–181. doi:10.17121/ressjournal.488

Twenge, J. M., & Campbell, W. K. (2018). Associations between screen time and lower psychological well-being among children and adolescents: Evidence from a population-based study. *Preventive Medicine Reports*, *12*, 271–283. doi:10.1016/j.pmedr.2018.10.003 PMID:30406005

Twenge, J. M., Joiner, T. E., Rogers, M. L., & Martin, G. N. (2018). Increases in Depressive Symptoms, Suicide-Related Outcomes, and Suicide Rates Among U.S. Adolescents After 2010 and Links to Increased New Media Screen Time. *Clinical Psychological Science*, *6*(1), 3–17. doi:10.1177/2167702617723376

Twenge, J. M., Martin, G. N., & Campbell, W. K. (2018). Decreases in psychological well-being among American adolescents after 2012 and links to screen time during the rise of smartphone technology. *Emotion (Washington, D.C.)*, *18*(6), 765–780. doi:10.1037/emo0000403 PMID:29355336

Twohig, M. P., & Crosby, J. M. (2010). Acceptance and commitment therapy as a treatment for problematic internet pornography viewing. *Behavior Therapy*, *41*(3), 285–295. doi:10.1016/j.beth.2009.06.002 PMID:20569778

Uğurlu, T. T., Şengül, C., & Şengül, C. (2012). Bağımlılık Psikofarmakolojisi. *Psikiyatride Güncel Yaklasimlar*, *4*(1), 37–50. doi:10.5455/cap.20120403

Ulubaş Hamurcu, A. (2022). The metaverse, online communities, and (real) urban space. *Urbani Izziv*, *33*(2), 73–81. doi:10.5379/urbani-izziv-en-2022-33-02-01

Ünal, M. (2017). *Management of Generations Y and Z* [Y ve Z Kuşaklarının Yönetimi]. Beta Basım Yayım Dağıtım A.Ş.

Uncu, B. A. (2018). Konda (2018) Seçmen Kümeleri: Ak Parti Seçmeni. *Konda*. https://konda.com.tr/uploads/konda-secmen-kumeleri-akparti-secmenleri-mayis2018-f3848f8d2137abf61eb8f9d2ab392e27a01c13f29fc7a5334ee3cc1336fd753c.pdf

UNICEF. (2017). *The State of The World's Children 2017 Children in a Digital World.* UNICEF.

Ünür, E. (2016). Geleneksel Medya'nın Sosyal Medyayı Nasıl Kullandığına İlişkin Bir İnceleme: Dizilerin Twitter Kullanımı. *Turkish Journal of Social Research*, *20*(1), 153–170.

Uslu, M. (2021). Türkiye'de Sosyal Medya Bağımlılığı ve Kullanımı Araştırması. *Turkish Academic Research Review*, 370-396.

Uslu, O. (2022). Causes and consequences of technology addiction: A review of information systems and information technology studies. *International Journal of Social Sciences and Education Research, 8*(3), 299–306. doi:10.24289/ijsser.1131136

Üstündağ, A. (2022). Çocukların Sosyal Medya, Akıllı Telefon ve Oyun Bağımlılığı Arasındaki İlişkinin İncelenmesi. *Bağımlılık Dergisi*, 316-326.

Üstündağ, A. (2022). Ergenlerin Instagram Bağımlılık Düzeyleri ile Psikolojik İhtiyaçları Arasındaki İlişki. *Bağımlılık Dergisi*, 8-21.

Ustundag, A., & Cevikcan, E. (2017). *Industry 4.0: Managing the Digital Transformation.* Springer.

Uysal, Z. (2021). *Dijital medya ve toplum.* İstanbul: Cinius yayınları.

Uzalac, A., & Cvjeticanin, B. (2008). *Digital culture: The changing dynamics.* Culturelink Publishing.

Üzmez, S. S. ve Büyükbeşe, T. (2021). Dijitalleşme sürecinde bilgi yönetiminin işletmelerin teknoloji uyumuna etkileri. *BEYDER, 16*(2), 117-127. . doi:10.54860/beyder.1028117

Uzunoğlu, A. (2021). Digital games and addiction. *Yeni Medya, 2021*(11), 116–131.

Uzunoğlu, S. (2015). Yeni medyada dijital emek sömürüsü: Tüketiciden Üreticiye yeni medya, yeni sömürü pratikleri [New media and new practices of exploitation: From consumer to prosumer]. *Intermedia International E-Journal, 2*(1), 181–194.

Vaala, S. E., & Bleakley, A. (2015). Monitoring, mediating, and modelling: Parental influence on adolescent computer and internet use in the United States. *Journal of Children and Media, 9*(1), 40–57. doi:10.1080/17482798.2015.997103

Välimäki, M., Athanasopoulou, C., Lahti, M., & Adams, C. E. (2016). Effectiveness of social media interventions for people with schizophrenia: A systematic review and meta-analysis. *Journal of Medical Internet Research, 18*(4), e92. doi:10.2196/jmir.5385 PMID:27105939

Vall-Roqué, H., Andrés, A., & Saldaña, C. (2021). The impact of COVID-19 lockdown on social network sites use, body image disturbances and self-esteem among adolescent and young women. *Progress in Neuro-Psychopharmacology & Biological Psychiatry, 110*, 110293. doi:10.1016/j.pnpbp.2021.110293 PMID:33662532

Valueprop. (2023). *5 Benefits of Face to Face Communication.* Value Prop. https://www.valueprop.com/blog/5-benefits-face-face-communication in 20.2.2023

Van den Eijnden, R. J. J. M., Lemmens, J. S., & Valkenburg, P. M. (2016). The Social Media Disorder Scale. *Computers in Human Behavior, 61*, 478–487. doi:10.1016/j.chb.2016.03.038

Van Dijck, J., & Poell, T. (2015). Social Media and The Transformation of Public Space. *Social Media + Society, 1*(2), 1–5. doi:10.1177/2056305115622482

Van Dijck, J., Poell, T., & De Waal, M. (2018). *The platform society: Public values in a connective world.* Oxford University Press., doi:10.1093/oso/9780190889760.001.0001

van Dijk, R., van der Valk, I. E., Vossen, H. G., Branje, S., & Deković, M. (2021). Problematic internet use in adolescents from divorced families: The role of family factors and adolescents' self-esteem. *International Journal of Environmental Research and Public Health, 18*(7), 3385. doi:10.3390/ijerph18073385 PMID:33805855

Van Rooij, A.J., Schoenmakers, T.M., Vermulst, A.A., Van Den Eijnden, R.J., & Van De Mheen, D. (2011). Online video game addiction: identification of addicted adolescent gamers. *Addiction, 106*(1), 205-12.

Van Rooij, A. J., Schoenmakers, T. M., Vermulst, A. A., Van Den Eijnden, R. J., & Van De Mheen, D. (2011). Online video game addiction: Identification of addicted adolescent gamers. *Addiction (Abingdon, England)*, *106*(1), 205–212. doi:10.1111/j.1360-0443.2010.03104.x PMID:20840209

Vatandaş, C. (2007). Toplumsal Cinsiyet ve Cinsiyet Rollerinin Algılanışı. *Sosyoloji Konferansları*, (35), 29–56.

Velioğlu, H. (2022). Endüstri 4.0 bağlamında siber güvenlik ile finansal tablolara ilişkin görüş oluşturma ve raporlama arasındaki ilişki. H. Şimşek, & M. Cihangir (Ed.) Değişim ve Geleceği Yönetmek. Holistence Publications.

Ventola, C. L. (2014). Social Media and Health Care Professionals: Benefits, Risks, and Best Practices. *P&T*, *39*(7), 492–520. PMID:25083128

Verma, A., Bhattacharya, P., Madhani, N., Trivedi, C., Bhushan, B., Tanwar, S., Sharma, G., Bokoro, P. N., & Sharma, R. (2022). Blockchain for industry 5.0: Vision, opportunities, key enablers, and future directions. *IEEE Access : Practical Innovations, Open Solutions*, *10*, 69160–69199. doi:10.1109/ACCESS.2022.3186892

Veugelers, R., & Cassiman, B. (2005). R&D cooperation between firms and universities. Some empirical evidence from Belgian manufacturing. *International Journal of Industrial Organization*, *23*(5-6), 355–379. doi:10.1016/j.ijindorg.2005.01.008

Vosoughi, S., Roy, D., & Aral, S. (2018). The spread of true and false news online. *Science*, *359*(6380), 1146–1151. doi:10.1126cience.aap9559 PMID:29590045

Vukosavljevic-Gvozden, T., Filipovic, S., & Opacic, G. (2015). The mediating role of symptoms of psychopathology between irrational beliefs and internet gaming addiction. *Journal of Rational-Emotive & Cognitive-Behavior Therapy*, *33*(4), 387–405. doi:10.100710942-015-0218-7

Wack, E., & Tantleff-Dunn, S. (2009). Relationships between electronic game play, obesity, and psychosocial functioning in young men. *Cyberpsychology & Behavior*, *12*(2), 241–244. doi:10.1089/cpb.2008.0151 PMID:19006465

Waisbord, S. (2004). *McTV: Understanding the Global Popularity of Television Formats*. SAGE Publications. doi:10.1177/1527476404268922

Walther, B., Morgenstern, M., & Hanewinkel, R. (2012). Co-occurrence of addictive behaviours: Personality factors related to substance use, gambling and computer gaming. *European Addiction Research*, *18*(4), 167–174. doi:10.1159/000335662 PMID:22398819

Wang, C., Pan, R., Wan, X., Tan, Y., Xu, L., Ho, C. S., & Ho, R. C. (2020). Immediate psychological responses and associated factors during the initial stage of the 2019 coronavirus disease (COVID-19) epidemic among the general population in China. *International Journal of Environmental Research and Public Health*, *17*(5), 1729. doi:10.3390/ijerph17051729 PMID:32155789

Wang, C.-W., Chan, C. L., Mak, K.-K., Ho, S.-Y., Wong, P. W., & Ho, R. T. (2014). Prevalence and correlates of video and internet gaming addiction among Hong Kong adolescents: A pilot study. *TheScientificWorldJournal*, *2014*, 2014. doi:10.1155/2014/874648 PMID:25032242

Wang, F., Lu, J., Lin, L., & Zhou, X. (2019). Mental health and risk behaviors of children in rural China with different patterns of parental migration: A cross-sectional study. *Child and Adolescent Psychiatry and Mental Health*, *13*(1), 1–9. doi:10.118613034-019-0298-8 PMID:31649750

Wang, F., Qin, R., Wang, X., & Hu, B. (2022). MetaSocieties in Metaverse: MetaEconomics and MetaManagement for MetaEnterprises and MetaCities. *IEEE Transactions on Computational Social Systems*, *9*(1), 1–6. doi:10.1109/TCSS.2022.3145165

Wang, Y., Gu, T., & Wang, S. (2019). Causes and characteristics of short video platform Internet community taking the TikTok short video application as an example. *IEEE International Conference on Consumer Electronics*. IEEE. 10.1109/ICCE-TW46550.2019.8992021

Wang, Y., Ko, E., & Wang, H. (2021). Augmented reality (AR) app use in the beauty product industry and consumer purchase intention. *Asia Pacific Journal of Marketing and Logistics*, *34*(1), 110–131. doi:10.1108/APJML-11-2019-0684

Wani, T. A., & Ali, S. W. (2015). Innovation diffusion theory. *Journal of general management research, 3*(2), 101-118.

Warburton, W. A. (2021). Should internet addiction and gaming addiction be categorized as disorders. In Masters of media: Controversies and solutions (pp. 43-58). Macquarie University.

Wartberg, L., Kriston, L., Kramer, M., Schwedler, A., Lincoln, T. M., & Kammerl, R. (2017). Internet gaming disorder in early adolescence: Associations with parental and adolescent mental health. *European Psychiatry*, *43*, 14–18. doi:10.1016/j.eurpsy.2016.12.013 PMID:28365463

Wartberg, L., Kriston, L., Zieglmeier, M., Lincoln, T., & Kammerl, R. (2019). A longitudinal study on psychosocial causes and consequences of Internet gaming disorder in adolescence. *Psychological Medicine*, *49*(2), 287–294. doi:10.1017/S003329171800082X PMID:29622057

Wassom, B. (2014). *Augmented Reality Law, Privacy, and Ethics: Law, Society, and Emerging AR Technologies*. Syngress., doi:10.1016/B978-0-12-800208-7.00003-X

Watson, J. B. (1913). Psychology as behaviourist views it. *Psychological Review*, *20*(2), 158–177. doi:10.1037/h0074428

We Are Social and Hootsuite. (2022). *Digital 2022 Global Overview Report*. Data Portal. Https://Datareportal.Com/Reports/Digital-2022-Global-Overview-Report. 2022.

Weber, R. P. (1989). *Basic Content Analysis*. Sage.

Wegmann, E., Oberst, U., Stodt, B., & Brand, M. (2017). Online-specific fear of missing out and Internet-use expectancies contribute to symptoms of Internet-communication disorder. *Addictive Behaviors Reports*, *5*, 33–42. doi:10.1016/j.abrep.2017.04.001 PMID:29450225

Weinstein, A. M. (2010). Computer and video game addiction—A comparison between game users and non-game users. *The American Journal of Drug and Alcohol Abuse*, *36*(5), 268–276. doi:10.3109/00952990.2010.491879 PMID:20545602

Westerman Gonnet, D., & Mcafee, A. (2014). *Leading Digital*. HBR.

WHO. (2018). *Public health implications of excessive use of the Internet and other communication and gaming platforms*. WHO. https://www.who.int/news/item/13-09-2018-public-health-implications-of-excessive-use-of-the-internet-and-other-communication-and-gaming-platforms

WHO. (2019). *ICD-11 - Disorders due to addictive behaviours 2019*. WHO. https://icd.who.int/browse11/l-m/en#/http%3a%2f%2fid.who.int%2ficd%2fentity%2f499894965. (accessed 30.12.2020)

WHO. (2019). *ICD-11 - Gaming disorder*. WHO. https://icd.who.int/browse11/l-m/en#/http%3a%2f%2fid.who.int%2ficd%2fentity%2f1448597234

*Why we play PUBG day-night? What are its psychological underpinnings ?* (2021, June 19). Times of India. https://timesofindia.indiatimes.com/readersblog/nothing-important/why-we-play-pubg-day-night-what-are-its-psychological-underpinnings-33843/

Widyanto, L., & McMurran, M. (2004). The Psychometric properties of the internet addiction test. *Cyberpsychology & Behavior*, *7*(4), 443–450. doi:10.1089/cpb.2004.7.443 PMID:15331031

Willard, N. (2007). *Cyberbullying and cyberthreats*. Research Press.

Wilmer, H. H., Sherman, L. E., & Chein, J. M. (2017). Smartphones and Cognition: A Review of Research Exploring the Links between Mobile Technology Habits and Cognitive Functioning. *Frontiers in Psychology*, *8*(APR), 605. doi:10.3389/fpsyg.2017.00605 PMID:28487665

Wilson, C. (2008). *Botnets, cybercrime, and cyberterrorism: Vulnerabilities and policy issues for congress.* CRS Report for Congress.

Winkler, A., Dörsing, B., Rief, W., Shen, Y., & Glombiewski, J. A. (2013). Treatment of internet addiction: A meta-analysis. *Clinical Psychology Review*, *33*(2), 317–329. doi:10.1016/j.cpr.2012.12.005 PMID:23354007

Wise, R. A. (2009). Roles for nigrostriatal-not just mesocorticolimbic-dopamine in reward and addiction. *Trends in Neurosciences*, *32*(10), 517–524. doi:10.1016/j.tins.2009.06.004 PMID:19758714

Wölfling, K., & Dominick, N. (2022). Using cognitive behavioral therapy as the select treatment approach for problematic Internet usage. *Current Opinion in Behavioral Sciences*, *45*, 101–121. doi:10.1016/j.cobeha.2022.101121

Wölfling, K., Müller, K. W., & Beutel, M. (2010). Reliability and validity of the Scale for the Assessment of Pathological Computer-Gaming (AICA-S). *Psychotherapie, Psychosomatik, Medizinische Psychologie*, 1–16. doi:10.1055-0030-1263145 PMID:20878599

Wolniczak, I., Cáceres-DelAguila, J. A., Palma-Ardiles, G., Arroyo, K. J., Solís-Visscher, R., Paredes-Yauri, S., Mego-Aquije, K., & Bernabe-Ortiz, A. (2013). Association between Facebook dependence and poor sleep quality: A study in a sample of undergraduate students in Peru. *PLoS One*, *8*(3), e59087. doi:10.1371/journal.pone.0059087 PMID:23554978

Wolniewicz, C. A., Tiamiyu, M. F., Weeks, J. W., & Elhai, J. D. (2018). Problematic smartphone use and relations with negative affect, fear of missing out, and fear of negative and positive evaluation. *Psychiatry Research*, *262*, 618–623. doi:10.1016/j.psychres.2017.09.058 PMID:28982630

Wong, I. L. K., & Lam, M. P. (2016). Gaming behavior and addiction among Hong Kong adolescents. *Asian Journal of Gambling Issues and Public Health*, *6*(1), 6. doi:10.118640405-016-0016-x PMID:27630813

Wongmonta, S. (2021). Marketing 5.0: The era of technology for humanity with a collaboration of humans and machines. *Nimitmai Review Journal*, *4*(1), 83–97.

Woods, H. C., & Scott, H. (2016). #Sleepyteens: Social media use in adolescence is associated with poor sleep quality, anxiety, depression and low self-esteem. *Journal of Adolescence*, *51*(1), 41–49. doi:10.1016/j.adolescence.2016.05.008 PMID:27294324

Wood, W., & Neal, D. T. (2016). Healthy through habit: Interventions for initiating & maintaining health behavior change. *Behavioral Science & Policy*, *2*(1), 71–83. doi:10.1353/bsp.2016.0008

World Health Organization (WHO). (2022). *Gaming disorder*. WHO. Https://Www.Who.Int/Standards/Classifications/Frequently-Asked-Questions/Gaming-Disorder

World Health Organization. (2022). *ICD-11 for Mortality and Morbidity Statistics*. WHO. https://icd.who.int/browse11/l-m/en

World Health Organization. (2023). ICD-11 for mortality and morbidity statistics (Version: 01/2023). *06 Mental, behavioural or neurodevelopmental disorders*. ICD. https://icd.who.int/browse11/l-m/en

Wright, J. (2011). The effects of video game play on academic performance. *Modern Psychological Studies, 17*(1), 37-44. https://scholar.utc.edu/mps/vol17/iss1/6

Wu, A. M. S., Cheung, V. I., Ku, L., & Hung, E. P. W. (2013). *Psychological risk factors of addiction to social networking sites among Chinese smartphone users.*

Wu, A. M. S., Lau, J. T. F., Cheng, K. M., Law, R. W., Tse, V. W. S., & Lau, M. M. C. (2018). Direct and interaction effects of co-existing familial risk factors and protective factors associated with internet addiction among Chinese students in Hong Kong. *The Journal of Early Adolescence*, *38*(4), 1–22. doi:10.1177/0272431616671826

Xie, J., Liu, X., & Dajun Zeng, D. (2018). Mining e-cigarette adverse events in social media using Bi-LSTM recurrent neural network with word embedding representation. *Journal of the American Medical Informatics Association : JAMIA*, *25*(1), 72–80. doi:10.1093/jamia/ocx045 PMID:28505280

Xiuqin, H., Huimin, Z., Mengchen, L., Jinan, W., Ying, Z., & Ran, T. (2010). Mental health, personality, and parental rearing styles of adolescents with Internet addiction disorder. *Cyberpsychology, Behavior, and Social Networking*, *13*(4), 401–406. doi:10.1089/cyber.2009.0222 PMID:20712498

Xu, X., Lu, Y., Vogel-Heuser, B., & Wang, L. (2021). Industry 4.0 and Industry 5.0—Inception, conception and perception. *Journal of Manufacturing Systems*, *61*, 530–535. doi:10.1016/j.jmsy.2021.10.006

Xu, Z., Turel, O., & Yuan, Y. (2012). Online game addiction among adolescents: Motivation and prevention factors. *European Journal of Information Systems*, *21*(3), 321–340. doi:10.1057/ejis.2011.56

Yalçın, C. (2003). Sosyolojik Bir Bakış Açısıyla İnternet. *Cumhuriyet Üniversitesi Edebiyat Fakültesi Sosyal Bilimler Dergisi*, *27*(1), 77–89.

Yalcin, S., & Bertiz, Y. (2019). Qualitative study on the effects of game addiction on university students. Science, Education [SEAT Journal]. *Art and Technology Journal*, *3*(1), 27–34.

Yali, Z., Sen, L., & Guoliang, Y. (2021). The relationship between social media use and fear of missing out: A meta-analysis. *Acta Psychologica Sinica*, *53*(3), 273–290.

Yang, S., Zhao, Y., & Ma, Y. (2019). Analysis of the reasons and development of short video application: Taking TikTok as an example. *9th International Conference on Information and Social Science*. IEEE.

Yanık, C., & Öztürk, M. (2014). Toplumsal hareketlerin dönüşümü üzerine bir değerlendirme. *Mukaddime*, *5*(1), 45–63.

Yankın, F. B. (2018). Dijital Dönüşüm Sürecinde Çalışma Yaşamı. *Trakya Üniversitesi İktisadi ve İdari Bilimler Fakültesi E-Dergi*, *7*(2), 1–38.

Yao, M. Z., He, J., Ko, D. M., & Pang, K. (2014). The influence of personality, parental behaviors, and self-esteem on Internet addiction: A study of Chinese college students. *Cyberpsychology, Behavior, and Social Networking*, *17*(2), 104–110. doi:10.1089/cyber.2012.0710 PMID:24003966

Yayman, E., & Bilgin, O. (2020). Relationship between social media addiction, game addiction and family functions. *International Journal of Evaluation and Research in Education, 9*, 979-986. doi:10.11591/ijere.v9i4.20680

Yee, N. (2006). Motivations for play in online games. *Cyberpsychology & Behavior*, *9*(6), 772–775. doi:10.1089/cpb.2006.9.772 PMID:17201605

Yee, N., Ducheneaut, N., & Nelson, L. (2012). Online gaming motivations scale: Development and validation. In *Proceedings of the SIGCHI Conference on Human Factors in Computing Systems*, Austin, TX. 10.1145/2207676.2208681

Yegen, C. (2014). Bir ijital aktivizm biçimi olarak slaktivizm: Change.org örneği. *Karadeniz Teknik Üniversitesi İletişim Araştırmaları Dergisi*, *4*(2), 84-108.

Yengin, D. (2019). Teknoloji bağımlılığı olarak dijital bağımlılık. *The Turkish Online Journal of Design, Art and Communication – TOJDAC, 9*(2), 130-144.

Yengin, D. (2019). Teknoloji Bağımlılığı Olarak Dijital Bağımlılık. *The Turkish Online Journal Of Design, Art and Communication- TOJDAC*, 130-144.

Yengin, D. (2019). Digital Addiction as Technology Addiction. *Turkish Online Journal of Design Art and Communication, 9*(2), 130–144. doi:10.7456/10902100/007

Yeşilay. (2022). *Technology addiction* [Teknoloji Bağımlılığı]. Yeşilay Yayınları.

Yetkin Cılızoğlu, G., & Çetinkaya, A. (2018). Zaman ve mekandan bağımsız katılım; örgütlü yurttaştan dijital bireye: Change.org örneği. *Journal of Human Sciences, 15*(4), 1944–1958. doi:10.14687/jhs.v15i4.5529

Yeung, K. (2018). Algorithmic regulation: A critical interrogation. *Regulation & Governance, 12*(4), 505–523. doi:10.1111/rego.12158

Yıldıran, Ö. Ü. (2009). Baudrillard Perspektifinden Bir Kitle İletişim ve Sanat Aracı Olarak Simülasyon Evreninde Televizyon. *Selçuk İletişim Dergisi, 5*(4), 201–218.

Yıldız, İ., & Kanak, M. (2021). Children's Digital Technology Usage and Parental Approaches: A Cross Sectional Study. *TJFMPC, 15*(2), 306–314. doi:10.21763/tjfmpc.797346

Yin, R. K. (1984). *Case study research: Design and methods*. Sage.

Young, K. S. (1996, August). *Internet addiction: The emergence of a new clinical disorder.* Paper presented at the American Psychological Association, Toronto, Canada.

Young, K. (1998). *Caught in the net: How to recognize the signs of internet addiction and a winning strategy for recovery*. John Wiley & Sons.

Young, K. (2009). Internet addiction: Diagnosis and treatment considerations. *Journal of Contemporary Psychotherapy, 39*(4), 241–246. doi:10.100710879-009-9120-x

Young, K. (2009). Understanding online gaming addiction and treatment issues for adolescents. *The American Journal of Family Therapy, 37*(5), 355–372. doi:10.1080/01926180902942191

Young, K. S. (1998). *Caught in the net: How to recognize the signs of internet addiction—and a winning strategy for recovery*. John Wiley & Sons.

Young, K. S. (1998). Internet Addiction: The Emergence of a New Clinical Disorder. *Cyberpsychology & Behavior, 1*(3), 237–244. doi:10.1089/cpb.1998.1.237

Young, K. S. (1999). Internet addiction: Evaluation and treatment. *Student BMJ, 7*, 351–352.

Young, K. S. (2007). Cognitive behavior therapy with Internet addicts: Treatment outcomes and implications. *Cyberpsychology & Behavior, 10*(5), 671–679. doi:10.1089/cpb.2007.9971 PMID:17927535

Yuan, G., Elhai, J. D., & Hall, B. J. (2021). The influence of depressive symptoms and fear of missing out on severity of problematic smartphone use and internet gaming disorder among Chinese young adults: A three-wave mediation model. *Addictive Behaviors, 112*, 106648. doi:10.1016/j.addbeh.2020.106648 PMID:32977268

Yüksel Avcılar, M., & Atalar, S. (2019). Narsistik Kişilik Özelliklerinin Sosyal Medya Bağımlılık Düzeyi ve Gösterişçi Tüketim Eğilimleri Üzerine Etkisinin Tespiti. *Opus, Uluslararası Toplum Araştırmaları Dergisi*, 1373-1407.

Yüksel, N., Soygür, H., Tural, Ü., & Demet, M. M. (2010). *Temel psikofarmakoloji*. Türkiye Psikiyatri Derneği Yayınları.

Yu, M., & Baxter, J. (2016). Australian children's screen time and participation in extracurricular activities. In *LSAC Annual Statistical Report 2015* (pp. 99–125). Australian Institute of Family Studies.

Zajac, K., Ginley, M. K., Chang, R., & Petry, N. M. (2017). Treatments for Internet gaming disorder and Internet addiction: A systematic review. *Psychology of Addictive Behaviors, 31*(8), 979–994. doi:10.1037/adb0000315 PMID:28921996

Zakharova, V. A., Chernov, I. V., Nazarenko, T. I., Pavlov, P. V., Lyubchenko, V. S., & Kulikova, V. S. (2020). Social health and environmental behavior of students in the digital age. *Cypriot Journal of Educational Science., 15*(5), 1288–1294. doi:10.18844/cjes.v15i5.5167

Zamani, E., Chashmi, M., & Hedayati, N. (2009). Effect of Addiction to Computer Games on Physical and Mental Health of Female and Male Students of Guidance School in City of Isfahan. *Addiction & Health, 1*(2), 98–104. PMID:24494091

Zengin, Y., & Zengin, R. B. (2022). Endüstri 5.0 döneminde pazarlamaya dair genel bir bakış. *Hacettepe Üniversitesi Sosyal Bilimler Dergisi, 4*(1), 111–138.

Zhang, J.-T., Yao, Y.-W., Potenza, M. N., Xia, C.-C., Lan, J., Liu, L., Wang, L.-J., Liu, B., Ma, S.-S., & Fang, X.-Y. (2016). Effects of craving behavioral intervention on neural substrates of cue-induced craving in Internet gaming disorder. *NeuroImage. Clinical, 12*, 591–599. doi:10.1016/j.nicl.2016.09.004 PMID:27699148

Zhang, L., Luo, T., Hao, W., Cao, Y., Yuan, M., & Liao, Y. (2022). Gaming Disorder Symptom Questionnaire: The development and validation of a screening tool for ICD-11 gaming disorder in adolescents. *Frontiers in Psychiatry, 13*, 1–12. doi:10.3389/fpsyt.2022.848157 PMID:35401279

Zhang, W., Zhao, S., Wan, X., & Yao, Y. (2021). Study on the effect of digital economy on high-quality economic development in China. *PLoS One, 16*(9), e0257365. doi:10.1371/journal.pone.0257365 PMID:34547019

Zhang, Y., Mei, S., Li, L., Chai, J., Li, J., & Du, H. (2015). The relationship between impulsivity and internet addiction in Chinese college students: A moderated mediation analysis of meaning in life and self-esteem. *PLoS One, 10*(7), e0131597. doi:10.1371/journal.pone.0131597 PMID:26171860

Zhong, X., Tao, R., Zu, S., Sha, S., & Yang, F. (2009). Effect of group psychological intervention in adolescents on Internet addiction. *Journal of Capital Medical University, 30*, 494–499.

Zhou, J. (2013). Digitalization and intelligentization of manufacturing industry. *Advances in Manufacturing, 1*(1), 1–7. doi:10.100740436-013-0006-5

Zhou, X. H., & Xing, J. (2021). The relationship between college students' online game addiction, family function and self-control. *Health, 13*(9), 910–919. doi:10.4236/health.2021.139070

Zhou, Z., Yuan, G., & Yao, J. (2012). Cognitive bases toward internet game-related pictures and executive deficits in individuals with an internet game addiction. *PLoS One, 7*(11), 1–9. doi:10.1371/journal.pone.0048961 PMID:23155434

Zhu, X., & Xiong, Z. (2022). Exploring association between social media addiction, fear of missing out, and self-presentation online among university students: A cross-sectional study. *Frontiers in Psychiatry, 13*(13), 896762. doi:10.3389/fpsyt.2022.896762 PMID:35633794

Zıvdır, P., & Karakul, A. (2023). Üniversite Öğrencilerinin Sosyal Medya Bağımlılığı Düzeyleri ve FOMO İlişkisi. *İnönü Üniversitesi Sağlık Hizmetleri Meslek Yüksekokulu Dergisi*, 1054-1067.

# About the Contributors

**Rengim Sine Nazlı** has been working in the fields of new media, journalism and communication studies. Since 2020, she is associate proffessor at Bolu Abant İzzet Baysal University, Department of Journalism.

**Gülşah Sarı** works as an Associate Professor at the Department of Journalism, in Aksaray University, Turkey. She became a Ph.D. in İstanbul University, Department of Radio Television and Cinema in 2016. She held a master degree in Marmara University, department of Cinema in 2010. She has published several papers in journals and books including women's studies, gender, digital communication, communication studies.

* * *

**Sevda Mutlu Akar** is an Associate Professor of the Department of Public Finance at Bandirma Onyedi Eylul University, Faculty of Economics and Administrative Sciences in Turkey since 2018. She earned her Ph.D. degree in public finance at Marmara University, Department of Public Finance, Institute of Social Sciences (Turkey). Her Ph.D. dissertation is titled "The Impact of Natural Disasters on Public Finance: Turkish Case (in Turkish, 2009-2013)". Her teaching and research are in the area of public economics, public finance, and budgeting. She has also worked on health expenditures, public policies, public expenditures, taxation, and time series analysis.

**Özge Akcaoğlu Erdem** received training in the field of Social Studies. She is currently studying for a master's degree in Communication Sciences at Bolu Abant İzzet Baysal University Graduate Education Institute. She is in the thesis stage.

**Mustafa Eren Akpınar**, born on October 27, 1998, graduated from Kocaeli University, Faculty of Communication, Department of Journalism in 2020. In the same year, he received a master's degree from Istanbul Aydın University Graduate Education Institute, Department of Journalism. He completed his master's degree in the same department in June 2022 and received a master's degree. Mustafa Eren Akpınar currently conducts research mainly in the fields of Social Media Studies, Gender Studies, Digital Communication, Communication Studies and Journalism and Media Studies.

**Antonia Armaou** graduated from the 2nd General High School of Agios Dimitrios (Athens). She holds a Bachelor Degree form the Department of Mathematics of the School of Positive and Technological Sciences of the University of Crete (2005) and a Master's Degree of "Educational Sciences" from the Faculty of Humanities of the Hellenic Open University (2022). Since 2006 she has been working as a Secondary Education Mathematics teacher. Her research interests concern the psycho-emotional development of children and adolescents as well as the didactic of Mathematics. For a number of years he was a member of the Algebra laboratory of the Standard Experimental Lyceum Evangelical School of Nea Smyrni (Athens).

**Fırat Ata** graduated from Selcuk University, Faculty of Communication, Department of Journalism in 2012. He completed his master's and doctoral studies at Selçuk University, Institute of Social Sciences, Department of Journalism. The author, who completed his master's degree (2012-2015) with his thesis titled "New Constructers of Truth in the New Media: Readers", completed his doctoral education (2017-2022) with his thesis titled "Verification in Local Internet Journalism: The Case of Hatay". Ata, is working Hatay Mustafa Kemal University, Antakya Vocational School Journalism Department.

**Betül Başer** is a research assistant who started at Cumhuriyet University, Faculty of Communication, Public Relations and Publicity Department in 2013 and graduated in 2017. In the same year, she started her graduate degree at Marmara University, Social Science Institute, Public Relations and Publicity Department and completed this program in 2020 with "The Role of Social Media Phenomena on Purchasing Decision of Z Generation Consumers: The Example of Youtubers" thesis. In the same year, she started her doctorate education at İstanbul University, Social Science Institute, Public Relations and Publicity Department and she continues her education and works as a research assistant at Ondokuz Mayıs University, Faculty of Communication, Public Relations and Publicity Department. Study fields: Public relations, new media, digital games and consumer behavior.

**Veysel Çakmak** was born in Aksaray in 1977. He graduated from Gazi University Faculty of Trade and Tourism Education in 1998. In 2008, he completed his graduate study and doctorate education at Selçuk University, the Institute of Social Sciences Public Relation Department. He worked at Selçuk University between 2001 and 20007 and he worked at Karamanoğlu Mehmet Bey University between 2007 and 2011. He is currently working as an Assistant Professor at Aksaray University Aksaray Vocational High School of Social Sciences. Çakmak has various articles on the fields of communication, public relations, and social media.

**Claúdio Cardoso** graduated in Psychology and a Master's student in Clinical Psychology course at the University of Trás-os-Montes e Alto Douro, researcher in the area of cyber abuse and social media, also with experience in the portuguese prison system.

**Ines Carvalho Relva** is an integrated member of the Research Center in Sports Sciences and Human Development (CIDESD), and collaborator member of the Centre for Research and Intervention in Education (CIIE).

**Selahattin Çavuş** graduated from the Journalism Department of Communication Faculty at Selçuk University in 2007. He received his Ph.D. degree at the Institute of Social Sciences, Department of Journalism in 2013. He worked as a lecturer at Ardahan University between the years 2011-2013. He worked at Aksaray University Faculty of Tourism between 2013-2017 Currently he is working as an associate professor in the Department of Journalism, at Aksaray University. His research topics include such as digital journalism, social media, technology addiction, privacy, and gaming.

**Umut Çıvgın** completed his Ph.D. in Clinical Psychology in 2020. He continues both his field and academic studies. He works as an Assistant Professor in the Department of Psychology at Bursa Technical University.

**Tuncay Dilci** is the founder of DIBAMDER.

**Ismail Ergen** received his M.F.A. (USA Proficiency in Arts) from the Academy of Art San Francisco and his Proficiency in Arts (Doctorate) from Arel University's Faculty of Fine Art. He has worked in advertising, art, and business-related industries throughout his career. He also founded a number of award-winning businesses in the United States, including a toy design company that can create next-generation 3D toys out of recyclable materials. He recently returned to Turkey to take a management job at Ambeent Inc, a Silicon Valley firm that develops next-generation AI algorithms for 5G and 6G technologies and was just awarded the coveted Horizon 2020 EIC SME Phase II grant. His thesis, "Digital Design Techniques with Developing Gaming Technologies: User Effects of Robotic Automation, Artificial Intelligence, and 3D Design," reflects his research interests. He's now working on methods for incorporating aggregated digital design into game design, as well as artificial intelligence, experience design, UX research, and user interface design.

**Mustafa Ersoy** is an associate professor in the Department of Educational Sciences at Sivas Cumhuriyet University Faculty of Education in Turkey. He conducts research on integrating technological innovations into education, personalized learning systems, artificial intelligence, metaverse, and technology addiction, which have gained popularity in recent years, and makes significant contributions to the literature in these areas. Dr. ERSOY has presented at numerous national and international conferences in Turkey and abroad and his articles have been published in international academic journals. He has also participated in national projects and provided consulting services in technology-focused personalized education. Through his research, Dr. ERSOY highlights the importance of effective use of technological innovations in education, emphasizing the necessity of technology integration in education for students to achieve more efficient and effective learning processes.

**Luísa Felício** has a bachelor's degree in Communication Sciences and is a Master's student in Digital Communication at ISCAP. She has focused on research related to the implications of social media in today's society, which is an area of interest for the author.

**Metin Hasde**, graduated from Gülhane Military Medical Faculty in 1985. He became a Public Health Specialist, also Occupational Physician in 1991 and a Military Hygiene Specialist in 1992. In 1993, he became an Assistant Professor in the Department of Public Health. He became Associate Professor of Public Health in 1996. He was appointed Professor in 2003. During this period, he served as GATA Board

Member and Secretary, GATA DOSE Board Member and Secretary, GATF Faculty Board Member, GATA Bulletin Editorial Board Member and GATA Ethics Committee Member. He is an Occupational Medicine and Occupational Safety Specialist Trainer by the Ministry of Labor and Social Security, a Member of the Public Health Commission of the Ministry of Health Medical Specialization Board Curriculum Formation and Standard Setting System (TUKMOS), and a Member of the "Immunization Advisory Board" of the Ministry of Health. He is still working as the Head of Health Sciences University, Gülhane Faculty of Medicine, Department of Public Health.

**Bhim Jyoti** is working as an Assistant Professor (Economics) in the School of Liberal Arts & Management, DIT University Dehradun. He did Post-Doctorate Research with EDI of India, Ahmedabad, Gujarat (India). He received MPhil (Economics) from DAVV Indore (India), and PhD (Economics) from IIT Indore (India. He has published several research papers in the diversified area such as climate change, agricultural productivity, assessment of food security; estimation of GFSI, development of environmental sustainability index (ESI) and its association with socio-economic indicators; measurement and determinants of entrepreneurship ecosystem, and dimension of sustainable development and its interlinkages with economic development.

**Tolga Karadas** is an English Teacher / Education Programming and Teaching Ph. D. Student at Sivas Cumhuriyet University.

**Mohid Khan** is a high school student from New Hampshire, USA. He dedicates most of his time to performing biological and psychological research and studying for science competitions, hoping that he will be in this field one day. He plays the trumpet, table tennis, and chess in his spare time.

**Özgün Arda Kuş** graduated from Maltepe University, Faculty of Communication, Department of Public Relations and Publicity and a double major from the Department of Psychology with 100% scholarship. He completed his master's degree in Okan University, Department of Business Administration, Sales-Marketing Department. He continues his doctoral education at Istanbul University, Department of Public Relations and Publicity, at the thesis stage. He has an internationally published work titled "The Concept of Mobile Marketing, Istanbul and a Research for Generation Y", compilation books titled "Digital State of Games 1 and 2" edited with Özge Uğurlu Akbaş, papers presented at international scientific meetings, and chapters and articles in various books. Özgün Arda Kuş's areas of work and interest are Digital games, alienation, mobile marketing, consumer behaviors and generations, mood disorders and behavioral addictions. He is a full member of the Turkish Psychological Association.

**Ana Paula Monteiro** is an integrate member of the Centre for Research and Intervention in Education (CIIE), Portugal.

**Senem Nart** is an Associate Professor of the Department of Maritime Business Management at Bandirma Onyedi Eylul Universit, Faculty of Maritime. She completed her undergraduate education in Economics and her master's degree in Business Administration. She received her Ph.D. degree from Balıkesir University Institute of Social Sciences, Business Administration program. In 2021, she received the title of associate professor in the field of management and strategy. She has national and international publications on leadership, talent in working life, organizational behavior, and organizational psychology.

**Paula Peres** is a full professor with habilitation in the doctoral area of e-Learning, a post-PhD in Education technologies and a PhD in area Information Systems. Master in computer science and graduate in Math Computer. She has a Post-graduation in adult education. She is currently teaching on the Information System scientific area in the School of Accounting and Administration of Porto / Polytechnic of Porto (ISCAP/P.PORTO). She was the pro-president for e-Learning of Polytechnic of Porto. She was responsible for the Training Center and Services of ISCAP/ Polytechnic of Porto. She was the coordinator of the Unit of eLearning and Pedagogical Innovation of P.PORTO (EIPP/P.PORTO). She is the responsible for the GAIE – Support Office in innovation and education She is a director of the Master in Assistance in Digital Communication. He is a member of the commission for distance learning at A3ES (Higher Education Assessment and Accreditation Agency). President and Member of different external evaluation commissions for the accreditation of study cycles taught at a distance. Member of GILT -Games, Interaction and Learning Technologies is a R&D unit hosted by the Porto Polytechnic since 2005.

**Ahmet Furkan Şahbaz**, a graduate of the English Language Teaching undergraduate program at the Faculty of Education, holds a master's degree in Curriculum and Instruction and is currently a doctoral student in the same department. His research focuses on the use of technology in foreign language teaching, particularly in the context of English language instruction.

**Çağrı Emin Şahin**, graduated from Istanbul University Faculty of Medicine in 2015. He worked as technical staff in various positions in Istanbul Public Health Directorate and as the manager of Sultangazi Community Health Center. He attended the two-year Field Epidemiology Training of the Ministry of Health. He completed his PhD in Public Health with his thesis titled "Evaluation of Cost-Effectiveness of HPV Vaccine for the National Vaccination Programme". He worked as a Public Health Manager at the Ministry of Health, General Directorate of Public Health, Department of Vaccine Preventable Diseases. In the Immunization Department, he carried out duties such as measles/rubella, congenital rubella syndrome surveillance, maternal neonatal tetanus surveillance contact person, adverse events following immunisation monitoring, vaccine safety and cold chain follow-up. He took part in various humanitarian and public health projects in Türkiye and abroad. He has first aid trainer and occupational medicine certificates. He is currently working as an Assistant Professor at the Department of Public Health, Gulhane Faculty of Medicine, University of Health Sciences.

**Luan Carlos Santos Silva** is an Associate Professor (since 2016) at the Faculty of Business Administration, Accounting Sciences and Economics of the Federal University of Grande Dourados (UFGD), Brazil. Doctor of Philosophy (Ph.D.), Production Engineering the Federal University of Rio Grande do Sul (UFRGS), Porto Alegre, Brazil. Master's degree, Production Engineering at the Federal University of Paraná (UTFPR), Ponta Grossa, Brazil. Bachelor's degree (Undergraduate degree), Business Administration at the Faculty of Discovery (FACESCO), Santa Cruz Cabrália, Brazil.

**Cüneyd İkbal Sarıoğlu,** who works as Assistant Professor Doctor at Kocaeli University Hereke Ömer İsmet Uzunyol Vocational School Foreign Trade Department, completed his undergraduate education at Atatürk University Business Administration Department, and his master's and doctorate degrees at Cumhuriyet University Social Sciences Institute Business Administration Department. The author conducts research and studies in the fields of consumer behavior, social media, digital marketing, service marketing, customer relations, sales management.

**Margarida Simões** is an Assistant Professor at the University of Trás-Os-Montes and Alto Douro. PhD in Psychology from the University of Beira Interior and member of the Center for Educational Research (CIIE) of the University of Porto. Specialist in Clinical Psychology with advanced specialization in Justice Psychology. Coordinator of the Forensic Psychological Assessment Unit (U.A.P.F.) of UTAD, where she carries out psychological examinations for courts and other organs of justice. Researcher in the area of clinical psychology and justice, namely psychopathy in adolescence, cyberbullying, and juvenile delinquency.

**Ajay Kumar Singh** has been worked with V.C.S.G., UUHF, College of Forestry, Ranichauri, Tehri Garhwal, Uttarakhand, India as Assistant Professor of Seed and Technology. She received MSc in Seed and Technology from CCS University Meerut and PhD in Seed and Technology from G. B. Pant University of Agriculture, Pantnagar, Uttarakhand. She has published several research articles in the seed and technology, plant growth, seed vigour, genetic variability, Biotechnological approaches, climate change and agricultural productivity.

**Hulya Sirin** graduated Cukurova University, School of Medicine in 1992, worked as a general practitioner in the field of primary health care and completed PhD program in Public Health at Gazi University in 2011. Between the years of 2003 and 2005, she worked as a researcher at Center for Injury Research and Control, University of Pittsburgh. She got training on Newborn Screening Program Policies at U.S. National Newborn Screening and Genetics Resource Center, University of Texas. She has worked as a program manager in newborn screening program at the General Directorate of Mother and Child Health and Family Planning between 2006 and 2010, and as a senior advisor at the General Directorate of Public Health between 2014 and 2018, Ministry of Health. Dr Sirin created a great experience on public health science at almost every level including primary care, policy making and academy. Since 2018, he enjoys sharing his knowledge and experience as an Associate Professor at Gülhane School of Medicine, University of Health Sciences.

**Ian Stark** is a Ph.D. student in Technical Communication and Rhetoric at Texas Tech University. With an interdisciplinary background in healthcare management and medical humanities, they conduct research on the administrative systems and rhetorical practices of mental health communication.

**Carla Schwengber ten Caten** is an Associate Professor at the Production Engineering Departmentof the Federal University of Rio Grande do Sul (UFRGS), Porto Alegre, Brazil. Doctor of Philosophy (Ph.D.), Materials Engineering the Federal University of Rio Grande do Sul (UFRGS), Porto Alegre, Brazil. Postdoctoral fellow at the University of Southern California (USC) in the USA

**İbrahim Toruk** graduated from Marmara University in 1990.He started his academic career as a research assistant at Selçuk University Communication Faculty and continues as a professor in the Journalism Department of the same faculty. His fields of study include Economic journalism, communication and media studies, and media ethics.

**Thanos Touloupis** is a Laboratory Teaching Staff (E.DI.P.) of "Educational Psychology" at the Department of Psychology of the University of Western Macedonia, as well as an adjunct faculty at the Hellenic Open University. He has graduated from the Department of Primary Education of the University of Thessaly, and followed Master's, Doctoral and Postdoctoral studies at the Department of Psychology of Aristotle University of Thessaloniki. His research work focuses on the problematic internet use among students with and without special educational needs, and on social-emotional factors, which trigger or are triggered by problematic internet use affecting the educational process. Additionally, he is interested in school-family collaboration to prevent/address the above issues in the school community. He has many years of teaching experience in General and Special Primary Education while he has worked in Higher Education as a contractual Lecturer/Academic Scholar in Greek and Cypriot Institutions, teaching undergraduate and postgraduate courses from the fields of Educational and School Psychology. His scientific work has been published and presented in international and Greek scientific journals and conferences respectively.

**Hasan Tutar** is instructer in Bolu Abant İzzet Baysal University. He is PhD in management and organization (2000, Atatürk University, Turkey); Associate Professor (2009, Sakarya University, Turkey); Professor (2013, Sakarya University, Turkey). His research interests include organizational strategy, organizational theories, human resource management, and organizational behavior.

**Aikaterini Vasiou** is an Assistant Professor of "Methodological approaches in Educational Psychology" in the Department of Primary Education at University of Crete. She holds a PhD in Educational Psychology from the University of Thessaly, while as part of an Excellence scholarship she conducted post-doctoral research in School Psychology and Counseling at the University of Western Macedonia. She has participated in an Experimental Study research program at the Kapodistrian University of Athens and in Mental Health research programs at the University of the Aegean. She has published her research in international and Greek journals and has made announcements at international and panhellenic psychology and educational conferences.

# Index

## A



## B



## C



## D

# E



# F



# G



# H

## I



## J



## L



## M



## N



## O

## W

## Ensure Quality Research is Introduced to the Academic Community

# Become an Evaluator for IGI Global Authored Book Projects

**The overall success of an authored book project is dependent on quality and timely manuscript evaluations.**

**Applications and Inquiries may be sent to:**
development@igi-global.com

Applicants must have a doctorate (or equivalent degree) as well as publishing, research, and reviewing experience. Authored Book Evaluators are appointed for one-year terms and are expected to complete at least three evaluations per term. Upon successful completion of this term, evaluators can be considered for an additional term.

If you have a colleague that may be interested in this opportunity, we encourage you to share this information with them.

www.ingramcontent.com/pod-product-compliance
Lightning Source LLC
LaVergne TN
LVHW080403011026
849161LV00009B/2339